# FIGHTER UNITS & PILOTS OF THE 8TH AIR FORCE

FIGHTER UNITS & PILOTS OF THE 8TH AIR FORCE:
*Volume 1: Day-to-Day Operations • Fighter Group Histories*
*Volume 2: Aerial Victory Lists • Ace Data*

# FIGHTER UNITS & PILOTS OF THE 8TH AIR FORCE

*September 1942 - May 1945*

## VOLUME 2
## Aerial Victories • Ace Data

Kent D. Miller

**Schiffer Military History**
Atglen, PA

**Dust jacket artwork by Steve Ferguson, Colorado Springs, CO.**

**BUD BY A HALF**
Shown is Capt. Walker "Bud" Mahurin leading his 63rd Fighter Squadron element down to strafe the landing field at Wesendorf, Germany on March 8, 1944. Two Focke-Wulf 190s and a Junkers Ju 88 were confirmed for him by his wingman after the mission, giving him 19 1/2 victories to date.

**Dedication**

These volumes are dedicated to my very patient and understanding wife, Hannah, and to my children, Evan and Jenna. Thank you for giving me the time to pursue my interest. They are also dedicated to all those who served in the 8th Air Force, and especially to those who paid the ultimate price for their country. God bless.

Kent D. Miller
Hicksville, Ohio
June 2000

Book design by Robert Biondi.


Library of Congress Catalog Number: 00-106806.



Printed in China.
ISBN: 0-7643-1242-1



Published by Schiffer Publishing Ltd.
4880 Lower Valley Road
Atglen, PA 19310
Phone: (610) 593-1777
FAX: (610) 593-2002
E-mail: Schifferbk@aol.com.
Visit our web site at: www.schifferbooks.com
Please write for a free catalog.
This book may be purchased from the publisher.
Please include $3.95 postage.
Try your bookstore first.

In Europe, Schiffer books are distributed by:
Bushwood Books
6 Marksbury Ave.
Kew Gardens
Surrey TW9 4JF
England
Phone: 44 (0)208 392-8585
FAX: 44 (0)208 392-9876
E-mail: Bushwd@aol.com.
Free postage in the UK. Europe: air mail at cost.
Try your bookstore first.

# Contents

# Introduction

The American 8th Air Force was the largest and most publicized organization in the Army Air Force during World War Two. Flying from bases in England for a little over three and a half years, the 8th's heavy bombers carried out a strategic bombing campaign against Germany. The fighter groups assigned to the 8th played a three part role: first and foremost was the escort and protection of the B-17's and B-24's; secondly, they were to hunt out and destroy the Luftwaffe, whether in aerial battles or by strafing German airfields; and thirdly, to act as a long-range striking arm against enemy transportation and defensive targets. While not as deeply involved in ground attacks as their counterparts in the 9th Air Force, the 8th's fighter pilots racked up an impressive score, with approximate claims of 4,374-2,979 locomotives, 6,970-24,971 railcars, 4,738-3,603 vehicles, 42-922 vessels (barges, tugs, ships, etc.), and 314-521 flak positions/towers. In addition, numerous other targets, including hangars, buildings, and bridges, were also destroyed or damaged.

Against the Luftwaffe, the 8th's pilots claimed 5160.6 aerial and 4108.75 ground victories, while total losses to all causes was 2,145 Spitfires, Thunderbolts, Lightnings, and Mustangs. A further 204 pilots were killed in accidents from the beginning of combat until the late summer of 1945. Not included in the latter number are the pilots who died while attached to the 495th and 496th Fighter Training Groups prior to being assigned to a combat unit.

The following volumes comprise a statistical summary of all fighter operations undertaken by the 8th Air Force's fighter units from September of 1942 through May of 1945. Not included are the units assigned to the 8th in mid-1942 which were eventually sent to North Africa with the 12th Air Force. While some sorties were flown and a few claims were made, the start of operations for this book begins with the formation of the 4th Fighter Group in September of 1942.

*Volume I* is a chronological listing of day-to-day operations with the following information for each date: groups involved, a short summary of the day's missions, air and ground claims, details of losses, strafing claims, pilots killed in accidents, and crash-landings, bail-outs, etc. Also, the beginning of Volume I has a number of tables covering the 8th's fighter operations. Of note is the scoring system used; 0-0-0 air is read as destroyed-probable-damaged while 0-0 ground is destroyed-damaged. Volume I also includes a breakdown of each group into individual mini-histories. Details include a short summary of the unit, Group and Squadron CO's, aircraft markings, a statistical history, scorers, list of day-to-day scoring and losses, pilot rosters, and representative aircraft.

*Volume II* is an alphabetical listing of all aerial victory scorers with their claims. Volume II also deals with all of the 8th Air Force aces. In addition to various tables and lists, each ace has his own section with information concerning combat career.

A great number of people, veterans and non-veterans alike, have helped me in putting this story together. They are listed here, in no particular order, with my sincerest thanks for their assistance. Unfortunately, a number of the veterans have passed away since their contribution and failed to see this end result. Again, thank you all: Frank Birtciel, Wilton Johnson, Clyde Taylor, Donald McGee, Joseph Myers, Frank McCauley, Randel Murphy, Harry Corey, Vernon Rafferty, Harold Comstock, Myron Becraft, George Butler, Robert Johnson, John McGinn, Fred Alexander, Sidney Hewett, Dale Karger, Charles Elmgren, Roy Evans, Edward Kier, Robert Winks, Walter Sharbo, Vic Byers, Ray Bank, Jack Ilfrey, Frank Emory, William Allen, Clifford Armstrong, Carroll Henry, Thomas Hayes, Wayne Blickenstaff, Leslie Smith, Ed Pogue, William Beyer, George Witzel, Arthur Jeffrey, Herb Rutland, Huie Lamb, Michael Yannell, John Truluck, Ken Hansen, James Carter, Richard Conner, Donald Henley, Russell Haworth, Vincent Zettler, Edward Kulik, Richard Peterson, Andrew Evans, William Jordan, John Kirk, David Thwaites, Lowell Einhaus, Richard Gibbs, Frank Gailer, Claude Chinn, Francis Harrington, Walter Cook, Richard Hewitt, Edwin Reinhardt, Ernest Hopcroft, William Wilkerson, Billy Edens, Horace Waggoner, Donald Baccus, Robert Wright, Clifford Ashby, Robert Hatter, Jack Price, Wallace Hopkins, George Doersch, Robert Wright, John Pugh, Jerome Nagel, Robert Schimanski, William Price, William Bailey, Ray Greenwood, Verne Hooker, Robert T. Green, William Tanner, Leedom John, Melville Hightshoe, Gerald Miller, Richard Davis, Ray Friend, John Taylor, Travis Greenwood, Norbert Fisher, George Sykes, Nelson Butler, Fred McClanahan, Joseph Fulton, Edward Beaumont, Roger Mooers, Jack Mengle, Max Victor, Lloyd Lamouria, Merle Olmsted, Robert Strobell, Jerry Brasher, Harvey Mace, Richard Thieme, Burton Newmark, Ray Shewfelt, Robert Unangst, Charles Whitefield, David James, Robert Cherry, Thaddeus Buszko, Peter Randall, James Heard, Don Olander, Richard J. Davis, Anthony Chardella, Robert Clark, Joseph DeShay, Vic Plassenthal, Amos Bomberger, Vernon Davis, Richard Shults, James Frolking, Clayborn Burleson, Avery Goodrich, Alvin Walther, Richard Ozinga, Reuben Curtis, James Seibert, Carl Tucker, Stephen Kefalas, John Earnest, Milford Hater, Harmon Wheeler, Robert Pinson, Robert Jensen, Millard Easton, Earl Storer, Irving Gittin, John Warner, George Roepke, Ray Hall, Robert Krull, Clyde Bergman, Leo Lester, Jenny Blue, Al Richards, Marc Hamel, James Reid, Mark Frailey, Ron Smith, Doug and Harold Daniel, Dave Raphael, Jack Johnston, Dave McCloskey, Mike Miller, James Underwood, Joe McGorry, Mrs. William J. Sykes, Mrs. Einar A. Malmstrom, Henry Selib, James Woolnough, David Knight, Melvin Jackson, Robert Foose, Tom Ivie, James Crow, Tom Frisque, Steve Knauff, William Hess, the USAF Museum, the USAF Historical Center, and the 8th Air Force Association. Finally, a very special thank you to Ted Damick, a friend and invaluable consultant on the 8th's fighter aircraft. To any others I have forgotten to mention, excuse me, but thank you for your help as well.

# PART THREE:
Aerial Victories

**Aal, Olger I., Lt.**
350th Ftr Sqn/353rd Ftr Grp

| *Sqn* | *Date* | *Claims* | *Location* | *A/C* |
|---|---|---|---|---|
| 350th | August 4, 1944 | Me-109 dest(air) | NE Hanover | P-47 |
| | August 29 | (2)Me-110 dest(grd) | Diest | P-47 |

1-0-0 air
2-0 ground

**Abbott, Earl L., Maj.**
328th Ftr Sqn/352nd Ftr Grp

| *Sqn* | *Date* | *Claims* | *Location* | *A/C* |
|---|---|---|---|---|
| 328th | January 29, 1944 | FW-190 dam(air) | Pelm | P-47 |
| | March 22 | (.25)FW-200 dest(air)* | Hesepe | P-47 |
| | April 29 | Me-109 dest(air) | Neuhaldenslaben | P-51 |
| | May 21 | u/i a/c dest(grd) | Alt Ruppin | P-51 |
| | | (2)u/i a/c dam(grd) | Alt Ruppin | P-51 |
| | May 29 | Me-109 dest(air) | Neubrandenburg | P-51 |
| | November 2 | (2)Me-109 dest(air) | Merseburg | P-51 |
| | November 21 | (.5)FW-190 dest(air)** | Merseburg | P-51 |

4.75-0-1 air
1-2 ground

* - shared with Lt. R.C. Brookins, Lt. J.F. Thornell, and Lt. E. Zellner of the 328th Ftr Sqn
** - shared with an unknown pilot

**Abel, Luther J., Lt.**
84th Ftr Sqn/78th Ftr Grp

| *Sqn* | *Date* | *Claims* | *Location* | *A/C* |
|---|---|---|---|---|
| 84th | February 5, 1944 | FW-190 dam(air) | Bernay | P-47 |
| | March 23 | Me-410 dest(grd) | Brussels | P-47 |
| | | (3)Me-410 dam(grd) | Brussels | P-47 |
| | March 30 | (.33)Do-217 dest(air)* | Twente/Enschede | P-47 |
| | June 10 | Me-109 dest(air) | La Ferte Mace | P-47 |

1.33-0-1 air
1-3 ground

* - shared with Lt. Q.L. Brown and Lt. E.S. Lang of the 84th Ftr Sqn

**Abel, Richard K., Lt.**
343rd Ftr Sqn/55th Ftr Grp

| *Sqn* | *Date* | *Claims* | *Location* | *A/C* |
|---|---|---|---|---|
| 343rd | April 9, 1945 | u/i a/c dest(grd) | Munich-Brunnthal | P-51 |

0-0-0 air
1-0 ground

**Abernathy, Robert B., Lt.**
82nd Ftr Sqn/78th Ftr Grp

| *Sqn* | *Date* | *Claims* | *Location* | *A/C* |
|---|---|---|---|---|
| 82nd | April 10, 1945 | Me-109 dest(grd) | Werder A/F | P-51 |
| | | Me-109 dam(grd) | Werder A/F | P-51 |
| | | u/i a/c dam(grd) | Werder A/F | P-51 |

0-0-0 air
1-2 ground

**Abernathy, Robert W., Capt.**
350th Ftr Sqn/353rd Ftr Grp

| *Sqn* | *Date* | *Claims* | *Location* | *A/C* |
|---|---|---|---|---|
| 350th | September 23, 1944 | Me-109 dest(air) | SE Arnheim | P-47 |
| | November 2 | Me-109 dest(air) | Merseburg | P-51 |
| | November 18 | (.5)u/i a/c dam(grd)* | Lechfeld | P-51 |
| | November 27 | FW-190 dam(air) | Brunswick | P-51 |
| | December 24 | (2)Me-109 dest(air) | Coblenz-Limburg | P-51 |
| | April 10, 1945 | Me-262 dest(air) | Dessau | P-51 |

5-0-1 air
0-0.5 ground

* - shared with Capt. W.J. Price of the 350th Ftr Sqn

**Achramowicz, Walter T., Lt.**
38th Ftr Sqn/55th Ftr Grp

| *Sqn* | *Date* | *Claims* | *Location* | *A/C* |
|---|---|---|---|---|
| 38th | April 9, 1945 | FW-190 dam(grd) | Munich-Brunnthal | P-51 |

0-0-0 air
0-1 ground

**Ackerly, Robert A., Maj.**
334th Ftr Sqn/4th Ftr Grp
335th Ftr Sqn/4th Ftr Grp
HdQts/4th Ftr Grp

| *Sqn* | *Date* | *Claims* | *Location* | *A/C* |
|---|---|---|---|---|
| HdQts | November 18, 1944 | Me-262 dest(grd) | Leipheim | P-51 |

0-0-0 air
1-0 ground

**Acosta, Argent J., Lt.**
383rd Ftr Sqn/364th Ftr Grp

| *Sqn* | *Date* | *Claims* | *Location* | *A/C* |
|---|---|---|---|---|
| 383rd | August 9, 1944 | u/i a/c dest(grd) | W/Munich | P-51 |
| | | u/i a/c dam(grd) | W/Munich | P-51 |
| | | Ju-88 dam(grd) | W/Munich | P-51 |
| | August 14 | (2)Me-410 dam(grd) | Memmingen | P-51 |
| | August 24 | Me-109 dest(air) | Seyda | P-51 |

1-0-0 air
1-4 ground

**Adamina, Robert E., Capt.**
82nd Ftr Sqn/78th Ftr Grp

| *Sqn* | *Date* | *Claims* | *Location* | *A/C* |
|---|---|---|---|---|
| 82nd | May 14, 1943 | FW-190 dest(air) | Antwerp | P-47 |

1-0-0 air
0-0 ground

**Adams, Charles W., Lt.**
360th Ftr Sqn/356th Ftr Grp

| *Sqn* | *Date* | *Claims* | *Location* | *A/C* |
|---|---|---|---|---|
| 360th | April 23, 1944 | (.5)Go-242 dam(grd)* | Hagenau | P-47 |
| | May 13 | FW-190 prob(air) | Kiel | P-47 |

0-1-0 air
0-0.5 ground

* - shared with Lt. R.C. L'Heureux of the 360th Ftr Sqn

**Adams, Donald E., Lt.**
343rd Ftr Sqn/55th Ftr Grp

| *Sqn* | *Date* | *Claims* | *Location* | *A/C* |
|---|---|---|---|---|
| 343rd | April 9, 1945 | Me-109 dest(grd) | Furtenfeld | P-51 |
| | | Me-410 dest(grd) | Munich-Brunnthal | P-51 |
| | | Me-109 dam(grd) | Furtenfeld | P-51 |
| | April 17 | Me-109 dam(grd) | Bautzen/Litten | P-51 |

0-0-0 air
2-2 ground

**Adams, Fletcher E., Capt.**
362nd Ftr Sqn/357th Ftr Grp

| *Sqn* | *Date* | *Claims* | *Location* | *A/C* |
|---|---|---|---|---|
| 362nd | February 22, 1944 | Me-109 dest(air) | NW Bernberg | P-51 |
| | March 18 | Me-109 dest(air) | NW Paris | P-51 |
| | April 11 | (2)Me-109 dest(air) | N/Magdeburg | P-51 |
| | April 24 | (3)Me-110 dest(air) | Munich | P-51 |
| | May 19 | (.5)Me-109 dest(air)* | Hagenow | P-51 |
| | May 27 | FW-190 dest(air) | N/Strasbourg | P-51 |
| | May 30 | (.5)Me-410 dest(air)** | W/Bernberg | P-51 |

9-0-0 air
0-0 ground

* - shared with Lt. A.J. Roberson of the 362nd Ftr Sqn
** - shared with Lt. G.M. O'Brien of the 362nd Ftr Sqn

**Adams, Louis W., Lt.**
77th Ftr Sqn/20th Ftr Grp

| Sqn | Date | Claims | Location | A/C |
|---|---|---|---|---|
| 77th | July 7, 1944 | Me-410 dest(air) | Oschersleben | P-38 |
| | | FW-190 dam(air) | Halle | P-38 |
| | July 29 | (2)Me-109 dest(air) | Gutersloh | P-51 |
| | August 16 | Me-109 dest(air) | Northeim | P-51 |
| | October 6 | Ar-196 dest(grd) | Bad Berg-Dievenow | P-51 |
| | | Do-18 dest(grd) | Bad Berg-Dievenow | P-51 |

4-0-1 air
2-0 ground

**Adams, Robert G., Lt.**
375th Ftr Sqn/361st Ftr Grp

| Sqn | Date | Claims | Location | A/C |
|---|---|---|---|---|
| 375th | November 26, 1944 | FW-190 dest(air) | Celle-Gifhorn | P-51 |
| | November 27 | Me-109 dam(air) | N/Munster | P-51 |

1-0-1 air
0-0 ground

**Adams, Thomas H., Capt.**
364th Ftr Sqn/357th Ftr Grp

| Sqn | Date | Claims | Location | A/C |
|---|---|---|---|---|
| 364th | December 5, 1944 | FW-190 dest(air) | NW Berlin | P-51 |
| | January 5, 1945 | (.5)FW-190 dest(air)* | N/Hanau | P-51 |
| | January 10 | Me-109 dest(air) | Paderborn A/F | P-51 |
| | | He-111 dest(grd) | Paderborn A/F | P-51 |
| | January 14 | (2)FW-190 dest(air) | Ludwigslust | P-51 |

4.5-0-0 air
1-0 ground

* - shared with Lt. I.E. Snedeker of the 364th Ftr Sqn

**Adkins, Boyd N., Lt.**
368th Ftr Sqn/359th Ftr Grp

| Sqn | Date | Claims | Location | A/C |
|---|---|---|---|---|
| 368th | October 24, 1944 | FW-190 dest(air) | Nordhausen | P-51 |
| | January 1, 1945 | FW-190 dest(air) | Havelburg | P-51 |

2-0-0 air
0-0 ground

**Adkins, Jesse O., Lt.**
374th Ftr Sqn/361st Ftr Grp

| Sqn | Date | Claims | Location | A/C |
|---|---|---|---|---|
| 374th | June 8, 1944 | Me-109 dest(air) | St. Pierre | P-51 |
| | July 25 | (.5)FW-190 dest(grd)* | N/Alencon | P-51 |
| | August 8 | FW-190 dam(air) | Evreux | P-51 |

1-0-1 air
0.5-0 ground

* - shared with Capt. R.E. Locke of the 374th Ftr Sqn

**Adrianse, Lyle A., Capt.**
63rd Ftr Sqn/56th Ftr Grp

| Sqn | Date | Claims | Location | A/C |
|---|---|---|---|---|
| 63rd | September 3, 1943 | FW-190 dest(air) | Romilly | P-47 |
| | November 5 | FW-190 dam(air) | Rheine-Munster | P-47 |
| | February 22, 1944 | Me-110 dest(air) | Raderborn | P-47 |

2-0-1 air
0-0 ground

**Aggers, William R., Lt.**
61st Ftr Sqn/56th Ftr Grp

| Sqn | Date | Claims | Location | A/C |
|---|---|---|---|---|
| 61st | December 11, 1943 | (.5)FW190 dest(air)* | Emden | P-47 |

0.5-0-0 air
0-0 ground

* - shared with Lt. D.F. Smith of the 61st Ftr Sqn

**Agnew, William M., Jr., Lt.**
350th Ftr Sqn/353rd Ftr Grp

| Sqn | Date | Claims | Location | A/C |
|---|---|---|---|---|
| 350th | March 2, 1945 | Me-109 prob(air) | Ruhland | P-51 |

0-1-0 air
0-0 ground

**Aheron, Frank R., Lt.**
62nd Ftr Sqn/56th Ftr Grp

| Sqn | Date | Claims | Location | A/C |
|---|---|---|---|---|
| 62nd | January 14, 1945 | Me-109 prob(air) | Magdeburg | P-47 |

0-1-0 air
0-0 ground

**Ahles, George N., Lt.**
351st Ftr Sqn/353rd Ftr Grp

| Sqn | Date | Claims | Location | A/C |
|---|---|---|---|---|
| 351st | June 8, 1944 | FW-190 dam(air) | Domfort | P-47 |

0-0-1 air
0-0 ground

**Aitken, John, Jr., Maj.**
504th Ftr Sqn/339th Ftr Grp
503rd Ftr Sqn/339th Ftr Grp
Earlier flew in the MTO with the 52nd Ftr Grp and claimed 1.5 kills; a Me-109 on April 7, 1943, and half a Ju-88 on April 9, 1943.

| Sqn | Date | Claims | Location | A/C |
|---|---|---|---|---|
| 503rd | August 5, 1944 | (2)FW-190 dest(air) | S/Hameln | P-51 |
| | September 11 | Me-109 dest(air) | Annaberg | P-51 |
| | | FW-190 dam(air) | Annaberg | P-51 |
| | September 13 | Ju-88 dest(grd) | Holzkirchen | P-51 |

3-0-1 air
1-0 ground

**Akard, Richard R., Lt.**
352nd Ftr Sqn/353rd Ftr Grp

| Sqn | Date | Claims | Location | A/C |
|---|---|---|---|---|
| 352nd | August 12, 1944 | FW-190 dest(grd) | S/Tournan | P-47 |

0-0-0 air
1-0 ground

**Alba, Michael, Lt.**
338th Ftr Sqn/55th Ftr Grp

| Sqn | Date | Claims | Location | A/C |
|---|---|---|---|---|
| 338th | September 12, 1944 | He-111 dest(grd) | Giessen | P-51 |
| | September 13 | Me-109 dest(air) | Eisenach-Gotha | P-51 |
| | November 2 | Me-109 dest(air) | Merseburg | P-51 |
| | | Me-109 dam(air) | Merseburg | P-51 |

2-0-1 air
1-0 ground

**Albert, Edgar J., Lt.**
351st Ftr Sqn/353rd Ftr Grp

| Sqn | Date | Claims | Location | A/C |
|---|---|---|---|---|
| 351st | September 23, 1943 | FW-190 dest(air) | S/Nantes | P-47 |

1-0-0 air
0-0 ground

**Albright, Clinton R., Lt.**
62nd Ftr Sqn/56th Ftr Grp

| Sqn | Date | Claims | Location | A/C |
|---|---|---|---|---|
| 62nd | April 10, 1945 | (.5)u/i a/c dest(grd)* | Muritz Lake | P-47 |
| | | Ju-88 dam(grd) | Muritz Lake | P-47 |

0-0-0 air
0.5-1 ground

* - shared with Lt. R.L. Garlich of the 355th Ftr Grp

**Albright, Edward M., Jr., Lt.**
63rd Ftr Sqn/56th Ftr Grp

| *Sqn* | *Date* | *Claims* | *Location* | *A/C* |
|---|---|---|---|---|
| 63rd | August 28, 1944 | He-111 dest(air) | N/Saarbrucken | P-47 |
| | September 5 | FW-190 dest(grd) | Gelnhausen | P-47 |
| | | Ju-52 dest(grd) | Gelnhausen | P-47 |
| | September 8 | u/i a/c dam(grd) | Euskirchen | P-47 |

1-0-0 air
2-1 ground

**Alcorn, Estel C., Lt.**
376th Ftr Sqn/361st Ftr Grp

| *Sqn* | *Date* | *Claims* | *Location* | *A/C* |
|---|---|---|---|---|
| 376th | February 25, 1944 | Me-109 dest(air) | Longuyon | P-47 |

1-0-0 air
0-0 ground

**Aldrich, Richard T., Lt.**
504th Ftr Sqn/339th Ftr Grp

| *Sqn* | *Date* | *Claims* | *Location* | *A/C* |
|---|---|---|---|---|
| 504th | April 16, 1945 | (2)Me-109 dest(grd) | Klatovy A/F | P-51 |
| | | (2)Me-109 dam(grd) | Klatovy A/F | P-51 |

0-0-0 air
2-2 ground

**Alexander, Arthur K., Lt.**
358th Ftr Sqn/355th Ftr Grp

| *Sqn* | *Date* | *Claims* | *Location* | *A/C* |
|---|---|---|---|---|
| 358th | December 5, 1944 | (1.5)FW-190 dest(air)* | Berlin | P-51 |

1.5-0-0 air
0-0 ground

* - shared with Maj. W.J. Hovde of the 358th Ftr Sqn

**Alexander, Fred H., Lt.**
77th Ftr Sqn/20th Ftr Grp

| *Sqn* | *Date* | *Claims* | *Location* | *A/C* |
|---|---|---|---|---|
| 77th | August 4, 1944 | He-111 dest(grd) | Putnitz | P-51 |
| | August 6 | (2)Me-109 dest(air) | Belzig | P-51 |
| | October 6 | (3)He-111 dest(grd) | Bad Berg-Dievenow | P-51 |
| | | He-115 dest(grd) | Bad Berg-Dievenow | P-51 |
| | | Do-18 dest(grd) | Bad Berg-Dievenow | P-51 |
| | | (2)He-111 dam(grd) | Bad Berg-Dievenow | P-51 |

2-0-0 air
6-2 ground

**Alfred, Carl R., Capt.**
336th Ftr Sqn/4th Ftr Grp

| *Sqn* | *Date* | *Claims* | *Location* | *A/C* |
|---|---|---|---|---|
| 336th | January 16, 1945 | (2)FW-190 dest(grd) | Neuhausen A/F | P-51 |
| | February 22 | Do-217 dest(grd) | Halberstadt | P-51 |
| | | Me-410 dest(grd) | Halberstadt | P-51 |
| | March 21 | (3)Do-217 dest(grd) | Achmer | P-51 |
| | | Do-217 dam(grd) | Achmer | P-51 |
| | | Me-109 dam(grd) | Achmer | P-51 |
| | April 16 | u/i a/c dest(grd) | Praha A/F | P-51 |
| | | u/i a/c dam(grd) | Praha A/F | P-51 |

0-0-0 air
8-3 ground

**Allen, Bernice A., Lt.**
503rd Ftr Sqn/339th Ftr Grp

| *Sqn* | *Date* | *Claims* | *Location* | *A/C* |
|---|---|---|---|---|
| 503rd | November 26, 1944 | FW-190 dam(air) | SE Dummer Lake | P-51 |
| | December 31 | FW-190 dest(air) | S/Hamburg | P-51 |

1-0-1 air
0-0 ground

**Allen, John T., Lt.**
61st Ftr Sqn/56th Ftr Grp

| *Sqn* | *Date* | *Claims* | *Location* | *A/C* |
|---|---|---|---|---|
| 61st | December 23, 1944 | FW-190 dam(air) | E/Bonn | P-47 |
| | April 13, 1945 | u/i a/c dam(grd) | Eggebeck A/F | P-47 |

0-0-1 air
0-1 ground

**Allen, Merle F., Lt.**
364th Ftr Sqn/357th Ftr Grp

| *Sqn* | *Date* | *Claims* | *Location* | *A/C* |
|---|---|---|---|---|
| 364th | June 20, 1944 | (.5)Fi-156 dest(air)* | Pasewalk | P-51 |
| | June 29 | (.5)Me-410 dest(air)** | NW Leipzig | P-51 |
| | | FW-190 dam(air) | SW Leipzig | P-51 |
| | September 13 | Me-109 dest(air) | E/Bad Frankenhausen | P-51 |

2-0-1 air
0-0 ground

* - shared with Lt. L.A. Fecher of the 364th Ftr Sqn
** - shared with LtCol. T.L. Hayes of HdQts, 357th Ftr Grp

**Allen, Raymond G., Lt.**
343rd Ftr Sqn/55th Ftr Grp

| *Sqn* | *Date* | *Claims* | *Location* | *A/C* |
|---|---|---|---|---|
| 343rd | April 9, 1945 | Me-410 dest(grd) | Munich-Brunnthal | P-51 |
| | April 16 | (.5)BV-140 dest(grd)* | Lake Chiem | P-51 |

0-0-0 air
1.5-0 ground

* - shared with Lt. L.D. Boring of the 343rd Ftr Sqn

**Allen, Robert K., Capt.**
384th Ftr Sqn/364th Ftr Grp

| *Sqn* | *Date* | *Claims* | *Location* | *A/C* |
|---|---|---|---|---|
| 384th | December 27, 1944 | (2.5)Me-109 dest(air)* | SW Coblenz | P-51 |
| | | FW-190 dam(air) | SW Coblenz | P-51 |
| | April 13, 1945 | (2)u/i a/c dest(grd) | Kaltenkirchen | P-51 |

2.5-0-1 air
2-0 ground

* - shared with Lt. W.S. Sagar of the 385th Ftr Sqn, 364th Ftr Grp

**Allen, Roscoe R., Lt.**
358th Ftr Sqn/355th Ftr Grp

| *Sqn* | *Date* | *Claims* | *Location* | *A/C* |
|---|---|---|---|---|
| 358th | January 15, 1945 | Me-110 dest(grd) | Landsberg A/F | P-51 |

0-0-0 air
1-0 ground

**Allen, William H., Lt.**
343rd Ftr Sqn/55th Ftr Grp

| *Sqn* | *Date* | *Claims* | *Location* | *A/C* |
|---|---|---|---|---|
| 343rd | September 5, 1944 | (5)Trainer dest(air) | N/Goppingen A/F | P-51 |

5-0-0 air
0-0 ground

**Allain, Leroy J., Jr., Lt.**
328th Ftr Sqn/352nd Ftr Grp

| *Sqn* | *Date* | *Claims* | *Location* | *A/C* |
|---|---|---|---|---|
| 328th | June 6, 1944 | (.5)FW-190 dest(air)* | SE Rouen | P-51 |

0.5-0-0 air
0-0 ground

* - shared with Lt. F.W. Horne of the 328th Ftr Sqn

**Allers, Lorne W., Lt.**
504th Ftr Sqn/339th Ftr Grp

| Sqn | Date | Claims | Location | A/C |
|---|---|---|---|---|
| 504th | December 31, 1944 | FW-190 dest(air) | Hamburg | P-51 |
| | April 10, 1945 | (2)Me-410 dest(grd) | N/Neuruppin | P-51 |
| | | Me-410 dam(grd) | N/Neuruppin | P-51 |
| | April 16 | Me-109 dest(grd) | Klatovy A/F | P-51 |
| | | (2)Me-109 dam(grd) | Klatovy A/F | P-51 |

1-0-0 air
3-3 ground

**Allinder, Thomas L., Lt.**
385th Ftr Sqn/364th Ftr Grp

| Sqn | Date | Claims | Location | A/C |
|---|---|---|---|---|
| 385th | November 26, 1944 | Me-109 prob(air) | Dummer Lake | P-51 |
| | December 31 | (.5)FW-190 dest(air)[*] | SW Hamburg | P-51 |

0.5-1-0 air
0-0 ground

[*] - shared with F/O C.L. Smart of the 385th Ftr Sqn

**Allison, Fred M., Capt.**
487th Ftr Sqn/352nd Ftr Grp

| Sqn | Date | Claims | Location | A/C |
|---|---|---|---|---|
| 487th | April 11, 1944 | Ju-88 dest(grd) | SW Berlin | P-51 |
| | | Ju-88 dam(grd) | SW Berlin | P-51 |
| | April 28 | He-111 dest(grd) | Bourges A/F | P-51 |
| | | u/i a/c dam(grd) | Bourges A/F | P-51 |
| | May 12 | (1.5)Me-109 dest(air)[*] | SE Coblenz | P-51 |
| | | Me-109 dam(grd) | SE Coblenz | P-51 |

1.5-0-0 air
2-3 ground

[*] - shared with Lt. R.K. Butler of the 487th Ftr Sqn

**Allison, Ralph T., Capt.**
350th Ftr Sqn/353rd Ftr Grp

| Sqn | Date | Claims | Location | A/C |
|---|---|---|---|---|
| 350th | August 28, 1944 | Me-410 dest(grd) | Wavre | P-47 |
| | September 21 | FW-190 prob(air) | SW Nijmegen | P-47 |

0-1-0 air
1-0 ground

**Allstaedt, Kenneth C., Lt.**
83rd Ftr Sqn/78th Ftr Grp

| Sqn | Date | Claims | Location | A/C |
|---|---|---|---|---|
| 83rd | April 10, 1944 | Trainer dest(grd) | Romorantin A/F | P-47 |
| | | FW-190 dest(grd) | Romorantin A/F | P-47 |
| | | Trainer dam(grd) | Romorantin A/F | P-47 |
| | April 25 | FW-190 dest(air) | S/Verdun | P-47 |
| | June 17 | (.5)FW-190 dest(air)[*] | Laigle | P-47 |

1.5-0-0 air
2-1 ground

[*] - shared with Lt. R.W. Oxley of the 83rd Ftr Sqn

**Alphonse, Louis G., Lt.**
359th Ftr Sqn/356th Ftr Grp

| Sqn | Date | Claims | Location | A/C |
|---|---|---|---|---|
| 359th | August 4, 1944 | Me-109 dest(air) | Selseingen-Ottersberg | P-47 |

1-0-0 air
0-0 ground

**Altschuler, Richard L., Capt.**
61st Ftr Sqn/56th Ftr Grp

| Sqn | Date | Claims | Location | A/C |
|---|---|---|---|---|
| 61st | February 11, 1944 | Me-110 dam(grd) | Rheims | P-47 |
| | February 20 | Me-110 dam(air) | Steinhuder Lake | P-47 |

0-0-1 air
0-1 ground

**Ambrose, Vincent W., Capt.**
370th Ftr Sqn/359th Ftr Grp

| Sqn | Date | Claims | Location | A/C |
|---|---|---|---|---|
| 370th | April 11, 1944 | Ju-88 dest(grd) | Gutersloh | P-47 |
| | June 10 | Me-109 dam(air) | Evreux | P-51 |

0-0-1 air
1-0 ground

**Ames, Kenneth, F/O**
352nd Ftr Sqn/353rd Ftr Grp

| Sqn | Date | Claims | Location | A/C |
|---|---|---|---|---|
| 352nd | August 1, 1944 | Me-410 dest(grd) | Laon/Couvron | P-47 |

0-0-0 air
1-0 ground

**Ammon, Robert H., Capt.**
503rd Ftr Sqn/339th Ftr Grp
504th Ftr Sqn/339th Ftr Grp
HdQts/339th Ftr Grp

| Sqn | Date | Claims | Location | A/C |
|---|---|---|---|---|
| 503rd | June 8, 1944 | FW-190 dest(air) | Fourges | P-51 |
| | | Me-109 dam(air) | Fourges | P-51 |
| | July 7 | Me-109 dam(air) | Leipzig | P-51 |
| | September 23 | (2)FW-190 dest(air) | SW Wesel | P-51 |
| | September 28 | (2)FW-190 dest(air) | SE Brunswick | P-51 |
| HdQts | April 16, 1945 | (4)Me-109 dest(grd) | NE Prague | P-51 |
| | | (3)Ju-88 dest(grd) | NE Prague | P-51 |
| | | FW-190 dest(grd) | NE Prague | P-51 |
| | | He-111 dest(grd) | NE Prague | P-51 |
| | | Ju-88 dam(grd) | NE Prague | P-51 |

5-0-2 air
9-1 ground

**Amoss, Dudley M., Lt.**
38th Ftr Sqn/55th Ftr Grp

| Sqn | Date | Claims | Location | A/C |
|---|---|---|---|---|
| 38th | September 12, 1944 | u/i a/c dest(grd) | Herzogenaurach | P-51 |
| | (.5)Ju-52 dest(grd)[*] | Herzogenaurach | P-51 | |
| | February 3, 1945 | (1.5)FW-58 dest(air)[**] | Templin | P-51 |
| | February 15 | Me-262 dest(air) | Amberg | P-51 |
| | March 21 | (3)FW-190 dest(air) | SW Munster | P-51 |

5.5-0-0 air
1.5-0 ground

[*] - shared with Lt. W.J. Reilly of the 38th Ftr Sqn
[**] - shared with Lt. L.F. Spiecker of the 38th Ftr Sqn

**Ananian, Stephen C., Lt.**
505th Ftr Sqn/339th Ftr Grp

| Sqn | Date | Claims | Location | A/C |
|---|---|---|---|---|
| 505th | February 9, 1945 | Me-262 dest(air) | Fulda | P-51 |
| | March 30 | Me-262 dam(air) | N/Luneburg | P-51 |
| | April 4 | Ju-88 dest(grd) | Tribsees | P-51 |
| | April 5 | Me-262 dam(air) | Boblingen | P-51 |

1-0-2 air
1-0 ground

**Andermatt, Eugene W., Lt.**
63rd Ftr Sqn/56th Ftr Grp

| Sqn | Date | Claims | Location | A/C |
|---|---|---|---|---|
| 63rd | October 12, 1944 | Me-109 prob(air) | Dummer Lake | P-47 |
| | April 10, 1945 | Me-262 dam(air) | Damm A/F | P-47 |

0-1-1 air
0-0 ground

**Anderson, Charles F., Capt.**
335th Ftr Sqn/4th Ftr Grp

| Sqn | Date | Claims | Location | A/C |
|---|---|---|---|---|
| 335th | January 30, 1944 | Me-109 dest(air) | Lingen | P-47 |
| | | Me-109 dam(air) | Lingen | P-47 |
| | February 10 | (.5)Me-109 prob(air)[*] | SW Hanover | P-47 |

| Sqn | Date | Claims | Location | A/C |
|---|---|---|---|---|
| | March 6 | Do-217 dest(air) | SE Brandenburg | P-51 |
| | March 21 | (1.5)FW-190 dest(air)[**] | N/Bordeaux | P-51 |
| | | (.5)FW-190 dest(grd)[**] | N/Bordeaux | P-51 |
| | | (.5)Ju-52 dest(grd)[**] | N/Bordeaux | P-51 |
| | March 27 | FW-190 dest(air) | W/Bordeaux | P-51 |
| | March 28 | u/i a/c dest(grd) | S/Dreux | P-51 |
| | March 29 | (2.5)FW-190 dest(air)[@] | Gifhorn | P-51 |
| | April 1 | Me-109 dam(air) | Antwerp | P-51 |
| | April 5 | (2)Si-204 dest(grd) | Brandenburg | P-51 |
| | April 8 | FW-190 dest(air) | Gifhorn | P-51 |
| | April 10 | (.5)Bu-131 dest(grd)[@@] | Romorantin A/F | P-51 |
| | April 12 | (2)Me-109 dest(air) | NW Brunswick | P-51 |
| | | Ju-88 dam(grd) | NW Brunswick | P-51 |
| | April 15 | He-177 dest(grd) | Hagenow | P-51 |
| | | He-177 dam(grd) | Hagenow | P-51 |

10-0.5-2 air
5.5-2 ground

[*] - shared with Lt. A.L. Schlegel of the 335th Ftr Sqn
[**] - all shared with Maj. G. Carpenter of the 335th Ftr Sqn
[@] - shared with an unknown pilot
[@@] - shared with an unknown pilot

**Anderson, Clarence E., Jr., Maj.**
363rd Ftr Sqn/357th Ftr Grp

| Sqn | Date | Claims | Location | A/C |
|---|---|---|---|---|
| 363rd | February 20, 1944 | Me-109 dam(air) | N/Dessau | P-51 |
| | March 8 | Me-109 dest(air) | NW Hanover | P-51 |
| | April 11 | Me-109 dest(air) | W/Hanover | P-51 |
| | | (.25)He-111 dest(air)[*] | W/Hanover | P-51 |
| | | Me-109 dam(air) | W/Hanover | P-51 |
| | April 30 | FW-190 dest(air) | SE Orleans | P-51 |
| | May 8 | FW-190 dest(air) | Soltau | P-51 |
| | May 12 | Me-109 dest(air) | NE Frankfurt | P-51 |
| | | Me-109 dest(grd) | NE Frankfurt | P-51 |
| | May 27 | (2)Me-109 dest(air) | N/Strasbourg | P-51 |
| | May 30 | Me-109 dest(air) | E/Schonebeck | P-51 |
| | June 29 | (3)FW-190 dest(air) | SW Leipzig | P-51 |
| | July 7 | Me-109 dest(air) | N/Leipzig | P-51 |
| | November 27 | (2)FW-190 dest(air) | Noyehauser A/F & Magdeburg | P-51 |
| | | FW-190 prob(air) | Magdeburg | P-51 |
| | December 5 | (2)FW-190 dest(air) | W/Berlin | P-51 |
| | | FW-190 prob(air) | W/Berlin | P-51 |

16.25-2-2 air
1-0 ground

[*] - shared with Lt. H.R. Kayser, Lt. E.K. Simpson, and Lt. C.K. Peters of the 363rd Ftr Sqn

**Anderson, Clifford, Lt.**
362nd Ftr Sqn/357th Ftr Grp

| Sqn | Date | Claims | Location | A/C |
|---|---|---|---|---|
| 362nd | August 18, 1944 | Me-109 dest(air) | NE Paris | P-51 |
| | November 27 | FW-190 dest(air) | S/Magdeburg | P-51 |

2-0-0 air
0-0 ground

**Anderson, Delynn E., Maj.**
79th Ftr Sqn/20th Ftr Grp

| Sqn | Date | Claims | Location | A/C |
|---|---|---|---|---|
| 79th | April 8, 1944 | (.2)He-177 dest(air)[*] | Salzwedel | P-38 |
| | | (2)He-177 dest(grd) | Salzwedel | P-38 |
| | May 24 | Me-109 dam(air) | Eberswalde | P-38 |

0.2-0-1 air
2-0 ground

[*] - shared with Maj. R.C. Franklin and Capt. R.P. Gatterdam of the 79th Ftr Sqn and Capt. E.C. Hedlund and Lt. R.H. Dettre of the 474th Ftr Grp, 9th Air Force (on D.S. to the 20th Ftr Grp)

**Anderson, Edward E., Lt.**
385th Ftr Sqn/364th Ftr Grp

| Sqn | Date | Claims | Location | A/C |
|---|---|---|---|---|
| 385th | April 17, 1945 | He-111 dest(grd) | Karlsbad | P-51 |
| | | He-111 dam(grd) | Karlsbad | P-51 |

0-0-0 air
1-1 ground

**Anderson, Edward W., Col.**
HdQts/4th Ftr Grp

| Sqn | Date | Claims | Location | A/C |
|---|---|---|---|---|
| HdQts | July 28, 1943 | (2)Me-109 dest(air) | E/Rotterdam | P-47 |

2-0-0 air
0-0 ground

**Anderson, Harry M., Lt.**
55th Ftr Sqn/20th Ftr Grp

| Sqn | Date | Claims | Location | A/C |
|---|---|---|---|---|
| 55th | August 25, 1944 | Ju-88 dest(grd) | Parow A/F | P-51 |

0-0-0 air
1-0 ground

**Anderson, John E., Lt.**
38th Ftr Sqn/55th Ftr Grp

| Sqn | Date | Claims | Location | A/C |
|---|---|---|---|---|
| 38th | April 16, 1945 | Do-217 dest(grd) | Munich-Brunnthal | P-51 |

0-0-0 air
1-0 ground

**Anderson, Lanoy D., Capt.**
338th Ftr Sqn/55th Ftr Grp

| Sqn | Date | Claims | Location | A/C |
|---|---|---|---|---|
| 338th | July 7, 1944 | (2)Me-109 dest(air) | Bernburg | P-38 |
| | August 10 | Me-109 dest(air) | Damville | P-51 |

3-0-0 air
0-0 ground

**Anderson, Millard O., Capt.**
38th Ftr Sqn/55th Ftr Grp

| Sqn | Date | Claims | Location | A/C |
|---|---|---|---|---|
| 38th | December 24, 1944 | Me-109 dest(air) | W/St. Vith | P-51 |
| | January 21, 1945 | (.5)u/i a/c dest(grd)[*] | Stuttgart/Boblingen | P-51 |
| | February 25 | Me-262 dest(air) | W/Giebelstadt | P-51 |
| | | FW-190 dest(grd) | Giebelstadt A/F | P-51 |
| | April 9 | u/i a/c dam(grd) | Munich-Brunnthal | P-51 |
| | April 10 | u/i a/c dest(grd) | Wesendorf | P-51 |

2-0-0 air
2.5-1 ground

[*] - shared with Lt. A.E. Carr of the 38th Ftr Sqn

**Anderson, Milton A., Lt.**
61st Ftr Sqn/56th Ftr Grp

| Sqn | Date | Claims | Location | A/C |
|---|---|---|---|---|
| 61st | May 14, 1943 | FW-190 dam(air) | NE Antwerp | P-47 |

0-0-1 air
0-0 ground

**Anderson, Richard B., Lt.**
63rd Ftr Sqn/56th Ftr Grp

| Sqn | Date | Claims | Location | A/C |
|---|---|---|---|---|
| 63rd | August 3, 1944 | FW-190 dest(air) | SW Sarreburg | P-47 |
| | September 5 | (2)Me-109 dest(air) | NE Coblenz | P-47 |
| | December 2 | Me-109 dest(air) | S/Marburg | P-47 |

4-0-0 air
0-0 ground

**Anderson, Richard D., Capt.**
375th Ftr Sqn/361st Ftr Grp

| Sqn | Date | Claims | Location | A/C |
|---|---|---|---|---|
| 375th | March 21, 1945 | Me-262 dest(air) | Belzig | P-51 |

1-0-0 air
0-0 ground

**Anderson, Robert H., Lt.**
82nd Ftr Sqn/78th Ftr Grp

| *Sqn* | *Date* | *Claims* | *Location* | *A/C* |
|---|---|---|---|---|
| 82nd | March 21, 1945 | Me-262 dest(air) | Giebelstadt | P-51 |

1-0-0 air
0-0 ground

**Anderson, Roy R., Lt.**
352nd Ftr Sqn/353rd Ftr Grp

| *Sqn* | *Date* | *Claims* | *Location* | *A/C* |
|---|---|---|---|---|
| 352nd | April 17, 1945 | Me-109 dam(grd) | Ganacker | P-51 |

0-0-0 air
0-1 ground

**Anderson, Russell J., Lt.**
335th Ftr Sqn/4th Ftr Grp

| *Sqn* | *Date* | *Claims* | *Location* | *A/C* |
|---|---|---|---|---|
| 335th | September 27, 1944 | FW-190 dam(air) | S/Kassel | P-51 |

0-0-1 air
0-0 ground

**Anderson, Stanley M., Capt.**
334th Ftr Sqn/4th Ftr Grp

| *Sqn* | *Date* | *Claims* | *Location* | *A/C* |
|---|---|---|---|---|
| 334th | October 2, 1942 | FW-190 dest(air) | SW Dunkirk | Spit |
| | December 15 | (.5)Ju-52 prob(air)* | SW Flushing | Spit |
| | January 14, 1943 | FW-190 dest(air) | W/Ostend | Spit |
| | January 22 | FW-190 dest(air) | W/Dunkirk | Spit |

3-0.5-0 air
0-0 ground

* - shared with Lt. R.O. Boock of the 334th Ftr Sqn

**Anderson, William C., Capt.**
335th Ftr Sqn/ 4th Ftr Grp
436th Ftr Sqn/479th Ftr Grp

| *Sqn* | *Date* | *Claims* | *Location* | *A/C* |
|---|---|---|---|---|
| 335th | November 18, 1944 | Me-262 dest(grd) | Leipheim | P-51 |
| | | Me-262 dam(grd) | Leipheim | P-51 |
| 436th | February 22, 1945 | He-111 dest(grd) | Halberstadt | P-51 |

0-0-0 air
2-1 ground

**Anderson, Woodrow W., Capt.**
486th Ftr Sqn/352nd Ftr Grp

| *Sqn* | *Date* | *Claims* | *Location* | *A/C* |
|---|---|---|---|---|
| 486th | April 11, 1944 | (.5)Ju-52 dest(air)* | W/Torgau | P-51 |
| | | Ju-88 dest(grd) | Lonnewitz | P-51 |
| | | Ju-88 dam(grd) | Lonnewitz | P-51 |
| | April 13 | Hs-123 dest(grd) | S/Stuttgart | P-51 |
| | April 24 | (2)Ju-88 dest(grd) | Ingolstadt | P-51 |
| | | Do-217 dest(grd) | Ingolstadt | P-51 |
| | | He-111 dest(grd) | Neuburg | P-51 |
| | April 30 | FW-190 dest(air) | Clermont-Ferrand | P-51 |
| | | (2)Me-110 dest(grd) | Clermont-Ferrand | P-51 |
| | May 13 | Me-109 dest(air) | Tribsees | P-51 |
| | | u/i a/c dest(grd) | Wangerooge | P-51 |
| | May 24 | Me-109 dest(air) | NW Berlin | P-51 |
| | May 28 | Me-109 dest(air) | Dessau | P-51 |

4.5-0-0 air
9-1 ground

* - shared with Lt. F.A. Cutler of the 486th Ftr Sqn

**Anderz, Tadeusz, Capt.**
61st Ftr Sqn/56th Ftr Grp

| *Sqn* | *Date* | *Claims* | *Location* | *A/C* |
|---|---|---|---|---|
| 61st | April 9, 1944 | Me-109 dest(air) | SE Kiel | P-47 |

1-0-0 air
0-0 ground

**Andrew, Lowell V., Capt.**
383rd Ftr Sqn/364th Ftr Grp

| *Sqn* | *Date* | *Claims* | *Location* | *A/C* |
|---|---|---|---|---|
| 383rd | February 3, 1945 | Me-262 dam(air) | S/Gardelegen | P-51 |
| | March 21 | Me-109 dam(grd) | Achmer | P-51 |
| | | Ju-88 dam(grd) | Achmer | P-51 |
| | April 16 | Me-410 dest(grd) | Marienbad | P-51 |

0-0-1 air
1-2 ground

**Andrew, Stephen W., Maj.**
486th Ftr Sqn/352nd Ftr Grp
Earlier flew in the PTO with the 49th Ftr Grp and claimed one kill, a Zero on April 27, 1942.

| *Sqn* | *Date* | *Claims* | *Location* | *A/C* |
|---|---|---|---|---|
| 486th | March 15, 1944 | Me-109 dest(air) | Aldensaal | P-47 |
| | April 11 | Ju-88 dest(grd) | Finsterwalde | P-51 |
| | | Ju-86 dest(grd) | Finsterwalde | P-51 |
| | April 13 | (.5)He-111 dest(grd)* | S/Stuttgart | P-51 |
| | April 20 | Me-109 dest(air) | E/Paris | P-51 |
| | April 24 | u/i a/c dest(grd) | Neuburg | P-51 |
| | | Ju-88 dam(grd) | Ingolstadt | P-51 |
| | April 25 | Ju-88 dest(grd) | Metz | P-51 |
| | April 28 | FW-200 dest(grd) | Chateaudun | P-51 |
| | April 30 | FW-190 dest(air) | Clermont | P-51 |
| | May 8 | FW-190 dest(air) | NE Hanover | P-51 |
| | May 12 | FW-190 dest(air) | Gotha | P-51 |
| | May 19 | Me-109 dest(air) | Rathenow | P-51 |
| | May 28 | Me-109 dest(air) | NE Dessau | P-51 |
| | May 30 | FW-190 dest(air) | Magdeburg | P-51 |
| | June 8 | FW-190 dam(grd) | Le Mans | P-51 |
| | June 20 | Ju-52 dest(grd) | Burg A/F | P-51 |

9-0-0 air
6.5-2 ground

* - shared with Lt. M.H. Cunningham of the 486th Ftr Sqn

**Andrews, Thomas J., Maj.**
334th Ftr Sqn/4th Ftr Grp

| *Sqn* | *Date* | *Claims* | *Location* | *A/C* |
|---|---|---|---|---|
| 334th | May 18, 1943 | Me-109 dest(air) | Blankenberge-Knocke | P-47 |

1-0-0 air
0-0 ground

**Ankeny, Harry R., Capt.**
362nd Ftr Sqn/357th Ftr Grp

| *Sqn* | *Date* | *Claims* | *Location* | *A/C* |
|---|---|---|---|---|
| 362nd | April 8, 1944 | Me-109 dest(air) | W/Brunswick | P-51 |
| | April 11 | (.5)Me-109 dest(air)* | NE Magdeburg | P-51 |
| | May 21 | Me-110 dam(grd) | Tarnewitz | P-51 |

1.5-0-0 air
0-1 ground

* - shared with Lt. J.B. England of the 362nd Ftr Sqn

**Antonides, William O., Lt.**
334th Ftr Sqn/4th Ftr Grp

| *Sqn* | *Date* | *Claims* | *Location* | *A/C* |
|---|---|---|---|---|
| 334th | February 27, 1945 | (2)Ju-88 dest(grd) | Weimar | P-51 |
| | March 22 | (2)FW-190 dam(air) | Eggersdorf A/F | P-51 |
| | April 16 | (2)Me-109 dest(grd) | Gablingen | P-51 |
| | | FW-190 dest(grd) | Gablingen | P-51 |
| | | Me-410 dest(grd) | Gablingen | P-51 |
| | | u/i a/c dest(grd) | Gablingen | P-51 |
| | | u/i a/c dam(grd) | Gablingen | P-51 |

0-0-2 air
7-1 ground

**Apple, George A., Lt.**
343rd Ftr Sqn/55th Ftr Grp

| *Sqn* | *Date* | *Claims* | *Location* | *A/C* |
|---|---|---|---|---|
| 343rd | April 9, 1945 | Me-109 dest(grd) | Munich-Brunnthal | P-51 |
| | | Me-410 dam(grd) | Munich-Brunnthal | P-51 |
| | April 16 | FW-190 dest(grd) | Ainring A/F | P-51 |
| | April 17 | FW-190 dest(grd) | Dresden | P-51 |

| Sqn | Date | Claims | Location | A/C |
|---|---|---|---|---|
| | | Ju-88 dest(grd) | Dresden | P-51 |

0-0-0 air
4-1 ground

**Aranyos, John A., Lt.**
63rd Ftr Sqn/56th Ftr Grp

| Sqn | Date | Claims | Location | A/C |
|---|---|---|---|---|
| 63rd | April 24, 1944 | Do-217 dest(grd) | Thalheim A/F | P-47 |
| | | Me-109 dest(grd) | Thalheim A/F | P-47 |
| | | Do-217 dam(grd) | Thalheim A/F | P-47 |
| | | Me-210 dam(grd) | Thalheim A/F | P-47 |

0-0-0 air
2-2 ground

**Archibald, David B., Lt.**
368th Ftr Sqn/359th Ftr Grp

| Sqn | Date | Claims | Location | A/C |
|---|---|---|---|---|
| 368th | August 25, 1944 | u/i a/c dest(grd) | Gustrow | P-51 |

0-0-0 air
1-0 ground

**Archibald, John M., Lt.**
436th Ftr Sqn/479th Ftr Grp

| Sqn | Date | Claims | Location | A/C |
|---|---|---|---|---|
| 436th | April 13, 1945 | FW-190 dest(grd) | Salzwedel | P-51 |
| | Me-110 dam(grd) | Salzwedel | P-51 | |

0-0-0 air
1-1 ground

**Ard, John M., Lt.**
350th Ftr Sqn/353rd Ftr Grp

| Sqn | Date | Claims | Location | A/C |
|---|---|---|---|---|
| 350th | November 10, 1944 | Bu-133 dest(grd) | Fulda | P-51 |

0-0-0 air
1-0 ground

**Armsby, Sherman, Lt.**
375th Ftr Sqn/361st Ftr Grp

| Sqn | Date | Claims | Location | A/C |
|---|---|---|---|---|
| 375th | June 20, 1944 | (.5)BV-138 dam(grd)[*] | Putnitz | P-51 |
| | | (.5)glider dam(grd)[*] | Putnitz | P-51 |
| | June 29 | (.5)Me-109 dest(air)[**] | SW Kothen | P-51 |
| | July 20 | (3)Me-109 dest(air) | N/Leipzig | P-51 |
| | August 5 | Me-109 dest(air) | N/Nienburg | P-51 |
| | August 15 | u/i a/c dest(grd) | Wittmunhafen | P-51 |
| | | (2)Me-110 dam(grd) | Wittmunhafen | P-51 |

4.5-0-0 air
1-3 ground

* - both shared with Lt. J.T. Thomas of the 375th Ftr Sqn
** - shared with Lt. R.C. Wright of the 375th Ftr Sqn

**Armstrong, Clifford F., Lt.**
352nd Ftr Sqn/353rd Ftr Grp

| Sqn | Date | Claims | Location | A/C |
|---|---|---|---|---|
| 352nd | February 8, 1944 | FW-190 dest(air) | St. Hubert | P-47 |
| | February 10 | Me-109 dest(air) | Lingen | P-47 |
| | June 8 | (1.5)FW-190 dest(grd)[*] | Angars | P-47 |
| | | (.5)Ju-52 dest(grd)[**] | Angars | P-47 |
| | June 10 | FW-190 dest(air) | SW Nantes/Gassicourt | P-47 |

3-0-0 air
2-0 ground

* - shared with Lt. H.Q. Waggoner of the 352nd Ftr Sqn
** - shared with Lt. H.O. Miller of the 352nd Ftr Sqn

**Armstrong, John L., Lt.**
79th Ftr Sqn/20th Ftr Grp

| Sqn | Date | Claims | Location | A/C |
|---|---|---|---|---|
| 79th | August 9, 1944 | FW-190 dam(air) | SW Ulm | P-51 |

0-0-1 air
0-0 ground

**Arnold, Guy E., Lt.**
343rd Ftr Sqn/55th Ftr Grp

| Sqn | Date | Claims | Location | A/C |
|---|---|---|---|---|
| 343rd | April 9, 1945 | Me-262 dest(grd) | Munich-Brunnthal | P-51 |
| | | Me-410 dest(grd) | Munich-Brunnthal | P-51 |
| | April 16 | Me-410 dam(grd) | Munich-Brunnthal | P-51 |
| | April 17 | (2)Fi-156 dest(grd) | Bautzen/Litten | P-51 |

0-0-0 air
4-1 ground

**Arnold, John A., Lt.**
63rd Ftr Sqn/56th Ftr Grp

| Sqn | Date | Claims | Location | A/C |
|---|---|---|---|---|
| 63rd | April 10, 1945 | FW-190 dest(grd) | Stendal | P-47 |
| | April 13 | u/i a/c dest(grd) | Eggebeck A/F | P-47 |
| | | He-111 dam(grd) | Eggebeck A/F | P-47 |
| | | u/i a/c dam(grd) | Eggebeck A/F | P-47 |

0-0-0 air
2-2 ground

**Arnold, Merlin A., Lt.**
504th Ftr Sqn/339th Ftr Grp
351st Ftr Sqn/353rd Ftr Grp

| Sqn | Date | Claims | Location | A/C |
|---|---|---|---|---|
| 351st | January 14, 1945 | (.5)Me-262 dam(air)[*] | E/Hanover | P-51 |

0-0-0.5 air
0-0 ground

* - shared with Lt. G.E. Markham of the 351st Ftr Sqn

**Arrendale, Harold E., Lt.**
364th Ftr Sqn/357th Ftr Grp

| Sqn | Date | Claims | Location | A/C |
|---|---|---|---|---|
| 364th | April 10, 1945 | Ju-88 dam(grd) | Neuruppin | P-51 |

0-0-0 air
0-1 ground

**Arthaud, Charles C., Lt.**
77th Ftr Sqn/20th Ftr Grp

| Sqn | Date | Claims | Location | A/C |
|---|---|---|---|---|
| 77th | February 20, 1944 | (.5)Me-109 dest(air)[*] | Brunswick | P-38 |
| | July 14 | (.5)FW-190 dest(air)[**] | SW Reims | P-38 |
| | August 16 | FW-190 dest(air) | Eisenach | P-51 |

2-0-0 air
0-0 ground

* - shared with Lt. T.M. Williams of the 77th Ftr Sqn
** - shared with Lt. E.C. Fiebelkorn of the 77th Ftr Sqn

**Arthur, Marvin W., Lt.**
334th Ftr Sqn/4th Ftr Grp

| Sqn | Date | Claims | Location | A/C |
|---|---|---|---|---|
| 334th | April 16, 1945 | Me-109 dest(grd) | Gablingen | P-51 |
| | | (.5)FW-190 dest(grd)[*] | Gablingen | P-51 |

0-0-0 air
1.5-0 ground

* - shared with Lt. M.L. Spencer of the 334th Ftr Sqn

**Ashby, Clifford T., Lt.**
361st Ftr Sqn/356th Ftr Grp

| Sqn | Date | Claims | Location | A/C |
|---|---|---|---|---|
| 361st | November 25, 1944 | (2)FW-190 dest(grd) | Zwickau | P-51 |
| | | FW-190 dam(grd) | Zwickau | P-51 |

| Sqn | Date | Claims | Location | A/C |
|---|---|---|---|---|
| | December 5 | FW-190 dest(air) | Eberswalde | P-51 |
| | | FW-190 prob(air) | Eberswalde | P-51 |
| | January 14, 1945 | (2.5)FW-190 dest(air)* | SW Dummer Lake | P-51 |

3.5-1-0 air
2-1 ground

* - shared with Lt. W.M. Baskin of the 361st Ftr Sqn

**Ashenmacher, Joseph M., Lt.**
368th Ftr Sqn/359th Ftr Grp

| *Sqn* | *Date* | *Claims* | *Location* | *A/C* |
|---|---|---|---|---|
| 368th | September 8, 1944 | Ju-52 dest(grd) | Cronberg | P-51 |
| | | Ju-52 dam(grd) | Cronberg | P-51 |

0-0-0 air
1-1 ground

**Askelson, Howard S., Capt.**
83rd Ftr Sqn/78th Ftr Grp

| *Sqn* | *Date* | *Claims* | *Location* | *A/C* |
|---|---|---|---|---|
| 83rd | June 22, 1943 | FW-190 dest(air) | Walcheren Island | P-47 |
| | November 26 | Me-109 dest(air) | Paris | P-47 |

2-0-0 air
0-0 ground

**Asper, Harold E., Lt.**
350th Ftr Sqn/353rd Ftr Grp

| *Sqn* | *Date* | *Claims* | *Location* | *A/C* |
|---|---|---|---|---|
| 350th | August 24, 1944 | Me-109 dest(air) | S/Hanover | P-47 |
| | September 23 | FW-190 dest(air) | SE Arnheim | P-47 |

2-0-0 air
0-0 ground

**Attebury, Raymond N., Lt.**
504th Ftr Sqn/339th Ftr Grp

| *Sqn* | *Date* | *Claims* | *Location* | *A/C* |
|---|---|---|---|---|
| 504th | June 7, 1944 | FW-190 dest(air) | Laval | P-51 |
| | | FW-190 dest(grd) | Laval | P-51 |
| | July 29 | FW-190 dest(air) | Naumberg | P-51 |

2-0-0 air
1-0 ground

**Auchincloss, Bayard C., Lt.**
350th Ftr Sqn/353rd Ftr Grp

| *Sqn* | *Date* | *Claims* | *Location* | *A/C* |
|---|---|---|---|---|
| 350th | July 9, 1944 | Me-109 dam(air) | E/Evreux | P-47 |
| | August 24 | Me-109 dest(air) | S/Hanover | P-47 |
| | August 27 | (1.5)FW-190 dest(grd)* | Verdun | P-47 |
| | | FW-190 dam(grd) | Verdun | P-47 |
| | September 21 | FW-190 dam(air) | SE Arnheim | P-47 |
| | September 23 | FW-190 dest(air) | SE Arnheim | P-47 |
| | | Me-109 dest(air) | SE Arnheim | P-47 |
| | | FW-190 prob(air) | SE Arnheim | P-47 |

3-1-2 air
1.5-1 ground

* - shared with Lt. J.L. Schilt of the 350th Ftr Sqn

**Auguste, Robert A., Lt.**
385th Ftr Sqn/364th Ftr Grp

| *Sqn* | *Date* | *Claims* | *Location* | *A/C* |
|---|---|---|---|---|
| 385th | November 26, 1944 | Ju-88 dest(grd) | SE Jade Bay | P-51 |

0-0-0 air
1-0 ground

**Austin, James P., Capt.**
354th Ftr Sqn/355th Ftr Grp

| *Sqn* | *Date* | *Claims* | *Location* | *A/C* |
|---|---|---|---|---|
| 354th | April 10, 1944 | Me-109 dest(grd) | Bourges | P-51 |
| | | u/i a/c dam(grd) | Bourges | P-51 |
| | April 11 | u/i a/c dam(grd) | Pyritz A/F | P-51 |

0-0-0 air
1-2 ground

**Ayer, William H., Lt.**
336th Ftr Sqn/4th Ftr Grp

| *Sqn* | *Date* | *Claims* | *Location* | *A/C* |
|---|---|---|---|---|
| 336th | April 16, 1945 | (2)u/i a/c dest(grd) | Praha A/F | P-51 |

0-0-0 air
2-0 ground

**Ayers, James W., Lt.**
334th Ftr Sqn/4th Ftr Grp

| *Sqn* | *Date* | *Claims* | *Location* | *A/C* |
|---|---|---|---|---|
| 334th | January 16, 1945 | (.5)He-177 dest(grd)* | Neuburg A/F | P-51 |
| | February 27 | (3)u/i a/c dest(grd) | Weimar | P-51 |
| | | (.5)Ju-52 dest(grd)** | Weimar | P-51 |
| | April 7 | Me-109 dest(air) | NE Duneberg | P-51 |
| | April 16 | Me-109 dest(grd) | Gablingen | P-51 |
| | | FW-190 dest(grd) | Gablingen | P-51 |
| | | u/i a/c dest(grd) | Gablingen | P-51 |

1-0-0 air
7-0 ground

* - shared with Lt. M.J. Kennedy of the 334th Ftr Sqn
** - shared with Lt. R.S. Voyles of the 334th Ftr Sqn

**Ayers, Jerry H., Capt.**
38th Ftr Sqn/55th Ftr Grp

| *Sqn* | *Date* | *Claims* | *Location* | *A/C* |
|---|---|---|---|---|
| 38th | November 5, 1943 | Do-217 prob(air) | W/Munster | P-38 |
| | November 29 | Me-109 dest(air) | W/Bremen | P-38 |

1-1-0 air
0-0 ground

**Ayers, Joseph B., Lt.**
487th Ftr Sqn/352nd Ftr Grp

| *Sqn* | *Date* | *Claims* | *Location* | *A/C* |
|---|---|---|---|---|
| 487th | September 10, 1944 | Ju-52 dest(grd) | Wortheim | P-51 |
| | | u/i a/c dest(grd) | Wortheim | P-51 |

0-0-0 air
2-0 ground

**Ayoub, Lee S., Capt.**
383rd Ftr Sqn/364th Ftr Grp

| *Sqn* | *Date* | *Claims* | *Location* | *A/C* |
|---|---|---|---|---|
| 383rd | April 15, 1944 | (.5)Me-109 dest(air)* | SE Bremen | P-38 |
| | May 25 | FW-190 dest(air) | Paris | P-38 |

1.5-0-0 air
0-0 ground

* - shared with Maj. G.F. Ceuleers of the 383rd Ftr Sqn

**Baccus, Donald A., LtCol.**
359th Ftr Sqn/356th Ftr Grp
HdQts/356th Ftr Grp
HdQts/359th Ftr Grp

| *Sqn* | *Date* | *Claims* | *Location* | *A/C* |
|---|---|---|---|---|
| 359th | November 29, 1943 | Me-109 dest(air) | NE Meppel | P-47 |
| | December 30 | FW-190 dam(air) | SE Menahould | P-47 |
| | January 11, 1944 | (.5)Me-110 dest(air)* | Steinhuder Lake | P-47 |
| | March 18 | (.25)Do-217 dam(grd)** | W/Nancy | P-47 |
| | April 1 | Me-410 dest(grd) | Dummer Lake | P-47 |
| HdQts | May 13 | (.5)FW-190 dest(air)@ | Kiel-Lubeck | P-47 |
| | | FW-190 dam(air) | Kiel-Lubeck | P-47 |
| | June 7 | Me-323 dest(grd) | Laval | P-47 |
| | July 27 | He-111 dest(grd) | Cormeilles-en-Vixen | P-47 |
| | November 26 | (2)Me-109 dest(air) | Dummer Lake | P-51 |
| | December 25 | Me-109 dest(air) | Bonn | P-51 |
| HdQts (359th) | April 17, 1945 | u/i a/c dest(grd) | Ganacker-Plattling | P-51 |
| | | Me-109 dam(grd) | Ganacker-Plattling | P-51 |

5-0-2 air
4-1.25 ground

[*] - shared with Lt. J.H. Wadlow of the 359th Ftr Sqn
[**] - shared with Lt. R.K. Holtz, Lt. W.C. O'Barr, and Lt. G.B. Peet of the 359th Ftr Sqn
[@] - shared with Lt. R.A. Coughenour of the 359th Ftr Sqn

**Bach, Glenn C., Capt.**
368th Ftr Sqn/359th Ftr Grp
369th Ftr Sqn/359th Ftr Grp

| *Sqn* | *Date* | *Claims* | *Location* | *A/C* |
|---|---|---|---|---|
| 368th | May 21, 1944 | (2)FW-190 dest(grd) | N/Grevesmuhlen | P-51 |
| | | (4)u/i a/c dam(grd) | N/Grevesmuhlen | P-51 |

0-0-0 air
2-4 ground

**Bachman, Darrell D., Lt.**
38th Ftr Sqn/55th Ftr Grp

| *Sqn* | *Date* | *Claims* | *Location* | *A/C* |
|---|---|---|---|---|
| 38th | April 9, 1945 | Me-262 dest(grd) | Munich-Brunnthal | P-51 |
| | | He-111 dam(grd) | Munich-Brunnthal | P-51 |
| | April 10 | Me-262 dam(air) | Galworde | P-51 |

0-0-1 air
1-1 ground

**Badger, James B., Lt.**
362nd Ftr Sqn/357th Ftr Grp

| *Sqn* | *Date* | *Claims* | *Location* | *A/C* |
|---|---|---|---|---|
| 362nd | May 27, 1944 | Me-109 dam(air) | N/Strasbourg | P-51 |

0-0-1 air
0-0 ground

**Bailey, Robert E., Lt.**
63rd Ftr Sqn/56th Ftr Grp

| *Sqn* | *Date* | *Claims* | *Location* | *A/C* |
|---|---|---|---|---|
| 63rd | April 13, 1945 | (2)Me-110 dest(grd) | Eggebeck A/F | P-47 |
| | | (2)Me-110 dam(grd) | Eggebeck A/F | P-47 |

0-0-0 air
2-2 ground

**Bailey, Thomas F., Capt.**
361st Ftr Sqn/356th Ftr Grp

| *Sqn* | *Date* | *Claims* | *Location* | *A/C* |
|---|---|---|---|---|
| 361st | January 5, 1944 | FW-190 prob(air) | S/Liege | P-47 |
| | May 13 | FW-190 dest(air) | Schwerin | P-47 |

1-1-0 air
0-0 ground

**Bailey, William B., LtCol.**
352nd Ftr Sqn/353rd Ftr Grp
HdQts/353rd Ftr Grp

| *Sqn* | *Date* | *Claims* | *Location* | *A/C* |
|---|---|---|---|---|
| 352nd | October 14, 1943 | Me-109 dest(air) | Eecloo | P-47 |
| HdQts | August 4, 1944 | (2)He-111 dest(grd) | Plantlunne | P-47 |
| | | Ju-88 dest(grd) | Plantlunne | P-47 |
| | March 2, 1945 | (2)FW-190 dest(air) | S/Wittenberg | P-51 |

3-0-0 air
3-0 ground

**Bain, Charles F., Lt.**
55th Ftr Sqn/20th Ftr Grp

| *Sqn* | *Date* | *Claims* | *Location* | *A/C* |
|---|---|---|---|---|
| 55th | August 25, 1944 | Ju-88 dest(grd) | Parow A/F | P-51 |
| | | Ju-88 dam(grd) | Parow A/F | P-51 |

0-0-0 air
1-1 ground

**Bain, Robert J., Lt.**
376th Ftr Sqn/361st Ftr Grp

| *Sqn* | *Date* | *Claims* | *Location* | *A/C* |
|---|---|---|---|---|
| 376th | September 27, 1944 | (2)FW-190 dam(air) | Eisenach | P-51 |
| | | Me-109 dam(air) | Eisenach | P-51 |

0-0-3 air
0-0 ground

**Baird, Robert J., Lt.**
435th Ftr Sqn/479th Ftr Grp

| *Sqn* | *Date* | *Claims* | *Location* | *A/C* |
|---|---|---|---|---|
| 435th | April 17, 1945 | Me-262 dest(grd) | Puchhoff | P-51 |

0-0-0 air
1-0 ground

**Baker, George F., Capt.**
368th Ftr Sqn/359th Ftr Grp

| *Sqn* | *Date* | *Claims* | *Location* | *A/C* |
|---|---|---|---|---|
| 368th | September 8, 1944 | (.5)Ju-52 dest(grd)[*] | Cronberg | P-51 |
| | September 11 | (2)FW-190 dest(air) | Halberstadt | P-51 |
| | November 2 | (.5)Me-109 dest(air)[**] | Quedlinburg | P-51 |
| | | Me-109 dam(air) | Quedlinburg | P-51 |
| | December 31 | (2)FW-190 dest(air) | SE Stade | P-51 |

4.5-0-1 air
0.5-0 ground

[*] - shared with Lt. R.E. Benefiel of the 368th Ftr Sqn
[**] - shared with Lt. O.R. Fladmark of the 368th Ftr Sqn

**Baker, Gordon E., Maj.**
62nd Ftr Sqn/56th Ftr Grp
61st Ftr Sqn/56th Ftr Grp

| *Sqn* | *Date* | *Claims* | *Location* | *A/C* |
|---|---|---|---|---|
| 62nd | July 4, 1944 | Me-109 dest(air) | Conches | P-47 |
| | | Me-109 dam(air) | Conches | P-47 |
| 61st | August 4 | (.5)u/i a/c dest(grd)[*] | Salenter Lake | P-47 |
| | August 28 | Ju-88 dest(grd) | Wach | P-47 |
| | September 8 | u/i a/c dest(grd) | Euskirchen | P-47 |

1-0-1 air
2.5-0 ground

[*] - shared with Lt. C.E. Westman of the 61st Ftr Sqn

**Baker, Harry B., Capt.**
55th Ftr Sqn/20th Ftr Grp

| *Sqn* | *Date* | *Claims* | *Location* | *A/C* |
|---|---|---|---|---|
| 55th | January 24, 1944 | FW-190 dam(air) | Courtrai | P-38 |
| | June 30 | Me-109 dest(air) | Dreux | P-38 |

1-0-1 air
0-0 ground

**Baker, Irvin C., Capt.**
77th Ftr Sqn/20th Ftr Grp

| *Sqn* | *Date* | *Claims* | *Location* | *A/C* |
|---|---|---|---|---|
| 77th | May 12, 1944 | Me-109 dest(air) | SW Kassel | P-38 |

1-0-0 air
0-0 ground

**Baker, Maurice F., Capt.**
362nd Ftr Sqn/357th Ftr Grp

| *Sqn* | *Date* | *Claims* | *Location* | *A/C* |
|---|---|---|---|---|
| 362nd | May 12, 1944 | Me-109 dest(air) | N/Wurzburg | P-51 |

1-0-0 air
0-0 ground

**Baker, Raymond G., Lt.**
358th Ftr Sqn/355th Ftr Grp

| Sqn | Date | Claims | Location | A/C |
|---|---|---|---|---|
| 358th | December 5, 1944 | (2)FW-190 dest(air) | Berlin | P-51 |
| | | FW-190 dam(air) | Berlin | P-51 |

2-0-1 air
0-0 ground

**Baker, Robert L., Lt.**
82nd Ftr Sqn/78th Ftr Grp

| Sqn | Date | Claims | Location | A/C |
|---|---|---|---|---|
| 82nd | April 12, 1944 | (.33)FW-190 dest(air)* | Malmedy | P-47 |
| | May 12 | FW-190 dest(air) | Coblenz | P-47 |
| | May 19 | Me-109 dam(air) | Dummer Lake | P-47 |
| | | Me-110 dest(grd) | Dummer Lake | P-47 |
| | | Me-110 dest(grd) | Plantlunne | P-47 |

1.33-0-1 air
2-0 ground

* - shared with Maj. L.P. Marshall and Lt. G.J. Lundigan of the 82nd Ftr Sqn

**Baker, Schuyler A., Lt.**
55th Ftr Sqn/20th Ftr Grp

| Sqn | Date | Claims | Location | A/C |
|---|---|---|---|---|
| 55th | January 14, 1945 | (1.5)FW-190 dest(air)* | Perleberg | P-51 |

1.5-0-0 air
0-0 ground

* - shared with an unknown pilot

**Baker, Wilson K., Lt.**
370th Ftr Sqn/359th Ftr Grp

| Sqn | Date | Claims | Location | A/C |
|---|---|---|---|---|
| 370th | July 20, 1944 | Me-109 dest(air) | Zeitz | P-51 |
| | | FW-190 dam(air) | Zeitz | P-51 |
| | August 4 | Me-110 dest(air) | Denmark | P-51 |

2-0-1 air
0-0 ground

**Ball, Edwin C., Lt.**
505th Ftr Sqn/339th Ftr Grp

| Sqn | Date | Claims | Location | A/C |
|---|---|---|---|---|
| 505th | June 21, 1944 | Me-410 dam(air) | N/Berlin | P-51 |

0-0-1 air
0-0 ground

**Ball, Melville R., Capt.**
504th Ftr Sqn/339th Ftr Grp

| Sqn | Date | Claims | Location | A/C |
|---|---|---|---|---|
| 504th | May 24, 1944 | Me-109 dam(air) | Berlin | P-51 |
| | June 8 | FW-190 dest(air) | Rennes | P-51 |
| | June 10 | Me-109 dam(air) | SE Le Havre | P-51 |

1-0-2 air
0-0 ground

**Ball, Sanborn N., Jr., Lt.**
62nd Ftr Sqn/56th Ftr Grp

| Sqn | Date | Claims | Location | A/C |
|---|---|---|---|---|
| 62nd | December 4, 1944 | (.5)u/i a/c dest(grd)* | Neuburg | P-47 |
| | December 23 | FW-190 dest(air) | Euskirchen | P-47 |
| | March 14, 1945 | (.5)Ar-234 dest(air)** | Coblenz | P-47 |
| | April 13 | (2)Do-217 dest(grd) | Eggebeck A/F | P-47 |
| | | He-111 dest(grd) | Eggebeck A/F | P-47 |

1.5-0-0 air
3.5-0 ground

* - shared with Lt. D. Henley of the 62nd Ftr Sqn
** - shared with Lt. W.S. Lear of the 62nd Ftr Sqn

**Ballard, Jerome J., Lt.**
504th Ftr Sqn/339th Ftr Grp

| Sqn | Date | Claims | Location | A/C |
|---|---|---|---|---|
| 504th | March 18, 1945 | FW-190 dest(air) | Barnstorf | P-51 |

1-0-0 air
0-0 ground

**Ballinger, Philip R., Lt.**
367th Ftr Sqn/358th Ftr Grp

| Sqn | Date | Claims | Location | A/C |
|---|---|---|---|---|
| 367th | January 30, 1944 | Me-109 dam(air) | E/Zwolle | P-47 |

0-0-1 air
0-0 ground

**Bancroft, William H., Jr., Lt.**
335th Ftr Sqn/4th Ftr Grp
2nd Scouting Force

| Sqn | Date | Claims | Location | A/C |
|---|---|---|---|---|
| 2nd | April 4, 1945 | Me-262 dam(air) | S/Ratzburg | P-51 |

0-0-1 air
0-0 ground

**Bank, Raymond M., Lt.**
364th Ftr Sqn/357th Ftr Grp

| Sqn | Date | Claims | Location | A/C |
|---|---|---|---|---|
| 364th | December 24, 1944 | Me-109 dest(air) | S/Kassel | P-51 |
| | January 14, 1945 | (3)FW-190 dest(air) | S/Schwerin | P-51 |
| | March 2 | Me-109 dest(air) | SE Magdeburg | P-51 |
| | | He-111 dam(grd) | E/Magdeburg | P-51 |

5-0-0 air
0-1 ground

**Bankey, Ernest E., Jr., Maj.**
383rd Ftr Sqn/364th Ftr Grp
385th Ftr Sqn/364th Ftr Grp
HdQts/364th Ftr Grp

| Sqn | Date | Claims | Location | A/C |
|---|---|---|---|---|
| 383rd | April 11, 1944 | Me-109 dest(air) | Halberstadt | P-38 |
| | April 29 | FW-190 prob(air) | Stendal | P-38 |
| 385th | May 20 | Ju-88 dam(grd) | Soissons | P-38 |
| | November 26 | Me-109 dest(air) | NE Dummer Lake | P-51 |
| | | Me-109 prob(air) | NE Dummer Lake | P-51 |
| HdQts | December 27 | (4)FW-190 dest(air) | Bonn | P-51 |
| | | (1.5)Me-109 dest(air)* | Bonn | P-51 |
| | April 16, 1945 | (2)Me-109 dest(air) | N/Nordingen | P-51 |
| | | (2)Ju-188 dest(grd) | Pocking | P-51 |
| | | Do-217 dest(grd) | Pocking | P-51 |
| | | (2)FW-190 dam(grd) | Pocking | P-51 |
| | | (2)Ju-188 dam(grd) | Pocking | P-51 |
| | April 17 | (2)He-111 dest(grd) | Karlsbad | P-51 |
| | | (2)He-111 dam(grd) | Karlsbad | P-51 |

9.5-2-0 air
6-7 ground

* - shared with F/O A.H. Goebel of the 352nd Ftr Grp

**Bannister, John J., Capt.**
383rd Ftr Sqn/364th Ftr Grp

| Sqn | Date | Claims | Location | A/C |
|---|---|---|---|---|
| 383rd | May 21, 1944 | (2)Ju-88 dam(grd) | Rechlin | P-38 |

0-0-0 air
0-2 ground

**Barab, Bernard R., Lt.**
357th Ftr Sqn/355th Ftr Grp

| Sqn | Date | Claims | Location | A/C |
|---|---|---|---|---|
| 357th | November 26, 1944 | Me-109 dest(air) | W/Gardelegen | P-51 |

1-0-0 air
0-0 ground

**Barber, Donald L., Capt.**
352nd Ftr Sqn/353rd Ftr Grp

| *Sqn* | *Date* | *Claims* | *Location* | *A/C* |
|---|---|---|---|---|
| 352nd | July 6, 1944 | FW-190 dest(air) | Evreux-Paris | P-47 |
| | August 4 | Me-109 dest(air) | E/Bremen | P-47 |

2-0-0 air
0-0 ground

**Barber, Kenneth E., Lt.**
368th Ftr Sqn/359th Ftr Grp

| *Sqn* | *Date* | *Claims* | *Location* | *A/C* |
|---|---|---|---|---|
| 368th | March 23, 1945 | (.5)Ar-196 dest(air)* | Salzwedel | P-51 |
| | April 13 | (3)Me-110 dest(grd) | Neumunster | P-51 |
| | | u/i a/c dest(grd) | Neumunster | P-51 |

0.5-0-0 air
4-0 ground

* - shared with Capt. G.A. Doersch of the 368th Ftr Sqn

**Barden, John L., Lt.**
334th Ftr Sqn/4th Ftr Grp

| *Sqn* | *Date* | *Claims* | *Location* | *A/C* |
|---|---|---|---|---|
| 334th | April 29, 1944 | (.5)Ju-52 dest(grd)* | Nordhausen | P-51 |

0-0-0 air
0.5-0 ground

* - shared with Lt. N. Megura of the 334th Ftr Sqn

**Barger, Clarence R., Lt.**
354th Ftr Sqn/355th Ftr Grp

| *Sqn* | *Date* | *Claims* | *Location* | *A/C* |
|---|---|---|---|---|
| 354th | March 6, 1944 | (.33)Me-109 dest(air)* | Dummer Lake | P-47 |
| | March 8 | (3)Ju-88 dest(grd) | Hesepe | P-47 |
| | April 13 | Do-217 dest(grd) | Oberpfaffenhofen | P-51 |
| | | Ju-88 dest(grd) | Oberpfaffenhofen | P-51 |
| | | Do-217 dam(grd) | Oberpfaffenhofen | P-51 |
| | | Ju-88 dam(grd) | Oberpfaffenhofen | P-51 |

0.33-0-0 air
5-2 ground

* - shared with Capt. W.J. Koraleski and Lt. N.J. Fortier of the 354th Ftr Sqn

**Barksy, William M., Lt.**
435th Ftr Sqn/479th Ftr Grp

| *Sqn* | *Date* | *Claims* | *Location* | *A/C* |
|---|---|---|---|---|
| 435th | April 18, 1945 | u/i a/c dam(grd) | Mettenheim | P-51 |

0-0-0 air
0-1 ground

**Barlow, Albert W., Lt.**
351st Ftr Sqn/353rd Ftr Grp

| *Sqn* | *Date* | *Claims* | *Location* | *A/C* |
|---|---|---|---|---|
| 351st | August 4, 1944 | Me-109 dest(air) | S/Bremen | P-47 |

1-0-0 air
0-0 ground

**Barnaby, Harold T., Capt.**
83rd Ftr Sqn/78th Ftr Grp

| *Sqn* | *Date* | *Claims* | *Location* | *A/C* |
|---|---|---|---|---|
| 83rd | December 20, 1943 | Me-109 dest(air) | SW Bremen | P-47 |
| | February 10, 1944 | Me-109 dest(air) | Lingen | P-47 |
| | | FW-190 dest(air) | Lingen | P-47 |
| | | Me-109 dam(air) | Lingen | P-47 |
| | November 26 | u/i a/c dest(grd) | Weisswarte A/F | P-47 |
| | March 22, 1945 | Me-262 dest(air) | Giebelstadt | P-51 |

4-0-1 air
1-0 ground

**Barnes, Ben B., Lt.**
361st Ftr Sqn/356th Ftr Grp

| *Sqn* | *Date* | *Claims* | *Location* | *A/C* |
|---|---|---|---|---|
| 361st | November 26, 1944 | FW-190 dam(air) | Osnabruck-Dummer Lake | P-51 |

0-0-1 air
0-0 ground

**Barnes, Chester A., Maj.**
383rd Ftr Sqn/364th Ftr Grp
HdQts/364th Ftr Grp

| *Sqn* | *Date* | *Claims* | *Location* | *A/C* |
|---|---|---|---|---|
| 383rd | April 12, 1944 | Me-109 dam(air) | W/Frankfurt | P-38 |
| | May 21 | Ju-88 dest(grd) | NW Renow | P-38 |
| | September 11 | Me-109 dam(air) | Sangerhausen | P-51 |
| | February 14, 1945 | FW-190 dest(air) | Chemnitz | P-51 |
| | April 16 | FW-190 dam(grd) | Marienbad | P-51 |
| | | Ju-52 dam(grd) | Marienbad | P-51 |

1-0-2 air
1-2 ground

**Barnes, George W., Lt.**
335th Ftr Sqn/4th Ftr Grp

| *Sqn* | *Date* | *Claims* | *Location* | *A/C* |
|---|---|---|---|---|
| 335th | February 21, 1944 | Ju-88 dam(air) | Havern | P-47 |

0-0-1 air
0-0 ground

**Barnes, Harry H., Lt.**
487th Ftr Sqn/352nd Ftr Grp

| *Sqn* | *Date* | *Claims* | *Location* | *A/C* |
|---|---|---|---|---|
| 487th | May 12, 1944 | (.5)Me-109 dest(air)* | Coburg | P-51 |
| | May 28 | Me-109 dest(air) | W/Leipzig | P-51 |
| | | Me-109 dam(air) | W/Leipzig | P-51 |
| | May 30 | Me-109 dest(air) | N/Halberstadt | P-51 |
| | June 10 | Me-109 dam(air) | NW Mortain | P-51 |

2.5-0-2 air
0-0 ground

* - shared with Lt. J.W. Galiga of the 328th Ftr Sqn, 352nd Ftr Grp

**Barnes, Thomas C., Lt.**
55th Ftr Sqn/20th Ftr Grp

| *Sqn* | *Date* | *Claims* | *Location* | *A/C* |
|---|---|---|---|---|
| 55th | October 6, 1944 | Do-24 dest(grd) | Kubitzer Bay | P-51 |
| | | Do-24 dam(grd) | Kubitzer Bay | P-51 |

0-0-0 air
1-1 ground

**Barnes, William H., Lt.**
338th Ftr Sqn/55th Ftr Grp

| *Sqn* | *Date* | *Claims* | *Location* | *A/C* |
|---|---|---|---|---|
| 338th | April 10, 1945 | FW-190 dest(grd) | Burg A/F | P-51 |
| | | (2)FW-190 dam(grd) | Burg A/F | P-51 |

0-0-0 air
1-2 ground

**Barnes, William H., Lt.**
61st Ftr Sqn/56th Ftr Grp

| *Sqn* | *Date* | *Claims* | *Location* | *A/C* |
|---|---|---|---|---|
| 61st | July 20, 1944 | (3)He-111 dest(grd) | Bassenheim A/F | P-47 |
| | | He-111 dam(grd) | Bassenheim A/F | P-47 |

0-0-0 air
3-1 ground

**Barnett, Louis E., Lt.**
368th Ftr Sqn/359th Ftr Grp

| *Sqn* | *Date* | *Claims* | *Location* | *A/C* |
|---|---|---|---|---|
| 368th | September 11, 1944 | (2)FW-190 dest(air) | Eisleben | P-51 |
| | | FW-190 prob(air) | Eisleben | P-51 |

2-1-0 air
0-0 ground

**Barnhart, Philip W., Lt.**
354th Ftr Sqn/355th Ftr Grp

| *Sqn* | *Date* | *Claims* | *Location* | *A/C* |
|---|---|---|---|---|
| 354th | April 4, 1945 | (.5)Do-24 dest(grd)[*] | Muritz Lake | P-51 |
| | April 9 | He-111 dest(grd) | Memmingen | P-51 |
| | April 10 | u/i a/c dest(grd) | Husum | P-51 |
| | | (2)FW-190 dam(grd) | Husum | P-51 |
| | | u/i a/c dam(grd) | Husum | P-51 |
| | | u/i a/c dam(grd) | Rechlin | P-51 |
| | | 0-0-0 air | | |
| | | 2.5-4 ground | | |

[*] - shared with Lt. C.E. Decklar of the 354th Ftr Sqn

**Barnhart, Robert E., Capt.**
360th Ftr Sqn/356th Ftr Grp

| *Sqn* | *Date* | *Claims* | *Location* | *A/C* |
|---|---|---|---|---|
| 360th | November 26, 1944 | Me-109 dam(air) | Dummer Lake | P-51 |
| | January 14, 1945 | FW-190 dest(air) | S/Osnabruck | P-51 |
| | March 14 | Ar-234 dest(air) | Bielfeld-Hildesheim | P-51 |
| | | 2-0-1 air | | |
| | | 0-0 ground | | |

**Barnum, Eugene E., Capt.**
61st Ftr Sqn/56th Ftr Grp

| *Sqn* | *Date* | *Claims* | *Location* | *A/C* |
|---|---|---|---|---|
| 61st | November 5, 1943 | FW-190 dest(air) | S/Rheine | P-47 |
| | January 30, 1944 | Me-210 dest(air) | Lingen | P-47 |
| | February 24 | FW-190 dam(air) | Kassel | P-47 |
| | February 25 | Me-109 dam(air) | Landau | P-47 |
| | | 2-0-2 air | | |
| | | 0-0 ground | | |

**Baron, Richard L., Lt.**
84th Ftr Sqn/78th Ftr Grp

| *Sqn* | *Date* | *Claims* | *Location* | *A/C* |
|---|---|---|---|---|
| 84th | August 17, 1944 | (.5)Me-109 dest(grd)[*] | W/Chaudun | P-47 |
| | | Me-109 dam(grd) | W/Chaudun | P-47 |
| | September 10 | He-111 dest(grd) | Meinbullen | P-47 |
| | | He-111 dam(grd) | Meinbullen | P-47 |
| | | 0-0-0 air | | |
| | | 1.5-2 ground | | |

[*] - shared with Capt. R.E. Smith of the 84th Ftr Sqn

**Barrentine, Emmett S., Lt.**
63rd Ftr Sqn/56th Ftr Grp

| *Sqn* | *Date* | *Claims* | *Location* | *A/C* |
|---|---|---|---|---|
| 63rd | April 10, 1945 | (2)Ju-88 dest(grd) | Neuruppin | P-47 |
| | | He-177 dam(grd) | Neuruppin | P-47 |
| | | Ju-88 dam(grd) | Neuruppin | P-47 |
| | April 13 | Me-110 dest(grd) | Eggebeck A/F | P-47 |
| | | (2)u/i a/c dam(grd) | Eggebeck A/F | P-47 |
| | | 0-0-0 air | | |
| | | 3-4 ground | | |

**Barrett, Fred H., Lt.**
61st Ftr Sqn/56th Ftr Grp

| *Sqn* | *Date* | *Claims* | *Location* | *A/C* |
|---|---|---|---|---|
| 61st | September 5, 1944 | (1.5)Me-210 dam(grd)[*] | Gelnhausen | P-47 |
| | March 31, 1945 | Me-262 dam(air) | Steinhuder Lake | P-47 |
| | April 10 | (2)Ju-88 dest(grd) | Oranienburg | P-47 |
| | | (3)Ju-88 dam(grd) | Oranienburg | P-47 |
| | | 0-0-1 air | | |
| | | 2-4.5 ground | | |

[*] - shared with Capt. P.A. Conger of the 61st Ftr Sqn

**Barrett, Lawrence J., Lt.**
504th Ftr Sqn/339th Ftr Grp

| *Sqn* | *Date* | *Claims* | *Location* | *A/C* |
|---|---|---|---|---|
| 504th | March 20, 1945 | He-111 dest(grd) | Grossenbrode | P-51 |
| | April 10 | (2)Ju-88 dest(grd) | N/Neuruppin | P-51 |
| | | (2)Me-410 dam(grd) | N/Neuruppin | P-51 |
| | April 17 | Ju-52 dest(grd) | Mauching | P-51 |
| | | 0-0-0 air | | |
| | | 4-2 ground | | |

**Barrett, Richard I., Lt.**
338th Ftr Sqn/55th Ftr Grp

| *Sqn* | *Date* | *Claims* | *Location* | *A/C* |
|---|---|---|---|---|
| 338th | September 11, 1944 | Me-109 dest(air) | S/Meiningen | P-51 |
| | November 26 | FW-190 dest(grd) | Vorden A/F | P-51 |
| | | 1-0-0 air | | |
| | | 1-0 ground | | |

**Barrie, Jack T., Lt.**
385th Ftr Sqn/364th Ftr Grp

| *Sqn* | *Date* | *Claims* | *Location* | *A/C* |
|---|---|---|---|---|
| 385th | December 27, 1944 | Me-109 dest(air) | SW Bonn | P-51 |
| | | 1-0-0 air | | |
| | | 0-0 ground | | |

**Barth, Merle B., Lt.**
368th Ftr Sqn/359th Ftr Grp

| *Sqn* | *Date* | *Claims* | *Location* | *A/C* |
|---|---|---|---|---|
| 368th | September 12, 1944 | Me-109 dest(air) | NW Wittenburg | P-51 |
| | October 24 | FW-190 dest(air) | Nordhausen | P-51 |
| | | 2-0-0 air | | |
| | | 0-0 ground | | |

Bartle, William G., Lt.
61st Ftr Sqn/56th Ftr Grp

| *Sqn* | *Date* | *Claims* | *Location* | *A/C* |
|---|---|---|---|---|
| 61st | April 13, 1945 | (2)Ju-88 dest(grd) | Eggebeck A/F | P-47 |
| | | Me-109 dam(grd) | Eggebeck A/F | P-47 |
| | | 0-0-0 air | | |
| | | 2-1 ground | | |

**Bartlett, Richard D., Lt.**
343rd Ftr Sqn/55th Ftr Grp

| *Sqn* | *Date* | *Claims* | *Location* | *A/C* |
|---|---|---|---|---|
| 343rd | September 5, 1944 | (2)He-111 dest(grd) | Stuttagrt/Echterdingen | P-51 |
| | | Me-110 dest(grd) | Stuttgart/Echter. | P-51 |
| | | Me-109 dam(grd) | Stuttgart/Echter. | P-51 |
| | | (.5)glider dam(grd)[*] | Stuttgart/Echter. | P-51 |
| | November 2 | (.5)Me-109 dest(air)[**] | SW Leipzig | P-51 |
| | | 0.5-0-0 air | | |
| | | 3-1.5 ground | | |

[*] - shared with Capt. D.A. Parker of the 343rd Ftr Sqn
[**] - shared with Lt. J. Eliades of the 343rd Ftr Sqn

**Bartley, James G., Lt.**
352nd Ftr Sqn/353rd Ftr Grp

| *Sqn* | *Date* | *Claims* | *Location* | *A/C* |
|---|---|---|---|---|
| 352nd | April 16, 1945 | (.5)Ju-88 dest(grd)[*] | Bad Aibling | P-51 |
| | | 0-0-0 air | | |
| | | 0.5-0 ground | | |

[*] - shared with Capt. H.B. Tordoff of the 352nd Ftr Sqn

**Barto, Vernon N., Lt.**
504th Ftr Sqn/339th Ftr Grp

| *Sqn* | *Date* | *Claims* | *Location* | *A/C* |
|---|---|---|---|---|
| 504th | December 31, 1944 | FW-190 dam(air) | Hamburg | P-51 |
| | March 20, 1945 | Me-262 dest(air) | Hamburg | P-51 |
| | April 7 | (.5)Me-109 dest(air)[*] | Celle | P-51 |
| | April 10 | (2)Ju-88 dest(grd) | N/Neuruppin | P-51 |

| Sqn | Date | Claims | Location | A/C |
|---|---|---|---|---|
| | | Ju-88 dam(grd) | N/Neuruppin | P-51 |
| | April 16 | Me-109 dest(grd) | Klatovy | P-51 |

1.5-0-1 air
3-1 ground

[*] - shared with Lt. L.A. Kunz of the 504th Ftr Sqn

**Baskin, Walter M., Lt.**
361st Ftr Sqn/356th Ftr Grp

| *Sqn* | *Date* | *Claims* | *Location* | *A/C* |
|---|---|---|---|---|
| 361st | January 14, 1945 | (1.5)FW-190 dest(air)[*] | SW Dummer Lake | P-51 |

1.5-0-0 air
0-0 ground

[*] - shared with Lt. C.T. Ashby of the 361st Ftr Sqn

**Bast, Victor E., Capt.**
61st Ftr Sqn/56th Ftr Grp

| *Sqn* | *Date* | *Claims* | *Location* | *A/C* |
|---|---|---|---|---|
| 61st | December 23, 1944 | FW-190 dest(air) | Coblenz | P-47 |
| | April 13, 1945 | (3)Ju-88 dest(grd) | Eggebeck A/F | P-47 |
| | | (2)Ju-88 dam(grd) | Eggebeck A/F | P-47 |
| | | (2)u/i a/c dam(grd) | Eggebeck A/F | P-47 |

1-0-0 air
3-4 ground

**Bateman, James A., Lt.**
487th Ftr Sqn/352nd Ftr Grp

| *Sqn* | *Date* | *Claims* | *Location* | *A/C* |
|---|---|---|---|---|
| 487th | December 26, 1944 | Me-109 dest(air) | SE St. Vith | P-51 |
| | December 27 | Me-109 dest(air) | SW Bonn | P-51 |

2-0-0 air
0-0 ground

**Bateman, Paul H., Lt.**
370th Ftr Sqn/359th Ftr Grp

| *Sqn* | *Date* | *Claims* | *Location* | *A/C* |
|---|---|---|---|---|
| 370th | March 4, 1944 | (.5)FW-190 dest(air)[*] | Bonn | P-47 |
| | | (.25)Me-109 dest(air)[**] | Bonn | P-47 |
| | April 24 | Me-109 dest(grd) | St. Dizier | P-47 |
| | | (.33)u/i a/c dest(grd)[@] | St. Dizier | P-47 |
| | May 19 | FW-190 dest(air) | Stendal | P-51 |

1.75-0-0 air
1.33-0 ground

[*] - shared with Maj. J.B. Murphy of the 370th Ftr Sqn
[**] - shared with Maj. J.B. Murphy, Lt. A.C. Porter, and Lt. R.S. Wetmore of the 370th Ftr Sqn
[@] - shared with Capt. S.R. Smith of HdQts, 359th Ftr Grp, and Lt. R.S. Wetmore of the 370th Ftr Sqn

**Bates, Arthur W., Lt.**
504th Ftr Sqn/339th Ftr Grp

| *Sqn* | *Date* | *Claims* | *Location* | *A/C* |
|---|---|---|---|---|
| 504th | November 26, 1944 | FW-190 dest(air) | S/Dummer Lake | P-51 |

1-0-0 air
0-0 ground

**Batson, Samuel K., Lt.**
63rd Ftr Sqn/56th Ftr Grp

| *Sqn* | *Date* | *Claims* | *Location* | *A/C* |
|---|---|---|---|---|
| 63rd | December 2, 1944 | Me-109 dest(air) | S/Marburg | P-47 |
| | December 23 | FW-190 dest(air) | NW Coblenz | P-47 |
| | December 25 | Me-109 dam(air) | SW Cologne | P-47 |

2-0-1 air
0-0 ground

**Bauer, Harold M., Lt.**
343rd Ftr Sqn/55th Ftr Grp

| *Sqn* | *Date* | *Claims* | *Location* | *A/C* |
|---|---|---|---|---|
| 343rd | December 31, 1943 | FW-190 dest(air) | Niort | P-38 |

1-0-0 air
0-0 ground

**Baugh, Donald P., F/O**
336th Ftr Sqn/4th Ftr Grp

| *Sqn* | *Date* | *Claims* | *Location* | *A/C* |
|---|---|---|---|---|
| 336th | April 16, 1945 | (5)Ju-88 dest(grd) | Praha | P-51 |

0-0-0 air
5-0 ground

**Baughman, Robert A., Lt.**
61st Ftr Sqn/56th Ftr Grp

| *Sqn* | *Date* | *Claims* | *Location* | *A/C* |
|---|---|---|---|---|
| 61st | November 18, 1944 | FW-190 dest(air) | E/Hanau | P-47 |
| | February 27, 1945 | (2)u/i a/c dest(grd) | Weimar A/F | P-47 |

1-0-0 air
2-0 ground

**Baughn, Richard A., Lt.**
383rd Ftr Sqn/364th Ftr Grp

| *Sqn* | *Date* | *Claims* | *Location* | *A/C* |
|---|---|---|---|---|
| 383rd | December 23, 1944 | FW-190 dest(air) | NW Trier | P-51 |
| | April 13, 1945 | (2)Ju-52 dest(grd) | Flensburg | P-51 |
| | | FW-190 dest(grd) | Flensburg | P-51 |
| | | Me-109 dam(grd) | Flensburg | P-51 |
| | | FW-190 dam(grd) | Flensburg | P-51 |
| | April 16 | (2)u/i a/c dam(grd) | Marienbad | P-51 |
| | April 17 | Me-262 dest(grd) | SE Pilzen | P-51 |

1-0-0 air
4-4 ground

**Bauman, Peter W., Jr., Lt.**
354th Ftr Sqn/355th Ftr Grp

| *Sqn* | *Date* | *Claims* | *Location* | *A/C* |
|---|---|---|---|---|
| 354th | November 5, 1943 | Me-109 dam(air) | NW Gelsenkirchen | P-47 |

0-0-1 air
0-0 ground

**Baylor, Melvin W., Capt.**
361st Ftr Sqn/356th Ftr Grp

| *Sqn* | *Date* | *Claims* | *Location* | *A/C* |
|---|---|---|---|---|
| 361st | January 14, 1945 | FW-190 dest(air) | SW Dummer Lake | P-51 |
| | | FW-190 prob(air) | SW Dummer Lake | P-51 |
| | February 14 | (2)FW-190 dest(air) | S/Chemnitz | P-51 |
| | | FW-190 dam(air) | S/Chemnitz | P-51 |

3-1-1 air
0-0 ground

**Beach, William E., Lt.**
352nd Ftr Sqn/353rd Ftr Grp

| *Sqn* | *Date* | *Claims* | *Location* | *A/C* |
|---|---|---|---|---|
| 352nd | April 17, 1945 | Me-109 dest(grd) | Ganacker | P-51 |
| | | (.5)He-111 dest(grd)[*] | Ganacker | P-51 |

0-0-0 air
1.5-0 ground

[*] - shared with Lt. B.J. Lancaster of the 352nd Ftr Sqn

**Beaird, Thomas E., Jr., Capt.**
HdQts/55th Ftr Grp

| *Sqn* | *Date* | *Claims* | *Location* | *A/C* |
|---|---|---|---|---|
| HdQts | November 13, 1943 | FW-190 dam(air) | W/Bremen | P-38 |
| | November 29 | Me-109 prob(air) | W/Bremen | P-38 |
| | February 5, 1944 | Me-109 dest(air) | Chartres | P-38 |

1-1-1 air
0-0 ground

**Beal, Elby J., Capt.**
368th Ftr Sqn/359th Ftr Grp

| *Sqn* | *Date* | *Claims* | *Location* | *A/C* |
|---|---|---|---|---|
| 368th | September 12, 1944 | Me-109 dest(air) | Gransee | P-51 |
| | December 24 | (2)FW-190 dest(air) | Cologne | P-51 |
| | | FW-190 prob(air) | Cologne | P-51 |

3-1-0 air
0-0 ground

**Beal, Harry E., Jr., Capt.**
362nd Ftr Sqn/357th Ftr Grp

| *Sqn* | *Date* | *Claims* | *Location* | *A/C* |
|---|---|---|---|---|
| 362nd | April 24, 1944 | (2)Me-110 dest(air) | E/Munich | P-51 |
| | | Me-110 dam(air) | E/Munich | P-51 |
| | August 28 | (.5)Ju-52 dest(grd)[*] | Trier | P-51 |
| | September 19 | Me-109 dam(air) | Ijsselstein | P-51 |

2-0-2 air
0.5-0 ground

* - shared with Lt. J.H. Sehl of the 362nd Ftr Sqn

**Beall, Charles E., Lt.**
338th Ftr Sqn/55th Ftr Grp

| *Sqn* | *Date* | *Claims* | *Location* | *A/C* |
|---|---|---|---|---|
| 338th | November 13, 1943 | FW-190 dest(air) | Bremen | P-38 |

1-0-0 air
0-0 ground

**Beason, Eugene M., Lt.**
62nd Ftr Sqn/56th Ftr Grp

| *Sqn* | *Date* | *Claims* | *Location* | *A/C* |
|---|---|---|---|---|
| 62nd | September 5, 1944 | FW-190 dest(grd) | Gelnhausen | P-47 |
| | | u/i a/c dam(grd) | Gelnhausen | P-47 |
| | October 5 | Me-110 dest(grd) | S/Geseke | P-47 |
| | December 4 | He-177 dest(grd) | Neuburg | P-47 |
| | | FW-190 dest(grd) | Neuburg | P-47 |
| | December 23 | Me-109 dest(air) | Euskirchen-Bonn | P-47 |

1-0-0 air
4-1 ground

**Beatie, Ernest D., Capt.**
335th Ftr Sqn/4th Ftr Grp

| *Sqn* | *Date* | *Claims* | *Location* | *A/C* |
|---|---|---|---|---|
| 335th | May 16, 1943 | FW-190 prob(air) | Walcheren | P-47 |
| | June 22 | FW-190 dest(air) | Beveland-Walcheren | P-47 |
| | | Me-109 dest(air) | Beveland-Walcheren | P-47 |

2-1-0 air
0-0 ground

**Beaty, Wendell W., Capt.**
358th Ftr Sqn/355th Ftr Grp

| *Sqn* | *Date* | *Claims* | *Location* | *A/C* |
|---|---|---|---|---|
| 358th | November 18, 1944 | Me-262 dest(grd) | Leipheim | P-51 |
| | March 1, 1945 | Me-262 dest(air) | Ingolstadt | P-51 |

1-0-0 air
1-0 ground

**Beaumont, Edward C., Lt.**
383rd Ftr Sqn/364th Ftr Grp

| *Sqn* | *Date* | *Claims* | *Location* | *A/C* |
|---|---|---|---|---|
| 383rd | August 9, 1944 | FW-190 dest(air) | Munich | P-51 |
| | August 24 | Me-109 dest(air) | Seyda | P-51 |
| | | Me-109 dam(air) | Seyda | P-51 |
| | November 2 | Me-109 dest(air) | Merseburg | P-51 |
| | | FW-190 dam(air) | Merseburg | P-51 |

3-0-2 air
0-0 ground

**Beavers, Edward H., Jr., Capt.**
503rd Ftr Sqn/339th Ftr Grp

| *Sqn* | *Date* | *Claims* | *Location* | *A/C* |
|---|---|---|---|---|
| 503rd | July 25, 1944 | FW-190 dest(air) | Etrepagny | P-51 |
| | September 23 | FW-190 dest(air) | SW Wesel | P-51 |
| | November 18 | Me-109 dest(air) | Mannheim | P-51 |
| | November 26 | (2)FW-190 dest(air) | SE Dummer Lake | P-51 |

5-0-0 air
0-0 ground

**Bebaeff, Nick P., Lt.**
343rd Ftr Sqn/55th Ftr Grp

| *Sqn* | *Date* | *Claims* | *Location* | *A/C* |
|---|---|---|---|---|
| 343rd | November 2, 1944 | Me-109 dest(air) | Naumberg | P-51 |

1-0-0 air
0-0 ground

**Bebout, Russell W., Lt.**
79th Ftr Sqn/20th Ftr Grp

| *Sqn* | *Date* | *Claims* | *Location* | *A/C* |
|---|---|---|---|---|
| 79th | June 28, 1944 | FW-190 dest(air) | Beaumont | P-38 |
| | August 9 | (2)FW-190 dest(air) | SW Ulm | P-51 |

3-0-0 air
0-0 ground

**Bechtelheimer, Wayne F., Lt.**
82nd Ftr Sqn/78th Ftr Grp

| *Sqn* | *Date* | *Claims* | *Location* | *A/C* |
|---|---|---|---|---|
| 82nd | February 28, 1945 | (.5)Me-262 dam(air)[*] | Hersfeld-Fulda | P-51 |
| | April 10 | u/i a/c dest(grd) | Werder | P-51 |

0-0-0.5 air
1-0 ground

* - shared with Lt. J.E. Parker of the 82nd Ftr Sqn

**Beck, Charles E., Capt.**
361st Ftr Sqn/356th Ftr Grp

| *Sqn* | *Date* | *Claims* | *Location* | *A/C* |
|---|---|---|---|---|
| 361st | November 26, 1944 | Me-109 dest(air) | Osnabruck-Dummer Lake | P-51 |

1-0-0 air
0-0 ground

**Beck, Harold F., Lt.**
82nd Ftr Sqn/78th Ftr Grp
84th Ftr Sqn/78th Ftr Grp

| *Sqn* | *Date* | *Claims* | *Location* | *A/C* |
|---|---|---|---|---|
| 84th | August 10, 1944 | (1.5)Ju-88 dest(grd)[*] | Conflans | P-47 |

0-0-0 air
1.5-0 ground

* - shared with Lt. W.K. Grimes of the 84th Ftr Sqn

**Becker, Marvin H., Lt.**
63rd Ftr Sqn/56th Ftr Grp

| *Sqn* | *Date* | *Claims* | *Location* | *A/C* |
|---|---|---|---|---|
| 63rd | March 6, 1944 | (.25)Me-109 dest(air)[*] | Minden-Osnabruck | P-47 |
| | March 8 | Me-109 dest(air) | E/Dummer Lake | P-47 |
| | March 15 | FW-190 dam(air) | Hanover | P-47 |
| | April 15 | He-111 dest(grd) | Flensburg | P-47 |
| | June 7 | (.5)FW-190 dest(air)[**] | Les Andelys-Craches | P-47 |
| | June 30 | Ju-88 dest(air) | S/Noyon | P-47 |

2.75-0-1 air
1-0 ground

* - shared with Col. H. Zemke of HdQts, 56th Ftr Grp, and Lt. D.V. Peters and Lt. C.W. Reed of the 63rd Ftr Sqn
** - shared with Lt. S.B. Dale of the 63rd Ftr Sqn

**Becker, Robert H., Capt.**
362nd Ftr Sqn/357th Ftr Grp

| *Sqn* | *Date* | *Claims* | *Location* | *A/C* |
|---|---|---|---|---|
| 362nd | February 25, 1944 | (1.5)Me-110 dest(air)[*] | Regensburg | P-51 |
| | April 13 | FW-190 dest(air) | S/Mannheim | P-51 |
| | April 30 | Me-109 dest(air) | S/Paris | P-51 |
| | May 30 | (3)Me-109 dest(air) | Bernburg | P-51 |
| | July 29 | (.5)Me-109 dest(air)[**] | W/Merseburg | P-51 |

7-0-0 air
0-0 ground

[*] - shared with Capt. A.M. Lingo of the 362nd Ftr Sqn
[**] - shared with Lt. T.W. Martinek of the 362nd Ftr Sqn

**Beckham, Walter C., Maj.**
351st Ftr Sqn/353rd Ftr Grp

| *Sqn* | *Date* | *Claims* | *Location* | *A/C* |
|---|---|---|---|---|
| 351st | August 24, 1943 | FW-190 dam(air) | N/Paris | P-47 |
| | September 23 | FW-190 dest(air) | S/Nantes | P-47 |
| | October 2 | FW-190 prob(air) | Emden | P-47 |
| | | Me-109 prob(air) | Emden | P-47 |
| | October 4 | Me-109 dest(air) | Malines | P-47 |
| | October 8 | FW-190 dam(air) | Rhede | P-47 |
| | October 10 | Me-110 dest(air) | Munster | P-47 |
| | | Me-110 dest(air) | Gransbergen | P-47 |
| | | Me-210 dest(air) | Munster | P-47 |
| | October 14 | (2)FW-190 dest(air) | Aachen | P-47 |
| | November 5 | Me-410 dest(air) | SW Gelsenkirchen | P-47 |
| | | FW-190 dam(air) | SW Gelsenkirchen | P-47 |
| | November 11 | FW-190 dest(air) | Dulmar | P-47 |
| | December 1 | (2)FW-190 dest(air) | Koln | P-47 |
| | January 14, 1944 | (.33)FW-190 dam(grd)[*] | Rosiers-en-Santerne | P-47 |
| | January 21 | (2)Me-109 dest(air) | St. Quentin | P-47 |
| | January 30 | Me-109 dest(air) | N/Deventer | P-47 |
| | February 3 | Me-109 dest(air) | S/Oldenburg | P-47 |
| | | FW-190 dest(air) | S/Oldenburg | P-47 |
| | February 8 | Me-109 dest(air) | E/St. Hubert | P-47 |
| | | FW-190 dest(air) | St. Hubert | P-47 |
| | February 13 | FW-190 dam(air) | Cambrai | P-47 |
| | February 22 | (.25)FW-190 dam(grd)[**] | NE Bonn | P-47 |
| | | (.25)FW-190 dam(grd)[**] | NE Bonn | P-47 |

18-2-4 air
0-0.83 ground

[*] - shared with Lt. C.L. Stafford of HdQts, 353rd Ftr Grp, and Lt. A.C. Duncan of the 361st Ftr Grp
[**] - both shared with Lt. F.N. Emory, Lt. G.B. Compton, and Lt. G.F. Perpente of the 351st Ftr Sqn

**Beckley, Samuel R., LtCol.**
83rd Ftr Sqn/78th Ftr Grp

| *Sqn* | *Date* | *Claims* | *Location* | *A/C* |
|---|---|---|---|---|
| 83rd | December 19, 1944 | Me-109 dam(air) | S/Coblenz | P-47 |

0-0-1 air
0-0 ground

**Beckman, Jack M., Capt.**
358th Ftr Sqn/355th Ftr Grp

| *Sqn* | *Date* | *Claims* | *Location* | *A/C* |
|---|---|---|---|---|
| 358th | April 5, 1944 | Me-109 dam(air) | Landsberg | P-51 |
| | | Do-217 dest(grd) | Landsberg | P-51 |
| | | Ju-88 dest(grd) | Landsberg | P-51 |
| | | (5)Do-217 dam(grd) | Landsberg | P-51 |
| | April 15 | Do-217 dest(grd) | Glienicke | P-51 |
| | | Do-217 dam(grd) | Glienicke | P-51 |
| | November 26 | FW-190 dest(air) | Hanover-Berlin | P-51 |
| | | FW-190 dam(air) | Hanover-Berlin | P-51 |

1-0-2 air
3-6 ground

**Becraft, Myron A., Lt.**
362nd Ftr Sqn/357th Ftr Grp

| *Sqn* | *Date* | *Claims* | *Location* | *A/C* |
|---|---|---|---|---|
| 362nd | March 2, 1945 | Me-109 dest(air) | Kamenz A/F | P-51 |
| | | (2)He-111 dest(grd) | Kamenz A/F | P-51 |
| | | (2)u/i a/c dest(grd) | Kamenz A/F | P-51 |
| | March 31 | Me-262 dam(air) | N/Juist Island | P-51 |

1-0-1 air
4-0 ground

**Beeler, Glenn D., Lt.**
354th Ftr Sqn/355th Ftr Grp

| *Sqn* | *Date* | *Claims* | *Location* | *A/C* |
|---|---|---|---|---|
| 354th | April 7, 1945 | FW-190 dest(air) | S/Bremen | P-51 |
| | April 13 | He-111 dest(grd) | Husum | P-51 |

1-0-0 air
1-0 ground

**Beeler, Hugh F., Lt.**
62nd Ftr Sqn/56th Ftr Grp

| *Sqn* | *Date* | *Claims* | *Location* | *A/C* |
|---|---|---|---|---|
| 62nd | April 13, 1945 | FW-190 dest(grd) | Eggebeck A/F | P-47 |
| | | He-111 dam(grd) | Eggebeck A/F | P-47 |

0-0-0 air
1-1 ground

**Beeson, Duane W., Capt.**
334th Ftr Sqn/4th Ftr Grp

| *Sqn* | *Date* | *Claims* | *Location* | *A/C* |
|---|---|---|---|---|
| 334th | May 18, 1943 | Me-109 dest(air) | Blankenberge-Ostend | P-47 |
| | June 26 | Me-109 dest(air) | W/Dieppe | P-47 |
| | July 28 | Me-109 dest(air) | E/Rotterdam | P-47 |
| | | FW-190 dam(air) | E/Rotterdam | P-47 |
| | October 2 | FW-190 dest(air) | E/Wilhelmshaven | P-47 |
| | October 8 | (2)Me-109 dest(air) | Meppel-Zwolle | P-47 |
| | | Me-109 dam(air) | Meppel-Zwolle | P-47 |
| | October 10 | FW-190 dam(air) | Arnheim | P-47 |
| | November 29 | Me-109 prob(air) | Bremen | P-47 |
| | January 14, 1944 | FW-190 dest(air) | Soissons | P-47 |
| | January 29 | Me-109 dest(air) | Aachen | P-47 |
| | | FW-190 dest(air) | Aachen | P-47 |
| | January 31 | Me-109 dest(air) | Gilze-Rijen | P-47 |
| | February 20 | FW-190 dest(air) | Aachen | P-47 |
| | February 25 | FW-190 dest(air) | Beckingen | P-47 |
| | February 28 | (.25)Ju-88 dest(grd)[*] | Soissons | P-51 |
| | March 5 | Me-109 dest(air) | S/Bordeaux | P-51 |
| | | (.5)FW-200 dest(grd)[**] | Bordeaux | P-51 |
| | | FW-200 dam(grd) | Bordeaux | P-51 |
| | March 18 | Me-109 dest(air) | E/Mannheim | P-51 |
| | March 23 | (2)Me-109 dest(air) | E/Munster | P-51 |
| | March 27 | (1.5)Ju-88 dest(grd)[@] | Cazaux A/F | P-51 |
| | | Hs-126 dest(grd) | Cazaux A/F | P-51 |
| | | Ju-88 dam(grd) | Cazaux A/F | P-51 |
| | April 1 | Me-109 dest(air) | N/Lake Constance | P-51 |
| | April 5 | (.33)Ju-88 dest(air)[@@] | Plaue A/F | P-51 |
| | | (1.5)Ju-88 dest(grd)[#] | Weissewarte/Bush | P-51 |
| | | Me-323 dam(grd) | Brandenburg-Briest | P-51 |
| | | Me-109 dam(grd) | Brandenburg-Briest | P-51 |
| | | (.25) of (5)Ju-52 dam(grd)[##] | Brandenburg-Briest | P-51 |

17.33-1-3 air
4.75-5.25 ground

[*] - shared with Lt. W.B. Smith and Lt. N. Megura of the 334th Ftr Sqn and Lt. V. Garrison of the 336th Ftr Sqn, 4th Ftr Grp
[**] - shared with an unknown pilot
[@] - shared with Lt. H.T. Biel of the 334th Ftr Sqn
[@@] - shared with Lt. H.T. Biel of the 334th Ftr Sqn and Lt. C.A. Fiedler of the 335th Ftr Sqn, 4th Ftr Grp
[#] - shared with an unknown pilot
[##] - all shared with Lt. C.D. Carr and Lt. H.T. Biel of the 334th Ftr Sqn and Lt. R.S. Tussey of the 336th Ftr Sqn

**Behling, George A., Lt.**
362nd Ftr Sqn/357th Ftr Grp

| *Sqn* | *Date* | *Claims* | *Location* | *A/C* |
|---|---|---|---|---|
| 362nd | December 24, 1944 | FW-190 dest(air) | Fulda | P-51 |

1-0-0 air
0-0 ground

**Behrend, William W., Capt.**
503rd Ftr Sqn/339th Ftr Grp

| *Sqn* | *Date* | *Claims* | *Location* | *A/C* |
|---|---|---|---|---|
| 503rd | August 6, 1944 | Me-109 dest(air) | S/Schweriner Lake | P-51 |
| | March 2, 1945 | Me-109 dam(air) | E/Magdeburg | P-51 |

1-0-1 air
0-0 ground

**Beise, Merlin E., Lt.**
357th Ftr Sqn/355th Ftr Grp

| *Sqn* | *Date* | *Claims* | *Location* | *A/C* |
|---|---|---|---|---|
| 357th | April 13, 1945 | He-111 dam(grd) | Schleswig | P-51 |
| | April 16 | FW-190 dest(grd) | SE Germany | P-51 |
| | | (2)FW-190 dam(grd) | SE Germany | P-51 |

0-0-0 air
1-3 ground

**Belk, Oscar M., Lt.**
61st Ftr Sqn/56th Ftr Grp

| *Sqn* | *Date* | *Claims* | *Location* | *A/C* |
|---|---|---|---|---|
| 61st | June 12, 1944 | Me-109 dest(air) | Quittebeuf | P-47 |

1-0-0 air
0-0 ground

**Bell, Thomas R., Capt.**
334th Ftr Sqn/4th Ftr Grp

| *Sqn* | *Date* | *Claims* | *Location* | *A/C* |
|---|---|---|---|---|
| 334th | February 25, 1945 | FW-190 dest(grd) | Rohrensee | P-51 |
| | | (.5)Me-110 dest(grd)[*] | Rohrensee | P-51 |
| | | (.5)Me-110 dest(grd)[*] | Rohrensee | P-51 |
| | | (.5)Me-410 dest(grd)[**] | Rohrensee | P-51 |
| | February 27 | (3)Me-109 dest(grd) | Weimar | P-51 |

0-0-0 air
5.5-0 ground

* - both shared with Lt. G.A. Denson of the 334th Ftr Sqn
** - shared with Lt. C.G. Payne of the 334th Ftr Sqn

**Belliveau, Robert E., Capt.**
84th Ftr Sqn/78th Ftr Grp

| *Sqn* | *Date* | *Claims* | *Location* | *A/C* |
|---|---|---|---|---|
| 84th | March 24, 1944 | Ju-52 dam(grd) | Beaumont-Sur-Oise | P-47 |
| | May 25 | FW-190 dam(air) | Chaumont | P-47 |

0-0-1 air
0-1 ground

**Benedict, Douglas B., Capt.**
55th Ftr Sqn/20th Ftr Grp

| *Sqn* | *Date* | *Claims* | *Location* | *A/C* |
|---|---|---|---|---|
| 55th | October 6, 1944 | Do-24 dest(grd) | Kubitzer Bay | P-51 |

0-0-0 air
1-0 ground

**Benefiel, Robert E., Capt.**
368th Ftr Sqn/359th Ftr Grp

| *Sqn* | *Date* | *Claims* | *Location* | *A/C* |
|---|---|---|---|---|
| 368th | September 8, 1944 | (.5)Ju-52 dest(grd)[*] | Cronberg | P-51 |
| | September 11 | (2)Me-109 dam(air) | Eisenach | P-51 |
| | December 23 | Me-109 dest(air) | Coblenz | P-51 |

1-0-2 air
0.5-0 ground

* - shared with Lt. G.F. Baker of the 368th Ftr Sqn

**Benjamin, Swift T., Lt.**
62nd Ftr Sqn/ 56th Ftr Grp
350th Ftr Sqn/353rd Ftr Grp

| *Sqn* | *Date* | *Claims* | *Location* | *A/C* |
|---|---|---|---|---|
| 350th | June 12, 1944 | Me-109 dam(air) | Dreux | P-47 |
| | June 27 | (.5)Me-109 dest(grd)[*] | Chalons | P-47 |
| | August 7 | Me-410 dest(grd) | SE Amiens | P-47 |
| | August 29 | (3)Me-109 dest(grd) | Diest | P-47 |
| | | (2)Me-410 dest(grd) | Diest | P-47 |
| | | (4)Me-109 dam(grd) | Diest | P-47 |
| | September 9 | Do-217 dest(air) | Hesepe A/F | P-47 |

1-0-1 air
6.5-4 ground

* - shared with Lt. M.V. Bledsoe of the 350th Ftr Sqn

**Bennett, Carroll W., Capt.**
504th Ftr Sqn/339th Ftr Grp

| *Sqn* | *Date* | *Claims* | *Location* | *A/C* |
|---|---|---|---|---|
| 504th | March 30, 1945 | Me-262 dest(air) | Hamburg | P-51 |
| | | Me-262 dam(air) | Hamburg | P-51 |
| | April 10 | (2)Me-410 dest(grd) | N/Neuruppin | P-51 |
| | | (2)Me-410 dam(grd) | N/Neuruppin | P-51 |

1-0-1 air
2-2 ground

**Bennett, Eugene E., Lt.**
62nd Ftr Sqn/56th Ftr Grp

| *Sqn* | *Date* | *Claims* | *Location* | *A/C* |
|---|---|---|---|---|
| 62nd | May 4, 1944 | (.5)FW-190 dest(air)[*] | Nordhausen | P-47 |

0.5-0-0 air
0-0 ground

* - shared with Lt. R.C. Cherry of the 62nd Ftr Sqn

**Bennett, John R., Maj.**
487th Ftr Sqn/352nd Ftr Grp

| *Sqn* | *Date* | *Claims* | *Location* | *A/C* |
|---|---|---|---|---|
| 487th | November 26, 1943 | (.5)Me-109 dest(air)[*] | E/Groningen | P-47 |
| | December 22 | (.5)Me-109 dest(air)[**] | E/Zwolle | P-47 |
| | | FW-190 dam(air) | E/Zwolle | P-47 |
| | April 13 | u/i a/c dam(grd) | SE Stuttgart | P-51 |
| | September 10 | Ju-52 dest(grd) | Wertheim | P-51 |
| | September 11 | FW-190 dest(air) | Gottingen-Nordhausen | P-51 |
| | | (2)Me-109 dam(air) | Gottingen-Nordhausen | P-51 |

2-0-3 air
1-1 ground

* - shared with Lt. R.H. Berkshire of the 487th Ftr Sqn
** - shared with Lt. E.B. McMahan of the 487th Ftr Sqn

**Bennett, Joseph H., Capt.**
360th Ftr Sqn/356th Ftr Grp
61st Ftr Sqn/ 56th Ftr Grp
336th Ftr Sqn/ 4th Ftr Grp

| *Sqn* | *Date* | *Claims* | *Location* | *A/C* |
|---|---|---|---|---|
| 360th | November 29, 1943 | Me-109 prob(air) | Meppel | P-47 |
| 61st | December 20 | Me-110 dest(air) | Falkenburg | P-47 |
| | January 11, 1944 | (2)Me-109 dam(air) | Schwastorf | P-47 |
| | January 29 | (1.5)Me-110 dest(air)[*] | Simmern | P-47 |
| | March 8 | (2)Me-109 dest(air) | E/Steinhuder Lake | P-47 |
| | | FW-190 dest(air) | Munstorf A/F | P-47 |
| 336th | April 8 | Me-109 dest(air) | Huden | P-51 |
| | May 22 | Me-109 prob(air) | Lubeck | P-51 |
| | May 25 | (2)Me-109 dest(air) | Strasbourg | P-51 |
| | | (2)FW-190 prob(air) | Strasbourg | P-51 |
| | | FW-190 dam(air) | Strasbourg | P-51 |

8.5-4-3 air
0-0 ground

* - shared with Lt. P. Neyland of the 61st Ftr Sqn

**Bennett, Wallace E., Capt.**
83rd Ftr Sqn/78th Ftr Grp

| *Sqn* | *Date* | *Claims* | *Location* | *A/C* |
|---|---|---|---|---|
| 83rd | July 31, 1944 | u/i a/c dest(grd) | Neustadt A/F | P-47 |
| | September 10 | (.5)He-111 dest(grd) | Germsheim | P-47 |

0-0-0 air
1.5-0 ground

* - shared with Lt. D.D. Hartley of the 83rd Ftr Sqn

**Bennette, Charles J., Lt.**
328th Ftr Sqn/352nd Ftr Grp

| *Sqn* | *Date* | *Claims* | *Location* | *A/C* |
|---|---|---|---|---|
| 328th | April 8, 1944 | u/i a/c dest(grd) | Quackenbruck | P-47 |
| | | (.5)Me-110 dest(grd)[*] | Quackenbruck | P-47 |
| | May 21 | He-111 dest(grd) | Alt Ruppin | P-51 |
| | | u/i a/c dest(grd) | Alt Ruppin | P-51 |
| | June 10 | Me-109 dest(air) | Bayeux | P-51 |

| Sqn | Date | Claims | Location | A/C |
|---|---|---|---|---|
| | | Me-109 dam(air) | Bayeux | P-51 |
| | July 29 | Me-109 dest(air) | Merseburg | P-51 |
| | | Me-109 dam(air) | Merseburg | P-51 |

2-0-2 air
3.5-0 ground

* - shared with Lt. M.V. Long of the 328th Ftr Sqn

**Benoit, Norman R., Capt.**
435th Ftr Sqn/479th Ftr Grp

| *Sqn* | *Date* | *Claims* | *Location* | *A/C* |
|---|---|---|---|---|
| 435th | October 7, 1944 | (.5)Me-109 dest(air)* | W/Chemnitz | P-51 |
| | December 5 | Me-262 dam(grd) | Bremen | P-51 |
| | December 6 | He-111 dam(grd) | W/Dummer Lake | P-51 |
| | December 25 | Me-109 dest(air) | SW Cologne | P-51 |
| | | Me-109 dam(air) | SW Cologne | P-51 |
| | January 21, 1945 | Me-262 dam(grd) | Leipheim | P-51 |
| | | Ju-88 dam(grd) | Leipheim | P-51 |
| | February 9 | FW-190 dest(air) | SW Brandenburg | P-51 |

2.5-0-1 air
0-4 ground

* - shared with Col. H. Zemke of HdQts, 479th Ftr Grp

**Benson, Arvid E., Lt.**
357th Ftr Sqn/355th Ftr Grp

| *Sqn* | *Date* | *Claims* | *Location* | *A/C* |
|---|---|---|---|---|
| 357th | January 21, 1944 | FW-190 dam(air) | NW Dourdan | P-47 |
| | April 5 | (2)Do-217 dam(grd) | Landsberg | P-51 |

0-0-1 air
0-2 ground

**Bentley, John M., Lt.**
376th Ftr Sqn/361st Ftr Grp

| *Sqn* | *Date* | *Claims* | *Location* | *A/C* |
|---|---|---|---|---|
| 376th | March 6, 1944 | FW-190 dest(air) | Lingen | P-47 |

1-0-0 air
0-0 ground

**Bergmann, Charles H., Maj.**
374th Ftr Sqn/361st Ftr Grp

| *Sqn* | *Date* | *Claims* | *Location* | *A/C* |
|---|---|---|---|---|
| 374th | June 4, 1944 | (.5)Me-109 dest(air)* | SE Mulun | P-51 |
| | June 8 | Me-109 dest(air) | St. Pierre | P-51 |

1.5-0-0 air
0-0 ground

* - shared with Lt. J.K. Wood of the 374th Ftr Sqn

**Bergstrom, Airus E., Capt.**
359th Ftr Sqn/356th Ftr Grp

| *Sqn* | *Date* | *Claims* | *Location* | *A/C* |
|---|---|---|---|---|
| 359th | June 7, 1944 | Me-109 dest(grd) | Laval | P-47 |

0-0-0 air
1-0 ground

**Berguson, Kenneth V., Lt.**
504th Ftr Sqn/339th Ftr Grp

| *Sqn* | *Date* | *Claims* | *Location* | *A/C* |
|---|---|---|---|---|
| 504th | March 20, 1945 | Me-262 dam(air) | Hamburg | P-51 |

0-0-1 air
0-0 ground

**Berkshire, Robert H., Lt.**
487th Ftr Sqn/352nd Ftr Grp

| *Sqn* | *Date* | *Claims* | *Location* | *A/C* |
|---|---|---|---|---|
| 487th | November 26, 1943 | (.5)Me-109 dest(air)* | E/Groningen | P-47 |
| | February 21, 1944 | Me-109 dam(air) | N/Osnabruck | P-47 |
| | April 9 | Ju-88 dest(grd) | Vechta | P-51 |
| | May 27 | (2)Me-109 dest(air) | Strasbourg | P-51 |
| | May 30 | Me-109 dest(air) | Magdeburg | P-51 |
| | | FW-190 dest(air) | Ulzen | P-51 |
| | June 20 | Me-410 dam(air) | Magdeburg | P-51 |

4.5-0-2 air
1-0 ground

* - shared with Lt. J.R. Bennett of the 487th Ftr Sqn

**Bernardo, George W., F/O**
343rd Ftr Sqn/55th Ftr Grp

| *Sqn* | *Date* | *Claims* | *Location* | *A/C* |
|---|---|---|---|---|
| 343rd | April 17, 1945 | (3)FW-190 dest(grd) | Dresden | P-51 |
| | | Ju-88 dest(grd) | Dresden | P-51 |
| | | (2)FW-190 dam(grd) | Dresden | P-51 |

0-0-0 air
4-2 ground

**Berndt, Harley E., F/O**
369th Ftr Sqn/359th Ftr Grp

| *Sqn* | *Date* | *Claims* | *Location* | *A/C* |
|---|---|---|---|---|
| 369th | March 18, 1945 | Me-109 dam(air) | Joachimsthal | P-51 |

0-0-1 air
0-0 ground

**Bernert, John R., Lt.**
374th Ftr Sqn/361st Ftr Grp

| *Sqn* | *Date* | *Claims* | *Location* | *A/C* |
|---|---|---|---|---|
| 374th | January 30, 1944 | Me-109 prob(air) | Rheine | P-47 |

0-1-0 air
0-0 ground

**Bernhard, Jack J., Lt.**
82nd Ftr Sqn/78th Ftr Grp

| *Sqn* | *Date* | *Claims* | *Location* | *A/C* |
|---|---|---|---|---|
| 82nd | March 30, 1944 | glider dam(grd) | Wesel | P-47 |
| | April 28 | (2)He-111 dam(grd) | Chateaudun | P-47 |

0-0-0 air
0-3 ground

**Bernoske, Robert, Lt.**
357th Ftr Sqn/355th Ftr Grp

| *Sqn* | *Date* | *Claims* | *Location* | *A/C* |
|---|---|---|---|---|
| 357th | December 1, 1943 | Me-109 prob(air) | W/Cologne | P-47 |
| | June 6 | Ju-87 dest(air) | NE Janville | P-51 |

1-1-0 air
0-0 ground

**Berry, Lawrence J., Lt.**
338th Ftr Sqn/55th Ftr Grp

| *Sqn* | *Date* | *Claims* | *Location* | *A/C* |
|---|---|---|---|---|
| 338th | June 14, 1944 | Me-109 dest(air) | Paris | P-38 |

1-0-0 air
0-0 ground

**Bertrand, John R., Maj.**
84th Ftr Sqn/78th Ftr Grp

| *Sqn* | *Date* | *Claims* | *Location* | *A/C* |
|---|---|---|---|---|
| 84th July 30, 1943 | | FW-190 dest(air) | Winterswijk | P-47 |

1-0-0 air
0-0 ground

**Beschen, Darrell A., Capt.**
79th Ftr Sqn/20th Ftr Grp

| *Sqn* | *Date* | *Claims* | *Location* | *A/C* |
|---|---|---|---|---|
| 79th | January 14, 1945 | Me-109 dest(air) | E/Wittenburg | P-51 |

| Sqn | Date | Claims | Location | A/C |
|---|---|---|---|---|
| | February 20 | (1.5)He-111 dest(grd)[*] | Weiden A/F | P-51 |
| | | He-111 dam(grd) | Weiden A/F | P-51 |

1-0-0 air
1.5-1 ground

* - shared with Lt. V.J. Rudnick of the 79th Ftr Sqn

**Best, Donald J., Lt.**
38th Ftr Sqn/55th Ftr Grp

| *Sqn* | *Date* | *Claims* | *Location* | *A/C* |
|---|---|---|---|---|
| 38th | April 9, 1945 | (3)He-280 dest(grd) | Munich-Brunnthal | P-51 |
| | April 10 | (2)He-111 dest(grd) | Wesendorf | P-51 |
| | | Me-109 dam(grd) | Wesendorf | P-51 |

0-0-0 air
5-1 ground

**Betounes, Samuel G., Lt.**
354th Ftr Sqn/355th Ftr Grp

| *Sqn* | *Date* | *Claims* | *Location* | *A/C* |
|---|---|---|---|---|
| 354th | July 7, 1944 | (.5)Ju-88 dest(air)[*] | Lingen | P-51 |
| | September 10 | (4)He-60 dam(grd) | Frankfurt | P-51 |

0.5-0-0 air
0-4 ground

* - shared with Lt. R.G. Taylor of the 354th Ftr Sqn

**Bettin, Norman F., Lt.**
383rd Ftr Sqn/364th Ftr Grp

| *Sqn* | *Date* | *Claims* | *Location* | *A/C* |
|---|---|---|---|---|
| 383rd | April 11, 1944 | Me-109 prob(air) | Halberstadt | P-38 |
| | May 22 | FW-190 dam(air) | SW Kiel | P-38 |

0-1-1 air
0-0 ground

**Bevington, Jack H., Lt.**
343rd Ftr Sqn/55th Ftr Grp

| *Sqn* | *Date* | *Claims* | *Location* | *A/C* |
|---|---|---|---|---|
| 343rd | April 16, 1945 | FW-190 dest(grd) | Ainring A/F | P-51 |

0-0-0 air
1-0 ground

**Bevins, Hiram O., Lt.**
61st Ftr Sqn/56th Ftr Grp

| *Sqn* | *Date* | *Claims* | *Location* | *A/C* |
|---|---|---|---|---|
| 61st | September 3, 1943 | Ju-88 prob(air) | Paris | P-47 |

0-1-0 air
0-0 ground

**Beyer, William R., Capt.**
376th Ftr Sqn/361st Ftr Grp

| *Sqn* | *Date* | *Claims* | *Location* | *A/C* |
|---|---|---|---|---|
| 376th | September 17, 1944 | Me-109 dest(air) | Hasselt-Wesel | P-51 |
| | September 27 | (5)FW-190 dest(air) | Eisenach | P-51 |
| | November 2 | FW-190 dest(air) | N/Erfurt | P-51 |
| | November 26 | Me-109 dest(air) | S/Ulzen | P-51 |
| | | FW-190 dest(air) | S/Ulzen | P-51 |

9-0-0 air
0-0 ground

**Biales, Albert T., Lt.**
61st Ftr Sqn/56th Ftr Grp

| *Sqn* | *Date* | *Claims* | *Location* | *A/C* |
|---|---|---|---|---|
| 61st | May 14, 1943 | FW-190 prob(air) | NW Antwerp | P-47 |

0-1-0 air
0-0 ground

**Biedul, Chester A., Lt.**
338th Ftr Sqn/55th Ftr Grp

| *Sqn* | *Date* | *Claims* | *Location* | *A/C* |
|---|---|---|---|---|
| 338th | July 7, 1944 | FW-190 dest(air) | W/Bernburg | P-38 |

1-0-0 air
0-0 ground

**Biel, Hipolitus T., Lt.**
334th Ftr Sqn/4th Ftr Grp

| *Sqn* | *Date* | *Claims* | *Location* | *A/C* |
|---|---|---|---|---|
| 334th | January 14, 1944 | FW-190 dest(air) | Cambrai | P-47 |
| | February 10 | Me-109 dest(air) | Hengelo | P-47 |
| | | Me-109 dam(air) | Hengelo | P-47 |
| | March 18 | Me-109 dam(air) | SE Mannheim | P-51 |
| | March 27 | (1.5)Ju-88 dest(grd)[*] | Cazaux A/F | P-51 |
| | | Me-410 dest(grd) | Cazaux A/F | P-51 |
| | | FW-190 dam(grd) | Cazaux A/F | P-51 |
| | March 29 | FW-190 dest(air) | Gifhorn | P-51 |
| | April 5 | (.33)Ju-88 dest(air)[**] | Plaue A/F | P-51 |
| | | He-111 dest(grd) | Brandenburg-Briest | P-51 |
| | | Ju-88 dam(grd) | Brandenburg-Briest | P-51 |
| | | (.25) of (5)Ju-52 dam(grd)[@] | Brandenburg-Briest | P-51 |
| | April 8 | Ju-52 dest(grd) | SW Celle | P-51 |
| | | Me-109 dam(grd) | SW Celle | P-51 |
| | | Ju-88 dam(grd) | SW Celle | P-51 |
| | April 10 | u/i a/c dest(grd) | Romorantin A/F | P-51 |
| | April 11 | Me-410 dest(air) | SE Stettin | P-51 |
| | | Me-110 dest(air) | SE Stettin | P-51 |
| | April 15 | (.5)Ju-52 dest(grd)[@@] | Magdeburg | P-51 |

5.33-0-2 air
6-5.25 ground

* - shared with Capt. D.W. Beeson of the 334th Ftr Sqn
** - shared with Capt. D.W. Beeson of the 334th Ftr Sqn and Lt. C.A. Fiedler of the 335th Ftr Sqn, 4th Ftr Grp
@ - all shared with Capt. D.W. Beeson and Lt. C.D. Carr of the 334th Ftr Sqn, and Lt. R.S. Tussey of the 336th Ftr Sqn, 4th Ftr Grp
@@ - shared with Capt. R.C. Care of the 334th Ftr Sqn

**Bielok, Adolph, Lt.**
487th Ftr Sqn/352nd Ftr Grp

| *Sqn* | *Date* | *Claims* | *Location* | *A/C* |
|---|---|---|---|---|
| 487th | April 20, 1944 | (.5)Me-109 dest(air)[*] | SE Paris | P-51 |

0.5-0-0 air
0-0 ground

* - shared with Lt. C.J. Luksic of the 487th Ftr Sqn

**Biggs, Oscar K., Lt.**
505th Ftr Sqn/339th Ftr Grp

| *Sqn* | *Date* | *Claims* | *Location* | *A/C* |
|---|---|---|---|---|
| 505th | March 1, 1945 | (.5)Ju-88 dest(grd)[*] | S/Feldkirchen | P-51 |
| | March 2 | (3)Do-217 dest(grd) | Mockern | P-51 |
| | | (2)Do-217 dam(grd) | Mockern | P-51 |
| | April 7 | (.5)Me-109 dest(air)[**] | NE Steinhuder Lake | P-51 |
| | April 10 | (4)Ju-88 dest(grd) | Wittstock | P-51 |
| | | (2)Ju-88 dam(grd) | Wittstock | P-51 |
| | April 16 | Me-109 dest(grd) | NE Prague | P-51 |
| | | Ju-88 dest(grd) | NE Prague | P-51 |
| | | u/i a/c dest(grd) | NE Prague | P-51 |
| | April 17 | Ju-88 dest(grd) | SE Pocking | P-51 |

0.5-0-0 air
11.5-4 ground

* - shared with Lt. B.B. Booth of the 505th Ftr Sqn
** - shared with LtCol. J.L. Thury of the 505th Ftr Sqn

**Bille, Henry S., Maj.**
357th Ftr Sqn/355th Ftr Grp

| *Sqn* | *Date* | *Claims* | *Location* | *A/C* |
|---|---|---|---|---|
| 357th | March 16, 1944 | Me-109 dam(air) | S/Reutlingen | P-51 |
| | April 13 | Me-109 dest(air) | Augsburg | P-51 |
| | | Me-323 dam(grd) | Crailsheim | P-51 |
| | April 24 | FW-190 dest(air) | NW Munich | P-51 |
| | August 16 | (2)Me-109 dest(air) | SE Hildesheim | P-51 |
| | September 12 | FW-190 dam(air) | NE Berlin | P-51 |
| | November 26 | Me-109 prob(air) | W/Gardelegen | P-51 |

| Sqn | Date | Claims | Location | A/C |
|---|---|---|---|---|
| | April 16, 1945 | (2)u/i a/c dest(grd) | Eger A/F | P-51 |
| | | He-177 dest(grd) | Eger A/F | P-51 |
| | | Ju-87 dest(grd) | Eger A/F | P-51 |
| | | (2)u/i a/c dam(grd) | Eger A/F | P-51 |
| | April 20 | (2)Me-109 dest(air) | Letnany A/F | P-51 |
| | | (2)Me-109 dam(air) | Letnany A/F | P-51 |

6-1-4 air
4-3 ground

**Bingham, Percy, Lt.**
83rd Ftr Sqn/78th Ftr Grp

| Sqn | Date | Claims | Location | A/C |
|---|---|---|---|---|
| 83rd | September 1, 1944 | (.5)Me-110 dest(air)* | Gilze-Rijen | P-47 |

0.5-0-0 air
0-0 ground

* - shared with F/O J.A. Moothart of the 83rd Ftr Sqn

**Binkley, Harold O., Capt.**
79th Ftr Sqn/20th Ftr Grp

| Sqn | Date | Claims | Location | A/C |
|---|---|---|---|---|
| 79th | August 5, 1944 | Me-109 dest(air) | Hamburg-Bremen | P-51 |
| | August 9 | FW-190 dest(air) | SW Ulm | P-51 |
| | | FW-190 dam(air) | SW Ulm | P-51 |
| | September 10 | Me-110 dest(grd) | SW Stuttgart | P-51 |
| | | u/i a/c dest(grd) | SW Stuttgart | P-51 |

2-0-1 air
2-0 ground

**Birch, William K., Lt.**
38th Ftr Sqn/55th Ftr Grp

| Sqn | Date | Claims | Location | A/C |
|---|---|---|---|---|
| 38th | November 25, 1943 | Me-109 prob(air) | NW Arras | P-38 |

0-1-0 air
0-0 ground

**Birtciel, Frank E., Capt.**
343rd Ftr Sqn/55th Ftr Grp

| Sqn | Date | Claims | Location | A/C |
|---|---|---|---|---|
| 343rd | March 22, 1945 | Me-262 dam(air) | Schwabisch Hall | P-51 |
| | April 9 | (2)He-111 dest(grd) | Munich-Brunnthal | P-51 |
| | | (2)Ju-88 dest(grd) | Munich-Brunnthal | P-51 |
| | | Me-109 dest(grd) | Munich-Brunnthal | P-51 |
| | | Ju-88 dam(grd) | Munich-Brunnthal | P-51 |

0-0-1 air
5-1 ground

**Biscayart, Jules D., Maj.**
436th Ftr Sqn/479th Ftr Grp

| Sqn | Date | Claims | Location | A/C |
|---|---|---|---|---|
| 436th | September 28, 1944 | (2)FW-190 dest(air) | W/Magdeburg | P-38 |

2-0-0 air
0-0 ground

**Bishop, Lynn P., Lt.**
79th Ftr Sqn/20th Ftr Grp

| Sqn | Date | Claims | Location | A/C |
|---|---|---|---|---|
| 79th | April 13, 1945 | (2)u/i a/c dam(grd) | Jagel-Hutzfeld | P-51 |

0-0-0 air
0-2 ground

**Bishop, Richard D., Lt.**
343rd Ftr Sqn/55th Ftr Grp

| Sqn | Date | Claims | Location | A/C |
|---|---|---|---|---|
| 343rd | September 11, 1944 | FW-190 dest(air) | Saalfeld | P-51 |
| | | FW-190 dam(air) | Saalfeld | P-51 |
| | | FW-190 dest(grd) | Saalfeld | P-51 |

1-0-1 air
1-0 ground

**Bixby, William K., II, Lt.**
352nd Ftr Sqn/353rd Ftr Grp

| Sqn | Date | Claims | Location | A/C |
|---|---|---|---|---|
| 352nd | March 21, 1945 | u/i a/c dest(grd) | Achmer | P-51 |
| | April 16 | Ar-196 dam(grd) | Pocking | P-51 |
| | | u/i a/c dam(grd) | Pocking | P-51 |

0-0-0 air
1-2 ground

**Black, Richard H., Lt.**
79th Ftr Sqn/20th Ftr Grp

| Sqn | Date | Claims | Location | A/C |
|---|---|---|---|---|
| 79th | April 8, 1944 | Ju-88 dest(grd) | Salzwedel | P-38 |
| | | u/i a/c dest(grd) | Salzwedel | P-38 |
| | January 14, 1945 | Me-109 dest(air) | E/Wittenberg | P-51 |
| | | Me-109 dam(air) | E/Wittenberg | P-51 |

1-0-1 air
2-0 ground

**Blackburn, George H., Lt.**
368th Ftr Sqn/359th Ftr Grp

| Sqn | Date | Claims | Location | A/C |
|---|---|---|---|---|
| 368th | February 28, 1945 | Me-109 dest(grd) | Gunzberg | P-51 |

0-0-0 air
1-0 ground

**Blair, Charles W., Jr., Capt.**
358th Ftr Sqn/355th Ftr Grp

| Sqn | Date | Claims | Location | A/C |
|---|---|---|---|---|
| 358th | March 2, 1944 | Me-109 dest(air) | NE Liege | P-47 |
| | May 4 | Me-109 dam(air) | SW Hanover | P-51 |

1-0-1 air
0-0 ground

**Blair, Floyd A., Lt.**
343rd Ftr Sqn/55th Ftr Grp

| Sqn | Date | Claims | Location | A/C |
|---|---|---|---|---|
| 343rd | September 5, 1944 | He-177 dest(grd) | Stuttgart/Echterdingen | P-51 |
| | | u/i a/c dam(grd) | Stuttgart/Echterdingen | P-51 |
| | | (.5)Ju-52 dam(grd)* | Stuttgart/Echterdingen | P-51 |
| | September 10 | u/i a/c dest(grd) | Illesheim | P-51 |

0-0-0 air
2-1.5 ground

* - shared with Capt. D.A. Parker of the 343rd Ftr Sqn

**Blake, Gordon J., Capt.**
61st Ftr Sqn/56th Ftr Grp

| Sqn | Date | Claims | Location | A/C |
|---|---|---|---|---|
| 61st | February 24, 1944 | FW-190 dest(air) | N/Minden | P-47 |
| | March 8 | FW-190 dest(air) | NE Steinhuder Lake | P-47 |

2-0-0 air
0-0 ground

**Blakeslee, Donald J.M., Col.**
336th Ftr Sqn/4th Ftr Grp
335th Ftr Sqn/4th Ftr Grp
HdQts/4th Ftr Grp
Earlier flew with 401, 411, 121, and 133 Sqns, RAF, and claimed 3 kills: a Me-109 on November 21, 1942 (401st); a FW-190 on August 18, 1942, and a Do-217 on August 19, 1942 (both with the 133rd).

| Sqn | Date | Claims | Location | A/C |
|---|---|---|---|---|
| 335th | April 15, 1943 | FW-190 dest(air) | Knocke | P-47 |
| | May 14 | FW-190 dest(air) | N/Knocke | P-47 |
| HdQts | December 20 | Me-110 dest(air)* | Bremen | P-51 |
| | January 7, 1944 | FW-190 dest(air) | Hosdin | P-47 |
| | March 6 | Me-210 dest(air) | Berlin | P-51 |
| | March 16 | Me-110 dam(air) | SW Munich | P-51 |
| | March 18 | FW-190 dest(air) | S/Augsburg | P-51 |
| | March 23 | FW-190 dam(air) | Osnabruck | P-51 |
| | April 5 | (2)Ju-88 dam(grd) | Brandenburg-Briest | P-51 |
| | | u/i a/c dam(grd) | Brandenburg-Briest | P-51 |

| | | | |
|---|---|---|---|
| April 18 | He-177 dest(grd) | Fassberg A/F | P-51 |
| | u/i a/c dam(grd) | Fassberg A/F | P-51 |
| April 22 | (2)Me-109 dest(air) | Kassel | P-51 |
| April 24 | (1.5)FW-190 dest(air)[**] | N/Worms | P-51 |
| | FW-190 dam(air) | N/Worms | P-51 |
| April 30 | (.5)Do-24 dest(grd)[@] | Lyon Anchorage | P-51 |
| May 29 | Me-410 dest(air) | N/Falkenburg | P-51 |
| | (2)Do-18 dam(grd) | Dievenow | P-51 |
| July 2 | Me-109 dest(air) | Budapest | P-51 |

11.5-0-3 air
1.5-6 ground

[*] - scored while leading the 354th Ftr Grp, 9th Air Force on one of that unit's early missions.
[**] - shared with Capt. A.L. Schlegel of the 335th Ftr Sqn
[@] - shared with Lt. J.A. Patteeuw of the 336th Ftr Sqn, 4th Ftr Grp

**Blanchard, James L., Lt.**
362nd Ftr Sqn/357th Ftr Grp

| *Sqn* | *Date* | *Claims* | *Location* | *A/C* |
|---|---|---|---|---|
| 362nd | September 18, 1944 | Me-109 dest(air) | Nijmegen | P-51 |

1-0-0 air
0-0 ground

**Blanchard, Merle E., Capt.**
338th Ftr Sqn/55th Ftr Grp

| *Sqn* | *Date* | *Claims* | *Location* | *A/C* |
|---|---|---|---|---|
| 338th | January 31, 1944 | Me-109 dest(air) | Goch | P-38 |
| | May 22 | FW-190 dest(air) | Neumunster | P-38 |
| | June 11 | Me-109 dam(air) | Beauvais | P-38 |
| | July 6 | Me-109 dam(air) | Laon | P-38 |

2-0-2 air
0-0 ground

**Blanchfield, Herbert J., Capt.**
334th Ftr Sqn/4th Ftr Grp

| *Sqn* | *Date* | *Claims* | *Location* | *A/C* |
|---|---|---|---|---|
| 334th | April 5, 1944 | (2)Do-217 dest(grd) | Brandenburg-Briest | P-51 |
| | | (.33)He-111 dest(grd)[*] | Brandenburg-Briest | P-51 |
| | | (2)Ju-52 dam(grd) | Brandenburg-Briest | P-51 |
| | April 10 | Hs-126 dest(grd) | Romorantin A/F | P-51 |
| | April 15 | Ju-88 dest(grd) | Hagenow | P-51 |

0-0-0 air
4.33-2 ground

[*] - shared with Lt. V.J. France and Lt. L.R. Pierce of the 334th Ftr Sqn

**Blanding, Leon M., Maj.**
335th Ftr Sqn/4th Ftr Grp
HdQts/4th Ftr Grp

| *Sqn* | *Date* | *Claims* | *Location* | *A/C* |
|---|---|---|---|---|
| 335th | July 28, 1943 | FW-190 dest(air) | SE Utrecht | P-47 |
| | | FW-190 dam(air) | SE Utrecht | P-47 |
| | March 8, 1944 | Me-109 dam(air) | Burg-Genthin | P-51 |
| | July 17 | Me-109 dam(air) | NE Munich | P-51 |

1-0-3 air
0-0 ground

**Blaylock, Donald C., Lt.**
358th Ftr Sqn/55th Ftr Grp

| *Sqn* | *Date* | *Claims* | *Location* | *A/C* |
|---|---|---|---|---|
| 358th | July 24, 1944 | Do-217 dest(grd) | Augsburg | P-51 |
| | | (3)Do-217 dam(grd) | Augsburg | P-51 |

0-0-0 air
1-3 ground

**Bledsoe, Marvin V., Capt.**
350th Ftr Sqn/353rd Ftr Grp

| *Sqn* | *Date* | *Claims* | *Location* | *A/C* |
|---|---|---|---|---|
| 350th | June 27, 1944 | (.5)Me-109 dest(grd)[*] | Chalons | P-47 |
| | August 7 | Me-410 dest(grd) | SE Amiens | P-47 |
| | August 29 | (2)Me-110 dest(grd) | Diest | P-47 |
| | | (2)Me-109 dest(grd) | Diest | P-47 |
| | | (2)Me-110 dam(grd) | Diest | P-47 |
| | | (2)Me-109 dam(grd) | Diest | P-47 |

0-0-0 air
5.5-4 ground

[*] - shared with Lt. S.T. Benjamin of the 350th Ftr Sqn

**Blewett, John E., Lt.**
359th Ftr Sqn/356th Ftr Grp

| *Sqn* | *Date* | *Claims* | *Location* | *A/C* |
|---|---|---|---|---|
| 359th | November 27, 1944 | Me-109 prob(air) | N/Munster | P-51 |

0-1-0 air
0-0 ground

**Blickenstaff, Wayne K., LtCol.**
350th Ftr Sqn/353rd Ftr Grp
HdQts/353rd Ftr Grp

| *Sqn* | *Date* | *Claims* | *Location* | *A/C* |
|---|---|---|---|---|
| 350th | December 1, 1943 | Me-109 dam(air) | Solingen | P-47 |
| | June 30, 1944 | Me-109 prob(air) | W/Chalons | P-47 |
| | | Me-109 dam(air) | W/Chalons | P-47 |
| | November 27 | (4)FW-190 dest(air) | Steinhuder Lake-Brunswick | P-51 |
| | February 22, 1945 | Me-262 dest(air) | Berlin | P-51 |
| | March 24 | (3)FW-190 dest(air) | NW Kassel | P-51 |
| | | (2)Me-109 dest(air) | NW Kassel | P-51 |

10-1-2 air
0-0 ground

**Bline, Brooks J., Capt.**
505th Ftr Sqn/339th Ftr Grp

| *Sqn* | *Date* | *Claims* | *Location* | *A/C* |
|---|---|---|---|---|
| 505th | April 7, 1945 | FW-190 dest(air) | SW Ulzen | P-51 |
| | April 17 | (2)Me-109 dest(grd) | SE Pocking | P-51 |
| | | (2)Ju-88 dest(grd) | SE Pocking | P-51 |

1-0-0 air
4-0 ground

**Blizzard, Robert V.E., Lt.**
504th Ftr Sqn/339th Ftr Grp

| *Sqn* | *Date* | *Claims* | *Location* | *A/C* |
|---|---|---|---|---|
| 504th | April 7, 1945 | Me-262 prob(air) | Celle | P-51 |
| | | Me-262 dam(air) | Celle | P-51 |
| | April 10 | (2)Me-410 dest(grd) | N/Neuruppin | P-51 |
| | | (2)Me-410 dam(grd) | N/Neuruppin | P-51 |
| | April 16 | (4)Me-109 dest(grd) | Klatovy | P-51 |

0-1-1 air
6-2 ground

**Blodgett, Burton O., Lt.**
61st Ftr Sqn/56th Ftr Grp

| *Sqn* | *Date* | *Claims* | *Location* | *A/C* |
|---|---|---|---|---|
| 61st | April 10, 1945 | Do-24 dest(grd) | Muritz Lake | P-47 |
| | April 13 | (3)Ju-88 dest(grd) | Eggebeck A/F | P-47 |
| | | u/i a/c dest(grd) | Eggebeck A/F | P-47 |
| | | (2)Ju-88 dam(grd) | Eggebeck A/F | P-47 |

0-0-0 air
5-2 ground

**Blodgett, Warren S., Lt.**
84th Ftr Sqn/78th Ftr Grp

| *Sqn* | *Date* | *Claims* | *Location* | *A/C* |
|---|---|---|---|---|
| 84th | February 3, 1945 | FW-190 dest(grd) | Luneburg A/F | P-51 |
| | April 16 | (2)Me-110 dest(grd) | Praha/Kakewice | P-51 |
| | | Ju-52 dest(grd) | Praha/Kakewice | P-51 |
| | | Me-110 dam(grd) | Praha/Kakewice | P-51 |

0-0-0 air
4-1 ground

**Bloodgood, Donald L., Lt.**
385th Ftr Sqn/364th Ftr Grp

| *Sqn* | *Date* | *Claims* | *Location* | *A/C* |
|---|---|---|---|---|
| 385th | December 27, 1944 | FW-190 dest(air) | SE Bonn | P-51 |
| | April 16, 1945 | (2)FW-190 dest(grd) | Pocking | P-51 |

1-0-0 air
2-0 ground

**Blossom. Robert J., Lt.**
82nd Ftr Sqn/78th Ftr Grp

| *Sqn* | *Date* | *Claims* | *Location* | *A/C* |
|---|---|---|---|---|
| 82nd | January 14, 1945 | FW-190 dam(air) | Cologne | P-51 |
| | March 24 | He-111 dam(grd) | Diepholz | P-51 |
| | April 10 | He-111 dest(grd) | Werder A/F | P-51 |
| | | Me-109 dam(grd) | Werder A/F | P-51 |
| | April 16 | Do-217 dest(grd) | Pilzen/Prague | P-51 |

0-0-1 air
2-2 ground

**Blount, Delbert F., Lt.**
338th Ftr Sqn/55th Ftr Grp

| *Sqn* | *Date* | *Claims* | *Location* | *A/C* |
|---|---|---|---|---|
| 338th | July 21, 1944 | (2)Me-109 dest(air) | NE Kempton | P-51 |
| | | Me-109 dam(air) | NE Kempton | P-51 |

2-0-1 air
0-0 ground

**Bluhm, Roy B., Jr., Capt.**
62nd Ftr Sqn/ 56th Ftr Grp
360th Ftr Sqn/356th Ftr Grp

| *Sqn* | *Date* | *Claims* | *Location* | *A/C* |
|---|---|---|---|---|
| 62nd | February 21, 1944 | Me-109 dest(air) | Zwolle | P-47 |
| | April 11 | u/i a/c dam(grd) | Schleswig | P-47 |
| | May 4 | Me-109 dam(air) | Dummer Lake | P-47 |

1-0-1 air
0-1 ground

**Blystone, Harry L., Lt.**
83rd Ftr Sqn/78th Ftr Grp

| *Sqn* | *Date* | *Claims* | *Location* | *A/C* |
|---|---|---|---|---|
| 83rd | April 10, 1944 | (2)u/i a/c dest(grd) | Romorantin A/F | P-47 |
| | July 6 | FW-190 dam(air) | Rambouillet | P-47 |

0-0-1 air
2-0 ground

**Bochkay, Donald H., Maj.**
363rd Ftr Sqn/357th Ftr Grp

| *Sqn* | *Date* | *Claims* | *Location* | *A/C* |
|---|---|---|---|---|
| 363rd | March 5, 1944 | (.33)FW-190 dest(air)[*] | S/Bordeaux | P-51 |
| | March 6 | (2)Me-110 dest(air) | W/Berlin | P-51 |
| | April 8 | Me-109 dest(air) | NW Braunsweig | P-51 |
| | April 11 | (.5)Me-109 dest(air)[**] | Magdeburg | P-51 |
| | April 24 | Me-109 dest(air) | NE Munich | P-51 |
| | June 29 | Me-109 dest(air) | Schoningen | P-51 |
| | July 5 | Me-109 dest(air) | SE Rouen | P-51 |
| | | FW-190 dest(air) | SE Rouen | P-51 |
| | July 25 | Me-109 dest(air) | Paris | P-51 |
| | | Me-109 dam(air) | Paris | P-51 |
| | July 29 | FW-190 dest(air) | SW Merseburg | P-51 |
| | December 5 | (2)FW-190 dest(air) | NE Berlin | P-51 |
| | February 9, 1945 | Me-262 dest(air) | Fulda | P-51 |
| | April 18 | Me-262 dest(air) | SW Prague | P-51 |

13.83-0-1 air
0-0 ground

[*] - shared with Lt. C.K. Peters and Lt. E.A. Rogers of the 363rd Ftr Sqn
[**] - shared with Lt. M.A. Postle of the 363rd Ftr Sqn

**Bocquin, Victor E., Lt.**
376th Ftr Sqn/361st Ftr Grp

| *Sqn* | *Date* | *Claims* | *Location* | *A/C* |
|---|---|---|---|---|
| 376th | August 4, 1944 | Ju-88 dest(grd) | Anklam | P-51 |
| | | Ju-88 dam(grd) | Anklam | P-51 |
| | September 12 | Me-109 dest(air) | NW Magdeburg | P-51 |
| | September 27 | (3)FW-190 dest(air) | Eisenach | P-51 |

4-0-0 air
1-1 ground

**Bodenhamer, Donald, Jr., Maj.**
83rd Ftr Sqn/78th Ftr Grp

| *Sqn* | *Date* | *Claims* | *Location* | *A/C* |
|---|---|---|---|---|
| 83rd | August 16, 1943 | Me-109 dam(air) | Woensdrecht | P-47 |

0-0-1 air
0-0 ground

**Bodiford, Hugh, Lt.**
338th Ftr Sqn/55th Ftr Grp

| *Sqn* | *Date* | *Claims* | *Location* | *A/C* |
|---|---|---|---|---|
| 338th | January 14, 1945 | Do-217 dam(grd) | SE Salzwedel | P-51 |
| | February 6 | Me-110 dam(grd) | Gerolzhofen A/F | P-51 |
| | April 10 | Fi-156 dest(air) | SE Luneburg | P-51 |
| | April 16 | (2)u/i a/c dest(grd) | N/Landshut | P-51 |
| | | He-111 dest(grd) | N/Landshut | P-51 |
| | April 17 | FW-190 dest(air) | SE Dresden | P-51 |

2-0-0 air
3-2 ground

**Boeckman, Rex C., Capt.**
82nd Ftr Sqn/78th Ftr Grp

| *Sqn* | *Date* | *Claims* | *Location* | *A/C* |
|---|---|---|---|---|
| 82nd | August 27, 1944 | He-111 dest(grd) | Chatel-Cherary | P-47 |

0-0-0 air
1-0 ground

**Bolefahr, Wayne N., Capt.**
368th Ftr Sqn/359th Ftr Grp

| *Sqn* | *Date* | *Claims* | *Location* | *A/C* |
|---|---|---|---|---|
| 368th | March 6, 1944 | Me-109 dest(air) | Dummer Lake | P-47 |
| | May 8 | Me-109 dest(air) | SE Bremen | P-51 |
| | | Me-109 dam(air) | SE Bremen | P-51 |

2-0-1 air
0-0 ground

**Bollwerk, Val W., Maj.**
338th Ftr Sqn/55th Ftr Grp

| *Sqn* | *Date* | *Claims* | *Location* | *A/C* |
|---|---|---|---|---|
| 338th | January 31, 1944 | Me-109 prob(air) | Geldern | P-38 |
| | February 10 | Me-110 dest(air) | Brunswick | P-38 |
| | March 18 | (3)Me-109 dam(air) | SE Strasbourg | P-38 |
| | May 21 | Hs-129 dest(grd) | Helmstedt | P-38 |
| | June 11 | Me-109 dest(air) | Beauvais | P-38 |

2-1-3 air
1-0 ground

**Bond, Charles R., Lt.**
61st Ftr Sqn/56th Ftr Grp

| *Sqn* | *Date* | *Claims* | *Location* | *A/C* |
|---|---|---|---|---|
| 61st | December 4, 1944 | (2)u/i a/c dam(grd) | Ingolstadt | P-47 |
| | April 10, 1945 | Ju-88 dest(grd) | Rechlin | P-47 |
| | | Do-24 dest(grd) | Muritz Lake | P-47 |
| | | Do-217 dam(grd) | Muritz Lake | P-47 |
| | | Ju-88 dam(grd) | Rechlin | P-47 |

0-0-0 air
2-4 ground

**Bond, John S., Lt.**
84th Ftr Sqn/78th Ftr Grp

| *Sqn* | *Date* | *Claims* | *Location* | *A/C* |
|---|---|---|---|---|
| 84th | February 3, 1945 | FW-190 dest(grd) | Luneburg A/F | P-51 |
| | | Me-410 dam(grd) | Luneburg A/F | P-51 |

0-0-0 air
1-1 ground

**Bond, Richard T., Lt.**
77th Ftr Sqn/20th Ftr Grp

| *Sqn* | *Date* | *Claims* | *Location* | *A/C* |
|---|---|---|---|---|
| 77th | January 29, 1944 | (.5)Me-210 dest(air)[*] | S/Coblenz | P-38 |

0.5-0-0 air
0-0 ground

[*] - shared with Lt. R.S. Flynn of the 77th Ftr Sqn

**Bonebrake, Robert R., Capt.**
83rd Ftr Sqn/78th Ftr Grp

| *Sqn* | *Date* | *Claims* | *Location* | *A/C* |
|---|---|---|---|---|
| 83rd | July 5, 1944 | FW-190 dam(air) | Evreux | P-47 |
| | July 19 | Do-217 dest(grd) | Linburg-Coblenz | P-47 |
| | August 10 | He-111 dest(grd) | Chateau-Salines | P-47 |
| | | Ju-52 dest(grd) | Chateau-Salines | P-47 |
| | November 26 | Me-109 dest(air) | S/Dummer Lake | P-47 |
| | December 19 | Me-109 dest(air) | S/Coblenz | P-47 |
| | | FW-190 dest(air) | S/Coblenz | P-47 |

3-0-1 air
3-0 ground

**Boock, Robert A., Lt.**
334th Ftr Sqn/4th Ftr Grp

| *Sqn* | *Date* | *Claims* | *Location* | *A/C* |
|---|---|---|---|---|
| 334th | December 15, 1942 | (.5)Ju-52 prob(air)[*] | SW Flushing | Spit |
| | January 14, 1943 | FW-190 dest(air) | W/Ostend | Spit |
| | January 22 | FW-190 dest(air) | NW Dunkirk | Spit |
| | April 15 | FW-190 dest(air) | Belgian Coast | P-47 |

3-0.5-0 air
0-0 ground

[*] - shared with Lt. S.M. Anderson of the 334th Ftr Sqn

**Boone, Walker L., Maj.**
82nd Ftr Sqn/ 78th Ftr Grp
350th Ftr Sqn/353rd Ftr Grp

| *Sqn* | *Date* | *Claims* | *Location* | *A/C* |
|---|---|---|---|---|
| 82nd | February 13, 1944 | Ju-88 dam(grd) | Bryes-Sud A/F | P-47 |
| | April 1 | (.33)u/i a/c dest(grd)[*] | Verdun | P-47 |
| | | (.33)u/i a/c dest(grd)[*] | Verdun | P-47 |
| | | (.13)Do-217 dest(grd)[**] | Verdun | P-47 |
| | | Me-410 dam(grd) | Verdun | P-47 |
| | | Ju-52 dam(grd) | Verdun | P-47 |
| 350th | November 26 | FW-190 dest(air) | Minden | P-51 |
| | November 27 | FW-190 dest(air) | Brunswick | P-51 |
| | | FW-190 prob(air) | Brunswick | P-51 |
| | February 27, 1945 | (2)FW-190 dest(grd) | Rohrensee | P-51 |
| | | (2)He-219 dest(grd) | Rohrensee | P-51 |
| | | Me-410 dest(grd) | Rohrensee | P-51 |
| | | Ju-188 dest(grd) | Rohrensee | P-51 |
| | | Ar-234 dest(grd) | Rohrensee | P-51 |
| | | (3)u/i a/c dam(grd) | Rohrensee | P-51 |
| | | FW-190 dam(grd) | Rohrensee | P-51 |
| | | He-219 dam(grd) | Rohrensee | P-51 |
| | March 2 | Me-109 dam(air) | Ruhland | P-51 |
| | March 21 | (4)Ar-234 dest(grd) | Achmer | P-51 |
| | | (4)Ar-234 dam(grd) | Achmer | P-51 |
| | | Me-109 dam(grd) | Achmer | P-51 |

2-1-1 air
11.79-13 ground

[*] - both shared with Lt. B.M. Watkins and Lt. C. Webb of the 82nd Ftr Sqn
[**] - shared with Capt. W.E. May, Lt. B.M. Watkins, Lt. J.J. Hockery, Lt. C.R. Clark, Lt. H.L. Eakes, Lt. R.V. Hearn, and F/O C.W. DeWitt of the 82nd Ftr Sqn

**Booth, Billy B., Lt.**
505th Ftr Sqn/339th Ftr Grp

| *Sqn* | *Date* | *Claims* | *Location* | *A/C* |
|---|---|---|---|---|
| 505th | March 1, 1945 | (.5)Ju-88 dest(grd)[*] | S/Feldkirchen | P-51 |

0-0-0 air
0.5-0 ground

[*] - shared with Lt. O.K. Biggs of the 505th Ftr Sqn

**Booth, Robert J., Lt.**
369th Ftr Sqn/359th Ftr Grp

| *Sqn* | *Date* | *Claims* | *Location* | *A/C* |
|---|---|---|---|---|
| 369th | January 30, 1944 | Me-109 dest(air) | Lingen | P-47 |
| | March 6 | FW-190 dest(air) | Quackenbruck | P-47 |
| | April 22 | FW-190 dest(air) | Hamm | P-47 |
| | April 25 | Me-109 dest(air) | Salmagne | P-47 |
| | May 8 | (2)Me-109 dest(air) | Mellensdorf-Drakenburg | P-51 |
| | | FW-190 dest(air) | Mellensdorf-Drakenburg | P-51 |
| | May 29 | FW-190 dest(air) | Stettner Haven | P-51 |
| | May 30 | Ju-88 dam(grd) | Harsleben | P-51 |

8-0-0 air
0-1 ground

**Borelli, Bernard, Capt.**
360th Ftr Sqn/356th Ftr Grp

| *Sqn* | *Date* | *Claims* | *Location* | *A/C* |
|---|---|---|---|---|
| 360th | March 8, 1944 | Me-109 dest(air) | NW Lingen | P-47 |
| | March 29 | Me-410 dam(grd) | Cloppenburg | P-47 |
| | November 26 | Me-109 dam(air) | Dummer Lake | P-51 |

1-0-1 air
0-1 ground

**Borg, Robert M., Lt.**
369th Ftr Sqn/359th Ftr Grp
370th Ftr Sqn/359th Ftr Grp

| *Sqn* | *Date* | *Claims* | *Location* | *A/C* |
|---|---|---|---|---|
| 370th | April 11, 1944 | (2)u/i a/c dam(grd) | Volkenrod | P-47 |

0-0-0 air
0-2 ground

**Boring, Lloyd D., Lt.**
343rd Ftr Sqn/55th Ftr Grp

| *Sqn* | *Date* | *Claims* | *Location* | *A/C* |
|---|---|---|---|---|
| 343rd | February 27, 1945 | (.5)Ju-88 dest(air)[*] | Nurnburg | P-51 |
| | April 9 | Me-109 dest(grd) | Munich-Brunnthal | P-51 |
| | | Me-410 dest(grd) | Munich-Brunnthal | P-51 |
| | | Me-109 dam(grd) | Munich-Brunnthal | P-51 |
| | April 16 | (.5)BV-140 dest(grd)[**] | Lake Chiem | P-51 |
| | April 17 | (2)Fi-156 dest(grd) | Bautzen/Litten | P-51 |
| | | FW-190 dest(grd) | Bautzen/Litten | P-51 |
| | | u/i a/c dest(grd) | Bautzen/Litten | P-51 |

0.5-0-0 air
6.5-1 ground

[*] - shared with Capt. R.L. Buttke of the 343rd Ftr Sqn
[**] - shared with Lt. R.G. Allen of the 343rd Ftr Sqn

**Born, David L., Lt.**
434th Ftr Sqn/479th Ftr Grp

| *Sqn* | *Date* | *Claims* | *Location* | *A/C* |
|---|---|---|---|---|
| 434th | February 14, 1945 | Me-109 dest(air) | SW Berlin | P-51 |
| | April 17 | (2)u/i a/c dest(grd) | Puchhoff | P-51 |
| | | Me-109 dest(grd) | Puchhoff | P-51 |

1-0-0 air
3-0 ground

**Bostrom, Ernest O., Capt.**
486th Ftr Sqn/352nd Ftr Grp

| *Sqn* | *Date* | *Claims* | *Location* | *A/C* |
|---|---|---|---|---|
| 486th | July 18, 1944 | Ju-88 dest(air) | SE Warnemunde | P-51 |
| | September 12 | FW-190 dest(air) | Berlin | P-51 |
| | November 2 | (2)Me-109 dest(air) | W/Halle | P-51 |
| | January 14, 1945 | FW-190 dest(air) | Almello | P-51 |

5-0-0 air
0-0 ground

**Bostwick, George E., Maj.**
62nd Ftr Sqn/56th Ftr Grp
63rd Ftr Sqn/56th Ftr Grp

| *Sqn* | *Date* | *Claims* | *Location* | *A/C* |
|---|---|---|---|---|
| 62nd | June 7, 1944 | Me-109 dest(air) | Grandvillers A/F | P-47 |
| | July 4 | (3)Me-109 dest(air) | Conches | P-47 |
| | | Me-109 dam(air) | Conches | P-47 |
| | July 6 | Me-109 dest(air) | Beaumont | P-47 |
| | September 8 | (3)FW-190 dest(grd) | Coblenz | P-47 |
| 63rd | January 29, 1945 | Me-410 dam(grd) | Berge A/F | P-47 |
| | March 25 | Me-262 dest(air) | Parchim A/F | P-47 |
| | April 7 | (2)Me-109 dest(air) | S/Bremen-Hamburg | P-47 |
| | | Me-262 dam(air) | S/Bremen-Hamburg | P-47 |
| | April 10 | (2)Ju-88 dest(grd) | Werder A/F | P-47 |
| | | (2)u/i a/c dest(grd) | Werder A/F | P-47 |

8-0-2 air
7-1 ground

**Bosworth, Robert R., Lt.**
82nd Ftr Sqn/78th Ftr Grp

| *Sqn* | *Date* | *Claims* | *Location* | *A/C* |
|---|---|---|---|---|
| 82nd | August 10, 1944 | Ju-88 dest(grd) | Verdun | P-47 |
| | September 10 | (4)Ju-88 dest(grd) | Meinbullen | P-47 |
| | October 7 | Me-109 dest(air) | Leipzig | P-47 |

1-0-0 air
5-0 ground

**Boteler, George G., Lt.**
83rd Ftr Sqn/78th Ftr Grp

| *Sqn* | *Date* | *Claims* | *Location* | *A/C* |
|---|---|---|---|---|
| 83rd | June 20, 1944 | (.5)Me-109 dest(air)[*] | Amiens | P-47 |
| | September 1 | Me-110 dest(air) | Gilze-Rijen | P-47 |

1.5-0-0 air
0-0 ground

[*] - shared with Lt. P.C. Holder of the 83rd Ftr Sqn

**Bouldin, Frank H., Lt.**
352nd Ftr Sqn/353rd Ftr Grp

| *Sqn* | *Date* | *Claims* | *Location* | *A/C* |
|---|---|---|---|---|
| 352nd | August 28, 1944 | Me-110 dest(air) | SE Brussels | P-47 |
| | November 27 | Me-109 dest(air) | Magdeburg | P-51 |
| | December 5 | FW-190 dest(air) | NE Berlin | P-51 |

3-0-0 air
0-0 ground

**Boulet, William P., Lt.**
354th Ftr Sqn/355th Ftr Grp

| *Sqn* | *Date* | *Claims* | *Location* | *A/C* |
|---|---|---|---|---|
| 354th | April 5, 1944 | FW-200 dest(grd) | Landsberg | P-51 |
| | | Do-217 dest(grd) | Landsberg | P-51 |
| | | (2)Do-217 dam(grd) | Landsberg | P-51 |
| | April 10 | He-111 dam(grd) | Bourges | P-51 |
| | April 11 | FW-44 dam(grd) | S/Wadu Lake | P-51 |
| | April 13 | He-177 dest(grd) | Oberpfaffenhofen | P-51 |
| | | Me-110 dam(grd) | Oberpfaffenhofen | P-51 |
| | April 24 | (2)Me-109 dest(air) | SE Munich | P-51 |
| | | (.5)Me-109 dest(air)[*] | SE Munich | P-51 |
| | | (.5)Me-109 dest(air)[**] | SE Munich | P-51 |
| | | Me-109 dam(air) | SE Munich | P-51 |

3-0-1 air
3-5 ground

[*] - shared with Capt. R.E. Woody of the 354th Ftr Sqn
[**] - shared with Lt. N.J. Fortier of the 354th Ftr Sqn

**Bour, William E., Capt.**
61st Ftr Sqn/56th Ftr Grp

| *Sqn* | *Date* | *Claims* | *Location* | *A/C* |
|---|---|---|---|---|
| 61st | September 5, 1944 | He-111 dam(grd) | Merzhausen | P-47 |

0-0-0 air
0-1 ground

**Bourque, Walter E., Lt.**
82nd Ftr Sqn/78th Ftr Grp

| *Sqn* | *Date* | *Claims* | *Location* | *A/C* |
|---|---|---|---|---|
| 82nd | March 19, 1945 | Me-109 dest(air) | Osnabruck | P-51 |
| | March 21 | Me-262 dest(air) | Giebelstadt | P-51 |
| | April 10 | Me-109 dest(grd) | Werder A/F | P-51 |
| | | Ju-52 dam(grd) | Werder A/F | P-51 |
| | | u/i a/c dam(grd) | Werder A/F | P-51 |

2-0-0 air
1-2 ground

**Boussu, Marvin F., Capt.**
368th Ftr Sqn/359th Ftr Grp

| *Sqn* | *Date* | *Claims* | *Location* | *A/C* |
|---|---|---|---|---|
| 368th | March 23, 1945 | He-111 dam(grd) | Salzwedel | P-51 |
| | April 9 | Me-262 dam(air) | Augsburg | P-51 |

0-0-1 air
0-1 ground

**Bowers, Arthur R., Lt.**
334th Ftr Sqn/4th Ftr Grp

| *Sqn* | *Date* | *Claims* | *Location* | *A/C* |
|---|---|---|---|---|
| 334th | February 25, 1945 | FW-190 dest(grd) | Rohrensee | P-51 |
| | | Me-110 dest(grd) | Rohrensee | P-51 |
| | | Me-410 dest(grd) | Rohrensee | P-51 |
| | April 16 | (2)Me-109 dest(grd) | Gablingen | P-51 |
| | | Ju-88 dest(grd) | Gablingen | P-51 |
| | | (3)Me-109 dam(grd) | Gablingen | P-51 |

0-0-0 air
6-3 ground

**Bowers, Clifford W., Lt.**
434th Ftr Sqn/479th Ftr Grp

| *Sqn* | *Date* | *Claims* | *Location* | *A/C* |
|---|---|---|---|---|
| 434th | January 1, 1945 | (.5)FW-190 dest(air)[*] | Nienburg | P-51 |
| | April 13 | (.5)u/i a/c dest(grd)[**] | Ratzburger Lake | P-51 |
| | | u/i a/c dam(grd) | Ratzburger Lake | P-51 |
| | April 18 | Me-109 dest(grd) | Ottingen | P-51 |
| | | Me-110 dest(grd) | Ottingen | P-51 |
| | | u/i a/c dest(grd) | Deiningen | P-51 |
| | | u/i a/c dam(grd) | Deiningen | P-51 |

0.5-0-0 air
3.5-2 ground

[*] - shared with LtCol. K.L. Riddle of HdQts, 479th Ftr Grp
[**] - shared with Lt. O.J. Huval of the 434th Ftr Sqn

**Bowers, Elmer O., Lt.**
384th Ftr Sqn/364th Ftr Grp

| *Sqn* | *Date* | *Claims* | *Location* | *A/C* |
|---|---|---|---|---|
| 384th | September 19, 1944 | (1.5)Me-109 dest(air)[*] | Duisenberg | P-51 |

1.5-0-0 air
0-0 ground

[*] - shared with F/O W.E. Randolph of the 384th Ftr Sqn

**Bowers, Glenn L., Lt.**
487th Ftr Sqn/352nd Ftr Grp

| *Sqn* | *Date* | *Claims* | *Location* | *A/C* |
|---|---|---|---|---|
| 487th | September 10, 1944 | Ju-52 dest(grd) | Wertheim | P-51 |

0-0-0 air
1-0 ground

**Bowers, James A., Lt.**
361st Ftr Sqn/356th Ftr Grp

| *Sqn* | *Date* | *Claims* | *Location* | *A/C* |
|---|---|---|---|---|
| 361st | November 26, 1944 | Me-109 dest(air) | Osnabruck-Dummer Lake | P-51 |
| | January 14, 1945 | FW-190 dam(air) | SW Dummer Lake | P-51 |
| | February 14 | (2)FW-190 dest(air) | S/Chemnitz | P-51 |

3-0-1 air
0-0 ground

**Bowles, Paul N., Lt.**
363rd Ftr Sqn/357th Ftr Grp

| Sqn | Date | Claims | Location | A/C |
|---|---|---|---|---|
| 363rd | April 19, 1945 | Me-262 dest(air) | Prague | P-51 |

1-0-0 air
0-0 ground

**Bowman, Ralph I., Capt.**
55th Ftr Sqn/20th Ftr Grp

| Sqn | Date | Claims | Location | A/C |
|---|---|---|---|---|
| 55th | August 9, 1944 | Me-109 dest(air) | S/Augsburg | P-51 |
| | October 6 | Do-24 dest(grd) | Kubitzer Bay | P-51 |
| | | Do-24 dam(grd) | Kubitzer Bay | P-51 |

1-0-0 air
1-1 ground

**Box, Norman L., Capt.**
385th Ftr Sqn/364th Ftr Grp

| Sqn | Date | Claims | Location | A/C |
|---|---|---|---|---|
| 385th | November 21, 1944 | (.5)FW-190 dest(air)* | SW Merseburg | P-51 |
| | | FW-190 dam(air) | SW Merseburg | P-51 |
| | January 29, 1945 | u/i a/c dam(grd) | Darmstadt | P-51 |

0.5-0-1 air
0-1 ground

* - shared with Lt. H.W. Head of the 385th Ftr Sqn

**Boyd, Raymond A., Lt.**
368th Ftr Sqn/359th Ftr Grp

| Sqn | Date | Claims | Location | A/C |
|---|---|---|---|---|
| 368th | December 24, 1944 | FW-190 dam(air) | Cologne | P-51 |

0-0-1 air
0-0 ground

**Boyd, Warren D., Lt.**
383rd Ftr Sqn/364th Ftr Grp

| Sqn | Date | Claims | Location | A/C |
|---|---|---|---|---|
| 383rd | May 24, 1944 | (.5)Do-217 dest(grd)* | SW Berlin | P-38 |
| | September 28 | FW-190 dest(air) | S/Magdeburg | P-51 |
| | | FW-190 dam(air) | S/Magdeburg | P-51 |

1-0-1 air
0.5-0 ground

* - shared with Lt. K.F. Nicholson of the 383rd Ftr Sqn

**Boyd, William H., Lt.**
503rd Ftr Sqn/339th Ftr Grp

| Sqn | Date | Claims | Location | A/C |
|---|---|---|---|---|
| 503rd | April 16, 1945 | Me-109 dam(grd) | Kralupy | P-51 |

0-0-0 air
0-1 ground

**Boyle, Alfred R., Lt.**
363rd Ftr Sqn/357th Ftr Grp

| Sqn | Date | Claims | Location | A/C |
|---|---|---|---|---|
| 363rd | February 21, 1944 | Me-109 dest(air) | E/Zwolle | P-51 |

1-0-0 air
0-0 ground

**Boyle, Herbert L., Lt.**
84th Ftr Sqn/78th Ftr Grp

| Sqn | Date | Claims | Location | A/C |
|---|---|---|---|---|
| 84th | May 19, 1944 | FW-190 dest(air) | Quackenbruck | P-47 |

1-0-0 air
0-0 ground

**Boyle, Mark K., Capt.**
62nd Ftr Sqn/56th Ftr Grp

| Sqn | Date | Claims | Location | A/C |
|---|---|---|---|---|
| 62nd | November 26, 1943 | (.5)Me-110 dest(air)* | Papenburg | P-47 |
| | March 16, 1944 | FW-190 prob(air) | St. Dizier | P-47 |
| | April 11 | u/i a/c dam(air) | Schleswig | P-47 |
| | | He-115 dest(grd) | Schleswig | P-47 |
| | April 13 | Me-109 dest(air) | Ludwigshafen | P-47 |

1.5-1-1 air
1-0 ground

* - shared with Capt. E.W. O'Neill of the 62nd Ftr Sqn

**Boyles, Frank R., Capt.**
335th Ftr Sqn/4th Ftr Grp
Earlier flew with 121 Sqn, RAF, and claimed one kill on July 31, 1942.

| Sqn | Date | Claims | Location | A/C |
|---|---|---|---|---|
| 335th | July 28, 1943 | FW-190 dest(air) | SE Utrecht | P-47 |
| | July 30 | FW-190 dest(air) | Zaltboomel | P-47 |

2-0-0 air
0-0 ground

**Bradford, Frank D., Lt.**
338th Ftr Sqn/55th Ftr Grp

| Sqn | Date | Claims | Location | A/C |
|---|---|---|---|---|
| 338th | December 24, 1944 | FW-190 dest(air) | E/Frankfurt | P-51 |
| | | FW-190 dam(air) | E/Frankfurt | P-51 |

1-0-1 air
0-0 ground

**Bradley, Robert T., Lt.**
354th Ftr Sqn/355th Ftr Grp

| Sqn | Date | Claims | Location | A/C |
|---|---|---|---|---|
| 354th | July 8, 1944 | Me-109 dest(grd) | SW Chalons | P-51 |

0-0-0 air
1-0 ground

**Bradner, Robert H., Lt.**
362nd Ftr Sqn/357th Ftr Grp

| Sqn | Date | Claims | Location | A/C |
|---|---|---|---|---|
| 362nd | April 18, 1945 | (.5)Me-262 dam(air)* | SW Prague/Ruzny | P-51 |

0-0-0.5 air
0-0 ground

* - shared with Lt. F.A. Dellorto of the 362nd Ftr Sqn

**Bradshaw, Robert D., Lt.**
359th Ftr Sqn/356th Ftr Grp

| Sqn | Date | Claims | Location | A/C |
|---|---|---|---|---|
| 359th | February 10, 1944 | (.33)FW-190 dest(air)* | Meppen | P-47 |
| | March 16 | u/i a/c dam(grd) | Dummer Lake | P-47 |

0.33-0-0 air
0-1 ground

* - shared with Capt. E.J. White and Lt. G.W. Engel of the 359th Ftr Sqn

**Brady, James E., F/O**
338th Ftr Sqn/55th Ftr Grp

| Sqn | Date | Claims | Location | A/C |
|---|---|---|---|---|
| 338th | April 16, 1945 | Me-109 dest(grd) | N/Landshut | P-51 |

0-0-0 air
1-0 ground

**Brainard, Wayne A., Lt.**
62nd Ftr Sqn/56th Ftr Grp

| Sqn | Date | Claims | Location | A/C |
|---|---|---|---|---|
| 62nd | October 10, 1943 | Me-210 dam(air) | Altenberge | P-47 |

0-0-1 air
0-0 ground

**Braley, Byron K., Lt.**
364th Ftr Sqn/357th Ftr Grp

| *Sqn* | *Date* | *Claims* | *Location* | *A/C* |
|---|---|---|---|---|
| 364th | September 18, 1944 | FW-190 dest(air) | N/Maastricht | P-51 |
| | September 19 | Me-109 dest(air) | E/Arnheim | P-51 |
| | December 24 | FW-190 dest(air) | S/Kassel | P-51 |
| | January 5, 1945 | Me-109 dest(grd) | Altenstadt A/F | P-51 |
| | April 16 | Me-109 dest(grd) | Muhldorf A/F | P-51 |
| | | Me-109 dam(grd) | Muhldorf A/F | P-51 |

3-0-0 air
2-1 ground

**Brandenburg, James H., Lt.**
335th Ftr Sqn/4th Ftr Grp

| *Sqn* | *Date* | *Claims* | *Location* | *A/C* |
|---|---|---|---|---|
| 335th | March 21, 1944 | (.5)Fi-156 dest(air)[*] | NE Bordeaux | P-51 |

0.5-0-0 air
0-0 ground

[*] - shared with Capt. K.G. Smith of the 335th Ftr Sqn

**Brashear, Warren H., Lt.**
486th Ftr Sqn/352nd Ftr Grp

| *Sqn* | *Date* | *Claims* | *Location* | *A/C* |
|---|---|---|---|---|
| 486th | June 20, 1944 | Ju-88 dest(grd) | N/Burg | P-51 |

0-0-0 air
1-0 ground

**Brasher, J.E., Lt.**
82nd Ftr Sqn/78th Ftr Grp

| *Sqn* | *Date* | *Claims* | *Location* | *A/C* |
|---|---|---|---|---|
| 82nd | February 6, 1944 | (2)He-111 dam(grd) | Orleans | P-47 |
| | February 11 | Me-109 dest(air) | NE Luxembourg | P-47 |
| | February 13 | Ju-88 dam(grd) | Bryes-Sud A/F | P-47 |
| | April 5 | Go-242 dam(grd) | Ruwer | P-47 |
| | April 8 | (.33)Ar-196 dest(grd)[*] | Trier | P-47 |
| | | (.2)Me-110 dest(grd)[**] | Trier | P-47 |
| | | (.2)Me-110 dest(grd)[**] | Trier | P-47 |
| | | (.2)Me-110 dest(grd)[**] | Trier | P-47 |
| | | Ju-52 dam(grd) | Trier | P-47 |
| | April 24 | Do-217 dest(grd) | Diest | P-47 |

1-0-0 air
1.93-5 ground

[*] - shared with Lt. R.A. Hewitt and Capt. N.D. Munson of the 82nd Ftr Sqn
[**] - all shared with Maj. J.J. Oberhansly, Capt. N.D. Munson, Lt. M.K. Woller, and F/O C.W. DeWitt of the 82nd Ftr Sqn

**Brearley, William C., Capt.**
359th Ftr Sqn/356th Ftr Grp

| *Sqn* | *Date* | *Claims* | *Location* | *A/C* |
|---|---|---|---|---|
| 359th | April 23, 1944 | Go-242 dam(grd) | Hagenau | P-47 |

0-0-0 air
0-1 ground

**Breathwit, Carl E., Capt.**
38th Ftr Sqn/55th Ftr Grp

| *Sqn* | *Date* | *Claims* | *Location* | *A/C* |
|---|---|---|---|---|
| 38th | December 24, 1944 | Me-109 dest(air) | W/St. Vith | P-51 |

1-0-0 air
0-0 ground

**Bricker, John B., Lt.**
376th Ftr Sqn/361st Ftr Grp

| *Sqn* | *Date* | *Claims* | *Location* | *A/C* |
|---|---|---|---|---|
| 376th | September 18, 1944 | Me-109 dest(air) | N/Schleswig | P-51 |
| | September 27 | FW-190 dest(air) | Eisenach | P-51 |
| | | FW-190 dam(air) | Eisenach | P-51 |
| | November 2 | FW-190 dest(air) | N/Erfurt | P-51 |
| | December 24 | Me-109 dest(air) | Wengerohr | P-51 |

4-0-1 air
0-0 ground

**Brien, Cleveland J., Jr., Lt.**
358th Ftr Sqn/355th Ftr Grp

| *Sqn* | *Date* | *Claims* | *Location* | *A/C* |
|---|---|---|---|---|
| 358th | June 8, 1944 | (.5)He-177 dest(air)[*] | N/Angoulieme | P-51 |

0.5-0-0 air
0-0 ground

[*] - shared with Lt. W.J. McGinty of the 358th Ftr Sqn

**Briggs, Earle W., Lt.**
328th Ftr Sqn/352nd Ftr Grp

| *Sqn* | *Date* | *Claims* | *Location* | *A/C* |
|---|---|---|---|---|
| 328th | June 21, 1944 | Me-410 dam(air) | Dahmsdorf | P-51 |
| | November 2 | Me-109 prob(air) | Merseburg | P-51 |
| | November 21 | FW-190 prob(air) | Merseburg | P-51 |

0-2-1 air
0-0 ground

**Bristow, William E., Capt.**
384th Ftr Sqn/364th Ftr Grp

| *Sqn* | *Date* | *Claims* | *Location* | *A/C* |
|---|---|---|---|---|
| 384th | June 25, 1944 | Me-109 dest(air) | E/Blois | P-38 |
| | | Me-109 dam(air) | E/Blois | P-38 |
| | September 11 | FW-190 dest(air) | Nordhausen | P-51 |
| | | Me-109 dest(air) | Nordhausen | P-51 |
| | November 21 | FW-190 dam(air) | SW Halle | P-51 |

3-0-2 air
0-0 ground

**Britt, Daniel T., Lt.**
487th Ftr Sqn/352nd Ftr Grp

| *Sqn* | *Date* | *Claims* | *Location* | *A/C* |
|---|---|---|---|---|
| 487th | December 20, 1943 | Me-109 dest(air) | NW Oosterwalde | P-47 |

1-0-0 air
0-0 ground

**Broach, Richard H., Capt.**
369th Ftr Sqn/359th Ftr Grp

| *Sqn* | *Date* | *Claims* | *Location* | *A/C* |
|---|---|---|---|---|
| 369th | March 4, 1944 | Me-109 prob(air) | Aachen | P-47 |
| | May 21 | (.5)u/i a/c dest(air)[*] | NW Klutz | P-51 |

0.5-1-0 air
0-0 ground

[*] - shared with Lt. R.B. Sander of the 369th Ftr Sqn

**Broadhead, Joseph E., LtCol.**
362nd Ftr Sqn/357th Ftr Grp

| *Sqn* | *Date* | *Claims* | *Location* | *A/C* |
|---|---|---|---|---|
| 362nd | February 25, 1944 | Me-109 dest(air) | Regensburg | P-51 |
| | March 6 | Me-110 dest(air) | E/Berlin | P-51 |
| | March 16 | Me-410 dam(air) | S/Stuttgart | P-51 |
| | March 29 | Me-109 dest(air) | Brunswick | P-51 |
| | April 22 | FW-190 dest(air) | N/Dummer Lake | P-51 |
| | | FW-190 dam(air) | N/Dummer Lake | P-51 |
| | April 30 | Me-109 dest(air) | S/Paris | P-51 |
| | May 28 | FW-190 dest(air) | NW Magdeburg | P-51 |
| | December 5 | FW-190 dest(air) | Berlin | P-51 |
| | January 14, 1945 | Me-109 dest(air) | NW Berlin | P-51 |

8-0-2 air
0-0 ground

**Brock, Charles L., Lt.**
335th Ftr Sqn/4th Ftr Grp

| Sqn | Date | Claims | Location | A/C |
|---|---|---|---|---|
| 335th | November 2, 1944 | Me-109 dest(air) | Merseburg | P-51 |

1-0-0 air
0-0 ground

**Brock, Thomas C., Lt.**
505th Ftr Sqn/339th Ftr Grp
351st Ftr Sqn/353rd Ftr Grp

| Sqn | Date | Claims | Location | A/C |
|---|---|---|---|---|
| 351st | November 18, 1944 | Ju-88 dam(grd) | Prittrishing | P-51 |
| | March 14, 1945 | Me-109 dest(air) | Luckenwalde | P-51 |

1-0-0 air
0-1 ground

**Bromschwig, Robert I., Lt.**
434th Ftr Sqn/479th Ftr Grp

| Sqn | Date | Claims | Location | A/C |
|---|---|---|---|---|
| 434th | January 1, 1945 | FW-190 dam(air) | Nienburg | P-51 |
| | March 31 | Me-262 dam(air) | Braunschwieg | P-51 |

0-0-2 air
0-0 ground

**Brooker, Beacham O., Jr., Lt.**
336th Ftr Sqn/4th Ftr Grp

| Sqn | Date | Claims | Location | A/C |
|---|---|---|---|---|
| 336th | February 25, 1945 | (.5)FW-190 prob(air)[*] | Kothen A/F | P-51 |
| | April 16 | (2)Me-410 dest(grd) | Praha | P-51 |
| | | (3)Me-110 dam(grd) | Praha | P-51 |
| | | Ju-52 dam(grd) | Praha | P-51 |
| | April 17 | Me-109 dam(grd) | Pilzen | P-51 |

0-0.5-0 air
2-5 ground

[*] - shared with Lt. P.M. Morgan of the 336th Ftr Sqn

**Brookins, Richard C., Lt.**
328th Ftr Sqn/352nd Ftr Grp

| Sqn | Date | Claims | Location | A/C |
|---|---|---|---|---|
| 328th | March 22, 1944 | (.25)FW-200 dest(air)[*] | Hesepe | P-47 |
| | April 8 | (.5)Me-210 dest(grd)[**] | Quackenbruck | P-47 |
| | | (.5)u/i a/c dest(grd)[**] | Quackenbruck | P-47 |
| | May 19 | Me-109 dest(air) | Wittenberg-Havelburg | P-51 |
| | May 30 | Me-109 dest(air) | Halberstadt | P-51 |
| | June 6 | FW-190 dest(air) | SE Rouen | P-51 |
| | | FW-190 dam(air) | SE Rouen | P-51 |
| | September 27 | FW-190 dest(air) | NW Frankfurt | P-51 |

4.25-0-1 air
1-0 ground

[*] - shared with Capt. E.L. Abbott, Lt. J.F. Thornell, and Lt. E. Zellner of the 328th Ftr Sqn
[**] - both shared with Lt. F.A. Yochim of the 328th Ftr Sqn

**Brooks, Joseph B., Lt.**
350th Ftr Sqn/353rd Ftr Grp

| Sqn | Date | Claims | Location | A/C |
|---|---|---|---|---|
| 350th | June 20, 1944 | Me-110 dest(grd) | Plantlunne | P-47 |
| | August 28 | (.5)Fi-156 dest(air)[*] | Verdun | P-47 |

0.5-0-0 air
1-0 ground

[*] - shared with LtCol. K.W. Gallup of the 350th Ftr Sqn

**Brooks, John A., III, LtCol.**
2nd Scouting Force

| Sqn | Date | Claims | Location | A/C |
|---|---|---|---|---|
| 2nd | February 9, 1945 | (2)Me-109 dest(air) | SE Magdeburg | P-51 |

2-0-0 air
0-0 ground

**Brooks, Norman E., Capt.**
61st Ftr Sqn/56th Ftr Grp

| Sqn | Date | Claims | Location | A/C |
|---|---|---|---|---|
| 61st | October 14, 1943 | Me-110 dest(air) | W/Aachen | P-47 |
| | March 8, 1944 | FW-190 dam(air) | Dummer Lake | P-47 |

1-0-1 air
0-0 ground

**Brooks, Philip, Maj.**
338th Ftr Sqn/55th Ftr Grp
HdQts/55th Ftr Grp

| Sqn | Date | Claims | Location | A/C |
|---|---|---|---|---|
| 338th | November 26, 1944 | FW-190 dam(grd) | Vorden | P-51 |
| | January 6, 1945 | Do-217 dest(grd) | Giebelstadt | P-51 |
| | January 13 | (.5)Do-217 dest(grd)[*] | Giebelstadt | P-51 |
| | February 25 | Me-109 dest(grd) | Illesheim | P-51 |
| | | Me-109 dam(grd) | Illesheim | P-51 |

0-0-0 air
2.5-2 ground

[*] - shared with Lt. F.R. Sharp of the 338th Ftr Sqn

**Brown, Alston L., Lt.**
359th Ftr Sqn/356th Ftr Grp

| Sqn | Date | Claims | Location | A/C |
|---|---|---|---|---|
| 359th | December 25, 1944 | FW-190 dam(air) | Bonn | P-51 |
| | February 14, 1945 | FW-190 dest(air) | Dresden-Chemnitz | P-51 |
| | | FW-190 dam(air) | Dresden-Chemnitz | P-51 |
| | February 25 | He-111 dam(grd) | Berndorf A/F | P-51 |

1-0-2 air
0-1 ground

**Brown, Carey H., Capt.**
370th Ftr Sqn/359th Ftr Grp

| Sqn | Date | Claims | Location | A/C |
|---|---|---|---|---|
| 370th | February 10, 1944 | Me-109 dest(air) | Zuider Zee | P-47 |

1-0-0 air
0-0 ground

**Brown, Carl F., Capt.**
334th Ftr Sqn/4th Ftr Grp

| Sqn | Date | Claims | Location | A/C |
|---|---|---|---|---|
| 334th | November 18, 1944 | (2)Me-262 dest(grd) | Leipheim | P-51 |
| | | Me-262 dam(grd) | Leipheim | P-51 |
| | December 2 | FW-190 dest(air) | Hottenbach | P-51 |
| | January 16, 1945 | (.5)Me-262 dest(grd)[*] | Neuburg | P-51 |

1-0-0 air
2.5-1 ground

[*] - shared with Lt. J.E. Jahnke of the 334th Ftr Sqn

**Brown, Charles R., Lt.**
84th Ftr Sqn/78th Ftr Grp

| Sqn | Date | Claims | Location | A/C |
|---|---|---|---|---|
| 84th | May 16, 1943 | (2)FW-190 dest(air) | Flushing | P-47 |

2-0-0 air
0-0 ground

**Brown, Gerald, Maj.**
38th Ftr Sqn/55th Ftr Grp
334th Ftr Sqn/ 4th Ftr Grp

| Sqn | Date | Claims | Location | A/C |
|---|---|---|---|---|
| 38th | November 13, 1943 | Me-109 dam(air) | Bremen | P-38 |
| | January 31, 1944 | Me-109 dest(air) | Venlo | P-38 |
| | March 18 | FW-190 dest(air) | Nancy | P-38 |
| | April 8 | Me-109 dest(air) | Lingen | P-38 |
| | April 15 | FW-190 dest(air) | Munster | P-38 |
| | | He-111 dest(air) | Munster | P-38 |

5-0-1 air
0-0 ground

**Brown, Harley L., Capt.**
55th Ftr Sqn/20th Ftr Grp

| *Sqn* | *Date* | *Claims* | *Location* | *A/C* |
|---|---|---|---|---|
| 55th | August 25, 1944 | Ju-88 dam(grd) | Parow A/F | P-51 |
| | November 2 | (2)FW-190 dest(air) | Halle-Merseburg | P-51 |
| | | Me-109 dest(air) | Halle-Merseburg | P-51 |
| | | Me-109 dam(air) | Halle-Merseburg | P-51 |
| | December 2 | FW-190 dest(air) | Coblenz-St. Goar | P-51 |
| | January 14, 1945 | (2)Me-109 dest(air) | Perleberg | P-51 |
| | | 6-0-1 air | | |
| | | 0-0 ground | | |

**Brown, Henry W., Capt.**
354th Ftr Sqn/355th Ftr Grp

| *Sqn* | *Date* | *Claims* | *Location* | *A/C* |
|---|---|---|---|---|
| 354th | March 8, 1944 | (3.5)Ju-88 dest(grd)[*] | Hesepe | P-47 |
| | | Me-110 dest(grd) | Hesepe | P-47 |
| | | (2)Ju-88 dam(grd) | Hesepe | P-47 |
| | March 18 | Me-109 dest(air) | Nancy | P-51 |
| | | Me-110 dam(air) | N/Munich | P-51 |
| | March 20 | FW-190 dam(air) | Coxyde | P-51 |
| | March 29 | FW-190 dest(air) | Brunswick | P-51 |
| | April 5 | (.5)Me-108 dest(air)[**] | Landsberg | P-51 |
| | | (.2)Do-217 dest(air)[@] | Landsberg | P-51 |
| | April 8 | (.5)Me-109 dest(air)[@@] | Sachau A/F | P-51 |
| | April 11 | FW-190 dest(air) | E/Berlin | P-51 |
| | | Ju-52 dest(grd) | Strasbourg | P-51 |
| | | Ju-88 dam(grd) | Strasbourg | P-51 |
| | April 13 | (2)Ju-88 dest(grd) | Oberpfaffenhofen | P-51 |
| | April 24 | (2)Me-109 dest(air) | S/Munich | P-51 |
| | April 29 | Me-109 dest(air) | Brunswick | P-51 |
| | May 13 | Me-210 dest(air) | Landsberg | P-51 |
| | September 10 | (6)He-60 dest(grd) | Frankfurt | P-51 |
| | September 11 | (3)Me-109 dest(air) | S/Kassel | P-51 |
| | September 18 | Me-109 dest(air) | Warsaw | P-51 |
| | | Me-109 dam(air) | Warsaw | P-51 |
| | | Ju-87 dam(grd) | Warsaw | P-51 |
| | September 27 | (2)FW-190 dest(air) | Eschwege | P-51 |
| | October 3 | Me-110 dest(grd) | Nordlingen | P-51 |
| | | 14.2-0-3 air | | |
| | | 14.5-4 ground | | |

[*] - shared with Capt. C.G. Johnston of the 354th Ftr Sqn
[**] - shared with Lt. C.W. Lenfest of the 354th Ftr Sqn
[@] - shared with Capt. C.G. Johnston, Capt. W.J. Koraleski, Lt. J.E. Duffy, and Lt. B.C. Williamson of the 354th Ftr Sqn
[@@] - shared with Capt. R.G. Kurtz of the 354th Ftr Sqn

**Brown, Jack D., Lt.**
63rd Ftr Sqn/56th Ftr Grp

| *Sqn* | *Date* | *Claims* | *Location* | *A/C* |
|---|---|---|---|---|
| 63rd | October 4, 1943 | Me-110 dest(air) | E/Duren | P-47 |
| | November 26 | FW-190 dam(air) | Friesoythe | P-47 |
| | | 1-0-1 air | | |
| | | 0-0 ground | | |

**Brown, Jack F., Capt.**
359th Ftr Sqn/356th Ftr Grp

| *Sqn* | *Date* | *Claims* | *Location* | *A/C* |
|---|---|---|---|---|
| 359th | February 25, 1945 | He-111 dest(grd) | Berndorf A/F | P-51 |
| | April 7 | Me-109 dest(air) | NE Steinhuder Lake | P-51 |
| | | 1-0-0 air | | |
| | | 1-0 ground | | |

**Brown, John I., III, Capt.**
82nd Ftr Sqn/78th Ftr Grp

| *Sqn* | *Date* | *Claims* | *Location* | *A/C* |
|---|---|---|---|---|
| 82nd | January 14, 1945 | Me-109 dam(air) | Cologne | P-51 |
| | April 16 | Ju-52 dest(grd) | Pilzen/Prague | P-51 |
| | | Ju-86 dam(grd) | Pilzen/Prague | P-51 |
| | | u/i a/c dam(grd) | Pilzen/Prague | P-51 |
| | | 0-0-1 air | | |
| | | 1-2 ground | | |

**Brown, John K., Capt.**
55th Ftr Sqn/20th Ftr Grp

| *Sqn* | *Date* | *Claims* | *Location* | *A/C* |
|---|---|---|---|---|
| 55th | January 14, 1945 | (2)FW-190 dest(air) | Perleberg | P-51 |
| | February 14 | (.5)Me-262 dam(air)[*] | Stuttgart | P-51 |
| | April 10 | Me-262 dest(air) | Neuruppin | P-51 |
| | | 3-0-0.5 air | | |
| | | 0-0 ground | | |

[*] - shared with Lt. K.D. McNeel of the 55th Ftr Sqn

**Brown, Kirby M., Lt.**
364th Ftr Sqn/357th Ftr Grp

| *Sqn* | *Date* | *Claims* | *Location* | *A/C* |
|---|---|---|---|---|
| 364th | August 6, 1944 | (.5)Ju-88 dest(air)[*] | NE Warsaw | P-51 |
| | | 0.5-0-0 air | | |
| | | 0-0 ground | | |

[*] - shared with Lt. N.J. Frederick of the 364th Ftr Sqn

**Brown, Lewis R., Lt.**
62nd Ftr Sqn/56th Ftr Grp

| *Sqn* | *Date* | *Claims* | *Location* | *A/C* |
|---|---|---|---|---|
| 62nd | September 8, 1944 | u/i a/c dest(grd) | Coblenz | P-47 |
| | September 21 | FW-190 dest(air) | Arnheim | P-47 |
| | October 15 | Me-109 dam(grd) | Rheine A/F | P-47 |
| | December 23 | (3)FW-190 prob(air) | Coblenz | P-47 |
| | | FW-190 dam(air) | Coblenz | P-47 |
| | | 1-3-1 air | | |
| | | 1-1 ground | | |

**Brown, Philip A., Lt.**
434th Ftr Sqn/479th Ftr Grp

| *Sqn* | *Date* | *Claims* | *Location* | *A/C* |
|---|---|---|---|---|
| 434th | December 25, 1944 | FW-190 dest(air) | SW Bonn | P-51 |
| | | FW-190 prob(air) | SW Bonn | P-51 |
| | February 20, 1945 | (.5)He-111 dest(grd)[*] | Windleschenlaibach | P-51 |
| | | (.5)He-111 dam(grd)[*] | Windleschenlaibach | P-51 |
| | April 13 | (.5)u/i a/c dest(grd)[**] | Ratzburger Lake | P-51 |
| | | u/i a/c dam(grd) | Ratzburger Lake | P-51 |
| | April 16 | u/i a/c dest(grd) | Erferding | P-51 |
| | | 1-1-0 air | | |
| | | 2-1.5 ground | | |

[*] - shared with Capt. D.J. Pierce of the 434th Ftr Sqn
[**] - shared with Lt. R.G. Simpson of the 434th Ftr Sqn

**Brown, Quince L., Maj.**
84th Ftr Sqn/78th Ftr Grp

| *Sqn* | *Date* | *Claims* | *Location* | *A/C* |
|---|---|---|---|---|
| 84th | September 27, 1943 | Me-109 dest(air) | NW Emden | P-47 |
| | January 4, 1944 | (2)FW-190 dest(air) | Coesfeld | P-47 |
| | January 5 | Me-109 dest(air) | La Rochelle | P-47 |
| | January 30 | Me-109 dest(air) | Rheine | P-47 |
| | March 15 | Me-109 dest(air) | W/Munster | P-47 |
| | March 16 | (2)Me-109 dest(air) | St. Dizier | P-47 |
| | | FW-190 dest(air) | St. Dizier | P-47 |
| | | Ju-88 dest(grd) | St. Dizier | P-47 |
| | | (2)u/i a/c dam(grd) | St. Dizier | P-47 |
| | March 23 | FW-190 dest(air) | Goch | P-47 |
| | March 30 | (.33)Do-217 dest(air)[*] | Twente/Enschede | P-47 |
| | April 12 | FW-190 dest(air) | Duren | P-47 |
| | September 1 | Me-109 dest(air) | Liege-Trier | P-47 |
| | | 12.33-0-0 air | | |
| | | 1-2 ground | | |

[*] - shared with Lt. L.J. Abel and Lt. E.S. Lang of the 84th Ftr Sqn

**Brown, Richard C., Lt.**
354th Ftr Sqn/355th Ftr Grp

| *Sqn* | *Date* | *Claims* | *Location* | *A/C* |
|---|---|---|---|---|
| 354th | April 11, 1944 | Ju-52 dest(grd) | Strasbourg | P-51 |
| | | He-111 dam(grd) | Strasbourg | P-51 |
| | April 13 | (2)Ju-88 dest(grd) | Oberpfaffenhofen | P-51 |

0-0-0 air
3-1 ground

**Brown, Robert B., Lt.**
503rd Ftr Sqn/339th Ftr Grp

| *Sqn* | *Date* | *Claims* | *Location* | *A/C* |
|---|---|---|---|---|
| 503rd | May 24, 1944 | (.5)Me-109 dest(air)[*] | SW Berlin | P-51 |
| | | (2)Me-109 dam(air) | SW Berlin | P-51 |

0.5-0-2 air
0-0 ground

[*] - shared with Lt. J. Wolfort of the 503rd Ftr Sqn

**Brown, Robert D., Capt.**
362nd Ftr Sqn/357th Ftr Grp

| *Sqn* | *Date* | *Claims* | *Location* | *A/C* |
|---|---|---|---|---|
| 362nd | February 25, 1944 | FW-190 dest(air) | Regensburg | P-51 |
| | April 30 | Me-109 dest(air) | S/Paris | P-51 |
| | May 27 | Me-109 dam(air) | Strasbourg | P-51 |

2-0-1 air
0-0 ground

**Brown, Robert D., Capt.**
343rd Ftr Sqn/55th Ftr Grp

| *Sqn* | *Date* | *Claims* | *Location* | *A/C* |
|---|---|---|---|---|
| 343rd | September 10, 1944 | He-111 dest(grd) | NE Augsburg | P-51 |
| | November 2 | Me-109 dest(air) | SE Leipzig | P-51 |
| | February 20, 1945 | Ju-88 dest(grd) | Giebelstadt | P-51 |

1-0-0 air
2-0 ground

**Brown, Robert H., Lt.**
358th Ftr Sqn/355th Ftr Grp

| *Sqn* | *Date* | *Claims* | *Location* | *A/C* |
|---|---|---|---|---|
| 358th | December 5, 1944 | FW-190 dest(air) | Berlin | P-51 |

1-0-0 air
0-0 ground

**Brown, Winfield H., Maj.**
82nd Ftr Sqn/78th Ftr Grp

| *Sqn* | *Date* | *Claims* | *Location* | *A/C* |
|---|---|---|---|---|
| 82nd | March 19, 1945 | Me-109 dest(air) | Osnabruck | P-51 |
| | | (.5)Ar-234 dest(air)[*] | Osnabruck | P-51 |
| | | (2)Me-109 dam(air) | Osnabruck | P-51 |
| | March 21 | (.5)Me-262 dest(air)[**] | Giebelstadt | P-51 |

2-0-2 air
0-0 ground

[*] - shared with Lt. H.H. Lamb of the 82nd Ftr Sqn
[**] - shared with Lt. A.A. Rosenblum of the 82nd Ftr Sqn

**Browning, James W., Capt.**
363rd Ftr Sqn/357th Ftr Grp

| *Sqn* | *Date* | *Claims* | *Location* | *A/C* |
|---|---|---|---|---|
| 363rd | April 24, 1944 | Me-109 dest(air) | N/Augsburg | P-51 |
| | May 27 | Me-109 dest(air) | Strasbourg | P-51 |
| | May 30 | Me-109 dest(air) | NE Schonebeck | P-51 |
| | June 29 | (1.5)Me-410 dest(air)[*] | SW Leipzig | P-51 |
| | | (.5)FW-190 dest(air)[**] | SW Leipzig | P-51 |
| | December 5 | Me-109 dest(air) | N/Berlin | P-51 |
| | January 14, 1945 | Me-109 dest(air) | N/Brandenburg | P-51 |
| | | (2)Me-109 prob(air) | N/Brandenburg | P-51 |
| | | Me-109 dam(air) | N/Brandenburg | P-51 |

7-2-1 air
0-0 ground

[*] - shared with Lt. W.S. Fennell of the 363rd Ftr Sqn
[**] - shared with Lt. R.W. Staudte of the 363rd Ftr Sqn

**Browning, Robert A., Lt.**
354th Ftr Sqn/355th Ftr Grp

| *Sqn* | *Date* | *Claims* | *Location* | *A/C* |
|---|---|---|---|---|
| 354th | March 29, 1944 | (.5)u/i a/c dam(grd)[*] | NE Brunswick | P-51 |
| | | (.5)u/i a/c dam(grd)[*] | NE Brunswick | P-51 |
| | April 13 | (2)Do-217 dest(grd) | Oberpfaffenhofen | P-51 |
| | April 20 | Ju-88 dam(grd) | Blois A/F | P-51 |

0-0-0 air
2-2 ground

[*] - both shared with Lt. R.B. Kaminski of the 357th Ftr Sqn, 355th Ftr Grp

**Brubaker, Thomas F., Capt.**
375th Ftr Sqn/361st Ftr Grp

| *Sqn* | *Date* | *Claims* | *Location* | *A/C* |
|---|---|---|---|---|
| 375th | June 29, 1944 | Me-109 dest(air) | SE Kothen | P-51 |
| | September 13 | u/i a/c dest(grd) | Schwabeich Hall | P-51 |
| | October 6 | Me-109 dest(air) | NW Berlin | P-51 |

2-0-0 air
1-0 ground

**Bruce, John L., Lt.**
361st Ftr Sqn/356th Ftr Grp

| *Sqn* | *Date* | *Claims* | *Location* | *A/C* |
|---|---|---|---|---|
| 361st | April 23, 1944 | Go-242 dam(grd) | Hagenau | P-47 |

0-0-0 air
0-1 ground

**Brucks, George R., Lt.**
77th Ftr Sqn/20th Ftr Grp

| *Sqn* | *Date* | *Claims* | *Location* | *A/C* |
|---|---|---|---|---|
| 77th | August 4, 1944 | Ju-88 dam(grd) | Barth | P-51 |

0-0-0 air
0-1 ground

**Bryan, Donald S., Maj.**
328th Ftr Sqn/352nd Ftr Grp

| *Sqn* | *Date* | *Claims* | *Location* | *A/C* |
|---|---|---|---|---|
| 328th | January 29, 1944 | (.5)FW-190 dest(air)[*] | Namur | P-47 |
| | January 30 | FW-190 dest(air) | Emmen | P-47 |
| | February 20 | (.33)Me-110 dest(air)[**] | Vogelsand | P-47 |
| | February 24 | Me-109 dest(air) | W/Dummer Lake | P-47 |
| | March 15 | Me-109 dest(air) | Heusden | P-47 |
| | April 10 | (.5)FW-190 dest(air)[@] | Dormans | P-51 |
| | September 27 | (2)Me-109 dest(air) | NW Frankfurt | P-51 |
| | | Me-109 dam(air) | NW Frankfurt | P-51 |
| | November 2 | (5)Me-109 dest(air) | Merseburg | P-51 |
| | | (2)Me-109 dam(air) | Merseburg | P-51 |
| | December 23 | FW-190 dest(air) | S/Liege | P-51 |
| | December 31 | Ar-234 dam(air) | S/Verviers | P-51 |
| | March 14, 1945 | Ar-234 dest(air) | Elsafthal | P-51 |

13.33-0-4 air
0-0 ground

[*] - shared with Lt. Q.L. Quinn of the 328th Ftr Sqn
[**] - shared with LtCol. R.W. Osborn of HdQts, 67th Ftr Wg, and Lt. D.T. Zimms of the 328th Ftr Sqn
[@] - shared with Lt. J.L. Laing of the 328th Ftr Sqn

**Bryan, Gillespie, Maj.**
HdQts/78th Ftr Grp

| *Sqn* | *Date* | *Claims* | *Location* | *A/C* |
|---|---|---|---|---|
| HdQts | April 16, 1945 | (2)u/i a/c dest(grd) | Praha/Kakewice | P-51 |
| | | Me-109 dest(grd) | Praha/Kakewice | P-51 |
| | | Ju-52 dest(grd) | Praha/Kakewice | P-51 |
| | | (3)u/i a/c dam(grd) | Praha/Kakewice | P-51 |
| | April 17 | (2)u/i a/c dest(grd) | W/Dresden | P-51 |
| | | (3)u/i a/c dam(grd) | W/Dresden | P-51 |

0-0-0 air
6-6 ground

**Bryan, William E., Jr., Maj.**
503rd Ftr Sqn/339th Ftr Grp

| *Sqn* | *Date* | *Claims* | *Location* | *A/C* |
|---|---|---|---|---|
| 503rd | May 21, 1944 | (2)u/i a/c dest(grd) | Pelenz-Meckau | P-51 |

| | | | | |
|---|---|---|---|---|
| | May 24 | (.5)FW-190 dest(air)* | Dannenburg | P-51 |
| | May 30 | (2)FW-190 dest(air) | Magdeburg | P-51 |
| | June 21 | Me-410 dest(air) | S/Stettin | P-51 |
| | | (.5)Me-410 prob(air)** | S/Stettin | P-51 |
| | August 5 | FW-190 dest(air) | S/Hameln | P-51 |
| | December 31 | FW-190 dest(air) | S/Hamburg | P-51 |
| | March 2, 1945 | FW-190 dest(air) | E/Magdeburg | P-51 |
| | | Me-109 dest(air) | E/Magdeburg | P-51 |
| | | FW-190 dam(air) | E/Magdeburg | P-51 |

7.5-0.5-1 air
2-0 ground

* - shared with Lt. E.H. Graham of the 503rd Ftr Sqn
** - shared with Lt. F.D. Talcott of the 503rd Ftr Sqn

**Bryant, John P., Lt.**
62nd Ftr Sqn/56th Ftr Grp

| *Sqn* | *Date* | *Claims* | *Location* | *A/C* |
|---|---|---|---|---|
| 62nd | November 26, 1943 | Me-110 dest(air) | Papenburg | P-47 |
| | February 22, 1944 | FW-190 dam(air) | Breda | P-47 |
| | March 15 | FW-190 dest(air) | Dummer Lake | P-47 |

2-0-1 air
0-0 ground

**Bryant, Madison L., Jr., Lt.**
374th Ftr Sqn/361st Ftr Grp

| *Sqn* | *Date* | *Claims* | *Location* | *A/C* |
|---|---|---|---|---|
| 374th | July 25, 1944 | (.5)Me-109 dest(grd)* | N/Alencon | P-51 |
| | September 18 | Me-109 dest(air) | SE Jagel A/F | P-51 |

1-0-0 air
0.5-0 ground

* - shared with Lt. H.B. Lederer of the 374th Ftr Sqn

**Buchanan, Ralph H., Lt.**
334th Ftr Sqn/4th Ftr Grp

| *Sqn* | *Date* | *Claims* | *Location* | *A/C* |
|---|---|---|---|---|
| 334th | April 7, 1945 | Me-109 dest(air) | SE Krummel | P-51 |
| | April 16 | FW-190 dest(grd) | Gablingen | P-51 |
| | | Me-410 dest(grd) | Gablingen | P-51 |
| | | (2)FW-190 dam(grd) | Gablingen | P-51 |
| | | Me-109 dam(grd) | Gablingen | P-51 |

1-0-0 air
2-3 ground

**Buchanan, William E., Lt.**
370th Ftr Sqn/359th Ftr Grp

| *Sqn* | *Date* | *Claims* | *Location* | *A/C* |
|---|---|---|---|---|
| 370th | September 11, 1944 | Me-109 dest(air) | Gotha | P-51 |
| | | Ju-88 dam(grd) | Gotha | P-51 |

1-0-0 air
0-1 ground

**Bucher, Oliver B., Jr., Capt.**
335th Ftr Sqn/4th Ftr Grp

| *Sqn* | *Date* | *Claims* | *Location* | *A/C* |
|---|---|---|---|---|
| 335th | April 16, 1945 | (2)Ju-52 dest(grd) | Praha/Letnany | P-51 |
| | | Me-410 dest(grd) | Praha | P-51 |
| | | Me-410 dam(grd) | Praha | P-51 |

0-0-0 air
3-1 ground

**Bucholz, Robert C., Lt.**
335th Ftr Sqn/4th Ftr Grp

| *Sqn* | *Date* | *Claims* | *Location* | *A/C* |
|---|---|---|---|---|
| 335th | February 25, 1945 | Ju-88 dam(grd) | NE Torgau | P-51 |
| | April 9 | (3)u/i a/c dest(grd) | Munich-Brunnthal | P-51 |

0-0-0 air
3-1 ground

**Buckles, Clifford R., Lt.**
357th Ftr Sqn/355th Ftr Grp

| *Sqn* | *Date* | *Claims* | *Location* | *A/C* |
|---|---|---|---|---|
| 357th | June 20, 1944 | (.5)Me-410 dest(air)* | Pomeranian Bay | P-51 |

0.5-0-0 air
0-0 ground

* - shared with Lt. L.B. Fuller of the 357th Ftr Sqn

**Bullers, Walter E., Lt.**
79th Ftr Sqn/20th Ftr Grp

| *Sqn* | *Date* | *Claims* | *Location* | *A/C* |
|---|---|---|---|---|
| 79th | October 6, 1944 | He-115 dest(grd) | Bad Berg-Dievenow | P-51 |
| | February 20, 1945 | He-111 dest(grd) | Weiden A/F | P-51 |
| | | (2)He-111 dam(grd) | Weiden A/F | P-51 |

0-0-0 air
2-2 ground

**Bundgaard, Carl H., Lt.**
505th Ftr Sqn/339th Ftr Grp

| *Sqn* | *Date* | *Claims* | *Location* | *A/C* |
|---|---|---|---|---|
| 505th | September 5, 1944 | Me-410 dam(grd) | Sinsheim | P-51 |
| | September 11 | (2)Ju-88 dest(grd) | Munich | P-51 |
| | | (3)Ju-52 dam(grd) | Munich | P-51 |
| | November 18 | Me-109 dest(air) | Neustadt | P-51 |
| | November 26 | FW-190 dest(air) | S/Hanover | P-51 |
| | | FW-190 dam(air) | S/Hanover | P-51 |
| | March 1, 1945 | Ju-88 dest(grd) | S/Feldkirchen | P-51 |

2-0-1 air
3-4 ground

**Bunte, Allen F., Lt.**
334th Ftr Sqn/4th Ftr Grp

| *Sqn* | *Date* | *Claims* | *Location* | *A/C* |
|---|---|---|---|---|
| 334th | March 8, 1944 | Fi-156 dest(air) | Brunswick | P-51 |
| | | Me-109 dam(air) | SW Berlin | P-51 |
| | March 23 | Me-109 dest(air) | Osnabruck-Herford | P-51 |
| | | Me-109 dam(air) | Osnabruck-Herford | P-51 |
| | March 29 | FW-190 dest(air) | Magdeburg | P-51 |

3-0-2 air
0-0 ground

**Bur, Thomas G., Lt.**
369th Ftr Sqn/359th Ftr Grp

| *Sqn* | *Date* | *Claims* | *Location* | *A/C* |
|---|---|---|---|---|
| 369th | September 18, 1944 | (.5)Me-109 dest(air)* | SE Munster | P-51 |

0.5-0-0 air
0-0 ground

* - shared with Lt. J.E. Keur of the 369th Ftr Sqn

**Burch, Harold W., Lt.**
505th Ftr Sqn/339th Ftr Grp

| *Sqn* | *Date* | *Claims* | *Location* | *A/C* |
|---|---|---|---|---|
| 505th | March 2, 1945 | (3)Do-217 dest(grd) | Mockern | P-51 |
| | April 10 | (3)Me-410 dest(grd) | Wittstock | P-51 |
| | | He-111 dest(grd) | Wittstock | P-51 |
| | | Me-410 dam(grd) | Wittstock | P-51 |
| | | u/i a/c dam(grd) | Wittstock | P-51 |
| | April 16 | Ju-52 dest(grd) | NE Prague | P-51 |
| | | Ju-88 dest(grd) | NE Prague | P-51 |
| | April 17 | (2)Do-217 dest(grd) | SE Pocking | P-51 |

0-0-0 air
11-2 ground

**Burden, Rex R., Lt.**
361st Ftr Sqn/356th Ftr Grp

| *Sqn* | *Date* | *Claims* | *Location* | *A/C* |
|---|---|---|---|---|
| 361st | November 26, 1944 | FW-190 dest(air) | Osnabruck-Dummer Lake | P-51 |

1-0-0 air
0-0 ground

**Burdick, Clinton D., Lt.**
361st Ftr Sqn/356th Ftr Grp

| *Sqn* | *Date* | *Claims* | *Location* | *A/C* |
|---|---|---|---|---|
| 361st | November 25, 1944 | FW-190 dest(grd) | Zwickau | P-51 |
| | December 5 | FW-190 dest(air) | Eberswalde | P-51 |
| | | FW-190 dam(air) | Eberswalde | P-51 |
| | January 14, 1945 | (2)FW-190 dest(air) | SW Dummer Lake | P-51 |
| | | (2)FW-190 dam(air) | SW Dummer Lake | P-51 |
| | February 20 | (2.5)Fi-156 dest(air)* | SE Bayreuth | P-51 |

5.5-0-3 air
1-0 ground

* - shared with Lt. E.L. Slanker of the 361st Ftr Sqn

**Burford, James E., Lt.**
55th Ftr Sqn/20th Ftr Grp

| *Sqn* | *Date* | *Claims* | *Location* | *A/C* |
|---|---|---|---|---|
| 55th | August 25, 1944 | BV-140 dest(grd) | Parow A/F | P-51 |
| | | Hs-126 dest(grd) | Parow A/F | P-51 |
| | | (2)Ju-88 dam(grd) | Parow A/F | P-51 |
| | | Ju-52 dam(grd) | Parow A/F | P-51 |

0-0-0 air
2-3 ground

**Burgess, Leslie I., Lt.**
335th Ftr Sqn/4th Ftr Grp

| *Sqn* | *Date* | *Claims* | *Location* | *A/C* |
|---|---|---|---|---|
| 335th | April 9, 1945 | Ju-88 dest(grd) | Munich-Brunnthal | P-51 |
| | | Ju-88 dam(grd) | Munich-Brunnthal | P-51 |
| | | u/i a/c dam(grd) | Munich-Brunnthal | P-51 |

0-0-0 air
1-2 ground

**Burgher, Russell L., Lt.**
83rd Ftr Sqn/78th Ftr Grp

| *Sqn* | *Date* | *Claims* | *Location* | *A/C* |
|---|---|---|---|---|
| 83rd | August 10, 1944 | He-111 dest(grd) | Chateau-Salines | P-47 |
| | | (.5)Ju-52 dest(grd)* | Chateau-Salines | P-47 |

0-0-0 air
1.5-0 ground

* - shared with Lt. J.S. Reems of the 83rd Ftr Sqn

**Burgsteiner, Will D., Capt.**
370th Ftr Sqn/359th Ftr Grp

| *Sqn* | *Date* | *Claims* | *Location* | *A/C* |
|---|---|---|---|---|
| 370th | April 11, 1944 | (4)FW-190 dest(grd) | Gutersloh | P-47 |
| | | FW-190 dam(grd) | Gutersloh | P-47 |
| | November 21 | FW-190 prob(air) | SW Merseburg | P-51 |

0-1-0 air
4-1 ground

**Burke, Sylvester V., Maj.**
63rd Ftr Sqn/56th Ftr Grp

| *Sqn* | *Date* | *Claims* | *Location* | *A/C* |
|---|---|---|---|---|
| 63rd | November 11, 1943 | Me-109 dest(air) | NW Munster | P-47 |
| | January 11, 1944 | Me-109 dest(air) | N/Osnabruck | P-47 |
| | | Me-109 dam(air) | N/Osnabruck | P-47 |
| | February 8 | Me-109 dam(air) | Quesnoy | P-47 |
| | February 11 | Me-109 dest(air) | Hody-Spa | P-47 |

3-0-2 air
0-0 ground

**Burkett, William R., Lt.**
351st Ftr Sqn/353rd Ftr Grp

| *Sqn* | *Date* | *Claims* | *Location* | *A/C* |
|---|---|---|---|---|
| 351st | October 10, 1943 | (.5)Me-210 dam(air)* | NW Munster | P-47 |

0-0-0.5 air
0-0 ground

* - shared with Capt. J.R. Walsh of the 351st Ftr Sqn

**Burkhard, Harold D., Lt.**
385th Ftr Sqn/364th Ftr Grp

| *Sqn* | *Date* | *Claims* | *Location* | *A/C* |
|---|---|---|---|---|
| 385th | May 24, 1944 | (.5)Do-217 dest(air)* | Gifhorn | P-38 |
| | | Go-242 dam(grd) | Gifhorn | P-38 |

0.5-0-0 air
0-1 ground

* - shared with Lt. R.C. Scott of the 385th Ftr Sqn

**Burlingame, Gordon S., Capt.**
352nd Ftr Sqn/353rd Ftr Grp

| *Sqn* | *Date* | *Claims* | *Location* | *A/C* |
|---|---|---|---|---|
| 352nd | September 5, 1944 | Do-217 dest(air) | Apeldoorn | P-47 |

1-0-0 air
0-0 ground

**Burnett, Paul E., Lt.**
334th Ftr Sqn/4th Ftr Grp

| *Sqn* | *Date* | *Claims* | *Location* | *A/C* |
|---|---|---|---|---|
| 334th | April 16, 1945 | u/i a/c dest(grd) | Gablingen | P-51 |

0-0-0 air
1-0 ground

**Burnett, William T., Lt.**
357th Ftr Sqn/355th Ftr Grp

| *Sqn* | *Date* | *Claims* | *Location* | *A/C* |
|---|---|---|---|---|
| 357th | April 10, 1945 | (.5)B-24 dest(grd)* | Rechlin/Larz | P-51 |
| | | Me-109 dam(grd) | Rechlin/Larz | P-51 |

0-0-0 air
0.5-1 ground

* - shared with Lt. R.W. Cooper of the 357th Ftr Sqn

**Burney, Philo M., Lt.**
334th Ftr Sqn/4th Ftr Grp

| *Sqn* | *Date* | *Claims* | *Location* | *A/C* |
|---|---|---|---|---|
| 334th | March 21, 1945 | Me-109 dest(grd) | Achmer | P-51 |

0-0-0 air
1-0 ground

**Burns, William H., Capt.**
338th Ftr Sqn/55th Ftr Grp

| *Sqn* | *Date* | *Claims* | *Location* | *A/C* |
|---|---|---|---|---|
| 338th | January 31, 1944 | Me-109 prob(air) | N/Venlo | P-38 |
| | September 12 | (.5)Me-109 dest(air)* | N/Frankfurt | P-51 |

0.5-1-0 air
0-0 ground

* - shared with Lt. R.C. Haworth of the 338th Ftr Sqn

**Burns, William W., Lt.**
361st Ftr Sqn/356th Ftr Grp

| *Sqn* | *Date* | *Claims* | *Location* | *A/C* |
|---|---|---|---|---|
| 361st | April 11, 1944 | Ju-88 dest(grd) | Gifhorn | P-47 |
| | | u/i a/c dam(grd) | Gifhorn | P-47 |

0-0-0 air
1-1 ground

**Burroughs, Vernon A., Lt.**
357th Ftr Sqn/355th Ftr Grp
334th Ftr Sqn/ 4th Ftr Grp

| *Sqn* | *Date* | *Claims* | *Location* | *A/C* |
|---|---|---|---|---|
| 357th | February 11, 1944 | FW-190 dest(air) | S/Koln | P-47 |
| | | Me-109 dam(air) | S/Koln | P-47 |
| | February 21 | FW-190 dam(air) | Dummer Lake | P-47 |
| | March 16 | Me-109 dest(air) | S/Reutlingen | P-51 |
| | March 28 | Fi-156 dest(grd) | Dijon | P-51 |

| Sqn | Date | Claims | Location | A/C |
|---|---|---|---|---|
| | | Ju-88 dam(grd) | Dijon | P-51 |
| | March 29 | FW-190 dest(air) | NE Brunswick | P-51 |
| | | FW-190 prob(air) | NE Brunswick | P-51 |
| | | (2)FW-190 dam(air) | NE Brunswick | P-51 |

3-1-4 air
1-1 ground

**Burt, Harold R., Lt.**
369th Ftr Sqn/359th Ftr Grp

| *Sqn* | *Date* | *Claims* | *Location* | *A/C* |
|---|---|---|---|---|
| 369th | August 5, 1944 | Me-109 dest(air) | Tarmstedt | P-51 |
| | September 12 | FW-190 dest(air) | NE Berlin | P-51 |

2-0-0 air
0-0 ground

**Burtner, Rene L., Capt.**
369th Ftr Sqn/359th Ftr Grp

| *Sqn* | *Date* | *Claims* | *Location* | *A/C* |
|---|---|---|---|---|
| 369th | August 18, 1944 | (3)Me-109 dest(grd) | St. Dizier | P-51 |
| | | Ju-88 dam(grd) | St. Dizier | P-51 |
| | | Ju-52 dam(grd) | St. Dizier | P-51 |

0-0-0 air
3-2 ground

**Burton, Herbert C., Capt.**
369th Ftr Sqn/359th Ftr Grp

| *Sqn* | *Date* | *Claims* | *Location* | *A/C* |
|---|---|---|---|---|
| 369th | May 8, 1944 | Me-109 dest(air) | Hermansburg | P-51 |
| | May 19 | (2)Me-109 dest(air) | Rathenow | P-51 |
| | June 20 | (.5)Me-410 dest(air)* | NW Putbus | P-51 |

3.5-0-0 air
0-0 ground

* - shared with Lt. G.M. Perrin of the 359th Ftr Sqn

**Burton, Robert E., Lt.**
368th Ftr Sqn/359th Ftr Grp
370th Ftr Sqn/359th Ftr Grp

| *Sqn* | *Date* | *Claims* | *Location* | *A/C* |
|---|---|---|---|---|
| 368th | April 24, 1944 | (.5)u/i a/c dest(grd)* | St. Dizier | P-47 |

0-0-0 air
0.5-0 ground

* - shared with Lt. R.B. Janney of the 368th Ftr Sqn

**Burwell, Orvil L., Capt.**
360th Ftr Sqn/356th Ftr Grp

| *Sqn* | *Date* | *Claims* | *Location* | *A/C* |
|---|---|---|---|---|
| 360th | September 13, 1944 | Me-410 dest(grd) | NW Stuttgart | P-47 |
| | | FW-190 dam(grd) | NW Stuttgart | P-47 |
| | April 18, 1945 | Me-262 dam(air) | Ingolstadt | P-51 |

0-0-1 air
1-1 ground

**Bush, Jerry P., Lt.**
503rd Ftr Sqn/339th Ftr Grp

| *Sqn* | *Date* | *Claims* | *Location* | *A/C* |
|---|---|---|---|---|
| 503rd | July 7, 1944 | (.5)Me-109 dest(air)* | Leipzig | P-51 |
| | August 28 | Ju-88 dest(grd) | Saverne | P-51 |

0.5-0-0 air
1-0 ground

* - shared with Capt. V. Wyatt of the 503rd Ftr Sqn

**Buskirk, Clair E., Capt.**
338th Ftr Sqn/55th Ftr Grp

| *Sqn* | *Date* | *Claims* | *Location* | *A/C* |
|---|---|---|---|---|
| 338th | January 5, 1944 | Me-109 dest(air) | Neumunster | P-38 |
| | November 26 | (.5)FW-190 dam(grd)* | Vorden | P-51 |
| | January 6, 1945 | Ju-88 dest(grd) | Giebelstadt | P-51 |

1-0-0 air
1-0.5 ground

* - shared with Lt. R.C. Herbst of the 338th Ftr Sqn

**Buszko, Thaddeus S., Capt.**
62nd Ftr Sqn/56th Ftr Grp

| *Sqn* | *Date* | *Claims* | *Location* | *A/C* |
|---|---|---|---|---|
| 62nd | February 25, 1944 | FW-190 dam(air) | Hamburg | P-47 |
| | March 16 | FW-190 dest(air) | St. Dizier | P-47 |

1-0-1 air
0-0 ground

**Butcher, Chester J., Lt.**
357th Ftr Sqn/355th Ftr Grp

| *Sqn* | *Date* | *Claims* | *Location* | *A/C* |
|---|---|---|---|---|
| 357th | February 21, 1944 | FW-190 dam(air) | Dummer Lake | P-47 |
| | March 27 | (2)Ju-88 dam(grd) | Biscarosse | P-51 |

0-0-1 air
0-2 ground

**Butiste, Leo F., F/O**
62nd Ftr Sqn/56th Ftr Grp

| *Sqn* | *Date* | *Claims* | *Location* | *A/C* |
|---|---|---|---|---|
| 62nd | December 31, 1944 | FW-190 dest(air) | Quackenbruck | P-47 |
| | | FW-190 dam(air) | Quackenbruck | P-47 |
| | | Me-109 dam(air) | Quackenbruck | P-47 |
| | April 10, 1945 | He-111 dest(grd) | Neuruppin | P-47 |
| | | u/i a/c dest(grd) | Neuruppin | P-47 |

1-0-2 air
2-0 ground

**Butler, Frederick, Capt.**
503rd Ftr Sqn/339th Ftr Grp

| *Sqn* | *Date* | *Claims* | *Location* | *A/C* |
|---|---|---|---|---|
| 503rd | March 2, 1945 | FW-190 prob(air) | E/Magdeburg | P-51 |
| | | Me-109 dam(air) | E/Magdeburg | P-51 |

0-1-1 air
0-0 ground

**Butler, George H., Lt.**
62nd Ftr Sqn/56th Ftr Grp

| *Sqn* | *Date* | *Claims* | *Location* | *A/C* |
|---|---|---|---|---|
| 62nd | June 8, 1944 | Me-109 dest(air) | St. Andre de L'Eure | P-47 |
| | July 5 | FW-190 dest(air) | N/Evreux | P-47 |
| | September 5 | FW-44 dest(air) | NE Gelnhausen | P-47 |
| | | (2)Me-109 dest(grd) | Gelnhausen | P-47 |
| | | FW-190 dest(grd) | Gelnhausen | P-47 |
| | September 10 | u/i a/c dam(grd) | Seligenstadt A/F | P-47 |

3-0-0 air
3-1 ground

**Butler, Nelson W., Lt.**
435th Ftr Sqn/479th Ftr Grp

| *Sqn* | *Date* | *Claims* | *Location* | *A/C* |
|---|---|---|---|---|
| 435th | August 18, 1944 | (.5)He-111 dest(grd)* | Nancy/Essey A/F | P-38 |
| | | (.5)He-111 dest(grd)* | Nancy/Essey A/F | P-38 |
| | September 26 | (2)Me-109 dest(air) | SW Munster | P-51 |
| | December 24 | FW-190 dest(air) | SE Liege | P-51 |

3-0-0 air
1-0 ground

* - both shared with Lt. V.E. Hooker of the 435th Ftr Sqn

**Butler, Reed B., Capt.**
357th Ftr Sqn/355th Ftr Grp
HdQts/355th Ftr Grp

| Sqn | Date | Claims | Location | A/C |
|---|---|---|---|---|
| 357th | March 28, 1944 | (2)Ju-88 dest(grd) | Dijon | P-51 |
| | | (2)Ju-88 dam(grd) | Dijon | P-51 |
| | | Go-242 dam(grd) | Dijon | P-51 |
| | April 5 | Ju-88 dest(grd) | Ottingen | P-51 |
| | April 24 | (.5)Me-109 dest(air)* | NE Munich | P-51 |

0.5-0-0 air
3-3 ground

* - shared with Lt. E.P. McNeff of the 357th Ftr Sqn

**Butler, Robert K., Lt.**
487th Ftr Sqn/352nd Ftr Grp

| Sqn | Date | Claims | Location | A/C |
|---|---|---|---|---|
| 487th | May 12, 1944 | (.5)Me-109 dest(air)* | SE Coblenz | P-51 |
| | May 29 | Me-109 dam(air) | Gustrow | P-51 |

0.5-0-1 air
0-0 ground

* - shared with Capt. F.M. Allison of the 487th Ftr Sqn

**Buttke, Robert L., Capt.**
343rd Ftr Sqn/55th Ftr Grp

| Sqn | Date | Claims | Location | A/C |
|---|---|---|---|---|
| 343rd | November 3, 1943 | (2)Me-109 dest(air) | E/Wilhelmshaven | P-38 |
| | February 10, 1944 | (2)Me-210 dest(air) | NW Brunswick | P-38 |
| | | Me-110 dam(air) | NW Brunswick | P-38 |
| | April 22 | Me-109 dest(air) | W/Hamm | P-38 |
| | | Me-109 dam(air) | W/Hamm | P-38 |
| | February 27, 1945 | (.5)Ju-88 dest(air)* | Nurnburg | P-51 |

5.5-0-2 air
0-0 ground

* - shared with Lt. L.D. Boring of the 343rd Ftr Sqn

**Butts, Will T., Capt.**
376th Ftr Sqn/361st Ftr Grp

| Sqn | Date | Claims | Location | A/C |
|---|---|---|---|---|
| 376th | May 29, 1944 | (.5)FW-190 dest(air)* | Schwerin | P-51 |
| | September 12 | Me-109 dest(air) | W/Magdeburg | P-51 |
| | September 18 | (.5)Me-109 dest(air)** | N/Schleswig | P-51 |
| | October 7 | Me-109 dest(air) | Merseburg | P-51 |

3-0-0 air
0-0 ground

* - shared with Capt. W.B. Frank of the 376th Ftr Sqn
** - shared with Lt. C.W. Hanley of the 376th Ftr Sqn

**Bux, Arthur J., Jr., Lt.**
61st Ftr Sqn/56th Ftr Grp

| Sqn | Date | Claims | Location | A/C |
|---|---|---|---|---|
| 61st | July 24, 1944 | (.5)Me-210 dest(grd)* | Villaroche A/F | P-47 |
| | | (.5)Me-210 dam(grd)* | Villaroche A/F | P-47 |

0-0-0 air
0.5-0.5 ground

* - both shared with LtCol. D.C. Schilling of HdQts, 56th Ftr Grp

**Byers, James F., Lt.**
84th Ftr Sqn/78th Ftr Grp

| Sqn | Date | Claims | Location | A/C |
|---|---|---|---|---|
| 84th | July 1, 1943 | FW-190 dest(air) | Brielle | P-47 |

1-0-0 air
0-0 ground

**Byers, John R., Lt.**
503rd Ftr Sqn/339th Ftr Grp

| Sqn | Date | Claims | Location | A/C |
|---|---|---|---|---|
| 503rd | April 16, 1945 | (3)Ju-88 dest(grd) | NE Prague | P-51 |
| | | Me-109 dest(grd) | NE Prague | P-51 |
| | | FW-190 dest(grd) | NE Prague | P-51 |

0-0-0 air
5-0 ground

**Byers, Vic L., Jr., Maj.**
351st Ftr Sqn/353rd Ftr Grp

| Sqn | Date | Claims | Location | A/C |
|---|---|---|---|---|
| 351st | January 14, 1944 | (.5)FW-190 dam(grd)* | Rosieres-en-Santerne | P-47 |
| | March 6 | (.5)FW-190 dest(air)** | SW Nienburg | P-47 |
| | March 29 | Ju-88 dam(grd) | SE Steinhuder Lake | P-47 |
| | July 9 | Me-109 dam(air) | Argentan | P-47 |
| | August 4 | Ju-88 dest(grd) | Plantlunne | P-47 |
| | August 11 | Me-109 dest(air) | S/Paris | P-47 |
| | March 2, 1945 | FW-190 dest(air) | Wittenberg | P-51 |
| | | Me-109 prob(air) | Wittenberg | P-51 |
| | April 16 | Fi-156 dest(grd) | Reichersberg | P-51 |
| | | FW-190 dest(grd) | Reichersberg | P-51 |
| | | Me-262 dam(grd) | Reichersberg | P-51 |

2.5-1-1 air
3-2.5 ground

* - shared with Lt. H.D. Milligan of the 351st Ftr Sqn
** - shared with Lt. J. Terzian of the 351st Ftr Sqn

**Bynum, Horace B., Lt.**
55th Ftr Sqn/20th Ftr Grp

| Sqn | Date | Claims | Location | A/C |
|---|---|---|---|---|
| 55th | August 25, 1944 | Ju-88 dest(grd) | Parow A/F | P-51 |
| | | Ju-52 dest(grd) | Parow A/F | P-51 |

0-0-0 air
2-0 ground

**Byrd, Markrel L., F/O**
79th Ftr Sqn/20th Ftr Grp

| Sqn | Date | Claims | Location | A/C |
|---|---|---|---|---|
| 79th | January 14, 1944 | (.5)FW-190 dest(air)* | Rouen | P-38 |

0.5-0-0 air
0-0 ground

* - shared with LtCol. B.M. Russell of HdQts, 20th Ftr Grp

**Caid, Vernon L., Lt.**
370th Ftr Sqn/359th Ftr Grp

| Sqn | Date | Claims | Location | A/C |
|---|---|---|---|---|
| 370th | November 21, 1944 | (2)FW-190 dest(air) | SW Merseburg | P-51 |
| | | FW-190 dam(air) | SW Merseburg | P-51 |

2-0-1 air
0-0 ground

**Calderon, Severino B., Lt.**
84th Ftr Sqn/78th Ftr Grp

| Sqn | Date | Claims | Location | A/C |
|---|---|---|---|---|
| 84th | July 19, 1944 | Do-217 dam(grd) | Eutingen | P-47 |
| | | Ju-87 dam(grd) | Eutingen | P-47 |
| | September 10 | (2)He-111 dam(grd) | Meinbullen | P-47 |

0-0-0 air
0-4 ground

**Caldwell, Merle F., Lt.**
504th Ftr Sqn/339th Ftr Grp

| Sqn | Date | Claims | Location | A/C |
|---|---|---|---|---|
| 504th | June 7, 1944 | FW-190 dest(grd) | Laval | P-51 |
| | July 7 | (2)Me-109 dest(air) | Eisleben | P-51 |
| | September 13 | FW-190 dest(grd) | Munich | P-51 |
| | | u/i a/c dest(grd) | Munich | P-51 |

2-0-0 air
3-0 ground

**Callaghan, Robert E., Lt.**
38th Ftr Sqn/55th Ftr Grp

| Sqn | Date | Claims | Location | A/C |
|---|---|---|---|---|
| 38th | July 7, 1944 | Me-410 dest(air) | Bernburg | P-38 |
| | September 12 | Ju-88 dam(grd) | Herzogenaurach | P-51 |

1-0-0 air
0-1 ground

**Callahan, Robert M., Capt.**
370th Ftr Sqn/359th Ftr Grp

| Sqn | Date | Claims | Location | A/C |
|---|---|---|---|---|
| 370th | April 11, 1944 | (5)FW-190 dam(grd) | Gutersloh | P-47 |
| | April 15 | Ju-88 dest(grd) | Oldenburg | P-47 |
| | April 25 | FW-190 dest(grd) | Bar Le Duc | P-47 |
| | May 21 | Ju-88 dest(grd) | Schwerin | P-51 |
| | | Ju-88 dam(grd) | Schwerin | P-51 |
| | July 24 | Fi-156 dest(air) | Ulm | P-51 |

1-0-0 air
3-6 ground

**Callans, Glenn G., Capt.**
352nd Ftr Sqn/353rd Ftr Grp

| Sqn | Date | Claims | Location | A/C |
|---|---|---|---|---|
| 352nd | February 8, 1944 | FW-190 dest(air) | St. Hubert | P-47 |
| | March 29 | Me-109 dest(air) | SW Bremen | P-47 |
| | January 16, 1945 | Me-163 dest(grd) | Deiningen | P-51 |
| | | Ju-88 dam(grd) | Deiningen | P-51 |

2-0-0 air
1-1 ground

**Callaway, David L., Lt.**
374th Ftr Sqn/361st Ftr Grp

| Sqn | Date | Claims | Location | A/C |
|---|---|---|---|---|
| 374th | May 29, 1944 | FW-190 dest(air) | Pitka | P-51 |
| | | FW-190 dam(air) | Pitka | P-51 |

1-0-1 air
0-0 ground

**Calvin, John D., Lt.**
84th Ftr Sqn/78th Ftr Grp

| Sqn | Date | Claims | Location | A/C |
|---|---|---|---|---|
| 84th | April 10, 1945 | u/i a/c dam(grd) | Ulzen | P-51 |

0-0-0 air
0-1 ground

**Campbell, John, Lt.**
328th Ftr Sqn/352nd Ftr Grp

| Sqn | Date | Claims | Location | A/C |
|---|---|---|---|---|
| 328th | May 21, 1944 | He-111 dest(grd) | Alt Ruppin | P-51 |
| | | Do-217 dam(grd) | Alt Ruppin | P-51 |

0-0-0 air
1-1 ground

**Campbell, John C., Jr., Lt.**
503rd Ftr Sqn/339th Ftr Grp

| Sqn | Date | Claims | Location | A/C |
|---|---|---|---|---|
| 503rd | April 17, 1945 | Me-262 dest(air) | Pokycany | P-51 |

1-0-0 air
0-0 ground

**Campbell, Raymond H., Capt.**
361st Ftr Sqn/356th Ftr Grp

| Sqn | Date | Claims | Location | A/C |
|---|---|---|---|---|
| 361st | December 5, 1944 | (2)FW-190 dest(air) | Eberswalde | P-51 |

2-0-0 air
0-0 ground

**Campbell, Robert D., Capt.**
63rd Ftr Sqn/56th Ftr Grp

| Sqn | Date | Claims | Location | A/C |
|---|---|---|---|---|
| 63rd | May 31, 1944 | FW-190 dam(air) | NW Kassel | P-47 |
| | August 15 | Me-109 dest(grd) | St. Trond | P-47 |

0-0-1 air
1-0 ground

**Campbell, Robert E., Lt.**
79th Ftr Sqn/20th Ftr Grp

| Sqn | Date | Claims | Location | A/C |
|---|---|---|---|---|
| 79th | August 5, 1944 | Me-109 dest(air) | Hamburg-Bremen | P-51 |
| | | Me-109 dam(air) | Hamburg-Bremen | P-51 |
| | August 16 | Me-109 dest(air) | S/Hanover | P-51 |

2-0-1 air
0-0 ground

**Campbell, Robert L., Lt.**
361st Ftr Sqn/356th Ftr Grp

| Sqn | Date | Claims | Location | A/C |
|---|---|---|---|---|
| 361st | April 23, 1944 | He-111 dam(grd) | Hagenau | P-47 |

0-0-0 air
0-1 ground

**Campi, Louis R., Lt.**
82nd Ftr Sqn/78th Ftr Grp

| Sqn | Date | Claims | Location | A/C |
|---|---|---|---|---|
| 82nd | April 10, 1945 | (2)Me-109 dest(grd) | Werder A/F | P-51 |
| | | FW-190 dest(grd) | Werder A/F | P-51 |
| | | (2)u/i a/c dam(grd) | Werder A/F | P-51 |

0-0-0 air
3-2 ground

**Candelaria, Richard G., Lt.**
435th Ftr Sqn/479th Ftr Grp

| Sqn | Date | Claims | Location | A/C |
|---|---|---|---|---|
| 435th | December 5, 1944 | (2)FW-190 dest(air) | NW Berlin | P-51 |
| | March 3, 1945 | (3)Me-109 dam(grd) | Dummer Lake | P-51 |
| | April 7 | (4)Me-109 dest(air) | SW Luneburg | P-51 |
| | | Me-262 prob(air) | SW Luneburg | P-51 |

6-1-0 air
0-3 ground

**Canizares, Arlington W., Lt.**
62nd Ftr Sqn/56th Ftr Grp

| Sqn | Date | Claims | Location | A/C |
|---|---|---|---|---|
| 62nd | March 16, 1944 | (.5)FW-190 dest(air)[*] | St. Dizier | P-47 |
| | | Me-109 dam(air) | St. Dizier | P-47 |
| | April 8 | (.5)Me-410 dest(grd)[**] | Quackenbruck | P-47 |
| | | (.5)Me-109 dest(grd)[**] | Quackenbruck | P-47 |
| | April 9 | (.5)Me-109 dest(air)[@] | Lubeck | P-47 |

1-0-1 air
1-0 ground

[*] - shared with Capt. L.A. Schreiber of the 62nd Ftr Sqn
[**] - both shared with Maj. L.A. Schreiber of the 62nd Ftr Sqn
[@] - shared with Maj. L.A. Schreiber of the 62nd Ftr Sqn

**Cannon, Joseph W., Lt.**
363rd Ftr Sqn/357th Ftr Grp

| Sqn | Date | Claims | Location | A/C |
|---|---|---|---|---|
| 363rd | March 19, 1945 | Me-262 dam(air) | E/Leipzig | P-51 |

0-0-1 air
0-0 ground

**Capp, Merle R., Lt.**
82nd Ftr Sqn/78th Ftr Grp
84th Ftr Sqn/78th Ftr Grp

| Sqn | Date | Claims | Location | A/C |
|---|---|---|---|---|
| 82nd | May 12, 1944 | FW-190 dest(air) | Coblenz | P-47 |
| | May 19 | Me-109 dest(air) | Dummer Lake | P-47 |

| | | | | |
|---|---|---|---|---|
| 84th | August 17 | (.5)Me-109 dest(grd)* | S/Hamm | P-47 |
| | September 10 | (3)He-111 dest(grd) | Meinbullen | P-47 |
| | | He-111 dam(grd) | Meinbullen | P-47 |

2-0-0 air
3.5-1 ground

* - shared with Lt. E.H. Schneider of the 84th Ftr Sqn

**Carbonneau, Henry J., Lt.**
351st Ftr Sqn/353rd Ftr Grp

| *Sqn* | *Date* | *Claims* | *Location* | *A/C* |
|---|---|---|---|---|
| 351st | June 8, 1944 | Me-109 dest(air) | Domfort | P-47 |

1-0-0 air
0-0 ground

**Carcione, Anthony R., Lt.**
62nd Ftr Sqn/56th Ftr Grp

| *Sqn* | *Date* | *Claims* | *Location* | *A/C* |
|---|---|---|---|---|
| 62nd | September 7, 1943 | Me-109 dest(air) | Tessel Island | P-47 |
| | October 10 | Me-109 dest(air) | Nienburg | P-47 |
| | November 26 | Me-210 dest(air) | Papenburg | P-47 |
| | January 30, 1944 | (.5)Ju-88 dest(air)* | Twente | P-47 |
| | February 22 | Me-109 dest(grd) | Eindhoven | P-47 |

3.5-0-0 air
1-0 ground

* - shared with Lt. S.B. Morrill of the 62nd Ftr Sqn

**Carder, John B., Capt.**
364th Ftr Sqn/357th Ftr Grp

| *Sqn* | *Date* | *Claims* | *Location* | *A/C* |
|---|---|---|---|---|
| 364th | February 22, 1944 | Me-109 dest(air) | Bernburg | P-51 |
| | | FW-190 dam(air) | The Hague | P-51 |
| | March 2 | Me-109 dest(air) | N/Frankfurt | P-51 |
| | March 6 | Me-109 dest(air) | E/Bremen | P-51 |
| | | Me-109 dam(grd) | Berlin | P-51 |
| | March 8 | FW-190 dest(air) | S/Berlin | P-51 |
| | April 11 | Me-109 dest(air) | NE Leipzig | P-51 |
| | April 19 | Me-109 dest(air) | SE Kassel | P-51 |
| | April 24 | Me-109 dest(air) | S/Munich | P-51 |

7-0-1 air
0-1 ground

**Care, Raymond C., Capt.**
334th Ftr Sqn/4th Ftr Grp

| **Sqn Air** | **Claims** | **Location** | **A/C** | |
|---|---|---|---|---|
| 334th | June 26, 1943 | Me-109 dest(air) | W/Dieppe | P-47 |
| | July 28 | FW-190 dest(air) | E/Rotterdam | P-47 |
| | August 16 | FW-190 dest(air) | N/Paris | P-47 |
| | | FW-190 prob(air) | N/Paris | P-47 |
| | February 21, 1944 | FW-190 dest(air) | Dummer Lake | P-47 |
| | April 8 | Me-109 dest(air) | Ulzen | P-51 |
| | April 11 | Me-110 dest(air) | SE Stettin | P-51 |
| | April 15 | (.5)Ju-52 dest(grd)* | Magdeburg | P-51 |

6-1-0 air
0.5-0 ground

* - shared with Lt. H.T. Biel of the 334th Ftr Sqn

**Carlisle, Guernsey I., Maj.**
363rd Ftr Sqn/357th Ftr Grp

| *Sqn* | *Date* | *Claims* | *Location* | *A/C* |
|---|---|---|---|---|
| 363rd | December 24, 1944 | Me-109 dest(air) | W/Coblenz | P-51 |

1-0-0 air
0-0 ground

**Carlone, Michele M., Lt.**
328th Ftr Sqn/352nd Ftr Grp

| *Sqn* | *Date* | *Claims* | *Location* | *A/C* |
|---|---|---|---|---|
| 328th | May 19, 1944 | (.5)Me-109 dest(air)* | Wittenberg | P-51 |

0.5-0-0 air
0-0 ground

* - shared with Capt. R.H. Sharp of the 328th Ftr Sqn

**Carlson, Charles E., Lt.**
62nd Ftr Sqn/56th Ftr Grp

| *Sqn* | *Date* | *Claims* | *Location* | *A/C* |
|---|---|---|---|---|
| 62nd | December 23, 1944 | FW-190 dest(air) | Euskirchen-Bonn | P-47 |

1-0-0 air
0-0 ground

**Carlson, Kendall E., Capt.**
336th Ftr Sqn/4th Ftr Grp

| *Sqn* | *Date* | *Claims* | *Location* | *A/C* |
|---|---|---|---|---|
| 336th | August 16, 1943 | FW-190 dam(air) | Paris | P-47 |
| | January 31, 1944 | Me-109 dest(air) | Gilze-Rijen | P-47 |
| | March 3 | Me-110 dest(air) | E/Hanover | P-51 |
| | March 16 | (2)Me-110 dest(air) | Kaufburen | P-51 |
| | March 18 | (2)He-111 dam(grd) | Ludwigshafen | P-51 |
| | April 5 | Ju-88 dest(grd) | Stendal | P-51 |
| | April 22 | (1.5)Me-109 dest(air)* | SW Kassel | P-51 |
| | | (2)Me-109 dam(air) | SW Kassel | P-51 |
| | January 16, 1945 | FW-190 dest(grd) | Neuhausen | P-51 |
| | | Ju-88 dest(grd) | Neuhausen | P-51 |
| | February 20 | (.5)FW-190 dest(air)** | N/Ingolstadt | P-51 |
| | February 25 | u/i a/c dest(grd) | Kothen | P-51 |

6-0-3 air
4-2 ground

* - shared with Lt. D.R. Emerson of the 336th Ftr Sqn
** - shared with Capt. J.H. Joiner of the 336th Ftr Sqn

**Carpenter, George, Maj.**
335th Ftr Sqn/4th Ftr Grp

| *Sqn* | *Date* | *Claims* | *Location* | *A/C* |
|---|---|---|---|---|
| 335th | May 4, 1943 | FW-190 dam(air) | Walcheren Island | P-47 |
| | July 28 | FW-190 dam(air) | SE Utrecht | P-47 |
| | December 1 | Ju-88 dam(air) | E/Cologne | P-47 |
| | February 6, 1944 | FW-190 dam(air) | Versaille | P-47 |
| | February 20 | Me-110 dam(air) | W/Coblenz | P-47 |
| | February 22 | FW-190 dest(air) | Erkelenz | P-47 |
| | March 16 | (2)Me-110 dest(air) | SW Munich | P-51 |
| | | FW-190 dam(air) | SW Munich | P-51 |
| | March 18 | Me-109 dest(air) | SE Saarbrucken | P-51 |
| | Me-109 prob(air) | SE Saarbrucken | P-51 | |
| | March 21 | (1.5)FW-190 dest(air)* | NE Bordeaux | P-51 |
| | | (.5)FW-190 dest(grd)* | N/Bordeaux | P-51 |
| | | (.5)Ju-52 dest(grd)* | N/Bordeaux | P-51 |
| | | Ju-52 dam(grd) | N/Bordeaux | P-51 |
| | March 27 | FW-190 dest(air) | SW Bordeaux | P-51 |
| | March 29 | Me-109 dest(air) | Gifhorn | P-51 |
| | | (.33)He-111 dest(air)** | Brunswick | P-51 |
| | | Me-109 dam(air) | Gifhorn | P-51 |
| | April 5 | u/i a/c dest(grd) | Berlin | P-51 |
| | April 8 | (2)FW-190 dest(air) | Celle | P-51 |
| | April 12 | Me-109 dest(air) | NW Brunswick | P-51 |
| | | Ju-88 dam(grd) | NW Brunswick | P-51 |
| | April 13 | FW-190 dest(air) | SW Schweinfurt | P-51 |
| | April 18 | Me-109 dest(air) | NW Nauen | P-51 |
| | | FW-190 dest(air) | Rathenow-Rauen | P-51 |

13.83-1-8 air
2-3 ground

* - all shared with Lt. C.F. Anderson of the 335th Ftr Sqn
** - shared with Lt. J.T. Godfrey and F/O F.W. Glover of the 336th Ftr Sqn, 4th Ftr Grp

**Carpenter, Jesse E., Jr., Capt.**
79th Ftr Sqn/20th Ftr Grp

| *Sqn* | *Date* | *Claims* | *Location* | *A/C* |
|---|---|---|---|---|
| 79th | July 9, 1944 | Ju-290 dest(air) | Moulons | P-38 |
| | August 9 | FW-190 dest(air) | SW Ulm | P-51 |
| | October 6 | He-115 dest(grd) | Bad Berg-Dievenow | P-51 |

2-0-0 air
1-0 ground

**Carpenter, Leroy A., Capt.**
336th Ftr Sqn/4th Ftr Grp

| Sqn | Date | Claims | Location | A/C |
|---|---|---|---|---|
| 336th | January 16, 1945 | FW-190 dest(grd) | Nordhausen | P-51 |
| | April 16 | Me-410 dest(grd) | Praha | P-51 |
| | | u/i a/c dam(grd) | Praha | P-51 |

0-0-0 air
2-1 ground

**Carr, Alfred E., Lt.**
38th Ftr Sqn/55th Ftr Grp

| Sqn | Date | Claims | Location | A/C |
|---|---|---|---|---|
| 38th | January 21, 1945 | (.5)u/i a/c dest(grd)* | Stuttgart/Boblingen | P-51 |
| | January 22 | Ju-88 dest(grd) | Hanover-Langenhagen | P-51 |
| | | Ju-88 dam(grd) | Hanover-Langenhagen | P-51 |

0-0-0 air
1.5-1 ground

* - shared with Lt. M.O. Anderson of the 38th Ftr Sqn

**Carr, Charles D., Lt.**
334th Ftr Sqn/4th Ftr Grp

| Sqn | Date | Claims | Location | A/C |
|---|---|---|---|---|
| 334th | March 5, 1944 | Ju-88 dam(grd) | Fontenet A/F | P-51 |
| | April 5 | Ju-52 dest(grd) | Brandenburg-Briest | P-51 |
| | | Ju-88 dam(grd) | Brandenburg-Briest | P-51 |
| | | (.25) of (5)Ju-52 dam(grd)* | Brandenburg-Briest | P-51 |

0-0-0 air
1-3.25 ground

* - all shared with Capt. D.W. Beeson and Lt. H.T. Biel of the 334th Ftr Sqn and Lt. R.S. Tussey of the 336th Ftr Sqn, 4th Ftr Grp

**Carr, Robert E., Lt.**
359th Ftr Sqn/356th Ftr Grp

| Sqn | Date | Claims | Location | A/C |
|---|---|---|---|---|
| 359th | November 27, 1944 | FW-190 prob(air) | N/Munster | P-51 |

0-1-0 air
0-0 ground

**Carr, Vernon D., Lt.**
505th Ftr Sqn/339th Ftr Grp

| Sqn | Date | Claims | Location | A/C |
|---|---|---|---|---|
| 505th | March 12, 1945 | (.5)Me-109 dest(air)* | Hellevad | P-51 |
| | April 10 | Do-217 dest(grd) | N/Neuruppin | P-51 |
| | | Ju-88 dest(grd) | N/Neuruppin | P-51 |
| | | (2)Me-410 dam(grd) | N/Neuruppin | P-51 |
| | April 16 | Do-217 dest(grd) | NE Prague | P-51 |
| | April 17 | Ju-88 dest(grd) | SE Pocking | P-51 |
| | | Me-109 dam(grd) | SE Pocking | P-51 |

0.5-0-0 air
4-3 ground

* - shared with Capt. O.P. Farmer of the 505th Ftr Sqn

**Carrington, William H., Lt.**
62nd Ftr Sqn/56th Ftr Grp

| Sqn | Date | Claims | Location | A/C |
|---|---|---|---|---|
| 62nd | April 13, 1945 | Ju-87 dest(grd) | Eggebeck A/F | P-47 |
| | | (2)Do-217 dam(grd) | Eggebeck A/F | P-47 |

0-0-0 air
1-2 ground

**Carroll, Arthur C., Capt.**
351st Ftr Sqn/353rd Ftr Grp
HdQts/353rd Ftr Grp

| Sqn | Date | Claims | Location | A/C |
|---|---|---|---|---|
| 351st | November 18, 1944 | He-111 dest(grd) | Lechfeld | P-51 |
| | | He-111 dam(grd) | Lechfeld | P-51 |
| | November 27 | FW-190 dest(air) | NE Steinhuder Lk. | P-51 |
| | | FW-190 dam(air) | NE Steinhuder Lk. | P-51 |

1-0-1 air
1-1 ground

**Carroll, Dennis A., Lt.**
62nd Ftr Sqn/56th Ftr Grp

| Sqn | Date | Claims | Location | A/C |
|---|---|---|---|---|
| 62nd | March 10, 1945 | (.5)FW-190 dest(air)* | Remagen | P-47 |
| | April 10 | Me-109 dest(grd) | Rechlin | P-47 |
| | | Ju-88 dest(grd) | Rechlin | P-47 |
| | April 13 | He-111 dam(grd) | Eggebeck A/F | P-47 |

0.5-0-0 air
2-1 ground

* - shared with Lt. D. Henley of the 62nd Ftr Sqn

**Carroll, Edward J., Lt.**
82nd Ftr Sqn/78th Ftr Grp

| Sqn | Date | Claims | Location | A/C |
|---|---|---|---|---|
| 82nd | April 10, 1945 | FW-190 dest(grd) | Werder A/F | P-51 |
| | | Ju-88 dest(grd) | Werder A/F | P-51 |
| | | u/i a/c dest(grd) | Werder A/F | P-51 |
| | | (5)u/i a/c dam(grd) | Werder A/F | P-51 |

0-0-0 air
3-5 ground

**Carson, Leonard K., Maj.**
362nd Ftr Sqn/357th Ftr Grp

| Sqn | Date | Claims | Location | A/C |
|---|---|---|---|---|
| 362nd | March 28, 1944 | (.5)Ju-88 dest(grd)* | S/Paris | P-51 |
| | April 8 | (.5)Me-109 dest(air)** | SW Brunswick | P-51 |
| | April 13 | FW-190 dest(air) | NW Mannheim | P-51 |
| | May 28 | FW-190 dest(air) | N/Magdeburg | P-51 |
| | May 30 | Me-410 dest(air) | W/Bernburg | P-51 |
| | June 20 | (.5)Me-110 dam(grd)@ | Neumunster | P-51 |
| | July 25 | FW-190 dest(air) | Paris | P-51 |
| | July 29 | Me-109 dest(air) | W/Merseburg | P-51 |
| | November 2 | Me-109 dest(air) | Naumberg | P-51 |
| | November 18 | Me-109 dest(grd) | Mengen A/F | P-51 |
| | November 25 | FW-44 dest(grd) | Maraburg | P-51 |
| | November 27 | (5)FW-190 dest(air) | S/Magdeburg | P-51 |
| | December 2 | (2)Me-109 dest(air) | Bingen | P-51 |
| | December 5 | Me-109 dest(air) | Berlin | P-51 |
| | December 24 | FW-190 dest(air) | Fulda | P-51 |
| | January 14, 1945 | (2)FW-190 dest(air) | NW Berlin | P-51 |
| | | Me-109 dest(air) | NW Berlin | P-51 |
| | March 31 | Me-262 dam(air) | N/Juist Island | P-51 |
| | April 17 | FW-200 dest(grd) | Prague/Ruzny | P-51 |
| | April 18 | (2)Me-262 dam(air) | Prague/Ruzny | P-51 |

18.5-0-3 air
3.5-0.5 ground

* - shared with Lt. A.E. Smith of the 362nd Ftr Sqn
** - shared with Lt. J.S. Coon of the 362nd Ftr Sqn
@ - shared with Lt. T.W. Martinek of the 362nd Ftr Sqn

**Cartee, James G., Lt.**
328th Ftr Sqn/352nd Ftr Grp

| Sqn | Date | Claims | Location | A/C |
|---|---|---|---|---|
| 328th | April 16, 1945 | (2)FW-190 dam(grd) | Landau | P-51 |

0-0-0 air
0-2 ground

**Carter, Clifford E., Lt.**
369th Ftr Sqn/359th Ftr Grp

| Sqn | Date | Claims | Location | A/C |
|---|---|---|---|---|
| 369th | February 10, 1944 | Me-109 dam(air) | Quackenbruck | P-47 |
| | March 26 | He-111 dam(grd) | Chateaudun | P-47 |
| | March 29 | (2)Me-410 dest(grd) | Dummer Lake | P-47 |
| | April 1 | Me-109 dam(air) | Dummer Lake | P-47 |

0-0-2 air
2-1 ground

**Carter, James R., Maj.**
61st Ftr Sqn/56th Ftr Grp

| Sqn | Date | Claims | Location | A/C |
|---|---|---|---|---|
| 61st | August 19, 1943 | Me-109 dam(air) | W/Gilze-Rijen | P-47 |
| | October 4 | Me-110 prob(air) | E/Aachen | P-47 |

| Sqn | Date | Claims | Location | A/C |
|---|---|---|---|---|
| | January 11, 1944 | Me-109 dest(air) | N/Osnabruck | P-47 |
| | | Me-109 prob(air) | N/Osnabruck | P-47 |
| | | Me-109 dam(air) | N/Osnabruck | P-47 |
| | January 30 | FW-190 dest(air) | Leeuwen | P-47 |
| | February 20 | Me-110 dest(air) | Steinhuder Lake | P-47 |
| | May 22 | FW-190 dest(air) | Hoperhofen A/F | P-47 |
| | | FW-190 prob(air) | Hoperhofen A/F | P-47 |
| | | FW-190 dam(air) | Hoperhofen A/F | P-47 |
| | July 4 | Me-109 dest(air) | W/Louviers | P-47 |
| | November 18 | Me-109 dest(air) | E/Hanau | P-47 |

6-3-3 air
0-0 ground

**Carter, Johnnie L., Lt.**
363rd Ftr Sqn/357th Ftr Grp

| Sqn | Date | Claims | Location | A/C |
|---|---|---|---|---|
| 363rd | December 5, 1944 | FW-190 dest(air) | N/Berlin | P-51 |
| | December 24 | Me-109 dest(air) | W/Coblenz | P-51 |
| | | FW-190 dest(air) | W/Coblenz | P-51 |
| | February 9, 1945 | Me-262 dest(air) | E/Giessen | P-51 |
| | March 19 | (2)Me-262 dam(air) | N/Chemnitz | P-51 |

4-0-2 air
0-0 ground

**Carter, Joseph D., Lt.**
486th Ftr Sqn/352nd Ftr Grp

| Sqn | Date | Claims | Location | A/C |
|---|---|---|---|---|
| 486th | September 12, 1944 | (.5)FW-190 dest(air)* | Kustrin | P-51 |
| | April 17, 1945 | (5)FW-190 dest(grd) | Plattling | P-51 |
| | | FW-190 dam(grd) | Plattling | P-51 |

0.5-0-0 air
5-1 ground

* - shared with Capt. H.J. Miklajcyk of the 486th Ftr Sqn

**Carter, Leonard D., Lt.**
368th Ftr Sqn/359th Ftr Grp

| Sqn | Date | Claims | Location | A/C |
|---|---|---|---|---|
| 368th | September 12, 1944 | FW-190 dest(air) | N/Berlin | P-51 |
| | | FW-190 dam(air) | N/Berlin | P-51 |
| | January 1, 1945 | FW-190 dam(air) | Havelburg | P-51 |

1-0-2 air
0-0 ground

**Carter, Lyle M., Lt.**
504th Ftr Sqn/339th Ftr Grp

| Sqn | Date | Claims | Location | A/C |
|---|---|---|---|---|
| 504th | April 4, 1945 | u/i a/c dam(grd) | Weimar | P-51 |
| | April 7 | Me-109 dest(air) | Celle | P-51 |
| | | Me-262 dam(air) | Celle | P-51 |
| | April 16 | (2)Me-109 dest(grd) | Klatovy | P-51 |
| | | (2)Me-109 dam(grd) | Klatovy | P-51 |

1-0-1 air
2-3 ground

**Carter, Raymond S., Maj.**
435th Ftr Sqn/479th Ftr Grp

| Sqn | Date | Claims | Location | A/C |
|---|---|---|---|---|
| 435th | August 5, 1944 | Me-109 dest(air) | S/Hamburg | P-38 |
| | | Me-109 prob(air) | S/Hamburg | P-38 |

1-1-0 air
0-0 ground

**Carter, Walter T., Capt.**
503rd Ftr Sqn/339th Ftr Grp

| Sqn | Date | Claims | Location | A/C |
|---|---|---|---|---|
| 503rd | May 19, 1944 | (3)u/i a/c dam(grd) | Steinhuder Lake | P-51 |

0-0-0 air
0-3 ground

**Carwell, Jackie L., Lt.**
62nd Ftr Sqn/56th Ftr Grp

| Sqn | Date | Claims | Location | A/C |
|---|---|---|---|---|
| 62nd | September 8, 1944 | Me-109 dest(grd) | Coblenz | P-47 |

0-0-0 air
1-0 ground

**Casagrande, Manuel L., Capt.**
383rd Ftr Sqn/364th Ftr Grp

| Sqn | Date | Claims | Location | A/C |
|---|---|---|---|---|
| 383rd | August 14, 1944 | (2)He-111 dest(grd) | Memmingen | P-51 |
| | | Ju-88 dest(grd) | Memmingen | P-51 |
| | | (2)He-111 dam(grd) | Memmingen | P-51 |
| | August 15 | Me-109 dest(air) | Mannheim | P-51 |

1-0-0 air
3-2 ground

**Casey, James F., Lt.**
84th Ftr Sqn/78th Ftr Grp

| Sqn | Date | Claims | Location | A/C |
|---|---|---|---|---|
| 84th | March 24, 1944 | u/i a/c dest(grd) | St. Dizier | P-47 |
| | June 8 | Me-109 dam(air) | W/Gourey | P-47 |

0-0-1 air
1-0 ground

**Casey, Lawrence R., Lt.**
83rd Ftr Sqn/78th Ftr Grp

| Sqn | Date | Claims | Location | A/C |
|---|---|---|---|---|
| 83rd | April 30, 1944 | FW-190 dam(air) | Dreux | P-47 |
| | May 25 | (.5)He-111 dest(grd)* | St. Dizier | P-47 |

0-0-1 air
0.5-0 ground

* - shared with Capt. A.M. Juchheim of the 83rd Ftr Sqn

**Cast, Frederick A., Lt.**
328th Ftr Sqn/352nd Ftr Grp

| Sqn | Date | Claims | Location | A/C |
|---|---|---|---|---|
| 328th | April 17, 1945 | (2)Me-109 dest(grd) | Plattling | P-51 |
| | | Me-109 dam(grd) | Plattling | P-51 |

0-0-0 air
2-1 ground

**Casteel, Barney P., Lt.**
63rd Ftr Sqn/56th Ftr Grp

| Sqn | Date | Claims | Location | A/C |
|---|---|---|---|---|
| 63rd | March 6, 1944 | Me-109 dam(air) | Steinhuder Lake | P-47 |
| | July 6 | FW-190 dest(air) | E/Chartres | P-47 |

1-0-1 air
0-0 ground

**Castle, Dorman L., Lt.**
38th Ftr Sqn/55th Ftr Grp

| Sqn | Date | Claims | Location | A/C |
|---|---|---|---|---|
| 38th | September 13, 1944 | Me-109 dest(air) | Erfurt | P-51 |
| | | Me-109 dam(air) | Erfurt | P-51 |

1-0-1 air
0-0 ground

**Castleberry, Marvin H., Lt.**
2nd Scouting Force

| Sqn | Date | Claims | Location | A/C |
|---|---|---|---|---|
| 2nd | March 31, 1945 | Me-262 dest(air) | SW Brunswick | P-51 |

1-0-0 air
0-0 ground

**Casto, Dayton C., Jr., Maj.**
375th Ftr Sqn/361st Ftr Grp

| *Sqn* | *Date* | *Claims* | *Location* | *A/C* |
|---|---|---|---|---|
| 375th | April 24, 1944 | Me-109 dest(grd) | Metz | P-47 |
| | June 7 | Me-109 dam(air) | Chartres | P-51 |

0-0-1 air
1-0 ground

**Cater, Emer H., Lt.**
368th Ftr Sqn/359th Ftr Grp

| *Sqn* | *Date* | *Claims* | *Location* | *A/C* |
|---|---|---|---|---|
| 368th | February 22, 1944 | Me-109 dest(air) | Hamm | P-47 |
| | March 6 | FW-190 dam(air) | Vechta | P-47 |

1-0-1 air
0-0 ground

**Cathers, Benjamin E., Capt.**
61st Ftr Sqn/56th Ftr Grp

| *Sqn* | *Date* | *Claims* | *Location* | *A/C* |
|---|---|---|---|---|
| 61st | September 5, 1944 | Ju-88 dest(grd) | Merzhausen | P-47 |
| | | u/i a/c dam(grd) | Merzhausen | P-47 |
| | November 18 | FW-190 prob(air) | Hanau | P-47 |

0-1-0 air
1-1 ground

**Caton, Horace E., Lt.**
350th Ftr Sqn/353rd Ftr Grp

| *Sqn* | *Date* | *Claims* | *Location* | *A/C* |
|---|---|---|---|---|
| 350th | November 10, 1944 | Bu-133 dest(grd) | Fulda | P-51 |
| | February 27, 1945 | Ju-88 dest(grd) | Rohrensee | P-51 |
| | | (2)Me-109 dam(grd) | Rohrensee | P-51 |

0-0-0 air
2-2 ground

**Caulfield, Peter A., Maj.**
83rd Ftr Sqn/78th Ftr Grp

| *Sqn* | *Date* | *Claims* | *Location* | *A/C* |
|---|---|---|---|---|
| 83rd | May 8, 1944 | Me-109 dam(air) | Verdun | P-47 |
| | June 6 | FW-190 dest(air) | Mayenne | P-47 |
| | January 14, 1945 | FW-190 dest(air) | N/Diephals | P-51 |

2-0-1 air
0-0 ground

**Cavallo, Anthony S., Lt.**
63rd Ftr Sqn/56th Ftr Grp

| *Sqn* | *Date* | *Claims* | *Location* | *A/C* |
|---|---|---|---|---|
| 63rd | January 29, 1944 | Me-210 dest(air) | SW Coblenz | P-47 |
| | | Me-210 prob(air) | SW Coblenz | P-47 |
| | February 24 | FW-190 dam(air) | Minden | P-47 |
| | March 16 | Me-109 dam(air) | Vitry | P-47 |
| | May 12 | (2)FW-190 dest(air) | Coblenz | P-47 |

3-1-2 air
0-0 ground

**Cavanaugh, Cornelius J., Lt.**
368th Ftr Sqn/359th Ftr Grp

| *Sqn* | *Date* | *Claims* | *Location* | *A/C* |
|---|---|---|---|---|
| 368th | August 8, 1944 | FW-190 dam(air) | Dreux | P-51 |

0-0-1 air
0-0 ground

**Cavanaugh, Dennis A., Lt.**
38th Ftr Sqn/55th Ftr Grp

| *Sqn* | *Date* | *Claims* | *Location* | *A/C* |
|---|---|---|---|---|
| 38th | April 7, 1945 | (.5)Me-109 dest(air)* | Celle | P-51 |

0.5-0-0 air
0-0 ground

* - shared with Lt. D.T. Menegay of the 38th Ftr Sqn

**Cavell, Everett W., Capt.**
55th Ftr Sqn/20th Ftr Grp

| *Sqn* | *Date* | *Claims* | *Location* | *A/C* |
|---|---|---|---|---|
| 55th | October 6, 1944 | Do-24 dest(grd) | Kubitzer Bay | P-51 |
| | | Do-24 dam(grd) | Kubitzer Bay | P-51 |

0-0-0 air
1-1 ground

**Cavender, James V., Jr., Lt.**
357th Ftr Sqn/355th Ftr Grp

| *Sqn* | *Date* | *Claims* | *Location* | *A/C* |
|---|---|---|---|---|
| 357th | November 2, 1944 | u/i a/c dest(grd) | Wernigerode A/F | P-51 |
| | January 15, 1945 | (2)Me-110 dam(grd) | Landsberg | P-51 |

0-0-0 air
1-2 ground

**Caviness, Roy B., LtCol.**
376th Ftr Sqn/361st Ftr Grp
HdQts/361st Ftr Grp

| *Sqn* | *Date* | *Claims* | *Location* | *A/C* |
|---|---|---|---|---|
| 376th | February 25, 1944 | FW-190 dam(air) | NE Metz | P-47 |
| | March 17 | u/i a/c dest(grd) | Chartres | P-47 |
| | August 18 | Ju-52 dest(grd) | Romilly-Sur-Seine | P-51 |
| HdQts | April 16, 1945 | Me-109 dest(grd) | Halndorf | P-51 |

0-0-1 air
3-0 ground

**Caywood, Herbert L., Lt.**
505th Ftr Sqn/339th Ftr Grp

| *Sqn* | *Date* | *Claims* | *Location* | *A/C* |
|---|---|---|---|---|
| 505th | April 10, 1945 | (3)Ju-88 dest(grd) | N/Neuruppin | P-51 |
| | | (2)Ju-88 dam(grd) | N/Neuruppin | P-51 |
| | April 16 | (3)Me-109 dest(grd) | NE Prague | P-51 |
| | | u/i a/c dest(grd) | NE Prague | P-51 |
| | | (2)Ju-88 dam(grd) | NE Prague | P-51 |
| | | Me-109 dam(grd) | NE Prague | P-51 |

0-0-0 air
7-5 ground

**Cedoz, Merle F., Lt.**
364th Ftr Sqn/357th Ftr Grp

| *Sqn* | *Date* | *Claims* | *Location* | *A/C* |
|---|---|---|---|---|
| 364th | April 16, 1945 | (2)u/i a/c dam(grd) | Muhldorf A/F | P-51 |

0-0-0 air
0-2 ground

**Ceraolo, Nunzio B., Lt.**
360th Ftr Sqn/356th Ftr Grp

| *Sqn* | *Date* | *Claims* | *Location* | *A/C* |
|---|---|---|---|---|
| 360th | November 26, 1944 | Me-109 dam(air) | Dummer Lake | P-51 |
| | April 13, 1945 | FW-190 dam(grd) | Schwerin | P-51 |

0-0-1 air
0-1 ground

**Ceglarski, George W., Capt.**
335th Ftr Sqn/4th Ftr Grp
2nd Scouting Force

| *Sqn* | *Date* | *Claims* | *Location* | *A/C* |
|---|---|---|---|---|
| 335th | September 13, 1944 | (2)u/i a/c dest(grd) | Gelsheim | P-51 |
| | | u/i a/c dam(grd) | Gelsheim | P-51 |
| 2nd | November 26 | FW-190 dest(air) | S/Hanover | P-51 |

1-0-0 air
2-1 ground

**Cernicky, Melvin L., Lt.**
504th Ftr Sqn/339th Ftr Grp

| Sqn | Date | Claims | Location | A/C |
|---|---|---|---|---|
| 504th | September 23, 1944 | FW-190 prob(air) | Venlo | P-51 |

0-1-0 air
0-0 ground

**Cesky, Charles J., Capt.**
328th Ftr Sqn/352nd Ftr Grp

| Sqn | Date | Claims | Location | A/C |
|---|---|---|---|---|
| 328th | July 29, 1944 | FW-190 dest(air) | Merseburg | P-51 |
| | August 6 | (2)Me-109 dest(air) | E/Luneburg | P-51 |
| | August 16 | (.5)Me-109 dest(air)[*] | W/Mehls | P-51 |
| | September 12 | FW-190 dest(air) | N/Pritzwalk | P-51 |
| | November 27 | Me-109 dest(air) | Hanover | P-51 |
| | December 25 | (3)FW-190 dest(air) | Maastricht | P-51 |

8.5-0-0 air
0-0 ground

[*] - shared with Capt. W.E. Hendrian of the 328th Ftr Sqn

**Ceuleers, George F., LtCol.**
383rd Ftr Sqn/364th Ftr Grp
HdQts/364th Ftr Grp

| Sqn | Date | Claims | Location | A/C |
|---|---|---|---|---|
| 383rd | March 8, 1944 | FW-190 dest(air) | Nienburg | P-38 |
| | | FW-190 dam(air) | Nienburg | P-38 |
| | April 15 | (.5)Me-109 dest(air)[*] | SE Bremen | P-38 |
| | August 9 | FW-190 dest(air) | Munich | P-51 |
| | | (2)FW-190 dam(air) | Munich | P-51 |
| | August 10 | Me-109 dest(air) | NW Paris | P-51 |
| | December 23 | (4)Me-109 dest(air) | NW Trier | P-51 |
| | January 1, 1945 | (2)Me-109 dest(air) | Hamburg | P-51 |
| | April 4 | Me-262 dest(air) | Hamburg-Dessau | P-51 |

10.5-0-3 air
0-0 ground

[*] - shared with Lt. L.S. Ayoub of the 383rd Ftr Sqn

**Chadwick, Lewis P., Lt.**
376th Ftr Sqn/361st Ftr Grp

| Sqn | Date | Claims | Location | A/C |
|---|---|---|---|---|
| 376th | November 26, 1944 | FW-190 prob(air) | E/Ulzen | P-51 |
| | April 16, 1945 | (3)Ju-52 dest(grd) | Reichersberg | P-51 |

0-1-0 air
3-0 ground

**Chalmers, Allen J., Lt.**
376th Ftr Sqn/361st Ftr Grp

| Sqn | Date | Claims | Location | A/C |
|---|---|---|---|---|
| 376th | April 16, 1945 | FW-190 dest(grd) | Reichersberg | P-51 |
| | April 17 | FW-190 dest(grd) | Pilzen | P-51 |

0-0-0 air
2-0 ground

**Champion, William N., Lt.**
384th Ftr Sqn/364th Ftr Grp

| Sqn | Date | Claims | Location | A/C |
|---|---|---|---|---|
| 384th | August 9, 1944 | (.5)FW-190 dest(air)[*] | Kaufburen | P-51 |
| | August 15 | (.5)FW-190 dest(air)[**] | W/Weichaden | P-51 |
| | | (.5)FW-190 dam(air)[**] | W/Weichaden | P-51 |

1-0-0.5 air
0-0 ground

[*] - shared with Lt. J.E. Wilson of the 384th Ftr Sqn
[**] - both shared with Lt. L.A. Johnson of the 384th Ftr Sqn

**Chandler, Harold D., Lt.**
362nd Ftr Sqn/357th Ftr Grp

| Sqn | Date | Claims | Location | A/C |
|---|---|---|---|---|
| 362nd | November 18, 1944 | Me-109 dam(grd) | Mengen A/F | P-51 |

0-0-0 air
0-1 ground

**Chandler, Richard E., Lt.**
374th Ftr Sqn/361st Ftr Grp

| Sqn | Date | Claims | Location | A/C |
|---|---|---|---|---|
| 374th | November 26, 1944 | FW-190 dest(air) | Wittingen | P-51 |

1-0-0 air
0-0 ground

**Chandler, Van E., Lt.**
336th Ftr Sqn/4th Ftr Grp

| Sqn | Date | Claims | Location | A/C |
|---|---|---|---|---|
| 336th | September 12, 1944 | FW-190 dest(air) | Weisbaden | P-51 |
| | | FW-190 dam(air) | Weisbaden | P-51 |
| | November 6 | FW-190 dest(air) | Minden | P-51 |
| | December 25 | FW-190 dest(air) | SW Coblenz | P-51 |
| | | Me-109 dest(air) | SW Coblenz | P-51 |
| | January 1, 1945 | Me-109 dest(air) | Ulzen | P-51 |
| | January 16 | (2)FW-190 dest(grd) | Neuhausen | P-51 |
| | | (2)Ju-52 dest(grd) | Neuhausen | P-51 |

5-0-1 air
4-0 ground

**Chapin, Walter F., Jr., F/O**
376th Ftr Sqn/361st Ftr Grp

| Sqn | Date | Claims | Location | A/C |
|---|---|---|---|---|
| 376th | September 12, 1944 | Me-109 prob(air) | W/Magdeburg | P-51 |
| | September 27 | (2)FW-190 dest(air) | Eisenach | P-51 |

2-1-0 air
0-0 ground

**Chapman, Gerald C., Lt.**
336th Ftr Sqn/4th Ftr Grp

| Sqn | Date | Claims | Location | A/C |
|---|---|---|---|---|
| 336th | July 7, 1944 | FW-190 dest(air) | Bernburg | P-51 |

1-0-0 air
0-0 ground

**Chapman, Harry M., Lt.**
376th Ftr Sqn/361st Ftr Grp

| Sqn | Date | Claims | Location | A/C |
|---|---|---|---|---|
| 376th | March 21, 1945 | Me-262 dest(air) | Dresden | P-51 |
| | April 16 | (2)u/i a/c dest(grd) | Reichersberg | P-51 |
| | April 17 | (2)FW-190 dam(grd) | Pilzen | P-51 |

1-0-0 air
2-2 ground

**Chapman, Hugh D., Capt.**
376th Ftr Sqn/361st Ftr Grp

| Sqn | Date | Claims | Location | A/C |
|---|---|---|---|---|
| 376th | May 8, 1944 | Me-109 dest(air) | Nienburg | P-47 |
| | June 25 | Me-109 dest(air) | Bernay | P-51 |
| | | (.5)Me-109 dam(air)[*] | Bernay | P-51 |

2-0-0.5 air
0-0 ground

[*] - shared with an unknown pilot

**Chapman, John M., Lt.**
357th Ftr Sqn/355th Ftr Grp

| Sqn | Date | Claims | Location | A/C |
|---|---|---|---|---|
| 357th | June 21, 1944 | Me-109 dest(air) | Juterbug | P-51 |
| | September 12 | (2)Me-410 dam(grd) | Wittstock | P-51 |
| | | Do-217 dam(grd) | Wittstock | P-51 |

1-0-0 air
0-3 ground

**Chase, Harold W., Capt.**
351st Ftr Sqn/353rd Ftr Grp

| Sqn | Date | Claims | Location | A/C |
|---|---|---|---|---|
| 351st | November 27, 1944 | Me-109 dest(air) | NE Steinhuder Lk. | P-51 |
| | | Me-109 dam(air) | NE Steinhuder Lk. | P-51 |
| | April 7 | Me-109 dest(air) | NE Steinhuder Lk. | P-51 |
| | April 16 | (4)FW-190 dest(grd) | Reichersberg | P-51 |
| | | FW-190 dam(grd) | Reichersberg | P-51 |

2-0-1 air
4-1 ground

**Chasko, Andrew, Lt.**
62nd Ftr Sqn/56th Ftr Grp

| Sqn | Date | Claims | Location | A/C |
|---|---|---|---|---|
| 62nd | December 4, 1944 | (.5)He-177 dest(grd)* | Neuburg | P-47 |
| | | (4)Me-262 dam(grd) | Neuburg | P-47 |
| | December 23 | Me-109 dest(air) | Euskirchen-Bonn | P-47 |
| | | FW-190 dam(air) | Euskirchen-Bonn | P-47 |

1-0-1 air
0.5-4 ground

* - shared with Lt. W.C. Daley of the 62nd Ftr Sqn

**Chatfield, Donald W., Lt.**
368th Ftr Sqn/359th Ftr Grp

| Sqn | Date | Claims | Location | A/C |
|---|---|---|---|---|
| 368th | July 24, 1944 | (2)u/i a/c dam(grd) | Ulm | P-51 |

0-0-0 air
0-2 ground

**Chattaway, William P., Capt.**
62nd Ftr Sqn/56th Ftr Grp

| Sqn | Date | Claims | Location | A/C |
|---|---|---|---|---|
| 62nd | April 15, 1944 | FW-190 dest(air) | Altona | P-47 |
| | | (2)FW-190 dam(air) | Altona | P-47 |

1-0-1 air
0-0 ground

**Chatterly, Archie W., Lt.**
334th Ftr Sqn/4th Ftr Grp

| Sqn | Date | Claims | Location | A/C |
|---|---|---|---|---|
| 334th | January 29, 1944 | Me-109 dest(air) | Aachen | P-47 |
| | March 6 | Me-110 dest(air) | W/Brandenburg | P-51 |
| | | Me-210 prob(air) | W/Brandenburg | P-51 |
| | | (2)u/i a/c dam(grd) | W/Brandenburg | P-51 |
| | | Ju-88 dam(grd) | W/Brandenburg | P-51 |
| | March 16 | Me-110 dest(air) | Munich | P-51 |
| | March 18 | Me-109 dest(air) | SE Mannheim | P-51 |
| | March 21 | (.5)FW-190 dest(air)* | NE Bordeaux | P-51 |
| | March 27 | Me-109 dest(grd) | Angouleme | P-51 |

4.5-1-0 air
1-3 ground

* - shared with Lt. N. Megura of the 334th Ftr Sqn

**Cheever, Donald W., Lt.**
362nd Ftr Sqn/357th Ftr Grp

| Sqn | Date | Claims | Location | A/C |
|---|---|---|---|---|
| 362nd | November 18, 1944 | Me-109 dest(grd) | Mengen A/F | P-51 |
| | January 14, 1945 | FW-190 dest(air) | NW Berlin | P-51 |

1-0-0 air
1-0 ground

**Cheney, James B., Maj.**
376th Ftr Sqn/361st Ftr Grp

| Sqn | Date | Claims | Location | A/C |
|---|---|---|---|---|
| 376th | May 29, 1944 | (.5)FW-190 dest(air)* | E/Schwerin | P-51 |
| | June 7 | FW-190 dest(air) | N/Chateaudun | P-51 |

1.5-0-0 air
0-0 ground

* - shared with Lt. E.B. Murdy of the 374th Ftr Sqn, 361st Ftr Grp

**Chenez, Gordon H., Lt.**
504th Ftr Sqn/339th Ftr Grp

| Sqn | Date | Claims | Location | A/C |
|---|---|---|---|---|
| 504th | March 20, 1945 | Ju-52 dam(grd) | Grossenbrode | P-51 |
| | April 10 | (2)Me-410 dest(grd) | N/Neuruppin | P-51 |
| | | (2)Me-410 dam(grd) | N/Neuruppin | P-51 |
| | April 16 | (3)Me-109 dest(grd) | Klatovy | P-51 |

0-0-0 air
5-3 ground

**Chennault, Claire P., Lt.**
376th Ftr Sqn/361st Ftr Grp

| Sqn | Date | Claims | Location | A/C |
|---|---|---|---|---|
| 376th | September 12, 1944 | Me-109 dest(air) | W/Magdeburg | P-51 |
| | December 26 | FW-190 dest(air) | Merzig | P-51 |

2-0-0 air
0-0 ground

**Cherry, Robert C., Lt.**
62nd Ftr Sqn/56th Ftr Grp

| Sqn | Date | Claims | Location | A/C |
|---|---|---|---|---|
| 62nd | March 8, 1944 | FW-190 dest(air) | Steinhuder Lake | P-47 |
| | | FW-190 prob(air) | Steinhuder Lake | P-47 |
| | | FW-190 dam(air) | Steinhuder Lake | P-47 |
| | May 4 | Me-410 dest(air) | Nordhausen | P-47 |
| | | (.5)FW-190 dest(air)* | Nordhausen | P-47 |
| | June 27 | Me-109 dest(air) | La Perthe | P-47 |
| | July 5 | FW-190 dest(air) | W/Paris | P-47 |

4.5-1-1 air
0-0 ground

* - shared with Lt. E.E. Bennett of the 62nd Ftr Sqn

**Chesney, Herbert A., Capt.**
383rd Ftr Sqn/364th Ftr Grp

| Sqn | Date | Claims | Location | A/C |
|---|---|---|---|---|
| 383rd | June 25, 1944 | (.5)Me-109 dam(grd)* | Angars | P-38 |
| | August 16 | Me-109 dest(air) | Mannheim | P-51 |

1-0-0 air
0-0.5 ground

* - shared with Lt. M.E. Coates of the 383rd Ftr Sqn

**Chesser, Alvin J., Lt.**
328th Ftr Sqn/352nd Ftr Grp

| Sqn | Date | Claims | Location | A/C |
|---|---|---|---|---|
| 328th | December 25, 1944 | FW-190 dest(air) | Maastricht | P-51 |

1-0-0 air
0-0 ground

**Chetneky, Steve J., Lt.**
503rd Ftr Sqn/339th Ftr Grp

| Sqn | Date | Claims | Location | A/C |
|---|---|---|---|---|
| 503rd | March 2, 1945 | Me-109 dest(air) | E/Magdeburg | P-51 |
| | | Me-109 dam(air) | E/Magdeburg | P-51 |
| | April 16 | (3)Me-109 dest(grd) | NE Prague | P-51 |
| | | (2)Ju-88 dest(grd) | NE Prague | P-51 |
| | | He-111 dest(grd) | NE Prague | P-51 |
| | | (2)Ju-88 dam(grd) | NE Prague | P-51 |
| | | Me-109 dam(grd) | NE Prague | P-51 |

1-0-1 air
6-3 ground

**Chetwood, Kenneth, Capt.**
83rd Ftr Sqn/ 78th Ftr Grp
350th Ftr Sqn/353rd Ftr Grp

| Sqn | Date | Claims | Location | A/C |
|---|---|---|---|---|
| 350th | January 30, 1944 | Me-110 prob(air) | Vechta | P-47 |
| | May 12 | (.5)Me-109 dest(air)* | Selters | P-47 |

0.5-1-0 air
0-0 ground

* - shared with Lt. W.F. Tanner of the 350th Ftr Sqn

**Chilton, Andrew L., Maj.**
HdQts/364th Ftr Grp

| *Sqn* | *Date* | *Claims* | *Location* | *A/C* |
|---|---|---|---|---|
| HdQts | April 29, 1944 | Me-109 prob(air) | Stendal | P-38 |
| | May 21 | Ju-88 dest(grd) | Hagenow | P-38 |
| | | Ju-52 dest(grd) | Hagenow | P-38 |

0-1-0 air
2-0 ground

**Chinn, Claude A., Lt.**
63rd Ftr Sqn/56th Ftr Grp

| *Sqn* | *Date* | *Claims* | *Location* | *A/C* |
|---|---|---|---|---|
| 63rd | September 5, 1944 | u/i a/c dest(grd) | Gelnhausen | P-47 |
| | November 18 | (3)Me-109 dest(grd) | Gross Ostheim | P-47 |
| | December 4 | (2)Me-262 dest(grd) | Neuburg | P-47 |
| | | Me-262 dam(grd) | Neuburg | P-47 |

0-0-0 air
6-1 ground

**Chioles, Constantine S., Capt.**
338th Ftr Sqn/55th Ftr Grp

| *Sqn* | *Date* | *Claims* | *Location* | *A/C* |
|---|---|---|---|---|
| 338th | April 10, 1945 | Me-262 dam(air) | SE Hanover | P-51 |

0-0-1 air
0-0 ground

**Chlevin, Edward, Lt.**
383rd Ftr Sqn/364th Ftr Grp

| *Sqn* | *Date* | *Claims* | *Location* | *A/C* |
|---|---|---|---|---|
| 383rd | March 18, 1945 | He-111 dest(air) | Schwerin | P-51 |
| | April 16 | FW-190 dest(grd) | Marienbad | P-51 |
| | | (.5)Do-217 dest(grd)* | Marienbad | P-51 |
| | | Do-217 dam(grd) | Marienbad | P-51 |
| | | Ju-52 dam(grd) | Marienbad | P-51 |

1-0-0 air
1.5-2 ground

* - shared with F/O J.J. Jacaruso of the 383rd Ftr Sqn

**Choate, George R., Lt.**
62nd Ftr Sqn/56th Ftr Grp

| *Sqn* | *Date* | *Claims* | *Location* | *A/C* |
|---|---|---|---|---|
| 62nd | October 5, 1944 | Me-110 dest(grd) | S/Geseke | P-47 |

0-0-0 air
1-0 ground

**Chrissinger, Donald E., Lt.**
55th Ftr Sqn/20th Ftr Grp

| *Sqn* | *Date* | *Claims* | *Location* | *A/C* |
|---|---|---|---|---|
| 55th | November 2, 1944 | Me-109 dest(air) | Halle | P-51 |

1-0-0 air
0-0 ground

**Christ, Charles M., LtCol.**
83rd Ftr Sqn/78th Ftr Grp
HdQts/78th Ftr Grp

| *Sqn* | *Date* | *Claims* | *Location* | *A/C* |
|---|---|---|---|---|
| HdQts | March 19, 1945 | Me-109 dest(air) | Osmabruck | P-51 |

1-0-0 air
0-0 ground

**Christensen, Fred J., Jr., Capt.**
62nd Ftr Sqn/56th Ftr Grp

| *Sqn* | *Date* | *Claims* | *Location* | *A/C* |
|---|---|---|---|---|
| 62nd | November 26, 1943 | Me-110 dest(air) | Papenburg | P-47 |
| | December 1 | Me-109 dest(air) | SE Roermond | P-47 |
| | January 5, 1944 | FW-190 dest(air) | Ans | P-47 |
| | February 4 | FW-190 dest(air) | Charleroi | P-47 |
| | February 11 | Me-109 dest(air) | Bierset | P-47 |
| | February 20 | Ju-88 dest(air) | Steinhuder Lake | P-47 |
| | | (.5)Do-217 dest(air)* | Steinhuder Lake | P-47 |
| | February 24 | FW-190 dam(grd) | Quackenbruck | P-47 |
| | | Me-110 dam(grd) | Quackenbruck | P-47 |
| | March 6 | FW-190 dest(air) | N/Dummer Lake | P-47 |
| | March 15 | (2)FW-190 dest(air) | Dummer Lake | P-47 |
| | | (2)FW-190 dam(air) | Dummer Lake | P-47 |
| | March 16 | (2)FW-190 dest(air) | St. Dizier | P-47 |
| | April 15 | (2)Me-109 dest(air) | Altona | P-47 |
| | June 27 | Me-109 dest(air) | Cambrai-Lens | P-47 |
| | July 5 | FW-190 dest(air) | N/Evreux | P-47 |
| | July 7 | (6)Ju-52 dest(air) | Gardelegen A/F | P-47 |

21.5-0-2 air
0-2 ground

* - shared with Lt. S.B. Morrill of the 62nd Ftr Sqn

**Christian, Thomas J.J., Jr., Col.**
HdQts/361st Ftr Grp

| *Sqn* | *Date* | *Claims* | *Location* | *A/C* |
|---|---|---|---|---|
| HdQts | March 17, 1944 | (.5)u/i a/c dam(grd)* | Chartres | P-47 |
| | June 20 | He-115 dest(grd) | Putnitz | P-51 |

0-0-0 air
1-0.5 ground

* - shared with Lt. C.A. Laxton of the 376th Ftr Sqn, 361st Ftr Grp

**Chubin, Peter, Lt.**
77th Ftr Sqn/20th Ftr Grp

| *Sqn* | *Date* | *Claims* | *Location* | *A/C* |
|---|---|---|---|---|
| 77th | April 8, 1944 | (3)Ju-88 dam(grd) | Salzwedel | P-38 |
| | July 7 | FW-190 dam(air) | Halle | P-38 |

0-0-1 air
0-3 ground

**Church, Robert C., Capt.**
335th Ftr Sqn/4th Ftr Grp

| *Sqn* | *Date* | *Claims* | *Location* | *A/C* |
|---|---|---|---|---|
| 335th | March 21, 1944 | FW-190 dam(grd) | NE Bordeaux | P-51 |
| | March 29 | Me-109 dest(air) | NE Gifhorn | P-51 |
| | May 29 | Me-109 dest(air) | Fehmarn Belt | P-51 |

2-0-0 air
0-1 ground

**Clague, Robert E., Lt.**
84th Ftr Sqn/78th Ftr Grp

| *Sqn* | *Date* | *Claims* | *Location* | *A/C* |
|---|---|---|---|---|
| 84th | September 10, 1944 | (.5)He-111 dest(grd)* | Meinbullen | P-47 |

0-0-0 air
0.5-0 ground

* - shared with Lt. M.T. Wilson of the 84th Ftr Sqn

**Claiville, Daniel L., Lt.**
351st Ftr Sqn/353rd Ftr Grp

| *Sqn* | *Date* | *Claims* | *Location* | *A/C* |
|---|---|---|---|---|
| 351st | June 24, 1944 | (.5)Me-109 dest(grd)* | Deelan | P-47 |

0-0-0 air
0.5-0 ground

* - shared with Capt. L.G. Hally of the 351st Ftr Sqn

**Clamp, Charles C., Jr., Lt.**
63rd Ftr Sqn/56th Ftr Grp

| *Sqn* | *Date* | *Claims* | *Location* | *A/C* |
|---|---|---|---|---|
| 63rd | December 20, 1943 | FW-190 prob(air) | Bremen | P-47 |

0-1-0 air
0-0 ground

**Clark, Alvin F., Lt.**
77th Ftr Sqn/20th Ftr Grp

| *Sqn* | *Date* | *Claims* | *Location* | *A/C* |
|---|---|---|---|---|
| 77th | March 18, 1944 | (1.5)Me-109 dest(air)* | Memmingen | P-38 |
| | July 7 | FW-190 dest(air) | Halle | P-38 |

2.5-0-0 air
0-0 ground

* - shared with LtCol. M.E. Hubbard of HdQts, 20th Ftr Grp

**Clark, Charles R., Lt.**
63rd Ftr Sqn/56th Ftr Grp

| *Sqn* | *Date* | *Claims* | *Location* | *A/C* |
|---|---|---|---|---|
| 63rd | December 23, 1944 | FW-190 dest(air) | NW Coblenz | P-47 |
| | April 13, 1945 | He-111 dest(grd) | Eggebeck A/F | P-47 |
| | | Ju-88 dest(grd) | Eggebeck A/F | P-47 |
| | | (2)Me-110 dam(grd) | Eggebeck A/F | P-47 |

1-0-0 air
2-2 ground

**Clark, Charles R., Capt.**
82nd Ftr Sqn/78th Ftr Grp

| *Sqn* | *Date* | *Claims* | *Location* | *A/C* |
|---|---|---|---|---|
| 82nd | January 24, 1944 | Me-110 dam(air) | Engheim | P-47 |
| | April 1 | (.13)Do-217 dest(grd)* | Verdun | P-47 |

0-0-1 air
0.13-0 ground

* - shared with Capt. W.L. Boone, Capt. W.E. May, Lt. B.M. Watkins, Lt. H.L. Eakes, Lt. J.J. Hockery, Lt. R.V. Hearn, and F/O C.W. DeWitt of the 82nd Ftr Sqn

**Clark, Eugene L., LtCol.**
HdQts/352nd Ftr Grp

| *Sqn* | *Date* | *Claims* | *Location* | *A/C* |
|---|---|---|---|---|
| HdQts | December 30, 1943 | (.33)Me-110 prob(air)* | Chalons | P-47 |
| | January 30, 1944 | (2)Me-109 prob(air) | W/Zuider Zee | P-47 |
| | | Me-109 dam(air) | W/Zuider Zee | P-47 |
| | February 4 | FW-190 dest(air) | Hasselt | P-47 |
| | April 8 | (2)Me-210 dest(grd) | Quackenbruck | P-47 |
| | May 19 | Me-109 dest(air) | NW Wittenburg | P-51 |

2-2.33-1 air
2-0 ground

* - shared with Lt. W.E. Hendrian and Lt. D.T. Zimms of the 328th Ftr Sqn, 352nd Ftr Grp

**Clark, Glenn R., Lt.**
328th Ftr Sqn/352nd Ftr Grp

| *Sqn* | *Date* | *Claims* | *Location* | *A/C* |
|---|---|---|---|---|
| 328th | May 12, 1944 | Me-109 dest(air) | Coburg | P-51 |
| | November 2 | (2)Me-109 dest(air) | Merseburg | P-51 |

3-0-0 air
0-0 ground

**Clark, Jack W., Lt.**
503rd Ftr Sqn/339th Ftr Grp
350th Ftr Sqn/353rd Ftr Grp

| *Sqn* | *Date* | *Claims* | *Location* | *A/C* |
|---|---|---|---|---|
| 350th | February 27, 1945 | (2)Me-110 dest(grd) | Rohrensee | P-51 |
| | | Me-109 dest(grd) | Rohrensee | P-51 |
| | | (2)Me-410 dam(grd) | Rohrensee | P-51 |
| | March 24 | (2)FW-190 dest(air) | NW Kassel | P-51 |
| | April 10 | (.5)Me-262 dest(air)* | Dessau | P-51 |

2.5-0-0 air
3-2 ground

* - shared with Lt. B.D. McMahan of the 350th Ftr Sqn

**Clark, James A., Jr., LtCol.**
334th Ftr Sqn/4th Ftr Grp
HdQts/4th Ftr Grp

| *Sqn* | *Date* | *Claims* | *Location* | *A/C* |
|---|---|---|---|---|
| 334th | October 2, 1942 | (.5)FW-190 dest(air)* | SE Calais | Spit |
| | April 15, 1943 | FW-190 dam(air) | Belgian Coast | P-47 |
| | August 12 | FW-190 dest(air) | Sittard | P-47 |
| | August 16 | (2)FW-190 dest(air) | N/Paris | P-47 |
| | September 9 | FW-190 dam(air) | NE Paris | P-47 |
| | October 8 | Me-109 dest(air) | Meppel-Zwolle | P-47 |
| | March 8, 1944 | Me-109 dest(air) | S/Berlin | P-51 |
| HdQts | March 21 | FW-190 dest(air) | Bordeaux | P-51 |
| | | FW-190 dest(grd) | Bordeaux | P-51 |
| | March 23 | Me-109 dest(air) | SE Steinhuder Lk. | P-51 |
| | | FW-190 dest(air) | SE Steinhuder Lk. | P-51 |
| | March 27 | (1.5)Ju-88 dest(grd)** | Cazaux A/F | P-51 |
| | March 29 | FW-190 dest(air) | Gifhorn | P-51 |
| | April 10 | (2)u/i a/c dest(grd) | Romorantin A/F | P-51 |
| | June 20 | Me-410 dest(air) | SW Anklam | P-51 |

10.5-0-2 air
4.5-0 ground

* - shared with W/Cdr. R.M.B. Duke-Woolley of the RAF
** - shared with Lt. D.R. Emerson of the 336th Ftr Sqn, 4th Ftr Grp

**Clark, James J., Lt.**
61st Ftr Sqn/56th Ftr Grp

| *Sqn* | *Date* | *Claims* | *Location* | *A/C* |
|---|---|---|---|---|
| 61st | May 22, 1944 | FW-190 dest(air) | Hoperhofen A/F | P-47 |
| | | FW-190 dam(air) | Hoperhofen A/F | P-47 |
| | September 5 | (.5)Me-110 dest(grd)* | Merzhausen | P-47 |
| | | FW-190 dam(grd) | Merzhausen | P-47 |
| | September 12 | Me-109 dest(air) | N/Brandenburg | P-47 |

2-0-1 air
0.5-1 ground

* - shared with Lt. C.C. Thomton of the 61st Ftr Sqn

**Clark, McCauley, Capt.**
38th Ftr Sqn/55th Ftr Grp
HdQts/55th Ftr Grp

| *Sqn* | *Date* | *Claims* | *Location* | *A/C* |
|---|---|---|---|---|
| 38th | September 3, 1944 | FW-190 dest(air) | Antwerp | P-51 |
| | September 5 | Me-109 dam(grd) | Stuttgart/Boblingen | P-51 |
| | | Ju-87 dam(grd) | Stuttgart/Boblingen | P-51 |
| | September 12 | (.5)Me-109 dest(air)* | N/Frankfurt | P-51 |
| | | Me-410 dam(grd) | Herzogenaurach | P-51 |
| | September 13 | Me-109 dest(air) | Erfurt | P-51 |
| | December 5 | FW-190 dest(air) | NE Berlin | P-51 |
| | January 14, 1945 | FW-190 dam(air) | NW Osnabruck | P-51 |
| HdQts | April 7 | Me-109 dest(air) | Celle | P-51 |

4.5-0-1 air
0-3 ground

* - shared with Capt. W.H. Burns of the 338th Ftr Sqn, 55th Ftr Grp

**Clark, William C., LtCol.**
HdQts/ 66th Ftr Wg
504th Ftr Sqn/339th Ftr Grp
HdQts/339th Ftr Grp

| *Sqn* | *Date* | *Claims* | *Location* | *A/C* |
|---|---|---|---|---|
| HdQts (66th) | January 14, 1945 | FW-190 dest(air) | S/Schwerin | P-51 |
| 504th | March 20 | u/i a/c dest(grd) | Grossenbrode | P-51 |
| | | He-111 dam(grd) | Grossenbrode | P-51 |
| HdQts | April 4 | Me-262 dam(air) | Parchim A/F | P-51 |
| | | u/i a/c dest(grd) | Weimar | P-51 |
| | | u/i a/c dam(grd) | Weimar | P-51 |
| | April 16 | (3)FW-190 dest(grd) | Klatovy | P-51 |
| | | (2)Me-109 dest(grd) | Klatovy | P-51 |
| | | Ju-52 dest(grd) | Klatovy | P-51 |
| | | FW-190 dam(grd) | Klatovy | P-51 |
| | | Me-109 dam(grd) | Klatovy | P-51 |

1-0-1 air
8-4 ground

**Clark, William D., Capt.**
61st Ftr Sqn/56th Ftr Grp

| *Sqn* | *Date* | *Claims* | *Location* | *A/C* |
|---|---|---|---|---|
| 61st | September 5, 1944 | Me-110 dest(grd) | Merzhausen | P-47 |
| | | Me-410 dest(grd) | Merzhausen | P-47 |

| | | | | |
|---|---|---|---|---|
| | | u/i a/c dam(grd) | Merzhausen | P-47 |
| | November 18 | FW-190 prob(air) | E/Hanau | P-47 |
| | | FW-190 dam(air) | E/Hanau | P-47 |
| | December 25 | FW-190 dest(air) | Cologne | P-47 |
| | April 4, 1945 | Me-262 dam(air) | Salzwedel | P-47 |

1-1-2 air
2-1 ground

**Claus, Robert P., Lt.**
334th Ftr Sqn/4th Ftr Grp

| *Sqn* | *Date* | *Claims* | *Location* | *A/C* |
|---|---|---|---|---|
| 334th | March 27, 1944 | Ju-88 dam(grd) | Cazaux A/F | P-51 |

0-0-0 air
0-1 ground

**Clayborne, Millard M., Capt.**
359th Ftr Sqn/356th Ftr Grp

| *Sqn* | *Date* | *Claims* | *Location* | *A/C* |
|---|---|---|---|---|
| 359th | April 23, 1944 | (.5)Go-242 dam(grd)* | Hagenau | P-47 |
| | | (.5)He-111 dam(grd)* | Hagenau | P-47 |
| | June 8 | FW-190 dest(air) | Beauvais/Nivillers | P-47 |
| | August 4 | Me-109 dest(air) | Selsingen | P-47 |

2-0-0 air
0-1 ground

* - shared with Lt. R.B. Warren of the 359th Ftr Sqn

**Clayton, Donald B., Capt.**
361st Ftr Sqn/356th Ftr Grp

| *Sqn* | *Date* | *Claims* | *Location* | *A/C* |
|---|---|---|---|---|
| 361st | June 8, 1944 | (.5)FW-190 dest(grd)* | Beauvais/Nivillers | P-47 |
| | August 12 | (.5)Ju-88 dest(air)** | Guise-Avesnes | P-47 |

0.5-0-0 air
0.5-0 ground

* - shared with Lt. H.E. Wiggins of the 361st Ftr Sqn
** - shared with Lt. E.C. Fremaux of the 361st Ftr Sqn

**Clemmons, Billy, Lt.**
38th Ftr Sqn/55th Ftr Grp

| *Sqn* | *Date* | *Claims* | *Location* | *A/C* |
|---|---|---|---|---|
| 38th | September 3, 1944 | FW-190 dest(air) | Antwerp | P-51 |
| | | FW-190 dam(air) | Antwerp | P-51 |
| | | Me-109 dam(grd) | Antwerp | P-51 |
| | September 13 | Me-109 dest(air) | Erfurt | P-51 |
| | January 15, 1945 | (.5)Ju-88 dest(air)* | SW Stuttgart | P-51 |
| | January 21 | (.5)u/i a/c dest(grd)** | Stuttgart/Boblingen | P-51 |
| | February 25 | Me-262 dest(air) | SE Mannheim | P-51 |

3.5-0-1 air
0.5-1 ground

* - shared with Lt. D.H. Courtney of the 38th Ftr Sqn
** - shared with F/O W.V. Totten of the 38th Ftr Sqn

**Clemons, Charles W., Lt.**
84th Ftr Sqn/78th Ftr Grp

| *Sqn* | *Date* | *Claims* | *Location* | *A/C* |
|---|---|---|---|---|
| 84th | March 19, 1945 | FW-190 dam(air) | Osnabruck | P-51 |

0-0-1 air
0-0 ground

**Cles, Leslie P., Capt.**
352nd Ftr Sqn/353rd Ftr Grp

| *Sqn* | *Date* | *Claims* | *Location* | *A/C* |
|---|---|---|---|---|
| 352nd | May 27, 1944 | Me-109 dest(grd) | Saverne | P-47 |
| | June 7 | Me-109 dest(grd) | Cormeilles-en-Vixen | P-47 |
| | | Me-110 dest(grd) | Cormeilles-en-Vixen | P-47 |
| | June 20 | Me-110 dest(grd) | Twente/Enschede | P-47 |
| | | Hs-129 dam(grd) | Twente/Enschede | P-47 |
| | July 30 | (2.5)u/i a/c dest(grd)* | Orleans/Bricy | P-47 |
| | November 2 | FW-190 prob(air) | Naumburg | P-51 |
| | November 8 | (.5)Ju-88 dam(grd)** | Plantlunne | P-51 |

0-1-0 air
6.5-1.5 ground

* - shared with Lt. W.J. Jordan of the 352nd Ftr Sqn
** - shared with Lt. J.R. Evans of the 352nd Ftr Sqn

**Clifton, Frank A., Lt.**
504th Ftr Sqn/339th Ftr Grp

| *Sqn* | *Date* | *Claims* | *Location* | *A/C* |
|---|---|---|---|---|
| 504th | April 16, 1945 | (2)Me-109 dest(grd) | Klatovy | P-51 |
| | | FW-190 dest(grd) | Klatovy | P-51 |
| | April 17 | Me-109 dest(grd) | Klatovy-Anberg | P-51 |
| | | Fi-156 dest(grd) | Klatovy-Anberg | P-51 |
| | | Ju-88 dest(grd) | Klatovy-Anberg | P-51 |

0-0-0 air
6-0 ground

**Clifton, Henry E., Jr., Capt.**
334th Ftr Sqn/4th Ftr Grp

| *Sqn* | *Date* | *Claims* | *Location* | *A/C* |
|---|---|---|---|---|
| 334th | September 11, 1944 | FW-190 dam(air) | Aschersleben | P-51 |
| | December 18 | Me-109 dest(air) | E/Dortmund | P-51 |
| | February 25, 1945 | (2)Me-109 dam(grd) | Kothen | P-51 |
| | February 27 | (3)Me-108 dest(grd) | Weimar | P-51 |

1-0-1 air
3-2 ground

**Clifon, Oscar B., Capt.**
38th Ftr Sqn/55th Ftr Grp

| *Sqn* | *Date* | *Claims* | *Location* | *A/C* |
|---|---|---|---|---|
| 38th | September 10, 1944 | Ju-88 dest(grd) | Kitzingen | P-51 |

0-0-0 air
1-0 ground

**Clinton, Philip J., Lt.**
61st Ftr Sqn/56th Ftr Grp

| *Sqn* | *Date* | *Claims* | *Location* | *A/C* |
|---|---|---|---|---|
| 61st | April 10, 1945 | Do-24 dest(grd) | Muritz Lake | P-47 |
| | | u/i a/c dam(grd) | Muritz Lake | P-47 |

0-0-0 air
1-1 ground

**Clotfelter, Raymond P., Lt.**
335th Ftr Sqn/4th Ftr Grp

| *Sqn* | *Date* | *Claims* | *Location* | *A/C* |
|---|---|---|---|---|
| 335th | January 31, 1944 | Me-109 dest(air) | Zevenbergen | P-47 |
| | February 21 | Me-110 dam(air) | Havern | P-47 |
| | March 8 | FW-190 dest(air) | Magdeburg | P-51 |

2-0-1 air
0-0 ground

**Cloud, Carl E., Capt.**
503rd Ftr Sqn/339th Ftr Grp

| *Sqn* | *Date* | *Claims* | *Location* | *A/C* |
|---|---|---|---|---|
| 503rd | September 11, 1944 | Me-109 dest(air) | Annaberg | P-51 |

1-0-0 air
0-0 ground

**Coates, Mark E., Lt.**
383rd Ftr Sqn/364th Ftr Grp

| *Sqn* | *Date* | *Claims* | *Location* | *A/C* |
|---|---|---|---|---|
| 383rd | June 25, 1944 | (.5)Me-109 dam(grd)* | Angars | P-38 |
| | August 9 | FW-190 dest(grd) | W/Munich | P-51 |
| | | Ju-88 dest(grd) | W/Munich | P-51 |
| | | Me-109 dam(grd) | W/Munich | P-51 |
| | November 21 | (2)FW-190 dest(air) | S/Nordhausen | P-51 |
| | | FW-190 dam(air) | S/Nordhausen | P-51 |

2-0-1 air
2-1.5 ground

* - shared with Lt. H.A. Chesney of the 383rd Ftr Sqn

**Cobb, William G., Lt.**
351st Ftr Sqn/353rd Ftr Grp

| *Sqn* | *Date* | *Claims* | *Location* | *A/C* |
|---|---|---|---|---|
| 351st | June 7, 1944 | Me-109 dest(air) | Beauvais/Tille | P-47 |
| | | 1-0-0 air | | |
| | | 0-0 ground | | |

**Coe, Charles S., Lt.**
503rd Ftr Sqn/339th Ftr Grp

| *Sqn* | *Date* | *Claims* | *Location* | *A/C* |
|---|---|---|---|---|
| 503rd | September 11, 1944 | (1.5)FW-190 dest(air)* | Annaberg | P-51 |
| | November 26 | FW-190 dest(air) | SE Dummer Lake | P-51 |
| | | 2.5-0-0 air | | |
| | | 0-0 ground | | |

* - shared with Lt. E.H. Graham of the 503rd Ftr Sqn

**Coen, Oscar H., LtCol.**
334th Ftr Sqn/ 4th Ftr Grp
336th Ftr Sqn/ 4th Ftr Grp
HdQts/356th Ftr Grp
Earlier flew with 71 Sqn, RAF, and claimed 1.5 kills.

| *Sqn* | *Date* | *Claims* | *Location* | *A/C* |
|---|---|---|---|---|
| 336th | October 2, 1942 | FW-190 dest(air) | SW Dunkirk | Spit |
| | January 22, 1943 | FW-190 dest(air) | W/Dunkirk | Spit |
| HdQts | January 21, 1944 | (.5)FW-190 dam(grd)* | St. Leger | P-47 |
| | February 10 | FW-190 dam(air) | NE Lingen | P-47 |
| | February 11 | (.5)Me-109 dest(air)** | NW Charleville | P-47 |
| | | 2.5-0-1 air | | |
| | | 0-0.5 ground | | |

* - shared with Lt. J.D. Henry of the 359th Ftr Sqn, 356th Ftr Grp
** - shared with Lt. G.B. Peet of the 359th Ftr Sqn

**Coenen, Joseph E., Lt.**
63rd Ftr Sqn/56th Ftr Grp

| *Sqn* | *Date* | *Claims* | *Location* | *A/C* |
|---|---|---|---|---|
| 63rd | September 27, 1943 | (2)FW-190 dest(air) | S/Juist Island | P-47 |
| | | 2-0-0 air | | |
| | | 0-0 ground | | |

**Coggeshall, Chester E., Capt.**
343rd Ftr Sqn/55th Ftr Grp

| *Sqn* | *Date* | *Claims* | *Location* | *A/C* |
|---|---|---|---|---|
| 343rd | April 16, 1945 | FW-190 dest(grd) | Ainring A/F | P-51 |
| | | 0-0-0 air | | |
| | | 1-0 ground | | |

**Cohen, Henry, Lt.**
343rd Ftr Sqn/55th Ftr Grp

| *Sqn* | *Date* | *Claims* | *Location* | *A/C* |
|---|---|---|---|---|
| 343rd | March 3, 1945 | (2)Me-109 dam(grd) | Prague/Letnany | P-51 |
| | April 17 | Me-109 dest(grd) | Bautzen/Litten | P-51 |
| | | 0-0-0 air | | |
| | | 1-2 ground | | |

**Coker, Joseph R., F/O**
505th Ftr Sqn/339th Ftr Grp

| *Sqn* | *Date* | *Claims* | *Location* | *A/C* |
|---|---|---|---|---|
| 505th | March 12, 1945 | Me-109 dest(air) | Hellevad | P-51 |
| | | Me-109 dam(air) | Hellevad | P-51 |
| | | 1-0-1 air | | |
| | | 0-0 ground | | |

**Colburn, James E., Lt.**
364th Ftr Sqn/357th Ftr Grp

| *Sqn* | *Date* | *Claims* | *Location* | *A/C* |
|---|---|---|---|---|
| 364th | June 14, 1944 | FW-190 dest(air) | E/Paris | P-51 |
| | | 1-0-0 air | | |
| | | 0-0 ground | | |

**Colby, Thomas W., Capt.**
486th Ftr Sqn/352nd Ftr Grp

| *Sqn* | *Date* | *Claims* | *Location* | *A/C* |
|---|---|---|---|---|
| 486th | April 11, 1944 | Ju-86 dest(grd) | SE Berlin | P-51 |
| | | (2)Ju-86 dam(grd) | SE Berlin | P-51 |
| | April 24 | (2)He-177 dest(grd) | Ingolstadt | P-51 |
| | | u/i a/c dam(grd) | Ingolstadt | P-51 |
| | May 19 | Me-109 dest(air) | Rathenow | P-51 |
| | | 1-0-0 air | | |
| | | 3-3 ground | | |

**Cole, Charles B., Capt.**
61st Ftr Sqn/56th Ftr Grp

| *Sqn* | *Date* | *Claims* | *Location* | *A/C* |
|---|---|---|---|---|
| 61st | April 10, 1945 | u/i a/c dest(grd) | Oranienburg | P-47 |
| | | (5)u/i a/c dam(grd) | Oranienburg | P-47 |
| | April 13 | Ju-88 dest(grd) | Eggebeck A/F | P-47 |
| | | u/i a/c dam(grd) | Eggebeck A/F | P-47 |
| | | 0-0-0 air | | |
| | | 2-6 ground | | |

**Cole, Charles H., Jr., Capt.**
77th Ftr Sqn/20th Ftr Grp
55th Ftr Sqn/20th Ftr Grp

| *Sqn* | *Date* | *Claims* | *Location* | *A/C* |
|---|---|---|---|---|
| 77th | January 14, 1945 | Me-109 dest(air) | Perleberg | P-51 |
| | February 9 | (6)FW-190 dest(grd) | Esperstadt A/F | P-51 |
| | | FW-190 dam(grd) | Esperstadt A/F | P-51 |
| 55th | February 25 | (4)FW-190 dest(air) | Stendal | P-51 |
| | | 5-0-0 air | | |
| | | 6-1 ground | | |

**Cole, Eugene, Capt.**
375th Ftr Sqn/361st Ftr Grp

| *Sqn* | *Date* | *Claims* | *Location* | *A/C* |
|---|---|---|---|---|
| 375th | April 8, 1944 | Me-109 dest(air) | Diepholz | P-47 |
| | | FW-190 prob(air) | N/Zwolle | P-47 |
| | April 25 | FW-190 dest(grd) | Nancy | P-47 |
| | | u/i a/c dam(grd) | Nancy | P-47 |
| | June 29 | Me-109 dest(air) | SE Kothen | P-51 |
| | | 2-1-0 air | | |
| | | 1-1 ground | | |

**Cole, Gene H., Lt.**
343rd Ftr Sqn/55th Ftr Grp

| *Sqn* | *Date* | *Claims* | *Location* | *A/C* |
|---|---|---|---|---|
| 343rd | September 10, 1944 | Me-109 dest(grd) | S/Augsburg | P-51 |
| | September 13 | Me-109 dest(air) | Eisenach-Gotha | P-51 |
| | | 1-0-0 air | | |
| | | 1-0 ground | | |

**Coleman, John B., Jr., Capt.**
328th Ftr Sqn/352nd Ftr Grp

| *Sqn* | *Date* | *Claims* | *Location* | *A/C* |
|---|---|---|---|---|
| 328th | December 22, 1943 | Me-110 dest(air) | Zwolle | P-47 |
| | January 5, 1944 | (.33)He-177 dest(air)* | La Ferte Bernard | P-47 |
| | January 29 | Me-109 dest(air) | Pelm | P-47 |
| | April 8 | (2)Me-110 dest(grd) | Quackenbruck | P-47 |
| | | u/i a/c dam(grd) | Quackenbruck | P-47 |
| | April 22 | (.5)Me-210 dest(grd)** | Dummer Lake | P-51 |
| | May 13 | (2)Me-109 dest(air) | Demmin | P-51 |
| | | 4.33-0-0 air | | |
| | | 2.5-1 ground | | |

* - shared with Maj. E.W. Stewart and Lt. R.H. Powell of the 328th Ftr Sqn
** - shared with Lt. Q.L. Quinn of the 328th Ftr Sqn

**Coleman, Ralph L., Lt.**
358th Ftr Sqn/355th Ftr Grp

| *Sqn* | *Date* | *Claims* | *Location* | *A/C* |
|---|---|---|---|---|
| 358th | May 4, 1944 | Me-109 dam(air) | SW Hanover | P-51 |

0-0-1 air
0-0 ground

**Coleman, Wayne L., Capt.**
82nd Ftr Sqn/78th Ftr Grp

| *Sqn* | *Date* | *Claims* | *Location* | *A/C* |
|---|---|---|---|---|
| 82nd | September 9, 1944 | (3)FW-190 dest(air) | Hersfeld | P-47 |
| | March 31, 1945 | Me-262 dest(air) | Stendal | P-51 |

4-0-0 air
0-0 ground

**Colletti, Anthony T., Lt.**
83rd Ftr Sqn/78th Ftr Grp

| *Sqn* | *Date* | *Claims* | *Location* | *A/C* |
|---|---|---|---|---|
| 83rd | March 19, 1945 | FW-190 dest(air) | Osnabruck | P-51 |
| | | Me-109 dam(air) | Osnabruck | P-51 |
| | April 16 | (4)Ju-87 dest(grd) | N/Prague | P-51 |
| | | FW-190 dest(grd) | N/Prague | P-51 |
| | | (2)FW-190 dam(grd) | N/Prague | P-51 |
| | | FW-200 dam(grd) | N/Prague | P-51 |
| | | u/i a/c dam(grd) | N/Prague | P-51 |

1-0-1 air
5-4 ground

**Collins, Preston B., Lt.**
374th Ftr Sqn/361st Ftr Grp

| *Sqn* | *Date* | *Claims* | *Location* | *A/C* |
|---|---|---|---|---|
| 374th | October 7, 1944 | Me-109 dest(air) | Naumburg | P-51 |

1-0-0 air
0-0 ground

**Collins, Robert J., Lt.**
359th Ftr Sqn/356th Ftr Grp

| *Sqn* | *Date* | *Claims* | *Location* | *A/C* |
|---|---|---|---|---|
| 359th | April 23, 1944 | (.5)He-111 dam(grd)* | Hagenau | P-47 |
| | April 27 | (.5)FW-190 dest(air)** | Reims | P-47 |

0.5-0-0 air
0-0.5 ground

* - shared with Maj. J.R. Thorne of HdQts, 356th Ftr Grp
** - shared with Capt. H.A. Ogden of HdQts, 356th Ftr Grp

**Collins, William F., Capt.**
369th Ftr Sqn/359th Ftr Grp

| *Sqn* | *Date* | *Claims* | *Location* | *A/C* |
|---|---|---|---|---|
| 369th | December 31, 1944 | (1.5)FW-190 dest(air)* | SW Hamburg | P-51 |
| | | (.5)FW-190 dest(air)* | SW Hamburg | P-51 |
| | February 22, 1945 | (2)Ju-88 dest(grd) | Parchim | P-51 |
| | | Ju-88 dam(grd) | Parchim | P-51 |
| | March 24 | (2)Me-109 dest(air) | Eikelon A/F | P-51 |
| | April 17 | FW-190 dest(grd) | W/Dresden | P-51 |

4-0-0 air
3-1 ground

* - both shared with Lt. A.B. Morris of the 369th Ftr Sqn

**Collins, Wilmer W., Lt.**
336th Ftr Sqn/4th Ftr Grp

| *Sqn* | *Date* | *Claims* | *Location* | *A/C* |
|---|---|---|---|---|
| 336th | March 21, 1945 | Me-410 dam(grd) | Achmer | P-51 |
| | | Do-217 dam(grd) | Achmer | P-51 |
| | April 10 | Me-262 dest(air) | Lubeck | P-51 |
| | April 16 | Me-109 dam(grd) | Praha | P-51 |
| | | Do-217 dam(grd) | Praha | P-51 |
| | April 17 | Me-110 dest(grd) | Pilzen | P-51 |

1-0-0 air
1-4 ground

**Colson, Charles C., Capt.**
357th Ftr Sqn/355th Ftr Grp

| *Sqn* | *Date* | *Claims* | *Location* | *A/C* |
|---|---|---|---|---|
| 357th | March 16, 1944 | Me-109 dest(air) | S/Reutlingen | P-51 |
| | March 27 | Ju-88 dam(grd) | Biscarosse A/F | P-51 |
| | October 6 | Me-109 dam(air) | W/Berlin | P-51 |
| | November 18 | (4)Me-262 dam(grd) | Leipheim | P-51 |
| | April 16, 1945 | Me-110 dest(grd) | Bad Aibling | P-51 |
| | | Ju-88 dest(grd) | Bad Aibling | P-51 |

1-0-1 air
2-5 ground

**Compton, Gordon B., Capt.**
351st Ftr Sqn/353rd Ftr Grp

| *Sqn* | *Date* | *Claims* | *Location* | *A/C* |
|---|---|---|---|---|
| 351st | October 4, 1943 | Me-109 dam(air) | Malines | P-47 |
| | February 22, 1944 | Ju-88 dest(air) | W/Diest | P-47 |
| | | FW-190 dest(grd) | NE Bonn | P-47 |
| | | (.25)FW-190 dam(grd)* | NE Bonn | P-47 |
| | | (.25)FW-190 dam(grd)* | NE Bonn | P-47 |
| | June 7 | (.5)Me-109 dest(air)** | E/Ribecourt | P-47 |
| | June 8 | FW-190 dest(air) | SW Angars | P-47 |
| | June 20 | Ju-88 dest(grd) | Plantlunne | P-47 |
| | | (.5)He-111 dam(grd)@ | Plantlunne | P-47 |
| | June 24 | Ju-52 dest(grd) | Deelan | P-47 |
| | November 18 | (2)Ju-88 dest(grd) | Lechfeld | P-51 |
| | | u/i a/c dam(grd) | Lechfeld | P-51 |
| | November 27 | FW-190 dest(air) | NE Steinhuder Lk. | P-51 |
| | February 22, 1945 | Me-262 dest(air) | Brandenburg | P-51 |
| | March 21 | Ar-234 dest(grd) | Achmer | P-51 |
| | April 5 | (3)Me-410 dest(grd) | Weiden | P-51 |
| | | Me-110 dest(grd) | Weiden | P-51 |
| | April 10 | Me-262 dest(air) | Dessau-Kothen | P-51 |
| | April 16 | (3)Ju-188 dest(grd) | Reichersberg | P-51 |
| | | (2)Ju-88 dest(grd) | Reichersberg | P-51 |
| | | (3)u/i a/c dam(grd) | Reichersberg | P-51 |

5.5-0-1 air
15-5 ground

* - both shared with Maj. W.C. Beckham, Lt. F.N. Emory, and Lt. G.F. Perpente of the 351st Ftr Sqn
** - shared with Col. G.E. Duncan of HdQts, 353rd Ftr Grp
@ - shared with Lt. J.L. Dwyer of the 351st Ftr Sqn

**Comstock, Harold E., Maj.**
63rd Ftr Sqn/56th Ftr Grp

| *Sqn* | *Date* | *Claims* | *Location* | *A/C* |
|---|---|---|---|---|
| 63rd | August 17, 1943 | Me-109 dest(air) | Ans | P-47 |
| | October 4 | Me-110 dest(air) | Bruhl | P-47 |
| | November 26 | Me-110 dest(air) | Friesoythe | P-47 |
| | | Me-110 dam(air) | Friesoythe | P-47 |
| | | FW-190 dam(air) | Friesoythe | P-47 |
| | November 29 | Me-109 prob(air) | Papenburg | P-47 |
| | January 29, 1944 | FW-190 dam(air) | W/Ostend | P-47 |
| | February 24 | FW-190 dam(air) | Peterhagen | P-47 |
| | September 16 | He-177 dest(grd) | Alhorn A/F | P-47 |
| | November 18 | He-111 dest(grd) | Gross Ostheim | P-47 |
| | December 23 | (2)FW-190 dest(air) | SW Bonn | P-47 |
| | | (2)FW-190 dam(air) | SW Bonn | P-47 |

5-1-6 air
2-0 ground

**Conard, Jule V., Lt.**
487th Ftr Sqn/352nd Ftr Grp

| *Sqn* | *Date* | *Claims* | *Location* | *A/C* |
|---|---|---|---|---|
| 487th | May 29, 1944 | (.5)Me-109 dest(air)* | Wolgast | P-51 |
| | June 27 | (2)FW-190 dest(air) | N/Noyon | P-51 |

2.5-0-0 air
0-0 ground

* - shared with Lt. G.T. Moran of the 487th Ftr Sqn

**Conger, Paul A., Maj.**
61st Ftr Sqn/56th Ftr Grp
63rd Ftr Sqn/56th Ftr Grp

| *Sqn* | *Date* | *Claims* | *Location* | *A/C* |
|---|---|---|---|---|
| 61st | December 11, 1943 | (2)Me-110 dest(air) | Langeroog Island | P-47 |
| | | Ju-88 dest(air) | Langeroog Island | P-47 |
| | | Me-110 dam(air) | Langeroog Island | P-47 |
| | April 15, 1944 | FW-190 dest(air) | Elmshorn | P-47 |
| | May 12 | (2)FW-190 dest(air) | N/Marburg | P-47 |
| | | FW-190 dam(air) | N/Marburg | P-47 |
| | August 28 | (.5)He-111 dest(air)[*] | S/Saarbrucken | P-47 |
| | September 5 | (1.5)Me-210 dam(grd)[**] | Gelnhausen | P-47 |
| 63rd | December 2 | (2)Me-109 dest(air) | S/Marburg | P-47 |
| | January 14, 1945 | Me-109 dest(air) | Stendal | P-47 |
| | | Me-109 dam(air) | Stendal | P-47 |
| | February 3 | Me-109 dest(air) | Friedersdorf A/F | P-47 |
| | | FW-190 dest(air) | Friedersdorf A/F | P-47 |
| | | Me-109 dam(air) | Friedersdorf A/F | P-47 |

11.5-0-4 air
0-1.5 ground

* - shared with Lt. J.M. Jure of the 61st Ftr Sqn
** - shared with Lt. F.H. Barrett of the 61st Ftr Sqn

**Conklin, Cyril D., Lt.**
364th Ftr Sqn/357th Ftr Grp

| *Sqn* | *Date* | *Claims* | *Location* | *A/C* |
|---|---|---|---|---|
| 364th | May 21, 1944 | (1.5)Me-109 dest(grd)[*] | S/Eichhof | P-51 |
| | May 27 | (2)Me-109 dest(air) | Colmar | P-51 |

2-0-0 air
1.5-0 ground

* - shared with Lt. H.R. Nowlin of the 364th Ftr Sqn

**Connaghan, Frank J., Lt.**
362nd Ftr Sqn/357th Ftr Grp

| *Sqn* | *Date* | *Claims* | *Location* | *A/C* |
|---|---|---|---|---|
| 362nd | April 24, 1944 | Me-110 dest(air) | Munich | P-51 |

1-0-0 air
0-0 ground

**Connelly, Dick D., Lt.**
370th Ftr Sqn/359th Ftr Grp

| *Sqn* | *Date* | *Claims* | *Location* | *A/C* |
|---|---|---|---|---|
| 370th | September 12, 1944 | FW-190 dest(air) | Magdeburg | P-51 |
| | | Me-109 dest(air) | S/Berlin | P-51 |
| | November 2 | Me-109 dest(air) | Erfurt-Weimar | P-51 |

3-0-0 air
0-0 ground

**Conner, Richard E., LtCol.**
82nd Ftr Sqn/78th Ftr Grp

| *Sqn* | *Date* | *Claims* | *Location* | *A/C* |
|---|---|---|---|---|
| 82nd | August 6, 1944 | (.5)Me-109 dest(air)[*] | Hamburg | P-47 |
| | August 27 | Me-110 dest(grd) | Thionville | P-47 |
| | September 9 | (.5)Me-109 dest(grd)[**] | Giessen | P-47 |
| | October 7 | Me-262 dest(air) | Osnabruck | P-47 |
| | October 12 | FW-190 dest(air) | Hamburg | P-47 |
| | November 21 | (2)Me-109 dest(air) | Hanover | P-47 |
| | | Ju-88 dest(grd) | Gutersloh | P-47 |
| | March 21, 1945 | Me-262 dest(grd) | Dresden | P-51 |
| | | (2)Me-262 dam(grd) | Dresden | P-51 |

4.5-0-0 air
3.5-2 ground

* - shared with Lt. J.B. Stallings of the 82nd Ftr Sqn
** - shared with Lt. D.C. Hart of the 82nd Ftr Sqn

**Conners, Arthur F., Lt.**
338th Ftr Sqn/55th Ftr Grp

| *Sqn* | *Date* | *Claims* | *Location* | *A/C* |
|---|---|---|---|---|
| 338th | April 10, 1945 | FW-190 dest(grd) | Burg A/F | P-51 |

0-0-0 air
1-0 ground

**Connor, Bertis A., Lt.**
505th Ftr Sqn/339th Ftr Grp

| *Sqn* | *Date* | *Claims* | *Location* | *A/C* |
|---|---|---|---|---|
| 505th | March 2, 1945 | (2)Do-217 dest(grd) | Mockern | P-51 |

0-0-0 air
2-0 ground

**Connors, Stanley W., Lt.**
335th Ftr Sqn/4th Ftr Grp

| *Sqn* | *Date* | *Claims* | *Location* | *A/C* |
|---|---|---|---|---|
| 335th | March 21, 1945 | u/i a/c dam(grd) | Achmer | P-51 |
| | April 9 | Me-410 dam(grd) | Munich-Brunnthal | P-51 |

0-0-0 air
0-2 ground

**Contos, George G., Lt.**
486th Ftr Sqn/352nd Ftr Grp

| *Sqn* | *Date* | *Claims* | *Location* | *A/C* |
|---|---|---|---|---|
| 486th | January 14, 1945 | (.5)FW-190 dest(air)[*] | Almelo | P-51 |
| | | (.5)FW-190 dest(air)[**] | Almelo | P-51 |
| | January 23 | (.5)Me-109 dest(air)[@] | SW Dusseldorf | P-51 |

1.5-0-0 air
0-0 ground

* - shared with Lt. J.D. Stearns of the 486th Ftr Sqn
** - shared with an unknown pilot
@ - shared with Capt. L.J. Vitek of the 486th Ftr Sqn

**Cook, Alfred B., Lt.**
374th Ftr Sqn/361st Ftr Grp

| *Sqn* | *Date* | *Claims* | *Location* | *A/C* |
|---|---|---|---|---|
| 374th | September 18, 1944 | Me-109 dest(grd) | Jagel A/F | P-51 |
| | | Me-109 dam(grd) | Jagel A/F | P-51 |

0-0-0 air
1-1 ground

**Cook, Emory C., Lt.**
368th Ftr Sqn/359th Ftr Grp

| *Sqn* | *Date* | *Claims* | *Location* | *A/C* |
|---|---|---|---|---|
| 368th | August 9, 1944 | Me-109 dam(air) | Munich | P-51 |
| | December 23 | Me-109 dest(air) | Coblenz | P-51 |

1-0-1 air
0-0 ground

**Cook, James R., Capt.**
360th Ftr Sqn/356th Ftr Grp

| *Sqn* | *Date* | *Claims* | *Location* | *A/C* |
|---|---|---|---|---|
| 360th | February 21, 1944 | Me-109 dam(air) | Celle | P-47 |

0-0-1 air
0-0 ground

**Cook, Walter V., Capt.**
62nd Ftr Sqn/56th Ftr Grp

| *Sqn* | *Date* | *Claims* | *Location* | *A/C* |
|---|---|---|---|---|
| 62nd | June 12, 1943 | FW-190 dest(air) | Ypres | P-47 |
| | October 10 | Me-210 dest(air) | Altenberge | P-47 |
| | November 11 | (2)FW-190 dest(air) | Bucholt | P-47 |
| | November 26 | (2)Me-110 dest(air) | Papenburg | P-47 |

6-0-0 air
0-0 ground

**Cooley, George W., Lt.**
335th Ftr Sqn/4th Ftr Grp

| *Sqn* | *Date* | *Claims* | *Location* | *A/C* |
|---|---|---|---|---|
| 335th | June 20, 1944 | Me-109 dest(air) | Politz | P-51 |
| | | Me-109 dam(air) | Politz | P-51 |
| | September 11 | (2)FW-190 dest(air) | Naumberg | P-51 |

3-0-1 air
0-0 ground

**Cooley, Warren C., Lt.**
359th Ftr Sqn/356th Ftr Grp

| Sqn | Date | Claims | Location | A/C |
|---|---|---|---|---|
| 359th | November 26, 1944 | (2)Me-109 dest(air) | NW Dummer Lake | P-51 |
| | December 26 | (2)FW-190 dest(air) | NE Bonn | P-51 |

4-0-0 air
0-0 ground

**Coon, John S., Lt.**
362nd Ftr Sqn/357th Ftr Grp

| Sqn | Date | Claims | Location | A/C |
|---|---|---|---|---|
| 362nd | April 8, 1944 | (.5)Me-109 dest(air)* | SW Brunswick | P-51 |
| | April 24 | Me-110 dam(air) | E/Munich | P-51 |

0.5-0-1 air
0-0 ground

* - shared with Lt. L.K. Carson of the 362nd Ftr Sqn

**Coonan, John F., Capt.**
38th Ftr Sqn/55th Ftr Grp
Earlier flew in the CBI with the 51st Ftr Grp and claimed one kill on February 25, 1943.

| Sqn | Date | Claims | Location | A/C |
|---|---|---|---|---|
| 38th | September 13, 1944 | Me-109 dest(air) | Erfurt | P-51 |
| | November 2 | (.5)FW-190 dest(air)* | W/Merseburg | P-51 |
| | January 3, 1945 | Ar-196 dest(air) | SE Ulm | P-51 |

2.5-0-0 air
0-0 ground

* - shared with Lt. D.H. Courtney of the 38th Ftr Sqn

**Coons, Merle M., Capt.**
38th Ftr Sqn/55th Ftr Grp

| Sqn | Date | Claims | Location | A/C |
|---|---|---|---|---|
| 38th | September 11, 1944 | Me-109 dest(air) | Erfurt | P-51 |
| | | Me-109 prob(air) | Erfurt | P-51 |
| | September 13 | Me-109 dest(air) | Erfurt | P-51 |
| | November 2 | FW-190 dest(air) | W/Merseburg | P-51 |
| | December 5 | Me-109 dest(air) | N/Berlin | P-51 |
| | | FW-190 dest(air) | N/Berlin | P-51 |

5-1-0 air
0-0 ground

**Cooper, Donald C., Lt.**
77th Ftr Sqn/20th Ftr Grp

| Sqn | Date | Claims | Location | A/C |
|---|---|---|---|---|
| 77th | February 10, 1944 | FW-190 dam(air) | N/Hanover | P-38 |

0-0-1 air
0-0 ground

**Cooper, James M., LtCol.**
83rd Ftr Sqn/ 78th Ftr Grp
361st Ftr Sqn/356th Ftr Grp

| Sqn | Date | Claims | Location | A/C |
|---|---|---|---|---|
| 83rd | July 1, 1943 | FW-190 dam(air) | Schouwen | P-47 |
| | July 29 | FW-190 dam(air) | Ghent | P-47 |

0-0-2 air
0-0 ground

**Cooper, Randolph W., Lt.**
357th Ftr Sqn/355th Ftr Grp

| Sqn | Date | Claims | Location | A/C |
|---|---|---|---|---|
| 357th | April 4, 1945 | Me-262 dam(air) | Ludwigslust | P-51 |
| | April 10 | (.5)B-24 dest(grd)* | Rechlin/Larz | P-51 |
| | April 13 | (1.5)He-111 dest(grd)** | Schleswig | P-51 |
| | | FW-200 dest(grd) | Schleswig | P-51 |
| | April 16 | He-177 dest(grd) | SE Germany | P-51 |
| | | FW-190 dest(grd) | SE Germany | P-51 |

0-0-1 air
5-0 ground

* - shared with Lt. W.T. Burnett of the 357th Ftr Sqn
** - shared with Lt. R.F. Misner of the 357th Ftr Sqn

**Cooper, Roy E., Lt.**
338th Ftr Sqn/55th Ftr Grp

| Sqn | Date | Claims | Location | A/C |
|---|---|---|---|---|
| 338th | April 16, 1945 | FW-190 dest(grd) | N/Landshut | P-51 |
| | April 17 | FW-190 dest(air) | SE Dresden | P-51 |

1-0-0 air
1-0 ground

**Corbett, Richard J., Lt.**
336th Ftr Sqn/4th Ftr Grp

| Sqn | Date | Claims | Location | A/C |
|---|---|---|---|---|
| 336th | January 16, 1945 | (2)Ju-87 dest(grd) | Neuhausen | P-51 |
| | | FW-190 dest(grd) | Neuhausen | P-51 |
| | February 25 | He-111 dest(grd) | Kothen | P-51 |
| | | He-111 dam(grd) | Kothen | P-51 |

0-0-0 air
4-1 ground

**Corbett, Richard K., Lt.**
84th Ftr Sqn/78th Ftr Grp

| Sqn | Date | Claims | Location | A/C |
|---|---|---|---|---|
| 84th | February 3, 1945 | (2)Ju-87 dam(grd) | Luneburg A/F | P-51 |
| | April 7 | (.5)Me-109 dest(air)* | NE Dummer Lake | P-51 |

0.5-0-0 air
0-2 ground

* - shared with Lt. H.R. Slack of the 84th Ftr Sqn

**Corbin, Luther L., Lt.**
504th Ftr Sqn/339th Ftr Grp

| Sqn | Date | Claims | Location | A/C |
|---|---|---|---|---|
| 504th | June 7, 1944 | FW-190 dest(grd) | Laval | P-51 |

0-0-0 air
1-0 ground

**Corcoran, Martin E., Lt.**
486th Ftr Sqn/352nd Ftr Grp

| Sqn | Date | Claims | Location | A/C |
|---|---|---|---|---|
| 486th | April 11, 1944 | Ju-88 dest(grd) | Lonnewitz | P-51 |
| | | Me-109 dam(grd) | Lonnewitz | P-51 |
| | | u/i a/c dam(grd) | Lonnewitz | P-51 |
| | April 15 | (2)FW-190 dest(air) | NE Vechta | P-51 |

2-0-0 air
1-2 ground

**Corey, Harry R., Capt.**
505th Ftr Sqn/339th Ftr Grp

| Sqn | Date | Claims | Location | A/C |
|---|---|---|---|---|
| 505th | April 4, 1945 | Me-262 dest(air) | Rostock | P-51 |
| | April 10 | (4)Ju-88 dest(grd) | Wittstock | P-51 |
| | | FW-189 dam(grd) | Wittstock | P-51 |
| | | Ju-88 dam(grd) | Wittstock | P-51 |
| | | Ju-52 dam(grd) | Wittstock | P-51 |
| | April 16 | (4)u/i a/c dest(grd) | NE Prague | P-51 |
| | April 17 | (2)Ju-188 dest(grd) | SE Pocking | P-51 |
| | | Me-109 dest(grd) | SE Pocking | P-51 |

1-0-0 air
11-3 ground

**Cornett, Jack B., Lt.**
359th Ftr Sqn/356th Ftr Grp

| Sqn | Date | Claims | Location | A/C |
|---|---|---|---|---|
| 359th | November 25, 1944 | Ju-88 dam(grd) | Ettinghausen | P-51 |
| | April 7, 1945 | FW-190 dest(air) | NE Steinhuder Lk. | P-51 |

1-0-0 air
0-1 ground

**Cornick, Raymond L., Lt.**
328th Ftr Sqn/352nd Ftr Grp

| *Sqn* | *Date* | *Claims* | *Location* | *A/C* |
|---|---|---|---|---|
| 328th | December 11, 1943 | Me-110 dest(air) | Drachten | P-47 |

1-0-0 air
0-0 ground

**Coronios, Harry, Lt.**
62nd Ftr Sqn/56th Ftr Grp

| *Sqn* | *Date* | *Claims* | *Location* | *A/C* |
|---|---|---|---|---|
| 62nd | October 8, 1943 | FW-190 dest(air) | Quackenbruck | P-47 |
| | | FW-190 dam(air) | Quackenbruck | P-47 |

1-0-1 air
0-0 ground

**Corrigan, Donald J., Lt.**
352nd Ftr Sqn/353rd Ftr Grp

| *Sqn* | *Date* | *Claims* | *Location* | *A/C* |
|---|---|---|---|---|
| 352nd | February 8, 1944 | FW-190 dest(air) | Libramont | P-47 |

1-0-0 air
0-0 ground

**Corson, Charles O., Lt.**
487th Ftr Sqn/352nd Ftr Grp

| *Sqn* | *Date* | *Claims* | *Location* | *A/C* |
|---|---|---|---|---|
| 487th | June 27, 1944 | FW-190 dest(air) | N/Noyon | P-51 |

1-0-0 air
0-0 ground

**Costello, Walter O., Lt.**
357th Ftr Sqn/355th Ftr Grp

| *Sqn* | *Date* | *Claims* | *Location* | *A/C* |
|---|---|---|---|---|
| 357th | July 20, 1944 | Me-109 prob(air) | W/Leipzig | P-51 |

0-1-0 air
0-0 ground

**Cota, Norman D., Jr., Maj.**
360th Ftr Sqn/356th Ftr Grp

| *Sqn* | *Date* | *Claims* | *Location* | *A/C* |
|---|---|---|---|---|
| 360th | May 21, 1944 | He-177 dest(air) | Stade A/F | P-47 |
| | July 25 | (.5)Me-109 dam(air)* | NW Paris | P-47 |

1-0-0.5 air
0-0 ground

* - shared with Lt. C.M. Taylor of the 360th Ftr Sqn

**Cotter, John A., Lt.**
357th Ftr Sqn/355th Ftr Grp

| *Sqn* | *Date* | *Claims* | *Location* | *A/C* |
|---|---|---|---|---|
| 357th | June 6, 1944 | Ju-87 dest(air) | NE Janville | P-51 |
| | July 7 | Me-410 dest(air) | S/Halle | P-51 |
| | July 24 | u/i a/c dest(grd) | Lechfeld | P-51 |
| | | Me-109 dam(grd) | Lechfeld | P-51 |
| | August 3 | Me-109 dest(air) | Baden Baden | P-51 |

3-0-0 air
1-1 ground

**Cotter, William W., Lt.**
359th Ftr Sqn/356th Ftr Grp

| *Sqn* | *Date* | *Claims* | *Location* | *A/C* |
|---|---|---|---|---|
| 359th | February 21, 1944 | Me-109 dest(air) | Hanover | P-47 |

1-0-0 air
0-0 ground

**Coughenour, Robert A., Jr., Lt.**
359th Ftr Sqn/356th Ftr Grp

| *Sqn* | *Date* | *Claims* | *Location* | *A/C* |
|---|---|---|---|---|
| 359th | May 13, 1944 | (.5)FW-190 dest(air)* | Kiel-Lubeck | P-47 |

0.5-0-0 air
0-0 ground

* - shared with LtCol. D.A. Baccus of HdQts, 356th Ftr Grp

**Coughran, Elmer H., Lt.**
79th Ftr Sqn/20th Ftr Grp

| *Sqn* | *Date* | *Claims* | *Location* | *A/C* |
|---|---|---|---|---|
| 79th | September 10, 1944 | (3)u/i a/c dest(grd) | SW Stuttgart | P-51 |

0-0-0 air
3-0 ground

**Coursey, Richard R., Jr., Capt.**
435th Ftr Sqn/479th Ftr Grp

| *Sqn* | *Date* | *Claims* | *Location* | *A/C* |
|---|---|---|---|---|
| 435th | September 26, 1944 | Me-109 dest(air) | SW Munster | P-51 |

1-0-0 air
0-0 ground

**Courtney, David H., Lt.**
38th Ftr Sqn/55th Ftr Grp

| *Sqn* | *Date* | *Claims* | *Location* | *A/C* |
|---|---|---|---|---|
| 38th | September 5, 1944 | Ju-87 dam(grd) | Stuttgart/Boblingen | P-51 |
| | November 2 | (.5)FW-190 dest(air)* | W/Merseburg | P-51 |
| | January 3, 1945 | (.5)Ar-196 dest(air)** | SE Ulm | P-51 |
| | January 15 | (.5)Ju-88 dest(air)@ | SW Stuttgart | P-51 |

1.5-0-0 air
0-1 ground

* - shared with Capt. J.F. Coonan of the 38th Ftr Sqn
** - shared with Lt. J.W. Kavanaugh of the 38th Ftr Sqn
@ - shared with Lt. B. Clemmons of the 38th Ftr Sqn

**Couse, Robert L., Lt.**
335th Ftr Sqn/4th Ftr Grp

| *Sqn* | *Date* | *Claims* | *Location* | *A/C* |
|---|---|---|---|---|
| 335th | April 9, 1945 | Ju-88 dam(grd) | Munich-Brunnthal | P-51 |
| | | u/i a/c dam(grd) | Munich-Brunnthal | P-51 |
| | April 16 | (2)Do-217 dest(grd) | Praha/Letnany | P-51 |
| | | Ju-88 dam(grd) | Praha/Letnany | P-51 |

0-0-0 air
2-3 ground

**Covault, Vern W., Lt.**
358th Ftr Sqn/355th Ftr Grp

| *Sqn* | *Date* | *Claims* | *Location* | *A/C* |
|---|---|---|---|---|
| 358th | July 8, 1944 | FW-190 dest(grd) | SW Chalons | P-51 |
| | | FW-190 dam(grd) | SW Chalons | P-51 |
| | July 19 | FW-190 prob(air) | Augsburg | P-51 |

0-1-0 air
1-1 ground

**Covelle, Lloyd K., Jr., Capt.**
84th Ftr Sqn/78th Ftr Grp

| *Sqn* | *Date* | *Claims* | *Location* | *A/C* |
|---|---|---|---|---|
| 84th | May 19, 1944 | Me-109 dest(air) | Nienburg | P-47 |
| | June 7 | Me-109 dest(air) | Montdidier | P-47 |

2-0-0 air
0-0 ground

**Cowen, Noah N., Lt.**
350th Ftr Sqn/353rd Ftr Grp

| *Sqn* | *Date* | *Claims* | *Location* | *A/C* |
|---|---|---|---|---|
| 350th | December 5, 1944 | FW-190 dest(air) | S/Steinhuder Lake | P-51 |

1-0-0 air
0-0 ground

**Cowie, Albert A., Lt.**
368th Ftr Sqn/359th Ftr Grp

| *Sqn* | *Date* | *Claims* | *Location* | *A/C* |
|---|---|---|---|---|
| 368th | March 3, 1945 | u/i a/c dam(grd) | Hanover | P-51 |

0-0-0 air
0-1 ground

**Cowley, John C., Lt.**
77th Ftr Sqn/20th Ftr Grp

| *Sqn* | *Date* | *Claims* | *Location* | *A/C* |
|---|---|---|---|---|
| 77th | March 20, 1945 | Me-262 dam(air) | E/Hamburg | P-51 |

0-0-1 air
0-0 ground

**Cox, Ralph L., Maj.**
370th Ftr Sqn/359th Ftr Grp
369th Ftr Sqn/359th Ftr Grp

| *Sqn* | *Date* | *Claims* | *Location* | *A/C* |
|---|---|---|---|---|
| 370th | November 2, 1944 | Me-109 dest(air) | Erfurt-Weimar | P-51 |
| | November 21 | (3)FW-190 dest(air) | SW Merseburg | P-51 |
| 369th | March 18, 1945 | FW-190 dest(air) | Joachimsthal | P-51 |

5-0-0 air
0-0 ground

**Cox, Raymond J., Lt.**
361st Ftr Sqn/356th Ftr Grp

| *Sqn* | *Date* | *Claims* | *Location* | *A/C* |
|---|---|---|---|---|
| 361st | February 20, 1945 | FW-190 dest(grd) | Windleschenlaibach | P-51 |
| | | (2)FW-190 dam(grd) | Bayreuth-Eindbach | P-51 |

0-0-0 air
1-2 ground

**Cox, W.A., Lt.**
357th Ftr Sqn/355th Ftr Grp

| *Sqn* | *Date* | *Claims* | *Location* | *A/C* |
|---|---|---|---|---|
| 357th | July 8, 1944 | Me-410 dam(grd) | SW Chalons | P-51 |

0-0-0 air
0-1 ground

**Craft, Charles W., Lt.**
351st Ftr Sqn/353rd Ftr Grp

| *Sqn* | *Date* | *Claims* | *Location* | *A/C* |
|---|---|---|---|---|
| 351st | August 4, 1944 | (2)Me-109 prob(air) | NE Bremen | P-47 |
| | August 12 | (.5)Ju-88 dam(grd)[*] | SW Coulommiers | P-47 |

0-2-0 air
0-0.5 ground

[*] - shared with Lt. H. Moretz of the 351st Ftr Sqn

**Craig, Horace C., Maj.**
62nd Ftr Sqn/56th Ftr Grp

| *Sqn* | *Date* | *Claims* | *Location* | *A/C* |
|---|---|---|---|---|
| 62nd | August 24, 1943 | FW-190 dam(air) | S/Paris | P-47 |
| | November 26 | Me-210 prob(air) | Papenburg | P-47 |
| | | Me-110 prob(air) | Papenburg | P-47 |
| | December 20 | Do-217 dest(air) | SE Bremen | P-47 |

1-2-1 air
0-0 ground

**Cramer, Darrell S., Maj.**
338th Ftr Sqn/55th Ftr Grp
HdQts/55th Ftr Grp
Earlier flew in the PTO with the 347th Ftr Grp and claimed half a kill, a Betty on November 1, 1943.

| *Sqn* | *Date* | *Claims* | *Location* | *A/C* |
|---|---|---|---|---|
| 338th | September 3, 1944 | FW-190 dest(air) | Brussels | P-51 |
| | September 11 | (1.5)Me-109 dest(air)[*] | S/Meiningen | P-51 |
| | September 13 | (1.5)Me-109 dest(air)[**] | Eisenach-Gotha | P-51 |
| | October 7 | Me-109 dest(air) | Leipzig | P-51 |
| | November 2 | (.5)Me-109 dest(air)[@] | SW Leipzig | P-51 |
| | November 26 | (2)FW-190 dest(grd) | Vorden A/F | P-51 |
| | | Me-109 dam(grd) | Vorden A/F | P-51 |
| | January 14, 1945 | Me-262 dam(air) | Parchim A/F | P-51 |
| | | Me-110 dam(grd) | SE Salzwedel | P-51 |
| | January 29 | Me-109 dest(air) | Ulzen | P-51 |

6.5-0-1 air
2-2 ground

[*] - shared with an unknown pilot
[**] - shared with Capt. E.S. Gregg of the 338th Ftr Sqn
[@] - shared with LtCol. E.G. Righetti of the 338th Ftr Sqn

**Crandell, Jack L., Lt.**
357th Ftr Sqn/355th Ftr Grp

| *Sqn* | *Date* | *Claims* | *Location* | *A/C* |
|---|---|---|---|---|
| 357th | June 24, 1944 | (2)Me-109 dest(grd) | E/Angars | P-51 |
| | | (3)Me-109 dam(grd) | E/Angars | P-51 |
| | August 16 | Me-109 dest(air) | SE Hildesheim | P-51 |

1-0-0 air
2-3 ground

**Crandell, Jack S., Lt.**
375th Ftr Sqn/361st Ftr Grp

| *Sqn* | *Date* | *Claims* | *Location* | *A/C* |
|---|---|---|---|---|
| 375th | April 27, 1944 | (.5)He-111 dest(grd)[*] | Etampes | P-47 |
| | June 16 | Ju-52 dest(grd) | Toussus/Le Noble | P-51 |
| | June 25 | (2)Me-109 dest(air) | N/Rouen | P-51 |

2-0-0 air
1.5-0 ground

[*] - shared with Lt. S.D. Rames of the 375th Ftr Sqn

**Cranfill, Niven K., LtCol.**
369th Ftr Sqn/359th Ftr Grp
368th Ftr Sqn/359th Ftr Grp
HdQts/359th Ftr Grp

| *Sqn* | *Date* | *Claims* | *Location* | *A/C* |
|---|---|---|---|---|
| 369th | January 30, 1944 | Me-109 dam(air) | Lingen | P-47 |
| | May 8 | (.5)Me-109 prob(air)[*] | SW Brunswick | P-51 |
| HdQts | August 16 | Me-109 dest(air) | Einbeck | P-51 |
| 368th | November 27 | (2)Me-109 dest(air) | W/Merseburg | P-51 |
| | | FW-190 dest(air) | W/Merseburg | P-51 |
| | March 19, 1945 | Me-262 dest(air) | Leipzig | P-51 |
| | | Me-262 dam(air) | Leipzig | P-51 |

5-0.5-2 air
0-0 ground

[*] - shared with Lt. B.M. Hagen of the 368th Ftr Sqn

**Crawford, Harold R., Lt.**
336th Ftr Sqn/4th Ftr Grp

| *Sqn* | *Date* | *Claims* | *Location* | *A/C* |
|---|---|---|---|---|
| 336th | February 22, 1945 | (3)FW-190 dest(grd) | Halberstadt | P-51 |
| | February 27 | u/i a/c dest(grd) | Weimar | P-51 |

0-0-0 air
4-0 ground

**Crawford, Kenneth I., Lt.**
38th Ftr Sqn/55th Ftr Grp

| *Sqn* | *Date* | *Claims* | *Location* | *A/C* |
|---|---|---|---|---|
| 38th | August 24, 1944 | Ju-88 dest(grd) | Burg A/F | P-51 |
| | September 11 | Me-109 dest(air) | S/Erfurt | P-51 |

1-0-0 air
1-0 ground

**Creamer, John N., Capt.**
335th Ftr Sqn/4th Ftr Grp

| *Sqn* | *Date* | *Claims* | *Location* | *A/C* |
|---|---|---|---|---|
| 335th | November 18, 1944 | (.5)Me-262 dest(air)* | S/Leipheim | P-51 |

0.5-0-0 air
0-0 ground

* - shared with Capt. J.C. Fitch of the 335th Ftr Sqn

**Creamer, Richard W., Lt.**
487th Ftr Sqn/352nd Ftr Grp

| *Sqn* | *Date* | *Claims* | *Location* | *A/C* |
|---|---|---|---|---|
| 487th | April 16, 1945 | Me-109 dest(grd) | Ganacker | P-51 |
| | | (2)FW-190 dam(grd) | Ganacker | P-51 |
| | | u/i a/c dam(grd) | Ganacker | P-51 |

0-0-0 air
1-3 ground

**Creekmur, Thomas C., Lt.**
350th Ftr Sqn/353rd Ftr Grp

| *Sqn* | *Date* | *Claims* | *Location* | *A/C* |
|---|---|---|---|---|
| 350th | August 4, 1944 | Me-109 dest(air) | E/Verdun | P-47 |

1-0-0 air
0-0 ground

**Creighton, Richard D., Lt.**
434th Ftr Sqn/479th Ftr Grp

| *Sqn* | *Date* | *Claims* | *Location* | *A/C* |
|---|---|---|---|---|
| 434th | December 25, 1944 | FW-190 dest(air) | SW Bonn | P-51 |
| | February 9, 1945 | Me-109 dest(air) | SE Magdeburg | P-51 |
| | | FW-190 prob(air) | SE Magdeburg | P-51 |
| | April 13 | (2)u/i a/c dam(grd) | Ratzburger Lake | P-51 |

2-1-0 air
0-2 ground

**Crenshaw, Claude J., Capt.**
369th Ftr Sqn/359th Ftr Grp

| *Sqn* | *Date* | *Claims* | *Location* | *A/C* |
|---|---|---|---|---|
| 369th | August 18, 1944 | Ju-88 dest(grd) | St. Dizier | P-51 |
| | | Ju-52 dest(grd) | St. Dizier | P-51 |
| | | Ju-88 dam(grd) | St. Dizier | P-51 |
| | September 11 | (2)Me-109 dest(air) | Kolleda | P-51 |
| | | u/i a/c dest(grd) | Kolleda | P-51 |
| | September 18 | Me-109 dest(air) | Dusseldorf | P-51 |
| | November 21 | (4)FW-190 dest(air) | Merseburg | P-51 |
| | | FW-190 prob(air) | Merseburg | P-51 |

7-1-0 air
3-1 ground

**Cresswell, Raymond H., Lt.**
504th Ftr Sqn/339th Ftr Grp

| *Sqn* | *Date* | *Claims* | *Location* | *A/C* |
|---|---|---|---|---|
| 504th | April 7, 1945 | Me-109 dest(air) | Celle | P-51 |
| | April 16 | Me-109 dest(grd) | Klatovy | P-51 |
| | | u/i a/c dest(grd) | Klatovy | P-51 |
| | | FW-190 dam(grd) | Klatovy | P-51 |
| | | u/i a/c dam(grd) | Klatovy | P-51 |

1-0-0 air
2-2 ground

**Cristadoro, Maurice A., Maj.**
HdQts/356th Ftr Grp
55th Ftr Sqn/ 20th Ftr Grp

| *Sqn* | *Date* | *Claims* | *Location* | *A/C* |
|---|---|---|---|---|
| 55th | February 25, 1945 | FW-190 dest(air) | Stendal | P-51 |

1-0-0 air
0-0 ground

**Crockett, James R., Lt.**
503rd Ftr Sqn/339th Ftr Grp

| *Sqn* | *Date* | *Claims* | *Location* | *A/C* |
|---|---|---|---|---|
| 503rd | May 19, 1944 | (2)Ju-52 dest(grd) | Ludwigslust | P-51 |

0-0-0 air
2-0 ground

**Croker, Robert C., Capt.**
504th Ftr Sqn/339th Ftr Grp

| *Sqn* | *Date* | *Claims* | *Location* | *A/C* |
|---|---|---|---|---|
| 504th | April 4, 1945 | (.5)Me-262 dest(air)* | Parchim A/F | P-51 |
| | April 10 | (2)Me-410 dest(grd) | N/Neuruppin | P-51 |
| | | (4)Me-410 dam(grd) | N/Neuruppin | P-51 |

0.5-0-0 air
2-4 ground

* - shared with Capt. K.B. Everson of the 504th Ftr Sqn

**Crombie, William S., Maj.**
385th Ftr Sqn/364th Ftr Grp

| *Sqn* | *Date* | *Claims* | *Location* | *A/C* |
|---|---|---|---|---|
| 385th | October 12, 1944 | Me-109 dest(air) | W/Bremen | P-51 |
| | November 2 | Me-109 dest(air) | Halle | P-51 |
| | December 31 | FW-190 dest(air) | Hamburg | P-51 |
| | January 1, 1945 | FW-190 dest(air) | SE Hamburg | P-51 |
| | March 21 | u/i a/c dam(grd) | Achmer | P-51 |
| | April 10 | Me-262 dest(grd) | Stendal | P-51 |
| | | u/i a/c dest(grd) | Stendal | P-51 |
| | | Ju-88 dest(grd) | Stendal | P-51 |
| | | (2)FW-190 dam(grd) | Stendal | P-51 |
| | | Ju-88 dam(grd) | Stendal | P-51 |

4-0-0 air
3-4 ground

**Cronin, Timothy J., Lt.**
334th Ftr Sqn/4th Ftr Grp

| *Sqn* | *Date* | *Claims* | *Location* | *A/C* |
|---|---|---|---|---|
| 334th | December 25, 1944 | (1.5)FW-190 dest(air)* | S/Bonn | P-51 |

1.5-0-0 air
0-0 ground

* - shared with Maj. P.W. McKennon of the 335th Ftr Sqn, 4th Ftr Grp

**Cross, James F., Lt.**
352nd Ftr Sqn/353rd Ftr Grp

| *Sqn* | *Date* | *Claims* | *Location* | *A/C* |
|---|---|---|---|---|
| 352nd | September 23, 1944 | FW-190 dest(air) | SE Arnheim | P-47 |

1-0-0 air
0-0 ground

**Cross, Richard G., Jr., Lt.**
354th Ftr Sqn/355th Ftr Grp

| *Sqn* | *Date* | *Claims* | *Location* | *A/C* |
|---|---|---|---|---|
| 354th | June 24, 1944 | Me-109 dest(grd) | Seiches | P-51 |
| | July 7 | (2)Me-410 dest(air) | Lingen | P-51 |
| | July 8 | (.5)Me-109 dest(grd)* | SW Chalons | P-51 |
| | | Me-410 dam(grd) | SW Chalons | P-51 |

2-0-0 air
1.5-1 ground

* - shared with Capt. N.J. Fortier of the 354th Ftr Sqn

**Crosthwait, Edwin M., Jr., Lt.**
63rd Ftr Sqn/56th Ftr Grp

| *Sqn* | *Date* | *Claims* | *Location* | *A/C* |
|---|---|---|---|---|
| 63rd | March 25, 1945 | Me-262 dest(air) | Parchim A/F | P-47 |

1-0-0 air
0-0 ground

**Crouch, Roy A., Lt.**
385th Ftr Sqn/364th Ftr Grp

| Sqn | Date | Claims | Location | A/C |
|---|---|---|---|---|
| 385th | August 9, 1944 | Me-109 dest(grd) | Gaukonigshafen | P-51 |
| | | Me-210 dest(grd) | Gaukonigshafen | P-51 |

0-0-0 air
2-0 ground

**Croy, Manford O., Jr., Capt.**
82nd Ftr Sqn/78th Ftr Grp

| Sqn | Date | Claims | Location | A/C |
|---|---|---|---|---|
| 82nd | August 28, 1944 | (.5)Me-262 dest(air)* | Termonde | P-47 |
| | November 26 | (2)Me-109 dest(air) | Rheine | P-47 |
| | April 16, 1945 | FW-190 dest(grd) | Pilzen/Prague | P-51 |

2.5-0-0 air
1-0 ground

* - shared with Maj. J. Myers of the 82nd Ftr Sqn

**Crum, Glenn, Lt.**
359th Ftr Sqn/356th Ftr Grp

| Sqn | Date | Claims | Location | A/C |
|---|---|---|---|---|
| 359th | November 27, 1944 | Me-109 dam(air) | N/Munster | P-51 |

0-0-1 air
0-0 ground

**Crump, James T., Capt.**
363rd Ftr Sqn/357th Ftr Grp

| Sqn | Date | Claims | Location | A/C |
|---|---|---|---|---|
| 363rd | December 5, 1944 | FW-190 prob(air) | N/Berlin | P-51 |
| | December 24 | Me-109 dest(air) | W/Coblenz | P-51 |

1-1-0 air
0-0 ground

**Crump, John W., Capt.**
360th Ftr Sqn/356th Ftr Grp

| Sqn | Date | Claims | Location | A/C |
|---|---|---|---|---|
| 360th | February 21, 1945 | FW-190 dam(grd) | NW Crailsheim | P-51 |

0-0-0 air
0-1 ground

**Cudd, John W., Jr., Lt.**
77th Ftr Sqn/20th Ftr Grp

| Sqn | Date | Claims | Location | A/C |
|---|---|---|---|---|
| 77th | April 10, 1945 | (.5)Me-262 dest(air)* | Berlin | P-51 |

0.5-0-0 air
0-0 ground

* - shared with F/O J. Rosenblum of the 77th Ftr Sqn

**Cullerton, William J., Lt.**
357th Ftr Sqn/355th Ftr Grp

| Sqn | Date | Claims | Location | A/C |
|---|---|---|---|---|
| 357th | August 16, 1944 | (2)Me-109 dest(air) | SE Hildesheim | P-51 |
| | August 26 | FW-200 dest(grd) | Speyer | P-51 |
| | September 12 | (3)u/i a/c dest(grd) | Schwartz A/F | P-51 |
| | | (2)Me-110 dest(grd) | Schwartz A/F | P-51 |
| | | (2)Ju-88 dest(grd) | Schwartz A/F | P-51 |
| | | Me-110 dam(grd) | Schwartz A/F | P-51 |
| | | Ju-88 dam(grd) | Schwartz A/F | P-51 |
| | November 2 | Me-109 dest(air) | Wernigerode | P-51 |
| | | FW-190 dest(air) | Wernigerode | P-51 |
| | | (6)u/i a/c dest(grd) | Wernigerode | P-51 |
| | March 30, 1945 | He-111 dest(grd) | Lowenstadt | P-51 |
| | April 4 | FW-190 dest(air) | Halberstadt | P-51 |

5-0-0 air
15-2 ground

**Culp, Harold F., Lt.**
354th Ftr Sqn/355th Ftr Grp

| Sqn | Date | Claims | Location | A/C |
|---|---|---|---|---|
| 354th | March 28, 1944 | (.5)Ju-88 dest(grd)* | Dijon | P-51 |

0-0-0 air
0.5-0 ground

* - shared with LtCol. G.J. Dix of HdQts, 355th Ftr Grp

**Culp, Jack H., Lt.**
361st Ftr Sqn/356th Ftr Grp

| Sqn | Date | Claims | Location | A/C |
|---|---|---|---|---|
| 361st | April 23, 1944 | Me-109 dest(grd) | Hagenau | P-47 |
| | May 4 | (2)FW-190 dest(air) | Hanover | P-47 |

2-0-0 air
1-0 ground

**Cummings, Donald M., Capt.**
38th Ftr Sqn/55th Ftr Grp
Earlier flew in the MTO with the 27th Ftr Grp and claimed one kill; a Ju-52 on October 1, 1943.

| Sqn | Date | Claims | Location | A/C |
|---|---|---|---|---|
| 38th | January 14, 1945 | Me-109 dest(air) | E/Wittenberg | P-51 |
| | February 25 | Me-262 dest(air) | Giebelstadt A/F | P-51 |
| | | Me-262 dest(air) | Leipheim A/F | P-51 |
| | March 24 | (.5)Me-109 dest(air)* | S/Sorest | P-51 |
| | April 7 | (2)Me-109 dest(air) | Celle | P-51 |

5.5-0-0 air
0-0 ground

* - shared with Lt. H.B. Mooers of the 38th Ftr Sqn

**Cummings, William J., Jr., Col.**
HdQts/355th Ftr Grp

| Sqn | Date | Claims | Location | A/C |
|---|---|---|---|---|
| HdQts | April 5, 1944 | (2)Do-217 dest(grd) | Munich | P-51 |
| | | Do-217 dam(grd) | Munich | P-51 |

0-0-0 air
2-1 ground

**Cummins, Charles R., Maj.**
375th Ftr Sqn/361st Ftr Grp

| Sqn | Date | Claims | Location | A/C |
|---|---|---|---|---|
| 375th | June 25, 1944 | Me-109 dest(air) | N/Lisieux | P-51 |
| | September 12 | Me-109 dest(air) | NE Magdeburg | P-51 |

2-0-0 air
0-0 ground

**Cundy, Arthur C., Lt.**
352nd Ftr Sqn/353rd Ftr Grp

| Sqn | Date | Claims | Location | A/C |
|---|---|---|---|---|
| 352nd | November 27, 1944 | Me-109 dest(air) | Magdeburg | P-51 |
| | December 24 | Me-109 dest(air) | Leacher Lake | P-51 |
| | January 14, 1945 | FW-190 dest(air) | SW Dummer Lake | P-51 |
| | March 2 | (2)FW-190 dest(air) | Dessau | P-51 |
| | | Me-109 dest(air) | Dessau | P-51 |

6-0-0 air
0-0 ground

**Cunnick, John W., III, Lt.**
38th Ftr Sqn/55th Ftr Grp

| Sqn | Date | Claims | Location | A/C |
|---|---|---|---|---|
| 38th | March 22, 1945 | Me-262 dest(air) | Lechfeld | P-51 |
| | April 7 | Me-109 dest(air) | Celle | P-51 |
| | April 9 | FW-190 dest(grd) | Munich-Brunnthal | P-51 |
| | | Me-262 dest(grd) | Munich-Brunnthal | P-51 |
| | | Ju-88 dest(grd) | Munich-Brunnthal | P-51 |
| | | FW-190 dam(grd) | Munich-Brunnthal | P-51 |
| | | Me-262 dam(grd) | Munich-Brunnthal | P-51 |
| | April 10 | He-111 dest(grd) | Wesendorf | P-51 |
| | | Me-109 dest(grd) | Wesendorf | P-51 |
| | | He-111 dam(grd) | Wesendorf | P-51 |
| | April 16 | (2)Me-109 dest(grd) | N/Landshut | P-51 |
| | | Me-109 dam(grd) | N/Landshut | P-51 |

2-0-0 air
7-4 ground

**Cunningham, Charles V., Capt.**
370th Ftr Sqn/359th Ftr Grp

| *Sqn* | *Date* | *Claims* | *Location* | *A/C* |
|---|---|---|---|---|
| 370th | April 29, 1944 | FW-190 prob(air) | Gehrden | P-47 |

0-1-0 air
0-0 ground

**Cunningham, Murdoch R., Lt.**
486th Ftr Sqn/352nd Ftr Grp

| *Sqn* | *Date* | *Claims* | *Location* | *A/C* |
|---|---|---|---|---|
| 486th | April 13, 1944 | (.5)He-111 dest(grd)* | S/Stuttgart | P-51 |
| | April 15 | FW-190 dest(air) | NE Vechta | P-51 |
| | April 25 | Hs-129 dest(grd) | Metz | P-51 |

1-0-0 air
1.5-0 ground

* - shared with Capt. S.W. Andrew of the 486th Ftr Sqn

**Curran, Arthur R., Lt.**
358th Ftr Sqn/355th Ftr Grp

| *Sqn* | *Date* | *Claims* | *Location* | *A/C* |
|---|---|---|---|---|
| 358th | December 12, 1944 | u/i a/c dest(grd) | Gotha | P-51 |
| | April 13, 1945 | FW-190 dest(grd) | Flensburg | P-51 |
| | | Ju-88 dest(grd) | Flensburg | P-51 |

0-0-0 air
3-0 ground

**Currie, William J., Lt.**
363rd Ftr Sqn/357th Ftr Grp

| *Sqn* | *Date* | *Claims* | *Location* | *A/C* |
|---|---|---|---|---|
| 363rd | April 19, 1945 | Me-262 dam(air) | Prague | P-51 |

0-0-1 air
0-0 ground

**Curry, William R., Lt.**
352nd Ftr Sqn/353rd Ftr Grp

| *Sqn* | *Date* | *Claims* | *Location* | *A/C* |
|---|---|---|---|---|
| 352nd | December 5, 1944 | FW-190 prob(air) | NE Berlin | P-51 |

0-1-0 air
0-0 ground

**Curtis, Joseph R., Capt.**
61st Ftr Sqn/56th Ftr Grp
63rd Ftr Sqn/56th Ftr Grp

| *Sqn* | *Date* | *Claims* | *Location* | *A/C* |
|---|---|---|---|---|
| 61st | June 13, 1943 | FW-190 dam(air) | S/Furnes | P-47 |
| 63rd | June 7, 1944 | FW-190 dest(air) | Lyons La Foret | P-47 |
| | July 4 | Me-109 dest(air) | Bernay-Evreux | P-47 |
| | | (.5)Me-109 dest(air)* | Conches | P-47 |
| | July 6 | Me-109 dest(air) | N/Evreux | P-47 |

3.5-0-1 air
0-0 ground

* - shared with Lt. W.R. Frederick of the 63rd Ftr Sqn

**Curtis, Victor N., Capt.**
352nd Ftr Sqn/353rd Ftr Grp

| *Sqn* | *Date* | *Claims* | *Location* | *A/C* |
|---|---|---|---|---|
| 352nd | June 20, 1944 | He-111 dest(grd) | Plantlunne | P-47 |
| | June 29 | (.5)He-111 dam(grd)* | Plantlunne | P-47 |
| | July 30 | u/i a/c dest(grd) | Orleans/Bricy | P-47 |

0-0-0 air
2-0.5 ground

* - shared with Lt. L. Hunt of the 352nd Ftr Sqn

**Cutler, Frank A., Capt.**
486th Ftr Sqn/352nd Ftr Grp

| *Sqn* | *Date* | *Claims* | *Location* | *A/C* |
|---|---|---|---|---|
| 486th | February 20, 1944 | (2)Me-109 dest(air) | Nivelles | P-47 |
| | | Me-110 dest(grd) | Nivelles | P-47 |
| | April 11 | (2)FW-190 dest(air) | W/Torgau | P-51 |
| | | (.5)Ju-52 dest(air)* | W/Torgau | P-51 |
| | | Ju-88 dest(grd) | Lonnewitz | P-51 |
| | | Ju-52 dam(grd) | Lonnewitz | P-51 |
| | April 13 | Me-109 dest(grd) | S/Stuttgart | P-51 |
| | May 8 | (2)Me-109 dest(air) | Gifhorn | P-51 |
| | May 13 | Me-109 dest(air) | Neubrandenburg | P-51 |

7.5-0-0 air
3-1 ground

* - shared with Lt. W.W. Anderson of the 486th Ftr Sqn

**Cwiklinski, Arthur C., Lt.**
334th Ftr Sqn/4th Ftr Grp

| *Sqn* | *Date* | *Claims* | *Location* | *A/C* |
|---|---|---|---|---|
| 334th | June 20, 1944 | (.5)Me-109 dest(air)* | E/Pasewalk | P-51 |
| | | Me-109 dam(air) | E/Pasewalk | P-51 |
| | August 18 | (2)Me-109 dest(air) | SW Beauvais | P-51 |
| | | Me-109 dam(air) | SW Beauvais | P-51 |

2.5-0-2 air
0-0 ground

* - shared with Capt. T.E. Joyce of the 334th Ftr Sqn

**Czapla, Eugene J., Lt.**
376th Ftr Sqn/361st Ftr Grp

| *Sqn* | *Date* | *Claims* | *Location* | *A/C* |
|---|---|---|---|---|
| 376th | August 18, 1944 | Ju-52 dest(grd) | Romilly-Sur-Seine | P-51 |

0-0-0 air
1-0 ground

**Dacci, William K., Lt.**
84th Ftr Sqn/78th Ftr Grp

| *Sqn* | *Date* | *Claims* | *Location* | *A/C* |
|---|---|---|---|---|
| 84th | June 20, 1944 | Me-109 dest(air) | Montdidier | P-47 |

1-0-0 air
0-0 ground

**Dade, Lucian A., Jr., LtCol.**
63rd Ftr Sqn/56th Ftr Grp
62nd Ftr Sqn/56th Ftr Grp
HdQts/56th Ftr Grp

| *Sqn* | *Date* | *Claims* | *Location* | *A/C* |
|---|---|---|---|---|
| 62nd | May 13, 1944 | FW-190 dest(air) | Lubeck | P-47 |
| | July 4 | (2)Me-109 dest(air) | Conches | P-47 |
| | | (2)Me-109 dam(air) | Conches | P-47 |
| HdQts | September 5 | (2)Me-210 dest(grd) | Gelnhausen | P-47 |
| | | He-111 dest(grd) | Gelnhausen | P-47 |
| | April 13, 1945 | (2)Me-110 dest(grd) | Eggebeck A/F | P-47 |
| | | u/i a/c dest(grd) | Eggebeck A/F | P-47 |
| | | Me-110 dam(grd) | Eggebeck A/F | P-47 |

3-0-2 air
6-1 ground

**Dale, Jack D., LtCol.**
HdQts/364th Ftr Grp
Earlier flew in the PTO with the 17th Pursuit Sqn claiming 2 kills, both Zeros, on February 25, 1942.

| *Sqn* | *Date* | *Claims* | *Location* | *A/C* |
|---|---|---|---|---|
| HdQts | August 15, 1944 | FW-190 dest(air) | W/Frankfurt | P-51 |

1-0-0 air
0-0 ground

**Dale, Samuel D., Lt.**
63rd Ftr Sqn/56th Ftr Grp

| Sqn | Date | Claims | Location | A/C |
|---|---|---|---|---|
| 63rd | April 24, 1944 | Me-109 dest(grd) | Thalheim | P-47 |
| | | FW-190 dest(grd) | Thalheim | P-47 |
| | | (.25)u/i a/c dam(grd)[*] | Thalheim | P-47 |
| | June 7 | (.5)FW-190 dest(air)[**] | Les Andelys-Craches | P-47 |

0.5-0-0 air
2-0.25 ground

[*] - shared with Lt. H.F. Warner, Lt. D.W. Marshall, and Lt. A.J. Wisniewski of the 63rd Ftr Sqn
[**] - shared with Lt. M.H. Becker of the 63rd Ftr Sqn

**Daley, William C., Capt.**
62nd Ftr Sqn/56th Ftr Grp

| Sqn | Date | Claims | Location | A/C |
|---|---|---|---|---|
| 62nd | December 4, 1944 | (.5)He-177 dest(grd)[*] | Neuburg | P-47 |
| | | Me-262 dam(grd) | Neuburg | P-47 |
| | December 23 | Me-109 dest(air) | Bonn-Coblenz | P-47 |
| | December 25 | (2)Me-109 dest(air) | Bonn-Coblenz | P-47 |
| | January 14, 1945 | Me-109 dest(air) | Rheine | P-47 |

4-0-0 air
0.5-1 ground

[*] - shared with Lt. A. Chasko of the 62nd Ftr Sqn

**Daley, William J., Maj.**
335th Ftr Sqn/4th Ftr Grp

| Sqn | Date | Claims | Location | A/C |
|---|---|---|---|---|
| 335th | October 2, 1942 | FW-190 dam(air) | E/Calais | Spit |

0-0-1 air
0-0 ground

**Dalton, William T., Lt.**
383rd Ftr Sqn/364th Ftr Grp

| Sqn | Date | Claims | Location | A/C |
|---|---|---|---|---|
| 383rd | August 14, 1944 | Me-410 dest(grd) | Memmingen | P-51 |
| | | He-111 dam(grd) | Memmingen | P-51 |

0-0-0 air
1-1 ground

**Daniel, Robert J., Lt.**
63rd Ftr Sqn/56th Ftr Grp

| Sqn | Date | Claims | Location | A/C |
|---|---|---|---|---|
| 63rd | September 5, 1944 | Me-109 dest(air) | NE Coblenz | P-47 |
| | | FW-190 dest(grd) | Gelnhausen | P-47 |
| | November 18 | (.5)u/i a/c dam(grd)[*] | Gross Otheim | P-47 |
| | December 23 | FW-190 dest(air) | NW Coblenz | P-47 |

2-0-0 air
1-0.5 ground

[*] - shared with Lt. R. Frederickson of the 63rd Ftr Sqn

**Daniell, Jack S., Lt.**
505th Ftr Sqn/339th Ftr Grp

| Sqn | Date | Claims | Location | A/C |
|---|---|---|---|---|
| 505th | November 26, 1944 | (5)FW-190 dest(air) | S/Hanover | P-51 |

5-0-0 air
0-0 ground

**Daniels, Richard H., Lt.**
368th Ftr Sqn/359th Ftr Grp

| Sqn | Date | Claims | Location | A/C |
|---|---|---|---|---|
| 368th | November 27, 1944 | FW-190 prob(air) | SE Hanover | P-51 |

0-1-0 air
0-0 ground

**Danner, Eldrid C., Lt.**
362nd Ftr Sqn/357th Ftr Grp

| Sqn | Date | Claims | Location | A/C |
|---|---|---|---|---|
| 362nd | April 10, 1945 | Ju-88 dest(grd) | Neuruppin | P-51 |
| | April 17 | u/i a/c dest(grd) | Prague/Ruzny | P-51 |

0-0-0 air
2-0 ground

**Dargan, Archie S., Jr., Lt.**
338th Ftr Sqn/55th Ftr Grp

| Sqn | Date | Claims | Location | A/C |
|---|---|---|---|---|
| 338th | March 18, 1945 | (2)FW-190 dest(air) | N/Giessen | P-51 |
| | April 10 | Me-410 dest(grd) | Burg A/F | P-51 |
| | | Me-410 dam(grd) | Burg A/F | P-51 |

2-0-0 air
1-1 ground

**Darling, Charles H., Lt.**
436th Ftr Sqn/479th Ftr Grp

| Sqn | Date | Claims | Location | A/C |
|---|---|---|---|---|
| 436th | February 22, 1945 | (2)Ju-88 dam(grd) | Halberstadt | P-51 |
| | April 13 | (2)FW-190 dest(grd) | Salzwedel | P-51 |
| | | Me-110 dam(grd) | Salzwedel | P-51 |
| | | u/i a/c dam(grd) | Salzwedel | P-51 |
| | April 16 | He-111 dest(grd) | Landstadt | P-51 |
| | April 17 | u/i a/c dest(grd) | Karlsbad | P-51 |

0-0-0 air
4-4 ground

**Darling, Richard E., Lt.**
338th Ftr Sqn/55th Ftr Grp

| Sqn | Date | Claims | Location | A/C |
|---|---|---|---|---|
| 338th | April 10, 1945 | (2)Me-410 dest(grd) | Burg A/F | P-51 |
| | April 16 | Me-109 dest(grd) | Erding | P-51 |
| | | (2)Me-109 dam(grd) | Erding | P-51 |

0-0-0 air
3-2 ground

**Daudistel, William H., Lt.**
434th Ftr Sqn/479th Ftr Grp

| Sqn | Date | Claims | Location | A/C |
|---|---|---|---|---|
| 434th | February 14, 1945 | Me-109 dest(air) | SW Berlin | P-51 |

1-0-0 air
0-0 ground

**Dauphin, Ray, Capt.**
62nd Ftr Sqn/56th Ftr Grp

| Sqn | Date | Claims | Location | A/C |
|---|---|---|---|---|
| 62nd | June 26, 1943 | FW-190 dam(air) | Dieppe | P-47 |
| | October 8 | FW-190 prob(air) | Quackenbruck | P-47 |
| | February 22, 1944 | Me-110 dam(air) | Paderborn | P-47 |

0-1-2 air
0-0 ground

**Davenport, John E., Lt.**
352nd Ftr Sqn/353rd Ftr Grp

| Sqn | Date | Claims | Location | A/C |
|---|---|---|---|---|
| 352nd | November 27, 1944 | (2)Me-109 dam(air) | Magdeburg | P-51 |
| | February 9, 1945 | He-111 dest(grd) | Kothen | P-51 |

0-0-2 air
1-0 ground

**Davis, Albert J., Capt.**
335th Ftr Sqn/4th Ftr Grp

| Sqn | Date | Claims | Location | A/C |
|---|---|---|---|---|
| 335th | September 12, 1944 | Me-109 dest(air) | NE Frankfurt | P-51 |
| | September 17 | (2)FW-190 dest(air) | Bocholt | P-51 |

3-0-0 air
0-0 ground

**Davis, Arnold E., Capt.**
374th Ftr Sqn/361st Ftr Grp

| *Sqn* | *Date* | *Claims* | *Location* | *A/C* |
|---|---|---|---|---|
| 374th | October 7, 1944 | Me-109 dest(air) | Naumberg | P-51 |

1-0-0 air
0-0 ground

**Davis, Clayton E., Capt.**
487th Ftr Sqn/352nd Ftr Grp

| *Sqn* | *Date* | *Claims* | *Location* | *A/C* |
|---|---|---|---|---|
| 487th | January 29, 1944 | FW-190 dest(air) | Malmedy | P-47 |
| | April 9 | (2)Ju-88 dest(grd) | Vechta | P-51 |
| | April 10 | (.5)Me-109 dest(air)* | SW Rheims | P-51 |
| | April 11 | Ju-52 dest(grd) | W/Berlin | P-51 |
| | April 22 | Ju-88 dest(grd) | N/Hanover | P-51 |
| | | Ju-88 dam(grd) | N/Hanover | P-51 |
| | April 30 | (3)u/i a/c dam(grd) | Vechta | P-51 |
| | May 8 | (3)Me-109 dest(air) | Brunswick | P-51 |
| | | (.5)FW-190 dest(air)** | Brunswick | P-51 |

5-0-0 air
4-4 ground

* - shared with Lt. E.B. McMahan of the 487th Ftr Sqn
** - shared with Lt. W.E. Fowler of the 487th Ftr Sqn

**Davis, Glendon V., Capt.**
364th Ftr Sqn/357th Ftr Grp

| *Sqn* | *Date* | *Claims* | *Location* | *A/C* |
|---|---|---|---|---|
| 364th | March 5, 1944 | (2)FW-200 dest(air) | Parthenay A/F | P-51 |
| | March 6 | Me-110 dest(air) | E/Berlin | P-51 |
| | | (.5)FW-190 dest(air)* | NW Berlin | P-51 |
| | March 8 | (.5)FW-190 dest(air)** | Dummer Lake | P-51 |
| | March 16 | Me-109 dest(air) | Ulm | P-51 |
| | | (.5)Me-110 dest(air)@ | Ulm | P-51 |
| | April 13 | Me-109 dest(air) | Frankfurt | P-51 |
| | April 19 | FW-190 dest(air) | S/Bliecherode | P-51 |

7.5-0-0 air
0-0 ground

* - shared with Lt. T.L. Harris of the 364th Ftr Sqn
** - shared with Lt. T.L. Harris of the 364th Ftr Sqn
@ - shared with Lt. R.A. Peterson of the 364th Ftr Sqn

**Davis, Harry L., Lt.**
336th Ftr Sqn/4th Ftr Grp

| *Sqn* | *Date* | *Claims* | *Location* | *A/C* |
|---|---|---|---|---|
| 336th | February 27, 1945 | Me-108 dest(grd) | Weimar A/F | P-51 |

0-0-0 air
1-0 ground

**Davis, Hubert I., Lt.**
83rd Ftr Sqn/78th Ftr Grp

| *Sqn* | *Date* | *Claims* | *Location* | *A/C* |
|---|---|---|---|---|
| 83rd | March 2, 1945 | Me-109 dest(air) | Burg A/F | P-51 |
| | | Me-109 dam(air) | Burg A/F | P-51 |
| | March 19 | (2)Me-109 dest(air) | Osnabruck | P-51 |

3-0-1 air
0-0 ground

**Davis, Jack E., Lt.**
77th Ftr Sqn/20th Ftr Grp

| *Sqn* | *Date* | *Claims* | *Location* | *A/C* |
|---|---|---|---|---|
| 77th | February 5, 1944 | (.33)FW-200 dest(air)* | Bourges A/F | P-38 |

0.33-0-0 air
0-0 ground

* - shared with LtCol. R.P. Montgomery of HdQts, 20th Ftr Grp, and Capt. P.J. Sabo of the 77th Ftr Sqn

**Davis, Jesse C., Jr., Maj.**
83rd Ftr Sqn/78th Ftr Grp

| *Sqn* | *Date* | *Claims* | *Location* | *A/C* |
|---|---|---|---|---|
| 83rd | July 1, 1943 | FW-190 dest(air) | Schouwen | P-47 |
| | September 27 | Me-109 dest(air) | Emden | P-47 |

2-0-0 air
0-0 ground

**Davis, Lonnie M., Capt.**
350th Ftr Sqn/353rd Ftr Grp

| *Sqn* | *Date* | *Claims* | *Location* | *A/C* |
|---|---|---|---|---|
| 350th | August 27, 1944 | (2)FW-190 dest(grd) | Verdun | P-47 |
| | | FW-190 dam(grd) | Verdun | P-47 |
| | September 23 | Me-109 dam(air) | SE Arnheim | P-47 |

0-0-1 air
2-1 ground

**Davis, Marvin L., Lt.**
336th Ftr Sqn/4th Ftr Grp

| *Sqn* | *Date* | *Claims* | *Location* | *A/C* |
|---|---|---|---|---|
| 336th | April 7, 1945 | Me-109 dest(air) | SW Bremen | P-51 |
| | April 16 | Me-110 dest(grd) | Praha | P-51 |
| | | (2)Me-110 dam(grd) | Praha | P-51 |

1-0-0 air
1-2 ground

**Davis, Ramon R., Lt.**
63rd Ftr Sqn/56th Ftr Grp

| *Sqn* | *Date* | *Claims* | *Location* | *A/C* |
|---|---|---|---|---|
| 63rd | November 18, 1944 | FW-190 dest(air) | E/Hanau | P-47 |
| | January 14, 1945 | Me-109 dest(air) | Munster | P-47 |
| | February 3 | Me-109 dam(air) | SE Berlin | P-47 |

2-0-1 air
0-0 ground

**Davis, Richard P., Lt.**
383rd Ftr Sqn/364th Ftr Grp

| *Sqn* | *Date* | *Claims* | *Location* | *A/C* |
|---|---|---|---|---|
| 383rd | August 9, 1944 | FW-190 dest(air) | Munich | P-51 |

1-0-0 air
0-0 ground

**Davis, Riegel W., Capt.**
62nd Ftr Sqn/56th Ftr Grp

| *Sqn* | *Date* | *Claims* | *Location* | *A/C* |
|---|---|---|---|---|
| 62nd | October 5, 1944 | Me-109 dest(grd) | S/Geseke | P-47 |
| | Ju-88 dest(grd) | S/Geseke | P-47 | |
| | | Me-109 dam(grd) | S/Geseke | P-47 |
| | December 2 | (2)Me-109 dest(air) | E/Coblenz | P-47 |

2-0-0 air
2-1 ground

**Davis, Robert O., Lt.**
336th Ftr Sqn/4th Ftr Grp

| *Sqn* | *Date* | *Claims* | *Location* | *A/C* |
|---|---|---|---|---|
| 336th | February 27, 1945 | Ju-88 dest(grd) | Weimar A/F | P-51 |
| | March 22 | FW-190 dest(air) | Funsterwalde A/F | P-51 |

1-0-0 air
1-0 ground

**Davis, William C., Capt.**
352nd Ftr Sqn/353rd Ftr Grp

| *Sqn* | *Date* | *Claims* | *Location* | *A/C* |
|---|---|---|---|---|
| 352nd | November 18, 1944 | (2)He-111 dest(grd) | Lechfeld | P-51 |
| | April 17, 1945 | (4)FW-190 dest(grd) | Ganacker | P-51 |
| | | FW-190 dam(grd) | Ganacker | P-51 |

0-0-0 air
6-1 ground

**Dawson, Melvin P., Lt.**
350th Ftr Sqn/353rd Ftr Grp

| *Sqn* | *Date* | *Claims* | *Location* | *A/C* |
|---|---|---|---|---|
| 350th | October 2, 1943 | Me-109 dam(air) | Emden | P-47 |

0-0-1 air
0-0 ground

**Day, Voorhis H., Lt.**
62nd Ftr Sqn/56th Ftr Grp

| *Sqn* | *Date* | *Claims* | *Location* | *A/C* |
|---|---|---|---|---|
| 62nd | August 17, 1943 | (2)Me-210 dam(air) | Ans | P-47 |

0-0-2 air
0-0 ground

**Dayhuff, Harry J., LtCol.**
82nd Ftr Sqn/78th Ftr Grp
HdQts/78th Ftr Grp
HdQts/ 4th Ftr Grp

| *Sqn* | *Date* | *Claims* | *Location* | *A/C* |
|---|---|---|---|---|
| 82nd | July 30, 1943 | Me-109 dest(air) | Haldern | P-47 |
| HdQts (78th) | January 29, 1944 | (.5)FW-190 dest(air)[*] | Coblenz | P-47 |

1.5-0-0 air
0-0 ground

[*] - shared with Lt. V.Y. Jones of the 82nd Ftr Sqn

**DeAnda, Louis, Lt.**
84th Ftr Sqn/78th Ftr Grp

| *Sqn* | *Date* | *Claims* | *Location* | *A/C* |
|---|---|---|---|---|
| 84th | February 3, 1945 | (2)FW-200 dest(grd) | Luneburg | P-51 |
| | | Hs-126 dest(grd) | Luneburg | P-51 |
| | April 16 | (3)Ju-52 dest(grd) | Praha/Kakewice | P-51 |

0-0-0 air
6-0 ground

**Deary, Ralph H., Lt.**
503rd Ftr Sqn/339th Ftr Grp

| *Sqn* | *Date* | *Claims* | *Location* | *A/C* |
|---|---|---|---|---|
| 503rd | May 21, 1944 | u/i a/c dest(grd) | Pelenz-Mackau | P-51 |
| | | (2)u/i a/c dam(grd) | Pelenz-Mackau | P-51 |

0-0-0 air
1-2 ground

**Decker, Edmund L., F/O**
361st Ftr Sqn/356th Ftr Grp

| *Sqn* | *Date* | *Claims* | *Location* | *A/C* |
|---|---|---|---|---|
| 361st | April 11, 1944 | (.25)Me-109 dest(grd)[*] | Gifhorn | P-47 |
| | | (.25)Ju-88 dest(grd)[*] | Gifhorn | P-47 |
| | April 13 | Me-110 dest(grd) | Bischwiller | P-47 |
| | June 7 | FW-190 dest(air) | SE Laval | P-47 |

1-0-0 air
1.5-0 ground

[*] - both shared with Col. E.A. Malmstrom of HdQts, 356th Ftr Grp, and Lt. R. Gibson and Lt. J.V. Jack of the 361st Ftr Sqn

**Decklar, Carl E., Lt.**
354th Ftr Sqn/355th Ftr Grp

| *Sqn* | *Date* | *Claims* | *Location* | *A/C* |
|---|---|---|---|---|
| 354th | January 14, 1945 | Me-109 dest(air) | E/Meppen | P-51 |
| | | FW-190 dest(air) | E/Meppen | P-51 |
| | March 22 | He-111 dam(grd) | Memmingen | P-51 |
| | April 4 | (.5)Do-24 dest(grd)[*] | Muritz Lake | P-51 |
| | April 8 | Me-109 dest(air) | Oberpfaffenhofen | P-51 |

3-0-0 air
0.5-1 ground

[*] - shared with Lt. P.W. Barnhart of the 354th Ftr Sqn

**Deeds, Alvin L., Lt.**
350th Ftr Sqn/353rd Ftr Grp

| *Sqn* | *Date* | *Claims* | *Location* | *A/C* |
|---|---|---|---|---|
| 350th | November 10, 1944 | Bu-133 dest(grd) | Fulda | P-51 |
| | November 18 | FW-190 dam(grd) | Lechfeld | P-51 |
| | December 5 | FW-190 dest(air) | S/Steinhuder Lake | P-51 |

1-0-0 air
1-1 ground

**Deen, Grover C., Lt.**
369th Ftr Sqn/359th Ftr Grp

| *Sqn* | *Date* | *Claims* | *Location* | *A/C* |
|---|---|---|---|---|
| 369th | September 12, 1944 | FW-190 dest(air) | NE Berlin | P-51 |
| | September 18 | FW-190 dest(air) | Kiefeld | P-51 |

2-0-0 air
0-0 ground

**DeGain, William J., Lt.**
84th Ftr Sqn/78th Ftr Grp

| *Sqn* | *Date* | *Claims* | *Location* | *A/C* |
|---|---|---|---|---|
| 84th | January 14, 1945 | Me-109 dest(air) | E/Cologne | P-51 |
| | March 19 | FW-190 dest(air) | Osnabruck | P-51 |
| | April 16 | u/i a/c dest(grd) | Praha/Kakewice | P-51 |
| | | (2)u/i a/c dam(grd) | Praha/Kakewice | P-51 |
| | | Ju-87 dam(grd) | Praha/Kakewice | P-51 |

2-0-0 air
1-3 ground

**DeGenaro, August V., Lt.**
82nd Ftr Sqn/78th Ftr Grp

| *Sqn* | *Date* | *Claims* | *Location* | *A/C* |
|---|---|---|---|---|
| 82nd | July 14, 1943 | FW-190 dest(air) | Amiens | P-47 |
| | | FW-190 prob(air) | Amiens | P-47 |
| | | FW-190 dam(air) | Amiens | P-47 |

1-1-1 air
0-0 ground

**Degenhart, Louis J., Lt.**
79th Ftr Sqn/20th Ftr Grp

| *Sqn* | *Date* | *Claims* | *Location* | *A/C* |
|---|---|---|---|---|
| 79th | April 10, 1945 | (2)u/i a/c dest(grd) | Werder A/F | P-51 |
| | | u/i a/c dam(grd) | Werder A/F | P-51 |

0-0-0 air
2-1 ground

**DeGeorge, John J., Jr., Lt.**
358th Ftr Sqn/355th Ftr Grp

| *Sqn* | *Date* | *Claims* | *Location* | *A/C* |
|---|---|---|---|---|
| 358th | February 5, 1944 | (.25)FW-190 dam(air)[*] | S/Tours | P-47 |
| | March 16 | Me-109 dest(air) | W/Augsburg | P-51 |
| | | (2)Me-109 dam(air) | W/Augsburg | P-51 |

1-0-2.25 air
0-0 ground

[*] - shared with Lt. H.J. Hoffman, Lt. J.H. McConnell, and Lt. J.H. Upchurch of the 358th Ftr Sqn

**Delager, Herman H., Lt.**
362nd Ftr Sqn/357th Ftr Grp

| *Sqn* | *Date* | *Claims* | *Location* | *A/C* |
|---|---|---|---|---|
| 362nd | November 27, 1944 | Me-109 dest(air) | S/Magdeburg | P-51 |
| | December 2 | Me-109 dest(air) | Bingen | P-51 |

2-0-0 air
0-0 ground

**Delhamer, Robert W., Lt.**
357th Ftr Sqn/355th Ftr Grp

| *Sqn* | *Date* | *Claims* | *Location* | *A/C* |
|---|---|---|---|---|
| 357th | January 15, 1945 | (2)Me-110 dest(grd) | Landsberg | P-51 |

| Sqn | Date | Claims | Location | A/C |
|---|---|---|---|---|
| | | u/i a/c dest(grd) | Landsberg | P-51 |
| | | Fi-156 dam(grd) | Landsberg | P-51 |
| | February 9 | (.5)Do-217 dam(air)* | Lonnewitz A/F | P-51 |

0-0-0.5 air
3-1 ground

* - shared with Lt. E.H. Riffle of the 357th Ftr Sqn

**Dellorto, Francis A., Lt.**
362nd Ftr Sqn/357th Ftr Grp

| *Sqn* | *Date* | *Claims* | *Location* | *A/C* |
|---|---|---|---|---|
| 362nd | April 18, 1945 | (.5)Me-262 dam(air)* | SW Prague/Ruzny | P-51 |

0-0-0.5 air
0-0 ground

* - shared with Lt. R.H. Bradner of the 362nd Ftr Sqn

**Deloach, Robert, Lt.**
338th Ftr Sqn/55th Ftr Grp

| *Sqn* | *Date* | *Claims* | *Location* | *A/C* |
|---|---|---|---|---|
| 338th | April 16, 1945 | He-111 dest(grd) | N/Landshut | P-51 |
| | April 17 | Fi-156 dam(grd) | Riess/Canitz | P-51 |
| | April 19 | Me-262 dest(air) | W/Prague | P-51 |

1-0-0 air
1-1 ground

**DeMerit, Merrill W., Lt.**
361st Ftr Sqn/356th Ftr Grp

| *Sqn* | *Date* | *Claims* | *Location* | *A/C* |
|---|---|---|---|---|
| 361st | February 10, 1944 | (.5)FW-190 dest(air)* | NE Lingen | P-47 |

0.5-0-0 air
0-0 ground

* - shared with Capt. J.N. Wood of the 361st Ftr Sqn

**DeMers, Raymond F., Lt.**
357th Ftr Sqn/355th Ftr Grp

| *Sqn* | *Date* | *Claims* | *Location* | *A/C* |
|---|---|---|---|---|
| 357th | March 28, 1944 | He-111 dest(grd) | Dijon | P-51 |
| | | (2)He-111 dam(grd) | Dijon | P-51 |
| | | Ju-88 dam(grd) | Dijon | P-51 |
| | April 13 | (.33)Me-110 dest(grd)* | Crailsheim | P-51 |
| | April 24 | (2)Me-109 dest(air) | NE Munich | P-51 |

2-0-0 air
1.33-3 ground

* - shared with Maj. E.W. Szaniawski and Lt. R.L. Norman of the 357th Ftr Sqn

**Dempsey, Peter, Capt.**
338th Ftr Sqn/55th Ftr Grp

| *Sqn* | *Date* | *Claims* | *Location* | *A/C* |
|---|---|---|---|---|
| 338th | January 5, 1944 | Me-109 dest(air) | Neumunster | P-38 |
| | May 21 | (2)Me-109 dest(grd) | Helmstedt | P-38 |
| | | (3)FW-190 dam(grd) | Helmstedt | P-38 |

1-0-0 air
2-3 ground

**Denman, John A., Capt.**
368th Ftr Sqn/359th Ftr Grp

| *Sqn* | *Date* | *Claims* | *Location* | *A/C* |
|---|---|---|---|---|
| 368th | April 13, 1945 | (4)Me-110 dest(grd) | Neumunster | P-51 |

0-0-0 air
4-0 ground

**Dennehy, Bernard L., Capt.**
376th Ftr Sqn/361st Ftr Grp

| *Sqn* | *Date* | *Claims* | *Location* | *A/C* |
|---|---|---|---|---|
| 376th | September 27, 1944 | FW-190 dam(air) | Eisenach | P-51 |
| | December 26 | FW-190 dest(air) | Merzig | P-51 |

1-0-1 air
0-0 ground

**Denson, Gordon A., Lt.**
334th Ftr Sqn/4th Ftr Grp

| *Sqn* | *Date* | *Claims* | *Location* | *A/C* |
|---|---|---|---|---|
| 334th | February 25, 1945 | (.5)Me-110 dest(grd)* | Rohrensee | P-51 |
| | | (.5)Me-110 dest(grd)* | Rohrensee | P-51 |
| | April 16 | (2)FW-190 dest(grd) | Gablingen | P-51 |
| | | Me-410 dest(grd) | Gablingen | P-51 |
| | | He-177 dest(grd) | Gablingen | P-51 |
| | | FW-190 dam(grd) | Gablingen | P-51 |
| | | Me-410 dam(grd) | Gablingen | P-51 |
| | | u/i a/c dam(grd) | Gablingen | P-51 |

0-0-0 air
5-3 ground

* - both shared with Capt. T.R. Bell of the 334th Ftr Sqn

**Derr, Warner P., Lt.**
384th Ftr Sqn/364th Ftr Grp

| *Sqn* | *Date* | *Claims* | *Location* | *A/C* |
|---|---|---|---|---|
| 384th | August 9, 1944 | FW-190 dam(grd) | Kaufburen | P-51 |

0-0-0 air
0-1 ground

**Detlefson, Heinz W., Lt.**
435th Ftr Sqn/479th Ftr Grp

| *Sqn* | *Date* | *Claims* | *Location* | *A/C* |
|---|---|---|---|---|
| 435th | August 18, 1944 | (.5)Ju-88 dest(grd)* | Nancy/Essey A/F | P-38 |
| | | He-111 dam(grd) | Nancy/Essey A/F | P-38 |

0-0-0 air
0.5-1 ground

* - shared with Lt. G.W. Gleason of the 434th Ftr Sqn, 479th Ftr Grp

**Des Voignes, Clair W., Capt.**
38th Ftr Sqn/55th Ftr Grp

| *Sqn* | *Date* | *Claims* | *Location* | *A/C* |
|---|---|---|---|---|
| 38th | November 5, 1943 | (.5)Me-109 dest(air)* | Nijmegen | P-38 |
| | | (.5)Me-109 prob(air)* | Winterswijk | P-38 |
| | May 22, 1944 | FW-190 dest(air) | Neumunster | P-38 |

1.5-0.5-0 air
0-0 ground

* - both shared with Capt. M.K. Shipman of the 38th Ftr Sqn

**DeVilliers, Donald J., Lt.**
83rd Ftr Sqn/78th Ftr Grp

| *Sqn* | *Date* | *Claims* | *Location* | *A/C* |
|---|---|---|---|---|
| 83rd | August 10, 1944 | He-111 dest(grd) | Chateau-Salines | P-47 |
| | April 16, 1945 | (2)Me-109 dest(grd) | N/Prague | P-51 |
| | | (2)Ju-87 dest(grd) | N/Prague | P-51 |
| | | He-111 dest(grd) | N/Prague | P-51 |
| | | (2)Me-109 dam(grd) | N/Prague | P-51 |
| | | (2)Ju-87 dam(grd) | N/Prague | P-51 |

0-0-0 air
6-4 ground

**DeVries, Paul K., Capt.**
363rd Ftr Sqn/357th Ftr Grp

| *Sqn* | *Date* | *Claims* | *Location* | *A/C* |
|---|---|---|---|---|
| 363rd | April 11, 1944 | Me-109 dest(air) | W/Magdeburg | P-51 |
| | May 12 | FW-190 dest(air) | NE Frankfurt | P-51 |

2-0-0 air
0-0 ground

**Devine, Gerald P., Lt.**
350th Ftr Sqn/353rd Ftr Grp

| Sqn | Date | Claims | Location | A/C |
|---|---|---|---|---|
| 350th | September 23, 1944 | FW-190 dest(air) | SE Arnheim | P-47 |
| | | FW-190 dam(air) | SE Arnheim | P-47 |

1-0-1 air
0-0 ground

**DeWitt, Charles W., Capt.**
82nd Ftr Sqn/78th Ftr Grp

| Sqn | Date | Claims | Location | A/C |
|---|---|---|---|---|
| 82nd | April 1, 1944 | (.13)Do-217 dest(grd)* | Verdun | P-47 |
| | | He-111 dam(grd) | Verdun | P-47 |
| | April 5 | (.33)Go-242 dest(grd)** | Ruwer | P-47 |
| | | (.33)DFS-230 dest(grd)** | Ruwer | P-47 |
| | April 8 | (.2)Me-110 dest(grd)@ | Trier | P-47 |
| | | (.2)Me-110 dest(grd)@ | Trier | P-47 |
| | | (.2)Me-110 dest(grd)@ | Trier | P-47 |
| | May 11 | u/i a/c dest(grd) | Dijon | P-47 |
| | | (3)u/i a/c dam(grd) | Dijon | P-47 |
| | May 19 | FW-190 dam(air) | Dummer Lake | P-47 |
| | May 28 | Ju-52 dam(grd) | Hanover | P-47 |

0-0-1 air
2.4-5 ground

* - shared with Capt. W.L. Boone, Capt. W.E. May, Lt. R.V. Hearn, Lt. B.M. Watkins, Lt. C.R. Clark, Lt. H.L. Eakes, and Lt. J.J. Hockery of the 82nd Ftr Sqn
** - both shared with Lt. H.L. Eakes and Lt. J.J. Hockery of the 82nd Ftr Sqn
@ - all shared with Maj. J.J. Oberhansly, Capt. N.D. Munson, Lt. J.E. Brasher, and Lt. M.K. Woller of the 82nd Ftr Sqn

**DeYoung, Arthur A., Capt.**
343rd Ftr Sqn/55th Ftr Grp

| Sqn | Date | Claims | Location | A/C |
|---|---|---|---|---|
| 343rd | April 24, 1944 | Me-109 dam(air) | NW Lake Constance | P-38 |

0-0-1 air
0-0 ground

**Diamond, Brack, Jr., Capt.**
335th Ftr Sqn/4th Ftr Grp

| Sqn | Date | Claims | Location | A/C |
|---|---|---|---|---|
| 335th | August 18, 1944 | Me-109 dest(air) | NE Paris | P-51 |
| | September 13 | (3)Hs-123 dest(grd) | Gelcheim | P-51 |

1-0-0 air
3-0 ground

**Diamond, Walker G., Lt.**
487th Ftr Sqn/352nd Ftr Grp

| Sqn | Date | Claims | Location | A/C |
|---|---|---|---|---|
| 487th | December 26, 1944 | Me-109 dest(air) | Ollheim | P-51 |
| | January 1, 1945 | FW-190 dest(air) | N/Liege | P-51 |
| | | FW-190 dam(air) | N/Liege | P-51 |

2-0-1 air
0-0 ground

**Dickey, Melvin N., Capt.**
336th Ftr Sqn/4th Ftr Grp

| Sqn | Date | Claims | Location | A/C |
|---|---|---|---|---|
| 336th | August 24, 1944 | (3)Ju-52 dest(grd) | NE Nordhausen | P-51 |
| | February 27, 1945 | Ju-87 dest(grd) | Weimar A/F | P-51 |
| | | C-47 dest(grd) | Weimar A/F | P-51 |

0-0-0 air
5-0 ground

**Dickmeyer, Robert A., Lt.**
334th Ftr Sqn/4th Ftr Grp

| Sqn | Date | Claims | Location | A/C |
|---|---|---|---|---|
| 334th | June 20, 1944 | Me-109 dest(air) | E/Pasewalk | P-51 |
| | September 12 | (.5)FW-190 dest(air)* | Weisbaden | P-51 |
| | November 6 | Me-109 dam(air) | Rheine | P-51 |

1.5-0-1 air
0-0 ground

* - shared with Lt. E.F. Hustwit of the 334th Ftr Sqn

**Dickson, James B., Lt.**
358th Ftr Sqn/355th Ftr Grp

| Sqn | Date | Claims | Location | A/C |
|---|---|---|---|---|
| 358th | February 20, 1944 | Me-109 dest(air) | Marienburg | P-47 |
| | March 6 | Me-109 dest(air) | N/Enschede | P-47 |
| | March 16 | Me-109 dest(air) | W/Augsburg | P-51 |
| | | Me-109 prob(air) | W/Augsburg | P-51 |

3-1-0 air
0-0 ground

**Diefenback, James A., Capt.**
505th Ftr Sqn/339th Ftr Grp

| Sqn | Date | Claims | Location | A/C |
|---|---|---|---|---|
| 505th | April 17, 1945 | Do-217 dest(grd) | SE Pocking | P-51 |
| | | u/i a/c dest(grd) | SE Pocking | P-51 |

0-0-0 air
2-0 ground

**Dilling, Donald K., Capt.**
487th Ftr Sqn/352nd Ftr Grp

| Sqn | Date | Claims | Location | A/C |
|---|---|---|---|---|
| 487th | November 26, 1943 | Me-109 dest(air) | E/Groningen | P-47 |
| | December 11 | Me-110 dest(air) | Leeuwarden | P-47 |
| | December 20 | Me-109 dest(air) | NW Oosterwalde | P-47 |

3-0-0 air
0-0 ground

**Dillon, Richard M., Capt.**
358th Ftr Sqn/355th Ftr Grp
1st Scouting Force

| Sqn | Date | Claims | Location | A/C |
|---|---|---|---|---|
| 358th | July 24, 1944 | Ju-88 dest(grd) | Augsburg | P-51 |
| | | u/i a/c dam(grd) | Augsburg | P-51 |
| | August 1 | Me-109 dest(air) | Chateaudun | P-51 |

1-0-0 air
1-1 ground

**Dinse, Charles W., Capt.**
350th Ftr Sqn/353rd Ftr Grp

| Sqn | Date | Claims | Location | A/C |
|---|---|---|---|---|
| 350th | November 13, 1943 | FW-190 dam(air) | Meppen | P-47 |
| | January 24, 1944 | (.5)Me-110 dest(air)* | Termonde | P-47 |
| | February 8 | FW-190 dest(air) | Luxembourg | P-47 |

1.5-0-1 air
0-0 ground

* - shared with Lt. R.A. Stearns of the 350th Ftr Sqn

**DiPaola, Albert R., Lt.**
436th Ftr Sqn/479th Ftr Grp

| Sqn | Date | Claims | Location | A/C |
|---|---|---|---|---|
| 436th | February 22, 1945 | FW-190 dam(grd) | Halberstadt | P-51 |

0-0-0 air
0-1 ground

**Dissette, Lawrence J., Capt.**
358th Ftr Sqn/355th Ftr Grp

| Sqn | Date | Claims | Location | A/C |
|---|---|---|---|---|
| 358th | April 5, 1944 | (2)Me-110 dest(grd) | Munich | P-51 |
| | | Me-110 dam(grd) | Landsberg | P-51 |
| | | DFS-230 dam(grd) | Landsberg | P-51 |
| | April 15 | Do-217 dest(grd) | Glienicke A/F | P-51 |
| | | u/i a/c dam(grd) | Glienicke A/F | P-51 |
| | May 1 | Me-109 dest(air) | Traben-Trarbach | P-51 |
| | April 16, 1945 | (2)FW-190 dest(grd) | Straubing | P-51 |
| | | (2)FW-190 dam(grd) | Straubing | P-51 |

1-0-0 air
5-5 ground

**Dittmer, Karl K., Lt.**
487th Ftr Sqn/352nd Ftr Grp

| Sqn | Date | Claims | Location | A/C |
|---|---|---|---|---|
| 487th | November 27, 1944 | Me-109 dest(air) | N/Hanover | P-51 |

1-0-0 air
0-0 ground

**Dix, Gerald J., LtCol.**
HdQts/355th Ftr Grp

| Sqn | Date | Claims | Location | A/C |
|---|---|---|---|---|
| HdQts | March 8, 1944 | FW-190 dest(air) | NE Osnabruck | P-47 |
| | March 28 | (.5)Ju-88 dest(grd)* | Dijon | P-51 |
| | April 24 | FW-190 dest(air) | NE Augsburg | P-51 |
| | | Me-109 dam(air) | NE Augsburg | P-51 |
| | May 13 | (2)Me-410 dest(air) | SE Landsberg | P-51 |
| | May 22 | Me-109 prob(air) | SW Kiel | P-51 |
| | June 6 | Ju-87 dam(air) | Chartres | P-51 |
| | | Ju-87 dest(grd) | Chartres | P-51 |

4-1-2 air
1.5-0 ground

* - shared with Lt. H.E. Culp of the 354th Ftr Sqn, 355th Ftr Grp

**Dixon, Clyde J., Lt.**
79th Ftr Sqn/20th Ftr Grp

| Sqn | Date | Claims | Location | A/C |
|---|---|---|---|---|
| 79th | September 10, 1944 | u/i a/c dam(grd) | SW Stuttgart | P-51 |

0-0-0 air
0-1 ground

**Dixon, Herbert S., Lt.**
374th Ftr Sqn/361st Ftr Grp

| Sqn | Date | Claims | Location | A/C |
|---|---|---|---|---|
| 374th | April 4, 1945 | Me-262 dam(air) | W/Berlin | P-51 |

0-0-1 air
0-0 ground

**Doersch, George A., Maj.**
370th Ftr Sqn/359th Ftr Grp
368th Ftr Sqn/359th Ftr Grp

| Sqn | Date | Claims | Location | A/C |
|---|---|---|---|---|
| 370th | February 22, 1944 | FW-190 dest(air) | Ahlen | P-47 |
| | April 11 | FW-190 dest(air) | Brunswick | P-47 |
| | April 15 | Ju-88 dam(air) | Varel | P-47 |
| | May 8 | FW-190 dest(air) | Eschede | P-51 |
| | | Me-109 dest(air) | Eschede | P-51 |
| | | FW-190 dam(air) | Eschede | P-51 |
| | May 21 | u/i a/c dam(grd) | Bruel | P-51 |
| | May 29 | (.5)FW-190 dest(air)* | Stettin | P-51 |
| | | (.5)FW-190 dest(air)** | Stettin | P-51 |
| | June 10 | Me-109 dest(air) | Evreux | P-51 |
| | October 6 | (2)FW-190 dest(air) | S/Stettin | P-51 |
| | | FW-190 dam(air) | S/Stettin | P-51 |
| | October 7 | (.5)BV-140 dest(grd)@ | Dievenow | P-51 |
| | January 14, 1945 | (2)FW-190 dest(air) | Vorden A/F | P-51 |
| 368th | March 23 | (.5)Ar-196 dest(air)@@ | Salzwedel | P-51 |
| | April 9 | FW-190 dest(grd) | Gernering A/F | P-51 |
| | | He-111 dam(grd) | Gernering A/F | P-51 |

10.5-0-3 air
1.5-2 ground

* - shared with Maj. J.B. Murphy of the 370th Ftr Sqn
** - shared with Lt. R.W. Siltamaki of the 370th Ftr Sqn
@ - shared with F/O J.E. McCoskey of the 370th Ftr Sqn
@@ - shared with Lt. K.L. Barber of the 368th Ftr Sqn

**Doleac, Cyril B., F/O**
487th Ftr Sqn/352nd Ftr Grp

| Sqn | Date | Claims | Location | A/C |
|---|---|---|---|---|
| 487th | August 6, 1944 | Me-109 dest(air) | Hamburg | P-51 |

1-0-0 air
0-0 ground

**Donahue, Duncan R., Capt.**
487th Ftr Sqn/352nd Ftr Grp

| Sqn | Date | Claims | Location | A/C |
|---|---|---|---|---|
| 487th | March 8, 1944 | Me-109 dam(air) | Meppen | P-47 |
| | April 22 | (.33)Ju-88 dest(air)* | Stade A/F | P-51 |

0.33-0-1 air
0-0 ground

* - shared with Maj. G.E. Preddy and Lt. J.P. Kessler of the 487th Ftr Sqn

**Donnell, John C., Jr., Lt.**
434th Ftr Sqn/479th Ftr Grp

| Sqn | Date | Claims | Location | A/C |
|---|---|---|---|---|
| 434th | November 2, 1944 | Me-109 dest(air) | SW Leipzig | P-51 |
| | February 9, 1945 | (2)Me-109 dam(air) | SE Magdeburg | P-51 |

1-0-2 air
0-0 ground

**Donovan, David A., Lt.**
358th Ftr Sqn/355th Ftr Grp

| Sqn | Date | Claims | Location | A/C |
|---|---|---|---|---|
| 358th | May 30, 1944 | Me-109 dest(air) | SE Brunswick | P-51 |
| | | (.5)FW-190 dest(air)* | SE Brunswick | P-51 |

1.5-0-0 air
0-0 ground

* - shared with an unknown pilot

**Dooley, Chester H., Lt.**
364th Ftr Sqn/357th Ftr Grp

| Sqn | Date | Claims | Location | A/C |
|---|---|---|---|---|
| 364th | May 13, 1944 | (.5)Me-410 dest(air)* | E/Grunberg | P-51 |
| | May 21 | Me-109 dest(grd) | S/Eichhof | P-51 |
| | | (.5)FW-44 dest(grd)** | S/Eichhof | P-51 |

0.5-0-0 air
1.5-0 ground

* - shared with Lt. R.M. Shaw of the 364th Ftr Sqn
** - shared with Capt. J.A. Storch of the 364th Ftr Sqn

**Doolittle, Gordon L., Capt.**
435th Ftr Sqn/479th Ftr Grp

| Sqn | Date | Claims | Location | A/C |
|---|---|---|---|---|
| 435th | December 5, 1944 | FW-190 dest(air) | NW Berlin | P-51 |
| | | FW-190 prob(air) | NW Berlin | P-51 |
| | | FW-190 dam(air) | NW Berlin | P-51 |
| | February 9, 1945 | Me-109 dest(air) | SE Magdeburg | P-51 |

2-1-1 air
0-0 ground

**Doss, Gene C., Lt.**
83rd Ftr Sqn/78th Ftr Grp

| Sqn | Date | Claims | Location | A/C |
|---|---|---|---|---|
| 83rd | April 16, 1945 | (5)Ju-87 dest(grd) | N/Prague | P-51 |
| | | Me-109 dam(grd) | N/Prague | P-51 |

0-0-0 air
5-1 ground

**Dougherty, Kenneth W., Capt.**
83rd Ftr Sqn/78th Ftr Grp

| Sqn | Date | Claims | Location | A/C |
|---|---|---|---|---|
| 83rd | August 19, 1943 | Me-109 dest(air) | Woensdrecht | P-47 |
| | February 22, 1944 | Me-109 dest(air) | Nijmegen | P-47 |
| | | Me-109 prob(air) | Nijmegen | P-47 |
| | February 25 | Me-109 dest(air) | Boekingen | P-47 |

3-1-0 air
0-0 ground

**Dougherty, Paul A., Jr., Lt.**
375th Ftr Sqn/361st Ftr Grp

| Sqn | Date | Claims | Location | A/C |
|---|---|---|---|---|
| 375th | January 25, 1945 | (.5)Me-110 dest(air)* | NE Mannheim | P-51 |
| | April 17 | u/i a/c dam(grd) | Eger A/F | P-51 |

0.5-0-0 air
0-1 ground

* - shared with F/O W.M. Hart of the 375th Ftr Sqn

**Dougherty, Wayne W., Lt.**
84th Ftr Sqn/78th Ftr Grp

| Sqn | Date | Claims | Location | A/C |
|---|---|---|---|---|
| 84th | September 27, 1943 | Me-109 prob(air) | NW Emden | P-47 |

0-1-0 air
0-0 ground

**Douglas, Ward H., Lt.**
358th Ftr Sqn/355th Ftr Grp

| Sqn | Date | Claims | Location | A/C |
|---|---|---|---|---|
| 358th | July 24, 1944 | FW-190 dest(grd) | Augsburg | P-51 |

0-0-0 air
1-0 ground

**Dowell, Charles W., Capt.**
HdQts/339th Ftr Grp

| Sqn | Date | Claims | Location | A/C |
|---|---|---|---|---|
| HdQts | November 21, 1944 | (.5)Me-109 dest(air)* | Munster | P-51 |

0.5-0-0 air
0-0 ground

* - shared with F/O C.W. Palmer of the 505th Ftr Sqn

**Downey, Edward J., F/O**
83rd Ftr Sqn/78th Ftr Grp

| Sqn | Date | Claims | Location | A/C |
|---|---|---|---|---|
| 83rd | February 10, 1944 | FW-190 dest(air) | Lingen | P-47 |

1-0-0 air
0-0 ground

**Downey, Lawrence E., Lt.**
374th Ftr Sqn/361st Ftr Grp

| Sqn | Date | Claims | Location | A/C |
|---|---|---|---|---|
| 374th | May 29, 1944 | FW-190 dest(air) | Pitka | P-51 |
| | | FW-190 dam(air) | Pitka | P-51 |
| | June 13 | Me-109 dest(air) | St. Brieuc | P-51 |

2-0-1 air
0-0 ground

**Downing, Andrew H., Lt.**
84th Ftr Sqn/78th Ftr Grp

| Sqn | Date | Claims | Location | A/C |
|---|---|---|---|---|
| 84th | May 16, 1943 | FW-190 dam(air) | E/Sluis | P-47 |

0-0-1 air
0-0 ground

**Downing, Harry L., Maj.**
82nd Ftr Sqn/78th Ftr Grp
84th Ftr Sqn/78th Ftr Grp

| Sqn | Date | Claims | Location | A/C |
|---|---|---|---|---|
| 84th | March 19, 1945 | Me-109 dest(air) | Osnabruck | P-51 |
| | | FW-190 dest(air) | Osnabruck | P-51 |

2-0-0 air
0-0 ground

**Doyle, Gray H., Capt.**
84th Ftr Sqn/78th Ftr Grp
HdQts/78th Ftr Grp

| Sqn | Date | Claims | Location | A/C |
|---|---|---|---|---|
| 84th | December 1, 1943 | (2)FW-190 prob(air) | Leige-Aachen | P-47 |
| | February 10, 1944 | Ju-88 dam(grd) | Soesterburg A/F | P-47 |
| HdQts | March 24 | Ju-52 dest(grd) | Beaumont-Sur-Oise | P-47 |
| | | Ju-52 dam(grd) | Beaumont-Sur-Oise | P-47 |
| | April 11 | Me-109 dam(air) | Hanover | P-47 |

0-2-1 air
1-2 ground

**Draftz, Robert C., Lt.**
487th Ftr Sqn/352nd Ftr Grp

| Sqn | Date | Claims | Location | A/C |
|---|---|---|---|---|
| 487th | July 19, 1944 | Me-109 dest(air) | Wolfratshausen | P-51 |

1-0-0 air
0-0 ground

**Drake, Olin P., Lt.**
368th Ftr Sqn/359th Ftr Grp

| Sqn | Date | Claims | Location | A/C |
|---|---|---|---|---|
| 368th | May 21, 1944 | He-111 dam(grd) | Wismar-Rostock | P-51 |
| | | Go-242 dam(grd) | Wismar-Rostock | P-51 |
| | June 10 | (2)Me-109 dest(air) | Evreux | P-51 |

2-0-0 air
0-2 ground

**Drake, Walter M., Lt.**
434th Ftr Sqn/479th Ftr Grp

| Sqn | Date | Claims | Location | A/C |
|---|---|---|---|---|
| 434th | August 18, 1944 | (2)Ju-88 dest(grd) | Nancy/Essey A/F | P-38 |
| | | FW-190 dest(grd) | Nancy/Essey A/F | P-38 |
| | September 26 | Me-109 dest(air) | SW Munster | P-38 |

1-0-0 air
3-0 ground

**Dregne, Irwin H., Col.**
HdQts/357th Ftr Grp

| Sqn | Date | Claims | Location | A/C |
|---|---|---|---|---|
| HdQts | March 5, 1944 | FW-190 dam(air) | SE Bordeaux | P-51 |
| | March 16 | Me-109 dest(air) | SW Munich | P-51 |
| | May 8 | FW-190 dam(air) | N/Hanover | P-51 |
| | May 12 | Me-109 dest(air) | NE Frankfurt | P-51 |
| | May 19 | Me-109 dest(air) | Wittenburg | P-51 |
| | May 21 | (1.5)Me-109 dest(grd)* | S/Eichhof | P-51 |
| | December 24 | Me-109 dest(air) | Coblenz | P-51 |
| | January 14, 1945 | Me-109 dest(air) | NW Brandenburg | P-51 |
| | | FW-190 dam(air) | NW Brandenburg | P-51 |
| | April 10 | (2)Me-262 dest(grd) | Neuruppin | P-51 |
| | | FW-190 dest(grd) | Neuruppin | P-51 |
| | | Ju-88 dam(grd) | Neuruppin | P-51 |
| | April 17 | Ju-88 dest(grd) | Prague/Ruzny | P-51 |
| | | (2)Ju-88 dam(grd) | Prague/Ruzny | P-51 |

5-0-3 air
5.5-3 ground

* - shared with Lt. M.A. Stanley of the 364th Ftr Sqn, 357th Ftr Grp

**Drew, Urban L., Lt.**
375th Ftr Sqn/361st Ftr Grp

| Sqn | Date | Claims | Location | A/C |
|---|---|---|---|---|
| 375th | June 16, 1944 | Ju-52 dest(grd) | Toussus/Le Noble | P-51 |
| | June 25 | Me-109 dest(air) | N/Lisieux | P-51 |
| | August 7 | Me-109 dam(air) | Chartres | P-51 |
| | August 25 | Me-109 dest(air) | SW Rostock | P-51 |
| | September 11 | Me-109 dest(air) | S/Gottingen | P-51 |
| | September 18 | He-111 dest(air) | Fehrman Belt | P-51 |
| | October 7 | (2)Me-262 dest(air) | Achmer A/F | P-51 |

6-0-1 air
1-0 ground

**Dripps, Paul S., Capt.**
343rd Ftr Sqn/55th Ftr Grp

| *Sqn* | *Date* | *Claims* | *Location* | *A/C* |
|---|---|---|---|---|
| 343rd | February 21, 1944 | Me-109 dam(air) | Ruhr Valley | P-38 |
| | September 5 | He-111 dest(grd) | Stuttgart/Echterdingen | P-51 |
| | | (2)He-111 dam(grd) | Stuttgart/Echterdingen | P-51 |
| | | 0-0-1 air | | |
| | | 1-2 ground | | |

**Drozd, Walter T., Lt.**
77th Ftr Sqn/20th Ftr Grp

| *Sqn* | *Date* | *Claims* | *Location* | *A/C* |
|---|---|---|---|---|
| 77th | April 10, 1945 | Me-262 dest(air) | Oranienburg | P-51 |
| | | 1-0-0 air | | |
| | | 0-0 ground | | |

**Drybrough, Thomas R., Lt.**
351st Ftr Sqn/353rd Ftr Grp

| *Sqn* | *Date* | *Claims* | *Location* | *A/C* |
|---|---|---|---|---|
| 351st | November 18, 1944 | FW-190 dest(grd) | Landsberg | P-51 |
| | November 27 | FW-190 dest(air) | NE Steinhuder Lk. | P-51 |
| | | FW-190 prob(air) | NE Steinhuder Lk. | P-51 |
| | April 16, 1945 | (2)FW-190 dest(grd) | Reichersberg | P-51 |
| | | u/i a/c dam(grd) | Reichersberg | P-51 |
| | | 1-1-0 air | | |
| | | 3-1 ground | | |

**Dubay, Elmo B., Capt.**
328th Ftr Sqn/352nd Ftr Grp

| *Sqn* | *Date* | *Claims* | *Location* | *A/C* |
|---|---|---|---|---|
| 328th | November 27, 1944 | Me-109 dest(air) | Hanover | P-51 |
| | January 24, 1945 | (.5)Me-109 dest(air)[*] | Duren | P-51 |
| | | 1.5-0-0 air | | |
| | | 0-0 ground | | |

[*] - shared with Lt. C.E. Goodman of the 328th Ftr Sqn

**Duderstadt, Ernest H., Capt.**
384th Ftr Sqn/364th Ftr Grp

| *Sqn* | *Date* | *Claims* | *Location* | *A/C* |
|---|---|---|---|---|
| 384th | November 21, 1944 | (.5)FW-190 dest(air)[*] | Mulhausen | P-51 |
| | December 27 | (2)FW-190 dest(air) | W/Coblenz | P-51 |
| | | Me-109 dest(air) | W/Coblenz | P-51 |
| | | 3.5-0-0 air | | |
| | | 0-0 ground | | |

[*] - shared with Lt. E.W. Farnsworth of the 384th Ftr Sqn

**Dudley, Charles A., Lt.**
61st Ftr Sqn/56th Ftr Grp

| *Sqn* | *Date* | *Claims* | *Location* | *A/C* |
|---|---|---|---|---|
| 61st | June 12, 1944 | Me-109 dam(air) | Evreux | P-47 |
| | | 0-0-1 air | | |
| | | 0-0 ground | | |

**Dudley, Lawrence M., Jr., Capt.**
358th Ftr Sqn/355th Ftr Grp

| *Sqn* | *Date* | *Claims* | *Location* | *A/C* |
|---|---|---|---|---|
| 358th | March 2, 1944 | (.5)FW-190 dest(air)[*] | SE Charleroi | P-47 |
| | April 5 | FW-44 dest(air) | Oberpfaffenhofen | P-51 |
| | | Me-110 dest(grd) | Landsberg | P-51 |
| | April 11 | Me-410 dest(air) | NE Berlin | P-51 |
| | | (.25)Me-410 dest(air)[**] | NE Berlin | P-51 |
| | | (.25)Ju-88 dest(air)[**] | NE Berlin | P-51 |
| | | 3-0-0 air | | |
| | | 1-0 ground | | |

[*] - shared with Lt. R.J. Fussell of the 358th Ftr Sqn
[**] - both shared with Lt. R.J. Fussell, Lt. W.V. Gresham, and Lt. D.M. Martyn of the 358th Ftr Sqn

**Duffie, Claire A.P., Maj.**
434th Ftr Sqn/479th Ftr Grp
436th Ftr Sqn/479th Ftr Grp

| *Sqn* | *Date* | *Claims* | *Location* | *A/C* |
|---|---|---|---|---|
| 434th | August 18, 1944 | (1.5)Ju-88 dest(grd)[*] | Nancy/Essey A/F | P-38 |
| | August 25 | (2)Me-109 dest(air) | Rostock | P-38 |
| | September 26 | Me-109 dest(air) | SW Munster | P-38 |
| | | (2)Me-109 dam(air) | SW Munster | P-38 |
| 436th | February 22, 1945 | (3)u/i a/c dam(grd) | Halberstadt | P-51 |
| | | Ju-88 dam(grd) | Halberstadt | P-51 |
| | April 16 | (4)FW-190 dest(grd) | Landstadt | P-51 |
| | April 17 | (2)Ju-87 dest(grd) | Karlsbad | P-51 |
| | | FW-190 dest(grd) | Karlsbad | P-51 |
| | | 3-0-2 air | | |
| | | 8.5-4 ground | | |

[*] - shared with Lt. R.K. Friend of the 435th Ftr Sqn, 479th Ftr Grp

**Duffy, James E., Jr., Capt.**
354th Ftr Sqn/355th Ftr Grp

| *Sqn* | *Date* | *Claims* | *Location* | *A/C* |
|---|---|---|---|---|
| 354th | January 21, 1944 | FW-190 dest(air) | NW Dourdan | P-47 |
| | March 16 | FW-190 dest(air) | W/Ulm | P-51 |
| | April 5 | (.2)Do-217 dest(air)[*] | Landsberg | P-51 |
| | | (5)Do-217 dam(grd) | Landsberg | P-51 |
| | | FW-44 dam(grd) | Landsberg | P-51 |
| | April 10 | He-111 dest(grd) | Bourges A/F | P-51 |
| | | W-34 dam(grd) | Bourges A/F | P-51 |
| | April 13 | Me-110 dest(grd) | Oberpfaffenhofen | P-51 |
| | | Do-217 dest(grd) | Oberpfaffenhofen | P-51 |
| | | (2)Me-210 dam(grd) | Oberpfaffenhofen | P-51 |
| | | He-111 dam(grd) | Oberpfaffenhofen | P-51 |
| | | Do-217 dam(grd) | Oberpfaffenhofen | P-51 |
| | November 18 | Me-262 dest(grd) | Leipheim | P-51 |
| | November 26 | FW-190 dest(air) | Gifhorn-Hanover | P-51 |
| | December 5 | FW-190 dest(air) | N/Berlin | P-51 |
| | February 9, 1945 | FW-190 dest(air) | SW Berlin | P-51 |
| | February 23 | (2)u/i a/c dest(grd) | Leipheim | P-51 |
| | | Me-262 dest(grd) | Leipheim | P-51 |
| | April 13 | Ju-88 dest(grd) | Husum | P-51 |
| | | u/i a/c dam(grd) | Husum | P-51 |
| | April 16 | u/i a/c dest(grd) | Landstadt | P-51 |
| | | 5.2-0-0 air | | |
| | | 9-12 ground | | |

[*] - shared with Capt. C.G. Johnston, Capt. W.J. Koraleski, Lt. H.W. Brown, and Lt. B.C. Williamson of the 354th Ftr Sqn

**DuFour, John G., Maj.**
336th Ftr Sqn/4th Ftr Grp

| *Sqn* | *Date* | *Claims* | *Location* | *A/C* |
|---|---|---|---|---|
| 336th | August 16, 1943 | Me-109 dest(air) | N/Paris | P-47 |
| | | Me-109 dam(air) | N/Paris | P-47 |
| | | 1-0-1 air | | |
| | | 0-0 ground | | |

**DuFresne, Roland J., Capt.**
357th Ftr Sqn/355th Ftr Grp

| *Sqn* | *Date* | *Claims* | *Location* | *A/C* |
|---|---|---|---|---|
| 357th | January 29, 1944 | (2)FW-190 dam(air) | W/Frankfurt | P-47 |
| | November 2 | (2)u/i a/c dest(grd) | Wernigerode | P-51 |
| | | 0-0-2 air | | |
| | | 2-0 ground | | |

**Dugan, Harry E., Jr., Lt.**
336th Ftr Sqn/4th Ftr Grp

| *Sqn* | *Date* | *Claims* | *Location* | *A/C* |
|---|---|---|---|---|
| 336th | September 11, 1944 | Me-109 dest(air) | Korbach | P-51 |
| | | 1-0-0 air | | |
| | | 0-0 ground | | |

**Dunaway, Kenneth P., Lt.**
83rd Ftr Sqn/78th Ftr Grp

| Sqn | Date | Claims | Location | A/C |
|---|---|---|---|---|
| 83rd | August 10, 1944 | He-111 dam(grd) | Chateau-Salines | P-47 |
| | | Ju-52 dam(grd) | Chateau-Salines | P-47 |

0-0-0 air
0-2 ground

**Duncan, Albert C., Lt.**
375th Ftr Sqn/361st Ftr Grp

| Sqn | Date | Claims | Location | A/C |
|---|---|---|---|---|
| 375th | January 14, 1944 | (.33)FW-190 dam(grd)* | Rosierres-en-Santerne | P-47 |

0-0-0 air
0-0.33 ground

* - shared with Lt. C.L. Stafford of HdQts, 353rd Ftr Grp, and Maj. W.C. Beckham of the 351st Ftr Sqn, 353rd Ftr Grp

**Duncan, Earl D., LtCol.**
487th Ftr Sqn/352nd Ftr Grp
328th Ftr Sqn/352nd Ftr Grp

| Sqn | Date | Claims | Location | A/C |
|---|---|---|---|---|
| 487th | November 27, 1944 | Me-109 dest(air) | Hameln | P-51 |
| 328th | February 22, 1945 | Me-262 dam(air) | Stendal | P-51 |
| | April 10 | (.5)Me-262 dest(air)* | Berlin | P-51 |
| | April 16 | Me-109 dam(grd) | Landau | P-51 |
| | April 17 | (2)Me-109 dest(grd) | Plattling | P-51 |

1.5-0-1 air
2-1 ground

* - shared with Maj. R.G. McAuliffe of the 328th Ftr Sqn

**Duncan, Glenn E., Col.**
HdQts/353rd Ftr Grp

| Sqn | Date | Claims | Location | A/C |
|---|---|---|---|---|
| HdQts | August 16, 1943 | FW-190 dam(air) | NW Paris | P-47 |
| | September 23 | FW-190 dest(air) | Nantes | P-47 |
| | October 2 | Me-109 dest(air) | Emden | P-47 |
| | | Me-109 prob(air) | Emden | P-47 |
| | October 4 | Me-109 dam(air) | Malines | P-47 |
| | November 5 | Me-109 dam(air) | Gelsenkirchen | P-47 |
| | November 11 | Me-109 dest(air) | Numansdorp | P-47 |
| | | FW-190 dest(air) | Munster | P-47 |
| | | Me-109 dam(air) | Numansdorp | P-47 |
| | December 20 | FW-190 dest(air) | Rastede | P-47 |
| | January 4, 1944 | FW-190 dam(air) | Sendenhorst | P-47 |
| | January 5 | Me-109 dest(air) | Eindhoven-Gilze-Rijen | P-47 |
| | January 21 | (.33)Do-217 dest(grd)* | Albert | P-47 |
| | January 24 | (2)Me-110 dest(air) | Tirlemont | P-47 |
| | February 5 | FW-190 dest(air) | Sancerre | P-47 |
| | February 22 | FW-190 dest(air) | Turnhout | P-47 |
| | | (.5)Ju-88 dest(grd)** | Bonn | P-47 |
| | February 24 | FW-190 dest(air) | Steinhuder Lake | P-47 |
| | | Ju-88 dam(grd) | Steinhuder Lake | P-47 |
| | March 6 | (2)FW-190 dest(air) | Steinhuder Lake | P-47 |
| | March 16 | (1.5)u/i a/c dam(grd)@ | Laon | P-47 |
| | March 29 | Me-110 dest(grd) | Dummer Lake | P-47 |
| | | B-17 dest(grd) | Dummer Lake | P-47 |
| | | (6)u/i a/c dam(grd) | Dummer Lake | P-47 |
| | | Me-210 dam(grd) | Dummer Lake | P-47 |
| | April 28 | u/i a/c dest(grd) | Chateaudun | P-47 |
| | | u/i a/c dam(grd) | Chateaudun | P-47 |
| | May 12 | FW-190 dest(air) | Wiesbaden | P-47 |
| | | (2)FW-190 dam(air) | Wiesbaden | P-47 |
| | June 7 | Ju-52 dest(air) | E/Ribecourt | P-47 |
| | | (.5)Me-109 dest(air)@@ | E/Ribecourt | P-47 |
| | June 12 | (3)Me-109 dest(air) | Evreux-Dreux | P-47 |
| | June 20 | (2)He-111 dest(grd) | Plantlunne | P-47 |
| | July 5, 1944 | Me-109 dest(air) | Pont Audemer | P-47 |
| | July 7 | He-111 dest(grd) | Wesendorf | P-47 |

19.5-1-7 air
6.83-10.5 ground

* - shared with Lt. W.W. Johnson and Lt. C.H. Sperry of the 352nd Ftr Sqn, 353rd Ftr Grp
** - shared with Maj. H.H. Holt, a D.S. pilot from the 366th Ftr Grp, 9th Air Force
@ - shared with Lt. J. Terzian of the 351st Ftr Sqn, 353rd Ftr Grp
@@ - shared with Capt. G.B. Compton of the 351st Ftr Sqn

**Duncan, John D., Capt.,**
376th Ftr Sqn/361st Ftr Grp

| Sqn | Date | Claims | Location | A/C |
|---|---|---|---|---|
| 376th | February 25, 1944 | Me-109 dest(air) | Courtrai | P-47 |

1-0-0 air
0-0 ground

**Duncan, John F., Lt.**
362nd Ftr Sqn/357th Ftr Grp

| Sqn | Date | Claims | Location | A/C |
|---|---|---|---|---|
| 362nd | January 14, 1945 | (2)FW-190 dest(air) | NW Berlin | P-51 |
| | February 25 | He-111 dest(grd) | Memmingen | P-51 |
| | March 2 | Me-109 dest(air) | NE Leipzig | P-51 |
| | | Me-109 dam(air) | NE Leipzig | P-51 |
| | March 24 | Me-109 dest(air) | W/Gutersloh | P-51 |
| | April 10 | (2)Me-210 dest(grd) | Neuruppin | P-51 |
| | | Me-110 dest(grd) | Neuruppin | P-51 |
| | | Me-262 dam(grd) | Neuruppin | P-51 |
| | April 17 | Me-109 dest(grd) | Prague/Ruzny | P-51 |
| | | Me-262 dest(grd) | Prague/Ruzny | P-51 |

4-0-1 air
6-1 ground

**Dungan, Charles W., Lt.**
77th Ftr Sqn/20th Ftr Grp

| Sqn | Date | Claims | Location | A/C |
|---|---|---|---|---|
| 77th | October 7, 1944 | Ju-88 dest(grd) | Peenemunde | P-51 |

0-0-0 air
1-0 ground

**Dunham, Richard W., Lt.**
82nd Ftr Sqn/78th Ftr Grp

| Sqn | Date | Claims | Location | A/C |
|---|---|---|---|---|
| 82nd | August 10, 1944 | Ju-88 dam(grd) | Verdun | P-47 |
| | September 9 | (.5)FW-190 dam(grd)* | Giessen | P-47 |

0-0-0 air
0-1.5 ground

* - shared with Lt. W.K. Grimes of the 84th Ftr Sqn, 78th Ftr Grp

**Dunlap, Elmer N., Lt.**
370th Ftr Sqn/359th Ftr Grp

| Sqn | Date | Claims | Location | A/C |
|---|---|---|---|---|
| 370th | April 11, 1944 | FW-190 dest(air) | Fallersleben | P-47 |
| | | FW-190 dam(air) | Fallersleben | P-47 |

1-0-1 air
0-0 ground

**Dunlop, William R., Lt.**
363rd Ftr Sqn/357th Ftr Grp

| Sqn | Date | Claims | Location | A/C |
|---|---|---|---|---|
| 363rd | September 15, 1944 | Do-24 dam(grd) | Cristianmund | P-51 |
| | September 18 | Me-109 dest(air) | Apeldoorn | P-51 |
| | September 19 | Me-109 dest(air) | W/Arnheim | P-51 |
| | December 24 | Me-109 dest(air) | W/Coblenz | P-51 |
| | January 14, 1945 | Me-109 dest(air) | N/Brandenburg | P-51 |

4-0-0 air
0-1 ground

**Dunn, Carl W., Lt.**
360th Ftr Sqn/356th Ftr Grp

| Sqn | Date | Claims | Location | A/C |
|---|---|---|---|---|
| 360th | February 10, 1944 | (.5)FW-190 dest(air)* | Ruhlertwist | P-47 |

0.5-0-0 air
0-0 ground

* - shared with Lt. L.F. Kress of the 360th Ftr Sqn

**Dunn, Donald R., Lt.**
436th Ftr Sqn/479th Ftr Grp

| *Sqn* | *Date* | *Claims* | *Location* | *A/C* |
|---|---|---|---|---|
| 436th | September 28, 1944 | (3)FW-190 dest(air) | W/Magdeburg | P-38 |

3-0-0 air
0-0 ground

**Dunn, John W., Lt.**
362nd Ftr Sqn/357th Ftr Grp

| *Sqn* | *Date* | *Claims* | *Location* | *A/C* |
|---|---|---|---|---|
| 362nd | April 10, 1945 | He-111 dest(grd) | Neuruppin | P-51 |
| | | Do-217 dest(grd) | Neuruppin | P-51 |
| | | (2)He-111 dam(grd) | Neuruppin | P-51 |
| | | FW-190 dam(grd) | Neuruppin | P-51 |

0-0-0 air
2-3 ground

**Dunn, Philip H., Capt.**
336th Ftr Sqn/4th Ftr Grp

| *Sqn* | *Date* | *Claims* | *Location* | *A/C* |
|---|---|---|---|---|
| 336th | March 3, 1944 | He-111 prob(air) | Bordeaux | P-51 |
| | | Me-210 dam(air) | Wittenberg | P-51 |

0-1-1 air
0-0 ground

**Dunn, William K., Lt.**
360th Ftr Sqn/356th Ftr Grp

| *Sqn* | *Date* | *Claims* | *Location* | *A/C* |
|---|---|---|---|---|
| 360th | November 26, 1944 | Me-109 dam(air) | Dummer Lake | P-51 |

0-0-1 air
0-0 ground

**Duppstadt, Arthur G., Lt.**
358th Ftr Sqn/355th Ftr Grp

| *Sqn* | *Date* | *Claims* | *Location* | *A/C* |
|---|---|---|---|---|
| 358th | July 19, 1944 | Ju-88 dest(grd) | Munich | P-51 |
| | | Glider dest(grd) | Munich | P-51 |
| | | Ju-88 dam(grd) | Munich | P-51 |

0-0-0 air
2-1 ground

**Dupree, Charles W., Lt.**
336th Ftr Sqn/4th Ftr Grp

| *Sqn* | *Date* | *Claims* | *Location* | *A/C* |
|---|---|---|---|---|
| 336th | September 11, 1944 | (2)FW-190 dest(grd) | Langensalza | P-51 |
| | September 27 | FW-190 dest(air) | SW Kassel | P-51 |

1-0-0 air
2-0 ground

**Dupuy, John K., Lt.**
361st Ftr Sqn/356th Ftr Grp

| *Sqn* | *Date* | *Claims* | *Location* | *A/C* |
|---|---|---|---|---|
| 361st | February 20, 1945 | Ju-88 dest(grd) | Windleschenlaibach | P-51 |
| | | (.5)u/i a/c dest(grd)* | Windleschenlaibach | P-51 |

0-0-0 air
1.5-0 ground

* - shared with Lt. J.C. Lindsay of the 361st Ftr Sqn

**Duquette, Eugene H., Lt.**
338th Ftr Sqn/55th Ftr Grp

| *Sqn* | *Date* | *Claims* | *Location* | *A/C* |
|---|---|---|---|---|
| 338th | February 15, 1945 | (.5)Hs-129 dest(air)* | Scharndau | P-51 |

0.5-0-0 air
0-0 ground

* - shared with Lt. C.D. Henry of the 338th Ftr Sqn

**Durant, Charles O., Jr., Lt.**
350th Ftr Sqn/353rd Ftr Grp

| *Sqn* | *Date* | *Claims* | *Location* | *A/C* |
|---|---|---|---|---|
| 350th | December 1, 1943 | Me-110 dam(air) | Solingen | P-47 |
| | March 26, 1944 | FW-190 dam(grd) | Chartres | P-47 |
| | April 10 | Me-110 dest(grd) | Villaroche | P-47 |

0-0-1 air
1-1 ground

**Durbin, Richard M., Capt.**
376th Ftr Sqn/361st Ftr Grp
HdQts/361st Ftr Grp

| *Sqn* | *Date* | *Claims* | *Location* | *A/C* |
|---|---|---|---|---|
| 376th | June 25, 1944 | Me-109 dest(air) | S/Le Havre | P-51 |
| | July 7 | FW-190 dam(air) | Halle | P-51 |

1-0-1 air
0-0 ground

**Dustin, Harry H., Lt.**
352nd Ftr Sqn/353rd Ftr Grp

| *Sqn* | *Date* | *Claims* | *Location* | *A/C* |
|---|---|---|---|---|
| 352nd | March 8, 1944 | FW-190 dest(air) | N/Dummer Lake | P-47 |

1-0-0 air
0-0 ground

**Dvorak, Edward J., Lt.**
343rd Ftr Sqn/55th Ftr Grp

| *Sqn* | *Date* | *Claims* | *Location* | *A/C* |
|---|---|---|---|---|
| 343rd | September 10, 1944 | (.5)Hs-126 dest(air)* | Schwabmunchen | P-51 |

0.5-0-0 air
0-0 ground

* - shared with Lt. G.D. Leslie of the 343rd Ftr Sqn

**Dvorak, William J., Capt.**
334th Ftr Sqn/4th Ftr Grp

| *Sqn* | *Date* | *Claims* | *Location* | *A/C* |
|---|---|---|---|---|
| 334th | November 18, 1944 | Me-262 dam(grd) | Leipheim | P-51 |
| | April 16, 1945 | u/i a/c dest(grd) | Gablingen | P-51 |
| | | (2)u/i a/c dam(grd) | Gablingen | P-51 |

0-0-0 air
1-3 ground

**Dwyer, John L., Lt.**
351st Ftr Sqn/353rd Ftr Grp

| *Sqn* | *Date* | *Claims* | *Location* | *A/C* |
|---|---|---|---|---|
| 351st | June 20, 1944 | (.5)He-111 dam(grd)* | Plantlunne | P-47 |

0-0-0 air
0-0.5 ground

* - shared with Capt. G.B. Compton of the 351st Ftr Sqn

**Dwyer, Robert H., Lt.**
383rd Ftr Sqn/364th Ftr Grp

| *Sqn* | *Date* | *Claims* | *Location* | *A/C* |
|---|---|---|---|---|
| 383rd | August 9, 1944 | (2)FW-190 dam(grd) | W/Munich | P-51 |
| | August 15 | Me-109 dest(air) | Frankfurt | P-51 |

1-0-0 air
0-2 ground

**Dye, James D., Capt.**
335th Ftr Sqn/4th Ftr Grp

| *Sqn* | *Date* | *Claims* | *Location* | *A/C* |
|---|---|---|---|---|
| 335th | March 5, 1944 | FW-190 dest(air) | Redon | P-51 |
| | March 6 | Do-217 dest(air) | SW Berlin | P-51 |
| | March 8 | Me-109 dest(air) | Luckenwalde | P-51 |
| | | FW-190 prob(air) | Dahme | P-51 |

3-1-0 air
0-0 ground

**Dyer, Raymond A., Lt.**
334th Ftr Sqn/4th Ftr Grp

| *Sqn* | *Date* | *Claims* | *Location* | *A/C* |
|---|---|---|---|---|
| 334th | November 18, 1944 | (4)Me-262 dam(grd) | Leipheim | P-51 |
| | April 4, 1945 | Me-262 dest(air) | SE Parchim | P-51 |
| | April 16 | FW-190 dest(grd) | Gablingen | P-51 |
| | | Me-109 dest(grd) | Gablingen | P-51 |
| | | u/i a/c dest(grd) | Gablingen | P-51 |
| | | FW-190 dam(grd) | Gablingen | P-51 |
| | | Me-109 dam(grd) | Gablingen | P-51 |
| | | Me-410 dam(grd) | Gablingen | P-51 |

1-0-0 air
3-7 ground

**Dyke, Samuel E., Lt.**
328th Ftr Sqn/352nd Ftr Grp

| *Sqn* | *Date* | *Claims* | *Location* | *A/C* |
|---|---|---|---|---|
| 328th | April 29, 1944 | (.5)FW-190 dest(air)* | Calvorde | P-51 |
| | May 21 | (2)He-111 dest(grd) | Alt Ruppin | P-51 |
| | June 21 | (.5)Me-410 dest(air)** | Dahmsdorf | P-51 |

1-0-0 air
2-0 ground

* - shared with Lt. F.W. Horne of the 328th Ftr Sqn
* - shared with Lt. J.F. Thornell of the 328th Ftr Sqn

**Eadline, Lloyd L., Lt.**
83rd Ftr Sqn/78th Ftr Grp

| *Sqn* | *Date* | *Claims* | *Location* | *A/C* |
|---|---|---|---|---|
| 83rd | October 15, 1944 | FW-190 dest(air) | Bohmte | P-47 |

1-0-0 air
0-0 ground

**Eakes, Harvey L., Lt.**
82nd Ftr Sqn/78th Ftr Grp

| *Sqn* | *Date* | *Claims* | *Location* | *A/C* |
|---|---|---|---|---|
| 82nd | April 1, 1944 | (.13)Do-217 dest(grd)* | Verdun | P-47 |
| | April 5 | (.33)Go-242 dest(grd)** | Ruwer | P-47 |
| | | (.33)DFS-230 dest(grd)** | Ruwer | P-47 |

0-0-0 air
0.79-0 ground

* - shared with Capt. W.L. Boone, Capt. W.E. May, Lt. B.M. Watkins, Lt. C.R. Clark, Lt. J.J. Hockery, Lt. R.V. Hearn, and F/O C.W. DeWitt of the 82nd Ftr Sqn
** - both shared with Lt. J.J. Hockery and F/O C.W. DeWitt of the 82nd Ftr Sqn

**Ealey, Robert E., Capt.**
83rd Ftr Sqn/78th Ftr Grp

| *Sqn* | *Date* | *Claims* | *Location* | *A/C* |
|---|---|---|---|---|
| 83rd | May 19, 1944 | Me-109 dest(air) | Lingen | P-47 |
| | June 10 | Me-109 dest(air) | Argentan | P-47 |

2-0-0 air
0-0 ground

**Eanes, John W., Capt.**
HdQts/353rd Ftr Grp

| *Sqn* | *Date* | *Claims* | *Location* | *A/C* |
|---|---|---|---|---|
| HdQts | September 23, 1944 | FW-190 dest(air) | SE Arnheim | P-47 |

1-0-0 air
0-0 ground

**Earley, John R., III, Lt.**
436th Ftr Sqn/479th Ftr Grp

| *Sqn* | *Date* | *Claims* | *Location* | *A/C* |
|---|---|---|---|---|
| 436th | April 13, 1945 | FW-190 dest(grd) | Salzwedel | P-51 |
| | | Me-110 dest(grd) | Salzwedel | P-51 |
| | | Me-410 dam(grd) | Salzwedel | P-51 |

0-0-0 air
2-1 ground

**Earnest, Wallace H., Lt.**
338th Ftr Sqn/55th Ftr Grp

| *Sqn* | *Date* | *Claims* | *Location* | *A/C* |
|---|---|---|---|---|
| 338th | July 7, 1944 | FW-190 dest(air) | W/Bernburg | P-38 |

1-0-0 air
0-0 ground

**Easterly, William S., Capt.**
357th Ftr Sqn/355th Ftr Grp

| *Sqn* | *Date* | *Claims* | *Location* | *A/C* |
|---|---|---|---|---|
| 357th | December 1, 1943 | Me-109 dam(air) | W/Cologne | P-47 |
| | March 6, 1944 | FW-190 dest(air) | E/Dummer Lake | P-47 |
| | April 11 | Ju-88 dest(grd) | Wensdorf A/F | P-51 |

1-0-1 air
1-0 ground

**Eaton, Alfred F., Capt.**
84th Ftr Sqn/78th Ftr Grp

| *Sqn* | *Date* | *Claims* | *Location* | *A/C* |
|---|---|---|---|---|
| 84th | July 1, 1944 | Me-109 dam(air) | St. Quentin | P-47 |
| | July 19 | (1.5)Do-217 dest(grd)* | Eutingen | P-47 |
| | | Me-410 dest(grd) | Eutingen | P-47 |

0-0-1 air
2.5-0 ground

* - shared with Maj. B.I. Mayo of the 84th Ftr Sqn

**Eaton, Wilbur B., Lt.**
335th Ftr Sqn/4th Ftr Grp

| *Sqn* | *Date* | *Claims* | *Location* | *A/C* |
|---|---|---|---|---|
| 335th | September 13, 1944 | Hs-123 dest(grd) | Gelcheim | P-51 |
| | November 18 | Me-262 dest(grd) | Leipheim | P-51 |
| | | Me-262 dam(grd) | Leipheim | P-51 |

0-0-0 air
2-1 ground

**Eaves, John B., Capt.**
62nd Ftr Sqn/56th Ftr Grp

| *Sqn* | *Date* | *Claims* | *Location* | *A/C* |
|---|---|---|---|---|
| 62nd | October 10, 1943 | Me-109 dest(air) | Altenberge | P-47 |
| | March 8, 1944 | (.5)FW-190 dest(air)* | Celle | P-47 |
| | May 19 | (2)FW-190 dest(air) | N/Hanover | P-47 |
| | October 5 | FW-190 dest(grd) | S/Geseke | P-47 |

3.5-0-0 air
1-0 ground

* - shared with Capt. M.J. Quirk of the 62nd Ftr Sqn

**Eckfeldt, Robert T., Lt.**
374th Ftr Sqn/361st Ftr Grp

| *Sqn* | *Date* | *Claims* | *Location* | *A/C* |
|---|---|---|---|---|
| 374th | April 8, 1944 | Me-109 dest(air) | Dummer Lake | P-47 |
| | May 29 | FW-190 dest(air) | Pitka | P-51 |
| | June 8 | Me-109 dest(air) | St. Pierre | P-51 |
| | June 29 | (4)FW-190 dest(grd) | Oschersleben | P-51 |
| | | (2.5)FW-190 dam(grd)* | Oschersleben | P-51 |

3-0-0 air
4-2.5 ground

* - shared with Lt. V.R. Richards of the 374th Ftr Sqn

**Edens, Billy G., Lt.**
62nd Ftr Sqn/56th Ftr Grp

| *Sqn* | *Date* | *Claims* | *Location* | *A/C* |
|---|---|---|---|---|
| 62nd | June 8, 1944 | (2)Me-109 dest(air) | St. Andre de L'Eure | P-47 |
| | | FW-190 dest(air) | St. Andre de L'Eure | P-47 |
| | July 5 | FW-190 dest(air) | N/Evreux | P-47 |

| Sqn | Date | Claims | Location | A/C |
|---|---|---|---|---|
| | July 7 | (3)Ju-52 dest(air) | Gardelegen A/F | P-47 |
| | August 4 | (2)He-111 dest(grd) | Plantlunne | P-47 |
| | | (2)He-111 dam(grd) | Plantlunne | P-47 |
| | September 8 | u/i a/c dest(grd) | Coblenz | P-47 |

7-0-0 air
3-2 ground

**Edens, Malcolm B., Capt.**
503rd Ftr Sqn/339th Ftr Grp

| *Sqn* | *Date* | *Claims* | *Location* | *A/C* |
|---|---|---|---|---|
| 503rd | November 26, 1944 | (2)FW-190 dest(air) | SE Dummer Lake | P-51 |

2-0-0 air
0-0 ground

**Edwards, David W., Lt.**
375th Ftr Sqn/361st Ftr Grp

| *Sqn* | *Date* | *Claims* | *Location* | *A/C* |
|---|---|---|---|---|
| 375th | August 5, 1944 | Me-109 dest(air) | S/Bremen | P-51 |

1-0-0 air
0-0 ground

**Edwards, Harry L., Lt.**
486th Ftr Sqn/352nd Ftr Grp

| *Sqn* | *Date* | *Claims* | *Location* | *A/C* |
|---|---|---|---|---|
| 486th | November 2, 1944 | Me-109 dest(air) | Merseburg | P-51 |
| | December 9 | Me-262 dest(air) | Kircheim | P-51 |

2-0-0 air
0-0 ground

**Edwards, John C., LtCol.**
HdQts/352nd Ftr Grp

| *Sqn* | *Date* | *Claims* | *Location* | *A/C* |
|---|---|---|---|---|
| HdQts | May 8, 1944 | FW-190 dam(air) | Neinburg | P-51 |
| | May 27 | Me-109 dest(air) | Karlsruhe | P-51 |
| | July 13 | Me-109 dest(air) | SE Strasbourg | P-51 |

2-0-1 air
0-0 ground

**Edwards, Robert F., Lt.**
385th Ftr Sqn/364th Ftr Grp

| *Sqn* | *Date* | *Claims* | *Location* | *A/C* |
|---|---|---|---|---|
| 385th | November 21, 1944 | FW-190 dest(air) | Eisleben | P-51 |

1-0-0 air
0-0 ground

**Edwards, Trevor A., Lt.**
62nd Ftr Sqn/56th Ftr Grp

| *Sqn* | *Date* | *Claims* | *Location* | *A/C* |
|---|---|---|---|---|
| 62nd | September 5, 1944 | FW-190 dest(grd) | Gelnhausen | P-47 |
| | | FW-190 dam(grd) | Gelnhausen | P-47 |

0-0-0 air
1-1 ground

**Egan, Joseph L., Jr., Capt.**
63rd Ftr Sqn/56th Ftr Grp

| *Sqn* | *Date* | *Claims* | *Location* | *A/C* |
|---|---|---|---|---|
| 63rd | August 19, 1943 | FW-190 dest(air) | Tholen Island | P-47 |
| | January 30, 1944 | Me-210 dest(air) | S/Quackenbruck | P-47 |
| | February 21 | Me-109 dest(air) | Elburg | P-47 |
| | February 22 | Me-109 dest(air) | Munster | P-47 |
| | | FW-190 dam(air) | Munster | P-47 |
| | March 15 | FW-190 dest(air) | Nienburg | P-47 |

5-0-1 air
0-0 ground

**Egeland, Howard B., Lt.**
362nd Ftr Sqn/357th Ftr Grp

| *Sqn* | *Date* | *Claims* | *Location* | *A/C* |
|---|---|---|---|---|
| 362nd | September 18, 1944 | Me-109 dest(air) | Nijmegen | P-51 |

1-0-0 air
0-0 ground

**Egenes, Hubert I., LtCol.**
362nd Ftr Sqn/357th Ftr Grp
HdQts/357th Ftr Grp
Earlier flew in the PTO with the 17th Prov. Sqn and 35th Ftr Grp claiming 1 kill on February 14, 1942.

| *Sqn* | *Date* | *Claims* | *Location* | *A/C* |
|---|---|---|---|---|
| 362nd | February 22, 1944 | FW-190 dam(air) | E/Magdeburg | P-51 |
| HdQts | March 6 | Me-110 dam(air) | W/Berlin | P-51 |
| | March 16 | (2)Me-109 dest(air) | SW Stuttgart | P-51 |

2-0-2 air
0-0 ground

**Eggleston, Troy L., Lt.**
82nd Ftr Sqn/78th Ftr Grp

| *Sqn* | *Date* | *Claims* | *Location* | *A/C* |
|---|---|---|---|---|
| 82nd | August 27, 1944 | (.5)He-111 dest(grd)* | Chatel-Cherary | P-47 |
| | September 10 | (3)He-111 dest(grd) | Meinbullen | P-47 |

0-0-0 air
3.5-0 ground

* - shared with Lt. R.L. Wolfe of the 82nd Ftr Sqn

**Einhaus, Lowell E., Capt.**
77th Ftr Sqn/20th Ftr Grp

| *Sqn* | *Date* | *Claims* | *Location* | *A/C* |
|---|---|---|---|---|
| 77th | February 9, 1945 | (6)FW-190 dest(grd) | Esperstadt A/F | P-51 |

0-0-0 air
6-0 ground

**Eisenhart, Lee D., Capt.**
504th Ftr Sqn/339th Ftr Grp

| *Sqn* | *Date* | *Claims* | *Location* | *A/C* |
|---|---|---|---|---|
| 504th | May 21, 1944 | FW-190 dest(grd) | W/Leipzig | P-51 |
| | June 29 | FW-190 dest(air) | Nordhausen | P-51 |

1-0-0 air
1-0 ground

**Eisenhut, Van C., Lt.**
376th Ftr Sqn/361st Ftr Grp

| *Sqn* | *Date* | *Claims* | *Location* | *A/C* |
|---|---|---|---|---|
| 376th | April 16, 1945 | FW-190 dest(grd) | Reichersberg | P-51 |
| | | Fi-156 dam(grd) | Halndorf | P-51 |

0-0-0 air
1-1 ground

**Ekstrom, Carl F., Capt.**
358th Ftr Sqn/355th Ftr Grp

| *Sqn* | *Date* | *Claims* | *Location* | *A/C* |
|---|---|---|---|---|
| 358th | October 4, 1943 | Me-109 dest(air) | Leige-Maastricht | P-47 |
| | December 1 | Me-109 dam(air) | Duren | P-47 |

1-0-1 air
0-0 ground

**Elder, John L., Jr., LtCol.**
357th Ftr Sqn/355th Ftr Grp

| *Sqn* | *Date* | *Claims* | *Location* | *A/C* |
|---|---|---|---|---|
| 357th | February 21, 1944 | FW-190 dest(air) | Dummer Lake | P-47 |
| | March 27 | Ju-88 dam(grd) | Biscarosse A/F | P-51 |
| | March 29 | FW-190 dest(air) | NE Brunswick | P-51 |
| | | FW-190 dam(air) | NE Brunswick | P-51 |
| | April 8 | (2)Ju-88 dest(grd) | Gifhorn | P-51 |
| | April 15 | Me-109 dest(air) | E/Celle | P-51 |
| | August 14 | Ju-88 dest(grd) | Saareburg | P-51 |
| | August 16 | (2)Me-109 dest(air) | SE Hildesheim | P-51 |
| | September 18 | Me-109 dest(air) | NW Warsaw | P-51 |

| Sqn | Date | Claims | Location | A/C |
|---|---|---|---|---|
| | November 2 | Me-109 dest(air) | Wernigerode | P-51 |
| | | (5)u/i a/c dest(grd) | Wernigerode | P-51 |
| | January 14, 1945 | Me-109 dest(air) | Munster | P-51 |
| | February 23 | Me-109 dest(grd) | Neuburg | P-51 |
| | | Me-109 dam(grd) | Neuburg | P-51 |
| | April 16 | (2)FW-190 dest(grd) | SE Germany | P-51 |
| | | (2)u/i a/c dest(grd) | SE Germany | P-51 |
| | | (3)u/i a/c dam(grd) | SE Germany | P-51 |

8-0-1 air
13-5 ground

**Elder, Robert A., LtCol.**
350th Ftr Sqn/353rd Ftr Grp
HdQts/353rd Ftr Grp

| *Sqn* | *Date* | *Claims* | *Location* | *A/C* |
|---|---|---|---|---|
| HdQts | March 24, 1945 | (4)FW-190 dest(air) | NW Kassel | P-51 |
| | | Me-109 dest(air) | NW Kassel | P-51 |
| | | Me-109 dam(air) | NW Kassel | P-51 |
| | April 16 | FW-190 dest(grd) | Pocking | P-51 |
| | | Ju-87 dest(grd) | Pocking | P-51 |
| | | (3)Ju-87 dam(grd) | Pocking | P-51 |
| | | Me-109 dam(grd) | Pocking | P-51 |

5-0-1 air
2-4 ground

**Elffner, Thomas H., Lt.**
335th Ftr Sqn/4th Ftr Grp

| *Sqn* | *Date* | *Claims* | *Location* | *A/C* |
|---|---|---|---|---|
| 335th | April 9, 1945 | (2)Me-410 dest(grd) | Munich-Brunnthal | P-51 |

0-0-0 air
2-0 ground

**Eliades, Jordan, Lt.**
343rd Ftr Sqn/55th Ftr Grp

| *Sqn* | *Date* | *Claims* | *Location* | *A/C* |
|---|---|---|---|---|
| 343rd | November 2, 1944 | (.5)Me-109 dest(air)* | SW Leipzig | P-51 |

0.5-0-0 air
0-0 ground

* - shared with Lt. R.D. Bartlett of the 343rd Ftr Sqn

**Elin, Herbert W., Lt.**
84th Ftr Sqn/78th Ftr Grp

| *Sqn* | *Date* | *Claims* | *Location* | *A/C* |
|---|---|---|---|---|
| 84th | September 1, 1944 | FW-190 dam(grd) | SW Antwerp | P-47 |

0-0-0 air
0-1 ground

**Ellingson, Bertrum E., Capt.**
360th Ftr Sqn/356th Ftr Grp

| *Sqn* | *Date* | *Claims* | *Location* | *A/C* |
|---|---|---|---|---|
| 360th | February 13, 1944 | Me-109 dest(air) | Chartres | P-47 |
| | December 25 | FW-190 dest(air) | S/Bonn | P-51 |
| | | Me-109 dest(air) | SW Bonn | P-51 |

3-0-0 air
0-0 ground

**Ellington, Paul M., Capt.**
335th Ftr Sqn/4th Ftr Grp

| *Sqn* | *Date* | *Claims* | *Location* | *A/C* |
|---|---|---|---|---|
| 335th | January 31, 1944 | Me-109 dest(air) | Overflakkee | P-47 |
| | February 20 | Me-110 dest(air) | Coblenz | P-47 |

2-0-0 air
0-0 ground

**Elliott, Frank B., LtCol.**
2nd Scouting Force

| *Sqn* | *Date* | *Claims* | *Location* | *A/C* |
|---|---|---|---|---|
| 2nd | March 1, 1945 | Me-262 dam(air) | Ingolstadt | P-51 |
| | April 16 | (2)u/i a/c dest(grd) | SE Germany | P-51 |
| | | FW-190 dest(grd) | SE Germany | P-51 |
| | | FW-190 dam(grd) | SE Germany | P-51 |

0-0-1 air
3-1 ground

**Elliott, Miles E., Lt.**
375th Ftr Sqn/361st Ftr Grp

| *Sqn* | *Date* | *Claims* | *Location* | *A/C* |
|---|---|---|---|---|
| 375th | June 20, 1944 | (.5)BV-138 dam(grd)* | Putnitz | P-51 |

0-0-0 air
0-0.5 ground

* - shared with Lt. W.D. Rogers of the 375th Ftr Sqn

**Elliott, Robert H., Lt.**
368th Ftr Sqn/359th Ftr Grp

| *Sqn* | *Date* | *Claims* | *Location* | *A/C* |
|---|---|---|---|---|
| 368th | April 9, 1945 | (2)Ju-88 dam(grd) | Munich | P-51 |

0-0-0 air
0-2 ground

**Elliott, Virgil L., Lt.**
62nd Ftr Sqn/56th Ftr Grp

| *Sqn* | *Date* | *Claims* | *Location* | *A/C* |
|---|---|---|---|---|
| 62nd | April 13, 1945 | (2)Do-217 dest(grd) | Eggebeck A/F | P-47 |
| | | Ju-88 dam(grd) | Eggebeck A/F | P-47 |

0-0-0 air
2-1 ground

**Ellis, Edmund E., Lt.**
61st Ftr Sqn/56th Ftr Grp

| *Sqn* | *Date* | *Claims* | *Location* | *A/C* |
|---|---|---|---|---|
| 61st | April 10, 1945 | Do-217 dest(grd) | Oranienburg | P-47 |
| | | He-177 dest(grd) | Oranienburg | P-47 |
| | | u/i a/c dest(grd) | Oranienburg | P-47 |
| | | (4)u/i a/c dam(grd) | Oranienburg | P-47 |

0-0-0 air
3-4 ground

**Ellison, Charles E., Lt.**
487th Ftr Sqn/352nd Ftr Grp

| *Sqn* | *Date* | *Claims* | *Location* | *A/C* |
|---|---|---|---|---|
| 487th | July 18, 1944 | (3)Ju-88 dest(air) | SE Rostock | P-51 |
| | August 25 | Me-110 dam(grd) | Neubrandenburg | P-51 |

3-0-0 air
0-1 ground

**Ellison, John C., Lt.**
354th Ftr Sqn/355th Ftr Grp

| *Sqn* | *Date* | *Claims* | *Location* | *A/C* |
|---|---|---|---|---|
| 354th | June 24, 1944 | (2)Me-109 dest(grd) | Seiches | P-51 |

0-0-0 air
2-0 ground

**Elmgren, Charles B., Lt.**
436th Ftr Sqn/479th Ftr Grp

| *Sqn* | *Date* | *Claims* | *Location* | *A/C* |
|---|---|---|---|---|
| 436th | April 16, 1945 | (4)FW-190 dest(grd) | Landstadt | P-51 |
| | April 17 | (2)Fi-156 dest(grd) | Karlsbad | P-51 |
| | | u/i a/c dest(grd) | Karlsbad | P-51 |

0-0-0 air
7-0 ground

**Elsey, George V., Capt.**
82nd Ftr Sqn/78th Ftr Grp

| Sqn | Date | Claims | Location | A/C |
|---|---|---|---|---|
| 82nd | March 19, 1945 | Me-109 dam(air) | Osnabruck | P-51 |
| | April 10 | FW-190 dest(grd) | Werder A/F | P-51 |
| | April 16 | Me-109 dest(grd) | Pilzen/Prague | P-51 |
| | | Me-109 dam(grd) | Pilzen/Prague | P-51 |

0-0-1 air
2-1 ground

**Eluhow, Raymond, Lt.**
352nd Ftr Sqn/353rd Ftr Grp

| Sqn | Date | Claims | Location | A/C |
|---|---|---|---|---|
| 352nd | July 30, 1944 | (2)u/i a/c dest(grd) | Orleans-Bricy | P-47 |
| | August 12 | (.5)u/i a/c dest(grd)[*] | E/Paris | P-47 |

0-0-0 air
2.5-0 ground

[*] - shared with Lt. W.J. Jordan of the 352nd Ftr Sqn

**Emerson, Donald R., Capt.**
336th Ftr Sqn/4th Ftr Grp

| Sqn | Date | Claims | Location | A/C |
|---|---|---|---|---|
| 336th | March 21, 1944 | FW-190 prob(air) | SW Evreux | P-51 |
| | March 27 | (.5)Ju-88 dest(grd)[*] | Cazaux A/F | P-51 |
| | April 5 | (.5)Ju-88 dest(grd)[**] | Stendal | P-51 |
| | | (.5)Ju-88 dest(grd)[***] | Stendal | P-51 |
| | | Ju-88 dam(grd) | Stendal | P-51 |
| | April 18 | Me-109 dest(grd) | Wazendorf A/F | P-51 |
| | April 22 | (.5)Me-109 dest(air)[@] | SW Kassel | P-51 |
| | May 29 | (.5)Me-110 dest(air)[@@] | N/Falkenberg | P-51 |
| | | Do-18 dam(grd) | N/Falkenberg | P-51 |
| | June 20 | FW-190 dest(air) | S/Anklam | P-51 |
| | July 2 | (.5)Me-109 dest(air)[#] | W/Budapest | P-51 |
| | November 18 | Me-109 dam(grd) | Leipheim | P-51 |
| | December 25 | (2)FW-190 dest(air) | SW Coblenz | P-51 |

4.5-1-0 air
2.5-3 ground

[*] - shared with Maj. J.A. Clark of HdQts, 4th Ftr Grp
[**] - shared with Maj. J.A. Goodson of the 336th Ftr Sqn
[***] - shared with an unknown pilot
[@] - shared with Lt. K.E. Carlson of the 336th Ftr Sqn
[@@] - shared with Lt. C.J. Netting of the 336th Ftr Sqn
[#] - shared with Capt. D.H. Higgins of the 352nd Ftr Grp

**Emory, Frank N., Capt.**
351st Ftr Sqn/353rd Ftr Grp

| Sqn | Date | Claims | Location | A/C |
|---|---|---|---|---|
| 351st | November 5, 1943 | Me-210 dam(air) | Rheinburg | P-47 |
| | February 10, 1944 | FW-190 dest(air) | Lingen | P-47 |
| | February 22 | (.25)FW-190 dam(grd)[*] | NE Bonn | P-47 |
| | | (.25)FW-190 dam(grd)[*] | NE Bonn | P-47 |
| | June 8 | FW-190 dest(air) | SW Angars | P-47 |
| | March 21, 1945 | (2)Me-109 dest(grd) | Achmer | P-51 |
| | | FW-190 dam(grd) | Achmer | P-51 |
| | | u/i a/c dam(grd) | Achmer | P-51 |
| | April 9 | (2)Me-262 dest(grd) | S/Neubiberg | P-51 |
| | | Me-410 dest(grd) | S/Neubiberg | P-51 |
| | | u/i a/c dest(grd) | S/Neubiberg | P-51 |
| | April 16 | (2)FW-190 dest(grd) | Reichersberg | P-51 |
| | | Ju-87 dest(grd) | Reichersberg | P-51 |
| | | u/i a/c dest(grd) | Reichersberg | P-51 |
| | | FW-190 dam(grd) | Reichersberg | P-51 |
| | | Me-110 dam(grd) | Reichersberg | P-51 |

2-0-1 air
10-4.5 ground

[*] - both shared with Maj. W.C. Beckham, Lt. G.B. Compton, and Lt. G.F. Perpente of the 351st Ftr Sqn

**Engel, Gardner W., Capt.**
359th Ftr Sqn/356th Ftr Grp

| Sqn | Date | Claims | Location | A/C |
|---|---|---|---|---|
| 359th | February 10, 1944 | (.33)FW-190 dest(air)[*] | Meppen | P-47 |
| | March 6 | Me-109 prob(air) | Nienburg | P-47 |
| | June 7 | Ju-52 dest(grd) | Laval | P-47 |

0.33-1-0 air
1-0 ground

[*] - shared with Capt. E.J. White and Lt. R.D. Bradshaw of the 359th Ftr Sqn

**Engelbreit, Joseph C., Capt.**
357th Ftr Sqn/355th Ftr Grp

| Sqn | Date | Claims | Location | A/C |
|---|---|---|---|---|
| 357th | May 21, 1944 | (.5)Me-108 dest(air)[*] | W/Schwerin | P-51 |
| | | Do-217 dest(grd) | SE Schwerin | P-51 |
| | | (2)Do-217 dam(grd) | SE Schwerin | P-51 |
| | November 2 | u/i a/c dest(grd) | Wernigerode | P-51 |

0.5-0-0 air
2-2 ground

[*] - shared with Lt. W.E. MacFarlane of the 357th Ftr Sqn

**Engelhorn, Homer M., Capt.**
361st Ftr Sqn/356th Ftr Grp

| Sqn | Date | Claims | Location | A/C |
|---|---|---|---|---|
| 361st | May 19, 1944 | Me-109 dest(air) | Quackenbruck | P-47 |

1-0-0 air
0-0 ground

**England, John B., Maj.**
362nd Ftr Sqn/357th Ftr Grp

| Sqn | Date | Claims | Location | A/C |
|---|---|---|---|---|
| 362nd | March 8, 1944 | Me-109 dest(air) | Steinhuder Lake | P-51 |
| | March 16 | Me-110 dest(air) | S/Stuttgart | P-51 |
| | April 11 | (.5)Me-109 dest(air)[*] | NE Magdeburg | P-51 |
| | April 13 | FW-190 dest(air) | W/Mannheim | P-51 |
| | April 24 | (3)Me-110 dest(air) | S/Munich | P-51 |
| | May 27 | Me-109 dest(air) | N/Strasbourg | P-51 |
| | August 18 | (.5)Me-109 dest(air)[**] | NE Paris | P-51 |
| | September 13 | (2.5)Me-109 dest(air)[@] | S/Nordhausen | P-51 |
| | October 6 | (2)Me-109 dest(air) | NW Berlin | P-51 |
| | | Me-109 dam(air) | NW Berlin | P-51 |
| | November 18 | Me-109 dest(grd) | Mengen A/F | P-51 |
| | November 27 | (4)FW-190 dest(air) | S/Magdeburg | P-51 |
| | January 14, 1945 | Me-109 dest(air) | NW Berlin | P-51 |

17.5-0-1 air
1-0 ground

[*] - shared with Lt. H.R. Ankeny of the 362nd Ftr Sqn
[**] - shared with Lt. W.N. Perry of the 362nd Ftr Sqn
[@] - shared with Lt. S.G. Fuller of the 362nd Ftr Sqn

**Erb, Russell W., Jr., Lt.**
343rd Ftr Sqn/55th Ftr Grp

| Sqn | Date | Claims | Location | A/C |
|---|---|---|---|---|
| 343rd | November 2, 1944 | Me-109 dest(air) | W/Merseburg | P-51 |

1-0-0 air
0-0 ground

**Erby, Philip A., Lt.**
343rd Ftr Sqn/55th Ftr Grp

| Sqn | Date | Claims | Location | A/C |
|---|---|---|---|---|
| 343rd | March 21, 1945 | FW-190 dest(grd) | Hopsten A/F | P-51 |
| | March 30 | Me-262 dam(air) | SW Lubeck A/F | P-51 |
| | April 17 | FW-190 dest(air) | Kamenz A/F | P-51 |

1-0-1 air
1-0 ground

**Erfkamp, Willard G., Lt.**
385th Ftr Sqn/364th Ftr Grp

| Sqn | Date | Claims | Location | A/C |
|---|---|---|---|---|
| 385th | July 6, 1944 | FW-190 dam(air) | Chalons | P-38 |
| | August 9 | Me-210 dest(grd) | Gaukonigshafen | P-51 |
| | | Me-210 dam(grd) | Gaukonigshafen | P-51 |
| | October 7 | (.5)Me-163 dest(air)[*] | Brux | P-51 |
| | December 23 | (2)Me-109 dest(air) | Luxembourg | P-51 |

2.5-0-1 air
1-1 ground

[*] - shared with Capt. E.A. Taylor of the 385th Ftr Sqn

**Erickson, Earl E., Lt.**
503rd Ftr Sqn/339th Ftr Grp

| *Sqn* | *Date* | *Claims* | *Location* | *A/C* |
|---|---|---|---|---|
| 503rd | May 21, 1944 | u/i a/c dest(grd) | Pelenz-Meckau | P-51 |
| | September 5 | (.5)Me-109 dest(air)[*] | Schaffhausen | P-51 |
| | September 11 | FW-190 dest(air) | Annaberg | P-51 |
| | | FW-190 prob(air) | Annaberg | P-51 |

1.5-1-0 air
1-0 ground

[*] - shared with Lt. N. Ostrow of the 503rd Ftr Sqn

**Erickson, Juel E., Lt.**
357th Ftr Sqn/355th Ftr Grp

| *Sqn* | *Date* | *Claims* | *Location* | *A/C* |
|---|---|---|---|---|
| 357th | September 12, 1944 | FW-190 dam(air) | E/Muritz Lake | P-51 |
| | November 2 | (4)u/i a/c dest(grd) | Wernigerode | P-51 |

0-0-1 air
4-0 ground

**Erickson, Milton F., Lt.**
361st Ftr Sqn/356th Ftr Grp

| *Sqn* | *Date* | *Claims* | *Location* | *A/C* |
|---|---|---|---|---|
| 361st | January 24, 1944 | (.5)FW-190 dest(air)[*] | Ghent-Bruges | P-47 |

0.5-0-0 air
0-0 ground

[*] - shared with Lt. R.H. Gansberg of the 361st Ftr Sqn

**Erickson, Robert E., Lt.**
38th Ftr Sqn/55th Ftr Grp

| *Sqn* | *Date* | *Claims* | *Location* | *A/C* |
|---|---|---|---|---|
| 38th | November 26, 1943 | FW-190 dam(air) | W/Bremen | P-38 |
| | November 29 | Me-109 dam(air) | W/Bremen | P-38 |

0-0-2 air
0-0 ground

**Erickson, Wayne R., Lt.**
343rd Ftr Sqn/55th Ftr Grp

| *Sqn* | *Date* | *Claims* | *Location* | *A/C* |
|---|---|---|---|---|
| 343rd | March 3, 1945 | Me-110 dest(grd) | Prague/Letnany | P-51 |
| | | Me-109 dam(grd) | Prague/Letnany | P-51 |
| | | Ju-88 dam(grd) | Prague/Letnany | P-51 |

0-0-0 air
1-2 ground

**Ernst, Carl V., Capt.**
436th Ftr Sqn/479th Ftr Grp

| *Sqn* | *Date* | *Claims* | *Location* | *A/C* |
|---|---|---|---|---|
| 436th | December 23, 1944 | Me-109 dest(air) | Cologne | P-51 |
| | April 16, 1945 | He-111 dest(grd) | Landstadt | P-51 |

1-0-0 air
1-0 ground

**Eshelman, Francis L., Lt.**
357th Ftr Sqn/355th Ftr Grp

| *Sqn* | *Date* | *Claims* | *Location* | *A/C* |
|---|---|---|---|---|
| 357th | May 28, 1944 | Me-109 dest(air) | N/Limburg | P-51 |
| | July 7 | Me-109 dam(air) | Nordhausen | P-51 |

1-0-1 air
0-0 ground

**Eskridge, John R., Lt.**
338th Ftr Sqn/55th Ftr Grp

| *Sqn* | *Date* | *Claims* | *Location* | *A/C* |
|---|---|---|---|---|
| 338th | August 10, 1944 | Me-109 dest(air) | Damville | P-51 |

1-0-0 air
0-0 ground

**Ethridge, Jack R., Lt.**
338th Ftr Sqn/55th Ftr Grp

| *Sqn* | *Date* | *Claims* | *Location* | *A/C* |
|---|---|---|---|---|
| 338th | April 17, 1945 | (.5)u/i a/c dest(grd)[*] | Leipzig | P-51 |

0-0-0 air
0.5-0 ground

[*] - shared with Maj. E.E. Ryan of the 338th Ftr Sqn

**Ettleson, Charles C., Capt.**
369th Ftr Sqn/359th Ftr Grp
368th Ftr Sqn/359th Ftr Grp

| *Sqn* | *Date* | *Claims* | *Location* | *A/C* |
|---|---|---|---|---|
| 369th | February 10, 1944 | Me-109 dest(air) | Dummer Lake | P-47 |
| | March 29 | u/i a/c dam(grd) | Dummer Lake | P-47 |
| | May 8 | Me-109 dest(air) | Hermansburg | P-51 |
| | May 12 | (.5)u/i a/c dest(grd)[*] | Thamsbruck A/F | P-51 |
| | | u/i a/c dam(grd) | Thamsbruck A/F | P-51 |
| | May 19 | (.5)Me-109 dest(air)[**] | NW Berlin | P-51 |
| 368th | February 9, 1945 | u/i a/c dam(grd) | Halle | P-51 |

2.5-0-0 air
0.5-3 ground

[*] - shared with Lt. R.L. Thacker of the 369th Ftr Sqn
[**] - shared with Lt. E. Zellner of the 352nd Ftr Grp

**Eubanks, Jack O., Lt.**
385th Ftr Sqn/364th Ftr Grp

| *Sqn* | *Date* | *Claims* | *Location* | *A/C* |
|---|---|---|---|---|
| 385th | August 15, 1944 | Me-109 dest(air) | Frankfurt | P-51 |
| | August 25 | Ju-88 dest(grd) | Anklam | P-51 |

1-0-0 air
1-0 ground

**Euler, Howard A., Capt.**
375th Ftr Sqn/361st Ftr Grp

| *Sqn* | *Date* | *Claims* | *Location* | *A/C* |
|---|---|---|---|---|
| 375th | April 4, 1945 | Me-262 dam(air) | S/Hamburg | P-51 |

0-0-1 air
0-0 ground

**Evans, Andrew J., Jr., LtCol.**
HdQts/357th Ftr Grp

| *Sqn* | *Date* | *Claims* | *Location* | *A/C* |
|---|---|---|---|---|
| HdQts | November 27, 1944 | FW-190 dest(air) | S/Magdeburg | P-51 |
| | January 14, 1945 | (2)FW-190 dest(air) | NW Brandenburg | P-51 |
| | | (2)Me-109 dest(air) | NW Brandenburg | P-51 |
| | March 24 | Me-109 dest(air) | W/Gutersloh | P-51 |
| | April 10 | He-111 dest(grd) | Neuruppin | P-51 |
| | | Me-210 dest(grd) | Neuruppin | P-51 |
| | | He-111 dam(grd) | Neuruppin | P-51 |
| | | Me-210 dam(grd) | Neuruppin | P-51 |
| | | Do-217 dam(grd) | Neuruppin | P-51 |
| | | He-177 dam(grd) | Neuruppin | P-51 |

6-0-0 air
2-4 ground

**Evans, James R., Lt.**
352nd Ftr Sqn/353rd Ftr Grp

| *Sqn* | *Date* | *Claims* | *Location* | *A/C* |
|---|---|---|---|---|
| 352nd | November 8, 1944 | (.5)Ju-88 dam(grd)[*] | Plantlunne | P-51 |
| | November 27 | Me-109 dest(air) | Magdeburg | P-51 |
| | December 5 | (2)FW-190 dest(air) | NE Berlin | P-51 |
| | | FW-190 prob(air) | NE Berlin | P-51 |
| | January 14, 1945 | (.5)u/i a/c dam(grd)[**] | Brandenburg-Briest | P-51 |
| | | (.5)u/i a/c dam(grd)[**] | Brandenburg-Briest | P-51 |
| | February 23 | He-177 dest(grd) | Kitzingen | P-51 |
| | | (.5)Me-110 dest(grd)[@] | Kitzingen | P-51 |

3-1-0 air
1.5-1.5 ground

[*] - shared with Capt. L.P. Cles of the 352nd Ftr Sqn
[**] - both shared with F/O R.C. Hassell of the 352nd Ftr Sqn
[@] - shared with Lt. L.O. Pletz of the 352nd Ftr Sqn

**Evans, Roy W., LtCol.**
335th Ftr Sqn/ 4th Ftr Grp
HdQts/359th Ftr Grp

| *Sqn* | *Date* | *Claims* | *Location* | *A/C* |
|---|---|---|---|---|
| 335th | November 21, 1942 | Fi-156 dest(air) | SE Furnes | Spit |
| | July 28, 1943 | Me-109 dest(air) | W/Arnheim | P-47 |
| | | FW-190 dam(air) | W/Arnheim | P-47 |
| | August 16 | Me-109 dest(air) | S/Paris | P-47 |
| | September 6 | FW-190 dest(air) | N/Chateau Thierry | P-47 |
| | October 8 | Me-109 dest(air) | SW Oldenburg | P-47 |
| HdQts | November 26, 1944 | Me-109 dest(air) | Kassel | P-51 |
| | | Me-109 dam(air) | Kassel | P-51 |

6-0-2 air
0-0 ground

**Everett, Harold M., Lt.**
505th Ftr Sqn/339th Ftr Grp

| *Sqn* | *Date* | *Claims* | *Location* | *A/C* |
|---|---|---|---|---|
| 505th | May 9, 1944 | Me-109 dest(air) | Vouziers | P-51 |
| | | Me-109 dam(air) | Vouziers | P-51 |
| | May 21 | (.5)Ju-88 dest(air)* | Schwepnitz | P-51 |
| | May 24 | (2)FW-190 dest(air) | St. Quentin | P-51 |

3.5-0-1 air
0-0 ground

* - shared with Lt. W.F. Mudge of the 505th Ftr Sqn

**Everson, Kirke B., Capt.**
504th Ftr Sqn/339th Ftr Grp

| *Sqn* | *Date* | *Claims* | *Location* | *A/C* |
|---|---|---|---|---|
| 504th | April 4, 1945 | (.5)Me-262 dest(air)* | Parchim A/F | P-51 |
| | April 7 | Me-109 dest(air) | Celle | P-51 |
| | April 10 | (3)Me-410 dest(grd) | N/Neuruppin | P-51 |
| | | (3)Me-410 dam(grd) | N/Neuruppin | P-51 |
| | | (2)Me-110 dam(grd) | N/Neuruppin | P-51 |
| | April 16 | (3)FW-190 dest(grd) | Klatovy | P-51 |
| | April 17 | (2)Me-109 dest(grd) | Klatovy/Anberg | P-51 |
| | | (2)Fi-156 dest(grd) | Klatovy/Anberg | P-51 |
| | | (2)Ju-88 dest(grd) | Klatovy/Anberg | P-51 |
| | | Me-210 dest(grd) | Klatovy/Anberg | P-51 |

1.5-0-0 air
13-5 ground

* - shared with Lt. R.C. Croker of the 504th Ftr Sqn

**Ewing, Philip H., Lt.**
505th Ftr Sqn/339th Ftr Grp

| *Sqn* | *Date* | *Claims* | *Location* | *A/C* |
|---|---|---|---|---|
| 505th | May 27, 1944 | Fi-156 dest(grd) | Frankfurt | P-51 |
| | | u/i a/c dest(grd) | Frankfurt | P-51 |

0-0-0 air
2-0 ground

**Fagg, James W., Lt.**
77th Ftr Sqn/20th Ftr Grp

| *Sqn* | *Date* | *Claims* | *Location* | *A/C* |
|---|---|---|---|---|
| 77th | April 8, 1944 | Ju-88 dam(grd) | Salzwedel | P-38 |

0-0-0 air
0-1 ground

**Fahringer, John C., Capt.**
63rd Ftr Sqn/56th Ftr Grp

| *Sqn* | *Date* | *Claims* | *Location* | *A/C* |
|---|---|---|---|---|
| 63rd | December 2, 1944 | (2)Me-109 dest(air) | S/Marburg | P-47 |
| | February 3, 1945 | Me-109 dest(air) | SE Berlin | P-47 |
| | | (2)Me-109 dam(air) | SE Berlin | P-47 |
| | | FW-190 dam(air) | SE Berlin | P-47 |
| | April 5 | Me-262 dest(air) | N/Regensburg | P-47 |
| | April 10 | (4)FW-190 dam(grd) | Stendal | P-47 |
| | April 16 | Ju-88 dam(grd) | Ingolstadt | P-47 |

4-0-3 air
0-5 ground

**Fair, Gene R., Lt.**
343rd Ftr Sqn/55th Ftr Grp

| *Sqn* | *Date* | *Claims* | *Location* | *A/C* |
|---|---|---|---|---|
| 343rd | April 22, 1944 | Me-109 dest(air) | W/Hamm | P-38 |

1-0-0 air
0-0 ground

**Fairweather, Paul D., Lt.**
364th Ftr Sqn/357th Ftr Grp

| *Sqn* | *Date* | *Claims* | *Location* | *A/C* |
|---|---|---|---|---|
| 364th | April 13, 1944 | (.5)Me-109 dest(air)* | Donauworth | P-51 |
| | May 27 | Me-109 dest(air) | Strasbourg | P-51 |

1.5-0-0 air
0-0 ground

* - shared with Lt. R.C. Smith of the 364th Ftr Sqn

**Faison, Edward L., Capt.**
361st Ftr Sqn/356th Ftr Grp

| *Sqn* | *Date* | *Claims* | *Location* | *A/C* |
|---|---|---|---|---|
| 361st | May 13, 1944 | FW-190 prob(air) | Schwerin | P-47 |
| | August 4 | Me-109 dest(air) | Bremen-Hamburg | P-47 |

1-1-0 air
0-0 ground

**Falkner, George E., LtCol.**
436th Ftr Sqn/479th Ftr Grp

| *Sqn* | *Date* | *Claims* | *Location* | *A/C* |
|---|---|---|---|---|
| 436th | April 17, 1945 | u/i a/c dest(grd) | Karlsbad | P-51 |

0-0-0 air
1-0 ground

**Fall, Mack D., Lt.**
79th Ftr Sqn/20th Ftr Grp

| *Sqn* | *Date* | *Claims* | *Location* | *A/C* |
|---|---|---|---|---|
| 79th | January 30, 1944 | (.5)Do-217 dest(air)* | Minden | P-38 |

0.5-0-0 air
0-0 ground

* - shared with Capt. R.P. Gatterdam of the 79th Ftr Sqn

**Falvey, Harold W., F/O**
354th Ftr Sqn/355th Ftr Grp

| *Sqn* | *Date* | *Claims* | *Location* | *A/C* |
|---|---|---|---|---|
| 354th | November 26, 1944 | FW-190 dam(air) | Gifhorn | P-51 |
| | January 15, 1945 | FW-190 dest(grd) | Landsberg | P-51 |
| | | u/i a/c dest(grd) | Landsberg | P-51 |
| | | u/i a/c dam(grd) | Landsberg | P-51 |
| | March 22 | Me-262 dest(grd) | Kitzingen | P-51 |
| | | Me-109 dest(grd) | Wurzburg | P-51 |
| | | Me-262 dam(grd) | Kitzingen | P-51 |
| | April 9 | (.5)Ju-88 dest(grd)* | Memmingen | P-51 |
| | April 10 | Ju-52 dest(grd) | Rechlin/Larz | P-51 |
| | | (.5)He-111 dest(grd)** | Rechlin/Larz | P-51 |
| | | (4)u/i a/c dam(grd) | Rechlin/Larz | P-51 |
| | April 13 | FW-190 dest(grd) | Husum | P-51 |
| | | Ju-88 dest(grd) | Husum | P-51 |
| | | Ju-88 dam(grd) | Husum | P-51 |

0-0-1 air
8-7 ground

* - shared with Lt. J. Jabara of the 354th Ftr Sqn
** - shared with F/O T.R. Hixon of the 354th Ftr Sqn

**Farington, Fred E., Lt.**
334th Ftr Sqn/4th Ftr Grp

| *Sqn* | *Date* | *Claims* | *Location* | *A/C* |
|---|---|---|---|---|
| 334th | March 22, 1945 | FW-190 dest(air) | Furstenwalde A/F | P-51 |

1-0-0 air
0-0 ground

**Farley, Robert H., Lt.**
383rd Ftr Sqn/364th Ftr Grp

| *Sqn* | *Date* | *Claims* | *Location* | *A/C* |
|---|---|---|---|---|
| 383rd | November 21, 1944 | (2)FW-190 dest(air) | Meiningen | P-51 |

2-0-0 air
0-0 ground

**Farmer, James M., Capt.**
84th Ftr Sqn/78th Ftr Grp

| *Sqn* | *Date* | *Claims* | *Location* | *A/C* |
|---|---|---|---|---|
| 84th | November 9, 1944 | Fi-156 dest(grd) | Hanover | P-51 |
| | February 3, 1945 | Ju-87 dest(grd) | Luneburg A/F | P-51 |

0-0-0 air
2-0 ground

**Farmer, Owen P., Capt.**
505th Ftr Sqn/339th Ftr Grp

| *Sqn* | *Date* | *Claims* | *Location* | *A/C* |
|---|---|---|---|---|
| 505th | May 21, 1944 | u/i a/c dam(air) | Oschatz | P-51 |
| | June 27 | (.5)FW-190 dest(air)* | Paris | P-51 |
| | July 31 | (3)u/i a/c dam(grd) | Holzkirchen | P-51 |
| | September 10 | u/i a/c dest(grd) | Weizenburg | P-51 |
| | March 12, 1945 | (1.5)Me-109 dest(air)** | Hellevad | P-51 |
| | April 10 | (2)Ju-88 dest(grd) | N/Neuruppin | P-51 |
| | April 16 | Me-109 dest(grd) | NE Prague | P-51 |
| | | u/i a/c dest(grd) | NE Prague | P-51 |

2-0-1 air
5-3 ground

* - shared with Lt. W.G. Fish of the 505th Ftr Sqn
** - shared with Lt. V.D. Carr of the 505th Ftr Sqn

**Farmer, William L., Lt.**
359th Ftr Sqn/356th Ftr Grp

| *Sqn* | *Date* | *Claims* | *Location* | *A/C* |
|---|---|---|---|---|
| 359th | March 6, 1944 | Me-109 dest(air) | Nienburg | P-47 |
| | April 23 | (.5)Go-242 dam(grd)* | Hagenau | P-47 |
| | May 13 | FW-190 dest(air) | Kiel-Lubeck | P-47 |

2-0-0 air
0-0.5 ground

* - shared with Lt. C.F. Krowiak of the 359th Ftr Sqn

**Farney, Robert J., Lt.**
375th Ftr Sqn/361st Ftr Grp

| *Sqn* | *Date* | *Claims* | *Location* | *A/C* |
|---|---|---|---|---|
| 375th | November 26, 1944 | FW-190 dest(air) | S/Steinhuder Lake | P-51 |
| | January 2, 1945 | Me-109 dest(air) | W/Stuttgart | P-51 |
| | January 25 | Me-109 dest(air) | SE Speyer | P-51 |
| | April 4 | Me-262 dam(air) | S/Hamburg | P-51 |

3-0-1 air
0-0 ground

**Farnsworth, Everett W., Lt.**
384th Ftr Sqn/364th Ftr Grp

| *Sqn* | *Date* | *Claims* | *Location* | *A/C* |
|---|---|---|---|---|
| 384th | November 21, 1944 | (.5)FW-190 dest(air)* | Mulhausen | P-51 |
| | November 30 | Me-109 dest(air) | SE Zeitz | P-51 |
| | December 5 | FW-190 dest(air) | NW Berlin | P-51 |

2.5-0-0 air
0-0 ground

* - shared with Lt. E.H. Duderstadt of the 384th Ftr Sqn

**Farnum, Waldo B., Lt.**
375th Ftr Sqn/361st Ftr Grp

| *Sqn* | *Date* | *Claims* | *Location* | *A/C* |
|---|---|---|---|---|
| 375th | November 26, 1944 | FW-190 dam(air) | NE Steinhuder Lk. | P-51 |

0-0-1 air
0-0 ground

**Farrar, Donald R., Capt.**
375th Ftr Sqn/361st Ftr Grp

| *Sqn* | *Date* | *Claims* | *Location* | *A/C* |
|---|---|---|---|---|
| 375th | January 2, 1945 | Me-109 dest(air) | W/Stuttgart | P-51 |

1-0-0 air
0-0 ground

**Farrell, Everett N., Capt.**
385th Ftr Sqn/364th Ftr Grp

| *Sqn* | *Date* | *Claims* | *Location* | *A/C* |
|---|---|---|---|---|
| 385th | November 2, 1944 | Me-109 dest(air) | N/Merseburg | P-51 |
| | November 21 | FW-190 dest(air) | S/Merseburg | P-51 |
| | December 5 | (2)FW-190 dam(air) | N/Berlin | P-51 |
| | December 27 | Me-109 dest(air) | SE Bonn | P-51 |
| | | FW-190 dest(air) | SE Bonn | P-51 |
| | April 5, 1945 | Me-262 dam(grd) | SW Nurnburg | P-51 |

4-0-2 air
0-1 ground

**Farrell, Thomas P., Capt.**
385th Ftr Sqn/364th Ftr Grp

| *Sqn* | *Date* | *Claims* | *Location* | *A/C* |
|---|---|---|---|---|
| 385th | November 21, 1944 | (.5)FW-190 dest(air)* | Erfurt | P-51 |
| | December 5 | FW-190 dest(air) | N/Berlin | P-51 |
| | December 23 | (2)FW-190 dest(air) | W/Trier | P-51 |
| | March 21, 1945 | FW-190 dest(grd) | Achmer | P-51 |
| | | (3)Ju-188 dam(grd) | Achmer | P-51 |

3.5-0-0 air
1-3 ground

* - shared with Lt. S.L. Lett of the 385th Ftr Sqn

**Faulkner, Robert S., Capt.**
384th Ftr Sqn/364th Ftr Grp

| *Sqn* | *Date* | *Claims* | *Location* | *A/C* |
|---|---|---|---|---|
| 384th | December 27, 1944 | FW-190 dest(air) | S/Coblenz | P-51 |
| | December 31 | (.5)FW-190 dest(air)* | SW Hamburg | P-51 |
| | April 13, 1945 | u/i a/c dam(grd) | Kaltenkirchen | P-51 |

1.5-0-0 air
0-1 ground

* - shared with Lt. D.L. Leftwich of the 384th Ftr Sqn

**Fay, William C., Capt.**
77th Ftr Sqn/20th Ftr Grp

| *Sqn* | *Date* | *Claims* | *Location* | *A/C* |
|---|---|---|---|---|
| 77th | February 9, 1945 | (3)FW-190 dest(grd) | Esperstadt A/F | P-51 |
| | February 20 | W-34 dest(air) | Straubing | P-51 |

1-0-0 air
3-0 ground

**Fecher, Louis A., Lt.**
364th Ftr Sqn/357th Ftr Grp

| *Sqn* | *Date* | *Claims* | *Location* | *A/C* |
|---|---|---|---|---|
| 364th | June 20, 1944 | (.5)Me-109 dest(air)* | Pasewalk | P-51 |

0.5-0-0 air
0-0 ground

* - shared with Maj. J.A. Storch of the 364th Ftr Sqn

**Fees, Edwin W., Lt.**
358th Ftr Sqn/355th Ftr Grp

| *Sqn* | *Date* | *Claims* | *Location* | *A/C* |
|---|---|---|---|---|
| 358th | April 9, 1945 | Me-110 dest(grd) | Heilfingen | P-51 |
| | April 13 | (.5)He-111 dest(grd)* | Schleswig | P-51 |
| | | He-111 dam(grd) | Schleswig | P-51 |

0-0-0 air
1.5-1 ground

* - shared with Lt. C.C. Patrinely of the 358th Ftr Sqn

**Feller, Charles H., Capt.**
375th Ftr Sqn/361st Ftr Grp

| *Sqn* | *Date* | *Claims* | *Location* | *A/C* |
|---|---|---|---|---|
| 375th | April 27, 1944 | He-111 dam(grd) | Etampes | P-47 |

0-0-0 air
0-1 ground

**Fennell, William S., Lt.**
363rd Ftr Sqn/357th Ftr Grp

| *Sqn* | *Date* | *Claims* | *Location* | *A/C* |
|---|---|---|---|---|
| 363rd | June 29, 1944 | (.5)Me-410 dest(air)* | SW Leipzig | P-51 |
| | July 7 | Me-109 dest(air) | N/Leipzig | P-51 |
| | September 18 | (.5)Me-109 dest(air)** | W/Arnheim | P-51 |

2-0-0 air
0-0 ground

* - shared with Capt. J.W. Browning of the 363rd Ftr Sqn
** - shared with Lt. R.S. Fifield of the 363rd Ftr Sqn

**Ferguson, John W., Jr., Capt.**
62nd Ftr Sqn/56th Ftr Grp

| *Sqn* | *Date* | *Claims* | *Location* | *A/C* |
|---|---|---|---|---|
| 62nd | August 4, 1944 | (.5)He-111 dest(grd)* | Plantlunne | P-47 |
| | November 18 | FW-190 dest(air) | E/Hanau | P-47 |

1-0-0 air
0.5-0 ground

* - shared with Col. H. Zemke of HdQts, 56th Ftr Grp

**Fernandes, Irwin W., Lt.**
77th Ftr Sqn/20th Ftr Grp

| *Sqn* | *Date* | *Claims* | *Location* | *A/C* |
|---|---|---|---|---|
| 77th | April 8, 1944 | Do-217 dest(grd) | Salzwedel | P-38 |
| | | (.33)u/i a/c dest(grd)* | Salzwedel | P-38 |
| | | (.5)Ju-52 dam(grd)** | Salzwedel | P-38 |
| | July 7 | FW-190 dest(air) | Halle | P-38 |
| | | FW-190 dam(air) | Halle | P-38 |

1-0-1 air
1.33-0.5 ground

* - shared with Capt. J.M. Morris and Lt. W.F. Kuemmerle of the 77th Ftr Sqn
** - shared with Lt. B.N. Rader of the 77th Ftr Sqn

**Fernandez, Joseph P., Lt.**
334th Ftr Sqn/4th Ftr Grp

| *Sqn* | *Date* | *Claims* | *Location* | *A/C* |
|---|---|---|---|---|
| 334th | May 29, 1944 | (.5)Do-18 dam(grd)* | Dievenow | P-51 |
| | | (.5)Do-18 dam(grd)* | Dievenow | P-51 |
| | June 6 | (.5)FW-190 dest(air)** | Evreux | P-51 |

0.5-0-0 air
0-1 ground

* - both shared with Capt. W.M. Sobanski of the 334th Ftr Sqn
** - shared with Lt. J.T. Simon of the 334th Ftr Sqn

**Ferrell, Arthur K., Lt.**
350th Ftr Sqn/353rd Ftr Grp

| *Sqn* | *Date* | *Claims* | *Location* | *A/C* |
|---|---|---|---|---|
| 350th | November 18, 1944 | He-111 dest(grd) | Lechfeld | P-51 |
| | | He-111 dam(grd) | Lechfeld | P-51 |

0-0-0 air
1-1 ground

**Ferrell, Clarence I., Lt.**
503rd Ftr Sqn/339th Ftr Grp

| *Sqn* | *Date* | *Claims* | *Location* | *A/C* |
|---|---|---|---|---|
| 503rd | April 16, 1945 | (4)Ju-88 dest(grd) | NE Prague | P-51 |
| | | (2)FW-190 dam(grd) | NE Prague | P-51 |

0-0-0 air
4-2 ground

**Fetrow, Gene B., Capt.**
335th Ftr Sqn/4th Ftr Grp

| *Sqn* | *Date* | *Claims* | *Location* | *A/C* |
|---|---|---|---|---|
| 335th | October 2, 1942 | FW-190 dest(air) | SW Dunkirk | Spit |
| | December 6 | FW-190 prob(air) | NE Gris Nez | Spit |
| | January 22, 1943 | FW-190 dam(air) | NW Dunkirk | Spit |

1-1-1 air
0-0 ground

**Fickel, Paul D., Lt.**
503rd Ftr Sqn/339th Ftr Grp

| *Sqn* | *Date* | *Claims* | *Location* | *A/C* |
|---|---|---|---|---|
| 503rd | August 6, 1944 | Me-109 dest(air) | S/Schweriner Lake | P-51 |

1-0-0 air
0-0 ground

**Fiebelkorn, Ernest C., Capt.**
77th Ftr Sqn/20th Ftr Grp

| *Sqn* | *Date* | *Claims* | *Location* | *A/C* |
|---|---|---|---|---|
| 77th | April 8, 1944 | u/i a/c dest(grd) | Salzwedel | P-38 |
| | | (2)Ju-88 dam(grd) | Salzwedel | P-38 |
| | April 30 | Me-410 dest(grd) | Bricy A/F | P-38 |
| | July 14 | (.5)FW-190 dest(air)* | SW Reims | P-38 |
| | August 5 | Me-109 dest(air) | S/Hamburg | P-51 |
| | September 28 | (3)Me-109 dest(air) | S/Magdeburg | P-51 |
| | | FW-190 dest(air) | S/Magdeburg | P-51 |
| | | Me-109 dam(air) | S/Magdeburg | P-51 |
| | November 2 | (3)Me-109 dest(air) | N/Leipzig | P-51 |
| | November 8 | (.5)Me-262 dest(air)** | Dummer Lake | P-51 |

9-0-1 air
2-2 ground

* - shared with Lt. C.C. Arthaud of the 77th Ftr Sqn
** - shared with Lt. E.R. Haydon of the 357th Ftr Grp

**Fiedler, Clemens A., Lt.**
335th Ftr Sqn/4th Ftr Grp

| *Sqn* | *Date* | *Claims* | *Location* | *A/C* |
|---|---|---|---|---|
| 335th | February 20, 1944 | Me-110 dest(air) | Coblenz | P-47 |
| | | Me-110 dam(air) | Coblenz | P-47 |
| | March 8 | Me-109 dam(air) | NE Berlin | P-51 |
| | March 21 | FW-190 dest(grd) | Lans de Bassac | P-51 |
| | March 29 | Me-109 dest(air) | N/Brunswick | P-51 |
| | April 5 | (.33)Ju-88 dest(air)* | Plaue A/F | P-51 |
| | | (2)Ju-88 dam(grd) | Plaue A/F | P-51 |
| | | u/i a/c dam(grd) | Plaue A/F | P-51 |
| | April 8 | (2)Me-109 dest(air) | Wolfenbuttel | P-51 |

4.33-0-2 air
1-3 ground

* - shared with Capt. D.W. Beeson and Lt. H.T. Biel of the 334th Ftr Sqn

**Fieg, Lothar, Lt.**
328th Ftr Sqn/352nd Ftr Grp

| *Sqn* | *Date* | *Claims* | *Location* | *A/C* |
|---|---|---|---|---|
| 328th | April 29, 1944 | u/i a/c dam(grd) | Burg A/F | P-51 |
| | May 21 | (3)u/i a/c dam(grd) | Alt Ruppin | P-51 |
| | November 21 | Me-109 prob(air) | W/Merseburg | P-51 |

0-1-0 air
0-4 ground

**Field, Herbert K., Lt.**
351st Ftr Sqn/353rd Ftr Grp

| *Sqn* | *Date* | *Claims* | *Location* | *A/C* |
|---|---|---|---|---|
| 351st | April 22, 1944 | FW-190 dest(air) | N/Hamm | P-47 |
| | June 7 | Me-109 dest(air) | Beauvais/Tille | P-47 |

2-0-0 air
0-0 ground

**Fields, James E., Lt.**
62nd Ftr Sqn/56th Ftr Grp

| *Sqn* | *Date* | *Claims* | *Location* | *A/C* |
|---|---|---|---|---|
| 62nd | February 4, 1944 | FW-190 dest(air) | Charleroi | P-47 |
| | February 22 | (.5)FW-190 dest(air)* | Breda | P-47 |
| | | (.5)FW-190 dest(air)** | Breda | P-47 |
| | March 8 | FW-190 dest(air) | Steinhuder Lake | P-47 |
| | | FW-190 dam(air) | Steinhuder Lake | P-47 |
| | March 15 | FW-190 dest(air) | Dummer Lake | P-47 |

4-0-1 air
0-0 ground

* - shared with Capt. M.J. Quirk of the 62nd Ftr Sqn
** - shared with Capt. L.A. Schreiber of the 62nd Ftr Sqn

**Fiery, Elmer N., Capt.**
383rd Ftr Sqn/364th Ftr Grp

| *Sqn* | *Date* | *Claims* | *Location* | *A/C* |
|---|---|---|---|---|
| 383rd | December 27, 1944 | (2)FW-190 dest(air) | Frankfurt | P-51 |
| | | FW-190 dam(air) | Frankfurt | P-51 |

2-0-1 air
0-0 ground

**Fifield, Robert S., Capt.**
363rd Ftr Sqn/357th Ftr Grp

| *Sqn* | *Date* | *Claims* | *Location* | *A/C* |
|---|---|---|---|---|
| 363rd | September 18, 1944 | (.5)Me-109 dest(air)* | W/Arnheim | P-51 |
| | March 19, 1945 | Me-262 dest(air) | E/Leipzig | P-51 |
| | April 19 | Me-262 dest(air) | Prague | P-51 |

2.5-0-0 air
0-0 ground

* - shared with Lt. W.S. Fennell of the 363rd Ftr Sqn

**Fillipow, Edwin J., Lt.**
436th Ftr Sqn/479th Ftr Grp

| *Sqn* | *Date* | *Claims* | *Location* | *A/C* |
|---|---|---|---|---|
| 436th | September 5, 1944 | (2)FW-190 dam(grd) | Bad Nauheim | P-38 |

0-0-0 air
0-2 ground

**Fink, Frank M., Lt.**
335th Ftr Sqn/4th Ftr Grp

| *Sqn* | *Date* | *Claims* | *Location* | *A/C* |
|---|---|---|---|---|
| 335th | August 16, 1943 | FW-190 dest(air) | NW Paris | P-47 |

1-0-0 air
0-0 ground

**Finley, Daniel L., Lt.**
364th Ftr Sqn/357th Ftr Grp

| *Sqn* | *Date* | *Claims* | *Location* | *A/C* |
|---|---|---|---|---|
| 364th | June 20, 1944 | Me-109 dam(air) | Pasewalk | P-51 |
| | July 14 | Me-109 dest(air) | Valence | P-51 |

1-0-1 air
0-0 ground

**Finnesey, Robert V., Lt.**
358th Ftr Sqn/355th Ftr Grp

| *Sqn* | *Date* | *Claims* | *Location* | *A/C* |
|---|---|---|---|---|
| 358th | April 7, 1945 | Me-262 dam(air) | SE Bremen | P-51 |
| | April 13 | (.5)He-111 dest(grd)* | Schleswig | P-51 |

0-0-1 air
0.5-0 ground

* - shared with Lt. W.J. Schlect of the 358th Ftr Sqn

**Fiorito, Leonard J., Capt.**
503rd Ftr Sqn/339th Ftr Grp

| *Sqn* | *Date* | *Claims* | *Location* | *A/C* |
|---|---|---|---|---|
| 503rd | May 21, 1944 | Me-109 dest(grd) | Pelenz-Mackau | P-51 |
| | | Ju-88 dam(grd) | Pelenz-Mackau | P-51 |
| | June 15 | Me-109 dest(air) | Montiers | P-51 |
| | August 4 | FW-190 dest(air) | SW Hamburg | P-51 |

2-0-0 air
1-1 ground

**Fish, Frank A., Lt.**
83rd Ftr Sqn/78th Ftr Grp

| *Sqn* | *Date* | *Claims* | *Location* | *A/C* |
|---|---|---|---|---|
| 83rd | December 19, 1944 | Me-109 dest(air) | S/Coblenz | P-47 |

1-0-0 air
0-0 ground

**Fish, Wesley G., Lt.**
505th Ftr Sqn/339th Ftr Grp

| *Sqn* | *Date* | *Claims* | *Location* | *A/C* |
|---|---|---|---|---|
| 505th | June 27, 1944 | (.5)FW-190 dest(air)* | Paris | P-51 |

0.5-0-0 air
0-0 ground

* - shared with Lt. O.P. Farmer of the 505th Ftr Sqn

**Fisher, Donald C., Lt.**
383rd Ftr Sqn/364th Ftr Grp

| *Sqn* | *Date* | *Claims* | *Location* | *A/C* |
|---|---|---|---|---|
| 383rd | December 31, 1944 | FW-190 dest(air) | NW Hamburg | P-51 |
| | April 16, 1945 | FW-190 dest(grd) | Marienbad | P-51 |
| | April 19 | FW-190 dest(air) | Lubben | P-51 |

2-0-0 air
1-0 ground

**Fisher, Walter A., Lt.**
343rd Ftr Sqn/55th Ftr Grp

| *Sqn* | *Date* | *Claims* | *Location* | *A/C* |
|---|---|---|---|---|
| 343rd | April 17, 1945 | (2)FW-190 dest(grd) | Dresden | P-51 |
| | | (2)Me-410 dest(grd) | Dresden | P-51 |

0-0-0 air
4-0 ground

**Fitch, John C., Capt.**
335th Ftr Sqn/4th Ftr Grp

| *Sqn* | *Date* | *Claims* | *Location* | *A/C* |
|---|---|---|---|---|
| 335th | November 18, 1944 | (.5)Me-262 dest(air)* | S/Leipheim | P-51 |
| | | Me-109 dest(grd) | Leipheim | P-51 |

0.5-0-0 air
1-0 ground

* - shared with Lt. J.M. Creamer of the 335th Ftr Sqn

**Flack, James O., Lt.**
368th Ftr Sqn/359th Ftr Grp

| *Sqn* | *Date* | *Claims* | *Location* | *A/C* |
|---|---|---|---|---|
| 368th | September 11, 1944 | (.5)Me-109 dest(air)* | Eisenach | P-51 |

0.5-0-0 air
0-0 ground

* - shared with Lt. C.M. Lambright of the 368th Ftr Sqn

**Fladmark, Oscar R., Capt.**
368th Ftr Sqn/359th Ftr Grp

| *Sqn* | *Date* | *Claims* | *Location* | *A/C* |
|---|---|---|---|---|
| 368th | August 28, 1944 | Ju-88 dest(grd) | Saarbrucken | P-51 |
| | November 2 | (.5)Me-109 dest(air)* | Quedlinburg | P-51 |

0.5-0-0 air
1-0 ground

* - shared with Capt. G.F. Baker of the 368th Ftr Sqn

**Flagg, Walter L., Capt.**
63rd Ftr Sqn/56th Ftr Grp

| *Sqn* | *Date* | *Claims* | *Location* | *A/C* |
|---|---|---|---|---|
| 63rd | July 5, 1944 | Me-109 dest(air) | Evreux | P-47 |
| | | Me-109 dam(air) | Evreux | P-47 |
| | August 28 | Me-109 dest(air) | Charleroi | P-47 |
| | April 10, 1945 | (2)Do-217 dest(grd) | Werder A/F | P-47 |
| | | Me-109 dest(grd) | Werder A/F | P-47 |
| | | u/i a/c dest(grd) | Werder A/F | P-47 |
| | | Me-109 dam(grd) | Werder A/F | P-47 |
| | April 13 | FW-190 dest(grd) | Eggebeck A/F | P-47 |
| | | Ju-88 dest(grd) | Eggebeck A/F | P-47 |
| | | FW-190 dam(grd) | Eggebeck A/F | P-47 |

2-0-1 air
6-2 ground

**Fleming, Edward F., Capt.**
84th Ftr Sqn/78th Ftr Grp

| *Sqn* | *Date* | *Claims* | *Location* | *A/C* |
|---|---|---|---|---|
| 84th | December 11, 1943 | Me-109 dam(air) | SW Groningen | P-47 |

0-0-1 air
0-0 ground

**Fleming, Lawrence J., Lt.**
38th Ftr Sqn/55th Ftr Grp

| *Sqn* | *Date* | *Claims* | *Location* | *A/C* |
|---|---|---|---|---|
| 38th | April 16, 1945 | Do-217 dest(grd) | Munich-Brunnthal | P-51 |

0-0-0 air
1-0 ground

**Fleming, Philip E., Capt.**
62nd Ftr Sqn/56th Ftr Grp

| *Sqn* | *Date* | *Claims* | *Location* | *A/C* |
|---|---|---|---|---|
| 62nd | April 13, 1945 | (3)Do-217 dest(grd) | Eggebeck A/F | P-47 |
| | | He-111 dest(grd) | Eggebeck A/F | P-47 |

0-0-0 air
4-0 ground

**Fletcher, Jack M., Lt.**
354th Ftr Sqn/355th Ftr Grp

| *Sqn* | *Date* | *Claims* | *Location* | *A/C* |
|---|---|---|---|---|
| 354th | March 22, 1945 | Me-109 dest(grd) | Wurzburg | P-51 |
| | April 10 | (2)u/i a/c dest(grd) | Rechlin/Larz | P-51 |
| | April 16 | (2)u/i a/c dest(grd) | Eger A/F | P-51 |
| | | u/i a/c dam(grd) | Eger A/F | P-51 |

0-0-0 air
5-1 ground

**Fletcher, Westwood H., Jr., Capt.**
360th Ftr Sqn/356th Ftr Grp

| *Sqn* | *Date* | *Claims* | *Location* | *A/C* |
|---|---|---|---|---|
| 360th | February 24, 1944 | Me-109 dam(air) | SW Aachen | P-47 |
| | August 4 | (2)Me-109 dest(air) | SW Hamburg | P-47 |
| | September 1 | (.5)Ju-52 dest(grd)* | SE Nancy | P-47 |
| | September 13 | FW-190 dest(grd) | NW Stuttgart | P-47 |
| | | Me-410 dam(grd) | NW Stuttgart | P-47 |

2-0-1 air
1.5-1 ground

* - shared with Lt. J.T. Romine of the 360th Ftr Sqn

**Fling, Roy T., Capt.**
63rd Ftr Sqn/56th Ftr Grp

| *Sqn* | *Date* | *Claims* | *Location* | *A/C* |
|---|---|---|---|---|
| 63rd | August 12, 1944 | Me-109 dest(air) | Maubeuge | P-47 |

1-0-0 air
0-0 ground

**Flowers, Raymond R., Capt.**
77th Ftr Sqn/20th Ftr Grp

| *Sqn* | *Date* | *Claims* | *Location* | *A/C* |
|---|---|---|---|---|
| 77th | October 6, 1944 | (2.5)Do-18 dest(grd)* | Bad Berg-Dievenow | P-51 |

0-0-0 air
2.5-0 ground

* - shared with Lt. J.M. Garner of the 77th Ftr Sqn

**Flynn, Robert S., Lt.**
77th Ftr Sqn/20th Ftr Grp

| *Sqn* | *Date* | *Claims* | *Location* | *A/C* |
|---|---|---|---|---|
| 77th | January 29, 1944 | (.5)Me-210 dest(air)* | S/Coblenz | P-38 |

0.5-0-0 air
0-0 ground

* - shared with Lt. R.T. Bond of the 77th Ftr Sqn

**Flynt, William F., Lt.**
384th Ftr Sqn/364th Ftr Grp

| *Sqn* | *Date* | *Claims* | *Location* | *A/C* |
|---|---|---|---|---|
| 384th | December 5, 1944 | (.5)FW-190 dest(air)* | NW Berlin | P-51 |
| | December 23 | Me-109 dest(air) | Luxembourg | P-51 |

1.5-0-0 air
0-0 ground

* - shared with Lt. D.L. Leftwich of the 384th Ftr Sqn

**Fogarty, Edward M., Lt.**
352nd Ftr Sqn/353rd Ftr Grp

| *Sqn* | *Date* | *Claims* | *Location* | *A/C* |
|---|---|---|---|---|
| 352nd | October 10, 1943 | (.33)Me-110 dam(air)* | Amersfoort | P-47 |
| | October 20 | Me-109 prob(air) | Sittard | P-47 |

0-1-0.33 air
0-0 ground

* - shared with Lt. R.V. Keywan and Lt. W.H. Junttila of the 352nd Ftr Sqn

**Folger, John M., Lt.**
354th Ftr Sqn/355th Ftr Grp

| *Sqn* | *Date* | *Claims* | *Location* | *A/C* |
|---|---|---|---|---|
| 354th | July 19, 1944 | FW-190 dest(air) | Biberach | P-51 |
| | July 20 | Me-109 dam(air) | W/Oschatz | P-51 |

1-0-1 air
0-0 ground

**Folwell, Nathan T., Capt.**
503rd Ftr Sqn/339th Ftr Grp

| *Sqn* | *Date* | *Claims* | *Location* | *A/C* |
|---|---|---|---|---|
| 503rd | May 19, 1944 | (3)Me-109 dam(grd) | Pritzwalk | P-51 |
| | | u/i a/c dam(grd) | Pritzwalk | P-51 |

0-0-0 air
0-4 ground

**Fong, Frank S., Lt.**
369th Ftr Sqn/359th Ftr Grp

| *Sqn* | *Date* | *Claims* | *Location* | *A/C* |
|---|---|---|---|---|
| 369th | March 27, 1944 | FW-190 dest(air) | Gallardson | P-47 |

1-0-0 air
0-0 ground

**Ford, Delmar R., Lt.**
376th Ftr Sqn/361st Ftr Grp

| *Sqn* | *Date* | *Claims* | *Location* | *A/C* |
|---|---|---|---|---|
| 376th | November 26, 1944 | FW-190 dest(air) | S/Ulzen | P-51 |

1-0-0 air
0-0 ground

**Ford, John C., Capt.**
384th Ftr Sqn/364th Ftr Grp

| *Sqn* | *Date* | *Claims* | *Location* | *A/C* |
|---|---|---|---|---|
| 384th | March 8, 1944 | FW-190 dest(air) | NE Brunswick | P-38 |
| | March 29 | Me-109 dest(air) | Rheine/Enschede | P-38 |
| | May 21 | Ju-88 dest(grd) | Parchim-Hagenow | P-38 |
| | June 25 | (.5)Me-109 dest(air) | E/Blois | P-38 |

2.5-0-0 air
1-0 ground

* - shared with Lt. C. Hatfield of the 383rd Ftr Sqn, 364th Ftr Grp

**Ford, Joseph S., Capt.**
55th Ftr Sqn/20th Ftr Grp

| *Sqn* | *Date* | *Claims* | *Location* | *A/C* |
|---|---|---|---|---|
| 55th | August 25, 1944 | Ju-88 dest(grd) | Parow A/F | P-51 |
| | | Ju-52 dest(grd) | Parow A/F | P-51 |
| | | Ju-88 dam(grd) | Parow A/F | P-51 |
| | February 20, 1945 | Me-109 prob(air) | S/Nurnburg | P-51 |
| | | (2)Me-109 dest(grd) | S/Nurnburg | P-51 |

0-1-0 air
4-1 ground

**Forehand, Willard F., Lt.**
357th Ftr Sqn/355th Ftr Grp

| *Sqn* | *Date* | *Claims* | *Location* | *A/C* |
|---|---|---|---|---|
| 357th | February 9, 1945 | Ju-88 dest(grd) | Kothen A/F | P-51 |
| | | u/i a/c dam(grd) | Kothen A/F | P-51 |
| | February 23 | Me-262 dam(grd) | Neuburg | P-51 |
| | April 7 | Me-109 dest(air) | SE Hamburg | P-51 |

1-0-0 air
1-2 ground

**Forehand, William C., Maj.**
368th Ftr Sqn/359th Ftr Sqn

| *Sqn* | *Date* | *Claims* | *Location* | *A/C* |
|---|---|---|---|---|
| 368th | May 30, 1944 | Me-109 dest(air) | Dessau | P-51 |

1-0-0 air
0-0 ground

**Forga, James H., Jr., Lt.**
487th Ftr Sqn/352nd Ftr Grp

| *Sqn* | *Date* | *Claims* | *Location* | *A/C* |
|---|---|---|---|---|
| 487th | August 25, 1944 | Me-109 dest(grd) | Neubrandenburg | P-51 |
| | September 11 | (2)FW-190 dest(air) | Gottingen A/F | P-51 |
| | | Me-109 dest(air) | Gottingen A/F | P-51 |

3-0-0 air
1-0 ground

**Forker, George W., Lt.**
357th Ftr Sqn/355th Ftr Grp

| *Sqn* | *Date* | *Claims* | *Location* | *A/C* |
|---|---|---|---|---|
| 357th | June 24, 1944 | Me-109 dest(grd) | NE Angars | P-51 |
| | July 8 | Me-109 dest(grd) | SW Chalons | P-51 |
| | August 14 | Ju-88 dest(grd) | Sarrebourg | P-51 |

0-0-0 air
3-0 ground

**Forkin, Thomas J., Capt.**
352nd Ftr Sqn/353rd Ftr Grp

| *Sqn* | *Date* | *Claims* | *Location* | *A/C* |
|---|---|---|---|---|
| 352nd | March 29, 1944 | (2)Me-109 dest(air) | SW Bremen | P-47 |
| | | Me-109 dam(air) | SW Bremen | P-47 |
| | August 27 | (.5)FW-190 dest(grd)* | Metz | P-47 |
| | | Ju-88 dam(grd) | Metz | P-47 |
| | | (.5)Me-109 dam(grd)* | Metz | P-47 |

2-0-1 air
0.5-1.5 ground

* - both shared with LtCol. B. Rimerman of HdQts, 353rd Ftr Grp

**Forsblad, Richard W., Capt.**
38th Ftr Sqn/55th Ftr Grp

| *Sqn* | *Date* | *Claims* | *Location* | *A/C* |
|---|---|---|---|---|
| 38th | November 5, 1943 | FW-190 dam(air) | E/Rotterdam | P-38 |
| | July 21, 1944 | Me-109 dest(air) | Munich | P-51 |

1-0-1 air
0-0 ground

**Forsyth, Frank A., Lt.**
359th Ftr Sqn/356th Ftr Grp

| *Sqn* | *Date* | *Claims* | *Location* | *A/C* |
|---|---|---|---|---|
| 359th | April 23, 1944 | (.5)Go-242 dam(grd)* | Hagenau | P-47 |
| | August 18 | FW-190 dest(air) | Beauvais | P-47 |
| | December 5 | FW-190 dest(air) | Muritz Lake-Berlin | P-51 |
| | | FW-190 prob(air) | Muritz Lake-Berlin | P-51 |

2-1-0 air
0-0.5 ground

* - shared with Capt. H.A. Ogden of HdQts, 356th Ftr Grp

**Fortier, Norman J., Maj.**
354th Ftr Sqn/355th Ftr Grp

| *Sqn* | *Date* | *Claims* | *Location* | *A/C* |
|---|---|---|---|---|
| 354th | March 6, 1944 | (.33)Me-109 dest(air)* | Dummer Lake | P-47 |
| | March 29 | u/i a/c dest(grd) | Dummer Lake | P-47 |
| | April 24 | (1.5)Me-109 dest(air)** | Munich | P-51 |
| | | Me-109 dam(air) | Munich | P-51 |
| | May 1 | FW-190 dam(air) | Trier | P-51 |
| | May 13 | FW-190 dest(air) | NE Bremen | P-51 |
| | | Ju-88 dest(air) | N/Landsberg | P-51 |
| | June 6 | Ju-87 dest(air) | Chartres | P-51 |
| | July 8 | (.5)Me-109 dest(grd)@ | SW Chalons | P-51 |
| | July 20 | Me-109 dest(air) | W/Oschatz | P-51 |
| | July 24 | Me-262 dam(grd) | Lechfeld | P-51 |
| | November 18 | (2)Me-262 dest(grd) | Leipheim | P-51 |
| | | u/i a/c dam(grd) | Leipheim | P-51 |
| | January 15, 1945 | Ju-52 dest(grd) | Oberpfaffenhofen | P-51 |
| | | Ju-52 dam(grd) | Oberpfaffenhofen | P-51 |
| | April 16 | u/i a/c dest(grd) | Eger A/F | P-51 |

5.83-0-2 air
5.5-3 ground

* - shared with Capt. W.J. Koraleski and F/O C.R. Barger of the 354th Ftr Sqn
** - shared with Lt. W.P. Boulet of the 354th Ftr Sqn
@ - shared with Lt. R.G. Cross of the 354th Ftr Sqn

**Foster, Hugh O., Lt.**
83rd Ftr Sqn/78th Ftr Grp

| *Sqn* | *Date* | *Claims* | *Location* | *A/C* |
|---|---|---|---|---|
| 83rd | October 15, 1944 | Me-262 dam(air) | Bohmte | P-47 |

0-0-1 air
0-0 ground

**Foster, Justus D., Capt.**
61st Ftr Sqn/56th Ftr Grp

| *Sqn* | *Date* | *Claims* | *Location* | *A/C* |
|---|---|---|---|---|
| 61st | December 1, 1943 | FW-190 dest(air) | Beverloo | P-47 |
| | January 11, 1944 | Me-109 dest(air) | NE Osnabruck | P-47 |
| | | Me-109 dam(air) | NE Osnabruck | P-47 |
| | February 20 | Me-110 prob(air) | Steinhuder Lake | P-47 |
| | | Me-110 dam(air) | Steinhuder Lake | P-47 |

2-1-2 air
0-0 ground

**Foster, Kenneth E., F/O**
334th Ftr Sqn/4th Ftr Grp

| *Sqn* | *Date* | *Claims* | *Location* | *A/C* |
|---|---|---|---|---|
| 334th | November 18, 1944 | Me-262 dam(grd) | Leipheim | P-51 |

0-0-0 air
0-1 ground

**Foster, Thomas J., Lt.**
357th Ftr Sqn/355th Ftr Grp

| *Sqn* | *Date* | *Claims* | *Location* | *A/C* |
|---|---|---|---|---|
| 357th | May 24, 1944 | Me-109 dest(air) | Kyritz | P-51 |

1-0-0 air
0-0 ground

**Fowle, James M., Capt.**
384th Ftr Sqn/364th Ftr Grp

| *Sqn* | *Date* | *Claims* | *Location* | *A/C* |
|---|---|---|---|---|
| 384th | November 2, 1944 | Me-109 dest(air) | S/Merseburg | P-51 |
| | November 26 | FW-190 dest(air) | SE Dummer Lake | P-51 |
| | December 23 | (4)Me-109 dest(air) | NW Trier | P-51 |
| | December 31 | (2)FW-190 dest(air) | SW Hamburg | P-51 |
| | February 6, 1945 | Ar-234 dam(air) | SE Zuider Zee | P-51 |

8-0-1 air
0-0 ground

**Fowler, William E., Lt.**
487th Ftr Sqn/352nd Ftr Grp

| *Sqn* | *Date* | *Claims* | *Location* | *A/C* |
|---|---|---|---|---|
| 487th | April 11, 1944 | Me-110 dam(grd) | Stendal | P-51 |
| | April 22 | Me-110 dest(grd) | Hanover | P-51 |
| | May 8 | (.5)FW-190 dest(air)* | Brunswick | P-51 |
| | July 18 | (2)Me-109 dest(air) | Demmin | P-51 |

2.5-0-0 air
1-1 ground

* - shared with Capt. C.E. Davis of the 487th Ftr Sqn

**Foy, Robert W., Maj.**
363rd Ftr Sqn/357th Ftr Grp
HdQts/357th Ftr Grp

| *Sqn* | *Date* | *Claims* | *Location* | *A/C* |
|---|---|---|---|---|
| 363rd | May 19, 1944 | (3)Me-109 dest(air) | NW Brandenburg | P-51 |
| | June 29 | (2)Me-109 dest(air) | SW Leipzig | P-51 |
| | | FW-190 dest(air) | SW Leipzig | P-51 |
| | July 25 | FW-190 dest(air) | SE Paris | P-51 |
| | November 18 | Me-109 dest(air) | Villingen A/F | P-51 |
| | | Me-109 dam(air) | Villingen A/F | P-51 |
| | | Me-109 dest(grd) | Villingen A/F | P-51 |
| | | (3)Me-109 dam(grd) | Villingen A/F | P-51 |
| HdQts | December 2 | Ju-88 dest(air) | NE Coblenz | P-51 |
| | December 23 | Me-109 dest(air) | Wetzlar A/F | P-51 |
| | | Ju-88 dest(air) | Wetzlar A/F | P-51 |
| | January 14, 1945 | (2)FW-190 dest(air) | NW Berlin | P-51 |
| | | FW-190 dest(grd) | Berlin | P-51 |
| | February 9 | Me-262 dam(air) | Fulda | P-51 |
| | February 28 | Ju-88 dest(grd) | Lubeck/Blankensee | P-51 |
| | | FW-200 dam(grd) | Lubeck/Blankensee | P-51 |
| | | Me-109 dam(grd) | Lubeck/Blankensee | P-51 |
| | March 19 | Me-262 dest(air) | W/Giessen | P-51 |
| | March 24 | Me-109 dest(air) | N/Gutersloh | P-51 |

15-0-2 air
3-5 ground

**Frakes, Robert L., Lt.**
77th Ftr Sqn/20th Ftr Grp

| *Sqn* | *Date* | *Claims* | *Location* | *A/C* |
|---|---|---|---|---|
| 77th | February 5, 1944 | (.33)He-111 dest(air)* | Bourges A/F | P-38 |

0.33-0-0 air
0-0 ground

* - shared with Lt. M.J. Gilbertson and Lt. J.M. Morris of the 77th Ftr Sqn

**France, Victor J., Capt.**
334th Ftr Sqn/4th Ftr Grp

| *Sqn* | *Date* | *Claims* | *Location* | *A/C* |
|---|---|---|---|---|
| 334th | December 11, 1943 | Me-109 dest(air) | Leeuwarden | P-47 |
| | January 29, 1944 | FW-190 dest(air) | Hasselt | P-47 |
| | February 6 | FW-190 dam(air) | W/Paris | P-47 |
| | February 10 | FW-190 dest(air) | Lingen | P-47 |
| | March 8 | Me-109 dest(air) | Stendal | P-51 |
| | March 21 | (2)FW-190 dest(grd) | Bordeaux | P-51 |
| | March 27 | Ju-52 dest(grd) | Cazaux A/F | P-51 |
| | | Ju-88 dest(grd) | Cazaux A/F | P-51 |
| | | Ju-88 dam(grd) | Cazaux A/F | P-51 |
| | April 5 | (.33)He-111 dest(grd)* | Brandenburg-Briest | P-51 |
| | | FW-190 dam(grd) | Brandenburg-Briest | P-51 |
| | | Ju-52 dam(grd) | Brandenburg-Briest | P-51 |
| | April 18 | (.33)Me-109 dest(air)** | Fassberg A/F | P-51 |

4.33-0-1 air
4.33-3 ground

* - shared with Lt. L.R. Pierce and Lt. H.J. Blanchfield of the 334th Ftr Sqn
** - shared with Lt. N. Megura and Lt. G.C. Siems of the 334th Ftr Sqn

**Francis, Robert M., Capt.**
369th Ftr Sqn/359th Ftr Grp

| *Sqn* | *Date* | *Claims* | *Location* | *A/C* |
|---|---|---|---|---|
| 369th | February 21, 1945 | Me-410 dam(grd) | Schweinfurt | P-51 |

0-0-0 air
0-1 ground

**Frank, Wallace B., Capt.**
376th Ftr Sqn/361st Ftr Grp

| *Sqn* | *Date* | *Claims* | *Location* | *A/C* |
|---|---|---|---|---|
| 376th | April 26, 1944 | Ju-88 dest(grd) | Montdidier | P-47 |
| | May 8 | FW-190 dam(air) | Nienburg | P-47 |
| | May 29 | (.5)FW-190 dest(air)* | Schwerin | P-51 |
| | | FW-190 dam(air) | Schwerin | P-51 |

0.5-0-2 air
1-0 ground

* - shared with Lt. W.T. Butts of the 376th Ftr Sqn

**Frank, William J., Lt.**
351st Ftr Sqn/353rd Ftr Grp

| *Sqn* | *Date* | *Claims* | *Location* | *A/C* |
|---|---|---|---|---|
| 351st | June 12, 1944 | (.5)Me-109 dest(air)* | SW Paris | P-47 |

0.5-0-0 air
0-0 ground

* - shared with LtCol. B. Rimerman of HdQts, 353rd Ftr Grp

**Franklin, Dewey R., Lt.**
55th Ftr Sqn/20th Ftr Grp

| *Sqn* | *Date* | *Claims* | *Location* | *A/C* |
|---|---|---|---|---|
| 55th | August 9, 1944 | Me-109 dam(air) | S/Augsburg | P-51 |

0-0-1 air
0-0 ground

**Franklin, George W., Lt.**
351st Ftr Sqn/353rd Ftr Grp

| *Sqn* | *Date* | *Claims* | *Location* | *A/C* |
|---|---|---|---|---|
| 351st | June 7, 1944 | Me-109 dest(air) | Beauvais/Tille | P-47 |
| | | (2)Me-109 dam(air) | Beauvais/Tille | P-47 |
| | June 25 | Me-410 dest(grd) | Bourges | P-47 |
| | July 7 | FW-190 dest(grd) | Wesendorf | P-47 |

1-0-2 air
2-0 ground

**Franklin, Melvin C., Lt.**
336th Ftr Sqn/4th Ftr Grp

| *Sqn* | *Date* | *Claims* | *Location* | *A/C* |
|---|---|---|---|---|
| 336th | April 16, 1945 | (2)Ju-52 dest(grd) | Praha | P-51 |
| | | u/i a/c dam(grd) | Praha | P-51 |

0-0-0 air
2-1 ground

**Franklin, R.C., Jr., Maj.**
343rd Ftr Sqn/55th Ftr Grp
79th Ftr Sqn/20th Ftr Grp

| *Sqn* | *Date* | *Claims* | *Location* | *A/C* |
|---|---|---|---|---|
| 79th | March 18, 1944 | Me-110 dest(air) | Ulm | P-38 |
| | April 8 | Me-109 dest(air) | Salzwedel | P-38 |

| Sqn | Date | Claims | Location | A/C |
|---|---|---|---|---|
| | | (.2)He-177 dest(air)[*] | Salzwedel | P-38 |
| | April 23 | He-111 dest(grd) | Chateaudun A/F | P-38 |

2.2-0-0 air
1-0 ground

[*] - shared with Capt. D.E. Anderson and Capt. R.P. Gatterdam of the 79th Ftr Sqn and Capt. E.C. Hedlund and Lt. R.H. Dettre, D.S. pilots from the 474th Ftr Grp, 9th Air Force

**Frascotti, Robert C., Lt.**
486th Ftr Sqn/352nd Ftr Grp

| Sqn | Date | Claims | Location | A/C |
|---|---|---|---|---|
| 486th | April 13, 1944 | Me-110 dest(grd) | S/Stuttgart | P-51 |
| | | FW-190 dest(grd) | S/Stuttgart | P-51 |

0-0-0 air
2-0 ground

**Fraser, Thomas E., Lt.**
334th Ftr Sqn/4th Ftr Grp

| Sqn | Date | Claims | Location | A/C |
|---|---|---|---|---|
| 334th | May 21, 1944 | (2)Ju-88 dam(grd) | Buch A/F | P-51 |
| | | u/i a/c dam(grd) | Buch A/F | P-51 |
| | May 24 | FW-190 dest(air) | E/Hamburg | P-51 |

1-0-0 air
0-3 ground

**Frazer, Robert B., Lt.**
334th Ftr Sqn/4th Ftr Grp

| Sqn | Date | Claims | Location | A/C |
|---|---|---|---|---|
| 334th | October 8, 1943 | Me-109 dam(air) | Meppel-Zwolle | P-47 |
| | November 3 | Me-109 prob(air) | Lemmer | P-47 |

0-1-1 air
0-0 ground

**Frazier, John F., Lt.**
61st Ftr Sqn/56th Ftr Grp

| Sqn | Date | Claims | Location | A/C |
|---|---|---|---|---|
| 61st | December 23, 1944 | (2)FW-190 dest(air) | Coblenz | P-47 |

2-0-0 air
0-0 ground

**Frederick, Nicholas J., Lt.**
364th Ftr Sqn/357th Ftr Grp

| Sqn | Date | Claims | Location | A/C |
|---|---|---|---|---|
| 364th | May 24, 1944 | (.5)u/i a/c dest(grd)[*] | St. Lagar | P-51 |
| | June 20 | Me-109 dest(air) | Pasewalk | P-51 |
| | | (.5)Fi-156 dest(air)[**] | Pasewalk | P-51 |
| | July 14 | Me-109 dest(air) | Valence | P-51 |
| | August 6 | (.5)Ju-88 dest(air)[@] | NE Warsaw | P-51 |

3-0-0 air
0.5-0 ground

[*] - shared with Capt. R.A. Peterson of the 364th Ftr Sqn
[**] - shared with Lt. M.F. Allen of the 364th Ftr Sqn
[@] - shared with Lt. K.M. Brown of the 364th Ftr Sqn

**Frederick, Walter R., Lt.**
63rd Ftr Sqn/56th Ftr Grp

| Sqn | Date | Claims | Location | A/C |
|---|---|---|---|---|
| 63rd | April 9, 1944 | He-115 dest(grd) | Schleswig | P-47 |
| | | He-115 dam(grd) | Schleswig | P-47 |
| | June 14 | (3)Me-109 dam(air) | S/Soissons | P-47 |
| | July 4 | (.5)Me-109 dest(air)[*] | Conches | P-47 |
| | | FW-190 dam(air) | N/Chateaudun | P-47 |

0.5-0-4 air
1-1 ground

[*] - shared with Lt. J.R. Curtis of the 63rd Ftr Sqn

**Fredericks, Harold H., Lt.**
336th Ftr Sqn/4th Ftr Grp

| Sqn | Date | Claims | Location | A/C |
|---|---|---|---|---|
| 336th | April 30, 1944 | (.5)u/i a/c dest(grd)[*] | Valence A/F | P-51 |
| | May 13 | Me-109 prob(air) | SE Canabruck | P-51 |
| | April 4, 1945 | (.5)Me-262 dest(air)[**] | S/Ludwigslust | P-51 |
| | | Me-262 dam(air) | S/Ludwigslust | P-51 |
| | April 16 | (2)Ju-88 dest(grd) | Praha/Letnany | P-51 |
| | | Me-110 dest(grd) | Praha/Letnany | P-51 |
| | | Me-110 dam(grd) | Praha/Letnany | P-51 |
| | April 17 | Ju-87 dam(grd) | Pilzen | P-51 |

0.5-1-1 air
3.5-2 ground

[*] - shared with Lt. F.W. Glover of the 336th Ftr Sqn
[**] - shared with Lt. M.J. Kennedy of the 334th Ftr Sqn, 4th Ftr Grp

**Frederickson, Russell, Lt.**
63rd Ftr Sqn/56th Ftr Grp

| Sqn | Date | Claims | Location | A/C |
|---|---|---|---|---|
| 63rd | September 8, 1944 | Me-110 dam(grd) | Euskirchen | P-47 |
| | November 18 | (.5)u/i a/c dam(grd)[*] | Gross Otheim | P-47 |
| | November 27 | (2)Me-109 dest(air) | SE Dummer Lake | P-47 |
| | December 2 | Me-109 dest(air) | S/Marburg | P-47 |
| | | Me-109 prob(air) | S/Marburg | P-47 |

3-1-0 air
0-1.5 ground

[*] - shared with Lt. R.J. Daniel of the 63rd Ftr Sqn

**Freeburger, Edward P., Lt.**
335th Ftr Sqn/4th Ftr Grp

| Sqn | Date | Claims | Location | A/C |
|---|---|---|---|---|
| 335th | March 5, 1944 | (.5)FW-200 dest(air)[*] | Bergerac A/F | P-51 |

0.5-0-0 air
0-0 ground

[*] - shared with Capt. K.G. Smith of the 335th Ftr Sqn

**Freedman, David I., Lt.**
55th Ftr Sqn/20th Ftr Grp

| Sqn | Date | Claims | Location | A/C |
|---|---|---|---|---|
| 55th | November 2, 1944 | Me-109 dest(air) | Halle | P-51 |
| | | Me-109 dam(air) | Halle | P-51 |

1-0-1 air
0-0 ground

**Freedman, Roswell, LtCol.**
375th Ftr Sqn/361st Ftr Grp
376th Ftr Sqn/361st Ftr Grp

| Sqn | Date | Claims | Location | A/C |
|---|---|---|---|---|
| 376th | April 17, 1945 | u/i a/c dest(grd) | Pilzen | P-51 |

0-0-0 air
1-0 ground

**Freeman, Cecil M., Lt.**
486th Ftr Sqn/352nd Ftr Grp

| Sqn | Date | Claims | Location | A/C |
|---|---|---|---|---|
| 486th | September 12, 1944 | Me-109 dest(air) | Kyritz | P-51 |

1-0-0 air
0-0 ground

**Freeman, Lucian W., F/O**
335th Ftr Sqn/4th Ftr Grp

| Sqn | Date | Claims | Location | A/C |
|---|---|---|---|---|
| 335th | April 16, 1945 | He-177 dam(grd) | Praha/Letnany | P-51 |

0-0-0 air
0-1 ground

**Fremaux, Edward C., Capt.**
361st Ftr Sqn/356th Ftr Grp

| Sqn | Date | Claims | Location | A/C |
|---|---|---|---|---|
| 361st | April 23, 1944 | He-111 dam(grd) | Hagenau | P-47 |
| | August 12 | (.5)Ju-88 dest(air)* | Guise-Avesnes | P-47 |
| | | (.5)Ju-88 dest(air)** | Guise-Avesnes | P-47 |

1-0-0 air
0-1 ground

* - shared with Capt. D.B. Clayton of the 361st Ftr Sqn
** - shared with Lt. R.W. Gillette of the 361st Ftr Sqn

**French, Carl H., Lt.**
503rd Ftr Sqn/339th Ftr Grp

| Sqn | Date | Claims | Location | A/C |
|---|---|---|---|---|
| 503rd | March 2, 1945 | Me-109 dam(air) | E/Magdeburg | P-51 |
| | April 17 | Me-109 dest(grd) | Kleesdorf A/F | P-51 |

0-0-1 air
1-0 ground

**French, David J., Lt.**
486th Ftr Sqn/352nd Ftr Grp

| Sqn | Date | Claims | Location | A/C |
|---|---|---|---|---|
| 486th | July 18, 1944 | Me-410 dest(air) | NE Berlin | P-51 |
| | | (3)Me-410 dam(air) | NE Berlin | P-51 |
| | August 5 | (2)Me-109 dest(air) | Wilhelmshaven | P-51 |
| | | Me-109 dam(air) | Wilhelmshaven | P-51 |

3-0-4 air
0-0 ground

**French, Lloyd J., Capt.**
503rd Ftr Sqn/339th Ftr Grp

| Sqn | Date | Claims | Location | A/C |
|---|---|---|---|---|
| 503rd | November 26, 1944 | FW-190 dest(air) | SE Dummer Lake | P-51 |

1-0-0 air
0-0 ground

**Frey, Jesse R., Capt.**
362nd Ftr Sqn/357th Ftr Grp

| Sqn | Date | Claims | Location | A/C |
|---|---|---|---|---|
| 362nd | December 24, 1944 | FW-190 dest(air) | Fulda | P-51 |
| | January 14, 1945 | Me-109 dest(air) | NW Berlin | P-51 |

2-0-0 air
0-0 ground

**Frey, Royal D., Lt.**
55th Ftr Sqn/20th Ftr Grp

| Sqn | Date | Claims | Location | A/C |
|---|---|---|---|---|
| 55th | January 29, 1944 | Me-110 dest(air) | Undenheim | P-38 |
| | February 10 | Me-110 dest(air) | Celle | P-38 |

2-0-0 air
0-0 ground

**Friend, Raymond K., Capt.**
435th Ftr Sqn/479th Ftr Grp

| Sqn | Date | Claims | Location | A/C |
|---|---|---|---|---|
| 435th | August 18, 1944 | (.5)Ju-88 dest(grd)* | Nancy/Essey A/F | P-38 |
| | | (3)He-111 dam(grd) | Nancy/Essey A/F | P-38 |
| | September 26 | Me-109 dest(air) | SW Munster | P-51 |
| | | Me-109 dam(air) | SW Munster | P-51 |

1-0-1 air
0.5-3 ground

* - shared with Capt. C.A.P. Duffie of the 434th Ftr Sqn, 479th Ftr Grp

**Frisch, Robert J., Lt.**
503rd Ftr Sqn/339th Ftr Grp

| Sqn | Date | Claims | Location | A/C |
|---|---|---|---|---|
| 503rd | March 2, 1945 | Me-109 dam(air) | E/Magdeburg | P-51 |
| | April 10 | (4)Ju-88 dest(grd) | N/Neuruppin | P-51 |
| | | Ju-88 dam(grd) | N/Neuruppin | P-51 |
| | | u/i a/c dam(grd) | N/Neuruppin | P-51 |
| | April 16 | Me-109 dam(grd) | Kralupy | P-51 |
| | April 17 | Me-262 dest(grd) | Klatovy | P-51 |
| | | Ju-88 dest(grd) | Klatovy | P-51 |

0-0-1 air
6-3 ground

**Frolking, James E., Lt.**
436th Ftr Sqn/479th Ftr Grp

| Sqn | Date | Claims | Location | A/C |
|---|---|---|---|---|
| 436th | September 5, 1944 | FW-190 dest(grd) | Bad Nauheim | P-38 |
| | | FW-190 dam(grd) | Bad Nauheim | P-38 |
| | September 28 | FW-190 dam(air) | W/Magdeburg | P-38 |

0-0-1 air
1-1 ground

**Frost, R.B., Lt.**
435th Ftr Sqn/479th Ftr Grp

| Sqn | Date | Claims | Location | A/C |
|---|---|---|---|---|
| 435th | April 16, 1945 | (2)u/i a/c dam(grd) | S/Pocking | P-51 |

0-0-0 air
0-2 ground

**Fruechtenicht, Richard W., Capt.**
55th Ftr Sqn/20th Ftr Grp

| Sqn | Date | Claims | Location | A/C |
|---|---|---|---|---|
| 55th | January 14, 1945 | FW-190 dam(air) | Perleberg | P-51 |
| | February 25 | Me-109 dest(air) | Dummer Lake | P-51 |
| | | Me-109 dam(air) | Dummer Lake | P-51 |

1-0-2 air
0-0 ground

**Fruh, Robert K., Lt.**
338th Ftr Sqn/55th Ftr Grp

| Sqn | Date | Claims | Location | A/C |
|---|---|---|---|---|
| 338th | February 10, 1944 | Me-110 dest(air) | Brunswick | P-38 |
| | March 18 | Me-109 dest(air) | E/French Border | P-38 |
| | | (2)Me-109 prob(air) | E/French Border | P-38 |
| | September 11 | Me-109 dest(air) | S/Meiningen | P-51 |

3-2-0 air
0-0 ground

**Frum, Rollin W., F/O**
487th Ftr Sqn/352nd Ftr Grp

| Sqn | Date | Claims | Location | A/C |
|---|---|---|---|---|
| 487th | April 17, 1945 | (3)FW-190 dest(grd) | Plattling | P-51 |
| | | (2)FW-190 dam(grd) | Plattling | P-51 |

0-0-0 air
3-2 ground

**Fry, David M., Lt.**
343rd Ftr Sqn/55th Ftr Grp

| Sqn | Date | Claims | Location | A/C |
|---|---|---|---|---|
| 343rd | September 10, 1944 | He-111 dest(grd) | NE Augsburg | P-51 |
| | | He-111 dam(grd) | NE Augsburg | P-51 |

0-0-0 air
1-1 ground

**Fry, Dwight A., Lt.**
350th Ftr Sqn/353rd Ftr Grp

| Sqn | Date | Claims | Location | A/C |
|---|---|---|---|---|
| 350th | September 27, 1943 | Me-109 dest(air) | W/Emden | P-47 |
| | October 14 | FW-190 dest(air) | Duren | P-47 |

2-0-0 air
0-0 ground

**Fry, Edward R., Lt.**
364th Ftr Sqn/357th Ftr Grp

| Sqn | Date | Claims | Location | A/C |
|---|---|---|---|---|
| 364th | February 28, 1945 | (2)u/i a/c dest(grd) | Lubeck/Blankensee | P-51 |

0-0-0 air
2-0 ground

**Frye, James E., Lt.**
351st Ftr Sqn/353rd Ftr Grp

| Sqn | Date | Claims | Location | A/C |
|---|---|---|---|---|
| 351st | January 14, 1945 | Me-109 dest(air) | NE Hanover | P-51 |
| | March 3 | Me-262 dam(air) | SE Hamburg | P-51 |

1-0-1 air
0-0 ground

**Fryer, Earl R., Capt.**
38th Ftr Sqn/55th Ftr Grp

| Sqn | Date | Claims | Location | A/C |
|---|---|---|---|---|
| 38th | August 24, 1944 | Ju-88 dest(grd) | Burg A/F | P-51 |
| | September 11 | (3)Me-109 dest(air) | S/Erfurt | P-51 |
| | November 2 | FW-190 dest(air) | Merseburg | P-51 |

4-0-0 air
1-0 ground

**Fuller, Leonard B., Lt.**
357th Ftr Sqn/355th Ftr Grp

| Sqn | Date | Claims | Location | A/C |
|---|---|---|---|---|
| 357th | June 6, 1944 | Ju-87 dest(air) | NE Janville | P-51 |
| | | Ju-87 prob(air) | NE Janville | P-51 |
| | | Ju-87 dam(air) | NE Janville | P-51 |
| | June 20 | (.5)Me-410 dest(air)* | Pomeranian Bay | P-51 |
| | July 7 | Me-410 dest(air) | Halle-Nordhausen | P-51 |

2.5-1-1 air
0-0 ground

* - shared with Lt. C.R. Buckles of the 357th Ftr Sqn

**Fuller, Samuel G., Lt.**
362nd Ftr Sqn/357th Ftr Grp

| Sqn | Date | Claims | Location | A/C |
|---|---|---|---|---|
| 362nd | September 13, 1944 | (.5)Me-109 dest(air)* | S/Nordhausen | P-51 |

0.5-0-0 air
0-0 ground

* - shared with Capt. J.B. England of the 362nd Ftr Sqn

**Fulton, Joseph O., Lt.**
504th Ftr Sqn/339th Ftr Grp
351st Ftr Sqn/353rd Ftr Grp

| Sqn | Date | Claims | Location | A/C |
|---|---|---|---|---|
| 351st | March 14, 1945 | Me-109 dest(air) | Luckenwalde | P-51 |
| | April 16 | FW-190 dest(grd) | Reichersberg | P-51 |
| | | Ju-88 dest(grd) | Reichersberg | P-51 |
| | | Ju-88 dam(grd) | Reichersberg | P-51 |

1-0-0 air
2-1 ground

**Funcheon, Donald M., Lt.**
61st Ftr Sqn/56th Ftr Grp

| Sqn | Date | Claims | Location | A/C |
|---|---|---|---|---|
| 61st | February 11, 1944 | Me-110 dam(grd) | Rheims | P-47 |
| | February 20 | (2)Me-110 dam(air) | Steinhuder Lake | P-47 |
| | February 21 | Me-109 dest(air) | Zuider Zee | P-47 |
| | February 24 | FW-190 dest(air) | Holzminden | P-47 |
| | | FW-190 prob(air) | Holzminden | P-47 |
| | February 25 | Me-109 dest(air) | Landau | P-47 |

3-1-2 air
0-1 ground

**Funk, George E., Lt.**
338th Ftr Sqn/55th Ftr Grp

| Sqn | Date | Claims | Location | A/C |
|---|---|---|---|---|
| 338th | July 7, 1944 | (.5)Me-109 dest(air)* | W/Bernburg | P-38 |
| | September 19 | Me-109 dam(air) | S/Dusseldorf | P-51 |

0.5-0-1 air
0-0 ground

* - shared with Capt. O.E. Goodman of the 338th Ftr Sqn

**Furneaux, John W., Lt.**
351st Ftr Sqn/353rd Ftr Grp

| Sqn | Date | Claims | Location | A/C |
|---|---|---|---|---|
| 351st | June 25, 1944 | Me-410 dest(grd) | Bourges | P-47 |
| | July 9 | Me-109 dest(air) | Argentan | P-47 |

1-0-0 air
1-0 ground

**Furness, Joseph F., Capt.**
350th Ftr Sqn/353rd Ftr Grp

| Sqn | Date | Claims | Location | A/C |
|---|---|---|---|---|
| 350th | January 24, 1944 | Me-110 dest(air) | Tirlemont | P-47 |
| | June 12 | (2)Me-109 dest(air) | SW Paris | P-47 |

3-0-0 air
0-0 ground

**Furr, William W., Lt.**
328th Ftr Sqn/352nd Ftr Grp

| Sqn | Date | Claims | Location | A/C |
|---|---|---|---|---|
| 328th | April 8, 1944 | Me-210 dest(grd) | Quackenbruck | P-47 |
| | April 15 | Me-110 dest(grd) | Diepholz | P-51 |
| | May 21 | Ju-52 dest(grd) | Alt Ruppin | P-51 |
| | May 24 | Me-109 dest(air) | W/Perleberg | P-51 |
| | May 27 | Me-109 dest(air) | S/Strasbourg | P-51 |
| | | Me-109 dam(air) | S/Strasbourg | P-51 |
| | May 30 | (1.5)FW-190 dest(air)* | Schoningen | P-51 |

3.5-0-1 air
3-0 ground

* - shared with an unknown pilot

**Fussell, Roscoe J., Capt.**
358th Ftr Sqn/355th Ftr Grp

| Sqn | Date | Claims | Location | A/C |
|---|---|---|---|---|
| 358th | March 2, 1944 | (.5)FW-190 dest(air)* | SE Charleroi | P-47 |
| | April 11 | (.5)Me-410 dest(air)** | NE Berlin | P-51 |
| | | (.25)Me-410 dest(air)@ | NE Berlin | P-51 |
| | | (.25)Ju-88 dest(air)@ | NE Berlin | P-51 |
| | April 19 | FW-190 dest(air) | SW Brunswick | P-51 |
| | January 15, 1945 | u/i a/c dest(grd) | Landsberg | P-51 |
| | | (2)u/i a/c dam(grd) | Landsberg | P-51 |

2.5-0-0 air
1-2 ground

* - shared with F/O L.M. Dudley of the 358th Ftr Sqn
** - shared with Lt. W.V. Gresham of the 358th Ftr Sqn
@ - both shared with Lt. W.V. Gresham, Lt. D.M. Martyn, and F/O L.M. Dudley of the 358th Ftr Sqn

**Gabreski, Francis S., LtCol.**
61st Ftr Sqn/56th Ftr Grp
HdQts/56th Ftr Grp

| Sqn | Date | Claims | Location | A/C |
|---|---|---|---|---|
| 61st | May 15, 1943 | FW-190 dam(air) | NE Rotterdam | P-47 |
| | August 24 | FW-190 dest(air) | Dreux | P-47 |
| | September 3 | FW-190 dest(air) | St. Germain | P-47 |
| | November 5 | FW-190 dest(air) | S/Rheine | P-47 |
| | | FW-190 dam(air) | S/Rheine | P-47 |
| | November 26 | (2)Me-110 dest(air) | SE Oldenburg | P-47 |
| | November 29 | (2)Me-109 dest(air) | NE Bremen | P-47 |
| | December 11 | Me-110 dest(air) | Esens | P-47 |
| HdQts | January 29, 1944 | Me-110 dest(air) | S/Coblenz | P-47 |
| | January 30 | Me-109 dest(air) | Lingen | P-47 |
| | | Me-210 dest(air) | Lingen | P-47 |
| | February 20 | (2)Me-110 dest(air) | W/Hanover | P-47 |

| Sqn | Date | Claims | Location | A/C |
|---|---|---|---|---|
| | | Me-110 dam(air) | W/Hanover | P-47 |
| | February 22 | FW-190 dest(air) | N/Lippstadt | P-47 |
| | | Do-217 dest(grd) | Eindhoven | P-47 |
| | March 8 | FW-190 dest(grd) | Weinstorf A/F | P-47 |
| | | (4)FW-190 dam(grd) | Weinstorf A/F | P-47 |
| | March 16 | (2)FW-190 dest(air) | Nancy | P-47 |
| | March 27 | (2)Me-109 dest(air) | NE Nantes | P-47 |
| | April 9 | (.5)u/i a/c dest(grd)* | Schleswig | P-47 |
| 61st | April 24 | He-111 dam(grd) | Frieburg | P-47 |
| | May 8 | Me-109 dest(air) | Celle | P-47 |
| | May 22 | (3)FW-190 dest(air) | Hoperhofen A/F | P-47 |
| | | FW-190 prob(air) | Hoperhofen A/F | P-47 |
| | June 7 | Me-109 dest(air) | E/Dreux | P-47 |
| | | FW-190 dest(air) | E/Dreux | P-47 |
| | June 12 | (2)Me-109 dest(air) | Evreux | P-47 |
| | June 27 | Me-109 dest(air) | La Perth A/F | P-47 |
| | July 5 | Me-109 dest(air) | Evreux | P-47 |
| | July 7 | He-111 dest(grd) | Bassenheim A/F | P-47 |

28-1-3 air
3.5-5 ground

* - shared with Lt. H.L. Matthew of the 63rd Ftr Sqn, 56th Ftr Grp

**Gadpaille, Warren J., Lt.**
354th Ftr Sqn/355th Ftr Grp

| Sqn | Date | Claims | Location | A/C |
|---|---|---|---|---|
| 354th | March 22, 1945 | He-111 dest(grd) | Memmingen | P-51 |

0-0-0 air
1-0 ground

**Gailer, Frank L., Jr., Lt.**
363rd Ftr Sqn/357th Ftr Grp

| Sqn | Date | Claims | Location | A/C |
|---|---|---|---|---|
| 363rd | September 13, 1944 | (.5)Me-109 dest(air)* | S/Kassel | P-51 |
| | September 18 | (.5)FW-190 dest(air)** | Arnheim | P-51 |
| | September 19 | (.5)Me-109 dest(air)@ | W/Arnheim | P-51 |
| | October 7 | FW-190 dest(air) | SW Zeitz | P-51 |
| | October 12 | Me-109 dest(air) | Hanover | P-51 |
| | November 18 | Me-109 dest(grd) | Mengen A/F | P-51 |
| | November 27 | (2)FW-190 dest(air) | SE Magdeburg | P-51 |

5.5-0-0 air
1-0 ground

* - shared with Lt. C.E. Yeager of the 363rd Ftr Sqn
** - shared with Capt. T.E. Hughes of the 363rd Ftr Sqn
@ - shared with Lt. H.O. Hand of the 363rd Ftr Sqn

**Gaines, Robert S., Capt.**
369th Ftr Sqn/359th Ftr Grp

| Sqn | Date | Claims | Location | A/C |
|---|---|---|---|---|
| 369th | September 11, 1944 | Me-109 prob(air) | Weimar | P-51 |
| | March 18, 1945 | Me-109 dest(air) | Joachimsthal | P-51 |

1-1-0 air
0-0 ground

**Galer, Donald V., Lt.**
354th Ftr Sqn/355th Ftr Grp

| Sqn | Date | Claims | Location | A/C |
|---|---|---|---|---|
| 354th | April 10, 1945 | u/i a/c dest(grd) | Memmingen | P-51 |
| | April 13 | He-111 dest(grd) | Husum | P-51 |
| | | Ju-88 dest(grd) | Husum | P-51 |
| | | u/i a/c dam(grd) | Husum | P-51 |
| | April 16 | Ju-88 dest(grd) | Eger A/F | P-51 |
| | | u/i a/c dest(grd) | Eger A/F | P-51 |
| | | (2)u/i a/c dam(grd) | Autobahn | P-51 |
| | | Me-109 dam(grd) | Autobahn | P-51 |
| | | Me-410 dam(grd) | Autobahn | P-51 |

0-0-0 air
5-5 ground

**Galiga, John W., Lt.**
328th Ftr Sqn/352nd Ftr Grp

| Sqn | Date | Claims | Location | A/C |
|---|---|---|---|---|
| 328th | May 8, 1944 | FW-190 prob(air) | Nienburg | P-51 |
| | May 12 | (.5)Me-109 dest(air)* | Coburg | P-51 |
| | June 21 | (.5)Me-410 dest(air)** | Dahmsdorf | P-51 |
| | July 18 | (2)Ju-88 dam(air) | Wismar | P-51 |

1-1-2 air
0-0 ground

* - shared with Lt. H.H. Barnes of the 487th Ftr Sqn, 352nd Ftr Grp
** - shared with Lt. E.L. Smith of the 328th Ftr Sqn

**Gallagher, Harold E., Lt.**
62nd Ftr Sqn/56th Ftr Grp

| Sqn | Date | Claims | Location | A/C |
|---|---|---|---|---|
| 62nd | April 15, 1944 | FW-190 dam(air) | Altona | P-47 |

0-0-1 air
0-0 ground

**Gallant, George E., Lt.**
84th Ftr Sqn/78th Ftr Grp

| Sqn | Date | Claims | Location | A/C |
|---|---|---|---|---|
| 84th | April 16, 1945 | Ju-52 dam(grd) | Praha/Kakewice | P-51 |

0-0-0 air
0-1 ground

**Gallant, Morris E., Lt.**
364th Ftr Sqn/357th Ftr Grp

| Sqn | Date | Claims | Location | A/C |
|---|---|---|---|---|
| 364th | December 5, 1944 | FW-190 dest(air) | NW Berlin | P-51 |

1-0-0 air
0-0 ground

**Gallup, Kenneth W., LtCol.**
350th Ftr Sqn/353rd Ftr Grp
HdQts/353rd Ftr Grp

| Sqn | Date | Claims | Location | A/C |
|---|---|---|---|---|
| HdQts | May 28, 1944 | Me-109 dest(air) | Gutersloh | P-47 |
| | June 8 | FW-190 dest(grd) | Le Mans | P-47 |
| | | FW-190 dam(grd) | Le Mans | P-47 |
| | June 12 | (2)Me-109 dest(air) | SW Paris | P-47 |
| 350th | June 27 | Me-109 dest(air) | Epernay | P-47 |
| | July 6 | Me-109 dest(air) | SW Limay | P-47 |
| | August 4 | Me-109 dest(air) | Neunkirchen | P-47 |
| | | Me-109 prob(air) | Neunkirchen | P-47 |
| | August 5 | Me-109 dest(air) | Rheine | P-47 |
| | August 11 | u/i a/c dest(grd) | Maraville | P-47 |
| | August 12 | (1.5)Fi-156 dest(air)* | Verdun | P-47 |
| | | (.5)He-111 dest(air)** | SE Arlon | P-47 |

9-1-0 air
2-1 ground

* - shared with Lt. J.B. Brooks of the 350th Ftr Sqn
** - shared with Lt. J.L. Schilt of the 350th Ftr Sqn

**Gangwish, Robert C., Lt.**
363rd Ftr Sqn/357th Ftr Grp

| Sqn | Date | Claims | Location | A/C |
|---|---|---|---|---|
| 363rd | May 27, 1944 | Me-109 prob(air) | SE Baden Baden | P-51 |

0-1-0 air
0-0 ground

**Gansberg, Raymond H., Capt.**
361st Ftr Sqn/356th Ftr Grp

| Sqn | Date | Claims | Location | A/C |
|---|---|---|---|---|
| 361st | January 24, 1944 | (.5)FW-190 dest(air)* | Ghent-Bruges | P-47 |
| | April 11 | (2)He-111 dest(grd) | Gifhorn | P-47 |
| | | (2)Ju-88 dest(grd) | Gifhorn | P-47 |
| | April 23 | He-111 dam(grd) | Hagenau | P-47 |
| | May 19 | Me-109 dest(air) | Quackenbruck | P-47 |
| | June 11 | Me-109 dest(air) | SW Bernay | P-47 |

2.5-0-0 air
4-1 ground

* - shared with Lt. M.F. Erickson of the 361st Ftr Sqn

**Garback, Alfred A., Lt.**
84th Ftr Sqn/78th Ftr Grp

| *Sqn* | *Date* | *Claims* | *Location* | *A/C* |
|---|---|---|---|---|
| 84th | September 10, 1944 | He-111 dest(grd) | Meinbullen | P-47 |
| | | He-111 dam(grd) | Meinbullen | P-47 |
| | February 3, 1945 | FW-190 dest(grd) | Luneburg | P-51 |
| | March 19 | (.5)Me-109 dest(air)* | Osnabruck | P-51 |

0.5-0-0 air
2-1 ground

* - shared with Lt. E.F. Smith of the 84th Ftr Sqn

**Gard, Jack L., Lt.**
77th Ftr Sqn/20th Ftr Grp

| *Sqn* | *Date* | *Claims* | *Location* | *A/C* |
|---|---|---|---|---|
| 77th | December 1, 1943 | FW-190 dest(air) | Coblenz | P-38 |

1-0-0 air
0-0 ground

**Garlich, Robert L., Lt.**
357th Ftr Sqn/355th Ftr Grp

| *Sqn* | *Date* | *Claims* | *Location* | *A/C* |
|---|---|---|---|---|
| 357th | January 15, 1945 | u/i a/c dam(grd) | Landsberg | P-51 |
| | February 23 | Me-163 dest(grd) | Neuburg | P-51 |
| | April 10 | (1.5)Do-24 dest(grd)* | Rechlin/Larz | P-51 |
| | | He-111 dest(grd) | Rechlin/Larz | P-51 |
| | April 13 | (2)He-111 dest(grd) | Schleswig | P-51 |
| | April 16 | Ju-87 dest(grd) | Eger A/F | P-51 |

0-0-0 air
6.5-1 ground

* - shared with F/O C.R. Albright of the 56th Ftr Grp

**Garlock, Karl H., Capt.**
338th Ftr Sqn/55th Ftr Grp

| *Sqn* | *Date* | *Claims* | *Location* | *A/C* |
|---|---|---|---|---|
| 338th | November 13, 1943 | Me-210 dam(air) | Hagen | P-38 |

0-0-1 air
0-0 ground

**Garner, James M., Capt.**
77th Ftr Sqn/20th Ftr Grp

| *Sqn* | *Date* | *Claims* | *Location* | *A/C* |
|---|---|---|---|---|
| 77th | October 6, 1944 | (1.5)Do-18 dest(grd)* | Bad Berg-Dievenow | P-51 |
| | | Do-18 dam(grd) | Bad Berg-Dievenow | P-51 |
| | November 2 | (2)Me-109 dest(air) | N/Leipzig | P-51 |
| | December 2 | FW-190 dest(air) | Coblenz | P-51 |

3-0-0 air
1.5-1 ground

* - shared with Lt. R.R. Flowers of the 77th Ftr Sqn

**Garnett, Joseph K., Lt.**
338th Ftr Sqn/55th Ftr Grp

| *Sqn* | *Date* | *Claims* | *Location* | *A/C* |
|---|---|---|---|---|
| 338th | May 20, 1944 | FW-190 dest(air) | Sens | P-38 |
| | July 6 | Me-109 dest(air) | Laon | P-38 |
| | July 7 | FW-190 dest(air) | W/Bernburg | P-38 |

3-0-0 air
0-0 ground

**Garrett, Richard C., Capt.**
77th Ftr Sqn/20th Ftr Grp

| *Sqn* | *Date* | *Claims* | *Location* | *A/C* |
|---|---|---|---|---|
| 77th | January 29, 1944 | Me-110 dam(air) | W/Frankfurt | P-38 |

0-0-1 air
0-0 ground

**Garrison, Vermont, Lt.**
336th Ftr Sqn/4th Ftr Grp

| *Sqn* | *Date* | *Claims* | *Location* | *A/C* |
|---|---|---|---|---|
| 336th | December 16, 1943 | (.33)Ju-88 dest(air)* | E/Zuider Zee | P-47 |
| | January 7, 1944 | FW-190 dam(air) | Le Chateau | P-47 |
| | January 14 | (2)FW-190 dest(air) | Compiegne | P-47 |
| | January 31 | Me-109 dest(air) | Gilze-Rijen | P-47 |
| | February 6 | FW-190 dest(air) | Beauvais-Marigny | P-47 |
| | February 10 | Me-109 dest(air) | Dummer Lake | P-47 |
| | February 20 | FW-190 dam(air) | Malmedy | P-47 |
| | February 25 | FW-190 dest(air) | Luxembourg | P-47 |
| | February 28 | (.25)Ju-88 dest(grd)** | Soissons | P-51 |
| | March 3 | FW-190 dest(air) | NW Berlin | P-51 |
| | | Me-110 prob(air) | NW Berlin | P-51 |
| | | Me-110 dam(air) | NW Berlin | P-51 |

7.33-1-3 air
0.25-0 ground

* - shared with Capt. D.S. Gentile and Lt. L.H. Norley of the 336th Ftr Sqn
** - shared with Capt. D.W. Beeson, Lt. N. Megura, and Lt. W.B. Smith of the 334th Ftr Sqn, 4th Ftr Grp

**Garvey, Charles J., Lt.**
360th Ftr Sqn/356th Ftr Grp

| *Sqn* | *Date* | *Claims* | *Location* | *A/C* |
|---|---|---|---|---|
| 360th | February 11, 1944 | FW-190 dest(air) | S/Albert | P-47 |

1-0-0 air
0-0 ground

**Garvin, Leo C., Lt.**
334th Ftr Sqn/4th Ftr Grp

| *Sqn* | *Date* | *Claims* | *Location* | *A/C* |
|---|---|---|---|---|
| 334th | February 27, 1945 | Me-108 dest(grd) | Weimar | P-51 |

0-0-0 air
1-0 ground

**Gasser, James A., Lt.**
362nd Ftr Sqn/357th Ftr Grp

| *Sqn* | *Date* | *Claims* | *Location* | *A/C* |
|---|---|---|---|---|
| 362nd | January 14, 1945 | FW-190 dest(air) | NW Berlin | P-51 |

1-0-0 air
0-0 ground

**Gaston, Jack T., Lt.**
383rd Ftr Sqn/364th Ftr Grp

| *Sqn* | *Date* | *Claims* | *Location* | *A/C* |
|---|---|---|---|---|
| 383rd | November 26, 1944 | (.5)Me-109 dest(air)* | Dummer Lake | P-51 |

0.5-0-0 air
0-0 ground

* - shared with Lt. G.E. Smith of the 383rd Ftr Sqn

**Gates, Thomas L., Maj.**
362nd Ftr Sqn/357th Ftr Grp

| *Sqn* | *Date* | *Claims* | *Location* | *A/C* |
|---|---|---|---|---|
| 362nd | July 30, 1944 | Me-109 dest(air) | NW Paris | P-51 |
| | | Me-109 dam(air) | NW Paris | P-51 |
| | September 18 | Me-109 dest(air) | Nijmegen | P-51 |

2-0-1 air
0-0 ground

**Gates, William N., Capt.**
435th Ftr Sqn/479th Ftr Grp

| *Sqn* | *Date* | *Claims* | *Location* | *A/C* |
|---|---|---|---|---|
| 435th | August 3, 1944 | B-24 dest(grd) | Ensisheim | P-38 |

0-0-0 air
1-0 ground

**Gatlin, Wayne C., Lt.**
360th Ftr Sqn/356th Ftr Grp

| *Sqn* | *Date* | *Claims* | *Location* | *A/C* |
|---|---|---|---|---|
| 360th | April 10, 1945 | Me-262 dest(air) | Oranienburg | P-51 |
| | April 18 | (.33)Me-262 dam(air)* | Ingolstadt | P-51 |

1-0-0.33 air
0-0 ground

* - shared with Lt. L.B. Proctor and Lt. G.W. Seanor of the 360th Ftr Sqn

**Gatterdam, Richard P., Maj.**
79th Ftr Sqn/20th Ftr Grp
55th Ftr Sqn/20th Ftr Grp

| *Sqn* | *Date* | *Claims* | *Location* | *A/C* |
|---|---|---|---|---|
| 79th | January 29, 1944 | FW-190 prob(air) | Coblenz | P-38 |
| | January 30 | (.5)Me-210 dest(air)* | Brunswick | P-38 |
| | April 8 | (.2)He-177 dest(air)** | Salzwedel | P-38 |
| | October 6 | (2.5)He-115 dest(grd)@ | Bad Berg-Dievenow | P-51 |
| | November 2 | Me-109 dest(air) | SW Merseburg | P-51 |
| 55th | January 14, 1945 | (2)FW-190 dest(air) | Perleburg | P-51 |

3.7-1-0 air
2.5-0 ground

* - shared with Lt. J.T. Martin of the 79th Ftr Sqn
** - shared with Maj. R.C. Franklin and Capt. D.E. Anderson of the 79th Ftr Sqn and Capt. E.C. Hedlund and Lt. R.H. Dettre of the 474th Ftr Grp, 9th Air Force (on D.S. to the 20th)
@ - shared with Lt. M.G. Ingebrigsten of the 79th Ftr Sqn

**Gawienowski, John J., Lt.**
384th Ftr Sqn/364th Ftr Grp

| *Sqn* | *Date* | *Claims* | *Location* | *A/C* |
|---|---|---|---|---|
| 384th | August 9, 1944 | (.5)FW-190 dest(air)* | Kaufburen | P-51 |
| | | (.5)Trainer dest(air)* | Kaufburen | P-51 |
| | | Me-109 dam(grd) | Schongen | P-51 |
| | August 24 | Me-109 dest(air) | E/Hamburg | P-51 |

2-0-0 air
0-1 ground

* - both shared with Lt. F.T. Kozloski of the 384th Ftr Sqn

**Geary, Edward H., Lt.**
343rd Ftr Sqn/55th Ftr Grp

| *Sqn* | *Date* | *Claims* | *Location* | *A/C* |
|---|---|---|---|---|
| 343rd | April 9, 1945 | Me-109 dest(grd) | Munich-Brunnthal | P-51 |
| | | Me-109 dam(grd) | Munich-Brunnthal | P-51 |
| | April 17 | Me-410 dest(grd) | Bautzen/Litten | P-51 |
| | | Me-410 dam(grd) | Bautzen/Litten | P-51 |

0-0-0 air
2-2 ground

**Gebhardt, William P., Lt.**
338th Ftr Sqn/55th Ftr Grp

| *Sqn* | *Date* | *Claims* | *Location* | *A/C* |
|---|---|---|---|---|
| 338th | September 19, 1944 | Me-109 dest(air) | S/Dusseldorf | P-51 |

1-0-0 air
0-0 ground

**Geiger, Clarence W., Lt.**
351st Ftr Sqn/353rd Ftr Grp

| *Sqn* | *Date* | *Claims* | *Location* | *A/C* |
|---|---|---|---|---|
| 351st | April 16, 1945 | (2)u/i a/c dest(grd) | Reichersberg | P-51 |

0-0-0 air
2-0 ground

**Geiger, Everett E., Lt.**
55th Ftr Sqn/20th Ftr Grp

| *Sqn* | *Date* | *Claims* | *Location* | *A/C* |
|---|---|---|---|---|
| 55th | February 22, 1944 | Z.506 dest(air) | Cleve | P-38 |

1-0-0 air
0-0 ground

**Gelsone, Frank E., Lt.**
357th Ftr Sqn/355th Ftr Grp

| *Sqn* | *Date* | *Claims* | *Location* | *A/C* |
|---|---|---|---|---|
| 357th | April 16, 1945 | FW-190 dest(grd) | SE Germany | P-51 |
| | | (.5)Me-109 dest(grd)* | SE Germany | P-51 |
| | | (2)Me-109 dam(grd) | SE Germany | P-51 |

0-0-0 air
1.5-2 ground

* - shared with Lt. E.H. Whitney of the 357th Ftr Sqn

**Gendron, Leo F., Lt.**
375th Ftr Sqn/361st Ftr Grp

| *Sqn* | *Date* | *Claims* | *Location* | *A/C* |
|---|---|---|---|---|
| 375th | April 4, 1945 | (4)Me-262 dam(air) | S/Hamburg | P-51 |

0-0-4 air
0-0 ground

**Gentile, Don S., Capt.**
336th Ftr Sqn/4th Ftr Grp
Earlier flew with 133 Sqn, RAF, and claimed 2 kills; a FW-190 and Ju-88 on August 19, 1942.

| *Sqn* | *Date* | *Claims* | *Location* | *A/C* |
|---|---|---|---|---|
| 336th | March 12, 1943 | FW-190 dam(air) | Audruieg | Spit |
| | August 16 | Me-109 dam(air) | Paris | P-47 |
| | December 16 | (.33)Ju-88 dest(air)* | E/Zuider Zee | P-47 |
| | January 5, 1944 | FW-190 dest(air) | W/Tours | P-47 |
| | January 14 | (2)FW-190 dest(air) | Compiegne | P-47 |
| | February 25 | FW-190 dest(air) | SE Luxembourg | P-47 |
| | March 3 | (2)FW-190 dest(air) | Wittenburg | P-51 |
| | | Do-217 dam(air) | Wittenburg | P-51 |
| | March 8 | (3.5)Me-109 dest(air)** | Berlin | P-51 |
| | March 18 | FW-190 dest(air) | Augsburg | P-51 |
| | March 23 | (2)Me-109 dest(air) | Munster | P-51 |
| | March 27 | (2)Me-110 dest(grd) | Cazaux A/F | P-51 |
| | March 29 | (2)FW-190 dest(air) | Brunswick | P-51 |
| | | Me-109 dest(air) | Brunswick | P-51 |
| | April 1 | Me-109 dest(air) | SW Stuttgart | P-51 |
| | April 5 | (3)Ju-88 dest(grd) | Stendal | P-51 |
| | | (.5)Ju-88 dest(grd)@ | Stendal | P-51 |
| | | (.5)Ju-88 dest(grd)@@ | Stendal | P-51 |
| | April 8 | (3)FW-190 dest(air) | Ruhrburg | P-51 |

19.83-0-3 air
6-0 ground

* - shared with Lt. V. Garriosn and Lt. L.H. Norley of the 336th Ftr Sqn
** - shared with Lt. J.T. Godfrey of the 336th Ftr Sqn
@ - shared with Lt. J.T. Godfrey of the 336th Ftr Sqn
@@ - shared with Maj. J.A. Goodson of the 336th Ftr Sqn

**George, William H., Capt.**
335th Ftr Sqn/4th Ftr Grp

| *Sqn* | *Date* | *Claims* | *Location* | *A/C* |
|---|---|---|---|---|
| 335th | April 9, 1945 | (2)Me-410 dam(grd) | Munich-Brunnthal | P-51 |

0-0-0 air
0-2 ground

**Gerard, Francis R., Capt.**
503rd Ftr Sqn/339th Ftr Grp

| *Sqn* | *Date* | *Claims* | *Location* | *A/C* |
|---|---|---|---|---|
| 503rd | August 16, 1944 | Me-109 dest(air) | Gotha | P-51 |
| | September 11 | (3)Me-109 dest(air) | Annaberg | P-51 |
| | | FW-190 dest(air) | Annaberg | P-51 |
| | | Me-109 dam(air) | Annaberg | P-51 |
| | March 2, 1945 | (2)Me-109 dest(air) | E/Magdeburg | P-51 |
| | | Me-109 dam(air) | E/Magdeburg | P-51 |
| | March 18 | FW-190 dest(air) | Dummer Lake | P-51 |

8-0-2 air
0-0 ground

**Gerbe, William T., Jr., Lt.**
486th Ftr Sqn/352nd Ftr Grp

| *Sqn* | *Date* | *Claims* | *Location* | *A/C* |
|---|---|---|---|---|
| 486th | September 12, 1944 | (2)Me-109 dest(air) | Kyritz | P-51 |
| | November 1 | (.5)Me-262 dest(air)* | E/Arnheim-Hengelo | P-51 |

2.5-0-0 air
0-0 ground

* - shared with Lt. W.R. Groce of the 56th Ftr Grp

**Geren, Lloyd F., Lt.**
62nd Ftr Sqn/56th Ftr Grp

| *Sqn* | *Date* | *Claims* | *Location* | *A/C* |
|---|---|---|---|---|
| 62nd | December 23, 1944 | (.5)FW-190 dest(air)* | Euskirvhen-Bonn | P-47 |
| | April 13, 1945 | (4)He-111 dest(grd) | Eggebeck A/F | P-47 |
| | | (3)He-111 dam(grd) | Eggebeck A/F | P-47 |

0.5-0-0 air
4-3 ground

* - shared with Lt. D.A. Westover of the 62nd Ftr Sqn

**Gerick, Steven, Capt.**
61st Ftr Sqn/56th Ftr Grp

| *Sqn* | *Date* | *Claims* | *Location* | *A/C* |
|---|---|---|---|---|
| 61st | February 22, 1944 | Me-110 dam(air) | E/Paderborn | P-47 |
| | March 15 | Me-109 dest(air) | Dummer Lake | P-47 |
| | | Me-109 dam(air) | Dummer Lake | P-47 |
| | April 25 | Me-109 dest(grd) | Metz | P-47 |
| | May 12 | FW-190 dest(air) | NW Marburg | P-47 |
| | | Me-109 dam(air) | NW Marburg | P-47 |
| | June 7 | Me-109 dest(air) | SE Houdan | P-47 |
| | | Me-109 dam(air) | SE Houdan | P-47 |
| | June 12 | (2)Me-109 dest(air) | Evreux | P-47 |
| | | (4)Me-109 dam(air) | Evreux | P-47 |
| | June 27 | Me-109 dam(air) | Esternay | P-47 |
| | July 7 | u/i a/c dest(grd) | Peine A/F | P-47 |

5-0-9 air
2-0 ground

**Gerow, Arthur H., Lt.**
61st Ftr Sqn/56th Ftr Grp

| *Sqn* | *Date* | *Claims* | *Location* | *A/C* |
|---|---|---|---|---|
| 61st | November 18, 1944 | FW-190 dest(air) | E/Hanau | P-47 |
| | | FW-190 prob(air) | E/Hanau | P-47 |

1-1-0 air
0-0 ground

**Gerry, James L., Lt.**
338th Ftr Sqn/55th Ftr Grp

| *Sqn* | *Date* | *Claims* | *Location* | *A/C* |
|---|---|---|---|---|
| 338th | July 7, 1944 | FW-190 dest(air) | W/Bernburg | P-38 |
| | September 19 | Me-109 dest(air) | Cologne | P-51 |
| | November 26 | FW-190 dam(grd) | Vorden A/F | P-51 |

2-0-0 air
0-1 ground

**Gerst, Joseph L., Lt.**
486th Ftr Sqn/352nd Ftr Grp

| *Sqn* | *Date* | *Claims* | *Location* | *A/C* |
|---|---|---|---|---|
| 486th | May 24, 1944 | Me-109 dest(air) | N/Berlin | P-51 |

1-0-0 air
0-0 ground

**Gese, Albert L., Lt.**
77th Ftr Sqn/20th Ftr Grp

| *Sqn* | *Date* | *Claims* | *Location* | *A/C* |
|---|---|---|---|---|
| 77th | February 10, 1944 | Me-210 dam(air) | Brunswick | P-38 |
| | February 20 | FW-190 dam(air) | Brunswick-Gotha | P-38 |

0-0-2 air
0-0 ground

**Getz, Charles W., III, Capt.**
2nd Scouting Force

| *Sqn* | *Date* | *Claims* | *Location* | *A/C* |
|---|---|---|---|---|
| 2nd | March 1, 1945 | Me-262 dam(air) | Ingolstadt | P-51 |

0-0-1 air
0-0 ground

**Getz, Stuart H., Lt.**
61st Ftr Sqn/56th Ftr Grp

| *Sqn* | *Date* | *Claims* | *Location* | *A/C* |
|---|---|---|---|---|
| 61st | July 20, 1944 | (2)He-111 dest(grd) | Bassenheim A/F | P-47 |
| | | (2)He-111 dam(grd) | Bassenheim A/F | P-47 |
| | August 4 | (.5)u/i a/c dest(grd)* | Salenter Lake | P-47 |
| | September 12 | Me-109 dam(air) | N/Brandenburg | P-47 |
| | September 21 | (.5)FW-190 dest(air)** | Deventer | P-47 |

0.5-0-1 air
2.5-2 ground

* - shared with Lt. J.M. Jure of the 61st Ftr Sqn
** - shared with Lt. W.J. Osborne of the 61st Ftr Sqn

**Gevorkian, Samuel D., Capt.**
338th Ftr Sqn/55th Ftr Grp

| *Sqn* | *Date* | *Claims* | *Location* | *A/C* |
|---|---|---|---|---|
| 338th | November 2, 1944 | Me-109 dest(air) | NW Leipzig | P-51 |
| | December 24 | (.5)Me-109 dest(air)* | Friedburg | P-51 |
| | | (.5)FW-190 dest(air)* | Friedburg | P-51 |
| | April 10 | (2)Ju-88 dest(grd) | Burg A/F | P-51 |
| | | FW-190 dest(grd) | Burg A/F | P-51 |
| | April 16 | (3)FW-190 dest(grd) | N/Landshut | P-51 |
| | | (3)FW-190 dam(grd) | N/Landshut | P-51 |

2-0-0 air
6-3 ground

* - both shared with Lt. K.A. Lashbrook of the 338th Ftr Sqn

**Gibbs, Richard G., Lt.**
343rd Ftr Sqn/55th Ftr Grp

| *Sqn* | *Date* | *Claims* | *Location* | *A/C* |
|---|---|---|---|---|
| 343rd | February 3, 1945 | FW-190 dest(air) | Boizenburg | P-51 |
| | | Ju-88 dest(air) | Boizenburg | P-51 |
| | April 10 | He-111 dest(grd) | Burg A/F | P-51 |
| | | Ju-87 dam(grd) | Burg A/F | P-51 |
| | April 16 | (2)FW-190 dest(air) | Kamenz A/F | P-51 |

4-0-0 air
1-1 ground

**Gibson, Robert, Lt.**
361st Ftr Sqn/356th Ftr Grp

| *Sqn* | *Date* | *Claims* | *Location* | *A/C* |
|---|---|---|---|---|
| 361st | April 11, 1944 | (.25)Me-109 dest(grd)* | Gifhorn | P-47 |
| | | (.25)Ju-88 dest(grd)* | Gifhorn | P-47 |

0-0-0 air
0.5-0 ground

* - both shared with Col. E.A. Malmstrom of HdQts, 356th Ftr Grp, and Lt. J.V. Jack and F/O E.L. Decker of the 361st Ftr Sqn

**Gifford, Donald R., Lt.**
343rd Ftr Sqn/55th Ftr Grp

| *Sqn* | *Date* | *Claims* | *Location* | *A/C* |
|---|---|---|---|---|
| 343rd | April 9, 1945 | Me-410 dest(grd) | Munich-Brunnthal | P-51 |
| | | (2)Me-410 dam(grd) | Munich-Brunnthal | P-51 |

0-0-0 air
2-1 ground

**Gignac, Edward J., Maj.**
486th Ftr Sqn/352nd Ftr Grp
HdQts/352nd Ftr Grp

| *Sqn* | *Date* | *Claims* | *Location* | *A/C* |
|---|---|---|---|---|
| 486th | January 30, 1944 | (.5)Me-110 dest(air)* | Nordhorn | P-47 |
| | March 8 | Me-109 dest(air) | Minden | P-47 |

1.5-0-0 air
0-0 ground

* - shared with Lt. A.L. Marshall of the 486th Ftr Sqn

**Gilbert, Olin E., LtCol.**
83rd Ftr Sqn/78th Ftr Grp
HdQts/78th Ftr Grp
HdQts/66th Ftr Wg

| *Sqn* | *Date* | *Claims* | *Location* | *A/C* |
|---|---|---|---|---|
| 83rd | April 30, 1944 | FW-190 dest(air) | SW Paris | P-47 |
| | June 13 | FW-190 dest(air) | Orleans | P-47 |
| HdQts | August 10 | He-111 dest(grd) | Chateau-Salines | P-47 |
| (78th) | | u/i a/c dest(grd) | Chateau-Salines | P-47 |
| HdQts | April 16, 1945 | (3)FW-190 dest(grd) | Pilzen/Prague | P-51 |
| | | (1.5)Ju-87 dest(grd)* | Pilzen/Prague | P-51 |
| | | He-111 dest(grd) | Pilzen/Prague | P-51 |
| | | Ju-52 dest(grd) | Pilzen/Prague | P-51 |
| | | (2)u/i a/c dam(grd) | Pilzen/Prague | P-51 |
| | | FW-190 dam(grd) | Pilzen/Prague | P-51 |

2-0-0 air
8.5-3 ground

* - shared with Lt. D.J. Henahan of the 82nd Ftr Sqn, 78th Ftr Grp

**Gilbert, William T., Lt.**
362nd Ftr Sqn/357th Ftr Grp

| *Sqn* | *Date* | *Claims* | *Location* | *A/C* |
|---|---|---|---|---|
| 362nd | August 18, 1944 | (.5)FW-190 dam(grd)* | Rosieres A/F | P-51 |
| | October 6 | FW-190 dest(air) | NW Berlin | P-51 |
| | November 18 | (.5)He-111 dest(grd)** | Mengen A/F | P-51 |
| | November 27 | FW-190 dest(air) | S/Magdeburg | P-51 |
| | December 5 | Me-410 dam(grd) | Berlin | P-51 |
| | December 24 | (2)FW-190 dest(air) | Fulda | P-51 |

4-0-0 air
0.5-1.5 ground

* - shared with F/Lt. E.B.H. Woolley, a D.S. RAF pilot attached to the 362nd Ftr Sqn
** - shared with Lt. J.A. Kirla of the 362nd Ftr Sqn

**Gilbertson, Merle J., Maj.**
77th Ftr Sqn/20th Ftr Grp

| *Sqn* | *Date* | *Claims* | *Location* | *A/C* |
|---|---|---|---|---|
| 77th | January 30, 1944 | Do-217 dam(air) | Osnabruck | P-38 |
| | February 5 | (.33)He-111 dest(air)* | Bourges A/F | P-38 |
| | August 5 | Me-109 dest(air) | NW Hamburg | P-51 |
| | August 16 | Me-109 dest(air) | Mulhausen | P-51 |
| | January 14, 1945 | (.5)Me-109 dest(air)** | Perleberg | P-51 |
| | February 9 | (3)FW-190 dest(grd) | Esperstadt A/F | P-51 |
| | | Me-110 dam(grd) | Esperstadt A/F | P-51 |
| | April 16 | u/i a/c dest(grd) | Cham A/F | P-51 |

2.83-0-1 air
4-1 ground

* - shared with Lt. R.L. Frakes and Lt. J.M. Morris of the 77th Ftr Sqn
** - shared with Lt. J.P. Starke of the 77th Ftr Sqn

**Giller, Edward B., Maj.**
343rd Ftr Sqn/55th Ftr Grp

| *Sqn* | *Date* | *Claims* | *Location* | *A/C* |
|---|---|---|---|---|
| 343rd | November 13, 1943 | Ju-88 dest(air) | W/Bremen | P-38 |
| | February 25, 1944 | Me-410 dest(air) | SE Augsburg | P-38 |
| | April 9, 1945 | Me-262 dest(air) | Munich | P-51 |
| | | He-111 dest(grd) | Munich-Brunnthal | P-51 |
| | | Me-410 dest(grd) | Munich-Brunnthal | P-51 |
| | | Me-262 dest(grd) | Munich-Brunnthal | P-51 |
| | | Me-410 dam(grd) | Munich-Brunnthal | P-51 |
| | April 16 | He-111 dest(grd) | Munich-Brunnthal | P-51 |
| | | Me-109 dest(grd) | Munich-Brunnthal | P-51 |
| | | Ju-52 dest(grd) | Munich-Brunnthal | P-51 |
| | | Ju-88 dam(grd) | Munich-Brunnthal | P-51 |

3-0-0 air
6-2 ground

**Gillette, Richard W., Lt.**
361st Ftr Sqn/356th Ftr Grp

| *Sqn* | *Date* | *Claims* | *Location* | *A/C* |
|---|---|---|---|---|
| 361st | August 12, 1944 | (.5)Ju-88 dest(air)* | Guise-Avesnes | P-47 |

0.5-0-0 air
0-0 ground

* - shared with Lt. E.C. Fremaux of the 361st Ftr Sqn

**Gillette, Willard G., Lt.**
334th Ftr Sqn/4th Ftr Grp

| *Sqn* | *Date* | *Claims* | *Location* | *A/C* |
|---|---|---|---|---|
| 334th | May 24, 1944 | Me-109 dest(air) | NE Hamburg | P-51 |
| | June 20 | Ju-88 dest(air) | E/Pasewalk | P-51 |
| | | Do-217 dest(grd) | Neubrandenburg | P-51 |
| | | (.5)Ju-88 dest(grd)* | Neubrandenburg | P-51 |
| | July 7 | Me-109 dest(air) | Sangerhausen | P-51 |
| | | Me-109 prob(air) | Sangerhausen | P-51 |
| | | (2)Me-109 dam(air) | Sangerhausen | P-51 |
| | September 13 | FW-200 dam(grd) | Halle | P-51 |

3-1-2 air
1.5-1 ground

* - shared with Lt. C.H. Shilke of the 336th Ftr Sqn, 4th Ftr Grp

**Gilleland, Alvah G., Lt.**
357th Ftr Sqn/355th Ftr Grp

| *Sqn* | *Date* | *Claims* | *Location* | *A/C* |
|---|---|---|---|---|
| 357th | July 24, 1944 | Do-217 dest(grd) | Lechfeld | P-51 |
| | | Do-217 dam(grd) | Lechfeld | P-51 |
| | | FW-190 dam(grd) | Lechfeld | P-51 |

0-0-0 air
1-2 ground

**Gilliland, Leown A., Capt.**
383rd Ftr Sqn/364th Ftr Grp

| *Sqn* | *Date* | *Claims* | *Location* | *A/C* |
|---|---|---|---|---|
| 383rd | March 8, 1944 | FW-190 dest(air) | N/Rheine | P-38 |
| | | FW-190 dest(air) | N/Magdeburg | P-38 |
| | | FW-190 prob(air) | N/Magdeburg | P-38 |
| | | FW-190 dam(air) | N/Magdeburg | P-38 |

2-1-0 air
0-0 ground

**Gilmore, Chester R., Capt.**
368th Ftr Sqn/359th Ftr Grp

| *Sqn* | *Date* | *Claims* | *Location* | *A/C* |
|---|---|---|---|---|
| 368th | September 8, 1944 | Ju-52 dest(grd) | Cronberg | P-51 |
| | September 11 | FW-190 dest(air) | Eisleben | P-51 |

1-0-0 air
1-0 ground

**Giltner, Joseph H., Capt.**
363rd Ftr Sqn/357th Ftr Grp

| *Sqn* | *Date* | *Claims* | *Location* | *A/C* |
|---|---|---|---|---|
| 363rd | January 24, 1944 | FW-190 dest(air) | Brussels | P-51 |

1-0-0 air
0-0 ground

**Gimbel, Edward L., Capt.**
336th Ftr Sqn/4th Ftr Grp

| *Sqn* | *Date* | *Claims* | *Location* | *A/C* |
|---|---|---|---|---|
| 336th | April 16, 1945 | Me-110 dest(grd) | Praha | P-51 |
| | | (2)Me-110 dam(grd) | Praha | P-51 |

0-0-0 air
1-2 ground

**Ginn, Charles L., Lt.**
62nd Ftr Sqn/56th Ftr Grp

| *Sqn* | *Date* | *Claims* | *Location* | *A/C* |
|---|---|---|---|---|
| 62nd | February 22, 1944 | Do-217 dam(grd) | Eindhoven | P-47 |
| | March 16 | FW-190 dam(grd) | Burvinnes A/F | P-47 |

0-0-0 air
0-2 ground

**Girzi, Henry E., Jr., Lt.**
505th Ftr Sqn/339th Ftr Grp

| Sqn | Date | Claims | Location | A/C |
|---|---|---|---|---|
| 505th | November 26, 1944 | FW-190 dest(air) | S/Hanover | P-51 |

1-0-0 air
0-0 ground

**Gladych, Bolek M., Maj.**
61st Ftr Sqn/56th Ftr Grp
Earlier flew with the PAF and RAF claiming some 12 kills.

| Sqn | Date | Claims | Location | A/C |
|---|---|---|---|---|
| 61st | February 21, 1944 | (2)Me-109 dest(air) | Zuider Zee | P-47 |
| | March 6 | Me-109 dest(grd) | Vechta | P-47 |
| | March 8 | FW-190 dest(air) | Dummer Lake | P-47 |
| | | (3)FW-190 dam(grd) | Dummer Lake | P-47 |
| | March 27 | Me-109 dest(air) | S/Angars | P-47 |
| | April 25 | FW-190 dam(grd) | Metz | P-47 |
| | | Ju-88 dam(grd) | Metz | P-47 |
| | | u/i a/c dam(grd) | Metz | P-47 |
| | June 6 | Me-109 dest(air) | Croisy | P-47 |
| | June 7 | Me-109 dest(air) | SE Houdan | P-47 |
| | July 5 | Me-109 dest(air) | Evreux | P-47 |
| | August 12 | Ju-88 dest(air) | Cambrai | P-47 |
| | September 21 | (2)FW-190 dest(air) | E/Arnheim | P-47 |

10-0-0 air
1-6 ground

**Glankler, Francis T., Capt.**
375th Ftr Sqn/361st Ftr Grp

| Sqn | Date | Claims | Location | A/C |
|---|---|---|---|---|
| 375th | May 9, 1944 | Me-109 dam(grd) | Juvincourt | P-47 |

0-0-0 air
0-1 ground

**Glascow, Marvin W., Capt.**
383rd Ftr Sqn/364th Ftr Grp

| Sqn | Date | Claims | Location | A/C |
|---|---|---|---|---|
| 383rd | April 12, 1944 | FW-190 prob(air) | E/Frankfurt | P-38 |
| | May 8 | Me-109 dam(air) | NE Dummer Lake | P-38 |
| | May 21 | FW-190 dest(grd) | Rechlin | P-38 |
| | | Ju-88 dest(grd) | Rechlin | P-38 |
| | | (2)Ju-88 dam(grd) | Rechlin | P-38 |
| | August 9 | (2)Ju-88 dest(grd) | Munich | P-51 |
| | | (.5)u/i a/c dest(grd)* | Munich | P-51 |
| | September 12 | (2)FW-190 prob(air) | N/Berlin | P-51 |

0-3-1 air
4.5-2 ground

* - shared with Lt. P.J. Goldberg of the 383rd Ftr Sqn

**Glaser, Kenneth M., Lt.**
338th Ftr Sqn/55th Ftr Grp

| Sqn | Date | Claims | Location | A/C |
|---|---|---|---|---|
| 338th | July 6, 1944 | Me-109 dest(air) | Laon | P-38 |

1-0-0 air
0-0 ground

**Glass, Otey M., Jr., Capt.**
336th Ftr Sqn/4th Ftr Grp

| Sqn | Date | Claims | Location | A/C |
|---|---|---|---|---|
| 336th | June 20, 1944 | Me-109 dest(air) | S/Anklam | P-51 |
| | August 6 | (2)Ju-52 dest(grd) | SE Berlin | P-51 |
| | | Me-109 dam(grd) | SE Berlin | P-51 |
| | | Ju-52 dam(grd) | SE Berlin | P-51 |

1-0-0 air
2-2 ground

**Gleason, George W., Capt.**
434th Ftr Sqn/479th Ftr Grp

| Sqn | Date | Claims | Location | A/C |
|---|---|---|---|---|
| 434th | August 18, 1944 | FW-190 dest(grd) | Nancy/Essey A/F | P-38 |
| | | (.5)He-111 dest(grd)* | Nancy/Essey A/F | P-38 |
| | | (.5)He-111 dest(grd)* | Nancy/Essey A/F | P-38 |
| | | (.5)Ju-88 dest(grd)** | Nancy/Essey A/F | P-38 |
| | | FW-190 dam(grd) | Nancy/Essey A/F | P-38 |
| | September 26 | (3)Me-109 dest(air) | SW Munster | P-38 |
| | | Me-109 dam(air) | SW Munster | P-38 |
| | September 28 | Me-109 dest(air) | W/Halberstadt | P-51 |
| | | FW-190 dest(air) | W/Halberstadt | P-51 |
| | December 23 | (2)FW-190 dest(air) | SE Bonn | P-51 |
| | | FW-190 dam(air) | SE Bonn | P-51 |
| | December 25 | (3)FW-190 dest(air) | SW Bonn | P-51 |
| | February 9, 1945 | Me-109 dest(air) | SE Magdeburg | P-51 |
| | | FW-190 dest(air) | SE Magdeburg | P-51 |

12-0-2 air
2.5-2 ground

* - both shared with Lt. C.F. Monsell of the 435th Ftr Sqn, 479th Ftr Grp
** - shared with Lt. H.W. Detlefson of the 435th Ftr Sqn

**Gleason, Robert S., Lt.**
360th Ftr Sqn/356th Ftr Grp

| Sqn | Date | Claims | Location | A/C |
|---|---|---|---|---|
| 360th | August 4, 1944 | Me-109 dest(air) | SW Hamburg | P-47 |

1-0-0 air
0-0 ground

**Glessner, Milton F., Maj.**
374th Ftr Sqn/361st Ftr Grp
375th Ftr Sqn/361st Ftr Grp

| Sqn | Date | Claims | Location | A/C |
|---|---|---|---|---|
| 374th | November 26, 1944 | FW-190 dest(air) | Wittingen | P-51 |

1-0-0 air
0-0 ground

**Glover, Fred W., Maj.**
336th Ftr Sqn/4th Ftr Grp

| Sqn | Date | Claims | Location | A/C |
|---|---|---|---|---|
| 336th | March 6, 1944 | FW-190 prob(air) | W/Berlin | P-51 |
| | March 16 | (2)Me-110 dest(air) | Kaufburen | P-51 |
| | March 29 | FW-190 dest(air) | Brunswick | P-51 |
| | | (.33)He-111 dest(air)* | Brunswick | P-51 |
| | April 5 | (2)Ju-52 dest(grd) | Stendal | P-51 |
| | | (2)Ju-88 dam(grd) | Stendal | P-51 |
| | April 8 | FW-190 dest(air) | Ulzen | P-51 |
| | April 15 | Me-110 dest(grd) | Hagenow | P-51 |
| | | u/i a/c dam(grd) | Hagenow | P-51 |
| | April 30 | (1.5)u/i a/c dest(grd)** | Valence A/F | P-51 |
| | August 5 | Me-109 dest(air) | Gardelegen | P-51 |
| | August 6 | Me-109 dest(grd) | SE Berlin | P-51 |
| | November 2 | Me-163 dest(air) | E/Leipzig | P-51 |
| | November 21 | (3)Me-109 dest(air) | W/Merseburg | P-51 |
| | December 25 | FW-190 dest(air) | SW Coblenz | P-51 |
| | January 16, 1945 | (2)Ju-87 dest(grd) | Neuhausen | P-51 |
| | | FW-190 dest(grd) | Neuhausen | P-51 |
| | February 22 | Me-109 dest(grd) | Halberstadt | P-51 |
| | | Do-217 dest(grd) | Halberstadt | P-51 |
| | February 27 | (2)Me-109 dest(grd) | Weimar | P-51 |
| | | FW-190 dest(grd) | Weimar | P-51 |
| | April 17 | Ju-87 dest(grd) | Pilzen | P-51 |

10.33-1-0 air
14.5-3 ground

* - shared with Lt. J.T. Godfrey of the 336th Ftr Sqn and Maj. G. Carpenter of the 335th Ftr Sqn, 4th Ftr Grp
** - shared with Lt. H.H. Frederick of the 336th Ftr Sqn

**Godard, Claude G., Lt.**
82nd Ftr Sqn/78th Ftr Grp

| Sqn | Date | Claims | Location | A/C |
|---|---|---|---|---|
| 82nd | November 30, 1943 | Me-109 prob(air) | Eupen | P-47 |
| | April 1, 1944 | Ju-88 dam(grd) | Verdun | P-47 |

0-1-0 air
0-1 ground

**Godfrey, John T., Maj.**
336th Ftr Sqn/4th Ftr Grp

| *Sqn* | *Date* | *Claims* | *Location* | *A/C* |
|---|---|---|---|---|
| 336th | November 29, 1943 | Me-109 prob(air) | Bremen | P-47 |
| | December 1 | Me-109 dest(air) | Ruhr Valley | P-47 |
| | | Me-109 dam(air) | Ruhr Valley | P-47 |
| | December 22 | (1.5)Me-109 dest(air)[*] | W/Munster | P-47 |
| | March 2, 1944 | FW-190 dam(air) | SW Coblenz | P-51 |
| | March 6 | Me-109 dest(air) | N/Hanover | P-51 |
| | | FW-190 dam(air) | N/Hanover | P-51 |
| | March 8 | (2.5)Me-109 dest(air)[**] | Berlin | P-51 |
| | March 16 | Me-110 dest(air) | Kaufburen | P-51 |
| | March 23 | Me-109 dest(air) | Munster | P-51 |
| | March 29 | FW-190 dest(air) | Brunswick | P-51 |
| | | (.33)He-111 dest(air)[@] | Brunswick | P-51 |
| | | FW-190 prob(air) | Brunswick | P-51 |
| | April 5 | (1.5)Ju-88 dest(grd)[@@] | Stendal | P-51 |
| | | Me-110 dest(grd) | Stendal | P-51 |
| | | (2)Me-110 dam(grd) | Stendal | P-51 |
| | | (2)Ju-88 dam(grd) | Stendal | P-51 |
| | | Ju-52 dam(grd) | Stendal | P-51 |
| | April 9 | Me-410 dest(grd) | Lingen/Plantlunne | P-51 |
| | | (.33)Ju-88 dest(grd)[#] | Lingen/Plantlunne | P-51 |
| | | (.33)Ju-88 dest(grd)[#] | Lingen/Plantlunne | P-51 |
| | April 22 | (3)Me-109 dest(air) | SW Kassel | P-51 |
| | April 24 | FW-190 dest(air) | NW Ludwigshafen | P-51 |
| | | FW-190 dam(air) | NW Ludwigshafen | P-51 |
| | April 29 | Do-217 dest(grd) | Nordhausen | P-51 |
| | | (.5)Ju-52 dest(grd)[##] | Nordhausen | P-51 |
| | | (.5)Ju-52 dest(grd)[&] | Nordhausen | P-51 |
| | | Do-217 dam(grd) | Nordhausen | P-51 |
| | April 30 | (.5)Do-24 dest(grd)[&&] | Lyon Anchorage | P-51 |
| | August 5 | Me-109 dest(air) | N/Osnabruck | P-51 |
| | | (3)Ju-52 dest(grd) | SE Munden | P-51 |
| | | (3)Ju-52 dam(grd) | SE Munden | P-51 |
| | August 6 | Me-410 dest(air) | NE Berlin | P-51 |
| | | Me-109 dam(grd) | SE Berlin | P-51 |
| | August 24 | (4)Ju-52 dest(grd) | Nordhausen | P-51 |

16.33-2-4 air
13.67-10 ground

[*] - shared with Lt. V.H. Wynn of the 334th Ftr Sqn, 4th Ftr Grp
[**] - shared with Capt. D.S. Gentile of the 336th Ftr Sqn
[@] - shared with F/O F.W. Glover of the 336th Ftr Sqn and Maj. G. Carpenter of the 335th Ftr Sqn, 4th Ftr Grp
[@@] - shared with Capt. D.S. Gentile of the 336th Ftr Sqn
[#] - shared with Capt. J.R. Happel and Lt. P.W. McKennon of the 335th Ftr Sqn
[##] - shared with Lt. I.E. Grounds of the 336th Ftr Sqn
[&] - shared with Lt. J.A. Patteeuw of the 336th Ftr Sqn
[&&] - shared with Lt. T.K. McDill of the 336th Ftr Sqn

**Godwin, Lester B., Lt.**
335th Ftr Sqn/4th Ftr Grp

| *Sqn* | *Date* | *Claims* | *Location* | *A/C* |
|---|---|---|---|---|
| 335th | June 20, 1944 | (.5)Me-210 dest(air)[*] | Ratzburger Lake | P-51 |

0.5-0-0 air
0-0 ground

[*] - shared with Capt. G.I. Stanford of the 335th Ftr Sqn

**Goebel, Anthony H., F/O**
487th Ftr Sqn/352nd Ftr Grp

| *Sqn* | *Date* | *Claims* | *Location* | *A/C* |
|---|---|---|---|---|
| 487th | December 27, 1944 | (.5)Me-109 dest(air)[*] | Bonn | P-51 |
| | | (.5)Me-109 dest(air)[**] | SW Bonn | P-51 |

1-0-0 air
0-0 ground

[*] - shared with Capt. E.E. Bankey of the 364th Ftr Grp
[**] - shared with Maj. W.T. Halton of the 487th Ftr Sqn

**Goetz, Joseph, F/O**
62nd Ftr Sqn/56th Ftr Grp
335th Ftr Sqn/ 4th Ftr Grp

| *Sqn* | *Date* | *Claims* | *Location* | *A/C* |
|---|---|---|---|---|
| 335th | February 22, 1944 | (.5)Me-109 dest(air)[*] | SW Ooltgensplant | P-47 |
| | | (.5)FW-190 dam(air)[*] | Erkelenz | P-47 |

0.5-0-0.5 air
0-0 ground

[*] - shared with Lt. P.W. McKennon of the 335th Ftr Sqn

**Goff, Walter L., Capt.**
383rd Ftr Sqn/364th Ftr Grp
HdQts/364th Ftr Grp

| *Sqn* | *Date* | *Claims* | *Location* | *A/C* |
|---|---|---|---|---|
| HdQts | April 17, 1945 | Me-262 dest(air) | Pilzen | P-51 |

1-0-0 air
0-0 ground

**Gohsler, Harry R., Lt.**
359th Ftr Sqn/356th Ftr Grp

| *Sqn* | *Date* | *Claims* | *Location* | *A/C* |
|---|---|---|---|---|
| 359th | November 26, 1944 | Me-109 dest(air) | NW Dummer Lake | P-51 |
| | February 25, 1945 | He-111 dam(grd) | Berndorf | P-51 |
| | April 7 | Me-109 dest(air) | E/Steinhuder Lake | P-51 |
| | | Me-109 prob(air) | E/Steinhuder Lake | P-51 |

2-1-0 air
0-1 ground

**Gokey, John W., Capt.**
503rd Ftr Sqn/339th Ftr Grp

| *Sqn* | *Date* | *Claims* | *Location* | *A/C* |
|---|---|---|---|---|
| 503rd | November 26, 1944 | FW-190 dam(air) | SE Dummer Lake | P-51 |
| | March 2, 1945 | Me-109 dest(air) | E/Magdeburg | P-51 |
| | April 16 | Do-217 dest(grd) | Kralupy | P-51 |
| | | (3)u/i a/c dam(grd) | Kralupy | P-51 |

1-0-1 air
1-3 ground

**Goldberg, Paul J., Lt.**
383rd Ftr Sqn/364th Ftr Grp

| *Sqn* | *Date* | *Claims* | *Location* | *A/C* |
|---|---|---|---|---|
| 383rd | August 9, 1944 | (1.5)u/i a/c dest(grd)[*] | Munich | P-51 |
| | | u/i a/c dam(grd) | Muncih | P-51 |

0-0-0 air
1.5-1 ground

[*] - shared with Capt. M.W. Glascow of the 383rd Ftr Sqn

**Golden, John T., Lt.**
434th Ftr Sqn/479th Ftr Grp

| *Sqn* | *Date* | *Claims* | *Location* | *A/C* |
|---|---|---|---|---|
| 434th | February 14, 1945 | Me-109 dest(air) | SW Berlin | P-51 |
| | February 20 | (1.5)He-111 dest(grd)[*] | Windleschenlaibach | P-51 |
| | | (.5)FW-190 dam(grd)[*] | Windleschenlaibach | P-51 |
| | April 13 | u/i a/c dest(grd) | Ratzburger Lake | P-51 |
| | | (2)u/i a/c dam(grd) | Ratzburger Lake | P-51 |
| | April 16 | (3)u/i a/c dest(grd) | Reichersberg | P-51 |

1-0-0 air
5.5-2.5 ground

[*]both shared with Lt. R.B. Kline of the 434th Ftr Sqn

**Goldstein, George G., Lt.**
62nd Ftr Sqn/56th Ftr Grp

| *Sqn* | *Date* | *Claims* | *Location* | *A/C* |
|---|---|---|---|---|
| 62nd | September 16, 1943 | Me-109 dest(air) | Vitre | P-47 |
| | November 11 | FW-190 dest(air) | Munster | P-47 |

2-0-0 air
0-0 ground

**Gonnam, Jesse W., Capt.**
352nd Ftr Sqn/353rd Ftr Grp

| *Sqn* | *Date* | *Claims* | *Location* | *A/C* |
|---|---|---|---|---|
| 352nd | September 22, 1943 | Me-109 dest(air) | Schoonhaven | P-47 |
| | December 30 | (.5)Me-109 dest(air)[*] | Charleville | P-47 |
| | | Me-109 prob(air) | Charleville | P-47 |
| | | Me-109 dam(air) | Charleville | P-47 |
| | January 7, 1944 | (3)FW-190 dest(air) | Orleans | P-47 |

| Sqn | Date | Claims | Location | A/C |
|---|---|---|---|---|
| | March 16 | (.5)Me-110 dam(grd)[**] | Laon | P-47 |
| | | (.5)Me-110 dam(grd)[**] | Laon | P-47 |
| | | (.5)He-111 dam(grd)[**] | Laon | P-47 |

4.5-1-1 air
0-1.5 ground

[*] - shared with Lt. G.L. Willits of the 352nd Ftr Sqn
[**] - all shared with Lt. H. Herfurth of the 352nd Ftr Sqn

**Goodfleisch, Donald M., Capt.**
63rd Ftr Sqn/56th Ftr Grp

| Sqn | Date | Claims | Location | A/C |
|---|---|---|---|---|
| 63rd | June 26, 1943 | FW-190 prob(air) | E/Rouen | P-47 |
| | August 17 | Me-110 dam(air) | Ans | P-47 |
| | September 3 | FW-190 dest(air) | SE Paris | P-47 |
| | October 4 | Me-110 dest(air) | E/Duren | P-47 |
| | October 20 | FW-190 prob(air) | Dison | P-47 |
| | | FW-190 dam(air) | Chateau d'Ardenne | P-47 |

2-2-2 air
0-0 ground

**Goodman, Charles E., Lt.**
328th Ftr Sqn/352nd Ftr Grp

| Sqn | Date | Claims | Location | A/C |
|---|---|---|---|---|
| 328th | November 2, 1944 | (3)Me-109 dest(air) | Merseburg | P-51 |
| | December 25 | Me-109 dest(air) | SW Coblenz | P-51 |
| | January 24, 1945 | (.5)Me-109 dest(air)[*] | Duren | P-51 |
| | February 22 | Me-262 dam(air) | Stendal | P-51 |
| | April 16 | (2)Me-109 dest(grd) | Ganacker | P-51 |
| | | (4)Me-109 dam(grd) | Ganacker | P-51 |

4.5-0-1 air
2-4 ground

[*] - shared with Lt. E.B. Dubay of the 328th Ftr Sqn

**Goodman, Orville E., Capt.**
338th Ftr Sqn/55th Ftr Grp

| Sqn | Date | Claims | Location | A/C |
|---|---|---|---|---|
| 338th | July 6, 1944 | Me-109 dest(air) | Laon | P-38 |
| | July 7 | FW-190 dest(air) | W/Bernburg | P-38 |
| | | (.5)Me-109 dest(air)[*] | W/Bernburg | P-38 |

2.5-0-0 air
0-0 ground

[*] - shared with Lt. G.E. Funk of the 338th Ftr Sqn

**Goodson, James A., Maj.**
336th Ftr Sqn/4th Ftr Grp

| Sqn | Date | Claims | Location | A/C |
|---|---|---|---|---|
| 336th | June 22, 1943 | FW-190 dest(air) | NW Hulst | P-47 |
| | August 16 | (2)FW-190 dest(air) | Paris | P-47 |
| | | FW-190 dam(air) | Paris | P-47 |
| | September 3 | FW-190 prob(air) | Paris | P-47 |
| | January 7, 1944 | (2)FW-190 dest(air) | Bethune | P-47 |
| | March 16 | (2)Me-110 dest(air) | Kaufburen | P-51 |
| | March 18 | (2)He-111 dest(grd) | Mannheim | P-51 |
| | March 21 | Me-410 dest(grd) | Evreux | P-51 |
| | March 23 | (2)Me-109 dest(air) | Munster | P-51 |
| | March 29 | Ju-88 dest(air) | NE Brunswick | P-51 |
| | | (2)Ju-88 dest(grd) | NE Brunswick | P-51 |
| | April 5 | FW-190 dest(grd) | Stendal | P-51 |
| | | Ju-52 dest(grd) | Stendal | P-51 |
| | | Ju-88 dest(grd) | Stendal | P-51 |
| | | (.5)Ju-88 dest(grd)[*] | Stendal | P-51 |
| | | (.5)Ju-88 dest(grd)[**] | Stendal | P-51 |
| | | (.5)Ju-88 dest(grd)[@] | Stendal | P-51 |
| | April 10 | (4.5)u/i a/c dest(grd)[@@] | Romorantin A/F | P-51 |
| | | Hs-126 dest(grd) | Romorantin A/F | P-51 |
| | April 23 | (2)Me-109 dest(air) | Wienar Neustadt[#] | P-51 |
| | May 12 | Me-109 dest(air) | Kassel | P-51 |
| | May 25 | FW-190 dest(air) | Strasbourg | P-51 |

14-1-1 air
15-0 ground

[*] - shared with Capt. D.S. Gentile of the 336th Ftr Sqn
[**] - shared with Lt. D.R. Emerson of the 336th Ftr Sqn
[@] - shared with an unknown pilot
[@@] - shared with Lt. C.H. Shilke of the 336th Ftr Sqn
[#] - claimed while on D.S. to the 15th Air Force in Italy

**Goodwyn, John W., Capt.**
335th Ftr Sqn/4th Ftr Grp

| Sqn | Date | Claims | Location | A/C |
|---|---|---|---|---|
| 335th | March 21, 1944 | (.5)Ju-88 dest(grd)[*] | Langon | P-51 |
| | April 5 | (.5)He-111 dest(air)[**] | N/Brandenburg | P-51 |
| | | (2)Ju-88 dam(grd) | Brandenburg | P-51 |
| | May 1 | Me-109 dam(air) | Losheim | P-51 |
| | May 24 | Me-109 prob(air) | N/Hamburg | P-51 |
| | July 7 | Me-109 dest(air) | Bad Frankenhausen | P-51 |

1.5-1-1 air
0.5-2 ground

[*] - shared with Capt. H.D. Hively of the 334th Ftr Sqn, 4th Ftr Grp
[**] - shared with Lt. P.S. Riley of the 335th Ftr Sqn

**Gordon, Edwin A., Lt.**
362nd Ftr Sqn/357th Ftr Grp

| Sqn | Date | Claims | Location | A/C |
|---|---|---|---|---|
| 362nd | April 10, 1945 | (2)He-111 dest(grd) | Neuruppin | P-51 |

0-0-0 air
2-0 ground

**Gordon, Ray C., Lt.**
350th Ftr Sqn/353rd Ftr Grp

| Sqn | Date | Claims | Location | A/C |
|---|---|---|---|---|
| 350th | February 27, 1945 | (2)Me-110 dest(grd) | Rohrensee | P-51 |
| | | Ju-88 dest(grd) | Rohrensee | P-51 |
| | | (2)Me-110 dam(grd) | Rohrensee | P-51 |
| | | (2)Ju-88 dam(grd) | Rohrensee | P-51 |
| | April 16 | (3)FW-190 dest(grd) | Pocking | P-51 |

0-0-0 air
6-4 ground

**Gordon, Vincent P., Lt.**
343rd Ftr Sqn/55th Ftr Grp

| Sqn | Date | Claims | Location | A/C |
|---|---|---|---|---|
| 343rd | February 24, 1945 | Me-110 dam(grd) | Zwischenahn A/F | P-51 |
| | February 26 | FW-190 dest(grd) | S/Varel | P-51 |
| | March 3 | Me-109 dest(grd) | Prague/Letnany | P-51 |
| | | Ju-52 dest(grd) | Prague/Letnany | P-51 |
| | | (4)Me-109 dam(grd) | Prague/Letnany | P-51 |
| | April 9 | Do-217 dest(grd) | Furtenfeldbruck | P-51 |

0-0-0 air
4-5 ground

**Gordon, William P., Jr., Lt.**
62nd Ftr Sqn/56th Ftr Grp

| Sqn | Date | Claims | Location | A/C |
|---|---|---|---|---|
| 62nd | February 24, 1944 | FW-190 dest(air) | SW Hanover | P-47 |

1-0-0 air
0-0 ground

**Gore, Victor E., Lt.**
358th Ftr Sqn/355th Ftr Grp

| Sqn | Date | Claims | Location | A/C |
|---|---|---|---|---|
| 358th | January 15, 1945 | u/i a/c dest(grd) | Landsberg | P-51 |
| | | (2)u/i a/c dam(grd) | Landsberg | P-51 |
| | April 13 | (1.5)He-111 dest(grd)[*] | Schleswig | P-51 |

0-0-0 air
2.5-2 ground

[*] - shared with LtCol. C.H. Kinnard of HdQts, 355th Ftr Grp

**Gorian, Martin G., Lt.**
435th Ftr Sqn/479th Ftr Grp

| Sqn | Date | Claims | Location | A/C |
|---|---|---|---|---|
| 435th | September 26, 1944 | Me-109 dest(air) | SW Munster | P-51 |

1-0-0 air
0-0 ground

**Gossard, Philip D., Capt.**
435th Ftr Sqn/479th Ftr Grp

| *Sqn* | *Date* | *Claims* | *Location* | *A/C* |
|---|---|---|---|---|
| 435th | August 18, 1944 | He-111 dest(grd) | Nancy/Essey A/F | P-38 |
| | December 5 | FW-190 dest(air) | NW Berlin | P-51 |

1-0-0 air
1-0 ground

**Goth, Robert A., Lt.**
354th Ftr Sqn/355th Ftr Grp

| *Sqn* | *Date* | *Claims* | *Location* | *A/C* |
|---|---|---|---|---|
| 354th | February 23, 1945 | Ju-88 dam(grd) | Neuburg | P-51 |

0-0-0 air
0-1 ground

**Gould, Clifford C., Lt.**
38th Ftr Sqn/55th Ftr Grp

| *Sqn* | *Date* | *Claims* | *Location* | *A/C* |
|---|---|---|---|---|
| 38th | November 2, 1944 | Me-109 dest(air) | S/Merseburg | P-51 |
| | April 10, 1945 | (2)Me-109 dest(grd) | Wesendorf | P-51 |
| | | u/i a/c dest(grd) | Wesendorf | P-51 |
| | | Me-109 dam(grd) | Wesendorf | P-51 |
| | April 16 | (2)He-111 dest(grd) | N/Ansbach | P-51 |
| | | Me-109 dam(grd) | N/Ansbach | P-51 |

1-0-0 air
5-2 ground

**Gould, Norman D., Lt.**
62nd Ftr Sqn/56th Ftr Grp

| *Sqn* | *Date* | *Claims* | *Location* | *A/C* |
|---|---|---|---|---|
| 62nd | November 18, 1944 | Me-109 dest(air) | E/Hanau | P-47 |
| | December 4 | Me-262 dest(grd) | Neuburg | P-47 |
| | | Me-262 dam(grd) | Neuburg | P-47 |
| | December 23 | FW-190 dest(air) | Euskirchen | P-47 |
| | January 21, 1945 | (.5)Ju-52 dest(grd)* | Huntingen | P-47 |
| | March 10 | Me-109 dest(air) | Remagen | P-47 |
| | March 14 | Ar-234 dest(air) | Coblenz | P-47 |

4-0-0 air
1.5-1 ground

* - shared with LtCol. L.C. Smith of the 62nd Ftr Sqn

**Gover, Leroy, Maj.**
336th Ftr Sqn/4th Ftr Grp

| *Sqn* | *Date* | *Claims* | *Location* | *A/C* |
|---|---|---|---|---|
| 336th | May 14, 1943 | FW-190 prob(air) | S/St. Nicholas | P-47 |
| | | (2)FW-190 dam(air) | S/St. Nicholas | P-47 |
| | July 28 | FW-190 dest(air) | E/Rotterdam | P-47 |

1-1-2 air
0-0 ground

**Grabovski, Bruno J., Lt.**
486th Ftr Sqn/352nd Ftr Grp

| *Sqn* | *Date* | *Claims* | *Location* | *A/C* |
|---|---|---|---|---|
| 486th | November 30, 1944 | (2)FW-190 dam(grd) | W/Leipzig | P-51 |
| | | He-111 dam(grd) | W/Leipzig | P-51 |
| | December 5 | Me-262 dam(air) | Osnabruck | P-51 |

0-0-1 air
0-3 ground

**Graham, Clarence H., Lt.**
354th Ftr Sqn/355th Ftr Grp

| *Sqn* | *Date* | *Claims* | *Location* | *A/C* |
|---|---|---|---|---|
| 354th | June 6, 1944 | Ju-87 dest(grd) | Chartres | P-51 |
| | June 20 | Me-410 dest(air) | NW Stettin | P-51 |
| | July 8 | Me-109 dest(grd) | SW Chalons | P-51 |
| | | Me-109 dam(grd) | SW Chalons | P-51 |

1-0-0 air
2-1 ground

**Graham, Donald W., Col.**
HdQts/357th Ftr Grp

| *Sqn* | *Date* | *Claims* | *Location* | *A/C* |
|---|---|---|---|---|
| HdQts | February 5, 1944 | FW-190 dam(air) | Romilly-Sur-Seine | P-51 |
| | March 8 | FW-190 dest(air) | Berlin | P-51 |
| | | Me-109 dam(air) | Berlin | P-51 |

1-0-2 air
0-0 ground

**Graham, Ethelbert H., Jr., Lt.**
503rd Ftr Sqn/339th Ftr Grp

| *Sqn* | *Date* | *Claims* | *Location* | *A/C* |
|---|---|---|---|---|
| 503rd | May 24, 1944 | (.5)FW-190 dest(air)* | Annaberg | P-51 |
| | August 5 | Me-109 dam(air) | S/Hameln | P-51 |
| | September 11 | (.5)FW-190 dest(air)** | Annaberg | P-51 |
| | | (.5)Me-109 dest(air)@ | Annaberg | P-51 |

1.5-0-1 air
0-0 ground

* - shared with Lt. W.E. Bryan of the 503rd Ftr Sqn
** - shared with Lt. C.S. Coe of the 503rd Ftr Sqn
@ - shared with Lt. D.E. McClish of the 503rd Ftr Sqn

**Graham, Gerald E., Lt.**
505th Ftr Sqn/339th Ftr Grp

| *Sqn* | *Date* | *Claims* | *Location* | *A/C* |
|---|---|---|---|---|
| 505th | June 29, 1944 | (.5)Me-410 dest(air)* | Halle-S/Magdeburg | P-51 |
| | July 31 | (.5)Me-410 dest(grd)** | Holzkirchen | P-51 |
| | | u/i a/c dam(grd) | Holzkirchen | P-51 |
| | August 3 | Do-217 dest(grd) | Benestroff | P-51 |
| | September 5 | Me-410 dam(grd) | Sinsheim | P-51 |
| | September 11 | Me-410 dest(grd) | Munich | P-51 |
| | | Me-410 dam(grd) | Munich | P-51 |
| | | Do-217 dam(grd) | Munich | P-51 |
| | | Ju-88 dam(grd) | Munich | P-51 |

0.5-0-0 air
2.5-5 ground

* - shared with Lt. E.M. Johnson of the 505th Ftr Sqn
** - shared with Maj. J.L. Thury of the 505th Ftr Sqn

**Graham, Gordon M., LtCol.**
354th Ftr Sqn/355th Ftr Grp

| *Sqn* | *Date* | *Claims* | *Location* | *A/C* |
|---|---|---|---|---|
| 354th | December 25, 1944 | FW-190 dest(air) | NW Trier | P-51 |
| | | FW-190 prob(air) | NW Trier | P-51 |
| | December 31 | (2)FW-190 dest(air) | SW Hamburg | P-51 |
| | January 14, 1945 | (2)FW-190 dest(air) | E/Meppen | P-51 |
| | | FW-190 dam(air) | E/Meppen | P-51 |
| | January 15 | Ju-188 dest(grd) | Kotha | P-51 |
| | | (2)u/i a/c dam(grd) | Oberpfaffenhofen | P-51 |
| | February 23 | Me-109 dest(grd) | Naumberg | P-51 |
| | | FW-190 dam(grd) | Landsberg | P-51 |
| | | (.5)Ju-52 dam(grd)* | Schleswig | P-51 |
| | | (.5)Ju-52 dam(grd)* | Schleswig | P-51 |
| | | (.5)Ju-52 dam(grd)* | Schleswig | P-51 |
| | April 8 | (2)Me-109 dest(air) | Oberpfaffenhofen | P-51 |
| | April 9 | (2.5)He-111 dest(grd)** | Memmingen | P-51 |
| | April 10 | Me-109 dest(grd) | Rechlin/Larz | P-51 |
| | | B-24 dest(grd) | Rechlin/Larz | P-51 |
| | | (3)Me-109 dam(grd) | Rechlin/Larz | P-51 |
| | April 16 | (3)Ju-88 dest(grd) | Eger A/F | P-51 |

7-1-1 air
9.5-7.5 ground

* - all shared with Lt. D.B. Langley of the 354th Ftr Sqn
** - shared with Capt. A.S. White of the 354th Ftr Sqn

**Graham, Lindol F., Capt.**
79th Ftr Sqn/20th Ftr Grp

| *Sqn* | *Date* | *Claims* | *Location* | *A/C* |
|---|---|---|---|---|
| 79th | December 31, 1943 | FW-190 dam(air) | Bordeaux | P-38 |
| | January 14, 1944 | Me-109 dam(air) | Rouen | P-38 |

| Sqn | Date | Claims | Location | A/C |
|---|---|---|---|---|
| | January 29 | (3)FW-190 dest(air) | (1)Coblenz & | P-38 |
| | | | (2-3)E/Lille | P-38 |
| | February 20 | (2)Me-110 dest(air) | SW Brunswick | P-38 |
| | March 18 | (.5)Me-110 dest(air)* | Ulm | P-38 |

5.5-0-2 air
0-0 ground

* - shared with Lt. A.W. Heiden of the 79th Ftr Sqn

**Graham, Robert W., Lt.**
487th Ftr Sqn/352nd Ftr Grp

| Sqn | Date | Claims | Location | A/C |
|---|---|---|---|---|
| 487th | July 20, 1944 | He-111 dam(grd) | Nordhausen | P-51 |

0-0-0 air
0-1 ground

**Grainger, Lester M., Lt.**
350th Ftr Sqn/353rd Ftr Grp

| Sqn | Date | Claims | Location | A/C |
|---|---|---|---|---|
| 350th | September 23, 1944 | FW-190 dam(air) | SE Arnheim | P-47 |
| | November 2 | (2)Me-109 dest(air) | Merseburg | P-51 |

2-0-1 air
0-0 ground

**Granville, Chester W., Lt.**
435th Ftr Sqn/479th Ftr Grp

| Sqn | Date | Claims | Location | A/C |
|---|---|---|---|---|
| 435th | August 18, 1944 | He-111 dest(grd) | Nancy/Essey A/F | P-38 |
| | | Ju-88 dest(grd) | Nancy/Essey A/F | P-38 |

0-0-0 air
2-0 ground

**Grasshoff, Hans J., Capt.**
436th Ftr Sqn/479th Ftr Grp

| Sqn | Date | Claims | Location | A/C |
|---|---|---|---|---|
| 436th | July 24, 1944 | (.5)Me-109 dest(air)* | Evreux | P-38 |
| | August 8 | Me-109 dam(air) | S/Paris | P-38 |
| | September 5 | (4)FW-190 dest(grd) | Bad Nauheim | P-38 |
| | | FW-190 dam(grd) | Bad Nauheim | P-38 |
| | September 26 | Me-109 dest(air) | S/Munster | P-38 |
| | November 27 | FW-190 dest(air) | Osnabruck | P-51 |

2.5-0-1 air
4-1 ground

* - shared with Lt. H.P. Plunk of the 436th Ftr Sqn

**Graves, James F., F/O**
487th Ftr Sqn/352nd Ftr Grp

| Sqn | Date | Claims | Location | A/C |
|---|---|---|---|---|
| 487th | April 17, 1945 | u/i a/c dest(grd) | Plattling | P-51 |

0-0-0 air
1-0 ground

**Gravette, Edgar B., LtCol.**
504th Ftr Sqn/339th Ftr Grp

| Sqn | Date | Claims | Location | A/C |
|---|---|---|---|---|
| 504th | May 30, 1944 | FW-190 dest(air) | Magdeburg | P-51 |
| | | FW-190 dam(air) | Magdeburg | P-51 |

1-0-1 air
0-0 ground

**Gray, Frederic C., Jr., Col.**
HdQts/78th Ftr Grp

| Sqn | Date | Claims | Location | A/C |
|---|---|---|---|---|
| HdQts | June 6, 1944 | (.5)FW-190 dest(air)* | Mayenne | P-47 |

0.5-0-0 air
0-0 ground

* - shared with Lt. V.J. Massa of the 83rd Ftr Sqn, 78th Ftr Grp

**Gray, Rockford V., Maj.**
369th Ftr Sqn/359th Ftr Grp
HdQts/359th Ftr Grp

| Sqn | Date | Claims | Location | A/C |
|---|---|---|---|---|
| HdQts | January 29, 1944 | (.5)Me-110 dest(air)* | Dison | P-47 |
| | January 30 | Me-109 dest(air) | Haselunne | P-47 |

1.5-0-0 air
0-0 ground

* - shared with Lt. J.H. Oliphint of the 369th Ftr Sqn

**Green, George D., Lt.**
335th Ftr Sqn/4th Ftr Grp

| Sqn | Date | Claims | Location | A/C |
|---|---|---|---|---|
| 335th | December 24, 1944 | Me-109 prob(air) | W/Giessen | P-51 |
| | February 25, 1945 | Me-410 dam(grd) | Pretzech A/F | P-51 |
| | April 16 | (2)Ju-88 dest(grd) | Praha/Letnany | P-51 |
| | | Do-217 dest(grd) | Praha/Letnany | P-51 |
| | | u/i a/c dest(grd) | Praha/Letnany | P-51 |

0-1-0 air
4-1 ground

**Green, Robert T., Capt.**
83rd Ftr Sqn/78th Ftr Grp

| Sqn | Date | Claims | Location | A/C |
|---|---|---|---|---|
| 83rd | August 10, 1944 | (1.5)He-111 dest(grd)* | Chateau-Salines | P-47 |
| | | (.5)Ju-52 dest(grd)* | Chateau-Salines | P-47 |
| | October 15 | (3.5)FW-190 dest(air)** | Bohmte | P-47 |
| | April 7, 1945 | Me-109 dest(air) | Dummer Lake | P-51 |

4.5-0-0 air
2-0 ground

* - both shared with Capt. C.M. Peal of the 83rd Ftr Sqn
** - shared with Lt. J.S. Reems of the 83rd Ftr Sqn

**Greene, Franklin W., Maj.**
486th Ftr Sqn/352nd Ftr Grp

| Sqn | Date | Claims | Location | A/C |
|---|---|---|---|---|
| 486th | December 20, 1943 | Me-109 dest(air) | SW Emden | P-47 |
| | February 10, 1944 | Me-109 dam(air) | Enschede | P-47 |
| | May 13 | Me-109 dest(air) | Tribsees | P-51 |
| | December 27 | Me-109 dest(air) | SE Liege | P-51 |

3-0-1 air
0-0 ground

**Greene, Jack E., Lt.**
62nd Ftr Sqn/56th Ftr Grp

| Sqn | Date | Claims | Location | A/C |
|---|---|---|---|---|
| 62nd | April 15, 1944 | (3)FW-190 dam(air) | N/Hamburg | P-47 |
| | May 12 | Me-109 dest(air) | Frankfurt | P-47 |

1-0-3 air
0-0 ground

**Greenfield, Bernard, Lt.**
350th Ftr Sqn/353rd Ftr Grp

| Sqn | Date | Claims | Location | A/C |
|---|---|---|---|---|
| 350th | April 16, 1945 | Me-109 dest(grd) | Pocking | P-51 |
| | | FW-190 dest(grd) | Pocking | P-51 |
| | | Ju-87 dest(grd) | Pocking | P-51 |
| | | Me-109 dam(grd) | Pocking | P-51 |
| | | Ju-87 dam(grd) | Pocking | P-51 |
| | | u/i a/c dam(grd) | Pocking | P-51 |

0-0-0 air
3-3 ground

**Greenlease, Charles B., Lt.**
335th Ftr Sqn/4th Ftr Grp

| Sqn | Date | Claims | Location | A/C |
|---|---|---|---|---|
| 335th | April 16, 1945 | u/i a/c dest(grd) | Praha | P-51 |
| | | (5)u/i a/c dam(grd) | Praha | P-51 |

0-0-0 air
1-5 ground

**Greenwood, Raymond P., Lt.**
352nd Ftr Sqn/353rd Ftr Grp

| Sqn | Date | Claims | Location | A/C |
|---|---|---|---|---|
| 352nd | June 7, 1944 | Me-109 dest(grd) | Compiegne | P-47 |
| | June 20 | He-111 dest(grd) | Plantlunne | P-47 |
| | August 1 | Me-410 dest(grd) | Laon/Couvron | P-47 |
| | August 4 | (2)He-111 dest(grd) | Plantlunne | P-47 |
| | August 12 | (2)u/i a/c dest(grd) | E/Paris | P-47 |
| | | FW-190 dest(grd) | E/Paris | P-47 |

0-0-0 air
8-0 ground

**Greenwell, Howard K., Lt.**
357th Ftr Sqn/355th Ftr Grp

| Sqn | Date | Claims | Location | A/C |
|---|---|---|---|---|
| 357th | February 23, 1945 | Me-262 dam(grd) | Neuburg | P-51 |

0-0-0 air
0-1 ground

**Greer, Cyrus M., Lt.**
487th Ftr Sqn/352nd Ftr Grp

| Sqn | Date | Claims | Location | A/C |
|---|---|---|---|---|
| 487th | June 21, 1944 | Me-109 dam(air) | E/Magdeburg | P-51 |
| | July 1 | Me-109 dam(air) | St. Quentin | P-51 |
| | July 13 | Me-109 dam(air) | E/Schweighausen | P-51 |
| | July 20 | (2)He-111 dam(grd) | Nordhausen | P-51 |

0-0-3 air
0-2 ground

**Greer, Nile C., Capt.**
504th Ftr Sqn/339th Ftr Grp

| Sqn | Date | Claims | Location | A/C |
|---|---|---|---|---|
| 504th | March 21, 1945 | (.5)Me-262 dest(air)* | Wurzburg | P-51 |
| | April 4 | Me-262 dest(air) | Parchim | P-51 |

1.5-0-0 air
0-0 ground

* - shared with Lt. B.E. Langohr of the 504th Ftr Sqn

**Gregg, Eugene S., Capt.**
338th Ftr Sqn/55th Ftr Grp

| Sqn | Date | Claims | Location | A/C |
|---|---|---|---|---|
| 338th | September 13, 1944 | (.5)Me-109 dest(air)* | Eisenach-Gotha | P-51 |

0.5-0-0 air
0-0 ground

* - shared with Lt. D.S. Cramer of the 338th Ftr Sqn

**Grenning, Harold F., Jr., Lt.**
434th Ftr Sqn/479th Ftr Grp

| Sqn | Date | Claims | Location | A/C |
|---|---|---|---|---|
| 434th | August 18, 1944 | He-111 dest(grd) | Nancy/Essey A/F | P-38 |
| | | Ju-88 dest(grd) | Nancy/Essey A/F | P-38 |
| | | (2)Ju-88 dam(grd) | Nancy/Essey A/F | P-38 |
| | September 26 | Me-109 dest(air) | SW Munster | P-38 |

1-0-0 air
2-2 ground

**Gresham, Walter V., Jr., Maj.**
358th Ftr Sqn/355th Ftr Grp

| Sqn | Date | Claims | Location | A/C |
|---|---|---|---|---|
| 358th | March 2, 1944 | FW-190 dest(air) | SE Charleroi | P-47 |
| | March 16 | Me-109 dest(air) | W/Augsburg | P-51 |
| | April 5 | (2)He-111 dest(grd) | Munich | P-51 |
| | April 11 | (.5)Me-410 dest(air)* | NE Berlin | P-51 |
| | | (.25)Me-410 dest(air)** | NE Berlin | P-51 |
| | | (.25)Ju-88 dest(air)** | NE Berlin | P-51 |
| | May 4 | Me-109 prob(air) | SW Hanover | P-51 |
| | | Me-109 dam(air) | SW Hanover | P-51 |
| | August 15 | Me-109 dest(air) | NW Zwolle | P-51 |
| | April 10, 1945 | Me-262 dam(air) | W/Lubeck | P-51 |
| | April 17 | He-177 dest(grd) | Cheb A/F | P-51 |
| | | (3)u/i a/c dam(grd) | Eger A/F | P-51 |

4-1-2 air
3-3 ground

* - shared with Lt. R.J. Fussell of the 358th Ftr Sqn
** - both shared with Lt. R.J. Fussell, Lt. D.M. Martyn, and F/O L.M. Dudley of the 358th Ftr Sqn

**Griffin, Benjamin L., Lt.**
334th Ftr Sqn/4th Ftr Grp
336th Ftr Sqn/4th Ftr Grp

| Sqn | Date | Claims | Location | A/C |
|---|---|---|---|---|
| 336th | April 16, 1945 | (4)u/i a/c dest(grd) | Praha | P-51 |

0-0-0 air
4-0 ground

**Griffith, Walter B., Lt.**
504th Ftr Sqn/339th Ftr Grp

| Sqn | Date | Claims | Location | A/C |
|---|---|---|---|---|
| 504th | May 24, 1944 | Me-109 dest(air) | Berlin | P-51 |

1-0-0 air
0-0 ground

**Griffiths, Charles E., Jr., Capt.**
486th Ftr Sqn/352nd Ftr Grp

| Sqn | Date | Claims | Location | A/C |
|---|---|---|---|---|
| 486th | November 30, 1944 | Me-109 dest(air) | Glauchau | P-51 |

1-0-0 air
0-0 ground

**Grimes, Howard E., Lt.**
370th Ftr Sqn/359th Ftr Grp

| Sqn | Date | Claims | Location | A/C |
|---|---|---|---|---|
| 370th | May 29, 1944 | (2)FW-190 dest(air) | Stettin | P-51 |
| | May 30 | (.5)Me-109 dest(air)* | Dessau | P-51 |

2.5-0-0 air
0-0 ground

* - shared with an unknown pilot

**Grimes, Wilbur K., Capt.**
84th Ftr Sqn/78th Ftr Grp

| Sqn | Date | Claims | Location | A/C |
|---|---|---|---|---|
| 84th | August 10, 1944 | Me-109 dest(grd) | Conflans | P-47 |
| | | (.5)Ju-88 dest(grd)* | Conflans | P-47 |
| | September 9 | FW-190 dest(air) | Giessen | P-47 |
| | | (.5)FW-190 dam(air)** | Giessen | P-47 |

1-0-0.5 air
1.5-0 ground

* - shared with Lt. H.F. Beck of the 84th Ftr Sqn
** - shared with Lt. R.W. Dunham of the 82nd Ftr Sqn, 78th Ftr Grp

**Grimshaw, John L., Lt.**
384th Ftr Sqn/364th Ftr Grp

| Sqn | Date | Claims | Location | A/C |
|---|---|---|---|---|
| 384th | August 9, 1944 | Me-410 dam(grd) | Schongen | P-51 |
| | November 21 | FW-190 dest(air) | SW Merseburg | P-51 |
| | | Me-109 dam(air) | SW Merseburg | P-51 |

1-0-1 air
0-1 ground

*Anthony Rosatone, 352nd Fighter Squadron pilot who went MIA on January 18, 1945.*

*Ray Morris of the 354th Fighter Squadron with his crew.*

*Harold Daniel in his 351st Fighter Squadron P-47.*

*Daniel's YJ-M 42-28566 "Ticket Home."*

*Rear close-up of Daniel's YJ-M.*

*Second highest scorer in the 359th Fighter Group was George Doersch.*

*William Price with his 350th Fighter Squadron Mustang, LH-F 44-14419 "Janie."*

*George Baker of the 368th Fighter Squadron on CV-H 42-106809 "Liquidator."*

*George Bostwick in his 62nd Fighter Squadron P-47. On right is crewchief Joe Brennan.*

*Russell Haworth with his 338th Fighter Squadron P-51, CL-K 44-13642 "Krazy Kid."*

*Claude Crenshaw on his 369th Fighter Squadron P-51, IV-I 44-13606 "Louisiana Heat Wave."*

*357th Fighter Squadron ace Fred Haviland.*

*Longtime member of the 353rd Fighter Group William Bailey.*

*Another shot of top air scorer Francis Gabreski, 56th Fighter Group.*

*Left: George Gleason of the 434th Fighter Squadron with his crew; Left to right: Coakes (assistant), Gleason, Al Perdue (crewchief).*

*Top 20th Fighter Group ace Ernest Fiebelkorn.*

*Roy Evans, who earlier flew with the RAF and 4th Fighter Group, is seen here in his 359th Fighter Group Mustang.*

*Charles Cole of the 55th and 77th Fighter Squadrons.*

*Top 359th Fighter Group ace Ray Wetmore.*

*Right: Another shot of Wetmore after the January 14, 1945 mission.*

*Clarence Anderson of the 363rd Fighter Squadron.*

*338th Fighter Squadron ace Tom Schank on his CL-I 44-13668 "Rocky Mtn Canary."*

*Vernon Rafferty of the 350th Fighter Squadron.*

*The 361st Fighter Squadron's only "ace-in-a-day", Frank Morgan with his crew of QI-N 42-26459 "Portland Rose."*

*Right: William Stangel, 328th Fighter Squadron ace.*

*Wallace Hopkins, Operations Officer and later Deputy CO of the 361st Fighter Group.*

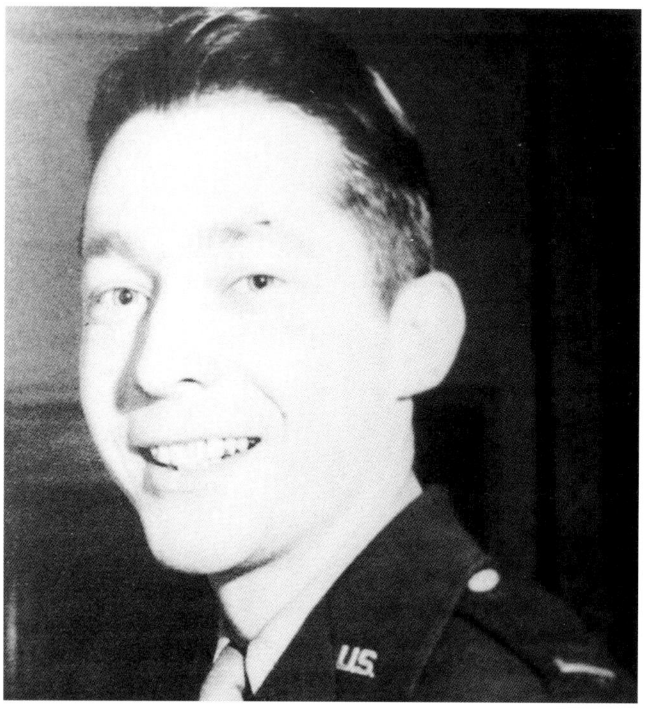


*505th Fighter Squadron "ace-in-a-day" Jack Daniell.*

*334th Fighter Squadron ace Howard Hively.*

*Arval Roberson and crew with his 362nd Fighter Squadron P-51, G4-A 44-13691 "Passion Wagon."*

*Sam Wicker of the 383rd Fighter Squadron who made ace on his last mission, December 31, 1944.*

*William Whisner of the 487th Fighter Squadron following the mission of November 21, 1944.*

*Boyd Jackson, 505th Fighter Squadron ace who was KIA on November 21, 1944.*

*High scoring 336th Fighter Squadron ace Fred Glover.*

*Robert York, 370th Fighter Squadron ace.*

*Dorian Ledington, 84th Fighter Squadron ace, who died only days before the war ended.*

*Joe Mason, CO of the 352nd Fighter Group, with his crew.*

*62nd Fighter Squadron ace Mike Jackson with his "Teddy."*

*505th Fighter Squadron CO and ace, Don Larson.*

*Ken Gallup of Headquarters, 353rd Fighter Group and the 350th Fighter Squadron.*

*Merle Capp of the 82nd and 84th Fighter Squadrons.*

*368th Fighter Squadron CO and ace Albert Tyrrell.*

*Charles Parmelee, 84th Fighter Squadron ace KIA September 10, 1944.*

William Maguire, 351st Fighter Squadron ace.

Number two strafer in the 8th Air Force was 505th Fighter Squadron CO Joe Thury.

Sam Beckley, CO of the 83rd Fighter Squadron.

Roy Osborn, CO of the 364th Fighter Group.

Charles Hoey, 352nd Fighter Squadron and Headquarters, 353rd Fighter Group.

Richard Rann, CO of the 359th Fighter Squadron.

*Don Vulgamore of the 376th Fighter Squadron.*

*Gerald Devine of the 350th Fighter Squadron with his "Mad Irishman."*

*Harvey Mace in a 362nd Fighter Squadron P-51D.*

*Rolfe Chickering with his 359th Fighter Squadron crew and OC-K 42-8588 "Gracie". Left to right: Tom Shafer (crewchief), Willard Gray (assistant), Henry Roberts (armorer).*

*Trio of 77th Fighter Squadron pilots on Fred Alexander's P-51, LC-H 44-13836 "It's The Kid!". Left to right: Alexander, Harold Gjolm, Hugh Jacobson.*

*Close-up of George Preddy's 328th Fighter Squadron P-51. Left is Art Snider (crewchief) with Sgt. Slade (photo section).*

*George Preddy's last P-51, PE-P 44-14906 "Cripes A'Mighty."*

*David Williams of the 384th Fighter Squadron.*

*Richard Olander, 505th Fighter Squadron ace.*

*Ray L. Shewfelt of the 479th Fighter Group and 2nd Scouting Force.*

352nd Fighter Squadron pilots, left to right: Maurice Morrison, Wilbert Junttila, Wilton Johnson, Glenn Callans.

More 352nd pilots, left to right: Wilbert Junttila, Wilton Johnson, William Bailey, and Glenn Callans.

William Cullerton of the 357th Fighter Squadron with his OS-X 44-13677 "Miss Steve."

359th Fighter Squadron P-51K of Jack Brown, OC-K 44-11366 "Bobby Socks."

Right: *Calvin Willruth's P-51 of the 335th Fighter Squadron, WD-Y 44-15028 "Dotty."*

Below: *Frank Birtciel's last P-51 of the 343rd Fighter Squadron, CY-A 44-13350 "Miss Velma."*

*Charles Yeager's last 363rd Fighter Squadron P-51, B6-Y 44-14888 "Glamorous Glen III."*

383rd Fighter Squadron P-51 getting ready for another mission.

Merle Gilbertson in his 77th Fighter Squadron P-51, LC-A 44-14822 "Sad Sack."

Carroll Ofsthun with his 363rd Fighter Squadron Mustang, B6-Y 44-14977 "The Count."

E9-O "Virginia" of the 376th Fighter Squadron.

Right: *Landing accident between a 369th Fighter Squadron P-51 and a truck, January 1, 1945.*

*Below: Darrell Beschen's MC-R 44-14337 "Bridget's Bunnion" of the 79th Fighter Squadron.*

*350th Fighter Squadron P-51 of William Tanner, LH-O 44-72212 "Prudence 7th."*

*Right: William Bailey's last 352nd Fighter Squadron P-51, SX-B 44-63684 "Double Trouble Two". Left to right are Marvin Martin (armorer), Olin Hertzog (aircraft), Bailey, Carl Buck (crewchief).*

*Below: 328th Fighter Squadron Mustang of William Stangel, PE-C 44-14015 "Stinky 2."*

*361st Fighter Squadron P-51 of Robert Wallace, QI-U 44-15066 "Ava Honey."*

**Grisham, Leon M., Lt.**
84th Ftr Sqn/78th Ftr Grp

| *Sqn* | *Date* | *Claims* | *Location* | *A/C* |
|---|---|---|---|---|
| 84th | February 3, 1945 | (3)FW-190 dest(grd) | Luneburg A/F | P-51 |

0-0-0 air
3-0 ground

**Griswold, Walter L., Jr., Lt.**
357th Ftr Sqn/355th Ftr Grp

| *Sqn* | *Date* | *Claims* | *Location* | *A/C* |
|---|---|---|---|---|
| 357th | April 16, 1945 | (.5)He-111 dest(grd)* | Bad Aibling | P-51 |
| | | He-111 dam(grd) | Bad Aibling | P-51 |
| | | Me-110 dam(grd) | Bad Aibling | P-51 |

0-0-0 air
0.5-2 ground

* - shared with Lt. R.O. Keuhl of the 357th Ftr Sqn

**Grizzle, Wiley, Lt.**
350th Ftr Sqn/353rd Ftr Grp

| *Sqn* | *Date* | *Claims* | *Location* | *A/C* |
|---|---|---|---|---|
| 350th | February 27, 1945 | (1.5)Me-410 dest(grd)* | Rohrensee | P-51 |
| | | FW-190 dam(grd) | Rohrensee | P-51 |
| | | u/i a/c dam(grd) | Rohrensee | P-51 |

0-0-0 air
1.5-2 ground

* - shared with Capt. H.G. Kolb of the 350th Ftr Sqn

**Groce, Walter R., Lt.**
63rd Ftr Sqn/56th Ftr Grp

| *Sqn* | *Date* | *Claims* | *Location* | *A/C* |
|---|---|---|---|---|
| 63rd | August 28, 1944 | He-111 dest(air) | N/Kaiserlautern | P-47 |
| | September 8 | Me-109 dam(grd) | Euskirchen | P-47 |
| | November 1 | (.5)Me-262 dest(air)* | E/Arnheim-Hengelo | P-47 |
| | December 2 | Me-109 dest(air) | S/Marburg | P-47 |
| | | Me-109 dam(air) | S/Marburg | P-47 |
| | December 4 | u/i a/c dam(grd) | Neuburg | P-47 |

3.5-0-1 air
0-2 ground

* - shared with Lt. W.T. Gerbe of the 352nd Ftr Grp

**Groshong, Douglas N., Lt.**
336th Ftr Sqn/4th Ftr Grp

| *Sqn* | *Date* | *Claims* | *Location* | *A/C* |
|---|---|---|---|---|
| 336th | November 21, 1944 | (2)Me-109 dest(air) | W/Merseburg | P-51 |
| | January 16, 1945 | FW-190 dest(grd) | Neuhausen | P-51 |
| | April 17 | Me-110 dest(grd) | Pilzen | P-51 |
| | | Ju-88 dam(grd) | Pilzen | P-51 |

2-0-0 air
2-1 ground

**Grounds, Duane, Lt.**
376th Ftr Sqn/361st Ftr Grp

| *Sqn* | *Date* | *Claims* | *Location* | *A/C* |
|---|---|---|---|---|
| 376th | April 16, 1945 | Ju-52 dam(grd) | Reichersberg | P-51 |

0-0-0 air
0-1 ground

**Grounds, Ira E., Capt.**
336th Ftr Sqn/4th Ftr Grp

| *Sqn* | *Date* | *Claims* | *Location* | *A/C* |
|---|---|---|---|---|
| 336th | April 29, 1944 | (.5)Ju-52 dest(grd)* | Nordhausen | P-51 |
| | May 25 | FW-190 dam(air) | Strasbourg | P-51 |
| | July 19 | (2)Me-109 dest(air) | E/Munchen | P-51 |
| | August 16 | Me-109 dest(air) | W/Magdeburg | P-51 |
| | August 25 | Me-109 prob(air) | SW Rostock | P-51 |
| | | (2)Me-109 dam(air) | SW Rostock | P-51 |

3-1-3 air
0.5-0 ground

* - shared with Lt. J.T. Godfrey of the 336th Ftr Sqn

**Grove, Francis M., Capt.**
336th Ftr Sqn/4th Ftr Grp

| *Sqn* | *Date* | *Claims* | *Location* | *A/C* |
|---|---|---|---|---|
| 336th | July 19, 1944 | Me-109 dest(air) | E/Munchen | P-51 |
| | September 11 | FW-190 dest(grd) | Langensalza | P-51 |
| | | (2)FW-190 dam(grd) | Langensalza | P-51 |
| | | Ju-188 dam(grd) | Langensalza | P-51 |
| | November 18 | (2)Me-262 dam(grd) | Leipheim | P-51 |

1-0-0 air
1-5 ground

**Grove, Lindsay W., Lt.**
352nd Ftr Sqn/353rd Ftr Grp

| *Sqn* | *Date* | *Claims* | *Location* | *A/C* |
|---|---|---|---|---|
| 352nd | January 16, 1945 | FW-190 dest(grd) | Deiningen | P-51 |
| | | Ju-88 dam(grd) | Deiningen | P-51 |
| | March 2 | Me-109 dest(air) | SE Berlin | P-51 |
| | April 16 | (2)He-111 dest(grd) | Pocking | P-51 |
| | | He-111 dam(grd) | Pocking | P-51 |
| | April 17 | FW-190 dest(grd) | Ganacker | P-51 |
| | | u/i a/c dam(grd) | Ganacker | P-51 |

1-0-0 air
4-3 ground

**Grow, Richard L., Lt.**
487th Ftr Sqn/352nd Ftr Grp

| *Sqn* | *Date* | *Claims* | *Location* | *A/C* |
|---|---|---|---|---|
| 487th | December 1, 1943 | (.5)Me-210 dest(air)* | S/Rheydt | P-47 |

0.5-0-0 air
0-0 ground

* - shared with Lt. V.K. Meroney of the 487th Ftr Sqn

**Gruber, William W., Lt.**
362nd Ftr Sqn/357th Ftr Grp

| *Sqn* | *Date* | *Claims* | *Location* | *A/C* |
|---|---|---|---|---|
| 362nd | March 2, 1945 | FW-190 dam(air) | NE Leipzig | P-51 |
| | March 24 | Me-109 dest(air) | W/Gutersloh | P-51 |

1-0-1 air
0-0 ground

**Gubana, Joseph L., Lt.**
79th Ftr Sqn/20th Ftr Grp

| *Sqn* | *Date* | *Claims* | *Location* | *A/C* |
|---|---|---|---|---|
| 79th | April 10, 1945 | Me-109 dest(grd) | Werder A/F | P-51 |
| | | Ju-88 dest(grd) | Werder A/F | P-51 |
| | | (2)u/i a/c dam(grd) | Werder A/F | P-51 |

0-0-0 air
2-2 ground

**Guckeyson, John W., Capt.**
375th Ftr Sqn/361st Ftr Grp

| *Sqn* | *Date* | *Claims* | *Location* | *A/C* |
|---|---|---|---|---|
| 375th | February 24, 1944 | Me-109 dest(air) | N/Loningen | P-47 |
| | March 8 | Me-109 dest(air) | Lemforde | P-47 |
| | April 15 | (.33)Ju-52 dest(grd)* | Fritzlar A/F | P-47 |
| | April 25 | Fi-156 dest(grd) | Nancy | P-47 |
| | | Ju-52 dest(grd) | Nancy | P-47 |
| | April 27 | (2)He-111 dam(grd) | Etampes | P-47 |
| | May 1 | (.5)Ju-188 dest(air)** | W/Verdun | P-47 |

2.5-0-0 air
2.33-2 ground

* - shared with Lt. S.D. Rames and Lt. W.A. Rautenbush of the 375th Ftr Sqn
** - shared with Lt. W.A. Rautenbush of the 375th Ftr Sqn

**Guernsey, Frank D., Maj.**
335th Ftr Sqn/ 4th Ftr Grp
504th Ftr Sqn/339th Ftr Grp

| *Sqn* | *Date* | *Claims* | *Location* | *A/C* |
|---|---|---|---|---|
| 504th | April 7, 1945 | FW-190 dest(air) | Celle | P-51 |
| | | Me-109 dam(air) | Celle | P-51 |

1-0-1 air
0-0 ground

**Guerrant, John, Lt.**
357th Ftr Sqn/355th Ftr Grp

| *Sqn* | *Date* | *Claims* | *Location* | *A/C* |
|---|---|---|---|---|
| 357th | May 22, 1944 | Me-109 dam(air) | Kiel | P-51 |

0-0-1 air
0-0 ground

**Guerrero, Thomas, Jr., Lt.**
63rd Ftr Sqn/56th Ftr Grp

| *Sqn* | *Date* | *Claims* | *Location* | *A/C* |
|---|---|---|---|---|
| 63rd | July 6, 1944 | FW-190 dest(air) | E/Chartres | P-47 |

1-0-0 air
0-0 ground

**Guggemos, Robert J., Lt.**
369th Ftr Sqn/359th Ftr Grp
368th Ftr Sqn/359th Ftr Grp

| *Sqn* | *Date* | *Claims* | *Location* | *A/C* |
|---|---|---|---|---|
| 369th | April 10, 1945 | Me-262 dest(air) | Gardelegen | P-51 |
| | | (2)Me-109 dest(grd) | Dennefeld | P-51 |

1-0-0 air
2-0 ground

**Guilfoyle, William A., Capt.**
82nd Ftr Sqn/78th Ftr Grp

| *Sqn* | *Date* | *Claims* | *Location* | *A/C* |
|---|---|---|---|---|
| 82nd | May 19, 1944 | (.5)He-111 dam(grd)* | Plantlunne | P-47 |

0-0-0 air
0-0.5 ground

* - shared with Lt. L.H. Hosford of the 82nd Ftr Sqn

**Gunner, Donald M., Lt.**
62nd Ftr Sqn/56th Ftr Grp

| *Sqn* | *Date* | *Claims* | *Location* | *A/C* |
|---|---|---|---|---|
| 62nd | April 10, 1945 | He-111 dest(grd) | Muritz Lake | P-47 |
| | April 13 | He-111 dest(grd) | Eggebeck A/F | P-47 |
| | | (2)He-111 dam(grd) | Eggebeck A/F | P-47 |

0-0-0 air
2-2 ground

**Gustke, Richard N., F/O**
350th Ftr Sqn/353rd Ftr Grp

| *Sqn* | *Date* | *Claims* | *Location* | *A/C* |
|---|---|---|---|---|
| 350th | February 27, 1945 | Me-410 dest(grd) | Rohrensee | P-51 |
| | | Ju-88 dest(grd) | Rohrensee | P-51 |
| | | (.5)FW-190 dest(grd)* | Rohrensee | P-51 |
| | | (4)u/i a/c dam(grd) | Rohrensee | P-51 |
| | March 21 | (4)Ar-234 dest(grd) | Achmer | P-51 |
| | | Me-109 dest(grd) | Achmer | P-51 |
| | | (4)Ar-234 dam(grd) | Achmer | P-51 |
| | March 24 | FW-190 dam(air) | NW Kassel | P-51 |
| | April 16 | (3)FW-190 dest(grd) | Pocking | P-51 |
| | | (2)Ju-87 dest(grd) | Pocking | P-51 |

0-0-1 air
12.5-8 ground

* - shared with Lt. J.D. McMullen of the 350th Ftr Sqn

**Gustke, Russell F., LtCol.**
HdQts/55th Ftr Grp
77th Ftr Sqn/20th Ftr Grp
HdQts/20th Ftr Grp
Earlier flew in the MTO with the 14th Ftr Grp and claimed one kill on December 5, 1942.

| *Sqn* | *Date* | *Claims* | *Location* | *A/C* |
|---|---|---|---|---|
| 77th | May 22, 1944 | FW-190 dest(air) | NW Kiel | P-38 |
| | November 4 | He-177 dam(grd) | SW Dummer Lake | P-51 |
| | December 2 | Me-109 dest(air) | Coblenz | P-51 |
| HdQts | March 24, 1945 | Ju-88 dam(grd) | Gutersloh | P-51 |

2-0-0 air
0-2 ground

**Guthrie, John L., Lt.**
350th Ftr Sqn/353rd Ftr Grp

| *Sqn* | *Date* | *Claims* | *Location* | *A/C* |
|---|---|---|---|---|
| 350th | March 21, 1945 | Me-109 dam(grd) | Achmer | P-51 |
| | March 24 | (3)Me-109 dest(air) | NW Kassel | P-51 |
| | | Me-109 dam(air) | NW Kassel | P-51 |
| | | FW-190 dam(air) | NW Kassel | P-51 |

3-0-2 air
0-1 ground

**Guy, John B., Lt.**
383rd Ftr Sqn/364th Ftr Grp

| *Sqn* | *Date* | *Claims* | *Location* | *A/C* |
|---|---|---|---|---|
| 383rd | March 30, 1945 | (.5)Me-262 dest(air)* | Brandenburg | P-51 |
| | April 13 | Me-109 dest(grd) | Flensburg | P-51 |
| | | Ju-52 dest(grd) | Flensburg | P-51 |
| | | FW-190 dam(grd) | Flensburg | P-51 |
| | | Ju-52 dam(grd) | Flensburg | P-51 |

0.5-0-0 air
2-2 ground

* - shared with an unknown pilot

**Guyton, William R., Lt.**
505th Ftr Sqn/339th Ftr Grp

| *Sqn* | *Date* | *Claims* | *Location* | *A/C* |
|---|---|---|---|---|
| 505th | April 10, 1945 | (2)Ju-88 dest(grd) | Wittstock | P-51 |
| | | Do-217 dest(grd) | Wittstock | P-51 |
| | April 16 | Me-109 dest(grd) | NE Prague | P-51 |
| | | Ju-88 dest(grd) | NE Prague | P-51 |

0-0-0 air
5-0 ground

**Haas, James H., Lt.**
368th Ftr Sqn/359th Ftr Grp

| *Sqn* | *Date* | *Claims* | *Location* | *A/C* |
|---|---|---|---|---|
| 368th | September 12, 1944 | FW-190 dest(air) | Pritzwalk | P-51 |

1-0-0 air
0-0 ground

**Hackney, Claude J., Jr., Capt.**
359th Ftr Sqn/356th Ftr Grp

| *Sqn* | *Date* | *Claims* | *Location* | *A/C* |
|---|---|---|---|---|
| 359th | December 5, 1944 | FW-190 dest(air) | Muritz Lake-Berlin | P-51 |
| | December 26 | FW-190 dest(air) | NE Bonn | P-51 |

2-0-0 air
0-0 ground

**Hagan, Benjamin M., Lt.**
368th Ftr Sqn/359th Ftr Grp

| *Sqn* | *Date* | *Claims* | *Location* | *A/C* |
|---|---|---|---|---|
| 368th | May 8, 1944 | (.5)Me-109 prob(air)* | SW Brunswick | P-51 |
| | May 21 | u/i a/c dest(grd) | Carlowe | P-51 |
| | | (2)u/i a/c dam(grd) | Carlowe | P-51 |
| | May 29 | Me-109 dest(air) | Ratzeburg | P-51 |

1-0.5-0 air
1-2 ground

* - shared with Capt. N.K. Cranfill of the 369th Ftr Sqn, 359th Ftr Grp

**Hagan, Harry N., Capt.**
336th Ftr Sqn/4th Ftr Grp

| *Sqn* | *Date* | *Claims* | *Location* | *A/C* |
|---|---|---|---|---|
| 336th | August 25, 1944 | Me-109 dest(air) | SW Rostock | P-51 |
| | January 16, 1945 | FW-190 dest(grd) | Neuhausen | P-51 |
| | | He-177 dest(grd) | Neuhausen | P-51 |
| | March 22 | FW-190 dest(air) | SE Berlin | P-51 |
| | April 16 | Me-109 dest(grd) | SW Pilzen | P-51 |

2-0-0 air
3-0 ground

**Hagan, Kenneth E., Capt.**
362nd Ftr Sqn/357th Ftr Grp

| *Sqn* | *Date* | *Claims* | *Location* | *A/C* |
|---|---|---|---|---|
| 362nd | March 6, 1944 | (.5)Me-110 dest(air)* | SW Berlin | P-51 |
| | | (.5)Me-110 dest(air)** | Berlin | P-51 |
| | May 28 | Me-410 dam(air) | N/Magdeburg | P-51 |

1-0-1 air
0-0 ground

* - shared with Lt. A.J. Roberson of the 362nd Ftr Sqn
** - shared with Lt. C.L. Williams of the 362nd Ftr Sqn

**Hagarty, Daniel D., Lt.**
82nd Ftr Sqn/78th Ftr Grp

| *Sqn* | *Date* | *Claims* | *Location* | *A/C* |
|---|---|---|---|---|
| 82nd | April 1, 1944 | (2)Do-217 dam(grd) | Verdun | P-47 |
| | April 12 | Ju-87 dest(air) | Sedan | P-47 |
| | | Ju-87 dam(air) | Sedan | P-47 |
| | May 12 | (2)FW-190 dest(air) | Trier | P-47 |

3-0-1 air
0-2 ground

**Hahn, Clifford B., Lt.**
82nd Ftr Sqn/78th Ftr Grp

| *Sqn* | *Date* | *Claims* | *Location* | *A/C* |
|---|---|---|---|---|
| 82nd | November 3, 1943 | Me-109 dest(air) | Barzal | P-47 |

1-0-0 air
0-0 ground

**Hahn, Peter J., Lt.**
384th Ftr Sqn/364th Ftr Grp

| *Sqn* | *Date* | *Claims* | *Location* | *A/C* |
|---|---|---|---|---|
| 384th | April 13, 1945 | FW-190 dam(grd) | Kaltenkirchen | P-51 |

0-0-0 air
0-1 ground

**Hahn, Robert F., Lt.**
351st Ftr Sqn/353rd Ftr Grp

| *Sqn* | *Date* | *Claims* | *Location* | *A/C* |
|---|---|---|---|---|
| 351st | April 7, 1945 | Me-109 dest(air) | Steinhuder Lake | P-51 |
| | April 16 | (4)Ju-88 dest(grd) | Reichersberg | P-51 |
| | | Ju-88 dam(grd) | Reichersberg | P-51 |

1-0-0 air
4-1 ground

**Haidle, Elmer E., Lt.**
503rd Ftr Sqn/339th Ftr Grp

| *Sqn* | *Date* | *Claims* | *Location* | *A/C* |
|---|---|---|---|---|
| 503rd | April 16, 1945 | (2)FW-190 dest(grd) | Kralupy | P-51 |
| | | FW-190 dam(grd) | Kralupy | P-51 |
| | | Me-109 dam(grd) | Kralupy | P-51 |

0-0-0 air
0-2 ground

**Haily, David R., Lt.**
338th Ftr Sqn/55th Ftr Grp

| *Sqn* | *Date* | *Claims* | *Location* | *A/C* |
|---|---|---|---|---|
| 338th | July 7, 1944 | FW-190 dest(air) | W/Bernburg | P-38 |
| | | Me-109 dam(air) | W/Bernburg | P-38 |

1-0-1 air
0-0 ground

**Hakonen, Howard H., Lt.**
350th Ftr Sqn/353rd Ftr Grp

| *Sqn* | *Date* | *Claims* | *Location* | *A/C* |
|---|---|---|---|---|
| 350th | February 27, 1945 | Me-410 dest(grd) | Rohrensee | P-51 |
| | | (.5)u/i a/c dest(grd)* | Rohrensee | P-51 |
| | | Me-410 dam(grd) | Rohrensee | P-51 |
| | March 24 | FW-190 prob(air) | NW Kassel | P-51 |

0-1-0 air
1.5-1 ground

* - shared with Capt. H.G. Kolb of the 350th Ftr Sqn

**Hale, Alfred R., Capt.**
359th Ftr Sqn/356th Ftr Grp

| *Sqn* | *Date* | *Claims* | *Location* | *A/C* |
|---|---|---|---|---|
| 359th | November 26, 1944 | FW-190 dest(air) | NW Dummer Lake | P-51 |
| | December 5 | FW-190 dam(air) | Muritz Lake-Berlin | P-51 |

1-0-1 air
0-0 ground

**Hall, George F., Capt.**
63rd Ftr Sqn/56th Ftr Grp

| *Sqn* | *Date* | *Claims* | *Location* | *A/C* |
|---|---|---|---|---|
| 63rd | August 17, 1943 | Me-109 prob(air) | Eupen-St. Nicholas | P-47 |
| | November 5 | Me-210 dest(air) | Enschede | P-47 |
| | January 30, 1944 | (2)Me-109 dest(air) | S/Quackenbruck | P-47 |
| | | (2)Me-109 dam(air) | S/Quackenbruck | P-47 |
| | February 22 | (2)Me-110 dest(air) | Raderborn | P-47 |
| | March 6 | FW-190 dest(air) | Ulzen | P-47 |

6-1-2 air
0-0 ground

**Hall, Glenn R., Capt.**
77th Ftr Sqn/20th Ftr Grp

| *Sqn* | *Date* | *Claims* | *Location* | *A/C* |
|---|---|---|---|---|
| 77th | February 9, 1945 | Me-109 dest(air) | Esperstadt A/F | P-51 |
| | | FW-190 dest(grd) | Esperstadt A/F | P-51 |
| | | Me-410 dam(grd) | Esperstadt A/F | P-51 |
| | | FW-190 dam(grd) | Esperstadt A/F | P-51 |
| | April 10 | Me-262 dam(air) | Werder A/F | P-51 |
| | | He-111 dest(grd) | Werder A/F | P-51 |
| | | Me-109 dest(grd) | Werder A/F | P-51 |
| | | He-111 dam(grd) | Werder A/F | P-51 |
| | | Ju-290 dam(grd) | Werder A/F | P-51 |

1-0-1 air
3-4 ground

**Hall, Robert L., Lt.**
487th Ftr Sqn/352nd Ftr Grp

| *Sqn* | *Date* | *Claims* | *Location* | *A/C* |
|---|---|---|---|---|
| 487th | April 30, 1944 | (3)u/i a/c dam(grd) | Clermont-Berrand | P-51 |

0-0-0 air
0-3 ground

**Hall, Thomas H., Jr., Lt.**
383rd Ftr Sqn/364th Ftr Grp

| *Sqn* | *Date* | *Claims* | *Location* | *A/C* |
|---|---|---|---|---|
| 383rd | August 9, 1944 | (2)Ju-88 dest(grd) | Munich | P-51 |
| | August 15 | (2)Me-109 dest(air) | Mannheim | P-51 |
| | November 2 | FW-190 dest(air) | Merseburg | P-51 |

3-0-0 air
2-0 ground

**Hallberg, Chester A., Capt.**
55th Ftr Sqn/20th Ftr Grp

| *Sqn* | *Date* | *Claims* | *Location* | *A/C* |
|---|---|---|---|---|
| 55th | January 29, 1944 | Me-110 dest(air) | Undenheim | P-38 |

| | February 20 | Me-110 dam(air) | NE Coblenz | P-38 |
|---|---|---|---|---|
| | March 18 | (.5)Me-110 dest(air)* | Memmingen | P-38 |
| | July 7 | Me-109 dest(air) | Halle | P-38 |

2.5-0-1 air
0-0 ground

* - shared with Capt. J.C. Serros of the 55th Ftr Sqn

**Halligan, James E., Jr., Lt.**
335th Ftr Sqn/4th Ftr Grp

| *Sqn* | *Date* | *Claims* | *Location* | *A/C* |
|---|---|---|---|---|
| 335th | April 16, 1945 | Me-110 dest(grd) | Praha | P-51 |
| | | FW-190 dest(grd) | Praha | P-51 |
| | | Ju-88 dest(grd) | Praha | P-51 |
| | | u/i a/c dest(grd) | Praha | P-51 |
| | | (4)u/i a/c dam(grd) | Praha | P-51 |
| | | Me-110 dam(grd) | Praha | P-51 |

0-0-0 air
4-5 ground

**Hallmark, John M., Capt.**
361st Ftr Sqn/356th Ftr Grp

| *Sqn* | *Date* | *Claims* | *Location* | *A/C* |
|---|---|---|---|---|
| 361st | October 7, 1944 | (3)Me-110 dam(grd) | Fritzlar | P-47 |

0-0-0 air
0-3 ground

**Hally, Lloyd G., Capt.**
351st Ftr Sqn/353rd Ftr Grp

| *Sqn* | *Date* | *Claims* | *Location* | *A/C* |
|---|---|---|---|---|
| 351st | June 24, 1944 | He-111 dest(grd) | Deelan | P-47 |
| | | (.5)Me-109 dest(grd)* | Deelan | P-47 |
| | August 4 | He-111 dest(grd) | Plantlunne | P-47 |
| | | Ju-88 dest(grd) | Plantlunne | P-47 |
| | August 27 | Ju-88 dest(grd) | NE Metz | P-47 |

0-0-0 air
4.5-0 ground

* - shared with Lt. D.L. Claiville of the 351st Ftr Sqn

**Halpin, Bernard C., Lt.**
77th Ftr Sqn/20th Ftr Grp

| *Sqn* | *Date* | *Claims* | *Location* | *A/C* |
|---|---|---|---|---|
| 77th | November 21, 1944 | Me-109 dest(air) | Munster | P-51 |

1-0-0 air
0-0 ground

**Halsey, Gilbert O., Maj.**
335th Ftr Sqn/4th Ftr Grp

| *Sqn* | *Date* | *Claims* | *Location* | *A/C* |
|---|---|---|---|---|
| 335th | May 16, 1943 | FW-190 dam(air) | Flushing | P-47 |

0-0-1 air
0-0 ground

**Halton, William T., LtCol.**
328th Ftr Sqn/352nd Ftr Grp
487th Ftr Sqn/352nd Ftr Grp

| *Sqn* | *Date* | *Claims* | *Location* | *A/C* |
|---|---|---|---|---|
| 328th | February 20, 1944 | Me-109 dest(air) | Louvain | P-47 |
| | April 22 | Ju-188 dam(grd) | Dummer Lake | P-51 |
| 487th | November 2 | Me-109 dest(air) | E/Merseburg | P-51 |
| | November 27 | Me-109 dest(air) | Hameln | P-51 |
| | December 26 | Me-109 dest(air) | SW Bonn | P-51 |
| | December 27 | (3.5)Me-109 dest(air)* | SW Bonn | P-51 |
| | January 1, 1945 | FW-190 dest(air) | N/Liege | P-51 |
| | January 24 | Me-109 dest(air) | SE Cologne | P-51 |
| | March 18 | Me-109 dest(air) | Bad Frienwalde | P-51 |
| | April 17 | FW-190 dest(grd) | Plattling | P-51 |
| | | Me-109 dest(grd) | Plattling | P-51 |
| | | (2)FW-190 dam(grd) | Plattling | P-51 |

10.5-0-0 air
2-3 ground

* - shared with F/O A.H. Goebel of the 487th Ftr Sqn

**Hambelton, Ted P., Capt.**
77th Ftr Sqn/20th Ftr Grp

| *Sqn* | *Date* | *Claims* | *Location* | *A/C* |
|---|---|---|---|---|
| 77th | October 7, 1944 | Ju-88 dam(grd) | Peenemunde | P-51 |
| | February 20, 1945 | Me-109 dam(grd) | Straubing | P-51 |

0-0-0 air
0-2 ground

**Hamilton, Ralph W., Capt.**
487th Ftr Sqn/352nd Ftr Grp

| *Sqn* | *Date* | *Claims* | *Location* | *A/C* |
|---|---|---|---|---|
| 487th | February 24, 1944 | Me-109 dam(air) | Enschede | P-47 |
| | April 22 | (3)He-111 dam(grd) | Salzwedel | P-51 |
| | April 28 | Ju-88 dest(grd) | Bourges | P-51 |
| | | u/i a/c dam(grd) | Bourges | P-51 |
| | May 27 | FW-190 dest(air) | Strasbourg | P-51 |
| | | FW-190 prob(air) | Strasbourg | P-51 |
| | May 29 | (2)u/i a/c dam(grd) | Jasmunder Bay | P-51 |
| | November 27 | (2)Me-109 dest(air) | Hameln | P-51 |
| | December 26 | Me-109 dest(air) | SW Bonn | P-51 |

4-1-1 air
1-6 ground

**Hamilton, Samuel D., Jr., Capt.**
61st Ftr Sqn/56th Ftr Grp

| *Sqn* | *Date* | *Claims* | *Location* | *A/C* |
|---|---|---|---|---|
| 61st | December 11, 1943 | (2)Me-110 dam(air) | NW Emden | P-47 |
| | February 6, 1944 | Me-109 dest(air) | Paris | P-47 |
| | February 20 | Me-110 prob(air) | Steinhuder Lake | P-47 |
| | | Me-109 dam(air) | Steinhuder Lake | P-47 |
| | March 6 | Me-109 dam(air) | NE Dummer Lake | P-47 |
| | March 18 | FW-190 dam(air) | Cambrai-Givet | P-47 |
| | April 9 | FW-190 dest(air) | NW Kiel | P-47 |
| | | (2)FW-190 dam(air) | NW Kiel | P-47 |

2-1-7 air
0-0 ground

**Hammett, Charles E., Capt.**
383rd Ftr Sqn/364th Ftr Grp

| *Sqn* | *Date* | *Claims* | *Location* | *A/C* |
|---|---|---|---|---|
| 383rd | December 23, 1944 | FW-190 dest(air) | NW Trier | P-51 |
| | February 14, 1945 | FW-190 prob(air) | Chemnitz | P-51 |
| | April 16 | Ju-52 dest(grd) | Marienbad | P-51 |
| | April 19 | FW-190 dest(air) | Lubben | P-51 |
| | | (.5)Do-217 dest(air)* | Lubben | P-51 |

2.5-1-0 air
1-0 ground

* - shared with F/O D. Healey of the 383rd Ftr Sqn

**Hancock, James H., Maj.**
38th Ftr Sqn/55th Ftr Grp

| *Sqn* | *Date* | *Claims* | *Location* | *A/C* |
|---|---|---|---|---|
| 38th | January 5, 1944 | FW-190 dest(air) | SW Kiel | P-38 |
| | | Me-109 prob(air) | SW Kiel | P-38 |
| | May 22 | FW-190 dest(air) | SW Kiel | P-38 |

2-1-0 air
0-0 ground

**Hand, Harold O., Lt.**
363rd Ftr Sqn/357th Ftr Grp

| *Sqn* | *Date* | *Claims* | *Location* | *A/C* |
|---|---|---|---|---|
| 363rd | September 13, 1944 | Me-109 dest(air) | E/Kassel | P-51 |
| | September 19 | (.5)Me-109 dest(air)* | W/Arnheim | P-51 |
| | November 2 | Me-109 dest(air) | E/Leipzig | P-51 |
| | | Me-109 dam(air) | E/Leipzig | P-51 |

2.5-0-1 air
0-0 ground

* - shared with Lt. F.L. Gailer of the 363rd Ftr Sqn

**Haning, Allen P., Lt.**
84th Ftr Sqn/78th Ftr Grp

| *Sqn* | *Date* | *Claims* | *Location* | *A/C* |
|---|---|---|---|---|
| 84th | September 10, 1944 | (2.5)He-111 dest(grd)* | Meinbullen | P-47 |
| | | He-111 dam(grd) | Meinbullen | P-47 |

0-0-0 air
2.5-1 ground

* - shared with Capt. R.E. Smith of the 84th Ftr Sqn

**Hanley, Claude, Jr., Lt.**
376th Ftr Sqn/361st Ftr Grp

| *Sqn* | *Date* | *Claims* | *Location* | *A/C* |
|---|---|---|---|---|
| 376th | September 18, 1944 | (.5)Me-109 dest(air)* | N/Schleswig | P-51 |
| | September 27 | FW-190 dest(air) | Eisenach | P-51 |
| | November 26 | FW-190 dest(air) | S/Ulzen | P-51 |

2.5-0-0 air
0-0 ground

* - shared with Lt. W.T. Butts of the 376th Ftr Sqn

**Hansard, Samuel E., Lt.**
338th Ftr Sqn/55th Ftr Grp

| *Sqn* | *Date* | *Claims* | *Location* | *A/C* |
|---|---|---|---|---|
| 338th | May 21, 1944 | Ju-88 dest(grd) | Magdeburg | P-38 |
| | August 10 | Me-109 dest(air) | Damville | P-51 |

1-0-0 air
1-0 ground

**Hanseman, Christopher J., Lt.**
505th Ftr Sqn/339th Ftr Grp

| *Sqn* | *Date* | *Claims* | *Location* | *A/C* |
|---|---|---|---|---|
| 505th | May 21, 1944 | (2)Trainer dest(air) | W/Dresden | P-51 |
| | | (.5)Ju-88 dest(air)* | W/Dresden | P-51 |
| | May 24 | (1.5)Me-109 dest(air)** | St. Gobain-Laon | P-51 |
| | June 10 | Me-109 dest(air) | Laigle | P-51 |
| | | Ju-88 dam(grd) | Laigle | P-51 |
| | July 19 | Ju-188 dest(grd) | SW Augsburg | P-51 |
| | | u/i a/c dest(grd) | SW Augsburg | P-51 |

5-0-0 air
2-1 ground

* - shared with Capt. L. Reid of the 505th Ftr Sqn
** - shared with an unknown pilot of the 503rd Ftr Sqn, 339th Ftr Grp

**Hansen, John W., Lt.**
434th Ftr Sqn/479th Ftr Grp

| *Sqn* | *Date* | *Claims* | *Location* | *A/C* |
|---|---|---|---|---|
| 434th | August 15, 1944 | Me-109 dest(air) | Steenwijk A/F | P-38 |
| | | (2)Me-109 dest(grd) | Steenwijk A/F | P-38 |
| | | Me-109 dam(grd) | Steenwijk A/F | P-38 |
| | | u/i a/c dam(grd) | Steenwijk A/F | P-38 |
| | August 18 | He-111 dest(grd) | Nancy/Essey A/F | P-38 |
| | | Ju-88 dest(grd) | Nancy/Essey A/F | P-38 |
| | | He-111 dam(grd) | Nancy/Essey A/F | P-38 |
| | September 26 | Me-109 dest(air) | SW Munster | P-38 |
| | | Me-109 dam(air) | SW Munster | P-38 |

2-0-1 air
4-3 ground

**Hansen, Kenneth J., Lt.**
436th Ftr Sqn/479th Ftr Grp

| *Sqn* | *Date* | *Claims* | *Location* | *A/C* |
|---|---|---|---|---|
| 436th | April 13, 1945 | (3)FW-190 dest(grd) | Salzwedel | P-51 |
| | | Me-110 dest(grd) | Salzwedel | P-51 |
| | April 17 | FW-189 dest(grd) | Karlsbad | P-51 |

0-0-0 air
5-0 ground

**Hanson, James R., Lt.**
505th Ftr Sqn/339th Ftr Grp

| *Sqn* | *Date* | *Claims* | *Location* | *A/C* |
|---|---|---|---|---|
| 505th | May 21, 1944 | (1.5)Trainer dest(air)* | Leipzig-Dresden | P-51 |
| | July 19 | Ju-188 dest(grd) | SW Augsburg | P-51 |

1.5-0-0 air
1-0 ground

* - shared with Lt. J.R. Starnes of the 505th Ftr Sqn

**Hanzo, Thomas A., Lt.**
79th Ftr Sqn/20th Ftr Grp

| *Sqn* | *Date* | *Claims* | *Location* | *A/C* |
|---|---|---|---|---|
| 79th | January 14, 1944 | (2)FW-190 dam(air) | S/Fecamp | P-38 |

0-0-2 air
0-0 ground

**Happel, James R., Maj.**
335th Ftr Sqn/4th Ftr Grp

| *Sqn* | *Date* | *Claims* | *Location* | *A/C* |
|---|---|---|---|---|
| 335th | August 16, 1943 | FW-190 dest(air) | Paris | P-47 |
| | January 30, 1944 | Me-109 prob(air) | Lingen | P-47 |
| | March 5 | FW-190 dam(air) | E/Bordeaux | P-51 |
| | March 27 | (.5)FW-190 dam(air)* | Libourne | P-51 |
| | April 8 | He-111 dest(air) | S/Ulzen | P-51 |
| | April 9 | (.33)Ju-88 dest(grd)** | Plantlunne | P-51 |
| | | (.33)Ju-88 dest(grd)** | Plantlunne | P-51 |
| | April 10 | (2)Bu-131 dest(grd) | Romorantin A/F | P-51 |
| | | (2)u/i a/c dest(grd) | Romorantin A/F | P-51 |
| | April 24 | FW-190 dest(air) | NE Worms | P-51 |
| | May 12 | Me-109 dest(air) | Giessen | P-51 |

4-1-1.5 air
4.67-0 ground

* - shared with Lt. A.L. Schlegel of the 335th Ftr Sqn
** - both shared with Lt. P.W. McKennon of the 335th Ftr Sqn and Lt. J.T. Godfrey of the 336th Ftr Sqn, 4th Ftr Grp

**Harbin, William R., Lt.**
352nd Ftr Sqn/353rd Ftr Grp

| *Sqn* | *Date* | *Claims* | *Location* | *A/C* |
|---|---|---|---|---|
| 352nd | April 16, 1945 | Ju-88 dam(grd) | Pocking | P-51 |

0-0-0 air
0-1 ground

**Hardee, Sellers S., Lt.**
357th Ftr Sqn/355th Ftr Grp

| *Sqn* | *Date* | *Claims* | *Location* | *A/C* |
|---|---|---|---|---|
| 357th | February 3, 1945 | Ju-88 dam(grd) | Gardelegen | P-51 |
| | February 9 | Ju-88 dest(grd) | Kothen | P-51 |
| | | Me-109 dam(grd) | Kothen | P-51 |
| | | Ju-52 dam(grd) | Kothen | P-51 |
| | February 23 | Me-109 dest(grd) | Neuburg | P-51 |

0-0-0 air
2-3 ground

**Hardin, William J., Lt.**
84th Ftr Sqn/78th Ftr Grp

| *Sqn* | *Date* | *Claims* | *Location* | *A/C* |
|---|---|---|---|---|
| 84th | June 7, 1944 | Me-109 dam(air) | Montdidier | P-47 |

0-0-1 air
0-0 ground

**Hardy, Preston B., Lt.**
334th Ftr Sqn/4th Ftr Grp

| *Sqn* | *Date* | *Claims* | *Location* | *A/C* |
|---|---|---|---|---|
| 334th | July 7, 1944 | Me-109 dest(air) | Blankenburg | P-51 |
| | | Me-109 prob(air) | Blankenburg | P-51 |
| | | (2)Me-109 dam(air) | Blankenburg | P-51 |
| | August 18 | Me-109 dest(air) | SW Beauvais | P-51 |
| | | Me-109 dam(air) | SW Beauvais | P-51 |

2-1-3 air
0-0 ground

**Hargreaves, Jack A., Capt.**
361st Ftr Sqn/356th Ftr Grp

| *Sqn* | *Date* | *Claims* | *Location* | *A/C* |
|---|---|---|---|---|
| 361st | August 18, 1944 | FW-190 dest(air) | Beauvais | P-47 |
| | | FW-190 prob(air) | Beauvais | P-47 |

1-1-0 air
0-0 ground

**Hargrove, Jasper E., Capt.**
385th Ftr Sqn/364th Ftr Grp

| *Sqn* | *Date* | *Claims* | *Location* | *A/C* |
|---|---|---|---|---|
| 385th | November 2, 1944 | Me-109 dest(air) | Halle | P-51 |
| | January 1, 1945 | (.5)FW-190 dest(air)* | Hamburg | P-51 |
| | March 21 | (2)FW-190 dam(grd) | Achmer | P-51 |
| | April 16 | Me-109 dest(grd) | Pocking | P-51 |
| | | Ju-87 dest(grd) | Pocking | P-51 |

1.5-0-0 air
2-2 ground

* - shared with Lt. F.X. Radley of the 385th Ftr Sqn

**Harker, Chester V., Capt.**
486th Ftr Sqn/352nd Ftr Grp

| *Sqn* | *Date* | *Claims* | *Location* | *A/C* |
|---|---|---|---|---|
| 486th | February 10, 1944 | Me-109 dam(air) | Enschede | P-47 |
| | April 24 | Do-217 dest(grd) | Ingolstadt | P-51 |
| | | Me-410 dest(grd) | Neuburg | P-51 |
| | | Ju-88 dam(grd) | Neuburg | P-51 |
| | April 25 | Me-110 dest(grd) | Metz | P-51 |
| | March 2, 1945 | FW-190 dam(grd) | Prague | P-51 |
| | | Me-410 dam(grd) | Prague | P-51 |

0-0-1 air
3-3 ground

**Harre, Charles W., Lt.**
334th Ftr Sqn/4th Ftr Grp

| *Sqn* | *Date* | *Claims* | *Location* | *A/C* |
|---|---|---|---|---|
| 334th | November 18, 1944 | (2)Me-262 dest(grd) | Leipheim | P-51 |
| | | (2)Me-262 dam(grd) | Leipheim | P-51 |
| | February 27, 1945 | Me-108 dest(grd) | Weimar | P-51 |
| | April 4 | Me-262 dam(air) | S/Parchim | P-51 |
| | April 16 | Me-109 dest(grd) | Gablingen | P-51 |
| | | (3)u/i a/c dam(grd) | Gablingen | P-51 |
| | | Me-109 dam(grd) | Gablingen | P-51 |

0-0-1 air
4-6 ground

**Harrell, John W., Maj.**
435th Ftr Sqn/479th Ftr Grp

| *Sqn* | *Date* | *Claims* | *Location* | *A/C* |
|---|---|---|---|---|
| 435th | November 27, 1944 | FW-190 dam(air) | SE Dummer Lake | P-51 |
| | December 25 | Me-109 dest(air) | SW Aachen | P-51 |

1-0-1 air
0-0 ground

**Harrington, Francis E., Lt.**
83rd Ftr Sqn/78th Ftr Grp

| *Sqn* | *Date* | *Claims* | *Location* | *A/C* |
|---|---|---|---|---|
| 83rd | September 10, 1944 | Me-410 dam(grd) | Germsheim | P-47 |
| | | Ju-87 dam(grd) | Germsheim | P-47 |
| | October 15 | FW-190 dam(air) | Bohmte | P-47 |
| | December 19 | Me-109 dest(air) | S/Coblenz | P-47 |
| | | FW-190 dest(air) | S/Coblenz | P-47 |
| | April 7, 1945 | Me-109 dest(air) | Dummer Lake | P-51 |
| | | FW-190 dest(air) | Dummer Lake | P-51 |
| | April 10 | (2)FW-190 dest(grd) | Werder A/F | P-51 |
| | | Ju-87 dest(grd) | Werder A/F | P-51 |
| | | u/i a/c dest(grd) | Werder A/F | P-51 |
| | | FW-190 dam(grd) | Werder A/F | P-51 |
| | | Ju-87 dam(grd) | Werder A/F | P-51 |
| | | u/i a/c dam(grd) | Werder A/F | P-51 |
| | April 16 | (2)u/i a/c dest(grd) | N/Prague | P-51 |
| | | Me-109 dest(grd) | N/Prague | P-51 |
| | | Me-262 dest(grd) | N/Prague | P-51 |
| | | (3)u/i a/c dam(grd) | N/Prague | P-51 |

4-0-1 air
8-8 ground

**Harrington, James C., Lt.**
358th Ftr Sqn/355th Ftr Grp

| *Sqn* | *Date* | *Claims* | *Location* | *A/C* |
|---|---|---|---|---|
| 358th | April 5, 1944 | (2)Me-110 dest(grd) | Munich | P-51 |
| | | (6)Me-110 dam(grd) | Munich | P-51 |
| | April 8 | (.5)Me-109 dest(air)* | E/Brunswick | P-51 |

0.5-0-0 air
2-6 ground

* - shared with Capt. E.L. Sluga of the 358th Ftr Sqn

**Harris, Delbert E., Lt.**
352nd Ftr Sqn/353rd Ftr Grp

| *Sqn* | *Date* | *Claims* | *Location* | *A/C* |
|---|---|---|---|---|
| 352nd | June 20, 1944 | u/i a/c dam(grd) | Plantlunne | P-47 |

0-0-0 air
0-1 ground

**Harris, Ollie E., Lt.**
362nd Ftr Sqn/357th Ftr Grp

| *Sqn* | *Date* | *Claims* | *Location* | *A/C* |
|---|---|---|---|---|
| 362nd | April 24, 1944 | Me-110 dam(air) | E/Munich | P-51 |
| | May 30 | Me-410 dest(air) | E/Bernburg | P-51 |

1-0-1 air
0-0 ground

**Harris, Ferris S., Lt.**
336th Ftr Sqn/4th Ftr Grp

| *Sqn* | *Date* | *Claims* | *Location* | *A/C* |
|---|---|---|---|---|
| 336th | April 30, 1944 | (.5)Do-24 dest(grd)* | Lyon S/P Base | P-51 |
| | June 20 | Do-217 dest(grd) | Neubrandenburg | P-51 |
| | | Do-217 dam(grd) | Neubrandenburg | P-51 |

0-0-0 air
1.5-1 ground

* - shared with Lt. W.E. Johnson of the 336th Ftr Sqn

**Harris, Shelby J., Capt.**
374th Ftr Sqn/361st Ftr Grp

| *Sqn* | *Date* | *Claims* | *Location* | *A/C* |
|---|---|---|---|---|
| 374th | July 5, 1944 | Ju-88 dest(grd) | Chateau Thierry | P-51 |

0-0-0 air
1-0 ground

**Harris, Thomas L., Capt.**
364th Ftr Sqn/357th Ftr Grp

| *Sqn* | *Date* | *Claims* | *Location* | *A/C* |
|---|---|---|---|---|
| 364th | March 6, 1944 | Me-110 dest(air) | E/Berlin | P-51 |
| | | (.5)FW-190 dest(air)* | NW Berlin | P-51 |
| | March 8 | (.5)FW-190 dest(air)** | Dummer Lake | P-51 |
| | April 19 | FW-190 dest(air) | S/Bliecherode | P-51 |
| | May 27 | (2)Me-109 dest(air) | Colmar | P-51 |
| | | Me-109 prob(air) | Colmar | P-51 |

5-1-0 air
0-0 ground

* - shared with Capt. G.V. Davis of the 364th Ftr Sqn
** - shared with Capt. G.V. Davis of the 364th Ftr Sqn

**Harrison, Charles R., Capt.**
62nd Ftr Sqn/56th Ftr Grp

| *Sqn* | *Date* | *Claims* | *Location* | *A/C* |
|---|---|---|---|---|
| 62nd | June 26, 1943 | FW-190 dest(air) | NE Rouen | P-47 |
| | August 17 | Me-110 dest(air) | Ans | P-47 |
| | February 21, 1944 | Me-109 dest(air) | Soesterburg | P-47 |

| Sqn | Date | Claims | Location | A/C |
|---|---|---|---|---|
| | April 9 | Me-109 dam(air) | Lubeck | P-47 |

3-0-1 air
0-0 ground

**Harry, G.P., Lt.**
504th Ftr Sqn/339th Ftr Grp

| Sqn | Date | Claims | Location | A/C |
|---|---|---|---|---|
| 504th | May 21, 1944 | Me-109 dam(air) | Leipzig | P-51 |
| | | Ju-87 dam(grd) | Leipzig | P-51 |

0-0-1 air
0-1 ground

**Hart, Cameron M., Capt.**
63rd Ftr Sqn/56th Ftr Grp

| Sqn | Date | Claims | Location | A/C |
|---|---|---|---|---|
| 63rd | September 5, 1944 | Me-109 dest(air) | NE Coblenz | P-47 |
| | | Me-109 prob(air) | NE Coblenz | P-47 |
| | | Me-109 dam(air) | NE Coblenz | P-47 |
| | December 23 | (2)FW-190 dest(air) | NW Coblenz | P-47 |
| | | FW-190 dam(air) | NW Coblenz | P-47 |
| | December 25 | Me-109 dest(air) | SE Cologne | P-47 |
| | February 3, 1945 | (2)FW-190 dest(air) | Friedersdorf A/F | P-47 |

6-1-2 air
0-0 ground

**Hart, Donald C., Capt.**
82nd Ftr Sqn/78th Ftr Grp

| Sqn | Date | Claims | Location | A/C |
|---|---|---|---|---|
| 82nd | September 9, 1944 | (.5)Me-109 dest(grd)* | Giessen | P-47 |
| | November 21 | Me-109 dam(air) | Hanover | P-47 |
| | | (.5)Ju-88 dest(grd)** | Gutersloh | P-47 |
| | November 26 | Me-109 dest(air) | Rheine | P-47 |
| | April 10, 1945 | FW-190 dam(grd) | Werder A/F | P-51 |
| | April 16 | (2)u/i a/c dam(grd) | Pilzen/Prague | P-51 |

1-0-1 air
1-3 ground

* - shared with Capt. R.E. Conner of the 82nd Ftr Sqn
** - shared with F/O H.R. Liebenrood of the 82nd Ftr Sqn

**Hart, Frederick L., Lt.**
435th Ftr Sqn/479th Ftr Grp

| Sqn | Date | Claims | Location | A/C |
|---|---|---|---|---|
| 435th | December 5, 1944 | FW-190 prob(air) | NW Berlin | P-51 |

0-1-0 air
0-0 ground

**Hart, Robert S., Capt.**
350th Ftr Sqn/353rd Ftr Grp

| Sqn | Date | Claims | Location | A/C |
|---|---|---|---|---|
| 350th | March 8, 1944 | FW-190 dest(air) | Dummer Lake-Steinhuder Lake | P-47 |
| | April 8 | u/i a/c dam(grd) | Hoperhofen | P-47 |

1-0-0 air
0-1 ground

**Hart, Wesley M., Jr., F/O**
375th Ftr Sqn/361st Ftr Grp

| Sqn | Date | Claims | Location | A/C |
|---|---|---|---|---|
| 375th | January 25, 1945 | (.5)Me-110 dest(air)* | NE Mannheim | P-51 |

0.5-0-0 air
0-0 ground

* - shared with Lt. P.A. Dougherty of the 375th Ftr Sqn

**Harte, Allan S., Jr., Capt.**
503rd Ftr Sqn/339th Ftr Grp

| Sqn | Date | Claims | Location | A/C |
|---|---|---|---|---|
| 503rd | May 21, 1944 | (2)Ju-88 dam(grd) | Riesa A/F | P-51 |
| | September 12 | Me-109 dest(air) | Magdeburg | P-51 |

1-0-0 air
0-2 ground

**Hartley, Alex S., Lt.**
351st Ftr Sqn/353rd Ftr Grp

| Sqn | Date | Claims | Location | A/C |
|---|---|---|---|---|
| 351st | June 7, 1944 | Me-109 dest(air) | Beauvais/Tille | P-47 |
| | | (2)Me-109 dam(air) | Beauvais/Tille | P-47 |
| | June 27 | Me-109 dest(air) | S/Chalons | P-47 |
| | August 4 | (2)Me-109 dest(air) | Steinhuder Lake-Dummer Lake | P-47 |

4-0-2 air
0-0 ground

**Hartley, Dunstan D., Lt.**
83rd Ftr Sqn/78th Ftr Grp

| Sqn | Date | Claims | Location | A/C |
|---|---|---|---|---|
| 83rd | September 10, 1944 | (.5)He-111 dest(grd)* | Germsheim | P-47 |

0-0-0 air
0.5-0 ground

* - shared with Lt. W.E. Bennett of the 83rd Ftr Sqn

**Hartley, Raymond E., Jr., Capt.**
HdQts/353rd Ftr Grp
351st Ftr Sqn/353rd Ftr Grp
Earlier flew in the MTO with the 325th Ftr Grp and claimed two kills: a FW-190 on January 21, 1944, and a Me-109 on April 12, 1944.

| Sqn | Date | Claims | Location | A/C |
|---|---|---|---|---|
| HdQts | March 24, 1945 | (2)FW-190 dest(air) | NW Kassel | P-51 |
| | | Me-109 dest(air) | NW Kassel | P-51 |
| | | Me-109 dam(air) | NW Kassel | P-51 |
| 351st | April 16 | (2)FW-200 dest(grd) | Reichersberg | P-51 |
| | | FW-190 dest(grd) | Reichersberg | P-51 |
| | | Ju-87 dest(grd) | Reichersberg | P-51 |

3-0-1 air
4-0 ground

**Hartnett, Vincent G., Capt.**
436th Ftr Sqn/479th Ftr Grp

| Sqn | Date | Claims | Location | A/C |
|---|---|---|---|---|
| 436th | September 5, 1944 | (2)FW-190 dest(grd) | Bad Nauheim | P-38 |
| | | FW-190 dam(grd) | Bad Nauheim | P-38 |

0-0-0 air
2-1 ground

**Hartney, Harold E., Jr., Lt.**
62nd Ftr Sqn/56th Ftr Grp

| Sqn | Date | Claims | Location | A/C |
|---|---|---|---|---|
| 62nd | May 8, 1944 | FW-190 dam(air) | Celle | P-47 |

0-0-1 air
0-0 ground

**Hartshorn, William W., Lt.**
61st Ftr Sqn/56th Ftr Grp

| Sqn | Date | Claims | Location | A/C |
|---|---|---|---|---|
| 61st | September 5, 1944 | FW-190 dam(grd) | Gelnhausen | P-47 |

0-0-0 air
0-1 ground

**Hass, Jene A., Lt.**
434th Ftr Sqn/479th Ftr Grp

| Sqn | Date | Claims | Location | A/C |
|---|---|---|---|---|
| 434th | July 6, 1944 | FW-190 prob(air) | Cambrai | P-38 |

0-1-0 air
0-0 ground

**Hassell, Robert C., Jr., Lt.**
352nd Ftr Sqn/353rd Ftr Grp

| *Sqn* | *Date* | *Claims* | *Location* | *A/C* |
|---|---|---|---|---|
| 352nd | January 14, 1945 | (.5)u/i a/c dam(grd)* | Brandenburg-Briest | P-51 |
| | | (.5)u/i a/c dam(grd)* | Brandenburg-Briest | P-51 |
| | April 17 | Me-109 dest(grd) | Ganacker | P-51 |
| | | Me-109 dam(grd) | Ganacker | P-51 |

0-0-0 air
1-2 ground

* - shared with Lt. J.R. Evans of the 352nd Ftr Sqn

**Hastin, James D., Lt.**
374th Ftr Sqn/361st Ftr Grp

| *Sqn* | *Date* | *Claims* | *Location* | *A/C* |
|---|---|---|---|---|
| 374th | January 30, 1944 | (.5)Me-109 dest(air)* | Rheine | P-47 |

0.5-0-0 air
0-0 ground

* - shared with Lt. H.B. Lederer of the 374th Ftr Sqn

**Hastings, William H., Lt.**
336th Ftr Sqn/4th Ftr Grp

| *Sqn* | *Date* | *Claims* | *Location* | *A/C* |
|---|---|---|---|---|
| 336th | April 16, 1945 | Me-110 dest(grd) | Praha | P-51 |
| | | Me-110 dam(grd) | Praha | P-51 |

0-0-0 air
1-1 ground

**Hatala, Paul R., Capt.**
364th Ftr Sqn/357th Ftr Grp

| *Sqn* | *Date* | *Claims* | *Location* | *A/C* |
|---|---|---|---|---|
| 364th | December 5, 1944 | Me-109 dest(air) | NW Berlin | P-51 |
| | January 14, 1945 | (2)FW-190 dest(air) | W/Berlin | P-51 |
| | March 2 | (.5)Me-109 dest(air)* | NE Leipzig | P-51 |
| | March 24 | (2)Me-109 dest(air) | W/Gutersloh | P-51 |

5.5-0-0 air
0-0 ground

* - shared with Lt. O.T. Ridley of the 362nd Ftr Sqn, 357th Ftr Grp

**Hatch, John J., Lt.**
351st Ftr Sqn/353rd Ftr Grp

| *Sqn* | *Date* | *Claims* | *Location* | *A/C* |
|---|---|---|---|---|
| 351st | June 8, 1944 | FW-190 dest(air) | SW Angars | P-47 |
| | June 17 | FW-190 dest(air) | Falaise | P-47 |
| | July 9 | (2)Me-109 dest(air) | Argentan | P-47 |

4-0-0 air
0-0 ground

**Hatfield, Clive, Lt.**
383rd Ftr Sqn/364th Ftr Sqn

| *Sqn* | *Date* | *Claims* | *Location* | *A/C* |
|---|---|---|---|---|
| 383rd | June 25, 1944 | (.5)Me-109 dest(air)* | E/Blois | P-38 |

0.5-0-0 air
0-0 ground

* - shared with Capt. J.C. Ford of the 384th Ftr Sqn, 364th Ftr Grp

**Hathorn, Vernon B., Maj.**
HdQts/339th Ftr Grp

| *Sqn* | *Date* | *Claims* | *Location* | *A/C* |
|---|---|---|---|---|
| HdQts | April 16, 1945 | (2)FW-190 dest(grd) | Klatovy | P-51 |
| | | Me-109 dest(grd) | Klatovy | P-51 |

0-0-0 air
3-0 ground

**Hathway, Randal B., Lt.**
83rd Ftr Sqn/78th Ftr Grp

| *Sqn* | *Date* | *Claims* | *Location* | *A/C* |
|---|---|---|---|---|
| 83rd | February 24, 1944 | Me-109 dest(air) | Furstenau | P-47 |
| | March 17 | u/i a/c dam(grd) | N/Reims | P-47 |
| | June 10 | FW-190 dam(grd) | Argentan | P-47 |

1-0-1 air
0-1 ground

**Hatter, Robert B., Capt.**
368th Ftr Sqn/359th Ftr Grp

| *Sqn* | *Date* | *Claims* | *Location* | *A/C* |
|---|---|---|---|---|
| 368th | May 21, 1944 | (6)u/i a/c dest(grd) | Grevesmuhlen | P-51 |
| | | (3)u/i a/c dam(grd) | Grevesmuhlen | P-51 |
| | May 29 | Me-109 dest(air) | Plau | P-51 |
| | September 12 | (2)FW-190 dest(air) | Liebenwalde | P-51 |

3-0-0 air
6-3 ground

**Hausenbauer, Edward P., Lt.**
383rd Ftr Sqn/364th Ftr Grp

| *Sqn* | *Date* | *Claims* | *Location* | *A/C* |
|---|---|---|---|---|
| 383rd | April 16, 1945 | Ju-52 dam(grd) | Marienbad | P-51 |

0-0-0 air
0-1 ground

**Hauver, Charles D., Capt.**
354th Ftr Sqn/355th Ftr Grp

| *Sqn* | *Date* | *Claims* | *Location* | *A/C* |
|---|---|---|---|---|
| 354th | November 26, 1944 | (2)FW-190 dest(air) | W/Hanover | P-51 |
| | December 25 | FW-190 dest(air) | NW Trier | P-51 |
| | | Me-109 dest(air) | NW Trier | P-51 |
| | December 31 | FW-190 dest(air) | SW Hamburg | P-51 |
| | | FW-190 dam(air) | SW Hamburg | P-51 |

5-0-1 air
0-0 ground

**Havighurst, Robert C., Lt.**
504th Ftr Sqn/339th Ftr Grp

| *Sqn* | *Date* | *Claims* | *Location* | *A/C* |
|---|---|---|---|---|
| 504th | April 4, 1945 | Me-262 dest(air) | Parchim | P-51 |

1-0-0 air
0-0 ground

**Haviland, Frederick R., Jr., Capt.**
357th Ftr Sqn/355th Ftr Grp

| *Sqn* | *Date* | *Claims* | *Location* | *A/C* |
|---|---|---|---|---|
| 357th | June 21, 1944 | Me-109 dest(air) | N/Magdeburg | P-51 |
| | June 24 | (3)Me-109 dest(grd) | E/Angars | P-51 |
| | July 7 | (2)Me-410 dest(air) | Halle | P-51 |
| | | Me-410 dam(air) | Halle | P-51 |
| | August 3 | FW-190 dest(air) | Sarrebourg | P-51 |
| | | Me-109 dam(air) | Sarrebourg | P-51 |
| | September 12 | (3)Ju-88 dest(grd) | Schwartz A/F | P-51 |
| | | Me-110 dam(grd) | Schwartz A/F | P-51 |
| | | Do-217 dam(grd) | Schwartz A/F | P-51 |
| | November 18 | (4)Me-262 dam(grd) | Leipheim | P-51 |
| | November 26 | FW-190 dest(air) | W/Gardelegen | P-51 |
| | | Me-109 dest(air) | W/Gardelegen | P-51 |

6-0-2 air
6-6 ground

**Hawkins, Anthony G., Capt.**
503rd Ftr Sqn/339th Ftr Grp

| *Sqn* | *Date* | *Claims* | *Location* | *A/C* |
|---|---|---|---|---|
| 503rd | December 31, 1944 | FW-190 dest(air) | S/Hamburg | P-51 |
| | | Me-262 dam(air) | S/Hamburg | P-51 |

1-0-1 air
0-0 ground

**Hawkins, William C., Lt.**
335th Ftr Sqn/4th Ftr Grp

| Sqn | Date | Claims | Location | A/C |
|---|---|---|---|---|
| 335th | March 21, 1944 | Me-110 dest(air) | Cozes | P-51 |

1-0-0 air
0-0 ground

**Hawkinson, Robert W., Capt.**
368th Ftr Sqn/359th Ftr Grp

| Sqn | Date | Claims | Location | A/C |
|---|---|---|---|---|
| 368th | May 30, 1944 | (.5)Me-109 dest(air)[*] | W/Dessau | P-51 |

0.5-0-0 air
0-0 ground

[*] - shared with Lt. J.B. Hunter of the 368th Ftr Sqn

**Hawley, Robert C., Lt.**
335th Ftr Sqn/4th Ftr Grp

| Sqn | Date | Claims | Location | A/C |
|---|---|---|---|---|
| 335th | April 9, 1945 | (2)u/i a/c dam(grd) | Munich-Brunnthal | P-51 |

0-0-0 air
0-2 ground

**Haworth, Russell C., Lt.**
338th Ftr Sqn/55th Ftr Grp

| Sqn | Date | Claims | Location | A/C |
|---|---|---|---|---|
| 338th | August 28, 1944 | (.5)DFS-230 dest(air)[*] | Dromersheim | P-51 |
| | September 11 | (2)Me-109 dest(air) | S/Meiningen | P-51 |
| | | Me-109 dam(air) | S/Meiningen | P-51 |
| | September 12 | (.5)Me-109 dest(air)[**] | Frankfurt | P-51 |
| | November 2 | Me-109 dest(air) | Merseburg | P-51 |
| | December 24 | Me-109 dest(air) | Vogelsburg | P-51 |

5-0-1 air
0-0 ground

[*] - shared with Lt. A.J. Ramm of the 338th Ftr Sqn
[**] - shared with Lt. C.C. Sherman of the 38th Ftr Sqn, 55th Ftr Grp

**Haydon, Edward R., Lt.**
364th Ftr Sqn/357th Ftr Grp

| Sqn | Date | Claims | Location | A/C |
|---|---|---|---|---|
| 364th | November 8, 1944 | (.5)Me-262 dest(air)[*] | Dummer Lake | P-51 |
| | November 18 | FW-190 dest(grd) | Neuhausen A/F | P-51 |

0.5-0-0 air
1-0 ground

[*] - shared with Lt. E.C. Fiebelkorn of the 20th Ftr Grp

**Hayes, Jack W., LtCol.**
HdQts/357th Ftr Grp

| Sqn | Date | Claims | Location | A/C |
|---|---|---|---|---|
| HdQts | April 17, 1945 | Me-262 dam(air) | SE Brux | P-51 |
| | April 19 | Me-262 dest(air) | W/Prague | P-51 |

1-0-1 air
0-0 ground

**Hayes, Thomas L., Jr., LtCol.**
364th Ftr Sqn/357th Ftr Grp
HdQts/357th Ftr Grp

| Sqn | Date | Claims | Location | A/C |
|---|---|---|---|---|
| 364th | February 24, 1944 | Me-109 prob(air) | NW Gotha | P-51 |
| | March 2 | Me-109 dest(air) | N/Frankfurt | P-51 |
| | March 6 | Me-109 dest(air) | E/Ulzen | P-51 |
| | March 8 | Me-410 dest(air) | W/Berlin | P-51 |
| | March 16 | Me-110 dest(air) | SE Stuttgart | P-51 |
| HdQts | April 19 | Me-109 dest(air) | S/Kassel | P-51 |
| | May 28 | Me-109 dest(air) | NW Magdeburg | P-51 |
| | June 29 | Me-109 dest(air) | W/Leipzig | P-51 |
| | | (.5)Me-410 dest(air)[*] | NW Leipzig | P-51 |
| | July 14 | Me-109 dest(air) | Valence | P-51 |

8.5-1-0 air
0-0 ground

[*] - shared with Lt. M.F. Allen of the 364th Ftr Sqn

**Haynes, Harry E., Capt.**
350th Ftr Sqn/353rd Ftr Grp

| Sqn | Date | Claims | Location | A/C |
|---|---|---|---|---|
| 350th | September 23, 1944 | Me-109 dest(air) | SE Arnheim | P-47 |
| | November 10 | Bu-133 dest(grd) | Fulda | P-51 |

1-0-0 air
1-0 ground

**Hazelett, Philip H., Lt.**
82nd Ftr Sqn/78th Ftr Grp

| Sqn | Date | Claims | Location | A/C |
|---|---|---|---|---|
| 82nd | April 1, 1944 | Ju-87 dest(grd) | Verdun | P-47 |
| | | u/i a/c dest(grd) | Verdun | P-47 |
| | April 5 | Go-242 dam(grd) | Ruwer | P-47 |
| | May 11 | Go-242 dam(grd) | Dijon | P-47 |
| | May 19 | Me-110 dest(grd) | Plantlunne | P-47 |

0-0-0 air
3-2 ground

**Head, Hayden W., Capt.**
385th Ftr Sqn/364th Ftr Grp

| Sqn | Date | Claims | Location | A/C |
|---|---|---|---|---|
| 385th | November 2, 1944 | Me-109 dam(air) | Merseburg | P-51 |
| | November 21 | (.5)FW-190 dest(air)[*] | SW Merseburg | P-51 |
| | November 25 | FW-190 dam(grd) | Fulda | P-51 |
| | December 27 | FW-190 dest(air) | NW Bonn | P-51 |
| | December 31 | FW-190 dest(air) | SE Hamburg | P-51 |
| | January 1, 1945 | FW-190 dest(air) | SE Hamburg | P-51 |
| | April 13 | Ju-88 dest(grd) | Tarnewitz | P-51 |

3.5-0-1 air
1-1 ground

[*] - shared with Lt. N.L. Box of the 385th Ftr Sqn

**Healey, Dana, Jr., F/O**
383rd Ftr Sqn/364th Ftr Grp

| Sqn | Date | Claims | Location | A/C |
|---|---|---|---|---|
| 383rd | April 16, 1945 | FW-190 dest(grd) | Marienbad | P-51 |
| | | Fi-156 dest(grd) | Marienbad | P-51 |
| | | Do-217 dam(grd) | Marienbad | P-51 |
| | | u/i a/c dam(grd) | Marienbad | P-51 |
| | April 19 | FW-190 dest(air) | Lubben | P-51 |
| | | (.5)Do-217 dest(air)[*] | Lubben | P-51 |

1.5-0-0 air
2-2 ground

[*] - shared with Capt. C.E. Hammett of the 383rd Ftr Sqn

**Heaton, Mack D., Lt.**
335th Ftr Sqn/4th Ftr Grp

| Sqn | Date | Claims | Location | A/C |
|---|---|---|---|---|
| 335th | April 9, 1945 | Fi-156 dest(grd) | Munich-Brunnthal | P-51 |
| | | u/i a/c dest(grd) | Munich-Brunnthal | P-51 |

0-0-0 air
2-0 ground

**Heaton, Robert L., Lt.**
354th Ftr Sqn/355th Ftr Grp

| Sqn | Date | Claims | Location | A/C |
|---|---|---|---|---|
| 354th | April 16, 1945 | He-111 dest(grd) | Eger A/F | P-51 |
| | | Ju-88 dest(air) | Eger A/F | P-51 |

0-0-0 air
2-0 ground

**Hearn, Roger V., Lt.**
82nd Ftr Sqn/78th Ftr Grp

| Sqn | Date | Claims | Location | A/C |
|---|---|---|---|---|
| 82nd | April 1, 1944 | (.13)Do-217 dest(grd)[*] | Verdun | P-47 |

0-0-0 air
0.13-0 ground

* - shared with Capt. W.L. Boone, Capt. W.E. May, Lt. C.R. Clark, Lt. H.L. Eakes, Lt. J.J. Hockery, Lt. B.M. Watkins, and F/O C.W. DeWitt of the 82nd Ftr Sqn

**Hedenburg, John W., Lt.**
436th Ftr Sqn/479th Ftr Grp

| *Sqn* | *Date* | *Claims* | *Location* | *A/C* |
|---|---|---|---|---|
| 436th | September 5, 1944 | u/i a/c dest(grd) | Hoehst Oberau | P-38 |
| | | u/i a/c dam(grd) | Hoehst Oberau | P-38 |

0-0-0 air
1-1 ground

**Hedler, Robert W., Lt.**
350th Ftr Sqn/353rd Ftr Grp

| *Sqn* | *Date* | *Claims* | *Location* | *A/C* |
|---|---|---|---|---|
| 350th | August 28, 1944 | He-111 dest(air) | SE Arlon | P-47 |
| | September 21 | (1.5)FW-190 dest(air)* | SE Arnheim | P-47 |

2.5-0-0 air
0-0 ground

* - shared with Lt. V.G. Rafferty of the 350th Ftr Sqn

**Hedrick, Walter O., Lt.**
360th Ftr Sqn/356th Ftr Grp

| *Sqn* | *Date* | *Claims* | *Location* | *A/C* |
|---|---|---|---|---|
| 360th | February 14, 1945 | FW-190 dam(air) | S/Chemnitz | P-51 |

0-0-1 air
0-0 ground

**Hedrick, William F., Capt.**
334th Ftr Sqn/4th Ftr Grp

| *Sqn* | *Date* | *Claims* | *Location* | *A/C* |
|---|---|---|---|---|
| 334th | July 2, 1944 | Me-109 dest(air) | Budapest | P-51 |
| | | Me-109 dam(air) | Budapest | P-51 |

1-0-1 air
0-0 ground

**Hegman, William T., Lt.**
82nd Ftr Sqn/78th Ftr Grp

| *Sqn* | *Date* | *Claims* | *Location* | *A/C* |
|---|---|---|---|---|
| 82nd | June 13, 1943 | FW-190 prob(air) | Armenteres | P-47 |
| | December 30 | Me-109 dest(air) | Reims | P-47 |

1-1-0 air
0-0 ground

**Hehn, William A., Lt.**
434th Ftr Sqn/479th Ftr Grp

| *Sqn* | *Date* | *Claims* | *Location* | *A/C* |
|---|---|---|---|---|
| 434th | August 9, 1944 | (2)He-111 dest(grd) | Nuneburg | P-38 |
| | | Ju-52 dam(grd) | Nuneburg | P-38 |

0-0-0 air
2-1 ground

**Heiden, Arthur W., Lt.**
79th Ftr Sqn/20th Ftr Grp

| *Sqn* | *Date* | *Claims* | *Location* | *A/C* |
|---|---|---|---|---|
| 79th | March 18, 1944 | (.5)Me-110 dest(air)* | Ulm | P-38 |
| | April 8 | (.5)He-111 dest(grd)** | Salzwedel | P-38 |
| | | Ju-88 dam(grd) | Salzwedel | P-38 |

0.5-0-0 air
0.5-1 ground

* - shared with Capt. L.F. Graham of the 79th Ftr Sqn
** - shared with Capt. E.C. Hedlund of the 474th Ftr Grp, 9th Air Force

**Heineman, Richard M., Lt.**
61st Ftr Sqn/56th Ftr Grp

| *Sqn* | *Date* | *Claims* | *Location* | *A/C* |
|---|---|---|---|---|
| 61st | April 25, 1944 | Me-109 dam(grd) | Metz | P-47 |
| | May 19 | FW-190 dest(air) | Halberstadt | P-47 |
| | May 22 | (2)FW-190 dest(air) | Hoperhofen A/F | P-47 |

3-0-0 air
0-1 ground

**Helding, Arnold G., Lt.**
434th Ftr Sqn/479th Ftr Grp

| *Sqn* | *Date* | *Claims* | *Location* | *A/C* |
|---|---|---|---|---|
| 434th | December 25, 1944 | FW-190 dest(air) | SW Bonn | P-51 |

1-0-0 air
0-0 ground

**Helfrecht, Kenneth G., Lt.**
335th Ftr Sqn/4th Ftr Grp

| *Sqn* | *Date* | *Claims* | *Location* | *A/C* |
|---|---|---|---|---|
| 335th | April 16, 1945 | (2)Me-410 dest(grd) | Gablingen | P-51 |
| | | (2)FW-190 dest(grd) | Gablingen | P-51 |
| | | He-177 dest(grd) | Gablingen | P-51 |
| | | (2)Ju-87 dam(grd) | Gablingen | P-51 |

0-0-0 air
5-2 ground

**Heller, Edwin L., Capt.**
486th Ftr Sqn/352nd Ftr Grp

| *Sqn* | *Date* | *Claims* | *Location* | *A/C* |
|---|---|---|---|---|
| 486th | April 23, 1944 | (.5)Ju-52 dest(grd)* | SE Paris | P-51 |
| | April 24 | (3)Me-110 dest(grd) | E/Neuburg | P-51 |
| | | (2)Ju-88 dest(grd) | E/Neuburg | P-51 |
| | | Ju-52 dest(grd) | E/Neuburg | P-51 |
| | | u/i a/c dest(grd) | E/Neuburg | P-51 |
| | | (4)Me-110 dam(grd) | E/Neuburg | P-51 |
| | | Ju-52 dam(grd) | E/Neuburg | P-51 |
| | May 8 | (2)Me-109 dest(air) | Gifhorn | P-51 |
| | May 28 | Me-109 dest(air) | Dessau | P-51 |
| | | (.5)Me-109 dest(air)** | Magdeburg | P-51 |
| | June 21 | Me-109 dest(air) | Brest-Litovsk | P-51 |
| | March 2, 1945 | FW-190 dest(air) | SE Leipzig | P-51 |
| | | FW-190 dam(air) | SE Leipzig | P-51 |
| | April 16 | (3)FW-190 dest(grd) | Ganacker | P-51 |
| | | (2)Ju-87 dest(grd) | Ganacker | P-51 |
| | | Me-109 dest(grd) | Ganacker | P-51 |
| | | Trainer dest(grd) | Ganacker | P-51 |

5.5-0-1 air
14.5-5 ground

* - shared with Lt. H.J. Miklajcyk of the 486th Ftr Sqn
** - shared with Lt. J.L. Lang of the 4th Ftr Grp

**Helmholz, Walter W., Jr., Lt.**
385th Ftr Sqn/364th Ftr Grp

| *Sqn* | *Date* | *Claims* | *Location* | *A/C* |
|---|---|---|---|---|
| 385th | April 10, 1945 | (2)Me-262 dest(grd) | Stendal | P-51 |
| | | FW-190 dest(grd) | Stendal | P-51 |
| | | FW-190 dam(grd) | Stendal | P-51 |

0-0-0 air
3-1 ground

**Henahan, Donald J., Lt.**
82nd Ftr Sqn/78th Ftr Grp

| *Sqn* | *Date* | *Claims* | *Location* | *A/C* |
|---|---|---|---|---|
| 82nd | April 16, 1945 | (2.5)Ju-87 dest(grd)* | Pilzen/Prague | P-51 |
| | | FW-190 dest(grd) | Pilzen/Prague | P-51 |
| | | Ju-52 dest(grd) | Pilzen/Prague | P-51 |
| | | FW-190 dam(grd) | Pilzen/Prague | P-51 |
| | | Ju-52 dam(grd) | Pilzen/Prague | P-51 |
| | | u/i a/c dam(grd) | Pilzen/Prague | P-51 |

0-0-0 air
4.5-3 ground

* - shared with LtCol. O.E. Gilbert of HdQts, 66th Ftr Wg

**Henderson, Everett A., Lt.**
63rd Ftr Sqn/56th Ftr Grp

| *Sqn* | *Date* | *Claims* | *Location* | *A/C* |
|---|---|---|---|---|
| 63rd | September 5, 1944 | FW-190 dest(grd) | Gelnhausen | P-47 |

0-0-0 air
1-0 ground

**Henderson, Harvey E., LtCol.**
503rd Ftr Sqn/339th Ftr Grp
HdQts/339th Ftr Grp

| *Sqn* | *Date* | *Claims* | *Location* | *A/C* |
|---|---|---|---|---|
| HdQts | November 26, 1944 | (2)FW-190 dest(air) | SE Dummer Lake | P-51 |

2-0-0 air
0-0 ground

**Henderson, Paul R., Lt.**
84th Ftr Sqn/78th Ftr Grp

| *Sqn* | *Date* | *Claims* | *Location* | *A/C* |
|---|---|---|---|---|
| 84th | April 16, 1945 | Ju-52 dam(grd) | Praha/Kakewice | P-51 |

0-0-0 air
0-1 ground

**Henderson, Richard L., Lt.**
486th Ftr Sqn/352nd Ftr Grp

| *Sqn* | *Date* | *Claims* | *Location* | *A/C* |
|---|---|---|---|---|
| 486th | December 27, 1944 | (2)Me-109 dest(air) | W/Bonn | P-51 |

2-0-0 air
0-0 ground

**Henderson, William D., Capt.**
335th Ftr Sqn/4th Ftr Grp

| *Sqn* | *Date* | *Claims* | *Location* | *A/C* |
|---|---|---|---|---|
| 335th | April 16, 1945 | (3)Me-109 dam(grd) | Praha | P-51 |
| | | u/i a/c dam(grd) | Praha | P-51 |

0-0-0 air
0-4 ground

**Hendrian, William E., Capt.**
328th Ftr Sqn/352nd Ftr Grp

| *Sqn* | *Date* | *Claims* | *Location* | *A/C* |
|---|---|---|---|---|
| 328th | December 30, 1943 | (.33)Me-110 prob(air)* | Chalons | P-47 |
| | April 8, 1944 | (2)Me-210 dest(grd) | Quackenbruck | P-47 |
| | | Me-210 dam(grd) | Quackenbruck | P-47 |
| | August 16 | (.5)Me-109 dest(air)** | W/Mehlis | P-51 |
| | September 11 | FW-190 dest(air) | E/Meiningen | P-51 |
| | November 21 | (.5)FW-190 dest(air)@ | Merseburg | P-51 |

2-0.33-0 air
2-1 ground

* - shared with LtCol. E.L. Clark of HdQts, 352nd Ftr Grp, and Lt. D.T. Zimms of the 328th Ftr Sqn
** - shared with Lt. C.J. Cesky of the 328th Ftr Sqn
@ - shared with Lt. J.F. Lambright of the 328th Ftr Sqn

**Hendricks, Howard F., Lt.**
77th Ftr Sqn/20th Ftr Grp

| *Sqn* | *Date* | *Claims* | *Location* | *A/C* |
|---|---|---|---|---|
| 77th | April 8, 1944 | (2)Ju-88 dam(grd) | Salzwedel | P-38 |

0-0-0 air
0-2 ground

**Hendrickson, Edwin M., Lt.**
357th Ftr Sqn/355th Ftr Grp

| *Sqn* | *Date* | *Claims* | *Location* | *A/C* |
|---|---|---|---|---|
| 357th | July 13, 1944 | Me-109 dest(air) | Sarrebourg | P-51 |
| | | Me-109 prob(air) | Sarrebourg | P-51 |

1-1-0 air
0-0 ground

**Hendrickson, Lauri A., Lt.**
434th Ftr Sqn/479th Ftr Grp

| *Sqn* | *Date* | *Claims* | *Location* | *A/C* |
|---|---|---|---|---|
| 434th | April 13, 1945 | FW-190 dest(grd) | Kaltenkirchen | P-51 |

0-0-0 air
1-0 ground

**Hendrickson, Robert H., Lt.**
434th Ftr Sqn/479th Ftr Grp

| *Sqn* | *Date* | *Claims* | *Location* | *A/C* |
|---|---|---|---|---|
| 434th | August 18, 1944 | (2)Ju-88 dest(grd) | Nancy/Essey A/F | P-38 |
| | | Ju-88 dam(grd) | Nancy/Essey A/F | P-38 |
| | September 5 | (2)Do-217 dest(grd) | Ettinghausen | P-38 |

0-0-0 air
4-1 ground

**Hendrix, George D., Lt.**
434th Ftr Sqn/479th Ftr Grp

| *Sqn* | *Date* | *Claims* | *Location* | *A/C* |
|---|---|---|---|---|
| 434th | August 9, 1944 | Ju-88 dest(grd) | Nuneburg | P-38 |
| | August 12 | Ju-88 dest(air) | Compiegne | P-38 |
| | August 15 | Me-109 dest(grd) | Steenwijk A/F | P-38 |
| | | (2)Me-109 dam(grd) | Steenwijk A/F | P-38 |
| | August 18 | Ju-88 dam(grd) | Nancy/Essey A/F | P-38 |
| | October 6 | FW-190 dam(air) | W/Berlin | P-51 |

1-0-1 air
2-3 ground

**Henley, Donald, Jr., Lt.**
62nd Ftr Sqn/56th Ftr Grp

| *Sqn* | *Date* | *Claims* | *Location* | *A/C* |
|---|---|---|---|---|
| 62nd | September 21, 1944 | FW-190 dest(air) | Arnheim | P-47 |
| | December 4 | (.5)u/i a/c dest(grd)* | Neuburg | P-47 |
| | January 14, 1945 | (1.5)Me-109 dest(air)** | Magdeburg | P-47 |
| | March 10 | (.5)FW-190 dest(air)@ | Remagen | P-47 |
| | April 10 | Ju-88 dest(grd) | Neuruppin | P-47 |
| | | Ju-88 dam(grd) | Neuruppin | P-47 |
| | April 13 | (2)He-111 dest(grd) | Eggebeck A/F | P-47 |
| | | Ju-87 dest(grd) | Eggebeck A/F | P-47 |
| | | (2)He-111 dam(grd) | Eggebeck A/F | P-47 |

3-0-0 air
4.5-3 ground

* - shared with Lt. S.N. Ball of the 62nd Ftr Sqn
** - shared with Lt. H.O. Womack of the 62nd Ftr Sqn
@ - shared with Lt. D.A. Carroll of the 62nd Ftr Sqn

**Hennessy, Thomas B., Lt.**
63rd Ftr Sqn/56th Ftr Grp

| *Sqn* | *Date* | *Claims* | *Location* | *A/C* |
|---|---|---|---|---|
| 63rd | April 13, 1945 | (2)Me-110 dest(grd) | Eggebeck A/F | P-47 |
| | | Me-110 dam(grd) | Eggebeck A/F | P-47 |

0-0-0 air
2-1 ground

**Henry, Carroll D., Capt.**
338th Ftr Sqn/55th Ftr Grp

| *Sqn* | *Date* | *Claims* | *Location* | *A/C* |
|---|---|---|---|---|
| 338th | November 26, 1944 | FW-190 dam(grd) | Vorden | P-51 |
| | January 13, 1945 | Me-109 dest(air) | W/Giebelstadt A/F | P-51 |
| | February 15 | (.5)Hs-129 dest(air)* | Scharndau | P-51 |
| | February 25 | FW-190 dest(grd) | Illesheim | P-51 |
| | | FW-190 dam(grd) | Illesheim | P-51 |
| | April 16 | (2)FW-190 dest(grd) | N/Landshut | P-51 |
| | April 17 | FW-190 dest(grd) | Riess/Canitz | P-51 |
| | | u/i a/c dest(grd) | Riess/Canitz | P-51 |

1.5-0-0 air
5-2 ground

* - shared with Lt. E.H. Duquette of the 338th Ftr Sqn

**Henry, John B., Jr., Col.**
HdQts/339th Ftr Grp

| *Sqn* | *Date* | *Claims* | *Location* | *A/C* |
|---|---|---|---|---|
| HdQts | March 30, 1945 | Me-262 prob(air) | SW Hamburg | P-51 |

0-1-0 air
0-0 ground

**Henry, Justus D., Lt.**
359th Ftr Sqn/356th Ftr Grp

| *Sqn* | *Date* | *Claims* | *Location* | *A/C* |
|---|---|---|---|---|
| 359th | January 21, 1944 | (.5)FW-190 dam(grd)* | St. Leger A/F | P-47 |
| | March 6 | FW-190 dam(air) | Nienburg | P-47 |
| | March 8 | Me-110 dest(grd) | Hesepe | P-47 |
| | | Me-110 dam(grd) | Hesepe | P-47 |

0-0-1 air
1-1.5 ground

* - shared with LtCol. O.H. Coen of HdQts, 356th Ftr Grp

**Henry, Raymond E., Lt.**
436th Ftr Sqn/479th Ftr Grp

| *Sqn* | *Date* | *Claims* | *Location* | *A/C* |
|---|---|---|---|---|
| 436th | February 22, 1945 | Ju-88 dest(grd) | Halberstadt | P-51 |
| | | He-111 dam(grd) | Halberstadt | P-51 |
| | April 16 | (3)FW-190 dest(grd) | Landstadt | P-51 |

0-0-0 air
4-1 ground

**Hepner, Neal, Lt.**
84th Ftr Sqn/78th Ftr Grp

| *Sqn* | *Date* | *Claims* | *Location* | *A/C* |
|---|---|---|---|---|
| 84th | April 16, 1945 | (2)Me-109 dest(grd) | Praha/Kakewice | P-51 |
| | | He-111 dest(grd) | Praha/Kakewice | P-51 |
| | | Ju-52 dest(grd) | Praha/Kakewice | P-51 |
| | | u/i a/c dest(grd) | Praha/Kakewice | P-51 |
| | | (2)Ju-52 dam(grd) | Praha/Kakewice | P-51 |
| | | Me-109 dam(grd) | Praha/Kakewice | P-51 |
| | | Ju-88 dam(grd) | Praha/Kakewice | P-51 |

0-0-0 air
5-4 ground

**Herb, John W., Lt.**
368th Ftr Sqn/359th Ftr Grp

| *Sqn* | *Date* | *Claims* | *Location* | *A/C* |
|---|---|---|---|---|
| 368th | April 13, 1945 | (2)Me-110 dest(grd) | Neumunster | P-51 |
| | | (2)Do-217 dest(grd) | Neumunster | P-51 |

0-0-0 air
4-0 ground

**Herbert, James H., Capt.**
77th Ftr Sqn/20th Ftr Grp

| *Sqn* | *Date* | *Claims* | *Location* | *A/C* |
|---|---|---|---|---|
| 77th | October 6, 1944 | Ar-196 dest(grd) | Bad Berg-Dievenow | P-51 |

0-0-0 air
1-0 ground

**Herbst, Richard C., Lt.**
338th Ftr Sqn/55th Ftr Grp

| *Sqn* | *Date* | *Claims* | *Location* | *A/C* |
|---|---|---|---|---|
| 338th | November 26, 1944 | (.5)FW-190 dam(grd)* | Vorden | P-51 |
| | April 10, 1945 | Me-262 dest(grd) | Burg A/F | P-51 |
| | April 16 | Me-109 dest(grd) | Erding | P-51 |

0-0-0 air
2-0.5 ground

* - shared with Capt. C.E. Buskirk of the 338th Ftr Sqn

**Hereford, Louis R., Lt.**
84th Ftr Sqn/78th Ftr Grp

| *Sqn* | *Date* | *Claims* | *Location* | *A/C* |
|---|---|---|---|---|
| 84th | January 14, 1945 | Me-109 dest(air) | SW Cologne | P-51 |

1-0-0 air
0-0 ground

**Herfurth, Herman, Lt.**
352nd Ftr Sqn/353rd Ftr Grp

| *Sqn* | *Date* | *Claims* | *Location* | *A/C* |
|---|---|---|---|---|
| 352nd | March 16, 1944 | (.5)Me-110 dam(grd)* | Laon | P-47 |
| | | (.5)Me-110 dam(grd)* | Laon | P-47 |
| | | (.5)Me-110 dam(grd)* | Laon | P-47 |
| | May 31 | Me-410 dam(grd) | Gutersloh | P-47 |

0-0-0 air
0-2.5 ground

* - all shared with Lt. J.W. Gonnam of the 352nd Ftr Sqn

**Herin, Reginald A., Lt.**
61st Ftr Sqn/ 56th Ftr Grp
360th Ftr Sqn/356th Ftr Grp

| *Sqn* | *Date* | *Claims* | *Location* | *A/C* |
|---|---|---|---|---|
| 61st | May 22, 1944 | FW-190 dest(air) | Hoperhofen A/F | P-47 |

1-0-0 air
0-0 ground

**Hermanson, Cephas, Lt.**
504th Ftr Sqn/339th Ftr Grp

| *Sqn* | *Date* | *Claims* | *Location* | *A/C* |
|---|---|---|---|---|
| 504th | April 7, 1945 | Me-109 prob(air) | Celle | P-51 |
| | April 10 | (3)Me-410 dest(grd) | N/Neuruppin | P-51 |
| | | (2)Me-410 dam(grd) | N/Neuruppin | P-51 |
| | April 16 | (2)Me-109 dest(grd) | Klatovy | P-51 |

0-1-0 air
5-2 ground

**Hermanson, Harry H., Lt.**
364th Ftr Sqn/357th Ftr Grp

| *Sqn* | *Date* | *Claims* | *Location* | *A/C* |
|---|---|---|---|---|
| 364th | April 11, 1944 | Me-109 dam(air) | NW Hanover | P-51 |
| | August 24 | Me-109 dest(air) | S/Brunswick | P-51 |

1-0-1 air
0-0 ground

**Hernandez, Victor M., Lt.**
352nd Ftr Sqn/353rd Ftr Grp

| *Sqn* | *Date* | *Claims* | *Location* | *A/C* |
|---|---|---|---|---|
| 352nd | November 18, 1944 | Ju-88 dest(grd) | Lechfeld | P-51 |

0-0-0 air
1-0 ground

**Herndon, Harvey V., Lt.**
384th Ftr Sqn/364th Ftr Grp

| *Sqn* | *Date* | *Claims* | *Location* | *A/C* |
|---|---|---|---|---|
| 384th | April 13, 1945 | Ju-88 dest(grd) | Kaltenkirchen | P-51 |

0-0-0 air
1-0 ground

**Herren, James M., Jr., LtCol.**
434th Ftr Sqn/479th Ftr Grp

| *Sqn* | *Date* | *Claims* | *Location* | *A/C* |
|---|---|---|---|---|
| 434th | August 18, 1944 | He-111 dest(grd) | Nancy/Essey A/F | P-38 |
| | | Ju-52 dest(grd) | Nancy/Essey A/F | P-38 |
| | September 26 | (3)Me-109 dest(air) | SW Munster | P-38 |
| | September 28 | Me-109 dest(air) | W/Halberstadt | P-51 |

4-0-0 air
2-0 ground

**Herrmann, Raymond F., Capt.**
504th Ftr Sqn/339th Ftr Grp

| Sqn | Date | Claims | Location | A/C |
|---|---|---|---|---|
| 504th | November 2, 1944 | FW-190 dest(air) | Mulhausen | P-51 |
| | December 31 | (2)FW-190 dest(air) | Hamburg | P-51 |

3-0-0 air
0-0 ground

**Herter, Glenn A., Lt.**
336th Ftr Sqn/4th Ftr Grp

| Sqn | Date | Claims | Location | A/C |
|---|---|---|---|---|
| 336th | February 25, 1944 | FW-190 dest(air) | SE Luxembourg | P-47 |
| | March 2 | FW-190 dest(air) | SW Coblenz | P-51 |
| | | FW-190 dam(air) | SW Coblenz | P-51 |

2-0-1 air
0-0 ground

**Hess, Leroy D., Lt.**
369th Ftr Sqn/359th Ftr Grp

| Sqn | Date | Claims | Location | A/C |
|---|---|---|---|---|
| 369th | June 12, 1944 | (2)FW-190 dest(air) | W/Paris | P-51 |

2-0-0 air
0-0 ground

**Hess, William P., Capt.**
384th Ftr Sqn/364th Ftr Grp

| Sqn | Date | Claims | Location | A/C |
|---|---|---|---|---|
| 384th | December 31, 1944 | (3)FW-190 dest(air) | SE Hamburg | P-51 |
| | | Ju-87 dest(grd) | SE Hamburg | P-51 |

3-0-0 air
1-0 ground

**Hewatt, Aubrey C., Lt.**
334th Ftr Sqn/4th Ftr Grp

| Sqn | Date | Claims | Location | A/C |
|---|---|---|---|---|
| 334th | May 21, 1944 | (.5)Bu-131 dest(air)* | Rathenow A/F | P-51 |

0.5-0-0 air
0-0 ground

* - shared with Lt. R.K. Hofer of the 334th Ftr Sqn

**Hewett, Sidney H., Capt.**
361st Ftr Sqn/356th Ftr Grp

| Sqn | Date | Claims | Location | A/C |
|---|---|---|---|---|
| 361st | January 21, 1944 | (.5)Ju-88 dest(air)* | Cambrai | P-47 |
| | January 24 | FW-190 dam(air) | Bruges-Ostend | P-47 |
| | February 13 | Me-109 dest(air) | SE Paris | P-47 |
| | | (2)FW-190 dam(air) | SE Paris | P-47 |
| | March 6 | Me-109 dest(air) | NW Steinhuder Lake | P-47 |
| | April 11 | (2)Ju-88 dest(grd) | Gifhorn | P-47 |
| | | (.5)FW-190 dest(grd)** | Gifhorn | P-47 |
| | | Ju-52 dam(grd) | Gifhorn | P-47 |

2.5-0-3 air
2.5-1 ground

* - shared with Lt. D.F. Thwaites of the 361st Ftr Sqn
** - shared with Lt. E.M. Parham of the 361st Ftr Sqn

**Hewitt, Richard A., Maj.**
82nd Ftr Sqn/78th Ftr Grp

| Sqn | Date | Claims | Location | A/C |
|---|---|---|---|---|
| 82nd | March 16, 1944 | Me-109 dest(air) | Strasbourg | P-47 |
| | | Me-109 dam(air) | Strasbourg | P-47 |
| | April 5 | Go-242 dam(grd) | Ruwer | P-47 |
| | April 8 | Ju-52 dest(grd) | Trier | P-47 |
| | | (.33)Ar-196 dest(grd)* | Trier | P-47 |
| | September 10 | (2)Ju-88 dest(grd) | Meinbullen | P-47 |
| | November 21 | Me-109 dest(air) | Hanover | P-47 |
| | March 19, 1945 | (2)Me-109 dest(air) | Osnabruck | P-51 |
| | April 17 | Me-262 dest(grd) | Prague | P-51 |

4-0-1 air
4.33-1 ground

* - shared with Capt. N.D. Munson and Lt. J.E. Brasher of the 82nd Ftr Sqn

**Hewit, Norton M., Lt.**
362nd Ftr Sqn/357th Ftr Grp

| Sqn | Date | Claims | Location | A/C |
|---|---|---|---|---|
| 362nd | April 10, 1945 | (2)He-111 dest(grd) | Neuruppin | P-51 |

0-0-0 air
2-0 ground

**Heyer, Sheldon L., Lt.**
487th Ftr Sqn/352nd Ftr Grp

| Sqn | Date | Claims | Location | A/C |
|---|---|---|---|---|
| 487th | August 6, 1944 | Me-109 dest(air) | Hamburg | P-51 |

1-0-0 air
0-0 ground

**Heyman, Richard M., Lt.**
384th Ftr Sqn/364th Ftr Grp

| Sqn | Date | Claims | Location | A/C |
|---|---|---|---|---|
| 384th | May 8, 1944 | Me-109 dest(air) | Steinhuder Lake | P-38 |
| | | Me-109 dam(air) | Steinhuder Lake | P-38 |

1-0-1 air
0-0 ground

**Heyn, Edward F., Lt.**
383rd Ftr Sqn/364th Ftr Grp

| Sqn | Date | Claims | Location | A/C |
|---|---|---|---|---|
| 383rd | December 23, 1944 | Me-109 dam(air) | NW Trier | P-51 |

0-0-1 air
0-0 ground

**Hicks, Barry R., Lt.**
374th Ftr Sqn/361st Ftr Grp

| Sqn | Date | Claims | Location | A/C |
|---|---|---|---|---|
| 374th | November 26, 1944 | FW-190 dest(air) | Wittingen | P-51 |
| | March 31, 1945 | FW-190 dest(air) | N/Frankfurt | P-51 |

2-0-0 air
0-0 ground

**Hicks, James R., F/O**
352nd Ftr Sqn/353rd Ftr Grp

| Sqn | Date | Claims | Location | A/C |
|---|---|---|---|---|
| 352nd | May 27, 1944 | Me-109 dam(air) | Saverne | P-47 |
| | June 7 | (2)FW-190 dest(grd) | Angars | P-47 |
| | | Ju-88 dest(grd) | Angars | P-47 |

0-0-1 air
3-0 ground

**Higginbottom, Foy E., Capt.**
83rd Ftr Sqn/78th Ftr Grp

| Sqn | Date | Claims | Location | A/C |
|---|---|---|---|---|
| 83rd | July 6, 1944 | FW-190 dest(air) | Rambouillet | P-47 |
| | July 19 | (2)Ju-188 dam(grd) | Linburg-Coblenz | P-47 |
| | October 15 | Do-217 dam(grd) | Munster | P-47 |
| | March 2, 1945 | Me-109 dest(air) | Burg A/F | P-51 |
| | | Me-109 prob(air) | Burg A/F | P-51 |
| | March 19 | (.5)Me-109 dest(air)* | Osnabruck | P-51 |
| | April 10 | Me-262 dam(grd) | Burg Bai Magdeburg | P-51 |

2.5-1-0 air
0-4 ground

* - shared with Lt. R.I. Kuehl of the 83rd Ftr Sqn

**Higgins, Donald H., Maj.**
486th Ftr Sqn/352nd Ftr Grp

| *Sqn* | *Date* | *Claims* | *Location* | *A/C* |
|---|---|---|---|---|
| 486th | May 13, 1944 | Me-109 dest(air) | Tribsees | P-51 |
| | July 2 | FW-190 dest(air) | W/Budapest | P-51 |
| | | (.5)Me-109 dest(air)* | W/Budapest | P-51 |
| | April 17, 1945 | (2)Ju-52 dest(grd) | Plattling | P-51 |
| | | Me-109 dest(grd) | Plattling | P-51 |
| | | Me-109 dam(grd) | Plattling | P-51 |

2.5-0-0 air
3-1 ground

* - shared with Lt. D.R. Emerson of the 4th Ftr Grp

**Higgins, Richard W., Lt.**
61st Ftr Sqn/56th Ftr Grp

| *Sqn* | *Date* | *Claims* | *Location* | *A/C* |
|---|---|---|---|---|
| 61st | April 10, 1945 | u/i a/c dest(grd) | Muritz Lake | P-47 |
| | | u/i a/c dam(grd) | Muritz Lake | P-47 |
| | April 13 | (2)Ju-88 dam(grd) | Eggebeck A/F | P-47 |

0-0-0 air
1-3 ground

**Higgins, Roy D., Lt.**
84th Ftr Sqn/78th Ftr Grp

| *Sqn* | *Date* | *Claims* | *Location* | *A/C* |
|---|---|---|---|---|
| 84th | February 22, 1945 | Ju-86 dam(grd) | Memmingen | P-51 |
| | March 1 | Me-109 dam(grd) | Boblingen | P-51 |
| | | u/i a/c dam(grd) | Boblingen | P-51 |

0-0-0 air
0-3 ground

**Highfield, Leroy B., Capt.**
351st Ftr Sqn/353rd Ftr Grp

| *Sqn* | *Date* | *Claims* | *Location* | *A/C* |
|---|---|---|---|---|
| 351st | April 16, 1945 | Me-110 dest(grd) | Reichersberg | P-51 |
| | | Ju-88 dest(grd) | Reichersberg | P-51 |
| | | He-111 dam(grd) | Reichersberg | P-51 |

0-0-0 air
2-1 ground

**Hightshoe, Melville W., Capt.**
350th Ftr Sqn/353rd Ftr Grp

| *Sqn* | *Date* | *Claims* | *Location* | *A/C* |
|---|---|---|---|---|
| 350th | August 7, 1944 | Me-410 dam(grd) | SE Amiens | P-47 |
| | | Me-109 dam(grd) | SE Amiens | P-47 |
| | August 29 | (2)Me-109 dest(grd) | Diest | P-47 |
| | | Me-410 dest(grd) | Diest | P-47 |
| | | (2)Me-109 dam(grd) | Diest | P-47 |
| | September 9 | Do-217 dam(grd) | Hesepe | P-47 |
| | November 18 | (2)He-177 dest(grd) | Lechfeld | P-51 |
| | | u/i a/c dest(grd) | Lechfeld | P-51 |
| | February 28, 1945 | (1.5)Me-110 dest(grd)* | S/Gotha | P-51 |
| | | Me-109 dest(grd) | S/Gotha | P-51 |
| | | Me-410 dest(grd) | S/Gotha | P-51 |
| | April 16 | (4)FW-190 dest(grd) | Pocking | P-51 |
| | | Me-109 dest(grd) | Pocking | P-51 |

0-0-0 air
14.5-5 ground

* - shared with Lt. J.D. McMullen of the 350th Ftr Sqn

**Hightower, Howard T., Lt.**
436th Ftr Sqn/479th Ftr Grp

| *Sqn* | *Date* | *Claims* | *Location* | *A/C* |
|---|---|---|---|---|
| 436th | September 28, 1944 | FW-190 dam(air) | W/Magdeburg | P-38 |

0-0-1 air
0-0 ground

**Hileman, James E., Lt.**
336th Ftr Sqn/4th Ftr Grp

| *Sqn* | *Date* | *Claims* | *Location* | *A/C* |
|---|---|---|---|---|
| 336th | November 21, 1944 | Me-109 prob(air) | W/Merseburg | P-51 |
| | | Me-109 dam(air) | W/Merseburg | P-51 |
| | February 25, 1945 | u/i a/c dest(grd) | Kothen | P-51 |

0-1-1 air
1-0 ground

**Hilgenburg, Raymond, Lt.**
351st Ftr Sqn/353rd Ftr Grp

| *Sqn* | *Date* | *Claims* | *Location* | *A/C* |
|---|---|---|---|---|
| 351st | November 27, 1944 | (.5)Me-109 dest(air)* | N/Dummer Lake | P-51 |

0.5-0-0 air
0-0 ground

* - shared with Lt. G.S. Montgomery of the 351st Ftr Sqn

**Hill, Archie W., Capt.**
82nd Ftr Sqn/78th Ftr Grp

| *Sqn* | *Date* | *Claims* | *Location* | *A/C* |
|---|---|---|---|---|
| 82nd | July 30, 1943 | FW-190 dam(air) | Haldern | P-47 |
| | October 24 | (.5)Me-109 dest(air)* | St. Gaillon | P-47 |

0.5-0-1 air
0-0 ground

* - shared with Capt. W.E. May of the 82nd Ftr Sqn

**Hill, Byron L., Lt.**
357th Ftr Sqn/355th Ftr Grp

| *Sqn* | *Date* | *Claims* | *Location* | *A/C* |
|---|---|---|---|---|
| 357th | March 6, 1944 | FW-190 dest(air) | W/Lingen | P-47 |
| | March 28 | He-111 dest(grd) | Dijon | P-51 |
| | | Do-217 dest(grd) | Dijon | P-51 |
| | | (2)Ju-88 dam(grd) | Dijon | P-51 |
| | | He-111 dam(grd) | Dijon | P-51 |
| | | Me-110 dam(grd) | Dijon | P-51 |
| | | u/i a/c dam(grd) | Dijon | P-51 |

1-0-0 air
2-5 ground

**Hill, Cowan S., Capt.**
385th Ftr Sqn/364th Ftr Grp

| *Sqn* | *Date* | *Claims* | *Location* | *A/C* |
|---|---|---|---|---|
| 385th | May 21, 1944 | (.5)He-111 dest(air)* | SE Luneburg | P-38 |
| | May 24 | (.5)Do-217 dest(air)** | Gifhorn | P-38 |
| | September 11 | Me-109 dest(air) | Sangerhausen | P-51 |
| | | FW-190 dest(air) | Sangerhausen | P-51 |

3-0-0 air
0-0 ground

* - shared with Lt. E.F. Izor of the 385th Ftr Sqn
** - shared with Lt. J.J. Pascoe of the 385th Ftr Sqn

**Hill, Francis R., Lt.**
328th Ftr Sqn/352nd Ftr Grp

| *Sqn* | *Date* | *Claims* | *Location* | *A/C* |
|---|---|---|---|---|
| 328th | November 2, 1944 | Me-109 dest(air) | Merseburg | P-51 |

1-0-0 air
0-0 ground

**Hill, Gordon F., Lt.**
383rd Ftr Sqn/364th Ftr Grp

| *Sqn* | *Date* | *Claims* | *Location* | *A/C* |
|---|---|---|---|---|
| 383rd | April 16, 1945 | (.5)FW-190 dest(grd)* | Marienbad | P-51 |
| | | FW-190 dam(grd) | Marienbad | P-51 |
| | April 17 | Me-262 dam(grd) | SE Pilzen | P-51 |

0-0-0 air
0.5-2 ground

* - shared with Capt. J.L. Truett of the 383rd Ftr Sqn

**Hill, Hershel L., Lt.**
362nd Ftr Sqn/357th Ftr Grp

| *Sqn* | *Date* | *Claims* | *Location* | *A/C* |
|---|---|---|---|---|
| 362nd | May 27, 1944 | Me-109 dest(air) | N/Strasbourg | P-51 |

1-0-0 air
0-0 ground

**Hill, Ralph S., Jr., Lt.**
503rd Ftr Sqn/339th Ftr Grp

| *Sqn* | *Date* | *Claims* | *Location* | *A/C* |
|---|---|---|---|---|
| 503rd | March 20, 1945 | (2)Me-262 dam(air) | Hamburg | P-51 |
| | April 16 | u/i a/c dest(grd) | Kralupy | P-51 |
| | | u/i a/c dam(grd) | Kralupy | P-51 |

0-0-2 air
1-1 ground

**Hillman, Howard K., Lt.**
357th Ftr Sqn/355th Ftr Grp

| *Sqn* | *Date* | *Claims* | *Location* | *A/C* |
|---|---|---|---|---|
| 357th | March 28, 1944 | Ju-88 dest(grd) | Dijon | P-51 |
| | | Me-109 dam(grd) | Dijon | P-51 |
| | | Me-210 dam(grd) | Dijon | P-51 |
| | | Ju-88 dam(grd) | Dijon | P-51 |
| | March 29 | FW-190 dam(air) | NE Brunswick | P-51 |
| | April 13 | Me-109 dest(air) | Augsburg | P-51 |

1-0-1 air
1-3 ground

**Hills, Robert L., Capt.**
334th Ftr Sqn/4th Ftr Grp

| *Sqn* | *Date* | *Claims* | *Location* | *A/C* |
|---|---|---|---|---|
| 334th | April 10, 1944 | u/i a/c dest(grd) | Romorantin A/F | P-51 |
| | April 11 | FW-190 dest(grd) | E/Stettin | P-51 |
| | | Ju-88 dest(grd) | E/Stettin | P-51 |
| | | FW-190 dam(grd) | E/Stettin | P-51 |

0-0-0 air
3-1 ground

**Himes, Ralph T., Maj.**
HdQts/78th Ftr Grp

| *Sqn* | *Date* | *Claims* | *Location* | *A/C* |
|---|---|---|---|---|
| HdQts | July 1, 1943 | FW-190 dam(air) | Gorderoode Island | P-47 |

0-0-1 air
0-0 ground

**Hinchey, James F., Lt.**
351st Ftr Sqn/353rd Ftr Grp

| *Sqn* | *Date* | *Claims* | *Location* | *A/C* |
|---|---|---|---|---|
| 351st | August 4, 1944 | Me-109 dam(air) | S/Bremen | P-47 |
| | August 12 | Ju-88 dest(grd) | SW Coulommiers | P-47 |
| | January 14, 1945 | (2)FW-190 dest(air) | NE Hanover | P-51 |
| | | Me-109 dest(air) | NE Hanover | P-51 |

3-0-1 air
1-0 ground

**Hiner, James W., Lt.**
343rd Ftr Sqn/55th Ftr Grp

| *Sqn* | *Date* | *Claims* | *Location* | *A/C* |
|---|---|---|---|---|
| 343rd | December 13, 1943 | Ju-88 dest(air) | NW Hamburg | P-38 |

1-0-0 air
0-0 ground

**Hines, Luther P., Jr., Lt.**
61st Ftr Sqn/56th Ftr Grp

| *Sqn* | *Date* | *Claims* | *Location* | *A/C* |
|---|---|---|---|---|
| 61st | November 18, 1944 | FW-190 dam(air) | E/Hanau | P-47 |

0-0-1 air
0-0 ground

**Hinman, Howard S., Lt.**
363rd Ftr Sqn/357th Ftr Grp

| *Sqn* | *Date* | *Claims* | *Location* | *A/C* |
|---|---|---|---|---|
| 363rd | March 16, 1944 | Ju-88 dam(air) | Ludwigshafen | P-51 |

0-0-1 air
0-0 ground

**Hipsher, Charles W., Lt.**
370th Ftr Sqn/359th Ftr Grp

| *Sqn* | *Date* | *Claims* | *Location* | *A/C* |
|---|---|---|---|---|
| 370th | May 19, 1944 | Me-109 dam(air) | Stendal | P-51 |
| | May 30 | (.5)Me-109 dest(air)[*] | Dessau | P-51 |

0.5-0-1 air
0-0 ground

[*] - shared with Lt. R.W. Siltamaki of the 370th Ftr Sqn

**Hiro, Edwin W., Maj.**
363rd Ftr Sqn/357th Ftr Grp

| *Sqn* | *Date* | *Claims* | *Location* | *A/C* |
|---|---|---|---|---|
| 363rd | February 22, 1944 | Me-109 dam(air) | Leopoldshall | P-51 |
| | April 24 | Me-109 dest(air) | SE Munich | P-51 |
| | May 19 | (2)Me-109 dest(air) | NW Brandenburg | P-51 |
| | | Me-109 dam(air) | NW Brandenburg | P-51 |
| | May 24 | FW-190 prob(air) | SE Berlin | P-51 |
| | May 28 | Me-109 prob(air) | N/Magdeburg | P-51 |
| | July 30 | Me-109 dest(air) | W/Paris | P-51 |
| | September 19 | Me-109 dest(air) | W/Arnheim | P-51 |

5-2-2 air
0-0 ground

**Hively, Howard D., Maj.**
334th Ftr Sqn/4th Ftr Grp

| *Sqn* | *Date* | *Claims* | *Location* | *A/C* |
|---|---|---|---|---|
| 334th | August 16, 1943 | FW-190 dest(air) | NW Paris | P-47 |
| | March 5, 1944 | (2)Me-109 dest(air) | Mont de Marson | P-51 |
| | March 21 | (.5)Ju-88 dest(grd)[*] | Langen A/F | P-51 |
| | March 23 | FW-190 dam(air) | Hereford | P-51 |
| | March 27 | Ju-88 dest(grd) | Cazaux A/F | P-51 |
| | May 9 | (2)Ju-88 dam(grd) | Riems/Champiegne | P-51 |
| | May 12 | Me-109 dest(air) | Plauen | P-51 |
| | May 19 | (3)Me-109 dest(air) | Lubeck-Schwerin | P-51 |
| | May 24 | Me-109 dest(air) | Hamburg | P-51 |
| | July 2 | (3)Me-109 dest(air) | Budapest | P-51 |
| | July 28 | Me-109 prob(air) | Nordhausen | P-51 |
| | November 18 | Me-262 dest(grd) | Leipheim | P-51 |
| | December 5 | FW-190 dest(air) | NW Nordhorn | P-51 |

12-1-1 air
2.5-2 ground

[*] - shared with Lt. J.W. Goodwyn of the 335th Ftr Sqn, 4th Ftr Grp

**Hixson, Thomas R., Jr., F/O**
354th Ftr Sqn/355th Ftr Grp

| *Sqn* | *Date* | *Claims* | *Location* | *A/C* |
|---|---|---|---|---|
| 354th | March 22, 1945 | He-111 dam(grd) | Memmingen | P-51 |
| | April 4 | u/i a/c dest(grd) | Muritz Lake | P-51 |
| | | (2)Ju-88 dam(grd) | Muritz Lake | P-51 |
| | April 10 | (.5)He-111 dest(grd)[*] | Rechlin/Larz | P-51 |
| | | (4)u/i a/c dam(grd) | Rechlin/Larz | P-51 |

0-0-0 air
1.5-7 ground

[*] - shared with F/O H.W. Falvey of the 354th Ftr Sqn

**Hjelm, Rex P., Lt.**
343rd Ftr Sqn/55th Ftr Grp

| *Sqn* | *Date* | *Claims* | *Location* | *A/C* |
|---|---|---|---|---|
| 343rd | June 11, 1944 | (2)FW-190 dest(air) | Clermont | P-38 |

2-0-0 air
0-0 ground

**Hobbs, Robert, Lt.**
376th Ftr Sqn/361st Ftr Grp

| Sqn | Date | Claims | Location | A/C |
|---|---|---|---|---|
| 376th | February 8, 1945 | (.5)He-111 dest(air)* | Erfurt | P-51 |

0.5-0-0 air
0-0 ground

* - shared with Lt. R.W. Ward of the 376th Ftr Sqn

**Hober, Joseph D., F/O**
357th Ftr Sqn/355th Ftr Grp

| Sqn | Date | Claims | Location | A/C |
|---|---|---|---|---|
| 357th | April 13, 1945 | He-111 dam(grd) | Schleswig | P-51 |

0-0-0 air
0-1 ground

**Hobert, Robert D., Capt.**
336th Ftr Sqn/4th Ftr Grp

| Sqn | Date | Claims | Location | A/C |
|---|---|---|---|---|
| 336th | February 6, 1944 | FW-190 dest(air) | Beauvais-Marigny | P-47 |
| | March 21 | FW-190 dest(air) | SW Evreux | P-51 |
| | March 27 | Ju-88 dam(grd) | Cazaux A/F | P-51 |
| | April 5 | (3)Ju-88 dest(grd) | Stendal | P-51 |
| | | Ju-88 dam(grd) | Stendal | P-51 |

2-0-0 air
3-2 ground

**Hobson, Kenneth L., Lt.**
369th Ftr Sqn/359th Ftr Grp

| Sqn | Date | Claims | Location | A/C |
|---|---|---|---|---|
| 369th | September 10, 1944 | u/i a/c dest(air) | NW Stuttgart | P-51 |
| | | u/i a/c dam(air) | NW Stuttgart | P-51 |

1-0-1 air
0-0 ground

**Hockery, John J., Capt.**
82nd Ftr Sqn/78th Ftr Grp

| Sqn | Date | Claims | Location | A/C |
|---|---|---|---|---|
| 82nd | January 24, 1944 | Me-110 dest(air) | Engheim | P-47 |
| | February 11 | Me-109 dest(air) | NW Luxembourg | P-47 |
| | February 20 | FW-190 dest(air) | Coblenz | P-47 |
| | March 24 | Ju-188 dest(air) | Paris | P-47 |
| | April 1 | (.13)Do-217 dest(grd)* | Verdun | P-47 |
| | April 5 | (.33)Go-242 dest(grd)** | Ruwer | P-47 |
| | | (.33)DFS-230 dest(grd)** | Ruwer | P-47 |
| | April 12 | Ju-87 dest(air) | Sedan | P-47 |
| | November 26 | (2)Me-109 dest(air) | Rheine | P-47 |
| | | FW-190 prob(air) | Rheine | P-47 |

7-1-0 air
0.8-0 ground

* - shared with Capt. W.L. Boone, Capt. W.E. May, Lt. B.M. Watkins, Lt. C.R. Clark, Lt. H.L. Eakes, Lt. R.V. Hearn, and F/O C.W. DeWitt of the 82nd Ftr Sqn
** - both shared with Lt. H.L. Eakes and F/O C.W. DeWitt of the 82nd Ftr Sqn

**Hockmeyer, Vincent, Capt.**
360th Ftr Sqn/356th Ftr Grp

| Sqn | Date | Claims | Location | A/C |
|---|---|---|---|---|
| 360th | April 23, 1944 | (1.5)Go-242 dam(grd)* | Hagenau | P-47 |

0-0-0 air
0-1.5 ground

* - shared with Lt. R.R. Withers of the 360th Ftr Sqn

**Hodge, Jack D., Lt.**
83rd Ftr Sqn/78th Ftr Grp

| Sqn | Date | Claims | Location | A/C |
|---|---|---|---|---|
| 83rd | March 2, 1945 | (2)Me-109 dest(air) | Burg A/F | P-51 |

2-0-0 air
0-0 ground

**Hodges, Fred S., Maj.**
369th Ftr Sqn/359th Ftr Grp

| Sqn | Date | Claims | Location | A/C |
|---|---|---|---|---|
| 369th | February 21, 1945 | FW-200 dam(grd) | Deiningen | P-51 |

0-0-0 air
0-1 ground

**Hodges, William R., Capt.**
370th Ftr Sqn/359th Ftr Grp

| Sqn | Date | Claims | Location | A/C |
|---|---|---|---|---|
| 370th | February 10, 1944 | (2)Me-109 dest(air) | E/Zuider Zee | P-47 |
| | March 4 | Me-109 prob(air) | Bonn | P-47 |
| | November 21 | (2)FW-190 dest(air) | SE Kassel | P-51 |
| | | FW-190 prob(air) | SE Kassel | P-51 |
| | | FW-190 dam(air) | SE Kassel | P-51 |
| | December 24 | FW-190 dest(air) | Bonn | P-51 |

5-2-1 air
0-0 ground

**Hoeflein, Robert W., Lt.**
61st Ftr Sqn/56th Ftr Grp

| Sqn | Date | Claims | Location | A/C |
|---|---|---|---|---|
| 61st | April 13, 1945 | Me-109 dest(grd) | Eggebeck A/F | P-47 |
| | | (2)Ju-88 dam(grd) | Eggebeck A/F | P-47 |
| | | u/i a/c dam(grd) | Eggebeck A/F | P-47 |

0-0-0 air
1-3 ground

**Hoelscher, William B., Lt.**
334th Ftr Sqn/4th Ftr Grp

| Sqn | Date | Claims | Location | A/C |
|---|---|---|---|---|
| 334th | November 18, 1944 | Me-262 dam(grd) | Leipheim | P-51 |
| | December 25 | FW-190 dest(air) | NE Trier | P-51 |
| | | (.5)Me-109 dest(air)* | NE Trier | P-51 |
| | | FW-190 dam(air) | NE Trier | P-51 |
| | March 21, 1945 | FW-190 dest(grd) | Achmer | P-51 |
| | April 7 | Me-109 dest(air) | SE Krummel | P-51 |
| | April 25 | Me-262 prob(air) | Prague/Ruzny A/F | P-51 |

2.5-1-1 air
1-1 ground

* - shared with Lt. V.R.T. Rentschler of the 334th Ftr Sqn

**Hoenselaar, Floyd J., Capt.**
384th Ftr Sqn/364th Ftr Grp

| Sqn | Date | Claims | Location | A/C |
|---|---|---|---|---|
| 384th | April 15, 1944 | Do-217 dam(grd) | Basbeck | P-38 |
| | | Ju-52 dam(grd) | Basbeck | P-38 |
| | April 29 | Me-109 dam(air) | Steinhuder Lake-Berlin | P-38 |

0-0-1 air
0-2 ground

**Hoeper, Paul E., Maj.**
343rd Ftr Sqn/55th Ftr Grp
HdQts/55th Ftr Grp

| Sqn | Date | Claims | Location | A/C |
|---|---|---|---|---|
| 343rd | February 10, 1944 | Me-210 dest(air) | Brunswick | P-38 |
| HdQts | April 10, 1945 | Me-262 dest(grd) | Burg A/F | P-51 |

1-0-0 air
1-0 ground

**Hoey, Charles J., Maj.**
352nd Ftr Sqn/353rd Ftr Grp

| Sqn | Date | Claims | Location | A/C |
|---|---|---|---|---|
| 352nd | September 22, 1943 | Me-109 dest(air) | SW Utrecht | P-47 |
| | October 8 | Me-109 dam(air) | Garrell | P-47 |
| | October 20 | Me-109 dam(air) | Sittard | P-47 |

1-0-2 air
0-0 ground

**Hofer, Ralph K., Lt.**
334th Ftr Sqn/4th Ftr Grp

| *Sqn* | *Date* | *Claims* | *Location* | *A/C* |
|---|---|---|---|---|
| 334th | October 8, 1943 | Me-109 dest(air) | NE Amsterdam | P-47 |
| | February 6, 1944 | Me-109 dest(air) | W/Paris | P-47 |
| | March 16 | Me-110 dest(air) | Munich | P-51 |
| | March 18 | (2)Me-109 dest(air) | SE Mannheim | P-51 |
| | March 21 | He-177 dest(grd) | Langen A/F | P-51 |
| | March 23 | FW-190 dest(air) | E/Hamm | P-51 |
| | | Me-109 dam(air) | E/Hamm | P-51 |
| | April 1 | Me-109 dest(air) | NW Lake Constance | P-51 |
| | April 8 | Me-109 dest(air) | Celle | P-51 |
| | April 11 | Me-110 dest(air) | SE Stettin | P-51 |
| | April 18 | (2)He-177 dest(grd) | Fassberg A/F | P-51 |
| | May 1 | Me-109 dest(air) | Koln | P-51 |
| | May 12 | (.5)Me-109 dest(air)[*] | N/Coburg | P-51 |
| | May 21 | (.5)Bu-131 dest(air)[**] | Rathenow A/F | P-51 |
| | | Bu-131 dest(grd) | Rathenow A/F | P-51 |
| | May 22 | Me-109 dest(air) | Hamburg | P-51 |
| | May 24 | (2)FW-190 dest(air) | E/Hamburg | P-51 |
| | May 28 | Me-109 dest(air) | Magdeburg | P-51 |
| | May 29 | (4)He-177 dest(grd) | Mackfitz A/F | P-51 |
| | May 30 | (2.5)FW-190 dest(grd)[@] | Oschersleben | P-51 |
| | May 31 | (3)Bu-131 dest(grd) | Luxeuil A/F | P-51 |
| | June 21 | Me-109 dam(air) | Siedlce | P-51 |

15-0-2 air
13.5-0 ground

[*] - shared with Lt. L.R. Pierce of the 334th Ftr Sqn
[**] - shared with Lt. A.C. Hewatt of the 334th Ftr Sqn
[@] - shared with Lt. F.C. Jones of the 335th Ftr Sqn, 4th Ftr Grp

**Hoffman, Garlyn C., Lt.**
354th Ftr Sqn/355th Ftr Grp

| *Sqn* | *Date* | *Claims* | *Location* | *A/C* |
|---|---|---|---|---|
| 354th | June 20, 1944 | Me-109 dest(air) | Rugen | P-51 |
| | July 24 | He-280 dest(grd) | Lechfeld | P-51 |

1-0-0 air
1-0 ground

**Hoffman, Harold J., Capt.**
358th Ftr Sqn/355th Ftr Grp

| *Sqn* | *Date* | *Claims* | *Location* | *A/C* |
|---|---|---|---|---|
| 358th | February 5, 1944 | (.25)FW-190 dam(air)[*] | S/Tours | P-47 |
| | March 2 | Me-109 dest(air) | NE Liege | P-47 |
| | April 5 | Me-110 dest(grd) | Munich | P-51 |
| | | u/i a/c dest(grd) | Munich | P-51 |
| | | (2)Do-217 dam(grd) | Munich | P-51 |
| | | (2)u/i a/c dam(grd) | Munich | P-51 |

1-0-0.25 air
2-4 ground

[*] - shared with Lt. J.J. DeGeorge, Lt. J.H. McConnell, and Lt. J.H. Upchurch of the 358th Ftr Sqn

**Hoffman, R.H., Lt.**
435th Ftr Sqn/479th Ftr Grp

| *Sqn* | *Date* | *Claims* | *Location* | *A/C* |
|---|---|---|---|---|
| 435th | April 17, 1945 | (2)Me-262 dest(grd) | Puchhoff | P-51 |
| | | Fi-156 dest(grd) | Puchhoff | P-51 |
| | | Me-262 dam(grd) | Puchhoff | P-51 |

0-0-0 air
3-1 ground

**Hoffman, Ted E., Lt.**
343rd Ftr Sqn/55th Ftr Grp

| *Sqn* | *Date* | *Claims* | *Location* | *A/C* |
|---|---|---|---|---|
| 343rd | September 5, 1944 | (4)Trainer dest(air) | N/Goppingen A/F | P-51 |

4-0-0 air
0-0 ground

**Hoffman, William R., Lt.**
63rd Ftr Sqn/56th Ftr Grp

| *Sqn* | *Date* | *Claims* | *Location* | *A/C* |
|---|---|---|---|---|
| 63rd | December 23, 1944 | FW-190 dest(air) | NW Coblenz | P-47 |
| | April 10, 1945 | (2)u/i a/c dest(grd) | Werder A/F | P-47 |

1-0-0 air
2-0 ground

**Hogan, Clifford F., Jr., Capt.**
385th Ftr Sqn/364th Ftr Grp

| *Sqn* | *Date* | *Claims* | *Location* | *A/C* |
|---|---|---|---|---|
| 385th | November 21, 1944 | u/i a/c dam(grd) | SE Eislebach | P-51 |
| | December 27 | FW-190 dest(air) | Laachen Lake | P-51 |
| | | FW-190 prob(air) | Laachen Lake | P-51 |

1-1-0 air
0-1 ground

**Hokinson, Leroy V., Jr., Lt.**
38th Ftr Sqn/55th Ftr Grp

| *Sqn* | *Date* | *Claims* | *Location* | *A/C* |
|---|---|---|---|---|
| 38th | January 31, 1944 | (2)FW-190 dest(air) | Eindhoven | P-38 |

2-0-0 air
0-0 ground

**Holden, Paul C., Lt.**
83rd Ftr Sqn/78th Ftr Grp

| *Sqn* | *Date* | *Claims* | *Location* | *A/C* |
|---|---|---|---|---|
| 83rd | March 30, 1944 | Me-109 dest(grd) | N/Venlo | P-47 |
| | April 10 | FW-190 dest(grd) | Romorantin A/F | P-47 |
| | | u/i a/c dam(grd) | Romorantin A/F | P-47 |
| | May 8 | Me-109 dam(air) | Verdun | P-47 |
| | May 19 | Me-109 dest(air) | Lingen | P-47 |
| | June 13 | Me-109 dest(air) | Orleans | P-47 |
| | June 20 | (.5)Me-109 dest(air)[*] | Amiens | P-47 |

2.5-0-1 air
2-1 ground

[*] - shared with Lt. G.G. Boteler of the 83rd Ftr Sqn

**Holderman, Eugene M., Capt.**
38th Ftr Sqn/55th Ftr Grp

| *Sqn* | *Date* | *Claims* | *Location* | *A/C* |
|---|---|---|---|---|
| 38th | July 7, 1944 | (2)Me-410 dest(air) | Bernburg | P-38 |
| | | Me-410 dam(air) | Bernburg | P-38 |
| | September 12 | (2)Ju-88 dam(grd) | Herzogenaurach | P-51 |
| | September 13 | Me-109 dest(air) | Erfurt | P-51 |

3-0-1 air
0-2 ground

**Holleman, Tunis H., Lt.**
38th Ftr Sqn/55th Ftr Grp

| *Sqn* | *Date* | *Claims* | *Location* | *A/C* |
|---|---|---|---|---|
| 38th | September 11, 1944 | Me-109 dest(air) | E/Meiningen | P-51 |
| | November 2 | FW-190 dest(air) | Merseburg | P-51 |

2-0-0 air
0-0 ground

**Holliday, Frank W., Lt.**
369th Ftr Sqn/359th Ftr Grp

| *Sqn* | *Date* | *Claims* | *Location* | *A/C* |
|---|---|---|---|---|
| 369th | August 5, 1944 | Me-109 dam(air) | Bremen-Hamburg | P-51 |
| | September 11 | Me-109 dest(air) | N/Erfurt | P-51 |

1-0-1 air
0-0 ground

**Hollingsworth, James M., Capt.**
434th Ftr Sqn/479th Ftr Grp
Earlier flew in the MTO with the 14th Ftr Grp and claimed 3 kills; a Do-217 on May 25, 1943; and Me-109's on June 24 and August 19, 1943.

| *Sqn* | *Date* | *Claims* | *Location* | *A/C* |
|---|---|---|---|---|
| 434th | August 28, 1944 | Do-217 dest(grd) | Sedan/Douzy A/F | P-38 |
| | September 5 | (4)Me-410 dest(grd) | Ettinghausen | P-38 |
| | | (2)Do-217 dest(grd) | Ettinghausen | P-38 |

| | Date | Claims | Location | A/C |
|---|---|---|---|---|
| | December 25 | Me-109 prob(air) | SW Bonn | P-51 |
| | | Me-109 dam(air) | SW Bonn | P-51 |

0-1-1 air
7-0 ground

**Hollins, John K., Capt.**
79th Ftr Sqn/20th Ftr Grp

| *Sqn* | *Date* | *Claims* | *Location* | *A/C* |
|---|---|---|---|---|
| 79th | February 20, 1945 | He-111 dest(grd) | Weiden A/F | P-51 |
| | | (2)He-111 dam(grd) | Weiden A/F | P-51 |
| | April 10 | Me-262 dest(air) | Neustadt | P-51 |

1-0-0 air
1-2 ground

**Hollis, Harold D., Lt.**
370th Ftr Sqn/359th Ftr Grp

| *Sqn* | *Date* | *Claims* | *Location* | *A/C* |
|---|---|---|---|---|
| 370th | March 4, 1944 | Me-109 dam(air) | Bonn | P-47 |
| | April 11 | Ju-88 dest(grd) | Volkenrod | P-47 |
| | April 15 | Ju-88 dest(grd) | Oldenburg | P-47 |
| | April 22 | FW-190 dest(air) | Hamm | P-47 |
| | May 11 | Me-410 dest(grd) | Reims | P-51 |

1-0-1 air
3-0 ground

**Hollister, Berkley E., Lt.**
434th Ftr Sqn/479th Ftr Grp

| *Sqn* | *Date* | *Claims* | *Location* | *A/C* |
|---|---|---|---|---|
| 434th | August 25, 1944 | (2)Me-109 dest(air) | Rostock | P-38 |
| | September 5 | (2)Ju-88 dest(grd) | Ettinghausen | P-38 |
| | December 5 | FW-190 prob(air) | Neuruppin | P-51 |

2-1-0 air
2-0 ground

**Holloway, John G., Capt.**
505th Ftr Sqn/339th Ftr Grp

| *Sqn* | *Date* | *Claims* | *Location* | *A/C* |
|---|---|---|---|---|
| 505th | July 25, 1944 | Me-109 dest(air) | Beauvais | P-51 |
| | August 4 | Me-109 dest(air) | S/Hamburg | P-51 |

2-0-0 air
0-0 ground

**Holly, Richard M., Capt.**
84th Ftr Sqn/78th Ftr Grp
Earlier flew in Iceland with the 50th Ftr Sqn and shared a FW-200 on August 5, 1943.

| *Sqn* | *Date* | *Claims* | *Location* | *A/C* |
|---|---|---|---|---|
| 84th | May 19, 1944 | Me-109 dest(air) | Nienburg | P-47 |

1-0-0 air
0-0 ground

**Holm, Willis A., Capt.**
359th Ftr Sqn/356th Ftr Grp

| *Sqn* | *Date* | *Claims* | *Location* | *A/C* |
|---|---|---|---|---|
| 359th | February 21, 1944 | Me-109 dam(air) | Hanover | P-47 |
| | May 13 | FW-190 prob(air) | Kiel-Lubeck | P-47 |

0-1-1 air
0-0 ground

**Holmberg, Paul E., Lt.**
362nd Ftr Sqn/357th Ftr Grp

| *Sqn* | *Date* | *Claims* | *Location* | *A/C* |
|---|---|---|---|---|
| 362nd | July 1, 1944 | Me-109 dest(air) | E/St. Quentin | P-51 |

1-0-0 air
0-0 ground

**Holms, Eldon, Lt.**
383rd Ftr Sqn/364th Ftr Grp

| *Sqn* | *Date* | *Claims* | *Location* | *A/C* |
|---|---|---|---|---|
| 383rd | April 13, 1945 | Me-109 dest(grd) | Flensburg | P-51 |
| | | (3)Me-109 dam(grd) | Flensburg | P-51 |

0-0-0 air
1-3 ground

**Holmes, Robert B., Lt.**
82nd Ftr Sqn/78th Ftr Grp
HdQts/78th Ftr Grp

| *Sqn* | *Date* | *Claims* | *Location* | *A/C* |
|---|---|---|---|---|
| HdQts | November 21, 1944 | Me-109 dest(air) | Hanover | P-47 |
| 82nd | April 16, 1945 | (5)u/i a/c dam(grd) | Pilzen/Prague | P-51 |

1-0-0 air
0-5 ground

**Holter, Paul C., Jr., Lt.**
374th Ftr Sqn/361st Ftr Grp

| *Sqn* | *Date* | *Claims* | *Location* | *A/C* |
|---|---|---|---|---|
| 374th | May 24, 1944 | Me-109 dam(air) | NE Berlin | P-51 |
| | June 8 | Me-109 dam(air) | St. Pierre | P-51 |
| | August 5 | Me-109 dest(air) | Hoperhofen | P-51 |

1-0-2 air
0-0 ground

**Holtmeier, Herbert R., Lt.**
61st Ftr Sqn/56th Ftr Grp

| *Sqn* | *Date* | *Claims* | *Location* | *A/C* |
|---|---|---|---|---|
| 61st | April 15, 1944 | Ju-88 dam(grd) | Flensburg | P-47 |

0-0-0 air
0-1 ground

**Holtz, Raymond K., Lt.**
359th Ftr Sqn/356th Ftr Grp

| *Sqn* | *Date* | *Claims* | *Location* | *A/C* |
|---|---|---|---|---|
| 359th | March 18, 1944 | (.25)Do-217 dam(grd)* | W/Nancy | P-47 |
| | April 27 | FW-190 dest(air) | Reims | P-47 |

1-0-0 air
0-0.25 ground

* - shared with Maj. D.A. Baccus, Lt. G.B. Peet, and Lt. W.C. O'Barr of the 359th Ftr Sqn

**Homeyer, Albert G., Capt.**
369th Ftr Sqn/359th Ftr Grp
368th Ftr Sqn/359th Ftr Grp

| *Sqn* | *Date* | *Claims* | *Location* | *A/C* |
|---|---|---|---|---|
| 368th | May 8, 1944 | Me-109 dam(air) | SE Bremen | P-51 |
| | May 21 | FW-190 dest(grd) | N/Grevesmuhlen | P-51 |
| | | FW-190 dam(grd) | N/Grevesmuhlen | P-51 |
| | | Ju-52 dam(grd) | N/Grevesmuhlen | P-51 |

0-0-1 air
1-2 ground

**Homuth, Robert H., Lt.**
335th Ftr Sqn/4th Ftr Grp

| *Sqn* | *Date* | *Claims* | *Location* | *A/C* |
|---|---|---|---|---|
| 335th | May 12, 1944 | Me-109 dest(air) | E/Giessen | P-51 |

1-0-0 air
0-0 ground

**Honaker, Stuart R., Lt.**
384th Ftr Sqn/364th Ftr Grp

| *Sqn* | *Date* | *Claims* | *Location* | *A/C* |
|---|---|---|---|---|
| 384th | April 10, 1945 | Do-217 dam(grd) | W/Berlin | P-51 |
| | | He-111 dam(grd) | W/Berlin | P-51 |

0-0-0 air
0-2 ground

**Honance, Eldie E., Lt.**
434th Ftr Sqn/479th Ftr Grp

| Sqn | Date | Claims | Location | A/C |
|---|---|---|---|---|
| 434th | April 18, 1945 | Me-109 dest(grd) | Deiningen | P-51 |
| | | Me-109 dam(grd) | Deiningen | P-51 |

0-0-0 air
1-1 ground

**Hood, Aubrey O., Lt.**
362nd Ftr Sqn/357th Ftr Grp

| Sqn | Date | Claims | Location | A/C |
|---|---|---|---|---|
| 362nd | May 12, 1944 | (.5)Me-109 dest(air)* | SE Frankfurt | P-51 |

0.5-0-0 air
0-0 ground

* - shared with Lt. T.E. Norris of the 362nd Ftr Sqn

**Hood, William K., Lt.**
383rd Ftr Sqn/364th Ftr Grp

| Sqn | Date | Claims | Location | A/C |
|---|---|---|---|---|
| 383rd | April 16, 1945 | Me-109 dest(grd) | Marienbad | P-51 |
| | | FW-190 dam(grd) | Marienbad | P-51 |
| | | Do-217 dam(grd) | Marienbad | P-51 |

0-0-0 air
1-2 ground

**Hooker, Freeman F., Lt.**
361st Ftr Sqn/356th Ftr Grp

| Sqn | Date | Claims | Location | A/C |
|---|---|---|---|---|
| 361st | October 7, 1944 | Me-110 dest(grd) | Fritzlar | P-47 |
| | | Me-110 dam(grd) | Fritzlar | P-47 |
| | | Me-410 dam(grd) | Fritzlar | P-47 |
| | January 14, 1945 | (2)FW-190 dest(air) | Dummer Lake | P-51 |
| | | Me-262 dam(grd) | Hesepe | P-51 |

2-0-0 air
1-3 ground

**Hooker, Verne E., Capt.**
435th Ftr Sqn/479th Ftr Grp

| Sqn | Date | Claims | Location | A/C |
|---|---|---|---|---|
| 435th | August 18, 1944 | (.5)He-111 dest(grd)* | Nancy/Essey A/F | P-38 |
| | | (.5)He-111 dest(grd)** | Nancy/Essey A/F | P-38 |
| | | Ju-88 dam(grd) | Nancy/Essey A/F | P-38 |
| | September 5 | He-111 dam(grd) | Hoehst Oberau | P-38 |
| | April 7, 1945 | Me-109 dest(air) | SE Bremen | P-51 |
| | | Me-262 dest(air) | SE Bremen | P-51 |
| | April 13 | (2)Ju-88 dest(grd) | Tarnewitz | P-51 |
| | | Ju-88 dam(grd) | Tarnewitz | P-51 |
| | April 16 | u/i a/c dest(grd) | S/Pocking | P-51 |
| | | Me-109 dam(grd) | S/Pocking | P-51 |
| | April 17 | u/i a/c dam(grd) | Puchhoff | P-51 |
| | April 18 | (2)u/i a/c dam(grd) | Mettenheim | P-51 |

2-0-0 air
4-7 ground

* - shared with Lt. C.F. Monsell of the 435th Ftr Sqn
** - shared with Lt. N.W. Butler of the 435th Ftr Sqn

**Hopcroft, Ernest J., Lt.**
436th Ftr Sqn/479th Ftr Grp

| Sqn | Date | Claims | Location | A/C |
|---|---|---|---|---|
| 436th | February 22, 1945 | He-111 dam(grd) | Halberstadt | P-51 |
| | April 13 | (2)Me-410 dest(grd) | Salzwedel | P-51 |
| | | Me-109 dest(grd) | Salzwedel | P-51 |
| | April 16 | He-111 dest(grd) | Landstadt | P-51 |
| | April 17 | FW-190 dest(grd) | Puchhoff | P-51 |
| | | Me-109 dest(grd) | Puchhoff | P-51 |
| | | Fi-156 dest(grd) | Puchhoff | P-51 |
| | | u/i a/c dam(grd) | Puchhoff | P-51 |

0-0-0 air
7-2 ground

**Hopkins, Wallace E., LtCol.**
HdQts/361st Ftr Grp

| Sqn | Date | Claims | Location | A/C |
|---|---|---|---|---|
| HdQts | May 29, 1944 | (2)FW-190 dest(air) | Pitka | P-51 |
| | June 29 | (4)FW-190 dest(grd) | Oschersleben | P-51 |
| | | (1.5)FW-190 dam(grd)* | Oschersleben | P-51 |
| | August 8 | (2)FW-190 dest(air) | Evreux | P-51 |

4-0-0 air
4-1.5 ground

* - shared with Lt. V.R. Richards of the 374th Ftr Sqn, 361st Ftr Grp

**Horman, Elmer H., Lt.**
383rd Ftr Sqn/364th Ftr Grp

| Sqn | Date | Claims | Location | A/C |
|---|---|---|---|---|
| 383rd | November 21, 1944 | FW-190 dest(air) | S/Nordhausen | P-51 |
| | February 22, 1945 | FW-190 dest(air) | SW Bremen | P-51 |
| | | (2)FW-190 dam(air) | SW Bremen | P-51 |
| | April 13 | (2)Ju-52 dest(grd) | Flensburg | P-51 |
| | | Ju-52 dam(grd) | Flensburg | P-51 |

2-0-2 air
2-1 ground

**Horne, Claude G., Capt.**
77th Ftr Sqn/20th Ftr Grp

| Sqn | Date | Claims | Location | A/C |
|---|---|---|---|---|
| 77th | April 8, 1944 | FW-190 dest(air) | Salzwedel | P-38 |
| | | (3)u/i a/c dam(grd) | Salzwedel | P-38 |
| | | Ju-88 dam(grd) | Salzwedel | P-38 |

1-0-0 air
0-4 ground

**Horne, Francis W., Capt.**
328th Ftr Sqn/352nd Ftr Grp

| Sqn | Date | Claims | Location | A/C |
|---|---|---|---|---|
| 328th | December 22, 1943 | Me-110 dest(air) | Zwolle | P-47 |
| | January 30, 1944 | (.5)FW-190 dest(air)* | Emmen | P-47 |
| | February 4 | FW-190 dest(air) | Brussels | P-47 |
| | April 29 | (.5)FW-190 dest(air)** | Calvorde | P-51 |
| | May 8 | FW-190 prob(air) | E/Bremen | P-51 |
| | May 13 | (2)FW-190 dest(air) | Demmin | P-51 |
| | May 21 | u/i a/c dest(grd) | Alt Ruppin | P-51 |
| | | He-111 dam(grd) | Alt Ruppin | P-51 |
| | June 6 | (.5)FW-190 dest(air)@ | SE Rouen | P-51 |

5.5-1-0 air
1-1 ground

* - shared with Lt. Q.L. Quinn of the 328th Ftr Sqn
** - shared with Lt. S.E. Dyke of the 328th Ftr Sqn
@ - shared with Lt. L.J. Allain of the 328th Ftr Sqn

**Horner, Kenneth R., Lt.**
385th Ftr Sqn/364th Ftr Grp

| Sqn | Date | Claims | Location | A/C |
|---|---|---|---|---|
| 385th | February 26, 1945 | (2)He-111 dest(grd) | SE Jade Bay | P-51 |
| | March 21 | Me-109 dest(grd) | Achmer | P-51 |
| | | Me-109 dam(grd) | Achmer | P-51 |
| | April 16 | Ju-188 dest(grd) | Pocking | P-51 |
| | | FW-190 dest(grd) | Pocking | P-51 |
| | | Ju-87 dest(grd) | Pocking | P-51 |
| | | FW-190 dam(grd) | Pocking | P-51 |

0-0-0 air
6-2 ground

**Hornick, Carl W., Lt.**
383rd Ftr Sqn/364th Ftr Grp

| Sqn | Date | Claims | Location | A/C |
|---|---|---|---|---|
| 383rd | April 13, 1945 | Me-109 dest(grd) | Flensburg | P-51 |
| | | Me-109 dam(grd) | Flensburg | P-51 |
| | | Ju-52 dam(grd) | Flensburg | P-51 |

0-0-0 air
1-2 ground

**Hosford, Lynn H., Lt.**
82nd Ftr Sqn/78th Ftr Grp

| *Sqn* | *Date* | *Claims* | *Location* | *A/C* |
|---|---|---|---|---|
| 82nd | May 19, 1944 | (.5)He-111 dam(grd)* | Plantlunne | P-47 |

0-0-0 air
0-0.5 ground

* - shared with Capt. W.A. Guilfoyle of the 82nd Ftr Sqn

**Hotchkiss, Courtlyn W., Lt.**
83rd Ftr Sqn/78th Ftr Grp

| *Sqn* | *Date* | *Claims* | *Location* | *A/C* |
|---|---|---|---|---|
| 83rd | February 22, 1944 | FW-190 dest(air) | Walcheren | P-47 |

1-0-0 air
0-0 ground

**Housholder, William T., Lt.**
385th Ftr Sqn/364th Ftr Grp

| *Sqn* | *Date* | *Claims* | *Location* | *A/C* |
|---|---|---|---|---|
| 385th | September 23, 1944 | FW-190 dest(air) | E/Arnheim | P-51 |
| | | Me-109 dam(air) | E/Arnheim | P-51 |
| | November 2 | Me-109 dest(air) | Halle | P-51 |
| | | Me-109 prob(air) | Halle | P-51 |

2-1-1 air
0-0 ground

**Houston, Byron G., Jr., Lt.**
354th Ftr Sqn/355th Ftr Grp

| *Sqn* | *Date* | *Claims* | *Location* | *A/C* |
|---|---|---|---|---|
| 354th | April 5, 1944 | Me-108 dam(air) | Landsberg | P-51 |
| | | (4)Do-217 dam(grd) | Landsberg | P-51 |
| | | Me-110 dam(grd) | Landsberg | P-51 |
| | April 8 | Me-109 dam(air) | Brunswick | P-51 |
| | April 20 | FW-190 dest(grd) | Blois A/F | P-51 |

0-0-2 air
1-5 ground

**Hovde, William J., Maj.**
358th Ftr Sqn/355th Ftr Grp

| *Sqn* | *Date* | *Claims* | *Location* | *A/C* |
|---|---|---|---|---|
| 358th | February 22, 1944 | FW-190 dest(air) | SE Munster | P-47 |
| | March 18 | (2)FW-190 dest(air) | Gunzburg-Augsburg | P-51 |
| | | FW-190 dam(air) | Gunzburg-Augsburg | P-51 |
| | March 28 | He-111 dam(grd) | Marigny | P-51 |
| | April 8 | Me-109 dest(air) | E/Brunswick | P-51 |
| | July 19 | Me-109 dest(air) | Augsburg | P-51 |
| | July 24 | Do-217 dest(grd) | Augsburg | P-51 |
| | | Ju-88 dest(grd) | Augsburg | P-51 |
| | December 5 | (4.5)FW-190 dest(air)* | Berlin | P-51 |
| | | Me-109 dest(air) | Berlin | P-51 |

10.5-0-1 air
2-1 ground

* - shared with Lt. A.K. Alexander of the 358th Ftr Sqn

**Howard, Harry F., Lt.**
505th Ftr Sqn/339th FtrGrp

| *Sqn* | *Date* | *Claims* | *Location* | *A/C* |
|---|---|---|---|---|
| 505th | March 2, 1945 | (3)Do-217 dest(grd) | Mockern | P-51 |

0-0-0 air
3-0 ground

**Howard, Herbert B., Capt.**
3rd Scouting Force

| *Sqn* | *Date* | *Claims* | *Location* | *A/C* |
|---|---|---|---|---|
| 3rd | December 24, 1944 | (2)Me-109 dest(air) | Frankfurt-Darmstadt | P-51 |
| | December 31 | FW-190 dest(air) | N/Steinhuder Lake | P-51 |

3-0-0 air
0-0 ground

**Howard, Ronald M., Capt.**
55th Ftr Sqn/20th Ftr Grp

| *Sqn* | *Date* | *Claims* | *Location* | *A/C* |
|---|---|---|---|---|
| 55th | August 25, 1944 | BV-140 dest(grd) | Parow A/F | P-51 |
| | | BV-140 dam(grd) | Parow A/F | P-51 |
| | October 6 | BV-140 dest(grd) | Kubitzer Bay | P-51 |
| | | Do-24 dest(grd) | Kubitzer Bay | P-51 |
| | | (3)BV-140 dam(grd) | Kubitzer Bay | P-51 |
| | February 22, 1945 | Me-262 dam(air) | Salzwedel | P-51 |

0-0-1 air
3-4 ground

**Howe, David W., Lt.**
334th Ftr Sqn/4th Ftr Grp

| *Sqn* | *Date* | *Claims* | *Location* | *A/C* |
|---|---|---|---|---|
| 334th | February 21, 1944 | FW-190 dest(air) | S/Dummer Lake | P-47 |
| | March 8 | Me-109 dest(air) | S/Berlin | P-51 |
| | March 29 | FW-190 dest(air) | NW Brunswick | P-51 |
| | April 10 | (.5)u/i a/c dest(grd)* | Romorantin A/F | P-51 |
| | April 18 | (2)Ju-52 dest(grd) | Juterbog A/F | P-51 |
| | | (.25) of (6)Ju-52 dam(grd)** | Juterbog A/F | P-51 |
| | April 24 | Me-109 dest(air) | Darmstadt | P-51 |
| | May 19 | Me-109 dest(air) | Neustadt Bay | P-51 |
| | September 28 | FW-190 dest(air) | NE Kassel | P-51 |

6-0-0 air
2.5-1.5 ground

* - shared with an unknown pilot
** - all shared with Lt. J.L. Lang, Lt. D.M. Malmsten, and Lt. S.W. Monroe of the 334th Ftr Sqn

**Howell, Horace P., Lt.**
364th Ftr Sqn/357th Ftr Grp

| *Sqn* | *Date* | *Claims* | *Location* | *A/C* |
|---|---|---|---|---|
| 364th | September 13, 1944 | (2)Me-109 dest(air) | E/Bad Frankenhausen | P-51 |

2-0-0 air
0-0 ground

**Howell, John C., Capt.**
364th Ftr Sqn/357th Ftr Grp

| *Sqn* | *Date* | *Claims* | *Location* | *A/C* |
|---|---|---|---|---|
| 364th | May 28, 1944 | Me-109 dest(air) | NW Magdeburg | P-51 |
| | May 30 | (.5)Me-410 dest(air)* | NW Bernburg | P-51 |
| | June 29 | Me-109 dest(air) | SW Leipzig | P-51 |
| | | FW-190 dam(air) | SW Leipzig | P-51 |

2.5-0-1 air
0-0 ground

* - shared with Lt. R.M. Shaw of the 364th Ftr Sqn

**Howell, Lester L., Lt.**
486th Ftr Sqn/352nd Ftr Grp

| *Sqn* | *Date* | *Claims* | *Location* | *A/C* |
|---|---|---|---|---|
| 486th | May 28, 1944 | Me-109 dest(air) | Dessau | P-51 |
| | June 20 | Me-109 dest(air) | Magdeburg | P-51 |
| | | He-177 dam(grd) | N/Burg | P-51 |

2-0-0 air
0-1 ground

**Hower, Earl W., Capt.**
55th Ftr Sqn/20th Ftr Grp

| *Sqn* | *Date* | *Claims* | *Location* | *A/C* |
|---|---|---|---|---|
| 55th | August 25, 1944 | BV-140 dest(grd) | Parow A/F | P-51 |
| | | Ju-88 dam(grd) | Parow A/F | P-51 |

0-0-0 air
1-1 ground

**Howes, Bernard H., Lt.**
343rd Ftr Sqn/55th Ftr Grp

| *Sqn* | *Date* | *Claims* | *Location* | *A/C* |
|---|---|---|---|---|
| 343rd | December 25, 1944 | (2)Me-109 dest(air) | SW Frankfurt | P-51 |
| | February 3, 1945 | (2)FW-190 dest(air) | Boizenburg | P-51 |

| Sqn | Date | Claims | Location | A/C |
|---|---|---|---|---|
| | | Ju-88 dest(air) | Boizenburg | P-51 |
| | February 19 | Me-108 dest(air) | S/Hameln | P-51 |
| | February 28 | FW-190 dest(grd) | SW Nurnburg | P-51 |
| | March 3 | Me-109 dest(grd) | Prague/Letnany | P-51 |
| | | Me-109 dam(grd) | Prague/Letnany | P-51 |
| | | Me-110 dam(grd) | Prague/Letnany | P-51 |
| | | Ju-88 dam(grd) | Prague/Letnany | P-51 |
| | | Ju-52 dam(grd) | Prague/Letnany | P-51 |

6-0-0 air
2-4 ground

**Howes, Osborn, Lt.**
364th Ftr Sqn/357th Ftr Grp

| *Sqn* | *Date* | *Claims* | *Location* | *A/C* |
|---|---|---|---|---|
| 364th | March 2, 1945 | Me-109 dest(air) | SE Magdeburg | P-51 |
| | | He-111 dest(grd) | E/Magdeburg | P-51 |
| | April 17 | Ju-88 dest(grd) | Prague/Ruzny | P-51 |

1-0-0 air
2-0 ground

**Howie, Donald E., Lt.**
350th Ftr Sqn/353rd Ftr Grp

| *Sqn* | *Date* | *Claims* | *Location* | *A/C* |
|---|---|---|---|---|
| 350th | March 21, 1945 | (2)FW-190 dest(grd) | Achmer | P-51 |

0-0-0 air
2-0 ground

**Hrico, George J., Lt.**
505th Ftr Sqn/339th Ftr Grp

| *Sqn* | *Date* | *Claims* | *Location* | *A/C* |
|---|---|---|---|---|
| 505th | May 25, 1944 | (.5)FW-190 dest(air)* | Paris | P-51 |
| | July 29 | (.5)Ju-52 dest(grd)** | NW Naumberg | P-51 |
| | September 13 | (2)u/i a/c dam(grd) | SE Munich | P-51 |

0.5-0-0 air
0.5-2 ground

* - shared with Lt. W.F. Mudge of the 505th Ftr Sqn
** - shared with Lt. W.A. Jones of the 505th Ftr Sqn

**Hubbard, Glenn A., Capt.**
364th Ftr Sqn/357th Ftr Grp

| *Sqn* | *Date* | *Claims* | *Location* | *A/C* |
|---|---|---|---|---|
| 364th | March 16, 1944 | Me-109 dam(air) | S/Stuttgart | P-51 |

0-0-1 air
0-0 ground

**Hubbard, Mark E., LtCol.**
HdQts/20th Ftr Grp
Earlier flew in the MTO with the 33rd Ftr Grp and claimed 4 kills; (2)Ju-88's on January 15, 1943; a Ju-87 on February 1, 1943; and a Me-109 on March 24, 1943.

| *Sqn* | *Date* | *Claims* | *Location* | *A/C* |
|---|---|---|---|---|
| HdQts | March 18, 1944 | (2.5)Me-109 dest(air)* | Memmingen | P-38 |
| | | Me-109 prob(air) | Memmingen | P-38 |

2.5-1-0 air
0-0 ground

* - shared with Lt. A.F. Clark of the 77th Ftr Sqn, 20th Ftr Grp

**Hubbell, William R., Lt.**
350th Ftr Sqn/353rd Ftr Grp

| *Sqn* | *Date* | *Claims* | *Location* | *A/C* |
|---|---|---|---|---|
| 350th | March 24, 1945 | Me-109 dest(air) | NW Kassel | P-51 |
| | | Me-109 prob(air) | NW Kassel | P-51 |

1-1-0 air
0-0 ground

**Hudson, Arthur R., Lt.**
328th Ftr Sqn/352nd Ftr Grp

| *Sqn* | *Date* | *Claims* | *Location* | *A/C* |
|---|---|---|---|---|
| 328th | November 2, 1944 | (4)Me-109 dest(air) | Merseburg | P-51 |

4-0-0 air
0-0 ground

**Hudson, Will M., Lt.**
504th Ftr Sqn/339th Ftr Grp

| *Sqn* | *Date* | *Claims* | *Location* | *A/C* |
|---|---|---|---|---|
| 504th | April 16, 1945 | (3)FW-190 dest(grd) | Klatovy | P-51 |
| | | Me-109 dest(grd) | Klatovy | P-51 |

0-0-0 air
4-0 ground

**Huff, Edgar J., Lt.**
63rd Ftr Sqn/56th Ftr Grp

| *Sqn* | *Date* | *Claims* | *Location* | *A/C* |
|---|---|---|---|---|
| 63rd | April 13, 1945 | u/i a/c dest(grd) | Eggebeck A/F | P-47 |
| | | Me-410 dam(grd) | Eggebeck A/F | P-47 |
| | | He-177 dam(grd) | Eggebeck A/F | P-47 |

0-0-0 air
1-2 ground

**Hughes, John L., Lt.**
384th Ftr Sqn/364th Ftr Grp

| *Sqn* | *Date* | *Claims* | *Location* | *A/C* |
|---|---|---|---|---|
| 384th | April 10, 1945 | He-111 dest(grd) | Oranienburg | P-51 |
| | | Me-109 dam(grd) | Oranienburg | P-51 |
| | April 17 | He-111 dest(grd) | Karlsbad | P-51 |
| | | He-111 dam(grd) | Karlsbad | P-51 |

0-0-0 air
2-2 ground

**Hughes, Melvin J., F/O**
63rd Ftr Sqn/56th Ftr Grp

| *Sqn* | *Date* | *Claims* | *Location* | *A/C* |
|---|---|---|---|---|
| 63rd | December 23, 1944 | FW-190 dest(air) | NW Coblenz | P-47 |
| | | FW-190 dam(air) | NW Coblenz | P-47 |

1-0-1 air
0-0 ground

**Hughes, Robert E., Lt.**
336th Ftr Sqn/4th Ftr Grp

| *Sqn* | *Date* | *Claims* | *Location* | *A/C* |
|---|---|---|---|---|
| 336th | April 5, 1944 | u/i a/c dam(grd) | Stendal | P-51 |
| | April 8 | FW-190 prob(air) | Ulzen | P-51 |
| | | Me-109 dam(air) | Ulzen | P-51 |

0-1-1 air
0-1 ground

**Hughes, Thomas E., Capt.**
363rd Ftr Sqn/357th Ftr Grp

| *Sqn* | *Date* | *Claims* | *Location* | *A/C* |
|---|---|---|---|---|
| 363rd | September 18, 1944 | (.5)FW-190 dest(air)* | Arnheim | P-51 |
| | November 2 | FW-190 dest(air) | E/Leipzig | P-51 |
| | | (2)FW-190 dam(air) | E/Leipzig | P-51 |

1.5-0-2 air
0-0 ground

* - shared with Lt. F.L. Gailer of the 363rd Ftr Sqn

**Huish, Heber M., Lt.**
354th Ftr Sqn/355th Ftr Grp

| *Sqn* | *Date* | *Claims* | *Location* | *A/C* |
|---|---|---|---|---|
| 354th | June 20, 1944 | (.5)Me-410 dest(air)* | Rugen | P-51 |

0.5-0-0 air
0-0 ground

* - shared with Lt. S.C. Williams of the 354th Ftr Sqn

**Hulderman, Robert E., Lt.**
354th Ftr Sqn/355th Ftr Grp

| *Sqn* | *Date* | *Claims* | *Location* | *A/C* |
|---|---|---|---|---|
| 354th | June 20, 1944 | Me-410 dam(air) | Bergen | P-51 |
| | June 24 | Me-109 dest(grd) | Seiches | P-51 |
| | July 5 | (.5)Ju-88 dest(grd)* | Chateauroux | P-51 |

0-0-1 air
1.5-0 ground

* - shared with LtCol. C.H. Kinnard of HdQts, 355th Ftr Grp

**Hull, James C., Capt.**
358th Ftr Sqn/355th Ftr Grp

| *Sqn* | *Date* | *Claims* | *Location* | *A/C* |
|---|---|---|---|---|
| 358th | November 29, 1943 | Me-109 dam(air) | Bremen | P-47 |

0-0-1 air
0-0 ground

**Hungate, Max B., Lt.**
351st Ftr Sqn/353rd Ftr Grp

| *Sqn* | *Date* | *Claims* | *Location* | *A/C* |
|---|---|---|---|---|
| 351st | June 7, 1944 | Me-109 dest(air) | Beauvais/Tille | P-47 |
| | June 27 | Me-109 dam(air) | SE Epernay | P-47 |
| | August 11 | Me-109 dest(air) | S/Paris | P-47 |

2-0-1 air
0-0 ground

**Hunt, Gilbert W., Lt.**
336th Ftr Sqn/4th Ftr Grp

| *Sqn* | *Date* | *Claims* | *Location* | *A/C* |
|---|---|---|---|---|
| 336th | September 12, 1944 | Me-109 dest(air) | NW Frankfurt | P-51 |

1-0-0 air
0-0 ground

**Hunt, Harlan F., Lt.**
504th Ftr Sqn/339th Ftr Grp

| *Sqn* | *Date* | *Claims* | *Location* | *A/C* |
|---|---|---|---|---|
| 504th | April 9, 1945 | Me-262 dam(air) | Leipzig | P-51 |
| | April 16 | FW-190 dest(grd) | Klatovy | P-51 |
| | | FW-190 dam(grd) | Klatovy | P-51 |
| | April 17 | Me-109 dest(grd) | Klatovy-Anberg | P-51 |
| | | FW-190 dest(grd) | Klatovy-Anberg | P-51 |
| | | Fi-156 dest(grd) | Klatovy-Anberg | P-51 |
| | | Ju-88 dest(grd) | Klatovy-Anberg | P-51 |

0-0-1 air
5-1 ground

**Hunt, Lloyd, Lt.**
352nd Ftr Sqn/353rd Ftr Grp

| *Sqn* | *Date* | *Claims* | *Location* | *A/C* |
|---|---|---|---|---|
| 352nd | June 29, 1944 | (.5)He-111 dam(grd)* | Plantlunne | P-47 |

0-0-0 air
0-0.5 ground

* - shared with Capt. V.N. Curtis of the 351st Ftr Sqn

**Hunt, Robert L., Lt.**
383rd Ftr Sqn/364th Ftr Grp

| *Sqn* | *Date* | *Claims* | *Location* | *A/C* |
|---|---|---|---|---|
| 383rd | February 22, 1945 | Me-262 dam(air) | Wittstock | P-51 |
| | March 30 | Me-262 dam(air) | Brandenburg | P-51 |
| | April 16 | u/i a/c dest(grd) | Marienbad | P-51 |
| | | FW-190 dam(grd) | Marienbad | P-51 |

0-0-2 air
1-1 ground

**Hunt, Robert S., Lt.**
384th Ftr Sqn/364th Ftr Grp

| *Sqn* | *Date* | *Claims* | *Location* | *A/C* |
|---|---|---|---|---|
| 384th | June 25, 1944 | Me-109 dest(air) | E/Blois | P-38 |

1-0-0 air
0-0 ground

**Hunt, William F., Capt.**
84th Ftr Sqn/78th Ftr Grp

| *Sqn* | *Date* | *Claims* | *Location* | *A/C* |
|---|---|---|---|---|
| 84th | April 8, 1944 | (3)Glider dam(grd) | NE Frankfurt | P-47 |
| | May 19 | Me-109 dest(air) | E/Nienburg | P-47 |

1-0-0 air
0-3 ground

**Hunter, Charles M., Lt.**
504th Ftr Sqn/339th Ftr Grp

| *Sqn* | *Date* | *Claims* | *Location* | *A/C* |
|---|---|---|---|---|
| 504th | August 16, 1944 | Me-109 dest(air) | Mulhausen | P-51 |

1-0-0 air
0-0 ground

**Hunter, Harry F., Lt.**
351st Ftr Sqn/353rd Ftr Grp

| *Sqn* | *Date* | *Claims* | *Location* | *A/C* |
|---|---|---|---|---|
| 351st | September 27, 1943 | Me-109 dest(air) | SW Emden | P-47 |
| | April 22, 1944 | FW-190 prob(air) | N/Hamm | P-47 |

1-1-0 air
0-0 ground

**Hunter, John B., Capt.**
368th Ftr Sqn/359th Ftr Grp

| *Sqn* | *Date* | *Claims* | *Location* | *A/C* |
|---|---|---|---|---|
| 368th | May 24, 1944 | (.5)Me-109 dest(air)* | NW Berlin | P-51 |
| | May 30 | (.5)Me-109 dest(air)** | W/Dessau | P-51 |
| | April 13, 1945 | He-111 dest(grd) | Luneburg | P-51 |
| | April 16 | Me-109 dest(grd) | E/Plattling | P-51 |
| | | (2)Me-109 dam(grd) | E/Plattling | P-51 |

1-0-0 air
2-2 ground

* - shared with Lt. V.E. Sansing of the 369th Ftr Sqn, 359th Ftr Grp
** - shared with Lt. R.W. Hawkinson of the 368th Ftr Sqn

**Hunter, John C., Capt.**
383rd Ftr Sqn/364th Ftr Grp

| *Sqn* | *Date* | *Claims* | *Location* | *A/C* |
|---|---|---|---|---|
| 383rd | November 21, 1944 | (2)FW-190 dest(air) | S/Nordhausen | P-51 |
| | | FW-190 dam(air) | S/Nordhausen | P-51 |
| | March 18, 1945 | FW-190 dest(air) | Schwerin | P-51 |
| | April 13 | (3)FW-190 dest(grd) | Flensburg | P-51 |
| | | (2)Ju-52 dest(grd) | Flensburg | P-51 |
| | | Me-110 dest(grd) | Flensburg | P-51 |
| | | (3)Ju-52 dam(grd) | Flensburg | P-51 |
| | | Me-109 dam(grd) | Flensburg | P-51 |

3-0-1 air
6-4 ground

**Hunter, Robert C., Jr., Lt.**
335th Ftr Sqn/4th Ftr Grp

| *Sqn* | *Date* | *Claims* | *Location* | *A/C* |
|---|---|---|---|---|
| 335th | April 9, 1945 | u/i a/c dest(grd) | Munich-Brunnthal | P-51 |
| | | (2)u/i a/c dam(grd) | Munich-Brunnthal | P-51 |
| | April 16 | (2)Do-217 dest(grd) | Praha/Letnany | P-51 |
| | | Ju-88 dest(grd) | Praha/Letnany | P-51 |

0-0-0 air
4-2 ground

**Hupe, Franklin E., Lt.**
84th Ftr Sqn/78th Ftr Grp
335th Ftr Sqn/ 4th Ftr Grp

| *Sqn* | *Date* | *Claims* | *Location* | *A/C* |
|---|---|---|---|---|
| 335th | March 23, 1944 | Me-109 dam(air) | E/Hanover | P-51 |

0-0-1 air
0-0 ground

**Hupp, Ellis E., Lt.**
505th Ftr Sqn/339th Ftr Grp

| *Sqn* | *Date* | *Claims* | *Location* | *A/C* |
|---|---|---|---|---|
| 505th | April 10, 1945 | Do-217 dest(grd) | N/Neuruppin | P-51 |
| | | Do-217 dam(grd) | N/Neuruppin | P-51 |
| | April 17 | Do-217 dest(grd) | SE Pocking | P-51 |

0-0-0 air
2-1 ground

**Hurlburt, Donald M., Lt.**
351st Ftr Sqn/353rd Ftr Grp

| *Sqn* | *Date* | *Claims* | *Location* | *A/C* |
|---|---|---|---|---|
| 351st | October 8, 1943 | (.5)Me-110 dest(air)* | Friesoythe | P-47 |

0.5-0-0 air
0-0 ground

* - shared with Capt. F.H. LeFebre of the 351st Ftr Sqn

**Hurley, James C., Lt.**
328th Ftr Sqn/352nd Ftr Grp

| *Sqn* | *Date* | *Claims* | *Location* | *A/C* |
|---|---|---|---|---|
| 328th | March 30, 1945 | Me-262 dest(air) | N/Magdeburg | P-51 |
| | April 17 | Me-109 dest(grd) | Plattling | P-51 |
| | | (2)Me-109 dam(grd) | Plattling | P-51 |

1-0-0 air
1-2 ground

**Hurley, William S., Jr., Capt.**
361st Ftr Sqn/356th Ftr Grp

| *Sqn* | *Date* | *Claims* | *Location* | *A/C* |
|---|---|---|---|---|
| 361st | June 22, 1944 | (.5)Me-109 dest(air)* | Evreux | P-47 |
| | August 4 | Me-109 dest(air) | Bremen-Hamburg | P-47 |
| | November 25 | FW-190 dest(grd) | Zwickau | P-51 |
| | | (2)FW-190 dam(grd) | Zwickau | P-51 |

1.5-0-0 air
1-2 ground

* - shared with Lt. G.L. Yoakum of the 361st Ftr Sqn

**Hurst, Carl P., Capt.**
83rd Ftr Sqn/78th Ftr Grp

| *Sqn* | *Date* | *Claims* | *Location* | *A/C* |
|---|---|---|---|---|
| 83rd | April 24, 1944 | Do-217 dam(grd) | Diest | P-47 |
| | | u/i a/c dam(grd) | Diest | P-47 |

0-0-0 air
0-2 ground

**Hurst, Wilford F., Capt.**
350th Ftr Sqn/353rd Ftr Grp

| *Sqn* | *Date* | *Claims* | *Location* | *A/C* |
|---|---|---|---|---|
| 350th | August 24, 1943 | FW-190 dest(air) | Rouen | P-47 |
| | October 10 | FW-190 dest(air) | Zutphen | P-47 |
| | November 5 | Me-109 dam(air) | W/Gelsenkirchen | P-47 |

2-0-1 air
0-0 ground

**Hurst, William M., Capt.**
55th Ftr Sqn/20th Ftr Grp

| *Sqn* | *Date* | *Claims* | *Location* | *A/C* |
|---|---|---|---|---|
| 55th | October 6, 1944 | (2)Do-24 dest(grd) | Kubitzer Bay | P-51 |
| | November 2 | Me-109 dest(air) | Halle | P-51 |
| | January 1, 1945 | Me-262 dam(air) | Magdeburg | P-51 |

1-0-1 air
2-0 ground

**Huskins, Samuel J., Capt.**
370th Ftr Sqn/359th Ftr Grp

| *Sqn* | *Date* | *Claims* | *Location* | *A/C* |
|---|---|---|---|---|
| 370th | November 2, 1944 | (.5)Me-109 dest(air)* | Erfurt-Weimar | P-51 |

0.5-0-0 air
0-0 ground

* - shared with an unknown pilot

**Hustead, Dallas J., Capt.**
385th Ftr Sqn/364th Ftr Grp

| *Sqn* | *Date* | *Claims* | *Location* | *A/C* |
|---|---|---|---|---|
| 385th | July 6, 1944 | FW-190 dam(air) | Chalons | P-38 |
| | August 9 | (2)Me-110 dest(grd) | Gaukonigshafen | P-51 |
| | | (3)Me-110 dam(grd) | Gaukonigshafen | P-51 |
| | | (.5)FW-200 dam(grd)* | Gaukonigshafen | P-51 |

0-0-1 air
2-3.5 ground

* - shared with Lt. R. Visconte of the 385th Ftr Sqn

**Huston, Dean M., Lt.**
487th Ftr Sqn/352nd Ftr Grp

| *Sqn* | *Date* | *Claims* | *Location* | *A/C* |
|---|---|---|---|---|
| 487th | September 10, 1944 | Ju-52 dest(grd) | Wertheim | P-51 |
| | November 27 | Me-109 dest(air) | Munster | P-51 |
| | January 1, 1945 | FW-190 dest(air) | N/Liege | P-51 |

2-0-0 air
1-0 ground

**Hustwit, Earl F., Lt.**
336th Ftr Sqn/4th Ftr Grp

| *Sqn* | *Date* | *Claims* | *Location* | *A/C* |
|---|---|---|---|---|
| 336th | September 12, 1944 | (1.5)FW-190 dest(air)* | Weisbaden | P-51 |
| | February 27, 1945 | Me-410 dest(grd) | Weimar | P-51 |

1.5-0-0 air
1-0 ground

* - shared with Lt. R.A. Dickmeyer of the 334th Ftr Sqn

**Huval, Ossie J., Lt.**
434th Ftr Sqn/479th Ftr Grp

| *Sqn* | *Date* | *Claims* | *Location* | *A/C* |
|---|---|---|---|---|
| 434th | February 21, 1945 | He-111 dest(grd) | Gotha | P-51 |
| | April 13 | (.5)u/i a/c dest(grd)* | Ratzburger Lake | P-51 |
| | | u/i a/c dam(grd) | Ratzburger Lake | P-51 |

0-0-0 air
1.5-1 ground

* - shared with Lt. C.W. Bowers of the 434th Ftr Sqn

**Huycke, Andre E., Capt.**
436th Ftr Sqn/479th Ftr Grp

| *Sqn* | *Date* | *Claims* | *Location* | *A/C* |
|---|---|---|---|---|
| 436th | September 5, 1944 | He-111 dest(grd) | Merzhausen | P-38 |
| | | He-111 dam(grd) | Merzhausen | P-38 |
| | | Do-217 dam(grd) | Merzhausen | P-38 |
| | December 23 | FW-190 dest(air) | Cologne | P-51 |

1-0-0 air
1-2 ground

**Hyde, Paul H., Jr., Capt.**
361st Ftr Sqn/356th Ftr Grp

| *Sqn* | *Date* | *Claims* | *Location* | *A/C* |
|---|---|---|---|---|
| 361st | November 5, 1943 | Me-109 dam(air) | Roermond | P-47 |

0-0-1 air
0-0 ground

**Hydorn, William H., Jr., Lt.**
82nd Ftr Sqn/78th Ftr Grp

| Sqn | Date | Claims | Location | A/C |
|---|---|---|---|---|
| 82nd | November 21, 1944 | FW-190 dam(air) | Hanover | P-47 |
| | February 9, 1945 | Me-262 prob(air) | Fulda | P-51 |

0-1-1 air
0-0 ground

**Hyman, Edward D., Lt.**
362nd Ftr Sqn/357th Ftr Grp

| Sqn | Date | Claims | Location | A/C |
|---|---|---|---|---|
| 362nd | December 24, 1944 | (2)FW-190 dest(air) | Fulda | P-51 |

2-0-0 air
0-0 ground

**Hynes, John A., Capt.**
351st Ftr Sqn/353rd Ftr Grp

| Sqn | Date | Claims | Location | A/C |
|---|---|---|---|---|
| 351st | March 14, 1945 | Me-109 dest(air) | Luckenwalde | P-51 |
| | April 9 | Me-262 dam(grd) | S/Neubiberg | P-51 |

1-0-0 air
0-1 ground

**Icard, Joseph W., Lt.**
62nd Ftr Sqn/56th Ftr Grp

| Sqn | Date | Claims | Location | A/C |
|---|---|---|---|---|
| 62nd | November 11, 1943 | FW-190 dest(air) | Munster | P-47 |
| | February 6, 1944 | FW-190 dam(air) | Albert | P-47 |
| | February 8 | Me-109 dest(air) | Cambrai | P-47 |
| | February 11 | Me-109 dest(air) | Bierset | P-47 |
| | February 21 | FW-190 dest(air) | Soesterberg | P-47 |
| | March 6 | FW-190 dest(air) | Dummer Lake | P-47 |

5-0-1 air
0-0 ground

**Iden, Paul S., Lt.**
335th Ftr Sqn/4th Ftr Grp

| Sqn | Date | Claims | Location | A/C |
|---|---|---|---|---|
| 335th | August 18, 1944 | Me-109 dest(air) | NE Paris | P-51 |

1-0-0 air
0-0 ground

**Iglesias, Victor D., Lt.**
357th Ftr Sqn/355th Ftr Grp

| Sqn | Date | Claims | Location | A/C |
|---|---|---|---|---|
| 357th | December 25, 1944 | FW-190 dest(air) | W/Coblenz | P-51 |
| | April 13, 1945 | (2)He-111 dest(grd) | Schleswig | P-51 |
| | April 20 | Me-109 dest(air) | Letnany A/F | P-51 |

2-0-0 air
2-0 ground

**Ilfrey, Jack M., Maj.**
79th Ftr Sqn/20th Ftr Grp
Earlier flew in the MTO with the 1st Ftr Grp claiming 6 kills

| Sqn | Date | Claims | Location | A/C |
|---|---|---|---|---|
| 94th | November 29, 1942 | Me-110 dest(air) | Gabes A/F | P-38 |
| | December 2 | (2)Me-109 dest(air) | Gabes A/F | P-38 |
| | December 26 | (2)FW-190 dest(air) | Bizerte | P-38 |
| | March 3, 1943 | Me-109 dest(air) | Bizerte | P-38 |
| 79th | May 24, 1944 | (2)Me-109 dest(air) | Eberswalde | P-38 |

2-0-0 air
0-0 ground

**Ingalls, Henry A., Lt.**
336th Ftr Sqn/4th Ftr Grp

| Sqn | Date | Claims | Location | A/C |
|---|---|---|---|---|
| 336th | September 11, 1944 | FW-190 dest(grd) | Langensalza | P-51 |

0-0-0 air
1-0 ground

**Ingebrigsten, Melbourne G., Capt.**
79th Ftr Sqn/20th Ftr Grp

| Sqn | Date | Claims | Location | A/C |
|---|---|---|---|---|
| 79th | October 6, 1944 | (1.5)He-115 dest(grd)* | Bad Berg-Dievenow | P-51 |

0-0-0 air
1.5-0 ground

* - shared with Capt. R.P. Gatterdam of the 79th Ftr Sqn

**Ingram, William J., Lt.**
338th Ftr Sqn/55th Ftr Grp

| Sqn | Date | Claims | Location | A/C |
|---|---|---|---|---|
| 338th | August 10, 1944 | Me-109 dest(air) | Damville | P-51 |
| | September 11 | (2.5)Me-109 dest(air)* | S/Meiningen | P-51 |
| | | Me-109 dam(air) | S/Meiningen | P-51 |

3.5-0-1 air
0-0 ground

* - shared with an unknown pilot

**Intravartola, Leonard V., Lt.**
328th Ftr Sqn/352nd Ftr Grp

| Sqn | Date | Claims | Location | A/C |
|---|---|---|---|---|
| 328th | November 21, 1944 | Me-109 dest(air) | W/Merseburg | P-51 |
| | | FW-190 dam(air) | W/Merseburg | P-51 |

1-0-1 air
0-0 ground

**Ireland, Robert N., Lt.**
350th Ftr Sqn/353rd Ftr Grp

| Sqn | Date | Claims | Location | A/C |
|---|---|---|---|---|
| 350th | October 2, 1943 | Me-109 dam(air) | Emden | P-47 |
| | December 1 | FW-190 prob(air) | Solingen | P-47 |
| | February 3, 1944 | Me-109 prob(air) | Wilhelmshaven | P-47 |

0-2-1 air
0-0 ground

**Irion, Robert E., Lt.**
505th Ftr Sqn/339th Ftr Grp

| Sqn | Date | Claims | Location | A/C |
|---|---|---|---|---|
| 505th | March 1, 1945 | (.5)Ju-88 dest(grd)* | S/Feldkirchen | P-51 |
| | | (.5)Ju-88 dest(grd)** | S/Feldkirchen | P-51 |
| | March 20 | Me-262 dest(air) | Schwerin | P-51 |
| | April 10 | (2)Ju-188 dest(grd) | Wittstock | P-51 |
| | | Do-217 dest(grd) | Wittstock | P-51 |
| | | Me-110 dam(grd) | Wittstock | P-51 |
| | April 17 | Me-110 dest(grd) | SE Pocking | P-51 |

1-0-0 air
5-1 ground

* - shared with Lt. B.B. Booth of the 505th Ftr Sqn
** - shared with Lt. O.K. Biggs of the 505th Ftr Sqn

**Irvin, John D., Maj.**
84th Ftr Sqn/78th Ftr Grp

| Sqn | Date | Claims | Location | A/C |
|---|---|---|---|---|
| 84th | May 16, 1943 | FW-190 dest(air) | E/Sluis | P-47 |
| | July 30 | FW-190 dest(air) | Winterswijk | P-47 |
| | | Me-109 dest(air) | Winterswijk | P-47 |
| | | FW-190 dam(air) | Winterswijk | P-47 |
| | September 27 | Me-109 dest(air) | NW Emden | P-47 |

4-0-1 air
0-0 ground

**Irvine, Chauncey S., Maj.**
369th Ftr Sqn/359th Ftr Grp
370th Ftr Sqn/359th Ftr Grp
HdQts/359th Ftr Grp

| *Sqn* | *Date* | *Claims* | *Location* | *A/C* |
|---|---|---|---|---|
| 369th | June 12, 1944 | Me-109 dam(grd) | W/Paris | P-51 |

0-0-0 air
0-1 ground

**Ista, Leroy W., Lt.**
352nd Ftr Sqn/353rd Ftr Grp

| *Sqn* | *Date* | *Claims* | *Location* | *A/C* |
|---|---|---|---|---|
| 352nd | November 5, 1943 | Me-109 dest(air) | Gelsenkirchen | P-47 |

1-0-0 air
0-0 ground

**Izor, Edward F., Capt.**
385th Ftr Sqn/364th Ftr Grp

| *Sqn* | *Date* | *Claims* | *Location* | *A/C* |
|---|---|---|---|---|
| 385th | May 21, 1944 | (.5)He-111 dest(air)* | SE Luneburg | P-38 |
| | August 25 | Me-210 dest(grd) | Anklam | P-51 |
| | | (2)Me-210 dam(grd) | Anklam | P-51 |
| | September 28 | FW-190 dest(air) | SW Magdeburg | P-51 |
| | November 2 | (3)Me-109 dest(air) | Halle | P-51 |

4.5-0-0 air
1-2 ground

* - shared with Lt. C.S. Hill of the 385th Ftr Sqn

**Jaaskelainen, William, Lt.**
505th Ftr Sqn/339th Ftr Grp

| *Sqn* | *Date* | *Claims* | *Location* | *A/C* |
|---|---|---|---|---|
| 505th | June 8, 1944 | FW-190 dest(air) | Rennes | P-51 |
| | September 11 | Ju-88 dest(grd) | Munich | P-51 |
| | | He-111 dam(grd) | Munich | P-51 |

1-0-0 air
1-1 ground

**Jabara, James, Lt.**
354th Ftr Sqn/355th Ftr Grp
Earlier flew in the ETO with the 363rd Ftr Grp, 9th Air Force, and claimed 1.5 kills, half a FW-190 on June 25, 1944, and a FW-190 on August 13, 1944.

| *Sqn* | *Date* | *Claims* | *Location* | *A/C* |
|---|---|---|---|---|
| 354th | March 22, 1945 | FW-190 dest(grd) | Wurzburg | P-51 |
| | | FW-190 dam(grd) | Wurzburg | P-51 |
| | April 9 | (.5)Ju-88 dest(grd)* | Memmingen | P-51 |
| | April 10 | (2)Me-410 dest(grd) | Rechlin/Larz | P-51 |
| | | (3)u/i a/c dam(grd) | Rechlin/Larz | P-51 |
| | April 13 | He-111 dest(grd) | Husum | P-51 |
| | | Me-109 dest(grd) | Husum | P-51 |
| | | Me-109 dam(grd) | Husum | P-51 |

0-0-0 air
5.5-5 ground

* - shared with F/O H.W. Falvey of the 354th Ftr Sqn

**Jacaruso, Joseph J., F/O**
383rd Ftr Sqn/364th Ftr Grp

| *Sqn* | *Date* | *Claims* | *Location* | *A/C* |
|---|---|---|---|---|
| 383rd | April 16, 1945 | (.5)Do-217 dest(grd)* | Marienbad | P-51 |
| | | u/i a/c dam(grd) | Marienbad | P-51 |

0-0-0 air
0.5-1 ground

* - shared with Lt. E. Chlevin of the 383rd Ftr Sqn

**Jack, Joseph V., Lt.**
361st Ftr Sqn/356th Ftr Grp

| *Sqn* | *Date* | *Claims* | *Location* | *A/C* |
|---|---|---|---|---|
| 361st | February 10, 1944 | FW-190 dest(air) | NE Lingen | P-47 |
| | April 11 | (.25)Me-109 dest(grd)* | Gifhorn | P-47 |
| | | (.25)Ju-88 dest(grd)* | Gifhorn | P-47 |

1-0-0 air
0.5-0 ground

* - both shared with Col. E.A. Malmstrom of HdQts, 356th Ftr Grp, and Lt. R. Gibson and F/O E.L. Decker of the 361st Ftr Sqn

**Jackson, Boyd O., Lt.**
505th Ftr Sqn/339th Ftr Grp

| *Sqn* | *Date* | *Claims* | *Location* | *A/C* |
|---|---|---|---|---|
| 505th | July 31, 1944 | FW-190 dest(grd) | Holzkirchen | P-51 |
| | September 10 | (2)u/i a/c dest(grd) | Weizenburg | P-51 |
| | | Ju-88 dest(grd) | Weizenburg | P-51 |
| | | (4)u/i a/c dam(grd) | Weizenburg | P-51 |
| | November 21 | Ju-88 dest(grd) | NE Munster | P-51 |

0-0-0 air
5-4 ground

**Jackson, Cameron E., Lt.**
383rd Ftr Sqn/364th Ftr Grp

| *Sqn* | *Date* | *Claims* | *Location* | *A/C* |
|---|---|---|---|---|
| 383rd | April 13, 1945 | (2)FW-190 dest(grd) | Flensburg | P-51 |
| | | FW-190 dam(grd) | Flensburg | P-51 |

0-0-0 air
2-1 ground

**Jackson, Carl E., Capt.**
HdQts/20th Ftr Grp
79th Ftr Sqn/20th Ftr Grp

| *Sqn* | *Date* | *Claims* | *Location* | *A/C* |
|---|---|---|---|---|
| HdQts | January 7, 1944 | (.5)Me-109 dam(air)* | Ludwigshafen | P-38 |
| 79th | February 10 | FW-190 dest(air) | N/Hanover | P-38 |
| | February 20 | (2)FW-190 dest(air) | SW Brunswick | P-38 |

3-0-0.5 air
0-0 ground

* - shared with Lt. V.R. Stockton of the 55th Ftr Sqn, 20th Ftr Grp

**Jackson, Donald G., Lt.**
38th Ftr Sqn/55th Ftr Grp

| *Sqn* | *Date* | *Claims* | *Location* | *A/C* |
|---|---|---|---|---|
| 38th | December 24, 1944 | FW-190 dest(air) | Coblenz | P-51 |

1-0-0 air
0-0 ground

**Jackson, Marion E., Capt.**
336th Ftr Sqn/4th Ftr Grp

| *Sqn* | *Date* | *Claims* | *Location* | *A/C* |
|---|---|---|---|---|
| 336th | September 26, 1942 | FW-190 dest(air) | Brest | Spit. |

1-0-0 air
0-0 ground

**Jackson, Michael J., Maj.**
62nd Ftr Sqn/56th Ftr Grp

| *Sqn* | *Date* | *Claims* | *Location* | *A/C* |
|---|---|---|---|---|
| 62nd | July 4, 1944 | Me-109 dest(air) | Conches | P-47 |
| | July 5 | FW-190 dam(air) | N/Evreux | P-47 |
| | July 7 | Ju-52 dest(air) | Gardelegen A/F | P-47 |
| | August 28 | Ju-88 dest(air) | Irsch | P-47 |
| | September 5 | (2)Ju-88 dest(grd) | Limburg | P-47 |
| | | (1.5)Me-210 dest(grd)* | Limburg | P-47 |
| | | Me-109 dest(grd) | Limburg | P-47 |
| | | (2)Ju-88 dam(grd) | Limburg | P-47 |
| | September 21 | FW-190 dest(air) | NE Arnheim | P-47 |
| | November 6 | Me-410 dam(air) | Deventer | P-47 |
| | November 18 | FW-190 dest(air) | E/Hanau | P-47 |
| | December 4 | Me-262 dest(grd) | Neuburg | P-47 |
| | | Me-262 dam(grd) | Neuburg | P-47 |
| | | FW-200 dam(grd) | Neuburg | P-47 |
| | December 25 | Me-109 dest(air) | Bonn-Coblenz | P-47 |
| | January 14, 1945 | Me-109 dest(air) | Rheine | P-47 |
| | | FW-190 dest(air) | Rheine | P-47 |

8-0-2 air
5.5-4 ground

* - shared with Lt. S.T. Murray of the 62nd Ftr Sqn

**Jackson, Norbert P., Lt.**
354th Ftr Sqn/355th Ftr Grp

| *Sqn* | *Date* | *Claims* | *Location* | *A/C* |
|---|---|---|---|---|
| 354th | July 8, 1944 | Me-109 dest(grd) | W/Chalons | P-51 |
| | November 26 | FW-190 dam(air) | S/Misburg | P-51 |

0-0-1 air
1-0 ground

**Jackson, Willie O., Jr., LtCol.**
486th Ftr Sqn/352nd Ftr Grp
328th Ftr Sqn/352nd Ftr Grp
HdQts/352nd Ftr Grp

| *Sqn* | *Date* | *Claims* | *Location* | *A/C* |
|---|---|---|---|---|
| 486th | February 20, 1944 | Me-109 dest(air) | Charleroi | P-47 |
| | | Me-109 dam(air) | Charleroi | P-47 |
| 328th | April 9 | FW-190 prob(air) | Dummer Lake | P-47 |
| 486th | July 18 | Me-109 dest(air) | N/Warnemunde | P-51 |
| | | Ju-88 dest(air) | N/Warnemunde | P-51 |
| | July 19 | Me-109 dest(air) | E/Munich | P-51 |
| | November 2 | Me-109 dam(air) | N/Merseburg | P-51 |
| | | FW-190 dam(air) | N/Merseburg | P-51 |
| | November 30 | Me-109 dest(air) | W/Chemnitz | P-51 |
| | December 27 | Me-109 dest(air) | SW Bonn | P-51 |
| HdQts | March 2, 1945 | FW-189 dest(air) | Prague | P-51 |
| | | (2)u/i a/c dam(grd) | Prague | P-51 |
| | April 16 | (2)Me-109 dest(grd) | Ganacker | P-51 |
| | | (2)FW-190 dest(grd) | Ganacker | P-51 |
| | | Me-109 dam(grd) | Ganacker | P-51 |
| | | u/i a/c dam(grd) | Ganacker | P-51 |

7-1-3 air
4-4 ground

**Jacobs, Jerome, Lt.**
364th Ftr Sqn/357th Ftr Grp

| *Sqn* | *Date* | *Claims* | *Location* | *A/C* |
|---|---|---|---|---|
| 364th | September 18, 1944 | FW-190 dest(air) | N/Maastricht | P-51 |
| | | Me-109 dest(air) | N/Maastricht | P-51 |
| | September 19 | Me-109 dest(air) | SE Arnheim | P-51 |

3-0-0 air
0-0 ground

**Jacobson, Donald J., Lt.**
354th Ftr Sqn/355th Ftr Grp

| *Sqn* | *Date* | *Claims* | *Location* | *A/C* |
|---|---|---|---|---|
| 354th | April 11, 1944 | (2)Ju-88 dest(grd) | Strasbourg | P-51 |
| | | FW-190 dam(grd) | Strasbourg | P-51 |
| | | Ju-88 dam(grd) | Strasbourg | P-51 |
| | May 13 | Me-410 dam(air) | Landsberg | P-51 |

0-0-1 air
2-2 ground

**Jacobson, Gail E., Lt.**
434th Ftr Sqn/479th Ftr Grp

| *Sqn* | *Date* | *Claims* | *Location* | *A/C* |
|---|---|---|---|---|
| 434th | December 5, 1944 | (2)FW-190 dest(air) | Neuruppin | P-51 |
| | December 23 | FW-190 dest(air) | SE Bonn | P-51 |
| | December 25 | FW-190 prob(air) | SW Bonn | P-51 |
| | February 21, 1945 | He-111 dest(grd) | Gotha | P-51 |
| | March 19 | (.5)FW-190 dest(air)* | Handorf A/F | P-51 |
| | April 7 | Me-109 dest(air) | Celle | P-51 |
| | April 16 | (2)FW-190 dest(grd) | Reichersberg | P-51 |
| | | FW-190 dam(grd) | Reichersberg | P-51 |
| | | Ju-88 dam(grd) | Reichersberg | P-51 |
| | April 18 | (2)Ju-88 dest(grd) | Ingolstadt | P-51 |
| | | FW-190 dest(grd) | Ottingen | P-51 |

4.5-1-0 air
6-2 ground

* - shared with Lt. F.M. Taylor of the 434th Ftr Sqn

**Jahnke, Jerome E., Lt.**
334th Ftr Sqn/4th Ftr Grp

| *Sqn* | *Date* | *Claims* | *Location* | *A/C* |
|---|---|---|---|---|
| 334th | January 16, 1945 | (.5)Me-262 dest(grd)* | Neuburg | P-51 |
| | March 22 | FW-190 dest(air) | Eggersdorf A/F | P-51 |

1-0-0 air
0.5-0 ground

* - shared with Lt. C.F. Brown of the 334th Ftr Sqn

**James, Eugene W., Lt.**
328th Ftr Sqn/352nd Ftr Grp

| *Sqn* | *Date* | *Claims* | *Location* | *A/C* |
|---|---|---|---|---|
| 328th | November 2, 1944 | (.5)Me-109 dest(air)* | Merseburg | P-51 |
| | | (.5)Me-109 dest(air)* | Merseburg | P-51 |

1-0-0 air
0-0 ground

* - both shared with Capt. W.J. Stangel of the 328th Ftr Sqn

**James, Frank B., Col.**
HdQts/55th Ftr Grp

| *Sqn* | *Date* | *Claims* | *Location* | *A/C* |
|---|---|---|---|---|
| HdQts | December 31, 1943 | FW-190 dest(air) | Niort | P-38 |

1-0-0 air
0-0 ground

**James, Harold M., Capt.**
384th Ftr Sqn/364th Ftr Grp

| *Sqn* | *Date* | *Claims* | *Location* | *A/C* |
|---|---|---|---|---|
| 384th | December 27, 1944 | Me-109 dam(air) | Bonn | P-51 |
| | December 31 | FW-190 dest(air) | SE Hamburg | P-51 |

1-0-1 air
0-0 ground

**James, Wayne W., Lt.**
357th Ftr Sqn/355th Ftr Grp

| *Sqn* | *Date* | *Claims* | *Location* | *A/C* |
|---|---|---|---|---|
| 357th | June 6, 1944 | Ju-87 dest(air) | NE Janville | P-51 |
| | | (2)Ju-87 dam(air) | NE Janville | P-51 |
| | | Ju-87 dest(grd) | NE Janville | P-51 |

1-0-2 air
1-0 ground

**Jamison, Gilbert L., Capt.**
385th Ftr Sqn/364th Ftr Grp

| *Sqn* | *Date* | *Claims* | *Location* | *A/C* |
|---|---|---|---|---|
| 385th | September 11, 1944 | (2)FW-190 dest(air) | SW Leipzig | P-51 |
| | September 13 | Me-109 dest(air) | SE Kassel | P-51 |
| | October 12 | FW-190 dest(air) | NE Bremen | P-51 |
| | November 25 | Me-109 dam(grd) | Fulda | P-51 |
| | December 27 | (3)FW-190 dest(air) | SW Bonn | P-51 |
| | | Me-109 dam(air) | E/Liege | P-51 |

7-0-1 air
0-1 ground

**Janicki, Zbigniew, F/Lt.**
61st Ftr Sqn/56th Ftr Grp (Attached from RAF)

| *Sqn* | *Date* | *Claims* | *Location* | *A/C* |
|---|---|---|---|---|
| 61st | June 7, 1944 | FW-190 prob(air) | S/Rouen | P-47 |
| | | FW-190 dam(air) | S/Rouen | P-47 |

0-1-1 air
0-0 ground

**Janney, Raymond B., II, Capt.**
368th Ftr Sqn/359th Ftr Grp

| *Sqn* | *Date* | *Claims* | *Location* | *A/C* |
|---|---|---|---|---|
| 368th | March 6, 1944 | FW-190 dam(air) | Dummer Lake-Steinhuder Lake | P-47 |

| Sqn | Date | Claims | Location | A/C |
|---|---|---|---|---|
| | March 8 | Me-109 dam(air) | N/Minden | P-47 |
| | April 24 | (.5)u/i a/c dest(grd)* | St. Dizier | P-47 |
| | April 30 | Me-410 dest(grd) | Bricy A/F | P-47 |
| | | Me-410 dam(grd) | Bricy A/F | P-47 |
| | May 19 | Me-109 dest(air) | Neuruppin | P-51 |

1-0-2 air
1.5-1 ground

* - shared with Lt. R.E. Burton of the 368th Ftr Sqn

**Janson, William H., Capt.**
63rd Ftr Sqn/56th Ftr Grp

| Sqn | Date | Claims | Location | A/C |
|---|---|---|---|---|
| 63rd | February 3, 1944 | Me-109 prob(air) | SE Ruhlertwist | P-47 |

0-1-0 air
0-0 ground

**Jarvis, William C., Lt.**
361st Ftr Sqn/356th Ftr Grp

| Sqn | Date | Claims | Location | A/C |
|---|---|---|---|---|
| 361st | November 26, 1944 | Me-109 dest(air) | Osnabruck-Dummer Lake | P-51 |
| | | FW-190 dam(air) | Osnabruck-Dummer Lake | P-51 |
| | January 14, 1945 | FW-190 dest(air) | SW Dummer Lake | P-51 |
| | February 20 | Ju-88 dest(grd) | Furth | P-51 |

2-0-1 air
1-0 ground

**Jeffrey, Arthur F., LtCol.**
434th Ftr Sqn/479th Ftr Grp

| Sqn | Date | Claims | Location | A/C |
|---|---|---|---|---|
| 434th | July 5, 1944 | FW-200 dest(air) | Cognac/Chateaubernard | P-38 |
| | July 29 | Me-163 dest(air) | Wilhelmshaven | P-38 |
| | August 15 | Me-109 dest(air) | Steenwijk A/F | P-38 |
| | August 28 | Ju-52 dest(air) | Sedan/Douzy A/F | P-38 |
| | October 7 | Me-109 dest(air) | S/Leipzig | P-51 |
| | November 2 | Me-109 dest(air) | Zeitz | P-51 |
| | December 5 | (3)FW-190 dest(air) | Neuruppin | P-51 |
| | | FW-190 dam(air) | Neuruppin | P-51 |
| | December 23 | (3)Me-109 dest(air) | SE Bonn | P-51 |
| | December 25 | Me-109 dest(air) | SW Bonn | P-51 |
| | February 14, 1945 | Me-109 dest(air) | SW Berlin | P-51 |
| | | Me-109 dam(air) | SW Berlin | P-51 |

14-0-2 air
0-0 ground

**Jenkins, Harold M., Lt.**
434th Ftr Sqn/479th Ftr Grp

| Sqn | Date | Claims | Location | A/C |
|---|---|---|---|---|
| 434th | December 25, 1944 | FW-190 dest(air) | SW Bonn | P-51 |

1-0-0 air
0-0 ground

**Jenkins, Jack S., LtCol.**
HdQts/55th Ftr Grp

| Sqn | Date | Claims | Location | A/C |
|---|---|---|---|---|
| HdQts | November 3, 1943 | Me-109 dest(air) | Spiekeroog Island | P-38 |
| | | FW-190 prob(air) | Wilhelmshaven | P-38 |
| | November 25 | FW-190 dest(air) | La Basse | P-38 |
| | January 11, 1944 | Me-210 dam(air) | Dummer Lake | P-38 |

2-1-1 air
0-0 ground

**Jenkins, Otto D., Lt.**
362nd Ftr Sqn/357th Ftr Grp

| Sqn | Date | Claims | Location | A/C |
|---|---|---|---|---|
| 362nd | September 13, 1944 | (1.5)Me-109 dest(air)* | S/Nordhausen | P-51 |
| | September 19 | Me-109 dest(air) | SE Ijsselstein | P-51 |
| | | FW-190 dest(air) | Ijsselstein | P-51 |
| | October 6 | FW-190 dest(air) | NW Berlin | P-51 |
| | November 18 | (2)Me-109 dest(grd) | Mengen A/F | P-51 |
| | December 24 | (4)FW-190 dest(air) | Fulda | P-51 |

8.5-0-0 air
2-0 ground

* - shared with Lt. J.A. Kirla of the 362nd Ftr Sqn

**Jennings, Edwin C., Capt.**
77th Ftr Sqn/20th Ftr Grp

| Sqn | Date | Claims | Location | A/C |
|---|---|---|---|---|
| 77th | February 9, 1945 | FW-190 dest(grd) | Esperstadt A/F | P-51 |

0-0-0 air
1-0 ground

**Jennings, Loton D., Jr., Lt.**
335th Ftr Sqn/4th Ftr Grp

| Sqn | Date | Claims | Location | A/C |
|---|---|---|---|---|
| 335th | April 9, 1945 | Ju-88 dest(grd) | Munich-Brunnthal | P-51 |
| | April 13 | He-115 dest(grd) | Ratzburger Lake | P-51 |
| | | u/i a/c dam(grd) | Ratzburger Lake | P-51 |
| | April 16 | (2)Me-210 dest(grd) | Praha A/F | P-51 |
| | | (2)Do-217 dest(grd) | Praha A/F | P-51 |

0-0-0 air
6-1 ground

**Jessup, John E., Lt.**
350th Ftr Sqn/353rd Ftr Grp

| Sqn | Date | Claims | Location | A/C |
|---|---|---|---|---|
| 350th | November 18, 1944 | Me-110 dest(grd) | Lechfeld | P-51 |
| | November 27 | FW-190 prob(air) | Brunswick | P-51 |
| | December 24 | Me-109 dest(air) | Leipzig | P-51 |

1-1-0 air
1-0 ground

**Jessup, Nelson R., Lt.**
487th Ftr Sqn/352nd Ftr Grp

| Sqn | Date | Claims | Location | A/C |
|---|---|---|---|---|
| 487th | November 2, 1944 | FW-190 dest(air) | Merseburg | P-51 |
| | November 21 | (2)FW-190 dest(air) | SW Merseburg | P-51 |
| | January 1, 1945 | FW-190 dest(air) | N/Liege | P-51 |

4-0-0 air
0-0 ground

**Jett, Shelby N., Lt.**
361st Ftr Sqn/356th Ftr Grp

| Sqn | Date | Claims | Location | A/C |
|---|---|---|---|---|
| 361st | November 25, 1944 | FW-190 dam(grd) | Zwickau | P-51 |
| | November 26 | (.5)Me-109 dest(air)* | Osnabruck-Dummer Lake | P-51 |

0.5-0-0 air
0-1 ground

* - shared with Capt. D.J. Strait of the 361st Ftr Sqn

**Jewell, David F., Jr., Capt.**
38th Ftr Sqn/55th Ftr Grp

| Sqn | Date | Claims | Location | A/C |
|---|---|---|---|---|
| 38th | September 12, 1944 | (.5)u/i a/c dest(grd)* | Herzogenaurach | P-51 |
| | November 2 | (.5)Me-109 dest(air)** | W/Merseburg | P-51 |
| | December 5 | FW-190 dest(air) | NE Berlin | P-51 |

1.5-0-0 air
0.5-0 ground

* - shared with Maj. A.B. Parsons of the 38th Ftr Sqn
** - shared with Lt. F.M. Matney of the 38th Ftr Sqn

**Jewell, Lyle J., Lt.**
374th Ftr Sqn/361st Ftr Grp

| Sqn | Date | Claims | Location | A/C |
|---|---|---|---|---|
| 374th | April 4, 1945 | Me-262 dam(air) | W/Berlin | P-51 |

0-0-1 air
0-0 ground

**Joel, Milton, Maj.**
38th Ftr Sqn/55th Ftr Grp

| *Sqn* | *Date* | *Claims* | *Location* | *A/C* |
|---|---|---|---|---|
| 38th | November 3, 1943 | (.5)FW-190 dest(air)* | Westerholt | P-38 |
| | | (2)FW-190 dam(air) | N/Wilhelmshaven | P-38 |
| | November 5 | Me-109 dest(air) | W/Ournheim | P-38 |
| | November 13 | Ju-88 dest(air) | Bremen | P-38 |
| | | Ju-88 prob(air) | Bremen | P-38 |
| | | Me-109 prob(air) | Bremen | P-38 |
| | | Me-109 dam(air) | Bremen | P-38 |

2.5-2-3 air
0-0 ground

* - shared with Lt. W.L. Kreft of the 38th Ftr Sqn

**John, Leedom K., Lt.**
338th Ftr Sqn/55th Ftr Grp

| *Sqn* | *Date* | *Claims* | *Location* | *A/C* |
|---|---|---|---|---|
| 338th | February 25, 1945 | Me-109 dest(grd) | Illesheim | P-51 |
| | | FW-190 dest(grd) | Illesheim | P-51 |
| | April 16 | (3)FW-200 dest(grd) | N/Landshut | P-51 |

0-0-0 air
5-0 ground

**Johnson, Clarence O., Capt.**
436th Ftr Sqn/479th Ftr Grp
487th Ftr Sqn/352nd Ftr Grp
Earlier flew in the MTO with the 82nd Ftr Grp and claimed 4 kills; a MC-202 on May 24, 1943, (2)FW-190 on August 20, 1943, and a Me-109 on September 2, 1943.

| *Sqn* | *Date* | *Claims* | *Location* | *A/C* |
|---|---|---|---|---|
| 436th | June 22, 1944 | Fi-156 dest(air) | Reims | P-38 |
| 487th | August 25 | He-177 dest(grd) | Neubrandenburg | P-51 |
| | | Hs-129 dam(grd) | Neubrandenburg | P-51 |
| | September 10 | (5)Ju-52 dest(grd) | Wertheim | P-51 |
| | September 11 | (2)Me-109 dest(air) | Gottingen | P-51 |

3-0-0 air
6-1 ground

**Johnson, Donald W., Capt.**
503rd Ftr Sqn/339th Ftr Grp

| *Sqn* | *Date* | *Claims* | *Location* | *A/C* |
|---|---|---|---|---|
| 503rd | November 26, 1944 | (3)FW-190 dest(air) | SE Dummer Lake | P-51 |

3-0-0 air
0-0 ground

**Johnson, Earl W., Lt.**
364th Ftr Sqn/357th Ftr Grp

| *Sqn* | *Date* | *Claims* | *Location* | *A/C* |
|---|---|---|---|---|
| 364th | January 14, 1945 | FW-190 dest(air) | NE Berlin | P-51 |

1-0-0 air
0-0 ground

**Johnson, Emory G., Lt.**
370th Ftr Sqn/359th Ftr Grp

| *Sqn* | *Date* | *Claims* | *Location* | *A/C* |
|---|---|---|---|---|
| 370th | October 7, 1944 | (.5)Ar-196 dam(grd)* | Dievenow | P-51 |
| | December 24 | (2)FW-190 dest(air) | Bonn | P-51 |
| | | (2)FW-190 dam(air) | Bonn | P-51 |
| | December 31 | (.5)Me-109 dest(air)** | Hanover | P-51 |

2.5-0-2 air
0-0.5 ground

* - shared with Lt. R.M. York of the 370th Ftr Sqn
** - shared with an unknown pilot

**Johnson, Evan M., V, Capt.**
505th Ftr Sqn/339th Ftr Grp

| *Sqn* | *Date* | *Claims* | *Location* | *A/C* |
|---|---|---|---|---|
| 505th | May 19, 1944 | (1.5)FW-190 dest(air)* | Gustrow | P-51 |
| | May 24 | FW-190 dest(air) | Berlin | P-51 |
| | June 10 | (.5)Ju-52 dest(air)** | Laigle | P-51 |
| | June 29 | (.5)Me-109 dest(air)@ | Halle-S/Magdeburg | P-51 |
| | | (.5)Me-410 dest(air)@@ | Halle-S/Magdeburg | P-51 |
| | September 5 | Me-410 dam(grd) | Sinsheim | P-51 |
| | November 18 | Me-109 dest(air) | Heilbronn | P-51 |
| | | Me-109 dam(air) | Heilbronn | P-51 |

5-0-1 air
0-1 ground

* - shared with Lt. J.R. Starnes of the 505th Ftr Sqn
** - shared with Capt. L. Reid of the 505th Ftr Sqn
@ - shared with Lt. A. Sirochman of the 505th Ftr Sqn
@@ - shared with Lt. G.E. Graham of the 505th Ftr Sqn

**Johnson, Gerald W., Maj.**
61st Ftr Sqn/ 56th Ftr Grp
360th Ftr Sqn/356th Ftr Grp
63rd Ftr Sqn/ 56th Ftr Grp

| *Sqn* | *Date* | *Claims* | *Location* | *A/C* |
|---|---|---|---|---|
| 61st | May 14, 1943 | FW-190 dam(air) | NE Antwerp | P-47 |
| | June 26 | FW-190 dest(air) | N/Dieppe | P-47 |
| | August 17 | (2)Me-109 dest(air) | Hasselt-Diest | P-47 |
| | | (.5)Me-110 dest(air)* | N/Liege | P-47 |
| | | Me-109 dam(air) | Hasselt-Diest | P-47 |
| | August 19 | Me-109 dest(air) | Gilze-Rijen | P-47 |
| | | Me-109 dam(air) | Gilze-Rijen | P-47 |
| | October 10 | Me-110 dest(air) | N/Munster | P-47 |
| | | Me-210 dest(air) | N/Munster | P-47 |
| | October 14 | FW-190 dest(air) | Eupen | P-47 |
| 360th | January 24, 1944 | FW-190 dest(air) | NE Ypres | P-47 |
| | | (.5)FW-190 dam(air)** | NE Ypres | P-47 |
| 63rd | February 21 | FW-190 dest(air) | NW Zwolle | P-47 |
| | February 22 | FW-190 prob(air) | SW Gutersloh | P-47 |
| | February 24 | FW-190 dest(air) | Minden | P-47 |
| | February 29 | Ju-52 dest(air) | Norderwijk | P-47 |
| | March 2 | Me-109 dest(air) | SE Aachen | P-47 |
| | March 6 | FW-190 dam(air) | Wenzendorf A/F | P-47 |
| | March 8 | (2)Me-109 dest(air) | Dummer Lake-Celle | P-47 |
| | March 15 | (2)Me-109 dest(air) | Nienburg | P-47 |

16.5-1-4.5 air
0-0 ground

* - shared with Lt. F.E. McCauley of the 61st Ftr Sqn
** - shared with Lt. W.G. Maxwell of the 360th Ftr Sqn

**Johnson, Herbert E., Jr., LtCol.**
77th Ftr Sqn/20th Ftr Grp
HdQts/20th Ftr Grp

| *Sqn* | *Date* | *Claims* | *Location* | *A/C* |
|---|---|---|---|---|
| 77th | November 26, 1943 | Do-217 dest(air) | S/Lemwerder A/F | P-38 |
| | February 11, 1944 | Me-109 dam(air) | Chateau d'Ardenne | P-38 |
| | February 20 | FW-190 dest(air) | Wernigerode | P-38 |
| | | FW-190 prob(air) | Wernigerode | P-38 |
| | April 8 | He-177 dest(air) | Salzwedel | P-38 |
| | | u/i a/c dest(grd) | Salzwedel | P-38 |
| | | Me-110 dam(grd) | Salzwedel | P-38 |
| | | u/i a/c dam(grd) | Salzwedel | P-38 |
| HdQts | July 5 | (.5)He-177 dest(air)* | Cognac | P-38 |

3.5-1-1 air
1-2 ground

* - shared with Lt. J.S. Reynolds of the 55th Ftr Sqn, 20th Ftr Grp

**Johnson, Jack V., Capt.**
384th Ftr Sqn/364th Ftr Grp

| *Sqn* | *Date* | *Claims* | *Location* | *A/C* |
|---|---|---|---|---|
| 384th | November 26, 1944 | Me-109 dest(air) | W/Steinhuder Lk. | P-51 |
| | | FW-190 dest(air) | W/Steinhuder Lk. | P-51 |

2-0-0 air
0-0 ground

**Johnson, James G., Lt.**
385th Ftr Sqn/364th Ftr Grp

| *Sqn* | *Date* | *Claims* | *Location* | *A/C* |
|---|---|---|---|---|
| 385th | April 13, 1945 | Ju-188 dest(grd) | E/Luneburg | P-51 |
| | | (.5)FW-190 dest(grd)* | E/Luneburg | P-51 |
| | | FW-190 dam(grd) | E/Luneburg | P-51 |
| | April 16 | (2)FW-190 dam(grd) | Pocking | P-51 |

0-0-0 air
1.5-3 ground

* - shared with Capt. A.B. McCormick of the 385th Ftr Sqn

**Johnson, James K., Lt.**
361st Ftr Sqn/356th Ftr Grp

| *Sqn* | *Date* | *Claims* | *Location* | *A/C* |
|---|---|---|---|---|
| 361st | May 4, 1944 | FW-190 dam(air) | Steinhuder Lake | P-47 |

0-0-1 air
0-0 ground

**Johnson, John H., Lt.**
83rd Ftr Sqn/78th Ftr Grp

| *Sqn* | *Date* | *Claims* | *Location* | *A/C* |
|---|---|---|---|---|
| 83rd | February 22, 1944 | FW-190 dest(air) | Dusseldorf | P-47 |
| | | FW-190 dam(air) | Dusseldorf | P-47 |

1-0-1 air
0-0 ground

**Johnson, Leonard D., Lt.**
357th Ftr Sqn/355th Ftr Grp

| *Sqn* | *Date* | *Claims* | *Location* | *A/C* |
|---|---|---|---|---|
| 357th | August 14, 1944 | Ju-88 dam(grd) | Sarreburg | P-51 |

0-0-0 air
0-1 ground

**Johnson, Louis A., Capt.**
384th Ftr Sqn/364th Ftr Grp

| *Sqn* | *Date* | *Claims* | *Location* | *A/C* |
|---|---|---|---|---|
| 384th | August 10, 1944 | Me-109 dest(air) | SW Paris | P-51 |
| | August 15 | (.5)FW-190 dest(air)* | W/Weichaden | P-51 |
| | | (.5)FW-190 dam(air)* | W/Weichaden | P-51 |

1.5-0-0.5 air
0-0 ground

* - both shared with Lt. W.N. Champion of the 384th Ftr Sqn

**Johnson, Marion D., F/O**
486th Ftr Sqn/352nd Ftr Grp

| *Sqn* | *Date* | *Claims* | *Location* | *A/C* |
|---|---|---|---|---|
| 486th | April 16, 1945 | Me-109 dest(grd) | Ganacker | P-51 |
| | | FW-190 dest(grd) | Ganacker | P-51 |
| | | (2)u/i a/c dam(grd) | Ganacker | P-51 |

0-0-0 air
2-2 ground

**Johnson, Martin H., Jr., Capt.**
375th Ftr Sqn/361st Ftr Grp

| *Sqn* | *Date* | *Claims* | *Location* | *A/C* |
|---|---|---|---|---|
| 375th | March 29, 1944 | FW-190 dest(grd) | Rheine | P-47 |
| | | Ju-88 dest(grd) | Rheine | P-47 |
| | April 18 | Ar-196 dest(grd) | Zwischenaschmer | P-47 |
| | April 24 | Me-109 dest(grd) | Metz | P-47 |
| | | FW-190 dest(grd) | Metz | P-47 |
| | | Me-110 dest(grd) | Metz | P-47 |
| | June 16 | Ju-52 dest(grd) | Toussus/Le Noble | P-51 |
| | June 21 | u/i a/c dest(grd) | Zwischenaschmer | P-51 |
| | August 15 | Ju-88 dest(grd) | Wittmunhafen | P-51 |
| | August 25 | Me-109 dest(air) | SW Rostock | P-51 |

1-0-0 air
9-0 ground

**Johnson, Ralph A., Maj.**
62nd Ftr Sqn/56th Ftr Grp

| *Sqn* | *Date* | *Claims* | *Location* | *A/C* |
|---|---|---|---|---|
| 62nd | September 7, 1943 | Me-109 dest(air) | Tessel Island | P-47 |
| | November 26 | (2)Me-110 dest(air) | Papenburg | P-47 |
| | December 1 | Me-109 dam(air) | SE Roermond | P-47 |

3-0-1 air
0-0 ground

**Johnson, Raymond G., Lt.**
503rd Ftr Sqn/339th Ftr Grp

| *Sqn* | *Date* | *Claims* | *Location* | *A/C* |
|---|---|---|---|---|
| 503rd | March 3, 1945 | Me-262 dam(air) | Celle | P-51 |
| | April 7 | FW-190 dest(air) | Celle | P-51 |

1-0-1 air
0-0 ground

**Johnson, Robert S., Maj.**
61st Ftr Sqn/56th Ftr Grp
62nd Ftr Sqn/56th Ftr Grp

| *Sqn* | *Date* | *Claims* | *Location* | *A/C* |
|---|---|---|---|---|
| 61st | June 13, 1943 | FW-190 dest(air) | SE Bergues | P-47 |
| | August 19 | Me-109 dest(air) | NE Woensdrecht | P-47 |
| | August 24 | FW-190 dam(air) | Evreux | P-47 |
| | October 8 | FW-190 dest(air) | Lingen | P-47 |
| | October 10 | FW-190 dest(air) | N/Munster | P-47 |
| | | Me-110 dest(air) | N/Munster | P-47 |
| | November 3 | Me-109 dest(air) | N/Ameland Island | P-47 |
| | December 22 | Me-109 dest(air) | N/Almelo | P-47 |
| | December 30 | FW-190 dest(air) | Soissons | P-47 |
| | December 31 | (2)FW-190 dest(air) | N/St. Gilles | P-47 |
| | January 5, 1944 | FW-190 dest(air) | N/Liege | P-47 |
| | January 21 | FW-190 dest(air) | N/Rouen | P-47 |
| | January 30 | Me-109 dest(air) | E/Lingen | P-47 |
| | | Me-210 dest(air) | E/Lingen | P-47 |
| | February 20 | (2)Me-110 dest(air) | W/Hanover | P-47 |
| | | (2)Me-110 dam(air) | W/Hanover | P-47 |
| | March 6 | FW-190 dest(air) | N/Dummer Lake | P-47 |
| | March 8 | (2)Me-109 dest(air) | NE Steinhuder Lk. | P-47 |
| | March 15 | (2)FW-190 dest(air) | Dummer Lake | P-47 |
| | | Me-109 dest(air) | Dummer Lake | P-47 |
| | April 9 | FW-190 dest(air) | NW Kiel | P-47 |
| | April 13 | (2)FW-190 dest(air) | Kaiserlautern | P-47 |
| 62nd | May 8 | Me-109 dest(air) | Brunswick-Hanover | P-47 |
| | | FW-190 dest(air) | Brunswick-Hanover | P-47 |

27-0-3 air
0-0 ground

**Johnson, Willard D., Lt.**
63rd Ftr Sqn/56th Ftr Grp

| *Sqn* | *Date* | *Claims* | *Location* | *A/C* |
|---|---|---|---|---|
| 63rd | March 27, 1944 | (.25)Do-217 dest(air)* | S/Chartres | P-47 |
| | April 15 | (.5)FW-190 dest(air)** | Flensburg-Husum | P-47 |
| | | He-111 dam(grd) | Flensburg | P-47 |

0.75-0-0 air
0-1 ground

* - shared with Maj. W.M. Mahurin, Lt. I.T. Porowski, and F/O S.J. Lowman of the 63rd Ftr Sqn
** - shared with Lt. S.O. Stamps of the 63rd Ftr Sqn

**Johnson, Warren E., Lt.**
336th Ftr Sqn/4th Ftr Grp

| *Sqn* | *Date* | *Claims* | *Location* | *A/C* |
|---|---|---|---|---|
| 336th | April 5, 1944 | (1.5)Ju-88 dest(grd)* | Stendal | P-51 |
| | | Ju-88 dam(grd) | Stendal | P-51 |
| | April 30 | (.5)Do-24 dest(grd)** | Lyon S/P Base | P-51 |

0-0-0 air
2-1 ground

* - shared with an unknown pilot
** - shared with Lt. F.S. Harris of the 336th Ftr Sqn

**Johnson, William E., Jr., Lt.**
360th Ftr Sqn/356th Ftr Grp

| *Sqn* | *Date* | *Claims* | *Location* | *A/C* |
|---|---|---|---|---|
| 360th | January 24, 1944 | Me-109 dest(air) | W/Bruges | P-47 |
| | February 10 | FW-190 dest(air) | Ruhlwert | P-47 |
| | March 29 | (2)Me-410 dest(grd) | Cloppenburg | P-47 |

2-0-0 air
2-0 ground

**Johnson, Wilton W., Maj.**
352nd Ftr Sqn/353rd Ftr Grp

| *Sqn* | *Date* | *Claims* | *Location* | *A/C* |
|---|---|---|---|---|
| 352nd | December 30, 1943 | FW-190 dest(air) | Charleville | P-47 |
| | January 21, 1944 | (.33)Do-217 dest(grd)* | Albert | P-47 |
| | May 19 | Me-109 dam(air) | SW Brunswick | P-47 |
| | December 5 | FW-190 dest(air) | NE Berlin | P-51 |
| | March 1, 1945 | Bu-181 dest(air) | Nordlingen | P-51 |
| | | (4)u/i a/c dam(grd) | Nordlingen | P-51 |
| | April 17 | (2)FW-190 dest(grd) | Muldorf | P-51 |
| | | (3)FW-190 dam(grd) | Muldorf | P-51 |
| | | Me-109 dam(grd) | Ganacker | P-51 |

3-0-1 air
2.33-8 ground

* - shared with Col. G.E. Duncan of HdQts, 353rd Ftr Grp, and Lt. C.H. Sperry of the 352nd Ftr Sqn

**Johnston, Ben D., Lt.**
357th Ftr Sqn/355th Ftr Grp

| *Sqn* | *Date* | *Claims* | *Location* | *A/C* |
|---|---|---|---|---|
| 357th | December 1, 1943 | Me-109 dest(air) | W/Cologne | P-47 |
| | | Me-109 dam(air) | W/Cologne | P-47 |
| | February 20, 1944 | Me-109 dest(air) | Siegen | P-47 |
| | February 21 | FW-190 dam(air) | Dummer Lake | P-47 |
| | March 28 | (2)Me-210 dest(grd) | Dijon | P-51 |
| | | Ju-88 dest(grd) | Dijon | P-51 |
| | | Me-109 dam(grd) | Dijon | P-51 |
| | | Me-210 dam(grd) | Dijon | P-51 |
| | | Ju-88 dam(grd) | Dijon | P-51 |
| | March 29 | (2)FW-190 dest(air) | Brunswick | P-51 |
| | | FW-190 dam(air) | Brunswick | P-51 |

4-0-3 air
3-3 ground

**Johnston, Curtis G., Capt.**
354th Ftr Sqn/355th Ftr Grp

| *Sqn* | *Date* | *Claims* | *Location* | *A/C* |
|---|---|---|---|---|
| 354th | March 8, 1944 | (.5)Ju-88 dest(grd)* | Hesepe | P-47 |
| | March 28 | Me-110 dest(grd) | Dijon | P-51 |
| | April 5 | (.2)Do-217 dest(air)** | Landsberg | P-51 |
| | April 11 | (2)Ju-88 dest(grd) | Strasbourg | P-51 |
| | | He-111 dest(grd) | Strasbourg | P-51 |

0.2-0-0 air
4.5-0 ground

* - shared with Lt. H.W. Brown of the 354th Ftr Sqn
** - shared with Capt. W.J. Koraleski, Lt. H.W. Brown, Lt. J.E. Duffy, and Lt. B.C. Williamson of the 354th Ftr Sqn

**Joiner, Joseph H., Capt.**
336th Ftr Sqn/4th Ftr Grp

| *Sqn* | *Date* | *Claims* | *Location* | *A/C* |
|---|---|---|---|---|
| 336th | September 11, 1944 | Me-109 dest(air) | Korbach | P-51 |
| | October 6 | Me-109 dest(air) | W/Berlin | P-51 |
| | November 18 | (.5)Me-262 dam(grd)* | Leipheim | P-51 |
| | | (.5)Me-262 dam(grd)* | Leipheim | P-51 |
| | | (.5)Me-262 dam(grd)* | Leipheim | P-51 |
| | January 16, 1945 | (4)FW-190 dest(grd) | Neuhausen A/F | P-51 |
| | February 20 | (1.5)FW-190 dest(grd)** | N/Ingolstadt | P-51 |

3.5-0-0 air
4-1.5 ground

* - all shared with Lt. H.A. Kaul of the 336th Ftr Sqn
** - shared with Capt. K.E. Carlson of the 336th Ftr Sqn

**Jones, Alma R., Lt.**
385th Ftr Sqn/364th Ftr Grp

| *Sqn* | *Date* | *Claims* | *Location* | *A/C* |
|---|---|---|---|---|
| 385th | October 12, 1944 | (3)FW-190 dest(air) | N/Bremen | P-51 |
| | | FW-190 dam(air) | N/Bremen | P-51 |

3-0-1 air
0-0 ground

**Jones, Carter L., Lt.**
363rd Ftr Sqn/357th Ftr Grp

| *Sqn* | *Date* | *Claims* | *Location* | *A/C* |
|---|---|---|---|---|
| 363rd | March 6, 1944 | Me-410 dam(air) | W/Berlin | P-51 |
| | March 22 | Me-109 dest(air) | Munster | P-51 |

1-0-1 air
0-0 ground

**Jones, Charles O., LtCol.**
338th Ftr Sqn/55th Ftr Grp
HdQts/55th Ftr Grp

| *Sqn* | *Date* | *Claims* | *Location* | *A/C* |
|---|---|---|---|---|
| 338th | December 13, 1943 | Me-109 dam(air) | N/Oldenburg | P-38 |
| | January 5, 1944 | Me-109 dest(air) | Neumunster | P-38 |

1-0-1 air
0-0 ground

**Jones, Cyril W., Lt.**
370th Ftr Sqn/359th Ftr Grp

| *Sqn* | *Date* | *Claims* | *Location* | *A/C* |
|---|---|---|---|---|
| 370th | August 9, 1944 | Me-109 dest(air) | Gunzburg | P-51 |
| | | Me-109 dam(air) | Gunzburg | P-51 |
| | August 16 | Me-163 dest(air) | SE Leipzig | P-51 |
| | September 11 | (4)Me-109 dest(air) | Gotha | P-51 |
| | | He-177 dest(grd) | Gotha | P-51 |
| | | Ju-88 dest(grd) | Gotha | P-51 |
| | | (2)Me-410 dam(grd) | Gotha | P-51 |
| | | (2)Ju-88 dam(grd) | Gotha | P-51 |
| | | (.5)He-177 dam(grd)* | Gotha | P-51 |
| | September 12 | (3)u/i a/c dest(grd) | S/Memmingen | P-51 |

6-0-1 air
5-4.5 ground

* - shared with Lt. W.C. Murray of the 370th Ftr Sqn

**Jones, Dale N., Capt.**
79th Ftr Sqn/20th Ftr Grp

| *Sqn* | *Date* | *Claims* | *Location* | *A/C* |
|---|---|---|---|---|
| 79th | January 14, 1945 | Me-109 dest(air) | E/Wittenberg | P-51 |
| | February 20 | He-111 dest(grd) | Weiden A/F | P-51 |
| | | He-111 dam(grd) | Weiden A/F | P-51 |

1-0-0 air
1-1 ground

**Jones, Donald F., Lt.**
360th Ftr Sqn/356th Ftr Grp

| *Sqn* | *Date* | *Claims* | *Location* | *A/C* |
|---|---|---|---|---|
| 360th | December 25, 1944 | FW-190 dam(air) | S/Bonn | P-51 |

0-0-1 air
0-0 ground

**Jones, Donald W., Lt.**
376th Ftr Sqn/361st Ftr Grp

| *Sqn* | *Date* | *Claims* | *Location* | *A/C* |
|---|---|---|---|---|
| 376th | April 16, 1945 | u/i a/c dest(grd) | Reichersberg | P-51 |

0-0-0 air
1-0 ground

**Jones, Edwards H., Lt.**
385th Ftr Sqn/364th Ftr Grp

| *Sqn* | *Date* | *Claims* | *Location* | *A/C* |
|---|---|---|---|---|
| 385th | April 16, 1945 | (3)FW-190 dam(grd) | Pocking | P-51 |
| | April 17 | (2)He-111 dam(grd) | Karlsbad | P-51 |

0-0-0 air
0-5 ground

**Jones, Frank C., Capt.**
335th Ftr Sqn/4th Ftr Grp

| *Sqn* | *Date* | *Claims* | *Location* | *A/C* |
|---|---|---|---|---|
| 335th | April 5, 1944 | (2)u/i a/c dest(grd) | SE Berlin | P-51 |
| | April 8 | Me-109 dam(air) | Wolfenbuttel | P-51 |
| | April 10 | (2)u/i a/c dam(grd) | Romorantin A/F | P-51 |

| Sqn | Date | Claims | Location | A/C |
|---|---|---|---|---|
| | April 12 | Me-109 dest(air) | Brunswick | P-51 |
| | April 15 | He-177 dest(grd) | Hagenow | P-51 |
| | April 22 | Me-109 dest(air) | Kassel | P-51 |
| | May 1 | Me-109 dest(air) | Zweibrucken | P-51 |
| | | Me-109 dam(air) | Zweibrucken | P-51 |
| | May 24 | Me-109 prob(air) | Hamburg | P-51 |
| | May 30 | (1.5)FW-190 dest(grd)* | Oschersleben | P-51 |
| | | FW-190 dam(grd) | Oschersleben | P-51 |
| | June 20 | Me-109 dest(air) | Stettin | P-51 |
| | June 21 | Me-109 dest(air) | Kobryn | P-51 |
| | | Me-109 dam(air) | Kobryn | P-51 |
| | August 8 | Ju-88 dest(grd) | Stravanger/Sola A/F | P-51 |

5-1-3 air
5.5-3 ground

* - shared with Lt. R.K. Hofer of the 334th Ftr Sqn, 4th Ftr Grp

**Jones, George W., Lt.**
505th Ftr Sqn/339th Ftr Grp

| Sqn | Date | Claims | Location | A/C |
|---|---|---|---|---|
| 505th | March 2, 1945 | Me-109 dam(air) | Osnabruck | P-51 |
| | March 3 | u/i a/c dest(grd) | E/Magdeburg | P-51 |

0-0-1 air
1-0 ground

**Jones, Grant L., Lt.**
385th Ftr Sqn/364th Ftr Grp

| Sqn | Date | Claims | Location | A/C |
|---|---|---|---|---|
| 385th | August 24, 1944 | (.5)Me-109 dest(air)* | Hamburg | P-51 |

0.5-0-0 air
0-0 ground

* - shared with Lt. E.A. Taylor of the 385th Ftr Sqn

**Jones, James M., Capt.**
62nd Ftr Sqn/56th Ftr Grp

| Sqn | Date | Claims | Location | A/C |
|---|---|---|---|---|
| 62nd | August 12, 1943 | FW-190 dam(air) | W/Maastricht | P-47 |
| | August 24 | FW-190 dest(air) | S/Paris | P-47 |
| | October 10 | FW-190 dest(air) | Altenberge | P-47 |
| | February 4, 1944 | FW-190 dam(air) | Charleroi | P-47 |
| | March 15 | FW-190 dest(air) | Dummer Lake | P-47 |
| | | FW-190 dam(air) | Dummer Lake | P-47 |
| | March 16 | FW-190 dam(air) | St. Dizier | P-47 |
| | April 8 | Ju-88 dest(grd) | Quackenbruck | P-47 |

3-0-4 air
1-0 ground

**Jones, John E., Lt.**
61st Ftr Sqn/56th Ftr Grp

| Sqn | Date | Claims | Location | A/C |
|---|---|---|---|---|
| 61st | April 10, 1945 | (2)Do-24 dest(grd) | Muritz Lake | P-47 |
| | | u/i a/c dest(grd) | Muritz Lake | P-47 |

0-0-0 air
3-0 ground

**Jones, Reps D., Capt.**
77th Ftr Sqn/20th Ftr Grp

| Sqn | Date | Claims | Location | A/C |
|---|---|---|---|---|
| 77th | November 2, 1944 | Me-109 dest(air) | Merseburg | P-51 |
| | | Me-109 prob(air) | Merseburg | P-51 |
| | January 14, 1945 | FW-190 dest(air) | Perleberg | P-51 |
| | February 9 | (4)FW-190 dest(grd) | Esperstadt A/F | P-51 |
| | | Me-109 dest(grd) | Esperstadt A/F | P-51 |
| | February 20 | u/i a/c dam(grd) | Straubing | P-51 |
| | March 2 | FW-190 dam(air) | Chemnitz | P-51 |

2-1-1 air
5-1 ground

**Jones, Robert, Lt.**
38th Ftr Sqn/55th Ftr Grp

| Sqn | Date | Claims | Location | A/C |
|---|---|---|---|---|
| 38th | January 3, 1945 | Ar-196 dest(air) | SE Ulm | P-51 |

1-0-0 air
0-0 ground

**Jones, Robert B., Jr., Lt.**
62nd Ftr Sqn/56th Ftr Grp

| Sqn | Date | Claims | Location | A/C |
|---|---|---|---|---|
| 62nd | April 10, 1945 | He-111 dest(grd) | Neuruppin | P-47 |
| | | He-111 dam(grd) | Neuruppin | P-47 |
| | April 13 | FW-190 dest(grd) | Eggebeck A/F | P-47 |
| | | He-111 desy(grd) | Eggebeck A/F | P-47 |
| | | (2)He-111 dam(grd) | Eggebeck A/F | P-47 |
| | | FW-190 dam(grd) | Eggebeck A/F | P-47 |
| | | Ju-88 dam(grd) | Eggebeck A/F | P-47 |

0-0-0 air
3-5 ground

**Jones, Thomas W., Lt.**
352nd Ftr Sqn/353rd Ftr Grp

| Sqn | Date | Claims | Location | A/C |
|---|---|---|---|---|
| 352nd | July 30, 1944 | u/i a/c dest(grd) | Orleans/Bricy | P-47 |
| | August 4 | (2)He-111 dest(grd) | Plantlunne | P-47 |
| | | u/i a/c dest(grd) | Plantlunne | P-47 |
| | August 12 | (2)He-111 dest(grd) | E/Paris | P-47 |
| | August 28 | (.5)Ju-88 dest(air)* | SE Luxembourg | P-47 |

0.5-0-0 air
6-0 ground

* - shared with Lt. B. Parker of the 352nd Ftr Sqn

**Jones, Vernon Y., Lt.**
82nd Ftr Sqn/78th Ftr Grp

| Sqn | Date | Claims | Location | A/C |
|---|---|---|---|---|
| 82nd | January 29, 1944 | (.5)FW-190 dest(air)* | Coblenz | P-47 |
| | | FW-190 prob(air) | Coblenz | P-47 |
| | February 10 | Me-109 dest(air) | Rheine | P-47 |

1.5-1-0 air
0-0 ground

* - shared with LtCol. H.J. Dayhuff of HdQts, 78th Ftr Grp

**Jones, William A., Lt.**
505th Ftr Sqn/339th Ftr Grp

| Sqn | Date | Claims | Location | A/C |
|---|---|---|---|---|
| 505th | May 9, 1944 | Me-109 dest(air) | Vouziers | P-51 |
| | June 8 | FW-190 dest(air) | Rennes | P-51 |
| | July 29 | (.5)Ju-52 dest(grd)* | NW Naumberg | P-51 |
| | September 10 | Ju-87 dest(grd) | Weizenburg | P-51 |
| | | u/i a/c dest(grd) | Weizenburg | P-51 |
| | | (.5)Me-109 dest(grd)** | Weizenburg | P-51 |
| | | (2)He-111 dam(grd) | Weizenburg | P-51 |
| | September 11 | Ju-88 dest(grd) | Munich | P-51 |
| | | Ju-52 dest(grd) | Munich | P-51 |
| | | Ju-88 dam(grd) | Munich | P-51 |

2-0-0 air
5-3 ground

* - shared with Lt. G.J. Hrico of the 505th Ftr Sqn
** - shared with Lt. C.R. Stewart of the 505th Ftr Sqn

**Jordan, Herbert H., Maj.**
435th Ftr Sqn/479th Ftr Grp
Earlier flew in the PTO with the 475th Ftr Grp and claimed one kill on September 4, 1943.

| Sqn | Date | Claims | Location | A/C |
|---|---|---|---|---|
| 435th | January 14, 1945 | Me-109 dest(air) | NW Wesel | P-51 |
| | February 9 | FW-190 dest(air) | W/Brandenburg | P-51 |

2-0-0 air
0-0 ground

**Jordan, William J., Capt.**
352nd Ftr Sqn/353rd Ftr Grp

| Sqn | Date | Claims | Location | A/C |
|---|---|---|---|---|
| 352nd | February 10, 1944 | Me-210 prob(air) | Lingen | P-47 |

| Sqn | Date | Claims | Location | A/C |
|---|---|---|---|---|
| | March 29 | Me-109 dest(air) | SW Bonn | P-47 |
| | July 30 | (2.5)u/i a/c dest(grd)* | Orleans/Bricy | P-47 |
| | August 4 | (.5)u/i a/c dest(grd)** | Plantlunne | P-47 |
| | August 12 | (.5)u/i a/c dest(grd)@ | E/Paris | P-47 |
| | November 18 | FW-190 dest(grd) | Lechfeld | P-51 |

1-1-0 air
4.5-0 ground

* - shared with Capt. L.P. Cles of the 352nd Ftr Sqn
** - shared with Lt. G.N. Porterfield of the 352nd Ftr Sqn
@ - shared with Lt. R. Eluhow of the 352nd Ftr Sqn

**Josey, Danford E., Lt.**
84th Ftr Sqn/78th Ftr Grp

| *Sqn* | *Date* | *Claims* | *Location* | *A/C* |
|---|---|---|---|---|
| 84th | April 16, 1945 | (2)FW-190 dest(grd) | Praha/Kakewice | P-51 |
| | | Me-109 dest(grd) | Praha/Kakewice | P-51 |
| | | He-111 dest(grd) | Praha/Kakewice | P-51 |
| | | (2)FW-190 dam(grd) | Praha/Kakewice | P-51 |
| | | Ju-52 dam(grd) | Praha/Kakewice | P-51 |
| | | u/i a/c dam(grd) | Praha/Kakewice | P-51 |
| | April 17 | FW-190 dest(grd) | W/Dresden | P-51 |
| | | Ju-88 dest(grd) | W/Dresden | P-51 |
| | | u/i a/c dest(grd) | W/Dresden | P-51 |
| | | FW-190 dam(grd) | W/Dresden | P-51 |
| | | Ju-88 dam(grd) | W/Dresden | P-51 |

0-0-0 air
8-6 ground

**Joyce, Thomas E., Cap.**
334th Ftr Sqn/4th Ftr Grp

| *Sqn* | *Date* | *Claims* | *Location* | *A/C* |
|---|---|---|---|---|
| 334th | May 29, 1944 | (.5)Do-18 dam(grd)* | Dievenow | P-51 |
| | June 20 | (.5)Me-109 dest(air)** | E/Pasewalk | P-51 |
| | July 7 | (2)Me-109 dest(air) | Aschersleben | P-51 |

2.5-0-0 air
0-0.5 ground

* - shared with Lt. M.H. Kolter of the 334th Ftr Sqn
** - shared with Lt. A.C. Cwiklinski of the 334th Ftr Sqn

**Juchheim, Alwin M., Capt.**
83rd Ftr Sqn/78th Ftr Grp

| *Sqn* | *Date* | *Claims* | *Location* | *A/C* |
|---|---|---|---|---|
| 83rd | February 22, 1944 | Me-109 dest(air) | E/Eindhoven | P-47 |
| | | FW-190 dam(air) | E/Eindhoven | P-47 |
| | February 24 | (2)Me-109 dest(air) | Furstenau | P-47 |
| | April 10 | (3)FW-190 dest(grd) | Romorantin A/F | P-47 |
| | | Hs-123 dest(grd) | Romorantin A/F | P-47 |
| | April 11 | FW-190 dest(air) | Luneburg | P-47 |
| | | FW-190 prob(air) | Luneburg | P-47 |
| | April 13 | FW-190 dest(air) | Beuchenburen | P-47 |
| | | FW-190 dest(grd) | Beuchenburen | P-47 |
| | April 24 | (.5)Me-110 dest(grd)* | Trier | P-47 |
| | | Me-110 dam(grd) | Trier | P-47 |
| | April 30 | (2)FW-190 dest(air) | Dreux | P-47 |
| | | FW-190 prob(air) | Dreux | P-47 |
| | | FW-190 dam(air) | Dreux | P-47 |
| | May 25 | Me-109 dest(air) | St. Dizier | P-47 |
| | | (.5)He-111 dest(grd)** | St. Dizier | P-47 |
| | May 27 | Me-109 dest(air) | Frieburg | P-47 |

9-2-2 air
6-1 ground

* - shared with Lt. V.J. Massa of the 83rd Ftr Sqn
** - shared with Lt. L.R. Casey of the 83rd Ftr Sqn

**Julian, William H., LtCol.**
83rd Ftr Sqn/ 78th Ftr Grp
504th Ftr Sqn/339th Ftr Grp

| *Sqn* | *Date* | *Claims* | *Location* | *A/C* |
|---|---|---|---|---|
| 83rd | May 14, 1943 | FW-190 dam(air) | St. Nicholas | P-47 |
| | December 30 | Me-109 dest(air) | Reims | P-47 |
| | December 31 | FW-190 dest(air) | NE Lorient | P-47 |
| | July 5, 1944 | FW-190 dest(air) | Evreux | P-47 |
| | March 2, 1945 | (2)Me-109 dest(air) | Burg A/F | P-51 |
| | | Me-109 dam(air) | Burg A/F | P-51 |
| 504th | April 10 | (2)Me-410 dest(grd) | N/Neuruppin | P-51 |
| | | (2)Me-410 dam(grd) | N/Neuruppin | P-51 |
| | April 16 | u/i a/c dest(grd) | Klatovy | P-51 |
| | | Me-109 dam(grd) | Klatovy | P-51 |
| | | FW-190 dam(grd) | Klatovy | P-51 |

5-0-2 air
3-4 ground

**Jungling, Enoch, Lt.**
335th Ftr Sqn/4th Ftr Grp

| *Sqn* | *Date* | *Claims* | *Location* | *A/C* |
|---|---|---|---|---|
| 335th | November 18, 1944 | Me-262 dam(grd) | Leipheim | P-51 |
| | April 4, 1945 | Me-262 dam(air) | NE Parchim | P-51 |

0-0-1 air
0-1 ground

**Juntilla, James O., Lt.**
357th Ftr Sqn/355th Ftr Grp

| *Sqn* | *Date* | *Claims* | *Location* | *A/C* |
|---|---|---|---|---|
| 357th | September 12, 1944 | (2)Ju-88 dest(grd) | Schwartz A/F | P-51 |
| | | Ju-52 dest(grd) | Schwartz A/F | P-51 |
| | | u/i a/c dest(grd) | Schwartz A/F | P-51 |
| | | (2)Ju-88 dam(grd) | Schwartz A/F | P-51 |
| | | (2)u/i a/c dam(grd) | Schwartz A/F | P-51 |

0-0-0 air
4-4 ground

**Junttila, Wilbert H., Maj.**
352nd Ftr Sqn/353rd Ftr Grp

| *Sqn* | *Date* | *Claims* | *Location* | *A/C* |
|---|---|---|---|---|
| 352nd | October 10, 1943 | (.33)Me-110 dam(air)* | Amersfoort | P-47 |
| | October 14 | Me-109 dest(air) | Turnhout | P-47 |
| | | Me-109 dam(air) | Turnhout | P-47 |
| | November 3 | Me-110 dest(air) | Wilhelmshaven | P-47 |
| | November 27, 1944 | Me-109 dam(air) | Magdeburg | P-51 |

2-0-2.33 air
0-0 ground

* - shared with Lt. E.M. Fogarty and Lt. R.V. Keywan of the 352nd Ftr Sqn

**Jure, James M., Lt.**
61st Ftr Sqn/56th Ftr Grp

| *Sqn* | *Date* | *Claims* | *Location* | *A/C* |
|---|---|---|---|---|
| 61st | May 13, 1944 | FW-190 dest(air) | NE Hamburg | P-47 |
| | June 27 | Me-109 dest(air) | Esternay | P-47 |
| | | Me-109 prob(air) | Esternay | P-47 |
| | August 4 | (.5)u/i a/c dest(grd)* | Salenter Lake | P-47 |
| | August 28 | (.5)He-111 dest(air)** | S/Saarbrucken | P-47 |
| | September 5 | He-111 dest(grd) | Merzhausen | P-47 |
| | | Ju-88 dam(grd) | Merzhausen | P-47 |
| | | u/i a/c dam(grd) | Merzhausen | P-47 |
| | September 12 | Me-109 dest(air) | N/Brandenburg | P-47 |

3.5-1-0 air
1.5-2 ground

* - shared with Lt. S.H. Getz of the 61st Ftr Sqn
** - shared with Capt. P.A. Conger of the 61st Ftr Sqn

**Jurgens, Fred H., Lt.**
79th Ftr Sqn/20th Ftr Grp

| *Sqn* | *Date* | *Claims* | *Location* | *A/C* |
|---|---|---|---|---|
| 79th | April 10, 1945 | (3)He-111 dest(grd) | Werder A/F | P-51 |
| | | (2)Si-204 dest(grd) | Werder A/F | P-51 |
| | | (2)Caudron dest(grd) | Werder A/F | P-51 |
| | | u/i a/c dest(grd) | Werder A/F | P-51 |

0-0-0 air
8-0 ground

**Just, Harry H., Lt.**
84th Ftr Sqn/78th Ftr Grp

| *Sqn* | *Date* | *Claims* | *Location* | *A/C* |
|---|---|---|---|---|
| 84th | March 30, 1944 | Me-323 dam(grd) | Deelan A/F | P-47 |

0-0-0 air
0-1 ground

**Juszczyk, Edmund J., Lt.**
364th Ftr Sqn/357th Ftr Grp

| *Sqn* | *Date* | *Claims* | *Location* | *A/C* |
|---|---|---|---|---|
| 364th | December 5, 1944 | FW-190 dest(air) | N/Berlin | P-51 |

1-0-0 air
0-0 ground

**Kaczynski, Henry J., Lt.**
361st Ftr Sqn/356th Ftr Grp

| *Sqn* | *Date* | *Claims* | *Location* | *A/C* |
|---|---|---|---|---|
| 361st | April 23, 1944 | (2)He-111 dam(grd) | Hagenau | P-47 |

0-0-0 air
0-2 ground

**Kahle, Dayne, Lt.**
361st Ftr Sqn/356th Ftr Grp

| *Sqn* | *Date* | *Claims* | *Location* | *A/C* |
|---|---|---|---|---|
| 361st | June 11, 1944 | Me-109 dest(air) | SW Bernay | P-47 |
| | June 15 | Me-109 dam(air) | SE Rouen | P-47 |
| | October 7 | Me-110 dest(grd) | Fritzlar | P-47 |
| | | (2)Me-110 dam(grd) | Fritzlar | P-47 |

1-0-1 air
1-2 ground

**Kalessa, Russell R., Lt.**
363rd Ftr Sqn/357th Ftr Grp

| *Sqn* | *Date* | *Claims* | *Location* | *A/C* |
|---|---|---|---|---|
| 363rd | April 10, 1945 | u/i a/c dest(grd) | Neuruppin | P-51 |
| | | u/i a/c dam(grd) | Neuruppin | P-51 |

0-0-0 air
0-1 ground

**Kaminski, Rudolph B., Lt.**
357th Ftr Sqn/355th Ftr Grp

| *Sqn* | *Date* | *Claims* | *Location* | *A/C* |
|---|---|---|---|---|
| 357th | March 28, 1944 | Ju-88 dam(grd) | Dijon | P-51 |
| | March 29 | FW-190 dest(air) | NE Brunswick | P-51 |
| | | (2)u/i a/c dam(grd) | NE Brunswick | P-51 |
| | | (.5)u/i a/c dam(grd)[*] | NE Brunswick | P-51 |
| | | (.5)u/i a/c dam(grd)[*] | NE Brunswick | P-51 |
| | April 5 | Me-110 dest(grd) | Deiningen | P-51 |

1-0-0 air
1-4 ground

[*] - both shared with Lt. R.A. Browning of the 357th Ftr Sqn

**Kammer, George D., Lt.**
350th Ftr Sqn/353rd Ftr Grp

| *Sqn* | *Date* | *Claims* | *Location* | *A/C* |
|---|---|---|---|---|
| 350th | February 28, 1945 | He-111 dam(grd) | Rohrensee | P-51 |

0-0-0 air
0-1 ground

**Kanaga, Robert H., Capt.**
334th Ftr Sqn/4th Ftr Grp

| *Sqn* | *Date* | *Claims* | *Location* | *A/C* |
|---|---|---|---|---|
| 334th | April 4, 1945 | Me-262 prob(air) | Schwerin | P-51 |

0-1-0 air
0-0 ground

**Kaplan, Albert B., Lt.**
354th Ftr Sqn/355th Ftr Grp

| *Sqn* | *Date* | *Claims* | *Location* | *A/C* |
|---|---|---|---|---|
| 354th | April 13, 1945 | He-111 dest(grd) | Husum | P-51 |
| | | FW-190 dam(grd) | Husum | P-51 |

0-0-0 air
1-1 ground

**Karger, Dale E., Lt.**
364th Ftr Sqn/357th Ftr Grp

| *Sqn* | *Date* | *Claims* | *Location* | *A/C* |
|---|---|---|---|---|
| 364th | December 5, 1944 | (2)FW-190 dest(air) | N/Berlin | P-51 |
| | December 24 | Me-109 dest(air) | S/Kassel | P-51 |
| | January 14, 1945 | Me-109 dest(air) | NW Berlin | P-51 |
| | January 20 | Me-262 dest(air) | N/Munich | P-51 |
| | March 2 | (.5)Me-109 dest(air)[*] | SE Magdeburg | P-51 |
| | | (4)u/i a/c dest(grd) | E/Magdeburg | P-51 |
| | | (2)Ju-88 dam(grd) | E/Magdeburg | P-51 |
| | | Ju-188 dam(grd) | E/Magdeburg | P-51 |
| | | u/i a/c dam(grd) | E/Magdeburg | P-51 |
| | March 24 | (2)Me-109 dest(air) | W/Gutersloh | P-51 |

7.5-0-0 air
4-4 ground

[*] - shared with Capt. R.G. Schimanski of the 364th Ftr Sqn

**Kasper, Billy D., Capt.**
368th Ftr Sqn/359th Ftr Grp

| *Sqn* | *Date* | *Claims* | *Location* | *A/C* |
|---|---|---|---|---|
| 368th | January 1, 1945 | Me-109 dest(air) | Stendal | P-51 |

1-0-0 air
0-0 ground

**Kassop, John W., Lt.**
61st Ftr Sqn/56th Ftr Grp

| *Sqn* | *Date* | *Claims* | *Location* | *A/C* |
|---|---|---|---|---|
| 61st | April 4, 1945 | Me-262 dam(air) | W/Hamburg | P-47 |

0-0-1 air
0-0 ground

**Kaul, Henry A., Lt.**
336th Ftr Sqn/4th Ftr Grp

| *Sqn* | *Date* | *Claims* | *Location* | *A/C* |
|---|---|---|---|---|
| 336th | November 18, 1944 | (.5)Me-262 dam(grd)[*] | Leipheim | P-51 |
| | | (.5)Me-262 dam(grd)[*] | Leipheim | P-51 |
| | | (.5)Me-262 dam(grd)[*] | Leipheim | P-51 |
| | January 16, 1945 | FW-190 dest(grd) | Neuhausen | P-51 |

0-0-0 air
1-1.5 ground

[*] - all shared with Lt. J.H. Joiner of the 336th Ftr Sqn

**Kavanaugh, John W., Capt.**
38th Ftr Sqn/55th Ftr Grp

| *Sqn* | *Date* | *Claims* | *Location* | *A/C* |
|---|---|---|---|---|
| 38th | December 5, 1944 | FW-190 dest(air) | NE Berlin | P-51 |
| | January 3, 1945 | (1.5)Ar-196 dest(air)[*] | SE Ulm | P-51 |
| | April 16 | Me-262 dest(grd) | Munich-Brunnthal | P-51 |
| | | u/i a/c dest(grd) | Munich-Brunnthal | P-51 |
| | | u/i a/c dam(grd) | Munich-Brunnthal | P-51 |

2.5-0-0 air
2-1 ground

[*] - shared with Lt. D.H. Courtney of the 38th Ftr Sqn

**Kayser, Henry R., Lt.**
363rd Ftr Sqn/357th Ftr Grp

| *Sqn* | *Date* | *Claims* | *Location* | *A/C* |
|---|---|---|---|---|
| 363rd | April 11, 1944 | Me-109 dest(air) | W/Hanover | P-51 |
| | | (.25)He-111 dest(air)[*] | W/Hanover | P-51 |

1.25-0-0 air
0-0 ground

[*] - shared with Capt. C.E. Anderson, Lt. E.K. Simpson, and Lt. W.B. Overstreet of the 363rd Ftr Sqn

**Keatley, Ivan H., Capt.**
82nd Ftr Sqn/78th Ftr Grp

| *Sqn* | *Date* | *Claims* | *Location* | *A/C* |
|---|---|---|---|---|
| 82nd | September 10, 1944 | He-111 dam(grd) | Meinbullen | P-47 |
| | November 26 | Me-109 dam(air) | Rheine | P-47 |
| | March 19, 1945 | (2)Me-109 dest(air) | Osnabruck | P-51 |

2-0-1 air
0-1 ground

**Kebelman, Frank L., Jr., Lt.**
328th Ftr Sqn/352nd Ftr Grp

| *Sqn* | *Date* | *Claims* | *Location* | *A/C* |
|---|---|---|---|---|
| 328th | July 18, 1944 | Me-109 dest(air) | Wismar | P-51 |
| | November 21 | (2)Me-109 dest(air) | Merseburg | P-51 |

3-0-0 air
0-0 ground

**Keeler, John W., Lt.**
63rd Ftr Sqn/56th Ftr Grp

| *Sqn* | *Date* | *Claims* | *Location* | *A/C* |
|---|---|---|---|---|
| 63rd | April 13, 1945 | Me-110 dest(grd) | Eggebeck A/F | P-47 |
| | | u/i a/c dest(grd) | Eggebeck A/F | P-47 |
| | | Me-410 dam(grd) | Eggebeck A/F | P-47 |

0-0-0 air
2-1 ground

**Keen, Robert J., Capt.**
61st Ftr Sqn/56th Ftr Grp
62nd Ftr Sqn/56th Ftr Grp

| *Sqn* | *Date* | *Claims* | *Location* | *A/C* |
|---|---|---|---|---|
| 61st | May 13, 1944 | (3)FW-190 dest(air) | W/Hagenow | P-47 |
| | | FW-190 prob(air) | W/Hagenow | P-47 |
| | July 5 | (3)Me-109 dest(air) | Evreux | P-47 |
| | | Me-109 dam(air) | Evreux | P-47 |
| | September 5 | (3)FW-190 dest(grd) | Gelnhausen | P-47 |
| | | (3)FW-190 dam(grd) | Gelnhausen | P-47 |
| | September 16 | Ju-88 dest(grd) | Dummer Lake | P-47 |

6-1-1 air
4-3 ground

**Keesey, John S., Capt.**
368th Ftr Sqn/359th Ftr Grp

| *Sqn* | *Date* | *Claims* | *Location* | *A/C* |
|---|---|---|---|---|
| 368th | August 8, 1944 | FW-190 dest(air) | Dreux | P-51 |
| | | (3)FW-190 dam(air) | Dreux | P-51 |
| | August 9 | FW-190 prob(air) | Munich | P-51 |
| | November 21 | FW-190 dam(air) | Erfurt | P-51 |

1-1-4 air
0-0 ground

**Kehrer, Merlin R., Lt.**
362nd Ftr Sqn/357th Ftr Grp

| *Sqn* | *Date* | *Claims* | *Location* | *A/C* |
|---|---|---|---|---|
| 362nd | February 25, 1944 | Ju-88 dest(air) | W/Schweinfurt | P-51 |

1-0-0 air
0-0 ground

**Keillor, Peter T., Capt.**
84th Ftr Sqn/78th Ftr Grp

| *Sqn* | *Date* | *Claims* | *Location* | *A/C* |
|---|---|---|---|---|
| 84th | April 10, 1945 | Ar-196 dest(grd) | Werder A/F | P-51 |
| | | Me-323 dest(grd) | Werder A/F | P-51 |
| | | Ar-196 dam(grd) | Werder A/F | P-51 |

0-0-0 air
2-1 ground

**Keirnan, John W., Lt.**
385th Ftr Sqn/364th Ftr Grp

| *Sqn* | *Date* | *Claims* | *Location* | *A/C* |
|---|---|---|---|---|
| 385th | April 16, 1945 | (2)Me-109 dest(grd) | Pocking | P-51 |
| | | Me-109 dam(grd) | Pocking | P-51 |

0-0-0 air
2-1 ground

**Keller, Frank J., Maj.**
434th Ftr Sqn/479th Ftr Grp

| *Sqn* | *Date* | *Claims* | *Location* | *A/C* |
|---|---|---|---|---|
| 434th | May 31, 1944 | Ju-88 dest(grd) | Humfield | P-38 |
| | August 9 | FW-200 dest(grd) | Nuneburg | P-38 |
| | | (.5)He-111 dam(grd)* | Nuneburg | P-38 |

0-0-0 air
2-0.5 ground

* - shared with Lt. T.D. Neely of the 434th Ftr Sqn

**Keller, Paul, Lt.**
82nd Ftr Sqn/78th Ftr Grp

| *Sqn* | *Date* | *Claims* | *Location* | *A/C* |
|---|---|---|---|---|
| 82nd | February 8, 1944 | He-111 dam(grd) | Paris | P-47 |

0-0-0 air
0-1 ground

**Kelley, Fred W., Capt.**
357th Ftr Sqn/355th Ftr Grp

| *Sqn* | *Date* | *Claims* | *Location* | *A/C* |
|---|---|---|---|---|
| 357th | November 5, 1943 | Me-109 dam(air) | Uden | P-47 |
| | June 6, 1944 | (2)Ju-87 dest(air) | NE Janville | P-51 |

2-0-1 air
0-0 ground

**Kelley, Wendell J., LtCol.**
HdQts/55th Ftr Grp

| *Sqn* | *Date* | *Claims* | *Location* | *A/C* |
|---|---|---|---|---|
| HdQts | September 3, 1944 | FW-190 dest(air) | Antwerp | P-51 |

1-0-0 air
0-0 ground

**Kelly, Dale E., Lt.**
369th Ftr Sqn/359th Ftr Grp

| *Sqn* | *Date* | *Claims* | *Location* | *A/C* |
|---|---|---|---|---|
| 369th | March 24, 1945 | (1.5)Me-109 dest(air)* | Eikelon A/F | P-51 |

1.5-0-0 air
0-0 ground

* - shared with Lt. H. Tenenbaum of the 369th Ftr Sqn

**Kelly, John J., Lt.**
369th Ftr Sqn/359th Ftr Grp

| *Sqn* | *Date* | *Claims* | *Location* | *A/C* |
|---|---|---|---|---|
| 369th | December 24, 1944 | Me-109 dest(air) | Vogelsand | P-51 |

1-0-0 air
0-0 ground

**Kelly, Joseph D., Lt.**
376th Ftr Sqn/361st Ftr Grp

| *Sqn* | *Date* | *Claims* | *Location* | *A/C* |
|---|---|---|---|---|
| 376th | March 29, 1944 | Ju-88 dam(grd) | Dummer Lake | P-47 |
| | April 1 | (2)Ju-88 dest(grd) | Gutersloh | P-47 |

0-0-0 air
2-1 ground

**Kelly, Marion C., Lt.**
376th Ftr Sqn/361st Ftr Grp

| *Sqn* | *Date* | *Claims* | *Location* | *A/C* |
|---|---|---|---|---|
| 376th | April 16, 1945 | Fi-156 dest(grd) | Reichersberg | P-51 |
| | April 17 | u/i a/c dest(grd) | Pilzen | P-51 |

0-0-0 air
2-0 ground

**Kelso, Duane F., Lt.**
79th Ftr Sqn/20th Ftr Grp

| *Sqn* | *Date* | *Claims* | *Location* | *A/C* |
|---|---|---|---|---|
| 79th | January 14, 1945 | Me-109 dest(air) | Wittenberge | P-51 |
| | | Me-109 dam(air) | Wittenberge | P-51 |

1-0-1 air
0-0 ground

**Kelsey, Joseph P., Capt.**
368th Ftr Sqn/359th Ftr Grp

| *Sqn* | *Date* | *Claims* | *Location* | *A/C* |
|---|---|---|---|---|
| 368th | July 24, 1944 | u/i a/c dam(grd) | Ulm | P-51 |

0-0-0 air
0-1 ground

**Kemp, William T., Lt.**
375th Ftr Sqn/361st Ftr Grp

| *Sqn* | *Date* | *Claims* | *Location* | *A/C* |
|---|---|---|---|---|
| 375th | July 20, 1944 | Me-109 dest(air) | N/Leipzig | P-51 |
| | | FW-190 dest(air) | N/Leipzig | P-51 |
| | August 7 | FW-190 dest(air) | Chartres | P-51 |
| | | FW-190 dam(air) | Chartres | P-51 |
| | | (.5)Me-109 dam(grd)* | Chartres | P-51 |
| | September 12 | (3)Me-109 dest(air) | NE Magdeburg | P-51 |

6-0-1 air
0-0.5 ground

* - shared with Lt. L.A. Wood of the 375th Ftr Sqn

**Kemper, George A., Jr., Lt.**
354th Ftr Sqn/355th Ftr Grp

| *Sqn* | *Date* | *Claims* | *Location* | *A/C* |
|---|---|---|---|---|
| 354th | January 14, 1945 | (2)FW-190 dest(air) | E/Meppen & SW Dummer Lake | P-51 |

2-0-0 air
0-0 ground

**Kennedy, Michael J., Lt.**
334th Ftr Sqn/4th Ftr Grp

| *Sqn* | *Date* | *Claims* | *Location* | *A/C* |
|---|---|---|---|---|
| 334th | January 16, 1945 | (.5)He-177 dest(grd)* | Neuburg | P-51 |
| | April 4 | (.5)Me-262 dest(air)** | S/Ludwigslust | P-51 |
| | April 16 | u/i a/c dest(grd) | Gablingen | P-51 |
| | | Ju-88 dam(grd) | Gablingen | P-51 |
| | | Ju-87 dam(grd) | Gablingen | P-51 |

0.5-0-0 air
1.5-2 ground

* - shared with Lt. J.W. Ayers of the 334th Ftr Sqn
** - shared with Lt. H.H. Fredericks of the 336th Ftr Sqn, 4th Ftr Grp

**Kenney, Harold M., Lt.**
363rd Ftr Sqn/357th Ftr Grp

| *Sqn* | *Date* | *Claims* | *Location* | *A/C* |
|---|---|---|---|---|
| 363rd | April 11, 1944 | FW-190 dest(air) | Steinhuder Lake | P-51 |
| | | FW-190 dam(air) | Steinhuder Lake | P-51 |

1-0-1 air
0-0 ground

**Kenney, James W., Lt.**
362nd Ftr Sqn/357th Ftr Grp

| *Sqn* | *Date* | *Claims* | *Location* | *A/C* |
|---|---|---|---|---|
| 362nd | September 13, 1944 | Me-109 dam(air) | S/Nordhausen | P-51 |
| | November 8 | Me-262 dest(air) | Quackenbruck | P-51 |

1-0-1 air
0-0 ground

**Kenney, Paul H., Lt.**
358th Ftr Sqn/355th Ftr Grp

| *Sqn* | *Date* | *Claims* | *Location* | *A/C* |
|---|---|---|---|---|
| 358th | February 22, 1944 | FW-190 dest(air) | SE Munster | P-47 |
| | March 16 | Me-109 dest(air) | W/Augsburg | P-51 |
| | | (3)Me-109 dam(air) | W/Augsburg | P-51 |
| | April 15 | Do-217 dest(grd) | Glienicke | P-51 |

2-0-3 air
1-0 ground

**Kenyon, Robert P., Capt.**
334th Ftr Sqn/4th Ftr Grp

| *Sqn* | *Date* | *Claims* | *Location* | *A/C* |
|---|---|---|---|---|
| 334th | March 27, 1944 | Do-217 dam(grd) | Cazaux A/F | P-51 |
| | | Ju-88 dam(grd) | Cazaux A/F | P-51 |
| | April 18 | He-111 dest(grd) | Fassberg A/F | P-51 |
| | April 19 | Me-109 dest(air) | Eschwege | P-51 |
| | May 28 | Me-109 dest(air) | Magdeburg | P-51 |

2-0-0 air
1-2 ground

**Keplinger, Eugene W., Capt.**
375th Ftr Sqn/361st Ftr Grp

| *Sqn* | *Date* | *Claims* | *Location* | *A/C* |
|---|---|---|---|---|
| 375th | August 8, 1944 | FW-190 dest(air) | Evreux | P-51 |
| | | FW-190 dam(air) | Evreux | P-51 |
| | December 2 | FW-190 dam(air) | Meinsenheim | P-51 |

1-0-2 air
0-0 ground

**Keppler, Charles N., Maj.**
84th Ftr Sqn/ 78th Ftr Grp
375th Ftr Sqn/361st Ftr Grp

| *Sqn* | *Date* | *Claims* | *Location* | *A/C* |
|---|---|---|---|---|
| 84th | December 1, 1943 | FW-190 dest(air) | Leige-Aachen | P-47 |
| 375th | February 22, 1944 | FW-190 dest(air) | NE Tilburg | P-47 |
| | | FW-190 dam(air) | NE Tilburg | P-47 |
| | March 8 | Me-109 dam(air) | Lemforde | P-47 |
| | April 8 | FW-190 dest(air) | NW Dummer Lake | P-47 |
| | April 27 | He-111 dam(grd) | Etampes | P-47 |
| | May 24 | Me-109 dam(air) | N/Berlin | P-51 |
| | June 20 | (1.5)glider dam(grd)* | Putnitz | P-51 |
| | | (.5)Me-110 dam(grd)* | Putnitz | P-51 |
| | November 27 | Me-109 dam(air) | Dummer Lake | P-51 |

3-0-4 air
0-3 ground

* - both shared with Lt. E.E. Neely of the 375th Ftr Sqn

**Kerch, Joseph F., Capt.**
357th Ftr Sqn/355th Ftr Grp

| *Sqn* | *Date* | *Claims* | *Location* | *A/C* |
|---|---|---|---|---|
| 357th | April 5, 1944 | (2)Me-110 dam(grd) | Ottingen | P-51 |
| | April 13 | Me-109 prob(air) | Augsburg | P-51 |
| | | (.33)Me-323 dest(grd)* | Crailsheim | P-51 |

0-1-0 air
0.33-2 ground

* - shared with Maj. E.W. Szaniawski and Lt. R.L. Norman of the 357th Ftr Sqn

**Kercher, Victor L., Capt.**
384th Ftr Sqn/364th Ftr Grp

| *Sqn* | *Date* | *Claims* | *Location* | *A/C* |
|---|---|---|---|---|
| 384th | May 22, 1944 | FW-190 dam(air) | SW Kiel | P-38 |
| | June 25 | (2)Me-109 dest(air) | E/Blois | P-38 |

2-0-1 air
0-0 ground

**Kerig, John A., Capt.**
383rd Ftr Sqn/364th Ftr Grp

| *Sqn* | *Date* | *Claims* | *Location* | *A/C* |
|---|---|---|---|---|
| 383rd | May 25, 1944 | FW-190 dam(air) | Dreux | P-38 |

0-0-1 air
0-0 ground

**Kerns, Leo H., Capt.**
77th Ftr Sqn/20th Ftr Grp

| *Sqn* | *Date* | *Claims* | *Location* | *A/C* |
|---|---|---|---|---|
| 77th | February 20, 1945 | Fi-156 dest(air) | N/Straubing | P-51 |
| | April 10 | Me-410 dest(grd) | Fassberg A/F | P-51 |

1-0-0 air
1-0 ground

**Kerr, John, Lt.**
383rd Ftr Sqn/364th Ftr Grp

| *Sqn* | *Date* | *Claims* | *Location* | *A/C* |
|---|---|---|---|---|
| 383rd | May 19, 1944 | FW-190 dam(air) | Trenemunde A/F | P-38 |

0-0-1 air
0-0 ground

**Kerr, Warren E., Jr., Capt.**
63rd Ftr Sqn/56th Ftr Grp

| *Sqn* | *Date* | *Claims* | *Location* | *A/C* |
|---|---|---|---|---|
| 63rd | April 9, 1944 | Ar-196 dest(grd) | Schleswig | P-47 |
| | April 24 | (2)Me-109 dest(grd) | Thalheim A/F | P-47 |
| | | Me-110 dest(grd) | Thalheim A/F | P-47 |
| | | Me-110 dam(grd) | Thalheim A/F | P-47 |
| | October 5 | Me-110 dest(grd) | S/Geseke | P-47 |

0-0-0 air
5-1 ground

**Kesler, Gilbert L., Lt.**
336th Ftr Sqn/4th Ftr Grp

| *Sqn* | *Date* | *Claims* | *Location* | *A/C* |
|---|---|---|---|---|
| 336th | January 1, 1945 | (.5)Me-109 dest(air)[*] | Ulzen | P-51 |
| | January 16 | FW-190 dest(grd) | Neuhausen | P-51 |
| | | He-177 dest(grd) | Neuhausen | P-51 |
| | February 27 | (2)Ju-52 dest(grd) | Weimar | P-51 |
| | | Me-109 dest(grd) | Weimar | P-51 |

0.5-0-0 air
5-0 ground

[*] - shared with Lt. A.O. Wallace of the 336th Ftr Sqn

**Kessler, John P., Capt.**
487th Ftr Sqn/352nd Ftr Grp

| *Sqn* | *Date* | *Claims* | *Location* | *A/C* |
|---|---|---|---|---|
| 487th | April 11, 1944 | FW-200 dest(grd) | SW Berlin | P-51 |
| | | Ju-52 dam(grd) | SW Berlin | P-51 |
| | April 22 | (.33)Ju-88 dest(air)[*] | Stade A/F | P-51 |
| | May 19 | Me-109 prob(air) | Ludwigslust | P-51 |
| | | Me-109 dam(air) | Ludwigslust | P-51 |
| | May 30 | Me-109 dest(air) | Halberstadt | P-51 |
| | | Me-109 prob(air) | Halberstadt | P-51 |
| | July 18 | Me-109 dam(air) | NE Rostock | P-51 |

1.33-2-2 air
1-1 ground

[*] - shared with Maj. G.E. Preddy and Lt. D.R. Donahue of the 487th Ftr Sqn

**Kester, John E., Lt.**
338th Ftr Sqn/55th Ftr Grp

| *Sqn* | *Date* | *Claims* | *Location* | *A/C* |
|---|---|---|---|---|
| 338th | November 2, 1944 | FW-190 dest(air) | W/Leipzig | P-51 |

1-0-0 air
0-0 ground

**Keuhl, Robert C., Lt.**
357th Ftr Sqn/355th Ftr Grp

| *Sqn* | *Date* | *Claims* | *Location* | *A/C* |
|---|---|---|---|---|
| 357th | April 16, 1945 | (.5)He-111 dest(grd)[*] | Bad Aibling | P-51 |
| | | He-111 dam(grd) | Bad Aibling | P-51 |
| | | Me-109 dam(grd) | Bad Aibling | P-51 |

0-0-0 air
0.5-2 ground

[*] - shared with Lt. W.L. Griswol of the 357th Ftr Sqn

**Keur, John E., Lt.**
369th Ftr Sqn/359th Ftr Grp

| *Sqn* | *Date* | *Claims* | *Location* | *A/C* |
|---|---|---|---|---|
| 369th | September 11, 1944 | Me-109 dest(air) | N/Erfurt | P-51 |
| | September 18 | (.5)Me-109 dest(air)[*] | SE Munster | P-51 |
| | December 24 | Me-109 dam(air) | Vogelsand | P-51 |

1.5-0-1 air
0-0 ground

[*] - shared with F/O T.G. Bur of the 369th Ftr Sqn

**Keywan, Richard V., Lt.**
352nd Ftr Sqn/353rd Ftr Grp

| *Sqn* | *Date* | *Claims* | *Location* | *A/C* |
|---|---|---|---|---|
| 352nd | October 10, 1943 | (.33)Me-110 dam(air)[*] | Amersfoort | P-47 |
| | October 14 | Me-109 dam(air) | Turnhout | P-47 |
| | June 7, 1944 | (1.5)Me-109 dam(grd)[**] | Compiegne | P-47 |
| | June 12 | Me-109 dest(air) | Evreux-Dreux | P-47 |
| | | (2)Me-109 dam(air) | Evreux-Dreux | P-47 |

1-0-3.33 air
0-1.5 ground

[*] - shared with Lt. E.M. Fogarty and Lt. W.H. Junttila of the 352nd Ftr Sqn
[**] - shared with Capt. J.N. Poindexter of the 352nd Ftr Sqn

**Kibler, Ralph E., Lt.**
368th Ftr Sqn/359th Ftr Grp
370th Ftr Sqn/359th Ftr Grp

| *Sqn* | *Date* | *Claims* | *Location* | *A/C* |
|---|---|---|---|---|
| 370th | February 10, 1944 | Me-109 dest(air) | E/Zuider Zee | P-47 |
| | April 11 | Me-109 dam(air) | Fallersleben | P-47 |
| | April 22 | (2)FW-190 dest(air) | Hamm | P-47 |

3-0-1 air
0-0 ground

**Kier, Edward L., Capt.**
55th Ftr Sqn/20th Ftr Grp

| *Sqn* | *Date* | *Claims* | *Location* | *A/C* |
|---|---|---|---|---|
| 55th | February 25, 1945 | (2)Me-109 dest(air) | Dummer Lake | P-51 |
| | April 10 | (5)Ju-88 dest(grd) | Berlin | P-51 |
| | | (4)Ju-88 dam(grd) | Berlin | P-51 |

2-0-0 air
5-4 ground

**Kiernan, Thomas, Jr., Lt.**
338th Ftr Sqn/55th Ftr Grp

| *Sqn* | *Date* | *Claims* | *Location* | *A/C* |
|---|---|---|---|---|
| 338th | January 29, 1945 | Me-109 dest(air) | NE Oldenburg | P-51 |
| | March 18 | FW-190 dest(air) | N/Giessen | P-51 |
| | April 17 | FW-190 dest(air) | S/Dresden | P-51 |

3-0-0 air
0-0 ground

**Kies, Clifford, Capt.**
79th Ftr Sqn/20th Ftr Grp

| *Sqn* | *Date* | *Claims* | *Location* | *A/C* |
|---|---|---|---|---|
| 79th | February 20, 1945 | He-111 dest(grd) | Weiden A/F | P-51 |
| | | (3)He-111 dam(grd) | Weiden A/F | P-51 |

0-0-0 air
1-3 ground

**Kilgo, Lee E., Capt.**
486th Ftr Sqn/352nd Ftr Grp

| Sqn | Date | Claims | Location | A/C |
|---|---|---|---|---|
| 486th | March 2, 1945 | (.5)FW-190 dest(air)[*] | Prague | P-51 |

0.5-0-0 air
0-0 ground

[*] - shared with Lt. E.L. Mundell of the 486th Ftr Sqn

**King, Ben H., Maj.**
436th Ftr Sqn/479th Ftr Grp
368th Ftr Sqn/359th Ftr Grp
Earlier flew in the PTO with the 347th Ftr Grp and claimed 3 kills; (2)Zeros on July 17, 1943, and a Zero on November 1, 1943.

| Sqn | Date | Claims | Location | A/C |
|---|---|---|---|---|
| 368th | September 11, 1944 | (2)FW-190 dest(air) | Eisleben | P-51 |
| | | Me-109 dest(air) | Eisleben | P-51 |
| | September 12 | Me-109 dest(air) | Gransee | P-51 |

4-0-0 air
0-0 ground

**King, David E., Lt.**
435th Ftr Sqn/479th Ftr Grp

| Sqn | Date | Claims | Location | A/C |
|---|---|---|---|---|
| 435th | February 9, 1945 | Me-109 dest(air) | SE Magdeburg | P-51 |

1-0-0 air
0-0 ground

**King, Herman E., Capt.**
370th Ftr Sqn/359th Ftr Grp
62nd Ftr Sqn/ 56th Ftr Grp

| Sqn | Date | Claims | Location | A/C |
|---|---|---|---|---|
| 62nd | May 12, 1944 | Me-109 dest(air) | Frankfurt | P-47 |
| | July 5 | FW-190 dam(air) | N/Evreux | P-47 |
| | September 5 | Me-110 dest(grd) | Merzhausen | P-47 |
| | | He-111 dest(grd) | Merzhausen | P-47 |
| | | Ju-88 dest(grd) | Merzhausen | P-47 |

1-0-1 air
3-0 ground

**King, Maynard R., Lt.**
343rd Ftr Sqn/55th Ftr Grp

| Sqn | Date | Claims | Location | A/C |
|---|---|---|---|---|
| 343rd | September 5, 1944 | Ju-87 dest(grd) | Goppingen | P-51 |
| | | Me-110 dam(grd) | Goppingen | P-51 |

0-0-0 air
1-1 ground

**King, Myles A., Lt.**
357th Ftr Sqn/355th Ftr Grp

| Sqn | Date | Claims | Location | A/C |
|---|---|---|---|---|
| 357th | April 24, 1944 | Me-109 dam(air) | NW Munich | P-51 |
| | May 21 | (2)Do-217 dest(grd) | SE Schwerin | P-51 |
| | | Do-217 dam(grd) | SE Schwerin | P-51 |

0-0-1 air
2-1 ground

**Kinkade, Orville A., Capt.**
351st Ftr Sqn/353rd Ftr Grp

| Sqn | Date | Claims | Location | A/C |
|---|---|---|---|---|
| 351st | September 27, 1943 | Me-109 dest(air) | SW Emden | P-47 |
| | | Me-109 dam(air) | SW Emden | P-47 |
| | October 8 | FW-190 dam(air) | SW Emden | P-47 |
| | October 14 | Me-109 dest(air) | Turnhout | P-47 |
| | November 5 | Me-109 dest(air) | W/Mors | P-47 |

3-0-2 air
0-0 ground

**Kinnaird, Eugene W., Lt.**
375th Ftr Sqn/361st Ftr Grp

| Sqn | Date | Claims | Location | A/C |
|---|---|---|---|---|
| 375th | March 8, 1944 | (.5)FW-190 dest(air)[*] | W/Dummer Lake | P-47 |
| | March 29 | (2)FW-190 dam(grd) | Dummer Lake | P-47 |
| | April 1 | Ju-88 dest(grd) | Gutersloh | P-47 |

0.5-0-0 air
1-2 ground

[*] - shared with LtCol. J.J. Kruzel of HdQts, 361st Ftr Grp

**Kinnard, Claiborne H., Jr., Col.**
360th Ftr Sqn/356th Ftr Grp
354th Ftr Sqn/355th Ftr Grp
HdQts/355th Ftr Grp
HdQts/ 4th Ftr Grp

| Sqn | Date | Claims | Location | A/C |
|---|---|---|---|---|
| 354th | March 29, 1944 | FW-190 dest(air) | SW Brunswick | P-51 |
| | April 5 | W-34 dest(air) | Landsberg | P-51 |
| | | (2)Do-217 dest(grd) | Landsberg | P-51 |
| | | Me-110 dest(grd) | Landsberg | P-51 |
| | | (2)Do-217 dam(grd) | Landsberg | P-51 |
| | April 10 | Ju-88 dest(grd) | Bourges | P-51 |
| | | u/i a/c dam(grd) | Bourges | P-51 |
| | April 13 | (3)Ju-88 dest(grd) | Oberpfaffenhofen | P-51 |
| | | Do-217 dest(grd) | Oberpfaffenhofen | P-51 |
| | | Do-217 dam(grd) | Oberpfaffenhofen | P-51 |
| | June 24 | (3)Me-109 dest(grd) | Seiches | P-51 |
| HdQts | July 5 | (.5)Ju-88 dest(grd)[*] | Chateauroux | P-51 |
| (355th) | July 7 | (2)Me-410 dest(air) | Lingen | P-51 |
| | | Me-109 dest(air) | Lingen | P-51 |
| HdQts | September 11 | Me-109 dest(air) | Halle | P-51 |
| (4th) | | Me-410 dest(grd) | Halle | P-51 |
| | September 13 | (2)Hs-123 dest(grd) | Gelcheim | P-51 |
| HdQts | April 13, 1945 | (2.5)He-111 dest(grd)[**] | Schleswig | P-51 |
| (355th) | April 20 | (2)Me-109 dest(air) | Prague/Letnany | P-51 |
| | | Me-109 dam(air) | Prague/Letnany | P-51 |

8-0-1 air
17-4 ground

[*] - shared with Lt. R.E. Hulderman of the 354th Ftr Sqn
[**] - shared with Lt. V.R. Gore of the 358th Ftr Sqn, 355th Ftr Grp

**Kinsolving, James E., Lt.**
82nd Ftr Sqn/78th Ftr Grp

| Sqn | Date | Claims | Location | A/C |
|---|---|---|---|---|
| 82nd | July 19, 1944 | Ju-52 dest(grd) | Stuttgart | P-47 |
| | | (.5)u/i a/c dest(grd)[*] | Stuttgart | P-47 |

0-0-0 air
1.5-0 ground

[*] - shared with Maj. N.D. Munson of the 82nd Ftr Sqn

**Kirby, Clarence B., Lt.**
384th Ftr Sqn/364th Ftr Grp

| Sqn | Date | Claims | Location | A/C |
|---|---|---|---|---|
| 384th | February 22, 1945 | (.5)Me-262 prob(air)[*] | Wittstock | P-51 |
| | | Me-262 dam(air) | Wittstock | P-51 |

0-0.5-1 air
0-0 ground

[*] - shared with Capt. R.W. Stevens of the 384th Ftr Sqn

**Kirby, Henry H., Jr., Maj.**
357th Ftr Sqn/355th Ftr Grp
HdQts/355th Ftr Grp

| Sqn | Date | Claims | Location | A/C |
|---|---|---|---|---|
| 357th | March 16, 1944 | Me-109 dam(air) | W/Augsburg | P-51 |
| | April 8 | Do-217 dest(grd) | Gifhorn | P-51 |
| | | Ju-88 dest(grd) | Gifhorn | P-51 |
| HdQts | September 18 | Me-109 dest(air) | NW Warsaw | P-51 |
| | March 1, 1945 | Me-262 dam(air) | Donauworth | P-51 |
| | March 30 | Me-109 dest(grd) | Lowenstadt | P-51 |
| | | FW-190 dest(grd) | Lowenstadt | P-51 |
| | | (.5)He-111 dam(grd)[*] | Lowenstadt | P-51 |
| | April 10 | Ju-88 dest(grd) | Rechlin/Larz | P-51 |
| | | (3)Ju-88 dam(grd) | Rechlin/Larz | P-51 |

1-0-2 air
5-3.5 ground

[*] - shared with Lt. H.I. Knight of the 357th Ftr Sqn

**Kirk, John A., III, Lt.**
83rd Ftr Sqn/78th Ftr Grp

| *Sqn* | *Date* | *Claims* | *Location* | *A/C* |
|---|---|---|---|---|
| 83rd | December 19, 1944 | Me-109 dest(air) | S/Coblenz | P-47 |
| | | FW-190 dest(air) | S/Coblenz | P-47 |
| | March 19, 1945 | Me-109 dest(air) | Osnabruck | P-51 |
| | March 21 | Me-262 dest(air) | Meiningen | P-51 |
| | April 10 | He-111 dest(grd) | Werder A/F | P-51 |
| | | Bu-133 dest(grd) | Werder A/F | P-51 |
| | April 16 | FW-190 dest(grd) | W/Prague | P-51 |
| | | Ju-87 dest(grd) | W/Prague | P-51 |
| | | Ju-88 dest(grd) | W/Prague | P-51 |
| | | u/i a/c dest(grd) | W/Prague | P-51 |
| | | (3)Ju-87 dam(grd) | W/Prague | P-51 |

4-0-0 air
6-3 ground

**Kirk, Robert J., Lt.**
357th Ftr Sqn/355th Ftr Grp

| *Sqn* | *Date* | *Claims* | *Location* | *A/C* |
|---|---|---|---|---|
| 357th | April 16, 1945 | Me-109 dest(grd) | SE Germany | P-51 |
| | | Me-109 dam(grd) | SE Germany | P-51 |

0-0-0 air
1-1 ground

**Kirla, John A., Capt.**
362nd Ftr Sqn/357th Ftr Grp

| *Sqn* | *Date* | *Claims* | *Location* | *A/C* |
|---|---|---|---|---|
| 362nd | September 13, 1944 | (1.5)Me-109 dest(air)[*] | S/Nordhausen | P-51 |
| | September 19 | Me-109 dest(air) | Ijsselstein | P-51 |
| | November 18 | (.5)He-111 dest(grd)[**] | Mengen A/F | P-51 |
| | December 5 | Me-109 dest(air) | Berlin | P-51 |
| | | FW-190 dest(air) | Berlin | P-51 |
| | December 24 | (3)FW-190 dest(air) | Fulda | P-51 |
| | January 14, 1945 | (2)Me-109 dest(air) | NW Berlin | P-51 |
| | | (2)FW-190 dest(air) | NW Berlin | P-51 |

11.5-0-0 air
0.5-0 ground

[*] - shared with F/O O.D. Jenkins of the 362nd Ftr Sqn
[**] - shared with Lt. W.T. Gilbert of the 362nd Ftr Sqn

**Kissel, William F., Capt.**
383rd Ftr Sqn/364th Ftr Grp

| *Sqn* | *Date* | *Claims* | *Location* | *A/C* |
|---|---|---|---|---|
| 383rd | April 13, 1945 | (4)Ju-52 dest(grd) | Flensburg | P-51 |
| | | (2)Me-109 dam(grd) | Flensburg | P-51 |
| | | Me-110 dam(grd) | Flensburg | P-51 |
| | | Ju-52 dam(grd) | Flensburg | P-51 |
| | April 17 | Me-262 dest(air) | Falkenst | P-51 |

1-0-0 air
4-4 ground

**Kitley, Edward T., Lt.**
83rd Ftr Sqn/78th Ftr Grp

| *Sqn* | *Date* | *Claims* | *Location* | *A/C* |
|---|---|---|---|---|
| 83rd | April 30, 1944 | (2)FW-190 dam(air) | Dreux | P-47 |
| | June 17 | FW-190 dest(air) | S/Laigle | P-47 |

1-0-2 air
0-0 ground

**Klaasen, Peter W., Lt.**
83rd Ftr Sqn/78th Ftr Grp

| *Sqn* | *Date* | *Claims* | *Location* | *A/C* |
|---|---|---|---|---|
| 83rd | March 19, 1945 | Me-109 dest(air) | Osnabruck | P-51 |
| | | Me-109 dam(air) | Osnabruck | P-51 |

1-0-1 air
0-0 ground

**Klank, Walter C., Jr., Lt.**
38th Ftr Sqn/55th Ftr Grp
3rd Scouting Force

| *Sqn* | *Date* | *Claims* | *Location* | *A/C* |
|---|---|---|---|---|
| 3rd | December 24, 1944 | Me-109 dest(air) | Frankfurt-Darmstadt | P-51 |

1-0-0 air
0-0 ground

**Klatt, Quintus, Lt.**
79th Ftr Sqn/20th Ftr Grp

| *Sqn* | *Date* | *Claims* | *Location* | *A/C* |
|---|---|---|---|---|
| 79th | August 9, 1944 | (2.5)FW-190 dest(air)[*] | SW Ulm | P-51 |

2.5-0-0 air
0-0 ground

[*] - shared with Lt. J.N. Reichard of the 79th Ftr Sqn

**Klaver, Ralph R., Lt.**
369th Ftr Sqn/359th Ftr Grp

| *Sqn* | *Date* | *Claims* | *Location* | *A/C* |
|---|---|---|---|---|
| 369th | April 10, 1945 | Me-262 dam(air) | Wittenberge | P-51 |

0-0-1 air
0-0 ground

**Klees, Paul H., Lt.**
375th Ftr Sqn/361st Ftr Grp

| *Sqn* | *Date* | *Claims* | *Location* | *A/C* |
|---|---|---|---|---|
| 375th | November 26, 1944 | FW-190 dest(air) | Celle-Gifhorn | P-51 |
| | | Me-109 dest(air) | Celle-Gifhorn | P-51 |

2-0-0 air
0-0 ground

**Kleineman, Bernard R., Lt.**
436th Ftr Sqn/479th Ftr Grp

| *Sqn* | *Date* | *Claims* | *Location* | *A/C* |
|---|---|---|---|---|
| 436th | April 13, 1945 | FW-190 dest(grd) | Salzwedel | P-51 |
| | | Me-110 dest(grd) | Salzwedel | P-51 |

0-0-0 air
2-0 ground

**Klem, Thomas J., Lt.**
369th Ftr Sqn/359th Ftr Grp

| *Sqn* | *Date* | *Claims* | *Location* | *A/C* |
|---|---|---|---|---|
| 369th | September 11, 1944 | Me-109 dam(air) | N/Leipzig | P-51 |

0-0-1 air
0-0 ground

**Klibbe, Frank W., Lt.**
61st Ftr Sqn/56th Ftr Grp

| *Sqn* | *Date* | *Claims* | *Location* | *A/C* |
|---|---|---|---|---|
| 61st | November 26, 1943 | Me-109 dest(air) | SE Oldenburg | P-47 |
| | January 30, 1944 | Me-109 dest(air) | Lingen | P-47 |
| | February 21 | Me-109 dest(air) | Zuider Zee | P-47 |
| | March 8 | FW-190 dest(air) | Steinhuder Lake | P-47 |
| | March 15 | FW-190 dest(air) | S/Barenburg | P-47 |
| | May 8 | Me-109 dest(air) | W/Celle | P-47 |
| | | FW-190 dest(grd) | W/Celle | P-47 |

7-0-0 air
0-0 ground

**Kline, Robert B., Lt.**
434th Ftr Sqn/479th Ftr Grp

| *Sqn* | *Date* | *Claims* | *Location* | *A/C* |
|---|---|---|---|---|
| 434th | September 28, 1944 | Me-109 dam(air) | W/Halberstadt | P-51 |
| | February 20, 1945 | (2)Do-217 dest(grd) | Windleschenlaibach | P-51 |
| | | (.5)He-111 dest(grd)[*] | Windleschenlaibach | P-51 |
| | | (.5)FW-190 dam(grd)[*] | Windleschenlaibach | P-51 |
| | April 13 | (.5)u/i a/c dest(grd)[**] | Ratzburger Lake | P-51 |

| Sqn | Date | Claims | Location | A/C |
|---|---|---|---|---|
| | | u/i a/c dam(grd) | Ratzburger Lake | P-51 |

0-0-1 air
3-1.5 ground

[*] - both shared with Lt. J.T. Golden of the 434th Ftr Sqn
[**] - shared with Lt. F.M. Taylor of the 434th Ftr Sqn

**Klink, John E., Lt.**
55th Ftr Sqn/20th Ftr Grp

| *Sqn* | *Date* | *Claims* | *Location* | *A/C* |
|---|---|---|---|---|
| 55th | August 6, 1944 | Do-217 dest(air) | Strausburg A/F | P-51 |

1-0-0 air
0-0 ground

**Knafelz, Albert P., Lt.**
62nd Ftr Sqn/56th Ftr Grp

| *Sqn* | *Date* | *Claims* | *Location* | *A/C* |
|---|---|---|---|---|
| 62nd | July 4, 1944 | Me-109 dest(air) | Conches | P-47 |
| | | Me-109 dam(air) | Conches | P-47 |

1-0-1 air
0-0 ground

**Knapp, Lester H., Lt.**
360th Ftr Sqn/356th Ftr Grp

| *Sqn* | *Date* | *Claims* | *Location* | *A/C* |
|---|---|---|---|---|
| 360th | April 23, 1944 | He-111 dest(grd) | Hagenau | P-47 |
| | | (1.5)Go-242 dam(grd)[*] | Hagenau | P-47 |

0-0-0 air
1-1.5 ground

[*] - shared with Capt. L.F. Kress of the 360th Ftr Sqn

**Knapp, Robert H., Lt.**
83rd Ftr Sqn/78th Ftr Grp

| *Sqn* | *Date* | *Claims* | *Location* | *A/C* |
|---|---|---|---|---|
| 83rd | January 24, 1944 | FW-190 dest(air) | Liege | P-47 |

1-0-0 air
0-0 ground

**Knight, George, Lt.**
505th Ftr Sqn/339th Ftr Grp

| *Sqn* | *Date* | *Claims* | *Location* | *A/C* |
|---|---|---|---|---|
| 505th | July 19, 1944 | (.5)Ju-188 dest(grd)[*] | SW Augsburg | P-51 |

0-0-0 air
0.5-0 ground

[*] - shared with Lt. W.H. Krauss of the 505th Ftr Sqn

**Knight, Harold I., Lt.**
357th Ftr Sqn/355th Ftr Grp

| *Sqn* | *Date* | *Claims* | *Location* | *A/C* |
|---|---|---|---|---|
| 357th | March 30, 1945 | He-111 dest(grd) | Lowenstadt | P-51 |
| | | (.5)He-111 dam(grd)[*] | Lowenstadt | P-51 |
| | April 16 | (2)FW-190 dest(grd) | SE Germany | P-51 |
| | | He-177 dam(grd) | SE Germany | P-51 |
| | | u/i a/c dam(grd) | SE Germany | P-51 |

0-0-0 air
3-2.5 ground

[*] - shared with Maj. H.H. Kirby of HdQts, 355th Ftr Grp

**Knoble, Joseph L., Capt.**
352nd Ftr Sqn/353rd Ftr Grp

| *Sqn* | *Date* | *Claims* | *Location* | *A/C* |
|---|---|---|---|---|
| 352nd | March 8, 1944 | FW-190 dest(air) | N/Dummer Lake | P-47 |
| | | FW-190 dam(air) | N/Dummer Lake | P-47 |
| | November 27 | Me-109 dest(air) | Magdeburg | P-51 |
| | December 5 | FW-190 dest(air) | NE Berlin | P-51 |

3-0-1 air
0-0 ground

**Knott, Clarence W., Capt.**
503rd Ftr Sqn/339th Ftr Grp

| *Sqn* | *Date* | *Claims* | *Location* | *A/C* |
|---|---|---|---|---|
| 503rd | May 24, 1944 | (.5)Me-109 dest(air)[*] | SW Soissons | P-51 |
| | | (.5)Me-109 dest(grd)[*] | SW Soissons | P-51 |
| | June 29 | FW-190 dest(air) | Eisleben | P-51 |

1.5-0-0 air
0.5-0 ground

[*] - both shared with Lt. C.E. Shake of the 503rd Ftr Sqn

**Knowling, William P., Lt.**
350th Ftr Sqn/353rd Ftr Grp

| *Sqn* | *Date* | *Claims* | *Location* | *A/C* |
|---|---|---|---|---|
| 350th | August 7, 1944 | Me-410 dest(grd) | SE Amiens | P-47 |
| | September 23 | Me-109 prob(air) | SE Arnheim | P-47 |

0-1-0 air
1-0 ground

**Knox, Baird M., Lt.**
62nd Ftr Sqn/56th Ftr Grp

| *Sqn* | *Date* | *Claims* | *Location* | *A/C* |
|---|---|---|---|---|
| 62nd | July 4, 1944 | Me-109 dest(air) | Conches | P-47 |
| | | Me-109 dam(air) | Conches | P-47 |
| | August 28 | He-111 dam(grd) | Jerny | P-47 |

1-0-1 air
0-1 ground

**Knupp, Daniel F., Lt.**
375th Ftr Sqn/361st Ftr Grp

| *Sqn* | *Date* | *Claims* | *Location* | *A/C* |
|---|---|---|---|---|
| 375th | September 12, 1944 | Me-109 dest(air) | NE Magdeburg | P-51 |

1-0-0 air
0-0 ground

**Knutty, Harold P., Lt.**
358th Ftr Sqn/355th Ftr Grp

| *Sqn* | *Date* | *Claims* | *Location* | *A/C* |
|---|---|---|---|---|
| 358th | April 9, 1945 | (.5)Me-110 dest(grd)[*] | Heilfingen | P-51 |
| | April 13 | Me-109 dest(grd) | Schleswig | P-51 |
| | | (.5)He-111 dest(grd)[**] | Schleswig | P-51 |
| | April 20 | (.5)Me-109 dest(air)[@] | Kbely | P-51 |

0.5-0-0 air
2-0 ground

[*] - shared with Lt. C.C. Patrinely of the 358th Ftr Sqn
[**] - shared with Lt. R.J. Nicodemus of the 358th Ftr Sqn
[@] - shared with Lt. K.L. Snook of the 358th Ftr Sqn

**Koch, Frank G., Lt.**
62nd Ftr Sqn/56th Ftr Grp

| *Sqn* | *Date* | *Claims* | *Location* | *A/C* |
|---|---|---|---|---|
| 62nd | April 10, 1945 | (2)u/i a/c dest(grd) | Neuruppin | P-51 |
| | | (4)u/i a/c dam(grd) | Neuruppin | P-51 |

0-0-0 air
2-4 ground

**Kocher, Donald C., Lt.**
364th Ftr Sqn/357th Ftr Grp

| *Sqn* | *Date* | *Claims* | *Location* | *A/C* |
|---|---|---|---|---|
| 364th | April 19, 1945 | Me-262 dam(air) | Dresden | P-51 |

0-0-1 air
0-0 ground

**Koczak, Alex S., Lt.**
360th Ftr Sqn/356th Ftr Grp

| *Sqn* | *Date* | *Claims* | *Location* | *A/C* |
|---|---|---|---|---|
| 360th | February 13, 1944 | FW-190 dest(air) | Dieppe | P-47 |

1-0-0 air
0-0 ground

**Koenig, Albert M., Lt.**
38th Ftr Sqn/55th Ftr Grp

| *Sqn* | *Date* | *Claims* | *Location* | *A/C* |
|---|---|---|---|---|
| 38th | September 5, 1944 | u/i a/c dam(grd) | Stuttgart/Boblingen | P-51 |

0-0-0 air
0-1 ground

**Koerber, James H., Lt.**
435th Ftr Sqn/479th Ftr Grp

| *Sqn* | *Date* | *Claims* | *Location* | *A/C* |
|---|---|---|---|---|
| 435th | April 18, 1945 | u/i a/c dest(grd) | Mettenheim | P-51 |

0-0-0 air
1-0 ground

**Kohler, Donald F., Lt.**
351st Ftr Sqn/353rd Ftr Grp

| *Sqn* | *Date* | *Claims* | *Location* | *A/C* |
|---|---|---|---|---|
| 351st | August 29, 1944 | u/i a/c dest(grd) | Chievres | P-47 |

0-0-0 air
1-0 ground

**Kolb, Herbert G., Capt.**
350th Ftr Sqn/353rd Ftr Grp

| *Sqn* | *Date* | *Claims* | *Location* | *A/C* |
|---|---|---|---|---|
| 350th | November 2, 1944 | FW-190 dam(air) | NW Merseburg | P-51 |
| | February 27, 1945 | (3)FW-190 dest(grd) | Rohrensee | P-51 |
| | | (1.5)Me-410 dest(grd)* | Rohrensee | P-51 |
| | | (.5)u/i a/c dest(grd)** | Rohrensee | P-51 |
| | | FW-190 dam(grd) | Rohrensee | P-51 |
| | April 16 | (5)FW-190 dest(grd) | Pocking | P-51 |
| | | (2)Me-109 dest(grd) | Pocking | P-51 |
| | | (1.5)Fi-156 dest(grd)@ | Pocking | P-51 |
| | | (.5)Fi-156 dest(grd)@ | Pocking | P-51 |
| | | (.5)Fi-156 dest(grd)@ | Pocking | P-51 |
| | | (2)Ju-87 dam(grd) | Pocking | P-51 |

0-0-1 air
14.5-3 ground

* - shared with Lt. W. Grizzle of the 350th Ftr Sqn
** - shared with Lt. H.H. Hakonen of the 350th Ftr Sqn
@ - all shared with Lt. B.D. McMahan of the 350th Ftr Sqn

**Kolbe, John E., Lt.**
335th Ftr Sqn/4th Ftr Grp

| *Sqn* | *Date* | *Claims* | *Location* | *A/C* |
|---|---|---|---|---|
| 335th | November 2, 1944 | Me-109 dest(air) | Leipzig | P-51 |
| | November 18 | Me-262 dest(grd) | Leipheim | P-51 |
| | November 21 | Me-109 dest(air) | NW Merseburg | P-51 |

2-0-0 air
1-0 ground

**Kolter, Mark H., Lt.**
334th Ftr Sqn/4th Ftr Grp

| *Sqn* | *Date* | *Claims* | *Location* | *A/C* |
|---|---|---|---|---|
| 334th | April 8, 1944 | (2)FW-190 dam(grd) | Celle | P-51 |
| | April 19 | Me-109 prob(air) | Eschwege-Kassel | P-51 |
| | May 28 | Me-109 dest(air) | Magdeburg | P-51 |
| | May 29 | Ar-196 dest(grd) | Dievenow | P-51 |
| | | (.5)Do-24 dam(grd)* | Dievenow | P-51 |

1-1-0 air
1-2.5 ground

* - shared with Capt. T.E. Joyce of the 334th Ftr Sqn

**Konantz, Walter J., Lt.**
338th Ftr Sqn/55th Ftr Grp

| *Sqn* | *Date* | *Claims* | *Location* | *A/C* |
|---|---|---|---|---|
| 338th | September 11, 1944 | Me-109 dest(air) | S/Meiningen | P-51 |
| | January 6, 1945 | Ju-88 dest(grd) | Giebelstadt | P-51 |
| | January 13 | Me-262 dest(air) | Giebelstadt A/F | P-51 |
| | January 29 | Me-109 dest(air) | NE Oldenburg | P-51 |

3-0-0 air
1-o ground

**Koontz, Glenn W., Capt.**
84th Ftr Sqn/78th Ftr Grp

| *Sqn* | *Date* | *Claims* | *Location* | *A/C* |
|---|---|---|---|---|
| 84th | July 30, 1943 | FW-190 dest(air) | Winterswijk | P-47 |
| | December 11 | Me-109 dest(air) | SW Groningen | P-47 |

2-0-0 air
0-0 ground

**Koraleski, Walter J., Capt.**
354th Ftr Sqn/355th Ftr Grp

| *Sqn* | *Date* | *Claims* | *Location* | *A/C* |
|---|---|---|---|---|
| 354th | March 6, 1944 | (2.33)Me-109 dest(air)* | Dummer Lake | P-47 |
| | March 16 | Me-109 dest(air) | Ulm | P-51 |
| | March 29 | FW-190 dest(air) | Brunswick | P-51 |
| | April 5 | (.5)Me-109 dest(air)** | Landsberg | P-51 |
| | | (.5)FW-44 dest(air)** | Landsberg | P-51 |
| | | (.2)Do-217 dest(air)@ | Landsberg | P-51 |
| | | Me-110 dam(grd) | Landsberg | P-51 |
| | | Do-217 dam(grd) | Landsberg | P-51 |

5.53-0-0 air
0-2 ground

* - shared with Lt. N.J. Fortier and F/O C.R. Barger of the 354th Ftr Sqn
** - both shared with Lt. R.E. Woody of the 354th Ftr Sqn
@ - shared with Capt. C.G. Johnston, Lt. H.W. Brown, Lt. J.E. Duffy, and Lt. B.C. Williamson of the 354th Ftr Sqn

**Korecky, James R., Lt.**
384th Ftr Sqn/364th Ftr Grp

| *Sqn* | *Date* | *Claims* | *Location* | *A/C* |
|---|---|---|---|---|
| 384th | June 25, 1944 | Me-109 dest(air) | E/Blois | P-38 |
| | | Me-109 dam(air) | E/Blois | P-38 |

1-0-1 air
0-0 ground

**Korhorn, Evert, Capt.**
361st Ftr Sqn/356th Ftr Grp

| *Sqn* | *Date* | *Claims* | *Location* | *A/C* |
|---|---|---|---|---|
| 361st | June 15, 1944 | Me-109 dam(air) | SE Rouen | P-47 |

0-0-1 air
0-0 ground

**Korinek, George, Lt.**
338th Ftr Sqn/55th Ftr Grp

| *Sqn* | *Date* | *Claims* | *Location* | *A/C* |
|---|---|---|---|---|
| 338th | January 31, 1944 | Me-109 dam(air) | N/Venlo | P-38 |
| | March 18 | Me-109 dest(air) | E/Frieburg | P-38 |

1-0-1 air
0-0 ground

**Korsmeyer, Willard J., Lt.**
83rd Ftr Sqn/78th Ftr Grp

| *Sqn* | *Date* | *Claims* | *Location* | *A/C* |
|---|---|---|---|---|
| 83rd | July 31, 1944 | u/i a/c dest(grd) | Neustadt A/F | P-47 |

0-0-0 air
1-0 ground

**Kortendick, Edward W., Lt.**
383rd Ftr Sqn/364th Ftr Grp

| Sqn | Date | Claims | Location | A/C |
|---|---|---|---|---|
| 383rd | February 22, 1945 | FW-190 dest(air) | S/Quackenbruck | P-51 |
| | | FW-190 dam(air) | S/Quackenbruck | P-51 |
| | April 13 | Me-109 dest(grd) | Flensburg | P-51 |
| | | Fi-156 dest(grd) | Flensburg | P-51 |
| | | (2)FW-190 dam(grd) | Flensburg | P-51 |
| | | Ju-52 dam(grd) | Flensburg | P-51 |

1-0-1 air
2-3 ground

**Kovach, Stephen C., Lt.**
375th Ftr Sqn/361st Ftr Grp

| Sqn | Date | Claims | Location | A/C |
|---|---|---|---|---|
| 375th | April 17, 1945 | (2)u/i a/c dam(grd) | Pilzen | P-51 |
| | | Ju-52 dam(grd) | Pilzen | P-51 |

0-0-0 air
0-3 ground

**Kovacs, Elmer A., Lt.**
361st Ftr Sqn/356th Ftr Grp

| Sqn | Date | Claims | Location | A/C |
|---|---|---|---|---|
| 361st | August 18, 1944 | FW-190 dest(air) | Beauvais | P-47 |

1-0-0 air
0-0 ground

**Kozacka, Arthur G., Lt.**
354th Ftr Sqn/355th Ftr Grp

| Sqn | Date | Claims | Location | A/C |
|---|---|---|---|---|
| 354th | April 13, 1945 | FW-190 dest(grd) | Husum | P-51 |
| | | (2)u/i a/c dam(grd) | Husum | P-51 |

0-0-0 air
1-2 ground

**Kozicki, Walter J., Capt.**
376th Ftr Sqn/361st Ftr Grp

| Sqn | Date | Claims | Location | A/C |
|---|---|---|---|---|
| 376th | May 29, 1944 | FW-190 dam(air) | Schwerin | P-51 |
| | November 26 | FW-190 prob(air) | S/Ulzen | P-51 |

0-1-1 air
0-0 ground

**Kozloski, Frank T., Lt.**
384th Ftr Sqn/364th Ftr Grp

| Sqn | Date | Claims | Location | A/C |
|---|---|---|---|---|
| 384th | August 9, 1944 | (.5)FW-190 dest(air)* | Kaufburen | P-51 |
| | | (.5)Trianer dest(air)* | Kaufburen | P-51 |
| | | FW-190 dam(grd) | Schongen | P-51 |

1-0-0 air
0-1 ground

* - both shared with Lt. J.J. Gawienowski of the 384th Ftr Sqn

**Kraft, Benedict E., Lt.**
351st Ftr Sqn/353rd Ftr Grp

| Sqn | Date | Claims | Location | A/C |
|---|---|---|---|---|
| 351st | October 14, 1943 | FW-190 dam(air) | Turnhout | P-47 |

0-0-1 air
0-0 ground

**Krambo, Victor P., Lt.**
343rd Ftr Sqn/55th Ftr Grp

| Sqn | Date | Claims | Location | A/C |
|---|---|---|---|---|
| 343rd | February 3, 1945 | He-111 dam(grd) | Stade A/F | P-51 |

0-0-0 air
0-1 ground

**Kramer, Harold W., Lt.**
84th Ftr Sqn/78th Ftr Grp

| Sqn | Date | Claims | Location | A/C |
|---|---|---|---|---|
| 84th | May 25, 1944 | FW-190 dam(grd) | Paris | P-47 |

0-0-0 air
0-1 ground

**Krauss, Richard E., Lt.**
503rd Ftr Sqn/339th Ftr Grp

| Sqn | Date | Claims | Location | A/C |
|---|---|---|---|---|
| 503rd | April 7, 1945 | Me-109 dest(air) | Celle | P-51 |

1-0-0 air
0-0 ground

**Krauss, William H., Capt.**
505th Ftr Sqn/339th Ftr Grp

| Sqn | Date | Claims | Location | A/C |
|---|---|---|---|---|
| 505th | July 19, 1944 | (.5)Ju-188 dest(grd)* | SW Augsburg | P-51 |
| | July 29 | (.5)Me-109 dest(air)** | NW Naumberg | P-51 |
| | September 10 | Ju-88 dam(grd) | Weizenburg | P-51 |
| | September 11 | (2)Me-410 dest(grd) | Munich | P-51 |
| | | Me-110 dest(grd) | Munich | P-51 |
| | | Ju-88 dest(grd) | Munich | P-51 |
| | | (3)Me-410 dam(grd) | Munich | P-51 |

0.5-0-0 air
4.5-4 ground

* - shared with Lt. G. Knight of the 505th Ftr Sqn
** - shared with Lt. J.R. Starnes of the 505th Ftr Sqn

**Kreft, Willard L., Lt.**
38th Ftr Sqn/55th Ftr Grp

| Sqn | Date | Claims | Location | A/C |
|---|---|---|---|---|
| 38th | November 3, 1943 | (.5)FW-190 dest(air)* | Westerholt-Wittmond | P-38 |

0.5-0-0 air
0-0 ground

* - shared with Maj. M. Joel of the 38th Ftr Sqn

**Kreger, Charles D., Lt.**
436th Ftr Sqn/479th Ftr Grp

| Sqn | Date | Claims | Location | A/C |
|---|---|---|---|---|
| 436th | April 17, 1945 | FW-190 dam(grd) | Puchhoff | P-51 |

0-0-0 air
0-1 ground

**Kress, Lester F., Capt.**
360th Ftr Sqn/356th Ftr Grp

| Sqn | Date | Claims | Location | A/C |
|---|---|---|---|---|
| 360th | January 24, 1944 | Me-109 dest(air) | NE Lille | P-47 |
| | February 10 | (.5)FW-190 dest(air)* | Ruhlertwist | P-47 |
| | April 23 | (1.5)Go-242 dam(grd)** | Hagenau | P-47 |

1.5-0-0 air
0-1.5 ground

* - shared with F/O C.W. Dunn of the 360th Ftr Sqn
** - shared with Lt. L.H. Knapp of the 360th Ftr Sqn

**Kritz, Stephen J., Lt.**
352nd Ftr Sqn/353rd Ftr Grp

| Sqn | Date | Claims | Location | A/C |
|---|---|---|---|---|
| 352nd | November 18, 1944 | FW-190 dam(grd) | Lechfeld | P-51 |

0-0-0 air
0-1 ground

**Krowiak, Casimir F., Lt.**
359th Ftr Sqn/356th Ftr Grp

| Sqn | Date | Claims | Location | A/C |
|---|---|---|---|---|
| 359th | April 23, 1944 | He-111 dam(grd) | Hagenau | P-47 |
| | | (.5)Go-242 dam(grd)* | Hagenau | P-47 |

0-0-0 air
0-1.5 ground

* - shared with Lt. W.L. Farmer of the 359th Ftr Sqn

**Krueger, Donald F., Lt.**
504th Ftr Sqn/339th Ftr Grp

| Sqn | Date | Claims | Location | A/C |
|---|---|---|---|---|
| 504th | April 10, 1945 | (2)Me-410 dam(grd) | N/Neuruppin | P-51 |
| | April 16 | FW-190 dest(grd) | Klatovy | P-51 |
| | | Me-109 dest(grd) | Klatovy | P-51 |
| | | FW-190 dam(grd) | Klatovy | P-51 |

0-0-0 air
2-3 ground

**Kruger, Charles H., Capt.**
369th Ftr Sqn/359th Ftr Grp

| Sqn | Date | Claims | Location | A/C |
|---|---|---|---|---|
| 369th | March 15, 1944 | Me-109 dest(air) | SW Hanover | P-47 |
| | | Me-109 prob(air) | SW Hanover | P-47 |
| | May 19 | Me-109 dest(air) | Rathenow | P-51 |

2-1-0 air
0-0 ground

**Kruzel, Joseph J., LtCol.**
HdQts/361st Ftr Grp
Earlier flew in the PTO with the 17th Pursuit Sqn and 49th Ftr Grp claiming 3 kills; a Nate on February 17, 1942, and single Zeros on February 19 and 20, 1942.

| Sqn | Date | Claims | Location | A/C |
|---|---|---|---|---|
| HdQts | February 22, 1944 | FW-190 dam(air) | SW Nijmegen | P-47 |
| | March 8 | (.5)FW-190 dest(air)* | W/Dummer Lake | P-47 |
| | April 29 | Me-109 dest(air) | Steinhuder Lake | P-47 |
| | June 13 | Me-109 dest(air) | St. Brieuc | P-51 |
| | June 25 | FW-190 dest(air) | N/Lisieux | P-51 |

3.5-0-1 air
0-0 ground

* - shared with Lt. E.W. Kinnaird of the 375th Ftr Sqn, 361st Ftr Grp

**Kubetin, William T., Lt.**
357th Ftr Sqn/355th Ftr Grp

| Sqn | Date | Claims | Location | A/C |
|---|---|---|---|---|
| 357th | April 16, 1945 | Me-109 dest(grd) | SE Germany | P-51 |

0-0-0 air
1-0 ground

**Kucheman, Henry B., Jr., Maj.**
354th Ftr Sqn/355th Ftr Grp

| Sqn | Date | Claims | Location | A/C |
|---|---|---|---|---|
| 354th | April 24, 1944 | (3)Me-109 dest(air) | NW Munich | P-51 |
| | June 20 | Me-410 dest(air) | NW Stettin | P-51 |
| | | Me-410 dam(air) | NW Stettin | P-51 |
| | June 24 | (2)Me-109 dam(grd) | Seiches | P-51 |
| | July 8 | (2)Me-410 dest(grd) | SW Chalons | P-51 |
| | | Me-109 dam(grd) | SW Chalons | P-51 |

4-0-1 air
2-3 ground

**Kuehl, Richard I., Lt.**
83rd Ftr Sqn/78th Ftr Grp

| Sqn | Date | Claims | Location | A/C |
|---|---|---|---|---|
| 83rd | March 2, 1945 | Me-109 dest(air) | Burg A/F | P-51 |
| | | Me-109 dam(air) | Burg A/F | P-51 |
| | March 19 | (.5)Me-109 dest(air)* | Osnabruck | P-51 |
| | April 7 | Me-109 dest(air) | Dummer Lake | P-51 |
| | April 10 | Me-410 dest(grd) | Brandenburg-Briest | P-51 |
| | | u/i a/c dam(grd) | Brandenburg-Briest | P-51 |

2.5-0-1 air
1-1 ground

* - shared with Capt. F.E. Higginbotham of the 83rd Ftr Sqn

**Kuemmerle, Walter F., Lt.**
77th Ftr Sqn/20th Ftr Grp

| Sqn | Date | Claims | Location | A/C |
|---|---|---|---|---|
| 77th | April 8, 1944 | (.33)u/i a/c dest(grd)* | Salzwedel | P-38 |
| | April 30 | Me-410 dest(grd) | Bricy A/F | P-38 |

0-0-0 air
1.33-0 ground

* - shared with Capt. J.M. Morris and Lt. I.W. Fernandes of the 77th Ftr Sqn

**Kuhlman, Robert M., Lt.**
504th Ftr Sqn/339th Ftr Grp

| Sqn | Date | Claims | Location | A/C |
|---|---|---|---|---|
| 504th | March 20, 1945 | FW-200 dest(grd) | Grossenbrode | P-51 |
| | | Ju-52 dam(grd) | Grossenbrode | P-51 |

0-0-0 air
1-1 ground

**Kuhn, Philip G., Lt.**
63rd Ftr Sqn/56th Ftr Grp

| Sqn | Date | Claims | Location | A/C |
|---|---|---|---|---|
| 63rd | February 3, 1945 | FW-190 dest(air) | Friedersdorf A/F | P-47 |
| | April 13 | (2)Me-410 dest(grd) | Eggebeck A/F | P-47 |
| | | FW-190 dest(grd) | Eggebeck A/F | P-47 |
| | | u/i a/c dest(grd) | Eggebeck A/F | P-47 |
| | | u/i a/c dam(grd) | Eggebeck A/F | P-47 |

1-0-0 air
4-1 ground

**Kulik, Edward R., Capt.**
83rd Ftr Sqn/78th Ftr Grp

| Sqn | Date | Claims | Location | A/C |
|---|---|---|---|---|
| 83rd | April 16, 1945 | (4)FW-190 dest(grd) | N/Prague | P-51 |
| | | Me-109 dest(grd) | N/Prague | P-51 |
| | | Ju-87 dest(grd) | N/Prague | P-51 |
| | | u/i a/c dest(grd) | N/Prague | P-51 |
| | | FW-190 dam(grd) | N/Prague | P-51 |

0-0-0 air
7-1 ground

**Kunz, Leonard A., Lt.**
504th Ftr Sqn/339th Ftr Grp

| Sqn | Date | Claims | Location | A/C |
|---|---|---|---|---|
| 504th | April 7, 1945 | (.5)Me-109 dest(air)* | Celle | P-51 |
| | April 10 | (2)Me-410 dest(grd) | N/Neuruppin | P-51 |
| | | (3)Me-410 dam(grd) | N/Neuruppin | P-51 |
| | April 16 | (2)FW-190 dam(grd) | Klatovy | P-51 |

0.5-0-0 air
2-5 ground

* - shared with Lt. V.N. Barto of the 504th Ftr Sqn

**Kurtz, Robert G., Capt.**
354th Ftr Sqn/355th Ftr Grp

| Sqn | Date | Claims | Location | A/C |
|---|---|---|---|---|
| 354th | April 5, 1944 | Do-217 dest(grd) | Landsberg | P-51 |
| | | (2)Do-217 dam(grd) | Landsberg | P-51 |
| | April 8 | (.5)Me-109 dest(air)* | Sachau A/F | P-51 |
| | April 10 | Do-217 dest(grd) | Bourges | P-51 |
| | | FW-190 dest(grd) | Bourges | P-51 |
| | April 11 | Ju-88 dam(grd) | Madu Lake | P-51 |
| | April 20 | He-111 dest(grd) | Blois A/F | P-51 |
| | | Ju-52 dest(grd) | Blois A/F | P-51 |

0.5-0-0 air
5-3 ground

* - shared with Lt. H.W. Brown of the 354th Ftr Sqn

**Kuykendall, Charles E., Lt.**
83rd Ftr Sqn/78th Ftr Grp

| *Sqn* | *Date* | *Claims* | *Location* | *A/C* |
|---|---|---|---|---|
| 83rd | September 1, 1944 | Me-110 dest(air) | Gilze-Rijen | P-47 |
| | | Me-110 dam(air) | Gilze-Rijen | P-47 |

1-0-1 air
0-0 ground

**Kyle, Frank A., Lt.**
363rd Ftr Sqn/357th Ftr Grp

| *Sqn* | *Date* | *Claims* | *Location* | *A/C* |
|---|---|---|---|---|
| 363rd | April 19, 1945 | Me-262 dam(air) | Prague | P-51 |

0-0-1 air
0-0 ground

**Kyle, James A., Capt.**
63rd Ftr Sqn/56th Ftr Grp

| *Sqn* | *Date* | *Claims* | *Location* | *A/C* |
|---|---|---|---|---|
| 63rd | September 5, 1944 | Me-109 dest(air) | NE Coblenz | P-47 |
| | September 21 | FW-190 dam(air) | NE Arnheim | P-47 |
| | October 15 | (.5)Me-109 dest(grd)* | Rheine | P-47 |

1-0-1 air
0.5-0 ground

* - shared with Lt. T.W. Saling of the 63rd Ftr Sqn

**Kyle, Thompson R., Lt.**
486th Ftr Sqn/352nd Ftr Grp

| *Sqn* | *Date* | *Claims* | *Location* | *A/C* |
|---|---|---|---|---|
| 486th | September 12, 1944 | Me-109 dam(air) | NW Berlin | P-51 |

0-0-1 air
0-0 ground

**Kyler, Russell S., Lt.**
61st Ftr Sqn/56th Ftr Grp

| *Sqn* | *Date* | *Claims* | *Location* | *A/C* |
|---|---|---|---|---|
| 61st | September 21, 1944 | FW-190 dest(air) | Deventer | P-47 |
| | November 18 | FW-190 dest(air) | E/Hanau | P-47 |
| | January 14, 1945 | Me-109 dest(air) | E/Rheine | P-47 |
| | April 10 | Me-109 dest(grd) | Muritz Lake | P-47 |
| | | u/i a/c dest(grd) | Muritz Lake | P-47 |
| | April 13 | (4)Ju-88 dest(grd) | Eggebeck A/F | P-47 |
| | | Me-410 dest(grd) | Eggebeck A/F | P-47 |

3-0-0 air
7-0 ground

**Kysely, Arvy F., Lt.**
368th Ftr Sqn/359th Ftr Grp

| *Sqn* | *Date* | *Claims* | *Location* | *A/C* |
|---|---|---|---|---|
| 368th | September 11, 1944 | FW-190 dam(air) | Weimar | P-51 |

0-0-1 air
0-0 ground

**Lacazette, Mario, Lt.**
358th Ftr Sqn/355th Ftr Grp

| *Sqn* | *Date* | *Claims* | *Location* | *A/C* |
|---|---|---|---|---|
| 358th | April 13, 1945 | (.5)He-111 dest(grd)* | Schleswig | P-51 |

0-0-0 air
0.5-0 ground

* - shared with Lt. W.B. Lister of the 358th Ftr Sqn

**LaCroix, Lucius G., Capt.**
374th Ftr Sqn/361st Ftr Grp
Earlier flew in the PTO with the 49th Ftr Grp and claimed one kill, a Zero, on November 30, 1942.

| *Sqn* | *Date* | *Claims* | *Location* | *A/C* |
|---|---|---|---|---|
| 374th | November 21, 1944 | FW-190 dest(air) | Jena | P-51 |
| | November 26 | FW-190 dam(air) | Wittingen | P-51 |

1-0-1 air
0-0 ground

**Lacy, Andrew C., Lt.**
334th Ftr Sqn/4th Ftr Grp

| *Sqn* | *Date* | *Claims* | *Location* | *A/C* |
|---|---|---|---|---|
| 334th | December 2, 1944 | FW-190 dam(air) | Hottenback | P-51 |

0-0-1 air
0-0 ground

**Lacy, Robert E., LtCol.**
384th Ftr Sqn/364th Ftr Grp

| *Sqn* | *Date* | *Claims* | *Location* | *A/C* |
|---|---|---|---|---|
| 384th | March 8, 1944 | FW-190 dam(air) | NE Brunswick | P-38 |
| | April 15 | (.33)BV-138 dest(grd)* | Elbe Estuary | P-38 |
| | April 29 | Me-109 dam(air) | N/Brandenburg | P-38 |
| | May 19 | He-111 dam(grd) | NW Schleswig | P-38 |
| | April 10, 1945 | Me-410 dest(grd) | Oranienburg | P-51 |
| | | He-177 dam(grd) | Oranienburg | P-51 |
| | April 16 | FW-190 dest(grd) | Pocking | P-51 |

0-0-2 air
2.33-2 ground

* - shared with Capt. C.W. Stapleton and Lt. D.J. Pick of the 384th Ftr Sqn

**Lacy, Roy P., Jr., Capt.**
374th Ftr Sqn/361st Ftr Grp

| *Sqn* | *Date* | *Claims* | *Location* | *A/C* |
|---|---|---|---|---|
| 374th | March 2, 1944 | Ju-88 dam(grd) | Chievres | P-47 |
| | April 8 | Me-109 dest(air) | N/Dummer Lake | P-47 |
| | June 13 | Me-109 dest(air) | St. Brieuc | P-51 |

2-0-0 air
0-1 ground

**Lacy, William O., Lt.**
82nd Ftr Sqn/78th Ftr Grp

| *Sqn* | *Date* | *Claims* | *Location* | *A/C* |
|---|---|---|---|---|
| 82nd | September 10, 1944 | (2)Ju-88 dest(grd) | Meinbullen | P-47 |
| | | (2)Ju-88 dam(grd) | Meinbullen | P-47 |

0-0-0 air
2-2 ground

**LaGrange, Jack, Jr., Lt.**
83rd Ftr Sqn/78th Ftr Grp

| *Sqn* | *Date* | *Claims* | *Location* | *A/C* |
|---|---|---|---|---|
| 83rd | September 1, 1944 | (.5)Me-110 dest(air)* | Gilze-Rijen | P-47 |
| | | (.5)Me-110 dest(air)** | Gilze-Rijen | P-47 |

1-0-0 air
0-0 ground

* - shared with Lt. P. Bingham of the 83rd Ftr Sqn
** - shared with F/O J.A. Moothart of the 83rd Ftr Sqn

**Lahke, William K., Lt.**
351st Ftr Sqn/353rd Ftr Grp

| *Sqn* | *Date* | *Claims* | *Location* | *A/C* |
|---|---|---|---|---|
| 351st | August 12, 1944 | Me-109 dest(grd) | SW Coulommiers | P-47 |
| | August 28 | Me-109 dest(air) | Dinan | P-47 |

1-0-0 air
1-0 ground

**Laho, Robert O., Lt.**
84th Ftr Sqn/78th Ftr Grp

| *Sqn* | *Date* | *Claims* | *Location* | *A/C* |
|---|---|---|---|---|
| 84th | November 9, 1944 | Ju-88 dam(grd) | Schenfheim A/F | P-47 |

0-0-0 air
0-1 ground

**Laing, D.H., Lt.**
369th Ftr Sqn/359th Ftr Grp

| *Sqn* | *Date* | *Claims* | *Location* | *A/C* |
|---|---|---|---|---|
| 369th | May 12, 1944 | u/i a/c dest(grd) | Thamsbruck | P-51 |

0-0-0 air
1-0 ground

**Laing, James L., Lt.**
328th Ftr Sqn/352nd Ftr Grp

| *Sqn* | *Date* | *Claims* | *Location* | *A/C* |
|---|---|---|---|---|
| 328th | April 10, 1944 | (.5)FW-190 dest(air)* | Dormans | P-47 |

0.5-0-0 air
0-0 ground

* - shared with Capt. D.S. Bryan of the 328th Ftr Sqn

**LaJeunesse, Oscar F., Lt.**
336th Ftr Sqn/4th Ftr Grp

| *Sqn* | *Date* | *Claims* | *Location* | *A/C* |
|---|---|---|---|---|
| 336th | March 29, 1944 | Ju-88 dam(air) | E/Hanover | P-51 |
| | | Ju-88 dest(grd) | E/Hanover | P-51 |
| | April 15 | He-177 dam(grd) | NE Hanover | P-51 |
| | May 30 | Me-109 dest(air) | Magdeburg | P-51 |

1-0-1 air
1-1 ground

**Lake, Joseph E., Lt.**
357th Ftr Sqn/355th Ftr Grp

| *Sqn* | *Date* | *Claims* | *Location* | *A/C* |
|---|---|---|---|---|
| 357th | January 15, 1945 | u/i a/c dam(grd) | Landsberg | P-51 |
| | April 13 | He-111 dam(grd) | Schleswig | P-51 |
| | April 16 | FW-190 dest(grd) | Erferding A/F | P-51 |

0-0-0 air
1-2 ground

**Lamb, Huie H., Jr., Lt.**
82nd Ftr Sqn/78th Ftr Grp

| *Sqn* | *Date* | *Claims* | *Location* | *A/C* |
|---|---|---|---|---|
| 82nd | October 12, 1944 | Me-109 dest(air) | Hamburg | P-47 |
| | October 15 | Me-262 dest(air) | Bohmte | P-47 |
| | March 19, 1945 | (.5)Ar-234 dest(air)* | Osnabruck | P-51 |
| | | Me-109 dam(air) | Osnabruck | P-51 |
| | | FW-190 dam(air) | Osnabruck | P-51 |
| | April 10 | Me-410 dest(grd) | Werder A/F | P-51 |
| | | Ju-52 dest(grd) | Werder A/F | P-51 |
| | | Ju-88 dest(grd) | Werder A/F | P-51 |
| | | Ju-52 dam(grd) | Werder A/F | P-51 |

2.5-0-2 air
3-1 ground

* - shared with Capt. W.H. Brown of the 82nd Ftr Sqn

**Lamb, James W., Lt.**
352nd Ftr Sqn/353rd Ftr Grp

| *Sqn* | *Date* | *Claims* | *Location* | *A/C* |
|---|---|---|---|---|
| 352nd | April 16, 1945 | Me-109 dest(grd) | Pocking | P-51 |
| | | Me-109 dam(grd) | Pocking | P-51 |
| | | u/i a/c dam(grd) | Pocking | P-51 |
| | April 17 | u/i a/c dest(grd) | Ganacker | P-51 |

0-0-0 air
2-2 ground

**Lamb, John T., Jr., Lt.**
82nd Ftr Sqn/78th Ftr Grp

| *Sqn* | *Date* | *Claims* | *Location* | *A/C* |
|---|---|---|---|---|
| 82nd | April 12, 1944 | Ju-87 dest(air) | Sedan | P-47 |
| | | Ju-87 dam(grd) | Sedan | P-47 |

1-0-0 air
0-1 ground

**Lamb, Robert A., Maj.**
61st Ftr Sqn/56th Ftr Grp
63rd Ftr Sqn/56th Ftr Grp

| *Sqn* | *Date* | *Claims* | *Location* | *A/C* |
|---|---|---|---|---|
| 61st | August 19, 1943 | FW-190 dest(air) | Breda | P-47 |
| | November 29 | Me-109 prob(air) | NE Bremen | P-47 |
| | December 11 | (3)Me-110 dest(air) | N/Langeroog Island | P-47 |
| | December 30 | FW-190 dam(air) | S/Soissons | P-47 |
| | February 6, 1944 | Me-109 dest(air) | Beauvais | P-47 |
| | February 20 | Ju-88 dest(air) | E/Minden | P-47 |
| | February 25 | Me-109 dest(air) | Landau | P-47 |

7-1-1 air
0-0 ground

**Lambright, Clarence M., Capt.**
368th Ftr Sqn/359th Ftr Grp

| *Sqn* | *Date* | *Claims* | *Location* | *A/C* |
|---|---|---|---|---|
| 368th | September 11, 1944 | (.5)Me-109 dest(air)* | Eisenach | P-51 |

0.5-0-0 air
0-0 ground

* - shared with Lt. J.D. Flack of the 368th Ftr Sqn

**Lambright, James F., Lt.**
328th Ftr Sqn/352nd Ftr Grp

| *Sqn* | *Date* | *Claims* | *Location* | *A/C* |
|---|---|---|---|---|
| 328th | November 21, 1944 | (.5)FW-190 dest(air)* | Merseburg | P-51 |
| | | FW-190 dam(air) | Merseburg | P-51 |
| | December 25 | Me-109 dest(air) | SW Coblenz | P-51 |
| | | Me-109 dam(air) | SW Coblenz | P-51 |

1.5-0-2 air
0-0 ground

* - shared with Capt. W.E. Hendrian of the 328th Ftr Sqn

**Lamer, Charles W., Capt.**
357th Ftr Sqn/355th Ftr Grp

| *Sqn* | *Date* | *Claims* | *Location* | *A/C* |
|---|---|---|---|---|
| 357th | August 16, 1944 | Me-109 dest(air) | SE Hildesheim | P-51 |
| | October 6 | (2)FW-190 dest(air) | W/Berlin | P-51 |

3-0-0 air
0-0 ground

**Lammie, Harold R., Lt.**
352nd Ftr Sqn/353rd Ftr Grp

| *Sqn* | *Date* | *Claims* | *Location* | *A/C* |
|---|---|---|---|---|
| 352nd | January 16, 1945 | Ju-88 dam(grd) | Deiningen | P-51 |
| | April 17 | FW-190 dam(grd) | Ganacker | P-51 |

0-0-0 air
0-2 ground

**Lamont, John W., Lt.**
370th Ftr Sqn/359th Ftr Grp

| *Sqn* | *Date* | *Claims* | *Location* | *A/C* |
|---|---|---|---|---|
| 370th | September 12, 1944 | (2)u/i a/c dest(grd) | S/Memmingen | P-51 |
| | November 21 | FW-190 dam(air) | SW Merseburg | P-51 |

0-0-1 air
2-0 ground

**Lancaster, Billy G., Lt.**
352nd Ftr Sqn/353rd Ftr Grp

| *Sqn* | *Date* | *Claims* | *Location* | *A/C* |
|---|---|---|---|---|
| 352nd | April 17, 1945 | Me-109 dest(grd) | Ganacker | P-51 |
| | | FW-190 dest(grd) | Ganacker | P-51 |
| | | (.5)He-111 dest(grd)* | Ganacker | P-51 |
| | | Me-109 dam(grd) | Ganacker | P-51 |

0-0-0 air
2.5-1 ground

* - shared with Lt. W.F. Beach of the 352nd Ftr Sqn

**Lancaster, Raymond R., Capt.**
370th Ftr Sqn/359th Ftr Grp

| Sqn | Date | Claims | Location | A/C |
|---|---|---|---|---|
| 370th | April 22, 1944 | FW-190 dest(air) | Hamm | P-47 |
| | | FW-190 dam(air) | Hamm | P-47 |
| | May 29 | Me-109 dest(air) | Stettin | P-51 |
| | | Me-109 prob(air) | Stettin | P-51 |

2-1-1 air
0-0 ground

**Lancaster, Robert T., Lt.**
369th Ftr Sqn/359th Ftr Grp

| Sqn | Date | Claims | Location | A/C |
|---|---|---|---|---|
| 369th | November 27, 1944 | Me-109 prob(air) | S/Hanover | P-51 |
| | March 24, 1945 | (2)Me-109 dest(air) | Eikelon A/F | P-51 |

2-1-0 air
0-0 ground

**Landers, John D., LtCol.**
38th Ftr Sqn/ 55th Ftr Grp
HdQts/357th Ftr Grp
HdQts/ 78th Ftr Grp
Earlier flew in the PTO with the 49th Ftr Grp and claimed 6 kills; (2)Sallys on April 4, 1942; a Zero on June 14 and July 30, 1942; and (2)Zeros on December 26, 1942.

| Sqn | Date | Claims | Location | A/C |
|---|---|---|---|---|
| 38th | May 21, 1944 | (.5)u/i a/c dest(grd)[*] | E/Helmstadt | P-38 |
| | | (.5)u/i a/c dest(grd)[*] | E/Helmstadt | P-38 |
| | June 25 | FW-190 dest(air) | SW Paris | P-38 |
| | | Me-109 dam(air) | SW Paris | P-38 |
| | July 7 | (3)Me-410 dest(air) | Bernburg | P-38 |
| | August 24 | (2)Ju-88 dest(grd) | Burg A/F | P-51 |
| | September 5 | Ju-88 dest(grd) | Stuttgart/Boblingen | P-51 |
| | | u/i a/c dam(grd) | Stuttgart/Boblingen | P-51 |
| HdQts | November 18 | Me-109 dest(air) | Villingen A/F | P-51 |
| (357th) | | Me-109 dest(grd) | Villingen A/F | P-51 |
| HdQts | March 2, 1945 | (2)Me-109 dest(air) | Burg A/F | P-51 |
| (78th) | March 19 | Me-109 dest(air) | Osnabruck | P-51 |
| | March 30 | (.5)Me-262 dest(air)[**] | Rendsburg | P-51 |
| | April 10 | (2)Me-109 dest(grd) | Werder A/F | P-51 |
| | | FW-190 dest(grd) | Werder A/F | P-51 |
| | | He-111 dest(grd) | Werder A/F | P-51 |
| | | Ju-188 dest(grd) | Werder A/F | P-51 |
| | | Ju-88 dest(grd) | Werder A/F | P-51 |
| | April 16 | (9)He-177 dest(grd) | Praha/Kakewice | P-51 |

8.5-0-1 air
20-1 ground

[*] - both shared with Lt. N.R. Tipton of the 38th Ftr Sqn
[**] - shared with Lt. T.V. Thain of the 84th Ftr Sqn, 78th Ftr Grp

**Landis, Keehn, Lt.**
363rd Ftr Sqn/357th Ftr Grp

| Sqn | Date | Claims | Location | A/C |
|---|---|---|---|---|
| 363rd | September 18, 1944 | Me-109 dest(air) | W/Arnheim | P-51 |

1-0-0 air
0-0 ground

**Landrum, Jack C., Lt.**
487th Ftr Sqn/352nd Ftr Grp

| Sqn | Date | Claims | Location | A/C |
|---|---|---|---|---|
| 487th | September 10, 1944 | Ju-52 dest(grd) | Wertheim | P-51 |

0-0-0 air
1-0 ground

**Landry, Robert B., Col.**
HdQts/56th Ftr Grp

| Sqn | Date | Claims | Location | A/C |
|---|---|---|---|---|
| HdQts | December 11, 1943 | Me-109 dest(air) | NE Emden | P-47 |

1-0-0 air
0-0 ground

**Lane, Howard A., Maj.**
376th Ftr Sqn/361st Ftr Grp

| Sqn | Date | Claims | Location | A/C |
|---|---|---|---|---|
| 376th | February 25, 1944 | FW-190 dest(air) | N/Metz | P-47 |

1-0-0 air
0-0 ground

**Lane, Thomas C., Lt.**
336th Ftr Sqn/4th Ftr Grp

| Sqn | Date | Claims | Location | A/C |
|---|---|---|---|---|
| 336th | September 12, 1944 | Me-109 dest(air) | Trier | P-51 |
| | | Me-109 dam(air) | Trier | P-51 |

1-0-1 air
0-0 ground

**Lane, Thomas S., Capt.**
368th Ftr Sqn/359th Ftr Grp

| Sqn | Date | Claims | Location | A/C |
|---|---|---|---|---|
| 368th | May 21, 1944 | (2)u/i a/c dest(grd) | N/Grevesmuhlen | P-51 |
| | | (3)u/i a/c dam(grd) | N/Grevesmuhlen | P-51 |

0-0-0 air
2-3 ground

**Lane, Warren J., Capt.**
HdQts/353rd Ftr Grp

| Sqn | Date | Claims | Location | A/C |
|---|---|---|---|---|
| HdQts | April 16, 1945 | FW-190 dest(grd) | Pocking | P-51 |

0-0-0 air
1-0 ground

**Lang, Ernest S., Lt.**
84th Ftr Sqn/78th Ftr Grp

| Sqn | Date | Claims | Location | A/C |
|---|---|---|---|---|
| 84th | February 5, 1944 | (.5)FW-190 dam(air)[*] | Bernay | P-47 |
| | March 2 | (.5)Ju-52 dest(grd)[**] | Chartres | P-47 |
| | | (.5)Hs-126 dest(grd)[**] | Chartres | P-47 |
| | March 8 | (.5)FW-190 dam(grd)[@] | Bohmte | P-47 |
| | March 16 | Me-210 dam(grd) | S/Nancy | P-47 |
| | | Me-110 dam(grd) | S/Nancy | P-47 |
| | March 17 | (.5)He-111 dam(grd)[@@] | Beauvais | P-47 |
| | March 30 | (.33)Do-217 dest(air)[#] | Twente/Enschede | P-47 |

0.33-0-0.5 air
1-3 ground

[*] - shared with Lt. P.E. Pompetti of the 84th Ftr Sqn
[**] - both shared with Lt. P.E. Pompetti of the 84th Ftr Sqn
[@] - shared with Lt. P.E. Pompetti of the 84th Ftr Sqn
[@@] - shared with Lt. P.E. Pompetti of the 84th Ftr Sqn
[#] - shared with Lt. L.J. Abel and Lt. Q.L. Brown of the 84th Ftr Sqn

**Lang, Joseph L., Capt.**
334th Ftr Sqn/4th Ftr Grp

| Sqn | Date | Claims | Location | A/C |
|---|---|---|---|---|
| 334th | April 18, 1944 | (3)Ju-52 dest(grd) | Juterbog | P-51 |
| | | (.25) of (6)Ju-52 dam(grd)[*] | Juterbog | P-51 |
| | April 30 | (.33)Me-110 dest(air)[**] | N/Lyon | P-51 |
| | | Me-110 dest(grd) | N/Lyon | P-51 |
| | | (2)Me-110 dam(grd) | Lyon | P-51 |
| | | He-111 dam(grd) | Lyon | P-51 |
| | May 19 | Me-109 dest(air) | Weismar | P-51 |
| | | u/i a/c dest(air) | Weismar | P-51 |
| | | Me-109 dam(air) | Weismar | P-51 |
| | May 24 | Me-109 dest(air) | N/Hamburg | P-51 |
| | May 28 | (1.5)Me-109 dest(air)[@] | Magdeburg | P-51 |
| | June 21 | Me-109 dest(air) | SE Warsaw | P-51 |
| | October 14 | (2)Me-109 dest(air) | Nancy/St. Dizier | P-51 |

7.83-0-1 air
4-4.5 ground

[*] - all shared with Lt. D.M. Malmsten, Lt. D.W. Howe, and Lt. S.W. Monroe of the 334th Ftr Sqn
[**] - shared with Capt. W.M. Sobanski and Lt. S.W. Monroe of the 334th Ftr Sqn
[@] - shared with Lt. E.L. Heller of the 352nd Ftr Grp

**Langdon, Lloyd M., Lt.**
63rd Ftr Sqn/56th Ftr Grp

| *Sqn* | *Date* | *Claims* | *Location* | *A/C* |
|---|---|---|---|---|
| 63rd | January 30, 1944 | (2)Me-109 dest(air) | S/Quackenbruck | P-47 |
| | | Me-109 dam(air) | S/Quackenbruck | P-47 |

2-0-1 air
0-0 ground

**Langley, Donald B., Lt.**
354th Ftr Sqn/355th Ftr Grp

| *Sqn* | *Date* | *Claims* | *Location* | *A/C* |
|---|---|---|---|---|
| 354th | March 22, 1945 | FW-190 dam(grd) | Wurzburg | P-51 |
| | March 30 | (.5)Ju-52 dam(grd)* | Schleswig | P-51 |
| | | (.5)Ju-52 dam(grd)* | Schleswig | P-51 |
| | | (.5)Ju-52 dam(grd)* | Schleswig | P-51 |
| | April 9 | He-111 dest(grd) | Memmingen | P-51 |
| | April 13 | (2)He-111 dest(grd) | Husum | P-51 |
| | | Me-109 dest(grd) | Husum | P-51 |
| | | (2)FW-190 dam(grd) | Husum | P-51 |

0-0-0 air
4-4.5 ground

* - all shared with LtCol. G.M. Graham of the 354th Ftr Sqn

**Langohr, Billy E., Lt.**
504th Ftr Sqn/339th Ftr Grp

| *Sqn* | *Date* | *Claims* | *Location* | *A/C* |
|---|---|---|---|---|
| 504th | March 21, 1945 | (.5)Me-262 dest(air)* | Wurzburg | P-51 |

0.5-0-0 air
0-0 ground

* - shared with Lt. N.C. Greer of the 504th Ftr Sqn

**Lanham, Wayne J., Lt.**
338th Ftr Sqn/55th Ftr Grp

| *Sqn* | *Date* | *Claims* | *Location* | *A/C* |
|---|---|---|---|---|
| 338th | August 28, 1944 | Do-217 dest(air) | Dromersheim | P-51 |

1-0-0 air
0-0 ground

**Lanius, John H., Lt.**
358th Ftr Sqn/355th Ftr Grp

| *Sqn* | *Date* | *Claims* | *Location* | *A/C* |
|---|---|---|---|---|
| 358th | April 9, 1945 | Me-110 dest(grd) | Heilfingen | P-51 |

0-0-0 air
1-0 ground

**Lanoue, Roland J., Lt.**
350th Ftr Sqn/353rd Ftr Grp

| *Sqn* | *Date* | *Claims* | *Location* | *A/C* |
|---|---|---|---|---|
| 350th | February 27, 1945 | (2)Me-410 dest(grd) | Rohrensee | P-51 |
| | | (2)u/i a/c dest(grd) | Rohrensee | P-51 |
| | | FW-190 dest(grd) | Rohrensee | P-51 |
| | | FW-190 dam(grd) | Rohrensee | P-51 |
| | February 28 | (3)Me-110 dest(grd) | S/Gotha | P-51 |
| | March 2 | Me-109 dest(air) | Ruhland | P-51 |
| | March 21 | (2)Ar-234 dest(grd) | Achmer | P-51 |
| | | He-111 dest(grd) | Achmer | P-51 |

1-0-0 air
11-1 ground

**Lanowski, Witold A., Capt.**
61st Ftr Sqn/56th Ftr Grp

| *Sqn* | *Date* | *Claims* | *Location* | *A/C* |
|---|---|---|---|---|
| 61st | May 22, 1944 | FW-190 dest(air) | Hopenhofen A/F | P-47 |
| | June 27 | Me-109 dest(air) | La Perth A/F | P-47 |
| | July 5 | Me-109 dest(air) | Conches A/F | P-47 |
| | November 18 | FW-190 dest(air) | E/Hanau | P-47 |

4-0-0 air
0-0 ground

**Lapham, Richard L., Lt.**
38th Ftr Sqn/55th Ftr Grp

| *Sqn* | *Date* | *Claims* | *Location* | *A/C* |
|---|---|---|---|---|
| 38th | September 13, 1944 | Me-109 dest(air) | Erfurt | P-51 |

1-0-0 air
0-0 ground

**Larrabee, Dale E., Lt.**
55th Ftr Sqn/20th Ftr Grp

| *Sqn* | *Date* | *Claims* | *Location* | *A/C* |
|---|---|---|---|---|
| 55th | June 30, 1944 | Me-109 dest(air) | Dreux | P-38 |

1-0-0 air
0-0 ground

**Larsen, Carl A., Lt.**
350th Ftr Sqn/353rd Ftr Grp

| *Sqn* | *Date* | *Claims* | *Location* | *A/C* |
|---|---|---|---|---|
| 350th | November 18, 1944 | He-111 dest(grd) | Lechfeld | P-51 |
| | | He-111 dam(grd) | Lechfeld | P-51 |
| | February 27, 1945 | (2)Me-410 dest(grd) | Rohrensee | P-51 |

0-0-0 air
3-1 ground

**Larsen, Frederick, Capt.**
77th Ftr Sqn/20th Ftr Grp

| *Sqn* | *Date* | *Claims* | *Location* | *A/C* |
|---|---|---|---|---|
| 77th | February 9, 1945 | (2)FW-190 dest(grd) | Esperstadt A/F | P-51 |
| | | u/i a/c dest(grd) | Esperstadt A/F | P-51 |

0-0-0 air
3-0 ground

**Larsen, Harry E., Lt.**
338th Ftr Sqn/55th Ftr Grp

| *Sqn* | *Date* | *Claims* | *Location* | *A/C* |
|---|---|---|---|---|
| 338th | January 29, 1944 | FW-190 dest(air) | Frankfurt | P-38 |
| | May 20 | FW-190 dest(air) | Sens | P-38 |

2-0-0 air
0-0 ground

**Larson, Delvin G., Lt.**
351st Ftr Sqn/353rd Ftr Grp

| *Sqn* | *Date* | *Claims* | *Location* | *A/C* |
|---|---|---|---|---|
| 351st | April 16, 1945 | (3)FW-190 dest(grd) | Reichersberg | P-51 |
| | | (4)FW-190 dam(grd) | Reichersberg | P-51 |

0-0-0 air
3-4 ground

**Larson, Donald A., Maj.**
505th Ftr Sqn/339th Ftr Grp

| *Sqn* | *Date* | *Claims* | *Location* | *A/C* |
|---|---|---|---|---|
| 505th | May 13, 1944 | FW-190 prob(air) | SE Lubeck | P-51 |
| | May 24 | (2)Me-109 dest(air) | Berlin | P-51 |
| | | FW-190 dest(air) | Berlin | P-51 |
| | | FW-190 dam(air) | Berlin | P-51 |
| | July 28 | Ju-52 dest(air) | Ansbach | P-51 |
| | August 3 | Do-217 dest(grd) | Benestroff | P-51 |
| | | FW-190 dest(grd) | Benestroff | P-51 |
| | August 4 | (2)Me-109 dest(air) | Ulzen-Celle | P-51 |
| | | Me-410 dest(grd) | E/Celle | P-51 |

6-1-1 air
3-0 ground

**Larson, Norman L., Lt.**
38th Ftr Sqn/55th Ftr Grp

| *Sqn* | *Date* | *Claims* | *Location* | *A/C* |
|---|---|---|---|---|
| 38th | November 2, 1944 | Me-109 dest(air) | W/Merseburg | P-51 |

1-0-0 air
0-0 ground

**Larson, Philip L., Capt.**
84th Ftr Sqn/78th Ftr Grp

| *Sqn* | *Date* | *Claims* | *Location* | *A/C* |
|---|---|---|---|---|
| 84th | October 10, 1943 | Me-110 dest(air) | Ochtrup | P-47 |
| | January 5, 1944 | Me-109 dest(air) | La Rochelle | P-47 |
| | November 26 | FW-190 dest(air) | Vorden A/F | P-47 |

3-0-0 air
0-0 ground

**Lasch, Ted F., F/O**
385th Ftr Sqn/364th Ftr Grp

| *Sqn* | *Date* | *Claims* | *Location* | *A/C* |
|---|---|---|---|---|
| 385th | April 10, 1945 | Ju-88 dest(grd) | Stendal | P-51 |

0-0-0 air
1-0 ground

**Lashbrook, Kenneth A., Lt.**
338th Ftr Sqn/55th Ftr Grp

| *Sqn* | *Date* | *Claims* | *Location* | *A/C* |
|---|---|---|---|---|
| 338th | December 24, 1944 | (.5)Me-109 dest(air)* | Friedburg | P-51 |
| | | (.5)FW-190 dest(air)* | Friedburg | P-51 |
| | February 20, 1945 | Me-109 dest(air) | Womding | P-51 |
| | April 10 | Me-262 dest(air) | Burg | P-51 |

3-0-0 air
0-0 ground

* - both shared with Lt. S.D. Gevorkian of the 338th Ftr Sqn

**Latimer, Joseph L., Capt.**
374th Ftr Sqn/361st Ftr Grp

| *Sqn* | *Date* | *Claims* | *Location* | *A/C* |
|---|---|---|---|---|
| 374th | January 30, 1944 | Me-109 dest(air) | Rheine | P-47 |

1-0-0 air
0-0 ground

**Lawhead, Douglas A., Capt.**
83rd Ftr Sqn/78th Ftr Grp

| *Sqn* | *Date* | *Claims* | *Location* | *A/C* |
|---|---|---|---|---|
| 83rd | July 5, 1944 | (2)FW-190 dam(air) | Evreux | P-47 |
| | July 6 | FW-190 prob(air) | Rambouillet | P-47 |

0-1-2 air
0-0 ground

**Lawrence, Edwin B., Lt.**
38th Ftr Sqn/55th Ftr Grp

| *Sqn* | *Date* | *Claims* | *Location* | *A/C* |
|---|---|---|---|---|
| 38th | September 12, 1944 | Me-109 dest(air) | Frankfurt | P-51 |

1-0-0 air
0-0 ground

**Lawrence, Floyd C., Jr., Capt.**
343rd Ftr Sqn/55th Ftr Grp

| *Sqn* | *Date* | *Claims* | *Location* | *A/C* |
|---|---|---|---|---|
| 343rd | September 5, 1944 | He-111 dest(grd) | Stuttgart/Echterdingen | P-51 |
| | September 10 | (2)Me-210 dest(grd) | Illesheim | P-51 |
| | | (4)Me-210 dam(grd) | Illesheim | P-51 |
| | February 24, 1945 | Ju-88 dest(grd) | Zwischenahn A/F | P-51 |
| | | u/i a/c dam(grd) | Zwischenahn A/F | P-51 |

0-0-0 air
4-5 ground

**Laxton, Cecil A., Lt.**
376th Ftr Sqn/361st Ftr Grp

| *Sqn* | *Date* | *Claims* | *Location* | *A/C* |
|---|---|---|---|---|
| 376th | March 17, 1944 | (.5)u/i a/c dam(grd)* | Chartres | P-47 |

0-0-0 air
0-0.5 ground

* - shared with Col. T.J.J. Christian of HdQts, 361st Ftr Grp

**Lay, Harry T., Capt.**
84th Ftr Sqn/78th Ftr Grp

| *Sqn* | *Date* | *Claims* | *Location* | *A/C* |
|---|---|---|---|---|
| 84th | July 1, 1944 | Me-109 dest(air) | St. Quentin | P-47 |
| | July 6 | FW-190 dest(air) | NW Paris | P-47 |

2-0-0 air
0-0 ground

**Layton, Caleb J., Lt.**
375th Ftr Sqn/361st Ftr Grp

| *Sqn* | *Date* | *Claims* | *Location* | *A/C* |
|---|---|---|---|---|
| 375th | December 23, 1944 | (2)FW-190 dest(air) | SE Bonn | P-51 |

2-0-0 air
0-0 ground

**Lazear, Earl R., Jr., Capt.**
486th Ftr Sqn/352nd Ftr Grp

| *Sqn* | *Date* | *Claims* | *Location* | *A/C* |
|---|---|---|---|---|
| 486th | July 19, 1944 | Me-109 prob(air) | NE Munich | P-51 |
| | September 12 | (3)Me-109 dest(air) | Kyritz | P-51 |
| | November 30 | Me-109 dest(air) | S/Merseburg | P-51 |
| | December 27 | Me-109 dest(air) | SW Bonn | P-51 |

5-1-0 air
0-0 ground

**Leaf, Dale B., Lt.**
336th Ftr Sqn/4th Ftr Grp
334th Ftr Sqn/4th Ftr Grp

| *Sqn* | *Date* | *Claims* | *Location* | *A/C* |
|---|---|---|---|---|
| 334th | June 26, 1943 | Me-109 dam(air) | W/Dieppe | P-47 |

0-0-1 air
0-0 ground

**Leaf, Leroy R., Jr., Lt.**
358th Ftr Sqn/355th Ftr Grp

| *Sqn* | *Date* | *Claims* | *Location* | *A/C* |
|---|---|---|---|---|
| 358th | April 13, 1945 | (.5)He-111 dest(grd)* | Schleswig | P-51 |

0-0-0 air
0.5-0 ground

* - shared with Lt. R.J. Nicodemus of the 358th Ftr Sqn

**Lear, Warren S., Lt.**
62nd Ftr Sqn/56th Ftr Grp

| *Sqn* | *Date* | *Claims* | *Location* | *A/C* |
|---|---|---|---|---|
| 62nd | December 23, 1944 | FW-190 dest(air) | Euskirchen | P-47 |
| | March 14, 1945 | (.5)Ar-234 dest(air)* | Coblenz | P-47 |

1.5-0-0 air
0-0 ground

* - shared with Lt. S.N. Ball of the 62nd Ftr Sqn

**Leatherman, Vernon A., Capt.**
351st Ftr Sqn/353rd Ftr Grp

| *Sqn* | *Date* | *Claims* | *Location* | *A/C* |
|---|---|---|---|---|
| 351st | April 24, 1944 | FW-190 prob(air) | Mannheim | P-47 |

0-1-0 air
0-0 ground

**Leathers, Wayne E., Capt.**
360th Ftr Sqn/356th Ftr Grp

| *Sqn* | *Date* | *Claims* | *Location* | *A/C* |
|---|---|---|---|---|
| 360th | April 27, 1944 | FW-190 dest(air) | Laon | P-47 |

1-0-0 air
0-0 ground

**Leavell, William A., Lt.**
384th Ftr Sqn/364th Ftr Grp

| *Sqn* | *Date* | *Claims* | *Location* | *A/C* |
|---|---|---|---|---|
| 384th | April 17, 1945 | He-111 dest(grd) | Karlsbad | P-51 |
| | | He-111 dam(grd) | Karlsbad | P-51 |

0-0-0 air
1-1 ground

**Lederer, Henry B., Capt.**
374th Ftr Sqn/361st Ftr Grp

| *Sqn* | *Date* | *Claims* | *Location* | *A/C* |
|---|---|---|---|---|
| 374th | January 30, 1944 | (.5)Me-109 dest(air)* | Rheine | P-47 |
| | July 25 | (.5)Me-109 dest(grd)** | N/Alencon | P-51 |
| | August 5 | Me-109 dest(air) | Hoperhofen | P-51 |
| | | Me-109 dam(air) | Hoperhofen | P-51 |

1.5-0-1 air
0.5-0 ground

* - shared with Lt. J.D. Hastin of the 374th Ftr Sqn
** - shared with Lt. M.L. Bryant of the 374th Ftr Sqn

**Ledington, Dorian, Capt.**
84th Ftr Sqn/78th Ftr Grp

| *Sqn* | *Date* | *Claims* | *Location* | *A/C* |
|---|---|---|---|---|
| 84th | June 7, 1944 | Me-109 dest(air) | Montdidier | P-47 |
| | June 10 | Me-109 dest(air) | La Ferte Mace | P-47 |
| | February 3, 1945 | (2)Me-410 dam(grd) | Luneburg A/F | P-51 |
| | April 16 | (2)Ju-52 dest(grd) | Praha/Kakewice | P-51 |
| | | u/i a/c dest(grd) | Praha/Kakewice | P-51 |
| | | Ju-52 dam(grd) | Praha/Kakewice | P-51 |

2-0-0 air
3-3 ground

**Lee, Charles M., Lt.**
357th Ftr Sqn/355th Ftr Grp

| *Sqn* | *Date* | *Claims* | *Location* | *A/C* |
|---|---|---|---|---|
| 357th | March 27, 1944 | Ju-88 dam(grd) | Biscarosse | P-51 |
| | March 29 | FW-190 prob(air) | NE Brunswick | P-51 |
| | April 5 | (3)Me-110 dam(grd) | Ottingen | P-51 |

0-1-0 air
0-4 ground

**Lee, Edward P., Lt.**
361st Ftr Sqn/356th Ftr Grp

| *Sqn* | *Date* | *Claims* | *Location* | *A/C* |
|---|---|---|---|---|
| 361st | April 13, 1944 | (4)He-111 dam(grd) | Hagenau | P-47 |

0-0-0 air
0-4 ground

**Lee, George S.H., Lt.**
350th Ftr Sqn/353rd Ftr Grp

| *Sqn* | *Date* | *Claims* | *Location* | *A/C* |
|---|---|---|---|---|
| 350th | December 24, 1944 | Me-109 dest(air) | Coblenz | P-51 |

1-0-0 air
0-0 ground

**Lee, Henry A., Lt.**
335th Ftr Sqn/4th Ftr Grp

| *Sqn* | *Date* | *Claims* | *Location* | *A/C* |
|---|---|---|---|---|
| 335th | April 9, 1945 | Me-410 dest(grd) | Munich-Brunnthal | P-51 |

0-0-0 air
1-0 ground

**Lee, John B., Lt.**
79th Ftr Sqn/20th Ftr Grp

| *Sqn* | *Date* | *Claims* | *Location* | *A/C* |
|---|---|---|---|---|
| 79th | April 10, 1945 | Ju-52 dest(grd) | Werder A/F | P-51 |
| | | Me-109 dam(grd) | Werder A/F | P-51 |
| | | Si-204 dam(grd) | Werder A/F | P-51 |

0-0-0 air
1-2 ground

**Lee, Louis W., Lt.**
350th Ftr Sqn/353rd Ftr Grp

| *Sqn* | *Date* | *Claims* | *Location* | *A/C* |
|---|---|---|---|---|
| 350th | March 2, 1945 | Me-109 dest(air) | Ruhland | P-51 |
| | | Me-109 dam(air) | Ruhland | P-51 |
| | March 24 | (2)FW-190 dest(air) | NW Kassel | P-51 |
| | | Me-109 dest(air) | NW Kassel | P-51 |
| | April 16 | (2)FW-190 dest(grd) | Pocking | P-51 |

4-0-1 air
2-0 ground

**LeFebre, Fred H., LtCol.**
351st Ftr Sqn/353rd Ftr Grp

| *Sqn* | *Date* | *Claims* | *Location* | *A/C* |
|---|---|---|---|---|
| 351st | October 8, 1943 | (.5)Me-110 dest(air)* | Friesoythe | P-47 |
| | December 22 | Me-109 dest(air) | Heerds | P-47 |
| | December 5, 1944 | FW-190 dest(air) | N/Berlin | P-51 |
| | | Me-109 dam(air) | N/Berlin | P-51 |

2.5-0-1 air
0-0 ground

* - shared with Lt. D.M. Hurlburt of the 351st Ftr Sqn

**LeFevre, Ferdinand E., Lt.**
79th Ftr Sqn/20th Ftr Grp

| *Sqn* | *Date* | *Claims* | *Location* | *A/C* |
|---|---|---|---|---|
| 79th | January 14, 1944 | Me-109 dam(air) | S/Rouen | P-38 |
| | February 10 | Me-210 dest(air) | Lingen | P-38 |
| | April 8 | Me-109 dest(air) | Salzwedel | P-38 |
| | | (2)Ju-88 dest(grd) | Salzwedel | P-38 |

2-0-1 air
2-0 ground

**Leeney, George H., Lt.**
434th Ftr Sqn/479th Ftr Grp

| *Sqn* | *Date* | *Claims* | *Location* | *A/C* |
|---|---|---|---|---|
| 434th | April 18, 1945 | FW-190 dest(grd) | Ottingen | P-51 |

0-0-0 air
1-0 ground

**Lefforge, Littleton L., Lt.**
384th Ftr Sqn/364th Ftr Grp

| *Sqn* | *Date* | *Claims* | *Location* | *A/C* |
|---|---|---|---|---|
| 384th | December 31, 1944 | FW-190 prob(air) | SW Hamburg | P-51 |
| | February 22, 1945 | Me-262 dam(air) | Stendal | P-51 |

0-1-1 air
0-0 ground

**Leftwich, Daniel L., Capt.**
384th Ftr Sqn/364th Ftr Grp

| *Sqn* | *Date* | *Claims* | *Location* | *A/C* |
|---|---|---|---|---|
| 384th | December 5, 1944 | (.5)FW-190 dest(air)* | NW Berlin | P-51 |
| | December 27 | (2)FW-190 dest(air) | W/Coblenz | P-51 |
| | December 31 | (.5)FW-190 dest(air)** | SW Hamburg | P-51 |
| | April 10, 1945 | Me-109 dam(grd) | Oranienburg | P-51 |
| | April 16 | FW-190 dest(grd) | Pocking | P-51 |

3-0-0 air
1-1 ground

* - shared with Lt. W.F. Flynt of the 384th Ftr Sqn
** - shared with Lt. R.S. Faulkner of the 384th Ftr Sqn

**Leidy, Robert M., Lt.**
360th Ftr Sqn/356th Ftr Grp

| *Sqn* | *Date* | *Claims* | *Location* | *A/C* |
|---|---|---|---|---|
| 360th | May 25, 1944 | Me-109 dest(air) | Neufchateau | P-47 |
| | September 1 | Me-109 dest(grd) | Le Culot | P-47 |
| | | Me-109 dam(grd) | Le Culot | P-47 |

1-0-0 air
1-1 ground

**Leinweber, Gerald F., Capt.**
38th Ftr Sqn/55th Ftr Grp

| *Sqn* | *Date* | *Claims* | *Location* | *A/C* |
|---|---|---|---|---|
| 38th | November 5, 1943 | Me-109 dest(air) | Rotterdam | P-38 |

1-0-0 air
0-0 ground

**Leitner, Frank W., Lt.**
352nd Ftr Sqn/353rd Ftr Grp

| *Sqn* | *Date* | *Claims* | *Location* | *A/C* |
|---|---|---|---|---|
| 352nd | April 16, 1945 | Me-109 dest(grd) | Bad Aibling | P-51 |
| | | Me-109 dam(grd) | Bad Aibling | P-51 |
| | | Me-110 dam(grd) | Bad Aibling | P-51 |
| | April 17 | FW-190 dam(grd) | Ganacker | P-51 |

0-0-0 air
1-3 ground

**Lemmens, Andrew T., Maj.**
368th Ftr Sqn/359th Ftr Grp
370th Ftr Sqn/359th Ftr Grp
HdQts/359th Ftr Grp

| *Sqn* | *Date* | *Claims* | *Location* | *A/C* |
|---|---|---|---|---|
| 368th | February 22, 1944 | Me-109 dest(air) | Hamm | P-47 |
| | April 24 | (.5)u/i a/c dest(grd)* | St. Dizier | P-47 |
| 370th | December 24 | FW-190 dest(air) | Bonn | P-51 |
| | December 31 | Me-109 dest(air) | Hanover | P-51 |

3-0-0 air
0.5-0 ground

* - shared with Capt. C.E. Mosse of the 368th Ftr Sqn

**LeMoyne, Harry F., Capt.**
359th Ftr Sqn/356th Ftr Grp

| *Sqn* | *Date* | *Claims* | *Location* | *A/C* |
|---|---|---|---|---|
| 359th | July 19, 1944 | Me-410 dam(grd) | Le Culot | P-47 |

0-0-0 air
0-1 ground

**Lenfest, Charles W., Maj.**
354th Ftr Sqn/355th Ftr Grp

| *Sqn* | *Date* | *Claims* | *Location* | *A/C* |
|---|---|---|---|---|
| 354th | March 16, 1944 | (1.5)Me-109 dest(air)* | NW Ulm | P-51 |
| | March 18 | (.5)Me-109 dest(air)** | NE Munich | P-51 |
| | | Me-109 dam(air) | NE Munich | P-51 |
| | March 29 | Me-108 dest(air) | Goslar A/F | P-51 |
| | | Trainer dest(grd) | Goslar A/F | P-51 |
| | April 5 | (.5)Me-108 dest(air)@ | Landsberg | P-51 |
| | | (4)Do-217 dam(grd) | Landsberg | P-51 |
| | August 3 | Me-109 dest(air) | E/Mannheim | P-51 |
| | August 6 | Me-109 dest(air) | S/Hamburg | P-51 |
| | October 3 | FW-190 dest(grd) | Nordlingen | P-51 |

5.5-0-1 air
2-4 ground

* - shared with Lt. T.F. Neal of the 354th Ftr Sqn
** - shared with Lt. L.G. Mendenhall of the 354th Ftr Sqn
@ - shared with Lt. H.W. Brown of the 354th Ftr Sqn

**Leo, Carl H., Capt.**
384th Ftr Sqn/364th Ftr Grp

| *Sqn* | *Date* | *Claims* | *Location* | *A/C* |
|---|---|---|---|---|
| 384th | March 5, 1944 | FW-190 dam(air) | N/Angouleme | P-38 |
| | August 9 | FW-190 dest(air) | Kaufburen | P-51 |

1-0-1 air
0-0 ground

**Leon, Ernest E., Lt.**
343rd Ftr Sqn/55th Ftr Grp

| *Sqn* | *Date* | *Claims* | *Location* | *A/C* |
|---|---|---|---|---|
| 343rd | April 9, 1945 | Ju-52 dest(grd) | Munich-Brunnthal | P-51 |
| | | Me-262 dam(grd) | Munich-Brunnthal | P-51 |

0-0-0 air
1-1 ground

**Leon, Jack D., Lt.**
55th Ftr Sqn/20th Ftr Grp

| *Sqn* | *Date* | *Claims* | *Location* | *A/C* |
|---|---|---|---|---|
| 55th | October 6, 1944 | Do-24 dest(grd) | Kubitzer Bay | P-51 |
| | | Do-24 dam(grd) | Kubitzer Bay | P-51 |
| | November 2 | Me-109 dest(air) | SW Merseburg | P-51 |
| | | Me-109 prob(air) | SW Merseburg | P-51 |
| | January 14, 1945 | (2)FW-190 dest(air) | Perleberg | P-51 |

3-1-0 air
1-1 ground

**Leon, Leonard, Lt.**
383rd Ftr Sqn/364th Ftr Grp

| *Sqn* | *Date* | *Claims* | *Location* | *A/C* |
|---|---|---|---|---|
| 383rd | April 13, 1945 | FW-190 dest(grd) | Flensburg | P-51 |
| | | Me-109 dam(grd) | Flensburg | P-51 |
| | | Ju-52 dam(grd) | Flensburg | P-51 |

0-0-0 air
1-2 ground

**Leonard, William J., Lt.**
338th Ftr Sqn/55th Ftr Grp

| *Sqn* | *Date* | *Claims* | *Location* | *A/C* |
|---|---|---|---|---|
| 338th | September 11, 1944 | Me-109 dest(air) | S/Meiningen | P-51 |
| | | Me-109 dam(air) | S/Meiningen | P-51 |

1-0-1 air
0-0 ground

**Leone, Frank J., Capt.**
343rd Ftr Sqn/55th Ftr Grp

| *Sqn* | *Date* | *Claims* | *Location* | *A/C* |
|---|---|---|---|---|
| 343rd | March 18, 1944 | FW-190 dam(air) | SE Strasbourg | P-38 |
| | June 11 | Me-109 prob(air) | Clermont | P-38 |

0-1-1 air
0-0 ground

**Lepore, Roscoe R., Lt.**
364th Ftr Sqn/357th Ftr Grp

| *Sqn* | *Date* | *Claims* | *Location* | *A/C* |
|---|---|---|---|---|
| 364th | February 28, 1945 | (4)u/i a/c dam(grd) | Lubeck/Blankensee | P-51 |
| | March 2 | (2)He-111 dest(grd) | E/Magdeburg | P-51 |

0-0-0 air
2-4 ground

**Leslie, Gus D., Lt.**
343rd Ftr Sqn/55th Ftr Grp

| *Sqn* | *Date* | *Claims* | *Location* | *A/C* |
|---|---|---|---|---|
| 343rd | September 5, 1944 | Ju-52 dest(grd) | Stuttgart/Echterdingen | P-51 |
| | September 10 | (.5)Hs-126 dest(air)* | Kitzingen A/F | P-51 |
| | November 2 | Me-109 dam(air) | Naumberg | P-51 |

0.5-0-1 air
1-0 ground

* - shared with Lt. E.J. Dvorak of the 343rd Ftr Sqn

**Lett, Sim L., Jr., Lt.**
385th Ftr Sqn/364th Ftr Grp

| *Sqn* | *Date* | *Claims* | *Location* | *A/C* |
|---|---|---|---|---|
| 385th | November 21, 1944 | (.5)FW-190 dest(air)* | Erfurt | P-51 |
| | December 23 | FW-190 dest(air) | NW Trier | P-51 |

1.5-0-0 air
0-0 ground

* - shared with Capt. T.P. Farrell of the 385th Ftr Sqn

**Levin, Emmanuel, Lt.**
383rd Ftr Sqn/364th Ftr Grp

| *Sqn* | *Date* | *Claims* | *Location* | *A/C* |
|---|---|---|---|---|
| 383rd | August 14, 1944 | (2)He-111 dest(grd) | Memmingen | P-51 |
| | | (3)He-111 dam(grd) | Memmingen | P-51 |

0-0-0 air
2-3 ground

**Lewin, Edward C., Capt.**
436th Ftr Sqn/479th Ftr Grp

| *Sqn* | *Date* | *Claims* | *Location* | *A/C* |
|---|---|---|---|---|
| 436th | September 5, 1944 | (2)FW-190 dest(grd) | Bad Nauheim | P-38 |
| | | Fi-156 dest(grd) | Bad Nauheim | P-38 |
| | | (2)u/i a/c dam(grd) | Bad Nauheim | P-38 |
| | December 23 | Me-109 dest(air) | NW Cologne | P-51 |

1-0-0 air
3-2 ground

**Lewis, Donald E., Lt.**
351st Ftr Sqn/353rd Ftr Grp

| *Sqn* | *Date* | *Claims* | *Location* | *A/C* |
|---|---|---|---|---|
| 351st | March 21, 1945 | Me-109 dest(grd) | Achmer | P-51 |
| | | Me-109 dam(grd) | Achmer | P-51 |

0-0-0 air
1-1 ground

**Lewis, Gordon H., Lt.**
62nd Ftr Sqn/56th Ftr Grp

| *Sqn* | *Date* | *Claims* | *Location* | *A/C* |
|---|---|---|---|---|
| 62nd | May 8, 1944 | FW-190 dest(air) | Oschersleben | P-47 |

1-0-0 air
0-0 ground

**Lewis, Ralph E., Lt.**
335th Ftr Sqn/4th Ftr Grp

| *Sqn* | *Date* | *Claims* | *Location* | *A/C* |
|---|---|---|---|---|
| 335th | October 6, 1944 | (.5)Me-410 dest(air)* | NW Heligoland | P-51 |

0.5-0-0 air
0-0 ground

* - shared with Lt. E.N. McCall of the 335th Ftr Sqn

**Lewis, Wilbur H., Capt.**
368th Ftr Sqn/359th Ftr Grp

| *Sqn* | *Date* | *Claims* | *Location* | *A/C* |
|---|---|---|---|---|
| 368th | September 11, 1944 | Me-109 dam(air) | Eisenach | P-51 |

0-0-1 air
0-0 ground

**Lewis, Willard H., Jr., Lt.**
79th Ftr Sqn/20th Ftr Grp

| *Sqn* | *Date* | *Claims* | *Location* | *A/C* |
|---|---|---|---|---|
| 79th | August 6, 1944 | Me-109 dest(air) | SW Berlin | P-51 |
| | | Me-109 dam(air) | SW Berlin | P-51 |

1-0-1 air
0-0 ground

**Lewis, William H., Capt.**
343rd Ftr Sqn/55th Ftr Grp

| *Sqn* | *Date* | *Claims* | *Location* | *A/C* |
|---|---|---|---|---|
| 343rd | September 5, 1944 | (5)Trainer dest(air) | N/Goppingen A/F | P-51 |
| | September 13 | Me-109 dest(air) | Eisenach-Gotha | P-51 |
| | | Me-109 dam(air) | Eisenach-Gotha | P-51 |
| | February 3, 1945 | Ju-88 dest(air) | Gartow | P-51 |

7-0-1 air
0-0 ground

**Leyser, Harry C., Lt.**
361st Ftr Sqn/356th Ftr Grp

| *Sqn* | *Date* | *Claims* | *Location* | *A/C* |
|---|---|---|---|---|
| 361st | March 6, 1944 | (.5)Me-109 dest(air)* | N/Steinhuder Lake | P-47 |
| | | (.5)Me-109 dam(air)* | N/Steinhuder Lake | P-47 |
| | April 11 | u/i a/c dam(grd) | Gifhorn | P-47 |

0.5-0-0.5 air
0-1 ground

* - both shared with Maj. W. Waller of the 361st Ftr Sqn

**L'Heureux, Robert C., Capt.**
360th Ftr Sqn/356th Ftr Grp

| *Sqn* | *Date* | *Claims* | *Location* | *A/C* |
|---|---|---|---|---|
| 360th | January 29, 1944 | FW-190 dest(air) | Louvain | P-47 |
| | April 23 | (.5)Go-242 dam(grd)* | Hagenau | P-47 |
| | May 19 | Me-109 dam(air) | Hanover | P-47 |

1-0-1 air
0-0.5 ground

* - shared wih Lt. C.W. Adams of the 360th Ftr Sqn

**Lichter, George, Capt.**
374th Ftr Sqn/361st Ftr Grp

| *Sqn* | *Date* | *Claims* | *Location* | *A/C* |
|---|---|---|---|---|
| 374th | January 30, 1944 | Me-109 dam(air) | Rheine | P-47 |
| | May 29 | FW-190 dest(air) | Pitka | P-51 |
| | | FW-190 prob(air) | Pitka | P-51 |
| | | FW-190 dam(air) | Pitka | P-51 |
| | July 5 | Ju-88 dam(grd) | Chateau Thierry | P-51 |
| | August 5 | Me-109 dest(air) | Hoperhofen | P-51 |

2-1-2 air
0-1 ground

**Liebenrood, Harold R., F/O**
82nd Ftr Sqn/78th Ftr Grp

| *Sqn* | *Date* | *Claims* | *Location* | *A/C* |
|---|---|---|---|---|
| 82nd | November 21, 1944 | (.5)Ju-88 dest(grd)* | Gutersloh | P-47 |
| | November 26 | Me-109 dest(air) | Rheine | P-47 |

1-0-0 air
0.5-0 ground

* - shared with Lt. D.C. Hart of the 82nd Ftr Sqn

**Liebold, Robert S., Lt.**
350th Ftr Sqn/353rd Ftr Grp

| *Sqn* | *Date* | *Claims* | *Location* | *A/C* |
|---|---|---|---|---|
| 350th | February 27, 1945 | Me-410 dest(grd) | Rohrensee | P-51 |
| | | Me-410 dam(grd) | Rohrensee | P-51 |

0-0-0 air
1-1 ground

**Lightfoot, Edward B., Jr., Lt.**
61st Ftr Sqn/56th Ftr Grp

| *Sqn* | *Date* | *Claims* | *Location* | *A/C* |
|---|---|---|---|---|
| 61st | April 10, 1945 | u/i a/c dest(grd) | Muritz Lake | P-47 |

0-0-0 air
1-0 ground

**Liles, Brooks J., Lt.**
343rd Ftr Sqn/55th Ftr Grp

| *Sqn* | *Date* | *Claims* | *Location* | *A/C* |
|---|---|---|---|---|
| 343rd | January 14, 1945 | FW-190 dest(air) | W/Salzwedel | P-51 |
| | February 3 | He-111 dest(grd) | Stade A/F | P-51 |

| Sqn | Date | Claims | Location | A/C |
|---|---|---|---|---|
| | | He-111 dam(grd) | Stade A/F | P-51 |
| | March 3 | Me-109 dest(grd) | Prague/Letnany | P-51 |
| | | (2)Me-109 dam(grd) | Prague/Letnany | P-51 |
| | | (2)Ju-52 dam(grd) | Prague/Letnany | P-51 |
| | | Ju-88 dam(grd) | Prague/Letnany | P-51 |

1-0-0 air
2-6 ground

**Linderer, Howard A., Lt.**
369th Ftr Sqn/359th Ftr Grp

| Sqn | Date | Claims | Location | A/C |
|---|---|---|---|---|
| 369th | March 16, 1944 | Me-109 dest(air) | St. Dizier | P-47 |

1-0-0 air
0-0 ground

**Lindsay, John C., Lt.**
361st Ftr Sqn/356th Ftr Grp

| Sqn | Date | Claims | Location | A/C |
|---|---|---|---|---|
| 361st | February 20, 1945 | FW-190 dest(grd) | Bayreuth-Eindbach | P-51 |
| | | (.5)u/i a/c dest(grd)* | Windleschenlaibach | P-51 |

0-0-0 air
1.5-0 ground

* - shared with F/O J.K. Dupuy of the 361st Ftr Sqn

**Lines, Ted E., Capt.**
335th Ftr Sqn/4th Ftr Grp

| Sqn | Date | Claims | Location | A/C |
|---|---|---|---|---|
| 335th | May 12, 1944 | Me-109 dest(air) | E/Frankfurt | P-51 |
| | August 24 | (2)Me-109 dest(air) | SE Emden | P-51 |
| | September 10 | (3)Me-109 dest(air) | Strasbourg | P-51 |
| | | Ju-88 dest(air) | S/Kaiserlautern | P-51 |
| | September 17 | (3)FW-190 dest(air) | Bocholt | P-51 |

10-0-0 air
0-0 ground

**Lingo, Arthur M., Capt.**
362nd Ftr Sqn/357th Ftr Grp

| Sqn | Date | Claims | Location | A/C |
|---|---|---|---|---|
| 362nd | February 25, 1944 | (.5)Me-110 dest(air)* | Regensburg | P-51 |
| | April 8 | Me-109 dest(air) | W/Brunswick | P-51 |

1.5-0-0 air
0-0 ground

* - shared with Lt. R.H. Becker of the 362nd Ftr Sqn

**Linn, Marcus C., Lt.**
384th Ftr Sqn/364th Ftr Grp
385th Ftr Sqn/364th Ftr Grp
Earlier flew in the MTO with the 1st Ftr Grp and claimed one kill on May 18, 1943.

| Sqn | Date | Claims | Location | A/C |
|---|---|---|---|---|
| 384th | March 8, 1944 | (2)Me-109 dam(air) | E/Steinhuder Lake | P-38 |

0-0-2 air
0-0 ground

**Lister, James E., Lt.**
63rd Ftr Sqn/56th Ftr Grp

| Sqn | Date | Claims | Location | A/C |
|---|---|---|---|---|
| 63rd | September 8, 1944 | (3)Ju-88 dam(grd) | Euskirchen | P-47 |
| | October 5 | Me-109 dam(air) | S/Geseke | P-47 |
| | October 12 | FW-190 dest(air) | Dummer Lake | P-47 |
| | November 27 | Me-109 dest(air) | SE Dummer Lake | P-47 |

2-0-1 air
0-3 ground

**Lister, Walter B., Lt.**
358th Ftr Sqn/355th Ftr Grp

| Sqn | Date | Claims | Location | A/C |
|---|---|---|---|---|
| 358th | April 13, 1945 | (.5)He-111 dest(grd)* | Schleswig | P-51 |

0-0-0 air
0.5-0 ground

* - shared with Lt. M. Lacazette of the 358th Ftr Sqn

**Littge, Raymond H., Capt.**
487th Ftr Sqn/352nd Ftr Grp

| Sqn | Date | Claims | Location | A/C |
|---|---|---|---|---|
| 487th | August 25, 1944 | (2)Me-210 dest(grd) | Neubrandenburg | P-51 |
| | | Me-109 dam(grd) | Neubrandenburg | P-51 |
| | September 11 | (2)Ju-88 dest(grd) | Gotha | P-51 |
| | | (2)Ju-88 dam(grd) | Gotha | P-51 |
| | November 27 | (2)Me-109 dest(air) | Hameln | P-51 |
| | December 26 | Me-109 dest(air) | Ollheim | P-51 |
| | December 27 | (3)FW-190 dest(air) | Nauen | P-51 |
| | January 1, 1945 | (2)FW-190 dest(air) | N/Liege | P-51 |
| | January 24 | Me-109 dest(air) | Bonn | P-51 |
| | February 21 | Ju-88 dam(grd) | SW Kassel | P-51 |
| | March 18 | (.5)Me-109 dest(air)* | Bad Frienwalde | P-51 |
| | March 25 | Me-262 dest(air) | Rechlin A/F | P-51 |
| | April 16 | (2)Me-109 dest(grd) | Ganacker | P-51 |
| | | Me-210 dest(grd) | Ganacker | P-51 |
| | | (3)Me-109 dam(grd) | Ganacker | P-51 |
| | | FW-190 dam(grd) | Ganacker | P-51 |
| | April 17 | (4)Me-109 dest(grd) | Plattling | P-51 |
| | | (2)Me-262 dest(grd) | Plattling | P-51 |

10.5-0-0 air
13-8 ground

* - shared with Lt. J.N. Wood of the 487th Ftr Sqn

**Little, Harry E., Lt.**
434th Ftr Sqn/479th Ftr Grp

| Sqn | Date | Claims | Location | A/C |
|---|---|---|---|---|
| 434th | August 18, 1944 | Ju-88 dest(grd) | Nancy/Essey A/F | P-38 |
| | | (.5)He-111 dest(grd)* | Nancy/Essey A/F | P-38 |
| | | (2)He-111 dam(grd) | Nancy/Essey A/F | P-38 |

0-0-0 air
1.5-2 ground

* - shared with Capt. G.K. Sykes of the 435th Ftr Sqn, 479th Ftr Grp

**Locke, Richard E., Capt.**
374th Ftr Sqn/361st Ftr Grp

| Sqn | Date | Claims | Location | A/C |
|---|---|---|---|---|
| 374th | July 25, 1944 | (.5)Me-109 dest(grd)* | N/Alencon | P-51 |

0-0-0 air
0.5-0 ground

* - shared with Lt. J.O. Adkins of the 374th Ftr Sqn

**Loehnert, Richard O., Lt.**
55th Ftr Sqn/20th Ftr Grp

| Sqn | Date | Claims | Location | A/C |
|---|---|---|---|---|
| 55th | July 7, 1944 | (2)Me-109 dest(air) | Halle | P-38 |

2-0-0 air
0-0 ground

**Logan, George H., Jr., Lt.**
336th Ftr Sqn/4th Ftr Grp

| Sqn | Date | Claims | Location | A/C |
|---|---|---|---|---|
| 336th | April 18, 1944 | (.5)FW-190 dest(grd)* | Wenzendorf | P-51 |
| | August 25 | Me-109 dest(air) | E/Schwerin | P-51 |

1-0-0 air
0.5-0 ground

* - shared with Lt. N. Van Wyk of the 336th Ftr Sqn

**London, Charles P., Capt.**
83rd Ftr Sqn/78th Ftr Grp

| Sqn | Date | Claims | Location | A/C |
|---|---|---|---|---|
| 83rd | May 14, 1943 | FW-190 prob(air) | NW Antwerp | P-47 |
| | June 22 | FW-190 dest(air) | W/Walcheren Isle | P-47 |

| Sqn | Date | Claims | Location | A/C |
|---|---|---|---|---|
| | June 29 | (2)Me-109 dest(air) | Gournay | P-47 |
| | July 14 | Me-109 dam(air) | Le Touquet | P-47 |
| | | FW-190 dam(air) | Le Touquet | P-47 |
| | July 30 | Me-109 dest(air) | Haltern | P-47 |
| | | FW-190 dest(air) | Haltern | P-47 |

5-1-2 air
0-0 ground

**Long, Marion V., Lt.**
328th Ftr Sqn/352nd Ftr Grp

| Sqn | Date | Claims | Location | A/C |
|---|---|---|---|---|
| 328th | February 20, 1944 | FW-190 dam(air) | Vogeland | P-47 |
| | April 8 | (.5)Me-110 dest(grd)* | Quackenbruck | P-47 |
| | | Me-110 dam(grd) | Quackenbruck | P-47 |
| | April 9 | FW-190 dest(air) | Osnabruck | P-47 |

1-0-1 air
0.5-1 ground

* - shared with Lt. C.J. Bennette of the 328th Ftr Sqn

**Long, Sylvester F., Lt.**
436th Ftr Sqn/479th Ftr Grp

| Sqn | Date | Claims | Location | A/C |
|---|---|---|---|---|
| 436th | April 13, 1945 | (2)FW-190 dest(grd) | Salzwedel | P-51 |

0-0-0 air
2-0 ground

**Long, Thurman C., Lt.**
357th Ftr Sqn/355th Ftr Grp

| Sqn | Date | Claims | Location | A/C |
|---|---|---|---|---|
| 357th | November 18, 1944 | (2)Me-262 dest(grd) | Leipheim | P-51 |
| | | (2)Me-262 dam(grd) | Leipheim | P-51 |
| | February 23, 1945 | Me-163 dam(grd) | Neuburg | P-51 |
| | February 25 | Ju-188 dest(grd) | Fassberg | P-51 |
| | March 31 | Ju-88 dest(grd) | Magdeburg | P-51 |
| | April 4 | (2)FW-190 dest(air) | Halberstadt | P-51 |

2-0-0 air
4-3 ground

**Long, William M., Maj.**
HdQts/353rd Ftr Grp

| Sqn | Date | Claims | Location | A/C |
|---|---|---|---|---|
| HdQts | March 31, 1945 | Me-109 dest(air) | Hanover | P-51 |

1-0-0 air
0-0 ground

**Lorance, Thomas, Jr., Lt.**
350th Ftr Sqn/353rd Ftr Grp

| Sqn | Date | Claims | Location | A/C |
|---|---|---|---|---|
| 350th | April 8, 1944 | FW-190 dam(grd) | Hoperhofen A/F | P-47 |

0-0-0 air
0-1 ground

**Loveless, Philip M., Jr., Capt.**
505th Ftr Sqn/339th Ftr Grp

| Sqn | Date | Claims | Location | A/C |
|---|---|---|---|---|
| 505th | November 26, 1944 | (.5)FW-190 dest(air)* | S/Hanover | P-51 |
| | April 16, 1945 | FW-190 dest(grd) | NE Prague | P-51 |
| | | Ju-87 dam(grd) | NE Prague | P-51 |
| | April 17 | (3)Do-217 dest(grd) | SE Pocking | P-51 |
| | | Me-109 dest(grd) | SE Pocking | P-51 |
| | | Do-217 dam(grd) | SE Pocking | P-51 |
| | | Ju-88 dam(grd) | SE Pocking | P-51 |

0.5-0-0 air
5-3 ground

* - shared with Lt. W.R. Phillippi of the 505th Ftr Sqn

**Lowell, John H., LtCol.**
384th Ftr Sqn/364th Ftr Grp
HdQts/364th Ftr Grp

| Sqn | Date | Claims | Location | A/C |
|---|---|---|---|---|
| 384th | March 6, 1944 | Me-109 dest(air) | W/Hanover | P-38 |
| | | Me-109 prob(air) | W/Hanover | P-38 |
| | March 8 | (2)FW-190 dest(air) | Stendal-Alt Ruppin | P-38 |
| | March 29 | Ju-52 dest(grd) | Osnabruck | P-38 |
| | | FW-190 dam(grd) | Osnabruck | P-38 |
| | April 9 | FW-190 dest(grd) | Bramsche/Rheine | P-38 |
| | | FW-190 dam(grd) | Bramsche/Rheine | P-38 |
| | May 21 | (2)Ju-52 dest(grd) | Parchim-Hagenow-Ludwigslust | P-38 |
| | | He-111 dest(grd) | Par.-Hag.-Lud. | P-38 |
| | | Ju-88 dest(grd) | Par.-Hag.-Lud. | P-38 |
| | | FW-190 dam(grd) | Par.-Hag.-Lud. | P-38 |
| HdQts | November 21 | FW-190 dest(air) | E/Leipzig | P-51 |
| | December 5 | (3)FW-190 dest(air) | N/Berlin | P-51 |
| | | FW-190 dam(air) | N/Berlin | P-51 |
| | December 27 | (.5)Me-109 dest(air)* | W/Coblenz | P-51 |
| | | Me-109 dam(air) | W/Coblenz | P-51 |
| | April 17, 1945 | He-111 dest(grd) | Karlsbad | P-51 |
| | | Me-262 dest(grd) | Karlsbad | P-51 |
| | | FW-200 dest(grd) | Karlsbad | P-51 |

7.5-1-2 air
9-3 ground

* - shared with Lt. S.J. Price of the 384th Ftr Sqn

**Lowery, Arthur L., Lt.**
503rd Ftr Sqn/339th Ftr Grp

| Sqn | Date | Claims | Location | A/C |
|---|---|---|---|---|
| 503rd | May 21, 1944 | u/i a/c dest(grd) | Pelenz-Mackau | P-51 |

0-0-0 air
1-0 ground

**Lowman, Samuel J., Lt.**
63rd Ftr Sqn/56th Ftr Grp

| Sqn | Date | Claims | Location | A/C |
|---|---|---|---|---|
| 63rd | March 27, 1944 | (.25)Do-217 dest(air)* | S/Chartres | P-47 |
| | April 15 | He-111 dest(grd) | Flensburg | P-47 |

0.25-0-0 air
1-0 ground

* - shared with Maj. W.M. Mahurin, Lt. W.D. Johnson, and Lt. I.T. Porowski of the 63rd Ftr Sqn

**Lowther, Donald G., Lt.**
334th Ftr Sqn/4th Ftr Grp

| Sqn | Date | Claims | Location | A/C |
|---|---|---|---|---|
| 334th | February 25, 1945 | Ju-88 dam(grd) | Kothen | P-51 |
| | April 10 | Ju-52 dest(grd) | Wittstock | P-51 |
| | April 16 | u/i a/c dest(grd) | Gablingen | P-51 |

0-0-0 air
2-1 ground

**Loyd, Daniel T., Lt.**
84th Ftr Sqn/78th Ftr Grp

| Sqn | Date | Claims | Location | A/C |
|---|---|---|---|---|
| 84th | June 7, 1944 | Me-109 dest(air) | Montdidier | P-47 |

1-0-0 air
0-0 ground

**Lubien, James J., Lt.**
368th Ftr Sqn/359th Ftr Grp

| Sqn | Date | Claims | Location | A/C |
|---|---|---|---|---|
| 368th | June 21, 1944 | (2)u/i a/c dam(grd) | E/Plau | P-51 |

0-0-0 air
0-2 ground

**Lucas, Paul J., Jr., Lt.**
335th Ftr Sqn/4th Ftr Grp

| Sqn | Date | Claims | Location | A/C |
|---|---|---|---|---|
| 335th | April 16, 1945 | (2)u/i a/c dam(grd) | Praha/Letnany | P-51 |

0-0-0 air
0-2 ground

**Luckett, Thomas B., Lt.**
38th Ftr Sqn/55th Ftr Grp

| Sqn | Date | Claims | Location | A/C |
|---|---|---|---|---|
| 38th | August 24, 1944 | Ju-88 dest(grd) | Burg A/F | P-51 |

0-0-0 air
1-0 ground

**Luckey, William J., Jr., Capt.**
84th Ftr Sqn/78th Ftr Grp

| Sqn | Date | Claims | Location | A/C |
|---|---|---|---|---|
| 84th | May 19, 1944 | Me-109 dest(air) | Nienburg | P-47 |
| | July 1 | Me-109 dest(air) | St. Quentin | P-47 |

2-0-0 air
0-0 ground

**Ludeke, Edward P., Lt.**
357th Ftr Sqn/355th Ftr Grp

| Sqn | Date | Claims | Location | A/C |
|---|---|---|---|---|
| 357th | February 9, 1945 | FW-190 dest(air) | Brandenburg | P-51 |
| | February 23 | (2)Me-163 dam(grd) | Neuburg | P-51 |

1-0-0 air
0-2 ground

**Ludwig, Donald E., Lt.**
82nd Ftr Sqn/78th Ftr Grp

| Sqn | Date | Claims | Location | A/C |
|---|---|---|---|---|
| 82nd | February 6, 1944 | (.5)He-111 dam(grd)[*] | Orleans | P-47 |
| | | (.5)Ju-52 dam(grd)[*] | Orleans | P-47 |

0-0-0 air
0-1 ground

[*] - shared with Lt. J.W. Wilkinson of the 82nd Ftr Sqn

**Ludwig, Vance P., Lt.**
63rd Ftr Sqn/56th Ftr Grp

| Sqn | Date | Claims | Location | A/C |
|---|---|---|---|---|
| 63rd | October 4, 1943 | (3)Me-110 dest(air) | E/Duren | P-47 |

3-0-0 air
0-0 ground

**Luksic, Carl J., Lt.**
487th Ftr Sqn/352nd Ftr Grp

| Sqn | Date | Claims | Location | A/C |
|---|---|---|---|---|
| 487th | April 9, 1944 | (3)Ju-88 dest(grd) | Dummer Lake | P-51 |
| | April 10 | (.5)FW-190 dest(air)[*] | SW Rheims | P-51 |
| | April 11 | (2)Ju-88 dest(grd) | W/Berlin | P-51 |
| | | He-111 dest(grd) | W/Berlin | P-51 |
| | | Me-110 dest(grd) | W/Berlin | P-51 |
| | | (3)Ju-88 dam(grd) | W/Berlin | P-51 |
| | April 20 | (1.5)Me-109 dest(air)[**] | SE Paris | P-51 |
| | May 8 | (3)FW-190 dest(air) | Brunswick | P-51 |
| | | (2)Me-109 dest(air) | Brunswick | P-51 |
| | May 13 | (.5)Ju-88 dest(air)[@] | E/Neubrandenburg | P-51 |
| | May 19 | Me-109 dest(air) | Ludwigslust | P-51 |

8.5-0-0 air
7-3 ground

[*] - shared with Maj. J.C. Meyer of the 487th Ftr Sqn
[**] - shared with Lt. A. Bielok of the 487th Ftr Sqn
[@] - shared with Lt. G.T. Moran of the 487th Ftr Sqn

**Lundigan, George J., Capt.**
82nd Ftr Sqn/78th Ftr Grp

| Sqn | Date | Claims | Location | A/C |
|---|---|---|---|---|
| 82nd | April 12, 1944 | (.33)FW-190 dest(air)[*] | Malmedy | P-47 |

0.33-0-0 air
0-0 ground

[*] - shared with Maj. L.P. Marshall and Lt. R.L. Baker of the 82nd Ftr Sqn

**Lundquist, Gustav E., Maj.**
486th Ftr Sqn/352nd Ftr Grp

| Sqn | Date | Claims | Location | A/C |
|---|---|---|---|---|
| 486th | July 29, 1944 | (2)Me-109 dest(air) | Magdeburg | P-51 |

2-0-0 air
0-0 ground

**Lunstrum, Richard M., Lt.**
434th Ftr Sqn/479th Ftr Grp

| Sqn | Date | Claims | Location | A/C |
|---|---|---|---|---|
| 434th | September 28, 1944 | FW-190 dest(air) | Halberstadt A/F | P-51 |

1-0-0 air
0-0 ground

**Lutz, Willis H., Lt.**
84th Ftr Sqn/78th Ftr Grp

| Sqn | Date | Claims | Location | A/C |
|---|---|---|---|---|
| 84th | November 26, 1944 | FW-190 dest(grd) | Vorden A/F | P-47 |
| | January 14, 1945 | FW-190 dest(air) | SW Cologne | P-51 |
| | | Me-109 dest(air) | SW Cologne | P-51 |
| | | (2)FW-190 dam(air) | SW Cologne | P-51 |
| | April 16 | He-111 dest(grd) | Praha/Kakewice | P-51 |
| | | (2)u/i a/c dam(grd) | Praha/Kakewice | P-51 |

2-0-2 air
2-2 ground

**Lux, Frank O., Capt.**
370th Ftr Sqn/359th Ftr Grp

| Sqn | Date | Claims | Location | A/C |
|---|---|---|---|---|
| 370th | August 9, 1944 | Me-109 dest(air) | Gunzburg | P-51 |
| | August 16 | Me-109 dest(air) | Erfurt | P-51 |
| | December 31 | (.5)Me-109 dest(air)[*] | Hanover | P-51 |

2.5-0-0 air
0-0 ground

[*] - shared with Lt. W.J. Rueschenberg of the 370th Ftr Sqn

**Lynch, James L., Lt.**
505th Ftr Sqn/339th Ftr Grp

| Sqn | Date | Claims | Location | A/C |
|---|---|---|---|---|
| 505th | May 21, 1944 | (1.5)Trainer dest(air)[*] | Riessa | P-51 |
| | | Do-217 dest(air) | Riessa | P-51 |
| | May 24 | Me-109 dest(grd) | Gifhorn | P-51 |

2.5-0-0 air
1-0 ground

[*] - shared with Lt. G.F. Perry of the 505th Ftr Sqn

**Lynch, William J., Lt.**
358th Ftr Sqn/355th Ftr Grp

| Sqn | Date | Claims | Location | A/C |
|---|---|---|---|---|
| 358th | April 9, 1945 | Me-110 dest(grd) | Heilfingen | P-51 |
| | | He-111 dest(grd) | Heilfingen | P-51 |
| | | u/i a/c dam(grd) | Heilfingen | P-51 |
| | April 16 | (2)FW-190 dest(grd) | Straubing | P-51 |
| | | Ju-88 dest(grd) | Straubing | P-51 |

0-0-0 air
5-1 ground

**Lyons, William S., Lt.**
357th Ftr Sqn/355th Ftr Grp

| Sqn | Date | Claims | Location | A/C |
|---|---|---|---|---|
| 357th | November 26, 1944 | Me-109 dest(air) | W/Gardelegen | P-51 |
| | February 9, 1945 | Me-109 dest(air) | Brandenburg | P-51 |
| | March 3 | Me-262 dam(air) | Brunswick | P-51 |

2-0-1 air
0-0 ground

**Mabie, Robert J., Capt.**
335th Ftr Sqn/4th Ftr Grp

| *Sqn* | *Date* | *Claims* | *Location* | *A/C* |
|---|---|---|---|---|
| 335th | November 18, 1944 | (2)Me-262 dam(grd) | Leipheim | P-51 |

0-0-0 air
0-2 ground

**MacClarence, William R., Lt.**
505th Ftr Sqn/339th Ftr Grp

| *Sqn* | *Date* | *Claims* | *Location* | *A/C* |
|---|---|---|---|---|
| 505th | April 4, 1945 | Me-410 dest(grd) | NE Tribsees | P-51 |
| | April 10 | (3)Ju-88 dest(grd) | N/Neuruppin | P-51 |
| | April 16 | (2)u/i a/c dest(grd) | NE Prague | P-51 |
| | April 17 | Ju-188 dest(grd) | SE Pocking | P-51 |
| | | He-111 dest(grd) | SE Pocking | P-51 |

0-0-0 air
8-0 ground

**MacConkey, Jack S., F/O**
358th Ftr Sqn/355th Ftr Grp

| *Sqn* | *Date* | *Claims* | *Location* | *A/C* |
|---|---|---|---|---|
| 358th | April 5, 1944 | (2)Do-217 dest(grd) | Munich | P-51 |
| | | (3)Do-217 dam(grd) | Munich | P-51 |
| | | Me-110 dam(grd) | Munich | P-51 |
| | April 15 | Do-217 dest(grd) | Glienicke | P-51 |
| | | Do-217 dam(grd) | Glienicke | P-51 |

0-0-0 air
3-5 ground

**MacDermott, James B., Lt.**
383rd Ftr Sqn/364th Ftr Grp

| *Sqn* | *Date* | *Claims* | *Location* | *A/C* |
|---|---|---|---|---|
| 383rd | May 22, 1944 | FW-190 dest(air) | Kiel | P-38 |
| | | FW-190 dam(air) | Kiel | P-38 |

1-0-1 air
0-0 ground

**Mace, Harvey F., Capt.**
362nd Ftr Sqn/357th Ftr Grp

| *Sqn* | *Date* | *Claims* | *Location* | *A/C* |
|---|---|---|---|---|
| 362nd | July 29, 1944 | Me-109 dest(air) | W/Merseburg | P-51 |
| | September 18 | Me-109 dest(air) | Nijmegen | P-51 |

2-0-0 air
0-0 ground

**MacFarlane, Walter E., Lt.**
357th Ftr Sqn/355th Ftr Grp

| *Sqn* | *Date* | *Claims* | *Location* | *A/C* |
|---|---|---|---|---|
| 357th | March 16, 1944 | Me-109 dam(air) | W/Augsburg | P-51 |
| | April 15 | u/i a/c dest(grd) | E/Celle | P-51 |
| | May 21 | (.5)Me-108 dest(air)* | W/Schwerin | P-51 |
| | | Do-217 dest(grd) | W/Schwerin | P-51 |
| | | (5)Do-217 dam(grd) | W/Schwerin | P-51 |
| | May 28 | Me-109 dest(air) | N/Limburg | P-51 |

1.5-0-1 air
2-5 ground

* - shared with Lt. J.C. Engelbreit of the 357th Ftr Sqn

**Machen, Evan J., Capt.**
77th Ftr Sqn/20th Ftr Grp

| *Sqn* | *Date* | *Claims* | *Location* | *A/C* |
|---|---|---|---|---|
| 77th | January 29, 1944 | Me-110 dest(air) | SW Frankfurt | P-38 |
| | April 8 | (2)Ju-88 dest(grd) | Salzwedel | P-38 |
| | | (2)Ju-88 dam(grd) | Salzwedel | P-38 |

1-0-0 air
2-2 ground

**MacKean, Robert G., Capt.**
486th Ftr Sqn/352nd Ftr Grp

| *Sqn* | *Date* | *Claims* | *Location* | *A/C* |
|---|---|---|---|---|
| 486th | April 24, 1944 | (3)Me-110 dest(grd) | Ingolstadt | P-51 |
| | | (2)Ju-88 dest(grd) | Ingolstadt | P-51 |

0-0-0 air
5-0 ground

**MaClay, Alfred B., Lt.**
374th Ftr Sqn/361st Ftr Grp

| *Sqn* | *Date* | *Claims* | *Location* | *A/C* |
|---|---|---|---|---|
| 374th | September 18, 1944 | Me-109 dest(grd) | Jagel A/F | P-51 |
| | | (4)Me-109 dam(grd) | Jagel A/F | P-51 |

0-0-0 air
1-4 ground

**Macurdy, Harold H., Lt.**
358th Ftr Sqn/355th Ftr Grp

| *Sqn* | *Date* | *Claims* | *Location* | *A/C* |
|---|---|---|---|---|
| 358th | December 1, 1943 | Me-109 prob(air) | NW Aachen | P-47 |
| | January 29, 1944 | Me-109 dest(air) | Coblenz | P-47 |
| | | FW-190 dest(air) | Liege | P-47 |

2-1-0 air
0-0 ground

**Madison, Garland F., Lt.**
368th Ftr Sqn/359th Ftr Grp

| *Sqn* | *Date* | *Claims* | *Location* | *A/C* |
|---|---|---|---|---|
| 368th | April 13, 1945 | Me-110 dest(grd) | Luneburg | P-51 |
| | | u/i a/c dest(grd) | Luneburg | P-51 |

0-0-0 air
2-0 ground

**Madole, William H., Capt.**
83rd Ftr Sqn/78th Ftr Grp

| *Sqn* | *Date* | *Claims* | *Location* | *A/C* |
|---|---|---|---|---|
| 83rd | July 1, 1943 | FW-190 dest(air) | Schouwen | P-47 |
| | July 30 | FW-190 dest(air) | Raesfeld | P-47 |
| | August 24 | (3)FW-190 dam(air) | Evreux | P-47 |

2-0-3 air
0-0 ground

**Madson, John A., Lt.**
350th Ftr Sqn/353rd Ftr Grp

| *Sqn* | *Date* | *Claims* | *Location* | *A/C* |
|---|---|---|---|---|
| 350th | February 28, 1945 | u/i a/c dest(grd) | S/Gotha | P-51 |
| | | Ju-88 dam(grd) | S/Gotha | P-51 |

0-0-0 air
1-1 ground

**Magel, David M., Lt.**
63rd Ftr Sqn/56th Ftr Grp

| *Sqn* | *Date* | *Claims* | *Location* | *A/C* |
|---|---|---|---|---|
| 63rd | December 2, 1944 | Me-109 dam(air) | S/Marburg | P-47 |

0-0-1 air
0-0 ground

**Magel, Robert W., F/O**
63rd Ftr Sqn/56th Ftr Grp

| *Sqn* | *Date* | *Claims* | *Location* | *A/C* |
|---|---|---|---|---|
| 63rd | July 4, 1944 | Me-109 dest(air) | SW Evreux | P-47 |

1-0-0 air
0-0 ground

**Maguire, William J., Capt.**
351st Ftr Sqn/353rd Ftr Grp

| Sqn | Date | Claims | Location | A/C |
|---|---|---|---|---|
| 351st | September 27, 1943 | Me-109 dest(air) | W/Emden | P-47 |
| | | Me-109 dam(air) | W/Emden | P-47 |
| | October 14 | FW-190 dest(air) | Flacher | P-47 |
| | June 7, 1944 | (2)Me-109 dest(air) | Beauvais/Tille | P-47 |
| | | Me-109 dam(air) | Beauvais/Tille | P-47 |
| | June 25 | Me-410 dest(grd) | Bourges | P-47 |
| | July 9 | Me-109 dest(air) | Argentan | P-47 |
| | March 14, 1945 | (2)Me-109 dest(air) | Luckenwalde | P-51 |

7-0-2 air
1-0 ground

**Mahany, Howard, Jr., Lt.**
343rd Ftr Sqn/55th Ftr Grp

| Sqn | Date | Claims | Location | A/C |
|---|---|---|---|---|
| 343rd | April 9, 1945 | He-111 dest(grd) | Munich-Brunnthal | P-51 |
| | | Me-262 dest(grd) | Munich-Brunnthal | P-51 |
| | | He-111 dam(grd) | Munich-Brunnthal | P-51 |
| | April 17 | (3)Me-410 dest(grd) | Dresden | P-51 |
| | | (2)FW-190 dest(grd) | Dresden | P-51 |
| | | (2)FW-190 dam(air) | Dresden | P-51 |

0-0-0 air
7-3 ground

**Mahurin, Walker M., Maj.**
63rd Ftr Sqn/56th Ftr Grp
Later flew in the PTO with the 3rd ACG and claimed a Dinah on January 14, 1945.

| Sqn | Date | Claims | Location | A/C |
|---|---|---|---|---|
| 63rd | August 17, 1943 | (2)FW-190 dest(air) | Eupen-St. Nicholas | P-47 |
| | September 9 | FW-190 dest(air) | S/Beauvais | P-47 |
| | October 4 | (3)Me-110 dest(air) | E/Duren | P-47 |
| | November 3 | Me-110 dest(air) | N/Juist | P-47 |
| | | (.5)Me-109 dest(air)* | N/Essens | P-47 |
| | November 26 | (3)Me-110 dest(air) | S/Oldenburg-Zuider Zee | P-47 |
| | | Me-110 prob(air) | S/Oldenburg-Zuider Zee | P-47 |
| | November 29 | Me-109 dest(air) | Leer-Papenburg | P-47 |
| | | Me-109 dam(air) | Leer-Papenburg | P-47 |
| | December 22 | (2)Me-109 dest(air) | Hesepe | P-47 |
| | January 30, 1944 | Ju-88 dest(air) | S/Quackenbruck | P-47 |
| | | Ju-88 prob(air) | S/Quackenbruck | P-47 |
| | February 3 | Me-109 dest(air) | SE Ruhlertwist | P-47 |
| | March 6 | FW-190 dest(air) | Wenzendorf A/F | P-47 |
| | | FW-190 prob(air) | Wenzendorf A/F | P-47 |
| | March 8 | (2)FW-190 dest(air) | Wesendorf A/F | P-47 |
| | | Ju-88 dest(air) | Wesendorf A/F | P-47 |
| | March 27 | (.25)Do-217 dest(air)** | S/Chartres | P-47 |

19.75-3-1 air
0-0 ground

* - shared with Lt. W.J. O'Connor of the 63rd Ftr Sqn
** - shared with Lt. W.D. Johnson, Lt. I.T. Porowski, and F/O S.J. Lowman of the 63rd Ftr Sqn

**Maisch, Joseph J., Jr., Lt.**
358th Ftr Sqn/355th Ftr Grp

| Sqn | Date | Claims | Location | A/C |
|---|---|---|---|---|
| 358th | July 24, 1944 | Do-217 dest(grd) | Augsburg | P-51 |
| | September 11 | (2)Me-109 dest(air) | Marburg | P-51 |

2-0-0 air
1-0 ground

**Major, Ross O., Lt.**
370th Ftr Sqn/359th Ftr Grp

| Sqn | Date | Claims | Location | A/C |
|---|---|---|---|---|
| 370th | February 10, 1944 | Me-109 dest(air) | E/Zuider Zee | P-47 |

1-0-0 air
0-0 ground

**Malarz, Chester, Capt.**
505th Ftr Sqn/339th Ftr Grp

| Sqn | Date | Claims | Location | A/C |
|---|---|---|---|---|
| 505th | September 10, 1944 | (2)Ju-88 dest(grd) | Weizenburg | P-51 |
| | | Me-410 dest(grd) | Weizenburg | P-51 |
| | | (3)He-111 dam(grd) | Weizenburg | P-51 |
| | | Ju-88 dam(grd) | Weizenburg | P-51 |
| | November 18 | (.5)Me-109 dest(air)* | Neustadt | P-51 |

0.5-0-0 air
3-4 ground

* - shared with Lt. G.T. Rich of the 505th Ftr Sqn

**Maldanado, Mario, Lt.**
55th Ftr Sqn/20th Ftr Grp

| Sqn | Date | Claims | Location | A/C |
|---|---|---|---|---|
| 55th | October 6, 1944 | Do-24 dest(grd) | Kubitzer Bay | P-51 |
| | | Do-24 dam(grd) | Kubitzer Bay | P-51 |

0-0-0 air
1-1 ground

**Maley, Ronald L., Lt.**
434th Ftr Sqn/479th Ftr Grp

| Sqn | Date | Claims | Location | A/C |
|---|---|---|---|---|
| 434th | August 18, 1944 | (2)He-111 dam(grd) | Nancy/Essey A/F | P-38 |
| | | FW-190 dam(grd) | Nancy/Essey A/F | P-38 |
| | September 10 | He-111 dam(grd) | Malmsheim | P-38 |
| | September 26 | Me-109 dest(air) | SW Munster | P-38 |
| | December 5 | FW-190 prob(air) | Neuruppin | P-51 |

1-1-0 air
0-4 ground

**Malmstedt, Roland M., Capt.**
343rd Ftr Sqn/55th Ftr Grp

| Sqn | Date | Claims | Location | A/C |
|---|---|---|---|---|
| 343rd | November 3, 1943 | Me-109 dam(air) | E/Wilhelmshaven | P-38 |
| | November 25 | Me-109 prob(air) | Lille | P-38 |
| | November 26 | Ju-88 dest(air) | NE Bremen | P-38 |

1-1-1 air
0-0 ground

**Malmsten, Donald M., Capt.**
334th Ftr Sqn/4th Ftr Grp

| Sqn | Date | Claims | Location | A/C |
|---|---|---|---|---|
| 334th | April 10, 1944 | u/i a/c dam(grd) | Romorantin A/F | P-51 |
| | April 18 | Ju-52 dest(grd) | Juterbog A/F | P-51 |
| | | (.25) of (6)Ju-52 dam(grd)* | Juterbog A/F | P-51 |
| | June 20 | Ju-88 dest(air) | Pasewalk | P-51 |
| | February 25, 1945 | (.5)FW-190 dest(air)** | Dessau | P-51 |
| | February 27 | (3)u/i a/c dest(grd) | Weimar | P-51 |
| | | (2)Ju-88 dest(grd) | Weimar | P-51 |
| | | Me-109 dest(grd) | Weimar | P-51 |
| | March 21 | (2)Me-109 dest(grd) | Achmer | P-51 |

1.5-0-0 air
9-2.5 ground

* - all shared with Lt. D.W. Howe, Lt. J.L. Lang, and Lt. S.W. Monroe of the 334th Ftr Sqn
** - shared with Lt. W.C. O'Bryan of the 334th Ftr Sqn

**Malmstrom, Einar A., Col.**
HdQts/356th Ftr Grp

| Sqn | Date | Claims | Location | A/C |
|---|---|---|---|---|
| HdQts | March 20, 1944 | Me-109 dest(air) | Charleville | P-47 |
| | April 11 | (2)Me-110 dest(grd) | Gifhorn | P-47 |
| | | (.25)Me-109 dest(grd)* | Gifhorn | P-47 |
| | | (.25)Ju-88 dest(grd)* | Gifhorn | P-47 |
| | April 23 | (3)He-111 dest(grd) | Hagenau | P-47 |

1-0-0 air
5.5-0 ground

* - both shared with Lt. J.V. Jack, Lt. R. Gibson, and F/O E.L. Decker of the 361st Ftr Sqn, 356th Ftr Grp

**Malone, Jay C., Capt.**
436th Ftr Sqn/479th Ftr Grp

| Sqn | Date | Claims | Location | A/C |
|---|---|---|---|---|
| 436th | February 21, 1945 | Ju-188 dam(grd) | Nordhausen | P-51 |
| | February 22 | Ju-88 dam(grd) | Halberstadt | P-51 |
| | April 13 | (2)FW-190 dest(grd) | Salzwedel | P-51 |
| | | Me-110 dest(grd) | Salzwedel | P-51 |
| | | (2)FW-190 dam(grd) | Salzwedel | P-51 |

| | | Me-410 dam(grd) | Salzwedel | P-51 |
|---|---|---|---|---|
| | April 16 | FW-190 dest(grd) | Landstedt | P-51 |

0-0-0 air
4-5 ground

**Maloney, John T., Lt.**
38th Ftr Sqn/55th Ftr Grp

| *Sqn* | *Date* | *Claims* | *Location* | *A/C* |
|---|---|---|---|---|
| 38th | April 9, 1945 | Me-262 dest(grd) | Munich-Brunnthal | P-51 |
| | | (2)u/i a/c dam(grd) | Munich-Brunnthal | P-51 |
| | April 10 | (2)Me-109 dest(grd) | Wesendorf | P-51 |
| | | FW-190 dest(grd) | Wesendorf | P-51 |
| | April 16 | Ju-52 dest(grd) | Bad Aibling | P-51 |
| | | u/i a/c dam(grd) | Bad Aibling | P-51 |

0-0-0 air
5-3 ground

**Maloney, Robert F., Capt.**
38th Ftr Sqn/55th Ftr Grp

| *Sqn* | *Date* | *Claims* | *Location* | *A/C* |
|---|---|---|---|---|
| 38th | November 13, 1943 | FW-190 dest(air) | Bremen | P-38 |
| | | FW-190 dam(air) | Bremen | P-38 |
| | November 25 | Me-109 dest(air) | Lille | P-38 |
| | | Me-109 prob(air) | Hazebrouck | P-38 |
| | September 5, 1944 | Ju-88 dest(grd) | Stuttgart/Boblingen | P-51 |
| | September 10 | Ju-88 dest(grd) | Kitzingen | P-51 |
| | December 24 | (.5)FW-190 dest(air)* | S/Coblenz | P-51 |

2.5-1-1 air
2-0 ground

* - shared with Lt. W.B. Staggs of the 38th Ftr Sqn

**Mann, Herbert R., Capt.**
354th Ftr Sqn/355th Ftr Grp

| *Sqn* | *Date* | *Claims* | *Location* | *A/C* |
|---|---|---|---|---|
| 354th | September 27, 1944 | (.5)Ju-88 dest(grd)* | Eschwege | P-51 |
| | February 23, 1945 | Ju-88 dest(grd) | Neuburg | P-51 |

0-0-0 air
1.5-0 ground

* - shared with LtCol. E.W. Stewart of HdQts, 355th Ftr Grp

**Manning, Cecil E., Capt.**
335th Ftr Sqn/4th Ftr Grp

| *Sqn* | *Date* | *Claims* | *Location* | *A/C* |
|---|---|---|---|---|
| 335th | February 10, 1944 | FW-190 dest(air) | SW Hanover | P-47 |
| | | FW-190 dam(air) | SW Hanover | P-47 |
| | March 6, 1944 | Do-217 dest(air) | SE Brandenburg | P-51 |
| | | Do-217 prob(air) | SE Brandenburg | P-51 |

2-1-1 air
0-0 ground

**Mansker, Joseph L., Capt.**
55th Ftr Sqn/20th Ftr Grp
HdQts/20th Ftr Grp

| *Sqn* | *Date* | *Claims* | *Location* | *A/C* |
|---|---|---|---|---|
| 55th | August 6, 1944 | FW-190 dest(air) | S/Brandenburg | P-51 |
| | August 25 | (5)Ju-88 dest(grd) | Parow A/F | P-51 |
| | | BV-140 dest(grd) | Parow A/F | P-51 |
| | | (3)Ju-88 dam(grd) | Parow A/F | P-51 |
| | October 6 | u/i a/c dest(grd) | Kubitzer Bay | P-51 |
| | November 2 | (2)Me-109 dest(air) | Halle-Merseburg | P-51 |
| | | Me-109 prob(air) | Halle-Merseburg | P-51 |

3-1-0 air
7-3 ground

**Manthos, Atlee G., Capt.**
363rd Ftr Sqn/357th Ftr Grp

| *Sqn* | *Date* | *Claims* | *Location* | *A/C* |
|---|---|---|---|---|
| 363rd | December 5, 1944 | FW-190 dam(air) | N/Berlin | P-51 |
| | March 19, 1945 | Me-262 dam(air) | E/Leipzig | P-51 |

0-0-2 air
0-0 ground

**Marangello, William A., Lt.**
61st Ftr Sqn/56th Ftr Grp

| *Sqn* | *Date* | *Claims* | *Location* | *A/C* |
|---|---|---|---|---|
| 61st | October 4, 1943 | Me-110 dest(air) | W/Aachen | P-47 |

1-0-0 air
0-0 ground

**Marchant, William S., Capt.**
352nd Ftr Sqn/353rd Ftr Grp

| *Sqn* | *Date* | *Claims* | *Location* | *A/C* |
|---|---|---|---|---|
| 352nd | February 25, 1944 | (.5)Me-110 dest(grd)* | Luxembourg | P-47 |
| | | Do-217 dam(grd) | Charleroi | P-47 |
| | May 19 | Me-109 dam(air) | SW Brunswick | P-47 |
| | May 25 | u/i a/c dest(grd) | N/Reims | P-47 |
| | | (3)Me-109 dam(grd) | N/Reims | P-47 |

0-0-1 air
1.5-4 ground

* - shared with Lt. W.F. Streit of the 352nd Ftr Sqn

**Marcotte, John C., Lt.**
63rd Ftr Sqn/56th Ftr Grp

| *Sqn* | *Date* | *Claims* | *Location* | *A/C* |
|---|---|---|---|---|
| 63rd | March 8, 1944 | FW-190 prob(air) | Dummer Lake | P-47 |

0-1-0 air
0-0 ground

**Maree, Howard P., Lt.**
351st Ftr Sqn/353rd Ftr Grp

| *Sqn* | *Date* | *Claims* | *Location* | *A/C* |
|---|---|---|---|---|
| 351st | September 13, 1944 | (.5)FW-200 dest(grd)* | Hellingen | P-47 |
| | January 14, 1945 | FW-190 dest(air) | SE Hamburg | P-51 |
| | | Me-109 dest(air) | SE Hamburg | P-51 |

2-0-0 air
0.5-0 ground

* - shared with Lt. H.D. Milligan of the 351st Ftr Sqn

**Marevka, Edward J., Lt.**
375th Ftr Sqn/361st Ftr Grp

| *Sqn* | *Date* | *Claims* | *Location* | *A/C* |
|---|---|---|---|---|
| 375th | September 13, 1944 | u/i a/c dest(grd) | Schwabeich Hall | P-51 |

0-0-0 air
1-0 ground

**Markel, Alfred H., Capt.**
334th Ftr Sqn/4th Ftr Grp

| *Sqn* | *Date* | *Claims* | *Location* | *A/C* |
|---|---|---|---|---|
| 334th | March 27, 1944 | (.5)Ju-88 dest(grd)* | Cazaux A/F | P-51 |
| | March 28 | Me-109 dam(grd) | W/Dreux | P-51 |
| | April 8 | FW-190 dest(air) | Celle | P-51 |
| | | Me-109 dam(air) | Celle | P-51 |
| | April 9 | u/i a/c dam(grd) | S/Osnabruck | P-51 |

1-0-1 air
0.5-2 ground

* - shared with Lt. N. Megura of the 334th Ftr Sqn

**Markham, Gene E., Capt.**
351st Ftr Sqn/353rd Ftr Grp

| *Sqn* | *Date* | *Claims* | *Location* | *A/C* |
|---|---|---|---|---|
| 351st | November 18, 1944 | Me-262 dam(air) | S/Augsburg | P-51 |
| | November 27 | FW-190 dest(air) | NE Steinhuder Lake | P-51 |
| | January 14, 1945 | (.5)Me-262 dam(air)* | E/Hanover | P-51 |
| | February 25 | FW-200 dam(grd) | Lechfeld | P-51 |
| | March 14, 1945 | (3)Me-109 dest(air) | Luckenwalde | P-51 |
| | April 7 | Me-109 dest(air) | E/Steinhuder Lake | P-51 |

| Sqn | Date | Claims | Location | A/C |
|---|---|---|---|---|
| | | Me-109 dam(air) | E/Steinhuder Lake | P-51 |

5-0-2.5 air
0-1 ground

* - shared with Lt. M.A. Arnold of the 351st Ftr Sqn

**Marlowe, Wendell H., Lt.**
434th Ftr Sqn/479th Ftr Grp

| Sqn | Date | Claims | Location | A/C |
|---|---|---|---|---|
| 434th | November 6, 1944 | (.5)FW-190 dest(grd)* | Hesepe | P-51 |

0-0-0 air
0.5-0 ground

* - shared with Lt. T.C. Olson of the 434th Ftr Sqn

**Marmon, Leon H., Lt.**
2nd Scouting Force

| Sqn | Date | Claims | Location | A/C |
|---|---|---|---|---|
| 2nd | November 26, 1944 | FW-190 dam(air) | S/Hanover | P-51 |

0-0-1 air
0-0 ground

**Marron, John T., Lt.**
368th Ftr Sqn/359th Ftr Grp

| Sqn | Date | Claims | Location | A/C |
|---|---|---|---|---|
| 368th | April 10, 1945 | Me-262 dam(air) | NW Gustrow | P-51 |
| | April 16 | (2)Me-109 dest(grd) | E/Plattling | P-51 |

0-0-1 air
2-0 ground

**Marsh, Halbert G., Lt.**
358th Ftr Sqn/355th Ftr Grp

| Sqn | Date | Claims | Location | A/C |
|---|---|---|---|---|
| 358th | April 16, 1945 | (5)FW-190 dest(grd) | Straubing | P-51 |
| | | (2)FW-190 dam(grd) | Straubing | P-51 |

0-0-0 air
5-2 ground

**Marsh, Lester C., Lt.**
503rd Ftr Sqn/339th Ftr Grp

| Sqn | Date | Claims | Location | A/C |
|---|---|---|---|---|
| 503rd | September 23, 1944 | FW-190 dest(air) | SW Wesel | P-51 |
| | November 18 | Me-109 dest(air) | Mannheim | P-51 |
| | November 26 | (3)FW-190 dest(air) | SE Dummer Lake | P-51 |
| | | FW-190 prob(air) | SE Dummer Lake | P-51 |
| | | FW-190 dam(air) | SE Dummer Lake | P-51 |

5-1-1 air
0-0 ground

**Marshall, Alfred L., Lt.**
486th Ftr Sqn/352nd Ftr Grp

| Sqn | Date | Claims | Location | A/C |
|---|---|---|---|---|
| 486th | January 30, 1944 | (.5)Me-110 dest(air)* | Nordhorn | P-47 |
| | April 11 | Ju-88 dam(grd) | Nehesdorf | P-51 |
| | | u/i a/c dam(grd) | Nehesdorf | P-51 |

0.5-0-0 air
0-2 ground

* - shared with Capt. E.J. Gignac of the 486th Ftr Sqn

**Marshall, Bert W., Jr., LtCol.**
354th Ftr Sqn/355th Ftr Grp
HdQts/355th Ftr Grp

| Sqn | Date | Claims | Location | A/C |
|---|---|---|---|---|
| 354th | June 6, 1944 | Ju-87 dest(air) | Chartres-Dire | P-51 |
| | June 20 | (2)Me-109 dest(air) | Bergen | P-51 |
| | July 28 | Me-109 dest(air) | Mulhausen | P-51 |
| | August 6 | Me-109 dest(air) | S/Hamburg | P-51 |
| | September 11 | (2)Me-109 dest(air) | S/Kassel | P-51 |
| | | Me-109 dam(air) | S/Kassel | P-51 |
| HdQts | April 13, 1945 | (2)u/i a/c dest(grd) | Husum A/F | P-51 |
| | | Me-109 dest(grd) | Husum A/F | P-51 |
| | | (2)u/i a/c dam(grd) | Husum A/F | P-51 |
| | | FW-190 dam(air) | Husum A/F | P-51 |

7-0-1 air
3-3 ground

**Marshall, Donald W., Lt.**
63rd Ftr Sqn/56th Ftr Grp

| Sqn | Date | Claims | Location | A/C |
|---|---|---|---|---|
| 63rd | April 24, 1944 | (.5)Me-210 dest(grd)* | Thalheim A/F | P-47 |
| | | (1.25)u/i a/c dam(grd)** | Thalheim A/F | P-47 |
| | | Me-109 dam(grd) | Thalheim A/F | P-47 |

0-0-0 air
0.5-2.25 ground

* - shared with Lt. A.J. Wisniewski of the 63rd Ftr Sqn
** - shared with Lt. S.B. Dale, Lt. H.F. Warner, and Lt. A.J. Wisniewski of the 63rd Ftr Sqn

**Marshall, Frank R., Jr., Capt.**
370th Ftr Sqn/359th Ftr Grp

| Sqn | Date | Claims | Location | A/C |
|---|---|---|---|---|
| 370th | November 27, 1944 | Me-109 dest(air) | Hanover | P-51 |

1-0-0 air
0-0 ground

**Marshall, Leonard P., LtCol.**
82nd Ftr Sqn/78th Ftr Grp
84th Ftr Sqn/78th Ftr Grp
HdQts/78th Ftr Grp

| Sqn | Date | Claims | Location | A/C |
|---|---|---|---|---|
| 82nd | April 12, 1944 | (.33)FW-190 dest(air)* | Malmedy | P-47 |
| 84th | November 9 | (2)He-111 dam(grd) | Schenfheim A/F | P-47 |
| | January 14, 1945 | Me-109 dest(air) | S/Cologne | P-51 |

1.33-0-0 air
0-2 ground

* - shared with Lt. R.L. Baker and Lt. G.J. Lundigan of the 82nd Ftr Sqn

**Marsiglia, Joseph P., Capt.**
338th Ftr Sqn/55th Ftr Grp

| Sqn | Date | Claims | Location | A/C |
|---|---|---|---|---|
| 338th | November 13, 1943 | Me-210 prob(air) | Hagen | P-38 |
| | November 29 | Me-109 dam(air) | E/Emmen | P-38 |

0-1-1 air
0-0 ground

**Martin, Allen G., Lt.**
368th Ftr Sqn/359th Ftr Grp

| Sqn | Date | Claims | Location | A/C |
|---|---|---|---|---|
| 368th | February 28, 1945 | Me-109 dest(grd) | Gunzberg | P-51 |

0-0-0 air
1-0 ground

**Martin, Jack T., Lt.**
79th Ftr Sqn/20th Ftr Grp

| Sqn | Date | Claims | Location | A/C |
|---|---|---|---|---|
| 79th | January 30, 1944 | (.5)Me-210 dest(air)* | Brunswick | P-38 |

0.5-0-0 air
0-0 ground

* - shared with Capt. R.P. Gatterdam of the 79th Ftr Sqn

**Martin, William D., Lt.**
354th Ftr Sqn/355th Ftr Grp

| Sqn | Date | Claims | Location | A/C |
|---|---|---|---|---|
| 354th | May 13, 1944 | Hs-129 dest(air) | Landsberg | P-51 |
| | June 20 | (2)Me-109 dest(air) | Rugen | P-51 |

| Sqn | Date | Claims | Location | A/C |
|---|---|---|---|---|
| | June 24 | (2)Me-109 dest(grd) | Angars | P-51 |
| | July 8 | Me-109 dest(grd) | SW Chalons | P-51 |
| | | (2)Me-109 dam(grd) | SW Chalons | P-51 |
| | August 6 | Me-109 dest(air) | S/Hamburg | P-51 |

4-0-0 air
3-2 ground

**Martinek, Thomas W., Lt.**
362nd Ftr Sqn/357th Ftr Grp

| Sqn | Date | Claims | Location | A/C |
|---|---|---|---|---|
| 362nd | June 20, 1944 | (.5)Me-110 dam(grd)* | Neumunster | P-51 |
| | July 29 | (.5)Me-109 dest(air)** | W/Merseburg | P-51 |
| | October 6 | FW-190 dest(air) | NW Berlin | P-51 |
| | | FW-190 prob(air) | NW Berlin | P-51 |
| | October 7 | (2)FW-190 dest(air) | SW Leipzig | P-51 |

3.5-1-0 air
0-0.5 ground

* - shared with Lt. L.K. Carson of the 362nd Ftr Sqn
** - shared with Capt. R.H. Becker of the 362nd Ftr Sqn

**Martinez, Manuel S., Capt.**
82nd Ftr Sqn/78th Ftr Grp

| Sqn | Date | Claims | Location | A/C |
|---|---|---|---|---|
| 82nd | September 27, 1943 | Me-109 dest(air) | Emden | P-47 |
| | December 22 | Me-109 dest(air) | Reims | P-47 |
| | January 4, 1944 | Me-109 dest(air) | Antwerp | P-47 |
| | | Me-110 dam(air) | Antwerp | P-47 |
| | January 29 | FW-190 dest(air) | Coblenz | P-47 |

4-0-1 air
0-0 ground

**Marts, Jay F., Lt.**
505th Ftr Sqn/339th Ftr Grp

| Sqn | Date | Claims | Location | A/C |
|---|---|---|---|---|
| 505th | August 28, 1944 | Ju-88 dest(grd) | Savernne | P-51 |
| | September 10 | (2)Me-410 dest(grd) | Weizenburg | P-51 |
| | | (2)He-111 dam(grd) | Weizenburg | P-51 |
| | | Ju-88 dam(grd) | Weizenburg | P-51 |
| | | u/i a/c dam(grd) | Weizenburg | P-51 |
| | March 2, 1945 | (2)Me-109 dest(air) | E/Magdeburg | P-51 |

2-0-0 air
3-4 ground

**Martyn, Donald M., Lt.**
358th Ftr Sqn/355th Ftr Grp

| Sqn | Date | Claims | Location | A/C |
|---|---|---|---|---|
| 358th | April 11, 1944 | (.25)Me-410 dest(air)* | NE Berlin | P-51 |
| | | (.25)Ju-88 dest(air)* | NE Berlin | P-51 |
| | May 4 | Me-109 dest(air) | SW Hanover | P-51 |
| | | Me-109 dam(air) | SW Hanover | P-51 |

1.5-0-1 air
0-0 ground

* - both shared with Lt. R.J. Fussell, Lt. W.V. Gresham, and F/O L.M. Dudley of the 358th Ftr Sqn

**Marvel, Thomas W., Lt.**
505th Ftr Sqn/339th Ftr Grp

| Sqn | Date | Claims | Location | A/C |
|---|---|---|---|---|
| 505th | March 1, 1945 | Ju-88 dest(grd) | S/Feldkirchen | P-51 |
| | April 10 | (3)Me-410 dest(grd) | N/Neuruppin | P-51 |
| | | Me-410 dam(grd) | N/Neuruppin | P-51 |
| | April 16 | Me-109 dest(grd) | NE Prague | P-51 |
| | | Ju-88 dest(grd) | NE Prague | P-51 |
| | April 17 | Me-109 dest(grd) | SE Pocking | P-51 |
| | | He-111 dest(grd) | SE Pocking | P-51 |
| | | u/i a/c dest(grd) | SE Pocking | P-51 |

0-0-0 air
9-1 ground

**Mason, Clair M., Capt.**
504th Ftr Sqn/339th Ftr Grp

| Sqn | Date | Claims | Location | A/C |
|---|---|---|---|---|
| 504th | April 7, 1945 | Me-262 dam(air) | Ulzen | P-51 |
| | April 10 | (2)Me-410 dest(grd) | N/Neuruppin | P-51 |
| | | Me-410 dam(grd) | N/Neuruppin | P-51 |

0-0-1 air
2-1 ground

**Mason, Joseph L., Col.**
HdQts/352nd Ftr Grp

| Sqn | Date | Claims | Location | A/C |
|---|---|---|---|---|
| HdQts | February 24, 1944 | Me-109 dest(air) | Schwagstorf | P-47 |
| | May 8 | FW-190 dest(air) | N/Nienburg | P-51 |
| | | FW-190 dam(air) | N/Nienburg | P-51 |
| | May 13 | (2)Me-109 dest(air) | Demnin-Friedland | P-51 |
| | | FW-190 dest(air) | Demnin-Friedland | P-51 |
| | | Me-109 dam(air) | Demnin-Friedland | P-51 |

5-0-2 air
0-0 ground

**Massa, Vincent J., Lt.**
83rd Ftr Sqn/78th Ftr Grp

| Sqn | Date | Claims | Location | A/C |
|---|---|---|---|---|
| 83rd | February 22, 1944 | Me-109 dam(air) | Aachen | P-47 |
| | April 24 | (.5)Me-110 dest(grd)* | Trier | P-47 |
| | June 6 | (.5)FW-190 dest(air)** | Mayenne | P-47 |

0.5-0-1 air
0.5-0 ground

* - shared with Lt. A.M. Juchheim of the 83rd Ftr Sqn
** - shared with Col. F.C. Gray of HdQts, 78th Ftr Grp

**Masters, Frank R., Lt.**
358th Ftr Sqn/355th Ftr Grp

| Sqn | Date | Claims | Location | A/C |
|---|---|---|---|---|
| 358th | November 26, 1944 | (3)FW-190 dest(air) | Hanover | P-51 |

3-0-0 air
0-0 ground

**Masters, Warren K., F/O**
385th Ftr Sqn/364th Ftr Grp

| Sqn | Date | Claims | Location | A/C |
|---|---|---|---|---|
| 385th | April 5, 1945 | Me-109 dest(grd) | SW Nurnburg | P-51 |
| | April 17 | He-111 dest(grd) | Karlsbad | P-51 |
| | | Ar-66 dest(grd) | Karlsbad | P-51 |

0-0-0 air
3-0 ground

**Mastin, Donald W., Lt.**
434th Ftr Sqn/479th Ftr Grp

| Sqn | Date | Claims | Location | A/C |
|---|---|---|---|---|
| 434th | April 17, 1945 | u/i a/c dest(grd) | Puchhoff | P-51 |

0-0-0 air
1-0 ground

**Mathews, Harold E., Lt.**
434th Ftr Sqn/479th Ftr Grp

| Sqn | Date | Claims | Location | A/C |
|---|---|---|---|---|
| 434th | August 9, 1944 | FW-200 dest(grd) | Nuneburg | P-38 |
| | September 5 | Ju-88 dest(grd) | Ettinghausen | P-38 |
| | September 10 | He-111 dam(grd) | Malmsheim | P-38 |
| | December 5 | FW-190 dest(air) | Neuruppin | P-51 |

1-0-0 air
2-1 ground

**Matney, Francis M., Lt.**
38th Ftr Sqn/55th Ftr Grp

| Sqn | Date | Claims | Location | A/C |
|---|---|---|---|---|
| 38th | September 5, 1944 | FW-190 dest(grd) | Stuttgart/Boblingen | P-51 |
| | September 11 | (2)Me-109 dest(air) | Erfurt | P-51 |

| Sqn | Date | Claims | Location | A/C |
|---|---|---|---|---|
| | November 2 | (.5)Me-109 dest(air)* | W/Merseburg | P-51 |
| | December 5 | FW-190 dest(air) | NE Berlin | P-51 |

3.5-0-0 air
1-0 ground

* - shared wih Lt. D.F. Jewell of the 38th Ftr Sqn

**Mattern, James L., Jr., Lt.**
82nd Ftr Sqn/78th Ftr Grp

| Sqn | Date | Claims | Location | A/C |
|---|---|---|---|---|
| 82nd | September 9, 1944 | FW-190 dam(air) | Coblenz | P-47 |

0-0-1 air
0-0 ground

**Matthew, Harold L., Lt.**
63rd Ftr Sqn/56th Ftr Grp

| Sqn | Date | Claims | Location | A/C |
|---|---|---|---|---|
| 63rd | April 9, 1944 | Me-109 dest(grd) | Jagel A/F | P-47 |
| | | (.5)u/i a/c dest(grd)* | Schleswig | P-47 |

0-0-0 air
1.5-0 ground

* - shared with LtCol. F.S. Gabreski of HdQts, 56th Ftr Grp

**Matthew, Harry L., Capt.**
369th Ftr Sqn/359th Ftr Grp

| Sqn | Date | Claims | Location | A/C |
|---|---|---|---|---|
| 369th | April 22, 1944 | FW-190 dest(air) | Ostbevern | P-47 |

1-0-0 air
0-0 ground

**Matthews, C.R., Lt.**
435th Ftr Sqn/479th Ftr Grp

| Sqn | Date | Claims | Location | A/C |
|---|---|---|---|---|
| 435th | April 17, 1945 | Me-262 dam(grd) | Puchhoff | P-51 |

0-0-0 air
0-1 ground

**Matthews, Joseph A., Lt.**
336th Ftr Sqn/4th Ftr Grp

| Sqn | Date | Claims | Location | A/C |
|---|---|---|---|---|
| 336th | January 22, 1943 | Me-109 dest(air) | Dunkirk | Spit |
| | August 16 | FW-190 dest(air) | St. Denis | P-47 |

2-0-0 air
0-0 ground

**Mau, Jerome R., Capt.**
374th Ftr Sqn/361st Ftr Grp

| Sqn | Date | Claims | Location | A/C |
|---|---|---|---|---|
| 374th | July 5, 1944 | Me-109 dest(air) | Amiens | P-51 |
| | | Me-109 dam(air) | Amiens | P-51 |
| | December 2 | (2)FW-190 dest(air) | Meinsenheim | P-51 |

3-0-1 air
0-0 ground

**Maul, Arthur C., Lt.**
61st Ftr Sqn/56th Ftr Grp

| Sqn | Date | Claims | Location | A/C |
|---|---|---|---|---|
| 61st | May 12, 1944 | Me-109 dest(air) | N/Marburg | P-47 |
| | June 12 | Me-109 dam(air) | Evreux | P-47 |
| | August 4 | Me-109 dest(air) | S/Hamburg | P-47 |

2-0-1 air
0-0 ground

**Mauldin, David L., Lt.**
61st Ftr Sqn/56th Ftr Grp

| Sqn | Date | Claims | Location | A/C |
|---|---|---|---|---|
| 61st | April 13, 1945 | Ju-88 dam(grd) | Eggebeck A/F | P-47 |
| | April 16 | (2)Me-109 dam(grd) | Muhldorf | P-47 |
| | | u/i a/c dam(grd) | Muhldorf | P-47 |

0-0-0 air
0-4 ground

**Mauldin, Thurman N., Lt.**
360th Ftr Sqn/356th Ftr Grp

| Sqn | Date | Claims | Location | A/C |
|---|---|---|---|---|
| 360th | April 9, 1945 | u/i a/c dam(grd) | Biberach A/F | P-51 |
| | April 10 | Me-262 prob(air) | Oranienburg | P-51 |

0-1-0 air
0-1 ground

**Maurice, Anthony, Capt.**
375th Ftr Sqn/361st Ftr Grp

| Sqn | Date | Claims | Location | A/C |
|---|---|---|---|---|
| 375th | November 8, 1944 | Me-262 dest(air) | W/Meppel | P-51 |
| | January 2, 1945 | (.5)Me-109 dest(air)* | W/Stuttgart | P-51 |
| | March 9 | FW-190 dest(air) | W/Giessen | P-51 |

2.5-0-0 air
0-0 ground

* - shared with Lt. G.R. Stockmeier of the 375th Ftr Sqn

**Max, Joseph H., Lt.**
357th Ftr Sqn/355th Ftr Grp

| Sqn | Date | Claims | Location | A/C |
|---|---|---|---|---|
| 357th | August 14, 1944 | (.5)Ju-88 dest(grd)* | Sarrebourg | P-51 |
| | November 18 | (2)Me-262 dam(grd) | Leipheim | P-51 |
| | November 26 | (2)FW-190 dest(air) | W/Gardelegen | P-51 |

2-0-0 air
0.5-2 ground

* - shared with Lt. W.A. Shade of the 357th Ftr Sqn

**Maxwell, Chester K., Capt.**
364th Ftr Sqn/357th Ftr Grp

| Sqn | Date | Claims | Location | A/C |
|---|---|---|---|---|
| 364th | September 19, 1944 | FW-190 dest(air) | SW Arnheim | P-51 |
| | | Me-109 dest(air) | SW Arnheim | P-51 |
| | January 14, 1945 | (3)FW-190 dest(air) | W/Berlin | P-51 |

5-0-0 air
0-0 ground

**Maxwell, DeWayne J., Capt.**
328th Ftr Sqn/352nd Ftr Grp

| Sqn | Date | Claims | Location | A/C |
|---|---|---|---|---|
| 328th | June 21, 1944 | Me-410 dam(air) | Dahmsdorf | P-51 |
| | November 2 | Me-109 dest(air) | Merseburg | P-51 |
| | November 21 | FW-190 dest(air) | Merseburg | P-51 |
| | | FW-190 dam(air) | Merseburg | P-51 |

2-0-2 air
0-0 ground

**Maxwell, Julius P., Capt.**
84th Ftr Sqn/78th Ftr Grp

| Sqn | Date | Claims | Location | A/C |
|---|---|---|---|---|
| 84th | March 16, 1944 | Me-109 dest(air) | St. Dizier | P-47 |
| | | Me-109 dam(air) | St. Dizier | P-47 |
| | December 31 | FW-190 dest(air) | Solingen | P-47 |

2-0-1 air
0-0 ground

**Maxwell, Robert A., Lt.**
343rd Ftr Sqn/55th Ftr Grp

| Sqn | Date | Claims | Location | A/C |
|---|---|---|---|---|
| 343rd | December 25, 1944 | Me-109 dest(air) | W/Coblenz | P-51 |

1-0-0 air
0-0 ground

**Maxwell, Wallace G., Lt.**
360th Ftr Sqn/356th Ftr Grp

| *Sqn* | *Date* | *Claims* | *Location* | *A/C* |
|---|---|---|---|---|
| 360th | January 24, 1944 | FW-190 dest(air) | N/Lille | P-47 |
| | | (.5)FW-190 dam(air)* | NE Ypres | P-47 |
| | February 13 | FW-190 dest(air) | Chartres | P-47 |
| | May 19 | Me-109 dest(air) | Nienburg | P-47 |

3-0-0.5 air
0-0 ground

* - shared with Maj. G.W. Johnson of the 360th Ftr Sqn

**May, John F., Lt.**
350th Ftr Sqn/353rd Ftr Grp

| *Sqn* | *Date* | *Claims* | *Location* | *A/C* |
|---|---|---|---|---|
| 350th | March 24, 1945 | (2)FW-190 dest(air) | NW Kassel | P-51 |

2-0-0 air
0-0 ground

**May, William E., LtCol.**
82nd Ftr Sqn/78th Ftr Grp
HdQts/78th Ftr Grp

| *Sqn* | *Date* | *Claims* | *Location* | *A/C* |
|---|---|---|---|---|
| 82nd | October 24, 1943 | (.5)Me-109 dest(air)* | St. Gaillon | P-47 |
| | April 1, 1944 | (.13)Do-217 dest(grd)** | Verdun | P-47 |
| | April 5 | Go-242 dam(grd) | Ruwer | P-47 |
| | April 9 | FW-190 dest(air) | Dummer Lake | P-47 |

1.5-0-0 air
0.13-1 ground

* - shared with Lt. A.W. Hill of the 82nd Ftr Sqn
** - shared with Capt. W.L. Boone, Lt. C.R. Clark, Lt. B.M. Watkins, Lt. J.J. Hockery, Lt. H.L. Eakes, Lt. R.V. Heran, and F/O C.W. DeWitt of the 82nd Ftr Sqn

**Mayden, James D., Col.**
HdQts/352nd Ftr Grp

| *Sqn* | *Date* | *Claims* | *Location* | *A/C* |
|---|---|---|---|---|
| HdQts | November 2, 1944 | Me-109 dest(air) | Merseburg | P-51 |
| | April 7, 1945 | Me-109 dest(air) | N/Minden | P-51 |
| | April 17 | (2)Me-109 dest(grd) | Plattling | P-51 |
| | | FW-190 dest(grd) | Plattling | P-51 |
| | | u/i a/c dest(grd) | Plattling | P-51 |
| | | (2)Me-109 dam(grd) | Plattling | P-51 |

2-0-0 air
4-2 ground

**Mayer, Raymond D., Lt.**
503rd Ftr Sqn/339th Ftr Grp

| *Sqn* | *Date* | *Claims* | *Location* | *A/C* |
|---|---|---|---|---|
| 503rd | September 11, 1944 | (2)Me-109 dest(air) | Annaberg | P-51 |
| | September 23 | FW-190 dest(air) | SW Wesel | P-51 |

3-0-0 air
0-0 ground

**Mayhew, Buran B., Lt.**
352nd Ftr Sqn/353rd Ftr Grp

| *Sqn* | *Date* | *Claims* | *Location* | *A/C* |
|---|---|---|---|---|
| 352nd | June 7, 1944 | FW-190 dam(grd) | Cormeilles-en-Vixen | P-47 |

0-0-0 air
0-1 ground

**Mayo, Benjamin I., Jr., LtCol.**
82nd Ftr Sqn/78th Ftr Grp
84th Ftr Sqn/78th Ftr Grp

| *Sqn* | *Date* | *Claims* | *Location* | *A/C* |
|---|---|---|---|---|
| 84th | June 7, 1944 | Me-109 dest(air) | Montdidier | P-47 |
| 82nd | June 20 | Me-109 dest(air) | Montdidier | P-47 |
| | July 1 | FW-190 dam(air) | St. Quentin | P-47 |
| 84th | July 19 | (1.5)Do-217 dest(grd)* | Eutingen | P-47 |
| | | u/i a/c dest(grd) | Eutingen | P-47 |
| | September 9 | (2)FW-190 dest(air) | Giessen | P-47 |

4-0-1 air
2.5-0 ground

* - shared with Capt. A.F. Eaton of the 84th Ftr Sqn

**McAdory, Louis M., Lt.**
352nd Ftr Sqn/353rd Ftr Grp

| *Sqn* | *Date* | *Claims* | *Location* | *A/C* |
|---|---|---|---|---|
| 352nd | April 17, 1945 | Me-109 dam(grd) | Ganacker | P-51 |

0-0-0 air
0-1 ground

**McAuley, Donald H., Maj.**
55th Ftr Sqn/20th Ftr Grp

| *Sqn* | *Date* | *Claims* | *Location* | *A/C* |
|---|---|---|---|---|
| 55th | January 24, 1944 | FW-190 dest(air) | Courtrai | P-38 |
| | | FW-190 prob(air) | Courtrai | P-38 |
| | March 18 | Me-109 dest(air) | Erding | P-38 |

2-1-0 air
0-0 ground

**McAuliffe, Richard G., Maj.**
328th Ftr Sqn/352nd Ftr Grp
Earlier flew in the MTO with the 82nd Ftr Grp and claimed 3 kills; singles on March 26, April 5, and April 10, 1943.

| *Sqn* | *Date* | *Claims* | *Location* | *A/C* |
|---|---|---|---|---|
| 328th | April 10, 1945 | (.5)Me-262 dest(air)* | Berlin-Wittenberg | P-51 |
| | April 16 | (2)FW-190 dam(grd) | Landau | P-51 |
| | April 17 | FW-190 dest(grd) | Plattling | P-51 |
| | | u/i a/c dam(grd) | Plattling | P-51 |

0.5-0-0 air
1-3 ground

* - shared with LtCol. E.D. Duncan of the 328th Ftr Sqn

**McArthur, John D., Lt.**
77th Ftr Sqn/20th Ftr Grp

| *Sqn* | *Date* | *Claims* | *Location* | *A/C* |
|---|---|---|---|---|
| 77th | May 11, 1944 | Ju-88 dest(grd) | Bretigny A/F | P-38 |

0-0-0 air
1-0 ground

**McBath, Charles T., Lt.**
63rd Ftr Sqn/56th Ftr Grp

| *Sqn* | *Date* | *Claims* | *Location* | *A/C* |
|---|---|---|---|---|
| 63rd | January 14, 1945 | (2)Me-109 dest(air) | Munster | P-47 |
| | April 7 | Me-109 dest(air) | N/Celle | P-47 |
| | April 10 | Ju-88 dam(grd) | Werder A/F | P-47 |
| | April 13 | Me-109 dest(grd) | Eggebeck A/F | P-47 |
| | | Me-109 dam(grd) | Eggebeck A/F | P-47 |
| | | He-111 dam(grd) | Eggebeck A/F | P-47 |

3-0-0 air
1-3 ground

**McCall, Elmer N., Lt.**
335th Ftr Sqn/4th Ftr Grp

| *Sqn* | *Date* | *Claims* | *Location* | *A/C* |
|---|---|---|---|---|
| 335th | October 6, 1944 | (.5)Me-410 dest(air)* | NW Heligoland | P-51 |
| | November 18 | Me-262 dam(grd) | Leipheim | P-51 |
| | | Me-109 dam(grd) | Leipheim | P-51 |

0.5-0-0 air
0-2 ground

* - shared with Lt. R.E. Lewis of the 335th Ftr Sqn

**McCall, Fred C., Lt.**
364th Ftr Sqn/357th Ftr Grp

| *Sqn* | *Date* | *Claims* | *Location* | *A/C* |
|---|---|---|---|---|
| 364th | December 5, 1944 | (2)FW-190 dest(air) | NW Berlin | P-51 |
| | December 24 | Me-109 dest(air) | E/Fulda | P-51 |
| | January 10, 1945 | He-111 dest(grd) | Paderborn | P-51 |

3-0-0 air
1-0 ground

**McCallister, David F., Lt.**
77th Ftr Sqn/20th Ftr Grp

| *Sqn* | *Date* | *Claims* | *Location* | *A/C* |
|---|---|---|---|---|
| 77th | March 2, 1945 | FW-190 dam(air) | Chemnitz | P-51 |

0-0-1 air
0-0 ground

**McCarthy, Lawrence E., Lt.**
328th Ftr Sqn/352nd Ftr Grp

| *Sqn* | *Date* | *Claims* | *Location* | *A/C* |
|---|---|---|---|---|
| 328th | February 20, 1944 | (2)Me-110 dest(air) | Blankenheim | P-47 |
| | | (2)Me-110 dam(air) | Blankenheim | P-47 |
| | June 12 | (.5)Me-109 dest(air)[*] | S/St. Malo | P-51 |

2.5-0-2 air
0-0 ground

[*] - shared with Lt. J.F. Thornell of the 328th Ftr Sqn

**McCasland, Darwin D., Lt.**
357th Ftr Sqn/355th Ftr Grp

| *Sqn* | *Date* | *Claims* | *Location* | *A/C* |
|---|---|---|---|---|
| 357th | March 6, 1944 | Me-109 dest(air) | E/Dummer Lake | P-47 |
| | March 29 | FW-190 dest(air) | Brunswick | P-51 |
| | | FW-190 prob(air) | Brunswick | P-51 |
| | April 8 | Ju-88 dest(grd) | Gifhorn | P-51 |
| | April 11 | (2)Ju-88 dest(grd) | Strasbourg | P-51 |
| | | FW-190 dam(grd) | Wensdorf | P-51 |

2-1-0 air
3-1 ground

**McCauley, Frank E., Lt.**
61st Ftr Sqn/56th Ftr Grp

| *Sqn* | *Date* | *Claims* | *Location* | *A/C* |
|---|---|---|---|---|
| 61st | August 17, 1943 | FW-190 dest(air) | Hasselt | P-47 |
| | | (.5)Me-110 dest(air)[*] | N/Liege | P-47 |
| | | FW-190 dam(air) | Hasselt | P-47 |
| | August 19 | Me-109 dest(air) | Oosterhout | P-47 |
| | | Me-109 dest(air) | Schoonhoven | P-47 |
| | October 4 | Me-110 dest(air) | E/Aachen | P-47 |
| | | Me-110 prob(air) | E/Aachen | P-47 |
| | October 14 | Me-110 dest(air) | W/Aachen | P-47 |

5.5-1-1 air
0-0 ground

[*] - shared with Capt. G.W. Johnson of the 61st Ftr Sqn

**McChrystal, Richard G., Capt.**
434th Ftr Sqn/479th Ftr Grp

| *Sqn* | *Date* | *Claims* | *Location* | *A/C* |
|---|---|---|---|---|
| 434th | September 26, 1944 | Me-109 dest(air) | SW Munster | P-38 |
| | | Me-109 dam(air) | SW Munster | P-38 |
| | December 5 | Me-109 dest(air) | Neuruppin | P-51 |
| | | Me-109 dam(air) | Neuruppin | P-51 |
| | February 9, 1945 | Me-109 dest(air) | SW Berlin | P-51 |

3-0-2 air
0-0 ground

**McClanahan, Fred C., Capt.**
385th Ftr Sqn/364th Ftr Grp

| *Sqn* | *Date* | *Claims* | *Location* | *A/C* |
|---|---|---|---|---|
| 385th | May 22, 1944 | (.5)FW-190 dam(air)[*] | Neumunster | P-38 |
| | July 6 | (2)FW-190 dam(air) | Chalons | P-38 |
| | August 9 | Me-109 dest(grd) | Gaukonigshafen | P-51 |
| | | Me-210 dest(grd) | Gaukonigshafen | P-51 |

0-0-2.5 air
2-0 ground

[*] - shared with Lt. H.H. Stubblefield of the 385th Ftr Sqn

**McClellan, William M., Lt.**
84th Ftr Sqn/78th Ftr Grp

| *Sqn* | *Date* | *Claims* | *Location* | *A/C* |
|---|---|---|---|---|
| 84th | April 17, 1945 | Me-410 dest(grd) | W/Dresden | P-51 |
| | | Ju-88 dest(grd) | W/Dresden | P-51 |
| | | u/i a/c dest(grd) | W/Dresden | P-51 |
| | | (3)u/i a/c dam(grd) | W/Dresden | P-51 |
| | | Me-410 dam(grd) | W/Dresden | P-51 |

0-0-0 air
3-4 ground

**McClish, Donald E., Capt.**
503rd Ftr Sqn/339th Ftr Grp

| *Sqn* | *Date* | *Claims* | *Location* | *A/C* |
|---|---|---|---|---|
| 503rd | September 11, 1944 | (.5)Me-109 dest(air)[*] | Annaberg | P-51 |
| | | (.5)FW-190 dest(air)[**] | Annaberg | P-51 |
| | | FW-190 prob(air) | Annaberg | P-51 |

1-1-0 air
0-0 ground

[*] - shared with Lt. E.H. Graham of the 503rd Ftr Sqn
[**] - shared with Capt. J.G. Robinson of the 503rd Ftr Sqn

**McClure, James H., Lt.**
350th Ftr Sqn/353rd Ftr Grp

| *Sqn* | *Date* | *Claims* | *Location* | *A/C* |
|---|---|---|---|---|
| 350th | April 16, 1945 | (2)Me-109 dest(grd) | Pocking | P-51 |
| | | FW-190 dest(grd) | Pocking | P-51 |
| | | FW-200 dest(grd) | Pocking | P-51 |
| | | Ju-88 dest(grd) | Pocking | P-51 |

0-0-0 air
5-0 ground

**McClure, Wendell A., Lt.**
62nd Ftr Sqn/56th Ftr Grp

| *Sqn* | *Date* | *Claims* | *Location* | *A/C* |
|---|---|---|---|---|
| 62nd | March 8, 1944 | FW-190 dam(air) | Minden | P-47 |
| | April 9 | (2)FW-190 dam(air) | Lubeck | P-47 |
| | April 20 | (.5)Ju-88 dest(air)[*] | NE Paris | P-47 |
| | May 31 | FW-190 dest(air) | Meldorf | P-47 |

1.5-0-3 air
0-0 ground

[*] - shared with Capt. F.D. Williamson of the 62nd Ftr Sqn

**McCollom, Francis N., Lt.**
358th Ftr Sqn/355th Ftr Grp

| *Sqn* | *Date* | *Claims* | *Location* | *A/C* |
|---|---|---|---|---|
| 358th | April 9, 1945 | Me-110 dest(grd) | Hailfingen | P-51 |
| | | He-111 dam(grd) | Hailfingen | P-51 |
| | April 16 | (2)FW-190 dest(grd) | Straubing | P-51 |
| | | Ju-88 dest(grd) | Straubing | P-51 |
| | | u/i a/c dest(grd) | Straubing | P-51 |

0-0-0 air
5-1 ground

**McCollom, Loren G., LtCol.**
61st Ftr Sqn/ 56th Ftr Grp
HdQts/353rd Ftr Grp

| *Sqn* | *Date* | *Claims* | *Location* | *A/C* |
|---|---|---|---|---|
| 61st | May 29, 1943 | Me-109 prob(air) | SE St. Moen | P-47 |
| | July 30 | Me-109 dam(air) | Arnheim | P-47 |
| HdQts | August 17 | Me-109 dest(air) | Diest | P-47 |
| | October 10 | Me-110 prob(air) | Rheine | P-47 |

1-2-1 air
0-0 ground

**McConnell, James H., Lt.**
358th Ftr Sqn/355th Ftr Grp

| *Sqn* | *Date* | *Claims* | *Location* | *A/C* |
|---|---|---|---|---|
| 358th | February 5, 1944 | (.25)FW-190 dam(air)* | S/Tours | P-47 |

0-0-0.25 air
0-0 ground

* - shared with Lt. H.J. Hoffman, Lt. J.J. DeGeorge, and Lt. J.H. Upchurch of the 358th Ftr Sqn

**McCoppin, William E., Lt.**
375th Ftr Sqn/361st Ftr Grp

| *Sqn* | *Date* | *Claims* | *Location* | *A/C* |
|---|---|---|---|---|
| 375th | November 26, 1944 | Me-109 dest(air) | NE Brunswick | P-51 |

1-0-0 air
0-0 ground

**McCord, Thomas A., Lt.**
336th Ftr Sqn/4th Ftr Grp

| *Sqn* | *Date* | *Claims* | *Location* | *A/C* |
|---|---|---|---|---|
| 336th | January 16, 1945 | FW-190 dest(grd) | Neuhausen | P-51 |
| | | Ju-87 dest(grd) | Neuhausen | P-51 |

0-0-0 air
2-0 ground

**McCormick, Arthur B., Capt.**
385th Ftr Sqn/364th Ftr Grp

| *Sqn* | *Date* | *Claims* | *Location* | *A/C* |
|---|---|---|---|---|
| 385th | November 2, 1944 | Me-109 dest(air) | Halle | P-51 |
| | | Me-109 dam(air) | Halle | P-51 |
| | November 21 | u/i a/c dest(grd) | Eisleben | P-51 |
| | November 26 | (4)Ju-88 dest(grd) | SE Jade Bay | P-51 |
| | January 29, 1945 | u/i a/c dam(grd) | Darmstadt | P-51 |
| | February 26 | (1.5)He-111 dest(grd)* | SE Jade Bay | P-51 |
| | April 13 | Do-217 dest(grd) | E/Luneburg | P-51 |
| | | Ju-188 dest(grd) | E/Luneburg | P-51 |
| | | (.5)FW-190 dest(grd)** | E/Luneburg | P-51 |
| | | Do-217 dam(grd) | E/Luneburg | P-51 |
| | | FW-190 dam(grd) | E/Luneburg | P-51 |

1-0-1 air
9-3 ground

* - shared with Lt. C.R. Roesch of the 385th Ftr Sqn
** - shared with Lt. J.G. Johnson of the 385th Ftr Sqn

**McCoskey, Jack E., Lt.**
370th Ftr Sqn/359th Ftr Grp

| *Sqn* | *Date* | *Claims* | *Location* | *A/C* |
|---|---|---|---|---|
| 370th | October 6, 1944 | FW-190 dest(air) | S/Stettin | P-51 |
| | October 7 | (.5)BV-140 dest(grd) | Dievenow | P-51 |
| | December 31 | Me-109 dam(air) | Hanover | P-51 |

1-0-1 air
0.5-0 ground

* - shared with Capt. G.A. Doersch of the 370th Ftr Sqn

**McCoy, Gordon A., Lt.**
383rd Ftr Sqn/364th Ftr Grp

| *Sqn* | *Date* | *Claims* | *Location* | *A/C* |
|---|---|---|---|---|
| 383rd | August 15, 1944 | Me-109 dest(air) | Frankfurt | P-51 |

1-0-0 air
0-0 ground

**McCubbin, James L., Lt.**
385th Ftr Sqn/364th Ftr Grp

| *Sqn* | *Date* | *Claims* | *Location* | *A/C* |
|---|---|---|---|---|
| 385th | November 21, 1944 | u/i a/c dest(grd) | SE Eisleben | P-51 |
| | | u/i a/c dam(grd) | SE Eisleben | P-51 |
| | December 2 | Me-109 dest(air) | Mannheim | P-51 |
| | December 5 | (2)FW-190 dest(air) | N/Berlin | P-51 |
| | | (2)FW-190 prob(air) | N/Berlin | P-51 |
| | January 1, 1945 | Me-109 dest(air) | SE Hamburg | P-51 |

4-2-0 air
1-1 ground

**McCullough, Philip E., Lt.**
360th Ftr Sqn/356th Ftr Grp

| *Sqn* | *Date* | *Claims* | *Location* | *A/C* |
|---|---|---|---|---|
| 360th | February 11, 1944 | FW-190 dest(air) | Marle | P-47 |
| | | FW-190 prob(air) | S/Albert | P-47 |
| | February 13 | Me-109 dam(air) | Chartres | P-47 |

1-1-1 air
0-0 ground

**McCully, Paul J., Jr., Capt.**
77th Ftr Sqn/20th Ftr Grp

| *Sqn* | *Date* | *Claims* | *Location* | *A/C* |
|---|---|---|---|---|
| 77th | September 28, 1944 | Me-109 dam(air) | S/Magdeburg | P-51 |

0-0-1 air
0-0 ground

**McCurry, Charles R., Lt.**
354th Ftr Sqn/355th Ftr Grp

| *Sqn* | *Date* | *Claims* | *Location* | *A/C* |
|---|---|---|---|---|
| 354th | September 11, 1944 | Ju-52 dest(grd) | S/Kassel | P-51 |

0-0-0 air
1-0 ground

**McDermott, William M., Lt.**
83rd Ftr Sqn/78th Ftr Grp

| *Sqn* | *Date* | *Claims* | *Location* | *A/C* |
|---|---|---|---|---|
| 83rd | February 22, 1944 | FW-190 dest(air) | Nijmegen | P-47 |
| | April 30 | (.5)FW-190 dest(air)* | Dreux | P-47 |
| | May 11 | FW-190 dam(air) | Montargis | P-47 |
| | May 25 | Me-109 dest(air) | St. Dizier | P-47 |
| | May 28 | (.5)Me-109 dest(air)** | Gardelegen | P-47 |

3-0-1 air
0-0 ground

* - shared with Lt. F. White of the 83rd Ftr Sqn
** - shared with Lt. F. White of the 83rd Ftr Sqn

**McDill, Thomas K., Lt.**
336th Ftr Sqn/4th Ftr Grp

| *Sqn* | *Date* | *Claims* | *Location* | *A/C* |
|---|---|---|---|---|
| 336th | April 24, 1944 | FW-190 dam(air) | NW Ludwigshafen | P-51 |
| | April 30 | (.5)Do-24 dest(grd)* | Lyon Anchorage | P-51 |
| | May 12 | Me-109 dest(air) | Kassel | P-51 |
| | May 25 | Me-109 dest(air) | Strasbourg | P-51 |

2-0-1 air
0.5-0 ground

* - shared with Capt. J.T. Godfrey of the 336th Ftr Sqn

**McDonald, James H., Lt.**
368th Ftr Sqn/359th Ftr Grp

| *Sqn* | *Date* | *Claims* | *Location* | *A/C* |
|---|---|---|---|---|
| 368th | April 16, 1945 | Me-109 dest(grd) | E/Plattling | P-51 |
| | | (2)Me-109 dam(grd) | E/Plattling | P-51 |

0-0-0 air
1-2 ground

**McDonald, Jerry R., Capt.**
338th Ftr Sqn/55th Ftr Grp

| *Sqn* | *Date* | *Claims* | *Location* | *A/C* |
|---|---|---|---|---|
| 338th | December 24, 1944 | Me-109 dest(air) | S/Coblenz | P-51 |
| | January 14, 1945 | Me-262 dest(grd) | Parchim | P-51 |

1-0-0 air
1-0 ground

**McDowell, Bert, Capt.**
338th Ftr Sqn/55th Ftr Grp

| *Sqn* | *Date* | *Claims* | *Location* | *A/C* |
|---|---|---|---|---|
| 338th | January 6, 1945 | Ju-88 dest(grd) | Giebelstadt | P-51 |
| | January 29 | Me-109 dam(air) | Ulzen | P-51 |
| | February 6 | Ju-88 dest(grd) | Gerolzhofen A/F | P-51 |

0-0-1 air
2-0 ground

**McDowell, Reginald C., Capt.**
361st Ftr Sqn/356th Ftr Grp

| *Sqn* | *Date* | *Claims* | *Location* | *A/C* |
|---|---|---|---|---|
| 361st | February 10, 1944 | FW-190 dest(air) | NE Lingen | P-47 |

1-0-0 air
0-0 ground

**McDuffie, Duncan M., Lt.**
83rd Ftr Sqn/78th Ftr Grp

| *Sqn* | *Date* | *Claims* | *Location* | *A/C* |
|---|---|---|---|---|
| 83rd | March 2, 1945 | (4)Me-109 dest(air) | Burg A/F | P-51 |
| | April 16 | (2)Me-109 dest(grd) | N/Prague | P-51 |
| | | (2)FW-190 dest(grd) | N/Prague | P-51 |
| | | Ju-87 dest(grd) | N/Prague | P-51 |

4-0-0 air
5-0 ground

**McElhare, William W., Lt.**
62nd Ftr Sqn/56th Ftr Grp

| *Sqn* | *Date* | *Claims* | *Location* | *A/C* |
|---|---|---|---|---|
| 62nd | June 6, 1944 | FW-190 dest(air) | Rambouillet | P-47 |
| | June 12 | Me-109 dam(air) | La Perth | P-47 |
| | July 4 | Me-109 dest(air) | Conches | P-47 |
| | | (3)Me-109 dam(air) | Conches | P-47 |

2-0-4 air
0-0 ground

**McElroy, James N., Capt.**
358th Ftr Sqn/355th Ftr Grp

| *Sqn* | *Date* | *Claims* | *Location* | *A/C* |
|---|---|---|---|---|
| 358th | April 5, 1944 | Me-110 dest(grd) | Munich | P-51 |
| | | Me-110 dam(grd) | Landsberg | P-51 |
| | April 15 | (5)Do-217 dest(grd) | Glienicke A/F | P-51 |
| | April 19 | Me-109 dam(air) | SW Brunswick | P-51 |
| | July 19 | FW-190 dest(air) | Augsburg | P-51 |
| | | FW-190 dam(air) | Augsburg | P-51 |
| | July 28 | Me-109 dest(air) | S/Merseburg | P-51 |
| | | FW-190 dest(air) | S/Merseburg | P-51 |
| | November 2 | Me-109 dam(air) | Merseburg | P-51 |
| | December 5 | FW-190 dest(air) | Berlin | P-51 |
| | | (3)FW-190 dam(air) | Berlin | P-51 |
| | February 27, 1945 | Do-217 dest(air) | SW Plauen | P-51 |

5-0-6 air
6-1 ground

**McElwee, Francis E., Lt.**
503rd Ftr Sqn/339th Ftr Grp

| *Sqn* | *Date* | *Claims* | *Location* | *A/C* |
|---|---|---|---|---|
| 503rd | March 18, 1945 | FW-190 dest(air) | Dummer Lake | P-51 |

1-0-0 air
0-0 ground

**McEntire, David W., Lt.**
487th Ftr Sqn/352nd Ftr Grp

| *Sqn* | *Date* | *Claims* | *Location* | *A/C* |
|---|---|---|---|---|
| 487th | April 11, 1944 | Ju-290 dam(grd) | SE Berlin | P-51 |
| | May 12 | Me-109 dest(air) | SE Coblenz | P-51 |

1-0-0 air
0-1 ground

**McFadden, Jack D., Capt.**
334th Ftr Sqn/4th Ftr Grp

| *Sqn* | *Date* | *Claims* | *Location* | *A/C* |
|---|---|---|---|---|
| 334th | July 7, 1944 | Me-109 dam(air) | Aschersleben | P-51 |
| | November 6 | Me-109 dest(air) | Rheine | P-51 |
| | November 18 | (2)Me-262 dam(grd) | Leipheim | P-51 |
| | December 2 | FW-190 dest(air) | Hottenback | P-51 |
| | February 27, 1945 | Me-108 dest(grd) | Weimar | P-51 |
| | | Ju-87 dest(grd) | Weimar | P-51 |
| | April 10 | Ju-88 dest(grd) | Wittstock | P-51 |

2-0-1 air
3-2 ground

**McFarlane, John D., Maj.**
336th Ftr Sqn/4th Ftr Grp

| *Sqn* | *Date* | *Claims* | *Location* | *A/C* |
|---|---|---|---|---|
| 336th | September 27, 1944 | FW-190 dest(air) | SE Kassel | P-51 |
| | February 22, 1945 | Do-217 dest(grd) | Halberstadt | P-51 |
| | February 27 | Me-108 dest(grd) | Weimar | P-51 |

1-0-0 air
2-0 ground

**McGarry, William T., Lt.**
352nd Ftr Sqn/353rd Ftr Grp

| *Sqn* | *Date* | *Claims* | *Location* | *A/C* |
|---|---|---|---|---|
| 352nd | June 7, 1944 | FW-190 dam(grd) | Cormeilles-en-Vixen | P-47 |

0-0-0 air
0-1 ground

**McGee, Donald C., Maj.**
363rd Ftr Sqn/357th Ftr Grp
364th Ftr Sqn/357th Ftr Grp
Earlier flew in the PTO with the 8th Ftr Grp and claimed 5 kills; a Zero on May 1, 1942; (2)Zeros on May 29, 1942; a Betty on April 12, 1943; and a Tony on September 15, 1943.

| *Sqn* | *Date* | *Claims* | *Location* | *A/C* |
|---|---|---|---|---|
| 363rd | March 2, 1945 | Me-109 dest(air) | NE Magdeburg | P-51 |
| | April 10 | Me-410 dest(grd) | Neuruppin | P-51 |
| | | He-111 dest(grd) | Neuruppin | P-51 |
| | | (2)u/i a/c dam(grd) | Neuruppin | P-51 |

1-0-0 air
2-2 ground

**McGeever, Thomas J., Capt.**
368th Ftr Sqn/359th Ftr Grp

| *Sqn* | *Date* | *Claims* | *Location* | *A/C* |
|---|---|---|---|---|
| 368th | February 24, 1944 | FW-190 dest(air) | Neuenhaus | P-47 |
| | March 15 | Me-109 prob(air) | Steinhuder Lake | P-47 |
| | | (2)Me-109 dam(air) | Steinhuder Lake | P-47 |
| | May 21 | Ju-52 dest(air) | Gadebusch | P-51 |
| | | u/i a/c dest(grd) | Gadebusch | P-51 |
| | November 21 | FW-190 dest(grd) | Gotha | P-51 |

2-1-2 air
2-0 ground

**McGehee, Fred S., Lt.**
369th Ftr Sqn/359th Ftr Grp

| *Sqn* | *Date* | *Claims* | *Location* | *A/C* |
|---|---|---|---|---|
| 369th | February 21, 1945 | FW-200 dam(grd) | Deiningen | P-51 |
| | | Me-410 dam(grd) | Deiningen | P-51 |
| | February 22 | (3)Ju-88 dam(grd) | Parchim | P-51 |
| | March 24 | (2)Me-109 dest(air) | Eikelon A/F | P-51 |

2-0-0 air
0-5 ground

**McGinley, William R., Lt.**
363rd Ftr Sqn/357th Ftr Grp

| Sqn | Date | Claims | Location | A/C |
|---|---|---|---|---|
| 363rd | March 16, 1944 | Me-109 prob(air) | S/Stuttgart | P-51 |

0-1-0 air
0-0 ground

**McGinn, John L., LtCol.**
338th Ftr Sqn/55th Ftr Grp
Earlier flew in the PTO with the 347th Ftr Grp and claimed 3 kills; Zeros on June 16, July 17, and November 1, 1943.

| Sqn | Date | Claims | Location | A/C |
|---|---|---|---|---|
| 338th | September 3, 1944 | FW-190 dest(air) | Brussels | P-51 |
| | September 11 | Me-109 dest(air) | S/Meiningen | P-51 |
| | | (2)Me-109 dam(air) | S/Meiningen | P-51 |

2-0-2 air
0-0 ground

**McGinnis, Keith R., Lt.**
38th Ftr Sqn/55th Ftr Grp

| Sqn | Date | Claims | Location | A/C |
|---|---|---|---|---|
| 38th | February 3, 1945 | (4)Fi-156 dest(grd) | Templin A/F | P-51 |
| | February 19 | FW-190 dest(air) | NW Ingolstadt | P-51 |
| | April 9 | (2)He-111 dest(grd) | Munich-Brunnthal | P-51 |
| | | He-111 dam(grd) | Munich-Brunnthal | P-51 |
| | April 10 | Me-262 dest(air) | Galworde | P-51 |

2-0-0 air
6-1 ground

**McGinty, William J., Lt.**
358th Ftr Sqn/355th Ftr Grp

| Sqn | Date | Claims | Location | A/C |
|---|---|---|---|---|
| 358th | March 2, 1944 | (.5)Me-109 dest(air)* | NE Liege | P-47 |
| | June 8 | (.5)He-177 dest(air)** | N/Angoulieme | P-51 |
| | July 8 | FW-190 dest(grd) | SW Chalons | P-51 |
| | | (2)FW-190 dam(grd) | SW Chalons | P-51 |

1-0-0 air
1-2 ground

* - shared with Maj. R.B. Myers of the 358th Ftr Sqn
** - shared with Lt. C.J. Brien of the 358th Ftr Sqn

**McGrattan, Bernard L., Capt.**
335th Ftr Sqn/4th Ftr Grp

| Sqn | Date | Claims | Location | A/C |
|---|---|---|---|---|
| 335th | February 22, 1944 | FW-190 dest(air) | Erkelenz | P-47 |
| | March 6 | Me-110 dest(air) | NE Magdeburg | P-51 |
| | March 18 | He-111 dest(air) | NE Augsburg | P-51 |
| | April 8 | Me-109 dest(air) | Wolfenbuttel | P-51 |
| | April 19 | Me-109 dest(air) | Eschwege | P-51 |
| | | (.5)FW-190 dest(air)* | Eschwege | P-51 |
| | April 24 | FW-190 dest(air) | Knocke | P-51 |
| | May 1 | Me-109 dest(air) | Losheim | P-51 |
| | May 29 | FW-190 dest(air) | Laaland Island | P-51 |

8.5-0-0 air
0-0 ground

* - shared with Lt. N. Megura of the 334th Ftr Sqn, 4th Ftr Grp

**McGraw, Charles L., Capt.**
351st Ftr Sqn/353rd Ftr Grp

| Sqn | Date | Claims | Location | A/C |
|---|---|---|---|---|
| 351st | September 13, 1944 | Do-217 dest(grd) | NW Stuttgart | P-47 |
| | April 7, 1945 | (3)Me-109 dest(air) | Steinhuder Lake | P-51 |
| | April 16 | He-111 dest(grd) | Reichersberg | P-51 |
| | | (2)He-111 dam(grd) | Reichersberg | P-51 |

3-0-0 air
2-2 ground

**McGuire, Allen G., Lt.**
84th Ftr Sqn/78th Ftr Grp

| Sqn | Date | Claims | Location | A/C |
|---|---|---|---|---|
| 84th | July 19, 1944 | Me-110 dest(grd) | Eutingen | P-47 |
| | | Do-217 dam(grd) | Eutingen | P-47 |
| | September 10 | (2)He-111 dest(grd) | Meinbullen | P-47 |
| | | (4)He-111 dam(grd) | Meinbullen | P-47 |

0-0-0 air
3-5 ground

**McGuire, Ivan L., Capt.**
364th Ftr Sqn/357th Ftr Grp

| Sqn | Date | Claims | Location | A/C |
|---|---|---|---|---|
| 364th | September 18, 1944 | FW-190 dest(air) | N/Maastricht | P-51 |
| | December 24 | FW-190 dest(air) | S/Kassel | P-51 |
| | March 3, 1945 | Me-262 dam(air) | S/Brunswick | P-51 |
| | April 7 | Me-109 dest(air) | NW Magdeburg | P-51 |
| | April 19 | (.5)Me-262 dest(air)* | S/Dresden | P-51 |

3.5-0-1 air
0-0 ground

* - shared with Lt. G.L. Weber of the 364th Ftr Sqn

**McHugh, Philip M.N., Lt.**
357th Ftr Sqn/355th Ftr Grp

| Sqn | Date | Claims | Location | A/C |
|---|---|---|---|---|
| 357th | June 24, 1944 | Me-109 dest(grd) | E/Angars | P-51 |
| | July 8 | (2)Me-410 dest(grd) | SW Chalons | P-51 |
| | | (3)Me-410 dam(grd) | SW Chalons | P-51 |
| | July 13 | Me-109 dam(air) | Sarrebourg | P-51 |
| | September 12 | (2)FW-190 dest(air) | E/Muritz Lake | P-51 |

2-0-1 air
3-3 ground

**McInnes, Robert L., Capt.**
370th Ftr Sqn/359th Ftr Grp

| Sqn | Date | Claims | Location | A/C |
|---|---|---|---|---|
| 370th | September 12, 1944 | (2)u/i a/c dest(grd) | S/Memmingen | P-51 |
| | | Ju-52 dest(grd) | S/Memmingen | P-51 |
| | | (4)u/i a/c dam(grd) | S/Memmingen | P-51 |
| | October 6 | FW-190 dest(air) | S/Stettin | P-51 |
| | | FW-190 dam(air) | S/Stettin | P-51 |

1-0-1 air
3-4 ground

**McIntosh, Fred B., Capt.**
62nd Ftr Sqn/56th Ftr Grp

| Sqn | Date | Claims | Location | A/C |
|---|---|---|---|---|
| 62nd | September 5, 1944 | FW-190 dest(grd) | Gelnhausen | P-47 |
| | | Me-110 dest(grd) | Limburg | P-47 |
| | | Me-210 dest(grd) | Limburg | P-47 |
| | | (2)Me-210 dam(grd) | Limburg | P-47 |
| | | (2)Ju-88 dam(grd) | Limburg | P-47 |
| | | Me-110 dam(grd) | Limburg | P-47 |
| | | FW-190 dam(grd) | Gelnhausen | P-47 |

0-0-0 air
3-6 ground

**McIntosh, John A., Lt.**
352nd Ftr Sqn/353rd Ftr Grp

| Sqn | Date | Claims | Location | A/C |
|---|---|---|---|---|
| 352nd | April 16, 1945 | He-111 dam(grd) | Pocking | P-51 |
| | April 17 | Me-109 dam(grd) | Ganacker | P-51 |

0-0-0 air
0-2 ground

**McIntosh, Robert J., Lt.**
84th Ftr Sqn/78th Ftr Grp

| Sqn | Date | Claims | Location | A/C |
|---|---|---|---|---|
| 84th | May 11, 1944 | FW-190 dest(air) | W/Orleans | P-47 |
| | | FW-190 dam(air) | W/Orleans | P-47 |
| | June 10 | FW-190 dest(air) | La Ferte Mace | P-47 |

2-0-1 air
0-0 ground

**McIntyre, Bryce W., Capt.**
364th Ftr Sqn/357th Ftr Grp

| Sqn | Date | Claims | Location | A/C |
|---|---|---|---|---|
| 364th | June 29, 1944 | He-177 dam(grd) | Leipzig | P-51 |
| | September 19 | Me-109 dest(air) | Emmerich | P-51 |
| | | FW-190 dest(air) | Emmerich | P-51 |

2-0-0 air
0-1 ground

**McIntyre, Winfield E., Capt.**
487th Ftr Sqn/352nd Ftr Grp

| Sqn | Date | Claims | Location | A/C |
|---|---|---|---|---|
| 487th | December 20, 1943 | Me-109 dest(air) | NW Oosterwolde | P-47 |

1-0-0 air
0-0 ground

**McKee, Daniel D., LtCol.**
370th Ftr Sqn/359th Ftr Grp
HdQts/359th Ftr Grp

| Sqn | Date | Claims | Location | A/C |
|---|---|---|---|---|
| 370th | March 2, 1944 | FW-190 dam(air) | Neufchateau | P-47 |
| | March 27 | FW-190 prob(air) | Chartres | P-47 |
| | | Me-109 dam(air) | Chartres | P-47 |
| | April 11 | Ju-88 dest(grd) | Volkenrod | P-47 |
| | | (2)Ju-88 dam(grd) | Volkenrod | P-47 |
| | April 15 | (2)Ju-88 dam(grd) | Oldenburg | P-47 |
| | November 21 | FW-190 dest(air) | SW Merseburg | P-51 |
| | April 13 | (2)Ar-196 dest(grd) | Schwerin Lake | P-51 |
| | April 17 | FW-190 dest(grd) | Ganacker-Plattling | P-51 |

1-1-2 air
4-4 ground

**McKee, John E., Lt.**
338th Ftr Sqn/55th Ftr Grp

| Sqn | Date | Claims | Location | A/C |
|---|---|---|---|---|
| 338th | July 7, 1944 | FW-190 dest(air) | W/Bernburg | P-38 |
| | | Me-109 prob(air) | W/Bernburg | P-38 |

1-1-0 air
0-0 ground

**McKenna, James P., F/O**
486th Ftr Sqn/352nd Ftr Grp

| Sqn | Date | Claims | Location | A/C |
|---|---|---|---|---|
| 486th | April 17, 1945 | FW-190 dest(grd) | Plattling | P-51 |
| | | Me-109 dest(grd) | Plattling | P-51 |
| | | Me-109 dam(grd) | Plattling | P-51 |
| | | FW-190 dam(grd) | Plattling | P-51 |
| | | u/i a/c dam(grd) | Plattling | P-51 |

0-0-0 air
2-3 ground

**McKenney, Paul H., Lt.**
84th Ftr Sqn/78th Ftr Grp

| Sqn | Date | Claims | Location | A/C |
|---|---|---|---|---|
| 84th | August 17, 1944 | (1.5)Me-109 dam(grd)[*] | W/Chaudun | P-47 |

0-0-0 air
0-1.5 ground

[*] - shared with Capt. R.E. Smith of the 84th Ftr Sqn

**McKennon, Pierce W., Maj.**
335th Ftr Sqn/4th Ftr Grp

| Sqn | Date | Claims | Location | A/C |
|---|---|---|---|---|
| 335th | July 30, 1943 | FW-190 dest(air) | Zaltboemel | P-47 |
| | December 11 | Me-109 dam(air) | Leeuwarden | P-47 |
| | February 20, 1944 | FW-190 dest(air) | Marburg | P-47 |
| | February 22 | (.5)Me-109 dest(air)[*] | SW Ooltgensplant | P-47 |
| | | (.5)FW-190 dam(air)[*] | Erkelenz | P-47 |
| | February 25 | FW-190 dest(air) | S/Luxembourg | P-47 |
| | March 6 | Me-109 dest(air) | S/Berlin | P-51 |
| | March 21 | FW-190 dest(air) | W/Landes de Bussac | P-51 |
| | March 28 | Ju-88 dam(grd) | S/Dreux | P-51 |
| | March 29 | Me-109 dest(air) | NE Brunswick | P-51 |
| | April 8 | FW-190 dest(air) | NW Brunswick | P-51 |
| | | FW-190 dam(air) | NW Brunswick | P-51 |
| | April 9 | (.33)Ju-88 dest(grd)[**] | Lingen-Plantlunne | P-51 |
| | | (.33)Ju-88 dest(grd)[**] | Lingen-Plantlunne | P-51 |
| | April 10 | u/i a/c dam(grd) | Romorantin A/F | P-51 |
| | April 13 | FW-190 dest(air) | SW Schweinfurt | P-51 |
| | April 18 | FW-190 dest(air) | Rathenow | P-51 |
| | April 19 | Me-109 dest(air) | Eschwege | P-51 |
| | December 25 | (.5)FW-190 dest(air)[@] | S/Bonn | P-51 |
| | February 25, 1945 | (2)u/i a/c dam(grd) | Pretzech | P-51 |
| | April 9 | (2)Ju-52 dest(grd) | Munich-Brunnthal | P-51 |
| | | Me-410 dest(grd) | Munich-Brunnthal | P-51 |
| | | Ju-52 dam(grd) | Munich-Brunnthal | P-51 |
| | April 16 | (2)Do-217 dest(grd) | Praha/Letnany | P-51 |
| | | u/i a/c dest(grd) | Praha/Letnany | P-51 |
| | | Me-410 dam(grd) | Praha/Letnany | P-51 |

11-0-2.5 air
6.67-6 ground

[*] - both shared with F/O J. Goetz of the 335th Ftr Sqn
[**] - both shared with Capt. J.R. Happel of the 335th Ftr Sqn and Lt. J.T. Godfrey of the 336th Ftr Sqn, 4th Ftr Grp
[@] - shared with Lt. T.J. Cronin of the 334th Ftr Sqn, 4th Ftr Grp

**McKeon, Joseph T., Capt.**
77th Ftr Sqn/20th Ftr Grp
55th Ftr Sqn/20th Ftr Grp
Earlier flew in the PTO with the 8th and 475th Ftr Grps claiming 5 kills; Zeros on December 7, 1942, and September 4, 22, and 24, 1943; and a Val on October 15, 1943.

| Sqn | Date | Claims | Location | A/C |
|---|---|---|---|---|
| 77th | August 16, 1944 | Me-109 dest(air) | Mulhausen | P-51 |
| | | FW-190 dam(air) | Mulhausen | P-51 |
| 55th | October 6 | (2)Do-24 dest(grd) | Kubitzer Bay | P-51 |

1-0-1 air
2-0 ground

**McKibben, Donald W., Lt.**
486th Ftr Sqn/352nd Ftr Grp

| Sqn | Date | Claims | Location | A/C |
|---|---|---|---|---|
| 486th | April 19, 1944 | Me-109 dest(air) | SE Kassel | P-51 |
| | April 23 | Ju-88 dest(grd) | SE Paris | P-51 |
| | July 18 | Me-109 prob(air) | N/Warnemunde | P-51 |

1-1-0 air
1-0 ground

**McKibben, Robert M., Lt.**
385th Ftr Sqn/364th Ftr Grp

| Sqn | Date | Claims | Location | A/C |
|---|---|---|---|---|
| 385th | November 21, 1944 | FW-190 dest(air) | W/Merseburg | P-51 |
| | December 31 | FW-190 dest(air) | SE Hamburg | P-51 |

2-0-0 air
0-0 ground

**McKinney, Thomas M., Capt.**
364th Ftr Sqn/357th Ftr Grp

| Sqn | Date | Claims | Location | A/C |
|---|---|---|---|---|
| 364th | March 6, 1944 | Me-110 dest(air) | Brandenburg | P-51 |
| | April 24 | Me-109 dest(air) | N/Augsburg | P-51 |
| | April 30 | (.5)Me-109 dest(air)[*] | S/Paris | P-51 |
| | May 12 | Me-109 dest(air) | NE Frankfurt | P-51 |

3.5-0-0 air
0-0 ground

[*] - shared with Lt. G.M. O'Brien of the 362nd Ftr Sqn, 357th Ftr Grp

**McLary, Maurice R., Maj.**
55th Ftr Sqn/20th Ftr Grp
77th Ftr Sqn/20th Ftr Grp

| Sqn | Date | Claims | Location | A/C |
|---|---|---|---|---|
| 55th | January 24, 1944 | FW-190 dest(air) | Courtrai | P-38 |
| | | FW-190 dam(air) | Courtrai | P-38 |
| | February 10 | Me-110 dest(air) | Gifhorn | P-38 |
| | | Me-410 dest(air) | Gifhorn | P-38 |

| Sqn | Date | Claims | Location | A/C |
|---|---|---|---|---|
| | | FW-190 dam(air) | Gifhorn | P-38 |
| | | Me-110 dam(air) | Gifhorn | P-38 |

3-0-3 air
0-0 ground

**McLaughlin, Grover H., Lt.**
351st Ftr Sqn/353rd Ftr Grp

| Sqn | Date | Claims | Location | A/C |
|---|---|---|---|---|
| 351st | June 7, 1944 | (2)Me-109 dest(air) | Beauvais-Tille | P-47 |
| | | Me-109 dest(grd) | Beauvais-Tille | P-47 |
| | | (3)Me-109 dam(grd) | Beauvais-Tille | P-47 |
| | June 8 | FW-190 prob(air) | Domfront | P-47 |
| | June 27 | Me-109 dam(air) | S/Chalons | P-47 |

2-1-1 air
1-3 ground

**McLaughlin, Harry B., Capt.**
360th Ftr Sqn/356th Ftr Grp

| Sqn | Date | Claims | Location | A/C |
|---|---|---|---|---|
| 360th | February 21, 1944 | Me-109 prob(air) | Celle | P-47 |
| | March 29 | Me-410 dest(grd) | Cloppenburg A/F | P-47 |

0-1-0 air
1-0 ground

**McLaurin, Grover G., Lt.**
436th Ftr Sqn/479th Ftr Grp

| Sqn | Date | Claims | Location | A/C |
|---|---|---|---|---|
| 436th | April 16, 1945 | (2)FW-190 dest(grd) | Landstadt | P-51 |

0-0-0 air
2-0 ground

**McLear, Robert M., Lt.**
354th Ftr Sqn/355th Ftr Grp

| Sqn | Date | Claims | Location | A/C |
|---|---|---|---|---|
| 354th | November 26, 1944 | (2)Me-109 dest(air) | Gifhorn-W/Hanover | P-51 |
| | April 16, 1945 | (2)u/i a/c dest(grd) | Autobahn | P-51 |

2-0-0 air
2-0 ground

**McLeod, Donald W., Maj.**
83rd Ftr Sqn/78th Ftr Grp

| Sqn | Date | Claims | Location | A/C |
|---|---|---|---|---|
| 83rd | June 10, 1944 | (2)Me-109 dest(air) | Lisieux | P-47 |
| | | (2)Me-109 dam(air) | Lisieux | P-47 |

2-0-2 air
0-0 ground

**McLeod, Michael J., Lt.**
354th Ftr Sqn/355th Ftr Grp

| Sqn | Date | Claims | Location | A/C |
|---|---|---|---|---|
| 354th | March 22, 1945 | Me-262 dam(grd) | Kitzingen | P-51 |
| | April 13 | u/i a/c dest(grd) | Husum A/F | P-51 |
| | | He-111 dam(grd) | Husum A/F | P-51 |
| | April 16 | u/i a/c dest(grd) | Eger A/F | P-51 |
| | | (3)u/i a/c dam(grd) | Eger A/F | P-51 |

0-0-0 air
2-5 ground

**McLoughlin, Edward J., Lt.**
335th Ftr Sqn/4th Ftr Grp

| Sqn | Date | Claims | Location | A/C |
|---|---|---|---|---|
| 335th | April 9, 1945 | u/i a/c dam(grd) | Munich-Brunnthal | P-51 |

0-0-0 air
0-1 ground

**McMahan, Bruce D., Lt.**
350th Ftr Sqn/353rd Ftr Grp

| Sqn | Date | Claims | Location | A/C |
|---|---|---|---|---|
| 350th | April 10, 1945 | (.5)Me-262 dest(air)* | Dessau | P-51 |
| | April 16 | (4)FW-190 dest(grd) | Pocking | P-51 |
| | | (.5)Fi-156 dest(grd)** | Pocking | P-51 |
| | | (.5)Fi-156 dest(grd)** | Pocking | P-51 |
| | | (.5)Hs-126 dest(grd)** | Pocking | P-51 |

0.5-0-0 air
5.5-0 ground

* - shared with Lt. J.W. Clark of the 350th Ftr Sqn
** - all shared with Capt. H.G. Kolb of the 350th Ftr Sqn

**McMahan, Darrell E., Lt.**
62nd Ftr Sqn/56th Ftr Grp

| Sqn | Date | Claims | Location | A/C |
|---|---|---|---|---|
| 62nd | July 4, 1944 | (.5)Me-109 dest(air)* | Conches | P-47 |
| | September 5 | (4)FW-190 dest(grd) | Gelnhausen | P-47 |
| | September 12 | Me-109 dest(air) | Sachau A/F | P-47 |

1.5-0-0 air
4-0 ground

**McMahan, Ernest B., Capt.**
487th Ftr Sqn/352nd Ftr Grp

| Sqn | Date | Claims | Location | A/C |
|---|---|---|---|---|
| 487th | December 22, 1943 | (.5)Me-109 dest(air)* | E/Zwolle | P-47 |
| | | FW-190 dam(air) | Lingen | P-47 |
| | April 9, 1944 | Ju-88 dest(grd) | Vechta | P-51 |
| | April 10 | (.5)Me-109 dest(air)** | SW Rheims | P-51 |
| | April 22 | Ju-88 dest(grd) | Stade A/F | P-51 |

1-0-1 air
2-0 ground

* - shared with Lt. J.R. Bennett of the 487th Ftr Sqn
** - shared with Capt. C.E. Davis of the 487th Ftr Sqn

**McMahan, Peter J., Lt.**
505th Ftr Sqn/339th Ftr Grp

| Sqn | Date | Claims | Location | A/C |
|---|---|---|---|---|
| 505th | June 6, 1944 | (2)Ju-87 dest(air) | Orleans | P-51 |
| | June 8 | (1.5)FW-190 dest(air)* | Rennes | P-51 |

3.5-0-0 air
0-0 ground

* - shared with Lt. J.R. Starnes of the 505th Ftr Sqn

**McManus, John B., LtCol.**
383rd Ftr Sqn/364th Ftr Grp

| Sqn | Date | Claims | Location | A/C |
|---|---|---|---|---|
| 383rd | April 29, 1944 | FW-190 prob(air) | Stendal | P-38 |
| | May 21 | Me-410 dest(grd) | NW Renow | P-38 |
| | August 14 | He-111 dest(grd) | Memmingen | P-51 |
| | | He-111 dam(grd) | Memmingen | P-51 |

0-1-0 air
2-1 ground

**McMinn, Evan D., Lt.**
61st Ftr Sqn/56th Ftr Grp

| Sqn | Date | Claims | Location | A/C |
|---|---|---|---|---|
| 61st | February 21, 1944 | Me-109 dest(air) | Zuider Zee | P-47 |
| | February 22 | FW-190 dest(air) | Lippstadt | P-47 |
| | March 6 | (2)Me-109 dam(grd) | Vechta | P-47 |
| | March 15 | Me-109 dam(air) | E/Dummer Lake | P-47 |
| | March 16 | FW-190 dest(air) | St. Dizier | P-47 |
| | April 15 | He-111 dest(grd) | Flensburg | P-47 |
| | | Me-210 dest(grd) | Flensburg | P-47 |
| | | He-111 dam(grd) | Flensburg | P-47 |
| | | Me-210 dam(grd) | Flensburg | P-47 |
| | May 22 | (2)FW-190 dest(air) | Rotenburg | P-47 |
| | | FW-190 dam(air) | Rotenburg | P-47 |

5-0-2 air
2-4 ground

**McMullen, James P., Lt.**
364th Ftr Sqn/357th Ftr Grp

| *Sqn* | *Date* | *Claims* | *Location* | *A/C* |
|---|---|---|---|---|
| 364th | April 19, 1945 | Me-262 dest(air) | Prague/Ruzny A/F | P-51 |

1-0-0 air
0-0 ground

**McMullen, Joseph D., Lt.**
350th Ftr Sqn/353rd Ftr Grp

| *Sqn* | *Date* | *Claims* | *Location* | *A/C* |
|---|---|---|---|---|
| 350th | February 27, 1945 | (1.5)FW-190 dest(grd)[*] | Rohrensee | P-51 |
| | | Ju-88 dest(grd) | Rohrensee | P-51 |
| | | FW-190 dam(grd) | Rohrensee | P-51 |
| | | Ju-88 dam(grd) | Rohrensee | P-51 |
| | February 28 | (1.5)Me-110 dest(grd)[**] | S/Gotha | P-51 |
| | March 21 | He-111 dest(grd) | Achmer | P-51 |
| | | Ar-234 dam(grd) | Achmer | P-51 |
| | April 16 | (5)FW-190 dest(grd) | Pocking | P-51 |

0-0-0 air
10-3 ground

[*] - shared with F/O R.N. Gustke of the 350th Ftr Sqn
[**] - shared with Lt. M.W. Hightshoe of the 350th Ftr Sqn

**McNally, Russell I., Lt.**
358th Ftr Sqn/355th Ftr Grp

| *Sqn* | *Date* | *Claims* | *Location* | *A/C* |
|---|---|---|---|---|
| 358th | July 8, 1944 | FW-190 dest(grd) | SW Chalons | P-51 |
| | July 24 | Ju-88 dest(grd) | Augsburg | P-51 |

0-0-0 air
2-0 ground

**McNary, Billy D., Lt.**
360th Ftr Sqn/356th Ftr Grp

| *Sqn* | *Date* | *Claims* | *Location* | *A/C* |
|---|---|---|---|---|
| 360th | April 13, 1945 | (2)FW-190 dam(grd) | Schwerin | P-51 |
| | | He-111 dam(grd) | Schwerin | P-51 |

0-0-0 air
0-3 ground

**McNeel, Kenneth D., Lt.**
55th Ftr Sqn/20th Ftr Grp

| *Sqn* | *Date* | *Claims* | *Location* | *A/C* |
|---|---|---|---|---|
| 55th | August 25, 1944 | (.5)Do-18 dest(grd)[*] | Parow A/F | P-51 |
| | October 6 | u/i a/c dest(grd) | Kubitzer Bay | P-51 |
| | January 14, 1945 | Me-262 dam(air) | Perleberg | P-51 |
| | February 14 | (.5)Me-262 dam(air)[**] | Stuttgart | P-51 |
| | February 20 | Me-109 dest(air) | Nurnburg | P-51 |

1-0-1.5 air
1.5-0 ground

[*] - shared with Lt. R.H. Riemensnider of the 55th Ftr Sqn
[**] - shared with Capt. J.K. Brown of the 55th Ftr Sqn

**McNeff, Edward P., Lt.**
357th Ftr Sqn/355th Ftr Grp

| *Sqn* | *Date* | *Claims* | *Location* | *A/C* |
|---|---|---|---|---|
| 357th | April 8, 1944 | Me-109 dam(air) | Gifhorn A/F | P-51 |
| | April 24 | (.5)Me-109 dest(air)[*] | NE Munich | P-51 |
| | June 24 | Me-109 dest(grd) | E/Angars | P-51 |
| | July 7 | Me-109 dest(air) | Nordhausen | P-51 |

1.5-0-1 air
1-0 ground

[*] - shared with Lt. R.B. Butler of the 357th Ftr Sqn

**McPharlin, Michael G.H., Maj.**
HdQts/339th Ftr Grp
Earlier flew with 71 Sqn, RAF, claiming 1.5 kills; (3)FW-190's shared on April 27, 1942.

| *Sqn* | *Date* | *Claims* | *Location* | *A/C* |
|---|---|---|---|---|
| HdQts | May 19, 1944 | (.5)Me-109 dest(air)[*] | Lubeck-Schwerin | P-51 |
| | | Me-109 dam(air) | Lubeck-Schwerin | P-51 |
| | May 28 | Me-109 dest(air) | Magdeburg | P-51 |
| | | Me-109 dam(air) | Magdeburg | P-51 |
| | May 29 | Do-18 dest(grd) | Dievenow | P-51 |
| | June 6 | FW-190 dam(air) | Evreux | P-51 |

1.5-0-3 air
1-0 ground

[*] - shared with Lt. J.F. Scott of the 4th Ftr Grp

**McTaggart, Elmer E., Capt.**
83rd Ftr Sqn/78th Ftr Grp

| *Sqn* | *Date* | *Claims* | *Location* | *A/C* |
|---|---|---|---|---|
| 83rd | May 14, 1943 | FW-190 dest(air) | SW Antwerp | P-47 |

1-0-0 air
0-0 ground

**McVay, James C., Lt.**
343rd Ftr Sqn/55th Ftr Grp

| *Sqn* | *Date* | *Claims* | *Location* | *A/C* |
|---|---|---|---|---|
| 343rd | December 24, 1944 | FW-190 dest(air) | S/Frankfurt | P-51 |
| | February 26, 1945 | Me-110 dest(grd) | S/Varel | P-51 |

1-0-0 air
1-0 ground

**Mead, Charles M., Lt.**
504th Ftr Sqn/339th Ftr Grp

| *Sqn* | *Date* | *Claims* | *Location* | *A/C* |
|---|---|---|---|---|
| 504th | November 18, 1944 | Me-109 dest(air) | Dachau | P-51 |

1-0-0 air
0-0 ground

**Mead, Edwin R., Lt.**
335th Ftr Sqn/4th Ftr Grp

| *Sqn* | *Date* | *Claims* | *Location* | *A/C* |
|---|---|---|---|---|
| 335th | January 30, 1944 | Me-109 prob(air) | Gronau | P-47 |

0-1-0 air
0-0 ground

**Meade, Donald J., Lt.**
338th Ftr Sqn/55th Ftr Grp

| *Sqn* | *Date* | *Claims* | *Location* | *A/C* |
|---|---|---|---|---|
| 338th | January 6, 1945 | Ju-88 dest(grd) | Giebelstadt | P-51 |
| | | u/i a/c dest(grd) | Giebelstadt | P-51 |

0-0-0 air
2-0 ground

**Meade, John W., Lt.**
359th Ftr Sqn/356th Ftr Grp

| *Sqn* | *Date* | *Claims* | *Location* | *A/C* |
|---|---|---|---|---|
| 359th | December 26, 1944 | FW-190 dest(air) | NE Bonn | P-51 |

1-0-0 air
0-0 ground

**Means, Billy C., Capt.**
435th Ftr Sqn/479th Ftr Grp

| *Sqn* | *Date* | *Claims* | *Location* | *A/C* |
|---|---|---|---|---|
| 435th | December 5, 1944 | Me-109 dest(air) | NW Berlin | P-51 |
| | March 3, 1945 | Me-109 dam(grd) | Dummer Lake | P-51 |

1-0-0 air
0-1 ground

**Mearns, William, Lt.**
343rd Ftr Sqn/55th Ftr Grp

| *Sqn* | *Date* | *Claims* | *Location* | *A/C* |
|---|---|---|---|---|
| 343rd | March 3, 1945 | Me-109 dam(grd) | Prague/Letnany | P-51 |

| Sqn | Date | Claims | Location | A/C |
|---|---|---|---|---|
| | | Ju-88 dam(grd) | Prague/Letnany | P-51 |
| | April 9 | Me-410 dam(grd) | Munich-Brunnthal | P-51 |

0-0-0 air
0-3 ground

**Medeiros, John L., Capt.**
364th Ftr Sqn/357th Ftr Grp

| *Sqn* | *Date* | *Claims* | *Location* | *A/C* |
|---|---|---|---|---|
| 364th | February 22, 1944 | Me-109 dest(air) | Bernburg | P-51 |
| | February 24 | FW-190 dest(air) | Gotha | P-51 |

2-0-0 air
0-0 ground

**Mednick, Harvey H., Lt.**
79th Ftr Sqn/20th Ftr Grp

| *Sqn* | *Date* | *Claims* | *Location* | *A/C* |
|---|---|---|---|---|
| 79th | January 14, 1944 | (.5)FW-190 prob(air)[*] | S/Fecamp | P-38 |
| | | FW-190 dam(air) | S/Fecamp | P-38 |

0-0.5-1 air
0-0 ground

[*] - shared with Maj. R.L. Ott of the 79th Ftr Sqn

**Megura, Nicholas, Capt.**
334th Ftr Sqn/4th Ftr Grp

| *Sqn* | *Date* | *Claims* | *Location* | *A/C* |
|---|---|---|---|---|
| 334th | February 28, 1944 | (.25)Ju-88 dest(grd)[*] | Soissons | P-51 |
| | March 4 | Me-109 dest(air) | NW Leipzig | P-51 |
| | March 6 | (2)Me-110 dest(air) | SW Berlin | P-51 |
| | | Me-110 dam(air) | SW Berlin | P-51 |
| | March 8 | Me-109 dest(air) | W/Berlin | P-51 |
| | | FW-190 dest(air) | W/Berlin | P-51 |
| | | FW-190 dam(air) | W/Berlin | P-51 |
| | | Ju-88 dam(air) | Ruhr | P-51 |
| | March 18 | Me-109 dest(air) | SE Mannheim | P-51 |
| | March 21 | (.5)FW-190 dest(air)[**] | NE Bordeaux | P-51 |
| | | He-177 dest(grd) | NE Bordeaux | P-51 |
| | March 23 | FW-190 dest(air) | Munster | P-51 |
| | March 27 | Me-109 dam(air) | Angars | P-51 |
| | | (.5)Ju-88 dest(grd)[@] | Cazaux A/F | P-51 |
| | | FW-190 dam(grd) | Cazaux A/F | P-51 |
| | April 1 | Me-109 dam(air) | NW Lake Constance | P-51 |
| | April 13 | FW-190 dest(air) | SE Mannheim | P-51 |
| | April 18 | (.33)Me-109 dest(air)[@@] | Fassberg A/F | P-51 |
| | | Ju-88 dam(grd) | Brandenburg | P-51 |
| | | u/i a/c dam(grd) | Brandenburg | P-51 |
| | April 19 | (.5)FW-190 dest(air)[#] | Eschwege | P-51 |
| | April 24 | (2)FW-190 dest(air) | S/Frankfurt | P-51 |
| | | FW-190 dam(air) | S/Frankfurt | P-51 |
| | April 29 | Ju-52 dest(grd) | Nordhausen | P-51 |
| | | (.5)Ju-52 dest(grd)[##] | Nordhausen | P-51 |
| | | (.5)Ju-52 dest(grd)[&] | Nordhausen | P-51 |
| | May 22 | (.5)Me-109 dest(air)[&&] | SW Kiel | P-51 |

11.83-0-6 air
3.75-3 ground

[*] - shared with Capt. D.W. Beeson and Lt. W.B. Smith of the 334th Ftr Sqn and Lt. V. Garrison of the 336th Ftr Sqn, 4th Ftr Grp
[**] - shared with Lt. A.W. Chatterly of the 334th Ftr Sqn
[@] - shared with Lt. A.H. Markel of the 334th Ftr Sqn
[@@] - shared with Capt. V.J. France and Lt. G.C. Siems of the 334th Ftr Sqn
[#] - shared with Lt. B.L. McGrattan of the 335th Ftr Sqn, 4th Ftr Grp
[##] - shared with Lt. J.L. Barden of the 334th Ftr Sqn
[&] - shared with Lt. S.W. Monroe of the 334th Ftr Sqn
[&&] - shared with an unknown P-38 pilot

**Meholic, James J., Capt.**
359th Ftr Sqn/356th Ftr Grp

| *Sqn* | *Date* | *Claims* | *Location* | *A/C* |
|---|---|---|---|---|
| 359th | March 6, 1944 | Me-109 dest(air) | Nienburg | P-47 |
| | March 15 | (.5)Me-109 dest(air)[*] | SE Nijmegen | P-47 |
| | April 1 | (.5)Me-410 dam(grd)[**] | Rheine | P-47 |
| | | (.5)Me-410 dam(grd)[**] | Rheine | P-47 |

1.5-0-0 air
0-1 ground

[*] - shared with Lt. H. Weber of the 359th Ftr Sqn
[**] - both shared with Lt. H. Weber of the 359th Ftr Sqn

**Meinzen, Robert W., Lt.**
55th Ftr Sqn/20th Ftr Grp

| *Sqn* | *Date* | *Claims* | *Location* | *A/C* |
|---|---|---|---|---|
| 55th | April 10, 1945 | Me-262 dam(air) | Neuruppin | P-51 |

0-0-1 air
0-0 ground

**Mejaski, Joseph W., Capt.**
369th Ftr Sqn/359th Ftr Grp

| *Sqn* | *Date* | *Claims* | *Location* | *A/C* |
|---|---|---|---|---|
| 369th | September 11, 1944 | (2)Ju-88 dest(grd) | S/Merseburg | P-51 |
| | | (3)Ju-88 dam(grd) | S/Merseburg | P-51 |

0-0-0 air
2-3 ground

**Mellen, Joseph E., Capt.**
354th Ftr Sqn/355th Ftr Grp

| *Sqn* | *Date* | *Claims* | *Location* | *A/C* |
|---|---|---|---|---|
| 354th | November 26, 1944 | FW-190 dest(air) | S/Misburg | P-51 |
| | April 7, 1945 | FW-190 dest(air) | S/Bremen | P-51 |
| | April 13 | (3)u/i a/c dest(grd) | Husum A/F | P-51 |
| | | (2)He-111 dest(grd) | Husum A/F | P-51 |
| | April 16 | He-111 dest(grd) | Eger A/F | P-51 |
| | | He-177 dest(grd) | Eger A/F | P-51 |
| | | Ju-88 dest(grd) | Eger A/F | P-51 |

2-0-0 air
8-0 ground

**Mendenhall, Lee G., Maj.**
354th Ftr Sqn/355th Ftr Grp

| *Sqn* | *Date* | *Claims* | *Location* | *A/C* |
|---|---|---|---|---|
| 354th | February 20, 1944 | Me-109 dam(air) | NE Bonn | P-47 |
| | March 18 | (.5)Me-109 dest(air)[*] | NE Munich | P-51 |
| | April 5 | (3)Ju-88 dest(grd) | Landsberg | P-51 |
| | | (3)Ju-88 dam(grd) | Landsberg | P-51 |

0.5-0-1 air
3-3 ground

[*] - shared with Lt. C.W. Lenfest of the 354th Ftr Sqn

**Menegay, Donald T., Lt.**
38th Ftr Sqn/55th Ftr Grp

| *Sqn* | *Date* | *Claims* | *Location* | *A/C* |
|---|---|---|---|---|
| 38th | February 25, 1945 | Me-262 dest(air) | W/Giebelstadt A/F | P-51 |
| | April 7 | (.5)Me-109 dest(air)[*] | Celle | P-51 |
| | April 10 | Ju-88 dest(grd) | Munich-Brunnthal | P-51 |

1.5-0-0 air
1-0 ground

[*] - shared with Lt. D.A. Cavanaugh of the 38th Ftr Sqn

**Mercer, Durward B., Lt.**
360th Ftr Sqn/356th Ftr Grp

| *Sqn* | *Date* | *Claims* | *Location* | *A/C* |
|---|---|---|---|---|
| 360th | April 27, 1944 | FW-190 dest(air) | Laon | P-47 |
| | | FW-190 dam(air) | Laon | P-47 |

1-0-1 air
0-0 ground

**Mercier, Donald L., Lt.**
343rd Ftr Sqn/55th Ftr Grp

| *Sqn* | *Date* | *Claims* | *Location* | *A/C* |
|---|---|---|---|---|
| 343rd | August 28, 1944 | He-111 dest(air) | SW Coblenz | P-51 |
| | September 10 | Me-109 dest(air) | NE Augsburg | P-51 |
| | November 2 | (.5)Me-109 dest(air)[*] | Erfurt-Weimar | P-51 |

1.5-0-0 air
1-0 ground

[*] - shared with Capt. S.J. Huskins of the 359th Ftr Grp

**Meredith, William B., Lt.**
336th Ftr Sqn/4th Ftr Grp

| Sqn | Date | Claims | Location | A/C |
|---|---|---|---|---|
| 336th | April 16, 1945 | Me-109 dest(grd) | Praha | P-51 |
| | April 17 | u/i a/c dest(grd) | Pilzen | P-51 |
| | | (2)Me-109 dam(grd) | Pilzen | P-51 |

0-0-0 air
2-2 ground

**Meroney, Virgil K., Capt.**
487th Ftr Sqn/352nd Ftr Grp

| Sqn | Date | Claims | Location | A/C |
|---|---|---|---|---|
| 487th | December 1, 1943 | Me-109 dest(air) | S/Rheydt | P-47 |
| | | (.5)Me-210 dest(air)* | S/Rheydt | P-47 |
| | December 4 | Me-109 dest(air) | Rotterdam-Utrecht | P-47 |
| | | (.5)FW-190 dest(air)** | Rotterdam-Utrecht | P-47 |
| | January 29, 1944 | FW-190 dest(air) | Malmedy | P-47 |
| | January 30 | Me-109 dest(air) | Zwolle | P-47 |
| | | Me-109 dam(air) | Zwolle | P-47 |
| | February 3 | FW-190 dest(air) | Groningen | P-47 |
| | February 10 | Me-109 dest(air) | Hengelo | P-47 |
| | March 8 | FW-190 dest(air) | Meppen | P-47 |
| | March 16 | Me-109 dest(air) | S/Bar de Luc | P-47 |

9-0-1 air
0-0 ground

* - shared with Lt. R.L. Grow of the 487th Ftr Sqn
** - shared with F/O J.L. Sweeney of the 487th Ftr Sqn

**Merrill, Wiley H., Jr., Lt.**
62nd Ftr Sqn/56th Ftr Grp

| Sqn | Date | Claims | Location | A/C |
|---|---|---|---|---|
| 62nd | April 15, 1944 | FW-190 dam(air) | Altona | P-47 |
| | July 4 | (2)Me-109 dest(air) | Conches | P-47 |
| | | Me-109 dam(air) | Conches | P-47 |

2-0-2 air
0-0 ground

**Merritt, George L., Jr., Maj.**
375th Ftr Sqn/361st Ftr Grp

| Sqn | Date | Claims | Location | A/C |
|---|---|---|---|---|
| 375th | February 22, 1944 | (2)FW-190 dest(air) | NE Tilburg | P-47 |
| | March 17 | Me-109 dest(grd) | Chartres | P-47 |
| | | Me-109 dam(grd) | Chartres | P-47 |
| | April 18 | Ju-88 dest(grd) | Zwischenaschmer | P-47 |
| | April 27 | He-111 dest(grd) | Etampes | P-47 |
| | May 8 | FW-190 dest(air) | N/Nienburg | P-47 |
| | May 24 | Me-109 dest(air) | NE Berlin | P-51 |
| | May 27 | FW-190 dest(air) | W/Lille | P-51 |
| | May 29 | (2)He-111 dest(grd) | Lackau-Juterbog | P-51 |
| | June 6 | Ju-88 dest(grd) | Tours | P-51 |

5-0-0 air
6-1 ground

**Messenger, Robert J., Lt.**
336th Ftr Sqn/4th Ftr Grp

| Sqn | Date | Claims | Location | A/C |
|---|---|---|---|---|
| 336th | January 5, 1944 | FW-190 dest(air) | Tours | P-47 |

1-0-0 air
0-0 ground

**Messinger, Richard A., Lt.**
83rd Ftr Sqn/78th Ftr Grp

| Sqn | Date | Claims | Location | A/C |
|---|---|---|---|---|
| 83rd | April 16, 1945 | (3)Ju-52 dest(grd) | N/Prague | P-51 |
| | | FW-190 dest(grd) | N/Prague | P-51 |
| | | (3)Ju-87 dam(grd) | N/Prague | P-51 |

0-0-0 air
4-3 ground

**Meteyer, Thomas O., Lt.**
358th Ftr Sqn/355th Ftr Grp

| Sqn | Date | Claims | Location | A/C |
|---|---|---|---|---|
| 358th | April 19, 1944 | Me-109 dest(air) | SW Brunswick | P-51 |

1-0-0 air
0-0 ground

**Metzger, Allen M., Lt.**
361st Ftr Sqn/356th Ftr Grp

| Sqn | Date | Claims | Location | A/C |
|---|---|---|---|---|
| 361st | November 29, 1943 | Me-109 dest(air) | Meppel | P-47 |

1-0-0 air
0-0 ground

**Meyer, Earl J., Lt.**
328th Ftr Sqn/352nd Ftr Grp

| Sqn | Date | Claims | Location | A/C |
|---|---|---|---|---|
| 328th | April 23, 1944 | Ju-88 dest(grd) | SE Paris | P-51 |
| | | Me-110 dam(grd) | SE Paris | P-51 |
| | April 28 | Ju-88 dam(grd) | Orleans-Bricy | P-51 |

0-0-0 air
1-2 ground

**Meyer, John C., LtCol.**
487th Ftr Sqn/352nd Ftr Grp
HdQts/352nd Ftr Grp

| Sqn | Date | Claims | Location | A/C |
|---|---|---|---|---|
| 487th | November 26, 1943 | Me-109 dest(air) | E/Groningen | P-47 |
| | | Me-109 prob(air) | E/Groningen | P-47 |
| | December 4 | Me-109 dest(air) | W/Utrecht | P-47 |
| | December 22 | Me-109 dest(air) | N/Lingen | P-47 |
| | April 10, 1944 | Me-109 dest(air) | SW Rheims | P-51 |
| | | (.5)FW-190 dest(air)* | SW Rheims | P-51 |
| | April 11 | FW-190 dest(grd) | S/Berlin | P-51 |
| | | Ju-88 dest(grd) | S/Berlin | P-51 |
| | | FW-200 dam(grd) | S/Berlin | P-51 |
| | | Ju-290 dam(grd) | S/Berlin | P-51 |
| | April 13 | (2)He-111 dest(grd) | S/Stuttgart | P-51 |
| | | Ju-52 dest(grd) | S/Stuttgart | P-51 |
| | April 22 | Me-210 dest(grd) | Stade A/F | P-51 |
| | | (2)He-111 dam(grd) | Stade A/F | P-51 |
| | May 8 | (3)Me-109 dest(air) | Brunswick-Hanover | P-51 |
| | May 12 | Me-109 dest(air) | SW Frankfurt | P-51 |
| | | He-177 dest(grd) | SW Frankfurt | P-51 |
| | August 25 | He-177 dest(grd) | Neubrandenburg | P-51 |
| | | Ju-52 dest(grd) | Neubrandenburg | P-51 |
| | | (2)u/i a/c dam(grd) | Neubrandenburg | P-51 |
| | September 10 | (3)Ju-52 dest(grd) | Wertheim | P-51 |
| | | u/i a/c dest(grd) | Wertheim | P-51 |
| | September 11 | (3)Me-109 dest(air) | Gottingen-Nordhausen | P-51 |
| | | FW-190 dest(air) | Gottingen-Nordhausen | P-51 |
| HdQts | November 21 | (3)FW-190 dest(air) | SW Merseburg | P-51 |
| | November 27 | Me-109 dest(air) | E/Munster | P-51 |
| | December 26 | (2.5)Me-109 dest(air)** | Uxheim | P-51 |
| | December 27 | (2)FW-190 dest(air) | SW Bonn | P-51 |
| | | (2)FW-190 dam(air) | SW Bonn | P-51 |
| | December 31 | Ar-234 dest(air) | Euskirchen | P-51 |
| | January 1, 1945 | (2)FW-190 dest(air) | N/Liege | P-51 |

24-1-2 air
13-6 ground

* - shared with Lt. C.J. Luksic of the 487th Ftr Sqn
** - shared with an unknown pilot

**Meyer, Robert J., LtCol.**
79th Ftr Sqn/20th Ftr Grp

| Sqn | Date | Claims | Location | A/C |
|---|---|---|---|---|
| 79th | January 14, 1944 | (2)Me-109 dam(air) | Rouen | P-38 |
| | February 10 | FW-190 dest(air) | N/Hanover | P-38 |
| | February 11 | Me-410 prob(air) | SW Frankfurt | P-38 |
| | August 9 | (2)FW-190 dest(air) | SW Ulm | P-51 |
| | | FW-190 dam(air) | SW Ulm | P-51 |
| | October 7 | (.5)He-115 dest(grd)* | Bad Berg-Dievenow | P-51 |
| | February 20, 1945 | Me-110 dam(grd) | Weiden A/F | P-51 |

3-1-3 air
0.5-1 ground

* - shared with Lt. Z. Wyman of the 79th Ftr Sqn

**Meyer, Victor W., Lt.**
503rd Ftr Sqn/339th Ftr Grp

| *Sqn* | *Date* | *Claims* | *Location* | *A/C* |
|---|---|---|---|---|
| 503rd | June 15, 1944 | FW-190 dest(air) | Montiers | P-51 |
| | June 29 | FW-190 dest(air) | Eisleben | P-51 |
| | | (.5)Me-410 dest(air)* | Eisleben | P-51 |
| | | Me-109 dam(air) | Eisleben | P-51 |

2.5-0-1 air
0-0 ground

* - shared with an unknown pilot of the 505th Ftr Sqn, 339th Ftr Grp

**Michaely, William D., Lt.**
363rd Ftr Sqn/357th Ftr Grp

| *Sqn* | *Date* | *Claims* | *Location* | *A/C* |
|---|---|---|---|---|
| 363rd | February 24, 1944 | FW-190 dest(air) | Gotha | P-51 |

1-0-0 air
0-0 ground

**Michel, Alvin, Lt.**
352nd Ftr Sqn/353rd Ftr Grp

| *Sqn* | *Date* | *Claims* | *Location* | *A/C* |
|---|---|---|---|---|
| 352nd | March 21, 1945 | (4)FW-190 dest(grd) | Achmer | P-51 |

0-0-0 air
4-0 ground

**Michel, Douglas, Capt.**
55th Ftr Sqn/20th Ftr Grp

| *Sqn* | *Date* | *Claims* | *Location* | *A/C* |
|---|---|---|---|---|
| 55th | April 10, 1945 | Me-262 dam(air) | Neuruppin | P-51 |

0-0-1 air
0-0 ground

**Michelena, Ralph L., Lt.**
358th Ftr Sqn/355th Ftr Grp

| *Sqn* | *Date* | *Claims* | *Location* | *A/C* |
|---|---|---|---|---|
| 358th | July 8, 1944 | FW-190 dest(grd) | SW Chalons | P-51 |
| | | FW-190 dam(grd) | SW Chalons | P-51 |
| | September 18 | Me-109 dest(air) | Warsaw | P-51 |
| | | Me-109 dam(air) | Warsaw | P-51 |

1-0-1 air
1-1 ground

**Michels, Kenneth M., Lt.**
357th Ftr Sqn/355th Ftr Grp

| *Sqn* | *Date* | *Claims* | *Location* | *A/C* |
|---|---|---|---|---|
| 357th | August 16, 1944 | Me-109 dest(air) | S/Hildesheim | P-51 |

1-0-0 air
0-0 ground

**Mickey, Melvin S., Lt.**
436th Ftr Sqn/479th Ftr Grp

| *Sqn* | *Date* | *Claims* | *Location* | *A/C* |
|---|---|---|---|---|
| 436th | August 5, 1944 | Me-109 dest(air) | NE Stendal | P-38 |

1-0-0 air
0-0 ground

**Middleton, Ellis S., Capt.**
350th Ftr Sqn/353rd Ftr Grp

| *Sqn* | *Date* | *Claims* | *Location* | *A/C* |
|---|---|---|---|---|
| 350th | July 9, 1944 | Me-109 dam(air) | Argentan | P-47 |
| | August 4 | Me-109 dest(air) | NE Soltau | P-47 |
| | September 23 | FW-190 dest(air) | SE Arnheim | P-47 |

2-0-1 air
0-0 ground

**Middleton, George A., Lt.**
328th Ftr Sqn/352nd Ftr Grp

| *Sqn* | *Date* | *Claims* | *Location* | *A/C* |
|---|---|---|---|---|
| 328th | June 15, 1944 | FW-190 dam(air) | Laigle | P-51 |

0-0-1 air
0-0-0 ground

**Mikalauskas, Kenneth E., Lt.**
358th Ftr Sqn/355th Ftr Grp

| *Sqn* | *Date* | *Claims* | *Location* | *A/C* |
|---|---|---|---|---|
| 358th | November 2, 1944 | FW-190 dest(air) | Merseburg | P-51 |

1-0-0 air
0-0 ground

**Miklajyck, Henry J., Capt.**
486th Ftr Sqn/352nd Ftr Grp

| *Sqn* | *Date* | *Claims* | *Location* | *A/C* |
|---|---|---|---|---|
| 486th | April 15, 1944 | FW-190 dest(air) | Vechta | P-51 |
| | April 23 | (.5)Ju-52 dest(grd)* | SE Paris | P-51 |
| | April 24 | Ju-52 dest(air) | E/Neuburg | P-51 |
| | | (3)Ju-88 dest(grd) | Neuburg | P-51 |
| | April 25 | Hs-129 dest(grd) | Metz | P-51 |
| | August 6 | (2)Me-109 dest(air) | SE Hamburg | P-51 |
| | September 12 | (1.5)FW-190 dest(air)** | Kustrin | P-51 |
| | | Ju-52 dest(grd) | Kustrin | P-51 |
| | November 2 | Me-109 dest(air) | Merseburg | P-51 |
| | | FW-190 dest(air) | Merseburg | P-51 |

7.5-0-0 air
5.5-0 ground

* - shared with Lt. E.L. Heller of the 486th Ftr Sqn
** - shared with Lt. J.D. Carter of the 486th Ftr Sqn

**Miles, Robert E., Lt.**
55th Ftr Sqn/20th Ftr Grp

| *Sqn* | *Date* | *Claims* | *Location* | *A/C* |
|---|---|---|---|---|
| 55th | June 28, 1944 | Me-109 dest(air) | Nivelles | P-38 |

1-0-0 air
0-0 ground

**Miles, Stanley G., Capt.**
486th Ftr Sqn/352nd Ftr Grp

| *Sqn* | *Date* | *Claims* | *Location* | *A/C* |
|---|---|---|---|---|
| 486th | April 11, 1944 | Ju-88 dest(grd) | SE Berlin | P-51 |
| | April 24 | Me-110 dest(grd) | Ingolstadt | P-51 |
| | | (3)u/i a/c dam(grd) | Ingolstadt | P-51 |
| | April 25 | FW-190 dest(grd) | Metz | P-51 |
| | May 13 | Me-109 dest(air) | Tribsees | P-51 |

1-0-0 air
3-3 ground

**Miley, Carl H., Maj.]**
336th Ftr Sqn/4th Ftr Grp

| *Sqn* | *Date* | *Claims* | *Location* | *A/C* |
|---|---|---|---|---|
| 336th | July 28, 1943 | Me-109 dest(air) | E/Rotterdam | P-47 |
| | | Me-109 prob(air) | E/Rotterdam | P-47 |
| | August 31 | (2)FW-190 dam(air) | N/Paris | P-47 |

1-1-2 air
0-0 ground

**Miller, Austin S., Lt.**
82nd Ftr Sqn/78th Ftr Grp

| *Sqn* | *Date* | *Claims* | *Location* | *A/C* |
|---|---|---|---|---|
| 82nd | October 7, 1944 | Me-109 dam(air) | Leipzig | P-47 |
| | March 19, 1945 | (2)Me-109 dest(air) | Osnabruck | P-51 |
| | April 10 | He-111 dest(grd) | Werder A/F | P-51 |
| | | FW-190 dam(grd) | Werder A/F | P-51 |
| | | u/i a/c dam(grd) | Werder A/F | P-51 |

2-0-1 air
1-2 ground

**Miller, Earl H., Lt.**
384th Ftr Sqn/364th Ftr Grp

| *Sqn* | *Date* | *Claims* | *Location* | *A/C* |
|---|---|---|---|---|
| 384th | November 21, 1944 | FW-190 dest(air) | NE Nordhausen | P-51 |
| | December 31 | (2)FW-190 dest(air) | Hamburg | P-51 |

3-0-0 air
0-0 ground

**Miller, Edwin H., Capt.**
83rd Ftr Sqn/78th Ftr Grp

| *Sqn* | *Date* | *Claims* | *Location* | *A/C* |
|---|---|---|---|---|
| 83rd | July 19, 1944 | (2)Ju-188 dest(grd) | Limburg-Coblenz | P-47 |
| | February 9, 1945 | Me-262 prob(air) | Fulda | P-51 |
| | March 21 | Me-262 dest(air) | Wittenberg | P-51 |

1-1-0 air
2-0 ground

**Miller, Fremont W., Lt.**
328th Ftr Sqn/352nd Ftr Grp

| *Sqn* | *Date* | *Claims* | *Location* | *A/C* |
|---|---|---|---|---|
| 328th | February 4, 1944 | FW-190 dest(air) | Brussels | P-47 |
| | March 15 | Me-109 dest(air) | Heusden | P-47 |
| | April 8 | Me-210 dest(grd) | Quackenbruck | P-47 |
| | April 10 | FW-190 dest(air) | Dormans | P-47 |

3-0-0 air
1-0 ground

**Miller, Gerald J., Lt.**
351st Ftr Sqn/353rd Ftr Grp

| *Sqn* | *Date* | *Claims* | *Location* | *A/C* |
|---|---|---|---|---|
| 351st | March 21, 1945 | (2)FW-190 dest(grd) | Achmer | P-51 |
| | | (2)FW-190 dam(grd) | Achmer | P-51 |
| | April 16 | (6)FW-190 dest(grd) | Reichersberg | P-51 |
| | | (2)Me-109 dest(grd) | Reichersberg | P-51 |
| | | Do-217 dest(grd) | Reichersberg | P-51 |

0-0-0 air
11-2 ground

**Miller, Harold O., Lt.**
352nd Ftr Sqn/353rd Ftr Grp

| *Sqn* | *Date* | *Claims* | *Location* | *A/C* |
|---|---|---|---|---|
| 352nd | June 8, 1944 | FW-190 dest(grd) | Angars | P-47 |
| | | (.5)Ju-88 dest(grd)* | Angars | P-47 |
| | June 12 | Me-109 dest(air) | Dreux | P-47 |
| | June 22 | Me-109 dest(air) | S/Rouen | P-47 |
| | June 27 | (2)Me-109 dam(air) | N/Troyes | P-47 |
| | August 4 | (2)He-111 dest(grd) | Plantlunne | P-47 |

2-0-2 air
3.5-0 ground

* - shared with Lt. C.F. Armstrong of the 352nd Ftr Sqn

**Miller, Harry L., Jr., Lt.**
328th Ftr Sqn/352nd Ftr Grp

| *Sqn* | *Date* | *Claims* | *Location* | *A/C* |
|---|---|---|---|---|
| 328th | February 20, 1944 | Me-110 dest(air) | Blankenheim | P-47 |
| | May 8 | Me-109 dam(air) | NE Bremen | P-51 |

1-0-1 air
0-0 ground

**Miller, Howard B., Lt.**
335th Ftr Sqn/4th Ftr Grp

| *Sqn* | *Date* | *Claims* | *Location* | *A/C* |
|---|---|---|---|---|
| 335th | April 16, 1945 | Do-217 dest(grd) | Praha/Letnany | P-51 |
| | | Ju-52 dest(grd) | Praha/Letnany | P-51 |
| | | Do-217 dam(grd) | Praha/Letnany | P-51 |
| | | Ju-52 dam(grd) | Praha/Letnany | P-51 |

0-0-0 air
2-2 ground

**Miller, Jack B., Lt.**
83rd Ftr Sqn/78th Ftr Grp

| *Sqn* | *Date* | *Claims* | *Location* | *A/C* |
|---|---|---|---|---|
| 83rd | July 19, 1944 | Ju-188 dest(grd) | Limburg-Coblenz | P-47 |
| | August 10 | u/i a/c dam(grd) | Chateau Salines | P-47 |

0-0-0 air
1-1 ground

**Miller, John H., Lt.**
2nd Scouting Force

| *Sqn* | *Date* | *Claims* | *Location* | *A/C* |
|---|---|---|---|---|
| 2nd | November 26, 1944 | FW-190 prob(air) | S/Hanover | P-51 |
| | | FW-190 dam(air) | S/Hanover | P-51 |

0-1-1 air
0-0 ground

**Miller, Kenneth J., Lt.**
357th Ftr Sqn/355th Ftr Grp

| *Sqn* | *Date* | *Claims* | *Location* | *A/C* |
|---|---|---|---|---|
| 357th | November 2, 1944 | (2)u/i a/c dest(grd) | Wernigerode | P-51 |

0-0-0 air
2-0 ground

**Miller, LaMarr J., Lt.**
383rd Ftr Sqn/364th Ftr Grp

| *Sqn* | *Date* | *Claims* | *Location* | *A/C* |
|---|---|---|---|---|
| 383rd | May 21, 1944 | Me-410 dam(grd) | NW Renow | P-38 |

0-0-0 air
0-1 ground

**Miller, Maurice W., Jr., Lt.**
336th Ftr Sqn/4th Ftr Grp

| *Sqn* | *Date* | *Claims* | *Location* | *A/C* |
|---|---|---|---|---|
| 336th | April 16, 1945 | u/i a/c dest(grd) | Praha | P-51 |

0-0-0 air
1-0 ground

**Miller, Richard C., Lt.**
359th Ftr Sqn/356th Ftr Grp

| *Sqn* | *Date* | *Claims* | *Location* | *A/C* |
|---|---|---|---|---|
| 359th | February 14, 1945 | FW-190 dam(air) | Dresden-Chemnitz | P-51 |

0-0-1 air
0-0 ground

**Miller, Richard I., Lt.**
82nd Ftr Sqn/78th Ftr Grp

| *Sqn* | *Date* | *Claims* | *Location* | *A/C* |
|---|---|---|---|---|
| 82nd | August 6, 1944 | Me-109 dam(air) | Hamburg | P-47 |

0-0-1 air
0-0 ground

**Miller, Robert J., Lt.**
334th Ftr Sqn/4th Ftr Grp

| *Sqn* | *Date* | *Claims* | *Location* | *A/C* |
|---|---|---|---|---|
| 334th | April 10, 1945 | u/i a/c dest(grd) | Wittstock | P-51 |

0-0-0 air
1-0 ground

**Miller, Robert J., Lt.**
486th Ftr Sqn/352nd Ftr Grp

| *Sqn* | *Date* | *Claims* | *Location* | *A/C* |
|---|---|---|---|---|
| 486th | July 18, 1944 | Me-410 dest(air) | S/Rostock | P-51 |
| | | Me-410 dam(air) | S/Rostock | P-51 |

1-0-1 air
0-0 ground

**Miller, Roy D., Lt.**
338th Ftr Sqn/55th Ftr Grp

| *Sqn* | *Date* | *Claims* | *Location* | *A/C* |
|---|---|---|---|---|
| 338th | September 13, 1944 | Me-109 dest(air) | Eisenach-Gotha | P-51 |
| | January 6, 1945 | Do-217 dest(grd) | Giebelstadt | P-51 |
| | January 13 | Me-262 dest(grd) | Giebelstadt | P-51 |
| | | Ju-88 dam(grd) | Giebelstadt | P-51 |
| | January 29 | Me-109 dest(air) | NE Oldenburg | P-51 |

2-0-0 air
2-1 ground

**Miller, William C., Jr., Lt.**
487th Ftr Sqn/352nd Ftr Grp

| *Sqn* | *Date* | *Claims* | *Location* | *A/C* |
|---|---|---|---|---|
| 487th | November 21, 1944 | FW-190 dam(air) | SW Merseburg | P-51 |
| | December 26 | Me-109 dest(air) | Veldenbor | P-51 |
| | | Me-109 dam(air) | Veldenbor | P-51 |

1-0-2 air
0-0 ground

**Milligan, Harry D., Lt.**
351st Ftr Sqn/353rd Ftr Grp

| *Sqn* | *Date* | *Claims* | *Location* | *A/C* |
|---|---|---|---|---|
| 351st | January 14, 1944 | (.5)FW-190 dam(grd)* | Rosiers-en-Santerne | P-47 |
| | September 13 | (.5)FW-200 dest(grd)* | Hellingen | P-47 |

0-0-0 air
0.5-0.5 ground

* - shared with Capt. V.L. Byers of the 351st Ftr Sqn
** - shared with Lt. H.P. Maree of the 351st Ftr Sqn

**Millikan, Willard W., Capt.**
336th Ftr Sqn/4th Ftr Grp

| *Sqn* | *Date* | *Claims* | *Location* | *A/C* |
|---|---|---|---|---|
| 336th | September 27, 1943 | FW-190 dest(air) | Potten | P-47 |
| | December 20, 1943 | Me-109 dest(air) | NW Bremen | P-47 |
| | February 10, 1944 | FW-190 dest(air) | N/Dummer Lake | P-47 |
| | March 3 | Me-110 dest(air) | Wittenburg | P-51 |
| | March 27 | He-177 dest(grd) | Cazaux A/F | P-51 |
| | April 8 | (3)Me-109 dest(air) | Ulzen | P-51 |
| | April 15 | He-177 dest(grd) | Hagenow | P-51 |
| | April 19 | Me-109 dest(air) | Eschwege | P-51 |
| | April 22 | (4)Me-109 dest(air) | SW Kassel | P-51 |
| | April 30 | Do-24 dam(grd) | Lyon Anchorage | P-51 |
| | May 22 | Me-109 dest(air) | NW Kiel | P-51 |

13-0-0 air
2-1 ground

**Mills, Henry L., Maj.**
334th Ftr Sqn/4th Ftr Grp

| *Sqn* | *Date* | *Claims* | *Location* | *A/C* |
|---|---|---|---|---|
| 334th | July 26, 1943 | FW-190 prob(air) | Brielle/Rotterdam | P-47 |
| | July 28 | FW-190 dam(air) | E/Rotterdam | P-47 |
| | August 16 | (2)FW-190 dest(air) | NW Paris | P-47 |
| | October 8 | Me-109 prob(air) | Meppel-Zwolle | P-47 |
| | January 29, 1944 | (2)Me-109 dest(air) | Aachen | P-47 |
| | February 20 | FW-190 dest(air) | Aachen | P-47 |
| | March 6 | FW-190 dest(air) | W/Brandenburg | P-51 |

6-2-1 air
0-0 ground

**Mills, Newell F., Jr., Lt.**
354th Ftr Sqn/355th Ftr Grp

| *Sqn* | *Date* | *Claims* | *Location* | *A/C* |
|---|---|---|---|---|
| 354th | January 14, 1945 | (2)Me-109 dest(air) | E/Meppen | P-51 |
| | | FW-190 dest(air) | E/Meppen | P-51 |
| | February 23 | u/i a/c dest(grd) | Neuburg | P-51 |

3-0-0 air
1-0 ground

**Mincemeyer, Allen J., Lt.**
354th Ftr Sqn/355th Ftr Grp

| *Sqn* | *Date* | *Claims* | *Location* | *A/C* |
|---|---|---|---|---|
| 354th | April 13, 1945 | He-111 dest(grd) | Husum A/F | P-51 |

0-0-0 air
1-0 ground

**Minchew, Leslie D., Capt.**
354th Ftr Sqn/355th Ftr Grp
357th Ftr Sqn/355th Ftr Grp
HdQts/355th Ftr Grp

| *Sqn* | *Date* | *Claims* | *Location* | *A/C* |
|---|---|---|---|---|
| 354th | March 28, 1944 | (.5)He-111 dest(grd)* | Dijon | P-51 |
| 357th | April 8 | Me-109 dest(air) | W/Brunswick | P-51 |
| | April 24 | Me-109 dam(air) | SW Munich | P-51 |
| | June 6 | Ju-87 dam(air) | NE Janville | P-51 |
| | June 20 | Me-109 dest(air) | Pomeranian Bay | P-51 |
| | July 7 | (2.5)Me-410 dest(air)** | Nordhausen | P-51 |
| | | (2)Me-410 dam(air) | Nordhausen | P-51 |
| | August 3 | Me-109 dest(air) | Baden Baden | P-51 |
| HdQts | February 9, 1945 | FW-190 dam(grd) | Kothen | P-51 |

5.5-0-4 air
0.5-1 ground

* - shared with Capt. T.F. Neal of the 354th Ftr Sqn
** - shared with an unknown P-38 pilot

**Mincik, Frank J., Lt.**
351st Ftr Sqn/353rd Ftr Grp

| *Sqn* | *Date* | *Claims* | *Location* | *A/C* |
|---|---|---|---|---|
| 351st | October 10, 1943 | Me-110 dam(air) | W/Munster | P-47 |

0-0-1 air
0-0 ground

**Mirando, Joseph E., Lt.**
38th Ftr Sqn/55th Ftr Grp

| *Sqn* | *Date* | *Claims* | *Location* | *A/C* |
|---|---|---|---|---|
| 38th | April 9, 1945 | (2)FW-190 dest(grd) | Munich-Brunnthal | P-51 |
| | | (2)FW-190 dam(grd) | Munich-Brunnthal | P-51 |

0-0-0 air
2-2 ground

**Mirsch, George E., Lt.**
336th Ftr Sqn/4th Ftr Grp

| *Sqn* | *Date* | *Claims* | *Location* | *A/C* |
|---|---|---|---|---|
| 336th | July 28, 1943 | FW-190 dam(air) | E/Rotterdam | P-47 |

0-0-1 air
0-0 ground

**Misner, Richard F., Lt.**
357th Ftr Sqn/355th Ftr Grp

| *Sqn* | *Date* | *Claims* | *Location* | *A/C* |
|---|---|---|---|---|
| 357th | February 9, 1945 | u/i a/c dam(grd) | Kothen | P-51 |
| | April 10 | Ju-88 dest(grd) | Rechlin/Larz | P-51 |
| | | Ju-88 dam(grd) | Rechlin/Larz | P-51 |
| | April 13 | (1.5)He-111 dest(grd)* | Schleswig | P-51 |
| | | He-111 dam(grd) | Schleswig | P-51 |
| | April 16 | (2)FW-190 dest(grd) | SE Germany | P-51 |
| | | (3)FW-190 dam(grd) | SE Germany | P-51 |

0-0-0 air
4.5-6 ground

* - shared with Lt. R.W. Cooper of the 357th Ftr Sqn

**Mitchell, Harold D., Capt.**
376th Ftr Sqn/361st Ftr Grp

| *Sqn* | *Date* | *Claims* | *Location* | *A/C* |
|---|---|---|---|---|
| 376th | October 7, 1944 | Me-109 dest(air) | Merseburg | P-51 |
| | November 2 | FW-190 dest(air) | N/Erfurt | P-51 |
| | December 2 | FW-190 dest(air) | Bingen | P-51 |

3-0-0 air
0-0 ground

**Mitchell, John R., Lt.**
351st Ftr Sqn/353rd Ftr Grp

| Sqn | Date | Claims | Location | A/C |
|---|---|---|---|---|
| 351st | June 7, 1944 | Me-109 dam(air) | Beauvais/Tille | P-47 |
| | June 8 | Me-109 dest(grd) | Angars | P-47 |
| | | He-111 dam(grd) | Breteuil | P-47 |

0-0-1 air
1-1 ground

**Mitchell, Lloyd W., Lt.**
362nd Ftr Sqn/357th Ftr Grp

| Sqn | Date | Claims | Location | A/C |
|---|---|---|---|---|
| 362nd | May 30, 1944 | Me-109 dest(air) | W/Bernburg | P-51 |

1-0-0 air
0-0 ground

**Mitchell, Raymond M., Capt.**
505th Ftr Sqn/339th Ftr Grp

| Sqn | Date | Claims | Location | A/C |
|---|---|---|---|---|
| 505th | September 10, 1944 | Ju-88 dam(grd) | Weizenburg | P-51 |
| | September 13 | Do-217 dest(grd) | SE Munich | P-51 |

0-0-0 air
1-1 ground

**Mitchell, Raymond R., Lt.**
328th Ftr Sqn/352nd Ftr Grp

| Sqn | Date | Claims | Location | A/C |
|---|---|---|---|---|
| 328th | December 25, 1944 | Me-109 dest(air) | SW Coblenz | P-51 |

1-0-0 air
0-0 ground

**Moats, Sanford K., Capt.**
487th Ftr Sqn/352nd Ftr Grp

| Sqn | Date | Claims | Location | A/C |
|---|---|---|---|---|
| 487th | July 18, 1944 | Ju-88 dest(air) | SE Rostock | P-51 |
| | July 21 | (.5)Me-109 dest(air)[*] | E/Munich | P-51 |
| | July 29 | Me-109 dest(air) | Merseburg | P-51 |
| | November 27 | Me-109 dest(air) | Munster | P-51 |
| | | Me-109 dam(air) | Munster | P-51 |
| | December 27 | FW-190 dest(air) | SW Bonn | P-51 |
| | January 1, 1945 | (4)FW-190 dest(air) | N/Liege | P-51 |

8.5-0-1 air
0-0 ground

[*] - shared with Maj. G.E. Preddy of the 487th Ftr Sqn

**Moe, Robert A., Lt.**
335th Ftr Sqn/4th Ftr Grp

| Sqn | Date | Claims | Location | A/C |
|---|---|---|---|---|
| 335th | April 9, 1945 | Do-217 dam(grd) | Munich-Brunnthal | P-51 |
| | | u/i a/c dam(grd) | Munich-Brunnthal | P-51 |

0-0-0 air
0-2 ground

**Moebius, Howard, Lt.**
364th Ftr Sqn/357th Ftr Grp

| Sqn | Date | Claims | Location | A/C |
|---|---|---|---|---|
| 364th | September 18, 1944 | FW-190 dest(air) | N/Maastricht | P-51 |
| | September 19 | (2)FW-190 dest(air) | SE Arnheim | P-51 |

3-0-0 air
0-0 ground

**Molnar, John E., Lt.**
354th Ftr Sqn/355th Ftr Grp

| Sqn | Date | Claims | Location | A/C |
|---|---|---|---|---|
| 354th | November 26, 1944 | FW-190 dest(air) | S/Misburg | P-51 |
| | | FW-190 dam(air) | S/Misburg | P-51 |
| | April 4, 1945 | BV-138 dest(grd) | Muritz Lake | P-51 |
| | April 16 | (2)Me-110 dest(grd) | Autobahn | P-51 |
| | | u/i a/c dam(grd) | Autobahn | P-51 |

1-0-1 air
3-1 ground

**Monahan, Harold L., Lt.**
357th Ftr Sqn/355th Ftr Grp

| Sqn | Date | Claims | Location | A/C |
|---|---|---|---|---|
| 357th | September 12, 1944 | FW-190 dest(air) | E/Muritz Lake | P-51 |
| | October 7 | FW-190 dest(air) | SW Leipzig | P-51 |
| | | Me-109 dest(grd) | SW Leipzig | P-51 |
| | | Ju-88 dam(grd) | SW Leipzig | P-51 |

2-0-0 air
1-1 ground

**Monahan, John D., Maj.**
385th Ftr Sqn/364th Ftr Grp

| Sqn | Date | Claims | Location | A/C |
|---|---|---|---|---|
| 385th | November 26, 1944 | FW-190 dest(air) | Uchte | P-51 |

1-0-0 air
0-0 ground

**Moncrieff, Rex E., Lt.**
77th Ftr Sqn/20th Ftr Grp

| Sqn | Date | Claims | Location | A/C |
|---|---|---|---|---|
| 77th | July 4, 1944 | Me-109 dest(grd) | Tours | P-38 |
| | July 29 | Me-109 dest(air) | Gutersloh | P-51 |
| | | Me-109 dam(air) | Gutersloh | P-51 |

1-0-1 air
1-0 ground

**Monroe, Shelton W., Maj.**
334th Ftr Sqn/4th Ftr Grp
335th Ftr Sqn/4th Ftr Grp
HdQts/4th Ftr Grp

| Sqn | Date | Claims | Location | A/C |
|---|---|---|---|---|
| 334th | March 27, 1944 | Me-410 dest(grd) | Cazaux A/F | P-51 |
| | April 8 | (1.5)FW-190 dest(air)[*] | Celle | P-51 |
| | | (.5)Me-109 dest(air)[*] | Celle | P-51 |
| | April 18 | (2)Ju-52 dest(grd) | Juterbog A/F | P-51 |
| | | (.25) of (6)Ju-52 dam(grd)[**] | Juterbog A/F | P-51 |
| | April 29 | (1.5)Ju-52 dest(grd)[@] | Nordhausen | P-51 |
| | April 30 | (.33)Me-110 dest(air)[@@] | N/Lyon | P-51 |
| | June 6 | FW-190 dest(air) | Evreux | P-51 |
| | June 20 | Me-109 dest(air) | E/Pasewalk | P-51 |
| | July 7 | FW-190 dam(air) | E/Nordhausen | P-51 |

4.33-0-1 air
4.5-1.5 ground

[*] - both shared with Lt. A.L. Schlegel of the 335th Ftr Sqn
[**] - all shared with Lt. D.W. Howe, Lt. J.L. Lang, and Lt. D.M. Malmsten of the 334th Ftr Sqn
[@] - shared with Lt. N. Megura of the 334th Ftr Sqn
[@@] - shared with Capt. W.M. Sobanski of the 334th Ftr Sqn

**Monsell, Charles F., Jr., Lt.**
435th Ftr Sqn/479th Ftr Grp

| Sqn | Date | Claims | Location | A/C |
|---|---|---|---|---|
| 435th | August 18, 1944 | (.5)He-111 dest(grd)[*] | Nancy/Essey A/F | P-38 |
| | | (.5)He-111 dest(grd)[**] | Nancy/Essey A/F | P-38 |
| | | (.5)He-111 dest(grd)[**] | Nancy/Essey A/F | P-38 |
| | September 26 | Me-109 dest(air) | SW Munster | P-51 |

1-0-0 air
1.5-0 ground

[*] - shared with Lt. V.E. Hooker of the 435th Ftr Sqn
[**] - both shared with Lt. G.W. Gleason of the 434th Ftr Sqn, 479th Ftr Grp

**Montgomery, Emery H., Maj.**
361st Ftr Sqn/356th Ftr Grp

| Sqn | Date | Claims | Location | A/C |
|---|---|---|---|---|
| 361st | January 21, 1944 | Me-109 dam(air) | NE Dunkirk | P-47 |
| | April 13 | (2)FW-190 dest(air) | Huy | P-47 |

2-0-1 air
0-0 ground

**Montgomery, George S., Lt.**
351st Ftr Sqn/353rd Ftr Grp

| *Sqn* | *Date* | *Claims* | *Location* | *A/C* |
|---|---|---|---|---|
| 351st | November 27, 1944 | (.5)Me-109 dest(air)* | NE Steinhuder Lake | P-51 |
| | March 14, 1945 | (2)Me-109 dest(air) | Luckenwalde | P-51 |

2.5-0-0 air
0-0 ground

* - shared with Lt. R. Hilgenburg of the 351st Ftr Sqn

**Montgomery, Gerald E., Maj.**
334th Ftr Sqn/4th Ftr Grp

| *Sqn* | *Date* | *Claims* | *Location* | *A/C* |
|---|---|---|---|---|
| 334th | January 14, 1944 | FW-190 dest(air) | Soissons | P-47 |
| | February 10 | Me-109 dest(air) | Emmerich | P-47 |
| | March 27 | (2)Ju-88 dest(grd) | Cazaux A/F | P-51 |
| | | FW-190 dest(grd) | Cazaux A/F | P-51 |
| | | Ju-52 dest(grd) | Cazaux A/F | P-51 |
| | | Ju-88 dam(grd) | Cazaux A/F | P-51 |
| | April 5 | (2)Ju-88 dest(grd) | Brandenburg-Briest | P-51 |
| | April 10 | (1.5)Bu-131 dest(grd)* | Romorantin A/F | P-51 |
| | April 15 | He-177 dest(grd) | Hagenow | P-51 |
| | | Ju-88 dest(grd) | Hagenow | P-51 |
| | September 11 | Me-109 dest(air) | Aschersleben | P-51 |
| | November 18 | Me-262 dest(grd) | Leipheim | P-51 |
| | | (4)Me-262 dam(grd) | Leipheim | P-51 |
| | February 27, 1945 | Do-217 dest(grd) | Weimar | P-51 |
| | | Me-108 dest(grd) | Weimar | P-51 |
| | | Ju-87 dest(grd) | Weimar | P-51 |
| | April 10 | Me-410 dest(grd) | Wittstock | P-51 |

3-0-0 air
14.5-5 ground

* - shared with Lt. G.C. Siems of the 334th Ftr Sqn

**Montgomery, Robert P., Col.**
HdQts/20th Ftr Grp

| *Sqn* | *Date* | *Claims* | *Location* | *A/C* |
|---|---|---|---|---|
| HdQts | January 5, 1944 | FW-190 dam(air) | W/Neumunster | P-38 |
| | February 5 | (.33)FW-200 dest(air)* | Bourges A/F | P-38 |
| | February 10 | FW-190 dam(air) | Nienburg | P-38 |
| | November 2 | (2)Me-109 dest(air) | Halle-Merseburg | P-51 |
| | | FW-190 dest(air) | Halle-Merseburg | P-51 |
| | April 10, 1945 | Si-204 dest(grd) | Werder A/F | P-51 |
| | | Ar-196 dest(grd) | Werder A/F | P-51 |
| | | Ju-52 dest(grd) | Werder A/F | P-51 |
| | | Do-217 dam(grd) | Werder A/F | P-51 |
| | | Si-204 dam(grd) | Werder A/F | P-51 |

3.33-0-2 air
3-2 ground

* - shared with Capt. P.J. Sabo and Lt. J.E. Davis of the 77th Ftr Sqn, 20th Ftr Grp

**Montgomery, William E., F/O**
328th Ftr Sqn/352nd Ftr Grp

| *Sqn* | *Date* | *Claims* | *Location* | *A/C* |
|---|---|---|---|---|
| 328th | July 18, 1944 | Ju-88 dam(air) | Wismar | P-51 |
| | September 27 | Me-109 dest(air) | NW Frankfurt | P-51 |

1-0-1 air
0-0 ground

**Montieth, Donald R., Lt.**
83rd Ftr Sqn/78th Ftr Grp

| *Sqn* | *Date* | *Claims* | *Location* | *A/C* |
|---|---|---|---|---|
| 83rd | April 10, 1945 | FW-190 dam(air) | Brandenburg-Briest | P-51 |

0-0-0 air
0-1 ground

**Mooers, Harold B., Lt.**
38th Ftr Sqn/55th Ftr Grp

| *Sqn* | *Date* | *Claims* | *Location* | *A/C* |
|---|---|---|---|---|
| 38th | January 14, 1945 | FW-190 dam(air) | NW Osnabruck | P-51 |
| | March 24 | (.5)Me-109 dest(air)* | S/Soest | P-51 |

0.5-0-1 air
0-0 ground

* - shared with Capt. D.M. Cummings of the 38th Ftr Sqn

**Mooers, James E., Lt.**
84th Ftr Sqn/78th Ftr Grp

| *Sqn* | *Date* | *Claims* | *Location* | *A/C* |
|---|---|---|---|---|
| 84th | February 3, 1945 | FW-200 dam(grd) | Luneburg | P-51 |
| | March 19 | FW-190 dest(air) | Osnabruck | P-51 |
| | April 16 | (2)Ju-52 dest(grd) | Praha/Kakewice | P-51 |
| | | Ju-88 dest(grd) | Praha/Kakewice | P-51 |
| | | (3)Ju-52 dam(grd) | Praha/Kakewice | P-51 |
| | | u/i a/c dam(grd) | Praha/Kakewice | P-51 |

1-0-0 air
3-5 ground

**Mooers, Roger B., Lt.**
38th Ftr Sqn/55th Ftr Grp

| *Sqn* | *Date* | *Claims* | *Location* | *A/C* |
|---|---|---|---|---|
| 38th | April 7, 1945 | Me-109 dest(air) | E/Celle | P-51 |

1-0-0 air
0-0 ground

**Mooney, William H., Lt.**
362nd Ftr Sqn/357th Ftr Grp

| *Sqn* | *Date* | *Claims* | *Location* | *A/C* |
|---|---|---|---|---|
| 362nd | October 6, 1944 | FW-190 dam(air) | NW Berlin | P-51 |

0-0-1 air
0-0 ground

**Moore, Clifford J., Jr., Maj.**
436th Ftr Sqn/479th Ftr Grp

| *Sqn* | *Date* | *Claims* | *Location* | *A/C* |
|---|---|---|---|---|
| 436th | August 5, 1944 | Me-109 dest(air) | NE Stendal | P-38 |
| | September 5 | u/i a/c dest(grd) | Bad Nauheim | P-38 |
| | | (2)FW-190 dam(grd) | Bad Nauheim | P-38 |
| | February 22, 1945 | Ju-52 dam(grd) | Halberstadt | P-51 |

1-0-0 air
1-3 ground

**Moore, Major L., Lt.**
375th Ftr Sqn/361st Ftr Grp

| *Sqn* | *Date* | *Claims* | *Location* | *A/C* |
|---|---|---|---|---|
| 375th | August 15, 1944 | Me-110 dam(grd) | Wittmunhafen | P-51 |

0-0-0 air
0-1 ground

**Moore, Patrick L., Lt.**
343rd Ftr Sqn/55th Ftr Grp

| *Sqn* | *Date* | *Claims* | *Location* | *A/C* |
|---|---|---|---|---|
| 343rd | February 3, 1945 | Ju-88 dest(air) | Boizenburg | P-51 |
| | March 21 | FW-190 dest(grd) | Hopsten A/F | P-51 |
| | March 30 | Me-262 dest(air) | Lubeck A/F | P-51 |

2-0-0 air
1-0 ground

**Moore, Robert N., Capt.**
363rd Ftr Sqn/357th Ftr Grp

| *Sqn* | *Date* | *Claims* | *Location* | *A/C* |
|---|---|---|---|---|
| 363rd | May 13, 1944 | Me-109 dest(air) | W/Hamburg | P-51 |
| | | Me-109 dam(air) | W/hamburg | P-51 |
| | May 30 | Me-109 dest(air) | NE Schonebeck | P-51 |
| | August 8 | Me-109 dest(air) | Crocil | P-51 |

3-0-1 air
0-0 ground

**Moore, Robert W., Capt.**
364th Ftr Sqn/357th Ftr Grp

| Sqn | Date | Claims | Location | A/C |
|---|---|---|---|---|
| 364th | April 10, 1945 | He-111 dest(grd) | Neuruppin | P-51 |

0-0-0 air
1-0 ground

**Moore, Thomas J., Lt.**
374th Ftr Sqn/361st Ftr Grp

| Sqn | Date | Claims | Location | A/C |
|---|---|---|---|---|
| 374th | September 18, 1944 | Me-109 dam(grd) | Jagel A/F | P-51 |
| | March 31, 1945 | FW-190 dest(air) | N/Frankfurt | P-51 |

1-0-0 air
0-1 ground

**Moore, Wayne L., Capt.**
374th Ftr Sqn/361st Ftr Grp

| Sqn | Date | Claims | Location | A/C |
|---|---|---|---|---|
| 374th | January 30, 1944 | Me-109 dam(air) | Rheine | P-47 |
| | March 6 | FW-190 dest(air) | Zuider Zee | P-47 |

1-0-1 air
0-0 ground

**Moore, William R., Lt.**
505th Ftr Sqn/339th Ftr Grp

| Sqn | Date | Claims | Location | A/C |
|---|---|---|---|---|
| 505th | September 10, 1944 | Ju-88 dest(grd) | Munich | P-51 |
| | September 13 | (.5)Ju-88 dest(grd)* | SE Munich | P-51 |

0-0-0 air
1.5-0 ground

* - shared with Lt. L.J. Powell of the 505th Ftr Sqn

**Moorhouse, Hugh J., Lt.**
364th Ftr Sqn/357th Ftr Grp

| Sqn | Date | Claims | Location | A/C |
|---|---|---|---|---|
| 364th | September 18, 1944 | FW-190 dest(air) | N/Maastricht | P-51 |

1-0-0 air
0-0 ground

**Moothart, James A., Lt.**
83rd Ftr Sqn/78th Ftr Grp

| Sqn | Date | Claims | Location | A/C |
|---|---|---|---|---|
| 83rd | August 10, 1944 | (.5)He-111 dest(grd)* | Chateau Salines | P-47 |
| | September 1 | (.5)Me-110 dest(air)** | Gilze-Rijen | P-47 |
| | | Me-110 dam(air) | Gilze-Rijen | P-47 |

0.5-0-1 air
0.5-0 ground

* - shared with Lt. G. Riccardo of the 83rd Ftr Sqn
** - shared with Lt. P. Bingham of the 83rd Ftr Sqn

**Moran, Glennon T., Lt.**
487th Ftr Sqn/352nd Ftr Grp

| Sqn | Date | Claims | Location | A/C |
|---|---|---|---|---|
| 487th | February 24, 1944 | Me-109 dest(air) | Enschede | P-47 |
| | | Me-109 dam(air) | Enschede | P-47 |
| | April 11 | Ju-88 dest(grd) | SE Berlin | P-51 |
| | | Ar-196 dam(grd) | SE Berlin | P-51 |
| | | Caudron dam(grd) | SE Berlin | P-51 |
| | | u/i a/c dam(grd) | SE Berlin | P-51 |
| | April 13 | Ju-88 dest(grd) | S/Stuttgart | P-51 |
| | | FW-190 dam(grd) | S/Stuttgart | P-51 |
| | May 13 | (.5)Ju-88 dest(air)* | E/Neubrandenburg | P-51 |
| | May 19 | Me-109 dest(air) | Ludwigslust | P-51 |
| | May 27 | (2)Me-109 dest(air) | Strasbourg | P-51 |
| | May 29 | (1.5)Me-109 dest(air)** | Wolgast | P-51 |
| | | FW-190 dest(air) | Gustrow | P-51 |
| | May 30 | Me-109 dest(air) | Ulzen | P-51 |
| | | FW-190 dest(air) | Ulzen | P-51 |
| | | FW-190 dam(air) | Ulzen | P-51 |
| | June 12 | Me-109 dest(air) | SW Rennes | P-51 |
| | June 21 | Me-109 dest(air) | E/Magdeburg | P-51 |
| | June 25 | Me-109 dest(air) | Soissons | P-51 |
| | | Me-109 dam(air) | Soissons | P-51 |
| | June 29 | Ju-52 dest(grd) | Burg A/F | P-51 |
| | August 5 | Me-109 dest(air) | S/Hamburg | P-51 |
| | August 25 | Me-210 dam(grd) | Neubrandenburg | P-51 |
| | | Caudron dam(grd) | Neubrandenburg | P-51 |

13-0-3 air
3-6 ground

* - shared with Lt. C.J. Luksic of the 487th Ftr Sqn
** - shared with Lt. J.V. Conard of the 487th Ftr Sqn

**Morehouse, Dean R., Lt.**
375th Ftr Sqn/361st Ftr Grp

| Sqn | Date | Claims | Location | A/C |
|---|---|---|---|---|
| 375th | April 9, 1944 | FW-190 dam(air) | NW Dummer Lake | P-47 |
| | April 24 | He-111 dam(grd) | Metz | P-47 |
| | May 29 | u/i a/c dest(grd) | Lackau-Juterbog | P-51 |
| | June 20 | (2)Glider dam(grd) | Putnitz | P-51 |
| | | Me-210 dam(grd) | Putnitz | P-51 |
| | July 7 | Me-109 dest(air) | N/Leipzig | P-51 |

1-0-1 air
1-4 ground

**Moretz, Hazel, Lt.**
351st Ftr Sqn/353rd Ftr Grp

| Sqn | Date | Claims | Location | A/C |
|---|---|---|---|---|
| 351st | August 4, 1944 | Me-109 dest(air) | S/Bremen | P-47 |
| | August 12 | (.5)Ju-88 dam(grd)* | SW Coulommiers | P-47 |

1-0-0 air
0-0.5 ground

* - shared with Lt. C.W. Craft of the 351st Ftr Sqn

**Morgan, David R., Lt.**
375th Ftr Sqn/361st Ftr Grp

| Sqn | Date | Claims | Location | A/C |
|---|---|---|---|---|
| 375th | June 20, 1944 | (2)Me-110 dam(grd) | Putnitz | P-51 |
| | July 7 | (.5)Me-109 dest(air)* | NW Leipzig | P-51 |
| | August 25 | Me-109 dest(air) | E/Wismar | P-51 |

1.5-0-0 air
0-2 ground

* - shared with Lt. R.J. Sobieski of the 375th Ftr Sqn

**Morgan, Frank A., Capt.**
361st Ftr Sqn/356th Ftr Grp

| Sqn | Date | Claims | Location | A/C |
|---|---|---|---|---|
| 361st | September 5, 1944 | (.5)He-111 dest(air)* | Twente/Enschede | P-47 |
| | February 20, 1945 | (3)u/i a/c dest(grd) | Windleschenlaibach | P-51 |
| | | Me-110 dest(grd) | Windleschenlaibach | P-51 |
| | | Ju-88 dest(grd) | Windleschenlaibach | P-51 |

0.5-0-0 air
5-0 ground

* - shared with Capt. D.F. Thwaites of the 361st Ftr Sqn

**Morgan, Paul M., Lt.**
336th Ftr Sqn/4th Ftr Grp

| Sqn | Date | Claims | Location | A/C |
|---|---|---|---|---|
| 336th | February 25, 1945 | (.5)FW-190 prob(air)* | Kothen A/F | P-51 |

0-0.5-0 air
0-0 ground

* - shared with Lt. B.O. Booker of the 336th Ftr Sqn

**Morgan, William B., Lt.**
334th Ftr Sqn/4th Ftr Grp

| Sqn | Date | Claims | Location | A/C |
|---|---|---|---|---|
| 334th | October 2, 1942 | FW-190 dam(air) | S/Nieuport | Spit |

0-0-1 air
0-0 ground

**Moroney, Edward J., Lt.**
357th Ftr Sqn/355th Ftr Grp

| *Sqn* | *Date* | *Claims* | *Location* | *A/C* |
|---|---|---|---|---|
| 357th | November 2, 1944 | Me-109 dest(air) | Wernigerode | P-51 |
| | | (2)u/i a/c dest(grd) | Wernigerode | P-51 |
| | November 18 | (3)Me-262 dam(grd) | Leipheim | P-51 |
| | November 26 | (2)FW-190 dest(air) | W/Gardelegen | P-51 |

3-0-0 air
2-3 ground

**Morrill, Stanley B., Capt.**
62nd Ftr Sqn/56th Ftr Grp

| *Sqn* | *Date* | *Claims* | *Location* | *A/C* |
|---|---|---|---|---|
| 62nd | November 26, 1943 | Me-109 dest(air) | Papenburg | P-47 |
| | | Me-109 dam(air) | Papenburg | P-47 |
| | December 11 | Me-109 dest(air) | Eelde | P-47 |
| | January 5, 1944 | Me-109 dest(air) | Duren | P-47 |
| | January 11 | Me-109 dest(air) | Bramsche | P-47 |
| | January 30 | (.5)Ju-88 dest(air)* | Twente | P-47 |
| | | Ju-88 dam(air) | Twente | P-47 |
| | February 4 | (2)FW-190 dam(air) | Charleroi | P-47 |
| | February 11 | Me-109 dest(air) | Dison | P-47 |
| | February 20 | Me-110 dest(air) | Steinhuder Lake | P-47 |
| | | (.5)Do-217 dest(air)** | Steinhuder Lake | P-47 |
| | | (6)Me-110 dam(grd) | Steinhuder Lake | P-47 |
| | February 24 | Me-109 dest(air) | E/Asnabruck | P-47 |
| | March 16 | FW-190 dest(air) | St. Dizier | P-47 |

9-0-4 air
0-6 ground

* - shared with Lt. A.R. Carcione of the 62nd Ftr Sqn
** - shared with Lt. F.J. Christensen of the 62nd Ftr Sqn

**Morris, Arthur B., Jr., Lt.**
369th Ftr Sqn/359th Ftr Grp

| *Sqn* | *Date* | *Claims* | *Location* | *A/C* |
|---|---|---|---|---|
| 369th | December 31, 1944 | (1.5)FW-190 dest(air)* | SW Hamburg | P-51 |
| | | (.5)FW-190 dest(air)* | SW Hamburg | P-51 |
| | February 21, 1945 | Ju-88 dest(grd) | Nordlingen | P-51 |
| | | Me-410 dam(grd) | Nordlingen | P-51 |

2-0-0 air
1-1 ground

* - both shared with Lt. W.F. Collins of the 369th Ftr Sqn

**Morris, George A., Lt.**
364th Ftr Sqn/357th Ftr Grp

| *Sqn* | *Date* | *Claims* | *Location* | *A/C* |
|---|---|---|---|---|
| 364th | September 18, 1944 | FW-190 dest(air) | N/Maastricht | P-51 |

1-0-0 air
0-0 ground

**Morris, Grady, Lt.**
343rd Ftr Sqn/55th Ftr Grp

| *Sqn* | *Date* | *Claims* | *Location* | *A/C* |
|---|---|---|---|---|
| 343rd | December 24, 1944 | FW-190 dest(air) | S/Frankfurt | P-51 |

1-0-0 air
0-0 ground

**Morris, Harold J., Lt.**
351st Ftr Sqn/353rd Ftr Grp
82nd Ftr Sqn/ 78th Ftr Grp
83rd Ftr Sqn/ 78th Ftr Grp

| *Sqn* | *Date* | *Claims* | *Location* | *A/C* |
|---|---|---|---|---|
| 351st | August 19, 1943 | Me-109 dam(air) | Gilze-Rijen | P-47 |
| | October 20 | Me-109 dam(air) | Duren | P-47 |
| 83rd | April 25, 1944 | (.5)FW-190 dest(air)* | S/Verdun | P-47 |

0.5-0-2 air
0-0 ground

* - shared with Lt. B.W. Sorenson of the 83rd Ftr Sqn

**Morris, Harry A., F/O**
351st Ftr Sqn/353rd Ftr Grp

| *Sqn* | *Date* | *Claims* | *Location* | *A/C* |
|---|---|---|---|---|
| 351st | March 21, 1945 | He-111 dest(grd) | Achmer | P-51 |
| | April 9 | Me-210 dest(grd) | S/Neubiberg | P-51 |
| | | Me-262 dam(grd) | S/Neubiberg | P-51 |
| | April 16 | Me-110 dest(grd) | Reichersberg | P-51 |
| | | (2)Me-109 dam(grd) | Reichersberg | P-51 |
| | | FW-190 dam(grd) | Reichersberg | P-51 |

0-0-0 air
3-4 ground

**Morris, James M., Capt.**
77th Ftr Sqn/20th Ftr Grp

| *Sqn* | *Date* | *Claims* | *Location* | *A/C* |
|---|---|---|---|---|
| 77th | February 5, 1944 | (.33)He-111 dest(air)* | Bourges A/F | P-38 |
| | February 8 | (2)FW-190 dest(air) | Sedan | P-38 |
| | | Me-109 dest(air) | Losheim | P-38 |
| | | Me-109 dest(air) | Denain | P-38 |
| | February 11 | Me-109 dest(air) | Giessen | P-38 |
| | February 24 | Me-110 dest(air) | Schweinfurt | P-38 |
| | April 8 | Me-410 dest(grd) | Salzwedel | P-38 |
| | | (.5)Ju-88 dest(grd)** | Salzwedel | P-38 |
| | | (.33)u/i a/c dest(grd)@ | Salzwedel | P-38 |
| | April 30 | He-177 dest(grd) | Bricy A/F | P-38 |
| | July 7 | Me-410 dest(air) | Leipzig-Halle | P-38 |

7.33-0-0 air
2.83-0 ground

* - shared with Lt. R.L. Frakes and Lt. M.J. Gilbertson of the 77th Ftr Sqn
** - shared with Lt. B.N. Rader of the 77th Ftr Sqn
@ - shared with Lt. I.W. Fernandes and Lt. W.F. Kuemmerle of the 77th Ftr Sqn

**Morris, Joseph A., LtCol.**
HdQts/353rd Ftr Grp

| *Sqn* | *Date* | *Claims* | *Location* | *A/C* |
|---|---|---|---|---|
| HdQts | August 16, 1943 | FW-190 dam(air) | NW Paris | P-47 |

0-0-1 air
0-0 ground

**Morris, Raymond S., Lt.**
354th Ftr Sqn/355th Ftr Grp

| *Sqn* | *Date* | *Claims* | *Location* | *A/C* |
|---|---|---|---|---|
| 354th | March 16, 1944 | Me-109 dest(air) | NW Ulm | P-51 |
| | March 28 | He-111 dest(grd) | Dijon | P-51 |
| | April 5 | Me-110 dest(grd) | Landsberg | P-51 |
| | | He-111 dest(grd) | Landsberg | P-51 |
| | | He-111 dam(grd) | Landsberg | P-51 |
| | April 13 | (2)Do-217 dest(grd) | Oberpfaffenhofen | P-51 |
| | | Do-217 dam(grd) | Oberpfaffenhofen | P-51 |
| | May 13 | (2)Me-410 dest(air) | E/Berlin | P-51 |
| | June 6 | (.5)Ju-87 dest(air)* | Chartres-Dire | P-51 |
| | June 24 | (3)Me-109 dest(grd) | Seiches | P-51 |
| | July 8 | Me-109 dest(grd) | SW Chalons | P-51 |
| | | Me-410 dest(grd) | SW Chalons | P-51 |

3.5-0-0 air
10-2 ground

* - shared with Lt. F.K. Taylor of the 354th Ftr Sqn

**Morris, Richard A., Lt.**
77th Ftr Sqn/20th Ftr Grp

| *Sqn* | *Date* | *Claims* | *Location* | *A/C* |
|---|---|---|---|---|
| 77th | April 10, 1945 | Me-410 dest(grd) | Fassberg A/F | P-51 |
| | | u/i a/c dest(grd) | Fassberg A/F | P-51 |

0-0-0 air
2-0 ground

**Morrison, Maurice, Lt.**
352nd Ftr Sqn/353rd Ftr Grp

| *Sqn* | *Date* | *Claims* | *Location* | *A/C* |
|---|---|---|---|---|
| 352nd | November 3, 1943 | Me-110 dest(air) | Wilhelmshaven | P-47 |
| | November 18, 1944 | Me-163 dest(grd) | Lechfeld | P-51 |
| | | He-177 dam(grd) | Lechfeld | P-51 |

1-0-0 air
1-1 ground

**Morrow, John W., Lt.**
434th Ftr Sqn/479th Ftr Grp

| *Sqn* | *Date* | *Claims* | *Location* | *A/C* |
|---|---|---|---|---|
| 434th | September 5, 1944 | Me-109 dest(grd) | Ettinghausen | P-38 |
| | September 26 | Me-109 dest(air) | SW Munster | P-38 |

1-0-0 air
1-0 ground

**Moseley, Mark L., Capt.**
62nd Ftr Sqn/56th Ftr Grp

| *Sqn* | *Date* | *Claims* | *Location* | *A/C* |
|---|---|---|---|---|
| 62nd | January 30, 1944 | Me-210 dam(air) | Hanskamp | P-47 |
| | March 8 | FW-190 dest(air) | Dummer Lake-Steinhuder Lake | P-47 |
| | | FW-190 dam(air) | Dummer Lake-Steinhuder Lake | P-47 |
| | March 15 | FW-190 dest(air) | Dummer Lake | P-47 |
| | June 7 | (.5)Ju-88 dest(air)* | St. Andre de L'Eure | P-47 |
| | June 8 | (2)FW-190 dest(air) | St. Andre de L'Eure | P-47 |
| | July 4 | Me-109 dest(air) | Conches | P-47 |
| | July 6 | Me-109 dest(air) | Beaumont | P-47 |

6.5-0-2 air
0-0 ground

* - shared with Lt. J.W. Pierce of the 62nd Ftr Sqn

**Mosse, Charles E., Capt.**
368th Ftr Sqn/359th Ftr Grp

| *Sqn* | *Date* | *Claims* | *Location* | *A/C* |
|---|---|---|---|---|
| 368th | March 4, 1944 | Me-109 dam(air) | Bonn | P-47 |
| | April 24 | (.5)u/i a/c dest(grd)* | St. Dizier | P-47 |
| | April 30 | Me-410 dest(grd) | Bricy A/F | P-47 |
| | May 19 | Me-109 dest(air) | NW Berlin | P-51 |

1-0-1 air
1.5-0 ground

* - shared with Lt. A.T. Lemmens of the 368th Ftr Sqn

**Motley, James L., Lt.**
352nd Ftr Sqn/353rd Ftr Grp

| *Sqn* | *Date* | *Claims* | *Location* | *A/C* |
|---|---|---|---|---|
| 352nd | August 27, 1944 | Me-109 dest(grd) | Metz | P-47 |

0-0-0 air
1-0 ground

**Mottis, Leonard H., Capt.**
375th Ftr Sqn/361st Ftr Grp

| *Sqn* | *Date* | *Claims* | *Location* | *A/C* |
|---|---|---|---|---|
| 375th | September 26, 1944 | u/i a/c dam(grd) | Achmer | P-51 |

0-0-0 air
0-1 ground

**Moulton, Howard N., Capt.**
334th Ftr Sqn/4th Ftr Grp

| *Sqn* | *Date* | *Claims* | *Location* | *A/C* |
|---|---|---|---|---|
| 334th | January 31, 1944 | (.5)Me-109 dest(air)* | Gilze-Rijen | P-47 |
| | March 6 | (.5)Me-110 dest(air)** | SW Berlin | P-51 |
| | | FW-190 dam(air) | SW Berlin | P-51 |
| | April 8 | Me-109 dest(air) | Celle | P-51 |

2-0-1 air
0-0 ground

* - shared with Capt. W.M. Sobanski of the 334th Ftr Sqn
** - shared with Lt. D.A. Van Epps of the 334th Ftr Sqn

**Mudge, Dick H., Jr., Capt.**
61st Ftr Sqn/56th Ftr Grp

| *Sqn* | *Date* | *Claims* | *Location* | *A/C* |
|---|---|---|---|---|
| 61st | May 15, 1943 | FW-190 dam(air) | NE Rotterdam | P-47 |
| | December 1 | Me-109 dest(air) | Ruhr Valley | P-47 |
| | March 8, 1944 | FW-190 dam(air) | S/Steinhuder Lake | P-47 |

1-0-2 air
0-0 ground

**Mudge, William F., Lt.**
505th Ftr Sqn/339th Ftr Grp

| *Sqn* | *Date* | *Claims* | *Location* | *A/C* |
|---|---|---|---|---|
| 505th | May 21, 1944 | (.5)Ju-88 dest(air)* | Schwepnitz | P-51 |
| | May 25 | (.5)FW-190 dest(air)** | Paris | P-51 |
| | June 6 | Ju-87 dest(air) | Orleans | P-51 |
| | July 19 | FW-190 dest(grd) | SW Augsburg | P-51 |
| | | Ju-188 dest(grd) | SW Augsburg | P-51 |
| | July 29 | Ju-52 dest(grd) | NW Naumberg | P-51 |
| | July 31 | FW-190 dest(grd) | Holzkirchen | P-51 |
| | | Me-110 dest(grd) | Holzkirchen | P-51 |
| | | Ju-88 dest(grd) | Holzkirchen | P-51 |
| | | (2)u/i a/c dam(grd) | Holzkirchen | P-51 |

2-0-0 air
6-2 ground

* - shared with Lt. H.M. Everett of the 505th Ftr Sqn
** - shared with Lt. G.J. Hrico of the 505th Ftr Sqn

**Mueller, Carl W., Capt.**
350th Ftr Sqn/353rd Ftr Grp

| *Sqn* | *Date* | *Claims* | *Location* | *A/C* |
|---|---|---|---|---|
| 350th | April 8, 1944 | u/i a/c dam(grd) | Hoperhofen | P-47 |

0-0-0 air
0-1 ground

**Muller, James B., Lt.**
505th Ftr Sqn/339th Ftr Grp

| *Sqn* | *Date* | *Claims* | *Location* | *A/C* |
|---|---|---|---|---|
| 505th | August 4, 1944 | (.5)Me-109 dest(air)* | Ulzen | P-51 |
| | | Me-410 dest(grd) | E/Celle | P-51 |
| | September 10 | Ju-88 dest(grd) | Weizenburg | P-51 |

0.5-0-0 air
2-0 ground

* - shared with Lt. A.E. Tongue of the 505th Ftr Sqn

**Muller, Wilbert, Lt.**
435th Ftr Sqn/479th Ftr Grp

| *Sqn* | *Date* | *Claims* | *Location* | *A/C* |
|---|---|---|---|---|
| 435th | August 18, 1944 | (2)Ju-88 dam(grd) | Nancy/Essey A/F | P-38 |

0-0-0 air
0-2 ground

**Mullins, Robert E., Lt.**
83rd Ftr Sqn/78th Ftr Grp

| *Sqn* | *Date* | *Claims* | *Location* | *A/C* |
|---|---|---|---|---|
| 83rd | July 1, 1944 | Me-109 dam(air) | Cambrai | P-47 |

0-0-1 air
0-0 ground

**Mullins, Walter H., Lt.**
55th Ftr Sqn/20th Ftr Grp

| *Sqn* | *Date* | *Claims* | *Location* | *A/C* |
|---|---|---|---|---|
| 55th | July 14, 1944 | FW-190 dest(air) | S/Nogent | P-38 |

1-0-0 air
0-0 ground

**Mulvany, Gerald M., Lt.**
436th Ftr Sqn/479th Ftr Grp

| *Sqn* | *Date* | *Claims* | *Location* | *A/C* |
|---|---|---|---|---|
| 436th | August 15, 1944 | (.5)B-24 dest(grd)* | N/Mulhosue | P-38 |
| | September 5 | (2)FW-190 dest(grd) | Bad Nauheim | P-38 |
| | | FW-190 dam(grd) | Bad Nauheim | P-38 |
| | September 26 | Me-109 dest(air) | S/Munster | P-38 |

1-0-0 air
2.5-1 ground

* - shared with Lt. T.E. Myers of the 436th Ftr Sqn

**Mundell, Earl L., Jr., Lt.**
486th Ftr Sqn/352nd Ftr Grp

| *Sqn* | *Date* | *Claims* | *Location* | *A/C* |
|---|---|---|---|---|
| 486th | July 19, 1944 | (2)Me-109 dest(air) | E/Munich | P-51 |
| | January 14, 1945 | FW-190 dest(air) | Almelo | P-51 |
| | March 2 | (.5)FW-190 dest(air)* | Prague | P-51 |

3.5-0-0 air
0-0 ground

* - shared with Capt. L.E. Kilgo of the 486th Ftr Sqn

**Mundy, John W., F/O**
84th Ftr Sqn/78th Ftr Grp

| *Sqn* | *Date* | *Claims* | *Location* | *A/C* |
|---|---|---|---|---|
| 84th | March 24, 1944 | Ju-52 dam(grd) | Beaumont-Sur-Oise | P-47 |
| | April 8 | FW-190 dam(air) | Antwerp | P-47 |

0-0-1 air
0-1 ground

**Munn, John W., Lt.**
385th Ftr Sqn/364th Ftr Grp

| *Sqn* | *Date* | *Claims* | *Location* | *A/C* |
|---|---|---|---|---|
| 385th | April 10, 1945 | FW-190 dest(grd) | Stendal | P-51 |
| | April 16 | FW-190 dest(grd) | Pocking | P-51 |
| | | (4)FW-190 dam(grd) | Pocking | P-51 |

0-0-0 air
2-4 ground

**Munson, Norman D., Maj.**
82nd Ftr Sqn/78th Ftr Grp

| *Sqn* | *Date* | *Claims* | *Location* | *A/C* |
|---|---|---|---|---|
| 82nd | November 3, 1943 | Me-109 dam(air) | Barzal | P-47 |
| | April 8, 1944 | Me-110 dest(grd) | Trier | P-47 |
| | | (.2)Me-110 dest(grd)* | Trier | P-47 |
| | | (.2)Me-110 dest(grd)* | Trier | P-47 |
| | | (.2)Me-110 dest(grd)* | Trier | P-47 |
| | | (.33)Ar-196 dest(grd)** | Trier | P-47 |
| | July 19 | (2.5)u/i a/c dest(grd)@ | Stuttgart | P-47 |

0-0-1 air
4.43-0 ground

* - all shared with Maj. J.J. Oberhansly, Lt. J.E. Brasher, Lt. M.K. Woller, and F/O C.W. DeWitt of the 82nd Ftr Sqn
** - shared with Lt. J.E. Brasher and Lt. R.A. Hewitt of the 82nd Ftr Sqn
@ - shared with Lt. J.R. Kinsolving of the 82nd Ftr Sqn

**Munson, Robert L., Lt.**
434th Ftr Sqn/479th Ftr Grp

| *Sqn* | *Date* | *Claims* | *Location* | *A/C* |
|---|---|---|---|---|
| 434th | April 7, 1945 | Me-109 dest(air) | Celle | P-51 |
| | April 16 | (2)FW-190 dest(grd) | Reichersberg | P-51 |
| | | FW-190 dam(grd) | Reichersberg | P-51 |

1-0-0 air
2-1 ground

**Murchake, John P., Jr., Lt.**
336th Ftr Sqn/4th Ftr Grp

| *Sqn* | *Date* | *Claims* | *Location* | *A/C* |
|---|---|---|---|---|
| 336th | April 16, 1945 | (2)Ju-88 dest(grd) | Praha | P-51 |
| | | Ju-88 dam(grd) | Praha | P-51 |

0-0-0 air
2-1 ground

**Murdoch, Raymond F., Lt.**
354th Ftr Sqn/355th Ftr Grp

| *Sqn* | *Date* | *Claims* | *Location* | *A/C* |
|---|---|---|---|---|
| 354th | December 30, 1943 | Me-109 prob(air) | Soissons | P-47 |
| | | Me-109 dam(air) | Soissons | P-47 |

0-1-1 air
0-0 ground

**Murdy, Edward B., Capt.**
374th Ftr Sqn/361st Ftr Grp

| *Sqn* | *Date* | *Claims* | *Location* | *A/C* |
|---|---|---|---|---|
| 374th | May 29, 1944 | (1.5)FW-190 dest(air)* | E/Schwerin | P-51 |
| | June 4 | Me-109 dam(air) | Mulun | P-51 |

1.5-0-1 air
0-0 ground

* - shared with Capt. J.B. Cheney of the 376th Ftr Sqn, 361st Ftr Grp

**Murphy, Alva C., Capt.**
362nd Ftr Sqn/357th Ftr Grp
364th Ftr Sqn/357th Ftr Grp

| *Sqn* | *Date* | *Claims* | *Location* | *A/C* |
|---|---|---|---|---|
| 362nd | November 18, 1944 | (2)Me-109 dest(grd) | Villingen A/F | P-51 |
| | November 27 | Me-109 dest(air) | S/Magdeburg | P-51 |
| | | FW-190 dest(air) | S/Magdeburg | P-51 |
| | December 2 | (2)Me-109 dest(air) | Bingen | P-51 |
| 364th | March 2, 1945 | (2)Me-109 dest(air) | SE Magdeburg | P-51 |

6-0-0 air
2-0 ground

**Murphy, Calvin J., Lt.**
434th Ftr Sqn/479th Ftr Grp

| *Sqn* | *Date* | *Claims* | *Location* | *A/C* |
|---|---|---|---|---|
| 434th | August 15, 1944 | Me-109 dest(grd) | Steenwijk A/F | P-38 |
| | | Me-109 dam(grd) | Steenwijk A/F | P-38 |
| | August 18 | FW-190 dest(grd) | Nancy/Essey A/F | P-38 |
| | | Ju-88 dam(grd) | Nancy/Essey A/F | P-38 |
| | September 5 | Me-410 dest(grd) | Ettinghausen | P-38 |

0-0-0 air
3-2 ground

**Murphy, Eugene, Capt.**
385th Ftr Sqn/364th Ftr Grp

| *Sqn* | *Date* | *Claims* | *Location* | *A/C* |
|---|---|---|---|---|
| 385th | December 31, 1944 | FW-190 dest(air) | Hamburg | P-51 |
| | February 25, 1945 | (.5)Ar-234 dest(air)* | Steinhuder Lake | P-51 |
| | April 17 | FW-190 dest(grd) | Karlsbad | P-51 |

1.5-0-0 air
1-0 ground

* - shared with Lt. R.E. White of the 385th Ftr Sqn

**Murphy, Jerome T., Lt.**
505th Ftr Sqn/339th Ftr Grp

| *Sqn* | *Date* | *Claims* | *Location* | *A/C* |
|---|---|---|---|---|
| 505th | April 10, 1945 | (3)Do-217 dest(grd) | Wittstock | P-51 |
| | | (2)Ju-88 dest(grd) | Wittstock | P-51 |
| | | (3)u/i a/c dam(grd) | Wittstock | P-51 |
| | April 17 | Me-109 dest(grd) | SE Pocking | P-51 |
| | | He-111 dest(grd) | SE Pocking | P-51 |
| | | (2)Me-109 dam(grd) | SE Pocking | P-51 |
| | | Ju-88 dam(grd) | SE Pocking | P-51 |

0-0-0 air
7-6 ground

**Murphy, John B., LtCol.**
370th Ftr Sqn/359th Ftr Grp
Earlier flew in Alaska with the 54th Ftr Sqn and claimed half a kill, a shared Mavis on June 3, 1942.

| *Sqn* | *Date* | *Claims* | *Location* | *A/C* |
|---|---|---|---|---|
| 370th | February 22, 1944 | Me-109 prob(air) | Hamm | P-47 |
| | February 24 | Me-109 dest(air) | Hardenbergh | P-47 |

| Sqn | Date | Claims | Location | A/C |
|---|---|---|---|---|
| | March 4 | (.5)FW-190 dest(air)* | Bonn | P-47 |
| | | (.25)Me-109 dest(air)** | Bonn | P-47 |
| | | Me-109 dam(air) | Bonn | P-47 |
| | May 29 | (1.5)FW-190 dest(air)@ | Stettin | P-51 |
| | July 21 | Me-109 dest(air) | Ammer Lake | P-51 |
| | August 9 | FW-190 dest(air) | Gunzburg | P-51 |
| | August 16 | Me-163 dest(air) | SE Leipzig | P-51 |

6.25-1-1 air
0-0 ground

* - shared with Lt. P.H. Bateman of the 370th Ftr Sqn
** - shared with Lt. P.H. Bateman, Lt. A.C. Porter, and Lt. R.S. Wetmore of the 370th Ftr Sqn
@ - shared with Lt. G.A. Doersch of the 370th Ftr Sqn

**Murphy, Michael L., Capt.**
383rd Ftr Sqn/364th Ftr Grp

| *Sqn* | *Date* | *Claims* | *Location* | *A/C* |
|---|---|---|---|---|
| 383rd | November 21, 1944 | FW-190 dam(air) | S/Nordhausen | P-51 |

0-0-1 air
0-0 ground

**Murphy, Randel L., Lt.**
63rd Ftr Sqn/56th Ftr Grp

| *Sqn* | *Date* | *Claims* | *Location* | *A/C* |
|---|---|---|---|---|
| 63rd | November 18, 1944 | FW-190 dest(grd) | Gross Ostheim | P-47 |
| | December 4 | FW-200 dam(grd) | Neuburg | P-47 |
| | December 23 | (2)FW-190 dest(air) | NW Coblenz | P-47 |
| | April 13, 1945 | (5)u/i a/c dest(grd) | Eggebeck A/F | P-47 |
| | | (3)He-111 dest(grd) | Eggebeck A/F | P-47 |
| | | FW-200 dest(grd) | Eggebeck A/F | P-47 |
| | | Me-210 dest(grd) | Eggebeck A/F | P-47 |
| | | u/i a/c dam(grd) | Eggebeck A/F | P-47 |

2-0-0 air
11-2 ground

**Murr, John N., Lt.**
434th Ftr Sqn/479th Ftr Grp

| *Sqn* | *Date* | *Claims* | *Location* | *A/C* |
|---|---|---|---|---|
| 434th | September 5, 1944 | (3)Me-110 dest(grd) | Ettinghausen | P-38 |
| | September 26 | Me-109 dest(air) | SW Munster | P-38 |
| | December 25 | FW-190 dest(air) | SW Bonn | P-51 |
| | | FW-190 prob(air) | SW Bonn | P-51 |
| | | FW-190 dam(air) | SW Bonn | P-51 |

2-1-1 air
3-0 ground

**Murray, Billy J., Lt.**
351st Ftr Sqn/353rd Ftr Grp

| *Sqn* | *Date* | *Claims* | *Location* | *A/C* |
|---|---|---|---|---|
| 351st | January 14, 1945 | Me-262 dest(air) | Wittenberg | P-51 |

1-0-0 air
0-0 ground

**Murray, Harold S., F/O**
351st Ftr Sqn/353rd Ftr Grp

| *Sqn* | *Date* | *Claims* | *Location* | *A/C* |
|---|---|---|---|---|
| 351st | April 16, 1945 | (2)FW-190 dest(grd) | Reichersberg | P-51 |

0-0-0 air
2-0 ground

**Murray, Steven T., Lt.**
62nd Ftr Sqn/56th Ftr Grp

| *Sqn* | *Date* | *Claims* | *Location* | *A/C* |
|---|---|---|---|---|
| 62nd | September 5, 1944 | (2)Fi-156 dest(grd) | Limburg | P-47 |
| | | (2)Ju-88 dest(grd) | Limburg | P-47 |
| | | (.5)Me-210 dest(grd)* | Limburg | P-47 |
| | | Me-109 dam(grd) | Limburg | P-47 |

0-0-0 air
4.5-1 ground

* - shared with Capt. M.J. Jackson of the 62nd Ftr Sqn

**Murray, Wallace C., Lt.**
370th Ftr Sqn/359th Ftr Grp

| *Sqn* | *Date* | *Claims* | *Location* | *A/C* |
|---|---|---|---|---|
| 370th | September 11, 1944 | Me-109 dest(air) | Gotha | P-51 |
| | | (2)Ju-88 dam(grd) | Gotha | P-51 |
| | | (.5)He-177 dam(grd)* | Gotha | P-51 |

1-0-0 air
0-2.5 ground

* - shared with Lt. C.W. Jones of the 370th Ftr Sqn

**Murrell, Robert E., Lt.**
77th Ftr Sqn/20th Ftr Grp

| *Sqn* | *Date* | *Claims* | *Location* | *A/C* |
|---|---|---|---|---|
| 77th | December 2, 1944 | FW-190 dest(air) | Coblenz | P-51 |

1-0-0 air
0-0 ground

**Mussey, Claude E., Lt.**
61st Ftr Sqn/56th Ftr Grp

| *Sqn* | *Date* | *Claims* | *Location* | *A/C* |
|---|---|---|---|---|
| 61st | February 20, 1944 | Me-110 dam(air) | Steinhuder Lake | P-47 |
| | February 21 | Me-109 dest(air) | Zuider Zee | P-47 |
| | March 8 | Me-109 dest(air) | E/Steinhuder Lake | P-47 |
| | | Ju-88 prob(air) | E/Steinhuder Lake | P-47 |

2-1-1 air
0-0 ground

**Muzzy, Raymond G., F/O**
368th Ftr Sqn/359th Ftr Grp

| *Sqn* | *Date* | *Claims* | *Location* | *A/C* |
|---|---|---|---|---|
| 368th | April 9, 1945 | (1.5)Me-262 dam(air)* | Augsburg | P-51 |

0-0-1.5 air
0-0 ground

* - shared with Lt. F. Rea of the 368th Ftr Sqn

**Myers, Joseph, Jr., LtCol.**
38th Ftr Sqn/55th Ftr Grp
82nd Ftr Sqn/78th Ftr Grp
HdQts/55th Ftr Grp

| *Sqn* | *Date* | *Claims* | *Location* | *A/C* |
|---|---|---|---|---|
| 38th | November 3, 1943 | FW-190 dam(air) | Wilhelmshaven | P-38 |
| | November 5 | Me-109 dest(air) | Arnheim | P-38 |
| | November 13 | Me-109 dest(air) | Bremen | P-38 |
| | | Ju-88 dam(air) | Bremen | P-38 |
| | December 31 | Me-109 dest(air) | N/Blaye et St. Luce | P-38 |
| 82nd | August 28, 1944 | (.5)Me-262 dest(air)* | Termonde | P-47 |
| | September 10 | (3)He-111 dest(grd) | Meinbullen | P-47 |
| | | He-111 dam(grd) | Meinbullen | P-47 |
| | October 7 | Me-109 dest(air) | Leipzig | P-47 |

4.5-0-2 air
3-1 ground

* - shared with Lt. M.O. Croy of the 82nd Ftr Sqn

**Myers, Raymond B., LtCol.**
358th Ftr Sqn/355th Ftr Grp

| *Sqn* | *Date* | *Claims* | *Location* | *A/C* |
|---|---|---|---|---|
| 358th | October 20, 1943 | FW-190 dest(air) | Ath | P-47 |
| | | FW-190 dam(air) | Ath | P-47 |
| | March 2, 1944 | (.5)Me-109 dest(air)* | NE Liege | P-47 |
| | April 5 | (2)Do-217 dest(grd) | Munich | P-51 |
| | | DFS-230 dest(grd) | Munich | P-51 |
| | | (6)Do-217 dam(grd) | Munich | P-51 |
| | April 11 | Me-410 dest(air) | W/Berlin | P-51 |
| | April 13 | FW-190 dest(air) | Nordlingen | P-51 |
| | April 15 | Do-217 dest(grd) | Glienicke | P-51 |
| | May 24 | Me-109 dest(air) | Berlin | P-51 |
| | | Me-109 dam(air) | Berlin | P-51 |

4.5-0-2 air
4-6 ground

* - shared with F/O W.J. McGinty of the 358th Ftr Sqn

**Myers, Robert W., Lt.**
376th Ftr Sqn/361st Ftr Grp

| *Sqn* | *Date* | *Claims* | *Location* | *A/C* |
|---|---|---|---|---|
| 376th | September 27, 1944 | FW-190 dest(air) | Eisenach | P-51 |
| | | FW-190 dam(air) | Eisenach | P-51 |

1-0-1 air
0-0 ground

**Myers, Thomas E., Capt.**
436th Ftr Sqn/479th Ftr Grp

| *Sqn* | *Date* | *Claims* | *Location* | *A/C* |
|---|---|---|---|---|
| 436th | August 15, 1944 | (.5)B-24 dest(grd)[*] | N/Mulhosue | P-38 |
| | October 6 | Me-109 dest(air) | E/Berlin | P-51 |
| | December 5 | (.5)FW-190 dest(air)[**] | N/Berlin | P-51 |
| | | Me-109 dam(air) | N/Berlin | P-51 |

1.5-0-1 air
0.5-0 ground

[*] - shared with Lt. G.M. Mulvany of the 436th Ftr Sqn
[**] - shared with Lt. P.C. Vasseur of the 436th Ftr Sqn

**Naedle, Scott L., Lt.**
HdQts/361st Ftr Grp

| *Sqn* | *Date* | *Claims* | *Location* | *A/C* |
|---|---|---|---|---|
| HdQts | April 8, 1944 | Me-109 dest(air) | W/Dummer Lake | P-47 |

1-0-0 air
0-0 ground

**Nagel, Jerome K., Lt.**
434th Ftr Sqn/479th Ftr Grp

| *Sqn* | *Date* | *Claims* | *Location* | *A/C* |
|---|---|---|---|---|
| 434th | April 7, 1945 | Me-109 dest(air) | Soltau | P-51 |
| | April 13 | Ju-88 dest(grd) | Kaltenkirchen | P-51 |
| | April 18 | FW-190 dest(grd) | Deiningen | P-51 |
| | | Me-109 dest(grd) | Deiningen | P-51 |
| | | Ju-88 dest(grd) | Ottingen | P-51 |

1-0-0 air
4-0 ground

**Narvis, Charles W., Lt.**
375th Ftr Sqn/361st Ftr Grp

| *Sqn* | *Date* | *Claims* | *Location* | *A/C* |
|---|---|---|---|---|
| 375th | September 12, 1944 | Me-109 dest(air) | NE Magdeburg | P-51 |
| | September 13 | u/i a/c dest(grd) | Schwabeich Hall | P-51 |
| | | u/i a/c dam(grd) | Schwabeich Hall | P-51 |

1-0-0 air
1-1 ground

**Naule, David L., Lt.**
435th Ftr Sqn/479th Ftr Grp

| *Sqn* | *Date* | *Claims* | *Location* | *A/C* |
|---|---|---|---|---|
| 435th | August 18, 1944 | He-111 dest(grd) | Nancy/Essey A/F | P-38 |

0-0-0 air
1-0 ground

**Nay, Martin N., Lt.**
505th Ftr Sqn/339th Ftr Grp

| *Sqn* | *Date* | *Claims* | *Location* | *A/C* |
|---|---|---|---|---|
| 505th | July 31, 1944 | u/i a/c dam(grd) | Holzkirchen | P-51 |

0-0-0 air
0-1 ground

**Naylor, James C., Lt.**
63rd Ftr Sqn/56th Ftr Grp

| *Sqn* | *Date* | *Claims* | *Location* | *A/C* |
|---|---|---|---|---|
| 63rd | April 10, 1945 | Me-109 dest(grd) | Werder A/F | P-47 |
| | | FW-190 dest(grd) | Werder A/F | P-47 |
| | | Do-217 dam(grd) | Werder A/F | P-47 |
| | | u/i a/c dam(grd) | Werder A/F | P-47 |

0-0-0 air
2-2 ground

**Neal, Thomas F., Jr., Capt.**
354th Ftr Sqn/355th Ftr Grp

| *Sqn* | *Date* | *Claims* | *Location* | *A/C* |
|---|---|---|---|---|
| 354th | November 13, 1943 | Me-109 dest(air) | W/Bremen | P-47 |
| | March 16, 1944 | (2.5)Me-109 dest(air)[*] | NW Ulm | P-51 |
| | March 18 | Me-109 dest(air) | NE Munich | P-51 |
| | March 28 | (.5)He-111 dest(grd)[**] | Dijon | P-51 |
| | April 10 | u/i a/c dam(grd) | Bourges | P-51 |

4.5-0-0 air
0.5-1 ground

[*] - shared with Lt. C.W. Lenfest of the 354th Ftr Sqn
[**] - shared with Lt. L.D. Minchew of the 357th Ftr Sqn, 355th Ftr Grp

**Nebinger, Edward M., Lt.**
360th Ftr Sqn/356th Ftr Grp

| *Sqn* | *Date* | *Claims* | *Location* | *A/C* |
|---|---|---|---|---|
| 360th | September 1, 1944 | (.5)Ju-52 dest(grd)[*] | W/Nancy | P-47 |
| | | (.5)Ju-52 dam(grd)[**] | W/Nancy | P-47 |

0-0-0 air
0.5-0.5 ground

[*] - shared with Lt. H.S. Olive of the 360th Ftr Sqn
[**] - shared with Lt. J.T. Romine of the 360th Ftr Sqn

**Neece, Richard D., LtCol.**
385th Ftr Sqn/364th Ftr Grp

| *Sqn* | *Date* | *Claims* | *Location* | *A/C* |
|---|---|---|---|---|
| 385th | August 25, 1944 | (2)Ju-88 dest(grd) | Anklam | P-51 |
| | September 28 | FW-190 dest(air) | S/Magdeburg | P-51 |

1-0-0 air
2-0 ground

**Neely, Elroy E., Capt.**
375th Ftr Sqn/361st Ftr Grp

| *Sqn* | *Date* | *Claims* | *Location* | *A/C* |
|---|---|---|---|---|
| 375th | June 20, 1944 | (1.5)glider dam(grd)[*] | Putnitz | P-51 |
| | | (.5)Me-110 dam(grd)[*] | Putnitz | P-51 |
| | June 29 | Me-109 dam(air) | SE Kothen | P-51 |
| | November 26 | (2)FW-190 dest(air) | S/Hanover | P-51 |
| | | FW-190 dam(air) | NE Brunswick | P-51 |

2-0-2 air
0-2 ground

[*] - both shared with Capt. C.N. Keppler of the 375th Ftr Sqn

**Neely, Tom D., Lt.**
434th Ftr Sqn/479th Ftr Grp

| *Sqn* | *Date* | *Claims* | *Location* | *A/C* |
|---|---|---|---|---|
| 434th | August 9, 1944 | He-111 dest(grd) | Nuneburg | P-38 |
| | | (.5)He-111 dam(grd)[*] | Nuneburg | P-38 |
| | September 5 | (2)Me-110 dest(grd) | Ettinghausen | P-38 |
| | | Ju-88 dest(grd) | Ettinghausen | P-38 |
| | December 23 | (2)FW-190 dest(air) | SE Bonn | P-51 |

2-0-0 air
4-0.5 ground

[*] - shared with Maj. F.J. Keller of the 434th Ftr Sqn

**Nelson, Ervin C., Jr., Lt.**
358th Ftr Sqn/355th Ftr Grp

| *Sqn* | *Date* | *Claims* | *Location* | *A/C* |
|---|---|---|---|---|
| 358th | April 16, 1945 | FW-190 dest(grd) | Straubing | P-51 |
| | | Ju-88 dam(grd) | Straubing | P-51 |

0-0-0 air
1-1 ground

**Nelson, James E., Lt.**
357th Ftr Sqn/355th Ftr Grp

| Sqn | Date | Claims | Location | A/C |
|---|---|---|---|---|
| 357th | November 18, 1944 | Me-262 dam(grd) | Leipheim | P-51 |

0-0-0 air
0-1 ground

**Nelson, James F., F/O**
384th Ftr Sqn/364th Ftr Grp

| Sqn | Date | Claims | Location | A/C |
|---|---|---|---|---|
| 384th | February 23, 1945 | (.5)Me-109 dest(air)* | Stuttgart | P-51 |

0.5-0-0 air
0-0 ground

* - shared with Capt. D.J. Pick of the 384th Ftr Sqn

**Nelson, Robert F., Lt.**
336th Ftr Sqn/4th Ftr Grp

| Sqn | Date | Claims | Location | A/C |
|---|---|---|---|---|
| 336th | April 1, 1944 | Ju-88 dam(grd) | Belgium | P-51 |
| | April 5 | Ju-88 dest(grd) | Brandenburg | P-51 |
| | | He-177 dam(grd) | Brandenburg | P-51 |
| | | Ju-88 dam(grd) | Brandenburg | P-51 |
| | April 10 | u/i a/c dest(grd) | Romorantin A/F | P-51 |
| | April 15 | Fi-156 dest(air) | Fassberg A/F | P-51 |
| | | (2)He-177 dest(grd) | Fassberg A/F | P-51 |
| | April 18 | Me-109 dest(grd) | Genthin A/F | P-51 |
| | | Me-109 dam(grd) | Genthin A/F | P-51 |
| | | Ju-88 dam(grd) | Genthin A/F | P-51 |
| | | u/i a/c dam(grd) | Genthin A/F | P-51 |

1-0-0 air
5-6 ground

**Netting, Conrad J., Lt.**
336th Ftr Sqn/4th Ftr Grp

| Sqn | Date | Claims | Location | A/C |
|---|---|---|---|---|
| 336th | April 24, 1944 | FW-190 dam(air) | NW Ludwigshafen | P-51 |
| | May 29 | (.5)Me-110 dest(air)* | N/Falkenberg | P-51 |
| | | (2)Do-18 dam(grd) | N/Falkenberg | P-51 |

0.5-0-1 air
0-2 ground

* - shared with Lt. D.R. Emerson of the 336th Ftr Sqn

**Newburg, Warren R., Lt.**
370th Ftr Sqn/359th Ftr Grp

| Sqn | Date | Claims | Location | A/C |
|---|---|---|---|---|
| 370th | May 21, 1944 | (2)Ju-88 dam(grd) | Schwerin | P-51 |
| | July 24 | Fi-156 dest(air) | Ulm | P-51 |

1-0-0 air
0-2 ground

**Newell, Frank C., Lt.**
62nd Ftr Sqn/56th Ftr Grp

| Sqn | Date | Claims | Location | A/C |
|---|---|---|---|---|
| 62nd | July 4, 1944 | (.5)Me-109 dest(air)* | Conches | P-47 |

0.5-0-0 air
0-0 ground

* - shared with Lt. D.E. McMahan of the 62nd Ftr Sqn

**Newell, William E., Lt.**
335th Ftr Sqn/4th Ftr Grp

| Sqn | Date | Claims | Location | A/C |
|---|---|---|---|---|
| 335th | March 29, 1944 | FW-190 prob(air) | Brunswick | P-51 |

0-1-0 air
0-0 ground

**Newhart, Dewey E., Capt.**
350th Ftr Sqn/353rd Ftr Grp

| Sqn | Date | Claims | Location | A/C |
|---|---|---|---|---|
| 350th | September 27, 1943 | (.5)Me-109 dest(air)* | Emden | P-47 |
| | | Me-109 dam(air) | Emden | P-47 |
| | October 8 | Me-210 dam(air) | Aschendorf | P-47 |
| | October 14 | FW-190 dam(air) | Duren | P-47 |
| | January 24, 1944 | Me-110 dest(air) | Termonde | P-47 |
| | | Me-109 dest(air) | Louvain-Beauvechain A/F | P-47 |
| | February 3 | Me-109 prob(air) | S/Oldenburg | P-47 |
| | | Me-109 dam(air) | S/Oldenburg | P-47 |

2.5-1-4 air
0-0 ground

* - shared with Lt. W.W. Odom of the 350th Ftr Sqn

**Newman, Robert A., Lt.**
352nd Ftr Sqn/353rd Ftr Grp

| Sqn | Date | Claims | Location | A/C |
|---|---|---|---|---|
| 352nd | October 14, 1943 | Me-109 dest(air) | Turnhout | P-47 |
| | | Me-109 dam(air) | Turnhout | P-47 |
| | November 3 | Me-110 dest(air) | Wilhelmshaven | P-47 |
| | December 1 | Me-210 dest(air) | Solingen | P-47 |
| | January 30, 1944 | Ju-88 dest(air) | Quackenbruck | P-47 |
| | February 22 | FW-190 dest(grd) | Antwerp | P-47 |

4-0-1 air
1-0 ground

**Newton, Madison H., Lt.**
370th Ftr Sqn/359th Ftr Grp

| Sqn | Date | Claims | Location | A/C |
|---|---|---|---|---|
| 370th | April 13, 1945 | (2)Ar-196 dest(grd) | Schwerin Lake | P-51 |

0-0-0 air
2-0 ground

**Newton, William M., Jr., Lt.**
352nd Ftr Sqn/353rd Ftr Grp

| Sqn | Date | Claims | Location | A/C |
|---|---|---|---|---|
| 352nd | August 26, 1944 | FW-190 dest(air) | S/Charleroi | P-47 |

1-0-0 air
0-0 ground

**Neyland, Praeger, Capt.**
61st Ftr Sqn/56th Ftr Grp

| Sqn | Date | Claims | Location | A/C |
|---|---|---|---|---|
| 61st | January 29, 1944 | (.5)Me-110 dest(air)* | Simmern | P-47 |
| | May 12 | Me-109 dam(air) | N/Marburg | P-47 |
| | May 22 | FW-190 dest(air) | Hoperhofen A/F | P-47 |
| | July 20 | He-111 dam(grd) | Bassenheim A/F | P-47 |

1.5-0-1 air
0-1 ground

* - shared with Capt. J.H. Bennett of the 61st Ftr Sqn

**Niccolai, Albert T., Lt.**
370th Ftr Sqn/359th Ftr Grp

| Sqn | Date | Claims | Location | A/C |
|---|---|---|---|---|
| 370th | February 22, 1944 | Me-109 dam(air) | Hamm | P-47 |

0-0-1 air
0-0 ground

**Nichols, Merle B., Maj.**
79th Ftr Sqn/20th Ftr Grp
77th Ftr Sqn/20th Ftr Grp
HdQts/20th Ftr Grp

| Sqn | Date | Claims | Location | A/C |
|---|---|---|---|---|
| 79th | January 4, 1944 | Do-217 dam(air) | Kiel | P-38 |
| | January 14 | FW-190 dest(air) | Rouen | P-38 |
| | February 11 | Me-410 dam(air) | W/Frankfurt | P-38 |
| | March 18 | Me-110 dest(air) | Ulm | P-38 |
| 77th: | January 14, 1945 | Me-109 dest(air) | Perleberg | P-51 |

3-0-2 air
0-0 ground

**Nicholson, Charles R., Lt.**
55th Ftr Sqn/20th Ftr Grp

| *Sqn* | *Date* | *Claims* | *Location* | *A/C* |
|---|---|---|---|---|
| 55th | February 25, 1945 | FW-190 dest(air) | Gardelegen | P-51 |

1-0-0 air
0-0 ground

**Nicholson, Kenneth F., Capt.**
383rd Ftr Sqn/364th Ftr Grp

| *Sqn* | *Date* | *Claims* | *Location* | *A/C* |
|---|---|---|---|---|
| 383rd | May 19, 1944 | FW-190 dam(air) | Lubeck Bay | P-38 |
| | May 22 | FW-190 dest(air) | SE Kiel | P-38 |
| | May 24 | (.5)Do-217 dest(grd)* | SW Berlin | P-38 |
| | May 25 | FW-190 dest(air) | Paris | P-38 |

2-0-1 air
0.5-0 ground

* - shared with Lt. W.D. Boyd of the 383rd Ftr Sqn

**Nickelbur, John M., Lt.**
351st Ftr Sqn/353rd Ftr Grp

| *Sqn* | *Date* | *Claims* | *Location* | *A/C* |
|---|---|---|---|---|
| 351st | November 27, 1944 | FW-190 dest(air) | NE Steinhuder Lake | P-51 |
| | | Me-109 dam(air) | NE Steinhuder L. | P-51 |
| | April 16, 1945 | (3)Ju-88 dest(grd) | Reichersberg | P-51 |
| | | (2)Ju-88 dam(grd) | Reichersberg | P-51 |

1-0-1 air
3-2 ground

**Nicodemus, Ralph J., Lt.**
358th Ftr Sqn/355th Ftr Grp

| *Sqn* | *Date* | *Claims* | *Location* | *A/C* |
|---|---|---|---|---|
| 358th | April 13, 1945 | (.5)He-111 dest(grd)* | Schleswig | P-51 |
| | | (.5)He-111 dest(grd)** | Schleswig | P-51 |

0-0-0 air
1-0 ground

* - shared with Lt. H.P. Knutty of the 358th Ftr Sqn
** - shared with Lt. L.R. Leaf of the 358th Ftr Sqn

**Niemi, Albert V., Capt.**
360th Ftr Sqn/356th Ftr Grp

| *Sqn* | *Date* | *Claims* | *Location* | *A/C* |
|---|---|---|---|---|
| 360th | January 24, 1944 | FW-190 dest(air) | N/Lille | P-47 |
| | | FW-190 dam(air) | N/Lille | P-47 |

1-0-1 air
0-0 ground

**Nolan, Francis A., Capt.**
62nd Ftr Sqn/56th Ftr Grp

| *Sqn* | *Date* | *Claims* | *Location* | *A/C* |
|---|---|---|---|---|
| 62nd | September 16, 1944 | He-111 dam(grd) | Dummer Lake | P-47 |
| | October 5 | Ju-88 dest(grd) | S/Geseke | P-47 |
| | December 4 | FW-200 dest(grd) | Neuburg | P-47 |
| | | Me-262 dam(grd) | Neuburg | P-47 |
| | December 31 | (2)FW-190 dest(air) | Quackenbruck | P-47 |

2-0-0 air
2-2 ground

**Nordquist, Dean A., Lt.**
62nd Ftr Sqn/56th Ftr Grp

| *Sqn* | *Date* | *Claims* | *Location* | *A/C* |
|---|---|---|---|---|
| 62nd | March 6, 1944 | FW-190 dam(air) | N/Dummer Lake | P-47 |

0-0-1 air
0-0 ground

**Norley, Louis H., Maj.**
334th Ftr Sqn/4th Ftr Grp
335th Ftr Sqn/4th Ftr Grp
336th Ftr Sqn/4th Ftr Grp

| *Sqn* | *Date* | *Claims* | *Location* | *A/C* |
|---|---|---|---|---|
| 336th | December 16, 1943 | (.33)Ju-88 dest(air)* | E/Zuider Zee | P-47 |
| | February 10, 1944 | Me-109 dest(air) | Dummer Lake | P-47 |
| | March 27 | Ju-88 dest(grd) | Cazaux A/F | P-51 |
| | April 8 | (3)FW-190 dest(air) | Ulzen | P-51 |
| | April 13 | FW-190 dest(air) | Schweinfurt | P-51 |
| | April 22 | (2)Me-109 dest(air) | SW Kassel | P-51 |
| 335th | September 17 | FW-190 dest(air) | Bocholt | P-51 |
| | November 2 | Me-163 dest(air) | SE Leipzig | P-51 |
| 334th | March 19, 1945 | Me-109 dest(air) | SE Frankfurt | P-51 |
| | April 16 | (2)FW-190 dest(grd) | Gablingen | P-51 |
| | | Ju-52 dest(grd) | Gablingen | P-51 |
| | | u/i a/c dest(grd) | Gablingen | P-51 |

10.33-0-0 air
5-0 ground

* - shared with Capt. D.S. Gentile and Lt. V. Garrison of the 336th Ftr Sqn

**Norman, Robert L., Lt.**
357th Ftr Sqn/355th Ftr Grp

| *Sqn* | *Date* | *Claims* | *Location* | *A/C* |
|---|---|---|---|---|
| 357th | February 21, 1944 | FW-190 dam(air) | Dummer Lake | P-47 |
| | March 8 | FW-190 dest(air) | Dummer Lake | P-51 |
| | April 5 | (2)Me-110 dam(grd) | Ottingen | P-51 |
| | April 13 | (.33)Me-110 dest(grd)* | Crailsheim | P-51 |
| | | (.33)Me-323 dest(grd)** | Crailsheim | P-51 |

1-0-1 air
0.67-2 ground

* - shared with Maj. E.W. Szaniawski and Lt. R.F. DeMers of the 357th Ftr Sqn
** - shared with Maj. E.W. Szaniawski and Capt. J.F. Kerch of the 357th Ftr Sqn

**Norris, Thomas E., Lt.**
362nd Ftr Sqn/357th Ftr Grp

| *Sqn* | *Date* | *Claims* | *Location* | *A/C* |
|---|---|---|---|---|
| 362nd | March 6, 1944 | Me-109 dam(air) | NE Berlin | P-51 |
| | May 12 | (1.5)Me-109 dest(air)* | SE Frankfurt | P-51 |
| | May 30 | Me-109 dam(air) | N/Celle | P-51 |
| | June 29 | Me-410 dest(air) | Naumberg | P-51 |

2.5-0-2 air
0-0 ground

* - shared with Lt. A.O. Hood of the 362nd Ftr Sqn

**North, Albert B., Lt.**
77th Ftr Sqn/20th Ftr Grp

| *Sqn* | *Date* | *Claims* | *Location* | *A/C* |
|---|---|---|---|---|
| 77th | February 20, 1945 | Me-108 dest(air) | Straubing | P-51 |
| | | Me-108 dest(grd) | Straubing | P-51 |
| | | Me-109 dest(grd) | Straubing | P-51 |
| | | u/i a/c dest(grd) | Straubing | P-51 |
| | | u/i a/c dam(grd) | Straubing | P-51 |
| | April 10 | Me-262 dest(air) | Oranienburg | P-51 |

2-0-0 air
3-1 ground

**Northrop, Leo W., Lt.**
486th Ftr Sqn/352nd Ftr Grp

| *Sqn* | *Date* | *Claims* | *Location* | *A/C* |
|---|---|---|---|---|
| 486th | June 21, 1944 | (2)Me-109 dest(air) | E/Warsaw | P-51 |

2-0-0 air
0-0 ground

**Nowlin, Hollis R., Lt.**
364th Ftr Sqn/357th Ftr Grp

| *Sqn* | *Date* | *Claims* | *Location* | *A/C* |
|---|---|---|---|---|
| 364th | March 8, 1944 | FW-190 dam(air) | Berlin | P-51 |
| | April 11 | Me-109 dest(air) | Hanover | P-51 |
| | May 21 | (1.5)Me-109 dest(grd)* | E/Eichhof | P-51 |
| | August 6 | Me-109 dam(air) | NE Warsaw | P-51 |

| Sqn | Date | Claims | Location | A/C |
|---|---|---|---|---|
| | August 7 | (1.5)Me-109 dest(air)[**] | Oswiecim | P-51 |

2.5-0-2 air
1.5-0 ground

[*] - shared with Lt. C.D. Conklin of the 364th Ftr Sqn
[**] - shared with Maj. J.A. Storch of the 364th Ftr Sqn

**Nunley, James A., Lt.**
84th Ftr Sqn/78th Ftr Grp

| Sqn | Date | Claims | Location | A/C |
|---|---|---|---|---|
| 84th | April 16, 1945 | Me-109 dam(grd) | Praha/Kakewice | P-51 |
| | | Me-110 dam(grd) | Praha/Kakewice | P-51 |

0-0-0 air
0-2 ground

**Nutter, Marion J., Capt.**
487th Ftr Sqn/352nd Ftr Grp

| Sqn | Date | Claims | Location | A/C |
|---|---|---|---|---|
| 487th | May 13, 1944 | Me-109 dest(air) | N/Neubrandenburg | P-51 |
| | December 26 | Me-109 dest(air) | SW Bonn | P-51 |
| | December 27 | (2)Me-109 dest(air) | SW Bonn | P-51 |

4-0-0 air
0-0 ground

**Nyman, Richard W., Capt.**
2nd Scouting Force

| Sqn | Date | Claims | Location | A/C |
|---|---|---|---|---|
| 2nd | March 31, 1945 | Me-262 dam(air) | SW Brunswick | P-51 |

0-0-1 air
0-0 ground

**Nystrom, Richard C., Capt.**
361st Ftr Sqn/356th Ftr Grp
HdQts/356th Ftr Grp

| Sqn | Date | Claims | Location | A/C |
|---|---|---|---|---|
| 361st | March 22, 1945 | He-111 dam(grd) | Plantlunne | P-51 |

0-0-0 air
0-1 ground

**Oakley, Robert G., Lt.**
370th Ftr Sqn/359th Ftr Grp

| Sqn | Date | Claims | Location | A/C |
|---|---|---|---|---|
| 370th | December 24, 1944 | FW-190 dest(air) | Bonn | P-51 |

1-0-0 air
0-0 ground

**O'Barr, William C., Lt.**
359th Ftr Sqn/356th Ftr Grp

| Sqn | Date | Claims | Location | A/C |
|---|---|---|---|---|
| 359th | February 10, 1944 | FW-190 dam(air) | Meppen | P-47 |
| | March 16 | (.5)Me-109 dest(air)[*] | SE St. Dizier | P-47 |
| | March 18 | Glider dam(grd) | W/Nancy | P-47 |
| | | (.25)Do-217 dam(grd)[**] | W/Nancy | P-47 |

0.5-0-1 air
0-1.25 ground

[*] - shared with Lt. R.B. Warren of the 359th Ftr Sqn
[**] - shared with Maj. D.A. Baccus, Lt. R.K. Holtz, and Lt. G.B. Peet of the 359th Ftr Sqn

**Oberhansly, Jack J., LtCol.**
82nd Ftr Sqn/78th Ftr Grp
HdQts/78th Ftr Grp
HdQts/ 4th Ftr Grp

| Sqn | Date | Claims | Location | A/C |
|---|---|---|---|---|
| 82nd | May 14, 1943 | FW-190 prob(air) | Antwerp | P-47 |
| | September 27 | Me-109 dest(air) | Emden | P-47 |
| | | Me-109 prob(air) | Emden | P-47 |
| | November 30 | FW-190 dest(air) | Eupen | P-47 |
| | February 22, 1944 | FW-190 dest(air) | Gilze-Rijen | P-47 |
| | | Me-109 dest(air) | Cologne | P-47 |
| | | (.5)FW-190 dest(air)[*] | Walcheren | P-47 |
| | | (.5)FW-190 dest(air)[*] | Walcheren | P-47 |
| | | Me-109 dam(air) | Cologne | P-47 |
| | April 8 | Me-109 dest(grd) | Trier | P-47 |
| | | (.2)Me-110 dest(grd)[**] | Trier | P-47 |
| | | (.2)Me-110 dest(grd)[**] | Trier | P-47 |
| | | (.2)Me-110 dest(grd)[**] | Trier | P-47 |
| | | Ju-52 dam(grd) | Trier | P-47 |
| HdQts (78th) | August 28 | Ju-88 dest(air) | Charleroi | P-47 |

6-2-1 air
1.6-1 ground

[*] - both shared with Lt. C.W. Hotchkiss of the 82nd Ftr Sqn
[**] - all shared with Capt. N.D. Munson, Lt. J.E. Brasher, Lt. M.K. Woller, and F/O C.W. DeWitt of the 82nd Ftr Sqn

**O'Brien, Gilbert M., Capt.**
362nd Ftr Sqn/357th Ftr Grp

| Sqn | Date | Claims | Location | A/C |
|---|---|---|---|---|
| 362nd | March 5, 1944 | FW-190 dest(air) | Bordeaux | P-51 |
| | | (.5)FW-190 dam(air)[*] | Bordeaux | P-51 |
| | April 11 | Me-109 dest(air) | Magdeburg | P-51 |
| | | (2)Me-109 dam(air) | Magdeburg | P-51 |
| | April 22 | FW-190 dest(air) | N/Dummer Lake | P-51 |
| | April 30 | (.5)Me-109 dest(air)[**] | S/Paris | P-51 |
| | May 27 | FW-190 dest(air) | N/Strasbourg | P-51 |
| | May 30 | Me-109 dest(air) | Celle | P-51 |
| | | (.5)Me-410 dest(air)[@] | W/Bernburg | P-51 |
| | July 29 | Me-109 dest(air) | W/Merseburg | P-51 |

7-0-2.5 air
0-0 ground

[*] - shared with Lt. A.E. Smith of the 362nd Ftr Sqn
[**] - shared with Lt. T.M. McKinney of the 364th Ftr Sqn, 357th Ftr Grp
[@] - shared with Capt. F.E. Adams of the 362nd Ftr Sqn

**O'Brien, Valentine A., Lt.**
383rd Ftr Sqn/364th Ftr Grp

| Sqn | Date | Claims | Location | A/C |
|---|---|---|---|---|
| 383rd | April 13, 1945 | Ju-52 dest(grd) | Flensburg | P-51 |
| | | (2)FW-190 dam(grd) | Flensburg | P-51 |

0-0-0 air
1-2 ground

**O'Brien, William R., Capt.**
363rd Ftr Sqn/357th Ftr Grp

| Sqn | Date | Claims | Location | A/C |
|---|---|---|---|---|
| 363rd | February 21, 1944 | Me-109 prob(air) | Bussum | P-51 |
| | March 5 | FW-190 prob(air) | N/Bordeaux | P-51 |
| | | FW-190 dam(air) | N/Bordeaux | P-51 |
| | March 6 | (.5)Me-110 dest(air)[*] | Berlin | P-51 |
| | May 12 | Me-109 dest(air) | N/Frankfurt | P-51 |
| | May 24 | Me-109 dest(air) | E/Berlin | P-51 |
| | May 27 | Me-109 dest(air) | Strasbourg | P-51 |
| | May 30 | (2)Me-109 dest(air) | NE Schonebeck | P-51 |

5.5-2-1 air
0-0 ground

[*] - shared with Lt. L.A. Ruder of the 364th Ftr Sqn, 357th Ftr Grp

**O'Bryan, William C., Lt.**
334th Ftr Sqn/4th Ftr Grp

| Sqn | Date | Claims | Location | A/C |
|---|---|---|---|---|
| 334th | February 25, 1945 | (.5)FW-190 dest(air)[*] | Dessau | P-51 |
| | April 16 | (3)u/i a/c dest(grd) | Gablingen | P-51 |

0.5-0-0 air
3-0 ground

[*] - shared with Lt. D.M. Malmsten of the 334th Ftr Sqn

**O'Connell, William P., Lt.**
385th Ftr Sqn/364th Ftr Grp

| Sqn | Date | Claims | Location | A/C |
|---|---|---|---|---|
| 385th | March 8, 1944 | Me-109 dest(air) | Belzig | P-38 |

1-0-0 air
0-0 ground

**O'Connor, Fred T., Lt.**
384th Ftr Sqn/364th Ftr Grp

| *Sqn* | *Date* | *Claims* | *Location* | *A/C* |
|---|---|---|---|---|
| 384th | March 2, 1945 | Me-262 dam(air) | NE Frankfurt | P-51 |

0-0-1 air
0-0 ground

**O'Connor, Wayne J., Lt.**
63rd Ftr Sqn/56th Ftr Grp

| *Sqn* | *Date* | *Claims* | *Location* | *A/C* |
|---|---|---|---|---|
| 63rd | September 27, 1943 | Me-109 dest(air) | Borkum Island | P-47 |
| | November 3 | (.5)Me-109 dest(air)* | N/Essens | P-47 |

1.5-0-0 air
0-0 ground

* - shared with Capt. W.M. Mahurin of the 63rd Ftr Sqn

**Odegard, John L., Capt.**
338th Ftr Sqn/55th Ftr Grp

| *Sqn* | *Date* | *Claims* | *Location* | *A/C* |
|---|---|---|---|---|
| 338th | February 10, 1944 | Me-110 dam(air) | Brunswick | P-38 |

0-0-1 air
0-0 ground

**Odom, William W., Lt.**
350th Ftr Sqn/353rd Ftr Grp

| *Sqn* | *Date* | *Claims* | *Location* | *A/C* |
|---|---|---|---|---|
| 350th | September 27, 1943 | (1.5)Me-109 dest(air)* | Emden | P-47 |

1.5-0-0 air
0-0 ground

* - shared with Capt. D.E. Newhart of the 350th Ftr Sqn

**O'Donnell, William J., Capt.**
335th Ftr Sqn/4th Ftr Grp

| *Sqn* | *Date* | *Claims* | *Location* | *A/C* |
|---|---|---|---|---|
| 335th | December 18, 1944 | Me-109 dest(air) | NE Frankfurt | P-51 |
| | April 13, 1945 | Ar-196 dest(grd) | Ratzburger Lake | P-51 |
| | April 16 | (2)u/i a/c dest(grd) | Praha/Letnany | P-51 |
| | | (2)u/i a/c dam(grd) | Praha/Letnany | P-51 |

1-0-0 air
3-2 ground

**Ofsthun, Carroll W., Lt.**
363rd Ftr Sqn/357th Ftr Grp

| *Sqn* | *Date* | *Claims* | *Location* | *A/C* |
|---|---|---|---|---|
| 363rd | April 19, 1945 | Me-262 dest(air) | SW Prague/Ruzny | P-51 |

1-0-0 air
0-0 ground

**Ogden, Frank M., III, Lt.**
63rd Ftr Sqn/56th Ftr Grp

| *Sqn* | *Date* | *Claims* | *Location* | *A/C* |
|---|---|---|---|---|
| 63rd | February 3, 1945 | FW-190 dest(air) | SE Berlin | P-47 |
| | April 7 | Me-109 prob(air) | S/Hamburg | P-47 |

1-1-0 air
0-0 ground

**Ogden, Frank A., Capt.**
359th Ftr Sqn/356th Ftr Grp
HdQts/356th Ftr Grp

| *Sqn* | *Date* | *Claims* | *Location* | *A/C* |
|---|---|---|---|---|
| HdQts | February 25, 1944 | (2)Me-109 dam(air) | Metz | P-47 |
| | April 1 | Me-410 dest(grd) | Rheine A/F | P-47 |
| | April 13 | Me-110 dest(grd) | Bishwiller A/F | P-47 |
| | | (2)Me-110 dam(grd) | Bishwiller A/F | P-47 |
| | April 23 | He-111 dest(grd) | Hagenau | P-47 |
| | | (.5)Go-242 dam(grd)* | Hagenau | P-47 |
| | April 27 | (.5)FW-190 dest(air)** | Reims | P-47 |

0.5-0-2 air
3-2.5 ground

* - shared with F/O F.A. Forsyth of the 359th Ftr Sqn
** - shared with Lt. R.J. Collins of the 359th Ftr Sqn

**Ogrom, Zeymow, Lt.**
436th Ftr Sqn/479th Ftr Grp

| *Sqn* | *Date* | *Claims* | *Location* | *A/C* |
|---|---|---|---|---|
| 436th | September 5, 1944 | (3)FW-190 dam(grd) | Bad Nauheim | P-38 |

0-0-0 air
0-3 ground

**Oiler, Frank E., Lt.**
84th Ftr Sqn/78th Ftr Grp

| *Sqn* | *Date* | *Claims* | *Location* | *A/C* |
|---|---|---|---|---|
| 84th | January 14, 1945 | FW-190 dest(air) | Cologne | P-51 |
| | | Me-109 dam(air) | Cologne | P-51 |
| | February 3 | Me-410 dest(grd) | Luneburg A/F | P-51 |
| | | Ju-88 dest(grd) | Luneburg A/F | P-51 |
| | | Me-410 dam(grd) | Luneburg A/F | P-51 |

1-0-1 air
2-1 ground

**Olander, Richard B., Capt.**
505th Ftr Sqn/339th Ftr Grp

| *Sqn* | *Date* | *Claims* | *Location* | *A/C* |
|---|---|---|---|---|
| 505th | May 27, 1944 | Me-109 dest(grd) | Reims | P-51 |
| | June 8 | (.5)FW-190 dest(air)* | Rennes | P-51 |
| | July 19 | Ju-188 dest(grd) | SW Augsburg | P-51 |
| | July 31 | Ju-87 dest(grd) | Holzkirchen | P-51 |
| | | u/i a/c dest(grd) | Holzkirchen | P-51 |
| | | u/i a/c dam(grd) | Holzkirchen | P-51 |
| | September 11 | u/i a/c dest(grd) | Munich | P-51 |
| | | (2)u/i a/c dam(grd) | Munich | P-51 |
| | September 12 | Me-109 dest(air) | Goslar | P-51 |

1.5-0-0 air
5-3 ground

* - shared with Lt. A. Sirochman of the 505th Ftr Sqn

**Olds, Robin, Maj.**
434th Ftr Sqn/479th Ftr Grp

| *Sqn* | *Date* | *Claims* | *Location* | *A/C* |
|---|---|---|---|---|
| 434th | August 14, 1944 | (2)FW-190 dest(air) | Montmirail | P-38 |
| | August 18 | (2)Ju-88 dest(grd) | Nancy/Essey A/F | P-38 |
| | | He-111 dest(grd) | Nancy/Essey A/F | P-38 |
| | August 25 | (3)Me-109 dest(air) | Rostock | P-38 |
| | October 6 | FW-190 dest(air) | W/Berlin | P-51 |
| | February 9, 1945 | Me-109 dest(air) | SE Magdeburg | P-51 |
| | February 14 | (2)Me-109 dest(air) | SW Berlin | P-51 |
| | | FW-190 dest(air) | SW Berlin | P-51 |
| | February 20 | Do-217 dest(grd) | Windleschenlaibach | P-51 |
| | | FW-190 dest(grd) | Windleschenlaibach | P-51 |
| | March 19 | Me-109 dest(air) | Handorf A/F | P-51 |
| | | FW-190 dest(air) | Handorf A/F | P-51 |
| | April 7 | Me-109 dest(air) | Dummer Lake-Bremen | P-51 |
| | | Me-262 dam(air) | Dummer Lake-Bremen | P-51 |
| | April 13 | Ar-234 dest(grd) | Lubeck | P-51 |
| | | Me-410 dam(grd) | Tarnewitz | P-51 |
| | April 16 | (2)Ju-87 dest(grd) | Reichersberg | P-51 |
| | | Me-109 dest(grd) | Reichersberg | P-51 |
| | | Me-110 dest(grd) | Reichersberg | P-51 |
| | | He-177 dest(grd) | Reichersberg | P-51 |

13-0-1 air
11-1 ground

**Oliphint, John H., Capt.**
369th Ftr Sqn/359th Ftr Grp

| Sqn | Date | Claims | Location | A/C |
|---|---|---|---|---|
| 369th | January 29, 1944 | (.5)Me-110 dest(air)[*] | Dison | P-47 |
| | March 26 | Me-110 dest(grd) | Chateaudun | P-47 |
| | | He-177 dam(grd) | Chateaudun | P-47 |
| | May 19 | Me-109 dest(air) | Wittengen | P-51 |

1.5-0-0 air
1-1 ground

[*] - shared with Maj. R.V. Gray of HdQts, 359th Ftr Grp

**Olive, Homer S., Lt.**
360th Ftr Sqn/356th Ftr Grp

| Sqn | Date | Claims | Location | A/C |
|---|---|---|---|---|
| 360th | September 1, 1944 | (.5)Ju-52 dest(grd)[*] | W/Nancy | P-47 |

0-0-0 air
0.5-0 ground

[*] - shared with Lt. E.M. Nebinger of the 360th Ftr Sqn

**Oliver, Leon, Lt.**
359th Ftr Sqn/356th Ftr Grp

| Sqn | Date | Claims | Location | A/C |
|---|---|---|---|---|
| 359th | December 5, 1944 | FW-190 dest(air) | Muritz Lake-Berlin | P-51 |
| | April 18, 1945 | Ar-234 dest(air) | Wertingen | P-51 |

2-0-0 air
0-0 ground

**Olson, Norman E., Capt.**
357th Ftr Sqn/355th Ftr Grp

| Sqn | Date | Claims | Location | A/C |
|---|---|---|---|---|
| 357th | November 7, 1943 | Me-210 dest(air) | Amiens | P-47 |
| | November 13 | Me-109 dest(air) | Zwolle | P-47 |
| | December 1 | Me-109 dam(air) | W/Cologne | P-47 |
| | February 5 | (2)Me-109 dest(air) | W/Vendome | P-47 |
| | February 20 | Me-109 dest(air) | Siegen | P-47 |
| | February 21 | FW-190 dest(air) | Dummer Lake | P-47 |
| | | FW-190 dam(air) | Dummer Lake | P-47 |
| | March 28 | He-111 dest(grd) | Dijon | P-51 |
| | | FW-190 dam(grd) | Dijon | P-51 |
| | April 8 | Ju-88 dest(grd) | Gifhorn | P-51 |

6-0-2 air
2-1 ground

**Olson, Thomas C., Lt.**
434th Ftr Sqn/479th Ftr Grp

| Sqn | Date | Claims | Location | A/C |
|---|---|---|---|---|
| 434th | August 18, 1944 | (1.5)He-111 dest(grd)[*] | Nancy/Essey A/F | P-38 |
| | | Me-109 dest(grd) | Nancy/Essey A/F | P-38 |
| | | Ju-88 dest(grd) | Nancy/Essey A/F | P-38 |
| | | (.5)FW-190 dest(grd)[**] | Nancy/Essey A/F | P-38 |
| | | He-111 dam(grd) | Nancy/Essey A/F | P-38 |
| | August 28 | FW-190 dest(air) | Sedan/Douzy A/F | P-38 |
| | | u/i a/c dam(grd) | Sedan/Douzy A/F | P-38 |
| | September 5 | (4)Do-217 dest(grd) | Ettinghausen | P-38 |
| | | Me-110 dest(grd) | Ettinghausen | P-38 |
| | November 6 | (.5)FW-190 dest(grd)[@] | Hesepe | P-51 |
| | November 27 | Me-410 dam(grd) | Vechta | P-51 |

1-0-0 air
9.5-3 ground

[*] - shared with Lt. N.W. Butler of the 435th Ftr Sqn, 479th Ftr Grp
[**] - shared with Lt. T.J. Sowerby of the 435th Ftr Sqn
[@] - shared with Lt. W.H. Marlowe of the 434th Ftr Sqn

**O'Nan, Robert G., Lt.**
487th Ftr Sqn/352nd Ftr Grp

| Sqn | Date | Claims | Location | A/C |
|---|---|---|---|---|
| 487th | April 10, 1944 | FW-190 dest(air) | SW Rheims | P-51 |
| | May 8 | Me-109 dest(air) | NE Brunswick | P-51 |

2-0-0 air
0-0 ground

**O'Neil, John F., Lt.**
38th Ftr Sqn/55th Ftr Grp

| Sqn | Date | Claims | Location | A/C |
|---|---|---|---|---|
| 38th | February 25, 1945 | Me-262 dest(air) | Giebelstadt A/F | P-51 |
| | | Me-262 dest(grd) | Giebelstadt A/F | P-51 |
| | March 9 | Me-262 dam(air) | Giebelstadt A/F | P-51 |
| | March 22 | Me-262 dest(grd) | Lechfeld A/F | P-51 |

1-0-1 air
2-0 ground

**O'Neill, Eugene W., Jr., Capt.**
62nd Ftr Sqn/56th Ftr Grp

| Sqn | Date | Claims | Location | A/C |
|---|---|---|---|---|
| 62nd | November 11, 1943 | FW-190 dest(air) | Munster | P-47 |
| | November 26 | FW-190 dest(air) | Papenburg | P-47 |
| | | (.5)Me-110 dest(air)[*] | Papenburg | P-47 |
| | December 20 | Me-109 dest(air) | Vegesack | P-47 |
| | February 6, 1944 | FW-190 dest(air) | Paris | P-47 |

4.5-0-0 air
0-0 ground

[*] - shared with Lt. M.K. Boyle of the 62nd Ftr Sqn

**O'Neill, Francis, Lt.**
350th Ftr Sqn/353rd Ftr Grp

| Sqn | Date | Claims | Location | A/C |
|---|---|---|---|---|
| 350th | March 21, 1945 | Ju-88 dest(grd) | Achmer | P-51 |
| | March 24 | Me-109 dest(air) | NW Kassel | P-51 |
| | | Me-109 dam(air) | NW Kassel | P-51 |

1-0-1 air
1-0 ground

**Onkey, John P., Lt.**
350th Ftr Sqn/353rd Ftr Grp

| Sqn | Date | Claims | Location | A/C |
|---|---|---|---|---|
| 350th | March 21, 1945 | Me-109 dest(grd) | Achmer | P-51 |

0-0-0 air
1-0 ground

**Opitz, William R., Lt.**
505th Ftr Sqn/339th Ftr Grp

| Sqn | Date | Claims | Location | A/C |
|---|---|---|---|---|
| 505th | June 8, 1944 | (.5)Do-217 dest(air)[*] | Laigle | P-51 |

0.5-0-0 air
0-0 ground

[*] - shared with Lt. A.A. Tower of the 505th Ftr Sqn

**O'Quinn, Percy C., Lt.**
359th Ftr Sqn/356th Ftr Grp

| Sqn | Date | Claims | Location | A/C |
|---|---|---|---|---|
| 359th | April 7, 1945 | Me-262 dam(air) | NE Steinhuder Lk. | P-51 |

0-0-1 air
0-0 ground

**Orcutt, Leon M., Jr., Lt.**
504th Ftr Sqn/339th Ftr Grp

| Sqn | Date | Claims | Location | A/C |
|---|---|---|---|---|
| 504th | April 9, 1945 | Me-262 dam(air) | Leipzig | P-51 |
| | April 17 | (6)Me-109 dest(grd) | Klatovy A/F | P-51 |
| | | (2)Ju-88 dest(grd) | Klatovy A/F | P-51 |

0-0-1 air
6-2 ground

**O'Regan, William T., Capt.**
334th Ftr Sqn/4th Ftr Grp

| Sqn | Date | Claims | Location | A/C |
|---|---|---|---|---|
| 334th | August 12, 1943 | Me-109 dest(air) | E/Sittard | P-47 |
| | | Me-109 prob(air) | E/Sittard | P-47 |

1-1-0 air
0-0 ground

**Orndorff, Roy W., Capt.**
383rd Ftr Sqn/364th Ftr Grp

| *Sqn* | *Date* | *Claims* | *Location* | *A/C* |
|---|---|---|---|---|
| 383rd | December 23, 1944 | (2)FW-190 dest(air) | NW Trier | P-51 |
| | December 31 | FW-190 dest(air) | SW Hamburg | P-51 |
| | April 13, 1945 | (2)Ju-52 dest(grd) | Flensburg | P-51 |
| | | Me-109 dest(grd) | Flensburg | P-51 |
| | | FW-190 dest(grd) | Flensburg | P-51 |
| | | Fi-156 dam(grd) | Flensburg | P-51 |
| | April 17 | Me-262 dest(air) | Praha A/F | P-51 |

4-0-0 air
4-1 ground

**Orwig, Eugene R., Capt.**
369th Ftr Sqn/359th Ftr Grp

| *Sqn* | *Date* | *Claims* | *Location* | *A/C* |
|---|---|---|---|---|
| 369th | May 21, 1944 | u/i a/c dest(grd) | Lubeck/Schwerin | P-51 |
| | | u/i a/c dam(grd) | Lubeck/Schwerin | P-51 |

0-0-0 air
1-1 ground

**Orzelek, Frank J., F/O**
350th Ftr Sqn/353rd Ftr Grp

| *Sqn* | *Date* | *Claims* | *Location* | *A/C* |
|---|---|---|---|---|
| 350th | November 26, 1944 | FW-190 dest(air) | SE Dummer Lake | P-51 |

1-0-0 air
0-0 ground

**Osborn, Roy W., Col.**
HdQts/67th Ftr Wg
HdQts/364th Ftr Grp

| *Sqn* | *Date* | *Claims* | *Location* | *A/C* |
|---|---|---|---|---|
| HdQts (67th) | February 20, 1944 | (1.33)Me-110 dest(air)[*] | Vogelsand | P-47 |
| HdQts (364th) | May 8 | FW-190 dest(air) | Steinhuder Lake | P-38 |
| | | Me-109 dam(air) | Steinhuder Lake | P-38 |
| | November 21 | FW-190 dest(air) | S/Merseburg | P-51 |

3.33-0-1 air
0-0 ground

[*] - shared with Capt. D.S. Bryan and Lt. D.T. Zimms of the 328th Ftr Sqn, 352nd Ftr Grp

**Osborne, William J., Lt.**
61st Ftr Sqn/56th Ftr Grp

| *Sqn* | *Date* | *Claims* | *Location* | *A/C* |
|---|---|---|---|---|
| 61st | September 21, 1944 | (.5)FW-190 dest(air)[*] | Deventer | P-47 |

0.5-0-0 air
0-0 ground

[*] - shared with Lt. S.H. Getz of the 61st Ftr Sqn

**O'Shea, James H., Lt.**
370th Ftr Sqn/359th Ftr Grp

| *Sqn* | *Date* | *Claims* | *Location* | *A/C* |
|---|---|---|---|---|
| 370th | September 11, 1944 | FW-190 dest(air) | Mulhausen | P-51 |

1-0-0 air
0-0 ground

**Ostrander, Paul S., Lt.**
84th Ftr Sqn/78th Ftr Grp

| *Sqn* | *Date* | *Claims* | *Location* | *A/C* |
|---|---|---|---|---|
| 84th | February 3, 1945 | (2)FW-190 dest(grd) | Luneburg A/F | P-51 |
| | | FW-190 dam(grd) | Luneburg A/F | P-51 |
| | March 19 | Me-109 dest(air) | Osnabruck | P-51 |
| | March 30 | Me-262 dest(grd) | Kaltenkirchen | P-51 |
| | | Me-262 dam(grd) | Kaltenkirchen | P-51 |

1-0-0 air
3-2 ground

**Ostrow, Nathan, Capt.**
503rd Ftr Sqn/339th Ftr Grp

| *Sqn* | *Date* | *Claims* | *Location* | *A/C* |
|---|---|---|---|---|
| 503rd | September 5, 1944 | (1.5)Me-109 dest(air)[*] | Schaffhausen | P-51 |

1.5-0-0 air
0-0 ground

[*] - shared with Lt. E.E. Erickson of the 503rd Ftr Sqn

**O'Sullivan, Walter R., Lt.**
504th Ftr Sqn/339th Ftr Grp

| *Sqn* | *Date* | *Claims* | *Location* | *A/C* |
|---|---|---|---|---|
| 504th | May 19, 1944 | FW-190 dest(air) | Berlin | P-51 |

1-0-0 air
0-0 ground

**Ott, Nelson T., Lt.**
351st Ftr Sqn/353rd Ftr Grp

| *Sqn* | *Date* | *Claims* | *Location* | *A/C* |
|---|---|---|---|---|
| 351st | June 12, 1944 | Me-109 dam(air) | SW Paris | P-47 |
| | June 25 | Me-410 dam(grd) | Bourges | P-47 |

0-0-1 air
0-1 ground

**Ott, Richard L., Maj.**
79th Ftr Sqn/20th Ftr Grp

| *Sqn* | *Date* | *Claims* | *Location* | *A/C* |
|---|---|---|---|---|
| 79th | January 14, 1944 | (.5)FW-190 prob(air)[*] | S/Fecamp | P-38 |
| | | FW-190 dam(air) | S/Fecamp | P-38 |
| | January 29 | Me-110 dest(air) | Mainz | P-38 |
| | | (.5)Me-210 dest(air)[**] | SW Frankfurt | P-38 |
| | January 30 | FW-190 dest(air) | Minden | P-38 |
| | | Do-217 dest(air) | Minden | P-38 |

3.5-0.5-1 air
0-0 ground

[*] - shared with Lt. H. Mednick of the 79th Ftr Sqn
[**] - shared with Lt. W.L. Whiteside of the 79th Ftr Sqn

**Overholt, David P., Lt.**
376th Ftr Sqn/361st Ftr Grp

| *Sqn* | *Date* | *Claims* | *Location* | *A/C* |
|---|---|---|---|---|
| 376th | September 12, 1944 | Me-109 dest(air) | W/Magdeburg | P-51 |
| | December 26 | FW-190 dest(air) | NW Merzig | P-51 |

2-0-0 air
0-0 ground

**Overstreet, William B., Lt.**
363rd Ftr Sqn/357th Ftr Grp

| *Sqn* | *Date* | *Claims* | *Location* | *A/C* |
|---|---|---|---|---|
| 363rd | April 11, 1944 | (.25)He-111 dest(air)[*] | W/Hanover | P-51 |
| | | (3)Me-109 dam(air) | W/Hanover | P-51 |
| | May 12 | Ju-52 dest(grd) | NE Frankfurt | P-51 |
| | June 29 | FW-190 dest(air) | SW Leipzig | P-51 |
| | July 29 | Me-109 dest(air) | W/Merseburg | P-51 |
| | | FW-190 dest(grd) | W/Merseburg | P-51 |
| | | Do-217 dam(grd) | W/Merseburg | P-51 |
| | | FW-190 dam(grd) | W/Merseburg | P-51 |

2.25-0-3 air
2-2 ground

[*] - shared with Capt. C.E. Anderson, Lt. H.R. Kayser, and Lt. E.K. Simpson of the 363rd Ftr Sqn

**Owens, Robert B., Lt.**
357th Ftr Sqn/355th Ftr Grp

| *Sqn* | *Date* | *Claims* | *Location* | *A/C* |
|---|---|---|---|---|
| 357th | April 16, 1945 | u/i a/c dest(grd) | SE Germany | P-51 |

0-0-0 air
1-0 ground

**Oxley, Daniel D., Lt.**
55th Ftr Sqn/20th Ftr Grp

| Sqn | Date | Claims | Location | A/C |
|---|---|---|---|---|
| 55th | August 25, 1944 | FW-190 dest(grd) | Parow A/F | P-51 |
| | | Ju-88 dam(grd) | Parow A/F | P-51 |
| | October 6 | (2)Do-24 dest(grd) | Kubitzer Bay | P-51 |

0-0-0 air
3-1 ground

**Oxley, Richard W., Lt.**
83rd Ftr Sqn/78th Ftr Grp

| Sqn | Date | Claims | Location | A/C |
|---|---|---|---|---|
| 83rd | June 17, 1944 | (.5)FW-190 dest(air)* | Laigle | P-47 |
| | July 19 | Ju-188 dam(grd) | Linburg-Coblenz | P-47 |

0.5-0-0 air
0-1 ground

**Packard, Hudson F., Lt.**
357th Ftr Sqn/355th Ftr Grp

| Sqn | Date | Claims | Location | A/C |
|---|---|---|---|---|
| 357th | March 28, 1944 | Ju-88 dest(grd) | Dijon | P-51 |
| | | (3)Ju-88 dam(grd) | Dijon | P-51 |
| | April 5 | Me-110 dest(grd) | Deiningen | P-51 |
| | | Me-110 dam(grd) | Deiningen | P-51 |

0-0-0 air
2-4 ground

**Padden, Walter, Lt.**
487th Ftr Sqn/352nd Ftr Grp

| Sqn | Date | Claims | Location | A/C |
|---|---|---|---|---|
| 487th | April 16, 1945 | (2)u/i a/c dest(grd) | Ganacker | P-51 |

0-0-0 air
2-0 ground

**Padgett, Cadmen V., Capt.**
335th Ftr Sqn/4th Ftr Grp

| Sqn | Date | Claims | Location | A/C |
|---|---|---|---|---|
| 335th | August 12, 1943 | Me-109 dest(air) | W/Duren | P-47 |
| | November 26 | Me-109 dest(air) | Rude | P-47 |

2-0-0 air
0-0 ground

**Page, Garnett D., Lt.**
350th Ftr Sqn/353rd Ftr Grp

| Sqn | Date | Claims | Location | A/C |
|---|---|---|---|---|
| 350th | March 2, 1945 | Me-109 dest(air) | Ruhland | P-51 |

1-0-0 air
0-0 ground

**Pagels, Roger E., Lt.**
363rd Ftr Sqn/357th Ftr Grp

| Sqn | Date | Claims | Location | A/C |
|---|---|---|---|---|
| 363rd | March 6, 1944 | Me-110 dest(air) | W/Berlin | P-51 |

1-0-0 air
0-0 ground

**Palmer, Gerald J., Capt.**
487th Ftr Sqn/352nd Ftr Grp

| Sqn | Date | Claims | Location | A/C |
|---|---|---|---|---|
| 487th | April 9, 1944 | Ju-88 dest(grd) | Vechta | P-51 |
| | May 30 | FW-190 dest(air) | Halberstadt | P-51 |
| | July 29 | Me-109 dest(air) | Merseburg | P-51 |

2-0-0 air
1-0 ground

**Palmer, Gerald W., Lt.**
505th Ftr Sqn/339th Ftr Grp

| Sqn | Date | Claims | Location | A/C |
|---|---|---|---|---|
| 505th | November 21, 1944 | (.5)Me-109 dest(air)* | Munster | P-51 |

0.5-0-0 air
0-0 ground

* - shared with Capt. C.W. Dowell of HdQts, 339th Ftr Grp

**Palopoli, Anthony A., Lt.**
83rd Ftr Sqn/78th Ftr Grp

| Sqn | Date | Claims | Location | A/C |
|---|---|---|---|---|
| 83rd | April 16, 1945 | (3)Ju-87 dest(grd) | N/Prague | P-51 |

0-0-0 air
3-0 ground

**Palson, Richard C.J., Lt.**
436th Ftr Sqn/479th Ftr Grp

| Sqn | Date | Claims | Location | A/C |
|---|---|---|---|---|
| 436th | April 13, 1945 | (2)He-111 dest(grd) | Salzwedel | P-51 |
| | | FW-190 dam(grd) | Salzwedel | P-51 |
| | | He-111 dam(grd) | Salzwedel | P-51 |
| | April 16 | (2)FW-190 dest(grd) | Landstadt | P-51 |
| | April 17 | (2)FW-190 dest(grd) | Puchhoff | P-51 |
| | | (2)Me-109 dest(grd) | Puchhoff | P-51 |

0-0-0 air
8-2 ground

**Paquet, Adolph A., Lt.**
360th Ftr Sqn/356th Ftr Grp

| Sqn | Date | Claims | Location | A/C |
|---|---|---|---|---|
| 360th | February 21, 1945 | FW-190 dam(grd) | NW Crailsheim | P-51 |
| | | W-34 dam(grd) | NW Crailsheim | P-51 |

0-0-0 air
0-2 ground

**Pardee, Harry W., Jr., Lt.**
358th Ftr Sqn/355th Ftr Grp

| Sqn | Date | Claims | Location | A/C |
|---|---|---|---|---|
| 358th | July 8, 1944 | FW-190 dest(grd) | SW Chalons | P-51 |
| | | (3)Me-109 dam(grd) | SW Chalons | P-51 |
| | July 24 | Do-217 dam(grd) | Augsburg | P-51 |

0-0-0 air
1-4 ground

**Parham, Ernest M., Lt.**
361st Ftr Sqn/356th Ftr Grp

| Sqn | Date | Claims | Location | A/C |
|---|---|---|---|---|
| 361st | April 11, 1944 | Ju-88 dest(grd) | Gifhorn | P-47 |
| | | (.5)FW-190 dest(grd)* | Gifhorn | P-47 |

0-0-0 air
1.5-0 ground

* - shared with Lt. S.H. Hewett of the 361st Ftr Sqn

**Parker, Bill, Lt.**
352nd Ftr Sqn/353rd Ftr Grp

| Sqn | Date | Claims | Location | A/C |
|---|---|---|---|---|
| 352nd | August 28, 1944 | (.5)Ju-88 dest(air)* | SE Luxembourg | P-47 |

0.5-0-0 air
0-0 ground

* - shared with Lt. T.W. Jones of the 352nd Ftr Sqn

**Parker, Douglas A., Capt.**
343rd Ftr Sqn/55th Ftr Grp

| Sqn | Date | Claims | Location | A/C |
|---|---|---|---|---|
| 343rd | September 5, 1944 | (.5)Ju-52 dam(grd)* | Stuttgart/Echterdingen | P-51 |

| Sqn | Date | Claims | Location | A/C |
|---|---|---|---|---|
| | | (.5)glider dam(grd)[**] | Stuttgart/Echterdingen | P-51 |
| | September 10 | He-111 dest(grd) | Illesheim | P-51 |
| | | Ju-88 dest(grd) | Illesheim | P-51 |
| | November 2 | Me-109 dest(air) | Weimar | P-51 |
| | December 11 | Me-410 dam(grd) | SE Kassel | P-51 |

1-0-0 air
2-2 ground

* - shared with Lt. F.A. Blair of the 343rd Ftr Sqn
** - shared with Lt. R.D. Butler of the 343rd Ftr Sqn

**Parker, Hunter D., Capt.**
360th Ftr Sqn/356th Ftr Grp

| Sqn | Date | Claims | Location | A/C |
|---|---|---|---|---|
| 360th | February 13, 1944 | FW-190 dest(air) | Chartres | P-47 |

1-0-0 air
0-0 ground

**Parker, James E., Lt.**
82nd Ftr Sqn/78th Ftr Grp

| Sqn | Date | Claims | Location | A/C |
|---|---|---|---|---|
| 82nd | February 28, 1945 | (.5)Me-262 dam(air)[*] | Hersfeld-Fulda | P-51 |
| | March 19 | FW-190 dest(air) | Osnabruck | P-51 |
| | | Ar-234 dest(air) | Osnabruck | P-51 |
| | | (3)FW-190 dam(air) | Osnabruck | P-51 |
| | April 16 | FW-190 dam(grd) | Pilzen/Prague | P-51 |

2-0-3.5 air
0-1 ground

* - shared with Lt. W.F. Bechtelheimer of the 82nd Ftr Sqn

**Parker, Thomas A., Lt.**
338th Ftr Sqn/55th Ftr Grp

| Sqn | Date | Claims | Location | A/C |
|---|---|---|---|---|
| 338th | June 14, 1944 | Me-109 dam(air) | Paris | P-38 |
| | July 7 | FW-190 dest(air) | SW Magdeburg | P-38 |
| | | Me-109 dest(air) | SW Magdeburg | P-38 |

2-0-1 air
0-0 ground

**Parks, Robert F., Lt.**
358th Ftr Sqn/355th Ftr Grp

| Sqn | Date | Claims | Location | A/C |
|---|---|---|---|---|
| 358th | April 13, 1945 | (2)FW-190 dest(grd) | Flensburg | P-51 |
| | | (2)He-111 dest(grd) | Flensburg | P-51 |
| | April 17 | u/i a/c dam(grd) | Eger A/F | P-51 |
| | April 20 | Me-109 dam(air) | Kbely | P-51 |

0-0-1 air
4-1 ground

**Parlee, Wendell F., Capt.**
328th Ftr Sqn/352nd Ftr Grp

| Sqn | Date | Claims | Location | A/C |
|---|---|---|---|---|
| 328th | March 16, 1944 | Me-109 dest(air) | Saulx | P-47 |

1-0-0 air
0-0 ground

**Parmelee, Charles E., Lt.**
84th Ftr Sqn/78th Ftr Grp

| Sqn | Date | Claims | Location | A/C |
|---|---|---|---|---|
| 84th | July 6, 1944 | FW-190 dest(air) | NW Paris | P-47 |
| | July 19 | Do-217 dest(grd) | Eutingen | P-47 |
| | August 11 | (2)Me-109 dest(air) | NW Paris | P-47 |
| | September 1 | FW-190 dest(grd) | SW Antwerp | P-47 |

3-0-0 air
2-0 ground

**Parsley, Adrian D., Capt.**
384th Ftr Sqn/364th Ftr Grp

| Sqn | Date | Claims | Location | A/C |
|---|---|---|---|---|
| 384th | May 8, 1944 | Me-109 dest(air) | Gifhorn-Steinhuder Lake | P-38 |

1-0-0 air
0-0 ground

**Parsons, Albert B., Maj.**
38th Ftr Sqn/55th Ftr Grp

| Sqn | Date | Claims | Location | A/C |
|---|---|---|---|---|
| 38th | September 5, 1944 | He-111 dest(grd) | Stuttgart/Boblingen | P-51 |
| | September 12 | (.5)u/i a/c dest(grd)[*] | Herzogenaurach | P-51 |
| | | Me-410 dam(grd) | Herzogenaurach | P-51 |
| | | Ju-87 dam(grd) | Herzogenaurach | P-51 |

0-0-0 air
1.5-2 ground

* - shared with Lt. D.F. Jewell of the 38th Ftr Sqn

**Parsons, James R., Lt.**
369th Ftr Sqn/359th Ftr Grp

| Sqn | Date | Claims | Location | A/C |
|---|---|---|---|---|
| 369th | September 11, 1944 | (2)Ju-88 dest(grd) | S/Merseburg | P-51 |
| | | (3)Ju-88 dam(grd) | S/Merseburg | P-51 |
| | September 18 | FW-190 dest(air) | Dieven | P-51 |

1-0-0 air
2-3 ground

**Parsons, James W., LtCol.**
369th Ftr Sqn/359th Ftr Grp
368th Ftr Sqn/359th Ftr Grp
HdQts/359th Ftr Grp

| Sqn | Date | Claims | Location | A/C |
|---|---|---|---|---|
| 369th | September 11, 1944 | Me-109 dest(air) | Kolleda | P-51 |
| HdQtsb | March 24, 1945 | Me-109 dest(air) | Eikelon A/F | P-51 |

2-0-0 air
0-0 ground

**Pasaka, Donald J., Lt.**
363rd Ftr Sqn/357th Ftr Grp

| Sqn | Date | Claims | Location | A/C |
|---|---|---|---|---|
| 363rd | September 19, 1944 | (2)Me-109 dest(air) | Anklam | P-51 |

2-0-0 air
0-0 ground

**Pascoe, Hershel T., Capt.**
363rd Ftr Sqn/357th Ftr Grp

| Sqn | Date | Claims | Location | A/C |
|---|---|---|---|---|
| 363rd | September 18, 1944 | Me-109 dest(air) | Arnheim | P-51 |

1-0-0 air
0-0 ground

**Pascoe, James J., Lt.**
385th Ftr Sqn/364th Ftr Grp

| Sqn | Date | Claims | Location | A/C |
|---|---|---|---|---|
| 385th | May 24, 1944 | (.5)Do-217 dest(air)[*] | Gifhorn | P-38 |
| | July 6 | FW-190 prob(air) | S/Chalons | P-38 |
| | September 11 | (2)FW-190 dest(air) | SW Leipzig | P-51 |
| | September 19 | FW-190 dest(air) | Arnheim | P-51 |
| | September 28 | FW-190 dam(air) | W/Magdeburg | P-51 |
| | November 2 | (2)Me-109 dest(air) | Halle | P-51 |

5.5-1-1 air
0-0 ground

* - shared with Lt. C.S. Hill of the 385th Ftr Sqn

**Patchen, Donald J., Lt.**
336th Ftr Sqn/4th Ftr Grp

| Sqn | Date | Claims | Location | A/C |
|---|---|---|---|---|
| 336th | April 5, 1944 | (2.5)Ju-88 dest(grd)[*] | Stendal | P-51 |

0-0-0 air
2.5-0 ground

* - shared with an unknown pilot

**Patelunas, Robert J., Lt.**
357th Ftr Sqn/355th Ftr Grp

| *Sqn* | *Date* | *Claims* | *Location* | *A/C* |
|---|---|---|---|---|
| 357th | April 16, 1945 | u/i a/c dest(grd) | SE Germany | P-51 |

0-0-0 air
1-0 ground

**Patrinely, Costa C., Lt.**
358th Ftr Sqn/355th Ftr Grp

| *Sqn* | *Date* | *Claims* | *Location* | *A/C* |
|---|---|---|---|---|
| 358th | April 9, 1945 | He-111 dest(grd) | Heilfingen | P-51 |
| | | (.5)Me-110 dest(grd)* | Heilfingen | P-51 |
| | April 13 | (.5)He-111 dest(grd)** | Schleswig | P-51 |

0-0-0 air
2-0 ground

* - shared with Lt. H.P. Knutty of the 358th Ftr Sqn
** - shared with Lt. E.W. Fees of the 358th Ftr Sqn

**Patteeuw, Joseph A., Capt.**
336th Ftr Sqn/4th Ftr Grp

| *Sqn* | *Date* | *Claims* | *Location* | *A/C* |
|---|---|---|---|---|
| 336th | April 29, 1944 | (.5)Ju-52 dest(grd)* | Nordhausen | P-51 |
| | April 30 | (.5)Do-24 dest(grd)** | Lyon S/P Base | P-51 |
| | August 6 | Me-410 dest(grd) | SE Berlin | P-51 |

0-0-0 air
2-0 ground

* - shared with Lt. J.T. Godfrey of the 336th Ftr Sqn
** - shared with Col. D.J.M. Blakeslee of HdQts, 4th Ftr Grp

**Patterson, C.H., Lt.**
336th Ftr Sqn/4th Ftr Grp

| *Sqn* | *Date* | *Claims* | *Location* | *A/C* |
|---|---|---|---|---|
| 336th | September 11, 1944 | FW-190 dest(grd) | Langensalza A/F | P-51 |

0-0-0 air
1-0 ground

**Patterson, Chet A., Maj.**
338th Ftr Sqn/55th Ftr Grp
HdQts/55th Ftr Grp

| *Sqn* | *Date* | *Claims* | *Location* | *A/C* |
|---|---|---|---|---|
| 338th | November 25, 1943 | FW-190 dest(air) | Lens | P-38 |
| | November 29 | Me-109 dest(air) | N/Emmen | P-38 |
| | January 31, 1944 | (2)Me-109 dest(air) | Goch & Kessel | P-38 |

4-0-0 air
0-0 ground

**Patterson, Gilbert T., Lt.**
354th Ftr Sqn/355th Ftr Grp

| *Sqn* | *Date* | *Claims* | *Location* | *A/C* |
|---|---|---|---|---|
| 354th | July 24, 1944 | He-280 dest(grd) | Lechfeld | P-51 |

0-0-0 air
1-0 ground

**Patterson, Roy L., Lt.**
62nd Ftr Sqn/56th Ftr Grp

| *Sqn* | *Date* | *Claims* | *Location* | *A/C* |
|---|---|---|---|---|
| 62nd | September 5, 1944 | (2)FW-190 dest(grd) | Gelnhausen | P-47 |
| | | u/i a/c dam(grd) | Gelnhausen | P-47 |
| | September 21 | FW-190 dest(air) | Arnheim | P-47 |
| | October 5 | Me-109 dest(grd) | S/Geseke | P-47 |
| | | Ju-88 dest(grd) | S/Geseke | P-47 |

1-0-0 air
4-1 ground

**Patterson, Warren S., Lt.**
61st Ftr Sqn/56th Ftr Grp

| *Sqn* | *Date* | *Claims* | *Location* | *A/C* |
|---|---|---|---|---|
| 61st | June 12, 1944 | Me-109 dam(air) | Evreux | P-47 |
| | June 27 | Me-109 dest(air) | Connentre | P-47 |
| | July 20 | He-111 dest(grd) | Bassenheim | P-47 |
| | | He-111 dam(grd) | Bassenheim | P-47 |

1-0-1 air
1-1 ground

**Pattillo, Charles C., Lt.**
486th Ftr Sqn/352nd Ftr Grp

| *Sqn* | *Date* | *Claims* | *Location* | *A/C* |
|---|---|---|---|---|
| 486th | March 2, 1945 | (2)u/i a/c dam(grd) | Prague | P-51 |
| | April 16 | (3)FW-190 dest(grd) | Ganacker | P-51 |
| | | (2)Me-109 dest(grd) | Ganacker | P-51 |
| | | Ju-88 dest(grd) | Ganacker | P-51 |
| | | (2)Me-109 dam(grd) | Ganacker | P-51 |
| | | FW-190 dam(grd) | Ganacker | P-51 |

0-0-0 air
6-5 ground

**Pattillo, Cuthbert A., Lt.**
487th Ftr Sqn/352nd Ftr Grp

| *Sqn* | *Date* | *Claims* | *Location* | *A/C* |
|---|---|---|---|---|
| 487th | April 10, 1945 | Me-262 dest(air) | E/Ulzen | P-51 |
| | April 16 | FW-190 dest(grd) | Ganacker | P-51 |
| | | Me-109 dest(grd) | Ganacker | P-51 |
| | | (2)FW-190 dam(grd) | Ganacker | P-51 |
| | | Me-109 dam(grd) | Ganacker | P-51 |

1-0-0 air
2-3 ground

**Patton, James O., Lt.**
84th Ftr Sqn/78th Ftr Grp

| *Sqn* | *Date* | *Claims* | *Location* | *A/C* |
|---|---|---|---|---|
| 84th | April 8, 1944 | u/i a/c dam(grd) | NE Frankfurt | P-47 |

0-0-0 air
0-1 ground

**Patton, Lee, Lt.**
369th Ftr Sqn/359th Ftr Grp

| *Sqn* | *Date* | *Claims* | *Location* | *A/C* |
|---|---|---|---|---|
| 369th | March 24, 1945 | (2)Me-109 dam(air) | Eikelon A/F | P-51 |

0-0-2 air
0-0 ground

**Patton, William W., Maj.**
376th Ftr Sqn/361st Ftr Grp

| *Sqn* | *Date* | *Claims* | *Location* | *A/C* |
|---|---|---|---|---|
| 376th | April 16, 1945 | Me-109 dest(grd) | Halndorf | P-51 |
| | | Me-109 dam(grd) | Halndorf | P-51 |
| | | u/i a/c dam(grd) | Halndorf | P-51 |
| | April 17 | (2)FW-190 dest(grd) | Pilzen | P-51 |

0-0-0 air
3-2 ground

**Paul, Robert H., Lt.**
505th Ftr Sqn/339th Ftr Grp

| *Sqn* | *Date* | *Claims* | *Location* | *A/C* |
|---|---|---|---|---|
| 505th | April 10, 1945 | (3)Do-217 dest(grd) | Wittstock | P-51 |
| | | (2)Ju-88 dest(grd) | Wittstock | P-51 |
| | | (2)Ju-88 dam(grd) | Wittstock | P-51 |
| | April 17 | Ju-88 dest(grd) | SE Pocking | P-51 |

0-0-0 air
6-2 ground

**Paulsen, Eugene A., Lt.**
486th Ftr Sqn/352nd Ftr Grp

| *Sqn* | *Date* | *Claims* | *Location* | *A/C* |
|---|---|---|---|---|
| 486th | March 2, 1945 | FW-190 dest(air) | Zwickau | P-51 |
| | | FW-190 prob(air) | Zwickau | P-51 |

1-1-0 air
0-0 ground

**Pavlock, Quentin S., Lt.**
434th Ftr Sqn/479th Ftr Grp

| *Sqn* | *Date* | *Claims* | *Location* | *A/C* |
|---|---|---|---|---|
| 434th | July 27, 1944 | (.5)Ju-88 dam(grd)[*] | Romilly | P-38 |
| | August 15 | Me-109 dest(air) | Steenwijk A/F | P-38 |
| | September 26 | (2)Me-109 dest(air) | SW Munster | P-38 |
| | | FW-190 dest(air) | SW Munster | P-38 |

4-0-0 air
0-0.5 ground

[*] - shared with Lt. W.H. Rodgers of the 434th Ftr Sqn

**Payne, Arlon D., Capt.**
77th Ftr Sqn/20th Ftr Grp

| *Sqn* | *Date* | *Claims* | *Location* | *A/C* |
|---|---|---|---|---|
| 77th | July 7, 1944 | FW-190 dam(air) | Halle | P-38 |

0-0-1 air
0-0 ground

**Payne, Carl G., Capt.**
334th Ftr Sqn/4th Ftr Grp

| *Sqn* | *Date* | *Claims* | *Location* | *A/C* |
|---|---|---|---|---|
| 334th | November 18, 1944 | Me-262 dest(grd) | Leipheim | P-51 |
| | | Me-262 dam(grd) | Leipheim | P-51 |
| | January 2, 1945 | (.5)Me-109 dest(air)[*] | Westerburg | P-51 |
| | | (.5)Me-109 dest(air)[**] | Westerburg | P-51 |
| | February 25 | Me-262 dest(air) | SE Naumberg | P-51 |
| | | (.5)Me-410 dest(grd)[@] | Rohrensee | P-51 |
| | February 27 | (2)Me-108 dest(grd) | Weimar A/F | P-51 |

2-0-0 air
3.5-1 ground

[*] - shared with Lt. A.J. Senecal of the 334th Ftr Sqn
[**] - shared with Lt. V.R.T. Rentschler of the 334th Ftr Sqn
[@] - shared with Capt. T.R. Bell of the 334th Ftr Sqn

**Peacock, Cecil M., Lt.**
434th Ftr Sqn/479th Ftr Grp

| *Sqn* | *Date* | *Claims* | *Location* | *A/C* |
|---|---|---|---|---|
| 434th | April 17, 1945 | (2)FW-190 dest(grd) | Puchhoff | P-51 |

0-0-0 air
2-0 ground

**Peacock, Fred W., Lt.**
360th Ftr Sqn/356th Ftr Grp

| *Sqn* | *Date* | *Claims* | *Location* | *A/C* |
|---|---|---|---|---|
| 360th | September 1, 1944 | (.5)Ju-52 dest(grd)[*] | SE Nancy | P-47 |

0-0-0 air
0.5-0 ground

[*] - shared with Lt. C.M. Taylor of the 360th Ftr Sqn

**Peal, Charles M., Capt.**
83rd Ftr Sqn/78th Ftr Grp

| *Sqn* | *Date* | *Claims* | *Location* | *A/C* |
|---|---|---|---|---|
| 83rd | February 24, 1944 | Me-109 dest(air) | Furstenau | P-47 |
| | March 30 | Me-410 dam(grd) | N/Venlo | P-47 |
| | April 10 | (3)Bu-133 dest(grd) | Romorantin A/F | P-47 |
| | | Me-109 dest(grd) | Romorantin A/F | P-47 |
| | | Bu-133 dam(grd) | Romorantin A/F | P-47 |
| | April 13 | FW-190 dest(air) | Beuchenbeuren | P-47 |
| | August 10 | (2.5)Ju-52 dest(grd)[*] | Chateau Salines | P-47 |
| | | (1.5)He-111 dest(grd)[*] | Chateau Salines | P-47 |

2-0-0 air
8-2 ground

[*] - both shared with Lt. R.T. Green of the 83rd Ftr Sqn

**Pearson, Richard P., Lt.**
354th Ftr Sqn/355th Ftr Grp

| *Sqn* | *Date* | *Claims* | *Location* | *A/C* |
|---|---|---|---|---|
| 354th | April 9, 1945 | He-111 dam(grd) | Memmingen | P-51 |
| | April 13 | Me-109 dest(grd) | Husum | P-51 |

0-0-0 air
1-1 ground

**Pederson, Douglas P., Lt.**
336th Ftr Sqn/4th Ftr Grp

| *Sqn* | *Date* | *Claims* | *Location* | *A/C* |
|---|---|---|---|---|
| 336th | February 27, 1945 | u/i a/c dest(grd) | Weimar | P-51 |
| | April 16 | (5)Ju-52 dest(grd) | Praha | P-51 |
| | | (3)Ju-52 dam(grd) | Praha | P-51 |

0-0-0 air
6-3 ground

**Pedigo, John H., Lt.**
367th Ftr Sqn/358th Ftr Grp

| *Sqn* | *Date* | *Claims* | *Location* | *A/C* |
|---|---|---|---|---|
| 367th | January 30, 1944 | Me-109 dam(air) | E/Zwolle | P-47 |

0-0-1 air
0-0 ground

**Peel, Eugene L., Lt.**
82nd Ftr Sqn/78th Ftr Grp

| *Sqn* | *Date* | *Claims* | *Location* | *A/C* |
|---|---|---|---|---|
| 82nd | March 22, 1945 | (.5)Me-262 dest(air)[*] | Ulm | P-51 |
| | April 10 | u/i a/c dest(grd) | Werder A/F | P-51 |
| | | (2)u/i a/c dam(grd) | Werder A/F | P-51 |
| | April 16 | u/i a/c dest(grd) | Pilzen/Prague | P-51 |
| | | FW-190 dam(grd) | Pilzen/Prague | P-51 |
| | | u/i a/c dam(grd) | Pilzen/Prague | P-51 |

0.5-0-0 air
2-4 ground

[*] - shared with Lt. M.B. Stutzman of the 82nd Ftr Sqn

**Peet, George B., Capt.**
359th Ftr Sqn/356th Ftr Grp

| *Sqn* | *Date* | *Claims* | *Location* | *A/C* |
|---|---|---|---|---|
| 359th | November 29, 1943 | Me-109 dam(air) | NE Meppel | P-47 |
| | February 11, 1944 | (.5)Me-109 dest(air)[*] | NW Charleville | P-47 |
| | March 18 | (.25)Do-217 dam(grd)[**] | W/Nancy | P-47 |
| | July 29 | He-111 dam(grd) | St. Andre de L'Eure | P-47 |
| | August 4 | Me-109 dest(air) | NE Bremen | P-47 |

1.5-0-1 air
0-1.25 ground

[*] - shared with LtCol. O.H. Coen of HdQts, 356th Ftr Grp
[**] - shared with Maj. D.A. Baccus, Lt. R.K. Holtz, and Lt. W.C. O'Barr of the 359th Ftr Sqn

**Pelon, Paul A., Jr., Lt.**
362nd Ftr Sqn/357th Ftr Grp

| *Sqn* | *Date* | *Claims* | *Location* | *A/C* |
|---|---|---|---|---|
| 362nd | December 24, 1944 | (2)FW-190 dest(air) | Fulda | P-51 |

2-0-0 air
0-0 ground

**Penn, Donald E., Maj.**
38th Ftr Sqn/55th Ftr Grp

| *Sqn* | *Date* | *Claims* | *Location* | *A/C* |
|---|---|---|---|---|
| 38th | April 15, 1944 | Ju-88 dest(grd) | Osnabruck | P-38 |
| | May 21 | Hs-129 dest(air) | Brunswick | P-38 |
| | June 14 | Me-109 dam(air) | S/Paris | P-38 |
| | December 24 | (2)Me-109 dam(air) | W/St. Vith | P-51 |
| | February 25, 1945 | Me-262 dest(air) | Giebelstadt A/F | P-51 |

2-0-3 air
1-0 ground

**Penny, Donald E., Lt.**
504th Ftr Sqn/339th Ftr Grp

| Sqn | Date | Claims | Location | A/C |
|---|---|---|---|---|
| 504th | August 6, 1944 | Me-109 dest(air) | Havelburg | P-51 |
| | November 2 | Me-109 dest(air) | Naumberg | P-51 |

2-0-0 air
0-0 ground

**Penrose, Richard C., Capt.**
504th Ftr Sqn/339th Ftr Grp

| Sqn | Date | Claims | Location | A/C |
|---|---|---|---|---|
| 504th | August 16, 1944 | Me-109 dest(air) | Mulhausen | P-51 |

1-0-0 air
0-0 ground

**Perez, William R., Jr., Lt.**
343rd Ftr Sqn/55th Ftr Grp

| Sqn | Date | Claims | Location | A/C |
|---|---|---|---|---|
| 343rd | September 5, 1944 | Trainer dest(air) | Goppingen A/F | P-51 |

1-0-0 air
0-0 ground

**Perkins, Donald D., Capt.**
335th Ftr Sqn/4th Ftr Grp

| Sqn | Date | Claims | Location | A/C |
|---|---|---|---|---|
| 335th | August 18, 1944 | Me-109 dest(air) | Beaumont-Sur-Oise | P-51 |

1-0-0 air
0-0 ground

**Perpente, George F., Lt.**
351st Ftr Sqn/353rd Ftr Grp

| Sqn | Date | Claims | Location | A/C |
|---|---|---|---|---|
| 351st | October 14, 1943 | Me-109 dam(air) | Turnhout | P-47 |
| | February 22, 1944 | (.25)FW-190 dam(grd)* | NE Bonn | P-47 |
| | | (.25)FW-190 dam(grd)* | NE Bonn | P-47 |

0-0-1 air
0-0.5 ground

* - both shared with Maj. W.C. Beckham, Lt. G.B. Compton, and Lt. F.N. Emory of the 351st Ftr Sqn

**Perrin, Grant M., Capt.**
369th Ftr Sqn/359th Ftr Grp

| Sqn | Date | Claims | Location | A/C |
|---|---|---|---|---|
| 369th | June 20, 1944 | (.5)Me-410 dest(air)* | NW Putbus | P-51 |
| | September 11 | (2)FW-190 dest(air) | Kolleda | P-51 |
| | | Me-109 prob(air) | Kolleda | P-51 |

2.5-1-0 air
0-0 ground

* - shared with Lt. H.C. Burton of the 369th Ftr Sqn

**Perrin, John P., Capt.**
361st Ftr Sqn/356th Ftr Grp

| Sqn | Date | Claims | Location | A/C |
|---|---|---|---|---|
| 361st | February 10, 1944 | FW-190 dest(air) | NE Lingen | P-47 |
| | | FW-190 dam(air) | NE Lingen | P-47 |
| | February 11 | FW-190 dam(air) | Charleville | P-47 |
| | April 23 | He-111 dam(grd) | Hagenau | P-47 |
| | May 4 | FW-190 dest(air) | Steinhuder Lake | P-47 |

2-0-2 air
0-1 ground

**Perron, Davis T., Capt.**
362nd Ftr Sqn/357th Ftr Grp

| Sqn | Date | Claims | Location | A/C |
|---|---|---|---|---|
| 362nd | March 6, 1944 | (2)FW-190 dest(air) | SW Berlin | P-51 |
| | | Me-210 dest(air) | SW Berlin | P-51 |

3-0-0 air
0-0 ground

**Perry, Alfred O., Lt.**
62nd Ftr Sqn/56th Ftr Grp

| Sqn | Date | Claims | Location | A/C |
|---|---|---|---|---|
| 62nd | December 23, 1944 | (2)FW-190 dest(air) | Bonn-Coblenz | P-47 |
| | December 26 | (2)FW-190 dest(air) | Coblenz | P-47 |
| | | FW-190 dam(air) | Coblenz | P-47 |

4-0-1 air
0-0 ground

**Perry, Emil F., Lt.**
354th Ftr Sqn/355th Ftr Grp

| Sqn | Date | Claims | Location | A/C |
|---|---|---|---|---|
| 354th | May 13, 1944 | FW-190 dest(air) | NE Bremen | P-51 |
| | | FW-190 prob(air) | NE Bremen | P-51 |
| | | FW-190 dam(air) | NE Bremen | P-51 |
| | May 24 | FW-190 dest(grd) | Cormeilles-en-Vixen | P-51 |
| | | FW-190 dam(grd) | Cormeilles-en-Vixen | P-51 |
| | June 24 | (2)Me-109 dest(grd) | Seiches | P-51 |
| | July 7 | Me-410 dest(air) | Lingen | P-51 |

2-1-1 air
3-1 ground

**Perry, Gordon F., Lt.**
505th Ftr Sqn/339th Ftr Grp

| Sqn | Date | Claims | Location | A/C |
|---|---|---|---|---|
| 505th | May 21, 1944 | (.5)Do-217 dest(air)* | Riessa | P-51 |

0.5-0-0 air
0-0 ground

* - shared with Lt. J.L. Lynch of the 505th Ftr Sqn

**Perry, Joseph H., Capt.**
61st Ftr Sqn/56th Ftr Grp

| Sqn | Date | Claims | Location | A/C |
|---|---|---|---|---|
| 61st | May 8, 1944 | FW-190 prob(air) | W/Celle | P-47 |
| | December 23 | (2)FW-190 dest(air) | Coblenz | P-47 |

2-1-0 air
0-0 ground

**Perry, Walter N., Jr., Capt.**
362nd Ftr Sqn/357th Ftr Grp

| Sqn | Date | Claims | Location | A/C |
|---|---|---|---|---|
| 362nd | August 18, 1944 | (.5)Me-109 dest(air)* | NE Paris | P-51 |
| | September 18 | Me-109 dest(air) | Nijmegen | P-51 |
| | September 19 | Me-109 dest(air) | Ijsselstein | P-51 |
| | October 6 | FW-190 dam(air) | NW Berlin | P-51 |

2.5-0-1 air
0-0 ground

* - shared with Capt. J.B. England of the 362nd Ftr Sqn

**Perryman, Allen A., Jr., Lt.**
360th Ftr Sqn/356th Ftr Grp

| Sqn | Date | Claims | Location | A/C |
|---|---|---|---|---|
| 360th | May 13, 1944 | FW-190 dam(air) | Kiel | P-47 |
| | May 19 | FW-190 dest(air) | SW Celle | P-47 |

1-0-1 air
0-0 ground

**Pesanka, John, Lt.**
505th Ftr Sqn/339th Ftr Grp

| Sqn | Date | Claims | Location | A/C |
|---|---|---|---|---|
| 505th | March 12, 1945 | Me-109 dest(air) | Hellevad | P-51 |

| Sqn | Date | Claims | Location | A/C |
|---|---|---|---|---|
| | April 16 | u/i a/c dest(grd) | NE Prague | P-51 |
| | April 17 | Me-109 dest(grd) | SE Pocking | P-51 |
| | | He-111 dest(grd) | SE Pocking | P-51 |

1-0-0 air
3-0 ground

**Peter, Lewis S., Jr., Maj.**
504th Ftr Sqn/339th Ftr Grp

| *Sqn* | *Date* | *Claims* | *Location* | *A/C* |
|---|---|---|---|---|
| 504th | May 30, 1944 | FW-190 prob(air) | Magdeburg | P-51 |
| | June 7 | FW-190 dest(air) | Laval | P-51 |

1-1-0 air
0-0 ground

**Peterburs, Joseph A., Lt.**
55th Ftr Sqn/20th Ftr Grp

| *Sqn* | *Date* | *Claims* | *Location* | *A/C* |
|---|---|---|---|---|
| 55th | April 10, 1945 | (5)u/i a/c dest(grd) | Berlin | P-51 |

0-0-0 air
5-0 ground

**Peters, Charles K., Capt.**
363rd Ftr Sqn/357th Ftr Grp

| *Sqn* | *Date* | *Claims* | *Location* | *A/C* |
|---|---|---|---|---|
| 363rd | March 5, 1944 | (.33)FW-190 dest(air)* | S/Bordeaux | P-51 |
| | April 11 | Me-109 dest(air) | Magdeburg | P-51 |
| | May 19 | Me-109 dest(air) | NW Brandenburg | P-51 |
| | | Me-109 dam(air) | NW Brandenburg | P-51 |
| | May 28 | Me-109 dest(air) | N/Magdeburg | P-51 |

3.33-0-1 air
0-0 ground

* - shared with Lt. D.H. Bochkay and Lt. E.A. Rogers of the 363rd Ftr Sqn

**Peters, Donald V., Lt.**
63rd Ftr Sqn/56th Ftr Grp

| *Sqn* | *Date* | *Claims* | *Location* | *A/C* |
|---|---|---|---|---|
| 63rd | March 6, 1944 | (.25)Me-109 dest(air)* | Minden-Osnabruck | P-47 |
| | March 15 | Me-109 dest(air) | Hanover | P-47 |
| | April 24 | Me-109 dest(grd) | Thalheim | P-47 |
| | | Me-210 dest(grd) | Thalheim | P-47 |
| | | (2)Me-109 dam(grd) | Thalheim | P-47 |
| | May 31 | FW-190 dest(air) | NW Kassel | P-47 |

2.25-0-0 air
2-2 ground

* - shared with Col. H. Zemke of HdQts, 56th Ftr Grp, and Lt. M.H. Becker and Lt. C.W. Reed of the 63rd Ftr Sqn

**Peters, John N., Lt.**
335th Ftr Sqn/4th Ftr Grp

| *Sqn* | *Date* | *Claims* | *Location* | *A/C* |
|---|---|---|---|---|
| 335th | September 11, 1944 | Me-109 prob(air) | NW Naumberg | P-51 |

0-1-0 air
0-0 ground

**Peters, Robert O., Lt.**
358th Ftr Sqn/355th Ftr Grp

| *Sqn* | *Date* | *Claims* | *Location* | *A/C* |
|---|---|---|---|---|
| 358th | July 20, 1944 | (2)FW-190 dest(air) | E/Leipzig | P-51 |
| | | Do-217 dest(air) | E/Leipzig | P-51 |
| | | He-111 dest(grd) | E/Leipzig | P-51 |
| | | Ju-88 dest(grd) | E/Leipzig | P-51 |

3-0-0 air
2-0 ground

**Peterson, Arman, Col.**
HdQts/78th Ftr Grp

| *Sqn* | *Date* | *Claims* | *Location* | *A/C* |
|---|---|---|---|---|
| HdQts | May 14, 1943 | FW-190 dam(air) | E/Flushing | P-47 |
| | May 16 | FW-190 dam(air) | E/Flushing | P-47 |
| | June 22 | FW-190 dest(air) | N/Walcheren Island | P-47 |

1-0-2 air
0-0 ground

**Peterson, Carl L., Lt.**
434th Ftr Sqn/479th Ftr Grp

| *Sqn* | *Date* | *Claims* | *Location* | *A/C* |
|---|---|---|---|---|
| 434th | August 18, 1944 | Ju-52 dest(grd) | Nancy/Essey A/F | P-38 |

0-0-0 air
1-0 ground

**Peterson, Chesley G., Col.**
HdQts/4th Ftr Grp
Earlier flew with 71 Sqn, RAF and claimed 6 kills: Me-109's on September 7 & 18, 1941; (2)FW-190 on April 27, 1942; FW-190 on June 1, 1942; Ju-88 on August 19, 1942.

| *Sqn* | *Date* | *Claims* | *Location* | *A/C* |
|---|---|---|---|---|
| HdQts | April 15, 1943 | FW-190 dest(air) | W/Ostend | P-47 |
| | May 14 | FW-190 prob(air) | W/St. Nicholas | P-47 |
| | | FW-190 dam(air) | W/St. Nicholas | P-47 |

1-1-1 air
0-0 ground

**Peterson, Clayton L., Maj.**
38th Ftr Sqn/55th Ftr Grp

| *Sqn* | *Date* | *Claims* | *Location* | *A/C* |
|---|---|---|---|---|
| 38th | September 12, 1944 | (.5)He-177 dam(grd)* | Herzogenaurach | P-51 |
| | April 16, 1945 | u/i a/c dam(grd) | Munich-Brunnthal | P-51 |

0-0-0 air
0-1.5 ground

* - shared with Lt. J.W. Silk of the 38th Ftr Sqn

**Peterson, James S., Lt.**
83rd Ftr Sqn/78th Ftr Grp

| *Sqn* | *Date* | *Claims* | *Location* | *A/C* |
|---|---|---|---|---|
| 83rd | April 10, 1945 | FW-190 dest(grd) | Hustedt A/F | P-51 |

0-0-0 air
1-0 ground

**Peterson, Kenneth D., Capt.**
336th Ftr Sqn/4th Ftr Grp

| *Sqn* | *Date* | *Claims* | *Location* | *A/C* |
|---|---|---|---|---|
| 336th | January 21, 1944 | FW-190 dam(air) | Douai | P-47 |
| | March 5 | FW-200 dest(air) | Bordeaux | P-51 |
| | | FW-200 dest(grd) | Bordeaux | P-51 |
| | March 29 | (2)FW-190 dest(air) | SW Brunswick | P-51 |

3-0-1 air
1-0 ground

**Peterson, Noble E., Capt.**
358th Ftr Sqn/355th Ftr Grp

| *Sqn* | *Date* | *Claims* | *Location* | *A/C* |
|---|---|---|---|---|
| 358th | April 5, 1944 | Ju-88 dest(grd) | Munich | P-51 |
| | | (3)Ju-88 dam(grd) | Munich | P-51 |
| | July 20 | Me-109 dest(air) | Dresden | P-51 |
| | | Me-109 dam(air) | Dresden | P-51 |
| | July 24 | Ju-88 dest(grd) | Augsburg | P-51 |

1-0-1 air
2-3 ground

**Peterson, Richard A., Maj.**
364th Ftr Sqn/357th Ftr Grp

| *Sqn* | *Date* | *Claims* | *Location* | *A/C* |
|---|---|---|---|---|
| 364th | March 5, 1944 | FW-190 dest(air) | Bordeaux | P-51 |
| | March 8 | FW-190 dam(air) | Berlin | P-51 |
| | March 16 | (.5)Me-110 dest(air)* | Ulm | P-51 |

| Sqn | Date | Claims | Location | A/C |
|---|---|---|---|---|
| | March 18 | Me-109 dest(air) | Augsburg | P-51 |
| | March 23 | Me-109 prob(air) | E/Brunswick | P-51 |
| | April 11 | Me-109 dest(air) | Magdeburg | P-51 |
| | April 24 | Me-109 dest(air) | Munich | P-51 |
| | April 30 | (2)FW-190 dest(air) | Auxerre | P-51 |
| | May 12 | (.5)FW-190 dest(air)[**] | NE Frankfurt | P-51 |
| | | FW-190 dam(air) | NE Frankfurt | P-51 |
| | May 13 | (1.5)Me-410 dest(air)[@] | E/Grunberg | P-51 |
| | May 24 | (.5)u/i a/c dest(grd)[@@] | St. Lagar | P-51 |
| | May 28 | Me-109 dest(air) | NW Magdeburg | P-51 |
| | July 1 | (2)Me-109 dest(air) | E/St. Quentin | P-51 |
| | October 6 | FW-190 dest(air) | W/Berlin | P-51 |
| | October 7 | Me-109 dest(air) | Jena | P-51 |
| | November 2 | FW-190 dest(air) | NW Merseburg | P-51 |
| | November 18 | Me-109 dest(air) | Neuhausen A/F | P-51 |
| | January 5, 1945 | (2)Ju-88 dest(grd) | Altenstadt A/F | P-51 |
| | | Me-109 dest(grd) | Altenstadt A/F | P-51 |

15.5-1-2 air
3.5-0 ground

[*] - shared with Capt. G.V. Davis of the 364th Ftr Sqn
[**] - shared with Capt. J.A. Storch of the 364th Ftr Sqn
[@] - shared with Lt. J.G. Sullivan of the 364th Ftr Sqn
[@@] - shared with Lt. N.J. Frederick of the 364th Ftr Sqn

**Petitt, Philip E., Capt.**
503rd Ftr Sqn/339th Ftr Grp

| Sqn | Date | Claims | Location | A/C |
|---|---|---|---|---|
| 503rd | November 26, 1944 | FW-190 dest(air) | SE Dummer Lake | P-51 |
| | April 7, 1945 | FW-190 dest(air) | Celle | P-51 |
| | | Me-262 dam(air) | Celle | P-51 |

2-0-1 air
0-0 ground

**Petterson, Lewis L., Lt.**
435th Ftr Sqn/479th Ftr Grp

| Sqn | Date | Claims | Location | A/C |
|---|---|---|---|---|
| 435th | November 27, 1944 | FW-190 dest(air) | NE Dummer Lake | P-51 |

1-0-0 air
0-0 ground

**Petticrew, Stanley S., Jr., Lt.**
505th Ftr Sqn/339th Ftr Grp
351st Ftr Sqn/353rd Ftr Grp

| Sqn | Date | Claims | Location | A/C |
|---|---|---|---|---|
| 351st | April 16, 1945 | Ju-88 dest(grd) | Reichersberg | P-51 |
| | | Me-109 dam(grd) | Reichersberg | P-51 |

0-0-0 air
1-1 ground

**Pettit, Kenneth L., Lt.**
55th Ftr Sqn/20th Ftr Grp

| Sqn | Date | Claims | Location | A/C |
|---|---|---|---|---|
| 55th | February 25, 1945 | Me-109 dest(air) | Dummer Lake | P-51 |

1-0-0 air
0-0 ground

**Petty, Raymond D., Lt.**
63rd Ftr Sqn/56th Ftr Grp

| Sqn | Date | Claims | Location | A/C |
|---|---|---|---|---|
| 63rd | November 26, 1943 | Me-110 dam(air) | Friesoythe | P-47 |

0-0-1 air
0-0 ground

**Pezda, Edwin F., Maj.**
369th Ftr Sqn/359th Ftr Grp
HdQts/359th Ftr Grp

| Sqn | Date | Claims | Location | A/C |
|---|---|---|---|---|
| 369th | August 5, 1944 | Me-109 dest(air) | Tarmstadt | P-51 |
| | August 18 | (2)Ju-88 dam(grd) | St. Dizier | P-51 |
| | February 21, 1945 | FW-200 dest(grd) | Schweinfurt | P-51 |

1-0-0 air
1-2 ground

**Phaneuf, Richard E., Lt.**
83rd Ftr Sqn/78th Ftr Grp

| Sqn | Date | Claims | Location | A/C |
|---|---|---|---|---|
| 83rd | April 10, 1945 | He-111 dest(grd) | Gardelegen | P-51 |
| | April 16 | (2)Ju-87 dest(grd) | N/Prague | P-51 |
| | | FW-190 dest(grd) | N/Prague | P-51 |
| | | Ju-52 dest(grd) | N/Prague | P-51 |
| | | (2)Ju-87 dam(grd) | N/Prague | P-51 |
| | | Me-109 dam(grd) | N/Prague | P-51 |
| | | He-111 dam(grd) | N/Prague | P-51 |

0-0-0 air
5-4 ground

**Pherson, Robert L., Capt.**
369th Ftr Sqn/359th Ftr Grp

| Sqn | Date | Claims | Location | A/C |
|---|---|---|---|---|
| 369th | January 30, 1944 | Ju-88 dam(air) | N/Lingen | P-47 |
| | March 6 | Me-109 dest(air) | Vechta | P-47 |
| | March 27 | Me-109 dest(air) | Gallardson | P-47 |

2-0-1 air
0-0 ground

**Philbrick, Charles H., Lt.**
436th Ftr Sqn/479th Ftr Grp

| Sqn | Date | Claims | Location | A/C |
|---|---|---|---|---|
| 436th | April 13, 1945 | Me-109 dest(grd) | Salzwedel | P-51 |
| | | FW-190 dest(grd) | Salzwedel | P-51 |
| | | (3)Me-109 dam(grd) | Salzwedel | P-51 |
| | | u/i a/c dam(grd) | Salzwedel | P-51 |
| | April 16 | Me-109 dest(grd) | Landstadt | P-51 |

0-0-0 air
3-4 ground

**Phillippi, William R., Lt.**
505th Ftr Sqn/339th Ftr Grp

| Sqn | Date | Claims | Location | A/C |
|---|---|---|---|---|
| 505th | November 26, 1944 | (1.5)FW-190 dest(air)[*] | S/Hanover | P-51 |
| | April 10, 1945 | (2)Ju-88 dest(grd) | N/Neuruppin | P-51 |

1.5-0-0 air
2-0 ground

[*] - shared with Lt. P.M. Loveless of the 505th Ftr Sqn

**Phillips, Baxter M., Lt.**
77th Ftr Sqn/20th Ftr Grp

| Sqn | Date | Claims | Location | A/C |
|---|---|---|---|---|
| 77th | April 13, 1945 | (.5)Me-110 dam(grd)[*] | E/Hamburg | P-51 |

0-0-0 air
0-0.5 ground

[*] - shared with Lt. H.J. Piatkiewicz of the 77th Ftr Sqn

**Phillips, Raymond G., Lt.**
328th Ftr Sqn/352nd Ftr Grp

| Sqn | Date | Claims | Location | A/C |
|---|---|---|---|---|
| 328th | February 20, 1944 | Me-110 dest(air) | Blankenheim | P-47 |
| | | Me-110 dam(air) | Blankenheim | P-47 |
| | | FW-190 dam(air) | Blankenheim | P-47 |
| | May 8 | Me-109 dest(air) | SE Nienburg | P-51 |
| | May 21 | FW-190 dest(grd) | Alt Ruppin | P-51 |
| | | Ju-52 dest(grd) | Alt Ruppin | P-51 |
| | | u/i a/c dest(grd) | Alt Ruppin | P-51 |
| | May 28 | Me-109 dam(air) | W/Magdeburg | P-51 |

2-0-3 air
3-0 ground

**Phillips, Samuel C., Maj.**
384th Ftr Sqn/364th Ftr Grp
385th Ftr Sqn/364th Ftr Grp
HdQts/364th Ftr Grp

| *Sqn* | *Date* | *Claims* | *Location* | *A/C* |
|---|---|---|---|---|
| 384th | March 6, 1944 | Me-109 dam(air) | W/Hanover | P-38 |
| | May 21 | He-111 dest(grd) | Parchim-Hagenau | P-38 |
| | | Ju-88 dam(grd) | Parchim-Hagenau | P-38 |
| | February 22, 1945 | Me-262 dam(air) | Stendal | P-51 |

0-0-2 air
1-1 ground

**Phipps, Laurel A., Capt.**
384th Ftr Sqn/364th Ftr Grp

| *Sqn* | *Date* | *Claims* | *Location* | *A/C* |
|---|---|---|---|---|
| 384th | February 22, 1945 | Me-262 dam(air) | Stendal | P-51 |

0-0-1 air
0-0 ground

**Piatkiewicz, Henry J., Lt.**
77th Ftr Sqn/20th Ftr Grp

| *Sqn* | *Date* | *Claims* | *Location* | *A/C* |
|---|---|---|---|---|
| 77th | February 20, 1945 | FW-44 dest(air) | Straubing | P-51 |
| | | (2)Me-110 dam(grd) | Straubing | P-51 |
| | April 13 | (.5)Me-110 dam(grd)* | E/Hamburg | P-51 |

1-0-0 air
0-2.5 ground

* - shared with Lt. B.M. Phillips of the 77th Ftr Sqn

**Pick, Douglas J., Maj.**
384th Ftr Sqn/364th Ftr Grp

| *Sqn* | *Date* | *Claims* | *Location* | *A/C* |
|---|---|---|---|---|
| 384th | April 15, 1944 | (.33)BV-138 dest(grd)* | Elbe Estuary | P-38 |
| | April 29 | FW-190 dam(air) | N/Brunswick | P-38 |
| | August 10 | Me-109 dest(air) | SW Paris | P-51 |
| | February 23, 1945 | (2.5)Me-109 dest(air)** | Stuttgart | P-51 |
| | | Me-109 dam(grd) | Stuttgart | P-51 |
| | April 10 | (.5)Me-262 dest(air)@ | Staaken A/F | P-51 |

4-0-1 air
0.33-1 ground

* - shared with Capt. R.E. Lacy and Capt. C.W. Stapleton of the 384thFtr Sqn
** - shared with F/O J.F. Nelson of the 384th Ftr Sqn
@ - shared with Lt. H.C. Schwartz of the 384th Ftr Sqn

**Pickering, Malcolm C., Lt.**
487th Ftr Sqn/352nd Ftr Grp

| *Sqn* | *Date* | *Claims* | *Location* | *A/C* |
|---|---|---|---|---|
| 487th | April 28, 1944 | Ju-88 dest(grd) | Bourges | P-51 |
| | | He-111 dam(grd) | Bourges | P-51 |
| | May 8 | FW-190 dest(air) | Nienburg | P-51 |
| | May 30 | FW-190 dest(air) | Halberstadt | P-51 |
| | June 29 | He-111 dest(grd) | Burg A/F | P-51 |
| | | Me-110 dam(grd) | Burg A/F | P-51 |
| | July 21 | Me-109 dest(air) | E/Munich | P-51 |
| | August 16 | FW-190 dest(air) | Plauen | P-51 |
| | September 10 | (2)u/i a/c dest(grd) | Wertheim | P-51 |

4-0-0 air
4-2 ground

**Pickering, William H., Lt.**
435th Ftr Sqn/479th Ftr Grp

| *Sqn* | *Date* | *Claims* | *Location* | *A/C* |
|---|---|---|---|---|
| 435th | September 26, 1944 | (2)Me-109 dest(air) | SW Munster | P-51 |

2-0-0 air
0-0 ground

**Pidduck, Stanley R., Maj.**
350th Ftr Sqn/353rd Ftr Grp

| *Sqn* | *Date* | *Claims* | *Location* | *A/C* |
|---|---|---|---|---|
| 350th | April 8, 1944 | Me-109 dam(grd) | Hoperhofen | P-47 |

0-0-0 air
0-1 ground

**Pierce, Donald J., Capt.**
336th Ftr Sqn/ 4th Ftr Grp
434th Ftr Sqn/479th Ftr Grp

| *Sqn* | *Date* | *Claims* | *Location* | *A/C* |
|---|---|---|---|---|
| 434th | February 14, 1945 | (2)Me-109 dam(air) | SW Berlin | P-51 |
| | February 20 | (.5)He-111 dest(grd)* | Windleschenlaibach | P-51 |
| | | (.5)He-111 dam(grd)* | Windleschenlaibach | P-51 |
| | April 13 | Ar-234 dest(grd) | Lubeck | P-51 |
| | | Ju-88 dam(grd) | Kaltenkirchen | P-51 |
| | April 16 | (2)Me-109 dest(grd) | Kirchen & Reichersberg | P-51 |
| | | FW-190 dest(grd) | Reichersberg | P-51 |
| | | Ju-88 dest(grd) | Reichersberg | P-51 |
| | | (2)Me-109 dam(grd) | Reichersberg | P-51 |
| | April 17 | (2)FW-190 dest(grd) | Puchhoff | P-51 |
| | | Me-109 dest(grd) | Landau | P-51 |
| | | Me-109 dam(grd) | Landau | P-51 |
| | | u/i a/c dam(grd) | Landau | P-51 |

0-0-2 air
8.5-5.5 ground

* - both shared with Lt. P.A. Brown of the 434th Ftr Sqn

**Pierce, Jack W., Lt.**
62nd Ftr Sqn/56th Ftr Grp

| *Sqn* | *Date* | *Claims* | *Location* | *A/C* |
|---|---|---|---|---|
| 62nd | June 7, 1944 | (.5)Ju-88 dest(air)* | St. Andre de L'Eure | P-47 |
| | July 5 | FW-190 dest(air) | N/Evreux | P-47 |
| | September 5 | FW-190 dest(grd) | Gelnhausen | P-47 |
| | | FW-190 dam(grd) | Gelnhausen | P-47 |
| | September 10 | He-111 dest(grd) | Seligenstadt A/F | P-47 |

1.5-0-0 air
2-1 ground

* - shared with Lt. M.L. Moseley of the 62nd Ftr Sqn

**Pierce, Joseph F., Capt.**
363rd Ftr Sqn/357th Ftr Grp

| *Sqn* | *Date* | *Claims* | *Location* | *A/C* |
|---|---|---|---|---|
| 363rd | March 6, 1944 | Me-110 dest(air) | W/Berlin | P-51 |
| | April 24 | Me-109 dest(air) | W/Munich | P-51 |
| | | Ju-88 dest(air) | W/Munich | P-51 |
| | April 29 | Me-109 dam(air) | Berlin | P-51 |
| | April 30 | (2)FW-190 dest(air) | NE Orleans | P-51 |
| | May 8 | FW-190 dest(air) | Soltau | P-51 |
| | May 12 | Me-109 dest(air) | NE Frankfurt | P-51 |
| | | Me-109 dest(grd) | NE Frankfurt | P-51 |

7-0-1 air
1-0 ground

**Pierce, Leonard R., Lt.**
334th Ftr Sqn/4th Ftr Grp

| *Sqn* | *Date* | *Claims* | *Location* | *A/C* |
|---|---|---|---|---|
| 334th | March 21, 1944 | Me-110 dam(grd) | Langon | P-51 |
| | March 23 | Me-109 dest(air) | Munster-Hamm | P-51 |
| | April 5 | Ju-88 dest(grd) | Brandenburg-Briest | P-51 |
| | | (.33)He-111 dest(grd)* | Brandenburg-Briest | P-51 |
| | April 24 | FW-190 dam(air) | N/Frankfurt | P-51 |
| | May 12 | (.5)Me-109 dest(air)** | N/Coburg | P-51 |

1.5-0-1 air
1.33-1 ground

* - shared with Lt. H.J. Blanchfield and Lt. V.J. France of the 334th 334th Ftr Sqn
** - shared with Lt. R.K. Hofer of the 334th Ftr Sqn

**Pierni, Donald J., Capt.**
336th Ftr Sqn/4th Ftr Grp

| *Sqn* | *Date* | *Claims* | *Location* | *A/C* |
|---|---|---|---|---|
| 336th | September 11, 1944 | (2)FW-190 dest(grd) | Langensalza A/F | P-51 |
| | November 18 | Me-262 dam(grd) | Leipheim | P-51 |
| | January 1, 1945 | Me-109 dest(air) | Ulzen | P-51 |

1-0-0 air
2-1 ground

**Pigg, Robert S., Lt.**
435th Ftr Sqn/479th Ftr Grp

| *Sqn* | *Date* | *Claims* | *Location* | *A/C* |
|---|---|---|---|---|
| 435th | August 18, 1944 | He-111 dest(grd) | Nancy/Essey A/F | P-38 |
| | | Ju-88 dest(grd) | Nancy/Essey A/F | P-38 |
| | | (4)He-111 dam(grd) | Nancy/Essey A/F | P-38 |
| | | Ju-88 dam(grd) | Nancy/Essey A/F | P-38 |

0-0-0 air
2-5 ground

**Pissanos, Spiros N., Lt.**
334th Ftr Sqn/4th Ftr Grp

| *Sqn* | *Date* | *Claims* | *Location* | *A/C* |
|---|---|---|---|---|
| 334th | May 21, 1943 | FW-190 dam(air) | Ghent | P-47 |
| | August 12 | Me-109 dest(air) | W/Walcheren | P-47 |
| | January 29, 1944 | (2)Me-109 dest(air) | Aachen | P-47 |
| | March 5 | (2)Me-109 dest(air) | Bordeaux | P-51 |

5-0-1 air
0-0 ground

**Pitts, Walter H., Lt.**
63rd Ftr Sqn/56th Ftr Grp

| *Sqn* | *Date* | *Claims* | *Location* | *A/C* |
|---|---|---|---|---|
| 63rd | September 21, 1944 | (2)FW-190 dest(air) | NE Arnheim | P-47 |

2-0-0 air
0-0 ground

**Pitz, Edwin R., Lt.**
77th Ftr Sqn/20th Ftr Grp

| *Sqn* | *Date* | *Claims* | *Location* | *A/C* |
|---|---|---|---|---|
| 77th | February 9, 1945 | (2)FW-190 dest(grd) | Esperstadt A/F | P-51 |
| | | Me-110 dam(grd) | Esperstadt A/F | P-51 |

0-0-0 air
2-1 ground

**Planchak, Eugene, Jr., Lt.**
55th Ftr Sqn/20th Ftr Grp

| *Sqn* | *Date* | *Claims* | *Location* | *A/C* |
|---|---|---|---|---|
| 55th | December 2, 1944 | (2)Me-109 dest(air) | Coblenz-St. Goar | P-51 |

2-0-0 air
0-0 ground

**Pleasant, Edward W., Capt.**
360th Ftr Sqn/356th Ftr Grp

| *Sqn* | *Date* | *Claims* | *Location* | *A/C* |
|---|---|---|---|---|
| 360th | September 1, 1944 | Ju-52 dest(grd) | SE Nancy | P-47 |
| | September 13 | Me-410 dam(grd) | NW Stuttgart | P-47 |
| | December 25 | FW-190 dest(air) | Bonn | P-51 |
| | | FW-190 dam(air) | Bonn | P-51 |

1-0-1 air
1-1 ground

**Plemmons, Charles E., Lt.**
358th Ftr Sqn/355th Ftr Grp

| *Sqn* | *Date* | *Claims* | *Location* | *A/C* |
|---|---|---|---|---|
| 358th | April 9, 1945 | He-111 dam(grd) | Heilfingen | P-51 |
| | April 16 | FW-190 dest(grd) | Straubing | P-51 |
| | | Me-110 dest(grd) | Straubing | P-51 |

0-0-0 air
2-1 ground

**Pletz, Leroy O., Lt.**
352nd Ftr Sqn/353rd Ftr Grp

| *Sqn* | *Date* | *Claims* | *Location* | *A/C* |
|---|---|---|---|---|
| 352nd | February 23, 1945 | He-111 dest(grd) | Kitzingen | P-51 |
| | | (.5)Me-110 dest(grd)* | Kitzingen | P-51 |
| | April 16 | He-111 dest(grd) | Bad Aibling | P-51 |
| | | (2)He-111 dam(grd) | Bad Aibling | P-51 |
| | April 17 | Me-109 dam(grd) | Ganacker | P-51 |

0-0-0 air
2.5-3 ground

* - shared with Lt. J.R. Evans of the 352nd Ftr Sqn

**Plezibat, John A., Lt.**
434th Ftr Sqn/479th Ftr Grp

| *Sqn* | *Date* | *Claims* | *Location* | *A/C* |
|---|---|---|---|---|
| 434th | April 16, 1945 | FW-190 dest(grd) | Reichersberg | P-51 |

0-0-0 air
1-0 ground

**Plunk, Henry P., Lt.**
436th Ftr Sqn/479th Ftr Grp

| *Sqn* | *Date* | *Claims* | *Location* | *A/C* |
|---|---|---|---|---|
| 436th | July 24, 1944 | (.5)Me-109 dest(air)* | Evreux | P-38 |

0.5-0-0 air
0-0 ground

* - shared with Lt. H.J. Grasshoff of the 436th Ftr Sqn

**Poage, Charles E., Jr., Lt.**
335th Ftr Sqn/4th Ftr Grp

| *Sqn* | *Date* | *Claims* | *Location* | *A/C* |
|---|---|---|---|---|
| 335th | September 13, 1944 | (3)Hs-123 dest(grd) | Gelcheim | P-51 |
| | December 25 | (2)FW-190 prob(air) | SE Duren | P-51 |

0-2-0 air
3-0 ground

**Pogue, Edward F., Lt.**
79th Ftr Sqn/20th Ftr Grp

| *Sqn* | *Date* | *Claims* | *Location* | *A/C* |
|---|---|---|---|---|
| 79th | February 20, 1945 | (2)He-111 dest(grd) | Weiden A/F | P-51 |
| | April 10 | (3)He-111 dest(grd) | Werder A/F | P-51 |
| | | Me-109 dest(grd) | Werder A/F | P-51 |
| | | He-111 dam(grd) | Werder A/F | P-51 |
| | | Me-109 dam(grd) | Werder A/F | P-51 |
| | April 13 | Me-109 dam(grd) | Jagel-Hutzfeld | P-51 |
| | | He-177 dam(grd) | Jagel-Hutzfeld | P-51 |

0-0-0 air
6-4 ground

**Poindexter, James N., Maj.**
352nd Ftr Sqn/353rd Ftr Grp

| *Sqn* | *Date* | *Claims* | *Location* | *A/C* |
|---|---|---|---|---|
| 352nd | September 23, 1943 | Me-109 dest(air) | NE Nantes | P-47 |
| | November 3 | Me-110 dest(air) | Wilhelmshaven | P-47 |
| | | Me-210 dest(air) | Wilhelmshaven | P-47 |
| | February 22, 1944 | (2)Me-109 dest(air) | NW Koln | P-47 |
| | February 24 | FW-190 dam(air) | Steinhuder Lake | P-47 |
| | May 30 | (2)FW-190 dest(air) | Peine | P-47 |
| | June 7 | Me-109 dest(grd) | Compiegne | P-47 |
| | | (1.5)Me-109 dam(grd)* | Compiegne | P-47 |
| | June 20 | He-111 dest(grd) | Plantlunne | P-47 |
| | August 1 | Me-410 dest(grd) | Laon/Couvron | P-47 |
| | November 18 | He-177 dest(grd) | Lechfeld | P-51 |
| | | He-177 dam(grd) | Lechfeld | P-51 |

7-0-1 air
4-2.5 ground

* - shared with Lt. R.V. Keywan of the 352nd Ftr Sqn

**Pollock, Robert H., Capt.**
79th Ftr Sqn/20th Ftr Grp

| *Sqn* | *Date* | *Claims* | *Location* | *A/C* |
|---|---|---|---|---|
| 79th | October 6, 1944 | u/i a/c dam(grd) | Bad Berg-Dievenow | P-51 |

| Sqn | Date | Claims | Location | A/C |
|---|---|---|---|---|
| | February 20, 1945 | (1.5)He-111 dest(grd) | Weiden A/F | P-51 |
| | | Me-410 dam(grd) | Weiden A/F | P-51 |

0-0-0 air
1.5-2 ground

[*] - shared with Lt. J.C. Santee of the 79th Ftr Sqn

**Pompetti, Peter E., Lt.**
84th Ftr Sqn/78th Ftr Grp

| *Sqn* | *Date* | *Claims* | *Location* | *A/C* |
|---|---|---|---|---|
| 84th | July 30, 1943 | Me-109 dest(air) | Didam | P-47 |
| | August 17 | Me-210 dest(air) | SE Aachen | P-47 |
| | September 27 | Me-109 dest(air) | NW Emden | P-47 |
| | | Me-110 dest(air) | NW Emden | P-47 |
| | December 1 | FW-190 dam(air) | Leige-Aachen | P-47 |
| | January 4, 1944 | Me-109 dest(air) | Coesfeld | P-47 |
| | | FW-190 dam(air) | Coesfeld | P-47 |
| | January 14 | Me-109 dam(air) | NE Lille | P-47 |
| | February 5 | (.5)Me-109 dam(air)[*] | Bernay | P-47 |
| | February 6 | Hs-129 dest(grd) | Orleans/Bricy | P-47 |
| | | Ju-88 dam(grd) | Orleans/Bricy | P-47 |
| | March 2 | (.5)Ju-52 dest(grd)[**] | Chartres | P-47 |
| | | (.5)Hs-126 dest(grd)[**] | Chartres | P-47 |
| | March 8 | (.5)FW-190 dam(grd)[@] | Bohmte | P-47 |
| | March 16 | Me-109 dam(grd) | S/Nancy | P-47 |
| | March 17 | (.5)He-111 dam(grd)[@@] | Beauvais | P-47 |

5-0-3.5 air
2-3 ground

[*] - shared with Lt. L.J. Abel of the 84th Ftr Sqn
[**] - both shared with Lt. E.S. Lang of the 84th Ftr Sqn
[@] - shared with Lt. E.S. Lang of the 84th Ftr Sqn
[@@] - shared with Lt. E.S. Lang of the 84th Ftr Sqn

**Pool, Lawrence W., Lt.**
367th Ftr Sqn/358th Ftr Grp

| *Sqn* | *Date* | *Claims* | *Location* | *A/C* |
|---|---|---|---|---|
| 367th | January 30, 1944 | Me-109 prob(air) | E/Zwolle | P-47 |

0-1-0 air
0-0 ground

**Poore, William L., Lt.**
385th Ftr Sqn/364th Ftr Grp

| *Sqn* | *Date* | *Claims* | *Location* | *A/C* |
|---|---|---|---|---|
| 385th | April 15, 1944 | Me-109 dam(air) | Vechta | P-38 |

0-0-1 air
0-0 ground

**Pope, William K., Lt.**
343rd Ftr Sqn/55th Ftr Grp

| *Sqn* | *Date* | *Claims* | *Location* | *A/C* |
|---|---|---|---|---|
| 343rd | September 5, 1944 | (2)He-177 dam(grd) | Goppingen | P-51 |

0-0-0 air
0-2 ground

**Popplewell, Joel I., Lt.**
61st Ftr Sqn/56th Ftr Grp

| *Sqn* | *Date* | *Claims* | *Location* | *A/C* |
|---|---|---|---|---|
| 61st | June 7, 1944 | Me-109 dest(air) | SE Houdan | P-47 |

1-0-0 air
0-0 ground

**Popy, Stephen W., Lt.**
374th Ftr Sqn/361st Ftr Grp

| *Sqn* | *Date* | *Claims* | *Location* | *A/C* |
|---|---|---|---|---|
| 374th | November 27, 1944 | Me-109 dest(air) | Dummer Lake | P-51 |

1-0-0 air
0-0 ground

**Porowski, Isadore T., Lt.**
63rd Ftr Sqn/56th Ftr Grp

| *Sqn* | *Date* | *Claims* | *Location* | *A/C* |
|---|---|---|---|---|
| 63rd | March 27, 1944 | (.25)Do-217 dest(air)[*] | S/Chartres | P-47 |

0.25-0-0 air
0-0 ground

[*] - shared with Maj. W.M. Mahurin, Lt. W.D. Johnson, and F/O S.J. Lowman of the 63rd Ftr Sqn

**Porter, Alan C., Lt.**
370th Ftr Sqn/359th Ftr Grp

| *Sqn* | *Date* | *Claims* | *Location* | *A/C* |
|---|---|---|---|---|
| 370th | March 4, 1944 | (.25)Me-109 dest(air)[*] | Bonn | P-47 |
| | April 11 | Ju-88 dam(grd) | Volkenrod | P-47 |
| | April 24 | Me-109 dest(grd) | St. Dizier | P-47 |

0.25-0-0 air
1-1 ground

[*] - shared with Maj. J.B. Murphy, Lt. P.H. Bateman, and Lt. R.S. Wetmore of the 370th Ftr Sqn

**Porter, Clair D., Lt.**
343rd Ftr Sqn/55th Ftr Grp

| *Sqn* | *Date* | *Claims* | *Location* | *A/C* |
|---|---|---|---|---|
| 343rd | April 24, 1944 | Me-109 dest(air) | NW Lake Constance | P-38 |
| | June 11 | FW-190 dest(air) | Clermont | P-38 |
| | | Me-109 dam(air) | Clermont | P-38 |

2-0-1 air
0-0 ground

**Porter, Fred S., Jr., Capt.**
361st Ftr Sqn/356th Ftr Grp

| *Sqn* | *Date* | *Claims* | *Location* | *A/C* |
|---|---|---|---|---|
| 361st | March 6, 1944 | Me-109 dest(air) | N/Steinhuder Lake | P-47 |
| | March 20 | Me-110 dam(grd) | N/Brussels | P-47 |

1-0-0 air
0-1 ground

**Porter, Paul P., Lt.**
343rd Ftr Sqn/55th Ftr Grp

| *Sqn* | *Date* | *Claims* | *Location* | *A/C* |
|---|---|---|---|---|
| 343rd | September 5, 1944 | (2)He-111 dam(grd) | Stuttgart/Echterdingen | P-51 |

0-0-0 air
0-2 ground

**Porterfield, George N., Lt.**
352nd Ftr Sqn/353rd Ftr Grp

| *Sqn* | *Date* | *Claims* | *Location* | *A/C* |
|---|---|---|---|---|
| 352nd | August 4, 1944 | (.5)u/i a/c dest(grd)[*] | Plantlunne | P-47 |
| | September 23 | FW-190 dest(air) | SE Arnheim | P-47 |
| | December 31 | FW-190 dest(air) | W/Coblenz | P-51 |

2-0-0 air
0.5-0 ground

[*] - shared with Lt. W.J. Jordan of the 352nd Ftr Sqn

**Postle, Maurice A., Lt.**
364th Ftr Sqn/357th Ftr Grp

| *Sqn* | *Date* | *Claims* | *Location* | *A/C* |
|---|---|---|---|---|
| 364th | April 11, 1944 | (.5)Me-109 dest(air)[*] | Magdeburg | P-51 |
| | April 13 | Me-109 dest(air) | Luxembourg | P-51 |

1.5-0-0 air
0-0 ground

[*] - shared with Lt. D.H. Bochkay of the 363rd Ftr Sqn, 357th Ftr Grp

**Potochnik, John F., Lt.**
383rd Ftr Sqn/364th Ftr Grp

*Starboard view of Irwin Dregne's 364th Fighter Squadron P-51, C5-Q 44-11678 "Jeanne/Ah Fung-Goo."*

*Daniel McKee on his 370th Fighter Squadron P-51, CS-A 44-14521.*

*Bert Marshall's 354th Fighter Squadron P-51, WR-B 44-72953 "Jane VII."*

*P-51D of the 2nd Scouting Force, YF-Q 44-63739 "Rugged Rebel V."*

Right: *486th Fighter Squadron P-51 of Earl Lazear, PZ-L 44-14877 "Pennie's Earl."*

*Harry Gohsler's 359th Fighter Squadron P-51, OC-Y 44-15138.*

*384th Fighter Squadron P-51 of John Lowell, 5Y-L 44-63262 "Penny 4."*

*Don Baccus in his 359th Fighter Group Mustang, CV-U 44-72746.*

*William Foard's 364th Fighter Squadron P-51, C5-A 44-15660 "Swamp Fox."*

*Joe Thury in his 505th Fighter Squadron P-51, 6N-C 44-72437 "Pauline."*

Right: Pair of 357th Fighter Squadron Mustangs in early 1945; OS-L 44-14314 "Sexless Stella/One More Time" was flown by Jack Dressler while Walt Griswold was the pilot of OS-U 44-14786 "Joereine II."

Below: B7-U 44-14139 of the 374th Fighter Squadron.

61st Fighter Squadron P-47M of Robert Hoeflein, HV-W 44-21187 "Lil Snorkey."

Right: Norman Fortier's WR-N 44-15373 of the 354th Fighter Squadron.

363rd Fighter Squadron P-51 of Joe Cannon, B6-B 44-72258 "Little Joe."

Robert Foy's 363rd Fighter Squadron P-51, B6-V 44-63621 "Little Shrimp."

*Above: Robert Garlich's 357th Fighter Squadron P-51, OS-S 44-14966 "Lucious Lu."*

*Right: Robert McIntosh and crew with their 369th Fighter Squadron P-51, IV-E 44-14127 "Dilbert" (port)"Lil Marge" (starboard) left to right are Robert Pollack (assistant), McIntosh, Floyd Myers (crewchief).*

*Below: 77th Fighter Squadron P-51, LC-Y 44-14632 "My Rosie."*

Right: John Lowell with his "Penny 4" of the 384th Fighter Squadron.

Below: 1st Scouting Force P-51 at a strip on the continent, 9H-Z 44-72239 "Zoom Zoozie."

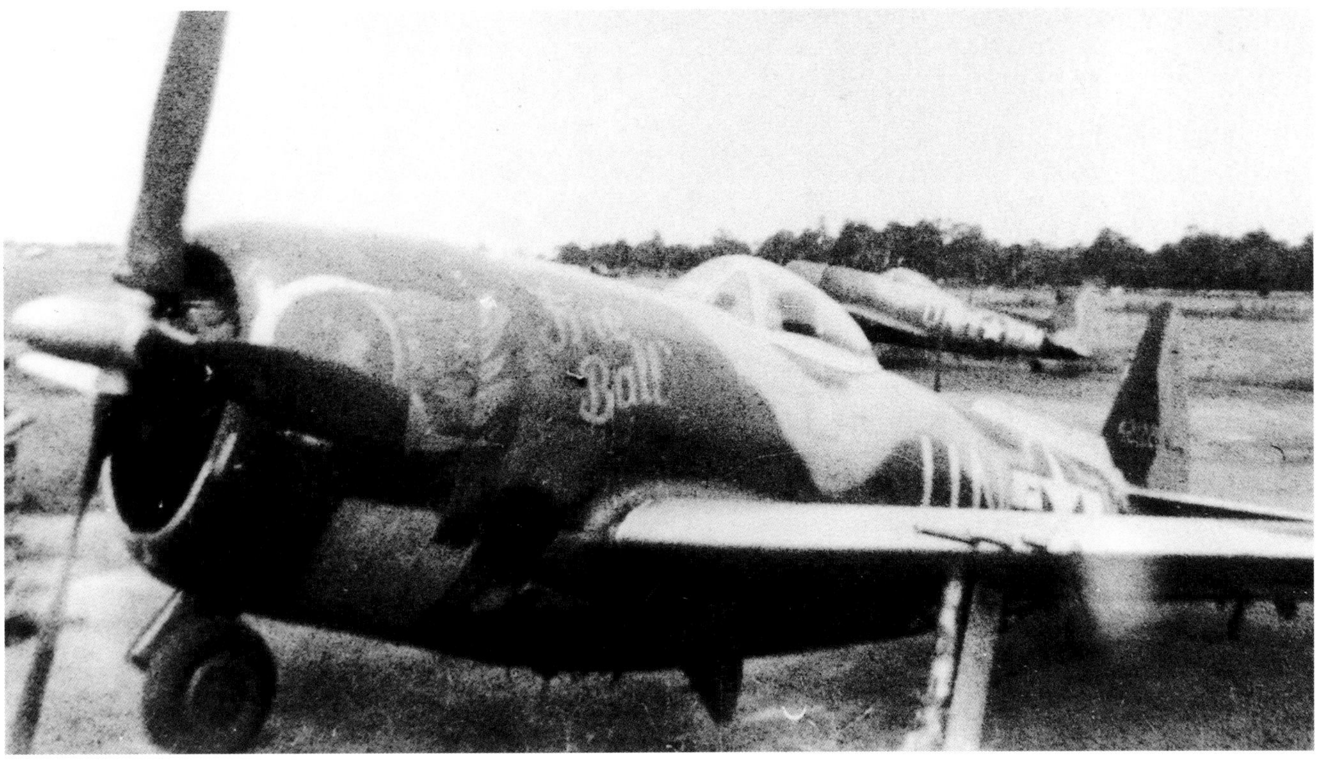

63rd Fighter Squadron P-47M of Philip Kuhn, UN-K 44-21225 "Fireball."

*Ray Wetmore in his 370th P-51 CS-L 44-14733 "Daddy's Girl."*

*360th Fighter Squadron P-51 of Nunzio Ceraolo, PI-L 44-63251 "Louise."*

*Right: 84th Fighter Squadron mount of John Landers, WZ-I 44-72218 "Big Beautiful Doll."*

*Below: 374th Fighter Squadron P-51 of Jack Joss, B7-Q 44-14957 "Darlin' Dora."*

*Richard Thieme's 505th Fighter Squadron P-51 prior to take-off, 6N-W 44-14705 "Boomerang!"*

*Right: Robert Montgomery in his LC-D 44-72519 "Gumpy" of the 77th Fighter Squadron.*

*Two 354th Fighter Squadron aces in flight towards war's end, WR-Y is 44-63764 "Dragon Wagon" with James Duffy and Norman Fortier is in WR-N 44-72361.*

*Glenn Duncan's final wartime P-51 of the 350th Fighter Squadron, LH-X 44-73060 "Dove of Peace VIII."*

*Above: 362nd Fighter Squadron P-51 of Leonard Carson, G4-C 44-11622 "Nooky Booky IV."*

*Right: Poor quality shot of an 84th Fighter Squadron P-51.*

Right: Ray Littge's 487th Fighter Squadron P-51, HO-M 44-11330 "E Pluribus Unum."

Below: Pair of 376th Fighter Squadron P-51's near war's end. In front is E9-V 44-14600 with war weary trainer E9-B in rear.

Robert Frisch in his 503rd Fighter Squadron P-51 D7-J 44-14118 "Worry Bird."

*361st Fighter Squadron P-51's heading home, February 14, 1945 First three planes are QI-T 44-15152 "Jersey Jerk" of Don Strait, QI-E 44-15666 "Jett Job" of Shelby Jett, and QI-A 44-15094 of Rex Burden.*

*Formation of 350th Fighter Squadron Mustangs in early 1945 Front four ships are LH-B, LH-P 44-15671 "Miss Ellen" of Harold Jung, LH-R 44-15137 "Baby Duck" of Herbert Kolb, and LH-I 44-14673 "Galloping Ghost."*

Above: Line-up of 368th Fighter Squadron P-51's with the first five planes being CV-Y 44-13776 "Kitten" of George Long, CV-N 44-14965 "Lady", CV-T 44-11758 "Silky" of John Denman, CV-Z 44-72281 "Happy 2" of James Way, and CV-Q 44-15717 "Wild Will" of James Parsons.

Right: Unidentified 505th Fighter Squadron crewmen with 6N-P 44-14052 "Mariam."

Below: Slightly fuzzy shot of a 505th Fighter Squadron Mustang down on March 25, 1945. 6N-R 44-13680 "The Roller."

Right: *Richard Gibbs' 343rd Fighter Squadron ship in the junkyard shortly after war's end.*

*Below: Four 370th Fighter Squadron P-51's heading for East Wretham in early 1945. CS-Z 44-14368, CS-C 44-72208, CS-T 44-15102 "Skeeter's Skooter", and CS-O 44-14518.*

*375th Fighter Squadron P-51 of John Johnston, E2-Y 44-14460.*

*Nice close showing the 356th Fighter Group nose markings. Pilot is Amos Bomberger of the 361st Fighter Squadron and the plane is QI-B 44-15081 "Carolyn's Vergeltungswaffe."*

*"The Mighty Myth", a 63rd Fighter Squadron P-47M with pilot Melvin Hughes.*

| Sqn | Date | Claims | Location | A/C |
|---|---|---|---|---|
| 383rd | May 25, 1944 | FW-190 dest(air) | SW Paris | P-38 |

1-0-0 air
0-0 ground

**Potthoff, John R., Lt.**
503rd Ftr Sqn/339th Ftr Grp

| Sqn | Date | Claims | Location | A/C |
|---|---|---|---|---|
| 503rd | April 17, 1945 | Ju-88 dam(grd) | Klatovy | P-51 |

0-0-0 air
0-1 ground

**Poutre, Lawrence, Capt.**
503rd Ftr Sqn/339th Ftr Grp

| Sqn | Date | Claims | Location | A/C |
|---|---|---|---|---|
| 503rd | March 2, 1945 | (2)Me-109 dest(air) | E/Magdeburg | P-51 |
| | | FW-190 dest(air) | E/Magdeburg | P-51 |
| | March 18 | FW-190 dam(air) | Dummer Lake | P-51 |
| | April 7 | Me-109 dest(air) | Celle | P-51 |

4-0-1 air
0-0 ground

**Powell, Everett W., Lt.**
83rd Ftr Sqn/78th Ftr Grp

| Sqn | Date | Claims | Location | A/C |
|---|---|---|---|---|
| 83rd | September 27, 1943 | Me-109 dest(air) | Emden | P-47 |

1-0-0 air
0-0 ground

**Powell, Homer C., Lt.**
376th Ftr Sqn/361st Ftr Grp

| Sqn | Date | Claims | Location | A/C |
|---|---|---|---|---|
| 376th | September 27, 1944 | (2)FW-190 dest(air) | Eisenach | P-51 |
| | December 26 | FW-190 dest(air) | N/Merzig | P-51 |

3-0-0 air
0-0 ground

**Powell, Lawrence J., Jr., Lt.**
505th Ftr Sqn/339th Ftr Grp

| Sqn | Date | Claims | Location | A/C |
|---|---|---|---|---|
| 505th | July 31, 1944 | Me-410 dest(grd) | Holzkirchen | P-51 |
| | | u/i a/c dam(grd) | Holzkirchen | P-51 |
| | August 4 | FW-190 dest(air) | S/Hamburg | P-51 |
| | | (.5)Me-109 dest(air)[*] | S/Hamburg | P-51 |
| | September 10 | Me-410 dest(grd) | Weizenburg | P-51 |
| | | Do-217 dest(grd) | Weizenburg | P-51 |
| | | (4)u/i a/c dam(grd) | Weizenburg | P-51 |
| | September 13 | (.5)Ju-88 dest(grd)[**] | SE Munich | P-51 |
| | September 23 | FW-190 dest(air) | Geldern-Weeze | P-51 |

2.5-0-0 air
3.5-5 ground

[*] - shared with Lt. A.E. Tongue of the 505th Ftr Sqn
[**] - shared with Lt. W.R. Moore of the 505th Ftr Sqn

**Powell, Robert H., Jr., Lt.**
328th Ftr Sqn/352nd Ftr Grp

| Sqn | Date | Claims | Location | A/C |
|---|---|---|---|---|
| 328th | December 22, 1943 | (.5)Me-110 dest(air)[*] | Zwolle | P-47 |
| | January 5, 1944 | (.33)He-177 dest(air)[**] | La Ferte Bernard | P-47 |
| | April 8 | Me-210 dest(grd) | Quackenbruck | P-47 |
| | | Me-210 dam(grd) | Quackenbruck | P-47 |
| | April 28 | Ju-88 dest(grd) | Herbouville | P-51 |
| | | (.5)Ju-88 dam(grd)[@] | Avord | P-51 |
| | May 21 | (2)He-111 dest(grd) | Alt Ruppin | P-51 |
| | | (2)He-111 dam(grd) | Alt Ruppin | P-51 |
| | June 21 | Me-410 dam(air) | Dahmsdorf | P-51 |
| | July 1 | Me-109 dam(air) | Bethune | P-51 |

0.83-0-2 air
4-3.5 ground

[*] - shared with Maj. E.W. Stewart of the 328th Ftr Sqn
[**] - shared with Maj. E.W. Stewart and Lt. J.B. Coleman of the 328th Ftr Sqn
[@] - shared with Capt. R.H. Sharp of the 328th Ftr Sqn

**Powers, Joseph H., Jr., Capt.**
61st Ftr Sqn/56th Ftr Grp
62nd Ftr Sqn/56th Ftr Grp

| Sqn | Date | Claims | Location | A/C |
|---|---|---|---|---|
| 61st | July 30, 1943 | Me-109 dest(air) | Arnheim | P-47 |
| | November 29 | Me-109 dest(air) | NE Bremen | P-47 |
| | December 11 | Me-110 dest(air) | N/Norderney Isle | P-47 |
| | | Me-109 dest(air) | N/Aurich | P-47 |
| | | Me-110 dam(air) | N/Aurich | P-47 |
| | December 20 | Me-109 dest(air) | NE Bremen | P-47 |
| | | (.5)Me-109 dam(air)[*] | NE Bremen | P-47 |
| | | (.5)Me-210 dam(air)[*] | NE Bremen | P-47 |
| | January 30, 1944 | FW-190 dest(air) | Meppen | P-47 |
| | February 6 | Me-109 dest(air) | Beauvais | P-47 |
| | February 24 | FW-190 dest(air) | Minden | P-47 |
| | March 15 | FW-190 dest(air) | Dummer Lake | P-47 |
| | | Me-109 dest(air) | Dummer Lake | P-47 |
| | | FW-190 dam(air) | Dummer Lake | P-47 |
| | March 16 | Me-109 dest(air) | St. Dizier | P-47 |
| | | FW-190 dam(air) | St. Dizier | P-47 |
| | March 18 | FW-190 dest(air) | Cambrai-Givet | P-47 |
| 62nd | April 9 | Me-109 dest(air) | S/Kiel | P-47 |
| | April 13 | Me-109 dam(air) | Ludwigshafen | P-47 |
| | May 4 | Me-109 dest(air) | Quackenbruck | P-47 |
| | May 12 | (.5)Me-109 dest(air)[**] | Frankfurt | P-47 |

14.5-0-5 air
0-0 ground

[*] - both shared with Lt. M.C. Wood of the 61st Ftr Sqn
[**] - shared with F/O J. Vitale of the 62nd Ftr Sqn

**Preddy, George E., Maj.**
487th Ftr Sqn/352nd Ftr Grp
328th Ftr Sqn/352nd Ftr Grp

| Sqn | Date | Claims | Location | A/C |
|---|---|---|---|---|
| 487th | December 1, 1943 | Me-109 dest(air) | S/Rheydt | P-47 |
| | December 22 | Me-410 dest(air) | E/Zuider Zee | P-47 |
| | January 29, 1944 | Me-109 dest(air) | Malmedy | P-47 |
| | April 11 | He-111 dest(grd) | SE Berlin | P-51 |
| | | He-111 dam(grd) | SE Berlin | P-51 |
| | April 13 | Bu-133 dest(grd) | SE Stuttgart | P-51 |
| | April 20 | Me-109 dam(air) | Beauvais-Chartres | P-51 |
| | April 22 | (.33)Ju-88 dest(air)[*] | Stade A/F | P-51 |
| | | Ju-52 dest(grd) | Salzwedel | P-51 |
| | April 28 | He-111 dam(grd) | Bourges | P-51 |
| | May 12 | (3)u/i a/c dam(grd) | Frankenhausen | P-51 |
| | May 13 | (2)Me-109 dest(air) | Neubrandenburg | P-51 |
| | May 30 | (2.5)Me-109 dest(air)[**] | Magdeburg | P-51 |
| | June 12 | Me-109 dest(air) | SW Rennes | P-51 |
| | June 20 | FW-190 dest(air) | E/Bernburg | P-51 |
| | | (.5)Me-410 dest(air)[@] | E/Bernburg | P-51 |
| | June 21 | Me-109 dest(air) | E/Magdeburg | P-51 |
| | June 29 | Ju-52 dest(grd) | Burg A/F | P-51 |
| | July 18 | (2)Ju-88 dest(air) | NE Rostock | P-51 |
| | | Me-109 dest(air) | NE Rostock | P-51 |
| | | Ju-88 prob(air) | NE Rostock | P-51 |
| | | (2)Ju-88 dam(air) | NE Rostock | P-51 |
| | July 20 | Me-410 dest(grd) | Nordhausen | P-51 |
| | | He-111 dam(grd) | Nordhausen | P-51 |
| | July 21 | (.5)Me-109 dest(air)[@@] | E/Munich | P-51 |
| | July 29 | Me-109 dest(air) | Naunberg | P-51 |
| | August 5 | Me-109 dest(air) | S/Hamburg | P-51 |
| | | Me-109 prob(air) | S/Hamburg | P-51 |
| | August 6 | (6)Me-109 dest(air) | Luneburg-Havelburg | P-51 |
| 328th | November 2 | Me-109 dest(air) | Merseburg | P-51 |
| | November 21 | Me-109 dest(air) | Merseburg | P-51 |
| | | Me-109 prob(air) | Merseburg | P-51 |
| | | Me-109 dam(air) | Merseburg | P-51 |
| | December 25 | (2)Me-109 dest(air) | SW Coblenz | P-51 |

26.83-3-4 air
5-6 ground

[*] - shared with Lt. D.R. Donahue and Lt. J.P. Kessler of the 487th Ftr Sqn
[**] - shared with Lt. W.T. Whisner of the 487th Ftr Sqn
[@] - shared with Lt. J.N. Wood of the 487th Ftr Sqn
[@@] - shared with Lt. S.K. Moats of the 487th Ftr Sqn

**Preddy, William R., Lt.**
503rd Ftr Sqn/339th Ftr Grp

| *Sqn* | *Date* | *Claims* | *Location* | *A/C* |
|---|---|---|---|---|
| 503rd | March 2, 1945 | FW-190 dest(air) | E/Magdeburg | P-51 |
| | | Me-109 prob(air) | E/Magdeburg | P-51 |
| | April 16 | u/i a/c dam(grd) | Kralupy | P-51 |

1-1-0 air
0-1 ground

**Prescott, Walter A.S., Lt.**
350th Ftr Sqn/353rd Ftr Grp

| *Sqn* | *Date* | *Claims* | *Location* | *A/C* |
|---|---|---|---|---|
| 350th | March 21, 1945 | Ju-88 dest(grd) | Achmer | P-51 |
| | | Ar-234 dam(grd) | Achmer | P-51 |
| | March 24 | (2)Me-109 dest(air) | NW Kassel | P-51 |
| | April 16 | (2)FW-190 dest(grd) | Pocking | P-51 |
| | | Me-109 dest(grd) | Pocking | P-51 |

2-0-0 air
4-1 ground

**Prewitt, Luster H., Lt.**
369th Ftr Sqn/359th Ftr Grp

| *Sqn* | *Date* | *Claims* | *Location* | *A/C* |
|---|---|---|---|---|
| 369th | January 29, 1944 | Me-110 dam(air) | Dison | P-47 |
| | January 30 | Ju-88 dam(air) | Haselunne | P-47 |

0-0-2 air
0-0 ground

**Price, Charles D., Lt.**
486th Ftr Sqn/352nd Ftr Grp

| *Sqn* | *Date* | *Claims* | *Location* | *A/C* |
|---|---|---|---|---|
| 486th | February 22, 1945 | Me-262 dest(air) | Wahrenholz | P-51 |
| | March 2 | FW-190 dest(air) | Zwebau | P-51 |
| | April 16 | He-111 dest(grd) | Ganacker | P-51 |
| | | Me-109 dest(grd) | Ganacker | P-51 |
| | | (3)u/i a/c dam(grd) | Ganacker | P-51 |

2-0-0 air
2-3 ground

**Price, Jack B., Lt.**
503rd Ftr Sqn/339th Ftr Grp

| *Sqn* | *Date* | *Claims* | *Location* | *A/C* |
|---|---|---|---|---|
| 503rd | May 21, 1944 | (2)Ju-88 dam(grd) | Pelenz A/F | P-51 |
| | September 11 | FW-190 dest(air) | Annaberg | P-51 |

1-0-0 air
0-2 ground

**Price, Jack C., Maj.**
84th Ftr Sqn/78th Ftr Grp
55th Ftr Sqn/20th Ftr Grp
HdQts/20th Ftr Grp

| *Sqn* | *Date* | *Claims* | *Location* | *A/C* |
|---|---|---|---|---|
| 84th | July 14, 1943 | FW-190 dest(air) | N/Abbeville | P-47 |
| | July 30 | (2)FW-190 dest(air) | Winterswijk | P-47 |
| | October 20 | Me-109 dam(air) | Dinant | P-47 |
| | November 26 | FW-190 dest(air) | Paris | P-47 |
| | | Me-109 dest(air) | Paris | P-47 |

5-0-1 air
0-0 ground

**Price, James T., Lt.**
361st Ftr Sqn/356th Ftr Grp

| *Sqn* | *Date* | *Claims* | *Location* | *A/C* |
|---|---|---|---|---|
| 361st | December 1, 1943 | FW-190 dest(air) | Brussels-Louvain | P-47 |
| | | FW-190 prob(air) | Brussels-Louvain | P-47 |

1-1-0 air
0-0 ground

**Price, Keith C., Lt.**
79th Ftr Sqn/20th Ftr Grp

| *Sqn* | *Date* | *Claims* | *Location* | *A/C* |
|---|---|---|---|---|
| 79th | August 9, 1944 | FW-190 dest(air) | SW Ulm | P-51 |
| | | FW-190 dam(air) | SW Ulm | P-51 |

1-0-1 air
0-0 ground

**Price, Stephen R., Lt.**
328th Ftr Sqn/352nd Ftr Grp

| *Sqn* | *Date* | *Claims* | *Location* | *A/C* |
|---|---|---|---|---|
| 328th | April 17, 1945 | Me-109 dest(grd) | Plattling | P-51 |
| | | Me-109 dam(grd) | Plattling | P-51 |

0-0-0 air
1-1 ground

**Price, Sterling J., Lt.**
384th Ftr Sqn/364th Ftr Grp

| *Sqn* | *Date* | *Claims* | *Location* | *A/C* |
|---|---|---|---|---|
| 384th | December 27, 1944 | (.5)Me-109 dest(air)* | W/Coblenz | P-51 |
| | February 22, 1945 | Me-262 dam(air) | Stendal | P-51 |
| | April 17 | Me-262 dam(air) | Karlsbad | P-51 |

0.5-0-2 air
0-0 ground

* - shared with LtCol. J.H. Lowell of HdQts, 364th Ftr Grp

**Price, William J., Maj.**
350th Ftr Sqn/353rd Ftr Grp

| *Sqn* | *Date* | *Claims* | *Location* | *A/C* |
|---|---|---|---|---|
| 350th | November 5, 1943 | Me-210 dest(air) | Ruhr Valley | P-47 |
| | August 28, 1944 | Me-410 dest(grd) | Wavre | P-47 |
| | | (2)Me-410 dam(grd) | Wavre | P-47 |
| | August 29 | (3)Me-109 dest(grd) | Diest | P-47 |
| | | Me-109 dam(grd) | Diest | P-47 |
| | September 23 | FW-190 dest(air) | SE Arnheim | P-47 |
| | November 18 | u/i a/c dest(air) | Lechfeld | P-51 |
| | | (.5)u/i a/c dam(grd)* | Lechfeld | P-51 |

3-0-0 air
4-3.5 ground

* - shared with Lt. R.W. Abernathy of the 350th Ftr Sqn

**Prichard, Joseph W., Lt.**
487th Ftr Sqn/352nd Ftr Grp

| *Sqn* | *Date* | *Claims* | *Location* | *A/C* |
|---|---|---|---|---|
| 487th | April 10, 1945 | (.5)Me-262 dest(air)* | Neuruppin | P-51 |

0.5-0-0 air
0-0 ground

* - shared with Lt. C.A. Ricci of the 487th Ftr Sqn

**Priest, Royce W., Lt.**
354th Ftr Sqn/355th Ftr Grp

| *Sqn* | *Date* | *Claims* | *Location* | *A/C* |
|---|---|---|---|---|
| 354th | September 11, 1944 | Me-109 dest(air) | S/Kassel | P-51 |
| | September 27 | FW-190 dest(air) | Eschwege | P-51 |
| | November 2 | Me-109 dest(air) | W/Naumberg | P-51 |
| | November 26 | (2)FW-190 dest(air) | Misburg | P-51 |

5-0-0 air
0-0 ground

**Proctor, Lawrence B., Jr., Lt.**
360th Ftr Sqn/356th Ftr Grp

| *Sqn* | *Date* | *Claims* | *Location* | *A/C* |
|---|---|---|---|---|
| 360th | April 18, 1945 | (.33)Me-262 dam(air)* | Ingolstadt | P-51 |

0-0-0.33 air
0-0 ground

* - shared with Lt. W.C. Gatlin and Lt. G.W. Seanor of the 360th Ftr Sqn

**Province, Gerald F., Lt.**
350th Ftr Sqn/353rd Ftr Grp

| Sqn | Date | Claims | Location | A/C |
|---|---|---|---|---|
| 350th | September 23, 1944 | FW-190 dest(air) | SE Arnheim | P-47 |

1-0-0 air
0-0 ground

**Pruden, Harry M., Jr., Lt.**
62nd Ftr Sqn/56th Ftr Grp

| Sqn | Date | Claims | Location | A/C |
|---|---|---|---|---|
| 62nd | November 29, 1943 | (.5)Me-210 dest(air)* | S/Oldenburg | P-47 |

0.5-0-0 air
0-0 ground

* - shared with Capt. L.A. Schreiber of the 62nd Ftr Sqn

**Pruitt, Sherman, Jr., Lt.**
62nd Ftr Sqn/56th Ftr Grp

| Sqn | Date | Claims | Location | A/C |
|---|---|---|---|---|
| 62nd | March 14, 1945 | Me-109 dest(air) | Frankfurt | P-47 |
| | April 13 | He-111 dam(grd) | Eggebeck A/F | P-47 |

1-0-0 air
0-1 ground

**Pryor, Thomas P., Lt.**
351st Ftr Sqn/353rd Ftr Grp

| Sqn | Date | Claims | Location | A/C |
|---|---|---|---|---|
| 351st | April 5, 1945 | (3)Me-410 dest(grd) | Weiden | P-51 |
| | | Me-110 dam(grd) | Weiden | P-51 |
| | April 16 | FW-190 dest(grd) | Reichersberg | P-51 |
| | | Do-217 dest(grd) | Reichersberg | P-51 |

0-0-0 air
5-1 ground

**Pubentz, Robert L., Capt.**
79th Ftr Sqn/20th Ftr Grp

| Sqn | Date | Claims | Location | A/C |
|---|---|---|---|---|
| 79th | November 2, 1944 | Me-109 dest(air) | SW Merseburg | P-51 |

1-0-0 air
0-0 ground

**Pugh, John F., Capt.**
362nd Ftr Sqn/357th Ftr Grp

| Sqn | Date | Claims | Location | A/C |
|---|---|---|---|---|
| 362nd | April 8, 1944 | Me-109 dest(air) | S/Brunswick | P-51 |
| | April 11 | Me-109 dest(air) | Magdeburg | P-51 |
| | May 27 | FW-190 dest(air) | N/Strasbourg | P-51 |
| | June 29 | Me-109 dest(air) | Naumberg | P-51 |
| | July 25 | Me-109 dest(air) | Versailles | P-51 |
| | August 7 | FW-190 dest(air) | Cracow | P-51 |

6-0-0 air
0-0 ground

**Purse, Franklin V., Lt.**
77th Ftr Sqn/20th Ftr Grp

| Sqn | Date | Claims | Location | A/C |
|---|---|---|---|---|
| 77th | February 9, 1945 | Me-109 dam(air) | Mulhausen | P-51 |

0-0-1 air
0-0 ground

**Pursell, Franklin R., Lt.**
83rd Ftr Sqn/78th Ftr Grp

| Sqn | Date | Claims | Location | A/C |
|---|---|---|---|---|
| 83rd | May 11, 1944 | FW-190 dest(air) | Montargis | P-47 |
| | June 10 | FW-190 dest(air) | Argentan | P-47 |
| | | FW-190 dam(air) | Argentan | P-47 |
| | July 6 | FW-190 dest(air) | Rambouillet | P-47 |

3-0-1 air
0-0 ground

**Pushcar, Carl J., Lt.**
384th Ftr Sqn/364th Ftr Grp

| Sqn | Date | Claims | Location | A/C |
|---|---|---|---|---|
| 384th | June 25, 1944 | Me-109 dam(air) | E/Blois | P-38 |

0-0-1 air
0-0 ground

**Putnam, John B., Jr., Lt.**
84th Ftr Sqn/78th Ftr Grp

| Sqn | Date | Claims | Location | A/C |
|---|---|---|---|---|
| 84th | May 11, 1944 | FW-190 dest(air) | Orleans | P-47 |
| | July 6 | FW-190 dest(air) | NW Paris | P-47 |
| | July 19 | Ju-188 dest(grd) | Eutingen | P-47 |

2-0-0 air
1-0 ground

**Putnam, Melvin D., Lt.**
83rd Ftr Sqn/78th Ftr Grp

| Sqn | Date | Claims | Location | A/C |
|---|---|---|---|---|
| 83rd | December 22, 1943 | Me-109 dest(air) | W/Munster | P-47 |
| | | Me-109 dam(air) | W/Munster | P-47 |

1-0-1 air
0-0 ground

**Pyeatt, Alvin F., III, Lt.**
362nd Ftr Sqn/357th Ftr Grp

| Sqn | Date | Claims | Location | A/C |
|---|---|---|---|---|
| 362nd | February 22, 1944 | Me-109 dest(air) | NW Bernburg | P-51 |
| | February 25 | FW-190 dest(air) | Regensburg | P-51 |

2-0-0 air
0-0 ground

**Pyle, William V., Lt.**
383rd Ftr Sqn/364th Ftr Grp

| Sqn | Date | Claims | Location | A/C |
|---|---|---|---|---|
| 383rd | February 22, 1945 | (2)FW-190 dam(air) | SW Bremen | P-51 |

0-0-2 air
0-0 ground

**Queal, Ralph W., Jr., Lt.**
383rd Ftr Sqn/364th Ftr Grp

| Sqn | Date | Claims | Location | A/C |
|---|---|---|---|---|
| 383rd | April 16, 1945 | Do-217 dam(grd) | Marienbad | P-51 |
| | April 19 | FW-190 dest(air) | Lubben | P-51 |
| | | FW-190 dam(air) | Lubben | P-51 |

1-0-1 air
0-1 ground

**Queen, Thomas W., Jr., Lt.**
63rd Ftr Sqn/56th Ftr Grp

| Sqn | Date | Claims | Location | A/C |
|---|---|---|---|---|
| 63rd | August 28, 1944 | Ju-88 dam(grd) | Bad Brommach | P-47 |
| | September 5 | Me-109 dam(air) | NE Coblenz | P-47 |
| | | FW-190 dest(grd) | Gelnhausen | P-47 |
| | | FW-190 dam(grd) | Gelnhausen | P-47 |
| | April 13, 1945 | (3)u/i a/c dest(grd) | Eggebeck A/F | P-47 |
| | | Me-410 dest(grd) | Eggebeck A/F | P-47 |

0-0-1 air
5-2 ground

**Quiggins, Richard S., Lt.**
22nd PRS/7th PRG

| Sqn | Date | Claims | Location | A/C |
|---|---|---|---|---|
| 22nd | February 25, 1945 | FW-190 dest(air) | Aschaffenberg | P-51 |

1-0-0 air
0-0 ground

**Quinn, Quentin L., Capt.**
328th Ftr Sqn/352nd Ftr Grp

| *Sqn* | *Date* | *Claims* | *Location* | *A/C* |
|---|---|---|---|---|
| 328th | January 29, 1944 | (.5)FW-200 dest(air)[*] | Namur | P-47 |
| | January 30 | (.5)FW-190 dest(air)[**] | Emmen | P-47 |
| | April 22 | (.5)Me-210 dest(grd)[@] | Dummer Lake | P-51 |
| | May 8 | Me-109 dest(air) | NW Bremen | P-51 |
| | | FW-190 prob(air) | NW Bremen | P-51 |

2-1-0 air
0.5-0 ground

[*] - shared with Lt. D.S. Bryan of the 328th Ftr Sqn
[**] - shared with Lt. F.W. Horne of the 328th Ftr Sqn
[@] - shared with Capt. J.B. Coleman of the 328th Ftr Sqn

**Quinn, Richard F., Lt.**
38th Ftr Sqn/55th Ftr Grp

| *Sqn* | *Date* | *Claims* | *Location* | *A/C* |
|---|---|---|---|---|
| 38th | April 16, 1945 | u/i a/c dam(grd) | Bad Aibling | P-51 |

0-0-0 air
0-1 ground

**Quinn, Russell G., Lt.**
77th Ftr Sqn/20th Ftr Grp

| *Sqn* | *Date* | *Claims* | *Location* | *A/C* |
|---|---|---|---|---|
| 77th | February 11, 1944 | Me-109 dam(air) | Chateau d'Ardenne | P-38 |

0-0-1 air
0-0 ground

**Quinn, William J., Capt.**
374th Ftr Sqn/361st Ftr Grp

| *Sqn* | *Date* | *Claims* | *Location* | *A/C* |
|---|---|---|---|---|
| 374th | October 7, 1944 | Me-109 dest(air) | Naumberg | P-51 |
| | November 6 | Me-262 dest(air) | Bessum | P-51 |

2-0-0 air
0-0 ground

**Quirk, Michael J., Capt.**
62nd Ftr Sqn/56th Ftr Grp

| *Sqn* | *Date* | *Claims* | *Location* | *A/C* |
|---|---|---|---|---|
| 62nd | August 19, 1943 | FW-190 dest(air) | Gilze-Rijen | P-47 |
| | October 8 | FW-190 dest(air) | Quackenbruck | P-47 |
| | December 20 | Me-109 dest(air) | S/Bremen | P-47 |
| | January 4, 1944 | FW-190 dest(air) | N/St. Gilles | P-47 |
| | January 11 | Me-109 prob(air) | Lingen | P-47 |
| | January 30 | Me-109 dest(air) | Almelo | P-47 |
| | | Me-109 dam(air) | Almelo | P-47 |
| | February 4 | FW-190 dest(air) | Charleroi | P-47 |
| | | Me-110 dest(air) | St. Omer | P-47 |
| | February 22 | (1.5)FW-190 dest(air)[*] | Breda | P-47 |
| | February 25 | FW-190 dest(air) | Homburg | P-47 |
| | March 8 | (.5)FW-190 dest(air)[**] | Celle | P-47 |
| | March 15 | FW-190 dest(air) | Dummer Lake | P-47 |
| | August 4 | (3)He-111 dam(grd) | Plantlunne | P-47 |
| | September 5 | (4)FW-190 dest(grd) | Gelnhausen | P-47 |
| | | (4)FW-190 dam(grd) | Gelnhausen | P-47 |
| | September 10 | He-111 dest(grd) | Seligenstadt | P-47 |

11-1-1 air
5-7 ground

[*] - shared with Lt. J.E. Fields of the 62nd Ftr Sqn
[**] - shared with Lt. J.B. Eaves of the 62nd Ftr Sqn

**Quist, Earl A., Lt.**
336th Ftr Sqn/4th Ftr Grp

| *Sqn* | *Date* | *Claims* | *Location* | *A/C* |
|---|---|---|---|---|
| 336th | September 12, 1944 | Me-109 prob(air) | NW Frankfurt | P-51 |

0-1-0 air
0-0 ground

**Racine, Rolland W., Lt.**
361st Ftr Sqn/356th Ftr Grp

| *Sqn* | *Date* | *Claims* | *Location* | *A/C* |
|---|---|---|---|---|
| 361st | January 11, 1944 | Me-110 dest(air) | NW Hanover | P-47 |

1-0-0 air
0-0 ground

**Rader, Benjamin N., Lt.**
77th Ftr Sqn/20th Ftr Grp

| *Sqn* | *Date* | *Claims* | *Location* | *A/C* |
|---|---|---|---|---|
| 77th | February 11, 1944 | Me-109 dest(air) | Giessen | P-38 |
| | April 8 | (.5)Ju-88 dest(grd)[*] | Salzwedel | P-38 |
| | | (.5)Ju-52 dam(grd)[**] | Salzwedel | P-38 |
| | August 4 | Ju-88 dam(grd) | Barth | P-51 |
| | August 6 | Me-109 dest(air) | Pitsdam | P-51 |

2-0-0 air
0.5-1.5 ground

[*] - shared with Capt. J.M. Morris of the 77th Ftr Sqn
[**] - shared with Lt. I.W. Fernandes of the 77th Ftr Sqn

**Rader, Franklin S., Lt.**
61st Ftr Sqn/56th Ftr Grp

| *Sqn* | *Date* | *Claims* | *Location* | *A/C* |
|---|---|---|---|---|
| 61st | April 13, 1945 | He-111 dest(grd) | Eggebeck A/F | P-47 |
| | | (2)He-111 dam(grd) | Eggebeck A/F | P-47 |

0-0-0 air
1-2 ground

**Radley, Francis X., Lt.**
385th Ftr Sqn/364th Ftr Grp

| *Sqn* | *Date* | *Claims* | *Location* | *A/C* |
|---|---|---|---|---|
| 385th | December 31, 1944 | FW-190 prob(air) | SE Hamburg | P-51 |
| | January 1, 1945 | (.5)FW-190 dest(air)[*] | Hamburg | P-51 |

0.5-1-0 air
0-0 ground

[*] - shared with Lt. J.E. Hargrove of the 385th Ftr Sqn

**Rafalovich, Alex, Lt.**
334th Ftr Sqn/4th Ftr Grp

| *Sqn* | *Date* | *Claims* | *Location* | *A/C* |
|---|---|---|---|---|
| 334th | November 3, 1943 | Me-109 dest(air) | NE Zuider Zee | P-47 |
| | January 14, 1944 | (.5)FW-190 dest(air)[*] | Soissons | P-47 |
| | February 21 | FW-190 dam(air) | Dummer Lake | P-47 |
| | March 6 | Me-109 dest(air) | Brandenburg | P-51 |
| | March 21 | (.5)Do-217 dest(grd)[**] | E/Bordeaux | P-51 |

2.5-0-1 air
0.5-0 ground

[*] - shared with Lt. E.D. Whalen of the 334th Ftr Sqn
[**] - shared with Capt. D.A. Van Epps of the 334th Ftr Sqn

**Rafferty, Vernon G., Capt.**
350th Ftr Sqn/353rd Ftr Grp

| *Sqn* | *Date* | *Claims* | *Location* | *A/C* |
|---|---|---|---|---|
| 350th | June 20, 1944 | (.5)He-111 dest(grd)[*] | Plantlunne | P-47 |
| | June 27 | Me-109 dam(grd) | Chalons | P-47 |
| | August 4 | (3)He-111 dest(grd) | Plantlunne | P-47 |
| | September 21 | (.5)FW-190 dest(air)[**] | SE Arnheim | P-47 |
| | September 23 | FW-190 dest(air) | SE Arnheim | P-47 |
| | | Me-109 dest(air) | SE Arnheim | P-47 |

2.5-0-0 air
3.5-1 ground

[*] - shared with LtCol. B. Rimerman of HdQts, 353rd Ftr Grp
[**] - shared with Lt. R.W. Hedler of the 350th Ftr Sqn

**Ragsdale, Raleigh S., Lt.**
360th Ftr Sqn/356th Ftr Grp

| Sqn | Date | Claims | Location | A/C |
|---|---|---|---|---|
| 360th | February 21, 1945 | (.5)He-111 dam(grd)* | S/Nurnberg | P-51 |

0-0-0 air
0-0.5 ground

* - shared with Lt. J.P. Weller of the 360th Ftr Sqn

**Ralston, Gilbert R., Jr., Capt.**
369th Ftr Sqn/359th Ftr Grp

| Sqn | Date | Claims | Location | A/C |
|---|---|---|---|---|
| 369th | September 11, 1944 | Me-109 dest(air) | Kolleda | P-51 |
| | | FW-190 dest(air) | Kolleda | P-51 |

2-0-0 air
0-0 ground

**Rames, Stanley D., Lt.**
375th Ftr Sqn/361st Ftr Grp

| Sqn | Date | Claims | Location | A/C |
|---|---|---|---|---|
| 375th | April 15, 1944 | (.33)Ju-52 dest(grd)* | Fritzlar | P-47 |
| | April 27 | (.5)He-111 dest(grd)** | Etampes | P-47 |
| | April 29 | Me-109 dest(air) | Steinhuder Lake | P-47 |

1-0-0 air
0.83-0 ground

* - shared with Capt. J.W. Guckeyson and Lt. W.A. Rautenbush of the 375th Ftr Sqn
** - shared with Lt. J.S. Crandell of the 375th Ftr Sqn

**Ramm, Albert J., Capt.**
338th Ftr Sqn/55th Ftr Grp

| Sqn | Date | Claims | Location | A/C |
|---|---|---|---|---|
| 338th | August 28, 1944 | (.5)DFS-230 dest(air)* | Dromersheim | P-51 |
| | November 26 | FW-190 dest(grd) | Vorden A/F | P-51 |
| | January 6, 1945 | (2)Ju-88 dest(grd) | Giebelstadt | P-51 |
| | | (2)u/i a/c dest(grd) | Giebelstadt | P-51 |

0.5-0-0 air
5-0 ground

* - shared with Lt. R.C. Haworth of the 338th Ftr Sqn

**Ramsdell, Fred L., Jr., Maj.**
357th Ftr Sqn/355th Ftr Grp

| Sqn | Date | Claims | Location | A/C |
|---|---|---|---|---|
| 357th | March 29, 1944 | FW-190 dest(air) | NE Brunswick | P-51 |

1-0-0 air
0-0 ground

**Ramser, Galen E., Capt.**
370th Ftr Sqn/359th Ftr Grp

| Sqn | Date | Claims | Location | A/C |
|---|---|---|---|---|
| 370th | December 31, 1944 | Me-109 prob(air) | Hanover | P-51 |

0-1-0 air
0-0 ground

**Randolph, Gaston M., Lt.**
368th Ftr Sqn/359th Ftr Grp

| Sqn | Date | Claims | Location | A/C |
|---|---|---|---|---|
| 368th | May 21, 1944 | (3)u/i a/c dam(grd) | Gadebusch | P-51 |

0-0-0 air
0-3 ground

**Randolph, John P., LtCol.**
HdQts/ 20th Ftr Grp
HdQts/359th Ftr Grp

| Sqn | Date | Claims | Location | A/C |
|---|---|---|---|---|
| HdQts | August 9, 1944 | Me-109 dest(air) | S/Augsburg | P-51 |
| (20th) | August 25 | Ju-88 dest(grd) | Parow A/F | P-51 |
| | | BV-140 dest(grd) | Parow A/F | P-51 |
| | | (2)Ju-88 dam(grd) | Parow A/F | P-51 |
| | October 6 | (2)Do-24 dest(grd) | Kubitzer Bay | P-51 |

1-0-0 air
4-2 ground

**Randolph, William E., Lt.**
384th Ftr Sqn/364th Ftr Grp

| Sqn | Date | Claims | Location | A/C |
|---|---|---|---|---|
| 384th | September 19, 1944 | (.5)Me-109 dest(air)* | Duisenburg | P-51 |
| | | (2)Me-109 dam(air) | Duisenburg | P-51 |
| | December 31 | (2)FW-190 dest(air) | S/Hamburg | P-51 |
| | February 22, 1945 | Me-262 dam(air) | Stendal | P-51 |

2.5-0-3 air
0-0 ground

* - shared with Lt. E.O. Bowers of the 384th Ftr Sqn

**Rankin, Chauncey H., Lt.**
358th Ftr Sqn/355th Ftr Grp

| Sqn | Date | Claims | Location | A/C |
|---|---|---|---|---|
| 358th | November 5, 1943 | Me-210 dam(air) | Alben | P-47 |

0-0-1 air
0-0 ground

**Rankin, Robert J., Capt.**
61st Ftr Sqn/56th Ftr Grp

| Sqn | Date | Claims | Location | A/C |
|---|---|---|---|---|
| 61st | February 6, 1944 | Me-109 dest(air) | Paris | P-47 |
| | March 15 | (2)Me-109 dest(air) | Dummer Lake | P-47 |
| | | Me-109 prob(air) | Dummer Lake | P-47 |
| | | FW-190 dam(air) | Dummer Lake | P-47 |
| | March 29 | Me-109 dest(air) | NE Nienburg | P-47 |
| | May 12 | (5)Me-109 dest(air) | NW Marburg | P-47 |
| | June 7 | Me-109 dest(air) | SE Senlis | P-47 |
| | | Me-109 dam(air) | SE Senlis | P-47 |

10-1-2 air
0-0 ground

**Rann, Richard A., Maj.**
359th Ftr Sqn/356th Ftr Grp

| Sqn | Date | Claims | Location | A/C |
|---|---|---|---|---|
| 359th | November 4, 1944 | Me-262 dam(air) | Lingen-Enschede | P-47 |
| | November 26 | (2)Me-109 dest(air) | NW Dummer Lake | P-51 |

2-0-1 air
0-0 ground

**Raphael, Jack L., Lt.**
336th Ftr Sqn/4th Ftr Grp

| Sqn | Date | Claims | Location | A/C |
|---|---|---|---|---|
| 336th | November 11, 1943 | FW-190 dam(air) | W/Hook of Holland | P-47 |

0-0-1 air
0-0 ground

**Rau, Harold J., Col.**
HdQts/356th Ftr Grp
HdQts/ 20th Ftr Grp

| Sqn | Date | Claims | Location | A/C |
|---|---|---|---|---|
| HdQts | April 8, 1944 | Me-109 dest(air) | Salzwedel | P-38 |
| (20th) | | (3)Ju-88 dest(grd) | Salzwedel | P-38 |
| | | Ju-52 dest(grd) | Salzwedel | P-38 |

1-0-0 air
4-0 ground

**Raub, Waldo C., Lt.**
486th Ftr Sqn/352nd Ftr Grp

| Sqn | Date | Claims | Location | A/C |
|---|---|---|---|---|
| 486th | June 20, 1944 | Me-109 dest(air) | Magdeburg | P-51 |

1-0-0 air
0-0 ground

**Rauk, Lloyd A., Capt.**
486th Ftr Sqn/352nd Ftr Grp

| *Sqn* | *Date* | *Claims* | *Location* | *A/C* |
|---|---|---|---|---|
| 486th | July 19, 1944 | (2)Me-109 dest(air) | E/Munich | P-51 |

2-0-0 air
0-0 ground

**Rautenbush, William A., Lt.**
375th Ftr Sqn/361st Ftr Grp

| *Sqn* | *Date* | *Claims* | *Location* | *A/C* |
|---|---|---|---|---|
| 375th | April 15, 1944 | u/i a/c dest(grd) | Fritzlar | P-47 |
| | | (.33)Ju-52 dest(grd)* | Fritzlar | P-47 |
| | April 24 | Ju-88 dest(grd) | Metz | P-47 |
| | May 1 | (.5)Ju-188 dest(air)** | W/Verdun | P-47 |

0.5-0-0 air
2.33-0 ground

* - shared with Capt. J.W. Guckeyson and Lt. S.D. Rames of the 375th Ftr Sqn
** - shared with Capt. J.W. Guckeyson of the 375th Ftr Sqn

**Rawley, Walter N., Lt.**
436th Ftr Sqn/479th Ftr Grp

| *Sqn* | *Date* | *Claims* | *Location* | *A/C* |
|---|---|---|---|---|
| 436th | April 16, 1945 | FW-190 dest(grd) | Landstadt | P-51 |

0-0-0 air
1-0 ground

**Rayborn, Garland, Lt.**
328th Ftr Sqn/352nd Ftr Grp

| *Sqn* | *Date* | *Claims* | *Location* | *A/C* |
|---|---|---|---|---|
| 328th | May 21, 1944 | (2)He-111 dest(grd) | Alt Ruppin | P-51 |

0-0-0 air
2-0 ground

**Raymond, Charles J., Lt.**
61st Ftr Sqn/56th Ftr Grp

| *Sqn* | *Date* | *Claims* | *Location* | *A/C* |
|---|---|---|---|---|
| 61st | November 18, 1944 | FW-190 dest(air) | E/Hanau | P-47 |
| | April 10, 1945 | Do-217 dest(grd) | Oranienburg | P-47 |
| | April 13 | u/i a/c dest(grd) | Eggebeck A/F | P-47 |
| | | (5)u/i a/c dam(grd) | Eggebeck A/F | P-47 |

1-0-0 air
2-5 ground

**Rea, Frank, Jr., Lt.**
368th Ftr Sqn/359th Ftr Grp

| *Sqn* | *Date* | *Claims* | *Location* | *A/C* |
|---|---|---|---|---|
| 368th | April 9, 1945 | (.5)Me-262 dam(air)* | Augsburg | P-51 |

0-0-0.5 air
0-0 ground

* - shared with F/O R.G. Muzzy of the 368th Ftr Sqn

**Read, Leighton M., Capt.**
335th Ftr Sqn/4th Ftr Grp

| *Sqn* | *Date* | *Claims* | *Location* | *A/C* |
|---|---|---|---|---|
| 335th | April 24, 1944 | FW-190 dest(air) | N/Worms | P-51 |
| | April 27 | u/i a/c dest(grd) | Toul | P-51 |

1-0-0 air
1-0 ground

**Redd, Howard E., Lt.**
364th Ftr Sqn/357th Ftr Grp

| *Sqn* | *Date* | *Claims* | *Location* | *A/C* |
|---|---|---|---|---|
| 364th | June 20, 1944 | Me-109 dam(air) | Pasewalk | P-51 |

0-0-1 air
0-0 ground

**Reed, Charles W., Lt.**
63rd Ftr Sqn/56th Ftr Grp

| *Sqn* | *Date* | *Claims* | *Location* | *A/C* |
|---|---|---|---|---|
| 63rd | November 5, 1943 | FW-190 dest(air) | Rheine-Munster | P-47 |
| | February 3, 1944 | Me-109 dest(air) | SE Ruhlertwist | P-47 |
| | March 6 | (.25)Me-109 dest(air)* | Minden-Osnabruck | P-47 |
| | April 15 | He-111 dest(grd) | Flensburg | P-47 |

2.25-0-0 air
1-0 ground

* - shared with Col. H. Zemke of HdQts, 56th Ftr Grp, and Lt. M.H. Becker and Lt. D.V. Peters of the 63rd Ftr Sqn

**Reed, Joseph E., Lt.**
358th Ftr Sqn/355th Ftr Grp

| *Sqn* | *Date* | *Claims* | *Location* | *A/C* |
|---|---|---|---|---|
| 358th | March 16, 1944 | (2)Me-109 dam(air) | W/Augsburg | P-51 |
| | April 5 | Me-109 dest(grd) | Munich | P-51 |
| | | Do-217 dest(grd) | Munich | P-51 |
| | April 11 | Me-109 dest(air) | N/Berlin | P-51 |

1-0-2 air
2-0 ground

**Reed, Richard I., Lt.**
335th Ftr Sqn/4th Ftr Grp

| *Sqn* | *Date* | *Claims* | *Location* | *A/C* |
|---|---|---|---|---|
| 335th | February 20, 1944 | (.5)Me-110 dest(air)* | Coblenz | P-47 |

0.5-0-0 air
0-0 ground

* - shared with Lt. P.S. Riley of the 335th Ftr Sqn

**Reed, Robert G., Lt.**
487th Ftr Sqn/352nd Ftr Grp

| *Sqn* | *Date* | *Claims* | *Location* | *A/C* |
|---|---|---|---|---|
| 487th | April 17, 1945 | (2)Me-109 dest(grd) | Plattling | P-51 |
| | | (3)Me-109 dam(grd) | Plattling | P-51 |

0-0-0 air
2-3 ground

**Reeder, Caleb L., Lt.**
62nd Ftr Sqn/56th Ftr Grp

| *Sqn* | *Date* | *Claims* | *Location* | *A/C* |
|---|---|---|---|---|
| 62nd | August 17, 1943 | Me-110 dest(air) | Ans | P-47 |
| | | Me-210 dam(air) | Ans | P-47 |
| | October 8 | FW-190 dam(air) | Quackenbruck | P-47 |
| | March 8, 1944 | (2)FW-190 prob(air) | Hanover | P-47 |

1-2-2 air
0-0 ground

**Reedy, Irving, Lt.**
357th Ftr Sqn/355th Ftr Grp

| *Sqn* | *Date* | *Claims* | *Location* | *A/C* |
|---|---|---|---|---|
| 357th | March 27, 1944 | (.5)Me-109 dest(air)* | Biscarosse A/F | P-51 |
| | April 5 | Ju-88 dest(grd) | Ottingen | P-51 |
| | | Me-109 dam(grd) | Ottingen | P-51 |
| | | Ju-88 dam(grd) | Ottingen | P-51 |

0.5-0-0 air
1-2 ground

* - shared with Capt. J.H. Wilson of the 357th Ftr Sqn

**Reems, Julian S., Capt.**
83rd Ftr Sqn/78th Ftr Grp

| *Sqn* | *Date* | *Claims* | *Location* | *A/C* |
|---|---|---|---|---|
| 83rd | July 31, 1944 | u/i a/c dest(grd) | Neustadt A/F | P-47 |
| | August 10 | He-111 dest(grd) | Chateau Salines | P-47 |
| | | (.5)Ju-52 dest(grd)* | Chateau Salines | P-47 |
| | October 15 | (1.5)FW-190 dest(air)** | Bohmte | P-47 |

1.5-0-0 air
2.5-0 ground

* - shared with Lt. R.L. Burgher of the 83rd Ftr Sqn
** - shared with Lt. R.T. Green of the 83rd Ftr Sqn

**Reese, Luther C., F/O**
370th Ftr Sqn/359th Ftr Grp

| *Sqn* | *Date* | *Claims* | *Location* | *A/C* |
|---|---|---|---|---|
| 370th | July 20, 1944 | Me-109 dam(air) | Zeitz | P-51 |
| | July 21 | Ju-88 dest(grd) | N/Landsberg | P-51 |

0-0-1 air
1-0 ground

**Reese, William C., Lt.**
364th Ftr Sqn/357th Ftr Grp

| *Sqn* | *Date* | *Claims* | *Location* | *A/C* |
|---|---|---|---|---|
| 364th | March 16, 1944 | Me-110 dest(air) | Augsburg | P-51 |
| | | Do-217 dest(air) | Augsburg | P-51 |
| | April 11 | Me-109 dest(air) | E/Hanover | P-51 |
| | April 24 | Me-109 dest(air) | Munich | P-51 |
| | May 12 | Me-109 dest(air) | N/Schweinfurt | P-51 |

5-0-0 air
0-0 ground

**Reese, William H., Lt.**
486th Ftr Sqn/352nd Ftr Grp

| *Sqn* | *Date* | *Claims* | *Location* | *A/C* |
|---|---|---|---|---|
| 486th | December 27, 1944 | (2)Me-109 dest(air) | SW Bonn | P-51 |
| | January 14, 1945 | (2)FW-190 dest(air) | Almello | P-51 |

4-0-0 air
0-0 ground

**Rege, Robert A., Lt.**
77th Ftr Sqn/20th Ftr Grp

| *Sqn* | *Date* | *Claims* | *Location* | *A/C* |
|---|---|---|---|---|
| 77th | February 28, 1945 | Me-109 dam(grd) | Gelsheim | P-51 |

0-0-0 air
0-1 ground

**Reichard, James N., Capt.**
79th Ftr Sqn/20th Ftr Grp
HdQts/20th Ftr Grp

| *Sqn* | *Date* | *Claims* | *Location* | *A/C* |
|---|---|---|---|---|
| 79th | August 9, 1944 | (.5)FW-190 dest(air)* | SW Ulm | P-51 |

0.5-0-0 air
0-0 ground

* - shared with Lt. Q. Klatt of the 79th Ftr Sqn

**Reichman, David M., Lt.**
486th Ftr Sqn/352nd Ftr Grp

| *Sqn* | *Date* | *Claims* | *Location* | *A/C* |
|---|---|---|---|---|
| 486th | July 18, 1944 | Ju-88 dest(air) | S/Rostock | P-51 |
| | March 2, 1945 | FW-190 dest(air) | Zwebau | P-51 |

2-0-0 air
0-0 ground

**Reid, Langhorne, Jr., Maj.**
505th Ftr Sqn/339th Ftr Grp

| *Sqn* | *Date* | *Claims* | *Location* | *A/C* |
|---|---|---|---|---|
| 505th | May 21, 1944 | (1.5)Ju-88 dest(air)* | W/Dresden | P-51 |
| | June 10 | (.5)Ju-52 dest(air)** | Laigle | P-51 |

2-0-0 air
0-0 ground

* - shared with Lt. C.J. Hanseman of the 505th Ftr Sqn
** - shared with Lt. E.M. Johnson of the 505th Ftr Sqn

**Reiff, William L., Lt.**
357th Ftr Sqn/355th Ftr Grp

| *Sqn* | *Date* | *Claims* | *Location* | *A/C* |
|---|---|---|---|---|
| 357th | July 8, 1944 | Me-109 dam(grd) | SW Chalons | P-51 |

0-0-0 air
0-1 ground

**Reihmer, Donald A., Capt.**
79th Ftr Sqn/20th Ftr Grp
77th Ftr Sqn/20th Ftr Grp

| *Sqn* | *Date* | *Claims* | *Location* | *A/C* |
|---|---|---|---|---|
| 77th | April 24, 1944 | (.5)Me-109 dest(air)* | Worms | P-38 |
| | April 29 | (2)Me-109 dam(air) | Wittenberg | P-38 |
| | May 11 | Ju-88 dest(grd) | Bretigny A/F | P-38 |

0.5-0-2 air
1-0 ground

* - shared with Lt. W.G. Schultz of the 55th Ftr Sqn, 20th Ftr Grp

**Reilly, William J., Lt.**
38th Ftr Sqn/55th Ftr Grp

| *Sqn* | *Date* | *Claims* | *Location* | *A/C* |
|---|---|---|---|---|
| 38th | June 25, 1944 | FW-190 dest(air) | SW Paris | P-38 |
| | July 7 | FW-190 dest(air) | Bernburg | P-38 |
| | September 12 | (.5)Ju-52 dest(grd)* | Herzogenaurach | P-51 |

2-0-0 air
0.5-0 ground

* - shared with F/O D.M. Amoss of the 38th Ftr Sqn

**Reinhardt, Edwin D., Lt.**
352nd Ftr Sqn/353rd Ftr Grp

| *Sqn* | *Date* | *Claims* | *Location* | *A/C* |
|---|---|---|---|---|
| 352nd | June 7, 1944 | Me-109 dest(grd) | Compiegne | P-47 |
| | June 20 | He-111 dest(grd) | Twente/Enschede | P-47 |
| | August 4 | Me-410 dest(grd) | Plantlunne | P-47 |
| | | He-111 dest(grd) | Plantlunne | P-47 |
| | August 12 | FW-190 dest(grd) | S/Tournan | P-47 |

0-0-0 air
5-0 ground

**Rensch, Richard J., Lt.**
360th Ftr Sqn/356th Ftr Grp

| *Sqn* | *Date* | *Claims* | *Location* | *A/C* |
|---|---|---|---|---|
| 360th | April 9, 1945 | u/i a/c dest(grd) | Biberach A/F | P-51 |
| | | (3)u/i a/c dam(grd) | Biberach A/F | P-51 |
| | | Me-109 dam(grd) | Biberach A/F | P-51 |

0-0-0 air
1-4 ground

**Rentschler, Victor R.T., Capt.**
334th Ftr Sqn/4th Ftr Grp

| *Sqn* | *Date* | *Claims* | *Location* | *A/C* |
|---|---|---|---|---|
| 334th | December 25, 1944 | FW-190 dest(air) | NE Trier | P-51 |
| | | (.5)Me-109 dest(air)* | NE Trier | P-51 |
| | | FW-190 dam(air) | NE Trier | P-51 |
| | January 2, 1945 | (.5)Me-109 dest(air)** | Westerburg | P-51 |

2-0-1 air
0-0 ground

* - shared with Lt. W.B. Hoelscher of the 334th Ftr Sqn
** - shared with Lt. C.G. Payne of the 334th Ftr Sqn

**Renwick, Donald D., LtCol.**
61st Ftr Sqn/56th Ftr Grp
HdQts/56th Ftr Grp

| *Sqn* | *Date* | *Claims* | *Location* | *A/C* |
|---|---|---|---|---|
| 61st | August 17, 1943 | Me-109 dest(air) | Liege | P-47 |
| | October 8 | FW-190 dam(air) | Lingen | P-47 |
| HdQts | April 13, 1945 | He-111 dest(grd) | Eggebeck A/F | P-47 |

1-0-1 air
1-0 ground

**Reust, Fred W., Lt.**
363rd Ftr Sqn/357th Ftr Grp

| *Sqn* | *Date* | *Claims* | *Location* | *A/C* |
|---|---|---|---|---|
| 363rd | March 8, 1944 | FW-190 dam(air) | SW Berlin | P-51 |

0-0-1 air
0-0 ground

**Rew, George R., LtCol.**
374th Ftr Sqn/361st Ftr Grp

| *Sqn* | *Date* | *Claims* | *Location* | *A/C* |
|---|---|---|---|---|
| 374th | June 6, 1944 | (.5)Me-109 dest(grd)* | Vendome | P-51 |
| | June 12 | FW-190 dest(grd) | Chateau Du Loir | P-51 |

0-0-0 air
1.5-0 ground

* - shared with Lt. V.R. Richards of the 374th Ftr Sqn

**Reynolds, Gardner H., Capt.**
503rd Ftr Sqn/339th Ftr Grp

| *Sqn* | *Date* | *Claims* | *Location* | *A/C* |
|---|---|---|---|---|
| 503rd | May 21, 1944 | u/i a/c dest(grd) | Pelenz-Mackau | P-51 |

0-0-0 air
1-0 ground

**Reynolds, Garth L., Capt.**
77th Ftr Sqn/20th Ftr Grp

| *Sqn* | *Date* | *Claims* | *Location* | *A/C* |
|---|---|---|---|---|
| 77th | November 2, 1944 | Me-109 dest(air) | Merseburg | P-51 |
| | February 9, 1945 | (2)FW-190 dest(grd) | Esperstadt A/F | P-51 |
| | | (2)Me-410 dest(grd) | Esperstadt A/F | P-51 |
| | February 20 | u/i a/c dest(air) | Straubing | P-51 |

2-0-0 air
4-0 ground

**Reynolds, Miron C., Lt.**
487th Ftr Sqn/352nd Ftr Grp

| *Sqn* | *Date* | *Claims* | *Location* | *A/C* |
|---|---|---|---|---|
| 487th | April 17, 1945 | FW-190 dest(grd) | Plattling | P-51 |
| | | Me-109 dest(grd) | Plattling | P-51 |

0-0-0 air
2-0 ground

**Reynolds, James S., Lt.**
55th Ftr Sqn/20th Ftr Grp

| *Sqn* | *Date* | *Claims* | *Location* | *A/C* |
|---|---|---|---|---|
| 55th | July 5, 1944 | (.5)He-177 dest(air)* | Cognac | P-38 |

0.5-0-0 air
0-0 ground

* - shared with LtCol. H.E. Johnson of HdQts, 20th Ftr Grp

**Reynolds, John R., Maj.**
HdQts/339th Ftr Grp

| *Sqn* | *Date* | *Claims* | *Location* | *A/C* |
|---|---|---|---|---|
| HdQts | July 25, 1944 | FW-190 dest(air) | Etrepagny | P-51 |
| | August 28 | (.5)Ju-88 dest(grd)* | Savernne | P-51 |

1-0-0 air
0.5-0 ground

* - shared with Lt. A.D. Young of the 505th Ftr Sqn, 339th Ftr Grp

**Rhodes, Harold W., Lt.**
38th Ftr Sqn/55th Ftr Grp

| *Sqn* | *Date* | *Claims* | *Location* | *A/C* |
|---|---|---|---|---|
| 38th | June 25, 1944 | Me-109 dest(air) | SW Paris | P-38 |

1-0-0 air
0-0 ground

**Riccardo, Gennaro, Lt.**
83rd Ftr Sqn/78th Ftr Grp

| *Sqn* | *Date* | *Claims* | *Location* | *A/C* |
|---|---|---|---|---|
| 83rd | April 13, 1944 | FW-190 dam(air) | Korbach | P-47 |
| | July 5 | FW-190 prob(air) | Evreux | P-47 |
| | July 19 | Ju-188 dest(grd) | Linburg-Coblenz | P-47 |
| | | Ju-188 dam(grd) | Linburg-Coblenz | P-47 |
| | August 10 | (.5)He-111 dest(grd)* | Chateau Salines | P-47 |
| | | u/i a/c dam(grd) | Chateau Salines | P-47 |

0-1-1 air
1.5-2 ground

* - shared with F/O J.A. Moothart of the 83rd Ftr Sqn

**Ricci, Carlo A., Lt.**
487th Ftr Sqn/352nd Ftr Grp

| *Sqn* | *Date* | *Claims* | *Location* | *A/C* |
|---|---|---|---|---|
| 487th | April 10, 1945 | (.5)Me-262 dest(air)* | Neuruppin | P-51 |

0.5-0-0 air
0-0 ground

* - shared with Lt. J.W. Prichard of the 487th Ftr Sqn

**Rice, Donald R., Lt.**
362nd Ftr Sqn/357th Ftr Grp

| *Sqn* | *Date* | *Claims* | *Location* | *A/C* |
|---|---|---|---|---|
| 362nd | February 24, 1944 | FW-190 dest(air) | E/Linz | P-51 |

1-0-0 air
0-0 ground

**Rice, George J., Capt.**
363rd Ftr Sqn/357th Ftr Grp

| *Sqn* | *Date* | *Claims* | *Location* | *A/C* |
|---|---|---|---|---|
| 363rd | December 5, 1944 | FW-190 dest(air) | N/Berlin | P-51 |
| | January 14, 1945 | Me-109 dest(air) | N/Brandenburg | P-51 |

2-0-0 air
0-0 ground

**Rice, John J., F/O**
505th Ftr Sqn/339th Ftr Grp

| *Sqn* | *Date* | *Claims* | *Location* | *A/C* |
|---|---|---|---|---|
| 505th | April 7, 1945 | Me-262 dam(air) | Ulzen | P-51 |
| | April 10 | (2)Do-217 dest(grd) | N/Neuruppin | P-51 |
| | | Do-217 dam(grd) | N/Neuruppin | P-51 |
| | April 16 | (2)Me-109 dest(grd) | NE Prague | P-51 |
| | | Ju-88 dest(grd) | NE Prague | P-51 |
| | | Me-109 dam(grd) | NE Prague | P-51 |
| | | Ju-88 dam(grd) | NE Prague | P-51 |

0-0-1 air
5-3 ground

**Rich, George T., Capt.**
505th Ftr Sqn/339th Ftr Grp

| *Sqn* | *Date* | *Claims* | *Location* | *A/C* |
|---|---|---|---|---|
| 505th | September 10, 1944 | FW-190 dest(grd) | Weizenburg | P-51 |
| | September 11 | (2)u/i a/c dest(grd) | Munich | P-51 |
| | | Me-410 dest(grd) | Munich | P-51 |
| | | Me-410 dam(grd) | Munich | P-51 |
| | November 18 | (.5)Me-109 dest(air)* | Neustadt | P-51 |
| | November 21 | Me-109 dest(air) | Warburg | P-51 |
| | March 30, 1945 | Me-262 dam(air) | N/Luneburg | P-51 |
| | April 4 | Do-217 dest(grd) | NE Tribsees | P-51 |

1.5-0-1 air
5-1 ground

* - shared with Lt. C. Malarz of the 505th Ftr Sqn

**Rich, Irving W., Lt.**
62nd Ftr Sqn/56th Ftr Grp

| *Sqn* | *Date* | *Claims* | *Location* | *A/C* |
|---|---|---|---|---|
| 62nd | April 13, 1945 | (2)Me-109 dam(grd) | Eggebeck A/F | P-47 |

0-0-0 air
0-2 ground

**Richards, Robert H., Lt.**
336th Ftr Sqn/4th Ftr Grp

| *Sqn* | *Date* | *Claims* | *Location* | *A/C* |
|---|---|---|---|---|
| 336th | January 14, 1944 | FW-190 dest(air) | Compiegne | P-47 |
| | January 21 | FW-190 dest(air) | Douai-Valenciennes | P-47 |
| | | FW-190 dam(air) | Douai-Valenciennes | P-47 |

2-0-1 air
0-0 ground

**Richards, Vernon R., Lt.**
374th Ftr Sqn/361st Ftr Grp

| *Sqn* | *Date* | *Claims* | *Location* | *A/C* |
|---|---|---|---|---|
| 374th | June 6, 1944 | (.5)Me-109 dest(grd)[*] | Vendome | P-51 |
| | June 25 | Me-109 dest(air) | S/Caen | P-51 |
| | | FW-190 dest(air) | S/Caen | P-51 |
| | June 29 | (3)FW-190 dest(grd) | Oschersleben | P-51 |
| | | (2)FW-190 dam(grd) | Oschersleben | P-51 |
| | | (.5)FW-190 dam(grd)[**] | Oschersleben | P-51 |
| | | (.5)FW-190 dam(grd)[@] | Oschersleben | P-51 |

2-0-0 air
3.5-3 ground

[*] - shared with Capt. G.R. Rew of the 374th Ftr Sqn
[**] - shared with LtCol. W.E. Hopkins of HdQts, 361st Ftr Grp
[@] - shared with Lt. R.T. Eckfeldt of the 374th Ftr Sqn

**Richardson, Stanley P., Lt.**
338th Ftr Sqn/55th Ftr Grp

| *Sqn* | *Date* | *Claims* | *Location* | *A/C* |
|---|---|---|---|---|
| 338th | June 11, 1944 | Me-109 dest(air) | Beauvais | P-38 |

1-0-0 air
0-0 ground

**Richason, Lee F., Capt.**
359th Ftr Sqn/356th Ftr Grp

| *Sqn* | *Date* | *Claims* | *Location* | *A/C* |
|---|---|---|---|---|
| 359th | November 29, 1943 | Me-109 dam(air) | NE Meppel | P-47 |
| | June 7, 1944 | Me-109 dest(grd) | Laval | P-47 |
| | | Ju-52 dest(grd) | Laval | P-47 |
| | | Me-109 dam(grd) | Laval | P-47 |
| | June 10 | FW-190 dest(grd) | SE Dreux | P-47 |
| | | FW-190 dam(grd) | SE Dreux | P-47 |
| | August 18 | (.5)FW-190 dam(air)[*] | Beauvais | P-47 |

0-0-1.5 air
3-2 ground

[*] - shared with Capt. J.D. Tarbutton of the 359th Ftr Sqn

**Richie, Arthur B., Capt.**
82nd Ftr Sqn/78th Ftr Grp

| *Sqn* | *Date* | *Claims* | *Location* | *A/C* |
|---|---|---|---|---|
| 82nd | July 30, 1943 | FW-190 dest(air) | Haldern | P-47 |

1-0-0 air
0-0 ground

**Richmond, Luther H., LtCol.**
486th Ftr Sqn/352nd Ftr Grp

| *Sqn* | *Date* | *Claims* | *Location* | *A/C* |
|---|---|---|---|---|
| 486th | April 15, 1944 | FW-190 dest(air) | E/Vechta | P-47 |

1-0-0 air
0-0 ground

**Riddle, Kyle L., Col.**
HdQts/479th Ftr Grp

| *Sqn* | *Date* | *Claims* | *Location* | *A/C* |
|---|---|---|---|---|
| HdQts | December 5, 1944 | FW-190 dest(air) | NW Berlin | P-51 |
| | | FW-190 dam(air) | NW Berlin | P-51 |
| | January 1, 1945 | (.5)FW-190 dest(air)[*] | Nienburg | P-51 |

1.5-0-1 air
0-0 ground

[*] - shared with Lt. C.W. Bowers of the 434th Ftr Sqn, 479th Ftr Grp

**Ridley, Oscar T., Lt.**
362nd Ftr Sqn/357th Ftr Grp

| *Sqn* | *Date* | *Claims* | *Location* | *A/C* |
|---|---|---|---|---|
| 362nd | March 2, 1945 | (.5)Me-109 dest(air)[*] | NE Leipzig | P-51 |

0.5-0-0 air
0-0 ground

[*] - shared with Capt. P.R. Hatala of the 364th Ftr Sqn, 357th Ftr Grp

**Riedel, William D., Capt.**
336th Ftr Sqn/4th Ftr Grp

| *Sqn* | *Date* | *Claims* | *Location* | *A/C* |
|---|---|---|---|---|
| 336th | January 16, 1945 | FW-190 dest(grd) | Neuhausen | P-51 |
| | March 21 | (2)u/i a/c dam(grd) | Achmer | P-51 |
| | March 22 | (2)FW-190 dest(air) | NE Ruhland | P-51 |

2-0-0 air
1-2 ground

**Riemensnider, Robert H., Maj.**
55th Ftr Sqn/20th Ftr Grp

| *Sqn* | *Date* | *Claims* | *Location* | *A/C* |
|---|---|---|---|---|
| 55th | August 25, 1944 | (1.5)Do-18 dest(grd)[*] | Parow A/F | P-51 |
| | | u/i a/c dest(grd) | Parow A/F | P-51 |
| | | Do-18 dam(grd) | Parow A/F | P-51 |

0-0-0 air
2.5-1 ground

[*] - shared with Lt. K.D. McNeel of the 55th Ftr Sqn

**Riffle, Elmer H., Lt.**
357th Ftr Sqn/355th Ftr Grp

| *Sqn* | *Date* | *Claims* | *Location* | *A/C* |
|---|---|---|---|---|
| 357th | November 2, 1944 | u/i a/c dest(grd) | Wernigerode | P-51 |
| | February 9, 1945 | (.5)Do-217 dam(air)[*] | Lonnewitz A/F | P-51 |
| | February 23 | Me-262 dest(grd) | Neuburg | P-51 |
| | April 4 | Ar-234 dest(air) | Magdeburg | P-51 |

1-0-0.5 air
2-0 ground

[*] - shared with Lt. R.W. Delhamer of the 357th Ftr Sqn

**Rigby, Alden P., Lt.**
487th Ftr Sqn/352nd Ftr Grp

| *Sqn* | *Date* | *Claims* | *Location* | *A/C* |
|---|---|---|---|---|
| 487th | September 10, 1944 | u/i a/c dest(grd) | Wertheim | P-51 |
| | November 27 | Me-109 dest(air) | Minden | P-51 |
| | January 1, 1945 | (2)FW-190 dest(air) | Liege | P-51 |
| | | (.5)Me-109 dest(air)[*] | Liege | P-51 |
| | | (.5)Me-109 dest(air)[*] | Liege | P-51 |

4-0-0 air
1-0 ground

[*] - both shared with an unknown pilot

**Righetti, Elwyn G., LtCol.**
338th Ftr Sqn/55th Ftr Grp
HdQts/55th Ftr Grp

| *Sqn* | *Date* | *Claims* | *Location* | *A/C* |
|---|---|---|---|---|
| 338th | November 2, 1944 | (.5)Me-109 dest(air)[*] | SW Leipzig | P-51 |
| | December 24 | (3)FW-190 dest(air) | SE Munster | P-51 |
| | | (2)FW-190 dam(air) | SE Munster | P-51 |
| | January 6, 1945 | (3)Ju-88 dest(grd) | Giebelstadt | P-51 |
| | January 13 | Me-109 dest(air) | W/Wurzburg | P-51 |
| | | Ju-88 dest(grd) | Giebelstadt | P-51 |
| HdQts | February 3 | (2)Ju-88 dest(air) | Boizenburg | P-51 |
| | | FW-190 dest(air) | Boizenburg | P-51 |

| Sqn | Date | Claims | Location | A/C |
|---|---|---|---|---|
| | | Ju-88 prob(air) | Boizenburg | P-51 |
| | March 21 | (2)FW-190 dest(grd) | Hopsten A/F | P-51 |
| | April 9 | (3)Me-262 dest(grd) | Munich-Brunnthal | P-51 |
| | | (2)u/i a/c dest(grd) | Munich-Brunnthal | P-51 |
| | | FW-190 dest(grd) | Munich-Brunnthal | P-51 |
| | | (2)u/i a/c dam(grd) | Munich-Brunnthal | P-51 |
| | April 16 | (3)He-111 dest(grd) | Bad Aibling | P-51 |
| | | (2)Ju-88 dest(grd) | Munich-Brunnthal | P-51 |
| | | Si-204 dest(grd) | Munich-Brunnthal | P-51 |
| | | (5)Si-204 dam(grd) | Munich-Brunnthal | P-51 |
| | | Fi-156 dam(grd) | Munich-Brunnthal | P-51 |
| | April 17 | (6)u/i a/c dest(grd) | Riess/Canitz | P-51 |
| | | (3)Me-109 dest(grd) | Riess/Canitz | P-51 |

7.5-1-2 air
27-8 ground

* - shared with Capt. D.S. Cramer of the 338th Ftr Sqn

**Riley, Harold S., Jr., Lt.**
487th Ftr Sqn/352nd Ftr Grp

| Sqn | Date | Claims | Location | A/C |
|---|---|---|---|---|
| 487th | December 20, 1943 | FW-190 dest(air) | NW Oosterwalde | P-47 |
| | December 22 | Me-109 prob(air) | E/Meppen | P-47 |

1-1-0 air
0-0 ground

**Riley, Paul S., Lt.**
335th Ftr Sqn/4th Ftr Grp

| Sqn | Date | Claims | Location | A/C |
|---|---|---|---|---|
| 335th | February 20, 1944 | (.5)Me-110 dest(air)* | Coblenz | P-47 |
| | March 4 | Me-109 prob(air) | NW Berlin | P-51 |
| | March 5 | Me-109 dam(air) | S/Bordeaux | P-51 |
| | March 16 | Me-110 dest(air) | SW Munich | P-51 |
| | | Me-110 dam(air) | SW Munich | P-51 |
| | March 29 | Me-109 dest(air) | E/Ulzen | P-51 |
| | April 5 | (.5)He-111 dest(air)** | N/Brandenburg | P-51 |
| | | (2)He-111 dest(grd) | N/Brandenburg | P-51 |
| | April 8 | FW-190 dest(air) | N/Brunswick | P-51 |
| | April 10 | Bu-131 dest(air) | Romorantin A/F | P-51 |
| | | Bu-131 dest(grd) | Romorantin A/F | P-51 |
| | April 22 | (.5)Me-109 dest(air)@ | SW Kassel | P-51 |
| | April 24 | FW-190 dest(air) | N/Mannheim | P-51 |
| | | FW-190 prob(air) | N/Mannheim | P-51 |

6.5-2-2 air
3-0 ground

* - shared with Lt. R.I. Reed of the 335th Ftr Sqn
** - shared with Lt. J.W. Goodwyn of the 335th Ftr Sqn
@ - shared with Lt. W.B. Smith of the 334th Ftr Sqn, 4th Ftr Grp

**Rimerman, Ben, LtCol.**
350th Ftr Sqn/353rd Ftr Grp
HdQts/353rd Ftr Grp
HdQts/ 55th Ftr Grp

| Sqn | Date | Claims | Location | A/C |
|---|---|---|---|---|
| 350th | September 27, 1943 | Me-109 dest(air) | S/Emden | P-47 |
| | October 14 | FW-190 dest(air) | Duren | P-47 |
| | November 5 | (2)FW-190 dam(air) | Dusseldorf & Munchen-Gladbach | P-47 |
| HdQts (353rd) | March 8, 1944 | FW-190 prob(air) | Hanover | P-47 |
| | June 12 | (1.5)Me-109 dest(air)* | S/Paris | P-47 |
| | June 20 | (.5)He-111 dest(grd)** | Plantlunne | P-47 |
| | | (2)u/i a/c dam(grd) | Plantlunne | P-47 |
| | August 2 | Me-109 dest(air) | S/Compiegne | P-47 |
| | August 12 | Ju-88 dest(grd) | SW Coulommiers | P-47 |
| | August 27 | (.5)FW-190 dest(grd)@ | Metz | P-47 |
| | | (.5)Me-109 dam(grd)@ | Metz | P-47 |
| | April 16, 1945 | (3)FW-190 dest(grd) | Reichersberg | P-51 |
| | | Me-109 dest(grd) | Reichersberg | P-51 |
| | | Me-108 dest(grd) | Reichersberg | P-51 |
| | | Ju-87 dest(grd) | Reichersberg | P-51 |

4.5-1-2 air
8-2.5 ground

* - shared with Lt. W.J. Frank of the 351st Ftr Sqn, 353rd Ftr Grp
** - shared with Lt. V.G. Rafferty of the 350th Ftr Sqn
@ - both shared with Lt. T.J. Forkin of the 352nd Ftr Sqn, 353rd Ftr Grp

**Rinebolt, Richard J., Lt.**
335th Ftr Sqn/4th Ftr Grp

| Sqn | Date | Claims | Location | A/C |
|---|---|---|---|---|
| 335th | September 11, 1944 | Me-109 dest(air) | NW Naumberg | P-51 |

1-0-0 air
0-0 ground

**Risk, Edward J., Lt.**
351st Ftr Sqn/353rd Ftr Grp

| Sqn | Date | Claims | Location | A/C |
|---|---|---|---|---|
| 351st | March 14, 1945 | Me-109 dest(air) | Luckenwalde | P-51 |
| | April 16 | FW-190 dest(grd) | Reichersberg | P-51 |

1-0-0 air
1-0 ground

**Rivers, Erskin H., Lt.**
385th Ftr Sqn/364th Ftr Grp

| Sqn | Date | Claims | Location | A/C |
|---|---|---|---|---|
| 385th | November 2, 1944 | FW-190 dam(air) | Merseburg | P-51 |

0-0-1 air
0-0 ground

**Roark, Frank H., Jr., Capt.**
79th Ftr Sqn/20th Ftr Grp

| Sqn | Date | Claims | Location | A/C |
|---|---|---|---|---|
| 79th | January 30, 1944 | (.5)Do-217 dest(air)* | Minden | P-38 |
| | August 9 | FW-190 dest(air) | SW Ulm | P-51 |

1.5-0-0 air
0-0 ground

* - shared with Lt. M.D. Fall of the 79th Ftr Sqn

**Roberson, Arval J., Lt.**
362nd Ftr Sqn/357th Ftr Grp

| Sqn | Date | Claims | Location | A/C |
|---|---|---|---|---|
| 362nd | March 6, 1944 | (.5)Me-110 dest(air)* | Berlin | P-51 |
| | March 16 | FW-190 prob(air) | SE Stuttgart | P-51 |
| | March 28 | Ju-88 dest(grd) | S/Paris | P-51 |
| | April 11 | Me-109 dest(air) | E/Magdeburg | P-51 |
| | May 19 | (.5)Me-109 dest(air)** | Hagenow | P-51 |
| | May 30 | (2)Me-109 dest(air) | NE Bernburg | P-51 |
| | September 19 | (2)Me-109 dest(air) | Ijsselstein | P-51 |

6-1-0 air
1-0 ground

* - shared with Lt. K.E. Hagen of the 362nd Ftr Sqn
** - shared with Capt. F.E. Adams of the 362nd Ftr Sqn

**Roberts, Eugene P., LtCol.**
84th Ftr Sqn/ 78th Ftr Grp
HdQts/ 78th Ftr Grp
HdQts/364th Ftr Grp

| Sqn | Date | Claims | Location | A/C |
|---|---|---|---|---|
| 84th | July 1, 1943 | FW-190 prob(air) | Goederoode Isle | P-47 |
| | July 30 | (2)FW-190 dest(air) | Winterswijk | P-47 |
| | | Me-109 dest(air) | Rhenon | P-47 |
| | August 17 | Me-110 dest(air) | SE Aachen | P-47 |
| | August 24 | Me-109 dest(air) | Rouen/Evreux | P-47 |
| | | FW-190 dest(air) | Rouen/Evreux | P-47 |
| HdQts (78th) | October 10 | Me-110 dest(air) | W/Enschede | P-47 |
| | | Me-210 dest(air) | W/Enschede | P-47 |
| | October 20 | Me-109 dest(air) | Dinant | P-47 |
| HdQts (364th) | April 16, 1945 | (3)Fi-156 dam(grd) | Marienbad | P-51 |

9-1-0 air
0-3 ground

**Roberts, Paul J., Lt.**
361st Ftr Sqn/356th Ftr Grp

| Sqn | Date | Claims | Location | A/C |
|---|---|---|---|---|
| 361st | October 7, 1944 | Me-110 dest(grd) | Fritzlar | P-47 |

0-0-0 air
1-0 ground

**Roberts, Robill W., Capt.**
61st Ftr Sqn/56th Ftr Grp

| *Sqn* | *Date* | *Claims* | *Location* | *A/C* |
|---|---|---|---|---|
| 61st | December 11, 1943 | Me-110 dest(air) | Langerooge Island | P-47 |
| | | Ju-88 dest(air) | Langerooge Island | P-47 |
| | | Ju-88 dam(air) | Langerooge Island | P-47 |

2-0-1 air
0-0 ground

**Roberts, Warner P., Lt.**
363rd Ftr Sqn/357th Ftr Grp

| *Sqn* | *Date* | *Claims* | *Location* | *A/C* |
|---|---|---|---|---|
| 363rd | December 24, 1944 | Me-109 dest(air) | W/Coblenz | P-51 |

1-0-0 air
0-0 ground

**Robertson, Lawrence J., Lt.**
77th Ftr Sqn/20th Ftr Grp

| *Sqn* | *Date* | *Claims* | *Location* | *A/C* |
|---|---|---|---|---|
| 77th | August 16, 1944 | Me-109 prob(air) | Altenburg | P-51 |
| | September 28 | (2)FW-190 dest(air) | Aschersleben | P-51 |

2-1-0 air
0-0 ground

**Robertson, Louis L., Capt.**
359th Ftr Sqn/356th Ftr Grp

| *Sqn* | *Date* | *Claims* | *Location* | *A/C* |
|---|---|---|---|---|
| 359th | December 5, 1944 | FW-190 prob(air) | N/Berlin | P-51 |

0-1-0 air
0-0 ground

**Robertson, Raynor E., Maj.**
352nd Ftr Sqn/353rd Ftr Grp

| *Sqn* | *Date* | *Claims* | *Location* | *A/C* |
|---|---|---|---|---|
| 352nd | November 5, 1943 | FW-190 dam(air) | Dinslaken | P-47 |
| | February 8, 1944 | FW-190 dest(air) | St. Hubert | P-47 |
| | March 8 | FW-190 dest(air) | N/Dummer Lake | P-47 |
| | | FW-190 dam(air) | N/Dummer Lake | P-47 |

2-0-2 air
0-0 ground

**Robey, Archie H., Lt.**
63rd Ftr Sqn/56th Ftr Grp

| *Sqn* | *Date* | *Claims* | *Location* | *A/C* |
|---|---|---|---|---|
| 63rd | October 20, 1943 | FW-190 dam(air) | S/Aachen | P-47 |
| | November 5 | FW-190 dam(air) | Rheine-Munster | P-47 |
| | January 11, 1944 | Me-109 dest(air) | N/Osnabruck | P-47 |
| | | Me-109 dam(air) | N/Osnabruck | P-47 |
| | March 8 | Me-109 dest(air) | Dummer Lake | P-47 |
| | March 15 | (2)FW-190 dest(air) | Vechta | P-47 |

4-0-3 air
0-0 ground

**Robinson, Allan T., Lt.**
358th Ftr Sqn/355th Ftr Grp

| *Sqn* | *Date* | *Claims* | *Location* | *A/C* |
|---|---|---|---|---|
| 358th | April 5, 1944 | (2)Do-217 dam(grd) | E/Schwerin | P-51 |
| | May 4 | Me-109 prob(air) | SW Hanover | P-51 |
| | | Me-109 dam(air) | SW Hanover | P-51 |
| | May 30 | FW-190 dest(air) | SE Hanover | P-51 |
| | | FW-190 dam(air) | SE Hanover | P-51 |

1-1-2 air
0-2 ground

**Robinson, Gilbert A., Lt.**
362nd Ftr Sqn/357th Ftr Grp

| *Sqn* | *Date* | *Claims* | *Location* | *A/C* |
|---|---|---|---|---|
| 362nd | March 2, 1945 | (4)He-111 dest(grd) | Kamenz A/F | P-51 |
| | | He-111 dam(grd) | Kamenz A/F | P-51 |
| | | u/i a/c dam(grd) | Kamenz A/F | P-51 |

0-0-0 air
4-2 ground

**Robinson, James G., Capt.**
503rd Ftr Sqn/339th Ftr Grp

| *Sqn* | *Date* | *Claims* | *Location* | *A/C* |
|---|---|---|---|---|
| 503rd | September 11, 1944 | (.5)FW-190 dest(air)* | Annaberg | P-51 |

0.5-0-0 air
0-0 ground

* - shared with Lt. D.E. McClish of the 503rd Ftr Sqn

**Robison, George W., Lt.**
350th Ftr Sqn/353rd Ftr Grp

| *Sqn* | *Date* | *Claims* | *Location* | *A/C* |
|---|---|---|---|---|
| 350th | February 28, 1945 | Me-410 dest(grd) | Sonneborn | P-51 |
| | March 24 | FW-190 dest(air) | NW Kassel | P-51 |

1-0-0 air
1-0 ground

**Rodebaugh, Charles R., Lt.**
2nd Scouting Force

| *Sqn* | *Date* | *Claims* | *Location* | *A/C* |
|---|---|---|---|---|
| 2nd | March 14, 1945 | Me-262 dest(air) | Coblenz | P-51 |

1-0-0 air
0-0 ground

**Rodgers, Francis H., Lt.**
357th Ftr Sqn/355th Ftr Grp

| *Sqn* | *Date* | *Claims* | *Location* | *A/C* |
|---|---|---|---|---|
| 357th | April 13, 1945 | He-111 dam(grd) | Schleswig | P-51 |

0-0-0 air
0-1 ground

**Rodgers, Robert E., Lt.**
361st Ftr Sqn/356th Ftr Grp

| *Sqn* | *Date* | *Claims* | *Location* | *A/C* |
|---|---|---|---|---|
| 361st | August 4, 1944 | Me-109 dam(air) | Bremen-Hamburg | P-47 |

0-0-1 air
0-0 ground

**Rodgers, William H., Lt.**
434th Ftr Sqn/479th Ftr Grp

| *Sqn* | *Date* | *Claims* | *Location* | *A/C* |
|---|---|---|---|---|
| 434th | July 29, 1944 | (.5)Ju-88 dam(grd)* | Romilly | P-38 |
| | August 18 | (4)Ju-88 dam(grd) | Nancy/Essey A/F | P-38 |

0-0-0 air
0-4.5 ground

* - shared with Lt. Q.S. Pavlock of the 434th Ftr Sqn

**Roe, Harry L., Lt.**
82nd Ftr Sqn/78th Ftr Grp

| *Sqn* | *Date* | *Claims* | *Location* | *A/C* |
|---|---|---|---|---|
| 82nd | April 10, 1945 | Do-217 dam(grd) | Werder A/F | P-51 |
| | April 16 | He-111 dam(grd) | Pilzen/Prague | P-51 |

0-0-0 air
0-2 ground

**Roesch, Clarence R., Jr., Lt.**
385th Ftr Sqn/364th Ftr Grp

| Sqn | Date | Claims | Location | A/C |
|---|---|---|---|---|
| 385th | December 23, 1944 | FW-190 dam(air) | Luxembourg | P-51 |
| | February 26, 1945 | (1.5)He-111 dest(grd)* | SE Jade Bay | P-51 |
| | April 16 | (2)FW-190 dest(grd) | Pocking | P-51 |
| | | FW-190 dam(grd) | Pocking | P-51 |

0-0-1 air
3.5-1 ground

* - shared with Lt. A.B. McCormick of the 385th Ftr Sqn

**Roff, Harry C., Jr., Lt.**
83rd Ftr Sqn/78th Ftr Grp

| Sqn | Date | Claims | Location | A/C |
|---|---|---|---|---|
| 83rd | December 1, 1943 | Me-110 prob(air) | Duren | P-47 |
| | December 31 | FW-190 dest(air) | NE Lorient | P-47 |
| | | FW-190 dam(air) | NE Lorient | P-47 |
| | January 4, 1944 | FW-190 dest(air) | Munster | P-47 |
| | February 10 | Me-109 dest(air) | Lingen | P-47 |
| | February 22 | FW-190 dam(air) | Nijmegen | P-47 |
| | February 24 | Me-109 prob(air) | Furstenau | P-47 |

3-2-2 air
0-0 ground

**Rogers, Charles E., Lt.**
328th Ftr Sqn/352nd Ftr Grp

| Sqn | Date | Claims | Location | A/C |
|---|---|---|---|---|
| 328th | November 2, 1944 | (2)Me-109 dest(air) | Merseburg | P-51 |

2-0-0 air
0-0 ground

**Rogers, Ellis A., Capt.**
363rd Ftr Sqn/357th Ftr Grp

| Sqn | Date | Claims | Location | A/C |
|---|---|---|---|---|
| 363rd | February 22, 1944 | Me-109 dest(air) | NW Schoningen | P-51 |
| | March 5 | Me-109 dest(air) | E/Bordeaux | P-51 |
| | | (.33)FW-190 dest(air)* | S/Bordeaux | P-51 |

2.33-0-0 air
0-0 ground

* - shared with Lt. D.H. Bochkay and Lt. C.K. Peters of the 363rd Ftr Sqn

**Rogers, John R., Lt.**
435th Ftr Sqn/479th Ftr Grp

| Sqn | Date | Claims | Location | A/C |
|---|---|---|---|---|
| 435th | February 9, 1945 | Me-109 dest(air) | SE Magdeburg | P-51 |
| | | Me-109 dam(air) | SE Magdeburg | P-51 |

1-0-1 air
0-0 ground

**Rogers, John S., Lt.**
385th Ftr Sqn/364th Ftr Grp

| Sqn | Date | Claims | Location | A/C |
|---|---|---|---|---|
| 385th | April 4, 1945 | Me-262 dam(air) | Fassberg A/F | P-51 |
| | April 17 | He-111 dest(grd) | Karlsbad | P-51 |
| | | Ju-52 dest(grd) | Karlsbad | P-51 |
| | | Ar-66 dest(grd) | Karlsbad | P-51 |
| | | (2)He-111 dam(grd) | Karlsbad | P-51 |

0-0-1 air
3-2 ground

**Rogers, Will D., Lt.**
375th Ftr Sqn/361st Ftr Grp

| Sqn | Date | Claims | Location | A/C |
|---|---|---|---|---|
| 375th | June 20, 1944 | (.5)BV-138 dam(grd)* | Putnitz | P-51 |
| | | (.5)FW-189 dam(grd)** | Putnitz | P-51 |
| | August 15 | Ju-88 dam(grd) | Wittmunhafen | P-51 |
| | September 18 | (.5)BV-138 dest(grd)@ | Bug S/P Base | P-51 |

0-0-0 air
0.5-2 ground

* - shared with Lt. M.E. Elliott of the 375th Ftr Sqn
** - shared with Lt. H.A. Spaulding of the 375th Ftr Sqn
@ - shared with Lt. L.C. Travis of the 375th Ftr Sqn

**Rohm, Richard A., Lt.**
505th Ftr Sqn/339th Ftr Grp

| Sqn | Date | Claims | Location | A/C |
|---|---|---|---|---|
| 505th | May 27, 1944 | Fi-156 dest(grd) | Frankfurt | P-51 |
| | August 4 | Ju-88 dest(grd) | E/Celle | P-51 |

0-0-0 air
2-0 ground

**Rohm, Robert F., Lt.**
83rd Ftr Sqn/78th Ftr Grp

| Sqn | Date | Claims | Location | A/C |
|---|---|---|---|---|
| 83rd | March 2, 1945 | Me-109 dam(air) | Burg A/F | P-51 |

0-0-1 air
0-0 ground

**Rohrs, John W., Lt.**
351st Ftr Sqn/353rd Ftr Grp

| Sqn | Date | Claims | Location | A/C |
|---|---|---|---|---|
| 351st | January 14, 1945 | (.5)Me-262 dest(air)* | E/Wittenberge | P-51 |

0.5-0-0 air
0-0 ground

* - shared with Lt. G.J. Rosen of the 351st Ftr Sqn

**Romano, Pasquale J., Lt.**
436th Ftr Sqn/479th Ftr Grp

| Sqn | Date | Claims | Location | A/C |
|---|---|---|---|---|
| 436th | April 17, 1945 | Ju-87 dest(grd) | Karlsbad | P-51 |
| | | u/i a/c dest(grd) | Karlsbad | P-51 |

0-0-0 air
2-0 ground

**Romine, Jack T., Capt.**
360th Ftr Sqn/356th Ftr Grp

| Sqn | Date | Claims | Location | A/C |
|---|---|---|---|---|
| 360th | September 1, 1944 | (.5)Ju-52 dest(grd)* | SE Nancy | P-47 |
| | | (.5)Ju-52 dam(grd)** | SE Nancy | P-47 |
| | September 9 | FW-190 dam(air) | W/Giessen | P-47 |

0-0-1 air
0.5-0.5 ground

* - shared with Lt. W.H. Fletcher of the 360th Ftr Sqn
** - shared with Lt. E.M. Nebinger of the 360th Ftr Sqn

**Roper, Richard C., Lt.**
363rd Ftr Sqn/357th Ftr Grp

| Sqn | Date | Claims | Location | A/C |
|---|---|---|---|---|
| 363rd | September 19, 1944 | (2)Me-109 dest(air) | W/Armheim | P-51 |
| | October 12 | (2)Me-109 dest(air) | Hanover | P-51 |

4-0-0 air
0-0 ground

**Rose, Robert T., Lt.**
352nd Ftr Sqn/353rd Ftr Grp

| Sqn | Date | Claims | Location | A/C |
|---|---|---|---|---|
| 352nd | April 16, 1945 | He-111 dest(grd) | Bad Aibling | P-51 |
| | | Ju-88 dam(grd) | Bad Aibling | P-51 |
| | April 17 | Ju-88 dest(grd) | Ganacker | P-51 |
| | | Me-109 dam(grd) | Ganacker | P-51 |
| | | Ju-88 dam(grd) | Ganacker | P-51 |

0-0-0 air
2-3 ground

**Rosen, George J., Lt.**
504th Ftr Sqn/339th Ftr Grp
351st Ftr Sqn/353rd Ftr Grp

| *Sqn* | *Date* | *Claims* | *Location* | *A/C* |
|---|---|---|---|---|
| 351st | January 14, 1945 | (.5)Me-262 dest(air)* | E/Wittenberge | P-51 |

0.5-0-0 air
0-0 ground

* - shared with Lt. J.W. Rohrs of the 351st Ftr Sqn

**Rosenberg, Alvin M., Lt.**
82nd Ftr Sqn/78th Ftr Grp

| *Sqn* | *Date* | *Claims* | *Location* | *A/C* |
|---|---|---|---|---|
| 82nd | April 16, 1945 | (2)FW-190 dam(grd) | Pilzen/Prague | P-51 |
| | | u/i a/c dam(grd) | Pilzen/Prague | P-51 |

0-0-0 air
0-3 ground

**Rosenberg, Joseph, Lt.**
350th Ftr Sqn/353rd Ftr Grp

| *Sqn* | *Date* | *Claims* | *Location* | *A/C* |
|---|---|---|---|---|
| 350th | September 27, 1943 | Me-109 dam(air) | Emden | P-47 |

0-0-1 air
0-0 ground

**Rosenblatt, Charles J., Maj.**
358th Ftr Sqn/355th Ftr Grp

| *Sqn* | *Date* | *Claims* | *Location* | *A/C* |
|---|---|---|---|---|
| 358th | March 16, 1944 | Me-109 dest(air) | NW Augsburg | P-51 |
| | April 5 | Do-217 dest(grd) | Landsberg | P-51 |
| | | (4)Do-217 dam(grd) | Landsberg | P-51 |

1-0-0 air
1-4 ground

**Rosenblum, Allen A., Lt.**
82nd Ftr Sqn/78th Ftr Grp

| *Sqn* | *Date* | *Claims* | *Location* | *A/C* |
|---|---|---|---|---|
| 82nd | November 21, 1944 | Me-109 dest(air) | Hanover | P-47 |
| | March 19, 1945 | FW-190 dest(air) | Osnabruck | P-51 |
| | | Me-109 dam(air) | Osnabruck | P-51 |
| | March 21 | (.5)Me-262 dest(air)* | Giebelstadt | P-51 |
| | April 17 | u/i a/c dest(grd) | Kralupy | P-51 |

2.5-0-1 air
1-0 ground

* - shared with Capt. W.H. Brown of the 82nd Ftr Sqn

**Rosenblum, Jerome, Lt.**
77th Ftr Sqn/20th Ftr Grp

| *Sqn* | *Date* | *Claims* | *Location* | *A/C* |
|---|---|---|---|---|
| 77th | April 10, 1945 | (.5)Me-262 dest(air)* | Berlin | P-51 |
| | April 17 | Me-262 dam(air) | S/Dresden | P-51 |

0.5-0-1 air
0-0 ground

* - shared with Lt. J.W. Cudd of the 77th Ftr Sqn

**Rosenhoff, Wayne E., Lt.**
343rd Ftr Sqn/55th Ftr Grp

| *Sqn* | *Date* | *Claims* | *Location* | *A/C* |
|---|---|---|---|---|
| 343rd | September 5, 1944 | He-111 dest(grd) | Stuttgart/Echterdingen | P-51 |
| | | He-111 dam(grd) | Stuttgart/Echterdingen | P-51 |
| | | Me-410 dam(grd) | Stuttgart/Echterdingen | P-51 |

0-0-0 air
1-2 ground

**Rosness, Joseph M., Capt.**
436th Ftr Sqn/479th Ftr Grp

| *Sqn* | *Date* | *Claims* | *Location* | *A/C* |
|---|---|---|---|---|
| 436th | September 5, 1944 | He-111 dam(grd) | Hoehst Oberau | P-38 |

0-0-0 air
0-1 ground

**Ross, Donald H., Lt.**
335th Ftr Sqn/ 4th Ftr Grp
363rd Ftr Sqn/357th Ftr Grp

| *Sqn* | *Date* | *Claims* | *Location* | *A/C* |
|---|---|---|---|---|
| 335th | October 8, 1943 | Me-210 dest(air) | Edewecht | P-47 |
| 363rd | February 20, 1944 | Me-109 dest(air) | Duben | P-51 |

2-0-0 air
0-0 ground

**Ross, Robert I., Lt.**
487th Ftr Sqn/352nd Ftr Grp

| *Sqn* | *Date* | *Claims* | *Location* | *A/C* |
|---|---|---|---|---|
| 487th | January 30, 1944 | Me-109 dest(air) | Zwolle | P-47 |
| | April 11 | FW-189 dest(grd) | SW Berlin | P-51 |
| | | Ju-52 dam(grd) | SW Berlin | P-51 |
| | | Ju-88 dam(grd) | SW Berlin | P-51 |
| | April 13 | Trainer dest(air) | SE Stuttgart | P-51 |
| | | u/i a/c dest(grd) | SE Stuttgart | P-51 |

2-0-0 air
2-2 ground

**Ross, Russell H., Lt.**
487th Ftr Sqn/352nd Ftr Grp

| *Sqn* | *Date* | *Claims* | *Location* | *A/C* |
|---|---|---|---|---|
| 487th | December 27, 1944 | FW-190 dest(air) | Mauen | P-51 |

1-0-0 air
0-0 ground

**Rossell, Roy M., Jr., Lt.**
434th Ftr Sqn/479th Ftr Grp

| *Sqn* | *Date* | *Claims* | *Location* | *A/C* |
|---|---|---|---|---|
| 434th | April 13, 1945 | Ar-234 dest(grd) | Lubeck | P-51 |

0-0-0 air
1-0 ground

**Rotzler, Charles M., Lt.**
63rd Ftr Sqn/56th Ftr Grp

| *Sqn* | *Date* | *Claims* | *Location* | *A/C* |
|---|---|---|---|---|
| 63rd | August 15, 1944 | Me-109 dam(grd) | St. Trond | P-47 |
| | September 5 | (2)FW-190 dest(grd) | Gelnhausen | P-47 |
| | | (2)FW-190 dam(grd) | Gelnhausen | P-47 |
| | | Me-109 dam(grd) | Gelnhausen | P-47 |
| | January 14, 1945 | Me-109 dest(air) | Munster | P-47 |

1-0-0 air
2-4 ground

**Roughgarden, James E., Lt.**
362nd Ftr Sqn/357th Ftr Grp

| *Sqn* | *Date* | *Claims* | *Location* | *A/C* |
|---|---|---|---|---|
| 362nd | April 11, 1944 | FW-190 dam(air) | NE Magdeburg | P-51 |
| | April 24 | (2)Me-110 dam(air) | E/Munich | P-51 |

0-0-3 air
0-0 ground

**Rouleau, Louis J., Jr., Lt.**
358th Ftr Sqn/355th Ftr Grp

| *Sqn* | *Date* | *Claims* | *Location* | *A/C* |
|---|---|---|---|---|
| 358th | April 13, 1945 | He-111 dest(grd) | Schleswig | P-51 |
| | April 16 | (2)FW-190 dam(grd) | Straubing | P-51 |

0-0-0 air
1-2 ground

**Rourke, Walter B., Lt.**
435th Ftr Sqn/479th Ftr Grp

| *Sqn* | *Date* | *Claims* | *Location* | *A/C* |
|---|---|---|---|---|
| 435th | April 13, 1945 | Ju-88 dest(grd) | Tarnewitz | P-51 |
| | | (2)Ju-88 dam(grd) | Tarnewitz | P-51 |

0-0-0 air
1-2 ground

**Routh, Sylvan R., Lt.**
435th Ftr Sqn/479th Ftr Grp

| *Sqn* | *Date* | *Claims* | *Location* | *A/C* |
|---|---|---|---|---|
| 435th | April 17, 1945 | Me-262 dest(grd) | Puchhoff | P-51 |

0-0-0 air
1-0 ground

**Rout, Bill C., Maj.**
504th Ftr Sqn/339th Ftr Grp

| *Sqn* | *Date* | *Claims* | *Location* | *A/C* |
|---|---|---|---|---|
| 504th | May 21, 1944 | (2)Me-109 dest(air) | Dobeln | P-51 |
| | July 7 | Me-109 dest(air) | Eisleben | P-51 |
| | August 16 | Me-109 dest(air) | Mulhausen | P-51 |
| | | Me-109 dam(air) | Mulhausen | P-51 |

4-0-1 air
0-0 ground

**Rowan, Chauncey, Lt.**
350th Ftr Sqn/353rd Ftr Grp

| *Sqn* | *Date* | *Claims* | *Location* | *A/C* |
|---|---|---|---|---|
| 350th | February 24, 1944 | FW-190 dest(air) | Steinhuder Lake | P-47 |

1-0-0 air
0-0 ground

**Rowbatham, Robert C., Lt.**
358th Ftr Sqn/355th Ftr Grp

| *Sqn* | *Date* | *Claims* | *Location* | *A/C* |
|---|---|---|---|---|
| 358th | April 16, 1945 | (3)FW-190 dest(grd) | Straubing | P-51 |
| | | (2)FW-190 dam(grd) | Straubing | P-51 |

0-0-0 air
3-2 ground

**Rowlett, Bruce W., Capt.**
375th Ftr Sqn/361st Ftr Grp

| *Sqn* | *Date* | *Claims* | *Location* | *A/C* |
|---|---|---|---|---|
| 375th | September 26, 1944 | FW-190 dest(grd) | Achmer | P-51 |
| | | He-177 dest(grd) | Achmer | P-51 |
| | | (2)FW-190 dam(grd) | Achmer | P-51 |

0-0-0 air
2-2 ground

**Rowlett, Lloyd E., Lt.**
77th Ftr Sqn/20th Ftr Grp

| *Sqn* | *Date* | *Claims* | *Location* | *A/C* |
|---|---|---|---|---|
| 77th | August 5, 1944 | Me-109 dam(air) | S/Hamburg | P-51 |
| | August 16 | Me-109 dest(air) | Mulhausen | P-51 |
| | November 2 | (2)Me-109 dest(air) | Merseburg | P-51 |

3-0-1 air
0-0 ground

**Roy, Frederick L., Lt.**
62nd Ftr Sqn/56th Ftr Grp

| *Sqn* | *Date* | *Claims* | *Location* | *A/C* |
|---|---|---|---|---|
| 62nd | February 22, 1944 | FW-190 dest(air) | Breda | P-47 |

1-0-0 air
0-0 ground

**Rubner, Chester H., Jr., Capt.**
359th Ftr Sqn/356th Ftr Grp

| *Sqn* | *Date* | *Claims* | *Location* | *A/C* |
|---|---|---|---|---|
| 359th | March 6, 1944 | Me-109 dest(air) | Nienburg | P-47 |
| | March 29 | Me-109 dest(air) | Steinhuder Lake | P-47 |

2-0-0 air
0-0 ground

**Ruch, Jay W., Capt.**
376th Ftr Sqn/361st Ftr Grp

| *Sqn* | *Date* | *Claims* | *Location* | *A/C* |
|---|---|---|---|---|
| 376th | December 26, 1944 | (.5)FW-190 dest(air)[*] | Merzig | P-51 |

0.5-0-0 air
0-0 ground

[*] - shared with Lt. G.R. Vanden Heuval of the 376th Ftr Sqn

**Rudd, Edward G., Capt.**
359th Ftr Sqn/356th Ftr Grp

| *Sqn* | *Date* | *Claims* | *Location* | *A/C* |
|---|---|---|---|---|
| 359th | March 20, 1945 | Me-262 dam(air) | Wesermunde-Hamburg | P-51 |

0-0-1 air
0-0 ground

**Ruder, Leroy A., Capt.**
364th Ftr Sqn/357th Ftr Grp

| *Sqn* | *Date* | *Claims* | *Location* | *A/C* |
|---|---|---|---|---|
| 364th | March 6, 1944 | (1.5)Me-110 dest(air)[*] | W/Berlin | P-51 |
| | April 11 | FW-190 dest(air) | NE Brunswick | P-51 |
| | May 19 | FW-190 dest(air) | N/Berlin | P-51 |
| | May 27 | Me-109 dest(air) | Strasbourg | P-51 |
| | May 28 | Me-109 dest(air) | NW Magdeburg | P-51 |

5.5-0-0 air
0-0 ground

[*] - shared with Capt. W.R. O'Brien of the 363rd Ftr Sqn, 357th Ftr Grp

**Rudnick, Vincent J., Lt.**
79th Ftr Sqn/20th Ftr Grp

| *Sqn* | *Date* | *Claims* | *Location* | *A/C* |
|---|---|---|---|---|
| 79th | February 20, 1945 | (.5)He-111 dest(grd)[*] | Weiden A/F | P-51 |
| | | He-111 dam(grd) | Weiden A/F | P-51 |

0-0-0 air
0.5-1 ground

[*] - shared with Lt. D.A. Beschen of the 79th Ftr Sqn

**Rueschenberg, Werner J., Lt.**
370th Ftr Sqn/359th Ftr Grp

| *Sqn* | *Date* | *Claims* | *Location* | *A/C* |
|---|---|---|---|---|
| 370th | December 31, 1944 | (.5)Me-109 dest(air)[*] | Hanover | P-51 |
| | January 14, 1945 | (.5)FW-190 dest(air)[**] | Vorden A/F | P-51 |

1-0-0 air
0-0 ground

[*] - shared with Capt. R.S. Wetmore of the 370th Ftr Sqn
[**] - shared with Capt. R.S. Wetmore of the 370th Ftr Sqn

**Ruland, James W., Lt.**
385th Ftr Sqn/364th Ftr Grp

| *Sqn* | *Date* | *Claims* | *Location* | *A/C* |
|---|---|---|---|---|
| 385th | April 4, 1945 | FW-190 dest(air) | Potsdam | P-51 |
| | April 17 | He-111 dam(grd) | Karlsbad | P-51 |

1-0-0 air
0-1 ground

**Ruscitto, James O., Capt.**
350th Ftr Sqn/353rd Ftr Grp

| Sqn | Date | Claims | Location | A/C |
|---|---|---|---|---|
| 350th | June 12, 1944 | Me-109 dest(air) | Dreux | P-47 |
| | | Me-109 dam(air) | Dreux | P-47 |
| | June 30 | Me-109 prob(air) | W/Chalons | P-47 |
| | August 4 | Me-109 dam(air) | Wenzendorf | P-47 |
| | August 11 | Me-109 dest(grd) | Maraville | P-47 |
| | August 28 | (2)Me-110 dest(air) | Wavre | P-47 |

3-1-2 air
1-0 ground

**Rushman, Glenn A., Lt.**
486th Ftr Sqn/352nd Ftr Grp

| Sqn | Date | Claims | Location | A/C |
|---|---|---|---|---|
| 486th | April 17, 1945 | (2)FW-190 dest(grd) | Plattling | P-51 |
| | | (2)FW-190 dam(grd) | Plattling | P-51 |

0-0-0 air
2-2 ground

**Russell, Barton M., Col.**
HdQts/20th Ftr Grp

| Sqn | Date | Claims | Location | A/C |
|---|---|---|---|---|
| HdQts | January 14, 1944 | (.5)FW-190 dest(air)[*] | Rouen | P-38 |

0.5-0-0 air
0-0 ground

[*] - shared with F/O M.L. Byrd of the 79th Ftr Sqn, 20th Ftr Grp

**Russell, Ernest E., Lt.**
84th Ftr Sqn/78th Ftr Grp

| Sqn | Date | Claims | Location | A/C |
|---|---|---|---|---|
| 84th | December 1, 1943 | FW-190 dam(air) | SE Aachen | P-47 |
| | March 16, 1944 | Me-110 dest(grd) | St. Dizier | P-47 |

0-0-1 air
1-0 ground

**Russell, Francis M., Capt.**
360th Ftr Sqn/356th Ftr Grp

| Sqn | Date | Claims | Location | A/C |
|---|---|---|---|---|
| 360th | May 19, 1944 | FW-190 dest(air) | Hanover | P-47 |

1-0-0 air
0-0 ground

**Russell, James W., Jr., Capt.**
335th Ftr Sqn/4th Ftr Grp

| Sqn | Date | Claims | Location | A/C |
|---|---|---|---|---|
| 335th | April 10, 1944 | u/i a/c dest(grd) | Romorantin A/F | P-51 |
| | | u/i a/c dam(grd) | Romorantin A/F | P-51 |
| | May 24 | Me-109 dest(air) | Hamburg-Lubeck | P-51 |
| | September 11 | Me-109 dest(air) | Erfurt | P-51 |
| | | Me-109 prob(air) | Erfurt | P-51 |
| | | FW-190 prob(air) | Erfurt | P-51 |

2-2-0 air
1-1 ground

**Rutan, Fred S., Jr., Lt.**
504th Ftr Sqn/339th Ftr Grp

| Sqn | Date | Claims | Location | A/C |
|---|---|---|---|---|
| 504th | July 29, 1944 | (2)Me-109 dest(air) | Naumburg | P-51 |

2-0-0 air
0-0 ground

**Ryan, Eugene E., Maj.**
343rd Ftr Sqn/55th Ftr Grp
338th Ftr Sqn/55th Ftr Grp

| Sqn | Date | Claims | Location | A/C |
|---|---|---|---|---|
| 343rd | November 3, 1943 | Me-109 dam(air) | Wilhelmshaven | P-38 |
| | November 13 | Me-109 dest(air) | W/Bremen | P-38 |
| | | FW-190 prob(air) | W/Bremen | P-38 |
| | November 25 | (2)Me-109 dam(air) | Lille | P-38 |
| | February 24, 1944 | FW-190 dam(air) | E/Gotha | P-38 |
| | February 25 | Me-410 prob(air) | Augsburg | P-38 |
| | April 22 | FW-190 dest(air) | W/Hamm | P-38 |
| 338th | April 16, 1945 | Me-262 dest(air) | Horsching A/F | P-51 |
| | | He-111 dest(grd) | N/Landshut | P-51 |
| | April 17 | (.5)u/i a/c dest(grd)[*] | Leipzig | P-51 |

3-2-4 air
1.5-0 ground

[*] - shared with Lt. J.R. Ethridge of the 338th Ftr Sqn

**Sabo, Paul J., Capt.**
77th Ftr Sqn/20th Ftr Grp

| Sqn | Date | Claims | Location | A/C |
|---|---|---|---|---|
| 77th | February 5, 1944 | (.33)FW-200 dest(air)[*] | Bourges A/F | P-38 |
| | February 10 | Me-110 dam(air) | Hanover | P-38 |
| | | Me-210 dam(air) | Hanover | P-38 |

0.33-0-2 air
0-0 ground

[*] - shared with LtCol. R.P. Montgomery of HdQts, 20th Ftr Grp, and Lt. J.E. Davis of the 77th Ftr Sqn

**Sadinski, John J., Lt.**
376th Ftr Sqn/361st Ftr Grp

| Sqn | Date | Claims | Location | A/C |
|---|---|---|---|---|
| 376th | November 2, 1944 | FW-190 dest(air) | N/Erfurt | P-51 |

1-0-0 air
0-0 ground

**Sagar, William S., Jr., Lt.**
385th Ftr Sqn/364th Ftr Grp

| Sqn | Date | Claims | Location | A/C |
|---|---|---|---|---|
| 385th | December 27, 1944 | FW-190 dest(air) | W/Coblenz | P-51 |
| | | (.5)Me-109 dest(air) | SW Coblenz | P-51 |
| | | Me-109 dam(air) | W/Coblenz | P-51 |

1.5-0-1 air
0-0 ground

[*] - shared with Lt. R.K. Allen of the 384th Ftr Sqn, 364th Ftr Grp

**Sainlar, Jerome J., Lt.**
504th Ftr Sqn/339th Ftr Grp

| Sqn | Date | Claims | Location | A/C |
|---|---|---|---|---|
| 504th | February 9, 1945 | Me-262 dam(air) | Meiningen | P-51 |

0-0-1 air
0-0 ground

**Saling, Thomas W., III, Lt.**
63rd Ftr Sqn/56th Ftr Grp

| Sqn | Date | Claims | Location | A/C |
|---|---|---|---|---|
| 63rd | October 15, 1944 | (.5)Me-109 dest(grd)[*] | Rheine A/F | P-47 |

0-0-0 air
0.5-0 ground

[*] - shared with Lt. J.A. Kyle of the 63rd Ftr Sqn

**Salinsky, Charles J., Lt.**
357th Ftr Sqn/355th Ftr Grp

| Sqn | Date | Claims | Location | A/C |
|---|---|---|---|---|
| 357th | June 21, 1944 | Me-109 dest(air) | N/Magdeburg | P-51 |
| | June 24 | (3)Me-109 dest(grd) | NE Angars | P-51 |
| | | (2)Me-109 dam(grd) | NE Angars | P-51 |
| | July 24 | Me-109 dam(grd) | Lechfeld | P-51 |
| | | u/i a/c dam(grd) | Lechfeld | P-51 |

1-0-0 air
3-4 ground

**Salsman, John J., Lt.**
364th Ftr Sqn/357th Ftr Grp

| Sqn | Date | Claims | Location | A/C |
|---|---|---|---|---|
| 364th | June 20, 1944 | Me-109 dest(air) | Pasewalk | P-51 |
| | July 29 | FW-190 dam(air) | Merseburg | P-51 |
| | October 7 | Me-109 dest(air) | SW Leipzig | P-51 |

2-0-1 air
0-0 ground

**Salter, G.M., Lt.**
435th Ftr Sqn/479th Ftr Grp

| Sqn | Date | Claims | Location | A/C |
|---|---|---|---|---|
| 435th | April 17, 1945 | u/i a/c dam(grd) | Puchhoff | P-51 |

0-0-0 air
0-1 ground

**Salze, Floyd W., Lt.**
435th Ftr Sqn/479th Ftr Grp

| Sqn | Date | Claims | Location | A/C |
|---|---|---|---|---|
| 435th | March 25, 1945 | Me-262 dam(air) | SE Hamburg | P-51 |
| | April 17 | Me-262 dest(grd) | Puchhoff | P-51 |

0-0-1 air
1-0 ground

**Sandborn, Dwaine A., Lt.**
364th Ftr Sqn/357th Ftr Grp

| Sqn | Date | Claims | Location | A/C |
|---|---|---|---|---|
| 364th | September 19, 1944 | Me-109 dest(air) | E/Arnheim | P-51 |

1-0-0 air
0-0 ground

**Sander, Robert B., Lt.**
369th Ftr Sqn/359th Ftr Grp

| Sqn | Date | Claims | Location | A/C |
|---|---|---|---|---|
| 369th | May 21, 1944 | (.5)u/i a/c dest(air)* | NW Klutz | P-51 |

0.5-0-0 air
0-0 ground

* - shared with Capt. R.H. Broach of the 369th Ftr Sqn

**Sanders, Donald J., Lt.**
354th Ftr Sqn/355th Ftr Grp

| Sqn | Date | Claims | Location | A/C |
|---|---|---|---|---|
| 354th | April 16, 1945 | u/i a/c dest(grd) | Eger A/F | P-51 |

0-0-0 air
1-0 ground

**Sandkaut, Henry D., Lt.**
383rd Ftr Sqn/364th Ftr Grp

| Sqn | Date | Claims | Location | A/C |
|---|---|---|---|---|
| 383rd | December 27, 1944 | FW-190 dest(air) | NW Frankfurt | P-51 |
| | April 13 | (2)Ju-52 dest(grd) | Flensburg | P-51 |
| | | Do-217 dam(grd) | Flensburg | P-51 |
| | | FW-190 dam(grd) | Flensburg | P-51 |

1-0-0 air
2-2 ground

**Sanford, William H., Lt.**
328th Ftr Sqn/352nd Ftr Grp

| Sqn | Date | Claims | Location | A/C |
|---|---|---|---|---|
| 328th | December 23, 1944 | FW-190 dest(air) | S/Liege | P-51 |
| | March 3, 1945 | Me-109 dest(air) | W/Dresden | P-51 |
| | April 16 | (2)FW-190 dest(grd) | Landau | P-51 |

2-0-0 air
2-0 ground

**Sansing, Virgal E., Lt.**
369th Ftr Sqn/359th Ftr Grp

| Sqn | Date | Claims | Location | A/C |
|---|---|---|---|---|
| 369th | May 24, 1944 | (1.5)Me-109 dest(air)* | NW Berlin | P-51 |

1.5-0-0 air
0-0 ground

* - shared with Lt. J.B. Hunter of the 368th Ftr Sqn, 359th Ftr Grp

**Santee, John C., Lt.**
79th Ftr Sqn/20th Ftr Grp

| Sqn | Date | Claims | Location | A/C |
|---|---|---|---|---|
| 79th | February 20, 1945 | (.5)He-111 dest(grd) | Weiden A/F | P-51 |
| | | He-111 dam(grd) | Weiden A/F | P-51 |

0-0-0 air
0.5-1 ground

* - shared with Lt. R.H. Pollock of the 79th Ftr Sqn

**Santos, Albert R., Lt.**
358th Ftr Sqn/355th Ftr Grp

| Sqn | Date | Claims | Location | A/C |
|---|---|---|---|---|
| 358th | May 30, 1944 | (2)FW-190 dest(air) | SE Brunswick | P-51 |

2-0-0 air
0-0 ground

**Sargent, Robert F., Capt.**
504th Ftr Sqn/339th Ftr Grp

| Sqn | Date | Claims | Location | A/C |
|---|---|---|---|---|
| 504th | March 30, 1945 | Me-262 dest(air) | Kaltenkirchen A/F | P-51 |
| | April 10 | (3)Me-410 dest(grd) | N/Neuruppin | P-51 |
| | | (2)Me-410 dam(grd) | N/Neuruppin | P-51 |

1-0-0 air
3-2 ground

**Sargent, Walter H., Lt.**
374th Ftr Sqn/361st Ftr Grp

| Sqn | Date | Claims | Location | A/C |
|---|---|---|---|---|
| 374th | June 7, 1944 | Ju-52 dest(grd) | Orleans/Bricy | P-51 |

0-0-0 air
1-0 ground

**Sarver, Frank A., Lt.**
354th Ftr Sqn/355th Ftr Grp

| Sqn | Date | Claims | Location | A/C |
|---|---|---|---|---|
| 354th | April 13, 1945 | FW-190 dest(grd) | Husum | P-51 |
| | | FW-190 dam(grd) | Husum | P-51 |

0-0-0 air
1-1 ground

**Satenstein, Marvin, Lt.**
343rd Ftr Sqn/55th Ftr Grp

| Sqn | Date | Claims | Location | A/C |
|---|---|---|---|---|
| 343rd | March 3, 1945 | (4)Me-109 dam(grd) | Prague/Letnany | P-51 |

0-0-0 air
0-4 ground

**Saunders, Ralph W., Lt.**
335th Ftr Sqn/4th Ftr Grp

| Sqn | Date | Claims | Location | A/C |
|---|---|---|---|---|
| 335th | March 29, 1944 | Me-109 dest(air) | Lingen | P-51 |
| | April 5 | Ju-52 dest(grd) | W/Brandenburg | P-51 |
| | | Me-110 dam(grd) | W/Brandenburg | P-51 |
| | | Ju-88 dam(grd) | W/Brandenburg | P-51 |

1-0-0 air
1-2 ground

**Savage, Morton R., Lt.**
334th Ftr Sqn/4th Ftr Grp

| *Sqn* | *Date* | *Claims* | *Location* | *A/C* |
|---|---|---|---|---|
| 334th | December 2, 1944 | Me-109 dam(air) | SE Bingen | P-51 |

0-0-1 air
0-0 ground

**Sawicki, Joseph F., Lt.**
505th Ftr Sqn/339th Ftr Grp

| *Sqn* | *Date* | *Claims* | *Location* | *A/C* |
|---|---|---|---|---|
| 505th | May 27, 1944 | Fi-156 dest(grd) | Frankfurt | P-51 |

0-0-0 air
1-0 ground

**Saylor, Henry B., Capt.**
385th Ftr Sqn/364th Ftr Grp

| *Sqn* | *Date* | *Claims* | *Location* | *A/C* |
|---|---|---|---|---|
| 385th | April 15, 1944 | Me-109 prob(air) | W/Hamburg | P-38 |

0-1-0 air
0-0 ground

**Scally, John J., Lt.**
334th Ftr Sqn/4th Ftr Grp

| *Sqn* | *Date* | *Claims* | *Location* | *A/C* |
|---|---|---|---|---|
| 334th | July 7, 1944 | Me-410 dest(air) | Sangerhausen | P-51 |

1-0-0 air
0-0 ground

**Scanlon, James J., Lt.**
335th Ftr Sqn/4th Ftr Grp

| *Sqn* | *Date* | *Claims* | *Location* | *A/C* |
|---|---|---|---|---|
| 335th | April 13, 1945 | (2)Ar-196 dam(grd) | Ratzburger Lake | P-51 |

0-0-0 air
0-2 ground

**Scarbrough, Milton G., Lt.**
335th Ftr Sqn/4th Ftr Grp

| *Sqn* | *Date* | *Claims* | *Location* | *A/C* |
|---|---|---|---|---|
| 335th | April 10, 1944 | u/i a/c dam(grd) | Romorantin A/F | P-51 |
| | April 15 | He-177 dam(grd) | Hagenow | P-51 |
| | April 24 | FW-190 prob(air) | S/Mannheim | P-51 |

0-1-0 air
0-2 ground

**Schallo, Philip L., Capt.**
77th Ftr Sqn/20th Ftr Grp
HdQts/20th Ftr Grp

| *Sqn* | *Date* | *Claims* | *Location* | *A/C* |
|---|---|---|---|---|
| 77th | November 2, 1944 | Me-109 dam(air) | N/Leipzig | P-51 |
| | February 9, 1945 | Me-109 dest(air) | Esperstadt A/F | P-51 |
| | | (2)FW-190 dest(grd) | Esperstadt A/F | P-51 |
| | | Me-410 dest(grd) | Esperstadt A/F | P-51 |

1-0-1 air
3-0 ground

**Schank, Thomas D., Lt.**
338th Ftr Sqn/55th Ftr Grp

| *Sqn* | *Date* | *Claims* | *Location* | *A/C* |
|---|---|---|---|---|
| 338th | June 11, 1944 | Me-109 dest(air) | Beauvais | P-38 |
| | July 25 | (2)Me-109 dest(air) | Dreux | P-38 |
| | | (3)Me-109 dam(air) | Dreux | P-38 |
| | September 13 | Me-109 dest(air) | Eisenach-Gotha | P-51 |
| | September 19 | Me-109 dest(air) | Cologne | P-51 |

5-0-3 air
0-0 ground

**Scharnberg, Russell C., Lt.**
359th Ftr Sqn/356th Ftr Grp

| *Sqn* | *Date* | *Claims* | *Location* | *A/C* |
|---|---|---|---|---|
| 359th | November 25, 1944 | Ju-88 dam(grd) | Ettinghausen | P-51 |

0-0-0 air
0-1 ground

**Scheible, Wilbur R., Maj.**
361st Ftr Sqn/356th Ftr Grp
HdQts/356th Ftr Grp

| *Sqn* | *Date* | *Claims* | *Location* | *A/C* |
|---|---|---|---|---|
| 361st | June 15, 1944 | Me-109 dest(air) | SE Rouen | P-47 |
| | October 7 | (2)Me-110 dest(grd) | Fritzlar | P-47 |
| | | Ju-88 dest(grd) | Fritzlar | P-47 |
| | | (4)Ju-88 dam(grd) | Fritzlar | P-47 |
| | November 26 | (3)Me-109 dest(air) | Osnabruck-Dummer Lake | P-51 |
| | | (2)Me-109 dam(air) | Osnabruck-Dummer Lake | P-51 |
| | December 5 | (2)FW-190 dest(air) | Eberswalde | P-51 |

6-0-2 air
3-4 ground

**Schilling, David C., Col.**
62nd Ftr Sqn/56th Ftr Grp
HdQts/56th Ftr Grp

| *Sqn* | *Date* | *Claims* | *Location* | *A/C* |
|---|---|---|---|---|
| HdQts | October 2, 1943 | Me-109 dest(air) | SE Groningen | P-47 |
| | | FW-190 dest(air) | NE Emden | P-47 |
| | October 4 | Me-110 dest(air) | E/Duren | P-47 |
| | October 8 | FW-190 dest(air) | Quackenbruck | P-47 |
| | October 10 | FW-190 dest(air) | Altenberg | P-47 |
| | November 26 | (2)FW-190 dest(air) | SE Oldenburg | P-47 |
| | | Me-210 dam(air) | SE Oldenburg | P-47 |
| | November 29 | (.5)FW-190 dest(air)[*] | S/Oldenburg | P-47 |
| | January 11, 1944 | FW-190 dest(air) | Osnabruck | P-47 |
| | | FW-190 dam(air) | Osnabruck | P-47 |
| | January 29 | Me-109 dest(air) | Bonn | P-47 |
| | March 8 | FW-190 dam(air) | Dummer Lake | P-47 |
| | | Me-210 dest(grd) | Dummer Lake | P-47 |
| | March 27 | Ju-52 dest(grd) | Chateaudun | P-47 |
| | March 29 | Me-109 dest(air) | NE Dummer Lake | P-47 |
| | | Me-109 dam(air) | NE Dummer Lake | P-47 |
| | April 9 | (2)FW-190 dest(air) | NE Schleswig | P-47 |
| | | FW-190 dam(air) | NE Schleswig | P-47 |
| | | W-34 dam(air) | Schleswig | P-47 |
| | | Ar-196 dest(grd) | Schleswig | P-47 |
| | April 13 | Me-109 dest(air) | Ludwigshafen | P-47 |
| | July 24 | (.5)Me-210 dest(grd)[**] | Villaroche | P-47 |
| | | (.5)Me-210 dam(grd)[**] | Villaroche | P-47 |
| | August 28 | He-111 dest(air) | S/Trier | P-47 |
| | September 5 | (2)FW-190 dest(grd) | Gelnhausen | P-47 |
| | | (2)u/i a/c dest(grd) | Gelnhausen | P-47 |
| | | FW-190 dam(grd) | Gelnhausen | P-47 |
| | September 21 | (3)FW-190 dest(air) | Lochen | P-47 |
| | October 5 | (3)Me-210 dest(grd) | S/Geseke | P-47 |
| | | (3)Me-210 dam(grd) | S/Geseke | P-47 |
| | December 23 | (3)Me-109 dest(air) | Euskirchen-Bonn | P-47 |
| | | (2)FW-190 dest(air) | Euskirchen-Bonn | P-47 |

22.5-0-6 air
10.5-4.5 ground

[*] - shared with Lt. F.D. Williamson of the 62nd Ftr Sqn
[**] - both shared with Lt. A.J. Bux of the 61st Ftr Sqn, 56th Ftr Grp

**Scheid, Adolph J., Lt.**
354th Ftr Sqn/355th Ftr Grp

| *Sqn* | *Date* | *Claims* | *Location* | *A/C* |
|---|---|---|---|---|
| 354th | April 13, 1945 | He-111 dam(grd) | Husum | P-51 |
| | | FW-190 dam(grd) | Husum | P-51 |
| | April 16 | Ju-88 dest(grd) | Autobahn | P-51 |

0-0-0 air
1-2 ground

**Schendel, Charles R., Lt.**
38th Ftr Sqn/55th Ftr Grp

| *Sqn* | *Date* | *Claims* | *Location* | *A/C* |
|---|---|---|---|---|
| 38th | April 9, 1945 | (2)u/i a/c dam(grd) | Munich-Brunnthal | P-51 |

0-0-0 air
0-2 ground

**Scherz, Willard G., Lt.**
63rd Ftr Sqn/56th Ftr Grp

| *Sqn* | *Date* | *Claims* | *Location* | *A/C* |
|---|---|---|---|---|
| 63rd | November 18, 1944 | FW-190 dam(air) | E/Hanau | P-47 |
| | December 23 | FW-190 dest(air) | NW Coblenz | P-47 |
| | | FW-190 prob(air) | NW Coblenz | P-47 |
| | | FW-190 dam(air) | NW Coblenz | P-47 |

1-1-2 air
0-0 ground

**Schilke, James F., Lt.**
367th Ftr Sqn/358th Ftr Grp

| *Sqn* | *Date* | *Claims* | *Location* | *A/C* |
|---|---|---|---|---|
| 367th | January 30, 1944 | Me-109 dest(air) | E/Zwolle | P-47 |

1-0-0 air
0-0 ground

**Schilt, John L., Lt.**
350th Ftr Sqn/353rd Ftr Grp

| *Sqn* | *Date* | *Claims* | *Location* | *A/C* |
|---|---|---|---|---|
| 350th | August 27, 1944 | (1.5)FW-190 dest(grd)* | Verdun | P-47 |
| | | FW-190 dam(grd) | Verdun | P-47 |
| | August 28 | (.5)He-111 dest(air)** | SE Arlon | P-47 |
| | September 21 | FW-190 dest(air) | S/Arnheim | P-47 |

1.5-0-0 air
1.5-1 ground

* - shared with Lt. B.C. Auchincloss of the 350th Ftr Sqn
** - shared with LtCol. K.W. Gallup of the 350th Ftr Sqn

**Schiltz, Glen D., Jr., Capt.**
63rd Ftr Sqn/56th Ftr Grp

| *Sqn* | *Date* | *Claims* | *Location* | *A/C* |
|---|---|---|---|---|
| 63rd | August 17, 1943 | (3)FW-190 dest(air) | Ans-St. Nicholas | P-47 |
| | | Me-210 dam(air) | Ans-St. Nicholas | P-47 |
| | October 4 | Me-110 dest(air) | E/Duren | P-47 |
| | October 10 | FW-190 dam(air) | W/Munster | P-47 |
| | December 11 | Me-210 dest(air) | Emden | P-47 |
| | January 11, 1944 | (3)Me-109 dest(air) | N/Osnabruck | P-47 |
| | February 21 | Me-109 dam(air) | Zuider Zee | P-47 |

8-0-3 air
0-0 ground

**Schimanski, Robert G., Capt.**
364th Ftr Sqn/357th Ftr Grp

| *Sqn* | *Date* | *Claims* | *Location* | *A/C* |
|---|---|---|---|---|
| 364th | September 13, 1944 | (.5)Me-109 dest(air)* | E/Bad Frankenhausen | P-51 |
| | November 27 | Me-109 dest(air) | S/Brandenburg | P-51 |
| | December 5 | FW-190 dest(air) | W/Berlin | P-51 |
| | December 24 | Me-109 dest(air) | Kassel | P-51 |
| | March 2, 1945 | (1.5)Me-109 dest(air)** | SE Magdeburg | P-51 |
| | | (2)He-111 dest(grd) | SE Magdeburg | P-51 |
| | March 24 | Me-109 dest(air) | W/Gutersloh | P-51 |
| | | Me-109 dam(air) | W/Gutersloh | P-51 |

6-0-1 air
2-0 ground

* - shared with Maj. J.A. Storch of the 364th Ftr Sqn
** - shared with Lt. D.E. Karger of the 364th Ftr Sqn

**Schlack, Robert F., Capt.**
361st Ftr Sqn/356th Ftr Grp

| *Sqn* | *Date* | *Claims* | *Location* | *A/C* |
|---|---|---|---|---|
| 361st | February 20, 1945 | Ju-88 dest(grd) | Furth | P-51 |
| | | (3)Ju-88 dam(grd) | Furth | P-51 |

0-0-0 air
1-3 ground

**Schlecht, Warner J., Lt.**
358th Ftr Sqn/355th Ftr Grp

| *Sqn* | *Date* | *Claims* | *Location* | *A/C* |
|---|---|---|---|---|
| 358th | April 13, 1945 | Me-109 dest(grd) | Schleswig | P-51 |
| | | (.5)He-111 dest(grd)* | Schleswig | P-51 |

0-0-0 air
1.5-0 ground

* - shared with Lt. R.V. Finnessey of the 358th Ftr Sqn

**Schlegel, Albert L., Capt.**
335th Ftr Sqn/4th Ftr Grp

| *Sqn* | *Date* | *Claims* | *Location* | *A/C* |
|---|---|---|---|---|
| 335th | October 2, 1943 | Me-109 dest(air) | SE Emden | P-47 |
| | | Me-109 dam(air) | SE Emden | P-47 |
| | February 10, 1944 | (.5)Me-109 prob(air)* | SW Hanover | P-47 |
| | February 24 | FW-190 prob(air) | NW Coblenz | P-47 |
| | March 8 | Me-109 prob(air) | NE Magdeburg | P-51 |
| | March 21 | He-111 dest(air) | S/Saintes | P-51 |
| | March 27 | (.5)FW-190 dam(air)** | Libourne | P-51 |
| | April 5 | He-111 dest(grd) | Brandenburg | P-51 |
| | | Ju-88 dest(grd) | Brandenburg | P-51 |
| | | Ju-52 dam(grd) | Brandenburg | P-51 |
| | | u/i a/c dam(grd) | Brandenburg | P-51 |
| | April 8 | (1.5)FW-190 dest(air)@ | Celle | P-51 |
| | | (.5)Me-109 dest(air)@ | Celle | P-51 |
| | | FW-190 dest(grd) | Brunswick | P-51 |
| | | FW-190 dam(grd) | Brunswick | P-51 |
| | April 10 | u/i a/c dest(grd) | Romorantin A/F | P-51 |
| | April 15 | He-177 dest(grd) | Hagenow | P-51 |
| | April 22 | (2)Me-109 dest(air) | S/Kassel | P-51 |
| | April 24 | (2.5)FW-190 dest(air)@@ | N/Worms | P-51 |

8.5-2.5-1.5 air
5-3 ground

* - shared with Lt. C.F. Anderson of the 335th Ftr Sqn
** - shared with Capt. J.R. Happel of the 335th Ftr Sqn
@ - both shared with Lt. S.W. Monroe of the 334th Ftr Sqn, 4th Ftr Grp
@@ - shared with Col. D.J.M. Blakeslee of HdQts, 4th Ftr Grp

**Schlieker, Robert L., Lt.**
362nd Ftr Sqn/357th Ftr Grp

| *Sqn* | *Date* | *Claims* | *Location* | *A/C* |
|---|---|---|---|---|
| 362nd | December 2, 1944 | Me-109 dest(air) | Bingen | P-51 |

1-0-0 air
0-0 ground

**Schmidt, George C., Lt.**
357th Ftr Sqn/355th Ftr Grp

| *Sqn* | *Date* | *Claims* | *Location* | *A/C* |
|---|---|---|---|---|
| 357th | February 9, 1945 | Me-109 dam(grd) | Kothen | P-51 |
| | February 23 | Me-110 dest(grd) | Neuburg | P-51 |

0-0-0 air
1-1 ground

**Schneider, Charles F., F/O**
364th Ftr Sqn/357th Ftr Grp

| *Sqn* | *Date* | *Claims* | *Location* | *A/C* |
|---|---|---|---|---|
| 364th | March 24, 1945 | Me-109 dest(air) | W/Gutersloh | P-51 |
| | | (2)Me-109 dam(air) | W/Gutersloh | P-51 |

1-0-2 air
0-0 ground

**Schneider, Edwin H., Lt.**
84th Ftr Sqn/78th Ftr Grp

| *Sqn* | *Date* | *Claims* | *Location* | *A/C* |
|---|---|---|---|---|
| 84th | August 17, 1944 | (.5)Me-109 dest(grd)* | S/Hamm | P-47 |

0-0-0 air
0.5-0 ground

* - shared with Lt. M.R. Capp of the 84th Ftr Sqn

**Schneider, Edwin O., Lt.**
82nd Ftr Sqn/78th Ftr Grp

| Sqn | Date | Claims | Location | A/C |
|---|---|---|---|---|
| 82nd | March 19, 1945 | Me-109 dest(air) | Osnabruck | P-51 |

1-0-0 air
0-0 ground

**Schneider, Kenneth C., Lt.**
338th Ftr Sqn/55th Ftr Grp

| Sqn | Date | Claims | Location | A/C |
|---|---|---|---|---|
| 338th | February 25, 1945 | FW-190 dam(grd) | Illesheim | P-51 |

0-0-0 air
0-1 ground

**Schneider, Robert, Lt.**
367th Ftr Sqn/358th Ftr Grp

| Sqn | Date | Claims | Location | A/C |
|---|---|---|---|---|
| 367th | January 30, 1944 | Me-109 prob(air) | E/Zwolle | P-47 |

0-1-0 air
0-0 ground

**Schoen, Donald W., Lt.**
352nd Ftr Sqn/353rd Ftr Grp

| Sqn | Date | Claims | Location | A/C |
|---|---|---|---|---|
| 352nd | February 23, 1945 | He-111 dest(grd) | Kitzingen | P-51 |
| | | Me-110 dest(grd) | Kitzingen | P-51 |
| | | Me-110 dam(grd) | Kitzingen | P-51 |

0-0-0 air
2-1 ground

**Schoenfeldt, Dean E., Lt.**
357th Ftr Sqn/355th Ftr Grp

| Sqn | Date | Claims | Location | A/C |
|---|---|---|---|---|
| 357th | March 16, 1944 | Me-109 dam(air) | S/Reutlingen | P-51 |
| | March 28 | Ju-88 dest(grd) | Dijon | P-51 |
| | | (2)Ju-88 dam(grd) | Dijon | P-51 |
| | April 11 | Ju-88 dest(grd) | Wensdorf A/F | P-51 |
| | | (2)Ju-88 dam(grd) | Wensdorf A/F | P-51 |

0-0-1 air
2-4 ground

**Scholz, Howard F., Lt.**
82nd Ftr Sqn/78th Ftr Grp

| Sqn | Date | Claims | Location | A/C |
|---|---|---|---|---|
| 82nd | July 1, 1944 | FW-190 dest(air) | Reims | P-47 |
| | September 9 | (2)FW-190 dest(air) | Giessen | P-47 |
| | | FW-190 dam(air) | Giessen | P-47 |
| | | Ju-88 dest(grd) | Munster | P-47 |

3-0-1 air
1-0 ground

**Schonenberg, Herman J., Lt.**
338th Ftr Sqn/55th Ftr Grp

| Sqn | Date | Claims | Location | A/C |
|---|---|---|---|---|
| 338th | September 3, 1944 | FW-190 dest(air) | Brussels | P-51 |
| | March 18, 1945 | FW-190 dest(air) | N/Giessen | P-51 |

2-0-0 air
0-0 ground

**Schreiber, Joseph, Lt.**
352nd Ftr Sqn/353rd Ftr Grp

| Sqn | Date | Claims | Location | A/C |
|---|---|---|---|---|
| 352nd | March 2, 1945 | Me-109 dest(air) | Magdeburg | P-51 |

1-0-0 air
0-0 ground

**Schreiber, Leroy A., Maj.**
61st Ftr Sqn/56th Ftr Grp
62nd Ftr Sqn/56th Ftr Grp

| Sqn | Date | Claims | Location | A/C |
|---|---|---|---|---|
| 61st | July 30, 1943 | (2)Me-109 dest(air) | Arnheim | P-47 |
| 62nd | August 24 | FW-190 dest(air) | S/Paris | P-47 |
| | October 8 | FW-190 dest(air) | Quackenbruck | P-47 |
| | November 11 | FW-190 dam(air) | Munster | P-47 |
| | November 29 | (.5)Me-210 dest(air)[*] | S/Oldenburg | P-47 |
| | February 8, 1944 | Me-109 prob(air) | Cambrai | P-47 |
| | February 11 | Me-109 dam(air) | Namur | P-47 |
| | February 20 | (3)Me-109 dest(air) | Steinhuder Lake | P-47 |
| | | Me-109 dam(air) | Steinhuder Lake | P-47 |
| | | Do-217 dam(grd) | Steinhuder Lake | P-47 |
| | February 21 | FW-190 dam(air) | Osnabruck | P-47 |
| | February 22 | (.5)FW-190 dest(air)[**] | Breda | P-47 |
| | March 8 | Me-109 dest(air) | Steinhuder Lake | P-47 |
| | | FW-190 dest(air) | Steinhuder Lake | P-47 |
| | March 16 | Me-109 dest(air) | St. Dizier | P-47 |
| | | (.5)FW-190 dest(air)[@] | St. Dizier | P-47 |
| | April 8 | (.5)Me-410 dest(grd)[@@] | Quackenbruck | P-47 |
| | | (.5)Me-109 dest(grd)[@@] | Quackenbruck | P-47 |
| | April 9 | (.5)Me-109 dest(air)[#] | Lubeck | P-47 |
| | | (3)Me-109 dam(grd) | Lubeck | P-47 |
| | April 15 | He-111 dest(grd) | Schleswig | P-47 |

12-1-4 air
2-4 ground

[*] - shared with Lt. H.M. Pruden of the 62nd Ftr Sqn
[**] - shared with Lt. J.E. Fields of the 62nd Ftr Sqn
[@] - shared with Lt. A.W. Canizares of the 62nd Ftr Sqn
[@@] - both shared with Lt. A.W. Canizares of the 62nd Ftr Sqn
[#] - shared with Lt. A.W. Canizares of the 62nd Ftr Sqn

**Schroeder, George Z., Capt.**
384th Ftr Sqn/364th Ftr Grp

| Sqn | Date | Claims | Location | A/C |
|---|---|---|---|---|
| 384th | December 31, 1944 | FW-190 dest(air) | Hamburg | P-51 |
| | April 5, 1945 | Me-262 dam(air) | N/Regensburg | P-51 |

1-0-1 air
0-0 ground

**Schrull, Edward W., Lt.**
360th Ftr Sqn/356th Ftr Grp

| Sqn | Date | Claims | Location | A/C |
|---|---|---|---|---|
| 360th | April 9, 1945 | FW-190 dam(grd) | Biberach | P-51 |
| | | u/i a/c dam(grd) | Biberach | P-51 |
| | April 10 | Me-262 dam(air) | Oranienburg | P-51 |

0-0-1 air
0-2 ground

**Schuh, Duerr H., Capt.**
487th Ftr Sqn/352nd Ftr Grp

| Sqn | Date | Claims | Location | A/C |
|---|---|---|---|---|
| 487th | September 11, 1944 | Me-109 dest(air) | Einbeck-Gottingen | P-51 |
| | November 2 | Me-109 dest(air) | Merseburg | P-51 |
| | December 26 | (3)Me-109 dest(air) | Veldenbor | P-51 |

5-0-0 air
0-0 ground

**Schutt, Ralph C., Lt.**
354th Ftr Sqn/355th Ftr Grp

| Sqn | Date | Claims | Location | A/C |
|---|---|---|---|---|
| 354th | April 10, 1944 | (2)Do-217 dam(grd) | Bourges | P-51 |
| | | u/i a/c dam(grd) | Bourges | P-51 |
| | April 11 | Me-108 dest(grd) | S/Madu Lake | P-51 |

0-0-0 air
1-3 ground

**Schwab, Warren A., Lt.**
354th Ftr Sqn/355th Ftr Grp

| Sqn | Date | Claims | Location | A/C |
|---|---|---|---|---|
| 354th | July 5, 1944 | Ju-88 dest(air) | Chateauroux | P-51 |

1-0-0 air
0-0 ground

**Schwartz, Harry C., Lt.**
384th Ftr Sqn/364th Ftr Grp

| *Sqn* | *Date* | *Claims* | *Location* | *A/C* |
|---|---|---|---|---|
| 384th | February 23, 1945 | (2)Me-109 dest(air) | Stuttgart | P-51 |
| | April 10 | (.5)Me-262 dest(air)[*] | Staaken A/F | P-51 |
| | | FW-200 dest(grd) | W/Berlin | P-51 |
| | April 16 | Ju-87 dest(grd) | Pocking | P-51 |
| | | (3)Me-109 dam(grd) | Pocking | P-51 |

2.5-0-0 air
2-3 ground

[*] - shared with Capt. D.J. Pick of the 384th Ftr Sqn

**Schwenke, William D., Lt.**
328th Ftr Sqn/352nd Ftr Grp

| *Sqn* | *Date* | *Claims* | *Location* | *A/C* |
|---|---|---|---|---|
| 328th | January 30, 1944 | Me-109 dest(air) | Ruhlertwist | P-47 |

1-0-0 air
0-0 ground

**Scordino, Anthony J., Lt.**
436th Ftr Sqn/479th Ftr Grp

| *Sqn* | *Date* | *Claims* | *Location* | *A/C* |
|---|---|---|---|---|
| 436th | February 22, 1945 | Ju-88 dest(grd) | Halberstadt | P-51 |
| | | (2)He-111 dam(grd) | Halberstadt | P-51 |

0-0-0 air
1-2 ground

**Scott, Donald H., Lt.**
434th Ftr Sqn/479th Ftr Grp

| *Sqn* | *Date* | *Claims* | *Location* | *A/C* |
|---|---|---|---|---|
| 434th | April 16, 1945 | u/i a/c dest(grd) | Erferding | P-51 |

0-0-0 air
1-0 ground

**Scott, James F., Lt.**
334th Ftr Sqn/4th Ftr Grp

| *Sqn* | *Date* | *Claims* | *Location* | *A/C* |
|---|---|---|---|---|
| 334th | May 19, 1944 | (.5)Me-109 dest(air)[*] | Lubeck-Schwerin | P-51 |
| | May 29 | Do-18 dam(grd) | Dievenow | P-51 |
| | May 30 | Me-109 dest(air) | Dessau-Bernburg | P-51 |
| | June 6 | FW-190 dest(air) | Evreux | P-51 |

2.5-0-0 air
0-1 ground

[*] - shared with Maj. M.G.H. McPharlin of HdQts, 339th Ftr Grp

**Scott, Kenneth J., Lt.**
376th Ftr Sqn/361st Ftr Grp

| *Sqn* | *Date* | *Claims* | *Location* | *A/C* |
|---|---|---|---|---|
| 376th | November 26, 1944 | FW-190 prob(air) | S/Ulzen | P-51 |
| | | FW-190 dam(air) | S/Ulzen | P-51 |
| | November 27 | Me-109 dest(air) | S/Munster | P-51 |
| | March 30, 1945 | Me-262 dest(air) | W/Rendsburg | P-51 |

2-1-1 air
0-0 ground

**Scott, Richard M., Capt.**
385th Ftr Sqn/364th Ftr Grp

| *Sqn* | *Date* | *Claims* | *Location* | *A/C* |
|---|---|---|---|---|
| 385th | March 15, 1944 | (.5)Me-109 dest(air)[*] | Dummer Lake | P-38 |
| | | (.5)FW-190 dest(air)[**] | Dummer Lake | P-38 |

1-0-0 air
0-0 ground

[*] - shared with Lt. J.D. Turner of the 385th Ftr Sqn
[**] - shared with Lt. J.C. Tallman of the 385th Ftr Sqn

**Scott, Robert M., Lt.**
79th Ftr Sqn/20th Ftr Grp

| *Sqn* | *Date* | *Claims* | *Location* | *A/C* |
|---|---|---|---|---|
| 79th | January 14, 1945 | Me-109 dam(air) | E/Wittenberg | P-51 |
| | February 20 | He-111 dest(grd) | Weiden A/F | P-51 |
| | | He-111 dam(grd) | Weiden A/F | P-51 |
| | April 17 | Me-262 dam(air) | SE Dresden | P-51 |

0-0-2 air
1-1 ground

**Scott, Roy C., Maj.**
385th Ftr Sqn/364th Ftr Grp

| *Sqn* | *Date* | *Claims* | *Location* | *A/C* |
|---|---|---|---|---|
| 385th | May 24, 1944 | (.5)Do-217 dest(air)[*] | Gifhorn | P-38 |

0.5-0-0 air
0-0 ground

[*] - shared with Lt. H.D. Burkhard of the 385th Ftr Sqn

**Scruggs, Harold W., LtCol.**
HdQts/339th Ftr Grp

| *Sqn* | *Date* | *Claims* | *Location* | *A/C* |
|---|---|---|---|---|
| HdQts | May 24, 1944 | (.5)FW-190 dest(air)[*] | NW Berlin | P-51 |
| | June 29 | (2)FW-190 dest(air) | Eisleben | P-51 |
| | | (2)FW-190 dam(air) | Eisleben | P-51 |

2.5-0-2 air
0-0 ground

[*] - shared with Lt. R.S. Whitelaw of the 503rd Ftr Sqn, 339th Ftr Grp

**Scrutchfield, Roy M., Capt.**
55th Ftr Sqn/20th Ftr Grp

| *Sqn* | *Date* | *Claims* | *Location* | *A/C* |
|---|---|---|---|---|
| 55th | April 23, 1944 | He-111 dest(grd) | Chateaudun A/F | P-38 |
| | | (2)u/i a/c dam(grd) | Chateaudun A/F | P-38 |
| | | Ju-87 dam(grd) | Chateaudun A/F | P-38 |
| | October 7 | Do-18 dest(grd) | Ribnitz A/F | P-51 |

0-0-0 air
2-3 ground

**Seanor, George W., Lt.**
360th Ftr Sqn/356th Ftr Grp

| *Sqn* | *Date* | *Claims* | *Location* | *A/C* |
|---|---|---|---|---|
| 360th | April 13, 1945 | Do-217 dam(grd) | Schwerin | P-51 |
| | April 18 | (.33)Me-262 dam(air)[*] | Ingolstadt | P-51 |

0-0-0.33 air
0-1 ground

[*] - shared with Lt. W.C. Gatlin and Lt. L.B. Proctor of the 360th Ftr Sqn

**Sears, Alex F., Capt.**
487th Ftr Sqn/352nd Ftr Grp

| *Sqn* | *Date* | *Claims* | *Location* | *A/C* |
|---|---|---|---|---|
| 487th | June 27, 1944 | FW-190 dest(air) | Noyon | P-51 |
| | July 29 | Me-109 dest(air) | W/Naumberg | P-51 |
| | August 5 | Me-109 dest(air) | S/Hamburg | P-51 |
| | September 11 | u/i a/c dest(grd) | Langensalza | P-51 |
| | December 26 | Me-109 dest(air) | Ollheim | P-51 |
| | January 1, 1945 | Me-109 dest(air) | N/Liege | P-51 |

5-0-0 air
1-0 ground

**Sears, Eugene E., Lt.**
434th Ftr Sqn/479th Ftr Grp

| *Sqn* | *Date* | *Claims* | *Location* | *A/C* |
|---|---|---|---|---|
| 434th | December 25, 1944 | Me-109 dest(air) | SW Bonn | P-51 |
| | February 20, 1945 | Do-217 dest(grd) | Windleschenlaibach | P-51 |

1-0-0 air
1-0 ground

**Sedman, Robert E., Maj.**
374th Ftr Sqn/361st Ftr Grp

| *Sqn* | *Date* | *Claims* | *Location* | *A/C* |
|---|---|---|---|---|
| 374th | January 30, 1944 | Me-109 dest(air) | Rheine | P-47 |
| | | Me-109 prob(air) | Rheine | P-47 |
| | March 6 | FW-190 dest(air) | Zuider Zee | P-47 |
| | April 8 | Me-109 dest(air) | N/Dummer Lake | P-47 |
| | May 21 | u/i a/c dest(grd) | Grossenheim A/F | P-51 |
| | | (2)u/i a/c dam(grd) | Grossenheim A/F | P-51 |

3-1-0 air
1-2 ground

**Seeley, Grant A., Capt.**
358th Ftr Sqn/355th Ftr Grp

| *Sqn* | *Date* | *Claims* | *Location* | *A/C* |
|---|---|---|---|---|
| 358th | April 16, 1945 | (2)FW-190 dest(grd) | Straubing | P-51 |
| | | Me-110 dam(grd) | Straubing | P-51 |
| | | u/i a/c dam(grd) | Straubing | P-51 |
| | April 20 | Me-109 prob(air) | Kbely A/F | P-51 |

0-1-0 air
2-2 ground

**Seeley, Howard L., Lt.**
83rd Ftr Sqn/78th Ftr Grp

| *Sqn* | *Date* | *Claims* | *Location* | *A/C* |
|---|---|---|---|---|
| 83rd | March 19, 1945 | (2)Me-109 dest(air) | Osnabruck | P-51 |
| | | FW-190 dam(air) | Osnabruck | P-51 |

2-0-1 air
0-0 ground

**Seely, Ralph S., Lt.**
343rd Ftr Sqn/55th Ftr Grp

| *Sqn* | *Date* | *Claims* | *Location* | *A/C* |
|---|---|---|---|---|
| 343rd | June 11, 1944 | Me-109 dest(air) | W/Beauvais | P-38 |

1-0-0 air
0-0 ground

**Segert, Albert L., F/O**
375th Ftr Sqn/361st Ftr Grp

| *Sqn* | *Date* | *Claims* | *Location* | *A/C* |
|---|---|---|---|---|
| 375th | April 17, 1945 | Ju-52 dam(grd) | Eger A/F | P-51 |

0-0-0 air
0-1 ground

**Sehl, James H., Lt.**
362nd Ftr Sqn/357th Ftr Grp

| *Sqn* | *Date* | *Claims* | *Location* | *A/C* |
|---|---|---|---|---|
| 362nd | August 28, 1944 | (.5)Ju-52 dest(grd)* | Trier | P-51 |
| | September 19 | Me-109 dest(air) | Ijsselstein | P-51 |

1-0-0 air
0.5-0 ground

* - shared with Capt. H.E. Beal of the 362nd Ftr Sqn

**Seifert, Paul F., Lt.**
55th Ftr Sqn/20th Ftr Grp

| *Sqn* | *Date* | *Claims* | *Location* | *A/C* |
|---|---|---|---|---|
| 55th | April 10, 1945 | He-111 dam(grd) | Werder A/F | P-51 |
| | | Me-110 dam(grd) | Werder A/F | P-51 |

0-0-0 air
0-2 ground

**Seitzinger, Bernard K., Capt.**
364th Ftr Sqn/357th Ftr Grp

| *Sqn* | *Date* | *Claims* | *Location* | *A/C* |
|---|---|---|---|---|
| 364th | September 18, 1944 | Me-109 dest(air) | N/Maastricht | P-51 |
| | | Me-109 dam(air) | N/Maastricht | P-51 |

1-0-1 air
0-0 ground

**Semon, Richard F., Lt.**
328th Ftr Sqn/352nd Ftr Grp

| *Sqn* | *Date* | *Claims* | *Location* | *A/C* |
|---|---|---|---|---|
| 328th | September 11, 1944 | FW-190 dest(air) | E/Meiningen | P-51 |

1-0-0 air
0-0 ground

**Senecal, Arthur J., Lt.**
334th Ftr Sqn/4th Ftr Grp

| *Sqn* | *Date* | *Claims* | *Location* | *A/C* |
|---|---|---|---|---|
| 334th | September 27, 1944 | Me-109 dest(air) | Giessen | P-51 |
| | November 18 | (2)Me-262 dam(grd) | Leipheim | P-51 |
| | January 2, 1945 | (.5)Me-109 dest(air)* | Westerburg | P-51 |

1.5-0-0 air
0-2 ground

* - shared with Lt. C.G. Payne of the 334th Ftr Sqn

**Sensibaugh, Zack S., Lt.**
335th Ftr Sqn/4th Ftr Grp

| *Sqn* | *Date* | *Claims* | *Location* | *A/C* |
|---|---|---|---|---|
| 335th | April 10, 1944 | u/i a/c dam(grd) | Romorantin A/F | P-51 |

0-0-0 air
0-1 ground

**Serros, Jerome C., Capt.**
55th Ftr Sqn/20th Ftr Grp

| *Sqn* | *Date* | *Claims* | *Location* | *A/C* |
|---|---|---|---|---|
| 55th | March 18, 1944 | (.5)Me-110 dest(air)* | Memmingen | P-38 |

0.5-0-0 air
0-0 ground

* - shared with Lt. C.A. Hallberg of the 55th Ftr Sqn

**Seth, Joseph A., Lt.**
383rd Ftr Sqn/364th Ftr Grp

| *Sqn* | *Date* | *Claims* | *Location* | *A/C* |
|---|---|---|---|---|
| 383rd | April 13, 1945 | Me-109 dest(grd) | Flensburg | P-51 |
| | | FW-190 dest(grd) | Flensburg | P-51 |
| | | Me-109 dam(grd) | Flensburg | P-51 |
| | April 16 | (2)Me-109 dest(grd) | Marienbad | P-51 |

0-0-0 air
4-1 ground

**Shackleford, William G., Capt.**
375th Ftr Sqn/361st Ftr Grp

| *Sqn* | *Date* | *Claims* | *Location* | *A/C* |
|---|---|---|---|---|
| 375th | July 7, 1944 | Me-109 dam(air) | N/Leipzig | P-51 |
| | August 5 | Do-217 dest(grd) | Alhorn | P-51 |
| | | (2)Me-163 dam(grd) | Alhorn | P-51 |

0-0-1 air
1-2 ground

**Shade, William A., Lt.**
357th Ftr Sqn/355th Ftr Grp

| *Sqn* | *Date* | *Claims* | *Location* | *A/C* |
|---|---|---|---|---|
| 357th | August 14, 1944 | Ju-88 dest(grd) | Vitry | P-51 |
| | | (.5)Ju-88 dest(grd)* | Sarrebourg | P-51 |

0-0-0 air
1.5-0 ground

* - shared with Lt. J. Max of the 357th Ftr Sqn

**Shafer, Dale E., Jr., LtCol.**
503rd Ftr Sqn/339th Ftr Grp

Earlier flew in the MTO with the 31st Ftr Grp and claimed 4 kills; a Me-109 on April 26, 1943; MC-202's on May 6 and June 10, 1943; and a FW-190 on September 10, 1943.

| *Sqn* | *Date* | *Claims* | *Location* | *A/C* |
|---|---|---|---|---|
| 503rd | November 18, 1944 | Me-109 dest(air) | Mannheim | P-51 |
| | December 5 | FW-190 dam(air) | S/Wittstock | P-51 |
| | March 18, 1945 | FW-190 dest(air) | Dummer Lake | P-51 |
| | | FW-190 dam(air) | Dummer Lake | P-51 |
| | April 10 | Me-109 dest(grd) | N/Neuruppin | P-51 |
| | | Ju-88 dest(grd) | N/Neuruppin | P-51 |
| | | (4)Ju-88 dam(grd) | N/Neuruppin | P-51 |
| | April 18 | Ar-234 dest(air) | Regensburg | P-51 |

3-0-2 air
2-4 ground

**Shaffer, Allen L., F/O**
79th Ftr Sqn/20th Ftr Grp

| *Sqn* | *Date* | *Claims* | *Location* | *A/C* |
|---|---|---|---|---|
| 79th | January 14, 1945 | Me-109 dest(air) | NW Berlin | P-51 |
| | February 20 | Me-110 dam(grd) | Weiden A/F | P-51 |

1-0-0 air
0-1 ground

**Shake, Clarence E., Lt.**
503rd Ftr Sqn/339th Ftr Grp

| *Sqn* | *Date* | *Claims* | *Location* | *A/C* |
|---|---|---|---|---|
| 503rd | May 24, 1944 | (.5)Me-109 dest(air)[*] | SW Soissons | P-51 |
| | | (.5)Me-109 dest(grd)[*] | SW Soissons | P-51 |

0.5-0-0 air
0.5-0 ground

* - shared with Lt. C.W. Knott of the 503rd Ftr Sqn

**Shane, Presson S., Capt.**
436th Ftr Sqn/479th Ftr Grp

| *Sqn* | *Date* | *Claims* | *Location* | *A/C* |
|---|---|---|---|---|
| 436th | April 13, 1945 | Me-410 dest(grd) | Salzwedel | P-51 |
| | | u/i a/c dest(grd) | Salzwedel | P-51 |
| | | Me-109 dam(grd) | Salzwedel | P-51 |
| | April 16 | (2)FW-190 dest(grd) | Landstadt | P-51 |
| | April 17 | Me-109 dest(grd) | Puchhoff | P-51 |

0-0-0 air
5-1 ground

**Shapleigh, Eliot H., Lt.**
335th Ftr Sqn/4th Ftr Grp

| *Sqn* | *Date* | *Claims* | *Location* | *A/C* |
|---|---|---|---|---|
| 335th | May 12, 1944 | (1.5)Me-109 dest(air)[*] | Giessen-Marburg | P-51 |

1.5-0-0 air
0-0 ground

* - shared with Lt. G.I. Stanford of the 335th Ftr Sqn

**Sharbo, Walter J., Lt.**
62nd Ftr Sqn/56th Ftr Grp

| *Sqn* | *Date* | *Claims* | *Location* | *A/C* |
|---|---|---|---|---|
| 62nd | December 25, 1944 | (2)Me-109 dest(air) | Bonn-Coblenz | P-47 |
| | April 10, 1945 | Me-262 dest(air) | Muritz Lake | P-47 |
| | | (2)He-111 dest(grd) | Neuruppin | P-47 |
| | | Ju-88 dam(grd) | Neuruppin | P-47 |

3-0-0 air
2-2 ground

**Sharp, Francis R., Lt.**
338th Ftr Sqn/55th Ftr Grp

| *Sqn* | *Date* | *Claims* | *Location* | *A/C* |
|---|---|---|---|---|
| 338th | January 13, 1945 | (.5)Do-217 dest(grd)[*] | Giebelstadt A/F | P-51 |
| | January 14 | Me-110 dest(grd) | SE Salzwedel | P-51 |

0-0-0 air
1.5-0 ground

* - shared with Lt. P. Brooks of the 338th Ftr Sqn

**Sharp, Robert H., Capt.**
328th Ftr Sqn/352nd Ftr Grp

| *Sqn* | *Date* | *Claims* | *Location* | *A/C* |
|---|---|---|---|---|
| 328th | February 24, 1944 | Me-109 dam(air) | Dummer Lake | P-47 |
| | April 28 | (.5)Ju-88 dam(grd)[*] | Avord A/F | P-51 |
| | May 19 | (.5)Me-109 dest(air)[**] | Wittenberg | P-51 |
| | May 21 | (2)Ju-88 dest(grd) | Alt Ruppin | P-51 |
| | | He-111 dam(grd) | Alt Ruppin | P-51 |
| | | u/i a/c dam(grd) | Alt Ruppin | P-51 |

0.5-0-1 air
2-2.5 ground

* - shared with Lt. R.H. Powell of the 328th Ftr Sqn
** - shared with Lt. M.M. Carlone of the 328th Ftr Sqn

**Sharp, Thoams S., Lt.**
334th Ftr Sqn/4th Ftr Grp

| *Sqn* | *Date* | *Claims* | *Location* | *A/C* |
|---|---|---|---|---|
| 334th | May 29, 1944 | Do-18 dam(grd) | Dievenow | P-51 |
| | May 30 | FW-190 dam(air) | W/Brandenburg | P-51 |
| | | (2)FW-190 dest(grd) | Oschersleben | P-51 |

0-0-1 air
2-1 ground

**Shaw, Bernell V., Lt.**
505th Ftr Sqn/339th Ftr Grp

| *Sqn* | *Date* | *Claims* | *Location* | *A/C* |
|---|---|---|---|---|
| 505th | August 3, 1944 | FW-190 dam(grd) | Benestroff | P-51 |
| | August 4 | Ju-88 dest(grd) | E/Celle | P-51 |

0-0-0 air
1-1 ground

**Shaw, Clifton, Maj.**
368th Ftr Sqn/359th Ftr Grp

| *Sqn* | *Date* | *Claims* | *Location* | *A/C* |
|---|---|---|---|---|
| 368th | January 29, 1944 | Me-110 dam(air) | Malmedy | P-47 |

0-0-1 air
0-0 ground

**Shaw, Robert M., Capt.**
364th Ftr Sqn/357th Ftr Grp

| *Sqn* | *Date* | *Claims* | *Location* | *A/C* |
|---|---|---|---|---|
| 364th | April 11, 1944 | Me-109 dest(air) | NE Brunswick | P-51 |
| | April 13 | Me-109 dest(air) | Frankfurt | P-51 |
| | April 24 | Me-109 prob(air) | SE Munich | P-51 |
| | May 13 | (.5)Me-410 dest(air)[*] | E/Grunberg | P-51 |
| | May 27 | Me-109 dest(air) | SW Strasbourg | P-51 |
| | | Me-109 dam(air) | SW Strasbourg | P-51 |
| | May 30 | (.5)Me-410 dest(air)[**] | NW Bernburg | P-51 |
| | June 14 | FW-190 dest(air) | E/Paris | P-51 |
| | | FW-190 dam(air) | E/Paris | P-51 |
| | July 5 | FW-190 dest(air) | SE Rouen | P-51 |
| | July 18 | Me-109 dam(air) | NW Rostock | P-51 |
| | August 6 | Me-109 dest(air) | N/Warsaw | P-51 |
| | September 18 | Me-109 dest(air) | N/Maastricht | P-51 |

8-1-3 air
0-0 ground

* - shared with Lt. C.H. Dooley of the 364th Ftr Sqn
** - shared with Lt. J.C. Howell of the 364th Ftr Sqn

**Shepard, Ernest B., Maj.**
384th Ftr Sqn/364th Ftr Grp
Earlier flew in the MTO with the 324th Ftr Grp and claimed 1.5 kills on July 9, 1943.

| *Sqn* | *Date* | *Claims* | *Location* | *A/C* |
|---|---|---|---|---|
| 384th | October 12, 1944 | Me-109 dest(air) | N/Bremen | P-51 |

1-0-0 air
0-0 ground

**Shepard, Thomas W., Jr., Lt.**
83rd Ftr Sqn/78th Ftr Grp

| *Sqn* | *Date* | *Claims* | *Location* | *A/C* |
|---|---|---|---|---|
| 83rd | June 24, 1943 | FW-190 dest(air) | Ostend | P-47 |

1-0-0 air
0-0 ground

**Sheridan, Dayton C., Lt.**
62nd Ftr Sqn/56th Ftr Grp

| *Sqn* | *Date* | *Claims* | *Location* | *A/C* |
|---|---|---|---|---|
| 62nd | July 4, 1944 | Me-109 dest(air) | Conches | P-47 |

1-0-0 air
0-0 ground

**Sherman, Clifford C., Lt.**
38th Ftr Sqn/55th Ftr Grp

| *Sqn* | *Date* | *Claims* | *Location* | *A/C* |
|---|---|---|---|---|
| 38th | August 28, 1944 | FW-190 dest(air) | Antwerp | P-51 |
| | September 11 | Me-109 dest(air) | Erfurt | P-51 |
| | September 12 | (1.5)Me-109 dest(air)[*] | Frankfurt | P-51 |
| | October 7 | Me-109 dest(air) | Leipzig | P-51 |

4.5-0-0 air
0-0 ground

* - shared with Lt. R.C. Haworth of the 338th Ftr Sqn, 55th Ftr Grp

**Shilke, Charles H., Lt.**
336th Ftr Sqn/4th Ftr Grp

| *Sqn* | *Date* | *Claims* | *Location* | *A/C* |
|---|---|---|---|---|
| 336th | April 10, 1944 | u/i a/c dest(grd) | Romorantin A/F | P-51 |
| | June 20 | Do-217 dest(grd) | Neubrandenburg | P-51 |
| | | (.5)Ju-88 dest(grd)[*] | Neubrandenburg | P-51 |

0-0-0 air
2.5-0 ground

* - shared with Lt. W.G. Gillette of the 336th Ftr Sqn

**Shipman, Mark K., LtCol.**
38th Ftr Sqn/55th Ftr Grp
HdQts/55th Ftr Grp
Earlier flew in the MTO with the 14th Ftr Grp and claimed one kill on November 22, 1942.

| *Sqn* | *Date* | *Claims* | *Location* | *A/C* |
|---|---|---|---|---|
| 38th | November 5, 1943 | Me-109 dest(air) | Doetinchem | P-38 |
| | | (.5)Me-109 dest(air)[*] | Nijmegen | P-38 |
| | | (.5)Me-109 prob(air)[*] | Winterswijk | P-38 |
| | January 5, 1944 | Me-109 dam(air) | E/Meldorf | P-38 |
| | January 31 | Me-109 prob(air) | N/Venlo | P-38 |
| HdQts | February 25 | Me-410 dam(air) | Augsburg | P-38 |

1.5-1.5-2 air
0-0 ground

* - both shared with Lt. C.W. Des Voignes of the 38th Ftr Sqn

**Shoffitt, Jimmy C., Capt.**
370th Ftr Sqn/359th Ftr Grp

| *Sqn* | *Date* | *Claims* | *Location* | *A/C* |
|---|---|---|---|---|
| 370th | August 16, 1944 | Me-163 dam(air) | Bohlen | P-51 |

0-0-1 air
0-0 ground

**Shope, Herbert K., Capt.**
82nd Ftr Sqn/78th Ftr Grp

| *Sqn* | *Date* | *Claims* | *Location* | *A/C* |
|---|---|---|---|---|
| 82nd | June 30, 1944 | Me-109 dest(grd) | Meilleray | P-47 |
| | August 6 | Me-109 dam(air) | Hamburg | P-47 |
| | September 9 | Ju-88 dest(grd) | Giessen | P-47 |
| | September 17 | Me-109 dest(grd) | Gilze-Rijen | P-47 |

0-0-1 air
3-0 ground

**Shriner, Fred F., Lt.**
435th Ftr Sqn/479th Ftr Grp

| *Sqn* | *Date* | *Claims* | *Location* | *A/C* |
|---|---|---|---|---|
| 435th | February 9, 1945 | Me-109 prob(air) | SE Magdeburg | P-51 |

0-1-0 air
0-0 ground

**Shultz, Floyd W., Lt.**
354th Ftr Sqn/355th Ftr Grp

| *Sqn* | *Date* | *Claims* | *Location* | *A/C* |
|---|---|---|---|---|
| 354th | September 11, 1944 | Me-109 dest(air) | S/Kassel | P-51 |
| | | (.5)FW-190 dest(grd)[*] | Marburg | P-51 |
| | November 26 | Me-109 dam(air) | Gifhorn-W/Hanover | P-51 |
| | | FW-190 dam(air) | Gifhorn-W/Hanover | P-51 |

1-0-2 air
0.5-0 ground

* - shared with Lt. R.S. White of the 354th Ftr Sqn

**Shultz, William G., Lt.**
55th Ftr Sqn/20th Ftr Grp

| *Sqn* | *Date* | *Claims* | *Location* | *A/C* |
|---|---|---|---|---|
| 55th | April 24, 1944 | (1.5)Me-109 dest(air)[*] | Worms | P-38 |

1.5-0-0 air
0-0 ground

* - shared with Capt. D.A. Reihmer of the 77th Ftr Sqn, 20th Ftr Grp

**Shupe, Arthur T., Lt.**
63rd Ftr Sqn/56th Ftr Grp

| *Sqn* | *Date* | *Claims* | *Location* | *A/C* |
|---|---|---|---|---|
| 63rd | April 10, 1945 | FW-190 dest(grd) | Stendal | P-47 |
| | | (2)FW-190 dam(grd) | Stendal | P-47 |

0-0-0 air
1-2 ground

**Shupe, Joseph E., Lt.**
370th Ftr Sqn/359th Ftr Grp

| *Sqn* | *Date* | *Claims* | *Location* | *A/C* |
|---|---|---|---|---|
| 370th | April 11, 1944 | Ju-88 dest(grd) | Volkenrod | P-47 |
| | | Ju-88 dam(grd) | Volkenrod | P-47 |
| | May 8 | (2)FW-190 dest(air) | Eschede | P-51 |
| | May 21 | (4)Ju-88 dest(grd) | Schwerin | P-51 |
| | | (3)Ju-88 dam(grd) | Schwerin | P-51 |

2-0-0 air
5-4 ground

**Siems, Grover C., Jr., Lt.**
334th Ftr Sqn/4th Ftr Grp

| *Sqn* | *Date* | *Claims* | *Location* | *A/C* |
|---|---|---|---|---|
| 334th | April 10, 1944 | (.5)Bu-131 dest(grd)[*] | Romorantin A/F | P-51 |
| | April 18 | (.33)Me-109 dest(air)[**] | Fassberg A/F | P-51 |
| | | u/i a/c dam(grd) | Fassberg A/F | P-51 |
| | May 9 | Ju-88 dest(grd) | Reims-Champiegne | P-51 |
| | May 12 | Me-109 dest(air) | Coburg | P-51 |
| | May 21 | (2)Me-210 dest(grd) | Rathenow | P-51 |
| | | (2)Me-210 dam(grd) | Rathenow | P-51 |
| | May 28 | FW-190 dest(air) | Magdeburg | P-51 |
| | June 6 | FW-190 dest(air) | Evreux A/F | P-51 |
| | July 2 | Me-109 dest(air) | Budapest | P-51 |

4.33-0-0 air
3.5-3 ground

* - shared with Lt. G.E. Montgomery of the 334th Ftr Sqn
** - shared with Capt. V.J. France and Lt. N. Megura of the 334th Ftr Sqn

**Silk, John W., Lt.**
38th Ftr Sqn/55th Ftr Grp

| *Sqn* | *Date* | *Claims* | *Location* | *A/C* |
|---|---|---|---|---|
| 38th | September 12, 1944 | Me-109 dest(air) | Frankfurt | P-51 |
| | | (.5)He-177 dam(grd)[*] | Herzogenaurach | P-51 |

1-0-0 air
0-0.5 ground

* - shared with Capt. C.L. Peterson of the 38th Ftr Sqn

**Silsby, Charles W., Capt.**
84th Ftr Sqn/78th Ftr Grp

| *Sqn* | *Date* | *Claims* | *Location* | *A/C* |
|---|---|---|---|---|
| 84th | July 30, 1943 | Me-109 dam(air) | Winterswijk | P-47 |
| | October 10 | Me-110 dest(air) | Ochtrup | P-47 |
| | | Me-210 dest(air) | Ochtrup | P-47 |

2-0-1 air
0-0 ground

**Siltamaki, Robert W., Lt.**
370th Ftr Sqn/359th Ftr Grp

| *Sqn* | *Date* | *Claims* | *Location* | *A/C* |
|---|---|---|---|---|
| 370th | May 29, 1944 | (.5)FW-190 dest(air)* | Stettin | P-51 |
| | May 30 | (.5)Me-109 dest(air)** | Dessau | P-51 |
| | July 21 | Ju-88 dest(grd) | N/Landsberg | P-51 |
| | | (3)He-111 dam(grd) | W/Munich | P-51 |
| | | (2)u/i a/c dam(grd) | W/Munich | P-51 |

1-0-0 air
1-5 ground

* - shared with Lt. G.A. Doersch of the 370th Ftr Sqn
** - shared with Lt. C.W. Hipsher of the 370th Ftr Sqn

**Silva, Stanley E., Capt.**
354th Ftr Sqn/355th Ftr Grp

| *Sqn* | *Date* | *Claims* | *Location* | *A/C* |
|---|---|---|---|---|
| 354th | December 5, 1944 | FW-190 dest(air) | N/Berlin | P-51 |
| | March 22, 1945 | (2)Me-262 dest(grd) | Kitzingen | P-51 |
| | | Me-109 dest(grd) | Kitzingen | P-51 |
| | | (3)Me-262 dam(grd) | Kitzingen | P-51 |
| | April 13 | (2)Me-109 dest(grd) | Husum | P-51 |
| | | He-111 dest(grd) | Husum | P-51 |
| | | Me-109 dam(grd) | Husum | P-51 |

1-0-0 air
6-4 ground

**Simanonok, Joseph E., Lt.**
77th Ftr Sqn/20th Ftr Grp

| *Sqn* | *Date* | *Claims* | *Location* | *A/C* |
|---|---|---|---|---|
| 77th | April 10, 1945 | Ju-88 dest(grd) | Oranienburg | P-51 |

0-0-0 air
1-0 ground

**Simon, Jack T., Lt.**
334th Ftr Sqn/4th Ftr Grp

| *Sqn* | *Date* | *Claims* | *Location* | *A/C* |
|---|---|---|---|---|
| 334th | June 6, 1944 | (.5)FW-190 dest(air)* | Evreux | P-51 |

0.5-0-0 air
0-0 ground

* - shared with Lt. J.P. Fernandez of the 334th Ftr Sqn

**Simon, Reuben, Capt.**
336th Ftr Sqn/4th Ftr Grp

| *Sqn* | *Date* | *Claims* | *Location* | *A/C* |
|---|---|---|---|---|
| 336th | April 5, 1944 | (2)u/i a/c dest(grd) | W/Brandenburg | P-51 |
| | April 8 | FW-190 dest(air) | Brunswick | P-51 |
| | April 22 | Me-109 dest(air) | SW Kassel | P-51 |

2-0-0 air
2-0 ground

**Simpson, Edward K., Capt.**
363rd Ftr Sqn/357th Ftr Grp

| *Sqn* | *Date* | *Claims* | *Location* | *A/C* |
|---|---|---|---|---|
| 363rd | April 11, 1944 | Me-109 dest(air) | W/Hanover | P-51 |
| | | (.25)He-111 dest(air)* | W/Hanover | P-51 |
| | May 27 | Me-109 dest(air) | Strasbourg | P-51 |
| | July 6 | Ju-88 dest(air) | N/Nordernay Island | P-51 |
| | July 7 | Me-109 dest(air) | N/Leipzig | P-51 |

4.25-0-0 air
0-0 ground

* - shared with Capt. C.E. Anderson, Lt. H.R. Kayser, and Lt. W.B. Overstreet of the 363rd Ftr Sqn

**Simpson, Richard G., Lt.**
434th Ftr Sqn/479th Ftr Grp

| *Sqn* | *Date* | *Claims* | *Location* | *A/C* |
|---|---|---|---|---|
| 434th | April 13, 1945 | (.5)u/i a/c dest(grd)* | Ratzburger Lake | P-51 |

0-0-0 air
0.5-0 ground

* - shared with Lt. P.A. Brown of the 434th Ftr Sqn

**Sims, Edward H., Lt.**
435th Ftr Sqn/479th Ftr Grp

| *Sqn* | *Date* | *Claims* | *Location* | *A/C* |
|---|---|---|---|---|
| 435th | January 21, 1945 | Ju-52 dam(grd) | Leipheim | P-51 |
| | April 4 | Me-262 dam(air) | W/Luneburg | P-51 |
| | April 17 | Me-262 dest(grd) | Puchhoff | P-51 |
| | April 18 | u/i a/c dam(grd) | Mettenheim | P-51 |

0-0-1 air
1-2 ground

**Sims, Hal B., Capt.**
338th Ftr Sqn/55th Ftr Grp

| *Sqn* | *Date* | *Claims* | *Location* | *A/C* |
|---|---|---|---|---|
| 338th | February 6, 1945 | (.5)Me-410 dest(grd)* | Gerolzhofen A/F | P-51 |
| | March 20 | u/i a/c dam(grd) | Aurich | P-51 |

0-0-0 air
0.5-1 ground

* - shared with Lt. R. DeLoach of the 338th Ftr Sqn

**Sirochman, Andrew, Lt.**
505th Ftr Sqn/339th Ftr Grp

| *Sqn* | *Date* | *Claims* | *Location* | *A/C* |
|---|---|---|---|---|
| 505th | June 8, 1944 | (.5)FW-190 dest(air)* | Rennes | P-51 |
| | June 29 | (.5)Me-109 dest(air)** | Halle-S/Magdeburg | P-51 |
| | July 19 | (.5)Ju-188 dest(grd)@ | SW Augsburg | P-51 |
| | August 3 | u/i a/c dest(grd) | Benestroff | P-51 |
| | | u/i a/c dam(grd) | Benestroff | P-51 |
| | August 4 | Ju-88 dest(grd) | E/Celle | P-51 |

1-0-0 air
2.5-1 ground

* - shared with Lt. R.B. Olander of the 505th Ftr Sqn
** - shared with Lt. E.M. Johnson of the 505th Ftr Sqn
@ - shared with Lt. R.H. Tannous of the 505th Ftr Sqn

**Sisson, Edward A., Jr., Lt.**
61st Ftr Sqn/56th Ftr Grp

| *Sqn* | *Date* | *Claims* | *Location* | *A/C* |
|---|---|---|---|---|
| 61st | April 15, 1944 | He-111 dest(grd) | Flensburg | P-47 |
| | | (2)Me-410 dam(grd) | Flensburg | P-47 |
| | June 16 | Me-109 dest(air) | Rouen | P-47 |

1-0-0 air
1-2 ground

**Sitzer, Saul, F/O**
363rd Ftr Sqn/357th Ftr Grp

| *Sqn* | *Date* | *Claims* | *Location* | *A/C* |
|---|---|---|---|---|
| 363rd | December 23, 1944 | Me-109 dest(air) | S/Ludwigshafen | P-51 |

1-0-0 air
0-0 ground

**Sjoblad, Edwin L., Lt.**
369th Ftr Sqn/359th Ftr Grp

| Sqn | Date | Claims | Location | A/C |
|---|---|---|---|---|
| 369th | August 5, 1944 | Me-109 dest(air) | Bremen | P-51 |

1-0-0 air
0-0 ground

**Slack, Henry R., IV, Lt.**
84th Ftr Sqn/78th Ftr Grp

| Sqn | Date | Claims | Location | A/C |
|---|---|---|---|---|
| 84th | March 19, 1945 | Me-109 dest(air) | Osnabruck | P-51 |
| | April 7 | (.5)Me-109 dest(air)* | NE Dummer Lake | P-51 |
| | April 10 | FW-190 dest(grd) | Werder | P-51 |
| | | Ju-87 dest(grd) | Werder | P-51 |
| | | Ju-52 dest(grd) | Werder | P-51 |
| | April 16 | (4)Ju-52 dest(grd) | Praha/Kakewice | P-51 |
| | | Ju-52 dam(grd) | Praha/Kakewice | P-51 |
| | | u/i a/c dam(grd) | Praha/Kakewice | P-51 |

1.5-0-0 air
7-2 ground

* - shared with Lt. R.K. Corbett of the 84th Ftr Sqn

**Sladek, Charles E., Lt.**
352nd Ftr Sqn/353rd Ftr Grp

| Sqn | Date | Claims | Location | A/C |
|---|---|---|---|---|
| 352nd | September 23, 1944 | FW-190 dest(air) | SE Arnheim | P-47 |

1-0-0 air
0-0 ground

**Slanker, Eldon L., Lt.**
361st Ftr Sqn/356th Ftr Grp

| Sqn | Date | Claims | Location | A/C |
|---|---|---|---|---|
| 361st | February 20, 1945 | (.5)Fi-156 dest(air)* | SE Bayreuth | P-51 |
| | | Fi-156 dam(air) | SE Bayreuth | P-51 |

0.5-0-1 air
0-0 ground

* - shared with Lt. C.D. Burdick of the 361st Ftr Sqn

**Slanker, Ted E., Capt.**
77th Ftr Sqn/20th Ftr Grp

| Sqn | Date | Claims | Location | A/C |
|---|---|---|---|---|
| 77th | September 28, 1944 | FW-190 dest(air) | S/Magdeburg | P-51 |
| | | FW-190 dam(air) | S/Magdeburg | P-51 |
| | | Me-210 dest(grd) | S/Magdeburg | P-51 |
| | November 4 | FW-190 dam(grd) | W/Munster | P-51 |

1-0-1 air
1-1 ground

**Slater, Harry B., Lt.**
82nd Ftr Sqn/78th Ftr Grp

| Sqn | Date | Claims | Location | A/C |
|---|---|---|---|---|
| 82nd | May 19, 1944 | Me-109 dam(air) | Dummer Lake | P-47 |
| | September 10 | (2)He-111 dest(grd) | Meinbullen | P-47 |
| | | He-111 dam(grd) | Meinbullen | P-47 |

0-0-1 air
2-1 ground

**Sloan, James R., Lt.**
363rd Ftr Sqn/357th Ftr Grp

| Sqn | Date | Claims | Location | A/C |
|---|---|---|---|---|
| 363rd | November 27, 1944 | FW-190 dest(air) | SW Magdeburg | P-51 |
| | December 24 | Me-109 dest(air) | W/Coblenz | P-51 |
| | January 14, 1945 | Me-109 dest(air) | N/Brandenburg | P-51 |

3-0-0 air
0-0 ground

**Sloan, James T., Lt.**
374th Ftr Sqn/361st Ftr Grp

| Sqn | Date | Claims | Location | A/C |
|---|---|---|---|---|
| 374th | April 9, 1945 | Me-262 dest(air) | SW Berlin | P-51 |
| | | Me-262 dam(air) | SW Berlin | P-51 |

1-0-1 air
0-0 ground

**Slovak, William R., Lt.**
505th Ftr Sqn/339th Ftr Grp

| Sqn | Date | Claims | Location | A/C |
|---|---|---|---|---|
| 505th | August 4, 1944 | Ju-88 dam(grd) | E/Celle | P-51 |
| | September 11 | Me-410 dest(grd) | Munich | P-51 |
| | | u/i a/c dest(grd) | Munich | P-51 |
| | | (2)Me-410 dam(grd) | Munich | P-51 |

0-0-0 air
2-3 ground

**Sluga, Emil L., LtCol.**
358th Ftr Sqn/355th Ftr Grp

| Sqn | Date | Claims | Location | A/C |
|---|---|---|---|---|
| 358th | November 5, 1943 | Me-210 dest(air) | Alben | P-47 |
| | April 8, 1944 | (1.5)Me-109 dest(air)* | E/Brunswick | P-51 |
| | April 11 | Me-109 dest(air) | NE Berlin | P-51 |
| | | Me-109 dam(air) | NE Berlin | P-51 |
| | November 26 | FW-190 dam(air) | Hanover | P-51 |

3.5-0-2 air
0-0 ground

* - shared with Lt. J.C. Harrington of the 358th Ftr Sqn

**Smart, Curtis L., Lt.**
385th Ftr Sqn/364th Ftr Grp

| Sqn | Date | Claims | Location | A/C |
|---|---|---|---|---|
| 385th | December 31, 1944 | (.5)FW-190 dest(air)* | SW Hamburg | P-51 |

0.5-0-0 air
0-0 ground

* - shared with Lt. T.L. Allinder of the 385th Ftr Sqn

**Smeltz, Kenneth C., Lt.**
55th Ftr Sqn/20th Ftr Grp

| Sqn | Date | Claims | Location | A/C |
|---|---|---|---|---|
| 55th | August 6, 1944 | FW-190 dest(air) | Schonfeld A/F | P-51 |
| | August 25 | (3)Ju-88 dest(grd) | Parow A/F | P-51 |
| | | (2)Ju-88 dam(grd) | Parow A/F | P-51 |
| | | BV-140 dam(grd) | Parow A/F | P-51 |
| | August 27 | Ju-88 dest(grd) | Habjeerg A/F | P-51 |

1-0-0 air
4-3 ground

**Smigel, Alfred J., Lt.**
436th Ftr Sqn/479th Ftr Grp

| Sqn | Date | Claims | Location | A/C |
|---|---|---|---|---|
| 436th | February 22, 1945 | He-111 dest(grd) | Halberstadt | P-51 |
| | | (2)Ju-88 dam(grd) | Halberstadt | P-51 |
| | April 16 | (2)FW-190 dest(grd) | Landstadt | P-51 |
| | | Me-109 dest(grd) | Landstadt | P-51 |
| | April 17 | u/i a/c dest(grd) | Karlsbad | P-51 |
| | | u/i a/c dam(grd) | Karlsbad | P-51 |

0-0-0 air
5-3 ground

**Smith, Alden E., Lt.**
362nd Ftr Sqn/357th Ftr Grp

| Sqn | Date | Claims | Location | A/C |
|---|---|---|---|---|
| 362nd | March 5, 1944 | (.5)FW-190 dam(air)* | Bordeaux | P-51 |
| | March 28 | (2.5)Ju-88 dest(grd)** | S/Paris | P-51 |
| | April 24 | Me-110 prob(air) | Munich | P-51 |
| | | Me-110 dam(air) | Munich | P-51 |
| | May 27 | Me-109 dest(air) | N/Strasbourg | P-51 |

| | Date | Claims | Location | A/C |
|---|---|---|---|---|
| | July 1 | Me-109 dam(air) | E/St. Quentin | P-51 |
| | July 30 | Me-109 dest(air) | NW Paris | P-51 |
| | August 28 | FW-190 dam(grd) | Trier | P-51 |
| | | Ju-52 dam(grd) | Trier | P-51 |

2-1-2.5 air
2.5-2 ground

[*] - shared with Lt. G.M. O'Brien of the 362nd Ftr Sqn
[**] - shared with Lt. L.K. Carson of the 362nd Ftr Sqn

**Smith, Bernard R., Lt.**
63rd Ftr Sqn/56th Ftr Grp

| *Sqn* | *Date* | *Claims* | *Location* | *A/C* |
|---|---|---|---|---|
| 63rd | October 4, 1943 | Me-110 dest(air) | Bruhl | P-47 |
| | November 29 | Me-109 dam(air) | Lathen | P-47 |
| | January 11, 1944 | FW-190 dest(air) | N/Osnabruck | P-47 |
| | March 8 | Me-110 dest(air) | NW Steinhuder Lake | P-47 |

3-0-1 air
0-0 ground

**Smith, Clyde D., Lt.**
334th Ftr Sqn/4th Ftr Grp

| *Sqn* | *Date* | *Claims* | *Location* | *A/C* |
|---|---|---|---|---|
| 334th | August 16, 1943 | (2)FW-190 dest(air) | SE Paris | P-47 |

2-0-0 air
0-0 ground

**Smith, Donovan F., Maj.**
61st Ftr Sqn/56th Ftr Grp

| *Sqn* | *Date* | *Claims* | *Location* | *A/C* |
|---|---|---|---|---|
| 61st | July 30, 1943 | Me-109 prob(air) | Nijmegen | P-47 |
| | December 11 | (2)Me-110 dest(air) | Emden | P-47 |
| | | (.5)FW-190 dest(air)[*] | Emden | P-47 |
| | | Me-110 dam(air) | Emden | P-47 |
| | February 20, 1944 | (2)Me-110 dest(air) | Steinhuder Lake | P-47 |
| | | Me-110 dam(air) | Steinhuder Lake | P-47 |
| | February 22 | FW-190 dest(air) | Lippstadt | P-47 |
| | July 20 | He-111 dest(grd) | Bassenheim A/F | P-47 |
| | | He-111 dam(grd) | Bassenheim A/F | P-47 |
| | September 16 | He-177 dest(grd) | Alhorn A/F | P-47 |

5.5-1-2 air
2-1 ground

[*] - shared with F/O W.R. Aggers of the 61st Ftr Sqn

**Smith, Elmer L., Lt.**
328th Ftr Sqn/352nd Ftr Grp

| *Sqn* | *Date* | *Claims* | *Location* | *A/C* |
|---|---|---|---|---|
| 328th | May 21, 1944 | He-111 dest(grd) | Alt Ruppin | P-51 |
| | | u/i a/c dam(grd) | Alt Ruppin | P-51 |
| | June 21 | (.5)Me-410 dest(air)[*] | Dahmsdorf | P-51 |
| | July 18 | Me-109 dest(air) | Wismar | P-51 |

1.5-0-0 air
1-1 ground

[*] - shared with Lt. J.W. Galiga of the 328th Ftr Sqn

**Smith, Eugene F., Lt.**
84th Ftr Sqn/78th Ftr Grp

| *Sqn* | *Date* | *Claims* | *Location* | *A/C* |
|---|---|---|---|---|
| 84th | March 19, 1945 | (.5)Me-109 dest(air)[*] | Osnabruck | P-51 |

0.5-0-0 air
0-0 ground

[*] - shared with Lt. A.A. Garback of the 84th Ftr Sqn

**Smith, Floyd W., Lt.**
505th Ftr Sqn/339th Ftr Grp

| *Sqn* | *Date* | *Claims* | *Location* | *A/C* |
|---|---|---|---|---|
| 505th | April 16, 1945 | FW-190 dest(grd) | NE Prague | P-51 |
| | | u/i a/c dam(grd) | NE Prague | P-51 |
| | April 17 | Me-109 dest(grd) | SE Pocking | P-51 |
| | | Ju-88 dest(grd) | SE Pocking | P-51 |

0-0-0 air
3-1 ground

**Smith, Fonzo D., Maj.**
335th Ftr Sqn/4th Ftr Grp
HdQts/4th Ftr Grp

| *Sqn* | *Date* | *Claims* | *Location* | *A/C* |
|---|---|---|---|---|
| 335th | June 22, 1943 | FW-190 dest(air) | Beveland-Walcheren | P-47 |
| | August 16 | FW-190 dest(air) | Paris | P-47 |
| | November 5 | FW-190 dest(air) | E/Eindhoven | P-47 |
| | November 29 | Me-109 prob(air) | Hude | P-47 |

3-1-0 air
0-0 ground

**Smith, Fred C., Capt.**
376th Ftr Sqn/361st Ftr Grp
362nd Ftr Sqn/357th Ftr Grp

| *Sqn* | *Date* | *Claims* | *Location* | *A/C* |
|---|---|---|---|---|
| 362nd | April 24, 1944 | Me-109 dest(air) | S/Munich | P-51 |
| | June 29 | FW-190 dest(air) | Naumberg | P-51 |
| | September 18 | Me-109 dest(air) | Nijmegen | P-51 |

3-0-0 air
0-0 ground

**Smith, George C., Lt.**
336th Ftr Sqn/4th Ftr Grp

| *Sqn* | *Date* | *Claims* | *Location* | *A/C* |
|---|---|---|---|---|
| 336th | September 27, 1944 | FW-190 dest(air) | S/Kassel | P-51 |
| | | Me-109 dest(air) | S/Kassel | P-51 |

2-0-0 air
0-0 ground

**Smith, George E., Lt.**
383rd Ftr Sqn/364th Ftr Grp

| *Sqn* | *Date* | *Claims* | *Location* | *A/C* |
|---|---|---|---|---|
| 383rd | November 26, 1944 | (.5)Me-109 dest(air)[*] | Dummer Lake | P-51 |
| | December 27 | FW-190 dam(air) | SW Frankfurt | P-51 |
| | April 13, 1945 | (2)FW-190 dest(grd) | Flensburg | P-51 |
| | | Ju-52 dest(grd) | Flensburg | P-51 |
| | | (2)FW-190 dam(grd) | Flensburg | P-51 |
| | | Ju-52 dam(grd) | Flensburg | P-51 |

0.5-0-1 air
3-3 ground

[*] - shared with Lt. J.T. Gaston of the 383rd Ftr Sqn

**Smith, Howard C., Capt.**
435th Ftr Sqn/479th Ftr Grp

| *Sqn* | *Date* | *Claims* | *Location* | *A/C* |
|---|---|---|---|---|
| 435th | August 18, 1944 | (4)He-111 dest(grd) | Nancy/Essey A/F | P-38 |

0-0-0 air
4-0 ground

**Smith, James B., Capt.**
359th Ftr Sqn/356th Ftr Grp

| *Sqn* | *Date* | *Claims* | *Location* | *A/C* |
|---|---|---|---|---|
| 359th | November 29, 1943 | Me-109 dest(air) | NE Meppel | P-47 |
| | | Me-109 prob(air) | NE Meppel | P-47 |
| | January 11, 1944 | Me-210 dest(air) | Steinhuder Lake | P-47 |
| | March 23 | Me-110 dam(grd) | W/Duren | P-47 |
| | March 29 | Me-109 prob(air) | Steinhuder Lake | P-47 |
| | April 8 | Do-217 dam(grd) | Salzbergen A/F | P-47 |

2-2-0 air
0-2 ground

**Smith, James D., Capt.**
376th Ftr Sqn/361st Ftr Grp

| *Sqn* | *Date* | *Claims* | *Location* | *A/C* |
|---|---|---|---|---|
| 376th | August 18, 1944 | Ju-88 dest(grd) | Romilly-Sur-Seine | P-51 |

0-0-0 air
1-0 ground

**Smith, Kenneth G., Capt.**
335th Ftr Sqn/4th Ftr Grp

| *Sqn* | *Date* | *Claims* | *Location* | *A/C* |
|---|---|---|---|---|
| 335th | July 30, 1943 | FW-190 dest(air) | Schouwen | P-47 |
| | March 5, 1944 | (.5)FW-200 dest(air)[*] | Bergerac A/F | P-51 |
| | March 8 | Me-110 dest(air) | Magdeburg | P-51 |
| | | Bu-181 dam(air) | Magdeburg | P-51 |
| | March 16 | Me-110 dest(air) | Wurm Lake | P-51 |
| | March 18 | FW-190 dest(air) | Gunzburg | P-51 |
| | March 21 | (.5)Fi-156 dest(air)[**] | NE Bordeaux | P-51 |

5-0-1 air
0-0 ground

[*] - shared with Lt. E.P. Freeburger of the 335th Ftr Sqn
[**] - shared with Lt. J.H. Brandenburg of the 335th Ftr Sqn

**Smith, Kenneth L., Lt.**
62nd Ftr Sqn/56th Ftr Grp

| *Sqn* | *Date* | *Claims* | *Location* | *A/C* |
|---|---|---|---|---|
| 62nd | January 14, 1945 | Me-109 dest(air) | Rheine | P-47 |

1-0-0 air
0-0 ground

**Smith, Leslie C., LtCol.**
61st Ftr Sqn/56th Ftr Grp
62nd Ftr Sqn/56th Ftr Grp
HdQts/56th Ftr Grp

| *Sqn* | *Date* | *Claims* | *Location* | *A/C* |
|---|---|---|---|---|
| 61st | July 30, 1943 | FW-190 dam(air) | Arnheim | P-47 |
| | January 21, 1944 | FW-190 dam(air) | NE Rouen | P-47 |
| | February 22 | (2)FW-190 dest(air) | Lippstadt | P-47 |
| | March 8 | FW-190 dam(air) | Steinhuder Lake | P-47 |
| | March 15 | Me-109 dest(air) | Dummer Lake-Solingen | P-47 |
| | March 27 | u/i a/c dam(grd) | Gael A/F | P-47 |
| | April 9 | Me-109 dest(air) | E/Neumunster | P-47 |
| | April 15 | He-111 dest(grd) | Flensburg | P-47 |
| | | He-111 dam(grd) | Flensburg | P-47 |
| | May 19 | (2)FW-190 dest(air) | N/Wernigerode | P-47 |
| 62nd | December 26 | FW-190 dest(air) | Coblenz | P-47 |
| | January 21, 1945 | Ju-88 dest(grd) | Thalheim | P-47 |
| | | (.5)Ju-52 dest(grd)[*] | Huntingen | P-47 |
| HdQts | February 27 | (2)u/i a/c dest(grd) | Weimar A/F | P-47 |
| | | (3)u/i a/c dam(grd) | Weimar A/F | P-47 |

7-0-3 air
4.5-5 ground

[*] - shared with Lt. N.D. Gould of the 62nd Ftr Sqn

**Smith, Martin H., Lt.**
84th Ftr Sqn/78th Ftr Grp

| *Sqn* | *Date* | *Claims* | *Location* | *A/C* |
|---|---|---|---|---|
| 84th | April 8, 1944 | (2)glider dam(grd) | NE Frankfurt | P-47 |

0-0-0 air
0-2 ground

**Smith, Raymond E., Jr., Maj.**
84th Ftr Sqn/78th Ftr Grp

| *Sqn* | *Date* | *Claims* | *Location* | *A/C* |
|---|---|---|---|---|
| 84th | January 5, 1944 | Me-109 dam(air) | La Rochelle | P-47 |
| | February 10 | Ju-88 dam(grd) | Soesterberg A/F | P-47 |
| | March 15 | Me-109 dest(air) | W/Munster | P-47 |
| | April 8 | glider dam(grd) | NE Frankfurt | P-47 |
| | August 17 | (.5)Me-109 dest(grd)[*] | W/Chaudun | P-47 |
| | | (.5)Me-109 dam(grd)[**] | W/Chaudun | P-47 |
| | September 10 | (4.5)He-111 dest(grd)[@] | Meinbullen | P-47 |
| | | He-111 dam(grd) | Meinbullen | P-47 |

1-0-1 air
5-3.5 ground

[*] - shared with Lt. R.L. Baron of the 84th Ftr Sqn
[**] - shared with Lt. P.H. McKenney of the 84th Ftr Sqn
[@] - shared with Lt. A.P. Haning of the 84th Ftr Sqn

**Smith, Richard C., Capt.**
364th Ftr Sqn/357th Ftr Grp

| *Sqn* | *Date* | *Claims* | *Location* | *A/C* |
|---|---|---|---|---|
| 364th | February 24, 1944 | Me-109 dest(air) | NW Gotha | P-51 |
| | March 6 | (2)He-111 dam(grd) | Ulzen | P-51 |
| | May 12 | FW-190 dest(air) | N/Frankfurt | P-51 |
| | June 20 | Me-109 dest(air) | N/Eberswalde | P-51 |

3-0-0 air
0-2 ground

**Smith, Robert C., Lt.**
364th Ftr Sqn/357th Ftr Grp

| *Sqn* | *Date* | *Claims* | *Location* | *A/C* |
|---|---|---|---|---|
| 364th | April 11, 1944 | Me-109 dest(air) | NE Magdeburg | P-51 |
| | April 13 | (.5)Me-109 dest(air)[*] | Donauworth | P-51 |
| | | Me-109 prob(air) | Frankfurt | P-51 |
| | May 8 | FW-190 dam(air) | S/Hanover | P-51 |
| | May 12 | FW-190 dest(air) | N/Frankfurt | P-51 |
| | May 21 | (3)Me-109 dest(grd) | S/Eichhof | P-51 |

2.5-1-1 air
3-0 ground

[*] - shared with Lt. P.D. Fairweather of the 364th Ftr Sqn

**Smith, Robert E., Lt.**
82nd Ftr Sqn/78th Ftr Grp

| *Sqn* | *Date* | *Claims* | *Location* | *A/C* |
|---|---|---|---|---|
| 82nd | January 14, 1945 | FW-190 dest(air) | Cologne | P-51 |

1-0-0 air
0-0 ground

**Smith, Robert L., Lt.**
364th Ftr Sqn/357th Ftr Grp

| *Sqn* | *Date* | *Claims* | *Location* | *A/C* |
|---|---|---|---|---|
| 364th | September 18, 1944 | (2)Me-109 dest(air) | N/Maastricht | P-51 |

2-0-0 air
0-0 ground

**Smith, Robert W., Maj.**
83rd Ftr Sqn/78th Ftr Grp

| *Sqn* | *Date* | *Claims* | *Location* | *A/C* |
|---|---|---|---|---|
| 83rd | July 19, 1944 | Ju-188 dest(grd) | Linburg-Coblenz | P-47 |
| | | (2)Ju-188 dam(grd) | Linburg-Coblenz | P-47 |

0-0-0 air
1-2 ground

**Smith, Roland W., F/O**
504th Ftr Sqn/339th Ftr Grp

| *Sqn* | *Date* | *Claims* | *Location* | *A/C* |
|---|---|---|---|---|
| 504th | April 10, 1945 | Me-410 dest(grd) | N/Neuruppin | P-51 |
| | | Ju-88 dam(grd) | N/Neuruppin | P-51 |
| | April 16 | FW-190 dest(grd) | Klatovy | P-51 |
| | | Me-109 dest(grd) | Klatovy | P-51 |

0-0-0 air
3-1 ground

**Smith, Roy O., Capt.**
385th Ftr Sqn/364th Ftr Grp

| *Sqn* | *Date* | *Claims* | *Location* | *A/C* |
|---|---|---|---|---|
| 385th | March 8, 1944 | Me-109 dam(air) | Gifhorn | P-38 |

0-0-1 air
0-0 ground

**Smith, Samuel R., Capt.**
370th Ftr Sqn/359th Ftr Grp
HdQts/359th Ftr Grp

| Sqn | Date | Claims | Location | A/C |
|---|---|---|---|---|
| 370th | April 11, 1944 | FW-190 prob(air) | Gutersloh | P-47 |
| | | (2)FW-190 dest(grd) | Gutersloh | P-47 |
| | | FW-190 dam(grd) | Gutersloh | P-47 |
| HdQts | April 24 | (1.33)u/i a/c dest(grd)[*] | St. Dizier | P-47 |

0-1-0 air
3.33-1 ground

[*] - shared with Lt. P.H. Bateman and Lt. R.S. Wetmore of the 370th Ftr Sqn

**Smith, Thomas P., Capt.**
370th Ftr Sqn/359th Ftr Grp

| Sqn | Date | Claims | Location | A/C |
|---|---|---|---|---|
| 370th | November 21, 1944 | (2)FW-190 dest(air) | SW Merseburg | P-51 |
| | | (2)FW-190 dam(air) | SW Merseburg | P-51 |

2-0-2 air
0-0 ground

**Smith, Thomas W., Jr., Lt.**
63rd Ftr Sqn/56th Ftr Grp

| Sqn | Date | Claims | Location | A/C |
|---|---|---|---|---|
| 63rd | April 10, 1945 | Ju-88 dest(grd) | Werder | P-47 |
| | | Ju-88 dam(grd) | Werder | P-47 |

0-0-0 air
1-1 ground

**Smith, Vernon A., Lt.**
63rd Ftr Sqn/56th Ftr Grp

| Sqn | Date | Claims | Location | A/C |
|---|---|---|---|---|
| 63rd | April 10, 1945 | Ju-88 dest(grd) | Werder | P-47 |
| | | u/i a/c dam(grd) | Werder | P-47 |
| | April 13 | (2)He-111 dest(grd) | Eggebeck A/F | P-47 |
| | | (2)Ju-88 dest(grd) | Eggebeck A/F | P-47 |
| | | (2)Ju-88 dam(grd) | Eggebeck A/F | P-47 |
| | | (2)u/i a/c dam(grd) | Eggebeck A/F | P-47 |

0-0-0 air
5-5 ground

**Smith, Walter S., Capt.**
487th Ftr Sqn/352nd Ftr Grp

| Sqn | Date | Claims | Location | A/C |
|---|---|---|---|---|
| 487th | November 27, 1944 | Me-109 dest(air) | Munster | P-51 |

1-0-0 air
0-0 ground

**Smith, William B., Capt.**
334th Ftr Sqn/4th Ftr Grp

| Sqn | Date | Claims | Location | A/C |
|---|---|---|---|---|
| 334th | February 28, 1944 | (.25)Ju-88 dest(grd)[*] | Soissons | P-51 |
| | March 27 | Me-109 dest(air) | Lake Biscarosse | P-51 |
| | | Me-109 dest(grd) | Angouleme | P-51 |
| | April 8 | FW-190 dest(air) | Celle | P-51 |
| | | FW-190 dam(air) | Celle | P-51 |
| | April 11 | (.5)Do-217 dest(air)[**] | SE Stettin | P-51 |
| | | Me-410 dam(air) | SE Stettin | P-51 |
| | | (2)FW-190 dest(grd) | Stettin | P-51 |
| | April 22 | (.5)Me-109 dest(air)[@] | SW Kassel | P-51 |
| | September 13 | u/i a/c dest(grd) | Schwabisch Hall | P-51 |

3-0-2 air
4.5-0 ground

[*] - shared with Capt. D.W. Beeson and Lt. N. Megura of the 334th Ftr Sqn and Lt. V. Garrison of the 336th Ftr Sqn, 4th Ftr Grp
[**] - shared with an unknown pilot
[@] - shared with Lt. P.S. Riley of the 334th Ftr Sqn

**Smith, William D., Capt.**
350th Ftr Sqn/353rd Ftr Grp

| Sqn | Date | Claims | Location | A/C |
|---|---|---|---|---|
| 350th | August 28, 1944 | He-111 dest(grd) | Verdun | P-47 |
| | August 29 | u/i a/c dest(grd) | Wavre | P-47 |

0-0-0 air
2-0 ground

**Smith, William F., Lt.**
61st Ftr Sqn/56th Ftr Grp

| Sqn | Date | Claims | Location | A/C |
|---|---|---|---|---|
| 61st | April 13, 1945 | Me-110 dest(grd) | Eggebeck A/F | P-47 |
| | | (2)u/i a/c dam(grd) | Eggebeck A/F | P-47 |

0-0-0 air
1-2 ground

**Smith, William W., Maj.**
55th Ftr Sqn/20th Ftr Grp
79th Ftr Sqn/20th Ftr Grp

| Sqn | Date | Claims | Location | A/C |
|---|---|---|---|---|
| 79th | August 9, 1944 | (2)FW-190 dest(air) | SW Ulm | P-51 |
| | | FW-190 dam(air) | SW Ulm | P-51 |

2-0-1 air
0-0 ground

**Smolinsky, Frank J., Lt.**
335th Ftr Sqn/4th Ftr Grp

| Sqn | Date | Claims | Location | A/C |
|---|---|---|---|---|
| 335th | November 19, 1942 | FW-190 dest(air) | SW Flushing | Spit |

1-0-0 air
0-0 ground

**Smutko, Leonard S., Lt.**
79th Ftr Sqn/20th Ftr Grp

| Sqn | Date | Claims | Location | A/C |
|---|---|---|---|---|
| 79th | January 14, 1944 | Me-109 dam(air) | Rouen | P-38 |

0-0-1 air
0-0 ground

**Snedeker, Irving E., Lt.**
364th Ftr Sqn/357th Ftr Grp

| Sqn | Date | Claims | Location | A/C |
|---|---|---|---|---|
| 364th | January 5, 1945 | (.5)FW-190 dest(air)[*] | N/Hanau | P-51 |
| | January 14 | FW-190 dest(air) | NW Berlin | P-51 |

1.5-0-0 air
0-0 ground

[*] - shared with Lt. T.H. Adams of the 364th Ftr Sqn

**Snell, Donald H., Capt.**
38th Ftr Sqn/55th Ftr Grp

| Sqn | Date | Claims | Location | A/C |
|---|---|---|---|---|
| 38th | June 14, 1944 | FW-190 dest(air) | Paris | P-38 |

1-0-0 air
0-0 ground

**Snell, Orrin C., Lt.**
334th Ftr Sqn/4th Ftr Grp

| Sqn | Date | Claims | Location | A/C |
|---|---|---|---|---|
| 334th | May 29, 1944 | Me-109 dest(air) | Cammin | P-51 |

1-0-0 air
0-0 ground

**Snodgrass, Fred E., Capt.**
77th Ftr Sqn/20th Ftr Grp

| Sqn | Date | Claims | Location | A/C |
|---|---|---|---|---|
| 77th | October 6, 1944 | (.5)Do-18 dest(grd)[*] | Bad Berg-Dievenow | P-51 |
| | | Do-18 dam(grd) | Bad Berg-Dievenow | P-51 |

0-0-0 air
0.5-1 ground

* - shared with Lt. D.W. Van Sickle of the 77th Ftr Sqn

**Snnok, Keo L., Lt.**
358th Ftr Sqn/355th Ftr Grp

| *Sqn* | *Date* | *Claims* | *Location* | *A/C* |
|---|---|---|---|---|
| 358th | April 20, 1945 | (.5)Me-109 dest(air)[*] | Kbely A/F | P-51 |

0.5-0-0 air
0-0 ground

* - shared with Lt. H.P. Knutty of the 358th Ftr Sqn

**Snow, Mitchell P., Lt.**
79th Ftr Sqn/20th Ftr Grp

| *Sqn* | *Date* | *Claims* | *Location* | *A/C* |
|---|---|---|---|---|
| 79th | April 8, 1944 | Me-109 dest(air) | Hermannsburg | P-38 |

1-0-0 air
0-0 ground

**Snyder, Alton B., Jr., Capt.**
375th Ftr Sqn/361st Ftr Grp

| *Sqn* | *Date* | *Claims* | *Location* | *A/C* |
|---|---|---|---|---|
| 375th | March 6, 1944 | FW-190 dest(air) | S/Quackenbruck | P-47 |
| | April 8 | Me-109 dest(air) | SW Dummer Lake | P-47 |
| | | FW-190 dest(air) | N/Zwolle | P-47 |

3-0-0 air
0-0 ground

**Snyder, Ralph B., Lt.**
352nd Ftr Sqn/353rd Ftr Grp

| *Sqn* | *Date* | *Claims* | *Location* | *A/C* |
|---|---|---|---|---|
| 352nd | April 17, 1945 | Me-109 dam(grd) | Ganacker | P-51 |

0-0-0 air
0-1 ground

**Sobanski, Winslow M., Maj.**
336th Ftr Sqn/4th Ftr Grp
334th Ftr Sqn/4th Ftr Grp

| *Sqn* | *Date* | *Claims* | *Location* | *A/C* |
|---|---|---|---|---|
| 334th | September 15, 1943 | FW-190 dam(air) | SW Paris | P-47 |
| | January 31, 1944 | (.5)Me-109 dest(air)[*] | Gilze-Rijen | P-47 |
| | February 21 | FW-190 prob(air) | S/Dummer Lake | P-47 |
| | March 29 | FW-190 dam(air) | Hanover | P-51 |
| | | Ju-52 dest(grd) | Steinhuder Lake | P-51 |
| | April 8 | Me-109 dam(air) | Celle | P-51 |
| | | FW-190 dam(grd) | Celle | P-51 |
| | April 11 | Me-110 dam(air) | SE Stettin | P-51 |
| | April 13 | FW-190 dest(air) | Ludwigshafen | P-51 |
| | April 30 | (.33)Me-110 dest(air)[**] | N/Lyon | P-51 |
| | | Me-110 dam(grd) | Lyon/Bron | P-51 |
| | May 28 | Me-109 dest(air) | Wittenberg-Magdeburg | P-51 |
| | May 29 | (.5)Do-18 dam(grd)[@] | Dievenow | P-51 |
| | | (.5)Do-18 dam(grd)[@] | Dievenow | P-51 |

2.83-1-4 air
1-3 ground

* - shared with Lt. H.N. Moulton of the 334th Ftr Sqn
** - shared with Lt. J.L. Lang and Lt. S.W. Monroe of the 334th Ftr Sqn
@ - both shared with Lt. J.P. Fernandez of the 334th Ftr Sqn

**Sobieski, Russell J., Lt.**
375th Ftr Sqn/361st Ftr Grp

| *Sqn* | *Date* | *Claims* | *Location* | *A/C* |
|---|---|---|---|---|
| 375th | April 8, 1944 | FW-190 prob(air) | N/Zwolle | P-47 |
| | July 7 | Me-410 dest(air) | NW Leipzig | P-51 |
| | | (.5)Me-109 dest(air)[*] | NW Leipzig | P-51 |

1.5-1-0 air
0-0 ground

* - shared with Lt. D.R. Morgan of the 375th Ftr Sqn

**Soehl, John E., Lt.**
384th Ftr Sqn/364th Ftr Grp

| *Sqn* | *Date* | *Claims* | *Location* | *A/C* |
|---|---|---|---|---|
| 384th | February 25, 1945 | FW-190 dest(air) | SW Ulzen | P-51 |
| | | FW-190 dam(air) | SW Ulzen | P-51 |
| | April 16 | (3)u/i a/c dest(grd) | Pocking | P-51 |

1-0-1 air
3-0 ground

**Sole, John R., Lt.**
84th Ftr Sqn/78th Ftr Grp

| *Sqn* | *Date* | *Claims* | *Location* | *A/C* |
|---|---|---|---|---|
| 84th | April 10, 1945 | u/i a/c dest(grd) | Ulzen | P-51 |
| | | u/i a/c dam(grd) | Ulzen | P-51 |
| | April 17 | (3)u/i a/c dest(grd) | W/Dresden | P-51 |
| | | (4)u/i a/c dam(grd) | W/Dresden | P-51 |

0-0-0 air
4-5 ground

**Sommer, Warren B., Lt.**
83rd Ftr Sqn/78th Ftr Grp

| *Sqn* | *Date* | *Claims* | *Location* | *A/C* |
|---|---|---|---|---|
| 83rd | September 10, 1944 | Me-410 dest(grd) | Germsheim | P-47 |
| | | FW-190 dest(grd) | Germsheim | P-47 |
| | October 15 | Me-109 dest(grd) | Fassberg A/F | P-47 |

0-0-0 air
3-0 ground

**Sooman, Woodrow F., Lt.**
336th Ftr Sqn/4th Ftr Grp

| *Sqn* | *Date* | *Claims* | *Location* | *A/C* |
|---|---|---|---|---|
| 336th | March 4, 1944 | Ju-52 dest(air) | Holmstedt | P-51 |
| | March 8 | Me-109 dam(air) | SW Berlin | P-51 |

1-0-1 air
0-0 ground

**Sorace, Kenneth J., Capt.**
343rd Ftr Sqn/55th Ftr Grp

| *Sqn* | *Date* | *Claims* | *Location* | *A/C* |
|---|---|---|---|---|
| 343rd | January 7, 1944 | Me-109 dam(air) | Ludwigshafen | P-38 |

0-0-1 air
0-0 ground

**Sorenson, Boyd W., Lt.**
83rd Ftr Sqn/78th Ftr Grp

| *Sqn* | *Date* | *Claims* | *Location* | *A/C* |
|---|---|---|---|---|
| 83rd | March 17, 1944 | (.5)Do-217 dest(grd)[*] | N/Reims | P-47 |
| | April 25 | (.5)FW-190 dest(air)[**] | S/Verdun | P-47 |
| | July 19 | (2)Ju-188 dest(grd) | Linburg-Coblenz | P-47 |
| | | Ju-188 dam(grd) | Linburg-Coblenz | P-47 |

0.5-0-0 air
2.5-1 ground

* - shared with Lt. W.H. Waldheim of the 83rd Ftr Sqn
** - shared with Lt. H.J. Morris of the 83rd Ftr Sqn

**Sorrells, Fred L., Lt.**
383rd Ftr Sqn/364th Ftr Grp

| *Sqn* | *Date* | *Claims* | *Location* | *A/C* |
|---|---|---|---|---|
| 383rd | September 28, 1944 | FW-190 dam(air) | S/Magdeburg | P-51 |
| | January 1, 1945 | Me-109 dest(air) | W/Stendal | P-51 |

1-0-1 air
0-0 ground

**Soule, Van H., Capt.**
38th Ftr Sqn/55th Ftr Grp

| *Sqn* | *Date* | *Claims* | *Location* | *A/C* |
|---|---|---|---|---|
| 38th | May 21, 1944 | (2)u/i a/c dam(grd) | E/Helmstedt | P-38 |

0-0-0 air
0-2 ground

**Sowerby, Theodore J., Capt.**
435th Ftr Sqn/479th Ftr Grp

| *Sqn* | *Date* | *Claims* | *Location* | *A/C* |
|---|---|---|---|---|
| 435th | August 18, 1944 | Ju-88 dest(grd) | Nancy/Essey A/F | P-38 |
| | | (.5)FW-190 dest(grd)* | Nancy/Essey A/F | P-38 |
| | | (2)He-111 dam(grd) | Nancy/Essey A/F | P-38 |
| | | Ju-88 dam(grd) | Nancy/Essey A/F | P-38 |
| | November 26 | FW-190 dest(air) | Minden | P-51 |
| | December 25 | FW-190 dest(air) | Bonn | P-51 |
| | January 21, 1945 | Ju-52 dest(grd) | Leipheim | P-51 |
| | | Ju-88 dest(grd) | Leipheim | P-51 |
| | April 13 | Ju-88 dest(grd) | Tarnewitz | P-51 |
| | | (4)Ju-88 dam(grd) | Tarnewitz | P-51 |
| | April 17 | (2)Me-262 dest(grd) | Puchhoff | P-51 |

2-0-0 air
6.5-7 ground

* - shared with Lt. T.C. Olson of the 434th Ftr Sqn, 479th Ftr Grp

**Spain, Frank O., Lt.**
385th Ftr Sqn/364th Ftr Grp

| *Sqn* | *Date* | *Claims* | *Location* | *A/C* |
|---|---|---|---|---|
| 385th | April 5, 1945 | FW-190 dam(grd) | SW Nurnburg | P-51 |
| | April 16 | FW-190 dest(grd) | Pocking | P-51 |
| | | Fi-156 dest(grd) | Pocking | P-51 |
| | | (3)Ju-87 dam(grd) | Pocking | P-51 |

0-0-0 air
2-4 ground

**Spalding, Robert P., Lt.**
82nd Ftr Sqn/78th Ftr Grp

| *Sqn* | *Date* | *Claims* | *Location* | *A/C* |
|---|---|---|---|---|
| 82nd | March 6, 1944 | FW-190 dest(air) | Barenburg | P-47 |

1-0-0 air
0-0 ground

**Spaulding, Howard A., Lt.**
375th Ftr Sqn/361st Ftr Grp

| *Sqn* | *Date* | *Claims* | *Location* | *A/C* |
|---|---|---|---|---|
| 375th | June 20, 1944 | (.5)FW-189 dam(grd)* | Putnitz | P-51 |
| | November 26 | (2)FW-190 dam(air) | Celle-Gifhorn | P-51 |

0-0-2 air
0-0.5 ground

* - shared with Lt. W.D. Rogers of the 375th Ftr Sqn

**Spaulding, Roger A., Lt.**
84th Ftr Sqn/78th Ftr Grp

| *Sqn* | *Date* | *Claims* | *Location* | *A/C* |
|---|---|---|---|---|
| 84th | April 10, 1945 | u/i a/c dest(grd) | Werder | P-51 |

0-0-0 air
1-0 ground

**Speer, Frank E., Lt.**
334th Ftr Sqn/4th Ftr Grp

| *Sqn* | *Date* | *Claims* | *Location* | *A/C* |
|---|---|---|---|---|
| 334th | May 21, 1944 | Ju-52 dest(grd) | Rathenow | P-51 |
| | | Ju-88 dest(grd) | Rathenow | P-51 |
| | May 24 | Me-109 dest(air) | E/Hamburg | P-51 |
| | May 29 | (3)He-177 dest(grd) | Mackfitz A/F | P-51 |

1-0-0 air
5-0 ground

**Spencer, Charles H., Capt.**
354th Ftr Sqn/355th Ftr Grp

| *Sqn* | *Date* | *Claims* | *Location* | *A/C* |
|---|---|---|---|---|
| 354th | March 19, 1945 | Me-262 dest(air) | Kitzingen | P-51 |

1-0-0 air
0-0 ground

**Spencer, Dale F., Lt.**
376th Ftr Sqn/361st Ftr Grp

| *Sqn* | *Date* | *Claims* | *Location* | *A/C* |
|---|---|---|---|---|
| 376th | May 29, 1944 | (4)Me-410 dest(air) | E/Schwerin | P-51 |
| | June 20 | (.5)BV-138 dest(grd)* | Putnitz | P-51 |
| | July 5 | (2)Me-109 dest(air) | Rouen-Evreux | P-51 |
| | | Me-109 dam(air) | Rouen-Evreux | P-51 |
| | July 7 | (2)Me-109 dest(air) | Wittenburg | P-51 |
| | September 12 | (1.5)Me-109 dest(air)** | W/Magdeburg | P-51 |

9.5-0-1 air
0.5-0 ground

* - shared with Lt. B.D. Welch of the 376th Ftr Sqn
** - shared with Lt. R.W. Ward of the 376th Ftr Sqn

**Spencer, Harold W., Lt.**
357th Ftr Sqn/355th Ftr Grp

| *Sqn* | *Date* | *Claims* | *Location* | *A/C* |
|---|---|---|---|---|
| 357th | June 24, 1944 | (2)Me-109 dest(grd) | E/Angars | P-51 |
| | August 16 | (2)Me-109 dest(air) | SE Hildesheim | P-51 |

2-0-0 air
2-0 ground

**Spencer, Herbert G., Lt.**
376th Ftr Sqn/361st Ftr Grp

| *Sqn* | *Date* | *Claims* | *Location* | *A/C* |
|---|---|---|---|---|
| 376th | April 16, 1945 | (3)Ju-52 dest(grd) | Reichersberg | P-51 |

0-0-0 air
3-0 ground

**Spencer, Milton L., Lt.**
334th Ftr Sqn/4th Ftr Grp

| *Sqn* | *Date* | *Claims* | *Location* | *A/C* |
|---|---|---|---|---|
| 334th | April 16, 1945 | (.5)FW-190 dest(grd)* | Gablingen | P-51 |

0-0-0 air
0.5-0 ground

* - shared with Lt. M.W. Arthur of the 334th Ftr Sqn

**Spencer, Richard S., Jr., Capt.**
436th Ftr Sqn/479th Ftr Grp

| *Sqn* | *Date* | *Claims* | *Location* | *A/C* |
|---|---|---|---|---|
| 436th | December 25, 1944 | (2)FW-190 dest(air) | SE Malmedy | P-51 |

2-0-0 air
0-0 ground

**Spencer, William G., Lt.**
334th Ftr Sqn/4th Ftr Grp

| *Sqn* | *Date* | *Claims* | *Location* | *A/C* |
|---|---|---|---|---|
| 334th | April 16, 1945 | FW-190 dest(grd) | Gablingen | P-51 |
| | | Me-109 dest(grd) | Gablingen | P-51 |
| | | u/i a/c dest(grd) | Gablingen | P-51 |

0-0-0 air
3-0 ground

**Spengler, William B., Lt.**
83rd Ftr Sqn/78th Ftr Grp

| *Sqn* | *Date* | *Claims* | *Location* | *A/C* |
|---|---|---|---|---|
| 83rd | March 19, 1945 | (2)Me-109 dam(air) | Osnabruck | P-51 |
| | April 16 | FW-190 dest(grd) | N/Prague | P-51 |
| | | (3)Ju-87 dam(grd) | N/Prague | P-51 |

0-0-2 air
1-3 ground

**Sperry, Clinton H., Lt.**
352nd Ftr Sqn/353rd Ftr Grp

| *Sqn* | *Date* | *Claims* | *Location* | *A/C* |
|---|---|---|---|---|
| 352nd | December 22, 1943 | Me-109 prob(air) | Canabruck | P-47 |
| | January 21, 1944 | (.33)Do-217 dest(grd)* | Albert | P-47 |
| | June 12 | Me-109 prob(air) | Dreux | P-47 |

0-2-0 air
0.33-0 ground

* - shared with LtCol. G.E. Duncan of HdQts, 353rd Ftr Grp, and Lt. W.W. Johnson of the 352nd Ftr Sqn

**Spicer, Henry R., Col.**
HdQts/357th Ftr Grp

| *Sqn* | *Date* | *Claims* | *Location* | *A/C* |
|---|---|---|---|---|
| HdQts | February 22, 1944 | Me-109 dest(air) | Bernburg | P-51 |
| | February 24 | Me-110 dest(air) | Erfurt | P-51 |
| | | Ju-88 dest(air) | Erfurt | P-51 |

3-0-0 air
0-0 ground

**Spieker, Lester F., Capt.**
38th Ftr Sqn/55th Ftr Grp

| *Sqn* | *Date* | *Claims* | *Location* | *A/C* |
|---|---|---|---|---|
| 38th | February 3, 1945 | (.5)FW-58 dest(air)* | Templin | P-51 |
| | March 24 | Me-109 dest(air) | S/Soest | P-51 |

1.5-0-0 air
0-0 ground

* - shared with Lt. D.M. Amoss of the 38th Ftr Sqn

**Splittsteeser, E.A., Lt.**
435th Ftr Sqn/479th Ftr Grp

| *Sqn* | *Date* | *Claims* | *Location* | *A/C* |
|---|---|---|---|---|
| 435th | April 18, 1945 | u/i a/c dam(grd) | Mettenheim | P-51 |

0-0-0 air
0-1 ground

**Spooner, Richard H., Lt.**
84th Ftr Sqn/78th Ftr Grp

| *Sqn* | *Date* | *Claims* | *Location* | *A/C* |
|---|---|---|---|---|
| 84th | November 9, 1944 | Ju-88 dam(grd) | Schenfheim A/F | P-47 |
| | January 14, 1945 | Me-109 dest(air) | SW Cologne | P-51 |
| | | FW-190 dest(air) | SW Cologne | P-51 |

2-0-0 air
0-1 ground

**Spradlin, Roy M., Capt.**
384th Ftr Sqn/364th Ftr Grp

| *Sqn* | *Date* | *Claims* | *Location* | *A/C* |
|---|---|---|---|---|
| 384th | April 29, 1944 | Me-109 prob(air) | Brandenburg | P-38 |
| | May 8 | (2)Me-109 dest(air) | Steinhuder Lake | P-38 |

2-1-0 air
0-0 ground

**Spriggs, Alfred G., Lt.**
350th Ftr Sqn/353rd Ftr Grp

| *Sqn* | *Date* | *Claims* | *Location* | *A/C* |
|---|---|---|---|---|
| 350th | February 27, 1945 | Me-109 dest(grd) | Rohrensee | P-51 |
| | | u/i a/c dest(grd) | Rohrensee | P-51 |

0-0-0 air
2-0 ground

**Squillaro, Raymond E., Lt.**
385th Ftr Sqn/364th Ftr Grp

| *Sqn* | *Date* | *Claims* | *Location* | *A/C* |
|---|---|---|---|---|
| 385th | March 8, 1944 | Me-109 dest(air) | W/Berlin | P-38 |

1-0-0 air
0-0 ground

**Stafford, Charles L., Capt.**
HdQts/353rd Ftr Grp

| *Sqn* | *Date* | *Claims* | *Location* | *A/C* |
|---|---|---|---|---|
| HdQts | January 14, 1944 | (.33)FW-190 dam(grd)* | Rosiers-en-Santerne | P-47 |
| | August 4 | Me-109 dest(air) | SE Bremen | P-47 |
| | | Me-109 dam(air) | SE Bremen | P-47 |
| | September 13 | (3)Me-109 dam(grd) | SW Stuttgart | P-47 |

1-0-1 air
0-0.33 ground

* - shared with Maj. W.C. Beckham of the 351st Ftr Sqn, 353rd Ftr Grp, and Lt. A.C. Duncan of the 375th Ftr Sqn, 361st Ftr Grp

**Staggers, Ted B., Lt.**
505th Ftr Sqn/339th Ftr Grp

| *Sqn* | *Date* | *Claims* | *Location* | *A/C* |
|---|---|---|---|---|
| 505th | July 31, 1944 | FW-190 dest(grd) | Holzkirchen | P-51 |
| | | u/i a/c dest(grd) | Holzkirchen | P-51 |
| | September 11 | Me-110 dest(grd) | Munich | P-51 |
| | | Ju-88 dest(grd) | Munich | P-51 |
| | | Me-110 dam(grd) | Munich | P-51 |
| | | He-111 dam(grd) | Munich | P-51 |
| | | Ju-88 dam(grd) | Munich | P-51 |

0-0-0 air
4-3 ground

**Staggs, William B., Capt.**
38th Ftr Sqn/55th Ftr Grp

| *Sqn* | *Date* | *Claims* | *Location* | *A/C* |
|---|---|---|---|---|
| 38th | December 24, 1944 | (.5)FW-190 dest(air)* | S/Coblenz | P-51 |
| | April 9, 1945 | (2)FW-190 dest(grd) | Munich-Brunnthal | P-51 |

0.5-0-0 air
2-0 ground

* - shared with Lt. R.F. Maloney of the 38th Ftr Sqn

**Staley, Charles W., Lt.**
369th Ftr Sqn/359th Ftr Grp

| *Sqn* | *Date* | *Claims* | *Location* | *A/C* |
|---|---|---|---|---|
| 369th | March 8, 1944 | FW-190 dam(air) | Nuiden | P-47 |

0-0-1 air
0-0 ground

**Stallings, James B., Lt.**
82nd Ftr Sqn/78th Ftr Grp

| *Sqn* | *Date* | *Claims* | *Location* | *A/C* |
|---|---|---|---|---|
| 82nd | August 6, 1944 | (.5)Me-109 dest(air)* | Hamburg | P-47 |

0.5-0-0 air
0-0 ground

* - shared with Capt. R.E. Conner of the 82nd Ftr Sqn

**Stallings, Robert L., Lt.**
335th Ftr Sqn/4th Ftr Grp

| *Sqn* | *Date* | *Claims* | *Location* | *A/C* |
|---|---|---|---|---|
| 335th | November 18, 1944 | Me-109 dam(grd) | Leipheim | P-51 |
| | December 18 | FW-190 dest(air) | NE Frankfurt | P-51 |

1-0-0 air
0-1 ground

**Stamps, Samuel O., Lt.**
63rd Ftr Sqn/56th Ftr Grp

| *Sqn* | *Date* | *Claims* | *Location* | *A/C* |
|---|---|---|---|---|
| 63rd | March 8, 1944 | Me-109 dam(air) | S/Dummer Lake | P-47 |
| | April 15 | (.5)FW-190 dest(air)* | Flensburg | P-47 |
| | | He-111 dam(grd) | Flensburg | P-47 |

0.5-0-1 air
0-1 ground

* - shared with Lt. W.D. Johnson of the 63rd Ftr Sqn

**Stanford, George I., Jr., Capt.**
335th Ftr Sqn/4th Ftr Grp

| Sqn | Date | Claims | Location | A/C |
|---|---|---|---|---|
| 335th | April 5, 1944 | (3)Ju-88 dam(grd) | Brandenburg | P-51 |
| | April 8 | Me-109 dest(air) | Gifhorn | P-51 |
| | April 10 | u/i a/c dest(grd) | Romorantin A/F | P-51 |
| | | u/i a/c dam(grd) | Romorantin A/F | P-51 |
| | May 12 | (.5)Me-109 dest(air)* | Giessen-Marburg | P-51 |
| | June 20 | (.5)Me-210 dest(air)** | Ratzburger Lake | P-51 |

3-0-0 air
1-4 ground

* - shared with Lt. E.H. Shapleigh of the 335th Ftr Sqn
** - shared with F/O L.B. Godwin of the 335th Ftr Sqn

**Stangel, William J., Capt.**
328th Ftr Sqn/352nd Ftr Grp

| Sqn | Date | Claims | Location | A/C |
|---|---|---|---|---|
| 328th | November 2, 1944 | (2)Me-109 dest(air) | Merseburg | P-51 |
| | | (.5)Me-109 dest(air)* | Merseburg | P-51 |
| | | (.5)Me-109 dest(air)* | Merseburg | P-51 |
| | December 25 | (2)Me-109 dest(air) | SW Coblenz | P-51 |

5-0-0 air
0-0 ground

* - both shared with Lt. E.W. James of the 328th Ftr Sqn

**Stanhope, Aubrey C., Lt.**
335th Ftr Sqn/4th Ftr Grp

| Sqn | Date | Claims | Location | A/C |
|---|---|---|---|---|
| 335th | May 14, 1943 | FW-190 dest(air) | NE Knocke | P-47 |
| | May 16 | FW-190 dam(air) | Walcheren Island | P-47 |
| | July 30 | FW-190 dest(air) | S/Arnheim | P-47 |
| | | FW-190 dam(air) | S/Arnheim | P-47 |
| | August 16 | Me-109 dest(air) | Melun-Paris | P-47 |
| | August 31 | FW-190 dam(air) | Glisy-Montdidier | P-47 |

3-0-3 air
0-0 ground

**Stanley, Morris A., Capt.**
364th Ftr Sqn/357th Ftr Grp

| Sqn | Date | Claims | Location | A/C |
|---|---|---|---|---|
| 364th | March 5, 1944 | FW-200 dest(air) | Parthenay A/F | P-51 |
| | March 6 | Me-110 dest(air) | Brandenburg | P-51 |
| | April 19 | FW-190 dest(air) | S/Bliecherode | P-51 |
| | May 21 | (1.5)Me-109 dest(grd)* | S/Eichhof | P-51 |
| | May 27 | (2)FW-190 dest(air) | Strasbourg | P-51 |

5-0-0 air
1.5-0 ground

* - shared with Maj. I.H. Dregne of HdQts, 357th Ftr Grp

**Stanton, O.N., Lt.**
354th Ftr Sqn/355th Ftr Grp

| Sqn | Date | Claims | Location | A/C |
|---|---|---|---|---|
| 354th | April 10, 1945 | u/i a/c dest(grd) | Wesendorf | P-51 |

0-0-0 air
1-0 ground

**Stapleton, Carl W., LtCol.**
384th Ftr Sqn/364th Ftr Grp
385th Ftr Sqn/364th Ftr Grp

| Sqn | Date | Claims | Location | A/C |
|---|---|---|---|---|
| 384th | April 15, 1944 | (.33)BV-138 dest(grd)* | Elbe Estuary | P-38 |
| 385th | May 20 | Ju-88 dest(grd) | Soissons | P-38 |
| | December 5 | FW-190 dest(air) | N/Berlin | P-51 |

1-0-0 air
1.33-0 ground

* - shared with Capt. R.E. Lacy and Lt. D.J. Pick of the 384th Ftr Sqn

**Staranick, Nicholas M., Capt.**
383rd Ftr Sqn/364th Ftr Grp

| Sqn | Date | Claims | Location | A/C |
|---|---|---|---|---|
| 383rd | August 14, 1944 | He-111 dam(grd) | Memmingen | P-51 |

0-0-0 air
0-1 ground

**Starck, Walter E., Capt.**
487th Ftr Sqn/352nd Ftr Grp

| Sqn | Date | Claims | Location | A/C |
|---|---|---|---|---|
| 487th | February 10, 1944 | Me-109 dest(air) | Arnheim | P-47 |
| | May 27 | Me-109 dest(air) | Strasbourg | P-51 |
| | June 20 | FW-190 prob(air) | NW Magdeburg | P-51 |
| | July 1 | Me-109 dest(air) | St. Quentin | P-51 |
| | | Me-109 dam(air) | St. Quentin | P-51 |
| | July 21 | Me-109 dest(air) | E/Munich | P-51 |
| | November 21 | FW-190 dam(air) | SW Leipzig | P-51 |
| | November 27 | (2)Me-109 dest(air) | Hameln | P-51 |
| | | Me-109 dest(air) | Osnabruck | P-51 |

7-1-2 air
0-0 ground

**Starke, John P., Lt.**
77th Ftr Sqn/20th Ftr Grp

| Sqn | Date | Claims | Location | A/C |
|---|---|---|---|---|
| 77th | January 14, 1945 | (.5)Me-109 dest(air)* | Perleberg | P-51 |
| | February 9 | FW-190 dest(grd) | Esperstadt A/F | P-51 |
| | | Me-410 dest(grd) | Esperstadt A/F | P-51 |

0.5-0-0 air
2-0 ground

* - shared with Capt. M.J. Gilbertson of the 77th Ftr Sqn

**Starkey, Rodney M., Lt.**
362nd Ftr Sqn/357th Ftr Grp

| Sqn | Date | Claims | Location | A/C |
|---|---|---|---|---|
| 362nd | March 6, 1944 | Me-109 dest(air) | Berlin | P-51 |
| | March 28 | Ju-88 dest(grd) | S/Paris | P-51 |
| | May 21 | Me-110 dam(grd) | Tarnewitz | P-51 |
| | | Ju-52 dam(grd) | Tarnewitz | P-51 |

1-0-0 air
1-2 ground

**Starnes, James R., Capt.**
505th Ftr Sqn/339th Ftr Grp

| Sqn | Date | Claims | Location | A/C |
|---|---|---|---|---|
| 505th | May 19, 1944 | (.5)FW-190 dest(air)* | Gustrow | P-51 |
| | May 21 | (.5)Trainer dest(air)** | Leipzig-Dresden | P-51 |
| | May 29 | FW-190 dest(air) | NE Stettin | P-51 |
| | June 8 | Me-109 dest(air) | Fourgeres | P-51 |
| | | (.5)FW-190 dest(air)@ | Rennes | P-51 |
| | July 11 | Trainer dest(grd) | NE Lake Constance | P-51 |
| | July 19 | Ju-188 dest(grd) | SW Augsburg | P-51 |
| | July 29 | (.5)Me-109 dest(air)@@ | NW Naumberg | P-51 |
| | July 31 | FW-190 dest(grd) | Holzkirchen | P-51 |
| | | u/i a/c dest(grd) | Holzkirchen | P-51 |
| | | FW-190 dam(grd) | Holzkirchen | P-51 |
| | August 4 | Me-109 dest(air) | S/Hamburg | P-51 |
| | March 2, 1945 | Me-109 dest(air) | E/Magdeburg | P-51 |
| | | u/i a/c dam(grd) | E/Magdeburg | P-51 |
| | March 3 | He-111 dest(grd) | E/Magdeburg | P-51 |
| | April 10 | Do-217 dest(grd) | N/Neuruppin | P-51 |
| | | (3)Do-217 dam(grd) | N/Neuruppin | P-51 |

6-0-0 air
6-5 ground

* - shared with Lt. E.M. Johnson of the 505th Ftr Sqn
** - shared with Lt. J.R. Hanson of the 505th Ftr Sqn
@ - shared with Lt. P.J. McMahan of the 505th Ftr Sqn
@@ - shared with Lt. W.H. Krauss of the 505th Ftr Sqn

**Starr, Albert B., Capt.**
354th Ftr Sqn/355th Ftr Grp

| *Sqn* | *Date* | *Claims* | *Location* | *A/C* |
|---|---|---|---|---|
| 354th | March 26, 1944 | u/i a/c dest(grd) | Chateaudun | P-47 |

0-0-0 air
1-0 ground

**Starr, John F., Lt.**
350th Ftr Sqn/353rd Ftr Grp

| *Sqn* | *Date* | *Claims* | *Location* | *A/C* |
|---|---|---|---|---|
| 350th | June 8, 1944 | He-111 dest(grd) | Breteuil | P-47 |
| | | (2)Me-109 dam(grd) | Breteuil | P-47 |
| | June 12 | Me-109 dam(air) | SW Paris | P-47 |

0-0-1 air
1-2 ground

**Staudte, Raymond W., Lt.**
363rd Ftr Sqn/357th Ftr Grp

| *Sqn* | *Date* | *Claims* | *Location* | *A/C* |
|---|---|---|---|---|
| 363rd | June 29, 1944 | (.5)FW-190 dest(air)* | SW Leipzig | P-51 |

0.5-0-0 air
0-0 ground

* - shared with Capt. J.W. Browning of the 363rd Ftr Sqn

**Staup, Homer A., Capt.**
370th Ftr Sqn/359th Ftr Grp

| *Sqn* | *Date* | *Claims* | *Location* | *A/C* |
|---|---|---|---|---|
| 370th | November 21, 1944 | (2)FW-190 dest(air) | SW Merseburg | P-51 |

2-0-0 air
0-0 ground

**Stearns, Richard A., Lt.**
350th Ftr Sqn/353rd Ftr Grp

| *Sqn* | *Date* | *Claims* | *Location* | *A/C* |
|---|---|---|---|---|
| 350th | November 5, 1943 | Me-210 dest(air) | Venlo | P-47 |
| | December 30 | Me-109 dam(air) | Charleville | P-47 |
| | January 24, 1944 | (.5)Me-110 dest(air)* | Termonde | P-47 |
| | February 24 | (2)FW-190 dest(air) | Obernkirchen | P-47 |

3.5-0-1 air
0-0 ground

* - shared with Capt. C.W. Dinse of the 350th Ftr Sqn

**Stearns, John D., Lt.**
486th Ftr Sqn/352nd Ftr Grp

| *Sqn* | *Date* | *Claims* | *Location* | *A/C* |
|---|---|---|---|---|
| 486th | September 12, 1944 | FW-190 dest(air) | S/Havelburg | P-51 |
| | January 14, 1945 | (.5)FW-190 dest(air)* | Almello | P-51 |

1.5-0-0 air
0-0 ground

* - shared with Lt. G.G. Contos of the 486th Ftr Sqn

**Stebelton, Samuel F., Capt.**
63rd Ftr Sqn/56th Ftr Grp

| *Sqn* | *Date* | *Claims* | *Location* | *A/C* |
|---|---|---|---|---|
| 63rd | April 13, 1945 | u/i a/c dest(grd) | Eggebeck A/F | P-47 |
| | | (3)u/i a/c dam(grd) | Eggebeck A/F | P-47 |

0-0-0 air
1-3 ground

**Steele, James F., Lt.**
335th Ftr Sqn/4th Ftr Grp

| *Sqn* | *Date* | *Claims* | *Location* | *A/C* |
|---|---|---|---|---|
| 335th | March 5, 1944 | FW-200 dest(air) | Bergerac A/F | P-51 |

1-0-0 air
0-0 ground

**Steiger, James A., Lt.**
364th Ftr Sqn/357th Ftr Grp

| *Sqn* | *Date* | *Claims* | *Location* | *A/C* |
|---|---|---|---|---|
| 364th | March 2, 1945 | Me-109 dest(air) | SW Magdeburg | P-51 |
| | April 10 | Ju-88 dest(grd) | Neuruppin | P-51 |
| | April 17 | Me-262 dest(air) | NE Prague | P-51 |

2-0-0 air
1-0 ground

**Steiger, Leroy A., F/O**
505th Ftr Sqn/339th Ftr Grp

| *Sqn* | *Date* | *Claims* | *Location* | *A/C* |
|---|---|---|---|---|
| 505th | April 16, 1945 | (3)FW-190 dest(grd) | NE Prague | P-51 |

0-0-0 air
3-0 ground

**Steinbacher, John R., Capt.**
384th Ftr Sqn/364th Ftr Grp

| *Sqn* | *Date* | *Claims* | *Location* | *A/C* |
|---|---|---|---|---|
| 384th | August 9, 1944 | FW-190 dest(air) | Kaufburen | P-51 |
| | November 21 | (2)FW-190 dam(air) | SW Halle | P-51 |

1-0-2 air
0-0 ground

**Steiner, DeLorn L., Lt.**
38th Ftr Sqn/55th Ftr Grp

| *Sqn* | *Date* | *Claims* | *Location* | *A/C* |
|---|---|---|---|---|
| 38th | November 5, 1943 | Do-217 dam(air) | Munster | P-38 |
| | November 25 | Me-109 dest(air) | Lille | P-38 |
| | January 5, 1944 | FW-190 dest(air) | SW Kiel | P-38 |

2-0-1 air
0-0 ground

**Stepelton, Mark H., Capt.**
364th Ftr Sqn/357th Ftr Grp

| *Sqn* | *Date* | *Claims* | *Location* | *A/C* |
|---|---|---|---|---|
| 364th | April 11, 1944 | (.5)FW-190 dest(air)* | Leipzig | P-51 |
| | May 21 | Me-109 dest(grd) | S/Eichhof | P-51 |
| | May 27 | Me-109 dest(air) | Strasbourg | P-51 |
| | June 29 | FW-190 dest(air) | W/Leipzig | P-51 |
| | July 14 | FW-190 dest(air) | Valence | P-51 |

3.5-0-0 air
1-0 ground

* - shared with Lt. C.D. Sumner of the 364th Ftr Sqn

**Steph, Walter B., Lt.**
436th Ftr Sqn/479th Ftr Grp

| *Sqn* | *Date* | *Claims* | *Location* | *A/C* |
|---|---|---|---|---|
| 436th | April 13, 1945 | FW-190 dest(grd) | Salzwedel | P-51 |
| | | Me-109 dam(grd) | Salzwedel | P-51 |
| | April 16 | Me-109 dest(grd) | Landstadt | P-51 |

0-0-0 air
2-1 ground

**Stephenson, Enoch B., Maj.**
503rd Ftr Sqn/339th Ftr Grp

| *Sqn* | *Date* | *Claims* | *Location* | *A/C* |
|---|---|---|---|---|
| 503rd | May 21, 1944 | Ju-88 dam(grd) | Riesa A/F | P-51 |
| | July 11 | Me-110 dam(air) | Landsberg | P-51 |
| | July 25 | Me-109 dest(air) | Etrepagny | P-51 |
| | August 6 | Me-109 dest(air) | S/Schweriner Lake | P-51 |

2-0-1 air
0-1 ground

**Stephenson, Stewart E., Lt.**
352nd Ftr Sqn/353rd Ftr Grp

| *Sqn* | *Date* | *Claims* | *Location* | *A/C* |
|---|---|---|---|---|
| 352nd | December 23, 1944 | Me-262 dam(air) | W/Magdeburg | P-51 |

0-0-1 air
0-0 ground

**Stepp, Malta L., Jr., Capt.**
336th Ftr Sqn/4th Ftr Grp
HdQts/4th Ftr Grp

| *Sqn* | *Date* | *Claims* | *Location* | *A/C* |
|---|---|---|---|---|
| 336th | May 14, 1943 | FW-190 dam(air) | W/Antwerp | P-47 |

0-0-1 air
0-0 ground

**Steppe, Edward J., Lt.**
334th Ftr Sqn/4th Ftr Grp

| *Sqn* | *Date* | *Claims* | *Location* | *A/C* |
|---|---|---|---|---|
| 334th | May 29, 1944 | Do-18 dam(grd) | Dievenow | P-51 |

0-0-0 air
0-1 ground

**Stern, John R., Capt.**
363rd Ftr Sqn/357th Ftr Grp

| *Sqn* | *Date* | *Claims* | *Location* | *A/C* |
|---|---|---|---|---|
| 363rd | December 5, 1944 | FW-190 dest(air) | N/Berlin | P-51 |
| | January 14, 1945 | (3)Me-109 dest(air) | N/Brandenburg | P-51 |
| | February 28 | Ju-88 dam(grd) | Lubeck-Blankensee | P-51 |

4-0-0 air
0-1 ground

**Stevens, Bradford V., Capt.**
504th Ftr Sqn/339th Ftr Grp

| *Sqn* | *Date* | *Claims* | *Location* | *A/C* |
|---|---|---|---|---|
| 504th | May 24, 1944 | Me-109 prob(air) | Berlin | P-51 |
| | | (2)Me-109 dam(air) | Berlin | P-51 |
| | May 30 | (2)FW-190 dest(air) | SE Brunswick | P-51 |
| | June 7 | FW-190 dest(grd) | Laval | P-51 |
| | September 12 | Me-109 dest(air) | Halbustalt | P-51 |

3-1-2 air
1-0 ground

**Stevens, Kent H., Lt.**
79th Ftr Sqn/20th Ftr Grp

| *Sqn* | *Date* | *Claims* | *Location* | *A/C* |
|---|---|---|---|---|
| 79th | May 24, 1944 | Me-109 dam(air) | Eberswalde | P-38 |

0-0-1 air
0-0 ground

**Stevens, Richard W., Capt.**
384th Ftr Sqn/364th Ftr Grp

| *Sqn* | *Date* | *Claims* | *Location* | *A/C* |
|---|---|---|---|---|
| 384th | November 8, 1944 | Me-262 dest(air) | Dummer Lake | P-51 |
| | December 27 | Me-109 dam(air) | Bonn | P-51 |
| | February 22, 1945 | (.5)Me-262 prob(air)* | Wittstock | P-51 |
| | February 23 | (2)Me-109 dest(air) | Stuttgart | P-51 |

3-0.5-1 air
0-0 ground

* - shared with Lt. C.B. Kirby of the 384th Ftr Sqn

**Stevens, WAlter R., Jr., Capt.**
375th Ftr Sqn/361st Ftr Grp

| *Sqn* | *Date* | *Claims* | *Location* | *A/C* |
|---|---|---|---|---|
| 375th | November 26, 1944 | FW-190 dest(air) | Celle-Gifhorn | P-51 |
| | April 17, 1945 | Ju-188 dest(grd) | Eger A/F | P-51 |

1-0-0 air
1-0 ground

**Stevenson, William J., Lt.**
62nd Ftr Sqn/56th Ftr Grp

| *Sqn* | *Date* | *Claims* | *Location* | *A/C* |
|---|---|---|---|---|
| 62nd | April 10, 1945 | Ju-88 dest(grd) | Neuruppin | P-51 |
| | | Ju-88 dam(grd) | Neuruppin | P-51 |
| | April 13 | (2)Ju-88 dest(grd) | Eggebeck A/F | P-51 |
| | | (3)Ju-88 dam(grd) | Eggebeck A/F | P-51 |

0-0-0 air
3-4 ground

**Stewart, Carl R., Lt.**
505th Ftr Sqn/56th Ftr Grp

| *Sqn* | *Date* | *Claims* | *Location* | *A/C* |
|---|---|---|---|---|
| 505th | July 31, 1944 | u/i a/c dest(grd) | Holzkirchen | P-51 |
| | | u/i a/c dam(grd) | Holzkirchen | P-51 |
| | September 10 | (2)Ju-88 dest(grd) | Weizenburg | P-51 |
| | | (.5)Me-109 dest(grd)* | Weizenburg | P-51 |
| | | (3)Ju-88 dam(grd) | Weizenburg | P-51 |

0-0-0 air
3.5-4 ground

* - shared with Lt. W.A. Jones of the 505th Ftr Sqn

**Stewart, David, Lt.**
79th Ftr sqn/20th Ftr Grp

| *Sqn* | *Date* | *Claims* | *Location* | *A/C* |
|---|---|---|---|---|
| 79th | April 10, 1945 | (3)Me-110 dest(grd) | Werder | P-51 |
| | | (2)FW-190 dest(grd) | Werder | P-51 |
| | | Me-109 dest(grd) | Werder | P-51 |
| | | He-111 dest(grd) | Werder | P-51 |

0-0-0 air
7-0 ground

**Stewart, Everett W., Col.**
328th Ftr Sqn/352nd Ftr Grp
HdQts/355th Ftr Grp
HdQts/ 4th Ftr Grp

| *Sqn* | *Date* | *Claims* | *Location* | *A/C* |
|---|---|---|---|---|
| 328th | December 22, 1943 | (.5)Me-110 dest(air)* | Zwolle | P-47 |
| | | Me-210 dam(air) | Zwolle | P-47 |
| | January 5, 1944 | (.33)He-177 dest(air)** | La Ferte Bernard | P-47 |
| HdQts | March 6 | Me-109 dest(air) | NW Hanover | P-47 |
| (355th) | March 16 | Me-109 dest(air) | Augsburg-Luneville | P-51 |
| | | Me-109 prob(air) | Augsburg-Luneville | P-51 |
| | | Me-109 dam(air) | Augsburg-Luneville | P-51 |
| | March 18 | Me-109 dest(air) | SW Munich | P-51 |
| | March 29 | (2)Me-108 dest(air) | E/Goslar A/F | P-51 |
| | | FW-190 dam(air) | S/Brunswick | P-51 |
| | | (2)Me-108 dam(grd) | Goslar A/F | P-51 |
| | April 11 | Me-410 dest(air) | NW Pyritz | P-51 |
| | | Ju-188 dest(air) | Schau | P-51 |
| | | (2)Ar-196 dam(grd) | Sorau | P-51 |
| | September 27 | (.5)Ju-88 dest(grd)@ | Eschwege | P-51 |
| | February 9, 1945 | Ju-188 dest(grd) | Kothen | P-51 |
| | | (2)Ju-188 dam(grd) | Kothen | P-51 |
| HdQts | March 3 | Me-262 dam(air) | Gardelegen | P-51 |

7.83-1-4 air
1.5-6 ground

* - shared with Lt. R.H. Powell of the 328th Ftr Sqn
** - shared with Lt. J.B. Coleman and Lt. R.H. Powell of the 328th Ftr Sqn
@ - shared with Lt. H.R. Mann of the 354th Ftr Sqn, 355th Ftr Grp

**Stewart, Henry M., II, Capt.**
487th Ftr Sqn/352nd Ftr Grp

| *Sqn* | *Date* | *Claims* | *Location* | *A/C* |
|---|---|---|---|---|
| 487th | September 11, 1944 | Ju-88 dest(grd) | Gotha | P-51 |
| | | (2)Ju-88 dam(grd) | Gotha | P-51 |
| | November 27 | Me-109 dest(air) | Hameln | P-51 |
| | January 1, 1945 | (3)Me-109 dest(air) | N/Liege | P-51 |

4-0-0 air
1-2 ground

**Stewart, James C., LtCol.**
HdQts/56th Ftr Grp
61st Ftr Sqn/56th Ftr Grp

| *Sqn* | *Date* | *Claims* | *Location* | *A/C* |
|---|---|---|---|---|
| HdQts | October 14, 1943 | Me-110 dam(air) | W/Aachen | P-47 |
| | October 18 | (.5)Me-210 dest(air)* | NE Maastricht | P-47 |
| | November 26 | Do-217 dest(air) | SE Oldenburg | P-47 |
| | January 5, 1944 | FW-190 dest(air) | SW Bonn | P-47 |
| 61st | February 11 | FW-190 dest(air) | Duren | P-47 |
| | February 22 | Me-109 dest(air) | SW Munster | P-47 |
| | February 24 | FW-190 dest(air) | Kassel | P-47 |
| | March 6 | (2)FW-190 dest(air) | N/Dummer Lake | P-47 |
| | March 8 | FW-190 dest(air) | S/Steinhuder Lake | P-47 |
| | | Me-110 dest(air) | S/Steinhuder Lake | P-47 |
| | March 15 | Me-109 dam(air) | Dummer Lake | P-47 |
| | March 20 | (2)Me-109 dest(air) | S/Charleville | P-47 |
| | | Me-109 prob(air) | S/Charleville | P-47 |
| HdQts | April 24 | Ju-87 dest(grd) | Thronville | P-47 |
| | | Ju-87 dam(grd) | Thronville | P-47 |
| | | u/i a/c dam(grd) | Thronville | P-47 |
| | April 29 | Me-109 dam(air) | W/Steinhuder Lake | P-47 |

11.5-1-3 air
1-2 ground

* - shared with Lt. M.C. Wood of the 61st Ftr Sqn

**Stewart, James C., Lt.**
376th Ftr Sqn/361st Ftr Grp

| *Sqn* | *Date* | *Claims* | *Location* | *A/C* |
|---|---|---|---|---|
| 376th | April 26, 1944 | Ju-88 dam(grd) | Montdidier | P-47 |

0-0-0 air
0-1 ground

**Stiefvater, Richard L., Capt.**
384th Ftr Sqn/364th Ftr Grp

| *Sqn* | *Date* | *Claims* | *Location* | *A/C* |
|---|---|---|---|---|
| 384th | September 19, 1944 | (.5)Me-109 dest(air)* | Duisenberg | P-51 |
| | October 12 | FW-190 dest(air) | N/Bremen | P-51 |
| | February 25, 1945 | FW-190 dam(air) | N/Gifhorn | P-51 |

1.5-0-1 air
0-0 ground

* - shared with Lt. B.W. Ward of the 384th Ftr Sqn

**Stier, Earl L., Capt.**
84th Ftr Sqn/78th Ftr Grp

| *Sqn* | *Date* | *Claims* | *Location* | *A/C* |
|---|---|---|---|---|
| 84th | January 14, 1945 | Me-109 dest(air) | SW Cologne | P-51 |
| | | Me-109 dam(air) | SW Cologne | P-51 |
| | February 3 | FW-190 dest(grd) | Luneburg | P-51 |
| | | Me-410 dest(grd) | Luneburg | P-51 |

1-0-1 air
2-0 ground

**Stiff, Edison G., Lt.**
352nd Ftr Sqn/353rd Ftr Grp

| *Sqn* | *Date* | *Claims* | *Location* | *A/C* |
|---|---|---|---|---|
| 352nd | December 20, 1943 | FW-190 prob(air) | Varel | P-47 |

0-1-0 air
0-0 ground

**Stiles, Bert, Lt.**
505th Ftr Sqn/339th Ftr Grp

| *Sqn* | *Date* | *Claims* | *Location* | *A/C* |
|---|---|---|---|---|
| 505th | November 26, 1944 | FW-190 dest(air) | S/Hanover | P-51 |

1-0-0 air
0-0 ground

**Stillwell, Frank M., Capt.**
503rd Ftr Sqn/339th Ftr Grp

| *Sqn* | *Date* | *Claims* | *Location* | *A/C* |
|---|---|---|---|---|
| 503rd | November 18, 1944 | Me-109 prob(air) | Mannheim | P-51 |
| | November 26 | FW-190 dest(air) | SE Dummer Lake | P-51 |

1-1-0 air
0-0 ground

**Stillwell, George W., Lt.**
82nd Ftr Sqn/78th Ftr Grp

| *Sqn* | *Date* | *Claims* | *Location* | *A/C* |
|---|---|---|---|---|
| 82nd | April 10, 1945 | Me-410 dest(grd) | Werder | P-51 |
| | | Me-410 dam(grd) | Werder | P-51 |
| | April 16 | FW-190 dest(grd) | Pilzen/Prague | P-51 |
| | | (4)Me-109 dam(grd) | Pilzen/Prague | P-51 |
| | | u/i a/c dam(grd) | Pilzen/Prague | P-51 |

0-0-0 air
2-6 ground

**Stish, Jerome R., Lt.**
61st Ftr Sqn/56th Ftr Grp

| *Sqn* | *Date* | *Claims* | *Location* | *A/C* |
|---|---|---|---|---|
| 61st | April 16, 1945 | u/i a/c dam(grd) | Muhldorf | P-47 |

0-0-0 air
0-1 ground

**Stitzer, Sidney G., Lt.**
55th Ftr Sqn/20th Ftr Grp

| *Sqn* | *Date* | *Claims* | *Location* | *A/C* |
|---|---|---|---|---|
| 55th | January 14, 1945 | FW-190 dest(air) | Perleberg | P-51 |

1-0-0 air
0-0 ground

**Stockman, Hervey S., Lt.**
504th Ftr Sqn/339th Ftr Grp

| *Sqn* | *Date* | *Claims* | *Location* | *A/C* |
|---|---|---|---|---|
| 504th | June 10, 1944 | Me-109 prob(air) | SE Le Havre | P-51 |
| | July 29 | Me-109 dest(air) | Merseburg-Naumberg | P-51 |
| | | Me-109 prob(air) | Merseburg-Naumberg | P-51 |
| | | Me-109 dam(air) | Merseburg-Naumberg | P-51 |
| | August 16 | Me-109 dest(air) | Mulhausen | P-51 |

2-2-1 air
0-0 ground

**Stockmeier, Glenn R., Capt.**
375th Ftr Sqn/361st Ftr Grp

| *Sqn* | *Date* | *Claims* | *Location* | *A/C* |
|---|---|---|---|---|
| 375th | January 2, 1945 | (.5)Me-109 dest(air)* | W/Stuttgart | P-51 |
| | March 31 | Me-262 dam(air) | Brunswick | P-51 |

0.5-0-1 air
0-0 ground

* - shared with Lt. A. Maurice of the 375th Ftr Sqn

**Stockton, Vincent R., Lt.**
55th Ftr Sqn/20th Ftr Grp

| *Sqn* | *Date* | *Claims* | *Location* | *A/C* |
|---|---|---|---|---|
| 55th | January 7, 1944 | (.5)Me-109 dam(air)* | Ludwigshafen | P-38 |

0-0-0.5 air
0-0 ground

* - shared with Capt. C.E. Jackson of HdQts, 20th Ftr Grp

**Stockton, William D., Lt.**
503rd Ftr Sqn/339th Ftr Grp

| *Sqn* | *Date* | *Claims* | *Location* | *A/C* |
|---|---|---|---|---|
| 503rd | September 11, 1944 | FW-190 dam(air) | Annaberg | P-51 |
| | September 13 | Ju-88 dest(grd) | Holzkirchen | P-51 |

0-0-1 air
1-0 ground

**Stokes, James E., Jr., Lt.**
83rd Ftr Sqn/78th Ftr Grp

| *Sqn* | *Date* | *Claims* | *Location* | *A/C* |
|---|---|---|---|---|
| 83rd | January 4, 1944 | FW-190 dest(air) | Munster | P-47 |

1-0-0 air
0-0 ground

**Stoll, Marvin B., Lt.**
486th Ftr Sqn/352nd Ftr Grp

| *Sqn* | *Date* | *Claims* | *Location* | *A/C* |
|---|---|---|---|---|
| 486th | July 18, 1944 | Ju-88 dest(air) | N/Warnemunde | P-51 |
| | September 12 | Me-109 dam(air) | Havelburg | P-51 |

1-0-1 air
0-0 ground

**Stolzy, Robert J., Lt.**
374th Ftr Sqn/361st Ftr Grp

| *Sqn* | *Date* | *Claims* | *Location* | *A/C* |
|---|---|---|---|---|
| 374th | February 24, 1944 | Me-109 dest(air) | Dummer Lake | P-47 |
| | | Me-110 dam(grd) | Hesepe A/F | P-47 |
| | June 7 | Ju-52 dest(grd) | Orleans/Bricy | P-51 |

1-0-0 air
1-1 ground

**Stone, James J., Jr., Col.**
83rd Ftr Sqn/78th Ftr Grp
HdQts/78th Ftr Grp

| *Sqn* | *Date* | *Claims* | *Location* | *A/C* |
|---|---|---|---|---|
| 83rd | May 14, 1943 | FW-190 dest(air) | NE St. Nicholas | P-47 |
| | July 1 | FW-190 prob(air) | W/Schouwen | P-47 |
| | July 30 | Me-109 dest(air) | Berkelo | P-47 |
| HdQts | February 20, 1944 | FW-190 dam(air) | Coblenz | P-47 |

2-1-1 air
0-0 ground

**Stone, Richard J., Lt.**
359th Ftr Sqn/356th Ftr Grp

| *Sqn* | *Date* | *Claims* | *Location* | *A/C* |
|---|---|---|---|---|
| 359th | March 21, 1945 | FW-190 dam(grd) | Achmer | P-51 |

0-0-0 air
0-1 ground

**Storch, John A., LtCol.**
364th Ftr Sqn/357th Ftr Grp

| *Sqn* | *Date* | *Claims* | *Location* | *A/C* |
|---|---|---|---|---|
| 364th | May 12, 1944 | (.5)FW-190 dest(air)[*] | NE Frankfurt | P-51 |
| | May 19 | Me-109 dest(air) | NE Salzwedel | P-51 |
| | May 21 | Me-109 dest(grd) | S/Eichhof | P-51 |
| | | (.5)FW-44 dest(grd)[**] | S/Eichhof | P-51 |
| | May 27 | (2)Me-109 dest(air) | Strasbourg | P-51 |
| | | (.5)FW-190 dest(air)[@] | Strasbourg | P-51 |
| | June 20 | (.5)Me-109 dest(air)[@@] | Pasewalk | P-51 |
| | August 6 | FW-190 dam(air) | Danzig | P-51 |
| | August 7 | (.5)Me-109 dest(air)[#] | Oswiecim | P-51 |
| | September 13 | (1.5)Me-109 dest(air)[##] | E/Bad Frankenhausen | P-51 |
| | January 14, 1945 | (2)FW-190 dest(air) | S/Schwerin | P-51 |
| | | Me-109 dest(air) | S/Schwerin | P-51 |
| | February 28 | (2)u/i a/c dam(grd) | Lubeck/Blankensee | P-51 |
| | March 24 | Me-109 dest(air) | W/Gutersloh | P-51 |

10.5-0-1 air
1.5-2 ground

[*] - shared with Capt. R.A. Peterson of the 364th Ftr Sqn
[**] - shared with Lt. C.H. Dooley of the 364th Ftr Sqn
[@] - shared with Lt. E. Zellner of the 352nd Ftr Grp
[@@] - shared with Lt. L.A. Fecher of the 364th Ftr Sqn
[#] - shared with Lt. H.R. Nowlin of the 364th Ftr Sqn
[##] - shared with Lt. R.G. Schimanski of the 364th Ftr Sqn

**Stott, Harold L., Lt.**
434th Ftr Sqn/479th Ftr Grp

| *Sqn* | *Date* | *Claims* | *Location* | *A/C* |
|---|---|---|---|---|
| 434th | April 16, 1945 | Ju-88 dest(grd) | Reichersberg | P-51 |
| | | Ju-88 dam(grd) | Reichersberg | P-51 |

0-0-0 air
1-1 ground

**Stott, John W., Lt.**
328th Ftr Sqn/352nd Ftr Grp

| *Sqn* | *Date* | *Claims* | *Location* | *A/C* |
|---|---|---|---|---|
| 328th | September 12, 1944 | FW-190 dest(air) | N/Pritzwalk | P-51 |

1-0-0 air
0-0 ground

**Stovall, Richard T., Capt.**
77th Ftr Sqn/20th Ftr Grp

| *Sqn* | *Date* | *Claims* | *Location* | *A/C* |
|---|---|---|---|---|
| 77th | October 7, 1944 | Ju-88 dest(grd) | Peenemunde | P-51 |

0-0-0 air
1-0 ground

**Stovall, William H., Jr., Lt.**
62nd Ftr Sqn/56th Ftr Grp

| *Sqn* | *Date* | *Claims* | *Location* | *A/C* |
|---|---|---|---|---|
| 62nd | December 23, 1944 | FW-190 dam(air) | Euskirchen-Bonn | P-47 |
| | December 31 | (2)FW-190 dest(air) | Burg Steinfort | P-47 |

2-0-1 air
0-0 ground

**Stover, Merton J., Lt.**
486th Ftr Sqn/352nd Ftr Grp

| *Sqn* | *Date* | *Claims* | *Location* | *A/C* |
|---|---|---|---|---|
| 486th | July 18, 1944 | Me-109 dam(air) | NE Berlin | P-51 |
| | March 2, 1945 | FW-190 prob(air) | Zwickau | P-51 |
| | | FW-190 dam(air) | Zwickau | P-51 |

0-1-2 air
0-0 ground

**Strachan, Robert W., Lt.**
357th Ftr Sqn/355th Ftr Grp

| *Sqn* | *Date* | *Claims* | *Location* | *A/C* |
|---|---|---|---|---|
| 357th | July 8, 1944 | Me-109 dest(grd) | SW Chalons | P-51 |

0-0-0 air
1-0 ground

**Strait, Donald J., Maj.**
361st Ftr Sqn/356th Ftr Grp

| *Sqn* | *Date* | *Claims* | *Location* | *A/C* |
|---|---|---|---|---|
| 361st | February 6, 1944 | FW-190 dest(air) | Paris-Soissons | P-47 |
| | February 10 | Me-109 dest(air) | NE Lingen | P-47 |
| | May 19 | Me-109 dest(air) | Quackenbruck | P-47 |
| | November 26 | (1.5)Me-109 dest(air)[*] | Osnabruck-Dummer Lake | P-51 |
| | December 5 | (2)FW-190 dest(air) | Eberswalde | P-51 |
| | December 25 | Me-109 dest(air) | SW Coblenz | P-51 |
| | January 14, 1945 | FW-190 dest(air) | SW Dummer Lake | P-51 |
| | February 14 | (2)FW-190 dest(air) | S/Chemnitz | P-51 |
| | February 20 | (3)Fi-156 dest(air) | SE Bayreuth | P-51 |

13.5-0-0 air
0-0 ground

[*] - shared with Lt. S.N. Jett of the 361st Ftr Sqn

**Stratford, John B., Jr., Capt.**
360th Ftr Sqn/356th Ftr Grp

| *Sqn* | *Date* | *Claims* | *Location* | *A/C* |
|---|---|---|---|---|
| 360th | January 24, 1944 | FW-190 dest(air) | SW Antwerp | P-47 |

1-0-0 air
0-0 ground

**Straub, George, Lt.**
436th Ftr Sqn/479th Ftr Grp

| *Sqn* | *Date* | *Claims* | *Location* | *A/C* |
|---|---|---|---|---|
| 436th | September 28, 1944 | FW-190 dest(air) | W/Magdeburg | P-38 |
| | | FW-190 dam(air) | W/Magdeburg | P-38 |

1-0-1 air
0-0 ground

**Strauch, Walter, Capt.**
343rd Ftr Sqn/55th Ftr Grp

| *Sqn* | *Date* | *Claims* | *Location* | *A/C* |
|---|---|---|---|---|
| 343rd | February 20, 1945 | (2)Me-109 dest(grd) | Giebelstadt A/F | P-51 |
| | April 16 | FW-190 dest(grd) | Ainring A/F | P-51 |
| | April 17 | FW-190 dest(air) | Kamenz A/F | P-51 |

1-0-0 air
3-0 ground

**Stream, Dale E., Lt.**
61st Ftr Sqn/56th Ftr Grp

| *Sqn* | *Date* | *Claims* | *Location* | *A/C* |
|---|---|---|---|---|
| 61st | March 18, 1944 | FW-190 dest(air) | Cambrai-Givet | P-47 |
| | March 20 | u/i a/c dest(grd) | Charleville | P-47 |

1-0-0 air
1-0 ground

**Street, William H., Lt.**
375th Ftr Sqn/361st Ftr Grp

| *Sqn* | *Date* | *Claims* | *Location* | *A/C* |
|---|---|---|---|---|
| 375th | December 23, 1944 | Me-109 dest(air) | SE Bonn | P-51 |
| | January 2, 1945 | Me-109 dest(air) | W/Stuttgart | P-51 |
| | April 4 | (2)Me-262 dam(air) | S/Hamburg | P-51 |

2-0-2 air
0-0 ground

**Streit, William F., Lt.**
352nd Ftr Sqn/353rd Ftr Grp

| *Sqn* | *Date* | *Claims* | *Location* | *A/C* |
|---|---|---|---|---|
| 352nd | September 23, 1943 | FW-190 dest(air) | Chateaubriant | P-47 |
| | | Me-109 dam(air) | Chateaubriant | P-47 |
| | October 14 | Me-109 dest(air) | Turnhout | P-47 |
| | January 30, 1944 | Ju-88 dam(air) | Quackenbruck | P-47 |
| | February 25 | (.5)Me-110 dest(grd)* | Luxembourg | P-47 |
| | | Ju-88 dam(grd) | Charleroi | P-47 |
| | March 29 | Me-109 dest(air) | SW Bremen | P-47 |

3-0-2 air
0.5-1 ground

* - shared with Lt. W.S. Marchant of the 352nd Ftr Sqn

**Strobel, Earle W., Lt.**
83rd Ftr Sqn/78th Ftr Grp

| *Sqn* | *Date* | *Claims* | *Location* | *A/C* |
|---|---|---|---|---|
| 83rd | April 10, 1945 | FW-190 dest(grd) | Werder | P-51 |
| | | u/i a/c dam(grd) | Werder | P-51 |
| | April 16 | (3)Ju-87 dest(grd) | N/Prague | P-51 |
| | | Me-109 dam(grd) | N/Prague | P-51 |

0-0-0 air
4-2 ground

**Strobell, Robert C., Lt.**
351st Ftr Sqn/353rd Ftr Grp

| *Sqn* | *Date* | *Claims* | *Location* | *A/C* |
|---|---|---|---|---|
| 351st | June 8, 1944 | FW-190 prob(air) | Domfort | P-47 |
| | July 9 | Me-109 dest(air) | Argentan | P-47 |

1-1-0 air
0-0 ground

**Strock, Frank E., Lt.**
79th Ftr Sqn/20th Ftr Grp

| *Sqn* | *Date* | *Claims* | *Location* | *A/C* |
|---|---|---|---|---|
| 79th | February 20, 1945 | (3)He-111 dest(grd) | Weiden A/F | P-51 |
| | | (2)He-111 dam(grd) | Weiden A/F | P-51 |

0-0-0 air
3-2 ground

**Strong, Roland W., Lt.**
505th Ftr Sqn/339th Ftr Grp

| *Sqn* | *Date* | *Claims* | *Location* | *A/C* |
|---|---|---|---|---|
| 505th | May 21, 1944 | Trainer dest(air) | Dresden | P-51 |
| | August 4 | Ju-88 dest(grd) | E/Celle | P-51 |

1-0-0 air
1-0 ground

**Struby, Joseph R., Capt.**
436th Ftr Sqn/479th Ftr Grp

| *Sqn* | *Date* | *Claims* | *Location* | *A/C* |
|---|---|---|---|---|
| 436th | December 23, 1944 | FW-190 dest(air) | E/Cologne | P-51 |

1-0-0 air
0-0 ground

**Stubblefield, Herman H., Capt.**
385th Ftr Sqn/364th Ftr Grp

| *Sqn* | *Date* | *Claims* | *Location* | *A/C* |
|---|---|---|---|---|
| 385th | May 22, 1944 | (.5)FW-190 dam(air)* | Neumunster | P-38 |
| | August 9 | Me-110 dest(grd) | Gaukonigshafen | P-51 |
| | | (4)Me-110 dam(grd) | Gaukonigshafen | P-51 |

0-0-0.5 air
1-4 ground

* - shared with Lt. F.C. McClanahan of the 385th Ftr Sqn

**Stuckrath, John M., Capt.**
384th Ftr Sqn/364th Ftr Grp

| *Sqn* | *Date* | *Claims* | *Location* | *A/C* |
|---|---|---|---|---|
| 384th | June 25, 1944 | FW-190 dest(air) | E/Blois | P-38 |
| | | FW-190 dam(air) | E/Blois | P-38 |
| | August 9 | FW-190 dest(air) | Kaufburen | P-51 |

2-0-1 air
0-0 ground

**Stump, Harold E., Maj.**
84th Ftr Sqn/78th Ftr Grp

| *Sqn* | *Date* | *Claims* | *Location* | *A/C* |
|---|---|---|---|---|
| 84th | September 27, 1943 | Me-109 dest(air) | NW Emden | P-47 |

1-0-0 air
0-0 ground

**Stump, Hassel D., Capt.**
351st Ftr Sqn/353rd Ftr Grp

| *Sqn* | *Date* | *Claims* | *Location* | *A/C* |
|---|---|---|---|---|
| 351st | November 3, 1943 | Me-109 dam(air) | SW Wilhelmshaven | P-47 |
| | Decemberc 23, 1944 | Me-262 dam(air) | Magdeburg-SE Hanover | P-51 |

0-0-2 air
0-0 ground

**Sturm, Jack D., Lt.**
357th Ftr Sqn/355th Ftr Grp

| *Sqn* | *Date* | *Claims* | *Location* | *A/C* |
|---|---|---|---|---|
| 357th | March 28, 1944 | He-111 dest(grd) | Dijon | P-51 |
| | | Ju-88 dest(grd) | Dijon | P-51 |
| | | (2)Ju-88 dam(grd) | Dijon | P-51 |
| | | He-111 dam(grd) | Dijon | P-51 |
| | April 5 | FW-200 dam(grd) | Ottingen | P-51 |
| | | Me-110 dam(grd) | Ottingen | P-51 |
| | | Ju-88 dam(grd) | Ottingen | P-51 |
| | | Ju-52 dam(grd) | Ottingen | P-51 |
| | April 13 | Me-109 dest(air) | Augsburg | P-51 |
| | | (.5)Me-323 dest(grd)* | Crailsheim | P-51 |

1-0-0 air
2.5-7 ground

* - shared with Capt. J.H. Wilson of the 357th Ftr Sqn

**Stutzman, Milton B., Lt.**
82nd Ftr Sqn/78th Ftr Grp

| *Sqn* | *Date* | *Claims* | *Location* | *A/C* |
|---|---|---|---|---|
| 82nd | March 22, 1945 | (.5)Me-262 dest(air)* | Ulm | P-51 |
| | April 10 | FW-190 dest(grd) | Werder | P-51 |
| | | He-111 dest(grd) | Werder | P-51 |
| | | (2)u/i a/c dam(grd) | Werder | P-51 |
| | April 16 | Me-109 dam(grd) | Pilzen/Prague | P-51 |

0.5-0-0 air
2-3 ground

* - shared with Lt. E.L. Peel of the 82nd Ftr Sqn

**Sublett, John L., Capt.**
362nd Ftr Sqn/357th Ftr Grp

| *Sqn* | *Date* | *Claims* | *Location* | *A/C* |
|---|---|---|---|---|
| 362nd | November 25, 1944 | FW-44 dest(grd) | Maraburg | P-51 |
| | November 27 | (3)FW-190 dest(air) | S/Magdeburg | P-51 |
| | January 14, 1945 | (2)Me-109 dest(air) | NW Berlin | P-51 |
| | March 2 | Me-109 dest(air) | NE Leipzig | P-51 |
| | | FW-190 dest(air) | NE Leipzig | P-51 |
| | March 3 | Me-262 dam(air) | NE Magdeburg | P-51 |
| | March 20 | Me-109 dest(air) | Quackenbruck | P-51 |

8-0-1 air
1-0 ground

**Sullivan, Clarence E., Capt.**
376th Ftr Sqn/361st Ftr Grp

| *Sqn* | *Date* | *Claims* | *Location* | *A/C* |
|---|---|---|---|---|
| 376th | June 20, 1944 | Do-24 dam(grd) | Putnitz | P-51 |
| | December 24 | Me-109 dest(air) | Wengerohr | P-51 |

1-0-0 air
0-1 ground

**Sullivan, Edward J., Lt.**
352nd Ftr Sqn/353rd Ftr Grp

| *Sqn* | *Date* | *Claims* | *Location* | *A/C* |
|---|---|---|---|---|
| 352nd | March 2, 1945 | FW-190 dest(air) | S/Wittenberg | P-51 |

1-0-0 air
0-0 ground

**Sullivan, James J., Capt.**
375th Ftr Sqn/361st Ftr Grp

| *Sqn* | *Date* | *Claims* | *Location* | *A/C* |
|---|---|---|---|---|
| 375th | November 26, 1944 | Me-109 dest(air) | Celle-Gifhorn | P-51 |
| | January 2, 1945 | Me-109 dest(air) | W/Stuttgart | P-51 |

2-0-0 air
0-0 ground

**Sullivan, Jeremiah J., Lt.**
338th Ftr Sqn/55th Ftr Grp

| *Sqn* | *Date* | *Claims* | *Location* | *A/C* |
|---|---|---|---|---|
| 338th | February 25, 1945 | FW-190 dest(grd) | Illesheim | P-51 |

0-0-0 air
1-0 ground

**Sullivan, John A., Lt.**
351st Ftr Sqn/353rd Ftr Grp

| *Sqn* | *Date* | *Claims* | *Location* | *A/C* |
|---|---|---|---|---|
| 351st | March 26, 1944 | Me-109 dam(grd) | Chartres | P-47 |

0-0-0 air
0-1 ground

**Sullivan, John A., Maj.**
435th Ftr Sqn/479th Ftr Grp
436th Ftr Sqn/479th Ftr Grp

| *Sqn* | *Date* | *Claims* | *Location* | *A/C* |
|---|---|---|---|---|
| 435th | July 24, 1944 | Me-109 dam(air) | SW Evreux | P-38 |
| 436th | September 5 | (2)Do-217 dam(grd) | Oberst Oberau | P-38 |
| | | He-111 dam(grd) | Bad Nauheim | P-38 |

0-0-1 air
0-3 ground

**Sullivan, Joseph G., Lt.**
364th Ftr Sqn/357th Ftr Grp

| *Sqn* | *Date* | *Claims* | *Location* | *A/C* |
|---|---|---|---|---|
| 364th | May 13, 1944 | FW-44 dest(air) | E/Grunberg | P-51 |
| | | (.5)Me-410 dest(air)* | E/Grunberg | P-51 |
| | | Me-410 dam(air) | E/Grunberg | P-51 |

1.5-0-1 air
0-0 ground

* - shared with Capt. R.A. Peterson of the 364th Ftr Sqn

**Sullivan, Walter A., Lt.**
385th Ftr Sqn/364th Ftr Grp

| *Sqn* | *Date* | *Claims* | *Location* | *A/C* |
|---|---|---|---|---|
| 385th | October 12, 1944 | FW-190 prob(air) | NE Bremen | P-51 |

0-1-0 air
0-0 ground

**Sumner, Charles D., Capt.**
364th Ftr Sqn/357th Ftr Grp

| *Sqn* | *Date* | *Claims* | *Location* | *A/C* |
|---|---|---|---|---|
| 364th | April 11, 1944 | (.5)FW-190 dest(air)* | Leipzig | P-51 |
| | April 24 | Me-109 dest(air) | Munich | P-51 |
| | May 12 | Me-109 dest(air) | NE Frankfurt | P-51 |
| | June 29 | Me-109 dest(air) | SW Leipzig | P-51 |
| | | FW-190 dest(air) | SW Leipzig | P-51 |
| | July 5 | FW-190 dam(air) | SE Evreux | P-51 |

4.5-0-1 air
0-0 ground

* - shared with Lt. M.H. Stepelton of the 364th Ftr Sqn

**Swanezy, John J., Jr., F/O**
352nd Ftr Sqn/353rd Ftr Grp

| *Sqn* | *Date* | *Claims* | *Location* | *A/C* |
|---|---|---|---|---|
| 352nd | August 4, 1944 | He-111 dest(grd) | Plantlunne | P-47 |
| | | Me-410 dest(grd) | Plantlunne | P-47 |

0-0-0 air
2-0 ground

**Swanson, William S., Lt.**
82nd Ftr Sqn/78th Ftr Grp

| *Sqn* | *Date* | *Claims* | *Location* | *A/C* |
|---|---|---|---|---|
| 82nd | November 3, 1943 | Me-109 dam(air) | Barzal | P-47 |
| | January 29, 1944 | FW-190 dest(air) | Coblenz | P-47 |

1-0-1 air
0-0 ground

**Swauger, Fred R., Lt.**
82nd Ftr Sqn/78th Ftr Grp

| *Sqn* | *Date* | *Claims* | *Location* | *A/C* |
|---|---|---|---|---|
| 82nd | April 16, 1945 | Me-109 dest(grd) | Pilzen/Prague | P-51 |

0-0-0 air
1-0 ground

**Sweat, Charles H., Lt.**
354th Ftr Sqn/355th Ftr Grp

| *Sqn* | *Date* | *Claims* | *Location* | *A/C* |
|---|---|---|---|---|
| 354th | November 5, 1943 | FW-190 dest(air) | NW Gelsenkirchen | P-47 |

1-0-0 air
0-0 ground

**Sweat, Dale S., Lt.**
83rd Ftr Sqn/78th Ftr Grp

| Sqn | Date | Claims | Location | A/C |
|---|---|---|---|---|
| 83rd | April 16, 1945 | (2)FW-190 dest(grd) | N/Prague | P-51 |
| | | (2)Ju-87 dest(grd) | N/Prague | P-51 |
| | | u/i a/c dest(grd) | N/Prague | P-51 |
| | | (2)FW-190 dam(grd) | N/Prague | P-51 |
| | | Ju-87 dam(grd) | N/Prague | P-51 |

0-0-0 air
5-3 ground

**Sweeney, Joseph L., Lt.**
487th Ftr Sqn/352nd Ftr Grp

| Sqn | Date | Claims | Location | A/C |
|---|---|---|---|---|
| 487th | December 4, 1943 | (.5)FW-190 dest(air)[*] | Rotterdam-Utrecht | P-47 |

0.5-0-0 air
0-0 ground

[*] - shared with Lt. V.K. Meroney of the 487th Ftr Sqn

**Swift, Blayne A., Lt.**
361st Ftr Sqn/356th Ftr Grp

| Sqn | Date | Claims | Location | A/C |
|---|---|---|---|---|
| 361st | May 13, 1944 | FW-190 dest(air) | S/Kiel | P-47 |

1-0-0 air
0-0 ground

**Swinson, Ronald O., Lt.**
486th Ftr Sqn/352nd Ftr Grp

| Sqn | Date | Claims | Location | A/C |
|---|---|---|---|---|
| 486th | April 16, 1945 | FW-190 dam(grd) | Ganacker | P-51 |

0-0-0 air
0-1 ground

**Sykes, George K., Capt.**
435th Ftr Sqn/479th Ftr Grp

| Sqn | Date | Claims | Location | A/C |
|---|---|---|---|---|
| 435th | August 5, 1944 | Me-109 dest(air) | S/Hamburg | P-38 |
| | | Me-109 dam(air) | S/Hamburg | P-38 |
| | August 18 | (1.5)He-111 dest(grd)[*] | Nancy/Essey A/F | P-38 |

1-0-1 air
1.5-0 ground

[*] - shared with Lt. H.C. Little of the 434th Ftr Sqn, 479th Ftr Grp

**Sykes, Henry S., Lt.**
487th Ftr Sqn/352nd Ftr Grp

| Sqn | Date | Claims | Location | A/C |
|---|---|---|---|---|
| 487th | April 16, 1945 | (3)u/i a/c dest(grd) | Ganacker | P-51 |
| | | Me-109 dest(grd) | Ganacker | P-51 |
| | | Fi-156 dest(grd) | Ganacker | P-51 |
| | | Me-109 dam(grd) | Ganacker | P-51 |
| | | u/i a/c dam(grd) | Ganacker | P-51 |

0-0-0 air
5-2 ground

**Sykes, William J., Lt.**
376th Ftr Sqn/361st Ftr Grp

| Sqn | Date | Claims | Location | A/C |
|---|---|---|---|---|
| 376th | September 27, 1944 | FW-190 dest(air) | Eisenach | P-51 |
| | | (2)Me-410 dest(grd) | Eisenach | P-51 |
| | November 2 | Me-109 dest(air) | N/Erfurt | P-51 |
| | | FW-190 dest(air) | N/Erfurt | P-51 |
| | November 27 | Me-109 dest(air) | S/Munster | P-51 |
| | | Me-109 prob(air) | S/Munster | P-51 |
| | | (2)Me-410 dest(grd) | Munster | P-51 |
| | | Me-110 dest(grd) | Munster | P-51 |
| | December 24 | Me-109 dest(air) | Wengerohr | P-51 |
| | | Me-109 prob(air) | Wengerohr | P-51 |

5-2-0 air
5-0 ground

**Sypher, Leroy H., Lt.**
375th Ftr Sqn/361st Ftr Grp

| Sqn | Date | Claims | Location | A/C |
|---|---|---|---|---|
| 375th | May 8, 1944 | Me-109 dest(air) | NE Steinhuder Lake | P-47 |
| | | Me-109 dam(air) | NE Steinhuder Lake | P-47 |

1-0-1 air
0-0 ground

**Szaniawski, Edward W., LtCol.**
357th Ftr Sqn/355th Ftr Grp

| Sqn | Date | Claims | Location | A/C |
|---|---|---|---|---|
| 357th | February 11, 1944 | (2)Me-109 dest(air) | S/Koln | P-47 |
| | March 28 | Me-110 dest(grd) | Dijon | P-51 |
| | | Me-410 dest(grd) | Dijon | P-51 |
| | | Ju-88 dest(grd) | Dijon | P-51 |
| | | (3)Ju-88 dam(grd) | Dijon | P-51 |
| | | Me-210 dam(grd) | Dijon | P-51 |
| | April 8 | Me-109 dest(air) | Meppen | P-51 |
| | | Me-109 dam(air) | Meppen | P-51 |
| | April 13 | Me-109 dest(air) | Augsburg | P-51 |
| | | Me-109 prob(air) | Augsburg | P-51 |
| | | Me-109 dam(air) | Augsburg | P-51 |
| | | (.33)Me-110 dest(grd)[*] | Crailsheim | P-51 |
| | | (.33)Me-323 dest(grd)[**] | Crailsheim | P-51 |

4-1-2 air
3.67-4 ground

[*] - shared with Lt. R.F. DeMers and Lt. R.L. Norman of the 357th Ftr Sqn
[**] - shared with Lt. J.F. Kerch and Lt. R.L. Norman of the 357th Ftr Sqn

**Tacon, Avelin P., Col.**
HdQts/359th Ftr Grp

| Sqn | Date | Claims | Location | A/C |
|---|---|---|---|---|
| HdQts | May 30, 1944 | FW-190 dam(grd) | Paderborn | P-51 |
| | July 24 | u/i a/c dam(grd) | Ulm | P-51 |

0-0-0 air
0-2 ground

**Talbot, Robert H., Lt.**
83rd Ftr Sqn/78th Ftr Grp

| Sqn | Date | Claims | Location | A/C |
|---|---|---|---|---|
| 83rd | March 19, 1945 | Me-109 dest(air) | Osnabruck | P-51 |
| | | Me-109 dam(air) | Osnabruck | P-51 |

1-0-1 air
0-0 ground

**Talcott, Franklin D., Lt.**
503rd Ftr Sqn/339th Ftr Grp

| Sqn | Date | Claims | Location | A/C |
|---|---|---|---|---|
| 503rd | June 21, 1944 | (.5)Me-410 prob(air)[*] | Stettin | P-51 |

0-0.5-0 air
0-0 ground

[*] - shared with Capt. W.E. Bryan of the 503rd Ftr Sqn

**Tallman, John C., Lt.**
385th Ftr Sqn/364th Ftr Grp

| Sqn | Date | Claims | Location | A/C |
|---|---|---|---|---|
| 385th | March 15, 1944 | (.5)FW-190 dest(air)[*] | Dummer Lake | P-38 |

0.5-0-0 air
0-0 ground

[*] - shared with Capt. R.M. Scott of the 385th Ftr Sqn

**Tally, Vernon B., Lt.**
HdQts/55th Ftr Grp
338th Ftr Sqn/55th Ftr Grp

| Sqn | Date | Claims | Location | A/C |
|---|---|---|---|---|
| 338th | April 10, 1945 | (2)Me-410 dest(grd) | Burg A/F | P-51 |

0-0-0 air
2-0 ground

**Tanner, William F., Maj.**
350th Ftr Sqn/353rd Ftr Grp

| *Sqn* | *Date* | *Claims* | *Location* | *A/C* |
|---|---|---|---|---|
| 350th | October 10, 1943 | FW-190 dest(air) | Hengelo | P-47 |
| | January 30, 1944 | FW-190 dest(air) | Zuider Zee | P-47 |
| | April 9 | He-115 dam(grd) | Eckenforder Bay | P-47 |
| | May 12 | (.5)Me-109 dest(air)* | Selters | P-47 |
| | June 12 | (2)Me-109 dest(air) | SW Paris | P-47 |
| | November 18 | He-177 dest(grd) | Lechfeld | P-51 |
| | December 5 | FW-190 dest(air) | S/Steinhuder Lake | P-51 |
| | | FW-190 dam(air) | S/Steinhuder Lake | P-51 |

5.5-0-1 air
1-1 ground

* - shared with Lt. K. Chetwood of the 350th Ftr Sqn

**Tannous, Richard H., Lt.**
505th Ftr Sqn/339th Ftr Grp

| *Sqn* | *Date* | *Claims* | *Location* | *A/C* |
|---|---|---|---|---|
| 505th | July 19, 1944 | (.5)Ju-188 dest(grd)* | SW Augsburg | P-51 |
| | September 10 | Me-410 dest(grd) | Weizenburg | P-51 |
| | | u/i a/c dest(grd) | Weizenburg | P-51 |
| | | (6)u/i a/c dam(grd) | Weizenburg | P-51 |
| | September 23 | FW-190 dest(air) | Geldern-Weeze | P-51 |
| | | FW-190 dam(air) | Geldern-Weeze | P-51 |

1-0-1 air
2.5-6 ground

* - shared with Lt. A. Sirochman of the 505th Ftr Sqn

**Tarbutton, Jean D., Capt.**
359th Ftr Sqn/356th Ftr Grp

| *Sqn* | *Date* | *Claims* | *Location* | *A/C* |
|---|---|---|---|---|
| 359th | August 18, 1944 | (.5)FW-190 dam(air)* | Beauvais | P-47 |
| | December 5 | (2)FW-190 dest(air) | NW Berlin | P-51 |

2-0-0.5 air
0-0 ground

* - shared with Lt. L.F. Richason of the 359th Ftr Sqn

**Taylor, Carter, Lt.**
63rd Ftr Sqn/56th Ftr Grp

| *Sqn* | *Date* | *Claims* | *Location* | *A/C* |
|---|---|---|---|---|
| 63rd | April 13, 1945 | Me-110 dest(grd) | Eggebeck A/F | P-47 |
| | | (2)Me-110 dam(grd) | Eggebeck A/F | P-47 |
| | | Me-109 dam(grd) | Eggebeck A/F | P-47 |

0-0-0 air
1-3 ground

**Taylor, Clyde E., Lt.**
84th Ftr Sqn/78th Ftr Grp

| *Sqn* | *Date* | *Claims* | *Location* | *A/C* |
|---|---|---|---|---|
| 84th | March 1, 1945 | u/i a/c dam(grd) | Boblingen | P-51 |
| | April 16 | (4)Ju-52 dest(grd) | Praha/Kakewice | P-51 |
| | | (3)Me-110 dest(grd) | Praha/Kakewice | P-51 |
| | | FW-190 dest(grd) | Praha/Kakewice | P-51 |
| | | He-111 dest(grd) | Praha/Kakewice | P-51 |
| | | FW-190 dam(grd) | Praha/Kakewice | P-51 |

0-0-0 air
9-2 ground

**Taylor, Clyde M., Lt.**
360th Ftr Sqn/356th Ftr Grp

| *Sqn* | *Date* | *Claims* | *Location* | *A/C* |
|---|---|---|---|---|
| 360th | July 25, 1944 | (.5)Me-109 dam(air)* | NW Paris | P-47 |
| | September 1 | (.5)Ju-52 dest(grd)** | W/Nancy | P-47 |

0-0-0.5 air
0.5-0 ground

* - shared with Capt. N.D. Cota of the 360th Ftr Sqn
** - shared with Lt. F.W. Peacock of the 360th Ftr Sqn

**Taylor, Elmer A., Capt.**
385th Ftr Sqn/364th Ftr Grp

| *Sqn* | *Date* | *Claims* | *Location* | *A/C* |
|---|---|---|---|---|
| 385th | May 21, 1944 | Me-210 dest(grd) | Schwerin-Luneburg | P-38 |
| | August 24 | (.5)Me-109 dest(air)* | Hamburg | P-51 |
| | September 28 | FW-190 dam(air) | W/Magdeburg | P-51 |
| | October 7 | (.5)Me-163 dest(air)** | Brux | P-51 |

1-0-1 air
1-0 ground

* - shared with Lt. G.L. Jones of the 385th Ftr Sqn
** - shared with Lt. W.G. Erfkamp of the 385th Ftr Sqn

**Taylor, Erle A., Lt.**
362nd Ftr Sqn/357th Ftr Grp

| *Sqn* | *Date* | *Claims* | *Location* | *A/C* |
|---|---|---|---|---|
| 362nd | September 13, 1944 | Me-109 dest(air) | S/Nordhausen | P-51 |

1-0-0 air
0-0 ground

**Taylor, Floyd K., Lt.**
354th Ftr Sqn/355th Ftr Grp

| *Sqn* | *Date* | *Claims* | *Location* | *A/C* |
|---|---|---|---|---|
| 354th | June 6, 1944 | (.5)Ju-87 dest(air)* | Chartres-Dire | P-51 |

0.5-0-0 air
0-0 ground

* - shared with Lt. R.S. Morris of the 354th Ftr Sqn

**Taylor, Frank M., Lt.**
434th Ftr Sqn/479th Ftr Grp

| *Sqn* | *Date* | *Claims* | *Location* | *A/C* |
|---|---|---|---|---|
| 434th | March 19, 1945 | (.5)FW-190 dest(air)* | Handorf A/F | P-51 |
| | April 13 | (.5)u/i a/c dest(grd)** | Ratzburger Lake | P-51 |
| | | (2)u/i a/c dam(grd) | Ratzburger Lake | P-51 |

0.5-0-0 air
0.5-2 ground

* - shared with Lt. G.E. Jacobson of the 434th Ftr Sqn
** - shared with Lt. R.B. Kline of the 434th Ftr Sqn

**Taylor, Guy P., Lt.**
487th Ftr Sqn/352nd Ftr Grp

| *Sqn* | *Date* | *Claims* | *Location* | *A/C* |
|---|---|---|---|---|
| 487th | August 5, 1944 | Me-109 dest(air) | S/Hamburg | P-51 |

1-0-0 air
0-0 ground

**Taylor, James E., Lt.**
363rd Ftr Sqn/357th Ftr Grp

| *Sqn* | *Date* | *Claims* | *Location* | *A/C* |
|---|---|---|---|---|
| 363rd | January 14, 1945 | Me-109 dest(air) | N/Brandenburg | P-51 |

1-0-0 air
0-0 ground

**Taylor, John E., Lt.**
384th Ftr Sqn/364th Ftr Grp

| *Sqn* | *Date* | *Claims* | *Location* | *A/C* |
|---|---|---|---|---|
| 384th | April 16, 1945 | FW-190 dest(grd) | Pocking | P-51 |
| | April 17 | He-111 dest(grd) | Karlsbad | P-51 |
| | | FW-200 dest(grd) | Karlsbad | P-51 |

0-0-0 air
3-0 ground

**Taylor, John K., Capt.**
79th Ftr Sqn/20th Ftr Grp

| *Sqn* | *Date* | *Claims* | *Location* | *A/C* |
|---|---|---|---|---|
| 79th | February 20, 1945 | Me-110 dam(grd) | Weiden A/F | P-51 |

0-0-0 air
0-1 ground

**Taylor, Lester G., Jr., Capt.**
369th Ftr Sqn/359th Ftr Grp

| *Sqn* | *Date* | *Claims* | *Location* | *A/C* |
|---|---|---|---|---|
| 369th | August 5, 1944 | FW-190 dest(air) | Tarmstedt | P-51 |

1-0-0 air
0-0 ground

**Taylor, Robert B., Lt.**
62nd Ftr Sqn/56th Ftr Grp

| *Sqn* | *Date* | *Claims* | *Location* | *A/C* |
|---|---|---|---|---|
| 62nd | September 16, 1943 | FW-190 dest(air) | Fourgeres | P-47 |
| | October 10 | FW-190 dest(air) | Altenberge | P-47 |
| | | FW-190 prob(air) | Altenberge | P-47 |

2-1-0 air
0-0 ground

**Taylor, Robert G., Lt.**
354th Ftr Sqn/355th Ftr Grp

| *Sqn* | *Date* | *Claims* | *Location* | *A/C* |
|---|---|---|---|---|
| 354th | June 20, 1944 | Me-410 dest(air) | Rugen | P-51 |
| | July 7 | (.5)Ju-88 dest(air)* | Lingen | P-51 |

1.5-0-0 air
0-0 ground

* - shared with Lt. S.G. Betounes of the 354th Ftr Sqn

**Taylor, Willis B., Capt.**
55th Ftr Sqn/20th Ftr Grp

| *Sqn* | *Date* | *Claims* | *Location* | *A/C* |
|---|---|---|---|---|
| 55th | January 7, 1944 | Me-109 dest(air) | Worms | P-38 |
| | February 10 | Me-109 dest(air) | NW Hanover | P-38 |
| | April 24 | Me-109 dest(air) | W/Worms | P-38 |
| | October 6 | Do-24 dest(grd) | Kubitzer Bay | P-51 |
| | | u/i a/c dest(grd) | Kubitzer Bay | P-51 |

3-0-0 air
2-0 ground

**Tazzia, Edward K., Lt.**
385th Ftr Sqn/364th Ftr Grp

| *Sqn* | *Date* | *Claims* | *Location* | *A/C* |
|---|---|---|---|---|
| 385th | July 6, 1944 | Me-109 dam(air) | Chalons | P-38 |
| | August 25 | Ju-88 dest(grd) | Anklam | P-51 |

0-0-1 air
1-0 ground

**Tear, Harry E., Lt.**
352nd Ftr Sqn/353rd Ftr Grp

| *Sqn* | *Date* | *Claims* | *Location* | *A/C* |
|---|---|---|---|---|
| 352nd | November 2, 1944 | Me-109 prob(air) | Naumberg | P-51 |

0-1-0 air
0-0 ground

**Teel, Thomas D., Lt.**
360th Ftr Sqn/356th Ftr Grp

| *Sqn* | *Date* | *Claims* | *Location* | *A/C* |
|---|---|---|---|---|
| 360th | August 4, 1944 | Me-109 dest(air) | SW Hamburg | P-47 |

1-0-0 air
0-0 ground

**Templin, John S., Lt.**
362nd Ftr Sqn/357th Ftr Grp

| *Sqn* | *Date* | *Claims* | *Location* | *A/C* |
|---|---|---|---|---|
| 362nd | September 13, 1944 | Me-109 dest(air) | S/Nordhausen | P-51 |
| | September 18 | Me-109 dest(air) | Nijmegen | P-51 |

2-0-0 air
0-0 ground

**Tenenbaum, Harold, Lt.**
369th Ftr Sqn/359th Ftr Grp

| *Sqn* | *Date* | *Claims* | *Location* | *A/C* |
|---|---|---|---|---|
| 369th | November 21, 1944 | FW-190 dest(air) | Merseburg | P-51 |
| | February 22, 1945 | Ju-88 dam(grd) | Schwerin | P-51 |
| | March 24 | (1.5)Me-109 dest(air)* | Eikelon A/F | P-51 |
| | April 10 | Me-262 dest(air) | Gardelegen A/F | P-51 |

3.5-0-0 air
0-1 ground

* - shared with Lt. D.E. Kelly of the 369th Ftr Sqn

**Tennant, John H., Capt.**
55th Ftr Sqn/20th Ftr Grp

| *Sqn* | *Date* | *Claims* | *Location* | *A/C* |
|---|---|---|---|---|
| 55th | November 2, 1944 | (2)FW-190 dest(air) | Halle-Merseburg | P-51 |
| | | Me-109 dest(air) | Halle-Merseburg | P-51 |

3-0-0 air
0-0 ground

**Terzian, Jack, Lt.**
351st Ftr Sqn/353rd Ftr Grp

| *Sqn* | *Date* | *Claims* | *Location* | *A/C* |
|---|---|---|---|---|
| 351st | March 6, 1944 | (.5)FW-190 dest(air)* | SW Nienburg | P-47 |
| | March 16 | (1.5)u/i a/c dam(grd)** | Laon | P-47 |
| | March 29 | u/i a/c dam(grd) | SE Steinhuder Lk. | P-47 |

0.5-0-0 air
0-2.5 ground

* - shared with Capt. V.L. Byers of the 351st Ftr Sqn
** - shared with Col. G.E. Duncan of HdQts, 353rd Ftr Grp

**Thacker, Robert L., Capt.**
369th Ftr Sqn/359th Ftr Grp

| *Sqn* | *Date* | *Claims* | *Location* | *A/C* |
|---|---|---|---|---|
| 369th | January 30, 1944 | Ju-88 dest(air) | Haselunne | P-47 |
| | | Ju-88 prob(air) | Haselunne | P-47 |
| | May 12 | (.5)u/i a/c dest(grd)* | Thamsbruck | P-51 |
| | May 29 | FW-190 dest(air) | Malchin | P-51 |

2-1-0 air
0.5-0 ground

* - shared with Capt. C.C. Ettlesen of the 369th Ftr Sqn

**Thain, Thomas V., Lt.**
84th Ftr Sqn/78th Ftr Grp

| *Sqn* | *Date* | *Claims* | *Location* | *A/C* |
|---|---|---|---|---|
| 84th | March 19, 1945 | Me-109 dest(air) | Osnabruck | P-51 |
| | March 30 | (.5)Me-262 dest(air)* | Rendsberg | P-51 |

1.5-0-0 air
0-0 ground

* - shared with LtCol. J.D. Landers of HdQts, 78th Ftr Grp

**Thibert, Henry G., Capt.**
504th Ftr Sqn/339th Ftr Grp

| *Sqn* | *Date* | *Claims* | *Location* | *A/C* |
|---|---|---|---|---|
| 504th | June 21, 1944 | Me-109 dest(air) | Soldin | P-51 |

1-0-0 air
0-0 ground

**Thieme, Richard C., Lt.**
505th Ftr Sqn/339th Ftr Grp

| *Sqn* | *Date* | *Claims* | *Location* | *A/C* |
|---|---|---|---|---|
| 505th | March 3, 1945 | Ju-88 dest(grd) | E/Magdeburg | P-51 |

0-0-0 air
1-0 ground

**Thistlethwaite, William T., Lt.**
HdQts/353rd Ftr Grp

| *Sqn* | *Date* | *Claims* | *Location* | *A/C* |
|---|---|---|---|---|
| HdQts | October 8, 1943 | FW-190 dam(air) | Rhede | P-47 |
| | January 21, 1944 | Me-109 dest(air) | St. Quentin | P-47 |

1-0-1 air
0-0 ground

**Thomas, Edward D., Lt.**
352nd Ftr Sqn/353rd Ftr Grp

| *Sqn* | *Date* | *Claims* | *Location* | *A/C* |
|---|---|---|---|---|
| 352nd | November 18, 1944 | Ju-88 dest(grd) | Lechfeld | P-51 |
| | | Me-163 dam(grd) | Lechfeld | P-51 |
| | | u/i a/c dam(grd) | Lechfeld | P-51 |

0-0-0 air
1-2 ground

**Thomas, John T., Lt.**
375th Ftr Sqn/361st Ftr Grp

| *Sqn* | *Date* | *Claims* | *Location* | *A/C* |
|---|---|---|---|---|
| 375th | June 20, 1944 | (.5)BV-138 dam(grd)* | Putnitz | P-51 |
| | | (.5)glider dam(grd)* | Putnitz | P-51 |
| | August 15 | Ju-88 dest(grd) | Wittmunhafen | P-51 |
| | | Ju-88 dam(grd) | Wittmunhafen | P-51 |

0-0-0 air
1-2 ground

* - both shared with Lt. S. Armsby of the 375th Ftr Sqn

**Thomas, William G., Capt.**
360th Ftr Sqn/356th Ftr Grp

| *Sqn* | *Date* | *Claims* | *Location* | *A/C* |
|---|---|---|---|---|
| 360th | February 21, 1945 | He-111 dam(grd) | S/Nurnberg | P-51 |

0-0-0 air
0-1 ground

**Thompson, Edward L., Lt.**
361st Ftr Sqn/356th Ftr Grp

| *Sqn* | *Date* | *Claims* | *Location* | *A/C* |
|---|---|---|---|---|
| 361st | July 6, 1944 | Me-109 dest(air) | Fontainbleau | P-47 |
| | August 18 | FW-190 dest(air) | Beauvais | P-47 |
| | | (2)FW-190 dam(air) | Beauvais | P-47 |
| | October 7 | Ju-88 dest(grd) | Fritzlar | P-47 |
| | | u/i a/c dest(grd) | Fritzlar | P-47 |
| | | Me-110 dam(grd) | Fritzlar | P-47 |
| | | Hs-123 dam(grd) | Fritzlar | P-47 |
| | | Ju-88 dam(grd) | Fritzlar | P-47 |

2-0-2 air
2-3 ground

**Thompson, Hilton O., Lt.**
434th Ftr Sqn/479th Ftr Grp

| *Sqn* | *Date* | *Claims* | *Location* | *A/C* |
|---|---|---|---|---|
| 434th | April 7, 1945 | Me-262 dest(air) | Luneberg | P-51 |
| | April 25 | Ar-234 dest(air) | Traunstein-Berchtesgaden | P-51 |

2-0-0 air
0-0 ground

**Thompson, Robert M., Lt.**
358th Ftr Sqn/355th Ftr Grp

| *Sqn* | *Date* | *Claims* | *Location* | *A/C* |
|---|---|---|---|---|
| 358th | July 19, 1944 | Me-109 dest(air) | Augsburg | P-51 |
| | July 21 | Me-109 prob(air) | Munich | P-51 |
| | September 12 | Me-109 dest(air) | Hanover | P-51 |

2-1-0 air
0-0 ground

**Thompson, Robert S., Lt.**
38th Ftr Sqn/55th Ftr Grp

| *Sqn* | *Date* | *Claims* | *Location* | *A/C* |
|---|---|---|---|---|
| 38th | January 5, 1944 | Me-109 dam(air) | SW Kiel | P-38 |

0-0-1 air
0-0 ground

**Thompson, Thomas H., Capt.**
436th Ftr Sqn/479th Ftr Grp

| *Sqn* | *Date* | *Claims* | *Location* | *A/C* |
|---|---|---|---|---|
| 436th | April 16, 1945 | He-111 dest(grd) | Landstedt | P-51 |

0-0-0 air
1-0 ground

**Thomson, Bryce H., Lt.**
369th Ftr Sqn/359th Ftr Grp

| *Sqn* | *Date* | *Claims* | *Location* | *A/C* |
|---|---|---|---|---|
| 369th | December 24, 1944 | Me-109 dest(air) | Vogelsand | P-51 |
| | March 24, 1945 | Me-109 dest(air) | Eikelon A/F | P-51 |

2-0-0 air
0-0 ground

**Thomson, Robert C., Maj.**
369th Ftr Sqn/359th Ftr Grp

| *Sqn* | *Date* | *Claims* | *Location* | *A/C* |
|---|---|---|---|---|
| 369th | February 3, 1944 | FW-190 dest(air) | Zuider Zee | P-47 |
| | May 19 | Me-109 dest(air) | Wittingen | P-51 |
| | February 21, 1945 | FW-190 dam(grd) | Nordlingen | P-51 |
| | | u/i a/c dam(grd) | Nordlingen | P-51 |
| | March 24 | (2)Me-109 dest(air) | Eikelon A/F | P-51 |

4-0-0 air
0-2 ground

**Thomton, Cleon C., Lt.**
61st Ftr Sqn/56th Ftr Grp

| *Sqn* | *Date* | *Claims* | *Location* | *A/C* |
|---|---|---|---|---|
| 61st | May 12, 1944 | Me-109 dest(air) | Marburg | P-47 |
| | July 20 | He-111 dam(grd) | Bassenheim A/F | P-47 |
| | September 5 | (.5)Me-110 dest(grd)* | Merzhausen | P-47 |
| | | u/i a/c dam(grd) | Merzhausen | P-47 |

1-0-0 air
0.5-2 ground

* - shared with Lt. J.J. Clark of the 61st Ftr Sqn

**Thorkelson, Robert L., Lt.**
363rd Ftr Sqn/357th Ftr Grp

| *Sqn* | *Date* | *Claims* | *Location* | *A/C* |
|---|---|---|---|---|
| 363rd | March 20, 1945 | FW-190 dest(air) | Dummer Lake | P-51 |

1-0-0 air
0-0 ground

**Thorn, Donald W., Lt.**
435th Ftr Sqn/479th Ftr Grp

| *Sqn* | *Date* | *Claims* | *Location* | *A/C* |
|---|---|---|---|---|
| 435th | April 17, 1945 | Me-262 dam(grd) | Puchhoff | P-51 |
| | | u/i a/c dam(grd) | Puchhoff | P-51 |

0-0-0 air
0-2 ground

**Thorne, James H., Maj.**
359th Ftr Sqn/356th Ftr Grp
HdQts/356th Ftr Grp

| Sqn | Date | Claims | Location | A/C |
|---|---|---|---|---|
| 359th | February 10, 1944 | FW-190 dest(air) | Meppen | P-47 |
| HdQts | March 29 | Me-109 dest(air) | Steinhuder Lake-Dummer Lake | P-47 |
| | April 23 | (.5)He-111 dam(grd)[*] | Hagenau | P-47 |

2-0-0 air
0-0.5 ground

[*] - shared with Lt. R.J. Collins of the 359th Ftr Sqn

**Thornell, John F., Jr., Capt.**
328th Ftr Sqn/352nd Ftr Grp

| Sqn | Date | Claims | Location | A/C |
|---|---|---|---|---|
| 328th | January 30, 1944 | Me-109 dest(air) | Ruhlertwist | P-47 |
| | | Me-109 dam(air) | Ruhlertwist | P-47 |
| | March 15 | (2)Me-109 dest(air) | Heusden | P-47 |
| | March 22 | (.25)FW-200 dest(air)[*] | Hesepe | P-47 |
| | April 10 | FW-190 dest(air) | Dormans | P-47 |
| | April 19 | (2)FW-190 dest(air) | SW Kassel | P-51 |
| | | FW-190 dam(air) | SW Kassel | P-51 |
| | May 8 | (3)Me-109 dest(air) | Nienburg | P-51 |
| | May 21 | (2)He-111 dest(grd) | Alt Ruppin | P-51 |
| | | He-177 dam(grd) | Alt Ruppin | P-51 |
| | May 27 | (2)Me-109 dest(air) | S/Strasbourg | P-51 |
| | May 28 | Me-109 dest(air) | W/Magdeburg | P-51 |
| | May 29 | (2)Me-109 dest(air) | N/Neubrandenburg | P-51 |
| | June 10 | (2)Me-109 dest(air) | Bayeux | P-51 |
| | June 12 | (.5)Me-109 dest(air)[**] | S/St. Malo | P-51 |
| | June 21 | (.5)Me-410 dest(air)[@] | Dahmsdorf | P-51 |

17.25-0-2 air
2-1 ground

[*] - shared with Capt. E.L. Abbott, Lt. R.C. Brookins, and Lt. E. Zellner of the 328th Ftr Sqn
[**] - shared with Lt. L.E. McCarthy of the 328th Ftr Sqn
[@] - shared with Lt. S.E. Dyke of the 328th Ftr Sqn

**Thorsen, Arthur L., Lt.**
38th Ftr Sqn/55th Ftr Grp

| Sqn | Date | Claims | Location | A/C |
|---|---|---|---|---|
| 38th | May 20, 1944 | FW-190 dam(air) | Troyes | P-38 |
| | September 11 | Me-109 dest(air) | SE Erfurt | P-51 |

1-0-1 air
0-0 ground

**Throop, Montgomery H., Jr., Maj.**
335th Ftr Sqn/ 4th Ftr Grp
363rd Ftr Sqn/357th Ftr Grp

| Sqn | Date | Claims | Location | A/C |
|---|---|---|---|---|
| 363rd | March 16, 1944 | Me-110 dest(air) | N/Lake Constance | P-51 |
| | April 11 | FW-190 dest(air) | N/Hanover | P-51 |
| | April 24 | Me-109 dest(air) | N/Munich | P-51 |
| | May 12 | FW-190 dam(air) | NE Frankfurt | P-51 |

3-0-1 air
0-0 ground

**Thury, Joseph L., LtCol.**
505th Ftr Sqn/339th Ftr Grp

| Sqn | Date | Claims | Location | A/C |
|---|---|---|---|---|
| 505th | May 27, 1944 | Fi-156 dest(grd) | Frankfurt | P-51 |
| | | He-111 dest(grd) | Frankfurt | P-51 |
| | | Fi-156 dam(grd) | Frankfurt | P-51 |
| | | u/i a/c dam(grd) | Frankfurt | P-51 |
| | May 29 | FW-190 dest(air) | NE Stettin | P-51 |
| | June 27 | FW-190 dest(air) | SE Paris | P-51 |
| | July 19 | Me-109 dest(grd) | SW Augsburg | P-51 |
| | | u/i a/c dest(grd) | SW Augsburg | P-51 |
| | July 31 | (2)u/i a/c dest(grd) | Holzkirchen | P-51 |
| | | (.5)Me-410 dest(grd)[*] | Holzkirchen | P-51 |
| | | u/i a/c dam(grd) | Holzkirchen | P-51 |
| | September 10 | Ju-52 dest(grd) | Weizenburg | P-51 |
| | | Ju-88 dest(grd) | Weizenburg | P-51 |
| | September 11 | (2)Ju-88 dest(grd) | Munich | P-51 |
| | | Me-109 dam(grd) | Munich | P-51 |
| | | Me-410 dam(grd) | Munich | P-51 |
| | | He-111 dam(grd) | Munich | P-51 |
| | | Ju-88 dam(grd) | Munich | P-51 |
| | March 1, 1945 | Ju-88 dest(grd) | S/Feldkirchen | P-51 |
| | March 3 | (3)Ju-88 dest(grd) | E/Magdeburg | P-51 |
| | | Do-217 dest(grd) | E/Magdeburg | P-51 |
| | | Ju-88 dam(grd) | E/Magdeburg | P-51 |
| | April 7 | (.5)Me-109 dest(air)[**] | NE Steinhuder Lk. | P-51 |
| | April 10 | (2)u/i a/c dest(grd) | N/Neuruppin | P-51 |
| | | Ju-88 dest(grd) | N/Neuruppin | P-51 |
| | | He-111 dam(grd) | N/Neuruppin | P-51 |
| | | u/i a/c dam(grd) | N/Neuruppin | P-51 |
| | April 16 | Me-109 dest(grd) | NE Prague | P-51 |
| | | Me-262 dest(grd) | NE Prague | P-51 |
| | April 17 | (2)Me-109 dest(grd) | SE Pocking | P-51 |
| | | (2)FW-190 dest(grd) | SE Pocking | P-51 |
| | | Ju-88 dest(grd) | SE Pocking | P-51 |
| | April 18 | Me-262 dam(air) | Tabor | P-51 |

2.5-0-1 air
25.5-10 ground

[*] - shared with Lt. G.E. Graham of the 505th Ftr Sqn
[**] - shared with Lt. O.K. Biggs of the 505th Ftr Sqn

**Thwaites, David F., Capt.**
361st Ftr Sqn/356th Ftr Grp

| Sqn | Date | Claims | Location | A/C |
|---|---|---|---|---|
| 361st | January 21, 1944 | (.5)Ju-88 dest(air)[*] | Cambrai | P-47 |
| | February 13 | Me-109 dest(air) | SW Paris | P-47 |
| | May 13 | FW-190 dest(air) | Hamburg | P-47 |
| | May 19 | FW-190 dest(air) | Quackenbruck-Brunswick | P-47 |
| | | (3)FW-190 dam(air) | Quackenbruck-Brunswick | P-47 |
| | May 25 | Me-109 dest(air) | Neufchateau | P-47 |
| | June 7 | Ju-52 dest(grd) | Laval | P-47 |
| | August 4 | Me-109 dest(air) | Bremen-Hamburg | P-47 |
| | September 5 | (.5)He-111 dest(air)[**] | Twente/Enschede | P-47 |

6-0-3 air
1-0 ground

[*] - shared with Lt. S.H. Hewett of the 361st Ftr Sqn
[**] - shared with Lt. F.A. Morgan of the 361st Ftr Sqn

**Tibor, Robert P., Lt.**
38th Ftr Sqn/55th Ftr Grp

| Sqn | Date | Claims | Location | A/C |
|---|---|---|---|---|
| 38th | June 25, 1944 | Me-109 dest(air) | SW Paris | P-38 |

1-0-0 air
0-0 ground

**Tilton, Elbert W., Lt.**
370th Ftr Sqn/359th Ftr Grp

| Sqn | Date | Claims | Location | A/C |
|---|---|---|---|---|
| 370th | July 24, 1944 | Fi-156 dest(air) | Neu Ulm | P-51 |
| | August 9 | Me-109 dest(air) | Gunzburg | P-51 |

2-0-0 air
0-0 ground

**Timony, Eugene J., Lt.**
63rd Ftr Sqn/56th Ftr Grp

| Sqn | Date | Claims | Location | A/C |
|---|---|---|---|---|
| 63rd | September 5, 1944 | FW-190 dest(air) | S/Coblenz | P-47 |
| | | (2)Bu-131 dest(grd) | Gelnhausen | P-47 |
| | | FW-190 dest(grd) | Gelnhausen | P-47 |
| | September 8 | Ju-88 dest(grd) | Euskirchen | P-47 |

1-0-0 air
4-0 ground

**Tingen, Clarence A., Lt.**
62nd Ftr Sqn/56th Ftr Grp

| Sqn | Date | Claims | Location | A/C |
|---|---|---|---|---|
| 62nd | April 10, 1945 | Ju-88 dest(grd) | Rechlin | P-47 |
| | | He-111 dam(grd) | Rechlin | P-47 |
| | | Ju-88 dam(grd) | Rechlin | P-47 |
| | April 16 | He-177 dest(grd) | Muhldorf | P-47 |

0-0-0 air
2-2 ground

**Tinkham, Edwin E., Lt.**
375th Ftr Sqn/361st Ftr Grp

| *Sqn* | *Date* | *Claims* | *Location* | *A/C* |
|---|---|---|---|---|
| 375th | March 31, 1945 | Me-262 dam(air) | Brunswick | P-51 |

0-0-1 air
0-0 ground

**Tinto, Anthony J., Capt.**
338th Ftr Sqn/55th Ftr Grp

| *Sqn* | *Date* | *Claims* | *Location* | *A/C* |
|---|---|---|---|---|
| 338th | February 24, 1944 | Me-109 dest(air) | W/Gotha | P-38 |
| | June 11 | Me-109 dest(air) | Beauvais | P-38 |

2-0-0 air
0-0 ground

**Tipps, John T., Lt.**
434th Ftr Sqn/479th Ftr Grp

| *Sqn* | *Date* | *Claims* | *Location* | *A/C* |
|---|---|---|---|---|
| 434th | July 6, 1944 | Me-109 dest(air) | Valenciennes | P-38 |
| | September 5 | Do-217 dest(grd) | Ettinghausen | P-38 |

1-0-0 air
1-0 ground

**Tipton, Noah R., Lt.**
38th Ftr Sqn/55th Ftr Grp

| *Sqn* | *Date* | *Claims* | *Location* | *A/C* |
|---|---|---|---|---|
| 38th | February 25, 1944 | Me-410 dam(air) | Augsburg | P-38 |
| | May 12 | FW-190 dest(air) | Wiesbaden | P-38 |
| | May 21 | (.5)u/i a/c dest(grd)* | E/Helmstadt | P-38 |
| | | (.5)u/i a/c dest(grd)* | E/Helmstadt | P-38 |

1-0-1 air
1-0 ground

* - both shared with Capt. J.D. Landers of the 38th Ftr Sqn

**Tischer, Frank L., Lt.**
343rd Ftr Sqn/55th Ftr Grp

| *Sqn* | *Date* | *Claims* | *Location* | *A/C* |
|---|---|---|---|---|
| 343rd | September 11, 1944 | Me-109 prob(air) | Sonneburg | P-38 |

0-1-0 air
0-0 ground

**Todd, Charles G., Lt.**
354th Ftr Sqn/355th Ftr Grp

| *Sqn* | *Date* | *Claims* | *Location* | *A/C* |
|---|---|---|---|---|
| 354th | March 22, 1945 | He-111 dest(grd) | Memmingen | P-51 |
| | April 16 | He-111 dest(grd) | Eger A/F | P-51 |
| | | He-111 dam(grd) | Eger A/F | P-51 |
| | | Ju-88 dam(grd) | Eger A/F | P-51 |

0-0-0 air
3-1 ground

**Todd, James M., Maj.**
376th Ftr Sqn/361st Ftr Grp
HdQts/361st Ftr Grp

| *Sqn* | *Date* | *Claims* | *Location* | *A/C* |
|---|---|---|---|---|
| 376th | February 25, 1944 | Me-109 dam(air) | SE St. Quentin | P-47 |
| HdQts | March 17 | Me-109 dam(grd) | Chartres | P-47 |

0-0-1 air
0-1 ground

**Todd, Theodore P., Jr., Lt.**
354th Ftr Sqn/355th Ftr Grp

| *Sqn* | *Date* | *Claims* | *Location* | *A/C* |
|---|---|---|---|---|
| 354th | November 18, 1944 | Me-262 dam(grd) | Leipheim | P-51 |

0-0-0 air
0-1 ground

**Tolby, William W., Jr., Lt.**
358th Ftr Sqn/355th Ftr Grp

| *Sqn* | *Date* | *Claims* | *Location* | *A/C* |
|---|---|---|---|---|
| 358th | February 25, 1945 | Me-109 dest(air) | E/Munster | P-51 |
| | | Me-109 dam(grd) | E/Munster | P-51 |

1-0-0 air
0-1 ground

**Tommie, Delton F., Lt.**
434th Ftr Sqn/479th Ftr Grp

| *Sqn* | *Date* | *Claims* | *Location* | *A/C* |
|---|---|---|---|---|
| 434th | April 16, 1945 | Me-109 dam(grd) | Reichersberg | P-51 |
| | | FW-190 dam(grd) | Reichersberg | P-51 |

0-0-0 air
0-2 ground

**Tongue, Arthur E., Jr., Lt.**
505th Ftr Sqn/339th Ftr Grp

| *Sqn* | *Date* | *Claims* | *Location* | *A/C* |
|---|---|---|---|---|
| 505th | August 4, 1944 | Me-109 dest(air) | Ulzen-Celle | P-51 |
| | | (.5)Me-109 dest(air)* | Ulzen | P-51 |
| | | (.5)Me-109 dest(air)** | S/Hamburg | P-51 |

2-0-0 air
0-0 ground

* - shared with Lt. J.B. Muller of the 505th Ftr Sqn
** - shared with Lt. L.J. Powell of the 505th Ftr Sqn

**Tonkin, Walter, Lt.**
83rd Ftr Sqn/78th Ftr Grp

| *Sqn* | *Date* | *Claims* | *Location* | *A/C* |
|---|---|---|---|---|
| 83rd | February 24, 1944 | FW-190 dest(air) | Furstenau | P-47 |
| | March 6 | Me-109 dam(air) | NE Dummer Lake | P-47 |

1-0-1 air
0-0 ground

**Tordoff, Harrison B., Capt.**
352nd Ftr Sqn/353rd Ftr Grp

| *Sqn* | *Date* | *Claims* | *Location* | *A/C* |
|---|---|---|---|---|
| 352nd | August 4, 1944 | (2)Me-109 dest(air) | E/Bremen | P-47 |
| | | He-111 dest(grd) | Plantlunne | P-47 |
| | | u/i a/c dest(grd) | Plantlunne | P-47 |
| | September 27 | Me-109 dest(air) | Hanau | P-47 |
| | March 31, 1945 | Me-262 dest(air) | Dessau | P-51 |
| | April 7 | Me-109 dest(air) | E/Hamburg | P-51 |
| | April 16 | Me-109 dest(grd) | Bad Aibling | P-51 |
| | | Do-217 dest(grd) | Bad Aibling | P-51 |
| | | (.5)Ju-88 dest(grd)* | Bad Aibling | P-51 |
| | | u/i a/c dam(grd) | Bad Aibling | P-51 |

5-0-0 air
4.5-1 ground

* - shared with Lt. J.G. Bartley of the 352nd Ftr Sqn

**Totten, Wesley V., F/O**
38th Ftr Sqn/55th Ftr Grp

| *Sqn* | *Date* | *Claims* | *Location* | *A/C* |
|---|---|---|---|---|
| 38th | January 21, 1945 | (.5)u/i a/c dest(grd)* | Stuttgart/Boblingen | P-51 |
| | January 22 | (2)Ju-88 dest(grd) | Hanover/Langenhagen | P-51 |
| | February 19 | FW-190 dest(grd) | Deiningen | P-51 |
| | | FW-190 dam(grd) | Deiningen | P-51 |
| | March 9 | Me-262 dam(air) | Prenzlau | P-51 |

0-0-1 air
3.5-1 ground

* - shared with Lt. B. Clemmons of the 38th Ftr Sqn

**Tower, Archie A., Maj.**
505th Ftr Sqn/339th Ftr Grp

| *Sqn* | *Date* | *Claims* | *Location* | *A/C* |
|---|---|---|---|---|
| 505th | June 8, 1944 | FW-190 dest(air) | Laigle | P-51 |
| | | (.5)Do-217 dest(air)* | Laigle | P-51 |

| | | | | |
|---|---|---|---|---|
| | July 19 | Ju-188 dest(grd) | SW Augsburg | P-51 |
| | September 10 | Ju-88 dest(grd) | Munich | P-51 |
| | | Ju-52 dest(grd) | Munich | P-51 |
| | | (2)He-111 dam(grd) | Munich | P-51 |
| | | Ju-88 dam(grd) | Munich | P-51 |
| | September 11 | (2)Ju-88 dest(grd) | Munich | P-51 |
| | | He-111 dest(grd) | Munich | P-51 |
| | | Me-410 dest(grd) | Munich | P-51 |
| | | Ju-87 dest(grd) | Munich | P-51 |
| | | (2)Ju-88 dam(grd) | Munich | P-51 |
| | March 24, 1945 | FW-190 dam(grd) | Ziegenhall | P-51 |
| | April 4 | (2)Me-410 dest(grd) | NE Tribsees | P-51 |
| | April 10 | (2)Do-217 dest(grd) | Wittstock | P-51 |
| | | (2)Me-410 dest(grd) | Wittstock | P-51 |
| | | (2)Hs-129 dest(grd) | Wittstock | P-51 |
| | | (2)Ju-88 dest(grd) | Wittstock | P-51 |
| | | Do-217 dam(grd) | Wittstock | P-51 |
| | | Me-410 dam(grd) | Wittstock | P-51 |

1.5-0-0 air
18-8 ground

* - shared with Lt. W.R. Opitz of the 505th Ftr Sqn

**Tracy, Richard M., Capt.**
55th Ftr Sqn/20th Ftr Grp

| *Sqn* | *Date* | *Claims* | *Location* | *A/C* |
|---|---|---|---|---|
| 55th | April 9, 1945 | Ju-88 dam(grd) | Munich | P-51 |
| | April 10 | Me-109 dest(grd) | Berlin | P-51 |
| | | Me-110 dest(grd) | Berlin | P-51 |
| | | Ju-52 dest(grd) | Berlin | P-51 |
| | | u/i a/c dest(grd) | Berlin | P-51 |

0-0-0 air
4-1 ground

**Travis, Lee C., Lt.**
375th Ftr Sqn/361st Ftr Grp

| *Sqn* | *Date* | *Claims* | *Location* | *A/C* |
|---|---|---|---|---|
| 375th | September 18, 1944 | (.5)BV-138 dest(grd)[*] | Bug S/P Base | P-51 |
| | November 26 | FW-190 dest(air) | NE Misburg | P-51 |

1-0-0 air
0.5-0 ground

* - shared with Lt. W.D. Rogers of the 375th Ftr Sqn

**Treff, Ernest H., Lt.**
61st Ftr Sqn/56th Ftr Grp

| *Sqn* | *Date* | *Claims* | *Location* | *A/C* |
|---|---|---|---|---|
| 61st | April 13, 1945 | (3)Ju-88 dest(grd) | Eggebeck A/F | P-47 |
| | | (5)Ju-88 dam(grd) | Eggebeck A/F | P-47 |

0-0-0 air
3-5 ground

**Trembarth, Floyd W., Lt.**
354th Ftr Sqn/355th Ftr Grp

| *Sqn* | *Date* | *Claims* | *Location* | *A/C* |
|---|---|---|---|---|
| 354th | June 24, 1944 | Me-109 dest(grd) | Seiches | P-51 |

0-0-0 air
1-0 ground

**Trester, John R., Lt.**
504th Ftr Sqn/339th Ftr Grp

| *Sqn* | *Date* | *Claims* | *Location* | *A/C* |
|---|---|---|---|---|
| 504th | July 29, 1944 | Me-109 prob(air) | Merseburg-Naumberg | P-51 |

0-1-0 air
0-0 ground

**Troge, Eldon F., Capt.**
359th Ftr Sqn/356th Ftr Grp

| *Sqn* | *Date* | *Claims* | *Location* | *A/C* |
|---|---|---|---|---|
| 359th | December 25, 1944 | FW-190 dest(air) | Bonn | P-51 |

1-0-0 air
0-0 ground

**Truett, Jesse L., Capt.**
383rd Ftr Sqn/364th Ftr Grp

| *Sqn* | *Date* | *Claims* | *Location* | *A/C* |
|---|---|---|---|---|
| 383rd | April 13, 1945 | (4)Ju-52 dest(grd) | Flensburg | P-51 |
| | | Do-217 dest(grd) | Flensburg | P-51 |
| | | Me-109 dam(grd) | Flensburg | P-51 |
| | | FW-190 dam(grd) | Flensburg | P-51 |
| | April 16 | Fi-156 dest(grd) | Marienbad | P-51 |
| | | (.5)FW-190 dest(grd)[*] | Marienbad | P-51 |
| | | Do-217 dam(grd) | Marienbad | P-51 |
| | | Fi-156 dam(grd) | Marienbad | P-51 |

0-0-0 air
6.5-4 ground

* - shared with Lt. G.F. Hill of the 383rd Ftr Sqn

**Truluck, John H., Capt.**
63rd Ftr Sqn/56th Ftr Grp

| *Sqn* | *Date* | *Claims* | *Location* | *A/C* |
|---|---|---|---|---|
| 63rd | August 17, 1943 | FW-190 dest(air) | Ans-St. Nicholas | P-47 |
| | | Me-210 dam(air) | Ans-St. Nicholas | P-47 |
| | September 27 | Me-109 dest(air) | Borkum Island | P-47 |
| | | FW-190 dest(air) | Borkum Island | P-47 |
| | November 26 | FW-190 dest(air) | Friesoythe | P-47 |
| | | Me-110 dam(air) | Friesoythe | P-47 |
| | February 24, 1944 | FW-190 dest(air) | Herford | P-47 |
| | March 8 | Me-109 dest(air) | Dummer Lake | P-47 |
| | March 15 | FW-190 dest(air) | Hanover | P-47 |
| | | Me-109 dam(air) | Hanover | P-47 |
| | April 24 | Do-217 dest(grd) | Thalheim A/F | P-47 |
| | | (3)Do-217 dam(grd) | Thalheim A/F | P-47 |

7-0-3 air
1-3 ground

**Trumble, Pershing B., Lt.**
63rd Ftr Sqn/56th Ftr Grp

| *Sqn* | *Date* | *Claims* | *Location* | *A/C* |
|---|---|---|---|---|
| 63rd | December 2, 1944 | Me-109 dest(air) | S/Marburg | P-47 |
| | December 23 | FW-190 dam(air) | NW Coblenz | P-47 |
| | January 14, 1945 | Me-109 dest(air) | Stendal | P-47 |
| | | Me-109 prob(air) | Stendal | P-47 |

2-1-1 air
0-0 ground

**Trybuszewski, Alfred J., Capt.**
385th Ftr Sqn/364th Ftr Grp

| *Sqn* | *Date* | *Claims* | *Location* | *A/C* |
|---|---|---|---|---|
| 385th | September 11, 1944 | (2)Me-109 dest(air) | W/Leipzig | P-51 |

2-0-0 air
0-0 ground

**Tucker, Charles E., Capt.**
62nd Ftr Sqn/56th Ftr Grp

| *Sqn* | *Date* | *Claims* | *Location* | *A/C* |
|---|---|---|---|---|
| 62nd | May 31, 1944 | FW-190 dest(air) | Meldorf | P-47 |
| | | FW-190 dam(air) | Melforf | P-47 |

1-0-1 air
0-0 ground

**Tucker, Dick F., Capt.**
359th Ftr Sqn/356th Ftr Grp

| *Sqn* | *Date* | *Claims* | *Location* | *A/C* |
|---|---|---|---|---|
| 359th | September 9, 1944 | He-111 dest(grd) | W/Bad Nauheim | P-47 |
| | November 26 | Me-109 dest(air) | NW Dummer Lake | P-51 |
| | | Me-109 dam(air) | NW Dummer Lake | P-51 |
| | November 27 | FW-190 dest(air) | N/Munster | P-51 |

2-0-1 air
1-0 ground

**Tulhoski, David C., Lt.**
354th Ftr Sqn/355th Ftr Grp

| *Sqn* | *Date* | *Claims* | *Location* | *A/C* |
|---|---|---|---|---|
| 354th | March 22, 1945 | FW-190 dest(grd) | Wurzburg | P-51 |

0-0-0 air
1-0 ground

**Tulloch, John F., Jr., Capt.**
358th Ftr Sqn/355th Ftr Grp

| *Sqn* | *Date* | *Claims* | *Location* | *A/C* |
|---|---|---|---|---|
| 358th | April 13, 1945 | (4)He-111 dest(grd) | Schleswig | P-51 |

0-0-0 air
4-0 ground

**Tumlin, Rupert M., Lt.**
351st Ftr Sqn/353rd Ftr Grp

| *Sqn* | *Date* | *Claims* | *Location* | *A/C* |
|---|---|---|---|---|
| 351st | April 24, 1944 | FW-190 dam(air) | Mannheim | P-47 |
| | June 12 | Me-109 dest(air) | SW Paris | P-47 |
| | | Me-109 dam(air) | SW Paris | P-47 |
| | July 7 | He-111 dest(grd) | Wesendorf | P-47 |

1-0-2 air
1-0 ground

**Turley, Grant M., Lt.**
82nd Ftr Sqn/78th Ftr Grp

| *Sqn* | *Date* | *Claims* | *Location* | *A/C* |
|---|---|---|---|---|
| 82nd | February 10, 1944 | (2)Me-109 dest(air) | Osnabruck | P-47 |
| | February 11 | Me-109 dest(air) | Verdun | P-47 |
| | | FW-190 dest(air) | Verdun | P-47 |
| | February 20 | FW-190 dest(air) | Coblenz | P-47 |
| | February 24 | Me-109 dest(air) | Dummer Lake | P-47 |

6-0-0 air
0-0 ground

**Turner, James D., Lt.**
385thn Ftr Sqn/364th Ftr Grp

| *Sqn* | *Date* | *Claims* | *Location* | *A/C* |
|---|---|---|---|---|
| 385th | March 15, 1944 | (.5)Me-109 dest(air)* | Dummer Lake | P-38 |

0.5-0-0 air
0-0 ground

* - shared with Capt. R.M. Scott of the 385th Ftr Sqn

**Tussey, Robert S., Lt.**
336th Ftr Sqn/4th Ftr Grp

| *Sqn* | *Date* | *Claims* | *Location* | *A/C* |
|---|---|---|---|---|
| 336th | March 8, 1944 | Ju-88 dest(air) | Magdeburg | P-51 |
| | March 29 | FW-190 prob(air) | SE Brunswick | P-51 |
| | April 5 | Me-110 dest(grd) | Stendal | P-51 |
| | | Ju-88 dam(grd) | Stendal | P-51 |
| | | (.25) of (5)Ju-52 dam(grd)* | Stendal | P-51 |

1-1-0 air
1-2.25 ground

* - all shared with Capt. D.W. Beeson, Lt. H.T. Biel, and Lt. C.D. Carr of the 334th Ftr Sqn, 4th Ftr Grp

**Tuttle, James M., Lt.**
352nd Ftr Sqn/353rd Ftr Grp

| *Sqn* | *Date* | *Claims* | *Location* | *A/C* |
|---|---|---|---|---|
| 352nd | August 4, 1944 | (2)u/i a/c dest(grd) | Plantlunne | P-47 |

0-0-0 air
2-0 ground

**Tyler, Gerald E., Capt.**
364th Ftr Sqn/357th Ftr Grp

| *Sqn* | *Date* | *Claims* | *Location* | *A/C* |
|---|---|---|---|---|
| 364th | June 29, 1944 | Me-109 dest(air) | SW Leipzig | P-51 |
| | July 5 | FW-190 dest(air) | SE Rouen | P-51 |
| | August 24 | Me-109 dest(air) | S/Brunswick | P-51 |
| | September 18 | (2)Me-109 dest(air) | N/Maastricht | P-51 |
| | | FW-190 dest(air) | N/Maastricht | P-51 |
| | September 19 | Me-109 dest(air) | E/Arnheim | P-51 |

7-0-0 air
0-0 ground

**Tyrrell, Albert R., LtCol.**
368th Ftr Sqn/359th Ftr Grp

| *Sqn* | *Date* | *Claims* | *Location* | *A/C* |
|---|---|---|---|---|
| 368th | February 24, 1944 | (2)FW-190 dest(air) | Neuenhaus | P-47 |
| | June 21 | Me-410 dest(grd) | Wittstock | P-51 |
| | | Me-110 dest(grd) | Wittstock | P-51 |
| | | FW-189 dest(grd) | Wittstock | P-51 |

2-0-0 air
3-0 ground

**Umla, Walter E., Lt.**
77th Ftr Sqn/20th Ftr Grp

| *Sqn* | *Date* | *Claims* | *Location* | *A/C* |
|---|---|---|---|---|
| 77th | April 10, 1945 | Ju-52 dest(grd) | Schonwalde A/F | P-51 |
| | | (2)Ju-52 dam(grd) | Schonwalde A/F | P-51 |

0-0-0 air
1-2 ground

**Unangst, Robert F., Lt.**
350th Ftr Sqn/353rd Ftr Grp

| *Sqn* | *Date* | *Claims* | *Location* | *A/C* |
|---|---|---|---|---|
| 350th | June 20, 1944 | Ju-88 dest(grd) | Plantlunne | P-47 |
| | August 14 | Ju-88 dest(air) | Chateau Thierry | P-47 |

1-0-0 air
1-0 ground

**Underwood, Wade F., Lt.**
335th Ftr Sqn/4th Ftr Grp

| *Sqn* | *Date* | *Claims* | *Location* | *A/C* |
|---|---|---|---|---|
| 335th | April 16, 1945 | FW-190 dest(grd) | Praha A/F | P-51 |
| | | Me-410 dest(grd) | Praha A/F | P-51 |
| | | u/i a/c dest(grd) | Praha A/F | P-51 |

0-0-0 air
3-0 ground

**Upchurch, James H., Lt.**
358th Ftr Sqn/355th Ftr Grp

| *Sqn* | *Date* | *Claims* | *Location* | *A/C* |
|---|---|---|---|---|
| 358th | February 5, 1944 | (.25)FW-190 dam(air)* | S/Tours | P-47 |

0-0-0.25 air
0-0 ground

* - shared with Lt. H.J. Hoffman, Lt. J.H. McConnell, and Lt. J.J. DeGeorge of the 358th Ftr Sqn

**Upp, Ronald J., Capt.**
361st Ftr Sqn/356th Ftr Grp

| *Sqn* | *Date* | *Claims* | *Location* | *A/C* |
|---|---|---|---|---|
| 361st | October 7, 1944 | (3.5)Ju-88 dam(grd)* | Fritzlar | P-47 |

0-0-0 air
0-3.5 ground

* - shared with Lt. H.E. Whitmore of the 361st Ftr Sqn

**Urban, Theodore J., Capt.**
360th Ftr Sqn/356th Ftr Grp

| *Sqn* | *Date* | *Claims* | *Location* | *A/C* |
|---|---|---|---|---|
| 360th | November 26, 1944 | Me-109 dest(air) | Dummer Lake | P-51 |
| | December 25 | FW-190 dam(air) | Bonn | P-51 |
| | January 14, 1945 | FW-190 dest(air) | S/Osnabruck | P-51 |

2-0-1 air
0-0 ground

**Uttwenweiler, Fred L., Capt.**
352nd Ftr Sqn/353rd Ftr Grp

| *Sqn* | *Date* | *Claims* | *Location* | *A/C* |
|---|---|---|---|---|
| 352nd | August 4, 1944 | (2)He-111 dest(grd) | Plantlunne | P-47 |
| | October 24, 1944 | (4)He-111 dest(grd) | N/Luxembourg | P-51 |
| | | (3)He-111 dam(grd) | N/Luxembourg | P-51 |

0-0-0 air
6-3 ground

**Valenta, Irvin E., Lt.**
62nd Ftr Sqn/56th Ftr Grp

| *Sqn* | *Date* | *Claims* | *Location* | *A/C* |
|---|---|---|---|---|
| 62nd | November 26, 1943 | (2)Me-110 dest(air) | Papenburg | P-47 |
| | | (2)Me-110 dam(air) | Papenburg | P-47 |
| | February 4, 1944 | FW-190 dam(air) | Charleroi | P-47 |
| | February 24 | FW-190 dam(air) | SW Hanover | P-47 |

2-0-4 air
0-0 ground

**Valluzzi, Arthur J., F/O**
434th Ftr Sqn/479th Ftr Grp

| *Sqn* | *Date* | *Claims* | *Location* | *A/C* |
|---|---|---|---|---|
| 434th | April 17, 1945 | (2)Me-109 dest(grd) | Puchhoff | P-51 |

0-0-0 air
2-0 ground

**Van Dyk, Warren V., Lt.**
82nd Ftr Sqn/78th Ftr Grp

| *Sqn* | *Date* | *Claims* | *Location* | *A/C* |
|---|---|---|---|---|
| 82nd | May 11, 1944 | (.5)He-111 dest(grd)* | Dijon | P-47 |
| | | (.5)Ju-52 dest(grd)** | Dijon | P-47 |

0-0-0 air
1-0 ground

* - shared with Capt. J.W. Wilkinson of the 82nd Ftr Sqn
** - shared with Lt. B.M. Watkins of the 82nd Ftr Sqn

**Van Epps, David A., Capt.**
334th Ftr Sqn/4th Ftr Grp

| *Sqn* | *Date* | *Claims* | *Location* | *A/C* |
|---|---|---|---|---|
| 334th | March 6, 1944 | (.5)Me-110 dest(air)* | W/Nienburg | P-51 |
| | | Me-110 dam(air) | W/Nienburg | P-51 |
| | | FW-190 dam(air) | W/Nienburg | P-51 |
| | | FW-190 dam(grd) | W/Nienburg | P-51 |
| | March 21 | (.5)Do-217 dest(grd)** | E/Bordeaux | P-51 |
| | March 29 | FW-190 dam(air) | Brunswick | P-51 |

0.5-0-3 air
0.5-1 ground

* - shared with Lt. H.N. Moulton of the 334th Ftr Sqn
** - shared with Lt. A. Rafalovich of the 334th Ftr Sqn

**Van Noy, George H., Jr., Capt.**
62nd Ftr Sqn/56th Ftr Grp

| *Sqn* | *Date* | *Claims* | *Location* | *A/C* |
|---|---|---|---|---|
| 62nd | June 8, 1944 | Me-109 dest(air) | St. Andre de L'Eure | P-47 |
| | September 10 | Ju-88 dam(grd) | Seligenstadt A/F | P-47 |

1-0-0 air
0-1 ground

**Van Sickle, Dick W., Capt.**
77th Ftr Sqn/20th Ftr Grp

| *Sqn* | *Date* | *Claims* | *Location* | *A/C* |
|---|---|---|---|---|
| 77th | October 6, 1944 | (.5)Do-18 dest(grd)* | Bad Berg-Dievenow | P-51 |
| | | Do-18 dam(grd) | Bad Berg-Dievenow | P-51 |
| | October 7 | u/i a/c dam(grd) | Peenemunde | P-51 |
| | January 14, 1945 | Me-109 prob(air) | Perleburg | P-51 |
| | February 20 | He-111 dam(grd) | Straubing | P-51 |

0-1-0 air
0.5-3 ground

* - shared with Lt. F.E. Snodgrass of the 77th Ftr Sqn

**Van Sickle, Frank L., Capt.**
77th Ftr Sqn/20th Ftr Grp

| *Sqn* | *Date* | *Claims* | *Location* | *A/C* |
|---|---|---|---|---|
| 77th | February 20, 1945 | Me-108 dest(air) | Straubing | P-51 |
| | | Me-108 dest(grd) | Straubing | P-51 |
| | | Fi-156 dest(grd) | Straubing | P-51 |
| | | u/i a/c dest(grd) | Straubing | P-51 |

1-0-0 air
3-0 ground

**Van Stryland, Robert G., Capt.**
376th Ftr Sqn/361st Ftr Grp

| *Sqn* | *Date* | *Claims* | *Location* | *A/C* |
|---|---|---|---|---|
| 376th | March 17, 1944 | Ju-88 dam(grd) | Chartres | P-47 |

0-0-0 air
0-1 ground

**Van Woert, Richard L., Lt.**
77th Ftr Sqn/20th Ftr Grp

| *Sqn* | *Date* | *Claims* | *Location* | *A/C* |
|---|---|---|---|---|
| 77th | September 28, 1944 | Me-109 dam(air) | S/Magdeburg | P-51 |

0-0-1 air
0-0 ground

**Van Wyk, Neil, Capt.**
336th Ftr Sqn/4th Ftr Grp
335th Ftr Sqn/4th Ftr Grp

| *Sqn* | *Date* | *Claims* | *Location* | *A/C* |
|---|---|---|---|---|
| 336th | April 10, 1944 | (4)u/i a/c dam(grd) | Romorantin A/F | P-51 |
| | April 18 | (.5)Me-109 dest(grd)* | Wenzendorf | P-51 |

0-0-0 air
0.5-4 ground

* - shared with Lt. G.H. Logan of the 336th Ftr Sqn

**Vanden Heuval, George R., Lt.**
376th Ftr Sqn/361st Ftr Grp

| *Sqn* | *Date* | *Claims* | *Location* | *A/C* |
|---|---|---|---|---|
| 376th | November 2, 1944 | FW-190 dest(air) | N/Erfurt | P-51 |
| | November 26 | (2)FW-190 dest(air) | S/Ulzen | P-51 |
| | December 24 | Me-109 dest(air) | Wengerohr | P-51 |
| | December 26 | (1.5)FW-190 dest(air)* | Merzig | P-51 |
| | April 16, 1945 | (2)FW-190 dest(grd) | Reichersberg | P-51 |
| | | Me-410 dest(grd) | Kircheim | P-51 |
| | | Ju-52 dam(grd) | Reichersberg | P-51 |

5.5-0-0 air
3-1 ground

* - shared with Capt. J.W. Ruch of the 376th Ftr Sqn

**Vander Vean, Cornelius, F/O**
328th Ftr Sqn/352nd Ftr Grp

| *Sqn* | *Date* | *Claims* | *Location* | *A/C* |
|---|---|---|---|---|
| 328th | April 17, 1945 | FW-190 dest(grd) | Plattling | P-51 |
| | | u/i a/c dest(grd) | Plattling | P-51 |
| | | (2)FW-190 dam(grd) | Plattling | P-51 |

0-0-0 air
2-2 ground

**Vandiver, Loy C., Lt.**
374th Ftr Sqn/361st Ftr Grp

| *Sqn* | *Date* | *Claims* | *Location* | *A/C* |
|---|---|---|---|---|
| 374th | March 2, 1944 | Ju-88 dam(grd) | Chievres | P-47 |
| | April 8 | Me-109 dest(air) | N/Dummer Lake | P-47 |

1-0-0 air
0-1 ground

**Vann, James F., Lt.**
385th Ftr Sqn/364th Ftr Grp

| Sqn | Date | Claims | Location | A/C |
|---|---|---|---|---|
| 385th | September 13, 1944 | Me-109 dest(air) | SE Kassel | P-51 |

1-0-0 air
0-0 ground

**Vasseur, Peter C., Lt.**
436th Ftr Sqn/479th Ftr Grp

| Sqn | Date | Claims | Location | A/C |
|---|---|---|---|---|
| 436th | December 5, 1944 | (.5)FW-190 dest(air)* | N/Berlin | P-51 |

0.5-0-0 air
0-0 ground

* - shared with Lt. T.E. Myers of the 436th Ftr Sqn

**Vear, Judd G., Lt.**
374th Ftr Sqn/361st Ftr Grp

| Sqn | Date | Claims | Location | A/C |
|---|---|---|---|---|
| 374th | November 2, 1944 | Me-109 dest(air) | N/Erfurt | P-51 |
| | November 26 | FW-190 dest(air) | Wittingen | P-51 |
| | | FW-190 dam(air) | Wittingen | P-51 |

2-0-1 air
0-0 ground

**Venell, Irvin E., Capt.**
350th Ftr Sqn/353rd Ftr Grp

| Sqn | Date | Claims | Location | A/C |
|---|---|---|---|---|
| 350th | August 24, 1943 | FW-190 dam(air) | Rouen | P-47 |

0-0-1 air
0-0 ground

**Vest, Boss E., Lt.**
63rd Ftr Sqn/56th Ftr Grp

| Sqn | Date | Claims | Location | A/C |
|---|---|---|---|---|
| 63rd | April 10, 1945 | Ju-88 dest(grd) | Stendal | P-47 |
| | | Me-109 dam(grd) | Stendal | P-47 |
| | April 16 | Ju-88 dest(grd) | Ingolstadt | P-47 |

0-0-0 air
2-1 ground

**Vickery, Duran M., Jr., Lt.**
354th Ftr Sqn/355th Ftr Grp

| Sqn | Date | Claims | Location | A/C |
|---|---|---|---|---|
| 354th | February 23, 1945 | Ju-88 dam(grd) | Neuburg A/F | P-51 |
| | April 13 | (3)He-111 dest(grd) | Husum A/F | P-51 |
| | | (2)He-111 dam(grd) | Husum A/F | P-51 |

0-0-0 air
3-3 ground

**Vickery, Joseph P., Lt.**
487th Ftr Sqn/352nd Ftr Grp

| Sqn | Date | Claims | Location | A/C |
|---|---|---|---|---|
| 487th | July 18, 1944 | (2)Ju-88 dam(air) | NE Rostock | P-51 |
| | November 2 | (2)Me-109 dest(air) | Merseburg | P-51 |

2-0-2 air
0-0 ground

**Vigna, Joseph J., Lt.**
358th Ftr Sqn/355th Ftr Grp

| Sqn | Date | Claims | Location | A/C |
|---|---|---|---|---|
| 358th | September 12, 1944 | FW-190 dam(air) | E/Berlin | P-51 |

0-0-1 air
0-0 ground

**Vincent, Roland L., Lt.**
354th Ftr Sqn/355th Ftr Grp

| Sqn | Date | Claims | Location | A/C |
|---|---|---|---|---|
| 354th | November 5, 1943 | Me-109 dam(air) | NW Gelsenkirchen | P-47 |
| | November 13 | Me-109 dest(air) | W/Meppen | P-47 |

1-0-1 air
0-0 ground

**Vineyard, Paul W., Jr., Lt.**
354th Ftr Sqn/355th Ftr Grp

| Sqn | Date | Claims | Location | A/C |
|---|---|---|---|---|
| 354th | March 22, 1945 | He-111 dest(grd) | Memmingen | P-51 |
| | April 7 | Me-109 dest(air) | SE Bremen | P-51 |

1-0-0 air
1-0 ground

**Visconte, Romildo, Capt.**
385th Ftr Sqn/364th Ftr Grp

| Sqn | Date | Claims | Location | A/C |
|---|---|---|---|---|
| 385th | May 21, 1944 | Ju-88 dest(grd) | Schwerin-Ludwigslust | P-38 |
| | August 9 | (3)Me-109 dest(grd) | Gaukonigshafen | P-51 |
| | | Me-110 dest(grd) | Gaukonigshafen | P-51 |
| | | Me-110 dam(grd) | Gaukonigshafen | P-51 |
| | | (.5)FW-200 dam(grd)* | Gaukonigshafen | P-51 |
| | September 23 | Me-109 dest(air) | Emmerich | P-51 |
| | | FW-190 dam(air) | Emmerich | P-51 |
| | October 12 | FW-190 dest(air) | NE Bremen | P-51 |
| | November 26 | Me-109 dest(air) | Hoyd | P-51 |
| | December 2 | FW-190 dest(air) | NW Ludwigshafen | P-51 |

4-0-1 air
5-1.5 ground

* - shared with Lt. D.J. Hustead of the 385th Ftr Sqn

**Visconti, Lawrence, Lt.**
384th Ftr Sqn/364th Ftr Grp

| Sqn | Date | Claims | Location | A/C |
|---|---|---|---|---|
| 384th | November 21, 1944 | FW-190 dest(air) | W/Merseburg | P-51 |

1-0-0 air
0-0 ground

**Vitale, Joseph, F/O**
62nd Ftr Sqn/56th Ftr Grp

| Sqn | Date | Claims | Location | A/C |
|---|---|---|---|---|
| 62nd | May 12, 1944 | (.5)Me-109 dest(air)* | Frankfurt | P-47 |

0.5-0-0 air
0-0 ground

* - shared with Capt. J.H. Powers of the 62nd Ftr Sqn

**Vitali, Chester A., Capt.**
360th Ftr Sqn/356th Ftr Grp

| Sqn | Date | Claims | Location | A/C |
|---|---|---|---|---|
| 360th | January 24, 1944 | (3)FW-190 dest(air) | NW Lille | P-47 |
| | | FW-190 dam(air) | NW Lille | P-47 |
| | May 19 | Me-109 dest(air) | Steinhuder Lake | P-47 |

4-0-1 air
0-0 ground

**Vitek, Lumir J., Capt.**
486th Ftr Sqn/352nd Ftr Grp

| Sqn | Date | Claims | Location | A/C |
|---|---|---|---|---|
| 486th | July 19, 1944 | (2)Me-109 dest(air) | Munich | P-51 |
| | | Me-109 dam(air) | Munich | P-51 |
| | November 2 | Me-109 dest(air) | SW Merseburg | P-51 |
| | January 23, 1945 | (.5)Me-109 dest(air)* | SW Dusseldorf | P-51 |

3.5-0-1 air
0-0 ground

* - shared with Lt. G.G. Contos of the 486th Ftr Sqn

**Vogel, Donald W., Lt.**
362nd Ftr Sqn/357th Ftr Grp

| Sqn | Date | Claims | Location | A/C |
|---|---|---|---|---|
| 362nd | May 30, 1944 | FW-190 dest(air) | Magdeburg | P-51 |

1-0-0 air
0-0 ground

**Vogel, Victor L., Lt.**
351st Ftr Sqn/353rd Ftr Grp

| Sqn | Date | Claims | Location | A/C |
|---|---|---|---|---|
| 351st | September 23, 1943 | Me-109 dam(air) | S/Rennes | P-47 |

0-0-1 air
0-0 ground

**Vogt, John W., Jr., Maj.**
63rd Ftr Sqn/ 56th Ftr Grp
360th Ftr Sqn/356th Ftr Grp

| Sqn | Date | Claims | Location | A/C |
|---|---|---|---|---|
| 63rd | August 19, 1943 | Me-109 dest(air) | Walcheren | P-47 |
| | October 4 | Me-110 dest(air) | E/Duren | P-47 |
| | October 20 | FW-190 dest(air) | N/Ans | P-47 |
| | February 21, 1944 | Me-110 dest(air) | N/Munster | P-47 |
| | February 22 | Me-110 dest(air) | Radeborn | P-47 |
| 360th | May 19 | FW-190 dest(air) | SW Celle | P-47 |
| | August 4 | (2)Me-109 dest(air) | SW Hamburg | P-47 |

8-0-0 air
0-0 ground

**Volkman, Robert R., Capt.**
376th Ftr Sqn/361st Ftr Grp

| Sqn | Date | Claims | Location | A/C |
|---|---|---|---|---|
| 376th | August 4, 1944 | Ju-88 dam(grd) | Anklam | P-51 |
| | September 27 | FW-190 dest(air) | Eisenach | P-51 |

1-0-0 air
0-1 ground

**Vomaske, Richard F., Lt.**
351st Ftr Sqn/353rd Ftr Grp

| Sqn | Date | Claims | Location | A/C |
|---|---|---|---|---|
| 351st | September 21, 1944 | Me-109 dest(air) | Arnheim-Nijmegen | P-47 |

1-0-0 air
0-0 ground

**Voss, Clyde K., Lt.**
383rd Ftr Sqn/364th Ftr Grp

| Sqn | Date | Claims | Location | A/C |
|---|---|---|---|---|
| 383rd | August 9, 1944 | FW-190 dest(air) | Munich | P-51 |
| | August 10 | Me-109 dest(air) | W/Paris | P-51 |
| | September 12 | FW-190 dest(air) | NE Berlin | P-51 |

3-0-0 air
0-0 ground

**Voss, John R., Lt.**
374th Ftr Sqn/361st Ftr Grp

| Sqn | Date | Claims | Location | A/C |
|---|---|---|---|---|
| 374th | November 6, 1944 | Me-262 dam(air) | Rehburg | P-51 |

0-0-1 air
0-0 ground

**Vossler, Richard G., Lt.**
359th Ftr Sqn/356th Ftr Grp

| Sqn | Date | Claims | Location | A/C |
|---|---|---|---|---|
| 359th | January 21, 1944 | Ju-88 prob(air) | St. Leger A/F | P-47 |
| | August 18 | FW-190 dest(air) | Beauvais | P-47 |
| | | FW-190 dam(air) | Beauvais | P-47 |

1-1-1 air
0-0 ground

**Voyles, Robert S., Lt.**
334th Ftr Sqn/4th Ftr Grp

| Sqn | Date | Claims | Location | A/C |
|---|---|---|---|---|
| 334th | February 27, 1945 | (.5)Ju-52 dest(grd)* | Weimar | P-51 |

0-0-0 air
0.5-0 ground

* - shared with Lt. J.W. Ayers of the 334th Ftr Sqn

**Vulgamore, Donald P., Lt.**
376th Ftr Sqn/361st Ftr Grp

| Sqn | Date | Claims | Location | A/C |
|---|---|---|---|---|
| 376th | September 12, 1944 | Me-109 dest(air) | W/Magdeburg | P-51 |
| | September 27 | FW-190 dest(air) | Eisenach | P-51 |
| | | Me-410 dest(grd) | Eisenach | P-51 |
| | | Me-410 dam(grd) | Eisenach | P-51 |

2-0-0 air
1-1 ground

**Wadlow, James H., Jr., Capt.**
359th Ftr Sqn/356th Ftr Grp

| Sqn | Date | Claims | Location | A/C |
|---|---|---|---|---|
| 359th | January 11, 1944 | (.5)Me-110 dest(air)* | Steinhuder Lake | P-47 |
| | March 8 | Me-110 dam(grd) | Hesepe | P-47 |

0.5-0-0 air
0-1 ground

* - shared with Maj. D.A. Baccus of the 359th Ftr Sqn

**Waggoner, Horace Q., Capt.**
352nd Ftr Sqn/353rd Ftr Grp

| Sqn | Date | Claims | Location | A/C |
|---|---|---|---|---|
| 352nd | May 27, 1944 | Do-217 dest(grd) | Saverne | P-47 |
| | June 7 | FW-190 dest(grd) | Cormeilles-en-Vixen | P-47 |
| | | (2)FW-190 dam(grd) | Cormeilles-en-Vixen | P-47 |
| | June 8 | (1.5)FW-190 dest(grd)* | Angars | P-47 |
| | June 20 | Hs-129 dam(grd) | Twente/Enschede | P-47 |
| | | Ju-88 dam(grd) | Plantlunne | P-47 |
| | December 24 | Me-109 dest(air) | SW Euskirchen | P-51 |
| | December 25 | Me-109 dest(air) | NE St. Vith | P-51 |
| | March 2, 1945 | (2)FW-190 dest(air) | Ruhland | P-51 |
| | | Me-109 dest(air) | Ruhland | P-51 |
| | April 17 | (3)Me-109 dest(grd) | Ganacker | P-51 |
| | | Ju-88 dest(grd) | Ganacker | P-51 |

5-0-0 air
7.5-4 ground

* - shared with Lt. H.O. Miller of the 352nd Ftr Sqn

**Wagner, Karl R., Lt.**
82nd Ftr Sqn/78th Ftr Grp

| Sqn | Date | Claims | Location | A/C |
|---|---|---|---|---|
| 82nd | April 1, 1944 | He-111 dest(grd) | Verdun | P-47 |
| | April 12 | FW-190 dest(air) | Malmedy | P-47 |
| | May 19 | Me-109 dam(air) | Dummer Lake | P-47 |

1-0-1 air
1-0 ground

**Waice, Francis J., Lt.**
38th Ftr Sqn/55th Ftr Grp

| Sqn | Date | Claims | Location | A/C |
|---|---|---|---|---|
| 38th | September 5, 1944 | FW-190 dam(grd) | Stuttgart/Boblingen | P-51 |
| | September 12 | Ju-88 dam(grd) | Herzogenaurach | P-51 |

0-0-0 air
0-2 ground

**Wakefield, J. Carroll, Capt.**
63rd Ftr Sqn/56th Ftr Grp

| Sqn | Date | Claims | Location | A/C |
|---|---|---|---|---|
| 63rd | May 12, 1944 | (3)Me-109 dest(air) | NW Frankfurt | P-47 |

3-0-0 air
0-0 ground

**Wakeland, John M., Lt.**
338th Ftr Sqn/55th Ftr Grp

| *Sqn* | *Date* | *Claims* | *Location* | *A/C* |
|---|---|---|---|---|
| 338th | July 7, 1944 | FW-190 dam(air) | W/Bernburg | P-38 |
| | September 11 | (2)Me-109 dest(air) | S/Meiningen | P-51 |
| | | Me-109 dam(air) | S/Meiningen | P-51 |
| | September 13 | Me-109 dest(air) | Eisenach-Gotha | P-51 |

3-0-2 air
0-0 ground

**Waldheim, William H., Lt.**
83rd Ftr Sqn/78th Ftr Grp

| *Sqn* | *Date* | *Claims* | *Location* | *A/C* |
|---|---|---|---|---|
| 83rd | February 10, 1944 | Me-109 dest(air) | Lingen | P-47 |
| | March 17 | (.5)Do-217 dest(grd)* | N/Reims | P-47 |
| | | (4)Bu-133 dam(grd) | N/Reims | P-47 |
| | | Do-217 dam(grd) | N/Reims | P-47 |

1-0-0 air
0.5-5 ground

* - shared with Lt. B.W. Sorenson of the 83rd Ftr Sqn

**Waldron, Karl M., Jr., Lt.**
487th Ftr Sqn/352nd Ftr Grp

| *Sqn* | *Date* | *Claims* | *Location* | *A/C* |
|---|---|---|---|---|
| 487th | November 2, 1944 | Me-109 dest(air) | Merseburg | P-51 |
| | November 21 | (2)FW-190 dest(air) | SW Merseburg | P-51 |
| | April 10, 1945 | Me-262 dam(air) | Salzwedel | P-51 |
| | April 16 | FW-190 dest(grd) | Ganacker | P-51 |
| | | Me-109 dest(grd) | Ganacker | P-51 |
| | April 17 | (2)FW-190 dest(grd) | Plattling | P-51 |
| | | (2)Me-109 dest(grd) | Plattling | P-51 |
| | | Fi-156 dest(grd) | Plattling | P-51 |
| | | (2)FW-190 dam(grd) | Plattling | P-51 |

3-0-1 air
7-2 ground

**Walker, John A., Capt.**
384th Ftr Sqn/364th Ftr Grp

| *Sqn* | *Date* | *Claims* | *Location* | *A/C* |
|---|---|---|---|---|
| 384th | September 13, 1944 | Me-262 dam(air) | S/Stralsand | P-51 |

0-0-1 air
0-0 ground

**Walker, John H., Jr., Lt.**
328th Ftr Sqn/352nd Ftr Grp

| *Sqn* | *Date* | *Claims* | *Location* | *A/C* |
|---|---|---|---|---|
| 328th | January 30, 1944 | Me-109 dest(air) | Ruhlertwist | P-47 |
| | February 4 | FW-190 dest(air) | Hasselt | P-47 |

2-0-0 air
0-0 ground

**Walker, Robert E., Lt.**
61st Ftr Sqn/56th Ftr Grp

| *Sqn* | *Date* | *Claims* | *Location* | *A/C* |
|---|---|---|---|---|
| 61st | November 18, 1944 | FW-190 dam(air) | E/Hanau | P-47 |
| | January 14, 1945 | Me-109 dest(air) | Rheine | P-47 |

1-0-1 air
0-0 ground

**Wallace, Alton J., Capt.**
486th Ftr Sqn/352nd Ftr Grp

| *Sqn* | *Date* | *Claims* | *Location* | *A/C* |
|---|---|---|---|---|
| 486th | April 15, 1944 | (2)FW-190 dest(air) | NE Vechta | P-51 |
| | April 24 | Do-217 dest(grd) | Neuburg | P-51 |
| | | Ju-88 dest(grd) | Ingolstadt | P-51 |
| | | (4)Ju-88 dam(grd) | Ingolstadt | P-51 |
| | | Me-109 dam(grd) | Neuburg | P-51 |
| | April 25 | Me-109 dest(grd) | Metz | P-51 |
| | August 16 | Me-109 dest(air) | Eisenach | P-51 |

3-0-0 air
3-5 ground

**Wallace, Alvin O., Lt.**
336th Ftr Sqn/4th Ftr Grp

| *Sqn* | *Date* | *Claims* | *Location* | *A/C* |
|---|---|---|---|---|
| 336th | January 1, 1945 | (.5)Me-109 dest(air)* | Ulzen | P-51 |
| | January 16 | FW-190 dest(grd) | Neuhausen | P-51 |

0.5-0-0 air
1-0 ground

* - shared with Lt. G.L. Kesler of the 336th Ftr Sqn

**Wallen, Robert D., Lt.**
362nd Ftr Sqn/357th Ftr Grp

| *Sqn* | *Date* | *Claims* | *Location* | *A/C* |
|---|---|---|---|---|
| 362nd | March 4, 1944 | Me-109 dest(air) | Berlin | P-51 |
| | May 30 | FW-190 dest(grd) | W/Bernburg | P-51 |

1-0-0 air
1-0 ground

**Waller, William, III, LtCol.**
361st Ftr Sqn/356th Ftr Grp

| *Sqn* | *Date* | *Claims* | *Location* | *A/C* |
|---|---|---|---|---|
| 361st | March 6, 1944 | (.5)Me-109 dest(air)* | N/Steinhuder Lake | P-47 |
| | | (.5)Me-109 dam(air)* | N/Steinhuder Lake | P-47 |
| | May 19 | Me-109 dam(air) | Dummer Lake | P-47 |

0.5-0-1.5 air
0-0 ground

* - both shared with Lt. H.C. Leyser of the 361st Ftr Sqn

**Walsh, Earl C., Lt.**
336th Ftr Sqn/4th Ftr Grp

| *Sqn* | *Date* | *Claims* | *Location* | *A/C* |
|---|---|---|---|---|
| 336th | July 7, 1944 | Me-109 dam(air) | Eisleben | P-51 |
| | November 6 | Me-109 prob(air) | Rheine | P-51 |
| | | Me-109 dam(air) | Rheine | P-51 |

0-1-2 air
0-0 ground

**Walsh, Francis T., Capt.**
350th Ftr Sqn/353rd Ftr Grp

| *Sqn* | *Date* | *Claims* | *Location* | *A/C* |
|---|---|---|---|---|
| 350th | January 30, 1944 | Me-110 dest(air) | Vechta | P-47 |
| | February 24 | FW-190 dest(air) | Steinhuder Lake | P-47 |

2-0-0 air
0-0 ground

**Walsh, Jack R., Capt.**
351st Ftr Sqn/353rd Ftr Grp

| *Sqn* | *Date* | *Claims* | *Location* | *A/C* |
|---|---|---|---|---|
| 351st | October 8, 1943 | FW-190 dam(air) | Wilhelmshaven | P-47 |
| | October 10 | (.5)Me-210 dam(air)* | NW Munster | P-47 |

0-0-1.5 air
0-0 ground

* - shared with Lt. W.R. Burkett of the 351st Ftr Sqn

**Walsh, Robert J., Lt.**
354th Ftr Sqn/355th Ftr Grp

| *Sqn* | *Date* | *Claims* | *Location* | *A/C* |
|---|---|---|---|---|
| 354th | February 23, 1945 | Me-109 dest(grd) | Neuburg | P-51 |

0-0-0 air
1-0 ground

**Wanda, Roy A., F/O**
486th Ftr Sqn/352nd Ftr Grp

| *Sqn* | *Date* | *Claims* | *Location* | *A/C* |
|---|---|---|---|---|
| 486th | April 17, 1945 | (2)FW-190 dest(grd) | Plattling | P-51 |
| | | Me-109 dest(grd) | Plattling | P-51 |
| | | (2)FW-190 dam(grd) | Plattling | P-51 |
| | | u/i a/c dam(grd) | Plattling | P-51 |

0-0-0 air
3-3 ground

**Warboys, Richard T., Lt.**
63rd Ftr Sqn/56th Ftr Grp

| *Sqn* | *Date* | *Claims* | *Location* | *A/C* |
|---|---|---|---|---|
| 63rd | September 5, 1944 | Me-109 dest(air) | NE Coblenz | P-47 |
| | | Me-109 dest(grd) | Gelnhausen | P-47 |

1-0-0 air
1-0 ground

**Ward, Bruce C., Capt.**
384th Ftr Sqn/364th Ftr Grp

| *Sqn* | *Date* | *Claims* | *Location* | *A/C* |
|---|---|---|---|---|
| 384th | September 19, 1944 | (.5)Me-109 dest(air)[*] | Dusseldorf | P-51 |
| | | Me-109 prob(air) | Dusseldorf | P-51 |
| | | Me-109 dam(air) | Dusseldorf | P-51 |

0.5-1-1 air
0-0 ground

[*] - shared with Lt. R.L. Stiefvater of the 384th Ftr Sqn

**Ward, Hugh A., Lt.**
335th Ftr Sqn/4th Ftr Grp

| *Sqn* | *Date* | *Claims* | *Location* | *A/C* |
|---|---|---|---|---|
| 335th | March 4, 1944 | Me-109 prob(air) | Berlin | P-51 |

0-1-0 air
0-0 ground

**Ward, Robert W., Capt.**
376th Ftr Sqn/361st Ftr Grp

| *Sqn* | *Date* | *Claims* | *Location* | *A/C* |
|---|---|---|---|---|
| 376th | September 12, 1944 | (.5)Me-109 dest(air)[*] | W/Magdeburg | P-51 |
| | September 27 | FW-190 dam(air) | Eisenach | P-51 |
| | November 27 | Me-109 dest(air) | W/Munster | P-51 |
| | February 8, 1945 | (.5)He-111 dest(air)[**] | Erfurt | P-51 |

2-0-1 air
0-0 ground

[*] - shared with Lt. D.F. Spencer of the 376th Ftr Sqn
[**] - shared with Lt. R. Hobbs of the 376th Ftr Sqn

**Warner, Clarence B., Lt.**
385th Ftr Sqn/364th Ftr Grp

| *Sqn* | *Date* | *Claims* | *Location* | *A/C* |
|---|---|---|---|---|
| 385th | March 8, 1944 | Me-109 dest(air) | Gifhorn | P-38 |

1-0-0 air
0-0 ground

**Warner, George O., Capt.**
385th Ftr Sqn/364th Ftr Grp

| *Sqn* | *Date* | *Claims* | *Location* | *A/C* |
|---|---|---|---|---|
| 385th | February 22, 1945 | (2)Me-262 dam(air) | W/Berlin | P-51 |
| | April 17 | (3)Me-262 dam(grd) | Praha | P-51 |

0-0-2 air
0-3 ground

**Warner, Harry F., Jr., Lt.**
63rd Ftr Sqn/56th Ftr Grp

| *Sqn* | *Date* | *Claims* | *Location* | *A/C* |
|---|---|---|---|---|
| 63rd | April 24, 1944 | Ju-87 dest(grd) | Thalheim | P-47 |
| | | (.25)u/i a/c dam(grd)[*] | Thalheim | P-47 |

0-0-0 air
1-0.25 ground

[*] - shared with Lt. D.W. Marshall, Lt. S.B. Dale, and Lt. A.J. Wisniewski of the 63rd Ftr Sqn

**Warren, Jack R., Capt.**
364th Ftr Sqn/357th Ftr Grp

| *Sqn* | *Date* | *Claims* | *Location* | *A/C* |
|---|---|---|---|---|
| 364th | February 22, 1944 | Me-109 dest(air) | Bernburg | P-51 |
| | March 8 | FW-190 dest(air) | SE Berlin | P-51 |
| | March 16 | (2)Me-110 dest(air) | Augsburg | P-51 |
| | | FW-190 dest(air) | Augsburg | P-51 |

5-0-0 air
0-0 ground

**Warren, Richard B., Lt.**
359th Ftr Sqn/356th Ftr Grp

| *Sqn* | *Date* | *Claims* | *Location* | *A/C* |
|---|---|---|---|---|
| 359th | March 16, 1944 | (.5)Me-109 dest(air)[*] | SE St. Dizier | P-47 |
| | April 1 | (2)Me-410 dest(grd) | Dummer Lake | P-47 |
| | April 23 | (.5)He-111 dam(grd)[**] | Hagenau | P-47 |
| | | (.5)Go-242 dam(grd)[**] | Hagenau | P-47 |

0.5-0-0 air
2-1 ground

[*] - shared with Lt. W.C. O'Barr of the 359th Ftr Sqn
[**] - both shared with Lt. M.M. Clayborne of the 359th Ftr Sqn

**Warren, Willard E., Lt.**
82nd Ftr Sqn/78th Ftr Grp

| *Sqn* | *Date* | *Claims* | *Location* | *A/C* |
|---|---|---|---|---|
| 82nd | September 10, 1944 | Ju-88 dest(grd) | Meinbullen | P-47 |
| | January 14, 1945 | (2)FW-190 dest(air) | Cologne | P-51 |

2-0-0 air
1-0 ground

**Wasil, Edwin E., Lt.**
55th Ftr Sqn/20th Ftr Grp

| *Sqn* | *Date* | *Claims* | *Location* | *A/C* |
|---|---|---|---|---|
| 55th | August 25, 1944 | (2)Do-18 dest(grd)[*] | Parow A/F | P-51 |

0-0-0 air
2-0 ground

**Wasylyk, Stephen, Lt.**
364th Ftr Sqn/357th Ftr Grp

| *Sqn* | *Date* | *Claims* | *Location* | *A/C* |
|---|---|---|---|---|
| 364th | February 28, 1945 | u/i a/c dest(grd) | Lubeck/Blankensee | P-51 |
| | March 24 | Me-109 dest(air) | W/Gutersloh | P-51 |

1-0-0 air
1-0 ground

**Waterman, Lloyd W., Lt.**
335th Ftr Sqn/4th Ftr Grp

| *Sqn* | *Date* | *Claims* | *Location* | *A/C* |
|---|---|---|---|---|
| 335th | March 6, 1944 | Me-110 dest(air) | SW Berlin | P-51 |
| | | Me-110 dam(air) | SW Berlin | P-51 |

1-0-1 air
0-0 ground

**Waters, Frank T., Lt.**
504th Ftr Sqn/339th Ftr Grp

| *Sqn* | *Date* | *Claims* | *Location* | *A/C* |
|---|---|---|---|---|
| 504th | June 7, 1944 | FW-190 dest(grd) | Laval | P-51 |

0-0-0 air
1-0 ground

**Waters, Glen L., Lt.**
367th Ftr Sqn/358th Ftr Grp

| Sqn | Date | Claims | Location | A/C |
|---|---|---|---|---|
| 367th | January 30, 1944 | Me-109 prob(air) | E/Zwolle | P-47 |

0-1-0 air
0-0 ground

**Waters, Phanor B., Lt.**
487th Ftr Sqn/352nd Ftr Grp

| Sqn | Date | Claims | Location | A/C |
|---|---|---|---|---|
| 487th | September 10, 1944 | (2)Ju-52 dest(grd) | Wertheim | P-51 |
| | September 11 | FW-190 dest(air) | Gottingen | P-51 |

1-0-0 air
2-0 ground

**Watkins, Benjamin M., Capt.**
82nd Ftr Sqn/78th Ftr Grp

| Sqn | Date | Claims | Location | A/C |
|---|---|---|---|---|
| 82nd | April 1, 1944 | (.13)Do-217 dest(grd)* | Verdun | P-47 |
| | | (.33)u/i a/c dest(grd)** | Verdun | P-47 |
| | | (.33)u/i a/c dest(grd)** | Verdun | P-47 |
| | | (2)u/i a/c dam(grd) | Verdun | P-47 |
| | April 11 | u/i a/c dam(grd) | Osnabruck | P-47 |
| | April 12 | Ju-87 dest(air) | Sedan | P-47 |
| | | (3)Ju-87 dam(grd) | Sedan | P-47 |
| | May 11 | (.5)Ju-52 dest(grd)@ | Dijon | P-47 |
| | | (3)u/i a/c dam(grd) | Dijon | P-47 |
| | May 12 | FW-190 dest(air) | Mannheim | P-47 |

2-0-0 air
1.3-9 ground

* - shared with Capt. W.L. Boone, Capt. W.E. May, Lt. C.R. Clark, Lt. H.L. Eakes, Lt. J.J. Hockery, Lt. R.V. Hearn, and F/O C.W. DeWitt of the 82nd Ftr Sqn
** - both shared with Capt. W.L. Boone and Lt. C. Webb of the 82nd Ftr Sqn
@ - shared with Lt. W.V. Van Dyk of the 82nd Ftr Sqn

**Watkins, David P., Lt.**
357th Ftr Sqn/355th Ftr Grp

| Sqn | Date | Claims | Location | A/C |
|---|---|---|---|---|
| 357th | February 23, 1945 | Me-163 dam(grd) | Neuburg | P-51 |
| | April 10 | He-111 dest(grd) | Rechlin/Larz | P-51 |
| | April 16 | Me-110 dest(grd) | Bad Aibling | P-51 |
| | | He-111 dest(grd) | Bad Aibling | P-51 |

0-0-0 air
3-1 ground

**Watkins, Robert N., Lt.**
358th Ftr Sqn/355th Ftr Grp

| Sqn | Date | Claims | Location | A/C |
|---|---|---|---|---|
| 358th | July 28, 1944 | Me-109 dam(air) | S/Merseburg | P-51 |

0-0-1 air
0-0 ground

**Watson, Harry J., Jr., Lt.**
79th Ftr Sqn/20th Ftr Grp

| Sqn | Date | Claims | Location | A/C |
|---|---|---|---|---|
| 79th | May 24, 1944 | Me-109 dam(air) | Eberswalde | P-38 |

0-0-1 air
0-0 ground

**Watson, Rodney P., Lt.**
55th Ftr Sqn/20th Ftr Grp

| Sqn | Date | Claims | Location | A/C |
|---|---|---|---|---|
| 55th | April 24, 1944 | Me-109 dest(air) | W/Worms | P-38 |

1-0-0 air
0-0 ground

**Watts, Cecil R., Capt.**
38th Ftr Sqn/55th Ftr Grp

| Sqn | Date | Claims | Location | A/C |
|---|---|---|---|---|
| 38th | February 5, 1944 | Me-109 dam(air) | Chartres | P-38 |
| | June 14 | Me-109 dest(air) | Paris | P-38 |
| | August 24 | Ju-88 dest(grd) | Burg A/F | P-51 |

1-0-1 air
1-0 ground

**Waymire, Harvey R., Lt.**
504th Ftr Sqn/339th Ftr Grp

| Sqn | Date | Claims | Location | A/C |
|---|---|---|---|---|
| 504th | June 15, 1944 | Me-109 dest(air) | Chateaudun | P-51 |

1-0-0 air
0-0 ground

**Weaver, Charles E., Capt.**
362nd Ftr Sqn/357th Ftr Grp

| Sqn | Date | Claims | Location | A/C |
|---|---|---|---|---|
| 362nd | September 19, 1944 | Me-109 dest(air) | S/Zuider Zee | P-51 |
| | November 18 | (2)Me-109 dest(grd) | Mengen A/F | P-51 |
| | November 27 | (2)FW-190 dest(air) | S/Magdeburg | P-51 |
| | | FW-190 prob(air) | S/Magdeburg | P-51 |
| | | FW-190 dam(air) | S/Magdeburg | P-51 |
| | December 23 | Me-109 dest(air) | N/Donauworth | P-51 |
| | January 14, 1945 | Me-109 dest(air) | NW Berlin | P-51 |
| | | FW-190 dest(air) | NW Berlin | P-51 |
| | February 25 | He-111 dest(grd) | Memmingen | P-51 |
| | | FW-190 dam(grd) | Memmingen | P-51 |
| | | Ju-88 dam(grd) | Memmingen | P-51 |
| | March 24 | Me-109 dest(air) | W/Gutersloh | P-51 |
| | April 18 | Me-262 dest(air) | Prague/Ruzny A/F | P-51 |

8-1-1 air
3-2 ground

**Weaver, William J., Lt.**
351st Ftr Sqn/353rd Ftr Grp

| Sqn | Date | Claims | Location | A/C |
|---|---|---|---|---|
| 351st | June 8, 1944 | FW-190 dest(air) | SW Angars | P-47 |
| | | FW-190 dam(air) | SW Angars | P-47 |

1-0-1 air
0-0 ground

**Webb, Calvin, Lt.**
82nd Ftr Sqn/78th Ftr Grp

| Sqn | Date | Claims | Location | A/C |
|---|---|---|---|---|
| 82nd | February 8, 1944 | (2)He-111 dam(grd) | Paris | P-47 |
| | February 11 | FW-190 dam(air) | Rouen | P-47 |
| | April 1 | (.33)u/i a/c dest(grd)* | Verdun | P-47 |
| | | (.33)u/i a/c dest(grd)* | Verdun | P-47 |

0-0-1 air
0.67-2 ground

* - both shared with Capt. W.L. Boone and Lt. B.M. Watkins of the 82nd Ftr Sqn

**Webb, Dallas W., LtCol.**
343rd Ftr Sqn/55th Ftr Grp
HdQts/55th Ftr Grp

| Sqn | Date | Claims | Location | A/C |
|---|---|---|---|---|
| 343rd | November 26, 1943 | Me-210 dest(air) | NE Bremen | P-38 |
| | January 31, 1944 | Me-109 dest(air) | NW Venlo | P-38 |
| HdQts | April 13 | Me-109 dam(air) | Donauworth | P-38 |

2-0-1 air
0-0 ground

**Webb, Dana A., Jr., F/O**
328th Ftr Sqn/352nd Ftr Grp

| Sqn | Date | Claims | Location | A/C |
|---|---|---|---|---|
| 328th | April 16, 1945 | FW-190 dest(grd) | Landau | P-51 |

0-0-0 air
1-0 ground

**Webb, Glenn M., Capt.**
79th Ftr Sqn/20th Ftr Grp

| *Sqn* | *Date* | *Claims* | *Location* | *A/C* |
|---|---|---|---|---|
| 79th | August 5, 1944 | Me-109 dam(air) | Hamburg-Bremen | P-51 |
| | November 2 | Me-109 dest(air) | SW Merseburg | P-51 |

1-0-1 air
0-0 ground

**Webb, Marcell E., Lt.**
358th Ftr Sqn/355th Ftr Grp

| *Sqn* | *Date* | *Claims* | *Location* | *A/C* |
|---|---|---|---|---|
| 358th | September 18, 1944 | Me-109 dam(air) | Warsaw | P-51 |

0-0-1 air
0-0 ground

**Webb, Roy A., Jr., LtCol.**
374th Ftr Sqn/361st Ftr Grp

| *Sqn* | *Date* | *Claims* | *Location* | *A/C* |
|---|---|---|---|---|
| 374th | January 30, 1944 | Me-109 dest(air) | Rheine | P-47 |
| | May 29 | FW-190 dest(air) | Pitka | P-51 |
| | June 13 | Me-109 dest(air) | St. Brieuc | P-51 |
| | June 25 | FW-190 dest(air) | S/Caen | P-51 |
| | June 29 | (5)FW-190 dest(grd) | Oschersleben | P-51 |
| | | FW-190 dam(grd) | Oschersleben | P-51 |

4-0-0 air
5-1 ground

**Weber, Carl W., Lt.**
328th Ftr Sqn/352nd Ftr Grp

| *Sqn* | *Date* | *Claims* | *Location* | *A/C* |
|---|---|---|---|---|
| 328th | April 17, 1945 | (3)Me-109 dest(grd) | Plattling | P-51 |
| | | u/i a/c dest(grd) | Plattling | P-51 |
| | | (2)FW-190 dam(grd) | Plattling | P-51 |

0-0-0 air
4-2 ground

**Weber, Gilman L., Lt.**
364th Ftr Sqn/357th Ftr Grp

| *Sqn* | *Date* | *Claims* | *Location* | *A/C* |
|---|---|---|---|---|
| 364th | November 2, 1944 | FW-190 dam(air) | NW Merseburg | P-51 |
| | March 24, 1945 | Me-109 dest(air) | W/Gutersloh | P-51 |
| | April 19 | (.5)Me-262 dest(air)[*] | S/Dresden | P-51 |

1.5-0-1 air
0-0 ground

[*] - shared with Capt. I.L. McGuire of the 364th Ftr Sqn

**Weber, Herbert, Capt.**
359th Ftr Sqn/356th Ftr Grp

| *Sqn* | *Date* | *Claims* | *Location* | *A/C* |
|---|---|---|---|---|
| 359th | March 15, 1944 | (.5)Me-109 dest(air)[*] | SE Nijmegen | P-47 |
| | April 1 | (.5)Me-410 dam(grd)[**] | Dummer Lake | P-47 |
| | | (.5)Me-410 dam(grd)[**] | Dummer Lake | P-47 |
| | May 19 | Me-109 dest(air) | Steinhuder Lake | P-47 |
| | July 19 | Me-410 dam(grd) | Le Culot | P-47 |

1.5-0-0 air
0-2 ground

[*] - shared with Lt. J.J. Meholic of the 359th Ftr Sqn
[**] - both shared with Lt. J.J. Meholic of the 359th Ftr Sqn

**Wegner, Gordon V., Lt.**
38th Ftr Sqn/55th Ftr Grp

| *Sqn* | *Date* | *Claims* | *Location* | *A/C* |
|---|---|---|---|---|
| 38th | September 10, 1944 | Ju-88 dam(grd) | Kitzingen A/F | P-51 |

0-0-0 air
0-1 ground

**Weidemann, John J., Lt.**
357th Ftr Sqn/355th Ftr Grp

| *Sqn* | *Date* | *Claims* | *Location* | *A/C* |
|---|---|---|---|---|
| 357th | February 23, 1945 | Me-163 dam(grd) | Neuburg | P-51 |
| | April 8 | Me-109 dest(grd) | Ansbach | P-51 |
| | | Me-109 dam(grd) | Ansbach | P-51 |
| | April 16 | FW-190 dest(grd) | SE Germany | P-51 |
| | | (3)FW-190 dam(grd) | SE Germany | P-51 |

0-0-0 air
2-5 ground

**Welch, Billy D., Lt.**
376th Ftr Sqn/361st Ftr Grp

| *Sqn* | *Date* | *Claims* | *Location* | *A/C* |
|---|---|---|---|---|
| 376th | June 20, 1944 | (.5)BV-138 dest(grd)[*] | Putnitz | P-51 |

0-0-0 air
0.5-0 ground

[*] - shared with Lt. D.F. Spencer of the 376th Ftr Sqn

**Welch, Fred S., Lt.**
384th Ftr Sqn/364th Ftr Grp

| *Sqn* | *Date* | *Claims* | *Location* | *A/C* |
|---|---|---|---|---|
| 384th | December 27, 1944 | Me-109 dest(air) | Coblenz | P-51 |

1-0-0 air
0-0 ground

**Welch, Robert E., Capt.**
343rd Ftr Sqn/55th Ftr Grp

| *Sqn* | *Date* | *Claims* | *Location* | *A/C* |
|---|---|---|---|---|
| 343rd | September 13, 1944 | Me-109 dest(air) | Eisenach-Gotha | P-51 |
| | | Me-109 dam(air) | Eisenach-Gotha | P-51 |
| | November 2 | Me-109 dest(air) | Naumberg | P-51 |
| | December 24 | Me-109 dest(air) | S/Duren | P-51 |
| | December 25 | (2)Me-109 dest(air) | W/Coblenz | P-51 |
| | March 21, 1945 | (2)FW-190 dest(grd) | Hopsten A/F | P-51 |
| | | Ju-88 dam(grd) | Rheine | P-51 |
| | April 9 | (2)Me-109 dest(grd) | Furtenfeldbruck | P-51 |
| | | (2)Me-410 dest(grd) | Munich-Brunnthal | P-51 |
| | | Me-262 dest(grd) | Munich-Brunnthal | P-51 |
| | | He-177 dest(grd) | Munich-Brunnthal | P-51 |
| | | Me-262 dam(grd) | Munich-Brunnthal | P-51 |
| | April 10 | (2)He-111 dest(grd) | Burg A/F | P-51 |
| | April 16 | Me-110 dest(grd) | Munich-Brunnthal | P-51 |
| | | Me-410 dest(grd) | Munich-Brunnthal | P-51 |
| | April 17 | FW-190 dest(air) | Kamenz A/F | P-51 |

6-0-1 air
12-2 ground

**Weller, Joel P., Lt.**
360th Ftr Sqn/356th Ftr Grp

| *Sqn* | *Date* | *Claims* | *Location* | *A/C* |
|---|---|---|---|---|
| 360th | February 21, 1945 | (.5)He-111 dam(grd)[*] | S/Nurnberg | P-51 |

0-0-0 air
0-0.5 ground

[*] - shared with Lt. R.S. Ragsdale of the 360th Ftr Sqn

**Wells, Lewis P., Lt.**
334th Ftr Sqn/4th Ftr Grp

| *Sqn* | *Date* | *Claims* | *Location* | *A/C* |
|---|---|---|---|---|
| 334th | February 27, 1945 | Me-109 dest(grd) | Weimar A/F | P-51 |

0-0-0 air
1-0 ground

**Wells, Trent H., Jr., Capt.**
384th Ftr Sqn/364th Ftr Grp

| *Sqn* | *Date* | *Claims* | *Location* | *A/C* |
|---|---|---|---|---|
| 384th | December 23, 1944 | Me-109 dest(air) | Luxembourg | P-51 |
| | December 31 | (2)FW-190 dest(air) | Hamburg | P-51 |

3-0-0 air
0-0 ground

**Wells, William W., Lt.**
55th Ftr Sq/20th Ftr Grp

| Sqn | Date | Claims | Location | A/C |
|---|---|---|---|---|
| 55th | August 25, 1944 | Me-410 dest(grd) | Parow A/F | P-51 |
| | | u/i a/c dest(grd) | Parow A/F | P-51 |
| | | (2)Ju-88 dam(grd) | Parow A/F | P-51 |
| | | u/i a/c dam(grd) | Parow A/F | P-51 |

0-0-0 air
2-3 ground

**Welsh, Stephen J., Lt.**
385th Ftr Sqn/364th Ftr Grp

| Sqn | Date | Claims | Location | A/C |
|---|---|---|---|---|
| 385th | May 21, 1944 | Ju-88 dest(grd) | Schwerin-Luneburg | P-38 |

0-0-0 air
1-0 ground

**Wendt, Eugene H., Lt.**
434th Ftr Sqn/479th Ftr Grp

| Sqn | Date | Claims | Location | A/C |
|---|---|---|---|---|
| 434th | September 28, 1944 | FW-190 dam(air) | W/Halberstadt | P-38 |
| | February 9, 1945 | Me-109 dest(air) | SE Magdeburg | P-51 |
| | | Me-109 dam(air) | SE Magdeburg | P-51 |
| | February 14 | (2)Me-109 dest(air) | SW Berlin | P-51 |
| | March 25 | Me-262 dest(air) | SW Hamburg | P-51 |

4-0-2 air
0-0 ground

**Wensch, Glenn W., Lt.**
486th Ftr Sqn/352nd Ftr Grp

| Sqn | Date | Claims | Location | A/C |
|---|---|---|---|---|
| 486th | September 12, 1944 | Me-109 dest(air) | Kyritz | P-51 |
| | April 16, 1945 | (2)FW-190 dest(grd) | Ganacker | P-51 |
| | April 17 | u/i a/c dest(grd) | Plattling | P-51 |
| | | FW-190 dam(grd) | Plattling | P-51 |
| | | u/i a/c dam(grd) | Plattling | P-51 |

1-0-0 air
3-2 ground

**Werder, Albert B., Lt.**
83rd Ftr Sqn/78th Ftr Grp

| Sqn | Date | Claims | Location | A/C |
|---|---|---|---|---|
| 83rd | March 16, 1944 | FW-190 dam(air) | Chievres | P-47 |

0-0-1 air
0-0 ground

**Werner, Leonard R., Lt.**
334th Ftr Sqn/4th Ftr Grp

| Sqn | Date | Claims | Location | A/C |
|---|---|---|---|---|
| 334th | September 11, 1944 | Me-109 dest(air) | Eisenach-Gotha | P-51 |
| | | FW-190 dam(air) | Eisenach-Gotha | P-51 |
| | October 6 | Me-109 dest(air) | Neuen | P-51 |
| | | FW-190 dam(air) | Neuen | P-51 |

2-0-2 air
0-0 ground

**Werternbaker, George L., LtCol.**
366th Ftr Sqn/358th Ftr Grp

| Sqn | Date | Claims | Location | A/C |
|---|---|---|---|---|
| 366th | January 30, 1944 | Me-109 dam(air) | Lingen | P-47 |

0-0-1 air
0-0 ground

**Wesling, Howard, Lt.**
364th Ftr Sqn/357th Ftr Grp

| Sqn | Date | Claims | Location | A/C |
|---|---|---|---|---|
| 364th | March 2, 1945 | He-111 dam(grd) | E/Magdeburg | P-51 |

0-0-0 air
0-1 ground

**Wesson, Warren M., Capt.**
82nd Ftr Sqn/78th Ftr Grp

| Sqn | Date | Claims | Location | A/C |
|---|---|---|---|---|
| 82nd | November 26, 1943 | FW-190 dest(air) | Beauvais | P-47 |
| | December 30 | Me-109 dest(air) | Reims | P-47 |
| | February 6, 1944 | FW-190 dest(air) | Orleans | P-47 |
| | | (2)He-111 dam(grd) | Orleans | P-47 |
| | February 8 | He-177 dest(grd) | Paris | P-47 |
| | | He-111 dest(grd) | Paris | P-47 |
| | February 10 | FW-190 dest(air) | Osnabruck | P-47 |
| | February 13 | Ju-88 dam(grd) | Bryes-Sud A/F | P-47 |

4-0-0 air
2-3 ground

**West, Rodney C., Lt.**
503rd Ftr Sqn/339th Ftr Grp

| Sqn | Date | Claims | Location | A/C |
|---|---|---|---|---|
| 503rd | June 21, 1944 | Me-410 dest(air) | Stettin | P-51 |

1-0-0 air
0-0 ground

**Westerveld, Robert, Lt.**
354th Ftr Sqn/355th Ftr Grp

| Sqn | Date | Claims | Location | A/C |
|---|---|---|---|---|
| 354th | April 13, 1945 | Me-109 dest(grd) | Husum | P-51 |

0-0-0 air
1-0 ground

**Westfall, Russell B., Capt.**
63rd Ftr Sqn/56th Ftr Grp

| Sqn | Date | Claims | Location | A/C |
|---|---|---|---|---|
| 63rd | February 3, 1944 | Me-109 dam(air) | SE Ruhlertwist | P-47 |

0-0-1 air
0-0 ground

**Westman, Carl E., Lt.**
61st Ftr Sqn/56th Ftr Grp

| Sqn | Date | Claims | Location | A/C |
|---|---|---|---|---|
| 61st | July 20, 1944 | He-111 dam(grd) | Bassenheim A/F | P-47 |
| | August 4 | (.5)u/i a/c dest(grd)* | Salenter Lake | P-47 |

0-0-0 air
0.5-1 ground

* - shared with Maj. G.E. Baker of the 61st Ftr Sqn

**Weston, Gordon L., F/O**
82nd Ftr Sqn/78th Ftr Grp

| Sqn | Date | Claims | Location | A/C |
|---|---|---|---|---|
| 82nd | November 21, 1944 | Me-109 prob(air) | Hanover | P-47 |

0-1-0 air
0-0 ground

**Westover, Donald A., Jr., Lt.**
62nd Ftr Sqn/56th Ftr Grp

| Sqn | Date | Claims | Location | A/C |
|---|---|---|---|---|
| 62nd | December 23, 1944 | (.5)FW-190 dest(air)* | Euskirchen-Bonn | P-47 |
| | | (2)FW-190 dam(air) | Euskirchen-Bonn | P-47 |
| | April 13, 1945 | (2)Do-217 dest(grd) | Eggebeck A/F | P-47 |
| | | FW-190 dest(grd) | Eggebeck A/F | P-47 |
| | | (2)Me-109 dam(grd) | Eggebeck A/F | P-47 |

0.5-0-2 air
3-2 ground

* - shared with Lt. L.F. Geren of the 62nd Ftr Sqn

**Westphal, Lawrence A., Lt.**
364th Ftr Sqn/357th Ftr Grp

| *Sqn* | *Date* | *Claims* | *Location* | *A/C* |
|---|---|---|---|---|
| 364th | March 24, 1945 | Me-109 dest(air) | W/Gutersloh | P-51 |

1-0-0 air
0-0 ground

**Wetmore, Ray S., Maj.**
370th Ftr Sqn/359th Ftr Grp

| *Sqn* | *Date* | *Claims* | *Location* | *A/C* |
|---|---|---|---|---|
| 370th | February 10, 1944 | Me-109 dest(air) | E/Zuider Zee | P-47 |
| | March 4 | (.25)Me-109 dest(air)[*] | Bonn | P-47 |
| | | Me-109 dam(air) | Bonn | P-47 |
| | March 16 | (2)FW-190 dest(air) | Sommesous | P-47 |
| | April 11 | (2)Ju-88 dest(grd) | Volkenrod | P-47 |
| | | Ju-88 dam(grd) | Volkenrod | P-47 |
| | April 22 | FW-190 dest(air) | Hamm | P-47 |
| | April 24 | Me-109 dest(grd) | St. Dizier | P-47 |
| | | (.33)u/i a/c dest(grd)[**] | St. Dizier | P-47 |
| | | Me-109 dam(grd) | St. Dizier | P-47 |
| | May 19 | (2)Me-109 dest(air) | Stendal | P-51 |
| | May 29 | (2)FW-190 dest(air) | Stettin | P-51 |
| | November 2 | (2)Me-109 dest(air) | Erfurt-Weimar | P-51 |
| | November 27 | (3)Me-109 dest(air) | SE Hanover | P-51 |
| | December 31 | (1.5)Me-109 dest(air)[@] | Hanover | P-51 |
| | January 1, 1945 | Me-109 dest(air) | Luneburg | P-51 |
| | January 14 | (4.5)FW-190 dest(air)[@@] | Vorden A/F | P-51 |
| | March 15 | Me-163 dest(air) | Wittenberg | P-51 |

21.25-0-1 air
3.33-2 ground

* - shared with Maj. J.B. Murphy, Lt. P.H. Bateman, and Lt. A.C. Porter of the 370th Ftr Sqn
** - shared with Capt. S.R. Smith of HdQts, 359th Ftr Grp, and Lt. P.H. Bateman of the 370th Ftr Sqn
@ - shared with Lt. W.J. Rueschenberg of the 370th Ftr Sqn
@@ - shared with Lt. W.J. Rueschenberg of the 370th Ftr Sqn

**Whalen, Edmund D., Lt.**
334th Ftr Sqn/4th Ftr Grp

| *Sqn* | *Date* | *Claims* | *Location* | *A/C* |
|---|---|---|---|---|
| 334th | January 14, 1944 | (1.5)FW-190 dest(air)[*] | Soissons | P-47 |
| | January 29 | Me-109 dest(air) | Aachen | P-47 |
| | March 6 | Me-110 dest(air) | Nienburg | P-51 |

3.5-0-0 air
0-0 ground

* - shared with Lt. A. Rafalovich of the 334th Ftr Sqn

**Whalen, William E., Lt.**
334th Ftr Sqn/4th Ftr Grp
2nd Scouting Force

| *Sqn* | *Date* | *Claims* | *Location* | *A/C* |
|---|---|---|---|---|
| 334th | August 18, 1944 | Me-109 dest(air) | Beauvais | P-51 |
| 2nd | November 26 | (3)FW-190 dest(air) | S/Hanover | P-51 |
| | February 9, 1945 | (2)Me-109 dest(air) | Dessau | P-51 |
| | | Me-109 prob(air) | Dessau | P-51 |
| | February 22 | (2)FW-190 dest(grd) | Thale A/F | P-51 |
| | | (3)FW-190 dam(grd) | Thale A/F | P-51 |

6-1-0 air
2-3 ground

**Whinnem, Donald Y., Lt.**
486th Ftr Sqn/352nd Ftr Grp

| *Sqn* | *Date* | *Claims* | *Location* | *A/C* |
|---|---|---|---|---|
| 486th | February 10, 1944 | Me-109 dam(air) | Enschede | P-47 |
| | April 13 | He-111 dest(grd) | S/Stuttgart | P-51 |
| | April 24 | (2)Ju-88 dest(grd) | Ingolstadt | P-51 |
| | | (6)Ju-88 dam(grd) | Ingolstadt | P-51 |
| | June 8 | (2)FW-190 dest(grd) | Le Mans | P-51 |
| | June 21 | Me-109 dest(air) | E/Warsaw | P-51 |
| | August 5 | Me-109 prob(air) | S/Hamburg | P-51 |
| | | Me-109 dam(air) | S/Hamburg | P-51 |

1-1-2 air
5-6 ground

**Whisner, William T., Capt.**
487th Ftr Sqn/352nd Ftr Grp

| *Sqn* | *Date* | *Claims* | *Location* | *A/C* |
|---|---|---|---|---|
| 487th | January 29, 1944 | FW-190 dest(air) | Malmedy | P-47 |
| | April 9 | (2)Ju-88 dest(grd) | Diepholz | P-47 |
| | April 30 | FW-190 dest(air) | Clermont-Ferrand | P-51 |
| | May 12 | Ju-52 dest(grd) | Frankenhausen | P-51 |
| | May 29 | FW-190 dest(air) | Gustrow | P-51 |
| | May 30 | (.5)Me-109 dest(air)[*] | Magdeburg | P-51 |
| | November 2 | Me-109 dest(air) | Merseburg | P-51 |
| | November 21 | (5)FW-190 dest(air) | SW Merseburg | P-51 |
| | | (2)FW-190 prob(air) | SW Merseburg | P-51 |
| | November 27 | (2)Me-109 dest(air) | Hameln | P-51 |
| | January 1, 1945 | (2)Me-109 dest(air) | N/Liege | P-51 |
| | | (2)FW-190 dest(air) | N/Liege | P-51 |

15.5-2-0 air
3-0 ground

* - shared with Maj. G.E. Preddy of the 487th Ftr Sqn

**White, Alvin S., Capt.**
354th Ftr Sqn/355th Ftr Grp

| *Sqn* | *Date* | *Claims* | *Location* | *A/C* |
|---|---|---|---|---|
| 354th | June 20, 1944 | Me-410 dam(air) | Bergen | P-51 |
| | April 4, 1945 | FW-190 dest(air) | Ludwigslust | P-51 |
| | April 9 | (.5)He-111 dest(grd)[*] | Memmingen | P-51 |

1-0-1 air
0.5-0 ground

* - shared with LtCol. G.M. Graham of the 354th Ftr Sqn

**White, Ernest J., Jr., LtCol.**
359th Ftr Sqn/356th Ftr Grp

| *Sqn* | *Date* | *Claims* | *Location* | *A/C* |
|---|---|---|---|---|
| 359th | November 29, 1943 | Me-109 dest(air) | NE Meppel | P-47 |
| | January 11, 1944 | Me-109 prob(air) | Lingen | P-47 |
| | February 10 | (.33)FW-190 dest(air)[*] | Meppen | P-47 |
| | February 21 | Me-109 dam(air) | Hanover | P-47 |

1.33-1-1 air
0-0 ground

* - shared with Lt. R.D. Bradshaw and Lt. G.W. Engel of the 359th Ftr Sqn

**White, Fred, Lt.**
83rd Ftr Sqn/78th Ftr Grp

| *Sqn* | *Date* | *Claims* | *Location* | *A/C* |
|---|---|---|---|---|
| 83rd | April 30, 1944 | (.5)Me-109 dest(air)[*] | Dreux | P-47 |
| | May 19 | Me-109 dest(air) | Lingen | P-47 |
| | May 28 | (.5)Me-109 dest(air)[**] | Gardelegen | P-47 |

2-0-0 air
0-0 ground

* - shared with Lt. W.M. McDermott of the 83rd Ftr Sqn
** - shared with Lt. W.M. McDermott of the 83rd Ftr Sqn

**White, Henry W., Jr., Capt.**
328th Ftr Sqn/352nd Ftr Grp

| *Sqn* | *Date* | *Claims* | *Location* | *A/C* |
|---|---|---|---|---|
| 328th | May 28, 1944 | FW-190 dest(air) | W/Magdeburg | P-51 |
| | July 18 | Me-109 dest(air) | Wismar | P-51 |

2-0-0 air
0-0 ground

**White, James N., Lt.**
487th Ftr Sqn/352nd Ftr Grp

| *Sqn* | *Date* | *Claims* | *Location* | *A/C* |
|---|---|---|---|---|
| 487th | March 18, 1945 | Me-109 dest(air) | E/Oder | P-51 |
| | April 17 | (2)Me-109 dest(grd) | Plattling | P-51 |
| | | FW-190 dest(grd) | Plattling | P-51 |
| | | Me-109 dam(grd) | Plattling | P-51 |
| | | FW-190 dam(grd) | Plattling | P-51 |

1-0-0 air
3-2 ground

**White, John C., Lt.**
338th Ftr Sqn/55th Ftr Grp

| *Sqn* | *Date* | *Claims* | *Location* | *A/C* |
|---|---|---|---|---|
| 338th | April 10, 1945 | Ar-234 dest(grd) | Burg A/F | P-51 |
| | April 16 | Me-109 dest(grd) | N/Landshut | P-51 |

0-0-0 air
2-0 ground

**White, Raymond S., Capt.**
376th Ftr Sqn/352nd Ftr Grp

| *Sqn* | *Date* | *Claims* | *Location* | *A/C* |
|---|---|---|---|---|
| 376th | February 22, 1944 | (2)FW-190 dam(air) | Cleve | P-47 |
| | July 7 | Me-109 dest(air) | Wittenburg | P-51 |
| | | FW-190 dest(air) | Wittenburg | P-51 |

2-0-2 air
0-0 ground

**White, Richard E., Capt.**
385th Ftr Sqn/364th Ftr Grp

| *Sqn* | *Date* | *Claims* | *Location* | *A/C* |
|---|---|---|---|---|
| 385th | February 25, 1945 | (.5)Ar-234 dest(air)* | Steinhuder Lake | P-51 |
| | April 17 | FW-200 dam(grd) | Karlsbad | P-51 |

0.5-0-0 air
0-1 ground

* - shared with Lt. E. Murphy of the 385th Ftr Sqn

**White, Richard M., Lt.**
357th Ftr Sqn/355th Ftr Grp

| *Sqn* | *Date* | *Claims* | *Location* | *A/C* |
|---|---|---|---|---|
| 357th | November 18, 1944 | Me-262 dam(grd) | Leipheim | P-51 |
| | March 22, 1945 | He-111 dest(grd) | Memmingen | P-51 |
| | | He-111 dam(grd) | Memmingen | P-51 |

0-0-0 air
1-2 ground

**White, Robert M., Lt.**
354th Ftr Sqn/355th Ftr Grp

| *Sqn* | *Date* | *Claims* | *Location* | *A/C* |
|---|---|---|---|---|
| 354th | September 11, 1944 | (1.5)FW-190 dest(grd)* | Marburg | P-51 |
| | February 22, 1945 | (2)Me-410 dest(grd) | Halberstadt | P-51 |
| | | FW-190 dam(grd) | Halberstadt | P-51 |

0-0-0 air
3.5-1 ground

* - shared with Lt. F.W. Schultz of the 354th Ftr Sqn

**Whitelaw, Richard S., Capt.**
503rd Ftr Sqn/339th Ftr Grp

| *Sqn* | *Date* | *Claims* | *Location* | *A/C* |
|---|---|---|---|---|
| 503rd | May 19, 1944 | (3)u/i a/c dam(grd) | Steinhuder Lake | P-51 |
| | May 21 | u/i a/c dam(grd) | Pelenz A/F | P-51 |
| | May 24 | (.5)FW-190 dest(air)* | NW Berlin | P-51 |
| | June 8 | FW-190 dest(air) | Rennes | P-51 |

1.5-0-0 air
0-4 ground

* - shared with Maj. H.W. Scruggs of the 503rd Ftr Sqn

**Whiteside, Walker L., Lt.**
77th Ftr Sqn/20th Ftr Grp

| *Sqn* | *Date* | *Claims* | *Location* | *A/C* |
|---|---|---|---|---|
| 77th | January 29, 1944 | Me-109 dest(air) | SW Frankfurt | P-38 |
| | | (.5)Me-210 dest(air)* | SW Frankfurt | P-38 |
| | April 8 | (4)Ju-88 dam(grd) | Salzwedel | P-38 |

1.5-0-0 air
0-4 ground

* - shared with Maj. R.L. Ott of the 79th Ftr Sqn, 20th Ftr Grp

**Whiting, Edmund J., Lt.**
328th Ftr Sqn/352nd Ftr Grp

| *Sqn* | *Date* | *Claims* | *Location* | *A/C* |
|---|---|---|---|---|
| 328th | May 8, 1944 | Me-109 prob(air) | Unter Lusz | P-51 |

0-1-0 air
0-0 ground

**Whitley, Edgar D., Lt.**
63rd Ftr Sqn/56th Ftr Grp

| *Sqn* | *Date* | *Claims* | *Location* | *A/C* |
|---|---|---|---|---|
| 63rd | August 17, 1943 | Me-110 dest(air) | Ans | P-47 |
| | | Me-110 dam(air) | Ans | P-47 |
| | August 19 | Me-109 dest(air) | Walcheren Island | P-47 |

2-0-1 air
0-0 ground

**Whitlow, Robert V., Capt.**
2nd Scouting Force

| *Sqn* | *Date* | *Claims* | *Location* | *A/C* |
|---|---|---|---|---|
| 2nd | November 26, 1944 | FW-190 dest(air) | S/Hanover | P-51 |
| | | FW-190 prob(air) | S/Hanover | P-51 |

1-1-0 air
0-0 ground

**Whitmore, Harold E., Lt.**
361st Ftr Sqn/356th Ftr Grp

| *Sqn* | *Date* | *Claims* | *Location* | *A/C* |
|---|---|---|---|---|
| 361st | October 7, 1944 | Ju-88 dest(grd) | Fritzlar | P-47 |
| | | (2.5)Ju-88 dam(grd)* | Fritzlar | P-47 |
| | November 26 | Me-109 dest(air) | Osnabruck-Dummer Lake | P-51 |
| | February 14, 1945 | (2)FW-190 dam(air) | S/Chemnitz | P-51 |
| | February 21 | Me-262 dest(air) | Stettin | P-51 |

2-0-2 air
1-2.5 ground

* - shared with Capt. R.J. Upp of the 361st Ftr Sqn

**Whitney, Emerson H., Lt.**
357th Ftr Sqn/355th Ftr Grp

| *Sqn* | *Date* | *Claims* | *Location* | *A/C* |
|---|---|---|---|---|
| 357th | April 16, 1945 | (1.5)Me-109 dest(grd)* | SE Germany | P-51 |

0-0-0 air
1.5-0 ground

* - shared with Lt. F.E. Gelsone of the 357th Ftr Sqn

**Whitney, James B., Lt.**
486th Ftr Sqn/352nd Ftr Grp

| *Sqn* | *Date* | *Claims* | *Location* | *A/C* |
|---|---|---|---|---|
| 486th | April 17, 1945 | Me-109 dest(grd) | Plattling | P-51 |
| | | Fi-156 dest(grd) | Plattling | P-51 |
| | | Me-109 dam(grd) | Plattling | P-51 |

0-0-0 air
2-1 ground

**Whitson, Richard N., Lt.**
361st Ftr Sqn/356th Ftr Grp

| *Sqn* | *Date* | *Claims* | *Location* | *A/C* |
|---|---|---|---|---|
| 361st | January 14, 1945 | FW-190 dam(air) | SW Dummer Lake | P-51 |

0-0-1 air
0-0 ground

**Wicker, Samuel J., Maj.**
383rd Ftr Sqn/364th Ftr Grp

| *Sqn* | *Date* | *Claims* | *Location* | *A/C* |
|---|---|---|---|---|
| 383rd | May 22, 1944 | (2)FW-190 dest(air) | SW Kiel | P-38 |
| | August 15 | Me-109 dest(air) | Frankfurt | P-51 |
| | December 31 | (4)FW-190 dest(air) | SW Hamburg | P-51 |

7-0-0 air
0-0 ground

**Wiehe, Robert K., Lt.**
351st Ftr Sqn/353rd Ftr Grp

| *Sqn* | *Date* | *Claims* | *Location* | *A/C* |
|---|---|---|---|---|
| 351st | November 27, 1944 | Me-109 dest(air) | NE Steinhuder Lk. | P-51 |
| | April 16, 1945 | He-111 dest(grd) | Reichersberg | P-51 |
| | | FW-190 dest(grd) | Reichersberg | P-51 |
| | | Me-109 dest(grd) | Reichersberg | P-51 |
| | | He-111 dam(grd) | Reichersberg | P-51 |

1-0-0 air
3-1 ground

**Wiens, Maynard J., Capt.**
338th Ftr Sqn/55th Ftr Grp

| *Sqn* | *Date* | *Claims* | *Location* | *A/C* |
|---|---|---|---|---|
| 338th | November 26, 1944 | FW-190 dest(grd) | Vorden A/F | P-51 |
| | | (2)FW-190 dam(grd) | Vorden A/F | P-51 |

0-0-0 air
1-2 ground

**Wiggin, Pierce L., Lt.**
336th Ftr Sqn/4th Ftr Grp

| *Sqn* | *Date* | *Claims* | *Location* | *A/C* |
|---|---|---|---|---|
| 336th | August 24, 1944 | Ju-52 dest(grd) | NE Nordhausen | P-51 |

0-0-0 air
1-0 ground

**Wiggins, Howard E., Capt.**
361st Ftr Sqn/356th Ftr Grp

| *Sqn* | *Date* | *Claims* | *Location* | *A/C* |
|---|---|---|---|---|
| 361st | June 8, 1944 | (.5)FW-190 dest(air)* | Beauvais/Nivillers | P-47 |
| | | (.5)FW-190 dest(grd)** | Beauvais/Nivillers | P-47 |
| | August 4 | (2)Me-109 dest(air) | Bremen-Hamburg | P-47 |
| | November 25 | FW-190 dest(grd) | Zwickau | P-51 |
| | | (3)FW-190 dam(grd) | Zwickau | P-51 |
| | November 26 | (2)FW-190 dest(air) | Osnabruck-Dummer Lake | P-51 |

4.5-0-0 air
1.5-3 ground

* - shared with Lt. G.L. Yoakum of the 361st Ftr Sqn
** - shared with Capt. D.B. Clayton of the 361st Ftr Sqn

**Wilcox, Richard H., Lt.**
504th Ftr Sqn/339th Ftr Grp

| *Sqn* | *Date* | *Claims* | *Location* | *A/C* |
|---|---|---|---|---|
| 504th | July 7, 1944 | (2)Me-109 dest(air) | Eisleben | P-51 |

2-0-0 air
0-0 ground

**Wiley, James H., Lt.**
338th Ftr Sqn/55th Ftr Grp

| *Sqn* | *Date* | *Claims* | *Location* | *A/C* |
|---|---|---|---|---|
| 338th | April 16, 1945 | He-111 dest(grd) | N/Landshut | P-51 |
| | April 17 | FW-190 dam(air) | Dresden | P-51 |

0-0-1 air
1-0 ground

**Wiley, Walter W., F/O**
370th Ftr Sqn/359th Ftr Grp

| *Sqn* | *Date* | *Claims* | *Location* | *A/C* |
|---|---|---|---|---|
| 370th | July 21, 1944 | Ju-88 dest(grd) | N/Landsberg | P-51 |
| | | (10)Ju-88 dam(grd) | N/Landsberg | P-51 |

0-0-0 air
1-10 ground

**Wilkerson, Samuel C., Jr., Capt.**
376th Ftr Sqn/361st Ftr Grp

| *Sqn* | *Date* | *Claims* | *Location* | *A/C* |
|---|---|---|---|---|
| 376th | June 7, 1944 | He-177 dest(air) | Vendome | P-51 |
| | June 20 | He-111 dest(grd) | Putnitz | P-51 |
| | August 4 | (2)Ju-88 dest(grd) | Anklam | P-51 |

1-0-0 air
3-0 ground

**Wilkerson, William F., Capt.**
62nd Ftr Sqn/56th Ftr Grp

| *Sqn* | *Date* | *Claims* | *Location* | *A/C* |
|---|---|---|---|---|
| 62nd | September 5, 1944 | He-111 dest(grd) | Limburg | P-47 |
| | October 5 | (2)He-111 dam(grd) | S/Geseke | P-47 |
| | | Me-109 dam(grd) | S/Geseke | P-47 |
| | November 18 | FW-190 dest(air) | E/Hanau | P-47 |
| | December 4 | He-111 dest(grd) | Neuburg | P-47 |
| | April 10, 1945 | Me-262 dam(air) | Muritz Lake | P-47 |
| | | (2)He-111 dest(grd) | Rechlin | P-47 |
| | | He-111 dam(grd) | Rechlin | P-47 |

1-0-1 air
4-4 ground

**Wilkes, Henry O., Lt.**
357th Ftr Sqn/355th Ftr Grp

| *Sqn* | *Date* | *Claims* | *Location* | *A/C* |
|---|---|---|---|---|
| 357th | November 2, 1944 | FW-190 dest(air) | S/Wernigerode A/F | P-51 |

1-0-0 air
0-0 ground

**Wilkins, John K., Jr., Capt.**
436th Ftr Sqn/479th Ftr Grp
2nd Scouting Force

| *Sqn* | *Date* | *Claims* | *Location* | *A/C* |
|---|---|---|---|---|
| 2nd | March 1, 1945 | Me-262 dest(air) | Ingolstadt | P-51 |

1-0-0 air
0-0 ground

**Wilkinson, James W., Capt.**
334th Ftr Sqn/ 4th Ftr Grp
82nd Ftr Sqn/78th Ftr Grp

| *Sqn* | *Date* | *Claims* | *Location* | *A/C* |
|---|---|---|---|---|
| 82nd | December 1, 1943 | Me-109 dest(air) | Eupen | P-47 |
| | February 6, 1944 | FW-190 dest(air) | Orleans | P-47 |
| | | (.5)He-111 dam(grd)* | Orleans | P-47 |
| | | (.5)Ju-52 dam(grd)* | Orleans | P-47 |
| | February 8 | (2)He-111 dam(grd) | Paris | P-47 |
| | February 20 | Me-109 dest(air) | Coblenz | P-47 |
| | March 6 | FW-190 dest(air) | Barenburg | P-47 |
| | March 30 | Glider dam(grd) | Wesel | P-47 |
| | April 5 | Ju-188 dam(grd) | Cambrai | P-47 |
| | April 11 | Ju-88 dest(grd) | Rheine | P-47 |
| | | (2)Ju-88 dam(grd) | Rheine | P-47 |
| | April 12 | (2)Me-109 dam(grd) | Florennes | P-47 |
| | May 11 | (.5)u/i a/c dest(grd)** | Dijon | P-47 |
| | | (2)u/i a/c dam(grd) | Dijon | P-47 |
| | | Go-242 dam(grd) | Dijon | P-47 |
| | May 12 | FW-190 dest(air) | Coblenz | P-47 |
| | May 19 | FW-190 dest(air) | Dummer Lake | P-47 |
| | | FW-190 dam(air) | Dummer Lake | P-47 |
| | May 25 | (.5)FW-190 dest(grd)@ | Metz | P-47 |
| | May 29 | FW-190 dam(grd) | Twente/Enschede | P-47 |

6-0-1 air
2-13 ground

* - both shared with Lt. D.E. Ludwig of the 82nd Ftr Sqn
** - shared with Lt. W.V. Van Dyk of the 82nd Ftr Sqn
@ - shared with Lt. R.E. Wilkinson of the 82nd Ftr Sqn

**Wilkinson, John C., Lt.**
374th Ftr Sqn/361st Ftr Grp

| *Sqn* | *Date* | *Claims* | *Location* | *A/C* |
|---|---|---|---|---|
| 374th | November 26, 1944 | FW-190 dest(air) | Wittingen | P-51 |
| | | FW-190 dam(air) | Wittingen | P-51 |

1-0-1 air
0-0 ground

**Wilkinson, Ruben E., Lt.**
82nd Ftr Sqn/78th Ftr Grp

| *Sqn* | *Date* | *Claims* | *Location* | *A/C* |
|---|---|---|---|---|
| 82nd | May 25, 1944 | (.5)FW-190 dest(grd)* | Metz | P-47 |

0-0-0 air
0.5-0 ground

* - shared with Capt. J.W. Wilkinson of the 82nd Ftr Sqn

**Williams, Bailey A., Capt.**
434th Ftr Sqn/479th Ftr Grp

| *Sqn* | *Date* | *Claims* | *Location* | *A/C* |
|---|---|---|---|---|
| 434th | July 5, 1944 | Ju-88 dam(grd) | Cognac/Chateaubernard | P-38 |
| | September 5 | (2)Do-217 dest(grd) | Ettinghausen | P-38 |

0-0-0 air
2-1 ground

**Williams, Benjamin G., Lt.**
357th Ftr Sqn/355th Ftr Grp

| *Sqn* | *Date* | *Claims* | *Location* | *A/C* |
|---|---|---|---|---|
| 357th | November 2, 1944 | (2)u/i a/c dest(grd) | Wernigerode A/F | P-51 |

0-0-0 air
2-0 ground

**Williams, Calvert L., Capt.**
362nd Ftr Sqn/357th Ftr Grp

| *Sqn* | *Date* | *Claims* | *Location* | *A/C* |
|---|---|---|---|---|
| 362nd | February 20, 1944 | Me-109 dest(air) | Leipzig | P-51 |
| | March 6 | (.5)Me-110 dest(air)* | SW Berlin | P-51 |
| | April 11 | FW-190 dam(air) | N/Magdeburg | P-51 |
| | April 24 | Me-109 dest(air) | NW Munich | P-51 |
| | May 27 | FW-190 dam(air) | N/Strasbourg | P-51 |
| | July 1 | Me-109 dest(air) | E/St. Quentin | P-51 |
| | August 28 | Ju-52 dest(grd) | Trier | P-51 |
| | September 18 | Me-109 prob(air) | Ijsselstein | P-51 |

3.5-1-2 air
1-0 ground

* - shared with Lt. K.E. Hagen of the 362nd Ftr Sqn

**Williams, Clarence T., Capt.**
38th Ftr Sqn/55th Ftr Grp

| *Sqn* | *Date* | *Claims* | *Location* | *A/C* |
|---|---|---|---|---|
| 38th | April 9, 1945 | (2)FW-190 dest(grd) | Munich-Brunnthal | P-51 |
| | | (2)FW-190 dam(grd) | Munich-Brunnthal | P-51 |
| | April 16 | Me-109 dam(grd) | Bad Aibling | P-51 |
| | | u/i a/c dam(grd) | Bad Aibling | P-51 |

0-0-0 air
2-4 ground

**Williams, David R., Lt.**
364th Ftr Sqn/357th Ftr Grp

| *Sqn* | *Date* | *Claims* | *Location* | *A/C* |
|---|---|---|---|---|
| 364th | January 14, 1945 | FW-190 dest(air) | W/Berlin | P-51 |
| | March 2 | (2)He-111 dest(grd) | E/Magdeburg | P-51 |
| | | (8)He-111 dam(grd) | E/Magdeburg | P-51 |
| | | u/i a/c dam(grd) | E/Magdeburg | P-51 |

1-0-0 air
2-9 ground

**Williams, David W., Lt.**
384th Ftr Sqn/364th Ftr Grp

| *Sqn* | *Date* | *Claims* | *Location* | *A/C* |
|---|---|---|---|---|
| 384th | June 25, 1944 | Me-109 prob(air) | E/Blois | P-38 |

0-1-0 air
0-0 ground

**Williams, Gene L., Lt.**
55th Ftr Sqn/20th Ftr Grp

| *Sqn* | *Date* | *Claims* | *Location* | *A/C* |
|---|---|---|---|---|
| 55th | April 10, 1945 | (4)Ju-88 dest(grd) | Berlin | P-51 |
| | | (4)Ju-88 dam(grd) | Berlin | P-51 |

0-0-0 air
4-4 ground

**Williams, James H., Lt.**
360th Ftr Sqn/356th Ftr Grp

| *Sqn* | *Date* | *Claims* | *Location* | *A/C* |
|---|---|---|---|---|
| 360th | August 4, 1944 | Me-109 dest(air) | S/Hamburg | P-47 |

1-0-0 air
0-0 ground

**Williams, Joseph R., Maj.**
354th Ftr Sqn/355th Ftr Grp
360th Ftr Sqn/356th Ftr Grp

| *Sqn* | *Date* | *Claims* | *Location* | *A/C* |
|---|---|---|---|---|
| 360th | March 8, 1944 | Me-109 dest(air) | NW Lingen | P-47 |

1-0-0 air
0-0 ground

**Williams, Kenneth S., Lt.**
486th Ftr Sqn/352nd Ftr Grp

| *Sqn* | *Date* | *Claims* | *Location* | *A/C* |
|---|---|---|---|---|
| 486th | February 20, 1944 | Me-109 dest(air) | Charleroi | P-47 |
| | April 13 | He-111 dam(grd) | S/Stuttgart | P-51 |

1-0-0 air
0-1 ground

**Williams, Kenneth T., Lt.**
343rd Ftr Sqn/55th Ftr Grp

| *Sqn* | *Date* | *Claims* | *Location* | *A/C* |
|---|---|---|---|---|
| 343rd | September 10, 1944 | He-111 dest(grd) | NE Augsburg | P-51 |
| | | Ju-88 dest(grd) | NE Augsburg | P-51 |

0-0-0 air
2-0 ground

**Williams, Monroe Q., Lt.**
351st Ftr Sqn/353rd Ftr Grp

| *Sqn* | *Date* | *Claims* | *Location* | *A/C* |
|---|---|---|---|---|
| 351st | August 27, 1944 | Me-109 dest(grd) | W/Metz | P-47 |

0-0-0 air
1-0 ground

**Williams, Morris C., Lt.**
376th Ftr Sqn/361st Ftr Grp

| *Sqn* | *Date* | *Claims* | *Location* | *A/C* |
|---|---|---|---|---|
| 376th | March 6, 1944 | FW-190 dest(air) | NW Dummer Lake | P-47 |
| | May 24 | Me-109 dest(air) | Berlin | P-51 |

2-0-0 air
0-0 ground

**Williams, Sumner C., Lt.**
354th Ftr Sqn/355th Ftr Grp

| *Sqn* | *Date* | *Claims* | *Location* | *A/C* |
|---|---|---|---|---|
| 354th | June 20, 1944 | (.5)Me-410 dest(air)* | Rugen | P-51 |
| | July 8 | Me-109 dest(grd) | SW Chalons | P-51 |
| | | Me-410 dest(grd) | SW Chalons | P-51 |
| | | Me-410 dam(grd) | SW Chalons | P-51 |

0.5-0-0 air
2-1 ground

* - shared with Lt. H.M. Huish of the 354th Ftr Grp

**Williams, Terrence M., Capt.**
77th Ftr Sqn/20th Ftr Grp

| *Sqn* | *Date* | *Claims* | *Location* | *A/C* |
|---|---|---|---|---|
| 77th | February 20, 1944 | FW-190 dest(air) | Brunswick | P-38 |
| | | (.5)Me-109 dest(air)* | Brunswick | P-38 |
| | | FW-190 dam(air) | Brunswick | P-38 |
| | | 1.5-0-1 air | | |
| | | 0-0 ground | | |

* - shared with Lt. C.C. Arthaud of the 77th Ftr Sqn

**Williams, Warren H., Lt.**
336th Ftr Sqn/4th Ftr Grp

| *Sqn* | *Date* | *Claims* | *Location* | *A/C* |
|---|---|---|---|---|
| 336th | September 25, 1944 | Ju-88 dest(grd) | Lippspringe | P-51 |
| | | 0-0-0 air | | |
| | | 1-0 ground | | |

**Williamson, Brady C., Capt.**
354th Ftr Sqn/355th Ftr Grp

| *Sqn* | *Date* | *Claims* | *Location* | *A/C* |
|---|---|---|---|---|
| 354th | March 20, 1944 | FW-190 dam(air) | Coxyde | P-51 |
| | March 28 | u/i a/c dam(grd) | Dijon | P-51 |
| | April 5 | W-34 dest(air) | Landsberg | P-51 |
| | | (.5)FW-44 dest(air)* | Landsberg | P-51 |
| | | (.2)Do-217 dest(air)** | Landsberg | P-51 |
| | | Do-217 dam(grd) | Landsberg | P-51 |
| | | FW-44 dam(grd) | Landsberg | P-51 |
| | April 13 | (2)Do-217 dest(grd) | Oberpfaffenhofen | P-51 |
| | | Do-217 dam(grd) | Oberpfaffenhofen | P-51 |
| | | u/i a/c dam(grd) | Oberpfaffenhofen | P-51 |
| | September 11 | FW-190 dest(grd) | S/Kassel | P-51 |
| | September 27 | FW-190 dest(grd) | Eschwege | P-51 |
| | | 1.7-0-1 air | | |
| | | 4-5 ground | | |

* - shared with Lt. R.E. Woody of the 354th Ftr Sqn
** - shared with Capt. C.G. Johnston, Capt. W.J. Koraleski, Lt. H.W. Brown, and Lt. J.E. Duffy of the 354th Ftr Sqn

**Williamson, Felix D., Maj.**
62nd Ftr Sqn/56th Ftr Grp

| *Sqn* | *Date* | *Claims* | *Location* | *A/C* |
|---|---|---|---|---|
| 62nd | November 29, 1943 | (.5)FW-190 dest(air)* | S/Oldenburg | P-47 |
| | December 22 | Me-109 dest(air) | W/Rheims | P-47 |
| | March 8, 1944 | FW-190 dest(air) | Minden | P-47 |
| | March 16 | FW-190 dest(air) | St. Dizier | P-47 |
| | April 20 | (.5)Ju-88 dest(air)** | NE Paris | P-47 |
| | December 23 | Me-109 dest(air) | Euskirchen | P-47 |
| | | FW-190 dest(air) | Euskirchen | P-47 |
| | January 14, 1945 | (4)Me-109 dest(air) | N/Burg | P-47 |
| | | FW-190 dest(air) | N/Burg | P-47 |
| | February 3 | FW-190 dest(air) | Berlin | P-47 |
| | | Me-109 dest(air) | Berlin | P-47 |
| | | FW-190 dam(air) | Berlin | P-47 |
| | | 13-0-1 air | | |
| | | 0-0 ground | | |

* - shared with LtCol. D.C. Schilling of HdQts, 56th Ftr Grp
** - shared with Lt. W.A. McClure of the 62nd Ftr Sqn

**Willis, Donald K., Maj.**
335th Ftr Sqn/4th Ftr Grp
HdQts/67th Ftr Wg

| *Sqn* | *Date* | *Claims* | *Location* | *A/C* |
|---|---|---|---|---|
| 67th | April 10, 1944 | u/i a/c dest(air) | Rotterdam | P-38 |
| | | 1-0-0 air | | |
| | | 0-0 ground | | |

**Willits, Gordon L., Lt.**
352nd Ftr Sqn/353rd Ftr Grp

| *Sqn* | *Date* | *Claims* | *Location* | *A/C* |
|---|---|---|---|---|
| 352nd | December 30, 1943 | (.5)Me-109 dest(air)* | Charleville | P-47 |
| | | 0.5-0-0 air | | |
| | | 0-0 ground | | |

* - shared with Lt. J.W. Gonnam of the 352nd Ftr Sqn

**Willruth, Calvin W., Capt.**
335th Ftr Sqn/4th Ftr Grp

| *Sqn* | *Date* | *Claims* | *Location* | *A/C* |
|---|---|---|---|---|
| 335th | December 24, 1944 | Me-109 dest(air) | W/Giessen | P-51 |
| | | 1-0-0 air | | |
| | | 0-0 ground | | |

**Wilsey, Edward L., Capt.**
374th Ftr Sqn/361st Ftr Grp

| *Sqn* | *Date* | *Claims* | *Location* | *A/C* |
|---|---|---|---|---|
| 374th | November 27, 1944 | Me-109 dest(air) | Dummer Lake | P-51 |
| | | 1-0-0 air | | |
| | | 0-0 ground | | |

**Wilson, Bruce B., Capt.**
383rd Ftr Sqn/364th Ftr Grp

| *Sqn* | *Date* | *Claims* | *Location* | *A/C* |
|---|---|---|---|---|
| 383rd | April 11, 1944 | Me-109 dam(air) | Halberstadt | P-38 |
| | May 21 | (2)Ju-88 dest(grd) | Rechlin | P-38 |
| | | Ju-88 dam(grd) | Rechlin | P-38 |
| | September 12 | FW-190 dest(air) | N/Berlin | P-51 |
| | | 1-0-1 air | | |
| | | 2-1 ground | | |

**Wilson, Cy, LtCol.**
55th Ftr Sqn/20th Ftr Grp
HdQts/20th Ftr Grp

| *Sqn* | *Date* | *Claims* | *Location* | *A/C* |
|---|---|---|---|---|
| HdQts | June 25, 1944 | Me-109 dest(air) | S/Paris | P-38 |
| | August 6 | FW-190 dam(air) | Potsdam | P-51 |
| | August 16 | Me-109 dest(air) | Eisenach | P-51 |
| | | FW-190 dest(air) | Eisenach | P-51 |
| | | 3-0-1 air | | |
| | | 0-0 ground | | |

**Wilson, Ernest L., Lt.**
385th Ftr Sqn/364th Ftr Grp

| *Sqn* | *Date* | *Claims* | *Location* | *A/C* |
|---|---|---|---|---|
| 385th | August 9, 1944 | Me-110 dest(grd) | Gaukonigshafen | P-51 |
| | | Me-210 dest(grd) | Gaukonigshafen | P-51 |
| | | (2)Me-110 dam(grd) | Gaukonigshafen | P-51 |
| | | 0-0-0 air | | |
| | | 2-2 ground | | |

**Wilson, John D., Lt.**
63rd Ftr Sqn/56th Ftr Grp

| *Sqn* | *Date* | *Claims* | *Location* | *A/C* |
|---|---|---|---|---|
| 63rd | October 4, 1943 | Me-110 dest(air) | E/Duren | P-47 |
| | November 5 | FW-190 dest(air) | Rheine-Munster | P-47 |
| | | 2-0-0 air | | |
| | | 0-0 ground | | |

**Wilson, John E., Lt.**
384th Ftr Sqn/364th Ftr Grp

| *Sqn* | *Date* | *Claims* | *Location* | *A/C* |
|---|---|---|---|---|
| 384th | August 9, 1944 | (.5)FW-190 dest(air)* | Kaufburen | P-51 |
| | | 0.5-0-0 air | | |
| | | 0-0 ground | | |

* - shared with Lt. W.N. Champion of the 384th Ftr Sqn

**Wilson, John H., Maj.**
357th Ftr Sqn/355th Ftr Grp

| Sqn | Date | Claims | Location | A/C |
|---|---|---|---|---|
| 357th | January 29, 1944 | FW-190 dest(air) | W/Frankfurt | P-47 |
| | March 27 | (.5)Me-109 dest(air)[*] | Biscarosse A/F | P-51 |
| | April 8 | Me-210 dest(grd) | Gifhorn A/F | P-51 |
| | April 13 | Me-109 dest(air) | Augsburg | P-51 |
| | | (.5)Me-323 dest(grd)[**] | Crailsheim | P-51 |
| | | Me-323 dam(grd) | Crailsheim | P-51 |
| | April 24 | Me-109 dest(air) | NW Munich | P-51 |
| | | Me-109 dam(air) | NW Munich | P-51 |
| | June 6 | Ju-87 dam(air) | NE Janville | P-51 |
| | November 18 | Me-262 dest(grd) | Leipheim | P-51 |
| | | Me-262 dam(grd) | Leipheim | P-51 |
| | January 15, 1945 | u/i a/c dest(grd) | Landsberg | P-51 |

3.5-0-2 air
3.5-2 ground

[*] - shared with Lt. I. Reedy of the 357th Ftr Sqn
[**] - shared with Lt. J.D. Sturm of the 357th Ftr Sqn

**Wilson, John P., Lt.**
503rd Ftr Sqn/339th Ftr Grp

| Sqn | Date | Claims | Location | A/C |
|---|---|---|---|---|
| 503rd | November 26, 1944 | (2)FW-190 dest(air) | SE Dummer Lake | P-51 |

2-0-0 air
0-0 ground

**Wilson, John W., Lt.**
370th Ftr Sqn/359th Ftr Grp

| Sqn | Date | Claims | Location | A/C |
|---|---|---|---|---|
| 370th | August 9, 1944 | Me-109 prob(air) | Gunzburg | P-51 |
| | September 11 | Me-109 dest(air) | Mulhausen | P-51 |
| | | FW-190 dam(air) | Mulhausen | P-51 |
| | December 24 | FW-190 dest(air) | Bonn | P-51 |

2-1-1 air
0-0 ground

**Wilson, Loren R., Lt.**
383rd Ftr Sqn/364th Ftr Grp

| Sqn | Date | Claims | Location | A/C |
|---|---|---|---|---|
| 383rd | May 21, 1944 | Me-323 dest(grd) | NW Renow | P-38 |
| | | Do-217 dam(grd) | NW Renow | P-38 |

0-0-0 air
1-1 ground

**Wilson, Louis L., Jr., Lt.**
367th Ftr Sqn/358th Ftr Grp

| Sqn | Date | Claims | Location | A/C |
|---|---|---|---|---|
| 367th | January 30, 1944 | Me-109 dest(air) | E/Zwolle | P-47 |
| | | Me-109 dam(air) | E/Zwolle | P-47 |

0-1-1 air
0-0 ground

**Wilson, Mark T., Jr., Lt.**
84th Ftr Sqn/78th Ftr Grp

| Sqn | Date | Claims | Location | A/C |
|---|---|---|---|---|
| 84th | September 10, 1944 | (.5)He-111 dest(grd)[*] | Meinbullen | P-47 |
| | | (4)He-111 dam(grd) | Meinbullen | P-47 |
| | January 14, 1945 | Me-109 dest(air) | SE Cologne | P-51 |

1-0-0 air
0.5-4 ground

[*] - shared with Lt. R.E. Clague of the 84th Ftr Sqn

**Wilson, William D., Lt.**
328th Ftr Sqn/352nd Ftr Grp

| Sqn | Date | Claims | Location | A/C |
|---|---|---|---|---|
| 328th | July 18, 1944 | Me-109 dam(air) | Wismar | P-51 |

0-0-1 air
0-0 ground

**Wilson, William F., Capt.**
385th Ftr Sqn/364th Ftr Grp

| Sqn | Date | Claims | Location | A/C |
|---|---|---|---|---|
| 385th | September 11, 1944 | (2)FW-190 dest(air) | W/Leipzig | P-51 |
| | | Me-109 dest(air) | W/Leipzig | P-51 |
| | December 5 | (2)FW-190 dest(air) | NW Berlin | P-51 |
| | | FW-190 dam(air) | NW Berlin | P-51 |

5-0-1 air
0-0 ground

**Winder, John H., II., Capt.**
350th Ftr Sqn/353rd Ftr Grp

| Sqn | Date | Claims | Location | A/C |
|---|---|---|---|---|
| 350th | November 26, 1944 | FW-190 dest(air) | Dummer Lake | P-51 |
| | November 27 | FW-190 dest(air) | Brunswick | P-51 |
| | December 24 | (2)Me-109 dest(air) | Coblenz-Limburg | P-51 |

4-0-0 air
0-0 ground

**Windham, James T., Capt.**
363rd Ftr Sqn/357th Ftr Grp

| Sqn | Date | Claims | Location | A/C |
|---|---|---|---|---|
| 363rd | January 14, 1945 | (.5)Me-109 dest(air)[*] | N/Brandenburg | P-51 |
| | March 20 | FW-190 dam(air) | Dummer Lake | P-51 |
| | | Ju-88 dam(grd) | Dummer Lake | P-51 |
| | April 7 | Me-109 dest(air) | Salzwedel | P-51 |

1.5-0-1 air
0-1 ground

[*] - shared with Lt. G.A. Zarnke of the 363rd Ftr Sqn

**Windmiller, Donald L., Capt.**
370th Ftr Sqn/359th Ftr Grp

| Sqn | Date | Claims | Location | A/C |
|---|---|---|---|---|
| 370th | November 27, 1944 | (2)Me-109 dest(air) | Hameln | P-51 |
| | February 22, 1945 | Me-410 dam(grd) | Pritzwalk | P-51 |

2-0-0 air
0-1 ground

**Wingfield, Hugh V., Lt.**
84th Ftr Sqn/78th Ftr Grp

| Sqn | Date | Claims | Location | A/C |
|---|---|---|---|---|
| 84th | April 16, 1945 | u/i a/c dest(grd) | Praha/Kakewice | P-51 |

0-0-0 air
1-0 ground

**Winkelman, Myer R., Lt.**
504th Ftr Sqn/339th Ftr Grp

| Sqn | Date | Claims | Location | A/C |
|---|---|---|---|---|
| 504th | August 6, 1944 | Me-109 dest(air) | Havelburg | P-51 |

1-0-0 air
0-0 ground

**Winks, Robert P., Lt.**
364th Ftr Sqn/357th Ftr Grp

| Sqn | Date | Claims | Location | A/C |
|---|---|---|---|---|
| 364th | November 18, 1944 | Me-109 dest(air) | Neuhausen A/F | P-51 |
| | December 24 | FW-190 dest(air) | Fulda | P-51 |
| | January 14, 1945 | (2)FW-190 dest(air) | SW Ludwigslust | P-51 |
| | | (.5)Me-109 dest(air)[*] | SW Ludwigslust | P-51 |
| | January 15 | Me-262 dest(air) | Shongau | P-51 |

5.5-0-0 air
0-0 ground

[*] - shared with an unknown pilot

**Winn, William, Jr., Lt.**
358th Ftr Sqn/355th Ftr Grp

| Sqn | Date | Claims | Location | A/C |
|---|---|---|---|---|
| 358th | July 8, 1944 | Me-109 dam(grd) | SW Chalons | P-51 |

0-0-0 air
0-1 ground

**Winski, Longfin M., Lt.**
61st Ftr Sqn/56th Ftr Grp

| Sqn | Date | Claims | Location | A/C |
|---|---|---|---|---|
| 61st | April 10, 1945 | He-115 dest(grd) | Muritz Lake | P-47 |
| | | (2)u/i a/c dam(grd) | Muritz Lake | P-47 |
| | April 13 | Ju-88 dest(grd) | Eggebeck A/F | P-47 |
| | | (2)Ju-88 dam(grd) | Eggebeck A/F | P-47 |
| | | Me-110 dam(grd) | Eggebeck A/F | P-47 |

0-0-0 air
2-5 ground

**Winters, Robert E., Capt.**
62nd Ftr Sqn/56th Ftr Grp

| Sqn | Date | Claims | Location | A/C |
|---|---|---|---|---|
| 62nd | September 5, 1944 | FW-190 dest(grd) | Gelnhausen | P-47 |
| | September 21 | FW-190 dest(air) | NE Arnheim | P-47 |
| | October 5 | Me-109 dest(grd) | S/Geseke | P-47 |
| | December 23 | Me-109 prob(air) | Euskirchen-Bonn | P-47 |
| | | FW-190 dam(air) | Euskirchen-Bonn | P-47 |
| | April 7, 1945 | Me-109 dest(air) | S/Hamburg | P-47 |
| | April 10 | u/i a/c dam(grd) | Rechlin | P-47 |

2-1-1 air
2-1 ground

**Wise, Robert E., Capt.**
83rd Ftr Sqn/78th Ftr Grp

| Sqn | Date | Claims | Location | A/C |
|---|---|---|---|---|
| 83rd | February 24, 1944 | FW-190 dest(air) | Furstenau | P-47 |
| | | u/i a/c dam(grd) | Furstenau | P-47 |
| | March 6 | Me-109 dam(air) | Dummer Lake | P-47 |
| | March 2, 1945 | Me-109 dam(air) | Burg A/F | P-51 |

1-0-2 air
0-1 ground

**Wisniewski, Adam J., Lt.**
63rd Ftr Sqn/56th Ftr Grp

| Sqn | Date | Claims | Location | A/C |
|---|---|---|---|---|
| 63rd | November 3, 1943 | Me-110 dam(air) | N/Juist | P-47 |
| | April 24, 1944 | (.5)Me-210 dest(grd)* | Thalheim | P-47 |
| | | Ju-87 dam(grd) | Thalheim | P-47 |
| | | (.25)u/i a/c dam(grd)** | Thalheim | P-47 |

0-0-1 air
0.5-1.25 ground

* - shared with Lt. D.W. Marshall of the 63rd Ftr Sqn
** - shared with Lt. D.W. Marshall, Lt. H.F. WArner, and Lt. S.B. Dale of the 63rd Ftr Sqn

**Withers, John C., Lt.**
505th Ftr Sqn/339th Ftr Grp

| Sqn | Date | Claims | Location | A/C |
|---|---|---|---|---|
| 505th | March 2, 1945 | (.5)Me-109 dest(air)* | E/Magdeburg | P-51 |
| | March 3 | Ju-88 dam(grd) | E/Magdeburg | P-51 |
| | April 10 | Ju-88 dest(grd) | N/Neuruppin | P-51 |
| | | (2)Ju-88 dam(grd) | N/Neuruppin | P-51 |

0.5-0-0 air
1-3 ground

* - shared with Lt. H.D. Ziegler of the 505th Ftr Sqn

**Withers, Raymond R., Capt.**
360th Ftr Sqn/356th Ftr Grp
359th Ftr Sqn/356th Ftr Grp

| Sqn | Date | Claims | Location | A/C |
|---|---|---|---|---|
| 360th | November 29, 1943 | Me-109 dest(air) | Meppel | P-47 |
| | April 23, 1944 | (1.5)Go-242 dam(grd)* | Hagenau | P-47 |
| | May 13 | FW-190 dest(air) | Kiel | P-47 |
| | May 19 | Me-109 dest(air) | Hanover | P-47 |
| | | Me-109 dam(air) | Hanover | P-47 |
| 359th | November 27 | Me-109 dest(air) | N/Munster | P-51 |

4-0-1 air
0-1.5 ground

* - shared with Lt. V. Hockmeyer of the 360th Ftr Sqn

**Witzel, George H., Lt.**
436th Ftr Sqn/479th Ftr Grp

| Sqn | Date | Claims | Location | A/C |
|---|---|---|---|---|
| 436th | February 21, 1945 | Ju-188 dam(grd) | Nordhausen | P-51 |
| | April 13 | (2)FW-190 dest(grd) | Salzwedel | P-51 |
| | | FW-190 dam(grd) | Salzwedel | P-51 |
| | | Me-110 dam(grd) | Salzwedel | P-51 |
| | April 16 | (3)FW-190 dest(grd) | Landstadt | P-51 |
| | April 17 | FW-190 dest(grd) | Karlsbad | P-51 |
| | | u/i a/c dest(grd) | Karlsbad | P-51 |

0-0-0 air
7-3 ground

**Woertz, Jack J., Lt.**
358th Ftr Sqn/355th Ftr Grp

| Sqn | Date | Claims | Location | A/C |
|---|---|---|---|---|
| 358th | November 29, 1943 | Me-109 dest(air) | W/Bremen | P-47 |

1-0-0 air
0-0 ground

**Wolf, Raymond E., Lt.**
363rd Ftr Sqn/357th Ftr Grp

| Sqn | Date | Claims | Location | A/C |
|---|---|---|---|---|
| 363rd | November 27, 1944 | FW-190 dest(air) | Noyehausen | P-51 |
| | January 14, 1945 | Me-109 dest(air) | N/Brandenburg | P-51 |
| | | Me-109 dam(air) | N/Brandenburg | P-51 |

2-0-1 air
0-0 ground

**Wolfe, Roland L., Capt.**
82nd Ftr Sqn/78th Ftr Grp

| Sqn | Date | Claims | Location | A/C |
|---|---|---|---|---|
| 82nd | March 6, 1944 | FW-190 dam(air) | Barenburg | P-47 |
| | April 28 | He-111 dam(grd) | Chateaudun | P-47 |
| | August 27 | (.5)He-111 dest(grd)* | Chatel-Cherary | P-47 |

0-0-1 air
0.5-1 ground

* - shared with Lt. T.L. Eggleston of the 82nd Ftr Sqn

**Wolfort, Joseph, Lt.**
503rd Ftr Sqn/339th Ftr Grp

| Sqn | Date | Claims | Location | A/C |
|---|---|---|---|---|
| 503rd | May 19, 1944 | u/i a/c dest(grd) | Ludwigslust | P-51 |
| | May 24 | (.5)Me-109 dest(air)* | SW Berlin | P-51 |
| | | Me-109 dam(air) | SW Berlin | P-51 |

0.5-0-1 air
1-0 ground

* - shared with Lt. R.B. Brown of the 503rd Ftr Sqn

**Woller, Myron K., Capt.**
82nd Ftr Sqn/78th Ftr Grp

| Sqn | Date | Claims | Location | A/C |
|---|---|---|---|---|
| 82nd | April 5, 1944 | Go-242 dam(grd) | Ruwer | P-47 |
| | | DFS-230 dam(grd) | Ruwer | P-47 |
| | April 8 | (.2)Me-110 dest(grd)* | Trier | P-47 |
| | | (.2)Me-110 dest(grd)* | Trier | P-47 |
| | | (.2)Me-110 dest(grd)* | Trier | P-47 |
| | | Ju-88 dam(grd) | Trier | P-47 |
| | May 19 | (2)Me-109 dest(air) | Dummer Lake | P-47 |

2-0-0 air
0.6-3 ground

[*] - all shared with Maj. J.J. Oberhansly, Capt. N.D. Munson, Lt. J.E. Brasher, and F/O C.W. DeWitt of the 82nd Ftr Sqn

**Wolski, Victor, Lt.**
436th Ftr Sqn/479th Ftr Grp

| *Sqn* | *Date* | *Claims* | *Location* | *A/C* |
|---|---|---|---|---|
| 436th | September 5, 1944 | (2)FW-190 dest(grd) | Bad Nauheim | P-38 |
| | | FW-190 dam(grd) | Bad Nauheim | P-38 |
| | September 28 | (3)FW-190 dest(air) | W/Magdeburg | P-38 |
| | | FW-190 dam(air) | W/Magdeburg | P-38 |

3-0-1 air
2-1 ground

**Womack, Herschel O., Lt.**
62nd Ftr Sqn/56th Ftr Grp

| *Sqn* | *Date* | *Claims* | *Location* | *A/C* |
|---|---|---|---|---|
| 62nd | September 5, 1944 | Me-210 dest(grd) | NE Coblenz | P-47 |
| | | Me-109 dam(grd) | NE Coblenz | P-47 |
| | | Ju-88 dam(grd) | NE Coblenz | P-47 |
| | January 14, 1945 | (.5)Me-109 dest(air)[*] | Magdeburg | P-47 |
| | April 10 | He-111 dest(grd) | Neuruppin | P-47 |

0.5-0-0 air
2-2 ground

[*] - shared with Lt. D. Henley of the 62nd Ftr Sqn

**Woock, Charles R., Lt.**
62nd Ftr Sqn/56th Ftr Grp
61st Ftr Sqn/56th Ftr Grp

| *Sqn* | *Date* | *Claims* | *Location* | *A/C* |
|---|---|---|---|---|
| 61st | December 4, 1944 | u/i a/c dest(grd) | Neuburg | P-47 |
| | December 23 | FW-190 prob(air) | E/Bonn | P-47 |
| | | (2)FW-190 dam(air) | E/Bonn | P-47 |

0-1-2 air
1-0 ground

**Wood, Eugene W., Lt.**
84th Ftr Sqn/78th Ftr Grp

| *Sqn* | *Date* | *Claims* | *Location* | *A/C* |
|---|---|---|---|---|
| 84th | September 10, 1944 | (2)He-111 dest(grd) | Meinbullen | P-47 |
| | | Fi-156 dest(grd) | Meinbullen | P-47 |
| | | (2)He-111 dam(grd) | Meinbullen | P-47 |

0-0-0 air
3-2 ground

**Wood, James N., LtCol.**
361st Ftr Sqn/356th Ftr Grp
360th Ftr Sqn/356th Ftr Grp

| *Sqn* | *Date* | *Claims* | *Location* | *A/C* |
|---|---|---|---|---|
| 361st | February 10, 1944 | (1.5)FW-190 dest(air)[*] | NE Lingen | P-47 |
| | May 4 | (3)FW-190 dest(air) | Steinhuder Lake | P-47 |

4.5-0-0 air
0-0 ground

[*] - shared with Lt. M.W. DeMerit of the 361st Ftr Sqn

**Wood, James N., Jr., Lt.**
487th Ftr Sqn/352nd Ftr Grp

| *Sqn* | *Date* | *Claims* | *Location* | *A/C* |
|---|---|---|---|---|
| 487th | June 20, 1944 | (.5)Me-410 dest(air)[*] | E/Bernburg | P-51 |
| | June 29 | He-111 dest(grd) | Burg | P-51 |
| | November 2 | Me-109 dest(air) | E/Merseburg | P-51 |
| | December 27 | FW-190 dest(air) | W/Mayen | P-51 |
| | March 18, 1945 | (.5)Me-109 dest(air)[*] | SE Bad Frienwalde | P-51 |

3-0-0 air
1-0 ground

[*] - shared with Maj. G.E. Preddy of the 487th Ftr Sqn
[**] - shared with Lt. R.H. Littge of the 487th Ftr Sqn

**Wood, Jefferson K., Lt.**
374th Ftr Sqn/361st Ftr Grp

| *Sqn* | *Date* | *Claims* | *Location* | *A/C* |
|---|---|---|---|---|
| 374th | June 4, 1944 | (.5)Me-109 dest(air)[*] | SE Mulun | P-51 |
| | July 5 | Me-109 dest(air) | Amiens | P-51 |

1.5-0-0 air
0-0 ground

[*] - shared with Capt. C.H. Bergmann of the 374th Ftr Sqn

**Wood, Joseph E., Lt.**
351st Ftr Sqn/353rd Ftr Grp

| *Sqn* | *Date* | *Claims* | *Location* | *A/C* |
|---|---|---|---|---|
| 351st | October 10, 1943 | Me-110 dam(air) | Metelen | P-47 |

0-0-1 air
0-0 ground

**Wood, Lawrence D., Capt.**
363rd Ftr Sqn/357th Ftr Grp

| *Sqn* | *Date* | *Claims* | *Location* | *A/C* |
|---|---|---|---|---|
| 363rd | May 9, 1944 | FW-190 dest(air) | Herenthals | P-51 |

1-0-0 air
0-0 ground

**Wood, Leonard A., Lt.**
375th Ftr Sqn/361st Ftr Grp

| *Sqn* | *Date* | *Claims* | *Location* | *A/C* |
|---|---|---|---|---|
| 375th | August 7, 1944 | (.5)Me-109 dam(grd)[*] | Chartres | P-51 |
| | November 2 | Me-109 dest(air) | S/Weiszenfels | P-51 |
| | November 26 | FW-190 dest(air) | S/Steinhuder Lake | P-51 |

2-0-0 air
0-0.5 ground

[*] - shared with Lt. W.T. Kemp of the 375th Ftr Sqn

**Wood, Melvin C., Lt.**
61st Ftr Sqn/56th Ftr Grp

| *Sqn* | *Date* | *Claims* | *Location* | *A/C* |
|---|---|---|---|---|
| 61st | October 18, 1943 | (.5)Me-210 dest(air)[*] | NE Maastricht | P-47 |
| | December 20 | (.5)Me-109 dam(air)[**] | NE Bremen | P-47 |
| | | (.5)Me-210 dam(air)[**] | NE Bremen | P-47 |
| | January 29, 1944 | Me-210 dest(air) | Simmern | P-47 |

1.5-0-1 air
0-0 ground

[*] - shared with Maj. J.C. Stewart of HdQts, 56th Ftr Grp
[**] - both shared with Lt. J.H. Powers of the 61st Ftr Sqn

**Wood, Robert T., Lt.**
504th Ftr Sqn/339th Ftr Grp

| *Sqn* | *Date* | *Claims* | *Location* | *A/C* |
|---|---|---|---|---|
| 504th | August 6, 1944 | Me-109 dest(air) | Havelburg-Pritzwalk | P-51 |

1-0-0 air
0-0 ground

**Wood, Thomas L., Lt.**
354th Ftr Sqn/355th Ftr Grp

| *Sqn* | *Date* | *Claims* | *Location* | *A/C* |
|---|---|---|---|---|
| 354th | November 18, 1944 | Me-262 dest(grd) | Leipheim | P-51 |
| | January 14, 1945 | Me-109 dest(air) | E/Meppen | P-51 |

1-0-0 air
1-0 ground

**Woods, Sidney S., LtCol.**
HdQts/479th Ftr Grp
HdQts/ 4th Ftr Grp
Earlier flew in the PTO with the 49th Ftr Grp and claimed 2 kills; a Betty on March 11, 1943, and an Oscar on July 28, 1943.

| Sqn | Date | Claims | Location | A/C |
|---|---|---|---|---|
| HdQts (479th) | September 5, 1944 | Ju-88 dest(grd) | Ettinghausen | P-38 |
| HdQts (4th) | March 22, 1945 | (5)FW-190 dest(air) | Furstenwalde-Eggersdorf | P-51 |
| | April 16 | (2)Ju-88 dest(grd) | Praha | P-51 |
| | | (5)Ju-88 dam(grd) | Praha | P-51 |

5-0-0 air
3-5 ground

**Woodside, Jackie D., Lt.**
383rd Ftr Sqn/364th Ftr Grp

| Sqn | Date | Claims | Location | A/C |
|---|---|---|---|---|
| 383rd | December 23, 1944 | Me-109 dest(air) | NW Trier | P-51 |
| | | Me-109 dam(air) | NW Trier | P-51 |
| | January 1, 1945 | Me-109 dest(air) | Hamburg | P-51 |

2-0-1 air
0-0 ground

**Woodson, Nelson B., Lt.**
358th Ftr Sqn/355th Ftr Grp

| Sqn | Date | Claims | Location | A/C |
|---|---|---|---|---|
| 358th | November 26, 1944 | FW-190 dam(air) | W/Hanover | P-51 |

0-0-1 air
0-0 ground

**Woodward, Donald T., Capt.**
376th Ftr Sqn/361st Ftr Grp

| Sqn | Date | Claims | Location | A/C |
|---|---|---|---|---|
| 376th | February 25, 1944 | Me-109 dam(air) | Verdun | P-47 |

0-0-1 air
0-0 ground

**Woody, Robert E., Capt.**
354th Ftr Sqn/355th Ftr Grp

| Sqn | Date | Claims | Location | A/C |
|---|---|---|---|---|
| 354th | April 5, 1944 | (.5)FW-44 dest(air)[*] | Landsberg | P-51 |
| | | (.5)FW-44 dest(air)[*] | Landsberg | P-51 |
| | | (.5)Me-109 dest(air)[**] | Landsberg | P-51 |
| | | Do-217 dam(grd) | Landsberg | P-51 |
| | | Me-110 dam(grd) | Landsberg | P-51 |
| | April 10 | He-111 dest(grd) | Bourges | P-51 |
| | | He-111 dam(grd) | Bourges | P-51 |
| | April 11 | Me-210 prob(air) | S/Madu Lake | P-51 |
| | | Ju-87 dam(grd) | S/Madu Lake | P-51 |
| | April 13 | Ju-88 dest(grd) | Oberpfaffenhofen | P-51 |
| | | Me-110 dam(grd) | Oberpfaffenhofen | P-51 |
| | April 19 | Me-109 dest(air) | Nordhausen | P-51 |
| | April 24 | (4.5)Me-109 dest(air)[@] | SE Munich | P-51 |
| | | Me-109 dam(air) | SE Munich | P-51 |

7-1-1 air
2-5 ground

[*] - both shared with Capt. W.J. Koraleski of the 354th Ftr Sqn
[**] - shared with Lt. B.C. Williamson of the 354th Ftr Sqn
[@] - shared with Lt. W.P. Boulet of the 354th Ftr Sqn

**Woolard, Marion L., Lt.**
354th Ftr Sqn/355th Ftr Grp

| Sqn | Date | Claims | Location | A/C |
|---|---|---|---|---|
| 354th | November 2, 1944 | Me-109 dest(air) | W/Naumberg | P-51 |

1-0-0 air
0-0 ground

**Woolery, James C., Lt.**
505th Ftr Sqn/339th Ftr Grp

| Sqn | Date | Claims | Location | A/C |
|---|---|---|---|---|
| 505th | March 1, 1945 | Do-217 dest(grd) | S/Feldkirchen | P-51 |
| | April 16 | (2)u/i a/c dest(grd) | NE Prague | P-51 |
| | | FW-190 dest(grd) | NE Prague | P-51 |
| | April 17 | Me-109 dest(grd) | SE Pocking | P-51 |
| | | Ju-88 dest(grd) | SE Pocking | P-51 |
| | | Me-109 dam(grd) | SE Pocking | P-51 |

0-0-0 air
6-1 ground

**Worth, Thomas H., Lt.**
358th Ftr Sqn/355th Ftr Grp

| Sqn | Date | Claims | Location | A/C |
|---|---|---|---|---|
| 358th | April 15, 1944 | Me-110 dam(grd) | Glienicke | P-51 |

0-0-0 air
0-1 ground

**Wren, William D., Lt.**
82nd Ftr Sqn/78th Ftr Grp

| Sqn | Date | Claims | Location | A/C |
|---|---|---|---|---|
| 82nd | June 13, 1943 | FW-190 prob(air) | Armentiers | P-47 |

0-1-0 air
0-0 ground

**Wright, Albert E., Capt.**
338th Ftr Sqn/55th Ftr Grp

| Sqn | Date | Claims | Location | A/C |
|---|---|---|---|---|
| 338th | November 26, 1944 | FW-190 dam(grd) | Vorden A/F | P-51 |
| | February 25, 1945 | FW-190 dest(grd) | Illesheim | P-51 |

0-0-0 air
1-1 ground

**Wright, Gilbert S., Lt.**
354th Ftr Sqn/355th Ftr Grp

| Sqn | Date | Claims | Location | A/C |
|---|---|---|---|---|
| 354th | June 20, 1944 | (2)Me-109 dest(air) | Bergen | P-51 |
| | June 24 | Me-109 dam(grd) | Seiches | P-51 |

2-0-0 air
0-1 ground

**Wright, Jimmie C., Lt.**
376th Ftr Sqn/361st Ftr Grp

| Sqn | Date | Claims | Location | A/C |
|---|---|---|---|---|
| 376th | February 22, 1944 | FW-190 dam(air) | S/Nijmegen | P-47 |
| | March 29 | Ju-88 dest(grd) | Dummer Lake | P-47 |
| | | (2)u/i a/c dam(grd) | Dummer Lake | P-47 |
| | April 1 | Ju-88 dest(grd) | Gutersloh | P-47 |
| | April 10 | Me-110 dest(grd) | Villaroche | P-47 |
| | | Me-110 dam(grd) | Villaroche | P-47 |

0-0-1 air
3-3 ground

**Wright, Lyle M., Lt.**
503rd Ftr Sqn/339th Ftr Grp

| Sqn | Date | Claims | Location | A/C |
|---|---|---|---|---|
| 503rd | May 21, 1944 | He-111 dest(air) | Riesa A/F | P-51 |
| | | Ju-88 dam(grd) | Riesa A/F | P-51 |
| | June 29 | Me-109 dam(air) | Leipzig | P-51 |
| | | Ju-88 dam(grd) | Leipzig | P-51 |

1-0-1 air
0-2 ground

**Wright, Melvin R., Lt.**
82nd Ftr Sqn/78th Ftr Grp

| Sqn | Date | Claims | Location | A/C |
|---|---|---|---|---|
| 82nd | July 30, 1943 | FW-190 dam(air) | Haldern | P-47 |
| | November 30 | Me-109 dam(air) | Eupen | P-47 |

0-0-2 air
0-0 ground

**Wright, Robert C., Capt.**
375th Ftr Sqn/361st Ftr Grp

| Sqn | Date | Claims | Location | A/C |
|---|---|---|---|---|
| 375th | May 29, 1944 | (2)Ju-52 dest(grd) | Lackau-Juterbog | P-51 |
| | | He-111 dest(grd) | Lackau-Juterbog | P-51 |

| Sqn | Date | Claims | Location | A/C |
|---|---|---|---|---|
| | | Ju-88 dest(grd) | Lackau-Juterbog | P-51 |
| | | Ju-88 dam(grd) | Lackau-Juterbog | P-51 |
| | June 29 | (1.5)Me-109 dest(air)* | SW Kothen | P-51 |
| | July 7 | (2)Me-109 dest(air) | N/Leipzig | P-51 |

3.5-0-0 air
4-0 ground

* - shared with Lt. S. Armsby of the 375th Ftr Sqn

**Wright, Roland R., Lt.**
364th Ftr Sqn/357th Ftr Grp

| Sqn | Date | Claims | Location | A/C |
|---|---|---|---|---|
| 364th | January 20, 1945 | Me-262 dest(air) | Lechfeld A/F | P-51 |
| | March 24 | Me-109 dest(air) | W/Gutersloh | P-51 |
| | | Me-109 dam(air) | W/Gutersloh | P-51 |

2-0-1 air
0-0 ground

**Wyatt, Harold A., Lt.**
362nd Ftr Sqn/357th Ftr Grp

| Sqn | Date | Claims | Location | A/C |
|---|---|---|---|---|
| 362nd | January 14, 1945 | FW-190 dest(air) | NW Berlin | P-51 |

1-0-0 air
0-0 ground

**Wyatt, James A., Lt.**
359th Ftr Sqn/356th Ftr Grp

| Sqn | Date | Claims | Location | A/C |
|---|---|---|---|---|
| 359th | May 13, 1944 | FW-190 prob(air) | Kiel-Lubeck | P-47 |
| | | FW-190 dam(air) | Kiel-Lubeck | P-47 |

0-1-1 air
0-0 ground

**Wyatt, Valdee, Capt.**
503rd Ftr Sqn/339th Ftr Grp

| Sqn | Date | Claims | Location | A/C |
|---|---|---|---|---|
| 503rd | June 15, 1944 | FW-190 dest(air) | Montiers | P-51 |
| | July 7 | (.5)Me-109 dest(air)* | Leipzig | P-51 |
| | July 25 | Me-109 dest(air) | Etrepagny | P-51 |

2.5-0-0 air
0-0 ground

* - shared with Lt. J.P. Bush of the 503rd Ftr Sqn

**Wyche, Wilton, Lt.**
38th Ftr Sqn/55th Ftr Grp

| Sqn | Date | Claims | Location | A/C |
|---|---|---|---|---|
| 38th | January 5, 1944 | Me-109 dam(air) | SW Kiel | P-38 |

0-0-1 air
0-0 ground

**Wyman, Burton C., Lt.**
335th Ftr Sqn/4th Ftr Grp

| Sqn | Date | Claims | Location | A/C |
|---|---|---|---|---|
| 335th | December 11, 1943 | Me-109 dam(air) | Harlingen | P-47 |

0-0-1 air
0-0 ground

**Wyman, Zell M., Lt.**
79th Ftr Sqn/20th Ftr Grp

| Sqn | Date | Claims | Location | A/C |
|---|---|---|---|---|
| 79th | October 6, 1944 | u/i a/c dest(grd) | Bad Berg-Dievenow | P-51 |
| | October 7 | (.5)He-115 dest(grd)* | Bad Berg-Dievenow | P-51 |

0-0-0 air
1.5-0 ground

* - shared with Capt. R.J. Meyer of the 79th Ftr Sqn

**Wynn, Vasseure H., Capt.**
334th Ftr Sqn/4th Ftr Grp

| Sqn | Date | Claims | Location | A/C |
|---|---|---|---|---|
| 334th | December 22, 1943 | (1.5)Me-109 dest(air)* | Eschede | P-47 |
| | March 2, 1944 | Me-109 dest(air) | S/Coblenz | P-51 |
| | March 27 | Do-217 dest(grd) | Cazaux | P-51 |
| | | Ju-88 dest(grd) | Cazaux | P-51 |

2.5-0-0 air
2-0 ground

* - shared with Lt. J.T. Godfrey of the 336th Ftr Sqn, 4th Ftr Grp

**Yannell, Michael P., Maj.**
360th Ftr Sqn/356th Ftr Grp
Earlier flew in the MTO with the 86th Ftr Grp, 12th Air Force claiming 2 kills; a FW-190 on September 9, 1943, and an u/i a/c on October 18, 1943.

| Sqn | Date | Claims | Location | A/C |
|---|---|---|---|---|
| 360th | November 26, 1944 | (2)Me-109 dest(air) | Dummer Lake | P-51 |
| | | (2)Me-109 dam(air) | Dummer Lake | P-51 |
| | February 23, 1945 | He-177 dest(grd) | Giebelstadt | P-51 |
| | | He-177 dam(grd) | Giebelstadt | P-51 |
| | April 9 | FW-190 dest(grd) | Biberach | P-51 |
| | | u/i a/c dest(grd) | Biberach | P-51 |
| | | Me-410 dam(grd) | Biberach | P-51 |
| | April 13 | FW-190 dest(grd) | Schwerin | P-51 |

2-0-2 air
4-2 ground

**Yarbrough, Walter R., Maj.**
79th Ftr Sqn/20th Ftr Grp

| Sqn | Date | Claims | Location | A/C |
|---|---|---|---|---|
| 79th | April 9, 1945 | Ju-88 dest(grd) | E/Munich | P-51 |
| | April 13 | (2)FW-190 dam(grd) | Jagel-Hutzfeld | P-51 |
| | | Ju-88 dam(grd) | Jagel-Hutzfeld | P-51 |

0-0-0 air
1-3 ground

**Yaryan, Jess O., Capt.**
79th Ftr Sqn/20th Ftr Grp

| Sqn | Date | Claims | Location | A/C |
|---|---|---|---|---|
| 79th | August 9, 1944 | FW-190 dest(air) | SW Ulm | P-51 |

1-0-0 air
0-0 ground

**Yeager, Charles E., Capt.**
363rd Ftr Sqn/357th Ftr Grp

| Sqn | Date | Claims | Location | A/C |
|---|---|---|---|---|
| 363rd | March 4, 1944 | Me-109 dest(air) | SE Kassel | P-51 |
| | | He-111 dam(air) | Wittenburg | P-51 |
| | September 13 | (.5)Me-109 dest(air)* | S/Kassel | P-51 |
| | October 12 | (5)Me-109 dest(air) | Steinhuder Lake-Hanover | P-51 |
| | November 6 | Me-262 dest(air) | E/Assen | P-51 |
| | | (2)Me-262 dam(air) | E/Assen | P-51 |
| | November 27 | (4)FW-190 dest(air) | SW Magdeburg | P-51 |

11.5-0-3 air
0-0 ground

* - shared with Lt. F.L. Gailer of the 363rd Ftr Sqn

**Yee Litt, Robert H., Lt.**
343rd Ftr Sqn/55th Ftr Grp

| Sqn | Date | Claims | Location | A/C |
|---|---|---|---|---|
| 343rd | September 11, 1944 | FW-190 dest(air) | Sonneburg | P-51 |

1-0-0 air
0-0 ground

**Yelton, Jack J., Lt.**
55th Ftr Sqn/20th Ftr Grp

| Sqn | Date | Claims | Location | A/C |
|---|---|---|---|---|
| 55th | March 6, 1944 | FW-190 dest(air) | Oldenburg | P-38 |
| | April 5 | FW-190 dest(air) | SW Hanover | P-38 |
| | | FW-200 dest(air) | SW Hanover | P-38 |

3-0-0 air
0-0 ground

**Yoakum, George L., Lt.**
361st Ftr Sqn/356th Ftr Grp

| *Sqn* | *Date* | *Claims* | *Location* | *A/C* |
|---|---|---|---|---|
| 361st | April 23, 1944 | (2)Go-242 dam(grd) | Hagenau | P-47 |
| | | Me-109 dam(grd) | Hagenau | P-47 |
| | June 8 | (.5)FW-190 dest(air)[*] | Beauvais/Nivillers | P-47 |
| | June 22 | (.5)Me-109 dest(air)[**] | Evreux | P-47 |

1-0-0 air
0-3 ground

* - shared with Lt. H.E. Wiggins of the 361st Ftr Sqn
** - shared with Lt. W.S. Hurley of the 361st Ftr Sqn

**Yochim, Fred A., Lt.**
328th Ftr Sqn/352nd Ftr Grp

| *Sqn* | *Date* | *Claims* | *Location* | *A/C* |
|---|---|---|---|---|
| 328th | February 4, 1944 | FW-190 dam(air) | Hasselt | P-47 |
| | March 15 | Me-109 prob(air) | Heusden | P-47 |
| | April 8 | (.5)Me-210 dest(grd)[*] | Quackenbruck | P-47 |
| | | (.5)u/i a/c dest(grd)[*] | Quackenbruck | P-47 |
| | April 9 | FW-190 dest(air) | Dummer Lake | P-47 |

1-1-1 air
1-0 ground

* - both shared with Lt. R.C. Brookins of the 328th Ftr Sqn

**Yocum, Denny L., F/O**
350th Ftr Sqn/353rd Ftr Grp

| *Sqn* | *Date* | *Claims* | *Location* | *A/C* |
|---|---|---|---|---|
| 350th | June 8, 1944 | Me-110 dest(grd) | Breteuil | P-47 |
| | | Me-110 dam(grd) | Breteuil | P-47 |
| | June 30 | (2)Me-109 dam(air) | W/Chalons | P-47 |

0-0-2 air
1-1 ground

**York, Robert M., Capt.**
370th Ftr Sqn/359th Ftr Grp

| *Sqn* | *Date* | *Claims* | *Location* | *A/C* |
|---|---|---|---|---|
| 370th | August 9, 1944 | Me-109 dest(air) | Gunzburg | P-51 |
| | October 7 | (.5)Ar-196 dam(grd)[*] | Dievenow | P-51 |
| | November 27 | (3)FW-190 dest(air) | Hanover | P-51 |
| | | FW-190 prob(air) | Hanover | P-51 |
| | January 1, 1945 | FW-190 dest(air) | Luneburg | P-51 |

5-1-0 air
0-0.5 ground

* - shared with Lt. E.G. Johnson of the 370th Ftr Sqn

**Yost, Byron P., Lt.**
384th Ftr Sqn/364th Ftr Grp

| *Sqn* | *Date* | *Claims* | *Location* | *A/C* |
|---|---|---|---|---|
| 384th | May 21, 1944 | Ju-52 dest(grd) | Parchim-Hagenow | P-38 |

0-0-0 air
1-0 ground

**Young, Allen D., Lt.**
505th Ftr Sqn/339th Ftr Grp

| *Sqn* | *Date* | *Claims* | *Location* | *A/C* |
|---|---|---|---|---|
| 505th | August 28, 1944 | (.5)Ju-88 dest(grd)[*] | Savernne | P-51 |
| | September 10 | (3)u/i a/c dest(grd) | Weizenburg | P-51 |

0-0-0 air
3.5-0 ground

* - shared with Maj. J.R. Reynolds of HdQts, 339th Ftr Grp

**Young, Donald A., Maj.**
335th Ftr Sqn/4th Ftr Grp

| *Sqn* | *Date* | *Claims* | *Location* | *A/C* |
|---|---|---|---|---|
| 335th | July 14, 1943 | FW-190 dam(air) | Amiens | P-47 |
| | July 30 | FW-190 dest(air) | SE Rotterdam | P-47 |
| | | FW-190 dam(air) | SE Rotterdam | P-47 |
| | August 16 | FW-190 dest(air) | Paris | P-47 |
| | | (2)FW-190 dam(air) | Paris | P-47 |

2-0-4 air
0-0 ground

**Young, Franklin W., Capt.**
336th Ftr Sqn/4th Ftr Grp

| *Sqn* | *Date* | *Claims* | *Location* | *A/C* |
|---|---|---|---|---|
| 336th | January 1, 1945 | Me-109 dest(air) | Ulzen | P-51 |
| | | Me-262 dest(air) | Ulzen | P-51 |

2-0-0 air
0-0 ground

**Young, William R., Lt.**
376th Ftr Sqn/361st Ftr Grp

| *Sqn* | *Date* | *Claims* | *Location* | *A/C* |
|---|---|---|---|---|
| 376th | October 7, 1944 | Me-109 dest(air) | Merseburg | P-51 |

1-0-0 air
0-0 ground

**Younglas, Donald A., Maj.**
367th Ftr Sqn/358th Ftr Grp

| *Sqn* | *Date* | *Claims* | *Location* | *A/C* |
|---|---|---|---|---|
| 367th | January 5, 1944 | Me-109 prob(air) | Belgium | P-47 |

0-1-0 air
0-0 ground

**Zacharie, Lloyd F., Lt.**
364th Ftr Sqn/357th Ftr Grp

| *Sqn* | *Date* | *Claims* | *Location* | *A/C* |
|---|---|---|---|---|
| 364th | April 10, 1945 | (2)He-111 dam(grd) | Neuruppin | P-51 |

0-0-0 air
0-2 ground

**Zarnke, Glenwood A., Lt.**
363rd Ftr Sqn/357th Ftr Grp

| *Sqn* | *Date* | *Claims* | *Location* | *A/C* |
|---|---|---|---|---|
| 363rd | January 14, 1945 | (.5)Me-109 dest(air)[*] | N/Brandenburg | P-51 |
| | April 19 | Me-262 dam(air) | Prague | P-51 |

0.5-0-1 air
0-0 ground

* - shared with Lt. J.T. Windham of the 363rd Ftr Sqn

**Zboinski, Dolphe C., Lt.**
82nd Ftr Sqn/78th Ftr Grp

| *Sqn* | *Date* | *Claims* | *Location* | *A/C* |
|---|---|---|---|---|
| 82nd | November 21, 1944 | Ju-88 dam(grd) | Gutersloh | P-47 |

0-0-0 air
0-1 ground

**Zeine, Donald A., Lt.**
504th Ftr Sqn/339th Ftr Grp

| *Sqn* | *Date* | *Claims* | *Location* | *A/C* |
|---|---|---|---|---|
| 504th | August 6, 1944 | Me-109 dest(air) | Havelburg | P-51 |

1-0-0 air
0-0 ground

**Zellman, Fred, Lt.**
436th Ftr Sqn/479th Ftr Grp

| *Sqn* | *Date* | *Claims* | *Location* | *A/C* |
|---|---|---|---|---|
| 436th | April 13, 1945 | Me-410 dest(grd) | Salzwedel | P-51 |

| Sqn | Date | Claims | Location | A/C |
|---|---|---|---|---|
| | | Me-109 dest(grd) | Salzwedel | P-51 |
| | | Me-109 dam(grd) | Salzwedel | P-51 |

0-0-0 air
2-1 ground

**Zellner, Edmond, Lt.**
328th Ftr Sqn/352nd Ftr Grp

| *Sqn* | *Date* | *Claims* | *Location* | *A/C* |
|---|---|---|---|---|
| 328th | March 22, 1944 | (.25)FW-200 dest(air)[*] | Hesepe | P-47 |
| | May 19 | (.5)Me-109 dest(air)[**] | Wittenburg-Havelburg | P-51 |
| | | Me-109 prob(air) | Wittenburg-Havelburg | P-51 |
| | May 21 | (2)He-111 dest(grd) | Alt Ruppin | P-51 |
| | May 24 | Me-109 dest(air) | W/Perleburg | P-51 |
| | May 27 | Me-109 dest(air) | S/Strasbourg | P-51 |
| | | (.5)FW-190 dest(air)[@] | S/Strasbourg | P-51 |

3.25-1-0 air
2-0 ground

* - shared with Capt. E.L. Abbott, Lt. R.C. Brookins, and Lt. J.F. Thornell of the 328th Ftr Sqn
** - shared with Capt. C.C. Ettlesen of the 359th Ftr Grp
@ - shared with Maj. J.A. Storch of the 357th Ftr Grp

**Zemke, Hubert, Col.**
HdQts/ 56th Ftr Grp
HdQts/479th Ftr Grp

| *Sqn* | *Date* | *Claims* | *Location* | *A/C* |
|---|---|---|---|---|
| HdQts | May 14, 1943 | FW-190 dam(air) | NE Antwerp | P-47 |
| (56th) | June 13 | (2)FW-190 dest(air) | Cassel | P-47 |
| | | FW-190 dam(air) | Cassel | P-47 |
| | August 17 | Me-110 dest(air) | St. Trond | P-47 |
| | August 19 | FW-190 dam(air) | Numensdorp | P-47 |
| | September 3 | FW-190 dest(air) | NW Romilly-Sur-Seine | P-47 |
| | October 2 | FW-190 dest(air) | Groningen | P-47 |
| | October 20 | FW-190 dest(air) | Eindhoven | P-47 |
| | November 5 | FW-190 dest(air) | Enschede-Rheine | P-47 |
| | February 11, 1944 | Me-109 dest(grd) | Rheims | P-47 |
| | | (2)Me-109 dam(grd) | Rheims | P-47 |
| | March 6 | (1.25)Me-109 dest(air)[*] | Minden/Osnabruck | P-47 |
| | | FW-190 dest(air) | Minden/Osnabruck | P-47 |
| | | FW-190 prob(air) | Minden/Osnabruck | P-47 |
| | March 16 | Me-109 dam(air) | Chalons | P-47 |
| | April 15 | (3)He-111 dest(grd) | Flensburg | P-47 |
| | | (3)He-111 dam(grd) | Flensburg | P-47 |
| | April 25 | (2)Ju-88 dest(grd) | Metz | P-47 |
| | May 12 | Me-109 dest(air) | SW Coblenz | P-47 |
| | May 31 | (2)FW-190 dest(air) | Gutersloh-Detmold | P-47 |
| | | FW-190 prob(air) | Gutersloh-Detmold | P-47 |
| | | FW-190 dam(air) | Gutersloh-Detmold | P-47 |
| | June 6 | FW-190 dest(air) | NE Bernay | P-47 |
| | June 7 | (2)FW-190 dest(air) | Chartres/Etampes | P-47 |
| | | FW-190 dam(air) | Chartres/Etampes | P-47 |
| | June 24 | Ju-88 dest(grd) | Sailly-Laurette | P-47 |
| | July 4 | Me-109 dam(air) | N/Conches A/F | P-47 |
| | August 4 | (1.5)He-111 dest(grd)[**] | Plantlunne | P-47 |
| | | (2)He-111 dam(grd) | Plantlunne | P-47 |
| HdQts | September 26 | (2)Me-109 dest(air) | Haltern | P-51 |
| (479th) | | Me-109 dam(air) | Haltern | P-51 |
| | October 7 | (.5)Me-109 dest(air)[@] | W/Chemnitz | P-51 |

17.75-2-8 air
8.5-7 ground

* - shared with Lt. M.H. Becker, Lt. D.V. Peters, and Lt. C.W. Reed of the 63rd Ftr Sqn, 56th Ftr Grp
** - shared with Lt. J.W. Ferguson of the 62nd Ftr Sqn, 56th Ftr Grp
@ - shared with Lt. N.R. Benoit of the 435th Ftr Sqn,479th Ftr Grp

**Zetterquist, Herman R., Capt.**
364th Ftr Sqn/357th Ftr Grp

| *Sqn* | *Date* | *Claims* | *Location* | *A/C* |
|---|---|---|---|---|
| 364th | December 5, 1944 | FW-190 dest(air) | N/Berlin | P-51 |

1-0-0 air
0-0 ground

**Zettler, Vincent V., Lt.**
364th Ftr Sqn/357th Ftr Grp

| *Sqn* | *Date* | *Claims* | *Location* | *A/C* |
|---|---|---|---|---|
| 364th | January 14, 1945 | FW-190 dam(air) | W/Berlin | P-51 |
| | March 2 | Me-109 dest(air) | SE Magdeburg | P-51 |
| | | (4)He-111 dest(grd) | S/Magdeburg | P-51 |
| | April 10 | (3)Ju-88 dest(grd) | Neuruppin | P-51 |

1-0-1 air
7-0 ground

**Ziegelbauer, Andrew, Lt.**
79th Ftr Sqn/20th Ftr Grp

| *Sqn* | *Date* | *Claims* | *Location* | *A/C* |
|---|---|---|---|---|
| 79th | Febraury 20, 1945 | (2)He-111 dest(grd) | Weiden A/F | P-51 |
| | | He-111 dam(grd) | Weiden A/F | P-51 |

0-0-0 air
2-1 ground

**Ziegler, Harry D., Lt.**
505th Ftr Sqn/339th Ftr Grp

| *Sqn* | *Date* | *Claims* | *Location* | *A/C* |
|---|---|---|---|---|
| 505th | March 1, 1945 | Ju-88 dest(grd) | S/Feldkirchen | P-51 |
| | March 2 | (.5)Me-109 dest(air)[*] | E/Magdeburg | P-51 |
| | March 3 | Ju-88 dest(grd) | E/Magdeburg | P-51 |

0.5-0-0 air
2-0 ground

* - shared with Lt. J.C. Withers of the 505th Ftr Sqn

**Zimms, David T., Lt.**
328th Ftr Sqn/352nd Ftr Grp

| *Sqn* | *Date* | *Claims* | *Location* | *A/C* |
|---|---|---|---|---|
| 328th | December 30, 1943 | (.33)Me-110 prob(air)[*] | Chalons | P-47 |
| | February 20, 1944 | (.33)Me-110 dest(air)[**] | Vogelsand | P-47 |
| | April 8 | Me-110 dest(grd) | Quackenbruck | P-47 |
| | May 27 | Me-109 dest(air) | S/Strasbourg | P-51 |

1.33-0.33-0 air
1-0 ground

* - shared with LtCol. E.L. Clark of Hdqts, 352nd Ftr Grp, and Lt. W.E. Hendrian of the 328th Ftr Sqn
** - shared with LtCol. R.W. Osborn of HdQts, 67th Ftr Wg, and Capt. D.S. Bryan of the 328th Ftr Sqn

**Ziska, Lawrence A., Lt.**
370th Ftr Sqn/359th Ftr Grp

| *Sqn* | *Date* | *Claims* | *Location* | *A/C* |
|---|---|---|---|---|
| 370th | August 27, 1944 | u/i a/c dest(air) | Munster | P-51 |
| | December 31 | (.5)Me-109 dest(air)[*] | Hanover | P-51 |

1.5-0-0 air
0-0 ground

* - shared with Lt. F.O. Lux of the 370th Ftr Sqn

**Zolner, John, Lt.**
350th Ftr Sqn/353rd Ftr Grp

| *Sqn* | *Date* | *Claims* | *Location* | *A/C* |
|---|---|---|---|---|
| 350th | March 8, 1944 | FW-190 dest(air) | Hanover | P-47 |

1-0-0 air
0-0 ground

**Zumwalt, Harding R., Lt.**
83rd Ftr Sqn/78th Ftr Grp

| *Sqn* | *Date* | *Claims* | *Location* | *A/C* |
|---|---|---|---|---|
| 83rd | February 22, 1944 | Me-109 dam(air) | Aachen | P-47 |
| | April 13 | FW-190 dam(air) | NE Trier | P-47 |

0-0-2 air
0-0 ground

# PART FOUR:
# Ace Data

## Introduction

During the Second World War, the United States had eleven Air Forces which actively engaged in operations against the Axis powers. Of those eleven, only three awarded credit to pilots for the destruction of enemy aircraft on the ground: the 8th Air Force in Europe, and the 10th and 14th Air Forces in the China-Burma-India Theater. The others (as well as the Navy and Marine Corps) kept scant records of individual ground scores and as such, most books dealing with the American aces exclude those with five or more combined air-ground victories. The author does not wish to get involved in the controversy over the definition of "ace" or to downgrade the accomplishments of the aerial aces of all services, but since the 8th Air Force did extend that recognition and this book deals solely with the 8th Air Force, the author has chosen to include these pilots in the fraternity of aces.

When the 8th Air Force first introduced this statistic in early 1944, it was meant as an incentive for the pilots to "hit the deck"; to strike the Luftwaffe anywhere it was found. Strafing of airfields was by no means an easy job; of the 8th's 2,145 losses, a good portion can be attributed to ground strafing hazards: flak (of all sorts and sizes), or collisions (with electric towers/wires, trees, etc., and in some cases, hitting the ground itself). Ask most 8th Air Force pilots and few will say they enjoyed strafing airfields. Individual flying skill, training, and tactics meant little when shooting up ground targets. It was not a case of pilot against pilot where the "best man" could win, it was a case of a pilot gambling his aircraft (and life) against a chance hit by a lucky flak gunner.

Critics of awarding ground kills point to the difficulty in determining if a plane was actually destroyed or not. It is true that gun camera film and eyewitnesses could not always definitely confirm a claim as destroyed. After over fifty years it would be impossible to totally confirm or disclaim each credit, but with fairly strict awarding procedures by higher authorities, most claims could be considered accurate.

Scores were accounted for by studying various official and unofficial documents. One major factor in final determination of scores was based on the 8th Fighter Command Victory Credit Board Final Assessment. This report was released in the Fall of 1945 and listed all claims made and whether confirmation was given or not. Where this report made obvious errors (there were some instances where claims were doubled in the final count and in other cases, names were misspelled which resulted in incorrect scores) corrections have been made.

The author will point out that there may possibly be errors, but overall, the scores presented should be accurate. The reader will notice a few scores are different from what has been accepted as fact over the years; please remember, however, that this is the first in-depth look at the 8th's air-ground aces in a number of years and not simply a re-hash of old information. If anyone has documented evidence contrary to what is printed, they are welcome to contact the author for future corrections.

### Aerial Aces of the 8th Air Force

| Name | Claims | Group | |
|---|---|---|---|
| Gabreski, Francis S., LtCol. | 28 | 56th | |
| Johnson, Robert S., Maj. | 27 | 56th | |
| Preddy, George E., Maj. | 26.83 | 352nd | |
| Meyer, John C., Col. | 24 | 352nd | |
| Schilling, David C., Col. | 22.5 | 56th | |
| Gentile, Don S., Capt. | 21.83 | 4th | 2 v RAF |
| Christensen Fred J., Jr., Capt. | 21.5 | 56th | |
| Wetmore, Ray S., Maj. | 21.25 | 359th | |
| Mahurin, Walker M., Maj. | 19.75 | 56th | |
| Duncan, Glenn E., Col. | 19.5 | 353rd | |
| Carson, Leonard K., Maj. | 18.5 | 357th | |
| Beckham, Walter C., Maj. | 18 | 353rd | |
| Zemke, Hubert, Col. | 17.75 | 56th | |
| | | 479th | |
| England, John B., Maj. | 17.5 | 357th | |
| Beeson, Duane W. Capt. | 17.33 | 4th | |
| Thornell, John F., Jr., Capt. | 17.25 | 352nd | |
| Johnson, Gerald W., Maj. | 16.5 | 56th | |
| | | 356th | |
| Godfrey, John T., Maj. | 16.33 | 4th | |
| Anderson, Clarence E., Jr., Maj. | 16.25 | 357th | |
| Peterson, Richard A., Maj. | 15.5 | 357th | |
| Whisner, William T., Capt. | 15.5 | 352nd | |
| Foy. Robert W., Maj. | 15 | 357th | |
| Hofer, Ralph K., Lt. | 15 | 4th | |
| Blakeslee, Donald J.M., Col. | 14.5 | 4th | 3 v RAF |
| Landers, John D., LtCol. | 14.5 | 55th | 6 v PTO |
| | | 78th | |
| | | 357th | |
| Powers, Joseph H., Capt. | 14.5 | 56th | |
| Brown, Henry W., Capt. | 14.2 | 355th | |
| Goodson, James A., Maj. | 14 | 4th | |
| Jeffrey, Arthur F., LtCol. | 14 | 479th | |
| Bochkay, Donald H., Maj. | 13.83 | 357th | |
| Carpenter, George, Maj. | 13.83 | 4th | |
| Strait, Donald J., Maj. | 13.5 | 356th | |
| Bryan, Donald S., Maj. | 13.33 | 352nd | |
| Millikan, Willard W., Capt. | 13 | 4th | |
| Moran, Glennon T., Lt. | 13 | 352nd | |
| Olds, Robin, Maj. | 13 | 479th | |
| Williamson, Felix D., Maj. | 13 | 56th | |
| Brown, Quince L., Maj. | 12.33 | 78th | |
| Gleason, George W., Capt. | 12 | 479th | |
| Hively, Howard D., Maj. | 12 | 4th | |
| Schreiber, Leroy A., Maj. | 12 | 56th | |
| Megura, Nicholas, Capt. | 11.83 | 4th | |
| Conger, Paul A., Maj. | 11.5 | 56th | |
| Kirla, John A., Capt. | 11.5 | 357th | |
| Stewart, James C., LtCol. | 11.5 | 56th | |
| Yeager, Charles E., Capt. | 11.5 | 357th | |
| McKennon, Pierce W., Maj. | 11 | 4th | |
| Quirk, Michael J., Capt. | 11 | 56th | |
| Ceuleers, George F., LtCol. | 10.5 | 364th | |
| Clark, James A., Jr., LtCol. | 10.5 | 4th | |
| Doersch, George A., Maj. | 10.5 | 359th | |
| Halton, William T., LtCol. | 10.5 | 352nd | |
| Hovde, William J., Maj. | 10.5 | 361st | |
| Littge, Raymond H., Capt. | 10.5 | 352nd | |
| Storch, John A., LtCol. | 10.5 | 357th | |
| Glover, Fred W., Maj. | 10.33 | 4th | |
| Norley, Louis H., Maj. | 10.33 | 4th | |
| Anderson, Charles F., Jr., Capt. | 10 | 4th | |
| Blickenstaff, Wayne K., LtCol. | 10 | 353rd | |
| Gladych, Bolek M., Maj. | 10 | 56th | |
| Lines, Ted E., Capt. | 10 | 4th | |
| Rankin, Robert J., Capt. | 10 | 56th | |
| Bankey, Ernest E., Jr., Maj. | 9.5 | 364th | |
| Spencer, Dale F., Lt. | 9.5 | 361st | |
| Adams, Fletcher E., Capt. | 9 | 357th | |
| Andrew, Stephen W., Maj. | 9 | 352nd | 1 v PTO |
| Beyer, William R., Capt. | 9 | 361st | |
| Fiebelkorn, Ernest C., Capt. | 9 | 20th | |
| Gallup, Kenneth W., LtCol. | 9 | 353rd | |
| Juchheim, Alwin M., Capt. | 9 | 78th | |
| Meroney, Virgil K., Capt. | 9 | 352nd | |
| Morrill, Stanley B., Capt. | 9 | 56th | |
| Roberts, Eugene P., LtCol. | 9 | 78th | |
| | | 364th | |
| Bennett, Joseph H., Capt. | 8.5 | 4th | |
| | | 56th | |
| | | 356th | |
| Cesky, Charles J., Capt. | 8.5 | 352nd | |
| Hayes, Thomas L., Jr., LtCol. | 8.5 | 357th | |
| Jenkins, Otto D., Lt. | 8.5 | 357th | |
| Luksic, Carl J., Lt. | 8.5 | 352nd | |
| McGrattan, Bernard L., Capt. | 8.5 | 4th | |
| Moats, Sanford K., Capt. | 8.5 | 352nd | |
| Schlegel, Albert L., Capt. | 8.5 | 4th | |
| Booth, Robert J., Lt. | 8 | 359th | |
| Bostwick, George E., Maj. | 8 | 56th | |
| Broadhead, Joseph E., LtCol. | 8 | 357th | |
| Elder, John L., Jr., LtCol. | 8 | 355th | |
| Fowle, James M., Capt. | 8 | 364th | |
| Gerard, Francis R., Capt. | 8 | 339th | |
| Ilfrey, Jack M., Maj. | 8 | 20th | 6 v PTO |
| Jackson, Michael J., Maj. | 8 | 56th | |
| Kinnard, Claiborne H., Jr., LtCol. | 8 | 4th | |
| | | 355th | |
| | | 356th | |
| Schiltz, Glen D., Jr., Capt. | 8 | 56th | |
| Shaw, Robert M., Capt. | 8 | 357th | |
| Sublett, John L., Capt. | 8 | 357th | |
| Vogt, John W., Jr., Maj. | 8 | 56th | |
| | | 356th | |
| Weaver, Charles E., Capt. | 8 | 357th | |
| Lang, Joseph L., Capt. | 7.83 | 4th | |
| Stewart, Everett W., Col. | 7.83 | 4th | |
| | | 352nd | |
| | | 355th | |
| Bryan, William E., Jr., Maj. | 7.5 | 339th | |
| Cutler, Frank A., Capt. | 7.5 | 352nd | |
| Davis, Glendon V., Capt. | 7.5 | 357th | |
| Karger, Dale E., Lt. | 7.5 | 357th | |
| Lowell, John H., LtCol. | 7.5 | 364th | |
| Miklajcyk, Henry J., Capt. | 7.5 | 352nd | |
| Righetti, Elwyn G., LtCol. | 7.5 | 55th | |
| Garrison, Vermont, Lt. | 7.33 | 4th | |
| Morris, James M., Capt. | 7.33 | 20th | |
| Becker, Robert H., Capt. | 7 | 357th | |
| Browning, James W., Capt. | 7 | 357th | |
| Carder, John B., Capt. | 7 | 357th | |
| Cramer, Darrell S., Maj. | 7 | 55th | 0.5 v PTO |
| Crenshaw, Claude J., Capt. | 7 | 359th | |
| Edens, Billy G., Lt. | 7 | 56th | |
| Graham, Gordon M., LtCol. | 7 | 355th | |
| Hockery, John J., Capt. | 7 | 78th | |
| Jackson, Willie O., Jr., LtCol. | 7 | 352nd | |
| Jamison, Gilbert L., Capt. | 7 | 364th | |
| Johnson, Clarence O., Capt. | 7 | 352nd | 4 v MTO |
| | | 479th | |
| King, Benjamin H., Maj. | 7 | 359th | 3 v PTO |
| | | 479th | |
| Klibbe, Frank W., Lt. | 7 | 56th | |
| Lamb, Robert A., Maj. | 7 | 56th | |
| Lewis, William H., Capt. | 7 | 55th | |
| Marshall, Bert W., Jr., LtCol. | 7 | 355th | |
| Maguire, William J., Capt. | 7 | 353rd | |
| O'Brien, Gilbert M., Capt. | 7 | 357th | |

| | | | |
|---|---|---|---|
| Peterson, Chesley G., Col. | 7 | 4th | 6 v RAF |
| Pierce, Joseph F., Lt. | 7 | 357th | |
| Poindexter, James N., Capt. | 7 | 353rd | |
| Shafer, Dale E., Jr., LtCol. | 7 | 339th | 4 v MTO |
| Smith, Leslie C., LtCol. | 7 | 56th | |
| Starck, Walter E., Capt. | 7 | 352nd | |
| Truluck, John H., Capt. | 7 | 56th | |
| Tyler, Gerald E., Capt. | 7 | 357th | |
| Wicker, Samuel J., Maj. | 7 | 364th | |
| Woods, Sidney S., LtCol. | 7 | 4th | 2 v PTO |
| | | 479th | |
| Woody, Robert E., Capt. | 7 | 355th | |
| Murphy, John B., LtCol. | 6.75 | 359th | 0.5 v Al |
| Cummings, Donald M., Capt. | 6.5 | 55th | 1 v MTO |
| Hubbard, Mark E., LtCol. | 6.5 | 20th | 4 v MTO |
| Kruzel, Joseph J., LtCol. | 6.5 | 361st | 3 v PTO |
| Moseley, Mark L., Capt. | 6.5 | 56th | |
| Riley, Paul S., Lt. | 6.5 | 4th | |
| Bille, Henry S., Maj. | 6 | 355th | |
| Brown, Harley L., Capt. | 6 | 20th | |
| Candelaria, Richard G., Lt. | 6 | 479th | |
| Care, Raymond C., Capt. | 6 | 4th | |
| Carlson, Kendall E., Capt. | 6 | 4th | |
| Carter, James R., Maj. | 6 | 56th | |
| Cook, Walter V., Capt. | 6 | 56th | |
| Cundy, Arthur C., Lt. | 6 | 353rd | |
| Drew, Urban L., Lt. | 6 | 361st | |
| Evans, Andrew J., Jr., LtCol. | 6 | 357th | |
| Evans, Roy W., LtCol. | 6 | 4th | |
| | | 359th | |
| Hall, George F., Capt. | 6 | 56th | |
| Hart, Cameron M., Capt. | 6 | 56th | |
| Haviland, Fred R., Jr., Capt. | 6 | 355th | |
| Howe, David W., Capt. | 6 | 4th | |
| Howes, Bernard H., Lt. | 6 | 55th | |
| Jones, Cyril W., Lt. | 6 | 359th | |
| Larson, Donald A., Maj. | 6 | 339th | |
| Keen, Robert J., Capt. | 6 | 56th | |
| Kemp, William T., Lt. | 6 | 361st | |
| McGee, Donald C., Maj. | 6 | 357th | 5 v PTO |
| McKeon, Joseph T., Capt. | 6 | 20th | 5 v PTO |
| Mills, Henry L., Maj. | 6 | 4th | |
| Murphy, Alva C., Capt. | 6 | 357th | |
| Oberhansly, Jack J., LtCol. | 6 | 4th | |
| | | 78th | |
| Olson, Norman E., Capt. | 6 | 355th | |
| Pugh, John F., Capt. | 6 | 357th | |
| Roberson, Arval J., Lt. | 6 | 357th | |
| Scheible, Wilbur R., Maj. | 6 | 356th | |
| Schimanski, Robert G., Capt. | 6 | 357th | |
| Starnes, James R., Capt. | 6 | 339th | |
| Thwaites, David F., Capt. | 6 | 356th | |
| Turley, Grant M., Lt. | 6 | 78th | |
| Welch, Robert E., Capt. | 6 | 55th | |
| Whalen, William E., Lt. | 6 | 2nd SF | |
| | | 4th | |
| Wilkinson, James W., Capt. | 6 | 4th | |
| | | 78th | |
| Fortier, Norman J., Maj. | 5.83 | 355th | |
| Koraleski, Walter J., Capt. | 5.53 | 355th | |
| Amoss, Dudley M., Lt. | 5.5 | 55th | |
| Buttke, Robert L., Capt. | 5.5 | 55th | |
| Burdick, Clinton D., Lt. | 5.5 | 356th | |
| Compton, Gordon B., Capt. | 5.5 | 353rd | |
| Gailer, Frank L., Jr., Lt. | 5.5 | 357th | |
| Graham, Lindol F., Capt. | 5.5 | 20th | |
| Hatala, Paul R., Capt. | 5.5 | 357th | |
| Heller, Edwin L., Capt. | 5.5 | 352nd | |
| Horne, Francis W., Capt. | 5.5 | 352nd | |
| Lenfest, Charles W., Maj. | 5.5 | 355th | |
| McCauley, Frank E., Lt. | 5.5 | 56th | |
| Minchew, Leslie D., Capt. | 5.5 | 355th | |
| O'Brien, William R., Capt. | 5.5 | 357th | |
| Pascoe, James J., Lt. | 5.5 | 364th | |
| Ruder, Leroy A., Capt. | 5.5 | 357th | |
| Smith, Donovan F., Maj. | 5.5 | 56th | |
| Tanner, William F., Maj. | 5.5 | 353rd | |
| Vanden Heuval, George R., Lt. | 5.5 | 361st | |
| Winks, Robert P., Capt. | 5.5 | 357th | |
| Biel, Hipolitus T., Lt. | 5.33 | 4th | |
| Duffy, James E., Jr., Capt. | 5.2 | 355th | |
| Abernathy, Robert W., Capt. | 5 | 353rd | |
| Allen, William H., Lt. | 5 | 55th | |
| Ammon, Robert H., Capt. | 5 | 339th | |
| Baccus, Donald A., LtCol. | 5 | 356th | |
| | | 359th | |
| Bank, Raymond M., Lt. | 5 | 357th | |
| Beavers, Edward H., Jr., Capt. | 5 | 339th | |
| Bostrom, Ernest O., Capt. | 5 | 352nd | |
| Brown, Gerald, Maj. | 5 | 4th | |
| | | 55th | |
| Chandler, Van E., Lt. | 5 | 4th | |
| Cole, Charles H., Capt. | 5 | 20th | |
| Comstock, Harold E., Maj. | 5 | 56th | |
| Coons, Merle M., Capt. | 5 | 55th | |
| Cox, Ralph L., Maj. | 5 | 359th | |
| Cranfill, Niven K., LtCol. | 5 | 359th | |
| Cullerton, William J., Lt. | 5 | 355th | |
| Davis, Clayton E., Capt. | 5 | 352nd | |
| Daniell, Jack S., Lt. | 5 | 339th | |
| Dregne, Irwin H., Col. | 5 | 357th | |
| Egan, Joseph L., Jr., Capt. | 5 | 56th | |
| Elder, Robert A., LtCol. | 5 | 353rd | |
| Gerick, Steven, Capt. | 5 | 56th | |
| Hanseman, Christopher J., Lt. | 5 | 339th | |
| Harris, Thomas L., Capt. | 5 | 357th | |
| Hartley, Raymond E., Jr., Capt. | 5 | 353rd | 2 v MTO |
| Hauver, Charles D., Capt. | 5 | 355th | |
| Haworth, Russell C., Lt. | 5 | 55th | |
| Hiro, Edwin W., Maj. | 5 | 357th | |
| Hodges, William R., Capt. | 5 | 359th | |
| Icard, Joseph W., Lt. | 5 | 56th | |
| Johnson, Evan M., V, Capt. | 5 | 339th | |
| Jones, Frank C., Capt. | 5 | 4th | |
| Julian, William H., LtCol. | 5 | 78th | |
| | | 339th | |
| Lazear, Earl R., Jr., Capt. | 5 | 352nd | |
| London, Charles P., Capt. | 5 | 78th | |
| Markham, Gene E., Capt. | 5 | 353rd | |
| Marsh, Lester C., Lt. | 5 | 339th | |
| Mason, Joseph L., Col. | 5 | 352nd | |
| Maxwell, Chester K., Capt. | 5 | 357th | |
| McElroy, James N., Capt. | 5 | 355th | |
| McGinn, John L., LtCol. | 5 | 55th | 3 v PTO |
| McMinn, Evan D., Lt. | 5 | 56th | |
| Merritt, George L., Maj. | 5 | 361st | |
| Pissanos, Spiros N., Capt. | 5 | 4th | |
| Pompetti, Peter E., Lt. | 5 | 78th | |
| Price, Jack C., Maj. | 5 | 20th | |
| | | 78th | |
| Priest, Royce W., Lt. | 5 | 355th | |
| Reese, William C., Lt. | 5 | 357th | |
| Schank, Thomas D., Lt. | 5 | 55th | |
| Schuh, Duerr H., Capt. | 5 | 352nd | |
| Sears, Alex F., Capt. | 5 | 352nd | |
| Smith, Kenneth G., Capt. | 5 | 4th | |
| Stangel, William J., Capt. | 5 | 352nd | |
| Stanley, Morris A., Capt. | 5 | 357th | |
| Sykes, William J., Lt. | 5 | 361st | |
| Tordoff, Harrison B., Capt. | 5 | 353rd | |
| Waggoner, Horace Q., Capt. | 5 | 353rd | |
| Warren, Jack R., Capt. | 5 | 357th | |
| Wilson, William F., Capt. | 5 | 364th | |
| York, Robert M., Capt. | 5 | 359th | |

**Air and Ground Aces of the 8th Air Force**

| Name | Air | Grd | Total | Group |
|---|---|---|---|---|
| Meyer, John C., LtCol. | 24 | 13 | 37 | 352nd |
| Landers, John D., LtCol. | 14.5 | 20 | 34.5 | 55th 6 v PTO |
| | | | | 78th |
| | | | | 357th |
| Righetti, Elwyn G., LtCol. | 7.5 | 27 | 34.5 | 55th |
| Schilling, David C., Col. | 22.5 | 10.5 | 33 | 56th |
| Preddy, George E., Maj. | 26.83 | 5 | 31.83 | 352nd |
| Gabreski, Francis S., LtCol. | 28 | 3 | 31 | 56th |
| Godfrey, John T., Maj. | 16.33 | 13.67 | 30 | 4th |
| Goodson, James A., Maj. | 14 | 15 | 29 | 4th |
| Brown, Henry W., Capt. | 14.2 | 14.5 | 28.7 | 355th |
| Hofer, Ralph K., Lt. | 15 | 13.5 | 28.5 | 4th |
| Thury, Joseph L., LtCol. | 2.5 | 25.5 | 28 | 339th |
| Gentile, Don S., Capt. | 21.83 | 6 | 27.83 | 4th 2 v RAF |
| Johnson, Robert S., Maj. | 27 | 0 | 27 | 56th |
| Duncan, Glenn E., Col. | 19.5 | 6.83 | 26.33 | 353rd |
| Zemke, Hubert, Col. | 17.75 | 8.5 | 26.25 | 56th |
| | | | | 479th |
| Kinnard, Claiborne H., LtCol. | 8 | 17 | 25 | 4th |
| | | | | 355th |
| | | | | 356th |
| Glover, Fred W., Maj. | 10.33 | 14.5 | 24.83 | 4th |
| Wetmore, Ray S., Maj. | 21.25 | 3.33 | 24.58 | 359th |
| Olds, Robin, Maj. | 13 | 11 | 24 | 479th |
| Littge, Raymond H., Capt. | 10.5 | 13 | 23.5 | 352nd |
| Beeson, Duane W., Capt. | 17.33 | 4.75 | 22.08 | 4th |
| Carson, Leonard K., Maj. | 18.5 | 3.5 | 22 | 357th |
| Christensen, Fred J., Capt. | 21.5 | 0 | 21.5 | 56th |
| Elder, John L., LtCol. | 8 | 13 | 21 | 355th |

| | | | | | |
|---|---|---|---|---|---|
| Compton, Gordon B., Capt. | 5.5 | 15 | 20.5 | 353rd | |
| Cullerton, William J., Lt. | 5 | 15 | 20 | 355th | |
| Heller, Edwin L., Capt. | 5.5 | 14.5 | 20 | 352nd | |
| Mahurin, Walker M., Maj. | 19.75 | 0 | 19.75 | 56th | |
| Tower, Archie A., Maj. | 1.5 | 18 | 19.5 | 339th | |
| Thornell, John F., Jr., Capt. | 17.25 | 2 | 19.25 | 352nd | |
| Peterson, Richard A., Maj. | 15.5 | 3.5 | 19 | 357th | |
| England, John B., Maj. | 17.5 | 1 | 18.5 | 357th | |
| Whisner, William T., Capt. | 15.5 | 3 | 18.5 | 352nd | |
| Beckham, Walter C., Maj. | 18 | 0 | 18 | 353rd | |
| Foy, Robert W., Maj. | 15 | 3 | 18 | 357th | |
| Welch, Robert E., Capt. | 6 | 12 | 18 | 55th | |
| McKennon, Pierce W., Maj. | 11 | 6.67 | 17.67 | 4th | |
| Montgomery, Gerald E., Maj. | 3 | 14.5 | 17.5 | 4th | |
| Anderson, Clarence E., Maj. | 16.25 | 1 | 17.25 | 357th | |
| Graham, Gordon M., LtCol. | 7 | 9.5 | 16.5 | 355th | |
| Johnson, Gerald W., Maj. | 16.5 | 0 | 16.5 | 56th<br>356th | |
| Lowell, John H., LtCol. | 7.5 | 9 | 16.5 | 364th | |
| Blakeslee, Donald J.M., Col. | 14.5 | 1.5 | 16 | 4th | 3 v RAF |
| Moran, Glennon T., Lt. | 13 | 3 | 16 | 352nd | |
| Quirk, Michael J., Capt. | 11 | 5 | 16 | 56th | |
| Carpenter, George, Maj. | 13.83 | 2 | 15.83 | 4th | |
| Megura, Nicholas, Capt. | 11.83 | 3.75 | 15.58 | 4th | |
| Anderson, Charles F., Capt. | 10 | 5.5 | 15.5 | 4th | |
| Andrew, Stephen W., Maj. | 9 | 6.5 | 15.5 | 352nd | 1 v PTO |
| Bankey, Ernest E., Jr., Maj. | 9.5 | 6 | 15.5 | 364th | |
| Luksoc, Carl J., Lt. | 8.5 | 7 | 15.5 | 352nd | |
| Norley, Louis H., Maj. | 10.33 | 5 | 15.33 | 4th | |
| Bostwick, George E., Maj. | 8 | 7 | 15 | 56th | |
| Clark, James A., Jr., LtCol. | 10.5 | 4.5 | 15 | 4th | |
| Juchheim, Alwin M., Capt. | 9 | 6 | 15 | 78th | |
| Millikan, Willard W., Capt. | 13 | 2 | 15 | 4th | |
| Everson, Kirke B., Capt. | 1.5 | 13 | 14.5 | 339th | |
| Gleason, George W., Capt. | 12 | 2.5 | 14.5 | 479th | |
| Hightshoe, Melville W., Capt. | 0 | 14.5 | 14.5 | 353rd | |
| Hively, Howard D., Maj. | 12 | 2.5 | 14.5 | 4th | |
| Kolb, Herbert G., Capt. | 0 | 14.5 | 14.5 | 353rd | |
| Powers, Joseph H., Capt. | 14.5 | 0 | 14.5 | 56th | |
| Duffy, James E., Jr. | 5.2 | 9 | 14.2 | 355th | |
| Ammon, Robert H., Capt. | 5 | 9 | 14 | 339th | |
| Jeffrey, Arthur F., LtCol. | 14 | 0 | 14 | 479th | |
| Schreiber, Leroy A., Maj. | 12 | 2 | 14 | 56th | |
| Bochkay, Donald H., Maj. | 13.83 | 0 | 13.83 | 357th | |
| Boone, Walker L., Maj. | 2 | 11.79 | 13.79 | 78th<br>353rd | |
| Anderson, Woodrow W., Capt. | 4.5 | 9 | 13.5 | 352nd | |
| Jackson, Michael J., Maj. | 8 | 5.5 | 13.5 | 56th | |
| Morris, Ray S., Lt. | 3.5 | 10 | 13.5 | 355th | |
| Schlegel, Albert L., Capt. | 8.5 | 5 | 13.5 | 4th | |
| Strait, Donald J., Maj. | 13.5 | 0 | 13.5 | 356th | |
| Brown, Quince L., Maj. | 12.33 | 1 | 13.33 | 78th | |
| Bryan, Donald S., Maj. | 13.33 | 0 | 13.33 | 352nd | |
| Johnson, Clarence O., Capt. | 7 | 6 | 13 | 352nd<br>479th | 4 v MTO |
| Miklajcyk, Henry J., Capt. | 7.5 | 5.5 | 13 | 352nd | |
| Murphy, Randel L., Lt. | 2 | 11 | 13 | 56th | |
| Williamson, Felix D., Maj. | 13 | 0 | 13 | 56th | |
| Gustke, Richard N., F/O | 0 | 12.5 | 12.5 | 353rd | |
| Halton, William T., LtCol. | 10.5 | 2 | 12.5 | 352nd | |
| Hovde, William J., Maj. | 10.5 | 2 | 12.5 | 355th | |
| Rimerman, Ben, Col. | 4.5 | 8 | 12.5 | 55th<br>353rd | |
| Stewart, James C., LtCol. | 11.5 | 1 | 12.5 | 56th | |
| Waggoner, Horace Q., Capt. | 5 | 7.5 | 12.5 | 353rd | |
| Biggs, Oscar K., Lt. | 0.5 | 11.5 | 12 | 339th | |
| Corey, Harry R., Capt. | 1 | 11 | 12 | 339th | |
| Doersch, George A., Maj. | 10.5 | 1.5 | 12 | 359th | |
| Emory, Frank N., Capt. | 2 | 10 | 12 | 353rd | |
| Harrington, Francis E., Lt. | 4 | 8 | 12 | 78th | |
| Haviland, Fred R., Jr., Capt. | 6 | 6 | 12 | 355th | |
| Kirla, John A., Capt. | 11.5 | 0.5 | 12 | 357th | |
| Lanoue, Roland J., Lt. | 1 | 11 | 12 | 353rd | |
| Starnes, James R., Capt. | 6 | 6 | 12 | 339th | |
| Storch, John A., LtCol. | 10.5 | 1.5 | 12 | 364th | |
| Lang, Joseph L., Capt. | 7.83 | 4 | 11.83 | 4th | |
| Conger, Paul A., Maj. | 11.5 | 0 | 11.5 | 56th | |
| Duffie, Claire A.P., Maj. | 3 | 8.5 | 11.5 | 479th | |
| Karger, Dale E., Lt. | 7.5 | 4 | 11.5 | 357th | |
| Smith, Leslie C., LtCol. | 7 | 4.5 | 11.5 | 56th | |
| Yeager, Charles E., Capt. | 11.5 | 0 | 11.5 | 357th | |
| Biel, Hipolitus T., Lt. | 5.33 | 6 | 11.33 | 4th | |
| Fortier, Norman J., Maj. | 5.83 | 5.5 | 11.33 | 355th | |
| Burch, Harold W., Lt. | 0 | 11 | 11 | 339th | |
| Cole, Charles H., Jr., Capt. | 5 | 6 | 11 | 20th | |
| Fiebelkorn, Ernest C., Capt. | 9 | 2 | 11 | 20th | |
| Gallup, Kenneth W., LtCol. | 9 | 2 | 11 | 353rd | |
| Gladych, Bolek M., Maj. | 10 | 1 | 11 | 56th | |
| Jackson, Willie O., Jr., LtCol | 7 | 4 | 11 | 352nd | |
| Jones, Cyril W., Lt. | 6 | 5 | 11 | 359th | |
| McElroy, James N., Capt. | 5 | 6 | 11 | 355th | |
| Merritt, George L., Maj. | 5 | 6 | 11 | 361st | |
| Miller, Gerald J., Lt. | 0 | 11 | 11 | 353rd | |
| Poindexter, James N., Maj. | 7 | 4 | 11 | 353rd | |
| Weaver, Charles E., Capt. | 8 | 3 | 11 | 357th | |
| Ceuleers, George F., LtCol. | 10.5 | 0 | 10.5 | 364th | |
| Cutler, Frank A., Capt. | 7.5 | 3 | 10.5 | 352nd | |
| Dregne, Irwin H., Col. | 5 | 5.5 | 10.5 | 357th | |
| Gilbert, Olin E., LtCol. | 2 | 8.5 | 10.5 | 78th<br>66th(FW) | |
| Jacobson, Gail E., Lt. | 4.5 | 6 | 10.5 | 479th | |
| Jenkins, Otto D., Lt. | 8.5 | 2 | 10.5 | 357th | |
| Jones, Frank C., Capt. | 5 | 5.5 | 10.5 | 4th | |
| Malmsten, Donald M., Capt. | 1.5 | 9 | 10.5 | 4th | |
| Olson, Thomas C., Lt. | 1 | 9.5 | 10.5 | 479th | |
| Morris, James M., Capt. | 7.33 | 2.83 | 10.16 | 20th | |
| Bille, Henry S., Maj. | 6 | 4 | 10 | 355th | |
| Blickenstaff, Wayne K., LtCol | 10 | 0 | 10 | 353rd | |
| Carson, Kendall E., Capt. | 6 | 4 | 10 | 4th | |
| Crenshaw, Claude E., Capt. | 7 | 3 | 10 | 359th | |
| Duncan, John F., Lt. | 4 | 6 | 10 | 357th | |
| Edens, Billy G., Lt. | 7 | 3 | 10 | 56th | |
| Hollingsworth, James M., Capt. | 3 | 7 | 10 | 479th | 3 v MTO |
| Johnson, Martin H., Capt. | 1 | 9 | 10 | 361st | |
| Keen, Robert J., Capt. | 6 | 4 | 10 | 56th | |
| Kirk, John A., III, Lt. | 4 | 6 | 10 | 78th | |
| Kyler, Russell S., Lt. | 3 | 7 | 10 | 56th | |
| Lines, Ted E., Capt. | 10 | 0 | 10 | 4th | |
| Mansker, Joseph L., Capt. | 3 | 7 | 10 | 20th | |
| Marshall, Bert W., Jr., LtCol. | 7 | 3 | 10 | 355th | |
| McCormick, Arthur B., Capt. | 1 | 9 | 10 | 364th | |
| McMullen, Joseph D., Lt. | 0 | 10 | 10 | 353rd | |
| Mellen, Joseph E., Capt. | 2 | 8 | 10 | 355th | |
| Peal, Charles M., Capt. | 2 | 8 | 10 | 78th | |
| Rankin, Robert J., Capt. | 10 | 0 | 10 | 56th | |
| Spencer, Dale F., Lt. | 9.5 | 0.5 | 10 | 361st | |
| Sykes, William J., Lt. | 5 | 5 | 10 | 361st | |
| Waldron, Karl M., Jr., Lt. | 3 | 7 | 10 | 352nd | |
| Woods, Sidney S., LtCol. | 7 | 3 | 10 | 4th<br>479th | 2 v PTO |
| Bryan, William E., Jr., Maj. | 7.5 | 2 | 9.5 | 339th | |
| Riley, Paul S., Lt. | 6.5 | 3 | 9.5 | 4th | |
| Tordoff, Harrison B., Capt. | 5 | 4.5 | 9.5 | 353rd | |
| Stewart, Everett W., Col. | 7.83 | 1.5 | 9.33 | 4th<br>352nd<br>355th | |
| Adams, Fletcher E., Capt. | 9 | 0 | 9 | 357th | |
| Baccus, Donald A., LtCol. | 5 | 4 | 9 | 356th<br>359th | |
| Beyer, William R., Capt. | 9 | 0 | 9 | 361st | |
| Chandler, Van E., Lt. | 5 | 4 | 9 | 4th | |
| Clark, William C., LtCol. | 1 | 8 | 9 | 66th(FW)<br>339th | |
| Cramer, Darrell S., Maj. | 7 | 2 | 9 | 55th | 0.5 v PTO |
| Cunnick, John W., III, Lt. | 2 | 7 | 9 | 55th | |
| Dade, Lucian A., LtCol. | 3 | 6 | 9 | 56th | |
| Davis, Clayton E., Capt. | 5 | 4 | 9 | 352nd | |
| Gevorkian, Samuel D., Capt. | 2 | 7 | 9 | 55th | |
| Giller, Edward B., Maj. | 3 | 6 | 9 | 55th | |
| Hartley, Raymond E., Capt. | 5 | 4 | 9 | 353rd | 2 v MTO |
| Hatter, Robert B., Capt. | 3 | 6 | 9 | 359th | |
| Hunter, John C., Capt. | 3 | 6 | 9 | 359th | |
| Larson, Donald A., Maj. | 6 | 3 | 9 | 339th | |
| Marvel, Thomas W., Lt. | 0 | 9 | 9 | 339th | |
| McDuffie, Duncan M., Lt. | 4 | 5 | 9 | 78th | |
| Meroney, Virgil K., Capt. | 9 | 0 | 9 | 352nd | |
| Morrill, Stanley B., Capt. | 9 | 0 | 9 | 56th | |
| Roberts, Eugene P., LtCol. | 9 | 0 | 9 | 78th<br>364th | |
| Scheible, Wilbur R., Maj. | 6 | 3 | 9 | 356th | |
| Shafer, Dale E., Jr., LtCol. | 7 | 2 | 9 | 339th | 4 v MTO |
| Sublett, John L., Capt. | 8 | 1 | 9 | 357th | |
| Taylor, Clyde E., Lt. | 0 | 9 | 9 | 78th | |
| Visconte, Romildo, Capt. | 4 | 5 | 9 | 364th | |
| Webb, Roy A., Jr., LtCol. | 4 | 5 | 9 | 361st | |
| Woody, Robert E., Capt. | 7 | 2 | 9 | 355th | |
| Monroe, Shelton W., Maj. | 4.33 | 4.5 | 8.83 | 4th | |
| France, Victor J., Capt. | 4.33 | 4.33 | 8.66 | 4th | |
| Happel, James R., Maj. | 4 | 4.66 | 8.66 | 4th | |
| Szaniawski, Edward W., LtCol. | 4 | 4.66 | 8.66 | 355th | |
| Bennett, Joseph H., Capt. | 8.5 | 0 | 8.5 | 4th<br>56th<br>356th | |
| Cesky, Charles J., Capt. | 8.5 | 0 | 8.5 | 352nd | |
| Hayes, Thomas L., Jr., LtCol. | 8.5 | 0 | 8.5 | 357th | |
| Howe, David W., Capt. | 6 | 2.5 | 8.5 | 4th | |

| | | | | | |
|---|---|---|---|---|---|
| McGrattan, Bernard L., Capt. | 8.5 | 0 | 8.5 | 4th | |
| Moats, Sanford K., Capt. | 8.5 | 0 | 8.5 | 352nd | |
| Myers, Raymond B., LtCol. | 4.5 | 4 | 8.5 | 355th | |
| Pierce, Donald J., Capt. | 0 | 8.5 | 8.5 | 4th<br>479th | |
| Slack, Henry R., IV, Lt. | 1.5 | 7 | 8.5 | 78th | |
| Sowerby, Theodore J., Capt. | 2 | 6.5 | 8.5 | 479th | |
| Vanden Heuval, George R., Lt. | 5.5 | 3 | 8.5 | 361st | |
| Hewitt, Richard A., Maj. | 4 | 4.33 | 8.33 | 78th | |
| Alexander, Fred H., Lt. | 2 | 6 | 8 | 20th | |
| Alfred, Carl R., Capt. | 0 | 8 | 8 | 4th | |
| Ayers, James W., Lt. | 1 | 7 | 8 | 4th | |
| Booth, Robert J., Lt. | 8 | 0 | 8 | 359th | |
| Broadhead, Joseph E., LtCol. | 8 | 0 | 8 | 357th | |
| Conner, Richard E., LtCol. | 4.5 | 3.5 | 8 | 78th | |
| Evans, Andrew J., Jr., LtCol. | 6 | 2 | 8 | 357th | |
| Falvey, Harold W., F/O | 0 | 8 | 8 | 355th | |
| Fowle, James M., Capt. | 8 | 0 | 8 | 364th | |
| Gerard, Francis R., Capt. | 8 | 0 | 8 | 339th | |
| Greenwood, Raymond P., Lt. | 0 | 8 | 8 | 353rd | |
| Hopkins, Wallace E., LtCol. | 4 | 4 | 8 | 361st | |
| Howes, Bernard H., Lt. | 6 | 2 | 8 | 55th | |
| Ilfrey, Jack M., Maj. | 8 | 0 | 8 | 20th | 6 v MTO |
| Josey, Danford E., Lt. | 0 | 8 | 8 | 78th | |
| Julian, William H., LtCol. | 5 | 3 | 8 | 78th<br>339th | |
| Jurgens, Fred H., Lt. | 0 | 8 | 8 | 20th | |
| MacClarence, William R., Lt. | 0 | 8 | 8 | 339th | |
| Maguire, William J., Capt. | 7 | 1 | 8 | 353rd | |
| McGee, Donald C., Maj. | 6 | 2 | 8 | 357th | 5 v PTO |
| McGinnis, Keith R., Lt. | 2 | 6 | 8 | 55th | |
| McKeon, Joseph T., Capt. | 6 | 2 | 8 | 20th | 5 v PTO |
| Mudge, William F., Jr., Lt. | 2 | 6 | 8 | 339th | |
| Murphy, Alva C., Capt. | 6 | 2 | 8 | 357th | |
| Olson, Norman E., Capt. | 6 | 2 | 8 | 355th | |
| Orcutt, Leon M., Jr., Lt. | 0 | 8 | 8 | 339th | |
| Orndorff, Roy W., Capt. | 4 | 4 | 8 | 364th | |
| Palson, Richard C.J., Lt. | 0 | 8 | 8 | 479th | |
| Pickering, Malcolm C., Lt. | 4 | 4 | 8 | 352nd | |
| Pierce, Joseph F., Lt. | 7 | 1 | 8 | 357th | |
| Schiltz, Glen D., Jr., Capt. | 8 | 0 | 8 | 56th | |
| Schimanski, Robert G., Capt. | 6 | 2 | 8 | 357th | |
| Shaw, Robert M., Capt. | 8 | 0 | 8 | 357th | |
| Truluck, John H., Capt. | 7 | 1 | 8 | 56th | |
| Vogt, John W., Jr., Maj. | 8 | 0 | 8 | 56th<br>356th | |
| Whalen, William E., Lt. | 6 | 2 | 8 | 2nd(SF)<br>4th | |
| Wilkinson, James W., Capt. | 6 | 2 | 8 | 4th<br>78th | |
| Yannell, Michael P., Maj. | 4 | 4 | 8 | 356th | 2 v MTO |
| Zettler, Vincent V., Lt. | 1 | 7 | 8 | 357th | |
| Siems, Grover C., Lt. | 4.33 | 3.5 | 7.83 | 4th | |
| Hockery, John J., Capt. | 7 | 0.8 | 7.8 | 78th | |
| Oberhansly, Jack J., LtCol. | 6 | 1.6 | 7.6 | 4th<br>78th | |
| Garrison, Vermont, Lt. | 7.33 | 0.25 | 7.58 | 4th | |
| Benjamin, Swift T., Lt. | 1 | 6.5 | 7.5 | 56th<br>353rd | |
| Davis, Glendon V., Capt. | 7.5 | 0 | 7.5 | 357th | |
| Henley, Donald, Jr., Lt. | 3 | 4.5 | 7.5 | 56th | |
| Joiner, Joseph H., Capt. | 3.5 | 4 | 7.5 | 4th | |
| Lenfest, Charles W., Jr., Maj. | 5.5 | 2 | 7.5 | 355th | |
| Myers, Joseph, Jr., Maj. | 4.5 | 3 | 7.5 | 55th<br>78th | |
| Smith, Donovan F., Maj. | 5.5 | 2 | 7.5 | 56th | |
| Wright, Robert C., Capt. | 3.5 | 4 | 7.5 | 361st | |
| Smith, William B., Capt. | 3 | 4.25 | 7.25 | 4th | |
| Amoss,Dudley M., Lt. | 5.5 | 1.5 | 7 | 55th | |
| Antonides, William O., Lt. | 0 | 7 | 7 | 4th | |
| Becker, Robert H., Capt. | 7 | 0 | 7 | 357th | |
| Boring, Lloyd D., Lt. | 0.5 | 6.5 | 7 | 55th | |
| Browning, James W., Capt. | 7 | 0 | 7 | 357th | |
| Carder, John B., Capt. | 7 | 0 | 7 | 357th | |
| Caywood, Herbert L., Lt. | 0 | 7 | 7 | 339th | |
| Chetneky, Steve J., Lt. | 0 | 7 | 7 | 339th | |
| Collins, William F., Capt. | 4 | 3 | 7 | 359th | |
| Comstock, Harold E., Maj. | 5 | 2 | 7 | 56th | |
| Crombie, William S., Maj. | 4 | 3 | 7 | 364th | |
| Drew, Urban L., Lt. | 6 | 1 | 7 | 361st | |
| Eckfeldt, Robert T., Lt. | 3 | 4 | 7 | 361st | |
| Elder, Robert A., LtCol. | 5 | 2 | 7 | 353rd | |
| Elmgren, Charles B., Lt. | 0 | 7 | 7 | 479th | |
| Emerson, Donald R., Capt. | 4.5 | 2.5 | 7 | 4th | |
| Farmer, Owen P., Capt. | 2 | 5 | 7 | 339th | |
| Gerick, Steven, Capt. | 5 | 2 | 7 | 56th | |
| Gresham, Walter V., Jr., Capt. | 4 | 3 | 7 | 355th | |
| Hanseman, Christopher J., Lt. | 5 | 2 | 7 | 339th | |
| Hopcroft, Ernest J., Lt. | 0 | 7 | 7 | 479th | |
| Jabara, James, Lt. | 1.5 | 5.5 | 7 | 355th | 1.5 v 9th AF |
| Jamison, Gilbert L., Capt. | 7 | 0 | 7 | 364th | |
| Johnston, Ben D., Jr., Lt. | 4 | 3 | 7 | 355th | |
| Jones, Reps D., Capt. | 2 | 5 | 7 | 20th | |
| Jones, William A., Lt. | 2 | 5 | 7 | 339th | |
| Kier, Edward L., Capt. | 2 | 5 | 7 | 20th | |
| King, Benjamin H., Maj. | 7 | 0 | 7 | 359th<br>479th | 3 v PTO |
| Klibbem Frank W., Lt. | 7 | 0 | 7 | 56th | |
| Kulik, Edward R., Capt. | 0 | 7 | 7 | 78th | |
| Lamb, Robert A., Maj. | 7 | 0 | 7 | 56th | |
| Lewis, William H., Capt. | 7 | 0 | 7 | 55th | |
| Mahany, Howard, Jr., Lt. | 0 | 7 | 7 | 55th | |
| Martin, William D., Lt. | 4 | 3 | 7 | 355th | |
| McMinn, Evan D., Lt. | 5 | 2 | 7 | 56th | |
| Murphy, Jerome T., Lt. | 0 | 7 | 7 | 339th | |
| O'Brien, Gilbert M., Capt. | 7 | 0 | 7 | 357th | |
| Peterson, Chesley G., Col. | 7 | 0 | 7 | 4th | 6 v RAF |
| Pompetti, Peter E., Lt. | 5 | 2 | 7 | 78th | |
| Price, William J., Maj. | 3 | 4 | 7 | 353rd | |
| Roberson, Arval J., Lt. | 6 | 1 | 7 | 357th | |
| Shupe, Joseph E., Lt. | 2 | 5 | 7 | 359th | |
| Silva, Stanley E., Capt. | 1 | 6 | 7 | 355th | |
| Starck, Walter E., Capt. | 7 | 0 | 7 | 352nd | |
| Stewart, David, Lt. | 0 | 7 | 7 | 20th | |
| Thwaites, David F., Capt. | 6 | 1 | 7 | 356th | |
| Tyler, Gerald E., Capt. | 7 | 0 | 7 | 357th | |
| Wicker, Samuel J., Maj. | 7 | 0 | 7 | 364th | |
| Wilson, John H., Jr., Maj. | 3.5 | 3.5 | 7 | 355th | |
| Witzel, George H., Lt. | 0 | 7 | 7 | 479th | |
| Coleman, John B., Jr., Capt. | 4.33 | 2.5 | 6.83 | 352nd | |
| Gilbertson, Merle J., Maj. | 2.83 | 4 | 6.83 | 20th | |
| Murphy, John B., LtCol. | 6.75 | 0 | 6.75 | 359th | 0.5 v Al |
| Burdick, Clinton D., Lt. | 5.5 | 1 | 6.5 | 356th | |
| Care, Raymond C., Capt. | 6 | 0.5 | 6.5 | 4th | |
| Cles, Leslie P., Capt. | 0 | 6.5 | 6.5 | 353rd | |
| Cummings, Donald M., Capt. | 6.5 | 0 | 6.5 | 55th | 1 v MTO |
| Furr, William W., Lt. | 3.5 | 3 | 6.5 | 352nd | |
| Gailer, Frank L., Jr., Lt. | 5.5 | 1 | 6.5 | 357th | |
| Gansberg, Raymond H., Capt. | 2.5 | 4 | 6.5 | 356th | |
| Garlich, Robert L., Lt. | 0 | 6.5 | 6.5 | 355th | |
| Golden, John T., Lt. | 1 | 5.5 | 6.5 | 479th | |
| Goodman, Charles E., Lt. | 4.5 | 2 | 6.5 | 352nd | |
| Grasshoff, Hans J., Capt. | 2.5 | 4 | 6.5 | 479th | |
| Green, Robert T., Capt. | 4.5 | 2 | 6.5 | 78th | |
| Henry, Carroll D., Capt. | 1.5 | 5 | 6.5 | 55th | |
| Horne, Francis W., Capt. | 5.5 | 1 | 6.5 | 352nd | |
| Hubbard, Mark E., LtCol. | 6.5 | 0 | 6.5 | 20th | 4 v MTO |
| Jones, Thomas W., Lt. | 0.5 | 6 | 6.5 | 353rd | |
| Kruzel, Joseph J., LtCol. | 6.5 | 0 | 6.5 | 361st | 3 v PTO |
| Malmstrom, Einar A., Col. | 1 | 5.5 | 6.5 | 356th | |
| Mayo, Ben I., Jr., LtCol. | 4 | 2.5 | 6.5 | 78th | |
| Moseley, Mark L., Capt. | 6.5 | 0 | 6.5 | 56th | |
| Olander, Richard B., Capt. | 1.5 | 5 | 6.5 | 339th | |
| Rich, George T., Capt. | 1.5 | 5 | 6.5 | 339th | |
| Stanley, Morris A., Capt. | 5 | 1.5 | 6.5 | 357th | |
| Tanner, William F., Maj. | 5.5 | 1 | 6.5 | 353rd | |
| Truett, Jesse L., Capt. | 0 | 6.5 | 6.5 | 364th | |
| Montgomery, Robert P., Col. | 3.33 | 3 | 6.33 | 20th | |
| Gatterdam, Richard P., Maj. | 3.7 | 2.5 | 6.2 | 20th | |
| Adams, Louis W., Lt. | 4 | 2 | 6 | 20th | |
| Bailey, William B., LtCol. | 3 | 3 | 6 | 353rd | |
| Blizzard, Robert V.E., Lt. | 0 | 6 | 6 | 339th | |
| Bonebrake, Robert R., Capt. | 3 | 3 | 6 | 78th | |
| Bosworth, Robert R., Lt. | 1 | 5 | 6 | 78th | |
| Boulet, William P., Lt. | 3 | 3 | 6 | 355th | |
| Bowers, Arthur R., Lt. | 0 | 6 | 6 | 4th | |
| Brown, Harley L., Capt. | 6 | 0 | 6 | 20th | |
| Bryan, Gillespie, Maj. | 0 | 6 | 6 | 78th | |
| Butler, George H., Lt. | 3 | 3 | 6 | 56th | |
| Candelaria, Richard G., Lt. | 6 | 0 | 6 | 479th | |
| Carter, James R., Maj. | 6 | 0 | 6 | 56th | |
| Chase, Harold W., Capt. | 2 | 4 | 6 | 353rd | |
| Chinn, Claude A., Lt. | 0 | 6 | 6 | 56th | |
| Clifton, Frank A., Lt. | 0 | 6 | 6 | 339th | |
| Colletti, Anthony T., Lt. | 1 | 5 | 6 | 78th | |
| Cook, Walter V., Capt. | 6 | 0 | 6 | 56th | |
| Cundy, Arthur C., Lt. | 6 | 0 | 6 | 353rd | |
| Davis, William C., Capt. | 0 | 6 | 6 | 353rd | |
| DeAnda, Louis, Lt. | 0 | 6 | 6 | 78th | |
| DeVilliers, Donald J., Lt. | 0 | 6 | 6 | 78th | |

| | | | | | |
|---|---|---|---|---|---|
| Dissette, Lawrence J., Capt. | 1 | 5 | 6 | 355th | |
| Einhaus, Lowell E., Capt. | 0 | 6 | 6 | 20th | |
| Evans, Roy W., LtCol. | 6 | 0 | 6 | 4th<br>359th | |
| Frisch, Robert J., Lt. | 0 | 6 | 6 | 339th | |
| Gordon, Ray C., Lt. | 0 | 6 | 6 | 353rd | |
| Gould, Clifford C., Lt. | 1 | 5 | 6 | 55th | |
| Hall, George F., Capt. | 6 | 0 | 6 | 56th | |
| Hansen, John W., Lt. | 2 | 4 | 6 | 479th | |
| Hart, Cameron M., Capt. | 6 | 0 | 6 | 56th | |
| Herren, James M., Jr., LtCol. | 4 | 2 | 6 | 479th | |
| Hooker, Verne E., Capt. | 2 | 4 | 6 | 479th | |
| Horner, Kenneth R., Lt. | 0 | 6 | 6 | 364th | |
| Irion, Robert E., Lt. | 1 | 5 | 6 | 339th | |
| Jennings, Loton D., Lt. | 0 | 6 | 6 | 4th | |
| Kemp, William T., Lt. | 6 | 0 | 6 | 361st | |
| Kirby, Henry H., Jr., Maj. | 1 | 5 | 6 | 355th | |
| Kucheman, Henry B., Jr., Maj. | 4 | 2 | 6 | 355th | |
| Lee, Louis W., Lt. | 4 | 2 | 6 | 353rd | |
| Long, Thurman C., Lt. | 2 | 4 | 6 | 355th | |
| Mayden, James D., Col. | 2 | 4 | 6 | 352nd | |
| McMahan, Bruce D., Lt. | 0.5 | 5.5 | 6 | 353rd | |
| Mills, Henry L., Maj. | 6 | 0 | 6 | 4th | |
| Minchew, Leslie D., Capt. | 5.5 | 0.5 | 6 | 355th | |
| Neely, Tom D., Lt. | 2 | 4 | 6 | 479th | |
| Nelson, Robert F., Lt. | 1 | 5 | 6 | 4th | |
| Pattillo, Charles C., Lt. | 0 | 6 | 6 | 352nd | |
| Paul, Robert H., Lt. | 0 | 6 | 6 | 339th | |
| Pederson, Douglas P., F/O | 0 | 6 | 6 | 4th | |
| Pogue, Edward F., Lt. | 0 | 6 | 6 | 20th | |
| Powell, Lawrence J., Jr., Lt. | 2.5 | 3.5 | 6 | 339th | |
| Prescott, Walter A.S., Lt. | 2 | 4 | 6 | 353rd | |
| Pugh, John F., Capt. | 6 | 0 | 6 | 357th | |
| Rafferty, Vernon G., Capt. | 2.5 | 3.5 | 6 | 353rd | |
| Reynolds, Garth L., Capt. | 2 | 4 | 6 | 20th | |
| Sears, Alexander F., Capt. | 5 | 1 | 6 | 352nd | |
| Smith, Raymond E., Maj. | 1 | 5 | 6 | 78th | |
| Speer, Frank E., Lt. | 1 | 5 | 6 | 4th | |
| Turley, Grant M., Lt. | 6 | 0 | 6 | 78th | |
| Uttwenweiler, Fred L., Capt. | 0 | 6 | 6 | 353rd | |
| Wallace, Alton J., Capt. | 3 | 3 | 6 | 352nd | |
| Wesson, Warren M., Capt. | 4 | 2 | 6 | 78th | |
| Whinnem, Donald Y., Lt. | 1 | 5 | 6 | 352nd | |
| Wiggins, Howard E., Capt. | 4.5 | 1.5 | 6 | 356th | |
| Woolery, James C., Lt. | 0 | 6 | 6 | 339th | |
| Abbott, Earl L., Maj. | 4.75 | 1 | 5.75 | 352nd | |
| Williamson, Brady C., Capt. | 1.7 | 4 | 5.7 | 355th | |
| Koraleski, Walter J., Capt. | 5.53 | 0 | 5.53 | 355th | |
| Adams, Thomas H., Capt. | 4.5 | 1 | 5.5 | 357th | |
| Aitken, John, Jr., Maj. | 4.5 | 1 | 5.5 | 339th | 1.5 v MTO |
| Armsby, Sherman, Lt. | 4.5 | 1 | 5.5 | 361st | |
| Ashby, Clifford T., Lt. | 3.5 | 2 | 5.5 | 356th | |
| Bell, Thomas R., Capt. | 0 | 5.5 | 5.5 | 4th | |
| Bennette, Charles J., Lt. | 2 | 3.5 | 5.5 | 352nd | |
| Berkshire, Robert H., Lt. | 4.5 | 1 | 5.5 | 352nd | |
| Bledsoe, Robert V., Capt. | 0 | 5.5 | 5.5 | 353rd | |
| Buttke, Robert L., Capt. | 5.5 | 0 | 5.5 | 55th | |
| Byers, Vic L., Jr., Maj. | 2.5 | 3 | 5.5 | 353rd | |
| Capp, Merle R., Lt. | 2 | 3.5 | 5.5 | 78th | |
| Carter, Joseph D., Lt. | 0.5 | 5 | 5.5 | 352nd | |
| Chatterly, Archie W., Capt. | 4.5 | 1 | 5.5 | 4th | |
| Clark, Jack W., Lt. | 2.5 | 3 | 5.5 | 353rd | |
| Dix, Gerald J., LtCol. | 4 | 1.5 | 5.5 | 355th | |
| Gould, Norman D., Lt. | 4 | 1.5 | 5.5 | 56th | |
| Graham, Lindol F., Capt. | 5.5 | 0 | 5.5 | 20th | |
| Hatala, Paul R., Capt. | 5.5 | 0 | 5.5 | 357th | |
| Higgins, Donald H., Maj. | 2.5 | 3 | 5.5 | 352nd | |
| Izor, Edward F., Capt. | 4.5 | 1 | 5.5 | 364th | |
| Jordan, William J., Capt. | 1 | 4.5 | 5.5 | 353rd | |
| Kesler, Gilbert L., Lt. | 0.5 | 5 | 5.5 | 4th | |
| Kurtz, Robert G., Capt. | 0.5 | 5 | 5.5 | 355th | |
| Lamb, Huie H., Jr., Lt. | 2.5 | 3 | 5.5 | 78th | |
| Loveless, Philip M., Capt. | 0.5 | 5 | 5.5 | 339th | |
| McCauley, Frank E., Lt. | 5.5 | 0 | 5.5 | 56th | |
| McMahan, Darrell E., Lt. | 1.5 | 4 | 5.5 | 56th | |
| Miller, Harold O., Lt. | 2 | 3.5 | 5.5 | 353rd | |
| Morgan, Frank A., Maj. | 0.5 | 5 | 5.5 | 356th | |
| O'Brien, William R., Capt. | 5.5 | 0 | 5.5 | 357th | |
| Pascoe, James J., Lt. | 5.5 | 0 | 5.5 | 364th | |
| Payne, Carl G., Capt. | 2 | 3.5 | 5.5 | 4th | |
| Ramm, Albert J., Capt. | 0.5 | 5 | 5.5 | 55th | |
| Richards, Vernon R., Lt. | 2 | 3.5 | 5.5 | 361st | |
| Ruder, Leroy A., Capt. | 5.5 | 0 | 5.5 | 357th | |
| Smith, Robert C., Lt. | 2.5 | 3 | 5.5 | 357th | |
| Winks, Robert P., Capt. | 5.5 | 0 | 5.5 | 357th | |
| Barger, Clarence R., Lt. | 0.33 | 5 | 5.33 | 355th | |
| Fiedler, Clemmons A., Lt. | 4.33 | 1 | 5.33 | 4th | |
| Johnson, Wilton W., Maj. | 3 | 2.33 | 5.33 | 353rd | |
| Brookins, Richard C., Lt. | 4.25 | 1 | 5.25 | 352nd | |
| Zellner, Edmond, Lt. | 3.25 | 2 | 5.25 | 352nd | |
| Abernathy, Robert W., Capt. | 5 | 0 | 5 | 353rd | |
| Allen, William H., Lt. | 5 | 0 | 5 | 55th | |
| Armstrong, Clifford F., Lt. | 3 | 2 | 5 | 353rd | |
| Baker, George F., Capt. | 4.5 | 0.5 | 5 | 359th | |
| Ball, Sanborn N., Jr., Lt. | 1.5 | 3.5 | 5 | 56th | |
| Bank, Raymond M., Lt. | 5 | 0 | 5 | 357th | |
| Barnaby, Harold T., Capt. | 4 | 1 | 5 | 78th | |
| Baugh, Donald P., F/O | 0 | 5 | 5 | 4th | |
| Baughn, Richard M., Lt. | 1 | 4 | 5 | 364th | |
| Beason, Eugene M., Lt. | 1 | 4 | 5 | 56th | |
| Beavers, Edward H., Jr., Capt. | 5 | 0 | 5 | 339th | |
| Becraft, Myron A., Lt. | 1 | 4 | 5 | 357th | |
| Best, Donald J., Lt. | 0 | 5 | 5 | 55th | |
| Birtciel, Frank E., Capt. | 0 | 5 | 5 | 55th | |
| Bline, Brooks J., Capt. | 1 | 4 | 5 | 339th | |
| Blodgett, Burton O., Lt. | 0 | 5 | 5 | 56th | |
| Bocquin, Victor E., Lt. | 4 | 1 | 5 | 361st | |
| Bodiford, Hugh, Lt. | 2 | 3 | 5 | 55th | |
| Bostrom, Ernest O., Capt. | 5 | 0 | 5 | 352nd | |
| Braley, Byron K., Lt. | 3 | 2 | 5 | 357th | |
| Brown, Gerald, Maj. | 5 | 0 | 5 | 4th<br>55th | |
| Bundgaard, Carl H., Lt. | 2 | 3 | 5 | 339th | |
| Byers, John R., Lt. | 0 | 5 | 5 | 339th | |
| Caldwell, Merle F., Lt. | 2 | 3 | 5 | 339th | |
| Chenez, Gordon H., Lt. | 0 | 5 | 5 | 339th | |
| Coons, Merle M., Capt. | 5 | 0 | 5 | 55th | |
| Cooper, Randolph W., Lt. | 0 | 5 | 5 | 355th | |
| Cox, Ralph L., Maj. | 5 | 0 | 5 | 359th | |
| Cranfill, Niven K., LtCol. | 5 | 0 | 5 | 359th | |
| Daniell, Jack S., Lt. | 5 | 0 | 5 | 339th | |
| Denson, Gordon A., Lt. | 0 | 5 | 5 | 4th | |
| Dickey, Melvin N., Capt. | 0 | 5 | 5 | 4th | |
| Doss, Gene C., Lt. | 0 | 5 | 5 | 78th | |
| Egan, Joseph L., Jr., Capt. | 5 | 0 | 5 | 56th | |
| Fletcher, Jack M., Lt. | 0 | 5 | 5 | 355th | |
| Fryer, Earl R., Capt. | 4 | 1 | 5 | 55th | |
| Galer, Donald, Lt. | 0 | 5 | 5 | 355th | |
| Gibbs, Richard G., Lt. | 4 | 1 | 5 | 55th | |
| Grove, Lindsay W., Lt. | 1 | 4 | 5 | 353rd | |
| Guyton, William R., Lt. | 0 | 5 | 5 | 339th | |
| Hagen, Harry N., Capt. | 2 | 3 | 5 | 4th | |
| Hahn, Robert F., Lt. | 1 | 4 | 5 | 353rd | |
| Hall, Thomas W., Jr., Lt. | 3 | 2 | 5 | 364th | |
| Hamilton, Ralph W., Capt. | 4 | 1 | 5 | 352nd | |
| Hansen, Kenneth J., Lt. | 0 | 5 | 5 | 479th | |
| Harris, Thomas L., Capt. | 5 | 0 | 5 | 357th | |
| Hauver, Charles D., Capt. | 5 | 0 | 5 | 355th | |
| Haworth, Russell C., Lt. | 5 | 0 | 5 | 55th | |
| Helfrecht, Kenneth G., Lt. | 0 | 5 | 5 | 4th | |
| Hepner, Neal, Lt. | 0 | 5 | 5 | 78th | |
| Hermanson, Cephas, Lt. | 0 | 5 | 5 | 339th | |
| Hewett, Sidney H., Capt. | 2.5 | 2.5 | 5 | 356th | |
| Hiro, Edwin W., Maj. | 5 | 0 | 5 | 357th | |
| Hobert, Robert D., Capt. | 2 | 3 | 5 | 4th | |
| Hodges, William R., Capt. | 5 | 0 | 5 | 359th | |
| Hunt, Harlan F., Lt. | 0 | 5 | 5 | 339th | |
| Icard, Joseph W., Lt. | 5 | 0 | 5 | 56th | |
| Jackson, Boyd O., Lt. | 0 | 5 | 5 | 339th | |
| John, Leedom K., Lt. | 0 | 5 | 5 | 55th | |
| Johnson, Evan M., V, Capt. | 5 | 0 | 5 | 339th | |
| Jure, James M., Lt. | 3.5 | 1.5 | 5 | 56th | |
| Kerr, Warren E., Capt. | 0 | 5 | 5 | 56th | |
| Kissell, William F., Capt. | 0 | 5 | 5 | 364th | |
| Krauss, William H., Capt. | 0.5 | 4.5 | 5 | 339th | |
| Kuhn, Philip G., Jr., Lt. | 1 | 4 | 5 | 56th | |
| Lazear, Earl R., Jr., Capt. | 5 | 0 | 5 | 352nd | |
| Ledington, Dorian, Capt. | 2 | 3 | 5 | 78th | |
| London, Charles P., Capt. | 5 | 0 | 5 | 78th | |
| Lynch, William J., Lt. | 0 | 5 | 5 | 355th | |
| MacKean, Robert G., Capt. | 0 | 5 | 5 | 352nd | |
| Maloney, John T., Lt. | 0 | 5 | 5 | 55th | |
| Markham, Gene E., Capt. | 5 | 0 | 5 | 353rd | |
| Marsh, Halbert G., Lt. | 0 | 5 | 5 | 355th | |
| Marsh, Lester C., Lt. | 5 | 0 | 5 | 339th | |
| Marts, Jay F., Lt. | 2 | 3 | 5 | 339th | |
| Mason, Joseph L., Col. | 5 | 0 | 5 | 352nd | |
| Maxwell, Chester K., Capt. | 5 | 0 | 5 | 357th | |
| McCasland, Darwin D., Lt. | 2 | 3 | 5 | 355th | |
| McClure, James H., Lt. | 0 | 5 | 5 | 353rd | |
| McCollom, Francis N., Lt. | 0 | 5 | 5 | 355th | |
| McCubbin, James L., Lt. | 4 | 1 | 5 | 364th | |
| McFadden, Jack D., Capt. | 2 | 3 | 5 | 4th | |
| McGinn, John L., LtCol. | 5 | 0 | 5 | 55th | 3 v PTO |
| McGraw, Charles L., Capt. | 3 | 2 | 5 | 353rd | |
| McHugh, Philip M.N., Lt. | 2 | 3 | 5 | 355th | |
| McKee, Daniel D., LtCol. | 1 | 4 | 5 | 359th | |
| Moroney. Edward J., Lt. | 3 | 2 | 5 | 355th | |

| | | | | |
|---|---|---|---|---|
| Murr, John N., Lt. | 2 | 3 | 5 | 479th |
| Nagel, Jerome K., Lt. | 1 | 4 | 5 | 479th |
| Neal, Thomas F., Jr., Capt. | 4.5 | 0.5 | 5 | 355th |
| Newman, Robert A., Lt. | 4 | 1 | 5 | 353rd |
| North, Albert B., Lt. | 2 | 3 | 5 | 20th |
| Parmelee, Charles E., Lt. | 3 | 2 | 5 | 78th |
| Patterson, Roy L., Lt. | 1 | 4 | 5 | 56th |
| Perry, Emil F., Lt. | 2 | 3 | 5 | 355th |
| Peterburs, Joseph A., Lt. | 0 | 5 | 5 | 20th |
| Peters, Robert O., Lt. | 3 | 2 | 5 | 355th |
| Phaneuf, Richard E., Lt. | 0 | 5 | 5 | 78th |
| Phillips, Raymond G., Lt. | 2 | 3 | 5 | 352nd |
| Pissanos, Spiros N., Capt. | 5 | 0 | 5 | 4th |
| Price, Jack C., Maj. | 5 | 0 | 5 | 20th<br>78th |
| Priest, Royce W., Lt. | 5 | 0 | 5 | 355th |
| Pryor, Thomas P., Jr., Lt. | 0 | 5 | 5 | 353rd |
| Queen, Thomas W., Jr., Lt. | 0 | 5 | 5 | 56th |
| Randolph, John P., Col. | 1 | 4 | 5 | 20th<br>359th |
| Rau, Harold J., Col. | 1 | 4 | 5 | 20th<br>356th |
| Reese, William C., Lt. | 5 | 0 | 5 | 357th |
| Reinhardt, Edwin D., Lt. | 0 | 5 | 5 | 353rd |
| Rice, John J., F/O | 0 | 5 | 5 | 339th |
| Rigby, Alden P., Lt. | 4 | 1 | 5 | 352nd |
| Schank, Thomas D., Lt. | 5 | 0 | 5 | 55th |
| Schuh, Duerr H., Capt. | 5 | 0 | 5 | 352nd |
| Shane, Presson S., Capt. | 0 | 5 | 5 | 479th |
| Sharbo, Walter J., Lt. | 3 | 2 | 5 | 56th |
| Smeltz, Kenneth C., Lt. | 1 | 4 | 5 | 20th |
| Smigel, Alfred J., Lt. | 0 | 5 | 5 | 479th |
| Smith, Kenneth G., Capt. | 5 | 0 | 5 | 4th |
| Smith, Vernon A., Lt. | 0 | 5 | 5 | 56th |
| Stangel, William J., Capt. | 5 | 0 | 5 | 352nd |
| Stewart, Henry M., II, Capt. | 4 | 1 | 5 | 352nd |
| Sweat, Dale S., Lt. | 0 | 5 | 5 | 78th |
| Sykes, Henry S., Lt. | 0 | 5 | 5 | 352nd |
| Taylor, Willis B., Capt. | 3 | 2 | 5 | 20th |
| Timony, Eugene J., Lt. | 1 | 4 | 5 | 56th |
| Tyrrell, Albert R., LtCol. | 2 | 3 | 5 | 359th |
| Warren, Jack R., Capt. | 5 | 0 | 5 | 357th |
| Wilkerson, William F., Capt. | 1 | 4 | 5 | 56th |
| Wilson, William F., Capt. | 5 | 0 | 5 | 364th |
| Wolski, Victor, Lt. | 3 | 2 | 5 | 479th |
| York, Robert M., Capt. | 5 | 0 | 5 | 359th |

**Aces of the 4th Fighter Group**

| Name | Air | Grd | Total | Sqn |
|---|---|---|---|---|
| Maj. John T. Godfrey | 16.33 | 13.67 | 30 | 336th |
| Maj. James A. Goodson | 14 | 15 | 29 | 336th |
| Lt. Ralph K. Hofer | 15 | 13.5 | 28.5 | 334th |
| Capt. Don S. Gentile | 21.83 | 6 | 27.83[*] | 336th |
| Maj. Fred W. Glover | 10.33 | 14.5 | 24.83 | 336th |
| Capt. Duane W. Beeson | 17.33 | 4.75 | 22.08 | 334th |
| Maj. Pierce W. McKennon | 11 | 6.67 | 17.67 | 335th |
| Maj. Gerald E. Montgomery | 3 | 14.5 | 17.5 | 334th |
| Col. Donald J.M. Blakeslee | 14.5 | 1.5 | 16[**] | 336th<br>335th<br>HdQts |
| Maj. George Carpenter | 13.83 | 2 | 15.83 | 335th |
| Capt. Nicholas Megura | 11.83 | 3.75 | 15.58 | 334th |
| Capt. Charles F. Anderson, Jr. | 10 | 5.5 | 15.5 | 335th |
| Maj. Louis H. Norley | 10.33 | 5 | 15.33 | 334th<br>335th<br>336th |
| LtCol. James A. Clark, Jr. | 10.5 | 4.5 | 15 | 334th<br>HdQts |
| Capt. Willard W. Millikan | 13 | 2 | 15 | 336th |
| Maj. Howard D. Hively | 12 | 2.5 | 14.5 | 334th |
| Capt. Albert L. Schlegel | 8.5 | 5 | 13.5 | 335th |
| Capt. Joseph L. Lang | 7.83 | 4 | 11.83 | 334th |
| Lt. Hipolitus T. Biel | 5.33 | 6 | 11.33 | 334th |
| Capt. Frank C. Jones | 5 | 5.5 | 10.5 | 335th |
| Capt. Donald M. Malmsten | 1.5 | 9 | 10.5 | 334th |
| Capt. Kendall E. Carlson | 6 | 4 | 10 | 336th |
| Capt. Ted E. Lines | 10 | 0 | 10 | 335th |
| LtCol. Sidney S. Woods | 7 | 3 | 10[***] | HdQts |
| Lt. Paul S. Riley | 6.5 | 3 | 9.5 | 335th |
| Lt. Van E. Chandler | 5 | 4 | 9 | 336th |
| Maj. Shelton W. Monroe | 4.33 | 4.5 | 8.83 | 334th<br>335th<br>HdQts |
| Maj. James R. Happel | 4 | 4.67 | 8.67 | 335th |
| Capt. Victor J. France | 4.33 | 4.33 | 8.66 | 334th |
| Capt. Joseph H. Bennett | 8.5 | 0 | 8.5[@] | 336th |
| Capt. David W. Howe | 6 | 2.5 | 8.5 | 334th |
| Capt. Bernard L. McGrattan | 8.5 | 0 | 8.5 | 335th |
| Capt. Carl R. Alfred | 0 | 8 | 8 | 336th |
| Lt. James W. Ayers | 1 | 7 | 8 | 334th |
| Lt. Grover C. Siems, Jr. | 4.33 | 3.5 | 7.83 | 334th |
| Lt. Vermont Garrison | 7.33 | 0.25 | 7.58 | 336th |
| Capt. Joseph H. Joiner | 3.5 | 4 | 7.5 | 336th |
| Capt. William B. Smith | 3 | 4.25 | 7.25 | 334th |
| Lt. William O. Antonides | 0 | 7 | 7 | 334th |
| Capt. Donald R. Emerson | 4.5 | 2.5 | 7 | 336th |
| LtCol. Chesley G. Peterson | 7 | 0 | 7[@@] | HdQts |
| Capt. Raymond C. Care | 6 | 0.5 | 6.5 | 334th |
| Lt. Arthur R. Bowers | 0 | 6 | 6 | 334th |
| LtCol. Roy W. Evans | 6 | 0 | 6[@@@] | 335th |
| Lt. Loton D. Jennings | 0 | 6 | 6 | 335th |
| Maj. Henry L. Mills | 6 | 0 | 6 | 334th |
| Lt. Robert F. Nelson | 1 | 5 | 6 | 336th |
| F/O Douglas P. Pederson | 0 | 6 | 6 | 336th |
| Lt. Frank E. Speer | 1 | 5 | 6 | 334th |
| Capt. Thomas R. Bell | 0 | 5.5 | 5.5 | 334th |
| Capt. Archie W. Chatterly | 4.5 | 1.5 | 5.5 | 334th |
| Lt. Gilbert L. Kesler | 0.5 | 5 | 5.5 | 336th |
| Capt. Carl G. Payne | 2 | 3.5 | 5.5 | 334th |
| Lt. Clemmons A. Fiedler | 4.33 | 1 | 5.33 | 335th |
| F/O Donald P. Baugh | 0 | 5 | 5 | 336th |
| Lt. Gordon A. Denson | 0 | 5 | 5 | 334th |
| Capt. Melvin N. Dickey | 0 | 5 | 5 | 336th |
| Capt. Harry N. Hagen | 2 | 3 | 5 | 336th |
| Lt. Kenneth G. Helfrecht | 0 | 5 | 5 | 334th |
| Capt. Robert D. Hobert | 2 | 3 | 5 | 336th |
| Capt. Jack D. McFadden | 0 | 5 | 5 | 334th |
| Capt. Spiros N. Pissanos | 5 | 0 | 5 | 334th |
| Capt. Kenneth G. Smith | 5 | 0 | 5 | 335th |
| Col. Claiborne H. Kinnard | 8 | 17 | 25[#] | HdQts |
| Col. Everett W. Stewart | 7.83 | 1.5 | 9.33[##] | HdQts |
| Lt. William E. Whalen | 6 | 2 | 8[###] | 334th |
| LtCol. Jack J. Oberhansly | 6 | 1.6 | 7.6[&] | HdQts |
| Maj. Gerald Brown | 5 | 0 | 5[&&] | 334th |

[*] - includes 2 air victories with the RAF
[**] - includes 3 air victories with the RAF
[***] - includes 2 air victories with the 49th Ftr Grp, PTO and 1 ground victory with the 479th Ftr Grp
[@] - includes 5 air victories with the 56th Ftr Grp
[@@] - includes 6 air victories with the RAF
[@@@] - includes 1 air victory with the 359th Ftr Grp
[#] - includes 7 air and 14 ground victories with the 355th Ftr Grp
[##] - all victories with the 352nd and 355th Ftr Grps
[###] - includes 5 air and 2 ground victories with the 2nd Scout Force
[&] - all victories with the 78th Ftr Grp
[&&] - all victories with the 55th Ftr Grp

**Aces of the 20th Fighter Group**

| Name | Air | Grd | Total | Sqn |
|---|---|---|---|---|
| Capt. Charles H. Cole | 5 | 6 | 11 | 55th<br>77th |
| Capt. Ernest C. Fielbelkorn | 9 | 2 | 11 | 77th |
| Capt. James M. Morris | 7.33 | 2.83 | 10.16 | 77th |
| Capt. Joseph L. Mansker | 3 | 7 | 10 | 55th |
| Lt. Fred H. Alexander | 2 | 6 | 8 | 77th |
| Maj. Jack M. Ilfrey | 8 | 0 | 8[*] | 79th |
| Lt. Fred H. Jurgens | 0 | 8 | 8 | 79th |
| Capt. Joseph T. McKeon | 6 | 2 | 8[**] | 55th<br>77th |
| Capt. Reps D. Jones | 2 | 5 | 7 | 77th |
| Capt. Edward L. Kier | 2 | 5 | 7 | 55th |
| Lt. David Stewart | 0 | 7 | 7 | 55th |
| Maj. Merle J. Gilbertson | 2.83 | 4 | 6.83 | 77th |
| LtCol. Mark E. Hubbard | 6.5 | 0 | 6.5[***] | HdQts |
| Col. Robert P. Montgomery | 3.33 | 3 | 6.33 | HdQts |
| Maj. Richard P. Gatterdam | 3.7 | 2.5 | 6.2 | 55th<br>79th |
| Lt. Louis W. Adams, Jr. | 4 | 2 | 6 | 77th |
| Capt. Harley L. Brown | 6 | 0 | 6 | 55th |
| Capt. Lowell E. Einhaus | 0 | 6 | 6 | 77th |
| Lt. Edward F. Pogue | 0 | 6 | 6 | 79th |
| Capt. Garth L. Reynolds | 2 | 4 | 6 | 77th |
| Capt. Lindol F. Graham | 5.5 | 0 | 5.5 | 79th |
| Lt. Albert B. North | 2 | 3 | 5 | 77th |
| Lt. Joseph A. Peterburs | 0 | 5 | 5 | 55th |
| LtCol. John P. Randolph | 1 | 4 | 5 | HdQts |
| Col. Harold J. Rau | 1 | 4 | 5 | HdQts |
| Lt. Kenneth C. Smeltz | 1 | 4 | 5 | 55th |
| Capt. Willis B. Taylor | 3 | 2 | 5 | 55th |
| Maj. Jack C. Price | 5 | 0 | 5[@] | 55th<br>HdQts |

[*] - includes 6 air victories with the 1st Ftr Grp, MTO
[**] - includes 5 air victories with the 475th Ftr Grp, PTO
[***] - includes 4 air victories with the 33rd Ftr Grp, MTO
[@] - all victories with the 78th Ftr Grp

### Aces of the 55th Fighter Group

| Name | Air | Grd | Total | Sqn |
|---|---|---|---|---|
| LtCol. John D. Landers | 14.5 | 20 | 34.5* | 38th |
| LtCol. Elwyn G. Righetti | 7.5 | 27 | 34.5 | 338th HdQts |
| Capt. Robert E. Welch | 6 | 12 | 18 | 343rd |
| Maj. Darrell S. Cramer | 7 | 2 | 9** | 338th |
| Lt. John W. Cunnick, III | 2 | 7 | 9 | 38th |
| Capt. Samuel D. Gevorkian | 2 | 7 | 9 | 338th |
| Maj. Edward B. Giller | 3 | 6 | 9 | 343rd |
| Lt. Bernard H. Howes | 6 | 2 | 8 | 343rd |
| Lt. Keith R. McGinnis | 2 | 6 | 8 | 38th |
| LtCol. Joseph Myers, Jr. | 4.5 | 3 | 7.5*** | 38th HdQts |
| Lt. Dudley M. Amoss | 5.5 | 1.5 | 7 | 38th |
| Lt. Lloyd D. Boring | 0.5 | 6.5 | 7 | 343rd |
| Capt. William H. Lewis | 7 | 0 | 7 | 343rd |
| Lt. Howard Mahany, Jr. | 0 | 7 | 7 | 343rd |
| Capt. Donald M. Cummings | 6.5 | 0 | 6.5@ | 38th |
| Capt. Carroll D. Henry | 1.5 | 5 | 6.5 | 338th |
| Lt. Clifford C. Gould | 1 | 5 | 6 | 38th |
| Capt. Robert L. Buttke | 5.5 | 0 | 5.5 | 343rd |
| Capt. Albert J. Ramm | 0.5 | 5 | 5.5 | 338th |
| Lt. William H. Allen | 5 | 0 | 5 | 343rd |
| Lt. Donald J. Best | 0 | 5 | 5 | 38th |
| Capt. Frank E. Birtciel | 0 | 5 | 5 | 343rd |
| Lt. Hugh Bodiford | 2 | 3 | 5 | 338th |
| Maj. Gerald Brown | 5 | 0 | 5 | 38th |
| Capt. Merle M. Coons | 5 | 0 | 5 | 38th |
| Capt. Earl R. Fryer | 4 | 1 | 5 | 38th |
| Lt. Richard G. Gibbs | 4 | 1 | 5 | 343rd |
| Lt. Russell C. Haworth | 5 | 0 | 5 | 338th |
| Lt. Leedom K. John | 0 | 5 | 5 | 338th |
| Lt. John T. Maloney | 0 | 5 | 5 | 38th |
| LtCol. John L. McGinn | 5 | 0 | 5@@ | 338th |
| Lt. Thomas D. Schank | 5 | 0 | 5 | 338th |
| Col. Ben Rimerman | 4.5 | 8 | 12.5@@@ | HdQts |

* - includes 6 air victories with the 49th Ftr Grp, PTO, and 4.5 air and 16 ground victories with the 78th and 357th Ftr Grps
** - includes 0.5 air victories with the 347th Ftr Grp, PTO
*** - includes 1.5 air and 3 ground victories with the 78th Ftr Grp
@ - includes 1 air victory with the 27th Ftr Grp, MTO
@@ - includes 3 air victories with the 347th Ftr Grp, PTO
@@@ - all victories with the 353rd Ftr Grp

### Aces of the 56th Fighter Group

| Name | Air | Grd | Total | Sqn |
|---|---|---|---|---|
| Col. David C. Schilling | 22.5 | 10.5 | 33 | 62nd HdQts |
| LtCol. Francis S. Gabreski | 28 | 3.5 | 31.5 | 61st HdQts |
| Maj. Robert S. Johnson | 27 | 0 | 27 | 61st 62nd |
| Col. Hubert Zemke | 17.75 | 8.5 | 26.25* | HdQts |
| Capt. Fred J. Christensen | 21.5 | 0 | 21.5 | 62nd |
| Maj. Walker M. Mahurin | 19.75 | 0 | 19.75 | 63rd |
| Maj. Gerald W. Johnson | 16.5 | 0 | 16.5** | 61st 63rd |
| Capt. Michael J. Quirk | 11 | 5 | 16 | 62nd |
| Maj. George E. Bostwick | 8 | 7 | 15 | 62nd 63rd |
| Capt. Joseph H. Powers | 14.5 | 0 | 14.5 | 61st 62nd |
| Maj. Leroy A. Schreiber | 12 | 2 | 14 | 61st 62nd |
| Maj. Michael J. Jackson | 8 | 5.5 | 13.5 | 62nd |
| Lt. Randel L. Murphy | 2 | 11 | 13 | 63rd |
| Maj. Felix D. Williamson | 13 | 0 | 13 | 62nd |
| LtCol. James C. Stewart | 11.5 | 1 | 12.5 | 61st HdQts |
| Maj. Paul A. Conger | 11.5 | 0 | 11.5 | 61st 63rd |
| LtCol. Leslie C. Smith | 7 | 4.5 | 11.5 | 61st 62nd HdQts |
| Maj. Bolek M. Gladych | 10 | 1 | 11 | 61st |
| Lt. Billy G. Edens | 7 | 3 | 10 | 62nd |
| Capt. Robert J. Keen | 6 | 4 | 10 | 61st 62nd |
| Lt. Russell S. Kyler | 3 | 7 | 10 | 61st |
| Capt. Robert J. Rankin | 10 | 0 | 10 | 61st |
| LtCol. Lucian A. Dade, Jr. | 3 | 6 | 9 | 62nd 63rd HdQts |
| Capt. Stanley B. Morrill | 9 | 0 | 9 | 62nd |
| Capt. Joseph H. Bennett | 8.5 | 0 | 8.5*** | 61st |
| Capt. Walter L. Flagg | 2 | 6 | 8 | 63rd |
| Capt. Glen D. Schiltz, Jr. | 8 | 0 | 8 | 63rd |
| Capt. John H. Truluck | 7 | 1 | 8 | 63rd |
| Maj. John W. Vogt, Jr. | 8 | 0 | 8@ | 63rd |
| Lt. Donald Henley, Jr. | 3 | 4.5 | 7.5 | 62nd |
| Maj. Donovan F. Smith | 5.5 | 2 | 7.5 | 61st |
| Maj. Harold E. Comstock | 5 | 2 | 7 | 63rd |
| Capt. Steven Gerick | 5 | 2 | 7 | 61st |
| Lt. Frank W. Klibbe | 7 | 0 | 7 | 61st |
| Maj. Robert A. Lamb | 7 | 0 | 7 | 61st 63rd |
| Lt. Evan D. McMinn | 5 | 2 | 7 | 61st |
| Capt. Mark L. Moseley | 6.5 | 0 | 6.5 | 62nd |
| Lt. George H. Butler | 3 | 3 | 6 | 62nd |
| Maj. James R. Carter | 6 | 0 | 6 | 61st |
| Lt. Claude A. Chinn | 0 | 6 | 6 | 63rd |
| Capt. Walter V. Cook | 6 | 0 | 6 | 62nd |
| Capt. George F. Hall | 6 | 0 | 6 | 63rd |
| Capt. Cameron M. Hart | 6 | 0 | 6 | 63rd |
| Lt. Norman D. Gould | 4 | 1.5 | 5.5 | 62nd |
| Lt. Frank E. McCauley | 5.5 | 0 | 5.5 | 61st |
| Lt. Darrell E. McMahan | 1.5 | 4 | 5.5 | 62nd |
| Lt. Sanborn N. Ball, Jr. | 1.5 | 3.5 | 5 | 62nd |
| Lt. Eugene M. Beason | 1 | 4 | 5 | 62nd |
| Lt. Burton O. Blodgett | 0 | 5 | 5 | 61st |
| Capt. Joseph L. Egan, Jr. | 5 | 0 | 5 | 63rd |
| Lt. Joseph W. Icard | 5 | 0 | 5 | 62nd |
| Lt. James M. Jure | 3.5 | 1.5 | 5 | 61st |
| Capt. Warren E. Kerr | 0 | 5 | 5 | 63rd |
| Lt. Philip G. Kuhn, Jr. | 1 | 4 | 5 | 63rd |
| Lt. Roy L. Patterson | 1 | 4 | 5 | 62nd |
| Lt. Thomas W. Queen, Jr. | 0 | 5 | 5 | 63rd |
| Lt. Walter J. Sharbo | 3 | 2 | 5 | 62nd |
| Lt. Vernon A. Smith | 0 | 5 | 5 | 63rd |
| Lt. Eugene J. Timony | 1 | 4 | 5 | 63rd |
| Capt. William F. Wilkerson | 1 | 4 | 5 | 62nd |

* - includes 2.5 air victories with the 479th Ftr Grp
** - includes 1 air victory with the 356th Ftr Grp
*** - includes 3 air victories with the 4th Ftr Grp
@ - includes 3 air victories with the 356th Ftr Grp

### Aces of the 78th Fighter Group

| Name | Air | Grd | Total | Sqn |
|---|---|---|---|---|
| LtCol. John D. Landers | 14.5 | 20 | 34.5* | HdQts |
| Capt. Alwin M. Juchheim | 9 | 6 | 15 | 83rd |
| Maj. Quince L. Brown | 12.33 | 1 | 13.33 | 84th |
| Lt. Francis E. Harrington | 4 | 8 | 12 | 83rd |
| LtCol. Olin E. Gilbert | 2 | 8.5 | 10.5** | 83rd HdQts |
| Lt. John A. Kirk, III | 4 | 6 | 10 | 83rd |
| Capt. Charles M. Peal | 2 | 8 | 10 | 83rd |
| Lt. Duncan M. McDuffie | 4 | 5 | 9 | 83rd |
| LtCol. Eugene P. Roberts | 9 | 0 | 9 | 84th HdQts |
| Lt. Clyde E. Taylor | 0 | 9 | 9 | 84th |
| Lt. Henry R. Slack, IV | 1.5 | 7 | 8.5 | 84th |
| Maj. Richard A. Hewitt | 4 | 4.33 | 8.33 | 82nd |
| LtCol. Richard E. Conner | 4.5 | 3.5 | 8 | 82nd |
| Lt. Danford E. Josey | 0 | 8 | 8 | 84th |
| LtCol. William H. Julian | 5 | 3 | 8*** | 83rd |
| Capt. James W. Wilkinson | 6 | 2 | 8 | 82nd |
| Capt. John J. Hockery | 7 | 0.8 | 7.8 | 82nd |
| LtCol. Jack J. Oberhansly | 6 | 1.6 | 7.6 | 82nd HdQts |
| LtCol. Joseph Myers, Jr. | 4.5 | 3 | 7.5@ | 82nd |
| Capt. Edward R. Kulik | 0 | 7 | 7 | 83rd |
| Lt. Peter E. Pompetti | 5 | 2 | 7 | 84th |
| Capt. Robert T. Green | 4.5 | 2 | 6.5 | 83rd |
| LtCol. Ben I. Mayo, Jr. | 4 | 2.5 | 6.5 | 82nd 84th |
| Capt. Robert R. Bonebrake | 3 | 3 | 6 | 83rd |
| Lt. Robert R. Bosworth | 1 | 5 | 6 | 82nd |
| Maj. Gillespie Bryan | 0 | 6 | 6 | HdQts |
| Lt. Anthony T. Colletti | 1 | 5 | 6 | 83rd |
| Lt. Louis DeAnda | 0 | 6 | 6 | 84th |
| Lt. Donald J. Devilliers | 0 | 6 | 6 | 83rd |
| Maj. Raymond E. Smith | 1 | 5 | 6 | 84th |
| Lt. Grant M. Turley | 6 | 0 | 6 | 82nd |
| Capt. Warren M. Wesson | 4 | 2 | 6 | 82nd |
| Lt. Merle R. Capp | 2 | 3.5 | 5.5 | 82nd 84th |
| Lt. Huie H. Lamb, Jr. | 2.5 | 3 | 5.5 | 82nd |
| Capt. Harold T. Barnaby | 4 | 1 | 5 | 83rd |
| Lt. Gene C. Doss | 0 | 5 | 5 | 83rd |

| Name | Air | Grd | Total | Sqn |
|---|---|---|---|---|
| Lt. Neal Hepner | 0 | 5 | 5 | 84th |
| Capt. Dorian Ledington | 2 | 3 | 5 | 84th |
| Capt. Charles P. London | 5 | 0 | 5 | 83rd |
| Lt. Charles E. Parmelee | 3 | 2 | 5 | 84th |
| Lt. Richard E. Phaneuf | 0 | 5 | 5 | 83rd |
| Maj. Jack C. Price | 5 | 0 | 5 | 84th |
| Lt. Dale S. Sweat | 0 | 5 | 5 | 83rd |

* - includes 6 air victories with the 49th Ftr Grp, PTO and 5 air and 5 ground victories with the 55th and 357th Ftr Grps
** - includes 6.5 victories with the 66th Ftr Wing
*** - includes 3 ground victories with the 339th Ftr Grp
@ - includes 3 air victories with the 55th Ftr Grp

**Aces of the 339th Fighter Group**

| Name | Air | Grd | Total | Sqn |
|---|---|---|---|---|
| LtCol. Joseph L. Thury | 2.5 | 25.5 | 28 | 505th |
| Maj. Archie A. Tower | 1.5 | 18 | 19.5 | 505th |
| Capt. Kirke B. Everson | 1.5 | 13 | 14.5 | 504th |
| Capt. Robert H. Ammon | 5 | 9 | 14 | 503rd<br>504th<br>HdQts |
| Lt. Oscar K. Biggs | 0.5 | 11.5 | 12 | 505th |
| Capt. Harry R. Corey | 1 | 11 | 12 | 505th |
| Capt. James R. Starnes | 6 | 6 | 12 | 505th |
| Lt. Harold W. Burch | 0 | 11 | 11 | 505th |
| Maj. William E. Bryan, Jr. | 7.5 | 2 | 9.5 | 503rd<br>HdQts |
| LtCol. William C. Clark | 1 | 8 | 9* | 504th<br>HdQts |
| Maj. Donald A. Larson | 6 | 3 | 9 | 505th |
| Lt. Thomas W. Marvel | 0 | 9 | 9 | 505th |
| LtCol. Dale E. Shafer, Jr. | 7 | 2 | 9** | 503rd |
| Capt. Francis R. Gerard | 8 | 0 | 8 | 503rd |
| LtCol. William H. Julian | 5 | 3 | 8*** | 504th |
| Lt. William R. MacClarence | 0 | 8 | 8 | 505th |
| Lt. William F. Mudge, Jr. | 2 | 6 | 8 | 505th |
| Lt. Leon M. Orcutt, Jr. | 0 | 8 | 8 | 504th |
| Lt. Herbert L. Caywood | 0 | 7 | 7 | 505th |
| Lt. Steve J. Chetneky | 1 | 6 | 7 | 503rd |
| Capt. Owen P. Farmer | 2 | 5 | 7 | 505th |
| Lt. Christopher J. Hanseman | 5 | 2 | 7 | 505th |
| Lt. William A. Jones | 2 | 5 | 7 | 505th |
| Lt. Jerome T. Murphy | 0 | 7 | 7 | 505th |
| Capt. Richard B. Olander | 1.5 | 5 | 6.5 | 505th |
| Capt. George T. Rich | 1.5 | 5 | 6.5 | 505th |
| Lt. Robert V.E. Blizzard | 0 | 6 | 6 | 504th |
| Lt. Frank A. Clifton | 0 | 6 | 6 | 504th |
| Lt. Robert J. Frisch | 0 | 6 | 6 | 503rd |
| Lt. Robert E. Irion | 1 | 5 | 6 | 505th |
| Lt. Robert H. Paul | 0 | 6 | 6 | 505th |
| Lt. Lawrence J. Powell, Jr. | 2.5 | 3.5 | 6 | 505th |
| Lt. James C. Woolery | 0 | 6 | 6 | 505th |
| Maj. John Aitken, Jr. | 4.5 | 1 | 5.5@ | 503rd<br>504th |
| Capt. Philip M. Loveless, Jr. | 0.5 | 5 | 5.5 | 505th |
| Capt. Edward H. Beavers, Jr. | 5 | 0 | 5 | 503rd |
| Capt. Brooks J. Bline | 1 | 4 | 5 | 505th |
| Lt. Carl H. Bundgaard | 2 | 3 | 5 | 505th |
| Lt. John R. Byers | 0 | 5 | 5 | 503rd |
| Lt. Merle F. Caldwell | 2 | 3 | 5 | 504th |
| Lt. Gordon H. Chenez | 0 | 5 | 5 | 504th |
| Lt. Jack S. Daniell | 5 | 0 | 5 | 505th |
| Lt. William R. Guyton | 0 | 5 | 5 | 505th |
| Lt. Cephas Hermanson | 0 | 5 | 5 | 504th |
| Lt. Harlan F. Hunt | 0 | 5 | 5 | 504th |
| Lt. Boyd O. Jackson | 0 | 5 | 5 | 505th |
| Capt. Evan M. Johnson, V | 5 | 0 | 5 | 505th |
| Capt. William H. Krauss | 0.5 | 4.5 | 5 | 505th |
| Lt. Lester C. Marsh | 5 | 0 | 5 | 503rd |
| Lt. Jay F. Marts | 2 | 3 | 5 | 505th |
| F/O John J. Rice | 0 | 5 | 5 | 505th |

* - includes 1 air victory with the 66th Ftr Wing
** - includes 4 air victories with the 31st Ftr Grp, MTO
*** - includes 5 air victories with the 78th Ftr Grp
@ - includes 1.5 air victories with the 52nd Ftr Grp, MTO

**Aces of the 352nd Fighter Group**

| Name | Air | Grd | Total | Sqn |
|---|---|---|---|---|
| LtCol. John C. Meyer | 24 | 13 | 37 | 487th<br>HdQts |
| Maj. George E. Preddy | 26.83 | 5 | 31.83 | 328th<br>487th |
| Capt. Raymond H. Littge | 10.5 | 13 | 23.5 | 487th |
| Capt. Edwin L. Heller | 5.5 | 14.5 | 20 | 486th |
| Capt. John F. Thornell, Jr. | 17.25 | 2 | 19.25 | 328th |
| Capt. William T. Whisner | 15.5 | 3 | 18.5 | 487th |
| Lt. Glennon T. Moran | 13 | 3 | 16 | 487th |
| Maj. Stephen W. Andrew | 9 | 6.5 | 15.5* | 486th |
| Lt. Carl J. Luksic | 8.5 | 7 | 15.5 | 487th |
| Capt. Woodrow W. Anderson | 4.5 | 9 | 13.5 | 486th |
| Maj. Donald S. Bryan | 13.33 | 0 | 13.33 | 328th |
| Capt. Clarence O. Johnson | 7 | 6 | 13** | 487th |
| Capt. Henry J. Miklajcyk | 7.5 | 5.5 | 13 | 486th |
| LtCol. William T. Halton | 10.5 | 2 | 12.5 | 328th<br>487th |
| LtCol. Willie O. Jackson, Jr. | 7 | 4 | 11 | 328th<br>486th<br>HdQts |
| Capt. Frank A. Cutler | 7.5 | 3 | 10.5 | 486th |
| Lt. Karl M. Waldron, Jr. | 3 | 7 | 10 | 487th |
| Col. Everett W. Stewart | 7.83 | 1.5 | 9.33*** | 328th |
| Capt. Clayton E. Davis | 5 | 4 | 9 | 487th |
| Capt. Virgil K. Meroney | 9 | 0 | 9 | 487th |
| Capt. Charles J. Cesky | 8.5 | 0 | 8.5 | 328th |
| Capt. Sanford K. Moats | 8.5 | 0 | 8.5 | 487th |
| Lt. Malcolm C. Pickering | 4 | 4 | 8 | 487th |
| Capt. Walter E. Starck | 7 | 0 | 7 | 487th |
| Capt. John B. Coleman, Jr. | 4.33 | 2.5 | 6.83 | 328th |
| Lt. William W. Furr | 3.5 | 3 | 6.5 | 328th |
| Lt. Charles E. Goodman | 4.5 | 2 | 6.5 | 328th |
| Capt. Francis W. Horne | 5.5 | 1 | 6.5 | 328th |
| Col. James D. Mayden | 2 | 4 | 6 | HdQts |
| Lt. Charles C. Pattillo | 0 | 6 | 6 | 486th |
| Capt. Alex F. Sears | 5 | 1 | 6 | 487th |
| Capt. Alton J. Wallace | 3 | 3 | 6 | 486th |
| Lt. Donald Y. Whinnem | 1 | 5 | 6 | 486th |
| Maj. Earl L. Abbott | 4.75 | 1 | 5.75 | 328th |
| Lt. Charles J. Bennette | 2 | 3.5 | 5.5 | 328th |
| Lt. Robert H. Berkshire | 4.5 | 1 | 5.5 | 487th |
| Lt. Joseph D. Carter | 0.5 | 5 | 5.5 | 486th |
| Maj. Donald H. Higgins | 2.5 | 3 | 5.5 | 486th |
| Lt. Richard C. Brookins | 4.25 | 1 | 5.25 | 328th |
| Lt. Edmond Zellner | 3.25 | 2 | 5.25 | 328th |
| Capt. Ernest O. Bostrom | 5 | 0 | 5 | 486th |
| Capt. Ralph W. Hamilton | 4 | 1 | 5 | 487th |
| Capt. Earl R. Lazear, Jr. | 5 | 0 | 5 | 486th |
| Capt. Robert G. MacKean | 0 | 5 | 5 | 486th |
| Col. Joseph L. Mason | 5 | 0 | 5 | HdQts |
| Lt. Raymond G. Phillips | 2 | 3 | 5 | 328th |
| Lt. Alden P. Rigby | 4 | 1 | 5 | 487th |
| Capt. Duerr H. Schuh | 5 | 0 | 5 | 487th |
| Capt. William J. Stangel | 5 | 0 | 5 | 328th |
| Capt. Henry M. Stewart, II | 4 | 1 | 5 | 487th |
| Lt. Henry S. Sykes | 0 | 5 | 5 | 487th |

* - includes 1 air victory with the 49th Ftr Grp, PTO
** - includes 4 air victories with the 82nd Ftr Grp, MTO, and 1 air victory with the 479th Ftr Grp
*** - includes 7 air and 1.5 ground victories with the 355th Ftr Grp

**Aces of the 353rd Fighter Group**

| Name | Air | Grd | Total | Sqn |
|---|---|---|---|---|
| Col. Glenn E. Duncan | 19.5 | 6.83 | 26.33 | HdQts |
| Capt. Gordon B. Compton | 5.5 | 15 | 20.5 | 351st |
| Maj. Walter C. Beckham | 18 | 0 | 18 | 351st |
| Capt. Melville W. Hightshoe | 0 | 14.5 | 14.5 | 350th |
| Capt. Herbert G. Kolb | 0 | 14.5 | 14.5 | 350th |
| Maj. Walker L. Boone | 2 | 11.79 | 13.79* | 350th |
| F/O Richard N. Gustke | 0 | 12.5 | 12.5 | 350th |
| Col. Ben Rimerman | 4.5 | 8 | 12.5 | 350th<br>HdQts |
| Capt. Horace Q. Waggoner | 5 | 7.5 | 12.5 | 352nd |
| Capt. Frank N. Emory | 2 | 10 | 12 | 351st |
| Lt. Roland J. Lanoue | 1 | 11 | 12 | 350th |
| LtCol. Kenneth W. Gallup | 9 | 2 | 11 | 350th<br>HdQts |
| Lt. Gerald J. Miller | 0 | 11 | 11 | 351st |
| Maj. James N. Poindexter | 7 | 4 | 11 | 352nd |
| LtCol. Wayne K. Blickenstaff | 10 | 0 | 10 | 350th<br>HdQts |
| Lt. Joseph D. McMullen | 0 | 10 | 10 | 350th |
| Capt. Harrison B. Tordoff | 5 | 4.5 | 9.5 | 352nd |
| Capt. Raymond E. Hartley | 5 | 4 | 9** | 351st<br>HdQts |
| Lt. Raymond P. Greenwood | 0 | 8 | 8 | 352nd |
| Capt. William J. Maguire | 7 | 1 | 8 | 351st |
| Lt. Swift T. Benjamin | 1 | 6.5 | 7.5 | 350th |
| LtCol. Robert A. Elder | 5 | 2 | 7 | 350th<br>HdQts |
| Maj. William J. Price | 3 | 4 | 7 | 350th |

| Name | Air | Grd | Total | Sqn |
|---|---|---|---|---|
| Capt. Leslie P. Cles | 0 | 6.5 | 6.5 | 352nd |
| Lt. Thomas W. Jones | 0.5 | 6 | 6.5 | 352nd |
| Maj. William F. Tanner | 5.5 | 1 | 6.5 | 350th |
| LtCol. William B. Bailey | 3 | 3 | 6 | 352nd<br>HdQts |
| Capt. Harold W. Chase | 2 | 4 | 6 | 351st |
| Lt. Arthur C. Cundy | 6 | 0 | 6 | 352nd |
| Capt. William C. Davis | 0 | 6 | 6 | 352nd |
| Lt. Ray C. Gordon | 0 | 6 | 6 | 350th |
| Lt. Louis W. Lee | 4 | 2 | 6 | 350th |
| Lt. Bruce D. McMahan | 0.5 | 5.5 | 6 | 350th |
| Capt. Fred L. Uttwenweiler | 0 | 6 | 6 | 352nd |
| Lt. Walter A.S. Prescott | 2 | 4 | 6 | 350th |
| Capt. Vernon G. Rafferty | 2.5 | 3.5 | 6 | 350th |
| Capt. Marvin V. Bledsoe | 0 | 5.5 | 5.5 | 350th |
| Maj. Vic L. Byers, Jr. | 2.5 | 3 | 5.5 | 351st |
| Lt. Jack W. Clark | 2.5 | 3 | 5.5 | 350th |
| Capt. William J. Jordan | 1 | 4.5 | 5.5 | 352nd |
| Lt. Harold O. Miller | 2 | 3.5 | 5.5 | 352nd |
| Maj. Wilton W. Johnson | 3 | 2.33 | 5.33 | 352nd |
| Capt. Robert W. Abernathy | 5 | 0 | 5 | 350th |
| Lt. Clifford F. Armstrong | 3 | 2 | 5 | 352nd |
| Lt. Lindsay W. Grove | 1 | 4 | 5 | 352nd |
| Lt. Robert F. Hahn | 1 | 4 | 5 | 351st |
| Capt. Gene E. Markham | 5 | 0 | 5 | 351st |
| Lt. James H. McClure | 0 | 5 | 5 | 350th |
| Capt. Charles L. McGraw | 3 | 2 | 5 | 351st |
| Lt. Robert A. Newman | 4 | 1 | 5 | 352nd |
| Lt. Thomas P. Pryor, Jr. | 0 | 5 | 5 | 351st |
| Lt. Edwin D. Reinhardt | 0 | 5 | 5 | 352nd |

* - includes 0.79 ground victories with the 78th Ftr Grp
** - includes 2 air victories with the 325th Ftr Grp, MTO

**Aces of the 355th Fighter Group**

| Name | Air | Grd | Total | Sqn |
|---|---|---|---|---|
| Capt. Henry W. Brown | 14.2 | 14.5 | 28.7 | 354th |
| Col. Claiborne H. Kinnard | 8 | 17 | 25* | 354th<br>HdQts |
| LtCol. John L. Elder | 8 | 13 | 21 | 357th |
| Lt. William J. Cullerton | 5 | 15 | 20 | 357th |
| LtCol. Gordon M. Graham | 7 | 9.5 | 16.5 | 354th |
| Capt. James E. Duffy, Jr. | 5.2 | 9 | 14.2 | 354th |
| Lt. Ray S. Morris | 3.5 | 10 | 13.5 | 354th |
| Maj. William J. Hovde | 10.5 | 2 | 12.5 | 358th |
| Capt. Fred R. Haviland | 6 | 6 | 12 | 357th |
| Maj. Norman J. Fortier | 5.83 | 5.5 | 11.33 | 354th |
| Capt. James N. McElroy | 5 | 6 | 11 | 358th |
| Maj. Henry S. Bille | 6 | 4 | 10 | 357th |
| LtCol. Bert W. Marshall, Jr. | 7 | 3 | 10 | 354th<br>HdQts |
| Capt. Joseph E. Mellen | 2 | 8 | 10 | 354th |
| Col. Everett W. Stewart | 7.83 | 1.5 | 9.33** | HdQts |
| Capt. Robert E. Woody | 7 | 2 | 9 | 354th |
| LtCol. Edward W. Szaniawski | 4 | 4.66 | 8.66 | 357th |
| LtCol. Raymond B. Myers | 4.5 | 4 | 8.5 | 358th |
| F/O Harold W. Falvey | 0 | 8 | 8 | 354th |
| Capt. Norman E. Olson | 6 | 2 | 8 | 357th |
| Maj. Charles W. Lenfest | 5.5 | 2 | 7.5 | 354th |
| Maj. Walter V. Gresham, Jr. | 4 | 3 | 7 | 358th |
| Lt. James Jabara | 1.5 | 5.5 | 7*** | 354th |
| Lt. Ben D. Johnston, Jr. | 4 | 3 | 7 | 357th |
| Lt. William D. Martin | 4 | 3 | 7 | 354th |
| Capt. Stanley E. Silva | 1 | 6 | 7 | 354th |
| Maj. John H. Wilson | 3.5 | 3.5 | 7 | 357th |
| Lt. Robert L. Garlich | 0 | 6.5 | 6.5 | 357th |
| Lt. William P. Boulet | 3 | 3 | 6 | 354th |
| Capt. Lawrence J. Dissette | 1 | 5 | 6 | 358th |
| Maj. Henry H. Kirby, Jr. | 1 | 5 | 6 | 357th<br>HdQts |
| Maj. Henry B. Kucheman, Jr. | 4 | 2 | 6 | 354th |
| Lt. Thurman C. Long | 2 | 4 | 6 | 357th |
| Capt. Leslie D. Minchew | 5.5 | 0.5 | 6 | 354th<br>357th<br>HdQts |
| Capt. Brady C. Williamson | 1.7 | 4 | 5.7 | 354th |
| Capt. Walter J. Koraleski | 5.53 | 0 | 5.53 | 354th |
| LtCol. Gerald J. Dix | 4 | 1.5 | 5.5 | HdQts |
| Capt. Robert G. Kurtz | 0.5 | 5 | 5.5 | 354th |
| Lt. Clarence R. Barger | 0.33 | 5 | 5.33 | 354th |
| Lt. Randolph W. Cooper | 0 | 5 | 5 | 357th |
| Lt. Jack M. Fletcher | 0 | 5 | 5 | 354th |
| Lt. Donald Galer | 0 | 5 | 5 | 354th |
| Capt. Charles D. Hauver | 5 | 0 | 5 | 354th |
| Lt. William J. Lynch | 0 | 5 | 5 | 358th |
| Lt. Halbert G. Marsh | 0 | 5 | 5 | 358th |
| Lt. Darwin D. McCasland | 2 | 3 | 5 | 357th |
| Lt. Francis N. McCollom | 0 | 5 | 5 | 358th |
| Lt. Philip M.N. McHugh | 2 | 3 | 5 | 357th |
| Lt. Edward J. Moroney | 2 | 3 | 5 | 357th |
| Capt. Thomas F. Neal, Jr. | 4.5 | 0.5 | 5 | 354th |
| Lt. Emil F. Perry | 2 | 3 | 5 | 354th |
| Lt. Robert O. Peters | 3 | 2 | 5 | 358th |
| Lt. Royce W. Priest | 5 | 0 | 5 | 354th |

* - includes 1 air and 3 ground victories with the 4th Ftr Grp
** - includes 0.83 air victory with the 352nd Ftr Grp
*** - includes 1.5 air victories with the 363rd Ftr Grp, 9th AF, ETO

**Aces of the 356th Fighter Group**

| Name | Air | Grd | Total | Sqn |
|---|---|---|---|---|
| Maj. Donald J. Strait | 13.5 | 0 | 13.5 | 361st |
| LtCol. Donald A. Baccus | 5 | 4 | 9* | 359th<br>HdQts |
| Maj. Wilbur R. Scheible | 6 | 3 | 9 | 361st<br>HdQts |
| Maj. Michael P. Yannell | 4 | 4 | 8** | 360th |
| Capt. David F. Thwaites | 6 | 1 | 7 | 361st |
| Lt. Clinton D. Burdick | 5.5 | 1 | 6.5 | 361st |
| Capt. Raymond H. Gansberg | 2.5 | 4 | 6.5 | 361st |
| Col. Einar A. Malmstrom | 1 | 5.5 | 6.5 | HdQts |
| Capt. Howard E. Wiggins | 4.5 | 1.5 | 6 | 361st |
| Lt. Clifford T. Ashby | 3.5 | 2 | 5.5 | 361st |
| Capt. Frank A. Morgan | 0.5 | 5 | 5.5 | 361st |
| Capt. Sidney H. Hewett | 2.5 | 2.5 | 5 | 361st |
| LtCol. Gerald W. Johnson | 16.5 | 0 | 16*** | 360th |
| Maj. John W. Vogt, Jr. | 8 | 0 | 8@ | 360th |

* - includes 1 ground victory with the 359th Ftr Grp
** - includes 2 air victories with the 86th Ftr Grp, MTO
*** - includes 15.5 air victories with the 56th Ftr Grp
@ - includes 5 air victories with the 56th Ftr Grp

**Aces of the 357th Fighter Group**

| Name | Air | Grd | Total | Sqn |
|---|---|---|---|---|
| Maj. Leonard K. Carson | 18.5 | 3.5 | 22 | 362nd |
| Maj. Richard A. Peterson | 15.5 | 3.5 | 19 | 364th |
| Maj. John B. England | 17.5 | 1 | 18.5 | 362nd |
| Maj. Robert W. Foy | 15 | 3 | 18 | 363rd<br>HdQts |
| Maj. Clarence E. Anderson | 16.25 | 1 | 17.25 | 363rd |
| Maj. Donald H. Bochkay | 13.83 | 0 | 13.83 | 363rd |
| Capt. John A. Kirla | 11.5 | 0.5 | 12 | 362nd |
| LtCol. John A. Storch | 10.5 | 1.5 | 12 | 364th |
| Lt. Dale E. Karger | 7.5 | 4 | 11.5 | 364th |
| Capt. Charles E. Yeager | 11.5 | 0 | 11.5 | 363rd |
| Capt. Charles E. Weaver | 8 | 3 | 11 | 362nd |
| Col. Irwin H. Dregne | 5 | 5.5 | 10.5 | HdQts |
| Lt. Otto D. Jenkins | 8.5 | 2 | 10.5 | 362nd |
| Lt. John F. Duncan | 4 | 6 | 10 | 362nd |
| Capt. Fletcher E. Adams | 9 | 0 | 9 | 362nd |
| Capt. John L. Sublett | 8 | 1 | 9 | 362nd |
| LtCol. Thomas L. Hayes, Jr. | 8.5 | 0 | 8.5 | 364th<br>HdQts |
| LtCol. Joseph E. Broadhead | 8 | 0 | 8 | 362nd<br>HdQts |
| LtCol. Andrew J. Evans, Jr. | 6 | 2 | 8 | HdQts |
| Maj. Donald C. McGee | 6 | 2 | 8* | 363rd<br>364th |
| Capt. Alva C. Murphy | 6 | 2 | 8 | 362nd<br>364th |
| Lt. Joseph F. Pierce | 7 | 1 | 8 | 363rd |
| Capt. Robert G. Schimanski | 6 | 2 | 8 | 364th |
| Capt. Robert M. Shaw | 8 | 0 | 8 | 364th |
| Lt. Vincent V. Zettler | 1 | 7 | 8 | 364th |
| Capt. Glendon V. Davis | 7.5 | 0 | 7.5 | 364th |
| Capt. Robert H. Becker | 7 | 0 | 7 | 362nd |
| Capt. James W. Browning | 7 | 0 | 7 | 363rd |
| Capt. John B. Carder | 7 | 0 | 7 | 364th |
| Capt. Gilbert M. O'Brein | 7 | 0 | 7 | 362nd |
| Lt. Arval J. Roberson | 6 | 1 | 7 | 362nd |
| Capt. Gerald E. Tyler | 7 | 0 | 7 | 364th |
| Lt. Frank L. Gailer, Jr. | 5.5 | 1 | 6.5 | 363rd |
| Capt. Morris A. Stanley | 5 | 1.5 | 6.5 | 364th |
| Capt. John F. Pugh | 6 | 0 | 6 | 362nd |
| Capt. Thomas H. Adams | 4.5 | 1 | 5.5 | 364th |
| Capt. Paul R. Hatala | 5.5 | 0 | 5.5 | 364th |
| Capt. William R. O'Brien | 5.5 | 0 | 5.5 | 363rd |
| Capt. Leroy A. Ruder | 5.5 | 0 | 5.5 | 364th |
| Lt. Robert C. Smith | 2.5 | 3 | 5.5 | 364th |
| Capt. Robert P. Winks | 5.5 | 0 | 5.5 | 364th |
| Lt. Raymond M. Bank | 5 | 0 | 5 | 364th |
| Lt. Myron A. Becraft | 1 | 4 | 5 | 362nd |

| Name | Air | Grd | Total | Sqn |
|---|---|---|---|---|
| Lt. Byron K. Braley | 3 | 2 | 5 | 364th |
| Capt. Thomas L. Harris | 5 | 0 | 5 | 364th |
| Maj. Edwin W. Hiro | 5 | 0 | 5 | 363rd |
| Capt. Chester K. Maxwell | 5 | 0 | 5 | 364th |
| Lt. William C. Reese | 5 | 0 | 5 | 364th |
| Capt. Jack R. Warren | 5 | 0 | 5 | 364th |
| LtCol. John D. Landers | 14.5 | 20 | 34.5[**] | HdQts |

[*] - includes 5 air victories with the 8th Ftr Grp, PTO
[**] - includes 6 air victories with the 49th Ftr Grp, PTO, and 7.5 air and19 ground victories with the 55th and 78th Ftr Grps

**Aces of the 359th Fighter Group**

| Name | Air | Grd | Total | Sqn |
|---|---|---|---|---|
| Maj. Ray S. Wetmore | 21.25 | 3.33 | 24.58 | 370th |
| Maj. George A. Doersch | 10.5 | 1.5 | 12 | 368th<br>370th |
| Lt. Cyril W. Jones | 6 | 5 | 11 | 370th |
| Capt. Claude J. Crenshaw | 7 | 3 | 10 | 369th |
| Capt. Robert B. Hatter | 3 | 6 | 9 | 368th |
| Lt. Robert J. Booth | 8 | 0 | 8 | 369th |
| Capt. William F. Collins | 4 | 3 | 7 | 369th |
| Maj. Benjamin H. King | 7 | 0 | 7[*] | 368th |
| Lt. Joseph E. Shupe | 2 | 5 | 7 | 370th |
| LtCol. John B. Murphy | 6.75 | 0 | 6.75[**] | 370th |
| Capt. George F. Baker | 4.5 | 0.5 | 5 | 368th |
| Maj. Ralph L. Cox | 5 | 0 | 5 | 369th<br>370th |
| LtCol. Niven K. Cranfill | 5 | 0 | 5 | 368th<br>369th<br>HdQts |
| Capt. William R. Hodges | 5 | 0 | 5 | 370th |
| LtCol. Daniel D. McKee | 1 | 4 | 5 | 370th<br>HdQts |
| LtCol. Albert R. Tyrrell | 2 | 3 | 5 | 368th |
| Capt. Robert M. York | 5 | 0 | 5 | 370th |
| LtCol. Donald A. Baccus | 5 | 4 | 9[***] | HdQts |
| LtCol. Roy W. Evans | 6 | 0 | 6[@] | HdQts |
| LtCol. John P. Randolph | 1 | 4 | 5[@@] | HdQts |

[*] - includes 3 air victories with the 347th Ftr Grp, PTO
[**] - includes 1/2 victory with the 54th Ftr Sqn, Alaska
[***] - includes 5 air and 3 ground victories with the 356th Ftr Grp
[@] - includes 5 air victories with the 4th Ftr Grp
[@@] - all victories with the 20th Ftr Grp

**Aces of the 361st Fighter Group**

| Name | Air | Grd | Total | Sqn |
|---|---|---|---|---|
| Maj. George L. Merritt | 5 | 6 | 11 | 375th |
| Capt. Martin H. Johnson, Jr. | 1 | 9 | 10 | 375th |
| Lt. Dale F. Spencer | 9.5 | 0.5 | 10 | 376th |
| Lt. William J. Sykes | 5 | 5 | 10 | 376th |
| Capt. William R. Beyer | 9 | 0 | 9 | 376th |
| LtCol. Roy A. Webb, Jr. | 4 | 5 | 9 | 374th |
| Lt. George R. Vanden Heuval | 5.5 | 3 | 8.5 | 376th |
| LtCol. Wallace E. Hopkins | 4 | 4 | 8 | HdQts |
| Capt. Robert C. Wright | 3.5 | 4 | 7.5 | 375th |
| Lt. Urban L. Drew | 6 | 1 | 7 | 375th |
| Lt. Robert T. Eckfeldt | 3 | 4 | 7 | 374th |
| LtCol. Joseph J. Kruzel | 6.5 | 0 | 6.5[*] | HdQts |
| Lt. William T. Kemp | 6 | 0 | 6 | 375th |
| Lt. Sherman Armsby | 4.5 | 1 | 5.5 | 375th |
| Lt. Vernon R. Richards | 2 | 3.5 | 5.5 | 374th |
| Lt. Victor E. Bocquin | 4 | 1 | 5 | 376th |

[*] - includes 3 air victories with the 17th Pur Sqn, PTO

**Aces of the 364th Fighter Group**

| Name | Air | Grd | Total | Sqn |
|---|---|---|---|---|
| LtCol. John H. Lowell | 7.5 | 9 | 16.5 | 384th<br>HdQts |
| Maj. Ernest E. Bankey, Jr. | 9.5 | 6 | 15.5 | 383rd<br>385th<br>HdQts |
| LtCol. George F. Ceuleers | 10.5 | 0 | 10.5 | 383rd |
| Capt. Arthur B. McCormick | 1 | 9 | 10 | 385th |
| Capt. John C. Hunter | 3 | 6 | 9 | 383rd |
| Capt. Romildo Visconte | 4 | 5 | 9 | 385th |
| Capt. James M. Fowle | 8 | 0 | 8 | 384th |
| Capt. Roy W. Orndorff | 4 | 4 | 8 | 383rd |
| Maj. William S. Crombie | 4 | 3 | 7 | 385th |
| Capt. Gilbert L. Jamison | 7 | 0 | 7 | 385th |
| Maj. Samuel J. Wicker | 7 | 0 | 7 | 383rd |
| Capt. Jesse L. Truett | 0 | 6.5 | 6.5 | 383rd |
| Lt. Kenneth R. Horner | 0 | 6 | 6 | 385th |
| Capt. Edward F. Izor | 4.5 | 1 | 5.5 | 385th |
| Lt. James J. Pascoe | 5.5 | 0 | 5.5 | 385th |
| Lt. Richard M. Baughn | 1 | 4 | 5 | 383rd |
| Lt. Thomas H. Hall | 3 | 2 | 5 | 383rd |
| Capt. William F. Kissell | 0 | 5 | 5 | 383rd |
| Lt. James L., McCubbin | 4 | 1 | 5 | 385th |
| Capt. William F. Wilson | 5 | 0 | 5 | 385th |
| LtCol. Eugene P. Roberts | 9 | 0 | 9[&*] | HdQts |

[*] - all victories with the 78th Ftr Grp

**Aces of the 479th Fighter Group**

| Name | Air | Grd | Total | Sqn |
|---|---|---|---|---|
| Maj. Robin Olds | 13 | 11 | 24 | 434th |
| Capt. George W. Gleason | 12 | 2.5 | 14.5 | 434th |
| LtCol. Arthur F. Jeffrey | 14 | 0 | 14 | 434th |
| Maj. Claire A.P. Duffie | 3 | 8.5 | 11.5 | 434th<br>436th |
| Lt. Gail E. Jacobson | 4.5 | 6 | 10.5 | 434th |
| Lt. Thomas C. Olson | 1 | 9.5 | 10.5 | 434th |
| Capt. James M. Hollingsworth | 3 | 7 | 10[*] | 434th |
| Capt. Donald J. Pierce | 0 | 8.5 | 8.5 | 434th |
| Capt. Theodore J. Sowerby | 2 | 6.5 | 8.5 | 435th |
| Lt. Richard C.J. Palson | 0 | 8 | 8 | 436th |
| Lt. Charles B. Elmgren, Jr. | 0 | 7 | 7 | 436th |
| Lt. Ernest J. Hopcroft | 0 | 7 | 7 | 436th |
| Lt. George H. Witzel | 0 | 7 | 7 | 436th |
| Lt. John T. Golden | 1 | 5.5 | 6.5 | 434th |
| Capt. Hans J. Grasshoff | 2.5 | 4 | 6.5 | 436th |
| Lt. Richard G. Candelaria | 6 | 0 | 6 | 435th |
| Lt. John W. Hansen | 2 | 4 | 6 | 434th |
| LtCol. James M. Herren, Jr. | 4 | 2 | 6 | 434th |
| Capt. Verne E. Hooker | 2 | 4 | 6 | 435th |
| Lt. Tom D. Neely | 2 | 4 | 6 | 434th |
| Lt. Kenneth J. Hansen | 0 | 5 | 5 | 436th |
| Lt. John N. Murr | 2 | 3 | 5 | 434th |
| Lt. Jerome K. Nagel | 1 | 4 | 5 | 434th |
| Capt. Presson S. Shane | 0 | 5 | 5 | 436th |
| Lt. Alfred J. Smigel | 0 | 5 | 5 | 436th |
| Lt. Victor Wolski | 3 | 2 | 5 | 436th |
| Col. Hubert Zemke | 17.75 | 8.5 | 26.25[**] | HdQts |
| Capt. Clarence O. Johnson | 7 | 6 | 13[***] | 436th |
| LtCol. Sidney S. Woods | 7 | 3 | 10[@] | HdQts |

[*] - includes 3 air victories with the 14th Ftr Grp, MTO
[**] - includes 15.25 air and 8.5 ground victories with the 56th Ftr Grp
[***] - includes 4 air victories with the 82nd Ftr Grp, MTO, and 2 air and 6 ground victories with the 352nd Ftr Grp
[@] - includes 2 air victories with the 49th Ftr Grp, PTO, and 5 air and 2 ground victories with the 4th Ftr Grp

**8th Air Force Aces By Month**

| Month | Aces | |
|---|---|---|
| May 1943 | 1 | |
| June | 0 | |
| July | 1 | |
| August | 1 | |
| September | 0 | |
| October | 9 | |
| November | 3 | |
| December | 3 | **1943 total 18** |
| January 1944 | 6 | |
| February | 19 | |
| March | 27 | |
| April | 63 | |
| May | 31 | |
| June | 24 | |
| July | 22 | |
| August | 19 | |
| September | 48 | |
| October | 11 | |
| November | 32 | |
| December | 29 | **1944 total 331** |
| January 1945 | 21 | |
| February | 22 | |
| March | 25 | |
| April | 146 | **1945 total 214** |

**overall total 563 plus 5 aces prior to service in the 8th Air Force**

**Aerial "Aces in a Day"**

| Date | Pilot | Claims | Group |
|---|---|---|---|
| May 8, 1944 | C.J. Luksic | 5 | 352nd |
| May 12 | R.J. Rankin | 5 | 56th |
| July 7 | F.J. Christensen | 6 | 56th |
| August 6 | G.E. Preddy | 6 | 352nd |
| September 5 | W.H. Allen | 5 | 55th |
| | W.H. Lewis | 5 | 55th |
| September 27 | W.R. Beyer | 5 | 361st |
| October 12 | C.E. Yeager | 5 | 357th |
| November 2 | D.S. Bryan | 5 | 352nd |
| November 21 | W.T. Whisner | 5 | 352nd |
| November 26 | J.S. Daniell | 5 | 339th |
| November 27 | L.K. Carson | 5 | 357th |
| December 5 | W.J. Hovde | 5.5 | 355th |
| December 23 | D.C. Schilling | 5 | 56th |
| December 27 | E.E. Bankey | 5.5 | 364th |
| January 14, 1945 | F.D. Williamson | 5 | 56th |
| March 22 | S.S. Woods | 5 | 4th |
| March 24 | W.K. Blickenstaff | 5 | 353rd |
| | R.A. Elder | 5 | 353rd |

**Combined Air-Ground "Aces in a Day"**

| Date | Pilot | Air | Grd | Total | Group |
|---|---|---|---|---|---|
| April 8, 1944 | H.J. Rau | 1 | 4 | 5 | 20th |
| July 20 | R.O. Peters | 3 | 2 | 5 | 355th |
| September 11 | C.W. Jones | 4 | 2 | 6 | 359th |
| November 2 | W.J. Cullerton | 2 | 6 | 8 | 355th |
| | J.L. Elder | 1 | 5 | 6 | 355th |
| March 2, 1945 | M.A. Becraft | 1 | 4 | 5 | 357th |
| | V.V. Zettler | 1 | 4 | 5 | 357th |
| April 16 | E.E. Bankey | 2 | 4 | 6 | 364th |

**Ground "Aces in a Day"**

| Date | Pilot | Claims | Group |
|---|---|---|---|
| April 10, 1944 | J.A. Goodson | 5.5 | 4th |
| April 15 | J.N. McElroy | 5 | 355th |
| April 24 | E.L. Heller | 7 | 352nd |
| | R.G. MacKean | 5 | 352nd |
| May 21 | R.B. Hatter | 6 | 359th |
| June 29 | R.A. Webb | 5 | 361st |
| August 25 | J.L. Mansker | 6 | 20th |
| August 29 | S.T. Benjamin | 5 | 353rd |
| September 5 | J.M. Hollingsworth | 6 | 479th |
| | T.C. Olson | 5 | 479th |
| September 10 | H.W. Brown | 6 | 355th |
| | C.O. Johnson | 5 | 352nd |
| September 11 | A.A. Tower | 5 | 339th |
| September 12 | W.J. Cullerton | 7 | 355th |
| October 6 | F.H. Alexander | 5 | 20th |
| November 2 | W.J. Cullerton | 6 | 355th |
| | J.L. Elder | 5 | 355th |
| February 9, 1945 | C.H. Cole | 6 | 20th |
| | L.E. Einhaus | 6 | 20th |
| February 20 | F.A. Morgan | 5 | 356th |
| February 27 | W.L. Boone | 7 | 353rd |
| | D.M. Malmsten | 6 | 4th |
| | H.G. Kolb | 5 | 353rd |
| | R.J. Lanoue | 5 | 353rd |
| March 21 | R.N. Gustke | 5 | 353rd |
| April 9 | E.G. Righetti | 6 | 55th |
| | R.E. Welch | 6 | 55th |
| | F.E. Birtciel | 5 | 55th |
| April 10 | F.H. Jurgens | 8 | 20th |
| | A.A. Tower | 8 | 339th |
| | D. Stewart | 7 | 20th |
| | J.D. Landers | 6 | 78th |
| | E.L. Kier | 5 | 20th |
| | J.T. Murphy | 5 | 339th |
| | R.H. Paul | 5 | 339th |
| April 13 | R.L. Murphy | 10 | 56th |
| | J.C. Hunter | 6 | 364th |
| | R.S. Kyler | 5 | 56th |
| | J.E. Mellen | 5 | 355th |
| | J.L. Truett | 5 | 364th |
| April 16 | H.G. Kolb | 9.5 | 353rd |
| | R.H. Ammon | 9 | 339th |
| | J.D. Landers | 9 | 78th |
| | G.J. Miller | 9 | 353rd |
| | C.E. Taylor | 9 | 78th |
| | E.L. Heller | 7 | 352nd |
| | O.E. Gilbert | 6.5 | 66th(FW) |
| | S.J. Chetneky | 6 | 339th |
| | W.C. Clark | 6 | 339th |
| | C.A. Pattillo | 6 | 352nd |
| | E.G. Righetti | 6 | 55th |
| | B. Rimerman | 6 | 353rd |
| | B.D. McMahan | 5.5 | 353rd |
| | W.O. Antonides | 5 | 4th |
| | D.P. Baugh | 5 | 4th |
| | J.R. Byers | 5 | 339th |
| | G.B. Compton | 5 | 353rd |
| | A.T. Colletti | 5 | 78th |
| | D.J. DeVilliers | 5 | 78th |
| | G.C. Doss | 5 | 78th |
| | R.N. Gustke | 5 | 353rd |
| | K.G. Helfrecht | 5 | 4th |
| | N. Hepner | 5 | 78th |
| | M.W. Hightshoe | 5 | 353rd |
| | D.E. Josey | 5 | 78th |
| | H.G. Marsh | 5 | 355th |
| | J.H. McClure | 5 | 353rd |
| | D.M. McDuffie | 5 | 78th |
| | J.D. McMullen | 5 | 353rd |
| | R. Olds | 5 | 479th |
| | D.P. Pederson | 5 | 4th |
| | D.S. Sweat | 5 | 78th |
| | H.S. Sykes | 5 | 352nd |
| April 17 | E.G. Righetti | 9 | 55th |
| | L.M. Orcutt | 8 | 339th |
| | K.B. Everson | 7 | 339th |
| | E.R. Kulik | 7 | 78th |
| | R.H. Littge | 6 | 352nd |
| | J.D. Carter | 5 | 352nd |
| | H. Mahany | 5 | 55th |
| | J.L. Thury | 5 | 339th |
| | K.M. Waldron | 5 | 352nd |

At least seven other aces flew with the 8th Air Force but gained all their kills with other units. In addition, one pilot began his combat tour with the 8th, where he claimed his initial victories, then went to the 9th Air Force and became an ace. While not technically 8th Air Force aces, the author feels they should be extended some recognition.

**Daley, William J., LtCol.** (Amarillo, TX)
Claimed 8 kills with 121 Sqn, RAF. Flew with the 4th Fighter Group until November of 1942, then later flew with the 9th Air Force as Deputy CO of the 371st Fighter Group. He was injured in a landing accident on September 10, 1944, and died two days later.

**Daymond, Gregory A., Maj.** (Burbank, CA)
Claimed 7 kills with 71 Sqn, RAF. Flew with the 4th Fighter Group until March of 1943.

**Donaldson, I.B. Jack, Maj.** (Kiefer, OK)
Claimed 5 kills with the 21st Pursuit Squadron and 49th Fighter Group in the Pacific. Flew 61 missions in the ETO with the 352nd Fighter Group.

**Edner, Seldon R., LtCol.** (San Jose, CA)
Claimed 5 kills with 121 and 133 Sqns, RAF. Flew with the 4th Fighter Group until becoming a POW on March 8, 1944.

**Gray, Rockford V., LtCol.** (Cincinnati, OH)
Claimed 1.5 kills with the 359th Fighter Group then transferred to the 9th Air Force's 365th Fighter Group in February of 1944. Claimed 2 kills with them, then went to the 371st Fighter Group and bagged 3 more. Killed in a landing accident on September 4, 1944.

**Kuentzal, Ward A., Lt.** (Delano, CA)
Claimed 7 kills with the 82nd Fighter Group in the MTO. Flew with the 479th Fighter Group until going MIA on June 19, 1944.

**McColpin, Carroll W., Col.** (Buffalo, NY)
Claimed 12 kills with 71, 121, and 133 Sqns, RAF. Flew with the 4th Fighter Group until November of 1942. Later served as CO of the 404th Fighter Group, 9th Air Force, and claimed 3 probables.

**White, Thomas A., Maj.** (Kelso, WA)
Claimed 6 kills with the 82nd Fighter Group in the MTO. Flew with the 55th Fighter Group until July of 1944.

...

The next section contains short combat biographies of each of the 8th Air Force aces. Information recorded for the pilots includes (where known):

a.) name, rank, total number of victories, and hometown
b.) combat unit assignment with dates of service
c.) number of combat missions and/or hours
d.) aircraft assigned to the pilot
e.) name of assigned groundcrew
f.) comments on combat in other theaters
g.) listing of all claims-kills, probables, and damaged-giving date, type of aircraft claimed, location, aircraft flown, and where applicable, the name(s) of other pilots involved in shared claims.

**Abbott, Earl L., Maj.** (5.75) Erie, PA
328th Ftr Sqn/352nd Ftr Grp Early 1943-January 24, 1945(KIA)
Downed by e/a near Aachen.
90 missions

P-47D PE-A 42-8435 "Sandra Lee"
P-47D PE-A 42-8653 "Flossie"
P-51B PE-A 42-106844 "Flossie II"
P-51D PE-A 44-14710 "Flossie III"
S/Sgt. Morrison-c/c
Sgt. Blanton-ac/c
Sgt. G.H. Vanander-arm.

| *Sqn* | *Date* | *Claims* | *Location* | *A/C* |
|---|---|---|---|---|
| 328th | January 29, 1944 | FW-190 dam(air) | Pelm | P-47 |
| | March 22 | (.25)FW-200 dest(air)* | Hesepe | P-47 |
| | April 29 | Me-109 dest(air) | Neuhaldensleben | P-51 |
| | May 21 | u/i a/c dest(grd) | Alt Ruppin | P-51 |
| | | (2)u/i a/c dam(grd) | Alt Ruppin | P-51 |
| | May 29 | Me-109 dest(air) | Neubrandenburg | P-51 |
| | November 2 | (2)Me-109 dest(air) | Merseburg | P-51 |
| | November 21 | (.5)FW-190 dest(air)** | Merseburg | P-51 |

4.75-0-1 air
1-2 ground

* - shared with Lt. R.C. Brookins, Lt. J.F. Thornell, and Lt. E. Zellner of the 328th Ftr Sqn
** - shared with an unknown P-51

**Abernathy, Robert W., Capt.** (5) Pulaski, TN
350th Ftr Sqn/353rd Ftr Grp August 1944-April 1945
71 missions, 321:20 hours

P-51D LH-G 44-14811 "Lady Gwen"
P-51D LH-G 44-15969 "Lady Gwen II"

| *Sqn* | *Date* | *Claims* | *Location* | *A/C* |
|---|---|---|---|---|
| 350th | September 23, 1944 | Me-109 dest(air) | SE Arnheim | P-47 |
| | November 2 | Me-109 dest(air) | Merseburg | P-51 |
| | November 18 | (.5)u/i a/c dam(grd)* | Lechfeld | P-51 |
| | November 27 | FW-190 dam(air) | Brunswick | P-51 |
| | December 24 | (2)Me-109 dest(air) | Coblenz-Limburg | P-51 |
| | April 10, 1945 | Me-262 dest(air) | Dessau | P-51 |

5-0-1 air
0-0.5 ground

* - shared with Capt. W.J. Price of the 350th Ftr Sqn

**Adams, Fletcher E., Capt.** (9) Ida, LA
362nd Ftr Sqn/357th Ftr Grp March 1943-May 30, 1944(KIA)
Hit by a Me-109 near Celle

P-51B G4-L 43-12468 "Southern Belle"

| *Sqn* | *Date* | *Claims* | *Location* | *A/C* |
|---|---|---|---|---|
| 362nd | February 22, 1944 | Me-109 dest(air) | NW Bernburg | P-51 |
| | March 18 | Me-109 dest(air) | NW Paris | P-51 |
| | April 11 | (2)Me-109 dest(air) | N/Magdeburg | P-51 |
| | April 24 | (3)Me-110 dest(air) | Munich | P-51 |
| | May 19 | (.5)Me-109 dest(air)* | Hagenow | P-51 |
| | May 27 | FW-190 dest(air) | N/Strasbourg | P-51 |
| | May 30 | (.5)Me-410 dest(air)** | W/Bernburg | P-51 |

9-0-0 air
0-0 ground

* - shared with Lt. A.J. Roberson of the 362nd Ftr Sqn
** - shared with Lt. G.M. O'Brien of the 362nd Ftr Sqn

**Adams, Louis W., Lt.** (6) Kingsville, TX
77th Ftr Sqn/20th Ftr Grp March 1944-November 1944
58 missions, 275:50 hours

P-38J LC-L
P-51D LC-L 44-13655
P-51D LC-L 44-14063 "Robb"

| *Sqn* | *Date* | *Claims* | *Location* | *A/C* |
|---|---|---|---|---|
| 77th | July 7, 1944 | Me-410 dest(air) | Oschersleben | P-38 |
| | | FW-190 dam(air) | Halle | P-38 |
| | July 29 | (2)Me-109 dest(air) | Gutersloh | P-51 |
| | August 16 | Me-109 dest(air) | Northeim | P-51 |
| | October 6 | Ar-196 dest(grd) | Bad Berg-Dievenow | P-51 |
| | | Do-18 dest | Bad Berg-Dievenow | P-51 |

4-0-1 air
2-0 ground

**Adams, Thomas H., Capt.** (5.5) Eldorado, AR
364th Ftr Sqn/357th Ftr Grp September 1944-June 1945

P-51D C5-L 44-64099 "Arkansas Traveler"

| *Sqn* | *Date* | *Claims* | *Location* | *A/C* |
|---|---|---|---|---|
| 364th | December 5, 1944 | FW-190 dest(air) | NW Berlin | P-51 |
| | January 5, 1945 | (.5)FW-190 dest(air)* | N/Hanau | P-51 |
| | January 10 | Me-109 dest(air) | Paderborn | P-51 |
| | | He-111 dest(grd) | Paderborn | P-51 |
| | January 14 | (2)FW-190 dest(air) | Ludwigslust | P-51 |

4.5-0-0 air
1-0 ground

* - shared with Lt. I.E. Snedeker of the 364th Ftr Sqn

**Aitken, John, Jr., Maj.** (5.5) Elberton, GA
504th Ftr Sqn/339th Ftr Grp States-May 1944
503rd Ftr Sqn/339th Ftr Grp May 1944-September 1944
Earlier flew with the 52nd Ftr Grp, 12th Air Force, in the MTO claiming one and a half kills: a Me-109 on April 7, 1943, and half of a Ju-88 on April 9, 1943.
270 hours

P-51B 5Q-
P-51C D7-A
P-51D D7-A 44-14004

| *Sqn* | *Date* | *Claims* | *Location* | *A/C* |
|---|---|---|---|---|
| 503rd | August 5, 1944 | (2)FW-190 dest(air) | S/Hameln | P-51 |
| | September 11 | Me-109 dest(air) | Annaberg | P-51 |
| | | FW-190 dam(air) | Annaberg | P-51 |
| | September 13 | Ju-88 dest(grd) | Holzkirchen | P-51 |

3-0-1 air
1-0 ground

**Alexander, Fred H., Lt.** (8) Seattle, WA
77th Ftr Sqn/20th Ftr Grp March 1944-October 1944
63 missions, 270:20 hours

P-38J No regular a/c
P-51D LC-H 44-13836 "It's The Kid!"
P-51D LC-M 44-13746 "It's The Kid!"
S/Sgt. Fred Frame-c/c
Sgt. Milton J. McAtee-ac/c

| *Sqn* | *Date* | *Claims* | *Location* | *A/C* |
|---|---|---|---|---|
| 77th | August 4, 1944 | He-111 dest(grd) | Putnitz | P-51 |
| | August 6 | (2)Me-109 dest(air) | Belzig | P-51 |
| | October 6 | (3)He-111 dest(grd) | Bad Berg-Dievenow | P-51 |
| | | He-115 dest(grd) | see above | P-51 |
| | | Do-18 dest(grd) | see above | P-51 |
| | | (2)He-111 dam(grd) | see above | P-51 |

2-0-0 air
6-2 ground

**Alfred, Carl R., Capt.** (8) Atwater, OH
336th Ftr Sqn/4th Ftr Grp July 1944-April 16, 1945(KIA)
Hit by flak at Praha Airfield.
83 missions

P-51D VF- 44-14552
P-51D VF- 44-72523
S/Sgt. Frank Blankschaen-c/c
Sgt. Roy Godfrey-ac/c
Sgt. Steinberg-arm.

| Sqn | Date | Claims | Location | A/C |
|---|---|---|---|---|
| 336th | January 16, 1945 | (2)FW-190 dest(grd) | Neuhausen A/F | P-51 |
| | February 22 | Do-217 dest(grd) | Halberstadt | P-51 |
| | | Me-410 dest(grd) | Halberstadt | P-51 |
| | March 21 | (3)Do-217 dest(grd) | Achmer | P-51 |
| | | Do-217 dam(grd) | Achmer | P-51 |
| | | Me-109 dam(grd) | Achmer | P-51 |
| | April 16 | u/i a/c dest(grd) | Praha A/F | P-51 |
| | | u/i a/c dam(grd) | Praha A/F | P-51 |

0-0-0 air
8-3 ground

**Allen, William H., Lt.** (5) Torrance, CA
343rd Ftr Sqn/55th Ftr Grp May 1944-October 1944
89 missions, 270 hours

P-38J CY-V 42-67966 "Pretty Patty"
P-51D CY-V 44-14049 "Pretty Patty II"
S/Sgt. Joseph Ruzika-c/c
Sgt. Gus E. Hoglund-ac/c

| Sqn | Date | Claims | Location | A/C |
|---|---|---|---|---|
| 343rd | September 5, 1944 | (5)Trainers dest(air) | N/Goppingen A/F | P-51 |

5-0-0 air
0-0 ground

**Ammon, Robert H., Capt.** (14) Sinking Springs, PA
503rd Ftr Sqn/339th Ftr Grp May 1944-January 1945
504th Ftr Sqn/339th Ftr Grp January 1945-March 1945
HdQts/339th Ftr Grp March 1945-EOW

P-51D D7-A 44-14004
P-51D 5Q-U"Annie Mae"

| Sqn | Date | Claims | Location | A/C |
|---|---|---|---|---|
| 503rd | June 8, 1944 | FW-190 dest(air) | Fourges | P-51 |
| | | Me-109 dam(air) | Fourges | P-51 |
| | July 7 | Me-109 dam(air) | Leipzig | P-51 |
| | September 23 | (2)FW-190 dest(air) | SW Wesel | P-51 |
| | September 28 | (2)FW-190 dest(air) | SE Brunswick | P-51 |
| HdQts | April 16, 1945 | (4)Me-109 dest(grd) | NE Prague | P-51 |
| | | (3)Ju-88 dest(grd) | NE Prague | P-51 |
| | | FW-190 dest(grd) | NE Prague | P-51 |
| | | He-111 dest(grd) | NE Prague | P-51 |
| | | Ju-88 dam(grd) | NE Prague | P-51 |

5-0-2 air
9-1 ground

**Amoss, Dudley M., Lt.** (7) Greenwich, CT
38th Ftr Sqn/55th Ftr Grp August 1944-March 21, 1945(POW)
Hit by flak near Hopsten.
59 missions

P-51D CG-B 44-13818 "Mah Ideel"

| Sqn | Date | Claims | Location | A/C |
|---|---|---|---|---|
| 38th | September 12, 1944 | u/i a/c dest(grd) | Herzogenaurach | P-51 |
| | | (.5)Ju-52 dest(grd)* | Herzogenaurach | P-51 |
| | February 3, 1945 | (1.5)FW-58 dest(air)** | Templin | P-51 |
| | February 15 | Me-262 dest(air) | Amberg | P-51 |
| | March 21 | (3)FW-190 dest(air) | SW Munster | P-51 |

5.5-0-0 air
1.5-0 ground

* - shared with Lt. W.J. Reilly of the 38th Ftr Sqn
** - shared with Lt. L.F. Spiecker of the 38th Ftr Sqn

**Anderson, Charles F., Jr., Capt.** (15.5) Gary, IN
335th Ftr Sqn/4th Ftr Grp August 1943-April 19, 1944(KIA)
Lost over Belgium for unknown reasons.

P-47D WD-L "Hell's Belle"
P-51B WD-L 43-7181

| Sqn | Date | Claims | Location | A/C |
|---|---|---|---|---|
| 335th | January 30, 1944 | Me-109 dest(air) | Lingen | P-47 |
| | | Me-109 dam(air) | Lingen | P-47 |
| | February 10 | (.5)Me-109 prob(air)* | SW Hanover | P-47 |
| | March 6 | Do-217 dest(air) | SE Brandenburg | P-51 |
| | March 21 | (1.5)FW-190 dest(air)** | N/Bordeaux | P-51 |
| | | (.5)FW-190 dest(grd)** | N/Bordeaux | P-51 |
| | | (.5)Ju-52 dest(grd)** | N/Bordeaux | P-51 |
| | March 27 | FW-190 dest(air) | W/Bordeaux | P-51 |
| | March 28 | u/i a/c dest(grd) | S/Dreux | P-51 |
| | March 29 | (2.5)FW-190 dest(air)@ | Gifhorn | P-51 |
| | April 1 | Me-109 dam(air) | Antwerp | P-51 |
| | April 5 | (2)Si-204 dest(grd) | Brandenburg | P-51 |
| | April 8 | FW-190 dest(air) | Gifhorn | P-51 |
| | April 10 | (.5)Bu-131 dest(grd)@@ | Romorantin | P-51 |
| | April 12 | (2)Me-109 dest(air) | NW Brunswick | P-51 |
| | | Ju-88 dam(grd) | NW Brunswick | P-51 |
| | April 15 | He-177 dest(grd) | Hagenow | P-51 |
| | | He-177 dam(grd) | Hagenow | P-51 |

10-0.5-2 air
5.5-2 ground

* - shared with Lt. A.L. Schlegel of the 335th Ftr Sqn
** - all shared with Maj. G. Carpenter of the 335th Ftr Sqn
@ - shared with an unknown pilot
@@ - shared with an unknown pilot

**Anderson, Clarence E., Jr., Maj.** (17.25) New Castle, CA
363rd Ftr Sqn/357th Ftr Grp February 1943-January 1945
116 missions, 480 hours

P-51B B6-S 43-6723 "Old Crow"
P-51B B6-S 43-24823 "Old Crow"
P-51D B6-S 44-14450 "Old Crow"
S/Sgt. Otto Heino-c/c
S/Sgt. Melvin Schueneman-c/c
Cpl. Leon Zimmerman-arm.

| Sqn | Date | Claims | Location | A/C |
|---|---|---|---|---|
| 363rd | February 20, 1944 | Me-109 dam(air) | N/Dessau | P-51 |
| | March 8 | Me-109 dest(air) | NW Hanover | P-51 |
| | April 11 | Me-109 dest(air) | W/Hanover | P-51 |
| | | (.25)He-111 dest(air)* | W/Hanover | P-51 |
| | | Me-109 dam(air) | W/Hanover | P-51 |
| | April 30 | FW-190 dest(air) | SE Orleans | P-51 |
| | May 8 | FW-190 dest(air) | Soltau | P-51 |
| | May 12 | Me-109 dest(air) | NE Frankfurt | P-51 |
| | | Me-109 dest(grd) | NE Frankfurt | P-51 |
| | May 27 | (2)Me-109 dest(air) | N/Strasbourg | P-51 |
| | May 30 | Me-109 dest(air) | E/Schonebeck | P-51 |
| | June 29 | (3)FW-190 dest(air) | SW Leipzig | P-51 |
| | July 7 | Me-109 dest(air) | N/Leipzig | P-51 |
| | November 27 | (2)FW-190 dest(air) | Magdeburg-Noyehausen A/F | P-51 |
| | | FW-190 prob(air) | Magdeburg | |
| | December 5 | (2)FW-190 dest(air) | W/Berlin | P-51 |
| | | FW-190 prob(air) | W/Berlin | P-51 |

16.25-2-2 air
1-0 ground

* - shared with Lt. H.R. Kayser, Lt. W.B. Overstreet, and Lt. E.K. Simpson of the 363rd Ftr Sqn

**Anderson, Woodrow W., Capt.** (13.5) Stockdale, TX
486th Ftr Sqn/352nd Ftr Grp September 1943-May 28, 1944(KIA)
Lost in a fight near Quedlinburg.

P-47D PZ-A
P-51B PZ-A 43-7000
P-51B PZ-A 42-106635 "Texas Blue Bonnet"

| Sqn | Date | Claims | Location | A/C |
|---|---|---|---|---|
| 486th | April 11, 1944 | (.5)Ju-52 dest(air)* | W/Torgau | P-51 |
| | | Ju-88 dest(grd) | Lonnewitz | P-51 |
| | | Ju-88 dam(grd) | Lonnewitz | P-51 |
| | April 13 | Hs-123 dest(grd) | S/Stuttgart | P-51 |
| | April 24 | (2)Ju-88 dest(grd) | Ingolstadt | P-51 |
| | | Do-217 dest(grd) | Ingolstadt | P-51 |
| | | He-111 dest(grd) | Neuburg | P-51 |
| | April 30 | FW-190 dest(air) | Clermont-Ferrand | P-51 |
| | | (2)Me-110 dest(grd) | Clermont-Ferrand | P-51 |
| | May 13 | Me-109 dest(air) | Tribsees | P-51 |
| | | u/i a/c dest(grd) | Wangerooge | P-51 |
| | May 24 | Me-109 dest(air) | NW Berlin | P-51 |
| | May 28 | Me-109 dest(air) | Dessau | P-51 |

4.5-0-0 air
9-1 ground

* - shared with Lt. F.A. Cutler of the 486th Ftr Sqn

**Andrew, Stephen W., Maj.** (15.5) Dallas, TX
486th Ftr Sqn/352nd Ftr Grp December 1942-July 2, 1944(POW)
Suffered mechanical failure near Budapest
Earlier flew with the 49th Ftr Grp, 5th Air Force, in the PTO, claiming one kill, a Zero, on April 27, 1942.
91 missions

P-47D PZ-A 42-8699 "Prairie Farmer"
P-51B PZ-A 42-106467
S/Sgt. Undo Rautio-c/c
Sgt. Carrazza-ac/c

| Sqn | Date | Claims | Location | A/C |
|---|---|---|---|---|
| 486th | March 15, 1944 | Me-109 dest(air) | Aldensaal | P-47 |
| | April 11 | Ju-88 dest(grd) | Finsterwalde | P-51 |
| | | Ju-86 dest(grd) | Finsterwalde | P-51 |
| | April 13 | (.5)He-111 dest(grd)[*] | S/Stuttgart | P-51 |
| | April 20 | Me-109 dest(air) | E/Paris | P-51 |
| | April 24 | u/i a/c dest(grd) | Neuburg | P-51 |
| | | Ju-88 dam(grd) | Ingolstadt | P-51 |
| | April 25 | Ju-88 dest(grd) | Metz | P-51 |
| | April 28 | FW-200 dest(grd) | Chateaudun | P-51 |
| | April 30 | FW-190 dest(air) | Clermont | P-51 |
| | May 8 | FW-190 dest(air) | NE Hanover | P-51 |
| | May 12 | FW-190 dest(air) | Gotha | P-51 |
| | May 19 | Me-109 dest(air) | Rathenow | P-51 |
| | May 28 | Me-109 dest(air) | NE Dessau | P-51 |
| | May 30 | FW-190 dest(air) | Magdeburg | P-51 |
| | June 8 | FW-190 dam(grd) | Le Mans | P-51 |
| | June 20 | Ju-52 dest(grd) | Burg A/F | P-51 |
| | | 9-0-0 air | | |
| | | 6.5-2 ground | | |

[*] - shared with Lt. M.H. Cunningham of the 486th Ftr Sqn

**Antonides, William O., Lt.** (7) Carbondale, CO
334th Ftr Sqn/4th Ftr Grp January 1945-September 1945
19 missions

P-51D QP-J

| Sqn | Date | Claims | Location | A/C |
|---|---|---|---|---|
| 334th | February 27, 1945 | (2)Ju-88 dest(grd) | Weimar | P-51 |
| | March 22 | (2)FW-190 dam(air) | Eggersdorf A/F | P-51 |
| | April 16 | (2)Me-109 dest(grd) | Gablingen | P-51 |
| | | FW-190 dest(grd) | see above | P-51 |
| | | Me-410 dest(grd) | see above | P-51 |
| | | u/i a/c dest(grd) | see above | P-51 |
| | | u/i a/c dam(grd) | see above | P-51 |
| | | 0-0-2 air | | |
| | | 7-1 ground | | |

**Armsby, Sherman, Lt.** (5.5) Baltimore, MD
375th Ftr Sqn/361st Ftr Grp April 1944-August 26, 1944(KIA)
Hit by flak in the Thionville-Trier area

P-51B E2-Y 42-106588

| Sqn | Date | Claims | Location | A/C |
|---|---|---|---|---|
| 375th | June 20, 1944 | (.5)BV-138 dam(grd)[*] | Putnitz | P-51 |
| | | (.5)Glider dam(grd)[*] | Putnitz | P-51 |
| | June 29 | (.5)Me-109 dest(air)[**] | SW Kothen | P-51 |
| | July 20 | (3)Me-109 dest(air) | N/Leipzig | P-51 |
| | August 5 | Me-109 dest(air) | N/Nienburg | P-51 |
| | August 15 | u/i a/c dest(grd) | Wittmunhafen | P-51 |
| | | (2)Me-110 dam(grd) | Wittmunhafen | P-51 |
| | | 4.5-0-0 air | | |
| | | 1-3 ground | | |

[*] - both shared with Lt. J.T. Thomas of the 375th Ftr Sqn
[**] - shared with Lt. R.C. Wright of the 375th Ftr Sqn

**Armstrong, Clifford F., Lt.** (5) New Baltimore, NY
352nd Ftr Sqn/353rd Ftr Grp December 1942-July 1944
91 missions, 301 hours

P-47D SX-F 42-7904 "8 Gun Melody"
P-47D SX-F 42-75622 "Hun Buster"
S/Sgt. Joseph F. Brandon-c/c
Sgt. Raymond A. Weinzgacz-ac/c
Cpl. Earl A. Dunn-arm.

| Sqn | Date | Claims | Location | A/C |
|---|---|---|---|---|
| 352nd | February 8, 1944 | FW-190 dest(air) | St. Hubert | P-47 |
| | February 10 | Me-109 dest(air) | Lingen | P-47 |
| | June 8 | (1.5)FW-190 dest(grd)[*] | Angars | P-47 |
| | | (.5)Ju-52 dest(grd)[**] | Angars | P-47 |
| | June 10 | FW-190 dest(air) | SW Nantes-Gassicourt | P-47 |
| | | 3-0-0 air | | |
| | | 2-0 ground | | |

[*] - shared with Lt. H.Q. Waggoner of the 352nd Ftr Sqn
[**] - shared with Lt. H.O. Miller of the 352nd Ftr Sqn

**Ashby, Clifford T., Lt.** (5.5) Nyssa, OR
361st Ftr Sqn/356th Ftr Grp June 1944-March 1945
77 missions, 313:30 hours

P-47D QI-M 42-76536 "Mary III"
P-51D QI-M 44-15073
S/Sgt. William H. McCormick-c/c

| Sqn | Date | Claims | Location | A/C |
|---|---|---|---|---|
| 361st | November 25, 1944 | (2)FW-190 dest(grd) | Zwickau | P-51 |
| | | FW-190 dam(grd) | Zwickau | P-51 |
| | December 5 | FW-190 dest(air) | Eberswalde | P-51 |
| | | FW-190 prob(air) | Eberswalde | P-51 |
| | January 14, 1945 | (2.5)FW-190 dest(air)[*] | SW Dummer Lake | P-51 |
| | | 3.5-1-0 air | | |
| | | 2-1 ground | | |

[*] - shared with Lt. W.M. Baskin of the 361st Ftr Sqn

**Ayers, James W., Lt.** (8) Tulsa, OK
334th Ftr Sqn/4th Ftr Grp June 1944-EOW

P-51B QP-K 43-6518
S/Sgt. William Rushing-c/c

| Sqn | Date | Claims | Location | A/C |
|---|---|---|---|---|
| 334th | January 16, 1945 | (.5)He-177 dest(grd)[*] | Neuburg | P-51 |
| | February 27 | (3)u/i a/c dest(grd) | Weimar | P-51 |
| | | (.5)Ju-52 dest(grd)[**] | Weimar | P-51 |
| | April 7 | Me-109 dest(air) | NE Duneburg | P-51 |
| | April 16 | Me-109 dest(grd) | Gablingen | P-51 |
| | | FW-190 dest(grd) | Gablingen | P-51 |
| | | u/i a/c dest(grd) | Gablingen | P-51 |
| | | 1-0-0 air | | |
| | | 7-0 ground | | |

[*] - shared with Lt. M.J. Kennedy of the 334th Ftr Sqn
[**] - shared with Lt. R.S. Voyles of the 334th Ftr Sqn

**Baccus, Donald A., LtCol.** (9) Los Angeles, CA
359th Ftr Sqn/356th Ftr Grp June 1943-April 1944
HdQts/356th Ftr Grp April 1944-April 1945
HdQts/359th Ftr Grp April 1945-September 1945
125 missions

P-47D OC-I 42-8568 "The Bloody Shaft"
P-47D OC-G 42-76583
P-51D OC-G 44-14993
P-51D CV-U 44-72746
T/Sgt. Ray J. Salicetti-c/c(356th)

| Sqn | Date | Claims | Location | A/C |
|---|---|---|---|---|
| 359th | November 29, 1943 | Me-109 dest(air) | NE Meppel | P-47 |
| | December 30 | FW-190 dam(air) | SE Menahould | P-47 |
| | January 11, 1944 | (.5)Me-110 dest(air)[*] | Steinhuder Lake | P-47 |
| | March 18 | (.25)Do-217 dam(grd)[**] | W/Nancy | P-47 |
| | April 1 | Me-410 dest(grd) | Dummer Lake | P-47 |
| HdQts | May 13 | (.5)FW-190 dest(air)[@] | Kiel-Lubeck | P-47 |
| | | FW-190 dam(air) | Kiel-Lubeck | P-47 |
| | June 7 | Me-323 dest(grd) | Laval | P-47 |
| | July 27 | He-111 dest(grd) | Cormeilles-en-Vixen | P-47 |
| | November 26 | (2)Me-109 dest(air) | Dummer Lake | P-51 |
| | December 25 | Me-109 dest(air) | Bonn | P-51 |
| HdQts | April 17, 1945 | u/i a/c dest(grd) | Ganacker-Plattling | P-51 |
| | | Me-109 dam(grd) | see above | P-51 |
| | | 5-0-2 air | | |
| | | 4-1.25 ground | | |

[*] - shared with Lt. J.H. Wadlow of the 359th Ftr Sqn
[**] - shared with Lt. R.K. Holtz, Lt. W.C. O'Barr, and Lt. G.B. Peet of the 359th Ftr Sqn
[@] - shared with Lt. R.L. Coughenour of the 359th Ftr Sqn

**Bailey, William B., LtCol.** (6) Rochester, NY
352nd Ftr Sqn/353rd Ftr Grp October 1942-July 1944
HdQts/353rd Ftr Grp July 1944-EOW
186 missions, 454:05 hours

P-47D SX-B "Butch"
P-47D SX-B 42-26459 "Butch II"
P-51D SX-B 44-14303 "Double Trouble"

P-51D SX-B 44-63684 "Double Trouble Two"
T/Sgt. Carl L. Buck-c/c
Sgt. Olin E. Hertzog-ac/c
Cpl. Marvin Martin-arm.

| Sqn | Date | Claims | Location | A/C |
|---|---|---|---|---|
| 352nd | October 14, 1943 | Me-109 dest(air) | Eecloo | P-47 |
| HdQts | August 4, 1944 | (2)He-111 dest(grd) | Plantlunne | P-47 |
| | | Ju-88 dest(grd) | Plantlunne | P-47 |
| | March 2, 1945 | (2)FW-190 dest(air) | S/Wittenburg | P-51 |

3-0-0 air
3-0 ground

**Baker, George F., Capt.** (5) Fulton, NY
368th Ftr Sqn/359th Ftr Grp August 1944-September 1945

P-51D CV-E 44-14081
P-51D CV-E 44-14500

| Sqn | Date | Claims | Location | A/C |
|---|---|---|---|---|
| 368th | September 8, 1944 | (.5)Ju-52 dest(grd)* | Cronberg | P-51 |
| | September 11 | (2)FW-190 dest(air) | Halberstadt | P-51 |
| | November 2 | (.5)Me-109 dest(air)** | Quedlinburg | P-51 |
| | | Me-109 dam(air) | Quedlinburg | P-51 |
| | December 31 | (2)FW-190 dest(air) | SE Stade | P-51 |

4.5-0-1 air
0.5-0 ground

* - shared with Lt. R.E. Benefiel of the 368th Ftr Sqn
** - shared with Lt. O.R. Fladmark of the 368th Ftr Sqn

**Ball, Sanborn N., Lt.** (5) Salem, MO
62nd Ftr Sqn/56th Ftr Grp November 1944-EOW

P-47M LM-R 44-21200

| Sqn | Date | Claims | Location | A/C |
|---|---|---|---|---|
| 62nd | December 4, 1944 | (.5)u/i a/c dest(grd)* | Neuburg | P-47 |
| | December 23 | FW-190 dest(air) | Euskirchen | P-47 |
| | March 14, 1945 | (.5)Ar-234 dest(air)** | Coblenz | P-47 |
| | April 13 | (2)Do-217 dest(grd) | Eggebeck A/F | P-47 |
| | | He-111 dest(grd) | Eggebeck A/F | P-47 |

1.5-0-0 air
3.5-0 ground

* - shared with Lt. D. Henley of the 62nd Ftr Sqn
** - shared with Lt. W.S. Lear of the 62nd Ftr Sqn

**Bank, Raymond M., Lt.** (5) Chicago, IL
364th Ftr Sqn/357th Ftr Grp September 1944-March 2, 1945(POW)
Hit by e/a southeast of Ruhland.
46 missions, 195 hours

P-51D C5-Y 44-15266 "Fireball"
S/Sgt. Randall Crawford-c/c

| Sqn | Date | Claims | Location | A/C |
|---|---|---|---|---|
| 364th | December 24, 1944 | Me-109 dest(air) | S/Kassel | P-51 |
| | January 14, 1945 | (3)FW-190 dest(air) | S/Schwerin | P-51 |
| | March 2 | Me-109 dest(air) | SE Magdeburg | P-51 |
| | | He-111 dam(grd) | E/Magdeburg | P-51 |

5-0-0 air
0-1 ground

**Bankey, Ernest E., Jr., Maj.** (15.5) Toledo, OH
383rd Ftr Sqn/364th Ftr Grp August 1943-April 1944
385th Ftr Sqn/364th Ftr Grp April 1944-December 1944
HdQts/364th Ftr Grp December 1944-July 1945

P-38J N2- "Lucky Lady"
P-38J 5E-B "Lucky Lady II"
P-38J 5E-B "Lucky Lady III"
P-51D 5E-B "Lucky Lady IV"
P-51D 5E-B "Lucky Lady V"
P-51D 5E-B 44-15019 "Lucky Lady VI"
P-51D 5E-B 44-73045 "Lucky Lady VII"
S/Sgt. Fay H. Thomas-c/c(385th)
Sgt. K.M. Dozier-ac/c(385th)
T/Sgt. Louis Crain-c/c(383rd)
Sgt. Alvin G. Baker-ac/c(383rd)

| Sqn | Date | Claims | Location | A/C |
|---|---|---|---|---|
| 383rd | April 11, 1944 | Me-109 dest(air) | Halberstadt | P-38 |
| | April 29 | FW-190 prob(air) | Stendal | P-38 |
| 385th | May 20 | Ju-88 dam(grd) | Soissons | P-38 |
| | November 26 | Me-109 dest(air) | NE Dummer Lake | P-51 |
| | | Me-109 prob(air) | NE Dummer Lake | P-51 |
| HdQts | December 27 | (4)FW-190 dest(air) | Bonn | P-51 |
| | | (1.5)Me-109 dest(air)* | Bonn | P-51 |
| | April 16, 1945 | (2)Me-109 dest(air) | N/Nordingen | P-51 |
| | | (2)Ju-188 dest(grd) | Pocking | P-51 |
| | | FW-190 dest(grd) | Pocking | P-51 |
| | | Do-217 dest(grd) | Pocking | P-51 |
| | | (2)FW-190 dam(grd) | Pocking | P-51 |
| | | (2)Ju-188 dam(grd) | Pocking | P-51 |
| | April 17 | (2)He-111 dest(grd) | Karlsbad | P-51 |
| | | (2)He-111 dam(grd) | Karlsbad | P-51 |

9.5-2-0 air
6-7 ground

* - shared with F/O A.H. Goebel of the 352nd Ftr Grp

**Barger, Clarence R., Lt.** (5.33) Allendale, MO
354th Ftr Sqn/355th Ftr Grp January 1944-May 28, 1944(KIA)
Hit by a Me-109 near Zerbst.
45 missions, 160 hours

P-47D WR-C 42-75275 "Hellen"
P-51B WR-C 43-6631 "Hellen 2nd"
S/Sgt. Julius Moseley-c/c

| Sqn | Date | Claims | Location | A/C |
|---|---|---|---|---|
| 354th | March 6, 1944 | (.33)Me-109 dest(air)* | Dummer Lake | P-47 |
| | March 8 | (3)Ju-88 dest(grd) | Hesepe | P-47 |
| | April 13 | Do-217 dest(grd) | Oberpfaffenhofen | P-51 |
| | | Ju-88 dest(grd) | see above | P-51 |
| | | Do-217 dam(grd) | see above | P-51 |
| | | Ju-88 dam(grd) | see above | P-51 |

0.33-0-0 air
5-2 ground

* - shared with Capt. W.J. Koraleski and Lt. N.J. Fortier of the 354th Ftr Sqn

**Barnaby, Harold T., Capt.** (5) Waco, TX
83rd Ftr Sqn/78th Ftr Grp February 1943-April 1945
106 missions

P-47D HL-I 42-7889
P-47D HL-I
P-51D HL-

| Sqn | Date | Claims | Location | A/C |
|---|---|---|---|---|
| 83rd | December 20, 1943 | Me-109 dest(air) | SW Bremen | P-47 |
| | February 10, 1944 | Me-109 dest(air) | Lingen | P-47 |
| | | FW-190 dest(air) | Lingen | P-47 |
| | | Me-109 dam(air) | Lingen | P-47 |
| | November 26 | u/i a/c dest(grd) | Weisswarte A/F | P-47 |
| | March 22, 1945 | Me-262 dest(air) | Giebelstadt | P-51 |

4-0-1 air
1-0 ground

**Baugh, Donald P., F/O** (5) Blanca, CA
336th Ftr Sqn/4th Ftr Grp November 1944-July 1945
38 missions

P-51D VF-U 44-14388

| Sqn | Date | Claims | Location | A/C |
|---|---|---|---|---|
| 336th | April 16, 1945 | (5)Ju-88 dest(grd) | Praha A/F | P-51 |

0-0-0 air
5-0 ground

**Baughn Richard M., Lt.** (5) Omaha, NE
383rd Ftr Sqn/364th Ftr Grp October 1944-EOW
49 missions

P-51D N2-B 44-15573 "The Snatch"

| Sqn | Date | Claims | Location | A/C |
|---|---|---|---|---|
| 383rd | December 23, 1944 | FW-190 dest(air) | NW Trier | P-51 |
| | April 13, 1945 | (2)Ju-52 dest(grd) | Flensburg | P-51 |
| | | FW-190 dest(grd) | see above | P-51 |
| | | Me-109 dam(grd) | see above | P-51 |

| Sqn | Date | Claims | Location | A/C |
|---|---|---|---|---|
| | | FW-190 dam(grd) | see above | P-51 |
| | April 16 | (2)u/i a/c dam(grd) | Marienbad | P-51 |
| | April 17 | Me-262 dest(grd) | SE Pilzen | P-51 |

1-0-0 air
4-4 ground

**Beason, Eugene M., Lt.** (5) Granite City, IL
62nd Ftr Sqn/56th Ftr Grp July 1944-January 1945

P-47D LM-P 42-26417

| Sqn | Date | Claims | Location | A/C |
|---|---|---|---|---|
| 62nd | September 5, 1944 | FW-190 dest(grd) | Gelnhausen | P-47 |
| | | u/i a/c dam(grd) | Gelnhausen | P-47 |
| | October 5 | Me-110 dest(grd) | S/Geseke | P-47 |
| | December 4 | He-177 dest(grd) | Neuburg | P-47 |
| | | FW-190 dest(grd) | Neuburg | P-47 |
| | December 23 | Me-109 dest(air) | Euskirchen-Bonn | P-47 |

1-0-0 air
4-1 ground

**Beavers, Edward H., Jr., Capt.** (5) Scranton, PA
503rd Ftr Sqn/339th Ftr Grp June 1944-November 27, 1944(KIA)
Hit by flak near Cologne.
43 missions

P-51D D7-Z 44-13980 "Shy Ann"
P-51D D7-Z 44-14525

| Sqn | Date | Claims | Location | A/C |
|---|---|---|---|---|
| 503rd | July 25, 1944 | FW-190 dest(air) | Etrepagny | P-51 |
| | September 23 | FW-190 dest(air) | SW Wesel | P-51 |
| | November 18 | Me-109 dest(air) | NE Mannheim | P-51 |
| | November 26 | (2)FW-190 dest(air) | SE Dummer Lake | P-51 |

5-0-0 air
0-0 ground

**Becker, Robert H., Capt.** (7) Hollywood, CA
362nd Ftr Sqn/357th Ftr Grp April 1943-September 1944

P-51B G4-O 43-6783 "Sebastian"
P-51D G4-O 44-13517 "Sebastian Jr."

| Sqn | Date | Claims | Location | A/C |
|---|---|---|---|---|
| 362nd | February 25, 1944 | (1.5)Me-110 dest(air)[*] | Regensburg | P-51 |
| | April 13 | FW-190 dest(air) | S/Mannheim | P-51 |
| | April 30 | Me-109 dest(air) | S/Paris | P-51 |
| | May 30 | (3)Me-109 dest(air) | Bernburg | P-51 |
| | July 29 | (.5)Me-109 dest(air) | W/Merseburg | P-51 |

7-0-0 air
0-0 ground

[*] - shared with Capt. A.M. Lingo of the 362nd Ftr Sqn
[**] - shared with Lt. T.W. Martinek of the 362nd Ftr Sqn

**Beckham, Walter C., Maj.** (18) DeFunick Springs, FL
351st Ftr Sqn/353rd Ftr Grp October 1944-February 22, 1944(POW)
Hit by flak near Bonn.
57 missions, 123 hours

P-47D YJ-X 42-8476 "Little Demon"
P-47D YJ-X 42-75226
S/Sgt. Henry Bush-c/c
Sgt. Marvin Eichstaedt-ac/c
Sgt. Richard Verity-arm.

| Sqn | Date | Claims | Location | A/C |
|---|---|---|---|---|
| 351st | August 24, 1943 | FW-190 dam(air) | N/Paris | P-47 |
| | September 23 | FW-190 dest(air) | S/Nantes | P-47 |
| | October 2 | FW-190 prob(air) | Emden | P-47 |
| | | Me-109 prob(air) | Emden | P-47 |
| | October 4 | Me-109 dest(air) | Malines | P-47 |
| | October 8 | FW-190 dam(air) | Rhede | P-47 |
| | October 10 | Me-110 dest(air) | Munster | P-47 |
| | | Me-110 dest(air) | Gransbergen | P-47 |
| | | Me-210 dest(air) | Munster | P-47 |
| | October 14 | (2)FW-190 dest(air) | Aachen | P-47 |
| | November 5 | Me-410 dest(air) | SW Gelsenkirchen | P-47 |
| | | FW-190 dam(air) | see above | P-47 |
| | November 11 | FW-190 dest(air) | Dulmar | P-47 |
| | December 1 | (2)FW-190 dest(air) | Koln | P-47 |
| | January 14, 1944 | (.33)FW-190 dam(grd)[*] | Rosiers-en-Santerne | P-47 |
| | January 21 | (2)Me-109 dest(air) | St. Quentin | P-47 |
| | January 30 | Me-109 dest(air) | N/Deventer | P-47 |
| | February 3 | Me-109 dest(air) | S/Oldenburg | P-47 |
| | | FW-190 dest(air) | S/Oldenburg | P-47 |
| | February 8 | Me-109 dest(air) | E/St. Hubert | P-47 |
| | | FW-190 dest(air) | St. Hubert | P-47 |
| | February 13 | FW-190 dam(air) | Cambrai | P-47 |
| | February 22 | (.25)FW-190 dam(grd)[**] | NE Bonn | P-47 |
| | | (.25)FW-190 dam(grd)[**] | NE Bonn | P-47 |

18-2-4 air
0-0.83 ground

[*] - shared with Lt. C.L. Stafford of HdQts, 353rd Ftr Grp and Lt. A.C. Duncan of the 361st Ftr Grp
[**] - both shared with Lt. F.N. Emory, Lt. G.B. Compton, and Lt. G.F. Perpente of the 351st Ftr Sqn

**Becraft, Myron A., Lt.** (5) Horseheads, NY
362nd Ftr Sqn/357th Ftr Grp October 1944-EOW
51 missions, 237:05 hours

P-51D G4-S 44-63221 "Moose"
S/Sgt. Joseph Sewell-c/c

| Sqn | Date | Claims | Location | A/C |
|---|---|---|---|---|
| 362nd | March 2, 1945 | Me-109 dest(air) | Kamenz A/F | P-51 |
| | | (2)He-111 dest(grd) | see above | P-51 |
| | | (2)u/i a/c dest(grd) | see above | P-51 |
| | March 31 | Me-262 dam(air) | N/Juist Island | P-51 |

1-0-1 air
4-0 ground

**Beeson, Duane W., Capt.** (22.08) Boise, ID
334th Ftr Sqn/4th Ftr Grp October 1942-April 5, 1944(POW)
Hit by flak at Brandenburg Airfield.
Earlier flew with 71 Sqn, RAF

Spitfire XR-J BL422
P-47D QP-B 42-7890 "Boise Bee"
P-51B QP-B 43-6819 "Bee"
S/Sgt. William Wahl-c/c

| Sqn | Date | Claims | Location | A/C |
|---|---|---|---|---|
| 334th | May 18, 1943 | Me-109 dest(air) | Blankenberge-Ostend | P-47 |
| | June 26 | Me-109 dest(air) | W/Dieppe | P-47 |
| | July 28 | Me-109 dest(air) | E/Rotterdam | P-47 |
| | | FW-190 dam(air) | see above | P-47 |
| | October 2 | FW-190 dest(air) | E/Wilhelmshaven | P-47 |
| | October 8 | (2)Me-109 dest(air) | Meppel-Zwolle | P-47 |
| | | Me-109 dam(air) | Meppel-Zwolle | P-47 |
| | October 10 | FW-190 dam(air) | Arnheim | P-47 |
| | November 29 | Me-109 prob(air) | Bremen | P-47 |
| | January 14, 1944 | FW-190 dest(air) | Soissons | P-47 |
| | January 29 | Me-109 dest(air) | Aachen | P-47 |
| | | FW-190 dest(air) | Aachen | P-47 |
| | January 31 | Me-109 dest(air) | Gilze-Rijen | P-47 |
| | February 20 | FW-190 dest(air) | Aachen | P-47 |
| | February 25 | FW-190 dest(air) | Beckingen | P-47 |
| | February 28 | (.25)Ju-88 dest(grd)[*] | Soissons | P-51 |
| | March 5 | Me-109 dest(air) | S/Bordeaux | P-51 |
| | | (.5)FW-200 dest(grd)[**] | Bordeaux | P-51 |
| | | FW-200 dam(grd) | Bordeaux | P-51 |
| | March 18 | Me-109 dest(air) | E/Mannheim | P-51 |
| | March 23 | (2)Me-109 dest(air) | E/Munster | P-51 |
| | March 27 | (1.5)Ju-88 dest(grd)[@] | Cazaux A/F | P-51 |
| | | Hs-126 dest(grd) | Cazaux A/F | P-51 |
| | | Ju-88 dam(grd) | Cazaux A/F | P-51 |
| | April 1 | Me-109 dest(air) | N/Lake Constance | P-51 |
| | April 5 | (.33)Ju-88 dest(air)[@@] | Plaue A/F | P-51 |
| | | (1.5)Ju-88 dest(grd)[#] | Weissewarte/Bush | P-51 |
| | | Me-323 dam(grd) | Brandenburg-Briest | P-51 |
| | | Me-109 dam(grd) | see above | P-51 |
| | | (.25) of (6)Ju-52 dam(grd)[##] | see above | P-51 |

17.33-1-3 air
4.75-5.25 ground

[*] - shared with Lt. W.B. Smith and Lt. N. Megura of the 334th Ftr Sqn and Lt. V. Garrison of the 336th Ftr Sqn, 4th Ftr Grp
[**] - shared with an unknown pilot
[@] - shared with Lt. H.T. Biel of the 334th Ftr Sqn
[@@] - shared with Lt. H.T. Biel of the 334th Ftr Sqn and Lt. C.A. Fiedler of the 335th Ftr Sqn, 4th Ftr Grp
[#] - shared with an unknown pilot
[##] - all shared with Lt. C.D. Carr and Lt. H.T. Biel of the 334th Ftr Sqn and Lt. R.S. Tussey of the 336th Ftr Sqn

**Bell, Thomas R., Capt.** (5.5) Shawboro, NC
334th Ftr Sqn/4th Ftr Grp September 1944-EOW

P-51D QP-G

| *Sqn* | *Date* | *Claims* | *Location* | *A/C* |
|---|---|---|---|---|
| 334th | February 25, 1945 | FW-190 dest(grd) | Rohrensee | P-51 |
| | | (.5)Me-110 dest(grd)[*] | see above | P-51 |
| | | (.5)Me-110 dest(grd)[*] | see above | P-51 |
| | | (.5)Me-410 dest(grd)[**] | see above | P-51 |
| | February 27 | (3)Me-109 dest(grd) | Weimar | P-51 |
| | | 0-0-0 air | | |
| | | 5.5-0 ground | | |

[*] - both shared with Lt. G.A. Denson of the 334th Ftr Sqn
[**] - shared with Lt. C.G. Payne of the 334th Ftr Sqn

**Benjamin, Swift T., Lt.** (7.5) Philadelphia, PA
62nd Ftr Sqn/ 56th Ftr Grp April 1944-May 1944
350th Ftr Sqn/353rd Ftr Grp May 1944-October 1944
73 missions, 270 hours

| *Sqn* | *Date* | *Claims* | *Location* | *A/C* |
|---|---|---|---|---|
| 350th | June 12, 1944 | Me-109 dam(air) | Dreux | P-47 |
| | June 27 | (.5)Me-109 dest(grd)[*] | Chalons | P-47 |
| | August 7 | Me-410 dest(grd) | SE Amiens | P-47 |
| | August 29 | (3)Me-109 dest(grd) | Diest | P-47 |
| | | (2)Me-410 dest(grd) | Diest | P-47 |
| | | (4)Me-109 dam(grd) | Diest | P-47 |
| | September 9 | Do-217 dest(air) | Hesepe | P-47 |
| | | 1-0-1 air | | |
| | | 6.5-4 ground | | |

[*] - shared with Lt. M.V. Bledsoe of the 350th Ftr Sqn

**Bennett, Joseph H., Capt.** (8.5) Morton, TX
360th Ftr Sqn/356th Ftr Grp March 1943-November 1943
61st Ftr Sqn/ 56th Ftr Grp November 1943-March 1944
336th Ftr Sqn/ 4th Ftr Grp March 1944-May 25, 1944(POW)
Hit by e/a near Strasbourg.
62 missions

P-47D PI- "Ann"
P-47D HV-L 42-751?? "Ann II"
P-51B VF-T 42-106686 "Ann III"
S/Sgt. John Ferra-c/c

| *Sqn* | *Date* | *Claims* | *Location* | *A/C* |
|---|---|---|---|---|
| 360th | November 29, 1943 | Me-109 prob(air) | Meppel | P-47 |
| 61st | December 20 | Me-110 dest(air) | Falkenburg | P-47 |
| | January 11, 1944 | (2)Me-109 dam(air) | Schwastorf | P-47 |
| | January 29 | (1.5)Me-110 dest(air)[*] | Simmern | P-47 |
| | March 8 | (2)Me-109 dest(air) | E/Steinhuder Lake | P-47 |
| | | FW-190 dest(air) | Munstorf A/F | P-47 |
| 336th | April 8 | Me-109 dest(air) | Huden | P-51 |
| | May 22 | Me-109 prob(air) | Lubeck | P-51 |
| | May 25 | (2)Me-109 dest(air) | Strasbourg | P-51 |
| | | (2)FW-190 prob(air) | see above | P-51 |
| | | FW-190 dam(air) | see above | P-51 |
| | | 8.5-4-3 air | | |
| | | 0-0 ground | | |

[*] - shared with Lt. P. Neyland of the 61st Ftr Sqn

**Bennette, Charles J., Lt.** (5.5) Oldtown, ME
328th Ftr Sqn/352nd Ftr Grp September 1943-August 1944

P-47D PE-O 42-8384
P-47D PE-O 42-75057
P-51B PE-O 42-106681 "The Maine-iacs"

| *Sqn* | *Date* | *Claims* | *Location* | *A/C* |
|---|---|---|---|---|
| 328th | April 8, 1944 | u/i a/c dest(grd) | Quackenbruck | P-47 |
| | | (.5)Me-110 dest(grd)[*] | see above | P-47 |
| | May 21 | He-111 dest(grd) | Alt Ruppin | P-51 |
| | | u/i a/c dest(grd) | see above | P-51 |
| | June 10 | Me-109 dest(air) | Bayeux | P-51 |
| | | Me-109 dam(air) | Bayeux | P-51 |
| | July 29 | Me-109 dest(air) | Merseburg | P-51 |
| | | Me-109 dam(air) | Merseburg | P-51 |
| | | 2-0-2 air | | |
| | | 3.5-0 ground | | |

[*] - shared with Lt. M.V. Long of the 328th Ftr Sqn

**Berkshire, Robert H., Lt.** (5.5) Tarzana, CA
487th Ftr Sqn/352nd Ftr Grp December 1942-June 26, 1944(MIA-E)
Hit by flak near Noyon.

P-47D HO-U 42-22515 "Brutal Lulu"
P-51B HO-U 43-6593 "Brutal Lulu"

| *Sqn* | *Date* | *Claims* | *Location* | *A/C* |
|---|---|---|---|---|
| 487th | November 26, 1943 | (.5)Me-109 dest(air)[*] | E/Groningen | P-47 |
| | February 21, 1944 | Me-109 dam(air) | N/Osnabruck | P-47 |
| | April 9 | Ju-88 dest(grd) | Vechta | P-51 |
| | May 27 | (2)Me-109 dest(air) | Strasbourg | P-51 |
| | May 30 | Me-109 dest(air) | Magdeburg | P-51 |
| | | FW-190 dest(air) | Ulzen | P-51 |
| | June 20 | Me-410 dam(air) | Magdeburg | P-51 |
| | | 4.5-0-2 air | | |
| | | 1-0 ground | | |

[*] - shared with Lt. J.R. Bennett of the 487th Ftr Sqn

**Best, Donald J., Lt.** (5) ????
38th Ftr Sqn/55th Ftr Grp February 1945-April 16, 1945(KIA)
Hit by flak at Munich-Brunnthal.
11 missions

No regular a/c or crew

| *Sqn* | *Date* | *Claims* | *Location* | *A/C* |
|---|---|---|---|---|
| 38th | April 9, 1945 | (3)He-280 dest(grd) | Munich-Brunnthal | P-51 |
| | April 10 | (2)He-111 dest(grd) | Wesendorf | P-51 |
| | | Me-109 dam(grd) | Wesendorf | P-51 |
| | | 0-0-0 air | | |
| | | 5-1 ground | | |

**Beyer, William R., Capt.** (9) Danville, IL
376th Ftr Sqn/361st Ftr Grp April 1944-December 1944
87 missions, 301 hours

P-51D E9-N 44-14144
S/Sgt. Ralph A. Nye-c/c

| *Sqn* | *Date* | *Claims* | *Location* | *A/C* |
|---|---|---|---|---|
| 376th | September 17, 1944 | Me-109 dest(air) | Hasselt-Wesel | P-51 |
| | September 27 | (5)FW-190 dest(air) | Eisenach | P-51 |
| | November 2 | FW-190 dest(air) | N/Erfurt | P-51 |
| | November 26 | Me-109 dest(air) | S/Ulzen | P-51 |
| | | FW-190 dest(air) | S/Ulzen | P-51 |
| | | 9-0-0 air | | |
| | | 0-0 ground | | |

**Biel, Hipolitus T., Lt.** (11.33) St. Paul, MN
334th Ftr Sqn/4th Ftr Grp September 1943-April 24, 1944(KIA)
Hit by e/a near Darmstadt.

P-47D QP-T
P-51B QP-T

| *Sqn* | *Date* | *Claims* | *Location* | *A/C* |
|---|---|---|---|---|
| 334th | January 14, 1944 | FW-190 dest(air) | Cambrai | P-47 |
| | February 10 | Me-109 dest(air) | Hengelo | P-47 |
| | | Me-109 dam(air) | Hengelo | P-47 |
| | March 18 | Me-109 dam(air) | SE Mannheim | P-51 |
| | March 27 | (1.5)Ju-88 dest(grd)[*] | Cazaux A/F | P-51 |
| | | Me-410 dest(grd) | see above | P-51 |
| | | FW-190 dam(grd) | see above | P-51 |
| | March 29 | FW-190 dest(air) | Gifhorn | P-51 |
| | April 5 | (.33)Ju-88 dest(air)[**] | Plaue A/F | P-51 |
| | | He-111 dest(grd) | Brandenburg-Briest | P-51 |
| | | Ju-88 dam(grd) | see above | P-51 |
| | | (.25) of (5)Ju-52 dam(grd)[@] | see above | P-51 |
| | April 8 | Ju-52 dest(grd) | SW Celle | P-51 |
| | | Me-109 dam(grd) | SW Celle | P-51 |
| | | Ju-88 dam(grd) | SW Celle | P-51 |
| | April 10 | u/i a/c dest(grd) | Romorantin A/F | P-51 |
| | April 11 | Me-410 dest(air) | SE Stettin | P-51 |
| | | Me-110 dest(air) | SE Stettin | P-51 |
| | April 15 | (.5)Ju-52 dest(grd)[@@] | Magdeburg | P-51 |
| | | 5.33-0-2 air | | |
| | | 6-5.25 ground | | |

[*] - shared with Capt. D.W. Beeson of the 334th Ftr Sqn
[**] - shared with Capt. D.W. Beeson of the 334th Ftr Sqn and Lt. C.A. Fiedler of the 335th Ftr Sqn, 4th Ftr Grp

@ - all shared with Capt. D.W. Beeson and Lt. C.D. Carr of the 334th Ftr Sqn and Lt. R.S. Tussey of the 336th Ftr Sqn, 4th Ftr Grp
@@ - shared with Capt. R.C. Care of the 334th Ftr Sqn

**Biggs, Oscar K., Lt.** (12) Wilmington, NC
505th Ftr Sqn/339th Ftr Grp February 1945-July 1945

P-51D 6N-E 44-72449 "Imogene"
S/Sgt. William G. Petrino-c/c
Sgt. Edmund J. Landry-ac/c

| *Sqn* | *Date* | *Claims* | *Location* | *A/C* |
|---|---|---|---|---|
| 505th | March 1, 1945 | (.5)Ju-88 dest(grd)* | S/Feldkirchen | P-51 |
| | March 2 | (3)Do-217 dest(grd) | Mockern | P-51 |
| | | (2)Do-217 dam(grd) | Mockern | P-51 |
| | April 7 | (.5)Me-109 dest(air)** | NE Steinhuder L. | P-51 |
| | April 10 | (4)Ju-88 dest(grd) | Wittstock | P-51 |
| | | (2)Ju-88 dam(grd) | Wittstock | P-51 |
| | April 16 | Me-109 dest(grd) | NE Prague | P-51 |
| | | Ju-88 dest(grd) | NE Prague | P-51 |
| | | u/i a/c dest(grd) | NE Prague | P-51 |
| | April 17 | Ju-88 dest(grd) | SE Pocking | P-51 |
| | | 0.5-0-0 air | | |
| | | 11.5-4 ground | | |

* - shared with Lt. B.B. Booth of the 505th Ftr Sqn
** - shared with LtCol. J.L. Thury of the 505th Ftr Sqn

**Bille, Henry S., Maj.** (10) Paradise, CA
357th Ftr Sqn/355th Ftr Grp February 1943-September 1945

P-47D OS-K 42-8397
P-51B OS-K
P-51B OS-K
P-51D OS-K 44-14314 "Prune Face"
S/Sgt. Charles J. Kawa-c/c

| *Sqn* | *Date* | *Claims* | *Location* | *A/C* |
|---|---|---|---|---|
| 357th | March 16, 1944 | Me-109 dam(air) | S/Reutlingen | P-51 |
| | April 13 | Me-109 dest(air) | Augsburg | P-51 |
| | | Me-323 dam(grd) | Crailsheim | P-51 |
| | April 24 | FW-190 dest(air) | NW Munich | P-51 |
| | August 16 | (2)Me-109 dest(air) | SE Hildesheim | P-51 |
| | September 12 | FW-190 dam(air) | NE Berlin | P-51 |
| | November 26 | Me-109 prob(air) | W/Gardelegen | P-51 |
| | April 16, 1945 | (2)u/i a/c dest(grd) | Eger A/F | P-51 |
| | | He-177 dest(grd) | Eger A/F | P-51 |
| | | Ju-87 dest(grd) | Eger A/F | P-51 |
| | | (2)u/i a/c dam(grd) | Eger A/F | P-51 |
| | April 20 | (2)Me-109 dest(air) | Letnany A/F | P-51 |
| | | (2)Me-109 dam(air) | Letnany A/F | P-51 |
| | | 6-1-4 air | | |
| | | 4-3 ground | | |

**Birtciel, Frank E., Capt.** (5) Sylvia, KS
343rd Ftr Sqn/55th Ftr Grp August 1943-April 1945
121 missions

P-38J CY-D 42-67872
P-51D CY-D 44-14561 "Miss Velma"
P-51D CY-A 44-13350 "Miss Velma"
S/Sgt. Bernard Fow-c/c
S/Sgt. John T. Grodski-ac/c
Sgt. Richard Martinson-arm.

| *Sqn* | *Date* | *Claims* | *Location* | *A/C* |
|---|---|---|---|---|
| 343rd | March 22, 1945 | Me-262 dam(air) | Schwabisch Hall | P-51 |
| | April 9 | (2)He-111 dest(grd) | Munich-Brunnthal | P-51 |
| | | (2)Ju-88 dest(grd) | see above | P-51 |
| | | Me-109 dest(grd) | see above | P-51 |
| | | Ju-88 dam(grd) | see above | P-51 |
| | | 0-0-1 air | | |
| | | 5-1 ground | | |

**Blakeslee, Donald J.M., Col.** (16) Fairport Harbor, OH
336th Ftr Sqn/4th Ftr Grp September 1942-November 1942
335th Ftr Sqn/4th Ftr Grp November 1942-May 1943
HdQts/4th Ftr Grp May 1943-November 1944
Earlier flew with 401, 411, 121, and 133 Sqns, RAF, claiming 3 kills: a Me-109 on November 22, 1941; a FW-190 on August 18, 1942; and a Ju-88 on August 19, 1942.

P-47D WD-C 42-7863
P-51B WD-C 43-6437
P-51B WD-C 42-106726
P-51D WD-C 44-13779
S/Sgt. Harry F. East-c/c

| *Sqn* | *Date* | *Claims* | *Location* | *A/C* |
|---|---|---|---|---|
| 335th | April 15, 1943 | FW-190 dest(air) | Knocke | P-47 |
| | May 14 | FW-190 dest(air) | N/Knocke | P-47 |
| HdQts | December 20 | Me-110 dest(air)* | Bremen | P-51 |
| | January 7, 1944 | FW-190 dest(air) | Hosdin | P-47 |
| | March 6 | Me-210 dest(air) | Berlin | P-51 |
| | March 16 | Me-110 dam(air) | SW Munich | P-51 |
| | March 18 | FW-190 dest(air) | S/Augsburg | P-51 |
| | March 23 | FW-190 dam(air) | Osnabruck | P-51 |
| | April 5 | (2)Ju-88 dam(grd) | Brandenburg-Briest | P-51 |
| | | u/i a/c dam(grd) | see above | P-51 |
| | April 18 | He-177 dest(grd) | Fassberg A/F | P-51 |
| | | u/i a/c dam(grd) | Fassberg A/F | P-51 |
| | April 22 | (2)Me-109 dest(air) | Kassel | P-51 |
| | April 24 | (1.5)FW-190 dest(air)** | N/Worms | P-51 |
| | | FW-190 dam(air) | N/Worms | P-51 |
| | April 30 | (.5)Do-24 dest(grd)@ | Lyon Anchorage | P-51 |
| | May 29 | Me-410 dest(air) | N/Falkenburg | P-51 |
| | | (2)Do-18 dam(grd) | Dievenow | P-51 |
| | July 2 | Me-109 dest(air) | Budapest | P-51 |
| | | 11.5-0-3 air | | |
| | | 1.5-6 ground | | |

* - scored while leading the 354th Ftr Grp, 9th Air Force
** - shared with Capt. A.L. Schlegel of the 335th Ftr Sqn
@ - shared with Lt. J.A. Patteeuw of the 336th Ftr Sqn

**Bledsoe, Marvin V., Capt.** (5.5) Los Angeles, CA
350th Ftr Sqn/353rd Ftr Grp June 1944-October 1944
70 missions, 270 hours

P-47D LH-J 42-26581 "Little Princess"

| *Sqn* | *Date* | *Claims* | *Location* | *A/C* |
|---|---|---|---|---|
| 350th | June 27, 1944 | (.5)Me-109 dest(grd)* | Chalons | P-47 |
| | August 7 | Me-410 dest(grd) | SE Amiens | P-47 |
| | August 29 | (2)Me-109 dest(grd) | Diest | P-47 |
| | | (2)Me-110 dest(grd) | Diest | P-47 |
| | | (2)Me-109 dam(grd) | Diest | P-47 |
| | | (2)Me-110 dam(grd) | Diest | P-47 |
| | | 0-0-0 air | | |
| | | 5.5-4 ground | | |

* - shared with Lt. S.T. Benjamin of the 350th Ftr Sqn

**Blickenstaff, Wayne K., LtCol.** (10) Chino, CA
350th Ftr Sqn/353rd Ftr Grp December 1942-April 1945
HdQts/353rd Ftr Grp April 1945-EOW
133 missions

P-47D LH-U 42-74647
P-47D LH-U 42-76320
P-47D LH-U 42-26402 "Soubrette"
P-51D LH-U "The Betty E"
P-51D LH-U 44-72374 "Betty-E"
S/Sgt. James B. Dibble-c/c

| *Sqn* | *Date* | *Claims* | *Location* | *A/C* |
|---|---|---|---|---|
| 350th | December 1, 1943 | Me-109 dam(air) | Solingen | P-47 |
| | June 30, 1944 | Me-109 prob(air) | W/Chalons | P-47 |
| | | Me-109 dam(air) | W/Chalons | P-47 |
| | November 27 | (4)FW-190 dest(air) | Steinhuder Lake-Brunswick | P-51 |
| | February 22, 1945 | Me-262 dest(air) | Berlin | P-51 |
| | March 24 | (3)FW-190 dest(air) | NW Kassel | P-51 |
| | | (2)Me-109 dest(air) | NW Kassel | P-51 |
| | | 10-1-2 air | | |
| | | 0-0 ground | | |

**Bline, Brooks J., Capt.** (5) Annapolis, IL
505th Ftr Sqn/339th Ftr Grp January 1945-July 1945

| *Sqn* | *Date* | *Claims* | *Location* | *A/C* |
|---|---|---|---|---|
| 505th | April 7, 1945 | FW-190 dest(air) | SW Ulzen | P-51 |
| | April 17 | (2)Me-109 dest(grd) | SE Pocking | P-51 |
| | | (2)Ju-88 dest(grd) | SE Pocking | P-51 |
| | | 1-0-0 air | | |
| | | 4-0 ground | | |

**Blizzard, Robert V.E., Lt.** (6) Detroit, MI
504th Ftr Sqn/339th Ftr Grp October 1944-July 1945

P-51B 5Q-O 42-106886 "Punkie"
P-51D 5Q-O 44-15499 "Punkie II"
S/Sgt. Jesse L. Russell-c/c
Sgt. William H. Courtney-ac/c
Sgt. Davis E. Hardee-arm.

| *Sqn* | *Date* | *Claims* | *Location* | *A/C* |
|---|---|---|---|---|
| 504th | April 7, 1945 | Me-262 prob(air) | Celle | P-51 |
| | | Me-262 dam(air) | Celle | P-51 |
| | April 10 | (2)Me-410 dest(grd) | N/Neuruppin | P-51 |
| | | (2)Me-410 dam(grd) | N/Neuruppin | P-51 |
| | April 16 | (4)Me-109 dest(grd) | Klatovy | P-51 |

0-1-1 air
6-2 ground

**Blodgett, Burton O., Lt.** (5) Detroit, MI
61st Ftr Sqn/56th Ftr Grp August 1944-EOW
31 missions

| *Sqn* | *Date* | *Claims* | *Location* | *A/C* |
|---|---|---|---|---|
| 61st | April 10, 1945 | Do-24 dest(grd) | Muritz Lake | P-47 |
| | April 13 | (3)Ju-88 dest(grd) | Eggebeck A/F | P-47 |
| | | u/i a/c dest(grd) | see above | P-47 |
| | | (2)Ju-88 dam(grd) | see above | P-47 |

0-0-0 air
5-2 ground

**Bochkay, Donald H., Maj.** (13.83) North Hollywood, CA
363rd Ftr Sqn/357th Ftr Grp April 1943-October 1945
123 missions, 510 hours

P-51B B6-F 43-6933 "Alice In Wonderland"
P-51C B6-F 42-103041 "Speedball Alice"
P-51D B6-F 44-13681
P-51D B6-F 44-15422
P-51D B6-F 44-72244
P-51D B6-F 44-72147
S/Sgt. R.A. Mills-c/c
Sgt. Roy Berridge-ac/c
Cpl. Russo-arm.

| *Sqn* | *Date* | *Claims* | *Location* | *A/C* |
|---|---|---|---|---|
| 363rd | March 5, 1944 | (.33)FW-190 dest(air)* | S/Bordeaux | P-51 |
| | March 6 | (2)Me-110 dest(air) | W/Berlin | P-51 |
| | April 8 | Me-109 dest(air) | NW Braunsweig | P-51 |
| | April 11 | (.5)Me-109 dest(air)** | Magdeburg | P-51 |
| | April 24 | Me-109 dest(air) | NE Munich | P-51 |
| | June 29 | Me-109 dest(air) | Schoningen | P-51 |
| | July 5 | FW-190 dest(air) | SE Rouen | P-51 |
| | | Me-109 dest(air) | SE Rouen | P-51 |
| | July 25 | Me-109 dest(air) | Paris | P-51 |
| | | Me-109 dam(air) | Paris | P-51 |
| | July 29 | FW-190 dest(air) | SW Merseburg | P-51 |
| | December 5 | (2)FW-190 dest(air) | NE Berlin | P-51 |
| | February 9, 1945 | Me-262 dest(air) | Fulda | P-51 |
| | April 18 | Me-262 dest(air) | SW Prague | P-51 |

13.83-0-1 air
0-0 ground

* - shared with Lt. C.K. Peters and Lt. E.A. Rogers of the 363rd Ftr Sqn
** - shared with Lt. M.A. Postle of the 364th Ftr Sqn, 357th Ftr Grp

**Bocquin, Victor E., Capt.** (5) Reading, KS
376th Ftr Sqn/361st Ftr Grp April 1944-November 1944

P-51B E9-G "Germicide"
P-51D E9-Q 44-14165
S/Sgt. Richard B. Schultz-c/c(G)
S/Sgt. Albert Godwich-c/c(Q)

| *Sqn* | *Date* | *Claims* | *Location* | *A/C* |
|---|---|---|---|---|
| 376th | August 4, 1944 | Ju-88 dest(grd) | Anklam | P-51 |
| | | Ju-88 dam(grd) | Anklam | P-51 |
| | September 12 | Me-109 dest(air) | NW Magdeburg | P-51 |
| | September 27 | (3)FW-190 dest(air) | Eisenach | P-51 |

4-0-0 air
1-1 ground

**Bodiford, Hugh, Lt.** (5) Montgomery, AL
338th Ftr Sqn/55th Ftr Grp October 1944-July 1945

P-51D CL-U
S/Sgt. Joseph Orebaugh-c/c
Sgt. John Lacalbo-ac/c
Cpl. Wes Miller-arm.

| *Sqn* | *Date* | *Claims* | *Location* | *A/C* |
|---|---|---|---|---|
| 338th | January 14, 1945 | Do-217 dam(grd) | SE Salzwedel | P-51 |
| | February 6 | Me-110 dam(grd) | Gerolzhofen | P-51 |
| | April 10 | Fi-156 dest(air) | SE Luneburg | P-51 |
| | April 16 | (2)u/i a/c dest(grd) | N/Landshut | P-51 |
| | | He-111 dest(grd) | N/Landshut | P-51 |
| | April 17 | FW-190 dest(air) | SE Dresden | P-51 |

2-0-0 air
3-2 ground

**Bonebrake, Robert R., Capt.** (6) Taylor, TX
83rd Ftr Sqn/78th Ftr Grp June 1944-January 1945

P-47D HL-E 42-25724
P-47D HL-E 44-19750

| *Sqn* | *Date* | *Claims* | *Location* | *A/C* |
|---|---|---|---|---|
| 83rd | July 5, 1944 | FW-190 dam(air) | Evreux | P-47 |
| | July 19 | Do-217 dest(grd) | Linburg-Coblenz | P-47 |
| | August 10 | He-111 dest(grd) | Chateau Salines | P-47 |
| | | Ju-52 dest(grd) | see above | P-47 |
| | November 26 | Me-109 dest(air) | S/Dummer Lake | P-47 |
| | December 19 | Me-109 dest(air) | S/Coblenz | P-47 |
| | | FW-190 dest(air) | S/Coblenz | P-47 |

3-0-1 air
3-0 ground

**Boone, Walker L., Maj.** (13.79) Wyandotte, OK
82nd Ftr Sqn/ 78th Ftr Grp July 1943-April 1944
350th Ftr Sqn/353rd Ftr Grp September 1944-March 1945

P-47D MX- "Margaret"
P-51D LH-E 44-14538 "Margaret Too"
P-51D LH-E "Margaret 3"

| *Sqn* | *Date* | *Claims* | *Location* | *A/C* |
|---|---|---|---|---|
| 82nd | February 13, 1944 | Ju-88 dam(grd) | Bryes-Sud A/F | P-47 |
| | April 1 | (.33)u/i a/c dest(grd)* | Verdun | P-47 |
| | | (.33)u/i a/c dest(grd)* | Verdun | P-47 |
| | | (.13)Do-217 dest(grd)** | Verdun | P-47 |
| | | Me-410 dam(grd) | Verdun | P-47 |
| | | Ju-52 dam(grd) | Verdun | P-47 |
| 350th | November 26 | FW-190 dest(air) | Minden | P-51 |
| | November 27 | FW-190 dest(air) | Brunswick | P-51 |
| | | FW-190 prob(air) | Brunswick | P-51 |
| | February 27, 1945 | (2)FW-190 dest(grd) | Rohrensee | P-51 |
| | | (2)He-219 dest(grd) | see above | P-51 |
| | | Me-410 dest(grd) | see above | P-51 |
| | | Ju-188 dest(grd) | see above | P-51 |
| | | Ar-234 dest(grd) | see above | P-51 |
| | | (3)u/i a/c dam(grd) | see above | P-51 |
| | | FW-190 dam(grd) | see above | P-51 |
| | | He-219 dam(grd) | see above | P-51 |
| | March 2 | Me-109 dam(air) | Ruhland | P-51 |
| | March 21 | (4)Ar-234 dest(grd) | Achmer | P-51 |
| | | (4)Ar-234 dam(grd) | Achmer | P-51 |
| | | Me-109 dam(grd) | Achmer | P-51 |

2-1-1 air
11.79-13 ground

* - shared with Lt. B.M. Watkins and Lt. C. Webb of the 82nd Ftr Sqn
** - shared with Capt. W.E. May, Lt. J.J. Hockery, Lt. B.M. Watkins, Lt. C.R. Clark, Lt. H.L. Eakes, Lt. R.V. Hearn, and F/O C.W. DeWitt of the 82nd Ftr Sqn

**Booth, Robert J., Lt.** (8) Waukesha, WI
369th Ftr Sqn/359th Ftr Grp April 1943-June 8, 1944(POW)
Hit by flak near La Fleche.

P-47D IV-F 42-8695 "Oily Boid"
P-51B IV-F 43-6757
P-51B IV-F 43-7199
S/Sgt. John W. Powell-c/c
Sgt. William E. Wall-ac/c
Sgt. Anthony R. Chentfant-arm.

| *Sqn* | *Date* | *Claims* | *Location* | *A/C* |
|---|---|---|---|---|
| 369th | January 30, 1944 | Me-109 dest(air) | Lingen | P-47 |
| | March 6 | FW-190 dest(air) | Quackenbruck | P-47 |
| | April 22 | FW-190 dest(air) | Hamm | P-47 |
| | April 25 | Me-109 dest(air) | Salmagne | P-47 |
| | May 8 | (2)Me-109 dest(air) | Mellensdorf-Drakenburg | P-51 |
| | | FW-190 dest(air) | see above | P-51 |
| | May 29 | FW-190 dest(air) | Stettner Haven | P-51 |
| | May 30 | Ju-88 dam(grd) | Harsleben | P-51 |

8-0-0 air
0-1 ground

**Boring, Lloyd D., Lt.** (7) Shelby, IN
343rd Ftr Sqn/55th Ftr Grp October 1944-April 1945

P-51D CY-D 44-15735 "Dizzy Jess"

| *Sqn* | *Date* | *Claims* | *Location* | *A/C* |
|---|---|---|---|---|
| 343rd | February 27, 1945 | (.5)Ju-88 dest(air)* | Nurnburg | P-51 |
| | April 9 | Me-109 dest(grd) | Munich-Brunnthal | P-51 |
| | | Me-410 dest(grd) | see above | P-51 |
| | | Me-109 dam(grd) | see above | P-51 |
| | April 16 | (.5)BV-140 dest(grd)** | Lake Chiem | P-51 |
| | April 17 | (2)Fi-156 dest(grd) | Bautzen/Litten | P-51 |
| | | FW-190 dest(grd) | see above | P-51 |
| | | u/i a/c dest(grd) | see above | P-51 |

0.5-0-0 air
6.5-1 ground

* - shared with Capt. R.L. Buttke of the 343rd Ftr Sqn
** - shared with Lt. R.G. Allen of the 343rd Ftr Sqn

**Bostrom, Ernest O., Capt.** (5) East Orange, NJ
486th Ftr Sqn/352nd Ftr Grp May 1944-April 1945

P-51D PZ-O 44-13929 "Little Marjorie"

| *Sqn* | *Date* | *Claims* | *Location* | *A/C* |
|---|---|---|---|---|
| 486th | July 18, 1944 | Ju-88 dest(air) | SE Warnemunde | P-51 |
| | September 12 | FW-190 dest(air) | Berlin | P-51 |
| | November 2 | (2)Me-109 dest(air) | W/Halle | P-51 |
| | January 14, 1945 | FW-190 dest(air) | Almelo | P-51 |

5-0-0 air
0-0 ground

**Bostwick, George E., Maj.** (15) Wausaw, WI
62nd Ftr Sqn/56th Ftr Grp April 1944-September 1944
63rd Ftr Sqn/56th Ftr Grp January 1945-EOW
92 missions, 390:55 hours

P-47D LM-G 42-26042 "Ugly Duckling"
P-47M UN-Z 44-21112
S/Sgt. Joseph A. Brennan-c/c(62nd)
Sgt. Andy A. Yourick-ac/c(62nd)
Sgt. Pasquale A. Fares-arm.(62nd)
S/Sgt. Max Victor-c/c(63rd)
Sgt. John C. Massey-arm.(63rd)

| *Sqn* | *Date* | *Claims* | *Location* | *A/C* |
|---|---|---|---|---|
| 62nd | June 7, 1944 | Me-109 dest(air) | Grandvillers A/F | P-47 |
| | July 4 | (3)Me-109 dest(air) | Conches | P-47 |
| | | Me-109 dam(air) | Conches | P-47 |
| | July 6 | Me-109 dest(air) | Beaumont | P-47 |
| | September 8 | (3)FW-190 dest(grd) | Coblenz | P-47 |
| 63rd | January 29, 1945 | Me-410 dam(grd) | Berge A/F | P-47 |
| | March 25 | Me-262 dest(air) | Parchim A/F | P-47 |
| | April 7 | (2)Me-109 dest(air) | S/Bremen-Hamburg | P-47 |
| | | Me-262 dam(air) | see above | P-47 |
| | April 10 | (2)Ju-88 dest(grd) | Werder A/F | P-47 |
| | | (2)u/i a/c dest(grd) | Werder A/F | P-47 |

8-0-2 air
7-1 ground

**Bosworth, Robert R., Lt.** (6) Oscaloosa, IA
82nd Ftr Sqn/78th Ftr Grp June 1944-November 1944

| *Sqn* | *Date* | *Claims* | *Location* | *A/C* |
|---|---|---|---|---|
| 82nd | August 10, 1944 | Ju-88 dest(grd) | Verdun | P-47 |
| | September 10 | (4)Ju-88 dest(grd) | Meinbullen | P-47 |
| | October 7 | Me-109 dest(air) | Leipzig | P-47 |

1-0-0 air
5-0 ground

**Boulet, William P., Lt.** (6) New Orleans, LA
354th Ftr Sqn/355th Ftr Grp States-April 26, 1944(POW)
Hit by fire from a B-17 near Clausthal.
47 missions, 165:10 hours

P-47D WR-E
P-51B WR-E 43-7153
S/Sgt. Yanavich-c/c

| *Sqn* | *Date* | *Claims* | *Location* | *A/C* |
|---|---|---|---|---|
| 354th | April 5, 1944 | FW-200 dest(grd) | Landsberg | P-51 |
| | | Do-217 dest(grd) | see above | P-51 |
| | | (2)Do-217 dam(grd) | see above | P-51 |
| | April 10 | He-111 dam(grd) | Bourges | P-51 |
| | April 11 | FW-44 dam(grd) | S/Madu Lake | P-51 |
| | April 13 | He-177 dest(grd) | Oberpfaffenhofen | P-51 |
| | | Me-110 dam(grd) | see above | P-51 |
| | April 24 | (2)Me-109 dest(air) | SE Munich | P-51 |
| | | (.5)Me-109 dest(air)* | see above | P-51 |
| | | (.5)Me-109 dest(air)** | see above | P-51 |
| | | Me-109 dam(air) | see above | P-51 |

3-0-1 air
3-5 ground

* - shared with Capt. R.E. Woody of the 354th Ftr Sqn
** - shared with Lt. N.J. Fortier of the 354th Ftr Sqn

**Bowers, Arthur R., Lt.** (6) Tiskilwa, IL
334th Ftr Sqn/4th Ftr Grp November 1944-EOW
30 missions

P-51D QP-S "Sweet Arlene"

| *Sqn* | *Date* | *Claims* | *Location* | *A/C* |
|---|---|---|---|---|
| 334th | February 25, 1945 | FW-190 dest(grd) | Rohrensee | P-51 |
| | | Me-110 dest(grd) | see above | P-51 |
| | | Me-410 dest(grd) | see above | P-51 |
| | April 16 | (2)Me-109 dest(grd) | Gablingen | P-51 |
| | | Ju-88 dest(grd) | see above | P-51 |
| | | (3)Me-109 dam(grd) | see above | P-51 |

0-0-0 air
6-3 ground

**Braley, Byron K., Lt.** (5) Chicago, IL
364th Ftr Sqn/357th Ftr Grp August 1944-September 1945

P-51D C5- "B.K.'s Battle Buggy"

| *Sqn* | *Date* | *Claims* | *Location* | *A/C* |
|---|---|---|---|---|
| 364th | September 18, 1944 | FW-190 dest(air) | N/Maastricht | P-51 |
| | September 19 | Me-109 dest(air) | E/Arnheim | P-51 |
| | December 24 | FW-190 dest(air) | S/Kassel | P-51 |
| | January 5, 1945 | Me-109 dest(grd) | Altenstadt | P-51 |
| | April 16 | Me-109 dest(grd) | Muhldorf A/F | P-51 |
| | | Me-109 dam(grd) | Muhldorf A/F | P-51 |

3-0-0 air
2-1 ground

**Broadhead, Joseph E., LtCol.** (8) Rupert, ID
362nd Ftr Sqn/357th Ftr Grp February 1943-April 1945

P-51B G4-V 43-12227 "Baby Mike"
P-51D G4-V 44-14798 "Master Mike"
Cpl. George H. Reid-arm.

| *Sqn* | *Date* | *Claims* | *Location* | *A/C* |
|---|---|---|---|---|
| 362nd | February 25, 1944 | Me-109 dest(air) | Regensburg | P-51 |
| | March 6 | Me-110 dest(air) | E/Berlin | P-51 |
| | March 16 | Me-410 dam(air) | S/Stuttgart | P-51 |
| | March 29 | Me-109 dest(air) | Brunswick | P-51 |
| | April 22 | FW-190 dest(air) | N/Dummer Lake | P-51 |
| | | FW-190 dam(air) | N/Dummer Lake | P-51 |
| | April 30 | Me-109 dest(air) | S/Paris | P-51 |
| | May 28 | FW-190 dest(air) | NW Magdeburg | P-51 |
| | December 5 | FW-190 dest(air) | Berlin | P-51 |
| | January 14, 1945 | Me-109 dest(air) | NW Berlin | P-51 |

8-0-2 air
0-0 ground

**Brookins, Richard C., Lt.** (5.25) Los Angeles, CA
328th Ftr Sqn/352nd Ftr Grp March 1944-October 1944

P-51B PE-D 43-7174 "The Duchess V"

| *Sqn* | *Date* | *Claims* | *Location* | *A/C* |
|---|---|---|---|---|
| 328th | March 22, 1944 | (.25)FW-200 dest(air)* | Hesepe | P-47 |
| | April 8 | (.5)Me-210 dest(grd)** | Quackenbruck | P-47 |
| | | (.5)u/i a/c dest(grd)** | see above | P-47 |
| | May 19 | Me-109 dest(air) | Wittenburg-Havelburg | P-51 |
| | May 30 | Me-109 dest(air) | Halberstadt | P-51 |
| | June 6 | FW-190 dest(air) | SE Rouen | P-51 |
| | | FW-190 dam(air) | SE Rouen | P-51 |
| | September 27 | FW-190 dest(air) | NW Frankfurt | P-51 |

4.25-0-1 air
1-0 ground

* - shared with Capt. E.L. Abbott, Lt. J.F. Thornell, and Lt. E. Zellner of the 328th Ftr Sqn
** - both shared with Lt. F.A. Yochim of the 328th Ftr Sqn

**Brown, Gerald, Maj.** (5) Phoenix, AZ
38th Ftr Sqn/55th Ftr Grp March 1943-April 1944
334th Ftr Sqn/ 4th Ftr Grp June 1944-October 1944

P-38H CG-G 42-67028
P-38J CG-G
P-51D QP-L

| *Sqn* | *Date* | *Claims* | *Location* | *A/C* |
|---|---|---|---|---|
| 38th | November 13, 1943 | Me-109 dam(air) | Bremen | P-38 |
| | January 31, 1944 | Me-109 dest(air) | Venlo | P-38 |
| | March 18 | FW-190 dest(air) | Nancy | P-38 |
| | April 8 | Me-109 dest(air) | Lingen | P-38 |
| | April 15 | FW-190 dest(air) | Munster | P-38 |
| | | He-111 dest(air) | Munster | P-38 |

5-0-1 air
0-0 ground

**Brown, Harley L., Capt.** (6) Wichita, KS
55th Ftr Sqn/20th Ftr Grp August 1944-March 1945
56 missions, 280:10 hours

P-51D KI-A 44-11205 "Be Good/Brownie's Ballroom"
S/Sgt. John H. Carpenter-c/c

| *Sqn* | *Date* | *Claims* | *Location* | *A/C* |
|---|---|---|---|---|
| 55th | August 25, 1944 | Ju-88 dam(grd) | Parow A/F | P-51 |
| | November 2 | (2)FW-190 dest(air) | Halle-Merseburg | P-51 |
| | | Me-109 dest(air) | see above | P-51 |
| | | Me-109 dam(air) | see above | P-51 |
| | December 2 | FW-190 dest(air) | Coblenz-St. Goar | P-51 |
| | January 14, 1945 | (2)Me-109 dest(air) | Perleberg | P-51 |

6-0-1 air
0-1 ground

**Brown, Henry W., Capt.** (28.7) Dallas, TX
354th Ftr Sqn/355th Ftr Grp September 1943-October 3, 1944(POW)
Hit by flak near Nordlingen.
72 missions

P-47D WR-Z 42-74703 "Baby"
P-51B WR-Z 42-106448 "Hun Hunter From Texas"
P-51D WR-Z 44-13305 "Hun Hunter From Texas"
S/Sgt. Mort Braun-c/c

| *Sqn* | *Date* | *Claims* | *Location* | *A/C* |
|---|---|---|---|---|
| 354th | March 8, 1944 | (3.5)Ju-88 dest(grd)* | Hesepe | P-47 |
| | | Me-110 dest(grd) | Hesepe | P-47 |
| | | (2)Ju-88 dam(grd) | Hesepe | P-47 |
| | March 18 | Me-109 dest(air) | Nancy | P-51 |
| | | Me-110 dam(air) | N/Munich | P-51 |
| | March 20 | FW-190 dam(air) | Coxyde | P-51 |
| | March 29 | FW-190 dest(air) | Brunswick | P-51 |
| | April 5 | (.5)Me-108 dest(air)** | Landsberg | P-51 |
| | | (.2)Do-217 dest(air)@ | Landsberg | P-51 |
| | April 8 | (.5)Me-109 dest(air)@@ | Sachau A/F | P-51 |
| | April 11 | FW-190 dest(air) | E/Berlin | P-51 |
| | | Ju-52 dest(grd) | Strasbourg | P-51 |
| | | Ju-88 dam(grd) | Strasbourg | P-51 |
| | April 13 | (2)Ju-88 dest(grd) | Oberpfaffenhofen | P-51 |
| | April 24 | (2)Me-109 dest(air) | S/Munich | P-51 |
| | April 29 | Me-109 dest(air) | Brunswick | P-51 |
| | May 13 | Me-210 dest(air) | Landsberg | P-51 |
| | September 10 | (6)He-60 dest(grd) | Frankfurt | P-51 |
| | September 11 | (3)Me-109 dest(air) | S/Kassel | P-51 |
| | September 18 | Me-109 dest(air) | Warsaw | P-51 |
| | | Me-109 dam(air) | Warsaw | P-51 |
| | | Ju-87 dam(grd) | Warsaw | P-51 |
| | September 27 | (2)FW-190 dest(air) | Eschwege | P-51 |
| | October 3 | Me-110 dest(grd) | Nordlingen | P-51 |

14.2-0-3 air
14.5-4 ground

* - shared with Capt. C.G. Johnston of the 354th Ftr Sqn
** - shared with Lt. C.W. Lenfest of the 354th Ftr Sqn
@ - shared with Capt. C.G. Johnston, Lt. W.J. Koraleski, Lt. J.E. Duffy, and Lt. B.C. Williamson of the 354th Ftr Sqn
@@ - shared with Capt. R.G. Kurtz of the 354th Ftr Sqn

**Brown, Quince L., Maj.** (13.33) Bristow, OK
84th Ftr Sqn/78th Ftr Grp June 1943-September 6, 1944(KIA)
Hit by flak near Vogelsand; was killed on the ground by an SS officer.
136 missions

P-47D WZ-J 42-74753 "Okie"
P-47D WZ-J 42-25698 "Okie II"
T/Sgt. Bill C. Jensen-c/c

| *Sqn* | *Date* | *Claims* | *Location* | *A/C* |
|---|---|---|---|---|
| 84th | September 27, 1943 | Me-109 dest(air) | NW Emden | P-47 |
| | January 4, 1944 | (2)FW-190 dest(air) | Coesfeld | P-47 |
| | January 5 | Me-109 dest(air) | La Rochelle | P-47 |
| | January 30 | Me-109 dest(air) | Rheine | P-47 |
| | March 15 | Me-109 dest(air) | W/Munster | P-47 |
| | March 16 | (2)Me-109 dest(air) | St. Dizier | P-47 |
| | | FW-190 dest(air) | see above | P-47 |
| | | Ju-88 dest(grd) | see above | P-47 |
| | | (2)u/i a/c dam(grd) | see above | P-47 |
| | March 23 | FW-190 dest(air) | Goch | P-47 |
| | March 30 | (.33)Do-217 dest(air)* | Twente/Enschede | P-47 |
| | April 12 | FW-190 dest(air) | Duren | P-47 |
| | September 1 | Me-109 dest(air) | Liege-Trier | P-47 |

12.33-0-0 air
1-2 ground

* - shared with Lt. L.J. Abel and Lt. E.S. Lang of the 84th Ftr Sqn

**Browning, James W., Capt.** (7) Syracuse, KS
363rd Ftr Sqn/357th Ftr Grp March 1943-February 9, 1945(KIA)
Last seen in a fight near Fulda.

P-51B B6-P 43-6563 "Gentleman Jim"
P-51D B6-P 44-14937 "Gentleman Jim"

| *Sqn* | *Date* | *Claims* | *Location* | *A/C* |
|---|---|---|---|---|
| 363rd | April 24, 1944 | Me-109 dest(air) | N/Augsburg | P-51 |
| | May 27 | Me-109 dest(air) | Strasbourg | P-51 |
| | May 30 | Me-109 dest(air) | NE Schonebeck | P-51 |
| | June 29 | (1.5)Me-410 dest(air)* | SW Leipzig | P-51 |
| | | (.5)FW-190 dest(air)** | SW Leipzig | P-51 |
| | December 5 | Me-109 dest(air) | N/Berlin | P-51 |
| | January 14, 1945 | Me-109 dest(air) | N/Brandenburg | P-51 |
| | | (2)Me-109 prob(air) | see above | P-51 |
| | | Me-109 dam(air) | see above | P-51 |

7-2-1 air
0-0 ground

* - shared with Lt. W.S. Fennell of the 363rd Ftr Sqn
** - shared with Lt. R.W. Staudte of the 363rd Ftr Sqn

**Bryan, Donald S. Maj.** (13.33) Paicines, CA
328th Ftr Sqn/352nd Ftr Grp March 1943-May 1945

P-47D PE-B 42-8381 "Little One"
P-51B PE-B 43-6894 "Little One II"
P-51D PE-B 44-14061 "Little One III"
S/Sgt. K.W. Noyes-c/c
Sgt. Bleckinger-ac/c
Sgt. Van Andel-arm.

| *Sqn* | *Date* | *Claims* | *Location* | *A/C* |
|---|---|---|---|---|
| 328th | January 29, 1944 | (.5)FW-190 dest(air)* | Namur | P-47 |
| | January 30 | FW-190 dest(air) | Emmen | P-47 |
| | February 20 | (.33)Me-110 dest(air)** | Vogelsand | P-47 |
| | February 24 | Me-109 dest(air) | W/Dummer Lake | P-47 |
| | March 15 | Me-109 dest(air) | Heusden | P-47 |
| | April 10 | (.5)FW-190 dest(air)@ | Dormans | P-47 |
| | September 27 | (2)Me-109 dest(air) | NW Frankfurt | P-51 |
| | | Me-109 dam(air) | NW Frankfurt | P-51 |
| | November 2 | (5)Me-109 dest(air) | Merseburg | P-51 |
| | | (2)Me-109 dam(air) | Merseburg | P-51 |
| | December 23 | FW-190 dest(air) | S/Liege | P-51 |

| | Date | Claims | Location | A/C |
|---|---|---|---|---|
| | December 31 | Ar-234 dam(air) | S/Verviers | P-51 |
| | March 14, 1945 | Ar-234 dest(air) | Elsafthal | P-51 |

13.33-0-4 air
0-0 ground

* - shared with Lt. Q.L. Quinn of the 328th Ftr Sqn
** - shared with LtCol. R.W. Osborn of the 67th Ftr Wg and Lt. D.T. Zimms of the 328th Ftr Sqn
@ - shared with Lt. J.L. Laing of the 328th Ftr Sqn

**Bryan, Gillespie, Maj.** (6) Winona, MS
HdQts/78th Ftr Grp March 1945-May 1945
8 missions

| Sqn | Date | Claims | Location | A/C |
|---|---|---|---|---|
| HdQts | April 16, 1945 | (2)u/i a/c dest(grd) | Praha/Kakewice | P-51 |
| | | Me-109 dest(grd) | see above | P-51 |
| | | Ju-52 dest(grd) | see above | P-51 |
| | | (3)u/i a/c dam(grd) | see above | P-51 |
| | April 17 | (2)u/i a/c dest(grd) | W/Dresden | P-51 |
| | | (3)u/i a/c dam(grd) | W/Dresden | P-51 |

0-0-0 air
6-6 ground

**Bryan, William E., Jr., Maj.** (9.5)Flint, MI
503rd Ftr Sqn/339th Ftr Grp States-March 1945
106 missions

P-51B D7-J 42-106798
P-51D D7-J 44-13601
P-51D D7-J 44-15074 "Big Noise"

| Sqn | Date | Claims | Location | A/C |
|---|---|---|---|---|
| 503rd | May 21, 1944 | (2)u/i a/c dest(grd) | Pelenz-Mackau | P-51 |
| | May 24 | (.5)FW-190 dest(air)* | Dannenburg | P-51 |
| | May 30 | (2)FW-190 dest(air) | Magdeburg | P-51 |
| | June 21 | Me-410 dest(air) | S/Stettin | P-51 |
| | | (.5)Me-410 prob(air)** | S/Stettin | P-51 |
| | August 5 | FW-190 dest(air) | S/Hameln | P-51 |
| | December 31 | FW-190 dest(air) | S/Hamburg | P-51 |
| | March 2, 1945 | FW-190 dest(air) | E/Magdeburg | P-51 |
| | | Me-109 dest(air) | see above | P-51 |
| | | FW-190 dam(air) | see above | P-51 |

7.5-0.5-1 air
2-0 ground

* - shared with Lt. E.H. Graham of the 503rd Ftr Sqn
** - shared with Lt. F.D. Talcott of the 503rd Ftr Sqn

**Bundgaard, Carl H., Lt.** (6) Withee, WI
505th Ftr Sqn/339th Ftr Grp June 1944-July 4, 1944(MIA-E)
Suffered m/f near Buzancals.
505th Ftr Sqn/339th Ftr Grp August 1944-March 1945

| Sqn | Date | Claims | Location | A/C |
|---|---|---|---|---|
| 505th | September 5, 1944 | Me-410 dam(grd) | Sinsheim | P-51 |
| | September 11 | (2)Ju-88 dest(grd) | Munich | P-51 |
| | | (3)Ju-52 dam(grd) | Munich | P-51 |
| | November 18 | Me-109 dest(air) | Neustadt | P-51 |
| | November 26 | FW-190 dest(air) | S/Hanover | P-51 |
| | | FW-190 dam(air) | S/Hanover | P-51 |
| | March 1, 1945 | Ju-88 dest(grd) | S/Feldkirchen | P-51 |

2-0-1 air
3-4 ground

**Burch, Harold W., Lt.** (11) Omaha, NE
505th Ftr Sqn/339th Ftr Grp February 1945-July 1945

P-51D 6N-D 44-72098

| Sqn | Date | Claims | Location | A/C |
|---|---|---|---|---|
| 505th | March 2, 1945 | (3)Do-217 dest(grd) | Mockern | P-51 |
| | April 10 | (3)Me-410 dest(grd) | Wittstock | P-51 |
| | | He-111 dest(grd) | see above | P-51 |
| | | Me-410 dam(grd) | see above | P-51 |
| | | u/i a/c dam(grd) | see above | P-51 |
| | April 16 | Ju-52 dest(grd) | NE Prague | P-51 |
| | | Ju-88 dest(grd) | NE Prague | P-51 |
| | April 17 | (2)Do-217 dest(grd) | SE Pocking | P-51 |

0-0-0 air
11-2 ground

**Burdick, Clinton D., Lt.** (6.5) Brooklyn, NY
361st Ftr Sqn/356th Ftr Grp October 1944-EOW
54 missions

P-51D QI-B 44-15310 "DoDo"
S/Sgt. Hugh G. Showers-c/c

| Sqn | Date | Claims | Location | A/C |
|---|---|---|---|---|
| 361st | November 25, 1944 | FW-190 dest(grd) | Zwickau A/F | P-51 |
| | December 5 | FW-190 dest(air) | Eberswalde | P-51 |
| | | FW-190 dam(air) | Eberswalde | P-51 |
| | January 14, 1945 | (2)FW-190 dest(air) | SW Dummer Lake | P-51 |
| | | (2)FW-190 dam(air) | see above | P-51 |
| | February 20 | (2.5)Fi-156 dest(air)* | SE Bayreuth | P-51 |

5.5-0-3 air
1-0 ground

* - shared with Lt. E.L. Slanker of the 361st Ftr Sqn

**Butler, George H. Lt.** (6) Los Angeles, CA
62nd Ftr Sqn/56th Ftr Grp April 1944-December 1944
76 missions, 286 hours

P-47D LM-B
P-47D LM-B 44-20615 "West O'The Rockies"

| Sqn | Date | Claims | Location | A/C |
|---|---|---|---|---|
| 62nd | June 8, 1944 | Me-109 dest(air) | St. Andre de L'Eure | P-47 |
| | July 5 | FW-190 dest(air) | N/Evreux | P-47 |
| | September 5 | FW-44 dest(air) | NE Gelnhausen | P-47 |
| | | (2)Me-109 dest(grd) | Gelnhausen | P-47 |
| | | FW-190 dest(grd) | Gelnhausen | P-47 |
| | September 10 | u/i a/c dam(grd) | Seligenstadt | P-47 |

3-0-0 air
3-1 ground

**Buttke, Robert L., Capt.** (5.5) Sacramento, CA
343rd Ftr Sqn/55th Ftr Grp March 1943-April 1945

P-38H CY-F 42-67047 "Lavenia"
P-38J CY-F "Lavenia"
P-51D CY-F 44-15025 "Beautiful Lavenia"
S/Sgt. Robert L. Pinson-c/c
Sgt. R.L. Potter-arm.

| Sqn | Date | Claims | Location | A/C |
|---|---|---|---|---|
| 343rd | November 3, 1943 | (2)Me-109 dest(air) | E/Wilhelmshaven | P-38 |
| | February 10, 1944 | (2)Me-210 dest(air) | NW Brunswick | P-38 |
| | | Me-110 dam(air) | NW Brunswick | P-38 |
| | April 22 | Me-109 dest(air) | W/Hamm | P-38 |
| | | Me-109 dam(air) | W/Hamm | P-38 |
| | February 27, 1945 | (.5)Ju-88 dest(air)* | Nurnburg | P-51 |

5.5-0-2 air
0-0 ground

* - shared with Lt. L.D. Boring of the 343rd Ftr Sqn

**Byers, John R., Lt.** (5) University City, MO
503rd Ftr Sqn/339th Ftr Grp March 1945-July 1945
20 missions

| Sqn | Date | Claims | Location | A/C |
|---|---|---|---|---|
| 503rd | April 16, 1945 | (3)Ju-88 dest(grd) | NE Prague | P-51 |
| | | FW-190 dest(grd) | NE Prague | P-51 |
| | | Me-109 dest(grd) | NE Prague | P-51 |

0-0-0 air
5-0 ground

**Byers, Vic L., Jr., Maj.** (5.5) Denison, IA
351st Ftr Sqn/353rd Ftr Grp December 1942-July 1945
113 missions, 406:25 hours

P-47D YJ-V 42-7958 "Hawkeye"
P-47D YJ-V 42-75863
P-47D YJ-V 43-25557
P-51D YJ-V 44-14593
P-51D YJ-V 44-15160
S/Sgt. Robert Lauletta-c/c

| Sqn | Date | Claims | Location | A/C |
|---|---|---|---|---|
| 351st | January 14, 1944 | (.5)FW-190 dam(grd)* | Rosieres-en-Santerne | P-47 |
| | March 6 | (.5)FW-190 dest(air)** | SW Nienburg | P-47 |

| | | | | |
|---|---|---|---|---|
| | March 29 | Ju-88 dam(grd) | SE Steinhuder L. | P-47 |
| | July 9 | Me-109 dam(air) | Argentan | P-47 |
| | August 4 | Ju-88 dest(grd) | Plantlunne | P-47 |
| | August 11 | Me-109 dest(air) | S/Paris | P-47 |
| | March 2, 1945 | FW-190 dest(air) | Wittenburg | P-51 |
| | | Me-109 prob(air) | Wittenburg | P-51 |
| | April 16 | FW-190 dest(grd) | Reichersberg | P-51 |
| | | Fi-156 dest(grd) | see above | P-51 |
| | | Me-262 dam(grd) | see above | P-51 |

2.5-1-1 air
3-2.5 ground

* - shared with Lt. H.D. Milligan of the 351st Ftr Sqn
** - shared with Lt. J. Terzian of the 351st Ftr Sqn

**Caldwell, Merle F., Lt.** (5) Greenville, PA
504th Ftr Sqn/339th Ftr Grp States-October 1944

P-51C 5Q-J 42-103737 "The Yankee Kid"
S/Sgt. James Taylor-c/c
Sgt. Americo Boccardi-ac/c
Sgt. Kenneth Willard-arm.

| *Sqn* | *Date* | *Claims* | *Location* | *A/C* |
|---|---|---|---|---|
| 504th | June 7, 1944 | FW-190 dest(grd) | Laval | P-51 |
| | July 7 | (2)Me-109 dest(air) | Eisleben | P-51 |
| | September 13 | FW-190 dest(grd) | Munich | P-51 |
| | | u/i a/c dest(grd) | Munich | P-51 |

2-0-0 air
3-0 ground

**Candelaria, Richard G., Lt.** (6) Los Angeles, CA
435th Ftr Sqn/479th Ftr Grp September 1944-April 13, 1945(POW)
Hit by flak near Tarnewitz.

P-51K J2-K 44-11755 "My Pride and Joy"
T/Sgt. Leslie A. Mullen-c/c
Sgt. Morris J. Gohring-arm.

| *Sqn* | *Date* | *Claims* | *Location* | *A/C* |
|---|---|---|---|---|
| 435th | December 5, 1944 | (2)FW-190 dest(air) | NW Berlin | P-51 |
| | March 3, 1945 | (3)Me-109 dam(grd) | Dummer Lake | P-51 |
| | April 7 | (4)Me-109 dest(air) | SW Luneburg | P-51 |
| | | Me-262 prob(air) | SW Luneburg | P-51 |

6-1-0 air
0-3 ground

**Capp, Merle R., Lt.** (5.5) Arlington, VA
82nd Ftr Sqn/78th Ftr Grp April 1944-July 1944
84th Ftr Sqn/78th Ftr Grp July 1944-September 1944
59 missions

P-47D MX-F
P-47D WZ-

| *Sqn* | *Date* | *Claims* | *Location* | *A/C* |
|---|---|---|---|---|
| 82nd | May 12, 1944 | FW-190 dest(air) | Coblenz | P-47 |
| | May 19 | Me-109 dest(air) | Dummer Lake | P-47 |
| 84th | August 17 | (.5)Me-109 dest(grd)* | S/Hamm | P-47 |
| | September 10 | (3)He-111 dest(grd) | Meinbullen | P-47 |
| | | He-111 dam(grd) | Meinbullen | P-47 |

2-0-0 air
3.5-1 ground

* - shared with Lt. E.H. Schneider of the 84th Ftr Sqn

**Carder, John B., Capt.** (7) Red Oak, IA
364th Ftr Sqn/357th Ftr Grp March 1943-May 12, 1944(POW)
Hit by e/a near Frankfurt.

P-51B C5-J
P-51B C5-J 42-106777 "Taxpayer's Delight"

| *Sqn* | *Date* | *Claims* | *Location* | *A/C* |
|---|---|---|---|---|
| 364th | February 22, 1944 | Me-109 dest(air) | Bernburg | P-51 |
| | | FW-190 dam(air) | The Hague | P-51 |
| | March 2 | Me-109 dest(air) | N/Frankfurt | P-51 |
| | March 6 | Me-109 dest(air) | E/Bremen | P-51 |
| | | Me-109 dam(grd) | Berlin | P-51 |
| | March 8 | FW-190 dest(air) | S/Berlin | P-51 |
| | April 11 | Me-109 dest(air) | NE Leipzig | P-51 |
| | April 19 | Me-109 dest(air) | SE Kassel | P-51 |
| | April 24 | Me-109 dest(air) | S/Munich | P-51 |

7-0-1 air
0-1 ground

**Care, Raymond C., Capt.** (6.5) Angola, IN
334th Ftr Sqn/4th Ftr Grp October 1942-February 1944
HdQts/65th Ftr Wg February 1944-April 1944
334th Ftr Sqn/4th Ftr Grp April 1944-April 15, 1944(POW)
Hit by flak in the Celle area.
Earlier flew with 71 Sqn, RAF
104 missions

Spitfire XR- "Calamity Jane"
P-47C QP-R 41-6404
P-47D QP-R 42-7981
P-51B QP-R 43-7183

| *Sqn* | *Date* | *Claims* | *Location* | *A/C* |
|---|---|---|---|---|
| 334th | June 26, 1943 | Me-109 dest(air) | W/Dieppe | P-47 |
| | July 28 | FW-190 dest(air) | E/Rotterdam | P-47 |
| | August 16 | FW-190 dest(air) | N/Paris | P-47 |
| | | FW-190 prob(air) | N/Paris | P-47 |
| | February 21, 1944 | FW-190 dest(air) | Dummer Lake | P-47 |
| | April 8 | Me-109 dest(air) | Ulzen | P-51 |
| | April 11 | Me-110 dest(air) | SE Stettin | P-51 |
| | April 15 | (.5)Ju-52 dest(grd)* | Magdeburg | P-51 |

6-1-0 air
0.5-0 ground

* - shared with Lt. H.T. Biel of the 334th Ftr Sqn

**Carlson, Kendall E., Capt.** (10) Red Bluff, CA
336th Ftr Sqn/4th Ftr Grp July 1943-February 25, 1945(POW)
Hit the ground while strafing at Kothen Airfield.

P-47C VF-E 41-6575
P-51B VF-E 43-6507
P-51K VF-E 44-11356
S/Sgt. W. Belcher-c/c
Sgt. Carl Anderson-ac/c

| *Sqn* | *Date* | *Claims* | *Location* | *A/C* |
|---|---|---|---|---|
| 336th | August 16, 1943 | FW-190 dam(air) | Paris | P-47 |
| | January 31, 1944 | Me-109 dest(air) | Gilze-Rijen | P-47 |
| | March 3 | Me-110 dest(air) | E/Hanover | P-51 |
| | March 16 | (2)Me-110 dest(air) | Kaufburen | P-51 |
| | March 18 | (2)He-111 dam(grd) | Ludwigshafen | P-51 |
| | April 5 | Ju-88 dest(grd) | Stendal | P-51 |
| | April 22 | (1.5)Me-109 dest(air)* | SW Kassel | P-51 |
| | | (2)Me-109 dam(air) | SW Kassel | P-51 |
| | January 16, 1945 | FW-190 dest(grd) | Neuhausen | P-51 |
| | | Ju-88 dest(grd) | Neuhausen | P-51 |
| | February 20 | (.5)FW-190 dest(air)** | Ingolstadt | P-51 |
| | February 25 | u/i a/c dest(grd) | Kothen A/F | P-51 |

6-0-3 air
4-2 ground

* - shared with Lt. D.R. Emerson of the 336th Ftr Sqn
** - shared with Capt. J.H. Joiner of the 336th Ftr Sqn

**Carpenter, George, Maj.** (15.83) Oil City, PA
335th Ftr Sqn/4th Ftr Grp September 1942-April 18, 1944(POW)
Hit by e/a near Rathenow.
Earlier flew with 121 Sqn, RAF
257 hours

Spitfire AV-X EN918
P-47C WD-I 41-6226
P-51B WD-I 43-6575 "Virginia"
P-51B WD-I 42-106675
S/Sgt. Walter Behm-c/c

| *Sqn* | *Date* | *Claims* | *Location* | *A/C* |
|---|---|---|---|---|
| 335th | May 4, 1943 | FW-190 dam(air) | Walcheren | P-47 |
| | July 28 | FW-190 dam(air) | SE Utrecht | P-47 |
| | December 1 | Ju-88 dam(air) | E/Cologne | P-47 |
| | February 6, 1944 | FW-190 dam(air) | Versailles | P-47 |
| | February 20 | Me-110 dam(air) | W/Coblenz | P-47 |
| | February 22 | FW-190 dest(air) | Erkelenz | P-47 |
| | March 16 | (2)Me-110 dest(air) | SW Munich | P-51 |
| | | FW-190 dam(air) | SW Munich | P-51 |
| | March 18 | Me-109 dest(air) | SE Saarbrucken | P-51 |
| | | Me-109 prob(air) | see above | P-51 |
| | March 21 | (1.5)FW-190 dest(air)* | NE Bordeaux | P-51 |

| Sqn | Date | Claims | Location | A/C |
|---|---|---|---|---|
| | | (.5)FW-190 dest(grd)[*] | N/Bordeaux | P-51 |
| | | (.5)Ju-52 dest(grd)[*] | see above | P-51 |
| | | Ju-52 dam(grd) | see above | P-51 |
| | March 27 | FW-190 dest(air) | SW Bordeaux | P-51 |
| | March 29 | Me-109 dest(air) | Gifhorn | P-51 |
| | | (.33)He-111 dest(air)[**] | Brunswick | P-51 |
| | | Me-109 dam(air) | Gifhorn | P-51 |
| | April 5 | u/i a/c dest(grd) | Berlin | P-51 |
| | April 8 | (2)FW-190 dest(air) | Celle | P-51 |
| | April 12 | Me-109 dest(air) | NW Brunswick | P-51 |
| | | Ju-88 dam(grd) | see above | P-51 |
| | April 13 | FW-190 dest(air) | SW Schweinfurt | P-51 |
| | April 18 | Me-109 dest(air) | NW Nauen | P-51 |
| | | FW-190 dest(air) | Rathenow-Nauen | P-51 |

13.83-1-8 air
2-3 ground

[*] - all shared with Lt. C.F. Anderson of the 335th Ftr Sqn
[**] - shared with Lt. J.T. Godfrey and F/O F.W. Glover of the 336th Ftr Sqn, 4th Ftr Grp

**Carson, Leonard K., Maj.** (22) Ayreshire, IA
362nd Ftr Sqn/357th Ftr Grp April 1943-November 1945
115 missions, 490:25 hours

P-51B G4-C 43-6634 "Nooky Booky"
P-51D G4-C 44-13316 "Nooky Booky II"
P-51D G4-C 44-14896 "Nooky Booky III"
P-51K G4-C 44-11622 "Nooky Booky IV"
S/Sgt. John W. Warner-c/c
Sgt. Livingstone Blauvelt-ac/c
Sgt. J. Williams-arm.

| *Sqn* | *Date* | *Claims* | *Location* | *A/C* |
|---|---|---|---|---|
| 362nd | March 28, 1944 | (.5)Ju-88 dest(grd)[*] | S/Paris | P-51 |
| | April 8 | (.5)Me-109 dest(air)[**] | SW Brunswick | P-51 |
| | April 13 | FW-190 dest(air) | NW Mannheim | P-51 |
| | May 28 | FW-190 dest(air) | N/Magdeburg | P-51 |
| | May 30 | Me-410 dest(air) | W/Bernburg | P-51 |
| | June 20 | (.5)Me-110 dam(grd)[@] | Neumunster | P-51 |
| | July 25 | FW-190 dest(air) | Paris | P-51 |
| | July 29 | Me-109 dest(air) | W/Merseburg | P-51 |
| | November 2 | Me-109 dest(air) | Naumberg | P-51 |
| | November 18 | Me-109 dest(grd) | Mengen A/F | P-51 |
| | November 25 | FW-44 dest(grd) | Maraburg | P-51 |
| | November 27 | (5)FW-190 dest(air) | S/Magdeburg | P-51 |
| | December 2 | (2)Me-109 dest(air) | Bingen | P-51 |
| | December 5 | Me-109 dest(air) | Berlin | P-51 |
| | December 24 | FW-190 dest(air) | Fulda | P-51 |
| | January 14, 1945 | (2)FW-190 dest(air) | NW Berlin | P-51 |
| | | Me-109 dest(air) | NW Berlin | P-51 |
| | March 31 | Me-262 dam(air) | N/Juist Island | P-51 |
| | April 17 | FW-200 dest(grd) | Prague/Ruzny | P-51 |
| | April 18 | (2)Me-262 dam(air) | Prague/Ruzny | P-51 |

18.5-0-3 air
3.5-0.5 ground

[*] - shared with Lt. A.E. Smith of the 362nd Ftr Sqn
[**] - shared with Lt. J.S. Coon of the 362nd Ftr Sqn
[@] - shared with Lt. T.W. Martinek of the 362nd Ftr Sqn

**Carter, James R., Maj.** (6) Palouse, WA
61st Ftr Sqn/56th Ftr Grp July 1942-May 1945
137 missions, 435 hours

P-47C HV-J
P-47D HV-J 42-7960
P-47M HV-C 44-21129
S/Sgt. Victor R. Laskowske-c/c
S/Sgt. Jack P. Fortson-c/c
S/Sgt. Joseph B. Gibson-c/c

| *Sqn* | *Date* | *Claims* | *Location* | *A/C* |
|---|---|---|---|---|
| 61st | August 19, 1943 | Me-109 dam(air) | W/Gilze-Rijen | P-47 |
| | October 4 | Me-110 prob(air) | E/Aachen | P-47 |
| | January 11, 1944 | Me-109 dest(air) | N/Osnabruck | P-47 |
| | | Me-109 prob(air) | see above | P-47 |
| | | Me-109 dam(air) | see above | P-47 |
| | January 30 | FW-190 dest(air) | Leeuwen | P-47 |
| | February 20 | Me-110 dest(air) | Steinhuder Lake | P-47 |
| | May 22 | FW-190 dest(air) | Hoperhofen A/F | P-47 |
| | | FW-190 prob(air) | see above | P-47 |
| | | FW-190 dam(air) | see above | P-47 |
| | July 4 | Me-109 dest(air) | W/Louviers | P-47 |
| | November 18 | Me-109 dest(air) | E/Hanau | P-47 |

6-3-3 air
0-0 ground

**Carter, Joseph D., Lt.** (5.5) Sherman, TX
486th Ftr Sqn/352nd Ftr Grp August 1944-EOW

| *Sqn* | *Date* | *Claims* | *Location* | *A/C* |
|---|---|---|---|---|
| 486th | September 12, 1944 | (.5)FW-190 dest(air)[*] | Kustrin | P-51 |
| | April 17, 1945 | (5)FW-190 dest(grd) | Plattling | P-51 |
| | | FW-190 dam(grd) | Plattling | P-51 |

0.5-0-0 air
5-1 ground

[*] - shared with Capt. H.J. Miklajcyk of the 486th Ftr Sqn

**Caywood, Herbert L., Lt.** (7) Los Angeles, CA
505th Ftr Sqn/339th Ftr Grp October 1944-April 1945

| *Sqn* | *Date* | *Claims* | *Location* | *A/C* |
|---|---|---|---|---|
| 505th | April 10, 1945 | (3)Ju-88 dest(grd) | N/Neuruppin | P-51 |
| | | (2)Ju-88 dam(grd) | N/Neuruppin | P-51 |
| | April 16 | (3)Me-109 dest(grd) | NE Prague | P-51 |
| | | u/i a/c dest(grd) | NE Prague | P-51 |
| | | (2)Ju-88 dam(grd) | NE Prague | P-51 |
| | | Me-109 dam(grd) | NE Prague | P-51 |

0-0-0 air
7-5 ground

**Cesky, Charles J., Capt.** (8.5) Baltimore, MD
328th Ftr Sqn/352nd Ftr Grp June 1944-January 1945

P-51D PE-L 44-13927 "Diann Ruth"
P-51D PE-L 44-13401 "Diann Ruth II"
S/Sgt. H.M. Miller-c/c
Sgt. J.A. Sullivan-ac/c

| *Sqn* | *Date* | *Claims* | *Location* | *A/C* |
|---|---|---|---|---|
| 328th | July 29, 1944 | FW-190 dest(air) | Merseburg | P-51 |
| | August 6 | (2)Me-109 dest(air) | E/Luneburg | P-51 |
| | August 16 | (.5)Me-109 dest(air)[*] | W/Mehlis | P-51 |
| | September 12 | FW-190 dest(air) | N/Pritzwalk | P-51 |
| | November 27 | Me-109 dest(air) | Hanover | P-51 |
| | December 25 | (3)FW-190 dest(air) | Maastricht | P-51 |

8.5-0-0 air
0-0 ground

[*] - shared with Capt. W.E. Hendrian of the 328th Ftr Sqn

**Ceuleers, George F., LtCol.** (10.5) Los Angeles, CA
383rd Ftr Sqn/364th Ftr Grp August 1943-May 1945
HdQts/364th Ftr Grp May 1945-July 1945
103 missions

P-38J N2-D 42-68043 "Connie & Butch, Inc."
P-51D N2-D 44-13971
P-51D N2-D 44-15020
P-51D N2-D 44-72719 "Constance"
T/Sgt. Alvin L. Archer-c/c
Cpl. Simpson-arm.

| *Sqn* | *Date* | *Claims* | *Location* | *A/C* |
|---|---|---|---|---|
| 383rd | March 8, 1944 | FW-190 dest(air) | Nienburg | P-38 |
| | | FW-190 dam(air) | Nienburg | P-38 |
| | April 15 | (.5)Me-109 dest(air)[*] | SE Bremen | P-38 |
| | August 9 | FW-190 dest(air) | Munich | P-51 |
| | | (2)FW-190 dam(air) | Munich | P-51 |
| | August 10 | Me-109 dest(air) | NW Paris | P-51 |
| | December 23 | (4)Me-109 dest(air) | NW Trier | P-51 |
| | January 1, 1945 | (2)Me-109 dest(air) | Hamburg | P-51 |
| | April 4 | Me-262 dest(air) | Hamburg-Dessau | P-51 |

10.5-0-0 air
0-0 ground

[*] - shared with Lt. L.S. Ayoub of the 383rd Ftr Sqn

**Chandler, Van E., Lt.** (9) Waxhachie, TX
336th Ftr Sqn/4th Ftr Grp June 1944-June 1945
74 missions

P-51B VF-U 43-24877
P-51D VF-U 44-14388 "Wheezy"

| *Sqn* | *Date* | *Claims* | *Location* | *A/C* |
|---|---|---|---|---|
| 336th | September 12, 1944 | FW-190 dest(air) | Weisbaden | P-51 |
| | | FW-190 dam(air) | Weisbaden | P-51 |
| | November 6 | FW-190 dest(air) | Minden | P-51 |

| | December 25 | Me-109 dest(air) | SW Coblenz | P-51 |
|---|---|---|---|---|
| | | FW-190 dest(air) | SW Coblenz | P-51 |
| | January 1, 1945 | Me-109 dest(air) | Ulzen | P-51 |
| | January 16 | (2)FW-190 dest(grd) | Neuhausen | P-51 |
| | | (2)Ju-52 dest(grd) | Neuhausen | P-51 |

5-0-1 air
4-0 ground

**Chase, Harold W., Capt.** (6) Bradford, VT
351st Ftr Sqn/353rd Ftr Grp October 1944-July 1945
48 missions

P-51D YJ-Z 44-14610

| *Sqn* | *Date* | *Claims* | *Location* | *A/C* |
|---|---|---|---|---|
| 351st | November 27, 1944 | Me-109 dest(air) | NE Steinhuder L. | P-51 |
| | | Me-109 dam(air) | see above | P-51 |
| | April 7, 1945 | Me-109 dest(air) | NE Steinhuder L. | P-51 |
| | April 16 | (4)FW-190 dest(grd) | Bad Aibling | P-51 |
| | | FW-190 dam(grd) | Bad Aibling | P-51 |

2-0-1 air
4-1 ground

**Chatterly, Archie W., Lt.** (5.5) San Diego, CA
334th Ftr Sqn/4th Ftr Grp January 1943-March 27, 1944(POW)
Hit by flak near Lake Biscarosse.

P-47C QP-G 41-6358 "Cal or Bust"
P-51B QP-G 43-6860

| *Sqn* | *Date* | *Claims* | *Location* | *A/C* |
|---|---|---|---|---|
| 334th | January 29, 1944 | Me-109 dest(air) | Aachen | P-47 |
| | March 6 | Me-110 dest(air) | W/Brandenburg | P-51 |
| | | Me-210 prob(air) | see above | P-51 |
| | | (2)u/i a/c dam(grd) | see above | P-51 |
| | | Ju-88 dam(grd) | see above | P-51 |
| | March 16 | Me-110 dest(air) | Munich | P-51 |
| | March 18 | Me-109 dest(air) | SE Mannheim | P-51 |
| | March 21 | (.5)FW-190 dest(air)* | NE Bordeaux | P-51 |
| | March 27 | Me-109 dest(grd) | Angouleme | P-51 |

4.5-0-1 air
1-3 ground

* - shared with Lt. N. Megura of the 334th Ftr Sqn

**Chenez, Gordon H., Lt.** (5) Lakewood, OH
504th Ftr Sqn/339th Ftr Grp October 1944-July 1945

| *Sqn* | *Date* | *Claims* | *Location* | *A/C* |
|---|---|---|---|---|
| 504th | March 20, 1945 | Ju-52 dam(grd) | Grossenbrode | P-51 |
| | April 10 | (2)Me-410 dest(grd) | N/Neuruppin | P-51 |
| | | (2)Me-410 dam(grd) | N/Neuruppin | P-51 |
| | April 16 | (3)Me-109 dest(grd) | Klatovy | P-51 |

0-0-0 air
5-3 ground

**Chetneky, Steve J., Lt.** (7) Trenton, NJ
503rd Ftr Sqn/339th Ftr Grp December 1944-June 1945
Earlier flew a tour as a bomber pilot with the 8th Air Force
26 missions

P-51D D7- "Hard Luck Jr."
Cpl. Al Hernandez-arm.

| *Sqn* | *Date* | *Claims* | *Location* | *A/C* |
|---|---|---|---|---|
| 503rd | March 2, 1945 | Me-109 dest(air) | E/Magdeburg | P-51 |
| | | Me-109 dam(air) | E/Magdeburg | P-51 |
| | April 16 | (3)Me-109 dest(grd) | NE Prague | P-51 |
| | | (2)Ju-88 dest(grd) | NE Prague | P-51 |
| | | He-111 dest(grd) | NE Prague | P-51 |
| | | (2)Ju-88 dam(grd) | NE Prague | P-51 |
| | | Me-109 dam(grd) | NE Prague | P-51 |

1-0-1 air
6-3 ground

**Chinn, Claude A., Lt.** (6) Kansas City, MO
63rd Ftr Sqn/56th Ftr Grp June 1944-December 1944
66 missions, 272:15 hours

P-47D UN-R 42-76468 "Ol Steel Butt"
P-47D UN-C 42-28741
S/Sgt. Robert W. Hull-c/c
Sgt. Virgil C. Stone-ac/c
Cpl. Malcolm V. Thaden-arm.

| *Sqn* | *Date* | *Claims* | *Location* | *A/C* |
|---|---|---|---|---|
| 63rd | September 5, 1944 | u/i a/c dest(grd) | Gelnhausen | P-47 |
| | November 18 | (3)Me-109 dest(grd) | Gross Ostheim | P-47 |
| | December 4 | (2)Me-262 dest(grd) | Neuburg | P-47 |
| | | Me-262 dam(grd) | Neuburg | P-47 |

0-0-0 air
6-1 ground

**Christensen, Fred J., Jr., Capt.** (21.5) Watertown, MA
62nd Ftr Sqn/56th Ftr Grp August 1943-September 1944
107 missions

P-47D LM-C 42-75207 "Rozzie Geth/Miss Fire"
P-47D LM-C 42-22628 "Rozzie Geth II/Miss Fire"
S/Sgt. Carl C. Connor-c/c
Cpl. Urbain C. Hymel-ac/c
PFC Thomas G. Myers-arm.
Cpl. William T. Floore-arm.

| *Sqn* | *Date* | *Claims* | *Location* | *A/C* |
|---|---|---|---|---|
| 62nd | November 26, 1943 | Me-110 dest(air) | Papenburg | P-47 |
| | December 1 | Me-109 dest(air) | SE Roermond | P-47 |
| | January 5, 1944 | FW-190 dest(air) | Ans | P-47 |
| | February 4 | FW-190 dest(air) | Charleroi | P-47 |
| | February 11 | Me-109 dest(air) | Bierset | P-47 |
| | February 20 | Ju-88 dest(air) | Steinhuder Lake | P-47 |
| | | (.5)Do-217 dest(air)* | see above | P-47 |
| | February 24 | FW-190 dam(grd) | Quackenbruck | P-47 |
| | | Me-110 dam(grd) | Quackenbruck | P-47 |
| | March 6 | FW-190 dest(air) | N/Dummer Lake | P-47 |
| | March 15 | (2)FW-190 dest(air) | Dummer Lake | P-47 |
| | | (2)FW-190 dam(air) | Dummer Lake | P-47 |
| | March 16 | (2)FW-190 dest(air) | St. Dizier | P-47 |
| | April 15 | (2)Me-109 dest(air) | Altona | P-47 |
| | June 27 | Me-109 dest(air) | Cambrai-Lens | P-47 |
| | July 5 | FW-190 dest(air) | N/Evreux | P-47 |
| | July 7 | (6)Ju-52 dest(air) | Gardelegen A/F | P-47 |

21.5-0-2 air
0-2 ground

* - shared with Lt. S.B. Morrill of the 62nd Ftr Sqn

**Clark, Jack W., Lt.** (5.5) Jacksonville, FL
503rd Ftr Sqn/339th Ftr Grp July 1944-October 1944
350th Ftr Sqn/353rd Ftr Grp October 1944-EOW
56 missions, 300:55 hours

| *Sqn* | *Date* | *Claims* | *Location* | *A/C* |
|---|---|---|---|---|
| 350th | February 27, 1945 | (2)Me-110 dest(grd) | Rohrensee | P-51 |
| | | Me-109 dest(grd) | see above | P-51 |
| | | (2)Me-410 dam(grd) | see above | P-51 |
| | March 24 | (2)FW-190 dest(air) | NW Kassel | P-51 |
| | April 10 | (.5)Me-262 dest(air)* | Dessau | P-51 |

2.5-0-0 air
3-2 ground

* - shared with Lt. B.D. McMahan of the 350th Ftr Sqn

**Clark, James A., Jr., LtCol.** (15) Westbury, NY
334th Ftr Sqn/4th Ftr Grp September 1942-March 1944
HdQts/4th Ftr Grp March 1944-September 1944
Earlier flew with 71 Sqn, RAF

Spitfire XR-
P-47C QP-W 41-6195
P-47D QP-W 42-75252
P-51B QP-W 43-6560
P-51B QP-W 42-106650
P-51D QP-W 44-13372
S/Sgt. Roderic Lonier-c/c
Sgt. L. Hendel-arm.

| *Sqn* | *Date* | *Claims* | *Location* | *A/C* |
|---|---|---|---|---|
| 334th | October 2, 1942 | (.5)FW-190 dest(air)* | SE Calais | Spit |
| | April 15, 1943 | FW-190 dam(air) | Belgian Coast | P-47 |
| | August 12 | FW-190 dest(air) | Sittard | P-47 |
| | August 16 | (2)FW-190 dest(air) | N/Paris | P-47 |
| | September 9 | FW-190 dam(air) | NE Paris | P-47 |

| Sqn | Date | Claims | Location | A/C |
|---|---|---|---|---|
| | October 8 | Me-109 dest(air) | Meppel-Zwolle | P-47 |
| | March 8, 1944 | Me-109 dest(air) | S/Berlin | P-51 |
| HdQts | March 21 | FW-190 dest(air) | Bordeaux | P-51 |
| | | FW-190 dest(grd) | Bordeaux | P-51 |
| | March 23 | Me-109 dest(air) | SE Steinhuder L. | P-51 |
| | | FW-190 dest(air) | see above | P-51 |
| | March 27 | (1.5)Ju-88 dest(grd)[**] | Cazaux A/F | P-51 |
| | March 29 | FW-190 dest(air) | Gifhorn | P-51 |
| | April 10 | (2)u/i a/c dest(grd) | Romorantin A/F | P-51 |
| | June 20 | Me-410 dest(air) | SW Anklam | P-51 |

10.5-0-2 air
4.5-0 ground

[*] - shared with W/Cdr. R.M.B. Duke-Woolley of the RAF
[**] - shared with Lt. D.R. Emerson of the 336th Ftr Sqn, 4th Ftr Grp

**Clark, William C., LtCol.** (9) Richmond, VA
HdQts/ 66th Ftr Wng [@]November 1944-January 1945
504th Ftr Sqn/339th Ftr Grp January 1945-March 1945
HdQts/339th Ftr Grp March 1945-September 1945

P-51D 5Q-C 44-64148 "Happy IV/Dolly"
S/Sgt. Bennie L. Kennedy-c/c

| Sqn | Date | Claims | Location | A/C |
|---|---|---|---|---|
| HdQts | January 14, 1945 | FW-190 dest(air) | S/Schwerin | P-51 |
| 504th | March 20 | u/i a/c dest(grd) | Grossenbrode | P-51 |
| | | He-111 dam(grd) | see above | P-51 |
| HdQts | April 4 | Me-262 dam(air) | Parchim A/F | P-51 |
| | | u/i a/c dest(grd) | Weimar | P-51 |
| | | u/i a/c dam(grd) | Weimar | P-51 |
| | April 16 | (3)FW-190 dest(grd) | Klatovy | P-51 |
| | | (2)Me-109 dest(grd) | Klatovy | P-51 |
| | | Ju-52 dest(grd) | Klatovy | P-51 |
| | | FW-190 dam(grd) | Klatovy | P-51 |
| | | Me-109 dam(grd) | Klatovy | P-51 |

1-0-1 air
8-4 ground

**Cles, Leslie P., Capt.** (6.5) Powell, WY
352nd Ftr Sqn/353rd Ftr Grp December 1942-November 8, 1944(POW)
Hit by flak at Plantlunne Airfield.
101 missions

P-47D SX-U 42-8522 "Betsy"
P-47D SX-U 42-25957 "Betsy"
P-51D SX-U 44-14831 "Pregnant Polecat"
S/Sgt. Ralph E. Raney-c/c
Sgt. Irving Gittin-ac/c
Sgt. Lester Marsh-arm.

| Sqn | Date | Claims | Location | A/C |
|---|---|---|---|---|
| 352nd | May 27, 1944 | Me-109 dest(grd) | Saverne | P-47 |
| | June 7 | Me-109 dest(grd) | Cormeilles-en-Vixen | P-47 |
| | | Me-110 dest(grd) | see above | P-47 |
| | June 20 | Me-110 dest(grd) | Twente/Enschede | P-47 |
| | | Hs-129 dam(grd) | Twente/Enschede | P-47 |
| | July 30 | (2.5)u/i a/c dest(grd)[*] | Orleans/Bricy | P-47 |
| | November 2 | FW-190 prob(air) | Naumberg | P-51 |
| | November 8 | (.5)Ju-88 dam(grd)[**] | Plantlunne | P-51 |

0-1-0 air
6.5-1.5 ground

[*] - shared with Lt. W.J. Jordan of the 352nd Ftr Sqn
[**] - shared with Lt. J.R. Evans of the 352nd Ftr Sqn

**Clifton, Frank A., Lt.** (6) Boise City, OK
504th Ftr Sqn/339th Ftr Grp March 1945-July 1945

| Sqn | Date | Claims | Location | A/C |
|---|---|---|---|---|
| 504th | April 16, 1945 | (2)Me-109 dest(grd) | Klatovy | P-51 |
| | | FW-190 dest(grd) | Klatovy | P-51 |
| | April 17 | Me-109 dest(grd) | Klatovy-Anberg | P-51 |
| | | Fi-156 dest(grd) | see above | P-51 |
| | | Ju-88 dest(grd) | see above | P-51 |

0-0-0 air
6-0 ground

**Cole, Charles H., Jr., Capt.** (11) St. Joseph, MO
77th Ftr Sqn/20th Ftr Grp September 1944-February 1945
55th Ftr Sqn/20th Ftr Grp February 1945-February 25, 1945(POW)
Hit by a FW-190 near Stendal.
43 missions, 227:25 hours

| Sqn | Date | Claims | Location | A/C |
|---|---|---|---|---|
| 77th | January 14, 1945 | Me-109 dest(air) | Perleberg | P-51 |
| | February 9 | (6)FW-190 dest(grd) | Esperstadt A/F | P-51 |
| | | FW-190 dam(grd) | see above | P-51 |
| 55th | February 25 | (4)FW-190 dest(air) | Stendal | P-51 |

5-0-0 air
6-1 ground

**Coleman, John B., Jr., Capt.** (6.83) Milwaukee, WI
328th Ftr Sqn/352nd Ftr Grp November 1942-October 5, 1944(MIA-E)
Suffered m/f near Tilburg.

P-47D PE-J 42-22529 "Mavourneen"
P-51B PE-J 43-7200
P-51B PE-J 43-24801
P-51C PE-J 42-103787
S/Sgt. G. Washoh-c/c
Sgt. Art C. Snyder-ac/c

| Sqn | Date | Claims | Location | A/C |
|---|---|---|---|---|
| 328th | December 22, 1943 | Me-110 dest(air) | Zwolle | P-47 |
| | January 5, 1944 | (.33)He-177 dest(air)[*] | La Ferte Bernard | P-47 |
| | January 29 | Me-109 dest(air) | Pelm | P-47 |
| | April 8 | (2)Me-110 dest(grd) | Quackenbruck | P-47 |
| | | u/i a/c dam(grd) | Quackenbruck | P-47 |
| | April 22 | (.5)Me-210 dest(grd)[**] | Dummer Lake | P-51 |
| | May 13 | (2)Me-109 dest(air) | Demnin | P-51 |

4.33-0-0 air
2.5-1 ground

[*] - shared with Maj. E.W. Stewart and Lt. R.H. Powell of the 328th Ftr Sqn
[**] - shared with Lt. Q.L. Quinn of the 328th Ftr Sqn

**Colletti, Anthony T., Lt.** (6) Rego Park, NY
83rd Ftr Sqn/78th Ftr Grp February 1945-July 1945
21 missions

| Sqn | Date | Claims | Location | A/C |
|---|---|---|---|---|
| 83rd | March 19, 1945 | FW-190 dest(air) | Osnabruck | P-51 |
| | | Me-109 dam(air) | Osnabruck | P-51 |
| | April 16 | (4)Ju-87 dest(grd) | N/Prague | P-51 |
| | | FW-190 dest(grd) | N/Prague | P-51 |
| | | (2)FW-190 dam(grd) | N/Prague | P-51 |
| | | FW-200 dam(grd) | N/Prague | P-51 |
| | | u/i a/c dam(grd) | N/Prague | P-51 |

1-0-1 air
5-4 ground

**Collins, William F., Capt.** (7) Janesville, WI
369th Ftr Sqn/359th Ftr Grp August 1944-September 1945

P-51D IV-V 44-13610
P-51D IV-Y 44-11350

| Sqn | Date | Claims | Location | A/C |
|---|---|---|---|---|
| 369th | December 31, 1944 | (1.5)FW-190 dest(air)[*] | SW Hamburg | P-51 |
| | | (.5)FW-190 dest(air) | SW Hamburg | P-51 |
| | February 22, 1945 | (2)Ju-88 dest(grd) | Parchim | P-51 |
| | | Ju-88 dam(grd) | Parchim | P-51 |
| | March 24 | (2)Me-109 dest(air) | Eikelon A/F | P-51 |
| | April 17 | FW-190 dest(grd) | W/Dresden | P-51 |

4-0-0 air
3-1 ground

[*] - shared with Lt. A.B. Morris of the 369th Ftr Sqn

**Compton, Gordon B., Capt.** (20.5) Dallas, TX
351st Ftr Sqn/353rd Ftr Grp October 1942-EOW
114 missions, 420 hours

P-47D YJ-O 42-25702 "Big Bouncer"
P-51D YJ-O 44-14808 "Little Bouncer"
P-51D YJ-O 44-72299 "Little Bouncer"
S/Sgt. George Finney-c/c
Sgt. J. Johnson-ac/c

| Sqn | Date | Claims | Location | A/C |
|---|---|---|---|---|
| 351st | October 4, 1943 | Me-109 dam(air) | Malines | P-47 |
| | February 22, 1944 | Ju-88 dest(air) | W/Diest | P-47 |
| | | FW-190 dest(grd) | NE Bonn | P-47 |
| | | (.25)FW-190 dam(grd)[*] | NE Bonn | P-47 |
| | | (.25)FW-190 dam(grd)[*] | NE Bonn | P-47 |

| Date | Claims | Location | A/C |
|---|---|---|---|
| June 7 | (.5)Me-109 dest(air)** | E/Ribecourt | P-47 |
| June 8 | FW-190 dest(air) | SW Angars | P-47 |
| June 20 | Ju-88 dest(grd) | Plantlunne | P-47 |
| | (.5)He-111 dam(grd)@ | Plantlunne | P-47 |
| June 24 | Ju-52 dest(grd) | Deelan | P-47 |
| November 18 | (2)Ju-88 dest(grd) | Lechfeld | P-51 |
| | u/i a/c dam(grd) | Lechfeld | P-51 |
| November 27 | FW-190 dest(air) | NE Steinhuder L. | P-51 |
| February 22, 1945 | Me-262 dest(air) | Brandenburg | P-51 |
| March 21 | Ar-234 dest(grd) | Achmer | P-51 |
| April 5 | (3)Me-410 dest(grd) | Weiden | P-51 |
| | Me-110 dest(grd) | Weiden | P-51 |
| April 10 | Me-262 dest(air) | Dessau-Kothen | P-51 |
| April 16 | (3)Ju-188 dest(grd) | Reichersberg | P-51 |
| | (2)Ju-88 dest(grd) | see above | P-51 |
| | (3)u/i a/c dam(grd) | see above | P-51 |

5.5-0-1 air
15-5 ground

* - both shared with Maj. W.C. Beckham, Lt. F.N. Emory, and Lt. G.F. Perpente of the 351st Ftr Sqn
** - shared with Col. G.E. Duncan of HdQts, 353rd Ftr Grp
@ - shared with Lt. J.L. Dwyer of the 351st Ftr Sqn

**Comstock, Harold E., Maj.** (7) Fresno, CA
63rd Ftr Sqn/56th Ftr Grp July 1942-January 1945
138 missions, 385 hours

P-47C UN-Y 41-6326
P-47D UN-Y 42-75870
P-47D UN-Y 44-19757
P-47D UN-Z 42-26413 "Happy Warrior"
S/Sgt. Max Victor-c/c
Sgt. Asa D. Maus-ac/c
Sgt. Harold L. Pittsford-arm.

| *Sqn* | *Date* | *Claims* | *Location* | *A/C* |
|---|---|---|---|---|
| 63rd | August 17, 1943 | Me-109 dest(air) | Ans | P-47 |
| | October 4 | Me-110 dest(air) | Bruhl | P-47 |
| | November 26 | Me-110 dest(air) | Friesoythe | P-47 |
| | | Me-110 dam(air) | see above | P-47 |
| | | FW-190 dam(air) | see above | P-47 |
| | November 29 | Me-109 prob(air) | Papenburg | P-47 |
| | January 29, 1944 | FW-190 dam(air) | W/Ostend | P-47 |
| | February 24 | FW-190 dam(air) | Peterhagen | P-47 |
| | September 16 | He-177 dest(grd) | Alhorn A/F | P-47 |
| | November 18 | He-111 dest(grd) | Gross Ostheim | P-47 |
| | December 23 | (2)FW-190 dest(air) | SW Bonn | P-47 |
| | | (2)FW-190 dam(air) | SW Bonn | P-47 |

5-1-6 air
2-0 ground

**Conger, Paul A., Maj.** (11.5) Piedmont, CA
61st Ftr Sqn/56th Ftr Grp July 1942-October 1944
63rd Ftr Sqn/56th Ftr Grp October 1944-March 1945
168 missions, 560 hours

P-47D HV-N 42-7880
P-47D HV-C 42-75435 "Hollywood High Hatter"
P-47D UN-P 44-19868
P-47M UN-P 44-21134 "Bernyce"
S/Sgt. Alex J. Schraut-c/c(61st)
Sgt. George Hundycz-ac/c(61st)
Cpl. James J. Kenney-ac/c(61st)
Cpl. Milton Greenberg-arm.(61st)
Cpl. William H. Milborn-arm.(63rd)

| *Sqn* | *Date* | *Claims* | *Location* | *A/C* |
|---|---|---|---|---|
| 61st | December 11, 1943 | (2)Me-110 dest(air) | Langeroog Island | P-47 |
| | | Ju-88 dest(air) | see above | P-47 |
| | | Me-110 dam(air) | see above | P-47 |
| | April 15, 1944 | FW-190 dest(air) | Elmshorn | P-47 |
| | May 12 | (2)FW-190 dest(air) | N/Marburg | P-47 |
| | | FW-190 dam(air) | N/Marburg | P-47 |
| | August 28 | (.5)He-111 dest(grd)* | S/Saarbrucken | P-47 |
| | September 5 | (1.5)Me-210 dam(grd)** | Gelnhausen | P-47 |
| 63rd | December 2 | (2)Me-109 dest(air) | S/Marburg | P-47 |
| | January 14, 1945 | Me-109 dest(air) | Stendal | P-47 |
| | | Me-109 dam(air) | Stendal | P-47 |
| | February 3 | Me-109 dest(air) | Friedersdorf A/F | P-47 |
| | | FW-190 dest(air) | see above | P-47 |
| | | Me-109 dest(air) | see above | P-47 |

11-0-4 air
0.5-1.5 ground

* - shared with Lt. J.M. Jure of the 61st Ftr Sqn
** - shared with Lt. F.H. Barrett of the 61st Ftr Sqn

**Conner, Richard E., LtCol.** (8) Vicksburg, MS
82nd Ftr Sqn/78th Ftr Grp May 1944-March 21, 1945(MIA-E)
Hit by flak near Lonnewitz.
82nd Ftr Sqn/78th Ftr Grp May 1945-May 1945

P-47D MX-Y 42-26475
P-51D MX-D 44-72233
S/Sgt. Gaston Basset-c/c

| *Sqn* | *Date* | *Claims* | *Location* | *A/C* |
|---|---|---|---|---|
| 82nd | August 6, 1944 | (.5)Me-109 dest(air)* | Hamburg | P-47 |
| | August 27 | Me-110 dest(grd) | Thionville | P-47 |
| | September 9 | (.5)Me-109 dest(grd)** | Giessen | P-47 |
| | October 7 | Me-262 dest(air) | Osnabruck | P-47 |
| | October 12 | FW-190 dest(air) | Hamburg | P-47 |
| | November 21 | (2)Me-109 dest(air) | Hanover | P-47 |
| | | Ju-88 dest(grd) | Gutersloh | P-47 |
| | March 21, 1945 | Me-262 dest(grd) | Dresden | P-51 |
| | | (2)Me-262 dam(grd) | Dresden | P-51 |

4.5-0-0 air
3.5-2 ground

* - shared with Lt. J.B. Stallings of the 82nd Ftr Sqn
** - shared with Lt. D.C. Hart of the 82nd Ftr Sqn

**Cook, Walter V., Capt.** (6) Cincinnati, OH
62nd Ftr Sqn/56th Ftr Grp Mid 1942-February 1944
66 missions

P-47C LM-W 41-6343 "Little Cookie"
S/Sgt. Tom B. Caddell-c/c

| *Sqn* | *Date* | *Claims* | *Location* | *A/C* |
|---|---|---|---|---|
| 62nd | June 12, 1943 | FW-190 dest(air) | Ypres | P-47 |
| | October 10 | Me-210 dest(air) | Altenberge | P-47 |
| | November 11 | (2)FW-190 dest(air) | Bocholt | P-47 |
| | November 26 | (2)Me-110 dest(air) | Papenburg | P-47 |

6-0-0 air
0-0 ground

**Coons, Merle M., Capt.** (5) Gresham, OR
38th Ftr Sqn/55th Ftr Grp June 1944-December 1944

P-51D CG-C 44-14068 "The Worry Bird"
S/Sgt. Duncan-c/c
Sgt. Holderman-ac/c
Cpl. Weens-arm.

| *Sqn* | *Date* | *Claims* | *Location* | *A/C* |
|---|---|---|---|---|
| 38th | September 11, 1944 | Me-109 dest(air) | Erfurt | P-51 |
| | | Me-109 prob(air) | Erfurt | P-51 |
| | September 13 | Me-109 dest(air) | Erfurt | P-51 |
| | November 2 | FW-190 dest(air) | W/Merseburg | P-51 |
| | December 5 | Me-109 dest(air) | N/Berlin | P-51 |
| | | FW-190 dest(air) | N/Berlin | P-51 |

5-1-0 air
0-0 ground

**Cooper, Randolph W., Lt.** (5) Jacksonville, FL
357th Ftr Sqn/355th Ftr Grp January 1945-June 11, 1945(KIAc)

| *Sqn* | *Date* | *Claims* | *Location* | *A/C* |
|---|---|---|---|---|
| 357th | April 4, 1945 | Me-262 dam(air) | Ludwigslust | P-51 |
| | April 10 | (.5)B-24 dest(grd)* | Rechlin/Larz | P-51 |
| | April 13 | (1.5)He-111 dest(grd)** | Schleswig | P-51 |
| | | FW-200 dest(grd) | Schleswig | P-51 |
| | April 16 | He-177 dest(grd) | SE Germany | P-51 |
| | | FW-190 dest(grd) | SE Germany | P-51 |

0-0-1 air
5-0 ground

* - shared with Lt. W.T. Burnett of the 357th Ftr Sqn
** - shared with Lt. R.F. Misner of the 357th Ftr Sqn

**Corey, Harry R., Capt.** (12) Niagara Fall, NY
505th Ftr Sqn/339th Ftr Grp September 1944-July 1945
64 missions, 326 hours

P-51D 6N-K 44-15647 "Maureen Ann"
S/Sgt. John E. Earnest-c/c
Sgt. George McFarlane-ac/c
Sgt. George Themascus-arm.

| Sqn | Date | Claims | Location | A/C |
|---|---|---|---|---|
| 505th | April 4, 1945 | Me-262 dest(air) | Rostock | P-51 |
| | April 10 | (4)Ju-88 dest(grd) | Wittstock | P-51 |
| | | FW-189 dam(grd) | see above | P-51 |
| | | Ju-88 dam(grd) | see above | P-51 |
| | | Ju-52 dam(grd) | see above | P-51 |
| | April 16 | (4)u/i a/c dest(grd) | NE Prague | P-51 |
| | April 17 | (2)Ju-188 dest(grd) | SE Pocking | P-51 |
| | | Me-109 dest(grd) | SE Pocking | P-51 |

1-0-0 air
11-3 ground

**Cox, Ralph L., Maj.** (5) Pasadena, CA
370th Ftr Sqn/359th Ftr Grp September 1944-February 1945
369th Ftr Sqn/359th Ftr Grp February 1945-September 1945

P-51D CS-H 44-14979
P-51D IV-N 44-72154
S/Sgt. Ernest J. Behm-c/c(369th)
Sgt. Anthony J. Castellano-ac/c(369th)
Sgt. Anthony C. Chardella-arm.(369th)

| Sqn | Date | Claims | Location | A/C |
|---|---|---|---|---|
| 370th | November 2, 1944 | Me-109 dest(air) | Erfurt-Weimar | P-51 |
| | November 21 | (3)FW-190 dest(air) | SW Merseburg | P-51 |
| 369th | March 18, 1945 | FW-190 dest(air) | Joachimsthal | P-51 |

5-0-0 air
0-0 ground

**Cramer, Darrell S., Maj.** (9) Ogden, UT
338th Ftr Sqn/55th Ftr Grp July 1944-February 1945
HdQts/55th Ftr Grp February 1945-June 1945
Earlier flew in the PTO with the 347th Ftr Grp claiming one-half kill; a shared Betty on November 1, 1943.
60 missions, 300 hours

P-51D CL-Z 44-14121 "Mick #5"
S/Sgt. Ralph W. Parkhurst-c/c
Sgt. George DeBanardi-ac/c
Sgt. Thomas Jung-arm.

| Sqn | Date | Claims | Location | A/C |
|---|---|---|---|---|
| 338th | September 3, 1944 | FW-190 dest(air) | Brussels | P-51 |
| | September 11 | (1.5)Me-109 dest(air)* | S/Meiningen | P-51 |
| | September 13 | (1.5)Me-109 dest(air)** | Eisenach-Gotha | P-51 |
| | October 7 | Me-109 dest(air) | Leipzig | P-51 |
| | November 2 | (.5)Me-109 dest(air)@ | SW Leipzig | P-51 |
| | November 26 | (2)FW-190 dest(grd) | Vorden A/F | P-51 |
| | | Me-109 dam(grd) | Vorden A/F | P-51 |
| | January 14, 1945 | Me-262 dam(air) | Parchim A/F | P-51 |
| | | Me-110 dam(grd) | SE Salzwedel | P-51 |
| | January 29 | Me-109 dest(air) | Ulzen | P-51 |

6.5-0-1 air
2-2 ground

* - shared with an unknown pilot
** - shared with Capt. E.S. Gregg of the 338th Ftr Sqn
@ - shared with LtCol. E.G. Righetti of the 338th Ftr Sqn

**Cranfill, Niven K., LtCol.** (5) Temple, TX
369th Ftr Sqn/359th Ftr Grp October 1943-July 1944
HdQts/359th Ftr Grp July 1944-August 1944
368th Ftr Sqn/359th Ftr Grp August 1944-April 1945
133 missions

P-47D IV-N 42-76465 "Deviless"
P-51B IV-N 42-106848 "Deviless 2nd"
P-51D IV-N 44-13390 "Deviless 3rd"
P-51D CV-Q 44-15100
P-51D CV-Q 44-15717
S/Sgt. Ernest Behm-c/c(N)
Sgt. Anthony Castellano-ac/c(N)
Sgt. Anthony C. Chardella-arm.(N)

| Sqn | Date | Claims | Location | A/C |
|---|---|---|---|---|
| 369th | January 30, 1944 | Me-109 dam(air) | Lingen | P-47 |
| | May 8 | (.5)Me-109 prob(air)* | SW Brunswick | P-51 |
| HdQts | August 16 | Me-109 dest(air) | Einbeck | P-51 |
| 368th | November 27 | (2)Me-109 dest(air) | W/Merseburg | P-51 |
| | | FW-190 dest(air) | W/Merseburg | P-51 |
| | March 19, 1945 | Me-262 dest(air) | Leipzig | P-51 |
| | | Me-262 dam(air) | Leipzig | P-51 |

5-0.5-2 air
0-0 ground

*-shared with Lt. B.M. Hagen of the 368th Ftr Sqn

**Crenshaw, Claude J., Capt.** (10) Monroe, LA
369th Ftr Sqn/359th Ftr Grp May 1944-December 1944
270 hours

P-51B IV-S 42-106689
P-51D IV-I 44-13606 "Louisiana Heat Wave"
P-51D IV-I 44-15016 "Heat Wave"
S/Sgt. George K. Abernathy-c/c
Cpl. Stanley Liest-arm.
Cpl. Nick Ratushey-arm.

| Sqn | Date | Claims | Location | A/C |
|---|---|---|---|---|
| 369th | August 18, 1944 | Ju-52 dest(grd) | St. Dizier | P-51 |
| | | Ju-88 dest(grd) | see above | P-51 |
| | | Ju-88 dam(grd) | see above | P-51 |
| | September 11 | (2)Me-109 dest(air) | Kolleda | P-51 |
| | | u/i a/c dest(grd) | Kolleda | P-51 |
| | September 18 | Me-109 dest(air) | Dusseldorf | P-51 |
| | November 21 | (4)FW-190 dest(air) | Merseburg | P-51 |
| | | FW-190 prob(air) | Merseburg | P-51 |

7-1-0 air
3-1 ground

**Crombie, William S., Maj.** (7) El Paso, TX
385th Ftr Sqn/364th Ftr Grp September 1944-EOW
62 missions

P-51D 5E-N 44-13994
P-51D 5E-N 44-72343
T/Sgt. Delbert K. McGraw-c/c
Sgt. Walter B. Gochenauer-arm.

| Sqn | Date | Claims | Location | A/C |
|---|---|---|---|---|
| 385th | October 12, 1944 | Me-109 dest(air) | W/Bremen | P-51 |
| | November 2 | Me-109 dest(air) | Halle | P-51 |
| | December 31 | FW-190 dest(air) | Hamburg | P-51 |
| | January 1, 1945 | FW-190 dest(air) | SE Hamburg | P-51 |
| | March 21 | u/i a/c dam(grd) | Achmer | P-51 |
| | April 10 | Me-262 dest(grd) | Stendal | P-51 |
| | | Ju-88 dest(grd) | Stendal | P-51 |
| | | u/i a/c dest(grd) | Stendal | P-51 |
| | | (2)FW-190 dam(grd) | Stendal | P-51 |
| | | Ju-88 dam(grd) | Stendal | P-51 |

4-0-0 air
3-4 ground

**Cullerton, William J., Lt.** (20) Chicago, IL
357th Ftr Sqn/355th Ftr Grp June 1944-April 8, 1945(POW-E)
Hit by flak near Ansbach; wounded by German troops but rescued by civilians.

P-51B OS-X
P-51D OS-X 44-13677 "Miss Steve"
S/Sgt. Jerome Seidl-c/c
Sgt. Woodnail-arm.

| Sqn | Date | Claims | Location | A/C |
|---|---|---|---|---|
| 357th | August 16, 1944 | (2)Me-109 dest(air) | SE Hildesheim | P-51 |
| | August 26 | FW-200 dest(grd) | Speyer | P-51 |
| | September 12 | (3)u/i a/c dest(grd) | Schwartz A/F | P-51 |
| | | (2)Me-110 dest(grd) | see above | P-51 |
| | | (2)Ju-88 dest(grd) | see above | P-51 |
| | | Me-110 dam(grd) | see above | P-51 |
| | | Ju-88 dam(grd) | see above | P-51 |
| | November 2 | Me-109 dest(air) | Wernigerode | P-51 |
| | | FW-190 dest(air) | see above | P-51 |
| | | (6)u/i a/c dest(grd) | see above | P-51 |
| | March 30, 1945 | He-111 dest(grd) | Lowenstadt | P-51 |
| | April 4 | FW-190 dest(air) | Halberstadt | P-51 |

5-0-0 air
15-2 ground

**Cummings, Donald M., Capt.** (6.5) Clayton, NY
38th Ftr Sqn/55th Ftr Grp December 1944-EOW
Earlier flew in the MTO with the 27th Ftr Grp, 12th Air Force, (117 missions) claiming a Ju-52 on October 1, 1943.
33 missions

P-51D CG-U 44-15192

| Sqn | Date | Claims | Location | A/C |
|---|---|---|---|---|
| 38th | January 14, 1945 | Me-109 dest(air) | E/Wittenburg | P-51 |

| | | | | |
|---|---|---|---|---|
| | February 25 | Me-262 dest(air) | Giebelstadt A/F | P-51 |
| | | Me-262 dest(air) | Leipheim A/F | P-51 |
| | March 24 | (.5)Me-109 dest(air)[*] | S/Soest | P-51 |
| | April 7 | (2)Me-109 dest(air) | Celle | P-51 |

5.5-0-0 air
0-0 ground

[*] - shared with Lt. H.B. Mooers of the 38th Ftr Sqn

**Cundy, Arthur C., Lt.** (6) Tallahassee, FL
352nd Ftr Sqn/353rd Ftr Grp August 1944-March 11, 1945(KIA)
Suffered m/f over the Channel.
69 missions

P-51D SX-B 44-15092 "Alabama Rammer Jammer"
S/Sgt. Magnus A. Geschwender-c/c
S/Sgt. Schelinger-c/c

| *Sqn* | *Date* | *Claims* | *Location* | *A/C* |
|---|---|---|---|---|
| 352nd | November 27, 1944 | Me-109 dest(air) | Magdeburg | P-51 |
| | December 24 | Me-109 dest(air) | Leacher Lake | P-51 |
| | January 14, 1945 | FW-190 dest(air) | SW Dummer Lake | P-51 |
| | March 2 | (2)FW-190 dest(air) | Dessau | P-51 |
| | | Me-109 dest(air) | Dessau | P-51 |

6-0-0 air
0-0 ground

**Cunnick, John W., III, Lt.** (9) Waco, TX
38th Ftr Sqn/55th Ftr Grp January 1945-EOW
37 missions

P-51D CG-
S/Sgt. Frank L. Younger-c/c

| *Sqn* | *Date* | *Claims* | *Location* | *A/C* |
|---|---|---|---|---|
| 38th | March 22, 1945 | Me-262 dest(air) | Lechfeld | P-51 |
| | April 7 | Me-109 dest(air) | Celle | P-51 |
| | April 9 | FW-190 dest(grd) | Munich-Brunnthal | P-51 |
| | | Me-262 dest(grd) | see above | P-51 |
| | | Ju-88 dest(grd) | see above | P-51 |
| | | FW-190 dam(grd) | see above | P-51 |
| | | Me-262 dam(grd) | see above | P-51 |
| | April 10 | He-111 dest(grd) | Wesendorf | P-51 |
| | | Me-109 dest(grd) | Wesendorf | P-51 |
| | | He-111 dam(grd) | Wesendorf | P-51 |
| | April 16 | (2)Me-109 dest(grd) | N/Landshut | P-51 |
| | | Me-109 dam(grd) | N/Landshut | P-51 |

2-0-0 air
7-4 ground

**Cutler, Frank A., Capt.** (10.5) Cleveland, OH
486th Ftr Sqn/352nd Ftr Grp December 1942-May 13, 1944(KIA)
Collided with a Me-109 near Grimmen.

P-47D PZ-P
P-51B PZ-P 43-6578 "Soldier's Vote"

| *Sqn* | *Date* | *Claims* | *Location* | *A/C* |
|---|---|---|---|---|
| 486th | February 20, 1944 | (2)Me-109 dest(air) | Nivelles | P-47 |
| | | Me-110 dest(grd) | Nivelles | P-47 |
| | April 11 | (2)FW-190 dest(air) | W/Torgau | P-51 |
| | | (.5)Ju-52 dest(air)[*] | W/Torgau | P-51 |
| | | Ju-88 dest(grd) | Lonnewitz | P-51 |
| | | Ju-52 dam(grd) | Lonnewitz | P-51 |
| | April 13 | Me-109 dest(grd) | S/Stuttgart | P-51 |
| | May 8 | (2)Me-109 dest(air) | Gifhorn | P-51 |
| | May 13 | Me-109 dest(air) | Neubrandenburg | P-51 |

7.5-0-0 air
3-1 ground

[*] - shared with Lt. W.W. Anderson of the 486th Ftr Sqn

**Dade, Lucian A., Jr., LtCol.** (9) Hopkinsville, KY
63rd Ftr Sqn/56th Ftr Grp Mid 1942-June 1943
HdQts/56th Ftr Grp June 1943-April 1944
62nd Ftr Sqn/56th Ftr Grp April 1944-August 1944
HdQts/56th Ftr Grp August 1944-August 1945

P-47C UN-P 41-6268
P-47D LM-P 42-75583
P-47D LM-P 42-25959
P-47D LM-P 42-26417
P-47M LM-P 44-21114

| *Sqn* | *Date* | *Claims* | *Location* | *A/C* |
|---|---|---|---|---|
| 62nd | May 13, 1944 | FW-190 dest(air) | Lubeck | P-47 |
| | July 4 | (2)Me-109 dest(air) | Conches | P-47 |
| | | (2)Me-109 dam(air) | Conches | P-47 |
| HdQts | September 5 | (2)Me-210 dest(grd) | Gelnhausen | P-47 |
| | | He-111 dest(grd) | Gelnhausen | P-47 |
| | April 13, 1945 | (2)Me-110 dest(grd) | Eggebeck A/F | P-47 |
| | | u/i a/c dest(grd) | Eggebeck A/F | P-47 |
| | | Me-110 dam(grd) | Eggebeck A/F | P-47 |

3-0-2 air
6-1 ground

**Daniell, Jack S., Lt.** (5) Birmingham, AL
505th Ftr Sqn/339th Ftr Grp July 1944-March 1945

P-51D 6N-K 44-14745 "Sweet'N Low Down"
S/Sgt. Albert J. Hermanson-c/c

| *Sqn* | *Date* | *Claims* | *Location* | *A/C* |
|---|---|---|---|---|
| 505th | November 26, 1944 | (5)FW-190 dest(air) | S/Hanover | P-51 |

5-0-0 air
0-0 ground

**Davis, Clayton E., Capt.** (9) Brookfield, VT
487th Ftr Sqn/352nd Ftr Grp Early 1943-August 17, 1944(MIA-E)
Hit by flak in the Noyon area.

P-47D HO-C "Marjorie"
P-51B HO-C 43-6805 "Marjorie II"
P-51D HO-C 44-13651

| *Sqn* | *Date* | *Claims* | *Location* | *A/C* |
|---|---|---|---|---|
| 487th | January 29, 1944 | FW-190 dest(air) | Malmedy | P-47 |
| | April 9 | (2)Ju-88 dest(grd) | Vechta | P-51 |
| | April 10 | (.5)Me-109 dest(air)[*] | SW Rheims | P-51 |
| | April 11 | Ju-52 dest(grd) | W/Berlin | P-51 |
| | April 22 | Ju-88 dest(grd) | N/Hanover | P-51 |
| | | Ju-88 dam(grd) | N/Hanover | P-51 |
| | April 30 | (3)u/i a/c dam(grd) | Vechta | P-51 |
| | May 8 | (3)Me-109 dest(air) | Brunswick | P-51 |
| | | (.5)FW-190 dest(air)[**] | Brunswick | P-51 |

5-0-0 air
4-4 ground

[*] - shared with Lt. E.B. McMahan of the 487th Ftr Sqn
[**] - shared with Lt. W.E. Fowler of the 487th Ftr Sqn

**Davis, Glendon V., Capt.** (7.5) Parma, ID
364th Ftr Sqn/357th Ftr Grp February 1943-April 28, 1944(MIA-E)
Suffered m/f near Bourges.

P-51B C5-O 43-6867 "Pregnant Polecat"

| *Sqn* | *Date* | *Claims* | *Location* | *A/C* |
|---|---|---|---|---|
| 364th | March 5, 1944 | (2)FW-200 dest(air) | Parthenay A/F | P-51 |
| | March 6 | Me-110 dest(air) | E/Berlin | P-51 |
| | | (.5)FW-190 dest(air)[*] | NW Berlin | P-51 |
| | March 8 | (.5)FW-190 dest(air)[**] | Dummer Lake | P-51 |
| | March 16 | Me-109 dest(air) | Ulm | P-51 |
| | | (.5)Me-110 dest(air)[@] | Ulm | P-51 |
| | April 13 | Me-109 dest(air) | Frankfurt | P-51 |
| | April 19 | FW-190 dest(air) | S/Bliecherode | P-51 |

7.5-0-0 air
0-0 ground

[*] - shared with Lt. T.L. Harris of the 364th Ftr Sqn
[**] - shared with Lt. T.L. Harris of the 364th Ftr Sqn
[@] - shared with Lt. R.A. Peterson of the 364th Ftr Sqn

**Davis, William C., Capt.** (6) Aurora, IL
352nd Ftr Sqn/353rd Ftr Grp July 1944-EOW
60 missions

P-51D SX-A 44-14642
P-51D SX-V 44-72392 "Aurora Haun' Dog, Feed It, It's Hungry!"

| *Sqn* | *Date* | *Claims* | *Location* | *A/C* |
|---|---|---|---|---|
| 352nd | November 18, 1944 | (2)He-111 dest(grd) | Lechfeld | P-51 |
| | April 17, 1945 | (4)FW-190 dest(grd) | Ganacker | P-51 |
| | | FW-190 dam(grd) | Ganacker | P-51 |

0-0-0 air
6-1 ground

*Mike Yannell's last 360th Fighter Squadron P-51, PI-Z "Audrey 4th."*

*Post-war shot of Roy Caviness' 78th Fighter Group P-51, WZ-I 44-14251 "Contrary Mary."*

*Herbert Kolb of the 350th Fighter Squadron with "Baby Duck."*

*Leedom John with his 338th Fighter Squadron P-51 "Ornery" and assistant crewchief Ernesto Gallego.*

*361st Fighter Squadron ace Wilbur Scheible with his crew. Left to right: Elwin Phillips (assistant), Scheible, and Mike Yahwak (crewchief).*

*Fred Jurgens in his 79th Fighter Squadron P-51.*

*487th Fighter Squadron ace Ray Littge.*

*Long serving Pacific and European ace John Landers in his "Big Beautiful Doll". Landers first flew with the 49th Fighter Group in the Pacific, then flew in the ETO with the 55th, 357th, and 78th Fighter Groups.*

*434th Fighter Squadron ace Jerome Nagel.*

*Former Pacific ace Don McGee who flew in the ETO with the 363rd and 364th Fighter Squadrons.*

*Last 360th Fighter Squadron CO and ace Mike Yannell.*

*James Jabara of the 354th Fighter Squadron; photo taken while Jabara was a member of the 363rd Fighter Group, 9th Air Force.*

*Melville Hightshoe, a top scoring 350th Fighter Squadron ace.*

*Verne Hooker, 435th Fighter Squadron ace.*

*357th Fighter Squadron ace William Cullerton with his crew. Left to right: unk., Jerome Seidl (crewchief), Cullerton, and Woodnail (armorer).*

*King of the strafers was Elwyn Righetti of the 55th Fighter Group.*

*Right: Top ace in the 356th Fighter Group was Don Strait.*

*Carroll Henry, 338th Fighter Squadron ace, with his P-51 CL-G 44-63227 "Little Trixie."*

*Francis Harrington of the 83rd Fighter Squadron with his crewchief Ed Wagner.*

*Charles Goodman with his 328th Fighter Squadron Mustang, PE-N 44-15530 "Family Tie."*

*Richard Phaneuf, 83rd Fighter Squadron ace.*

*Huie Lamb who became an ace with the 82nd Fighter Squadron.*

*Another 83rd Fighter Squadron ace, Dale Sweat.*

*Clinton Burdick of the 361st Fighter squadron with his QI-B 44-15310 "Do Do."*

*Record setting strafer Randel Murphy of the 63rd Fighter Squadron.*

*Top 364th Fighter Group air ace was George Ceuleers of the 383rd Fighter Squadron.*

*Niven Cranfill who made ace flying with the 359th Fighter Group.*

Randel Murphy (right) with Lucian Dade, both 56th Fighter Group aces.

Top 479th Fighter Group ace Robin Olds.

Late war ace Gillespie Bryan of the 78th Fighter Group.

William Julian, an ace who flew with the 83rd and 504th Fighter Squadrons.

*Gordon Graham with the 354th Fighter Squadron mascot.*

*Richard Gibbs (right) of the 343rd Fighter Squadron being congratulated by Jack Hayes, 55th Fighter Group CO.*

*Richard Gibbs with fellow 343rd flier John Gerig.*

*Two 351st Fighter Squadron aces with Tom Pryor on the left and Gerald Miller on the right.*

*Claiborne Kinnard on his 354th Fighter Squadron P-51 "Man O'War" Kinnard served with the 356th, 4th, and 355th Fighter Groups while in the ETO.*

*Another shot of Kinnard with his Mustang.*

*83rd Fighter Squadron ace John Kirk.*

*Vic Byers, CO and ace of the 351st Fighter Squadron.*

359th Fighter Group aces and enlisted men. Left to right are Ray Wetmore, Ernest DeGrave, August Berg, Dan McKee, and George Doersch.

Two 352nd Fighter Squadron aces with their crewchiefs, left to right: Edgar Wellborn, Horace Waggoner, Arthur Cundy, unk.

Five 353rd Fighter Group pilots following the mission of March 2, 1945. Left to right: Roland Lanoue, Walker Boone, Louis Lee, William Agnew (the only non-ace), William Bailey.

Charles Woods of the 375th Fighter Squadron.

Herb Rutland, a late war 360th Fighter Squadron replacement.

*Robert Hoeflein with his 61st Fighter Squadron P-47M "Lil Snorkey."*

*William DeGain in his 84th Fighter Squadron P-51 "Lee D."*

*John Balason of the 350th Fighter Squadron who was downed by flak and captured on February 22, 1945.*

*Richard Thieme of the 505th Fighter Squadron.*

*Jesse Walters, another 375th Fighter Squadron flier.*

*375th Fighter Squadron pilot John Johnston.*

*487th Fighter Squadron personnel in front of Alex Sears' P-51 Left to right: unk, unk, Sears, Russell Ross.*

**DeAnda, Louis, Lt.** (6) Bakerfield, CA
84th Ftr Sqn/78th Ftr Grp November 1944-July 1945
41 missions

P-51D WZ-K 44-15692
S/Sgt. James O. Tolleson-c/c

| *Sqn* | *Date* | *Claims* | *Location* | *A/C* |
|---|---|---|---|---|
| 84th | February 3, 1945 | (2)FW-200 dest(grd) | Luneburg | P-51 |
| | | Hs-126 dest(grd) | Luneburg | P-51 |
| | April 16 | (3)Ju-52 dest(grd) | Praha/Kakewice | P-51 |

0-0-0 air
6-0 ground

**Denson, Gordon A., Lt.** (5) Rockville, CT
334th Ftr Sqn/4th Ftr Grp January 1945-September 1945
24 missions, 126 hours
P-51D QP-E "Priscilla"

| *Sqn* | *Date* | *Claims* | *Location* | *A/C* |
|---|---|---|---|---|
| 334th | February 25, 1945 | (.5)Me-110 dest(grd)* | Rohrensee | P-51 |
| | | (.5)Me-110 dest(grd)* | Rohrensee | P-51 |
| | April 16 | (2)FW-190 dest(grd) | Gablingen | P-51 |
| | | Me-410 dest(grd) | Gablingen | P-51 |
| | | He-177 dest(grd) | Gablingen | P-51 |
| | | FW-190 dam(grd) | Gablingen | P-51 |
| | | Me-410 dam(grd) | Gablingen | P-51 |
| | | u/i a/c dam(grd) | Gablingen | P-51 |

0-0-0 air
5-3 ground

* - both shared with Capt. T.R. Bell of the 334th Ftr Sqn

**DeVillers, Donald J., Lt.** (6) Rochester, IL
83rd Ftr Sqn/78th Ftr Grp July 1944-July 1945

| *Sqn* | *Date* | *Claims* | *Location* | *A/C* |
|---|---|---|---|---|
| 83rd | August 10, 1944 | He-111 dest(grd) | Chateau Salines | P-47 |
| | April 16, 1945 | (2)Me-109 dest(grd) | N/Prague | P-51 |
| | | (2)Ju-87 dest(grd) | N/Prague | P-51 |
| | | He-111 dest(grd) | N/Prague | P-51 |
| | | (2)Me-109 dam(grd) | N/Prague | P-51 |
| | | (2)Ju-87 dam(grd) | N/Prague | P-51 |

0-0-0 air
6-4 ground

**Dickey, Melvin N., Capt.** (5) Tampa, FL
336th Ftr Sqn/4th Ftr Grp July 1944-June 1945
80 missions

P-51D VF-R "Betty Jane"
P-51D VF-R 44-13630 "Betty Jane II"

| *Sqn* | *Date* | *Claims* | *Location* | *A/C* |
|---|---|---|---|---|
| 336th | August 24, 1944 | (3)Ju-52 dest(grd) | NE Nordhausen | P-51 |
| | February 27, 1945 | Ju-87 dest(grd) | Weimar | P-51 |
| | | C-47 dest(grd) | Weimar | P-51 |

0-0-0 air
5-0 ground

**Dissette, Lawrence J., Capt.** (6) Buffalo, NY
358th Ftr Sqn/355th Ftr Grp May 1943-April 16, 1945(MIA-E)
Hit by flak at Straubing Airfield.
95 missions

P-47D YF-Q 42-22518 "Damn Yank"
P-51B YF-Q 42-106858 "Damn Yank II"
P-51D YF-Q "Damn Yank III"
P-51D YF-Q 44-14644 "Damn Yank IV"
S/Sgt. Claude McNeill-c/c

| *Sqn* | *Date* | *Claims* | *Location* | *A/C* |
|---|---|---|---|---|
| 358th | April 5, 1944 | (2)Me-110 dest(grd) | Munich | P-51 |
| | | Me-110 dam(grd) | Landsberg | P-51 |
| | | DFS-230 dam(grd) | Landsberg | P-51 |
| | April 15 | Do-217 dest(grd) | Glienicke | P-51 |
| | | u/i a/c dam(grd) | Glienicke | P-51 |
| | May 1 | Me-109 dest(air) | Traben-Trarbach | P-51 |
| | April 16, 1945 | (2)FW-190 dest(grd) | Straubing A/F | P-51 |
| | | (2)FW-190 dam(grd) | Straubing A/F | P-51 |

1-0-0 air
5-5 ground

**Dix, Gerald J., LtCol.** (5.5) Sullivan, IN
HdQts/355th Ftr Grp Early 1943-June 8, 1944(POW)
Suffered m/f near Niort.
Earlier flew in the PTO with the 17th Pursuit Sqn

P-47D YF-D
P-51B YF-D 43-7164
S/Sgt. Joseph A. Estrada-c/c

| *Sqn* | *Date* | *Claims* | *Location* | *A/C* |
|---|---|---|---|---|
| HdQts | March 8, 1944 | FW-190 dest(air) | NE Osnabruck | P-47 |
| | March 28 | (.5)Ju-88 dest(grd)* | Dijon | P-51 |
| | April 24 | FW-190 dest(air) | NE Augsburg | P-51 |
| | | Me-109 dam(air) | NE Augsburg | P-51 |
| | May 13 | (2)Me-410 dest(air) | SE Landsberg | P-51 |
| | May 22 | Me-109 prob(air) | SW Kiel | P-51 |
| | June 6 | Ju-87 dam(air) | Chartres | P-51 |
| | | Ju-87 dest(grd) | Chartres | P-51 |

4-1-2 air
1.5-0 ground

* - shared with Lt. H.E. Culp of the 354th Ftr Sqn, 355th Ftr Grp

**Doersch, George A., Maj.** (12) Seymour, WI
370th Ftr Sqn/359th Ftr Grp April 1943-February 1945
368th Ftr Sqn/359th Ftr Grp February 1945-September 1945
147 missions, 526:30 hours

P-47D CS-J 42-8552
P-51B CS-J 43-24810
P-51D CS-J 44-14948
P-51D CV-R 44-72067 "Ole Goat"
S/Sgt. Fred Schuster-c/c(370th)
Cpl. Scott Raeburn-arm.(370th)

| *Sqn* | *Date* | *Claims* | *Location* | *A/C* |
|---|---|---|---|---|
| 370th | February 22, 1944 | FW-190 dest(air) | Ahlen | P-47 |
| | April 11 | FW-190 dest(air) | Brunswick | P-47 |
| | April 15 | Ju-88 dam(air) | Varel | P-47 |
| | May 8 | Me-109 dest(air) | Eschede | P-51 |
| | | FW-190 dest(air) | Eschede | P-51 |
| | | FW-190 dam(air) | Eschede | P-51 |
| | May 21 | u/i a/c dam(grd) | Bruel | P-51 |
| | May 29 | (.5)FW-190 dest(air)* | Stettin | P-51 |
| | | (.5)FW-190 dest(air)** | Stettin | P-51 |
| | June 10 | Me-109 dest(air) | Evreux | P-51 |
| | October 6 | (2)FW-190 dest(air) | S/Stettin | P-51 |
| | | FW-190 dam(air) | S/Stettin | P-51 |
| | October 7 | (.5)BV-140 dest(grd)@ | Dievenow | P-51 |
| | January 14, 1945 | (2)FW-190 dest(air) | Vorden A/F | P-51 |
| 368th | March 23 | (.5)Ar-196 dest(air)@@ | Salzwedel | P-51 |
| | April 9 | FW-190 dest(grd) | Gernering | P-51 |
| | | He-111 dam(grd) | Gernering | P-51 |

10.5-0-3 air
1.5-2 ground

* - shared with LtCol. J.B. Murphy of the 370th Ftr Sqn
** - shared with Lt. R.W. Siltamaki of the 370th Ftr Sqn
@ - shared with F/O J.E. McCoskey of the 370th Ftr Sqn
@@ - shared with Lt. K.E. Barber of the 368th Ftr Sqn

**Doss, Gene C., Lt.** (5) McAlester, OK
83rd Ftr Sqn/78th Ftr Grp July 1944-EOW

| *Sqn* | *Date* | *Claims* | *Location* | *A/C* |
|---|---|---|---|---|
| 83rd | April 16, 1945 | (5)Ju-87 dest(grd) | N/Prague | P-51 |
| | | Me-109 dam(grd) | N/Prague | P-51 |

0-0-0 air
5-1 ground

**Dregne, Irwin H., Col.** (10.5) Viroqua, WI
HdQts/357th Ftr Grp May 1943-July 1945

P-51B C5-Q "Bobby Jeanne"
P-51D C5-Q 44-13408 "Bobby Jeanne"
P-51K C5-Q 44-11678 "Bobby Jeanne"
S/Sgt. Russell MacNeill-c/c
Sgt. James Enright-ac/c
Sgt. Eugene Shook-arm.

| *Sqn* | *Date* | *Claims* | *Location* | *A/C* |
|---|---|---|---|---|
| 364th | March 5, 1944 | FW-190 dam(air) | SE Bordeaux | P-51 |
| | March 16 | Me-109 dest(air) | SW Munich | P-51 |
| | May 8 | FW-190 dam(air) | N/Hanover | P-51 |

| | | | |
|---|---|---|---|
| May 12 | Me-109 dest(air) | NE Frankfurt | P-51 |
| May 19 | Me-109 dest(air) | Wittenburg | P-51 |
| May 21 | (1.5)Me-109 dest(grd)* | S/Eichhof | P-51 |
| December 24 | Me-109 dest(air) | Coblenz | P-51 |
| January 14, 1945 | Me-109 dest(air) | NW Brandenburg | P-51 |
| | FW-190 dam(air) | NW Brandenburg | P-51 |
| April 10 | (2)Me-262 dest(grd) | Neuruppin | P-51 |
| | FW-190 dest(grd) | see above | P-51 |
| | Ju-88 dam(grd) | see above | P-51 |
| April 17 | Ju-88 dest(grd) | Prague/Ruzny | P-51 |
| | (2)Ju-88 dam(grd) | Prague/Ruzny | P-51 |

5-0-3 air
5.5-3 ground

* - shared with Lt. M.A. Stanley of the 364th Ftr Sqn, 357th Ftr Grp

**Drew, Urban L., Lt.** (6) Detroit, MI
375th Ftr Sqn/361st Ftr Grp June 1944-November 1944
73 missions, 319 hours

P-51D E2-D 44-14164 "Detroit Miss"
S/Sgt. Vernon J. Davis-c/c

| *Sqn* | *Date* | *Claims* | *Location* | *A/C* |
|---|---|---|---|---|
| 375th | June 16, 1944 | Ju-52 dest(grd) | Toussus/Le Noble | P-51 |
| | June 25 | Me-109 dest(air) | S/Lisieux | P-51 |
| | August 7 | Me-109 dam(air) | Chartres | P-51 |
| | August 25 | Me-109 dest(air) | SW Rostock | P-51 |
| | September 11 | Me-109 dest(air) | S/Gottingen | P-51 |
| | September 18 | He-111 dest(air) | Fehrman Belt | P-51 |
| | October 7 | (2)Me-262 dest(air) | Achmer A/F | P-51 |

6-0-1 air
1-0 ground

**Duffie, Claire A.P., Maj.** (11.5) York, PA
434th Ftr Sqn/479th Ftr Grp October 1943-October 1944
436th Ftr Sqn/479th Ftr Grp Jaqnuary 1945-EOW

P-38J L2-A 43-28474 "Give'm Hell For H.L., Jr."
P-51D L2-A 44-14355 "Give'm Hell For H.L., Jr."
P-51D 9B-A 44-72516 "Give'm Hell For H.L., Jr."
T/Sgt. Joseph J. Pilcavage-c/c(434th)
Sgt. Art Daggett-ac/c(434th)
Cpl. David Nicol-arm.(434th)

| *Sqn* | *Date* | *Claims* | *Location* | *A/C* |
|---|---|---|---|---|
| 434th | August 18, 1944 | (1.5)Ju-88 dest(grd)* | Nancy/Essey A/F | P-38 |
| | August 25 | (2)Me-109 dest(air) | Rostock | P-38 |
| | September 26 | Me-109 dest(air) | SW Munster | P-38 |
| | | (2)Me-109 dam(air) | SW Munster | P-38 |
| 436th | February 22, 1945 | (3)u/i a/c dam(grd) | Halberstadt | P-51 |
| | | Ju-88 dam(grd) | Halberstadt | P-51 |
| | April 16 | (4)FW-190 dest(grd) | Landstadt | P-51 |
| | April 17 | (2)Ju-87 dest(grd) | Karlsbad | P-51 |
| | | FW-190 dest(grd) | Karlsbad | P-51 |

3-0-2 air
8.5-4 ground

* - shared with Lt. R.K. Friend of the 435th Ftr Sqn, 479th Ftr Grp

**Duffy, James E., Jr., Capt.** (14.2) Montclair, NJ
354th Ftr Sqn/355th Ftr Grp January 1943-EOW

P-47D WR-Y 42-74681
P-51B WR-Y 43-7182
P-51D WR-Y 44-14603
P-51D WR-Y 44-63764 "Dragon Wagon"
P-51D WR-Y 44-72186 "Dragon Wagon"
S/Sgt. Robert Baldwin-c/c

| *Sqn* | *Date* | *Claims* | *Location* | *A/C* |
|---|---|---|---|---|
| 354th | January 21, 1944 | FW-190 dest(air) | NW Dourdan | P-47 |
| | March 16 | FW-190 dest(air) | W/Ulm | P-51 |
| | April 5 | (.2)Do-217 dest(air)* | Landsberg | P-51 |
| | | (5)Do-217 dam(grd) | Landsberg | P-51 |
| | | FW-44 dam(grd) | Landsberg | P-51 |
| | April 10 | He-111 dest(grd) | Bourges | P-51 |
| | | W-34 dam(grd) | Bourges | P-51 |
| | April 13 | Me-110 dest(grd) | Oberpfaffenhofen | P-51 |
| | | Do-217 dest(grd) | see above | P-51 |
| | | (2)Me-210 dam(grd) | see above | P-51 |
| | | He-111 dam(grd) | see above | P-51 |
| | | Do-217 dam(grd) | see above | P-51 |
| | November 18 | Me-262 dest(grd) | Leipheim | P-51 |
| | November 26 | FW-190 dest(air) | Gifhorn-Hanover | P-51 |
| | December 5 | FW-190 dest(air) | N/Berlin | P-51 |
| | February 9, 1945 | FW-190 dest(air) | SW Berlin | P-51 |
| | February 23 | (2)u/i a/c dest(grd) | Leipheim | P-51 |
| | | Me-262 dest(grd) | Leipheim | P-51 |
| | April 13 | Ju-88 dest(grd) | Husum | P-51 |
| | | u/i a/c dam(grd) | Husum | P-51 |
| | April 16 | u/i a/c dest(grd) | Landstadt | P-51 |

5.2-0-0 air
9-12 ground

* - shared with Capt. C.G. Johnston, Capt. W.J. Koraleski, Lt. H.W. Brown, and Lt. B.C. Williamson of the 354th Ftr Sqn

**Duncan, Glenn E., Col.** (26.33) Houston, TX
HdQts/353rd Ftr Grp March 1943-July 7, 1944(MIA-E)
Hit by flak near Wesendorf.
HdQts/353rd Ftr Grp April 1945-September 1945
78 missions

P-47D LH-X 42-7988 "Dove of Peace"
P-47D LH-X 42-8634 "Dove of Peace"
P-47D LH-X 42-25506 "Dove of Peace"
P-47D LH-X 42-25971 "Dove of Peace"
P-51D LH-X 44-73060 "Dove of Peace"
T/Sgt. Richard Davidowski-c/c
Sgt. Frank Fiorito-ac/c

| *Sqn* | *Date* | *Claims* | *Location* | *A/C* |
|---|---|---|---|---|
| HdQts | August 16, 1943 | FW-190 dam(air) | NW Paris | P-47 |
| | September 23 | FW-190 dest(air) | Nantes | P-47 |
| | October 2 | Me-109 dest(air) | Emden | P-47 |
| | | Me-109 prob(air) | Emden | P-47 |
| | October 4 | Me-109 dam(air) | Malines | P-47 |
| | November 5 | Me-109 dam(air) | Gelsenkirchen | P-47 |
| | November 11 | Me-109 dest(air) | Numansdorp | P-47 |
| | | FW-190 dest(air) | Munster | P-47 |
| | | Me-109 dam(air) | Numansdorp | P-47 |
| | December 20 | FW-190 dest(air) | Rastede | P-47 |
| | January 4, 1944 | FW-190 dam(air) | Sendenhorst | P-47 |
| | January 5 | Me-109 dest(air) | Eindhoven-Gilze-Rijen | P-47 |
| | January 21 | (.33)Do-217 dest(grd)* | Albert | P-47 |
| | January 24 | (2)Me-110 dest(air) | Tirlemont | P-47 |
| | February 5 | FW-190 dest(air) | Sancerre | P-47 |
| | February 22 | FW-190 dest(air) | Turnhout | P-47 |
| | | (.5)Ju-88 dest(grd)** | Bonn | P-47 |
| | February 24 | FW-190 dest(air) | Steinhuder Lake | P-47 |
| | | Ju-88 dam(grd) | Steinhuder Lake | P-47 |
| | March 6 | (2)FW-190 dest(air) | Steinhuder Lake | P-47 |
| | March 16 | (1.5)u/i a/c dam(grd)@ | Laon | P-47 |
| | March 29 | Me-110 dest(grd) | Dummer Lake | P-47 |
| | | B-17 dest(grd) | see above | P-47 |
| | | (6)u/i a/c dam(grd) | see above | P-47 |
| | | Me-210 dam(grd) | see above | P-47 |
| | April 28 | u/i a/c dest(grd) | Chateaudun | P-47 |
| | | u/i a/c dam(grd) | Chateaudun | P-47 |
| | May 12 | FW-190 dest(air) | Wiesbaden | P-47 |
| | | (2)FW-190 dam(air) | Wiesbaden | P-47 |
| | June 7 | Ju-52 dest(air) | E/Ribecourt | P-47 |
| | | (.5)Me-109 dest(air)@@ | E/Ribecourt | P-47 |
| | June 12 | (3)Me-109 dest(air) | Evreux-Dreux | P-47 |
| | June 20 | (2)He-111 dest(grd) | Plantlunne | P-47 |
| | July 5 | Me-109 dest(air) | Pont Audemer | P-47 |
| | July 7 | He-111 dest(grd) | Wesendorf | P-47 |

19.5-1-7 air
6.83-10.5 ground

* - shared with Lt. W.W. Johnson and Lt. C.H. Sperry of the 352nd Ftr Sqn, 353rd Ftr Grp
** - shared with Maj. H.N. Holt of the 366th Ftr Grp, 9th Air Force
@ - shared with Lt. J. Terzian of the 351st Ftr Sqn, 353rd Ftr Grp
@@ - shared with Capt. G.B. Compton of the 351st Ftr Sqn

**Duncan, John F., Lt.** (10) Kokomo, IN
362nd Ftr Sqn/357th Ftr Grp November 1944-EOW

P-51D G4-Z 44-14612 "Hot Shot Charlie"
S/Sgt. George E. Roepke-c/c

| *Sqn* | *Date* | *Claims* | *Location* | *A/C* |
|---|---|---|---|---|
| 362nd | January 14, 1945 | (2)FW-190 dest(air) | NW Berlin | P-51 |
| | February 25 | He-111 dest(grd) | Memmingen | P-51 |
| | March 2 | Me-109 dest(air) | NE Leipzig | P-51 |
| | | Me-109 dam(air) | NE Leipzig | P-51 |
| | March 24 | Me-109 dest(air) | W/Gutersloh | P-51 |
| | April 10 | (2)Me-210 dest(grd) | Neuruppin | P-51 |
| | | Me-110 dest(grd) | see above | P-51 |

| Sqn | Date | Claims | Location | A/C |
|---|---|---|---|---|
| | | Me-262 dam(grd) | see above | P-51 |
| | April 17 | Me-262 dest(grd) | Prague/Ruzny | P-51 |
| | | Me-109 dest(grd) | Prague/Ruzny | P-51 |

4-0-1 air
6-1 ground

**Eckfeldt, Robert T., Lt.** (7) Belmont, MA
374th Ftr Sqn/361st Ftr Grp States-August 1944

P-47D B7-E 42-75522 "Bald Eagle"
P-51B B7-E 42-106811 "Bald Eagle II"
P-51B B7-E 42-106839 "Bald Eagle III"

| Sqn | Date | Claims | Location | A/C |
|---|---|---|---|---|
| 374th | April 8, 1944 | Me-109 dest(air) | Dummer Lake | P-47 |
| | May 29 | FW-190 dest(air) | Pitka | P-51 |
| | June 8 | Me-109 dest(air) | St. Pierre | P-51 |
| | June 29 | (4)FW-190 dest(grd) | Oschersleben | P-51 |
| | | (2.5)FW-190 dam(grd) | Oschersleben | P-51 |

3-0-0 air
4-2.5 ground

[*] - shared with Lt. V.R. Richards of the 374th Ftr Sqn

**Edens, Billy G., Lt.** (10) Tyrenza, AR
62nd Ftr Sqn/56th Ftr Grp April 1944-September 10, 1944(POW)
Hit by flak in the Trier area.
83 missions, 300 hours

P-47D LM-F 42-75093
P-47D LM-F 42-76363

| Sqn | Date | Claims | Location | A/C |
|---|---|---|---|---|
| 62nd | June 8, 1944 | (2)Me-109 dest(air) | St. Andre de L'Eure | P-47 |
| | | FW-190 dest(air) | see above | P-47 |
| | July 5 | FW-190 dest(air) | N/Evreux | P-47 |
| | July 7 | (3)Ju-52 dest(air) | Gardelegen | P-47 |
| | August 4 | (2)He-111 dest(grd) | Plantlunne | P-47 |
| | | (2)He-111 dam(grd) | Plantlunne | P-47 |
| | September 8 | Ju-88 dest(grd) | Coblenz | P-47 |

7-0-0 air
3-2 ground

**Egan, Joseph L., Jr., Capt.** (5) New York, NY
63rd Ftr Sqn/56th Ftr Grp Mid 1942-July 19, 1944(KIA)
Hit by flak northeast of Nancy.

P-47C UN-E 41-6584 "Holy Joe"
P-47D UN-E 42-75855

| Sqn | Date | Claims | Location | A/C |
|---|---|---|---|---|
| 63rd | August 19, 1943 | FW-190 dest(air) | Tholen Island | P-47 |
| | January 30, 1944 | Me-210 dest(air) | S/Quackenbruck | P-47 |
| | February 21 | Me-109 dest(air) | Elburg | P-47 |
| | February 22 | Me-109 dest(air) | Munster | P-47 |
| | | FW-190 dam(air) | Munster | P-47 |
| | March 15 | FW-190 dest(air) | Nienburg | P-47 |

5-0-1 air
0-0 ground

**Einhaus, Lowell E., Capt.** (6) Austin, MN
77th Ftr Sqn/20th Ftr Grp August 1944-February 1945
49 missions, 275:15 hours

P-51D LC-V 44-13918
S/Sgt. Clement J. Turchin-c/c
Sgt. James E.N. Carpenter-ac/c
Sgt. William W. Head-arm.

| Sqn | Date | Claims | Location | A/C |
|---|---|---|---|---|
| 77th | February 9, 1945 | (6)FW-190 dest(grd) | Esperstadt A/F | P-51 |

0-0-0 air
6-0 ground

**Elder, John L., LtCol.** (21) Ebensburg, PA
357th Ftr Sqn/355th Ftr Grp February 1943-September 1945

P-47D OS-R 42-8544 "Moon"
P-47D OS-R 42-22784 "Moon"
P-51B OS-R 43-6776 "Moon"
P-51B OS-R 42-106433 "Moon"
P-51B OS-R 42-106723
P-51D OS-R 44-63633
P-51D OS-R 44-73065
S/Sgt. William Mitchell-c/c

| Sqn | Date | Claims | Location | A/C |
|---|---|---|---|---|
| 357th | February 21, 1944 | FW-190 dest(air) | Dummer Lake | P-47 |
| | March 27 | Ju-88 dam(grd) | Biscarosse | P-51 |
| | March 29 | FW-190 dest(air) | NE Brunswick | P-51 |
| | | FW-190 dam(air) | NE Brunswick | P-51 |
| | April 8 | (2)Ju-88 dest(grd) | Gifhorn | P-51 |
| | April 15 | Me-109 dest(air) | E/Celle | P-51 |
| | August 14 | Ju-88 dest(grd) | Sarreburg | P-51 |
| | August 16 | (2)Me-109 dest(air) | SE Hildesheim | P-51 |
| | September 18 | Me-109 dest(air) | NW Warsaw | P-51 |
| | November 2 | Me-109 dest(air) | Wernigerode | P-51 |
| | | (5)u/i a/c dest(grd) | Wernigerode | P-51 |
| | January 14, 1945 | Me-109 dest(air) | Munster | P-51 |
| | February 23 | Me-109 dest(grd) | Neuburg | P-51 |
| | | Me-109 dam(grd) | Neuburg | P-51 |
| | April 16 | (2)FW-190 dest(grd) | SE Germany | P-51 |
| | | (2)u/i a/c dest(grd) | see above | P-51 |
| | | (3)u/i a/c dam(grd) | see above | P-51 |

8-0-1 air
13-5 ground

**Elder, Robert A., LtCol.** (7) Hernando, MS
HdQts/353rd Ftr Grp February 1945-April 1945
350th Ftr Sqn/353rd Ftr Grp April 1945-EOW
27 missions

P-51D LH-S 44-72736 "Miss Gamble"

| Sqn | Date | Claims | Location | A/C |
|---|---|---|---|---|
| HdQts | March 24, 1945 | (4)FW-190 dest(air) | NW Kassel | P-51 |
| | | Me-109 dest(air) | NW Kassel | P-51 |
| | | Me-109 dam(air) | NW Kassel | P-51 |
| 350th | April 16 | FW-190 dest(grd) | Pocking | P-51 |
| | | Ju-87 dest(grd) | Pocking | P-51 |
| | | (3)Ju-87 dam(grd) | Pocking | P-51 |
| | | Me-109 dam(grd) | Pocking | P-51 |

5-0-1 air
2-4 ground

**Elmgren, Charles B., Lt.** (7) Sheridan, WY
436th Ftr Sqn/479th Ftr Grp October 1944-July 1945
53 missions, 265:20 hours

P-51K 9B-P 44-11739
S/Sgt. Gordon Evian-c/c

| Sqn | Date | Claims | Location | A/C |
|---|---|---|---|---|
| 436th | April 16, 1945 | (4)FW-190 dest(grd) | Landstadt | P-51 |
| | April 17 | (2)Fi-156 dest(grd) | Karlsbad | P-51 |
| | | u/i a/c dest(grd) | Karlsbad | P-51 |

0-0-0 air
7-0 ground

**Emerson, Donald R., Capt.** (7) Pembina, ND
336th Ftr Sqn/4th Ftr Grp March 1944-December 25, 1944(KIA)
Hit by flak and crashed in Belgium
89 missions

P-51B VF-L 43-6889
P-51D VF-L 44-13317

| Sqn | Date | Claims | Location | A/C |
|---|---|---|---|---|
| 336th | March 21, 1944 | FW-190 prob(air) | SW Evreux | P-51 |
| | March 27 | (.5)Ju-88 dest(grd)[*] | Cazaux A/F | P-51 |
| | April 5 | (.5)Ju-88 dest(grd)[**] | Stendal | P-51 |
| | | (.5)Ju-88 dest(grd)[@] | Stendal | P-51 |
| | | Ju-88 dam(grd) | Stendal | P-51 |
| | April 18 | Me-109 dest(grd) | Wazendorf A/F | P-51 |
| | April 22 | (.5)Me-109 dest(air)[@@] | SW Kassel | P-51 |
| | May 29 | (.5)Me-110 dest(air)[#] | N/Falkenberg | P-51 |
| | | Do-18 dam(grd) | N/Falkenberg | P-51 |
| | June 20 | FW-190 dest(air) | S/Anklam | P-51 |
| | July 2 | (.5)Me-109 dest(air)[##] | W/Budapest | P-51 |
| | November 18 | Me-109 dam(grd) | Leipheim | P-51 |
| | December 25 | (2)FW-190 dest(air) | SW Coblenz | P-51 |

4.5-1-0 air
2.5-3 ground

[*] - shared with Maj. J.A. Clark of HdQts, 4th Ftr Grp
[**] - shared with Maj. J.A. Goodson of the 336th Ftr Sqn
[@] - shared with an unknown pilot
[@@] - shared with Lt. K.E. Carlson of the 336th Ftr Sqn
[#] - shared with Lt. C.J. Netting of the 336th Ftr Sqn
[##] - shared with Capt. D.H. Higgins of the 352nd Ftr Grp

**Emory, Frank N., Capt.** (12) Mt. Vernon, WA
351st Ftr Sqn/353rd Ftr Grp December 1942-April 1945
118 missions, 450:25 hours

P-47D YJ-E 42-8602 "Sis"
P-47D YJ-E 42-75815 "Sis II"
P-47D YJ-E "Sis III"
P-51D YJ-E 44-14573 "Sis IV"
S/Sgt. William H. Markey-c/c

| *Sqn* | *Date* | *Claims* | *Location* | *A/C* |
|---|---|---|---|---|
| 351st | November 5, 1943 | Me-210 dam(air) | Rheinburg | P-47 |
| | February 10, 1944 | FW-190 dest(air) | Lingen | P-47 |
| | February 22 | (.25)FW-190 dam(grd)[*] | NE Bonn | P-47 |
| | | (.25)FW-190 dam(grd)[*] | NE Bonn | P-47 |
| | June 8 | FW-190 dest(air) | SW Angars | P-47 |
| | March 21, 1945 | (2)Me-109 dest(grd) | Achmer | P-51 |
| | | FW-190 dam(grd) | Achmer | P-51 |
| | | u/i a/c dam(grd) | Achmer | P-51 |
| | April 9 | (2)Me-262 dest(grd) | S/Neubiberg | P-51 |
| | | Me-410 dest(grd) | S/Neubiberg | P-51 |
| | | u/i a/c dest(grd) | S/Neubiberg | P-51 |
| | April 16 | (2)FW-190 dest(grd) | Reichersberg | P-51 |
| | | Ju-87 dest(grd) | see above | P-51 |
| | | u/i a/c dest(grd) | see above | P-51 |
| | | FW-190 dam(grd) | see above | P-51 |
| | | Me-110 dam(grd) | see above | P-51 |

2-0-1 air
10-4.5 ground

[*] - both shared with Maj. W.C. Beckham, Lt. G.B. Compton, and Lt. G.F. Perpente of the 351st Ftr Sqn

**England, John B., Maj.** (18.5) Caruthersville, MO
362nd Ftr Sqn/357th Ftr Grp April 1943-February 1945
108 missions, 460 hours

P-51B G4-H
P-51B G4-H 42-106463 "U've Had It!"
P-51D G4-H 44-13735 "U've Had It!"
P-51D G4-E "Missouri Armada"
S/Sgt. John Currie-c/c
Sgt. Forrest Highland-ac/c

| *Sqn* | *Date* | *Claims* | *Location* | *A/C* |
|---|---|---|---|---|
| 362nd | March 8, 1944 | Me-109 dest(air) | Steinhuder Lake | P-51 |
| | March 16 | Me-110 dest(air) | S/Stuttgart | P-51 |
| | April 11 | (.5)Me-109 dest(air)[*] | NE Magdeburg | P-51 |
| | April 13 | FW-190 dest(air) | W/Mannheim | P-51 |
| | April 24 | (3)Me-110 dest(air) | S/Munich | P-51 |
| | May 27 | Me-109 dest(air) | N/Strasbourg | P-51 |
| | August 18 | (.5)Me-109 dest(air)[**] | NE Paris | P-51 |
| | September 13 | (2.5)Me-109 dest(air)[@] | S/Nordhausen | P-51 |
| | October 6 | (2)Me-109 dest(air) | NW Berlin | P-51 |
| | | Me-109 dam(air) | NW Berlin | P-51 |
| | November 18 | Me-109 dest(grd) | Mengen A/F | P-51 |
| | November 27 | (4)FW-190 dest(air) | S/Magdeburg | P-51 |
| | January 14, 1945 | Me-109 dest(air) | NW Berlin | P-51 |

17.5-0-1 air
1-0 ground

[*]-shared with Lt. H.R. Ankeny of the 362nd Ftr Sqn
[**]-shared with Lt. W.N. Perry of the 362nd Ftr Sqn
[@]-shared with Lt. S.G. Fuller of the 362nd Ftr Sqn

**Evans, Andrew J., Jr., LtCol.** (8) San Antonio, TX
HdQts/357th Ftr Grp October 1944-EOW
Earlier flew a tour in Iceland, no claims.
41 missions, 220 hours

P-51D G4-B 44-64051 "Little Sweetie 4"
S/Sgt. Ray A. Smith-c/c

| *Sqn* | *Date* | *Claims* | *Location* | *A/C* |
|---|---|---|---|---|
| HdQts | November 27, 1944 | FW-190 dest(air) | S/Magdeburg | P-51 |
| | January 14, 1945 | (2)FW-190 dest(air) | NW Brandenburg | P-51 |
| | | (2)Me-109 dest(air) | NW Brandenburg | P-51 |
| | March 24 | Me-109 dest(air) | W/Gutersloh | P-51 |
| | April 10 | He-111 dest(grd) | Neuruppin A/F | P-51 |
| | | Me-210 dest(grd) | see above | P-51 |
| | | He-111 dam(grd) | see above | P-51 |
| | | Me-210 dam(grd) | see above | P-51 |
| | | Do-217 dam(grd) | see above | P-51 |
| | | He-177 dam(grd) | see above | P-51 |

6-0-0 air
2-4 ground

**Evans, Roy W., LtCol.** (6) San Bernadino, CA
335th Ftr Sqn/4th Ftr Grp October 1942-February 1944
HdQts/359th Ftr Grp August 1944-February 14, 1945(POW)
Hit by flak near Dresden
Earlier flew with 71 Sqn, RAF

Spitfire AV-
P-47C WD-H 41-6206
P-47D WD-E 42-74686
P-51D IV-E 44-14988

| *Sqn* | *Date* | *Claims* | *Location* | *A/C* |
|---|---|---|---|---|
| 335th | November 21, 1942 | Fi-156 dest(air) | SE Furness | Spit |
| | July 28, 1943 | Me-109 dest(air) | W/Arnheim | P-47 |
| | | FW-190 dam(air) | W/Arnheim | P-47 |
| | August 16 | Me-109 dest(air) | S/Paris | P-47 |
| | September 6 | FW-190 dest(air) | N/Chateau Thierry | P-47 |
| | October 8 | Me-109 dest(air) | SW Oldenburg | P-47 |
| HdQts | November 26, 1944 | Me-109 dest(air) | Kassel | P-51 |
| | | Me-109 dam(air) | Kassel | P-51 |

6-0-2 air
0-0 ground

**Everson, Kirke B., Jr., Capt.** (14.5) Ft. Wetherell, RI
504th Ftr Sqn/339th Ftr Grp February 1945-July 1945

P-51D 5Q-E 44-14372 "Mary Beth"
S/Sgt. Greenberg-c/c

| *Sqn* | *Date* | *Claims* | *Location* | *A/C* |
|---|---|---|---|---|
| 504th | April 4, 1945 | (.5)Me-262 dest(air)[*] | Parchim A/F | P-51 |
| | April 7 | Me-109 dest(air) | Celle | P-51 |
| | April 10 | (3)Me-410 dest(grd) | N/Neuruppin | P-51 |
| | | (3)Me-410 dam(grd) | see above | P-51 |
| | | (2)Me-110 dam(grd) | see above | P-51 |
| | April 16 | (3)FW-190 dest(grd) | Klatovy | P-51 |
| | April 17 | (2)Me-109 dest(grd) | Klatovy-Anberg | P-51 |
| | | (2)Fi-156 dest(grd) | see above | P-51 |
| | | (2)Ju-88 dest(grd) | see above | P-51 |
| | | Me-210 dest(grd) | see above | P-51 |

1.5-0-0 air
13-5 ground

[*] - shared with Lt. R.C. Croker of the 504th Ftr Sqn

**Falvey, Harold W., F/O** (8) Bridgeport, CT
354th Ftr Sqn/355th Ftr Grp September 1944-June 1945

P-51D WR-E 44-15652
P-51D WR-E 44-63222

| *Sqn* | *Date* | *Claims* | *Location* | *A/C* |
|---|---|---|---|---|
| 354th | November 26, 1944 | FW-190 dam(air) | Gifhorn | P-51 |
| | January 15, 1945 | FW-190 dest(grd) | Landsberg | P-51 |
| | | u/i a/c dest(grd) | Landsberg | P-51 |
| | | u/i a/c dam(grd) | Landsberg | P-51 |
| | March 22 | Me-262 dest(grd) | Kitzingen | P-51 |
| | | Me-109 dest(grd) | Wurzburg | P-51 |
| | | Me-262 dam(grd) | Kitzingen | P-51 |
| | April 9 | (.5)Ju-88 dest(grd)[*] | Memmingen | P-51 |
| | April 10 | Ju-52 dest(grd) | Rechlin/Larz | P-51 |
| | | (.5)He-111 dest(grd)[**] | see above | P-51 |
| | | (4)He-111 dam(grd) | see above | P-51 |
| | April 13 | FW-190 dest(grd) | Husum | P-51 |
| | | Ju-88 dest(grd) | Husum | P-51 |
| | | Ju-88 dam(grd) | Husum | P-51 |

0-0-1 air
8-7 ground

[*] - shared with Lt. J. Jabara of the 354th Ftr Sqn
[**] - shared with F/O T.R. Hixon of the 354th Ftr Sqn

**Farmer, Owen P., Capt.** (7) Aberdeen, SD
505th Ftr Sqn/339th Ftr Grp States-June 1945

P-51B 6N-H
P-51D 6N-H 44-13946 "Dibbo"
P-51D 6N-H 44-13987 "Dibbo"
P-51D 6N-H 44-72084 "Dibbo"
P-51D 6N-H 44-72065 "Dibbo"

| Sqn | Date | Claims | Location | A/C |
|---|---|---|---|---|
| 505th | May 21, 1944 | u/i a/c dam(air) | Oschatz | P-51 |
| | June 27 | (.5)FW-190 dest(air)* | Paris | P-51 |
| | July 31 | (3)u/i a/c dam(grd) | Holzkirchen | P-51 |
| | September 10 | u/i a/c dest(grd) | Weizenburg | P-51 |
| | March 12, 1945 | (1.5)Me-109 dest(air)** | Hellevad | P-51 |
| | April 10 | (2)Ju-88 dest(grd) | N/Neuruppin | P-51 |
| | April 16 | Me-109 dest(grd) | NE Prague | P-51 |
| | | u/i a/c dest(grd) | NE Prague | P-51 |

2-0-1 air
5-3 ground

* - shared with Lt. W.G. Fish of the 505th Ftr Sqn
** - shared with Lt. V.D. Carr of the 505th Ftr Sqn

**Fiebelkorn, Ernest C., Capt.** (11) Los Angeles, CA
77th Ftr Sqn/20th Ftr Grp January 1944-December 1944
70 missions, 320:10 hours

P-38J LC-N 42-68068
P-51D LC-N 44-11161 "June Nite"
T/Sgt. Carl W. Tucker-c/c
Sgt. Nicholas Trynosky-ac/c
Sgt. Barney Yanchitis-arm.

| Sqn | Date | Claims | Location | A/C |
|---|---|---|---|---|
| 77th | April 8, 1944 | u/i a/c dest(grd) | Salzwedel | P-38 |
| | | (2)Ju-88 dam(grd) | Salzwedel | P-38 |
| | April 30 | Me-410 dest(grd) | Orleans/Bricy | P-38 |
| | July 14 | (.5)FW-190 dest(air)* | SW Reims | P-38 |
| | August 5 | Me-109 dest(air) | S/Hamburg | P-51 |
| | September 28 | (3)Me-109 dest(air) | S/Magdeburg | P-51 |
| | | FW-190 dest(air) | S/Magdeburg | P-51 |
| | | Me-109 dam(air) | S/Mahdeburg | P-51 |
| | November 2 | (3)Me-109 dest(air) | N/Leipzig | P-51 |
| | November 8 | (.5)Me-262 dest(air)** | Dummer Lake | P-51 |

9-0-1 air
2-2 ground

* - shared with Lt. C.C. Arthaud of the 77th Ftr Sqn
** - shared with Lt. E.R. Haydon of the 357th Ftr Grp

**Fiedler, Clemmons A., Lt.** (5.33) Fredericksburg, TX
335th Ftr Sqn/4th Ftr Grp August 1943-April 10, 1944(KIA)
Hit by flak at Romorantin Airfield.

P-47C WD-S 41-6185
P-51B WD-S 43-6579 "Snafu"

| Sqn | Date | Claims | Location | A/C |
|---|---|---|---|---|
| 335th | February 20, 1944 | Me-110 dest(air) | Coblenz | P-47 |
| | | Me-110 dam(air) | Coblenz | P-47 |
| | March 8 | Me-109 dam(air) | NE Berlin | P-51 |
| | March 21 | FW-190 dest(grd) | Lans de Bassac | P-51 |
| | March 29 | Me-109 dest(air) | N/Brunswick | P-51 |
| | April 5 | (.33)Ju-88 dest(air)* | Plaue A/F | P-51 |
| | | (2)Ju-88 dam(grd) | Plaue A/F | P-51 |
| | | u/i a/c dam(grd) | Plaue A/F | P-51 |
| | April 8 | (2)Me-109 dest(air) | Wolfenbuttel | P-51 |

4.33-0-2 air
1-3 ground

* - shared with Capt. D.W. Beeson and Lt. H.T. Biel of the 334th Ftr Sqn

**Flagg, Walter L., Capt.** (8) Conimicut, RI
63rd Ftr Sqn/56th Ftr Grp April 1944-June 1945
95 missions, 387 hours

P-47D UN-H 42-25317
P-47M UN-F 44-21140 "Shoot! You're Faded"

| Sqn | Date | Claims | Location | A/C |
|---|---|---|---|---|
| 63rd | July 5, 1944 | Me-109 dest(air) | Evreux | P-47 |
| | | Me-109 dam(air) | Evreux | P-47 |
| | August 28 | Me-109 dest(air) | Charleroi | P-47 |
| | April 10, 1945 | (2)Do-217 dest(grd) | Werder A/F | P-47 |
| | | Me-109 dest(grd) | see above | P-47 |
| | | u/i a/c dest(grd) | see above | P-47 |
| | | Me-109 dam(grd) | see above | P-47 |
| | April 13 | FW-190 dest(grd) | Eggebeck A/F | P-47 |
| | | Ju-88 dest(grd) | see above | P-47 |
| | | FW-190 dam(grd) | see above | P-47 |

2-0-1 air
6-2 ground

**Fletcher, Jack M., Lt.** (5) Moultrie, GA
354th Ftr Sqn/355th Ftr Grp November 1944-September 1945

P-51D WR-T

| Sqn | Date | Claims | Location | A/C |
|---|---|---|---|---|
| 354th | March 22, 1945 | Me-109 dest(grd) | Wurzburg | P-51 |
| | April 10 | (2)u/i a/c dest(grd) | Rechlin/Larz | P-51 |
| | April 16 | (2)u/i a/c dest(grd) | Eger A/F | P-51 |
| | | u/i a/c dam(grd) | Eger A/F | P-51 |

0-0-0 air
5-1 ground

**Fortier, Norman J., Maj.** (11.33) Nashua, NH
354th Ftr Sqn/355th Ftr Grp January 1943-September 1945
112 missions, 457 hours

P-47D WR-N
P-51B WR-N 42-106870 "Bud"
P-51C WR-N 42-103802 "Bud"
P-51D WR-N 44-15373
P-51D WR-N 44-72361
S/Sgt. McKibben-c/c

| Sqn | Date | Claims | Location | A/C |
|---|---|---|---|---|
| 354th | March 6, 1944 | (.33)Me-109 dest(air)* | Dummer Lake | P-47 |
| | March 29 | u/i a/c dest(grd) | Dummer Lake | P-47 |
| | April 24 | (1.5)Me-109 dest(air)** | Munich | P-51 |
| | | Me-109 dam(air) | Munich | P-51 |
| | May 1 | FW-190 dam(air) | Trier | P-51 |
| | May 13 | FW-190 dest(air) | NE Bremen | P-51 |
| | | Ju-88 dest(air) | N/Landsberg | P-51 |
| | June 6 | Ju-87 dest(air) | Chartres | P-51 |
| | July 8 | (.5)Me-109 dest(grd)@ | SW Chalons | P-51 |
| | July 20 | Me-109 dest(air) | W/Oschatz | P-51 |
| | July 24 | Me-262 dam(grd) | Lechfeld | P-51 |
| | November 18 | (2)Me-262 dest(grd) | Leipheim | P-51 |
| | | u/i a/c dam(grd) | Leipheim | P-51 |
| | January 15, 1945 | Ju-52 dest(grd) | Oberpfaffenhofen | P-51 |
| | | Ju-52 dam(grd) | Oberpfaffenhofen | P-51 |
| | April 16 | u/i a/c dest(grd) | Eger A/F | P-51 |

5.83-0-2 air
5.5-3 ground

* - shared with Capt. W.J. Koraleski and F/O C.R. Barger of the 354th Ftr Sqn
** - shared with Lt. W.P. Boulet of the 354th Ftr Sqn
@ - shared with Lt. R.G. Cross of the 354th Ftr Sqn

**Fowle, James M., Capt.** (8) San Francisco, CA
384th Ftr Sqn/364th Ftr Grp February 1944-April 1945

P-38J 5Y-J "Terry Claire"
P-51D 5Y-J 44-13829 "Terry Claire II"

| Sqn | Date | Claims | Location | A/C |
|---|---|---|---|---|
| 384th | November 2, 1944 | Me-109 dest(air) | S/Merseburg | P-51 |
| | November 26 | FW-190 dest(air) | SE Dummer Lake | P-51 |
| | December 23 | (4)Me-109 dest(air) | NW Trier | P-51 |
| | December 31 | (2)FW-190 dest(air) | SW Hamburg | P-51 |
| | February 6, 1945 | Ar-234 dam(air) | SE Zuider Zee | P-51 |

8-0-1 air
0-0 ground

**Foy, Robert W., Maj.** (18) Oswego, NY
363rd Ftr Sqn/357th Ftr Grp June 1943-November 1944
HdQts/357th Ftr Grp November 1944-April 1945

P-51B B6-V
P-51D B6-V 44-13712 "Reluctant Rebel"
P-51D B6-V 44-63621 "Little Shrimp"
S/Sgt. W.P. Sunderland-c/c

| Sqn | Date | Claims | Location | A/C |
|---|---|---|---|---|
| 363rd | May 19, 1944 | (3)Me-109 dest(air) | NW Brandenburg | P-51 |
| | June 29 | (2)Me-109 dest(air) | SW Leipzig | P-51 |

| Sqn | Date | Claims | Location | A/C |
|---|---|---|---|---|
| | | FW-190 dest(air) | SW Leipzig | P-51 |
| | July 25 | FW-190 dest(air) | SE Paris | P-51 |
| | November 18 | Me-109 dest(air) | Villingen A/F | P-51 |
| | | Me-109 dam(air) | see above | P-51 |
| | | Me-109 dest(grd) | see above | P-51 |
| | | (3)Me-109 dam(grd) | see above | P-51 |
| HdQts | December 2 | Ju-88 dest(air) | NE Coblenz | P-51 |
| | December 23 | Me-109 dest(air) | Wetzlar A/F | P-51 |
| | | Ju-88 dest(air) | Wetzlar A/F | P-51 |
| | January 14, 1945 | (2)FW-190 dest(air) | NW Berlin | P-51 |
| | | FW-190 dest(grd) | Berlin | P-51 |
| | February 9 | Me-262 dam(air) | Fulda | P-51 |
| | February 28 | Ju-88 dest(grd) | Lubeck-Blankensee | P-51 |
| | | FW-200 dam(grd) | see above | P-51 |
| | | Me-109 dam(grd) | see above | P-51 |
| | March 19 | Me-262 dest(air) | W/Giessen | P-51 |
| | March 24 | Me-109 dest(air) | N/Gutersloh | P-51 |

15-0-2 air
3-2 ground

**France, Victor J., Capt.** (8.66) Oklahoma City, OK
334th Ftr Sqn/4th Ftr Grp October 1942-April 18, 1944(KIA)
Hit the ground while chasing a Me-109 near Stendal.
Earlier flew with 71 Sqn, RAF

Spitfire XR-Q AD196 "Miss North Dallas"
P-47C QP-K 41-6414
P-47D QP-K 42-7876 "Miss Dallas"
P-51B QP-K 43-6832 "Miss Dallas"
S/Sgt. Don Allen-c/c
Sgt. Paul Fox-ac/c

| Sqn | Date | Claims | Location | A/C |
|---|---|---|---|---|
| 334th | December 11, 1943 | Me-109 dest(air) | Leeuwarden | P-47 |
| | January 29, 1944 | FW-190 dest(air) | Hasselt | P-47 |
| | February 6 | FW-190 dam(air) | W/Paris | P-47 |
| | February 10 | FW-190 dest(air) | Lingen | P-47 |
| | March 8 | Me-109 dest(air) | Stendal | P-51 |
| | March 21 | (2)FW-190 dest(grd) | Bordeaux | P-51 |
| | March 27 | Ju-52 dest(grd) | Cazaux A/F | P-51 |
| | | Ju-88 dest(grd) | see above | P-51 |
| | | Ju-88 dam(grd) | see above | P-51 |
| | April 5 | (.33)He-111 dest(grd)[*] | Brandenburg-Briest | P-51 |
| | | FW-190 dam(grd) | see above | P-51 |
| | | Ju-52 dam(grd) | see above | P-51 |
| | April 18 | (.33)Me-109 dest(air)[**] | Fassberg A/F | P-51 |

4.33-0-1 air
4.33-3 ground

[*] - shared with Lt. L.R. Pierce and Lt. H.J. Blanchfield of the 334th Ftr Sqn
[**] - shared with Lt. N. Megura and Lt. G.C. Siems of the 334th Ftr Sqn

**Frisch, Robert J., Lt.** (6) Cincinnati, OH
503rd Ftr Sqn/339th Ftr Grp October 1944-April 1945
53 missions

P-51D D7-J 44-14118 "Worry Bird"
P-51D D7-J 44-73287

| Sqn | Date | Claims | Location | A/C |
|---|---|---|---|---|
| 503rd | March 2, 1945 | Me-109 dam(air) | E/Magdeburg | P-51 |
| | April 10 | (4)Ju-88 dest(grd) | N/Neuruppin | P-51 |
| | | Ju-88 dam(grd) | see above | P-51 |
| | | u/i a/c dam(grd) | see above | P-51 |
| | April 16 | Me-109 dam(grd) | Kralupy | P-51 |
| | April 17 | Me-262 dest(grd) | Klatovy | P-51 |
| | | Ju-88 dest(grd) | Klatovy | P-51 |

0-0-1 air
6-3 ground

**Fryer, Earl R., Capt.** (5) Boyertown, PA
38th Ftr Sqn/55th Ftr Grp May 1944-November 8, 1944(KIA)
Hit by flak in the Hilversam area.

P-51D CG-Z 44-13804 "Spunktown"
T/Sgt. Prevost-c/c

| Sqn | Date | Claims | Location | A/C |
|---|---|---|---|---|
| 38th | August 24, 1944 | Ju-88 dest(grd) | Burg A/F | P-51 |
| | September 11 | (3)Me-109 dest(air) | S/Erfurt | P-51 |
| | November 2 | FW-190 dest(air) | Merseburg | P-51 |

4-0-0 air
1-0 ground

**Furr, William W., Lt.** (6.5) Raleigh, NC
328th Ftr Sqn/352nd Ftr Grp February 1944-June 5, 1944(MIA)
Suffered m/f near Merville.

P-47D PE-R 42-8563
P-51B PE-R 42-106460 "Lois"

| Sqn | Date | Claims | Location | A/C |
|---|---|---|---|---|
| 328th | April 8, 1944 | Me-210 dest(grd) | Quackenbruck | P-47 |
| | April 15 | Me-110 dest(grd) | Diepholz | P-51 |
| | May 21 | Ju-52 dest(grd) | Alt Ruppin | P-51 |
| | May 24 | Me-109 dest(air) | W/Perleburg | P-51 |
| | May 27 | Me-109 dest(air) | S/Strasbourg | P-51 |
| | | Me-109 dam(air) | S/Strasbourg | P-51 |
| | May 30 | (1.5)FW-190 dest(air)[*] | Schoningen | P-51 |

3.5-0-1 air
3-0 ground

[*] - shared with an unknown pilot

**Gabreski, Francis S., LtCol.** (31.5) Oil City, PA
61st Ftr Sqn/56th Ftr Grp February 1943-January 1944
HdQts/56th Ftr Grp January 1944-April 1944
61st Ftr Sqn/56th Ftr Grp April 1944-July 20, 1944(POW)
Hit the ground while strafing at Bassenheim.
Earlier flew in the PTO with the 45th Ftr Sqn, 7th Air Force, Hawaii.
166 missions (includes 13 while on D.S. with 315 Sqn, RAF)

P-47D HV-A 42-7871
P-47D HV-A 42-75510
P-47D HV-A 42-25864
P-47D HV-A 42-26418
S/Sgt. Ralph H. Safford-c/c
Sgt. Felix Shacki-ac/c
Sgt. Giuseppe DiFranza-arm.

| Sqn | Date | Claims | Location | A/C |
|---|---|---|---|---|
| 61st | May 15, 1943 | FW-190 dam(air) | NE Rotterdam | P-47 |
| | August 24 | FW-190 dest(air) | Dreux | P-47 |
| | September 3 | FW-190 dest(air) | St. Germain | P-47 |
| | November 5 | FW-190 dest(air) | S/Rheine | P-47 |
| | | FW-190 dam(air) | S/Rheine | P-47 |
| | November 26 | (2)Me-110 dest(air) | SE Oldenburg | P-47 |
| | November 29 | (2)Me-109 dest(air) | NE Bremen | P-47 |
| | December 11 | Me-110 dest(air) | Esens | P-47 |
| HdQts | January 29, 1944 | Me-110 dest(air) | S/Coblenz | P-47 |
| | January 30 | Me-109 dest(air) | Lingen | P-47 |
| | | Me-210 dest(air) | Lingen | P-47 |
| | February 20 | (2)Me-110 dest(air) | W/Hanover | P-47 |
| | | Me-110 dam(air) | W/Hanover | P-47 |
| | February 22 | FW-190 dest(air) | N/Lippstadt | P-47 |
| | | Do-217 dest(grd) | Eindhoven | P-47 |
| | March 8 | FW-190 dest(grd) | Weinstorf A/F | P-47 |
| | | (4)FW-190 dam(grd) | Weinstorf A/F | P-47 |
| | March 16 | (2)FW-190 dest(air) | Nancy | P-47 |
| | March 27 | (2)Me-109 dest(air) | NE Nantes | P-47 |
| | April 9 | (.5)u/i a/c dest(grd)[*] | Schleswig | P-47 |
| 61st | April 24 | He-111 dam(grd) | Frieburg A/F | P-47 |
| | May 8 | Me-109 dest(air) | Celle | P-47 |
| | May 22 | (3)FW-190 dest(air) | Hoperhofen A/F | P-47 |
| | | FW-190 prob(air) | Hoperhofen A/F | P-47 |
| | June 7 | Me-109 dest(air) | E/Dreux | P-47 |
| | | FW-190 dest(air) | E/Dreux | P-47 |
| | June 12 | (2)Me-109 dest(air) | Evreux | P-47 |
| | June 27 | Me-109 dest(air) | La Perth | P-47 |
| | July 5 | Me-109 dest(air) | Evreux | P-47 |
| | July 20 | He-111 dest(grd) | Bassenheim | P-47 |

28-1-3 air
3.5-5 ground

[*] - shared with Lt. H.L. Matthew of the 63rd Ftr Sqn, 56th Ftr Grp

**Gailer, Frank L., Jr., Lt.** (6.5) Long Island, NY
363rd Ftr Sqn/357th Ftr Grp August 1944-November 27, 1944(POW)
Hit by a P-51 near Magdeburg.
45 missions, 187:30 hours

P-51B B6- "Jeesil Peesil Mommy"
P-51K B6-A 44-11331 "Expectant"

| Sqn | Date | Claims | Location | A/C |
|---|---|---|---|---|
| 363rd | September 13, 1944 | (.5)Me-109 dest(air)[*] | S/Kassel | P-51 |
| | September 18 | (.5)FW-190 dest(air)[**] | Arnheim | P-51 |
| | September 19 | (.5)Me-109 dest(air)[@] | W/Arnheim | P-51 |
| | October 7 | FW-190 dest(air) | SW Zeitz | P-51 |
| | October 12 | Me-109 dest(air) | Hanover | P-51 |

| | | | |
|---|---|---|---|
| November 18 | Me-109 dest(grd) | Mengen A/F | P-51 |
| November 27 | (2)FW-190 dest(air) | SE Magdeburg | P-51 |

5.5-0-0 air
1-0 ground

* - shared with Lt. C.E. Yeager of the 363rd Ftr Sqn
** - shared with Capt. T.E. Hughes of the 363rd Ftr Sqn
@ - shared with Lt. H.O. Hand of the 363rd Ftr Sqn

**Galer, Donald V., Lt.** (5) Centralia, IL
354th Ftr Sqn/355th Ftr Grp November 1944-EOW

P-51D WR-O "Cherraine"

| *Sqn* | *Date* | *Claims* | *Location* | *A/C* |
|---|---|---|---|---|
| 354th | April 10, 1945 | u/i a/c dest(grd) | Memmingen | P-51 |
| | April 13 | He-111 dest(grd) | Husum | P-51 |
| | | Ju-88 dest(grd) | Husum | P-51 |
| | | u/i a/c dam(grd) | Husum | P-51 |
| | April 16 | Ju-88 dest(grd) | Eger A/F | P-51 |
| | | u/i a/c dest(grd) | Eger A/F | P-51 |
| | | (2)u/i a/c dam(grd) | Autobahn | P-51 |
| | | Me-109 dam(grd) | Autobahn | P-51 |
| | | Me-410 dam(grd) | Autobahn | P-51 |

0-0-0 air
5-5 ground

**Gallup, Kenneth W., LtCol.** (11) Clint, TX
HdQts/353rd Ftr Grp May 1944-June 1944
350th Ftr Sqn/353rd Ftr Grp June 1944-September 1944
HdQts/353rd Ftr Grp September 1944-November 1944
70 missions, 270 hours

P-47D LH-N 42-22275 "Rat-A-Dat"
P-47D LH-N 42-26525 "Rat-A-Dat 2"
P-47D LH-N 44-19562 "Rat-A-Dat 3"
P-47D LH-N 42-26634 "Rat-A-Dat"

| *Sqn* | *Date* | *Claims* | *Location* | *A/C* |
|---|---|---|---|---|
| HdQts | May 28, 1944 | Me-109 dest(air) | Gutersloh | P-47 |
| | June 8 | FW-190 dest(grd) | Le Mans | P-47 |
| | | FW-190 dam(grd) | Le Mans | P-47 |
| | June 12 | (2)Me-109 dest(air) | SW Paris | P-47 |
| 350th | June 27 | Me-109 dest(air) | Epernay | P-47 |
| | July 6 | Me-109 dest(air) | SW Limay | P-47 |
| | August 4 | Me-109 dest(air) | Neunkirchen | P-47 |
| | | Me-109 prob(air) | Neunkirchen | P-47 |
| | August 5 | Me-109 dest(air) | Rheine | P-47 |
| | August 11 | u/i a/c dest(grd) | Maraville | P-47 |
| | August 28 | (1.5)Fi-156 dest(air)* | Verdun | P-47 |
| | | (.5)He-111 dest(air)** | SE Arlon | P-47 |

9-1-0 air
2-1 ground

* - shared with Lt. J.B. Brooks of the 350th Ftr Sqn
** - shared with Lt. J.L. Schilt of the 350th Ftr Sqn

**Gansberg, Raymond H., Capt.** (6.5) Downers Grove, IL
361st Ftr Sqn/356th Ftr Grp March 1943-December 5, 1944(KIA)
Last seen in a fight northeast of Berlin
90 missions, 297:50 hours

P-47D QI-P 42-8440
P-47D QI-P 42-76177
P-51D QI-P 44-15109
S/Sgt. Edward S. Poplawski-c/c

| *Sqn* | *Date* | *Claims* | *Location* | *A/C* |
|---|---|---|---|---|
| 361st | January 24, 1944 | (.5)FW-190 dest(air)* | Ghent-Bruges | P-47 |
| | April 11 | (2)He-111 dest(grd) | Gifhorn | P-47 |
| | | (2)Ju-88 dest(grd) | Gifhorn | P-47 |
| | April 23 | He-111 dam(grd) | Hagenau | P-47 |
| | May 19 | Me-109 dest(air) | Quackenbruck | P-47 |
| | June 11 | Me-109 dest(air) | SW Bernay | P-47 |

2.5-0-0 air
4-1 ground

* - shared with Lt. M.F. Erickson of the 361st Ftr Sqn

**Garlich, Robert L., Lt.** (6.5) St. Louis, MO
357th Ftr Sqn/355th Ftr Grp November 1944-September 1945

P-51D OS-S 44-13734 "Lucious Lu"
P-51D OS-S 44-14966 "Lucious Lu II"
S/Sgt. William House-c/c

| *Sqn* | *Date* | *Claims* | *Location* | *A/C* |
|---|---|---|---|---|
| 357th | January 15, 1945 | u/i a/c dam(grd) | Landsberg | P-51 |
| | February 23 | Me-163 dest(grd) | Neuburg | P-51 |
| | April 10 | (1.5)Do-24 dest(grd)* | Muritz Lake | P-51 |
| | | He-111 dest(grd) | Rechlin/Larz | P-51 |
| | April 13 | (2)He-111 dest(grd) | Schleswig | P-51 |
| | April 16 | Ju-87 dest(grd) | Eger A/F | P-51 |

0-0-0 air
6.5-1 ground

* - shared with F/O C.R. Albright of the 56th Ftr Grp

**Garrison, Vermont, Lt.** (7.58) Mt. Victory, KY
336th Ftr Sqn/4th Ftr Grp September 1943-March 3, 1944(POW)
Hit by flak near Boulogne.

P-47D VF-H 42-74663
P-51B VF-H 43-6871

| *Sqn* | *Date* | *Claims* | *Location* | *A/C* |
|---|---|---|---|---|
| 336th | December 16, 1943 | (.33)Ju-88 dest(air)* | E/Zuider Zee | P-47 |
| | January 7, 1944 | FW-190 dam(air) | La Chateau | P-47 |
| | January 14 | (2)FW-190 dest(air) | Compiegne | P-47 |
| | January 31 | Me-109 dest(air) | Gilze-Rijen | P-47 |
| | February 6 | FW-190 dest(air) | Beauvais-Marigny | P-47 |
| | February 10 | Me-109 dest(air) | Dummer Lake | P-47 |
| | February 20 | FW-190 dam(air) | Malmedy | P-47 |
| | February 25 | FW-190 dest(air) | Luxembourg | P-47 |
| | February 28 | (.25)Ju-88 dest(grd)** | Soissons | P-51 |
| | March 3 | FW-190 dest(air) | NW Berlin | P-51 |
| | | Me-110 prob(air) | NW Berlin | P-51 |
| | | Me-110 dam(air) | NW Berlin | P-51 |

7.33-1-3 air
0.25-0 ground

* - shared with Capt. D.S. Gentile and Lt. L.H. Norley of the 336th Ftr Sqn
** - shared with Capt. D.W. Beeson, Lt. N. Megura, and Lt. W.B. Smith of the 334th Ftr Sqn, 4th Ftr Grp

**Gatterdam, Richard P., Maj.** (6.2) San Francisco, CA
79th Ftr Sqn/20th Ftr Grp October 1942-November 1944
55th Ftr Sqn/20th Ftr Grp November 1944-March 1945
91 missions, 430:10 hours

P-38J MC-G 42-67491
P-38J MC-G 42-68140 "Puddin"
P-51D MC-G 44-14003
P-51D KI-G 44-15327 "Puddin"
T/Sgt. Joseph Taylor-c/c(79th)

| *Sqn* | *Date* | *Claims* | *Location* | *A/C* |
|---|---|---|---|---|
| 79th | January 29, 1944 | FW-190 prob(air) | Coblenz | P-38 |
| | January 30 | (.5)Me-210 dest(air)* | Brunswick | P-38 |
| | April 8 | (.2)He-177 dest(air)** | Salzwedel | P-38 |
| | October 6 | (2.5)He-115 dest(grd)@ | Bad Berg-Dievenow | P-51 |
| | November 2 | Me-109 dest(air) | W/Merseburg | P-51 |
| 55th | January 14, 1945 | (2)Me-109 dest(air) | Perleburg | P-51 |

3.7-1-0 air
2.5-0 ground

* - shared with Lt. J.T. Martin of the 79th Ftr Sqn
** - shared with Maj. R.C. Franklin and Capt. D.E. Anderson of the 79th Ftr Sqn and Capt. E.C. Hedlund and Lt. R.H. Dettre of the 474th Ftr Grp, 9th Air Force
@ - shared with Lt. M.G. Ingebrigsten of the 79th Ftr Sqn

**Gentile, Don S., Capt.** (27.83) Piqua, OH
336th Ftr Sqn/4th Ftr Grp September 1942-April 1944
Earlier flew with 133 Sqn, RAF, and claimed 2 kills; a FW-190 and Ju-88 on August 19, 1942.
185 missions, 387 hours

Spitfire MD-T BL255 "Buckeye Don"
P-47D VF-T 42-8659 "Donnie Boy"
P-51B VF-T 43-6913 "Shangri-La"
S/Sgt. Lawrence Krantz-c/c
S/Sgt. John Ferra-ac/c
Sgt. J. Lammering-arm.

| *Sqn* | *Date* | *Claims* | *Location* | *A/C* |
|---|---|---|---|---|
| 336th | March 12, 1943 | FW-190 dam(air) | Audruieg | Spit |
| | August 16 | Me-109 dam(air) | Paris | P-47 |

| December 16 | (.33)Ju-88 dest(air)* | E/Zuider Zee | P-47 |
|---|---|---|---|
| January 5, 1944 | FW-190 dest(air) | W/Tours | P-47 |
| January 14 | (2)FW-190 dest(air) | Compiegne | P-47 |
| February 25 | FW-190 dest(air) | SE Luxembourg | P-47 |
| March 3 | (2)FW-190 dest(air) | Wittenburg | P-51 |
| | Do-217 dam(air) | Wittenburg | P-51 |
| March 8 | (3.5)Me-109 dest(air)** | Berlin | P-51 |
| March 18 | FW-190 dest(air) | Augsburg | P-51 |
| March 23 | (2)Me-109 dest(air) | Munster | P-51 |
| March 27 | (2)Me-110 dest(grd) | Cazaux A/F | P-51 |
| March 29 | (2)FW-190 dest(air) | Brunswick | P-51 |
| | Me-109 dest(air) | Brunswick | P-51 |
| April 1 | Me-109 dest(air) | SW Stuttgart | P-51 |
| April 5 | (3)Ju-88 dest(grd) | Stendal | P-51 |
| | (.5)Ju-88 dest(grd)@ | Stendal | P-51 |
| | (.5)Ju-88 dest(grd)@@ | Stendal | P-51 |
| April 8 | (3)FW-190 dest(air) | Ruhrburg | P-51 |

19.83-0-3 air
6-0 ground

* - shared with Lt. V. Garrison and Lt. L.H. Norley of the 336th Ftr Sqn
** - shared with Lt. J.T. Godfrey of the 336th Ftr Sqn
@ - shared with Lt. J.T. Godfrey of the 336th Ftr Sqn
@@ - shared with Maj. J.A. Goodson of the 336th Ftr Sqn

**Gerard, Francis R., Capt.** (8) Lyndhurst, NJ
503rd Ftr Sqn/339th Ftr Grp States-April 1945
80 missions, 420 hours

P-51B D7-U 42-106907
P-51B D7-U 42-106798
P-51D D7-U 44-13808
P-51D D7-U 44-15003

| *Sqn* | *Date* | *Claims* | *Location* | *A/C* |
|---|---|---|---|---|
| 503rd | August 16, 1944 | Me-109 dest(air) | Gotha | P-51 |
| | September 11 | (3)Me-109 dest(air) | Annaberg | P-51 |
| | | FW-190 dest(air) | Annaberg | P-51 |
| | | Me-109 dam(air) | Annaberg | P-51 |
| | March 2, 1945 | (2)Me-109 dest(air) | E/Magdeburg | P-51 |
| | | Me-109 dam(air) | E/Magdeburg | P-51 |
| | March 18 | FW-190 dest(air) | Dummer Lake | P-51 |

8-0-2 air
0-0 ground

**Gerick, Steven, Capt.** (7) Pittsburgh, PA
61st Ftr Sqn/56th Ftr Grp December 1943-August 1944

P-47D HV-O 42-26024 "Tally Ho Chaps!"
S/Sgt. Paul H. Blandford-c/c
Sgt. Fred R. Nelson-arm.

| *Sqn* | *Date* | *Claims* | *Location* | *A/C* |
|---|---|---|---|---|
| 61st | February 22, 1944 | Me-110 dam(air) | E/Paderborn | P-47 |
| | March 15 | Me-109 dest(air) | Dummer Lake | P-47 |
| | | Me-109 dam(air) | Dummer Lake | P-47 |
| | April 25 | Me-109 dest(grd) | Metz | P-47 |
| | May 12 | FW-190 dest(air) | NW Marburg | P-47 |
| | | Me-109 dam(air) | NW Marburg | P-47 |
| | June 7 | Me-109 dest(air) | SE Houdan | P-47 |
| | | Me-109 dam(air) | SE Houdan | P-47 |
| | June 12 | (2)Me-109 dest(air) | Evreux | P-47 |
| | | (4)Me-109 dam(air) | Evreux | P-47 |
| | June 27 | Me-109 dam(air) | Esternay | P-47 |
| | July 7 | u/i a/c dest(grd) | Peine A/F | P-47 |

5-0-9 air
2-0 ground

**Gevorkian, Samuel D., Capt.** (9) Pasadena, CA
338th Ftr Sqn/55th Ftr Grp July 1944-August 26, 1944(MIA-E)
Ran out of fuel near Truc Vert.
338th Ftr Sqn/55th Ftr Grp October 1944-August 8, 1945(KIAc)

P-51D CL-F 44-14156
S/Sgt. Curtis H. Payne-c/c
Sgt. Jack Trout-ac/c

| *Sqn* | *Date* | *Claims* | *Location* | *A/C* |
|---|---|---|---|---|
| 338th | November 2, 1944 | Me-109 dest(air) | NW Leipzig | P-51 |
| | December 24 | (.5)Me-109 dest(air)* | Friedburg | P-51 |
| | | (.5)FW-190 dest(air)* | Friedburg | P-51 |
| | April 10, 1945 | (2)Ju-88 dest(grd) | Burg A/F | P-51 |
| | | FW-190 dest(grd) | Burg A/F | P-51 |
| | April 16 | (3)FW-190 dest(grd) | N/Landshut | P-51 |
| | | (3)FW-190 dam(grd) | N/Landshut | P-51 |

2-0-0 air
6-3 ground

* - both shared with Lt. K.A. Lashbrook of the 338th Ftr Sqn

**Gibbs, Richard G., Lt.** (5) Nantucket, MA
343rd Ftr Sqn/55th Ftr Grp January 1945-EOW
42 missions, 192 hours
P-51D CY-Q 44-15314

| *Sqn* | *Date* | *Claims* | *Location* | *A/C* |
|---|---|---|---|---|
| 343rd | February 3, 1945 | FW-190 dest(air) | Boizenburg | P-51 |
| | | Ju-88 dest(air) | Boizenburg | P-51 |
| | April 10 | He-111 dest(grd) | Burg A/F | P-51 |
| | | Ju-87 dam(grd) | Burg A/F | P-51 |
| | April 17 | (2)FW-190 dest(air) | Kamenz A/F | P-51 |

4-0-0 air
1-1 ground

**Gilbert, Olin E., LtCol.** (10.5) Collinsville, IL
83rd Ftr Sqn/78th Ftr Grp November 1943-July 1944
HdQts/78th Ftr Grp July 1944-August 28, 1944(MIA-E)
Hit by flak near Valenciennes.
HdQts/78th Ftr Grp December 1944-March 1945
HdQts/66th Ftr Wg March 1945-EOW

P-47D HL-X 42-25837
P-47D HL-X 42-26449
P-51D HL-A 44-63216 "Anne-Nihilator"

| *Sqn* | *Date* | *Claims* | *Location* | *A/C* |
|---|---|---|---|---|
| 83rd | April 30, 1944 | FW-190 dest(air) | SW Paris | P-47 |
| | June 13 | FW-190 dest(air) | Orleans | P-47 |
| HdQts | August 10 | He-111 dest(grd) | Chateau Salines | P-47 |
| | | u/i a/c dest(grd) | Chateau Salines | P-47 |
| HdQts | April 16, 1945 | (3)FW-190 dest(grd) | Pilzen/Prague | P-51 |
| | | (1.5)Ju-87 dest(grd)* | see above | P-51 |
| | | He-111 dest(grd) | see above | P-51 |
| | | Ju-52 dest(grd) | see above | P-51 |
| | | (2)u/i a/c dam(grd) | see above | P-51 |
| | | FW-190 dam(grd) | see above | P-51 |

2-0-0 air
8.5-3 ground

* - shared with Lt. D.J. Henahan of the 82nd Ftr Sqn, 78th Ftr Grp

**Gilbertson, Merle J., Maj.** (6.83) Flora, ND
77th Ftr Sqn/20th Ftr Grp February 1943-EOW
100 missions, 434:35 hours

P-38J LC-P 42-67819
P-38J LC-P 42-68155 "Diamond Lil"
P-51D LC-A 44-14822 "Sad Sack"
T/Sgt. Carl W. Tucker-c/c(P)
Sgt. Milton J. McAtee-ac/c(P)
Sgt. Calvin M. Marin-ac/c(P)
Sgt. Barney Yonchitis-arm.(P)

| *Sqn* | *Date* | *Claims* | *Location* | *A/C* |
|---|---|---|---|---|
| 77th | January 30, 1944 | Do-217 dam(air) | Osnabruck | P-38 |
| | February 5 | (.33)He-111 dest(air)* | Bourges A/F | P-38 |
| | August 5 | Me-109 dest(air) | NW Hamburg | P-51 |
| | August 16 | Me-109 dest(air) | Mulhausen | P-51 |
| | January 14, 1945 | (.5)Me-109 dest(air)** | Perleburg | P-51 |
| | February 9 | (3)FW-190 dest(grd) | Esperstadt A/F | P-51 |
| | | Me-110 dam(grd) | Esperstadt A/F | P-51 |
| | April 16 | u/i a/c dest(grd) | Cham A/F | P-51 |

2.83-0-1 air
4-1 ground

* - shared with Lt. R.L. Frakes and Lt. J.M. Morris of the 77th Ftr Sqn
** - shared with Lt. J.P. Starke of the 77th Ftr Sqn

**Giller, Edward B., Maj.** (9) White Hall, IL
343rd Ftr Sqn/55th Ftr Grp February 1943-June 1945
115 missions, 420 hours

P-38J CY-G "The Millie G"
P-38J CY-G "The Millie G"
P-51D CY-G 44-14895 "The Millie G"

P-51D CY-G 44-15701 "The Millie G"
P-51D CY-G 44-63204 "The Millie G"
P-51D CY-G 44-72123 "The Millie G"
S/Sgt. James T. Marine-c/c
Sgt. John T. Grodoski-ac/c
Sgt. McGee-ac/c

| *Sqn* | *Date* | *Claims* | *Location* | *A/C* |
|---|---|---|---|---|
| 343rd | November 13, 1943 | Ju-88 dest(air) | W/Bremen | P-38 |
| | February 25, 1944 | Me-410 dest(air) | SE Augsburg | P-38 |
| | April 9, 1945 | Me-262 dest(air) | Munich | P-51 |
| | | He-111 dest(grd) | Munich-Brunnthal | P-51 |
| | | Me-410 dest(grd) | see above | P-51 |
| | | Me-262 dest(grd) | see above | P-51 |
| | | Me-410 dam(grd) | see above | P-51 |
| | April 16 | He-111 dest(grd) | Munich-Brunnthal | P-51 |
| | | Me-109 dest(grd) | see above | P-51 |
| | | Ju-52 dest(grd) | see above | P-51 |
| | | Ju-88 dam(grd) | see above | P-51 |

3-0-0 air
6-2 ground

**Gladych, Bolek M., Maj.** (11) Poland
61st Ftr Sqn/56th Ftr Grp February 1944-May 1945
Earlier flew with the PAF and RAF claiming at least 10 kills.

P-47D HV-M "Pengie"
P-47D HV-M 42-75224 "Pengie II"
P-47D HV-M 42-25836 "Pengie III"
P-47M HV-M 44-21127
S/Sgt. Richard C. Moffat-c/c

| *Sqn* | *Date* | *Claims* | *Location* | *A/C* |
|---|---|---|---|---|
| 61st | February 21, 1944 | (2)Me-109 dest(air) | Zuider Zee | P-47 |
| | March 6 | Me-109 dest(grd) | Vechta | P-47 |
| | March 8 | FW-190 dest(air) | Dummer Lake | P-47 |
| | | (3)FW-190 dam(grd) | Dummer Lake | P-47 |
| | March 27 | Me-109 dest(air) | S/Angars | P-47 |
| | April 25 | FW-190 dam(grd) | Metz | P-47 |
| | | Ju-88 dam(grd) | Metz | P-47 |
| | | u/i a/c dam(grd) | Metz | P-47 |
| | June 6 | Me-109 dest(air) | Croisy | P-47 |
| | June 7 | Me-109 dest(air) | SE Houdan | P-47 |
| | July 5 | Me-109 dest(air) | Evreux | P-47 |
| | August 12 | Ju-88 dest(air) | Cambrai | P-47 |
| | September 21 | (2)FW-190 dest(air) | E/Arnheim | P-47 |

10-0-0 air
1-6 ground

**Gleason, George W., Capt.** (14.5) Montrose, CA
434th Ftr Sqn/479th Ftr Grp May 1944-March 1945

P-38J L2-H
P-51D L2-H 44-14740 "Hot Toddy"
S/Sgt. Alfred M. Perdue-c/c
Sgt. Coakes-ac/c

| *Sqn* | *Date* | *Claims* | *Location* | *A/C* |
|---|---|---|---|---|
| 434th | August 18, 1944 | FW-190 dest(grd) | Nancy/Essey | P-38 |
| | | (.5)He-111 dest(grd)[*] | see above | P-38 |
| | | (.5)He-111 dest(grd)[*] | see above | P-38 |
| | | (.5)Ju-88 dest(grd)[**] | see above | P-38 |
| | | FW-190 dam(grd) | see above | P-38 |
| | September 26 | (3)Me-109 dest(air) | SW Munster | P-38 |
| | | Me-109 dam(air) | SW Munster | P-38 |
| | September 28 | Me-109 dest(air) | W/Halberstadt | P-51 |
| | | FW-190 dest(air) | W/Halberstadt | P-51 |
| | December 23 | (2)FW-190 dest(air) | SE Bonn | P-51 |
| | | FW-190 dam(air) | SE Bonn | P-51 |
| | December 25 | (3)FW-190 dest(air) | SW Bonn | P-51 |
| | February 9, 1945 | Me-109 dest(air) | SE Magdeburg | P-51 |
| | | FW-190 dest(air) | SE Magdeburg | P-51 |

12-0-2 air
2.5-1 ground

[*] - both shared with Lt. C.F. Monsell of the 435th Ftr Sqn, 479th Ftr Grp
[**] - shared with Lt. H.W. Detlefson of the 435th Ftr Sqn

**Glover, Fred W., Maj.** (24.83) Asheville, NC
336th Ftr Sqn/4th Ftr Grp February 1944-April 30, 1944(MIA-E)
Hit by flak near Valence Airfield.
336th Ftr Sqn/4th Ftr Grp June 1944-June 1945

P-51B VF-C 43-12214 "Rebel Queen"
P-51D VF-B 44-14787
P-51D VF-B 44-63153
S/Sgt. John Wilson-c/c(C)
Sgt. Norman Meyers-ac/c(C)
S/Sgt. Metcaffe-c/c(B)
Sgt. Edwin Marcotte-ac/c(B)

| *Sqn* | *Date* | *Claims* | *Location* | *A/C* |
|---|---|---|---|---|
| 336th | March 6, 1944 | FW-190 prob(air) | W/Berlin | P-51 |
| | March 16 | (2)Me-110 dest(air) | Kaufburen | P-51 |
| | March 29 | FW-190 dest(air) | Brunswick | P-51 |
| | | (.33)He-111 dest(air)[*] | Brunswick | P-51 |
| | April 5 | (2)Ju-52 dest(grd) | Stendal | P-51 |
| | | (2)Ju-88 dam(grd) | Stendal | P-51 |
| | April 8 | FW-190 dest(air) | Ulzen | P-51 |
| | April 15 | Me-110 dest(grd) | Hagenow | P-51 |
| | | u/i a/c dam(grd) | Hagenow | P-51 |
| | April 30 | (1.5)u/i a/c dest(grd)[**] | Valence A/F | P-51 |
| | August 5 | Me-109 dest(air) | Gardelegen | P-51 |
| | August 6 | Me-109 dest(air) | SE Berlin | P-51 |
| | November 2 | Me-163 dest(air) | E/Leipzig | P-51 |
| | November 21 | (3)Me-109 dest(air) | W/Merseburg | P-51 |
| | December 25 | FW-190 dest(air) | SW Coblenz | P-51 |
| | January 16, 1945 | (2)Ju-87 dest(grd) | Neuhausen | P-51 |
| | | FW-190 dest(grd) | Neuhausen | P-51 |
| | February 22 | Me-109 dest(grd) | Halberstadt | P-51 |
| | | Do-217 dest(grd) | Halberstadt | P-51 |
| | February 27 | (2)Me-109 dest(grd) | Weimar | P-51 |
| | | FW-190 dest(grd) | Weimar | P-51 |
| | April 17 | Ju-87 dest(grd) | Pilzen | P-51 |

10.33-1-0 air
14.5-3 ground

[*] - shared with Lt. J.T. Godfrey of the 336th Ftr Sqn and Maj. G. Carpenter of the 335th Ftr Sqn, 4th Ftr Grp
[**] - shared with Lt. H.H. Frederick of the 336th Ftr Sqn

**Godfrey, John T., Maj.** (30) Woonsocket, RI
336th Ftr Sqn/4th Ftr Grp September 1943-August 24, 1944(POW)
Hit by fire from a P-51 at Nordhausen.
Earlier served with the RCAF

P-47D VF-P 42-7884 "Reggie's Reply"
P-51B VF-P 43-6765
P-51B VF-P 42-106730 "Reggie's Reply"
S/Sgt. Lawrence Krantz-c/c
Sgt. Walter Smith-ac/c

| *Sqn* | *Date* | *Claims* | *Location* | *A/C* |
|---|---|---|---|---|
| 336th | November 29, 1943 | Me-109 prob(air) | Bremen | P-47 |
| | December 1 | Me-109 dest(air) | Ruhr Valley | P-47 |
| | | Me-109 dam(air) | Ruhr Valley | P-47 |
| | December 22 | (1.5)Me-109 dest(air)[*] | W/Munster | P-47 |
| | March 2, 1944 | FW-190 dam(air) | SW Coblenz | P-51 |
| | March 6 | Me-109 dest(air) | N/Hanover | P-51 |
| | | FW-190 dam(air) | N/Hanover | P-51 |
| | March 8 | (2.5)Me-109 dest(air)[**] | Berlin | P-51 |
| | March 16 | Me-110 dest(air) | Kaufburen | P-51 |
| | March 23 | Me-109 dest(air) | Munster | P-51 |
| | March 29 | FW-190 dest(air) | Brunswick | P-51 |
| | | (.33)He-111 dest(air)[@] | Brunswick | P-51 |
| | | FW-190 prob(air) | Brunswick | P-51 |
| | April 5 | (1.5)Ju-88 dest(grd)[@@] | Stendal | P-51 |
| | | Me-110 dest(grd) | Stendal | P-51 |
| | | (2)Me-110 dam(grd) | Stendal | P-51 |
| | | (2)Ju-88 dam(grd) | Stendal | P-51 |
| | | Ju-52 dam(grd) | Stendal | P-51 |
| | April 9 | Me-410 dest(grd) | Lingen/Plantlunn | P-51 |
| | | (.33)Ju-88 dest(grd)[#] | see above | P-51 |
| | | (.33)Ju-88 dest(grd)[#] | see above | P-51 |
| | April 22 | (3)Me-109 dest(air) | SW Kassel | P-51 |
| | April 24 | FW-190 dest(air) | NW Ludwigshafen | P-51 |
| | | FW-190 dam(air) | NW Ludwigshafen | P-51 |
| | April 29 | Do-217 dest(grd) | Nordhausen | P-51 |
| | | (.5)Ju-52 dest(grd)[##] | see above | P-51 |
| | | (.5)Ju-52 dest(grd)[&] | see above | P-51 |
| | | Do-217 dam(grd) | see above | P-51 |
| | April 30 | (.5)Do-24 dest(grd)[&&] | Lyon Anchorage | P-51 |
| | August 5 | Me-109 dest(air) | N/Osnabruck | P-51 |
| | | (3)Ju-52 dest(grd) | SE Munden | P-51 |
| | | (3)Ju-52 dam(grd) | SE Munden | P-51 |
| | August 6 | Me-410 dest(air) | NE Berlin | P-51 |
| | | Me-109 dam(grd) | SE Berlin | P-51 |
| | August 24 | (4)Ju-52 dest(grd) | Nordhausen | P-51 |

16.33-2-4 air
13.67-10 ground

* - shared with Lt. V.H. Wynn of the 334th Ftr Sqn, 4th Ftr Grp
** - shared with Capt. D.S. Gentile of the 336th Ftr Sqn
@ - shared with F/O F.W. Glover of the 336th Ftr Sqn and Maj. G. Carpenter of the 335th Ftr Sqn, 4th Ftr Grp
@@ - shared with Capt. D.S. Gentile of the 336th Ftr Sqn
# - both shared with Capt. J.R. Happel and Lt. P.W. McKennon of the 335th Ftr Sqn
##-shared with Lt. I.E. Grounds of the 336th Ftr Sqn
& - shared with Lt. J.A. Patteeuw of the 336th Ftr Sqn
&& - shared with Lt. T.K. McDill of the 336th Ftr Sqn

**Golden, John T., Lt.** (5.5) Nicalestes, OK
434th Ftr Sqn/479th Ftr Grp September 1944-April 16, 1945(POW)
Hit by flak near Reichersberg

P-51D L2-G 44-14856 "Junior"

| *Sqn* | *Date* | *Claims* | *Location* | *A/C* |
|---|---|---|---|---|
| 434th | February 14, 1945 | Me-109 dest(air) | SW Berlin | P-51 |
| | February 20 | (1.5)He-111 dest(grd)[*] | Windleschenlaibach | P-51 |
| | | (.5)FW-190 dam(grd)[*] | see above | P-51 |
| | April 13 | u/i a/c dest(grd) | Ratzburger Lake | P-51 |
| | | (2)u/i a/c dam(grd) | Ratzburger Lake | P-51 |
| | April 16 | (3)u/i a/c dest(grd) | Reichersberg | P-51 |
| | | 1-0-0 air | | |
| | | 5.5-2.5 ground | | |

* - both shared with Lt. R.B. Kline of the 434th Ftr Sqn

**Goodman, Charles E., Lt.** (6.5) Alhambra, CA
328th Ftr Sqn/352nd Ftr Grp August 1944-EOW

P-51D PE-N 44-15530 "Family Ties"

| *Sqn* | *Date* | *Claims* | *Location* | *A/C* |
|---|---|---|---|---|
| 328th | November 2, 1944 | (3)Me-109 dest(air) | Merseburg | P-51 |
| | December 25 | Me-109 dest(air) | SW Coblenz | P-51 |
| | January 24, 1945 | (.5)Me-109 dest(air)[*] | Duren | P-51 |
| | February 22 | Me-262 dam(air) | Stendal | P-51 |
| | April 16 | (2)Me-109 dest(grd) | Ganacker | P-51 |
| | | (4)Me-109 dam(grd) | Ganacker | P-51 |
| | | 4.5-0-1 air | | |
| | | 2-4 ground | | |

* - shared with Lt. E.B. Dubay of the 328th Ftr Sqn

**Goodson, James A., Maj.** (29) Toronto, CA
336th Ftr Sqn/4th Ftr Grp October 1942-June 20, 1944(POW)
Hit by flak near Neubrandenburg.
Earlier flew with 43 and 133 Sqns, RAF

Spitfire MD-
P-47D VF-W 42-7959
P-51B VF-B 43-24848
P-51D VF-B 44-13300
P-51D VF-B 44-13303
S/Sgt. Manny Green-c/c(W)
S/Sgt. Robert L. Gilbert-c/c(B)
Sgt. William Cassidy-ac/c(B)

| *Sqn* | *Date* | *Claims* | *Location* | *A/C* |
|---|---|---|---|---|
| 336th | June 22, 1943 | FW-190 dest(air) | NW Hulst | P-47 |
| | August 16 | (2)FW-190 dest(air) | Paris | P-47 |
| | | FW-190 dam(air) | Paris | P-47 |
| | September 3 | FW-190 prob(air) | Paris | P-47 |
| | January 7, 1944 | (2)FW-190 dest(air) | Bethune | P-47 |
| | March 16 | (2)Me-110 dest(air) | Kaufburen | P-51 |
| | March 18 | (2)He-111 dest(grd) | Mannheim | P-51 |
| | March 21 | Me-410 dest(grd) | Evreux | P-51 |
| | March 23 | (2)Me-109 dest(air) | Munster | P-51 |
| | March 29 | Ju-88 dest(air) | NE Brunswick | P-51 |
| | | (2)Ju-88 dest(grd) | NE Brunswick | P-51 |
| | April 5 | FW-190 dest(grd) | Stendal | P-51 |
| | | Ju-52 dest(grd) | Stendal | P-51 |
| | | Ju-88 dest(grd) | Stendal | P-51 |
| | | (.5)Ju-88 dest(grd)[*] | Stendal | P-51 |
| | | (.5)Ju-88 dest(grd)[**] | Stendal | P-51 |
| | | (.5)Ju-88 dest(grd)[@] | Stendal | P-51 |
| | April 10 | (4.5)u/i a/c dest(grd)[@@] | Romorantin | P-51 |
| | | Hs-126 dest(grd) | Romorantin | P-51 |
| | April 23 | (2)Me-109 dest(air)[#] | Wienar Neustadt | P-51 |
| | May 12 | Me-109 dest(air) | Kassel | P-51 |
| | May 25 | FW-190 dest(air) | Strasbourg | P-51 |
| | | 14-1-1 air | | |
| | | 15-0 ground | | |

* - shared with Capt. D.S. Gentile of the 336th Ftr Sqn
** - shared with Lt. D.R. Emerson of the 336th Ftr Sqn
@ - shared with an unknown pilot
@@ - shared with Lt. C.H. Shilke of the 336th Ftr Sqn
# - claimed while on D.S. with the 15th Air Force, MTO

**Gordon, Ray C., Lt.** (6) Ligonier, IN
350th Ftr Sqn/353rd Ftr Grp December 1944-EOW
27 missions

P-51D LH-N 44-72292 "Miss Florida"

| *Sqn* | *Date* | *Claims* | *Location* | *A/C* |
|---|---|---|---|---|
| 350th | February 27, 1945 | (2)Me-110 dest(grd) | Rohrensee | P-51 |
| | | Ju-88 dest(grd) | see above | P-51 |
| | | (2)Me-110 dam(grd) | see above | P-51 |
| | | (2)Ju-88 dam(grd) | see above | P-51 |
| | April 16 | (3)FW-190 dest(grd) | Pocking | P-51 |
| | | 0-0-0 air | | |
| | | 6-4 ground | | |

**Gould, Clifford C., Lt.** (6) Pleasant Ridge, MI
38th Ftr Sqn/55th Ftr Grp May 1944-EOW

P-51D CG-
T/Sgt. Michael Kwiatkowski-c/c
Sgt. Victor Pribyl-ac/c

| *Sqn* | *Date* | *Claims* | *Location* | *A/C* |
|---|---|---|---|---|
| 38th | November 2, 1944 | Me-109 dest(air) | S/Merseburg | P-51 |
| | April 10, 1945 | (2)Me-109 dest(grd) | Wesendorf | P-51 |
| | | u/i a/c dest(grd) | Wesendorf | P-51 |
| | | Me-109 dam(grd) | Wesendorf | P-51 |
| | April 16 | (2)He-111 dest(grd) | N/Ansbach | P-51 |
| | | Me-109 dam(grd) | N/Ansbach | P-51 |
| | | 1-0-0 air | | |
| | | 5-2 ground | | |

**Gould, Norman D., Lt.** (5.5) Erie, PA
62nd Ftr Sqn/56th Ftr Grp October 1944-EOW

P-47M LM-O 44-21210

| *Sqn* | *Date* | *Claims* | *Location* | *A/C* |
|---|---|---|---|---|
| 62nd | November 18, 1944 | Me-109 dest(air) | E/Hanau | P-47 |
| | December 4 | Me-262 dest(grd) | Neuburg | P-47 |
| | | Me-262 dam(grd) | Neuburg | P-47 |
| | December 23 | FW-190 dest(air) | Euskirchen | P-47 |
| | January 21, 1945 | (.5)Ju-52 dest(grd)[*] | Huntingen | P-47 |
| | March 10 | Me-109 dest(air) | Remagen | P-47 |
| | March 14 | Ar-234 dest(air) | Coblenz | P-47 |
| | | 4-0-0 air | | |
| | | 1.5-1 ground | | |

* - shared with LtCol. L.C. Smith of the 62nd Ftr Sqn

**Graham, Gordon M., LtCol.** (16.5) Taft, OK
354th Ftr Sqn/355th Ftr Grp September 1944-June 1945
73 missions, 368:05 hours

P-51D WR-F 44-15255 "Down For Double"
S/Sgt. James J. Murray-c/c
Sgt. Meyer-ac/c
Cpl. Mike Simon-arm.

| *Sqn* | *Date* | *Claims* | *Location* | *A/C* |
|---|---|---|---|---|
| 354th | December 25, 1944 | FW-190 dest(air) | NW Trier | P-51 |
| | | FW-190 prob(air) | NW Trier | P-51 |
| | December 31 | (2)FW-190 dest(air) | SW Hamburg | P-51 |
| | January 14, 1945 | (2)FW-190 dest(air) | E/Meppen | P-51 |
| | | FW-190 dam(air) | E/Meppen | P-51 |
| | January 15 | Ju-188 dest(grd) | Kotha | P-51 |
| | | (2)u/i a/c dam(grd) | Oberpfaffenhofen | P-51 |
| | February 23 | Me-109 dest(grd) | Naumberg | P-51 |
| | | FW-190 dam(grd) | Landsberg | P-51 |
| | March 30 | (.5)Ju-52 dam(grd)[*] | Schleswig | P-51 |
| | | (.5)Ju-52 dam(grd)[*] | Schleswig | P-51 |
| | | (.5)Ju-52 dam(grd)[*] | Schleswig | P-51 |
| | April 8 | (2)Me-109 dest(air) | Oberpfaffenhofen | P-51 |
| | April 9 | (2.5)He-111 dest(grd)[**] | Memmingen | P-51 |
| | April 10 | Me-109 dest(grd) | Rechlin/Larz | P-51 |
| | | B-24 dest(grd) | see above | P-51 |

| | Date | Claims | Location | A/C |
|---|---|---|---|---|
| | | (3)Me-109 dam(grd) | see above | P-51 |
| | April 16 | (3)Ju-88 dest(grd) | Eger A/F | P-51 |

7-1-1 air
9.5-7.5 ground

* - all shared with Lt. D.B. Langley of the 354th Ftr Sqn
** - shared with Capt. A.S. White of the 354th Ftr Sqn

**Graham, Lindol F., Capt.** (5.5) Ridgewood, NJ
79th Ftr Sqn/20th Ftr Grp October 1942-March 18, 1944(KIA)
Crashed while strafing a Me-110 he had just shot down near Ulm.
29 missions, 130:10 hours

P-38J MC-L 42-67926 "Susie"
P-38J MC-L 42-67497 "Susie"
S/Sgt. William Norris-c/c

| *Sqn* | *Date* | *Claims* | *Location* | *A/C* |
|---|---|---|---|---|
| 79th | December 31, 1943 | FW-190 dam(air) | Bordeaux | P-38 |
| | January 14, 1944 | Me-109 dam(air) | Rouen | P-38 |
| | January 29 | (2)FW-190 dest(air) | E/Lille | P-38 |
| | | FW-190 dest(air) | Coblenz | P-38 |
| | February 20 | (2)Me-110 dest(air) | SW Brunswick | P-38 |
| | March 18 | (.5)Me-110 dest(air)* | Ulm | P-38 |

5.5-0-2 air
0-0 ground

* - shared with Lt. A.W. Heiden of the 79th Ftr Sqn

**Grasshoff, Hans J., Capt.** (6.5) Los Angeles, CA
436th Ftr Sqn/479th Ftr Grp January 1944-December 1944
270 hours

P-38J 9B-J "Little Zippie"
P-51D 9B-J 44-14574 "Little Zippie"
T/Sgt. Walker-c/c
Sgt. Quinette-ac/c

| *Sqn* | *Date* | *Claims* | *Location* | *A/C* |
|---|---|---|---|---|
| 436th | July 24, 1944 | (.5)Me-109 dest(air)* | Evreux | P-38 |
| | August 8 | Me-109 dam(air) | S/Paris | P-38 |
| | September 5 | (4)FW-190 dest(grd) | Bad Nauheim | P-38 |
| | | FW-190 dam(grd) | Bad Nauheim | P-38 |
| | September 26 | Me-109 dest(air) | S/Munster | P-38 |
| | November 27 | FW-190 dest(air) | Osnabruck | P-51 |

2.5-0-1 air
4-1 ground

* - shared with Lt. H.P. Plunk of the 436th Ftr Sqn

**Green, Robert T., Capt.** (6.5) Long Beach, CA
83rd Ftr Sqn/78th Ftr Grp July 1944-April 1945
86 missions, 372 hours

P-47D HL-C 42-28518 "Green Hornet"
P-51K HL-K 44-11573 "Green Hornet"
S/Sgt. Walter Steinman-c/c
Cpl. J.A. Wolf-ac/c

| *Sqn* | *Date* | *Claims* | *Location* | *A/C* |
|---|---|---|---|---|
| 83rd | August 10, 1944 | (1.5)He-111 dest(grd)* | Salines | P-47 |
| | | (.5)Ju-52 dest(grd)* | Salines | P-47 |
| | October 15 | (3.5)FW-190 dest(air)** | Bohmte | P-47 |
| | April 7, 1945 | Me-109 dest(air) | Dummer Lake | P-51 |

4.5-0-0 air
2-0 ground

* - both shared with Capt. C.M. Peal of the 83rd Ftr Sqn
** - shared with Lt. J.S. Reems of the 83rd Ftr Sqn

**Greenwood, Ray P., Lt.** (8) Sandy, UT
352nd Ftr Sqn/353rd Ftr Grp May 1944-August 12, 1944(MIA-E)
Hit by flak near Paris.
65 missions, 245 hours

P-47D SX-O 42-26570

| *Sqn* | *Date* | *Claims* | *Location* | *A/C* |
|---|---|---|---|---|
| 352nd | June 7, 1944 | Me-109 dest(grd) | Compiegne | P-47 |
| | June 20 | He-111 dest(grd) | Plantlunne | P-47 |
| | August 1 | Me-410 dest(grd) | Laon/Couvron | P-47 |
| | August 4 | (2)He-111 dest(grd) | Plantlunne | P-47 |
| | August 12 | (2)u/i a/c dest(grd) | E/Paris | P-47 |
| | | FW-190 dest(grd) | E/Paris | P-47 |

0-0-0 air
8-0 ground

**Gresham, Walter V., Jr., Maj.** (7) Portsmouth, VA
358th Ftr Sqn/355th Ftr Grp January 1943-May 1945
113 missions

P-47D YF-T 42-8498 "Trigger"
P-51B YF-T 43-6592 "Trigger II"
P-51D YF-T 44-14230 "Trigger III"
S/Sgt. F.J. Coradggio-c/c
Sgt. David Kendall-ac/c

| *Sqn* | *Date* | *Claims* | *Location* | *A/C* |
|---|---|---|---|---|
| 358th | March 2, 1944 | FW-190 dest(air) | SE Charleroi | P-47 |
| | March 16 | Me-109 dest(air) | W/Augsburg | P-51 |
| | April 5 | (2)He-111 dest(grd) | Munich | P-51 |
| | April 11 | (.5)Me-410 dest(air)* | NE Berlin | P-51 |
| | | (.25)Ju-88 dest(air)** | NE Berlin | P-51 |
| | | (.25)Me-410 dest(air)** | NE Berlin | P-51 |
| | May 4 | Me-109 prob(air) | SW Hanover | P-51 |
| | | Me-109 dam(air) | SW Hanover | P-51 |
| | August 15 | Me-109 dest(air) | NW Zwolle | P-51 |
| | April 10, 1945 | Me-262 dam(air) | W/Lubeck | P-51 |
| | April 17 | He-177 dest(grd) | Cheb A/F | P-51 |
| | | (3)u/i a/c dam(grd) | Eger A/F | P-51 |

4-1-2 air
3-3 ground

* - shared with Lt. R.J. Fussell of the 358th Ftr Sqn
** - both shared with Lt. R.J. Fussell, Lt. D.M. Martyn, and F/O L.M. Dudley of the 358th Ftr Sqn

**Grove, Lindsay W., Lt.** (5) New Hartford, NY
352nd Ftr Sqn/353rd Ftr Grp December 1944-EOW
32 missions, 180 hours

P-51D SX-D "Miss Jackie"
P-51D SX-D 44-14963 "Miss Jackie II"

| *Sqn* | *Date* | *Claims* | *Location* | *A/C* |
|---|---|---|---|---|
| 352nd | January 16, 1945 | FW-190 dest(grd) | Deiningen | P-51 |
| | | Ju-88 dam(grd) | Deiningen | P-51 |
| | March 2 | Me-109 dest(air) | SE Berlin | P-51 |
| | April 16 | (2)He-111 dest(grd) | Pocking | P-51 |
| | | He-111 dam(grd) | Pocking | P-51 |
| | April 17 | FW-190 dest(grd) | Ganacker | P-51 |
| | | u/i a/c dam(grd) | Ganacker | P-51 |

1-0-0 air
4-3 ground

**Gustke, Richard N., F/O** (12.5) Battle Creek, MI
350th Ftr Sqn/353rd Ftr Grp December 1944-EOW
26 missions

P-51D LH-

| *Sqn* | *Date* | *Claims* | *Location* | *A/C* |
|---|---|---|---|---|
| 350th | February 27, 1945 | Me-410 dest(grd) | Rohrensee | P-51 |
| | | Ju-88 dest(grd) | see above | P-51 |
| | | (.5)FW-190 dest(grd)* | see above | P-51 |
| | | (4)u/i a/c dam(grd) | see above | P-51 |
| | March 21 | (4)Ar-234 dest(grd) | Achmer | P-51 |
| | | Me-109 dest(grd) | Achmer | P-51 |
| | | (4)Ar-234 dam(grd) | Achmer | P-51 |
| | March 24 | FW-190 dam(air) | NW Kassel | P-51 |
| | April 16 | (3)FW-190 dest(grd) | Pocking | P-51 |
| | | (2)Ju-87 dest(grd) | Pocking | P-51 |

0-0-1 air
12.5-8 ground

* - shared with Lt. J.D. McMullen of the 350th Ftr Sqn

**Guyton, William R., Lt.** (5) Pittsburgh, PA
505th Ftr Sqn/339th Ftr Sqn March 1945-September 1945

P-51D 6N-I "Eileen"

| *Sqn* | *Date* | *Claims* | *Location* | *A/C* |
|---|---|---|---|---|
| 505th | April 10, 1945 | (2)Ju-88 dest(grd) | Wittstock | P-51 |
| | | Do-217 dest(grd) | Wittstock | P-51 |

| Sqn | Date | Claims | Location | A/C |
|---|---|---|---|---|
| | April 16 | Me-109 dest(grd) | NE Prague | P-51 |
| | | Ju-88 dest(grd) | NE Prague | P-51 |

0-0-0 air
5-0 ground

**Hagen, Harry N., Capt.** (5) Yorkville, OH
336th Ftr Sqn/4th Ftr Grp June 1944-May 1945
87 missions

P-51D VF-Y 44-14317 "Duke"
P-51D VF-Y 44-72053
S/Sgt. Edwin Rowe-c/c

| *Sqn* | *Date* | *Claims* | *Location* | *A/C* |
|---|---|---|---|---|
| 336th | August 25, 1944 | Me-109 dest(air) | SW Rostock | P-51 |
| | January 16, 1945 | FW-190 dest(grd) | Neuhausen | P-51 |
| | | He-177 dest(grd) | Neuhausen | P-51 |
| | March 22 | FW-190 dest(air) | SE Berlin | P-51 |
| | April 16 | Me-109 dest(grd) | SW Pilzen | P-51 |

2-0-0 air
3-0 ground

**Hahn, Robert F., Lt.** (5) Weissport, PA
351st Ftr Sqn/353rd Ftr Grp October 1944-July 1945
50 missions

P-51D YJ-H 44-14658

| *Sqn* | *Date* | *Claims* | *Location* | *A/C* |
|---|---|---|---|---|
| 351st | April 7, 1945 | Me-109 dest(air) | Steinhuder Lake | P-51 |
| | April 16 | (4)Ju-88 dest(grd) | Reichersberg | P-51 |
| | | Ju-88 dam(grd) | Reichersberg | P-51 |

1-0-0 air
4-1 ground

**Hall, George F., Capt.** (6) West Palm Beach, FL
63rd Ftr Sqn/56th Ftr Grp July 1942-October 1944
299 hours

P-47C UN-F
P-47D UN-F 42-75266

| *Sqn* | *Date* | *Claims* | *Location* | *A/C* |
|---|---|---|---|---|
| 63rd | August 17, 1943 | Me-109 prob(air) | Eupen-St. Nicholas | P-47 |
| | November 5 | Me-210 dest(air) | Enschede | P-47 |
| | January 30, 1944 | (2)Me-109 dest(air) | S/Quackenbruck | P-47 |
| | | (2)Me-109 dam(air) | see above | P-47 |
| | February 22 | (2)Me-110 dest(air) | Raderborn | P-47 |
| | March 6 | FW-190 dest(air) | Ulzen | P-47 |

6-1-2 air
0-0 ground

**Hall, Thomas H., Jr., Lt.** (5) Miami, FL
383rd Ftr Sqn/364th Ftr Grp April 1944-November 1944
270 hours

P-38J N2-Q
P-51D N2-Q 44-13854

| *Sqn* | *Date* | *Claims* | *Location* | *A/C* |
|---|---|---|---|---|
| 383rd | August 9, 1944 | (2)Ju-88 dest(grd) | Munich | P-51 |
| | August 15 | (2)Me-109 dest(air) | Mannheim | P-51 |
| | November 2 | FW-190 dest(air) | Merseburg | P-51 |

3-0-0 air
2-0 ground

**Halton, William T., LtCol.** (12.5) Brooklyn, NY
328th Ftr Sqn/352nd Ftr Grp Late 1942-October 1944
487th Ftr Sqn/352nd Ftr Grp October 1944-EOW
186 missions, 561 hours

P-47D PE-T 42-8439 "Slender, Tender, & Tall"
P-51B PE-T 42-106717 "Slender, Tender, & Tall"
P-51D PE-T 44-13996 "Slender, Tender, & Tall"
P-51D HO-T 44-13557 "Slender, Tender, & Tall"
P-51D HO-T 44-14812 "Slender, Tender, & Tall"

| *Sqn* | *Date* | *Claims* | *Location* | *A/C* |
|---|---|---|---|---|
| 328th | February 20, 1944 | Me-109 dest(air) | Louvain | P-47 |
| | April 22 | Ju-188 dam(grd) | Dummer Lake | P-51 |
| 487th | November 2 | Me-109 dest(air) | E/Merseburg | P-51 |
| | November 27 | Me-109 dest(air) | Hameln | P-51 |
| | December 26 | Me-109 dest(air) | SW Bonn | P-51 |
| | December 27 | (3.5)Me-109 dest(air)* | SW Bonn | P-51 |
| | January 1, 1945 | FW-190 dest(air) | N/Liege | P-51 |
| | January 24 | Me-109 dest(air) | SE Cologne | P-51 |
| | March 18 | Me-109 dest(air) | Bad Frienwalde | P-51 |
| | April 17 | FW-190 dest(grd) | Plattling | P-51 |
| | | Me-109 dest(grd) | Plattling | P-51 |
| | | (2)FW-190 dam(grd) | Plattling | P-51 |

10.5-0-0 air
2-3 ground

* - shared with F/O A.H. Goebel of the 487th Ftr Sqn

**Hamilton, Ralph W., Capt.** (5) Des Moines, IA
487th Ftr Sqn/352nd Ftr Grp January 1943-March 1945
130 missions, 461:25 hours

P-47D HO-H 42-22457 "Frances B"
P-51B HO-H 43-6754 "Frances B, Too!"
P-51D HO-H 44-14668 "Jeanne M"

| *Sqn* | *Date* | *Claims* | *Location* | *A/C* |
|---|---|---|---|---|
| 487th | February 24, 1944 | Me-109 dam(air) | Enschede | P-47 |
| | April 22 | (3)He-111 dam(grd) | Salzwedel | P-51 |
| | April 28 | Ju-88 dest(grd) | Bourges | P-51 |
| | | u/i a/c dam(grd) | Bourges | P-51 |
| | May 27 | FW-190 dest(air) | Strasbourg | P-51 |
| | | FW-190 prob(air) | Strasbourg | P-51 |
| | May 29 | (2)u/i a/c dam(grd) | Jasmunder Bay | P-51 |
| | November 27 | (2)Me-109 dest(air) | Hameln | P-51 |
| | December 26 | Me-109 dest(air) | SW Bonn | P-51 |

4-1-1 air
1-6 ground

**Hanseman, Chris J., Lt.** (7) Mondovi, WI
505th Ftr Sqn/339th Ftr Grp States-July 29, 1944(KIA)
Hit the ground while strafing near Naumberg.

P-51B 6N-H"Eleanor"
P-51B 6N-H"Eleanor II"
P-51B 6N-H"Eleanor III"
P-51D 6N-H 44-13556 "Eleanor IV"
S/Sgt. Clarence B. Shockley-c/c
Sgt. Thomas H. Collins-ac/c
Sgt. Forrest W. Lukehart-arm.

| *Sqn* | *Date* | *Claims* | *Location* | *A/C* |
|---|---|---|---|---|
| 505th | May 21, 1944 | (2)Trainer dest(air) | W/Dresden | P-51 |
| | | (.5)Ju-88 dest(air)* | W/Dresden | P-51 |
| | May 24 | (1.5)Me-109 dest(air)** | St. Gobain-Laon | P-51 |
| | June 10 | Me-109 dest(air) | Laigle | P-51 |
| | | Ju-88 dam(grd) | Laigle | P-51 |
| | July 19 | Ju-188 dest(grd) | SW Augsburg | P-51 |
| | | u/i a/c dest(grd) | SW Augsburg | P-51 |

5-0-0 air
2-1 ground

* - shared with Capt. L. Reid of the 505th Ftr Sqn
** - shared with an unknown pilot of the 503rd Ftr Sqn, 339th Ftr Grp

**Hansen, John W., Lt.** (6) Altedena, CA
434th Ftr Sqn/479th Ftr Grp January 1944-November 1944

P-38J L2-B 43-28349
P-51D L2-B 44-15325 "Swanee Jr."

| *Sqn* | *Date* | *Claims* | *Location* | *A/C* |
|---|---|---|---|---|
| 434th | August 15, 1944 | Me-109 dest(air) | Steenwijk A/F | P-38 |
| | | (2)Me-109 dest(grd) | see above | P-38 |
| | | Me-109 dam(grd) | see above | P-38 |
| | | u/i a/c dam(grd) | see above | P-38 |
| | August 18 | He-111 dest(grd) | Nancy/Essey A/F | P-38 |
| | | Ju-88 dest(grd) | see above | P-38 |
| | | He-111 dam(grd) | see above | P-38 |
| | September 26 | Me-109 dest(air) | SW Munster | P-38 |
| | | Me-109 dam(air) | SW Munster | P-38 |

2-0-1 air
4-3 ground

**Hansen, Kenneth J., Lt.** (5) Arapahoe, WY
436th Ftr Sqn/479th Ftr Grp October 1944-EOW
38 missions, 187:20 hours

P-51D 9B-
S/Sgt. Kenneth Paulson-c/c

| Sqn | Date | Claims | Location | A/C |
|---|---|---|---|---|
| 436th | April 13, 1945 | (3)FW-190 dest(grd) | Salzwedel | P-51 |
| | | Me-110 dest(grd) | Salzwedel | P-51 |
| | April 17 | FW-189 dest(grd) | Karlsbad | P-51 |

0-0-0 air
5-0 ground

**Happel, James R., Maj.** (8.66) Paulsboro, NJ
335th Ftr Sqn/4th Ftr Grp October 1942-June 1944
Earlier flew with 121 Sqn, RAF

Spitfire AV-
P-47C WD-X 41-6182
P-51B WD-X 43-6784

| Sqn | Date | Claims | Location | A/C |
|---|---|---|---|---|
| 335th | August 16, 1943 | FW-190 dest(air) | Paris | P-47 |
| | January 30, 1944 | Me-109 prob(air) | Lingen | P-47 |
| | March 5 | FW-190 dam(air) | E/Bordeaux | P-51 |
| | March 27 | (.5)FW-190 dam(air)* | Libourne | P-51 |
| | April 8 | He-111 dest(air) | S/Ulzen | P-51 |
| | April 9 | (.33)Ju-88 dest(grd)** | Lingen/Plantlunne | P-51 |
| | | (.33)Ju-88 dest(grd)** | see above | P-51 |
| | April 10 | (2)Bu-131 dest(grd) | Romorantin A/F | P-51 |
| | | (2)u/i a/c dest(grd) | see above | P-51 |
| | April 24 | FW-190 dest(air) | NE Worms | P-51 |
| | May 12 | Me-109 dest(air) | Giessen | P-51 |

4-1-1.5 air
4.66-0 ground

* - shared with Lt. A.L. Schlegel of the 335th Ftr Sqn
** - both shared with Lt. P.W. McKennon of the 335th Ftr Sqn and Lt. J.T. Godfrey of the 336th Ftr Sqn, 4th Ftr Grp

**Harrington, Francis E., Lt.** (12) Randolph, MA
83rd Ftr Sqn/78th Ftr Grp May 1944-April 1945
73 missions, 350 hours

P-47D HL-I "Boston Bean"
P-51D HL-I 44-15586 "Boston Bean"
S/Sgt. Edward Wagner-c/c

| Sqn | Date | Claims | Location | A/C |
|---|---|---|---|---|
| 83rd | September 10, 1944 | Me-410 dam(grd) | Germsheim | P-47 |
| | | Ju-87 dam(grd) | Germsheim | P-47 |
| | October 15 | FW-190 dam(air) | Bohmte | P-47 |
| | December 19 | Me-109 dest(air) | S/Coblenz | P-47 |
| | | FW-190 dest(air) | S/Coblenz | P-47 |
| | April 7, 1945 | Me-109 dest(air) | Dummer Lake | P-51 |
| | | FW-190 dest(air) | Dummer Lake | P-51 |
| | April 10 | (2)FW-190 dest(grd) | Werder A/F | P-51 |
| | | Ju-87 dest(grd) | see above | P-51 |
| | | u/i a/c dest(grd) | see above | P-51 |
| | | FW-190 dam(grd) | see above | P-51 |
| | | Ju-87 dam(grd) | see above | P-51 |
| | | u/i a/c dam(grd) | see above | P-51 |
| | April 16 | (2)u/i a/c dest(grd) | N/Prague | P-51 |
| | | Me-109 dest(grd) | N/Prague | P-51 |
| | | Me-262 dest(grd) | N/Prague | P-51 |
| | | (3)u/i a/c dam(grd) | N/Prague | P-51 |

4-0-1 air
8-8 ground

**Harris, Thomas L., Capt.** (5) Santa Paula, CA
364th Ftr Sqn/357th Ftr Grp July 1943-May 27, 1944(POW)
Collided with a P-51 near Strasbourg.

P-51B C5-S 43-6653 "Lil Red's Rocket"
S/Sgt. Paul E. Slentz-c/c

| Sqn | Date | Claims | Location | A/C |
|---|---|---|---|---|
| 364th | March 6, 1944 | Me-110 dest(air) | E/Berlin | P-51 |
| | | (.5)FW-190 dest(air)* | NW Berlin | P-51 |
| | March 8 | (.5)FW-190 dest(air)** | Dummer Lake | P-51 |
| | April 19 | FW-190 dest(air) | S/Bleicherode | P-51 |
| | May 27 | (2)Me-109 dest(air) | Colmar | P-51 |
| | | Me-109 prob(air) | Colmar | P-51 |

5-1-0 air
0-0 ground

* - shared with Capt. G.V. Davis of the 364th Ftr Sqn
** - shared with Capt. G.V. Davis of the 364th Ftr Sqn

**Hart, Cameron M., Capt.** (6) Westfield, NJ
63rd Ftr Sqn/56th Ftr Grp June 1944-April 1945
60 missions

P-47D UN-B 42-26299
P-47D UN-B 44-19937
S/Sgt. Louis E. White-c/c
Cpl. Walter C. Scheide-arm.

| Sqn | Date | Claims | Location | A/C |
|---|---|---|---|---|
| 63rd | September 5, 1944 | Me-109 dest(air) | NE Coblenz | P-47 |
| | | Me-109 prob(air) | NE Coblenz | P-47 |
| | | Me-109 dam(air) | NE Coblenz | P-47 |
| | December 23 | (2)FW-190 dest(air) | NW Coblenz | P-47 |
| | | FW-190 dam(air) | NW Coblenz | P-47 |
| | December 25 | Me-109 dest(air) | SE Cologne | P-47 |
| | February 3, 1945 | (2)FW-190 dest(air) | Friedersdorf A/F | P-47 |

6-1-2 air
0-0 ground

**Hartley, Raymond E., Capt.** (9) Kansas City, MO
HdQts/353rd Ftr Grp February 1945-April 1945
351st Ftr Sqn/353rd Ftr Grp April 1945-EOW
Earlier flew in the MTO with the 325th Ftr Grp, 15th Air Force, claiming 2 kills: a FW-190 on January 21, 1944 and a Me-109 on April 12, 1944.
12 missions

No regular a/c or crew

| Sqn | Date | Claims | Location | A/C |
|---|---|---|---|---|
| HdQts | March 24, 1945 | (2)FW-190 dest(air) | NW Kassel | P-51 |
| | | Me-109 dest(air) | NW Kassel | P-51 |
| | | Me-109 dam(air) | NW Kassel | P-51 |
| 351st | April 16 | (2)FW-200 dest(grd) | Reichersberg | P-51 |
| | | FW-190 dest(grd) | see above | P-51 |
| | | Ju-87 dest(grd) | see above | P-51 |

3-0-1 air
4-0 ground

**Hatala, Paul R., Capt.** (5.5) Cleveland, OH
364th Ftr Sqn/357th Ftr Grp August 1944-EOW
66 missions

P-51D C5-B "Jeanne"
S/Sgt. Richard Eagen-c/c

| Sqn | Date | Claims | Location | A/C |
|---|---|---|---|---|
| 364th | December 5, 1944 | FW-190 dest(air) | NW Berlin | P-51 |
| | January 14, 1945 | (2)FW-190 dest(air) | W/Berlin | P-51 |
| | March 2 | (.5)Me-109 dest(air)* | NE Leipzig | P-51 |
| | March 24 | (2)Me-109 dest(air) | W/Gutersloh | P-51 |

5.5-0-0 air
0-0 ground

* - shared with Lt. O.T. Ridley of the 362nd Ftr Sqn, 357th Ftr Grp

**Hatter, Robert B., Capt.** (9) Ottawa, IL
368th Ftr Sqn/359th Ftr Grp April 1944-October 1944
63 missions, 270 hours

P-51C CV-H 42-103197
S/Sgt. Oscar Schaller-c/c
Sgt. Samuel Dailey-arm.

| Sqn | Date | Claims | Location | A/C |
|---|---|---|---|---|
| 368th | May 21, 1944 | (6)u/i a/c dest(grd) | Grevesmuhlen | P-51 |
| | | (3)u/i a/c dam(grd) | see above | P-51 |
| | May 29 | Me-109 dest(air) | Plau | P-51 |
| | September 12 | (2)FW-190 dest(air) | Liebenwalde | P-51 |

3-0-0 air
6-3 ground

**Hauver, Charles D., Capt.** (5) Poughkeepsie, NY
354th Ftr Sqn/355th Ftr Grp July 1944-December 1944

P-51B WR-R 43-6943 "Patricia"
P-51D WR-R 44-14090 "Princess Pat"
P-51D WR-R 44-14704 "Princess Pat II"

| Sqn | Date | Claims | Location | A/C |
|---|---|---|---|---|
| 354th | November 26, 1944 | (2)FW-190 dest(air) | W/Hanover | P-51 |
| | December 25 | FW-190 dest(air) | NW Trier | P-51 |
| | | Me-109 dest(air) | NW Trier | P-51 |
| | December 31 | FW-190 dest(air) | SW Hamburg | P-51 |
| | | FW-190 dam(air) | SW Hamburg | P-51 |

5-0-1 air
0-0 ground

**Haviland, Fred R., Jr., Capt.** (12) Chicago, IL
357th Ftr Sqn/355th Ftr Grp May 1944-November 1944
HdQts/355th Ftr Grp November 1944-January 1945

P-51C OS-H 42-103753
P-51D OS-H 44-14402 "Barbara"
S/Sgt. Gale Torrey-c/c

| Sqn | Date | Claims | Location | A/C |
|---|---|---|---|---|
| 357th | June 21, 1944 | Me-109 dest(air) | N/Magdeburg | P-51 |
| | June 24 | (3)Me-109 dest(grd) | E/Angars | P-51 |
| | July 7 | (2)Me-410 dest(air) | Halle | P-51 |
| | | Me-410 dam(air) | Halle | P-51 |
| | August 3 | FW-190 dest(air) | Saarebourg | P-51 |
| | | Me-109 dam(air) | Saarebourg | P-51 |
| | September 12 | (3)Ju-88 dest(grd) | Schwartz A/F | P-51 |
| | | Me-110 dam(grd) | see above | P-51 |
| | | Do-217 dam(grd) | see above | P-51 |
| | November 18 | (4)Me-262 dam(grd) | Leipheim | P-51 |
| | November 26 | FW-190 dest(air) | W/Gardelegen | P-51 |
| | | Me-109 dest(air) | W/Gardelegen | P-51 |

6-0-2 air
6-6 ground

**Haworth, Russell C., Lt.** (5) Cedar Hill, TX
338th Ftr Sqn/55th Ftr Grp July 1944-December 1944
64 missions

P-51D CL-K 44-13642 "Krazy Kid"
S/Sgt. George W. Clark-c/c
Sgt. Ernesto Gallego-ac/c
Sgt. Toney R. Todey-arm.

| Sqn | Date | Claims | Location | A/C |
|---|---|---|---|---|
| 338th | August 28, 1944 | (.5)DFS-230 dest(air)[*] | Dromersheim | P-51 |
| | September 11 | (2)Me-109 dest(air) | S/Meiningen | P-51 |
| | | Me-109 dam(air) | see above | P-51 |
| | September 12 | (.5)Me-109 dest(air)[**] | S/Frankfurt | P-51 |
| | November 2 | Me-109 dest(air) | Merseburg | P-51 |
| | December 24 | Me-109 dest(air) | Vogelsburg | P-51 |

5-0-1 air
0-0 ground

[*] - shared with Lt. A.J. Ramm of the 338th Ftr Sqn
[**] - shared with Lt. C.C. Sherman of the 38th Ftr Sqn, 55th Ftr Grp

**Hayes, Thomas L., Jr., LtCol.** (8.5) Brooks, OR
364th Ftr Sqn/357th Ftr Grp May 1943-March 1944
HdQts/357th Ftr Grp March 1944-August 1944
Earlier flew in the PTO with the 20th Pursuit Sqn
78 missions, 300 hours

P-51B C5-N "Frenesi"
P-51D C5-N 44-13318 "Frenesi"
S/Sgt. Robert Krull-c/c
Sgt. Gene Barsalow-ac/c
Sgt. Fred Keiper-arm.

| Sqn | Date | Claims | Location | A/C |
|---|---|---|---|---|
| 364th | February 24, 1944 | Me-109 prob(air) | NW Gotha | P-51 |
| | March 2 | Me-109 dest(air) | N/Frankfurt | P-51 |
| | March 6 | Me-109 dest(air) | E/Ulzen | P-51 |
| | March 8 | Me-410 dest(air) | W/Berlin | P-51 |
| | March 16 | Me-110 dest(air) | SE Stuttgart | P-51 |
| HdQts | April 19 | Me-109 dest(air) | S/Kassel | P-51 |
| | May 28 | Me-109 dest(air) | NW Magdeburg | P-51 |
| | June 29 | Me-109 dest(air) | W/Leipzig | P-51 |
| | | (.5)Me-410 dest(air)[*] | NW Leipzig | P-51 |
| | July 14 | Me-109 dest(air) | Valence | P-51 |

8.5-1-0 air
0-0 ground

[*] - shared with Lt. M.F. Allen of the 364th Ftr Sqn

**Helfrecht, Kenneth G., Lt.** (5) Madison, WI
334th Ftr Sqn/4th Ftr Grp October 1944-September 1945
47 missions

P-51D QP-R 44-14110 "Georgie"
P-51D QP-K "Georgie"
S/Sgt. R. Lewis-c/c(R)
S/Sgt. William Rushing-c/c(K)

| Sqn | Date | Claims | Location | A/C |
|---|---|---|---|---|
| 334th | April 16, 1945 | (2)Me-410 dest(grd) | Gablingen | P-51 |
| | | (2)FW-190 dest(grd) | see above | P-51 |
| | | He-177 dest(grd) | see above | P-51 |
| | | (2)Ju-87 dam(grd) | see above | P-51 |

0-0-0 air
5-2 ground

**Heller, Edwin L., Capt.** (20) Schneeksville, PA
486th Ftr Sqn/352nd Ftr Grp March 1943-May 1945
520 hours

P-47D PZ-H 42-75183 "Happy"
P-51B PZ-H 43-6704 "Hell-er-Bust"
P-51D PZ-H 44-14696 "Hell-er-Bust"
S/Sgt. Charles Agee-c/c

| Sqn | Date | Claims | Location | A/C |
|---|---|---|---|---|
| 486th | April 23, 1944 | (.5)Ju-52 dest(grd)[*] | SE Paris | P-51 |
| | April 24 | (3)Me-110 dest(grd) | E/Neuburg-Bokingen | P-51 |
| | | (2)Ju-88 dest(grd) | see above | P-51 |
| | | Ju-52 dest(grd) | see above | P-51 |
| | | u/i a/c dest(grd) | see above | P-51 |
| | | (4)Me-110 dam(grd) | see above | P-51 |
| | | Ju-52 dam(grd) | see above | P-51 |
| | May 8 | (2)Me-109 dest(air) | Gifhorn | P-51 |
| | May 28 | Me-109 dest(air) | Dessau | P-51 |
| | | (.5)Me-109 dest(air)[**] | Magdeburg | P-51 |
| | June 21 | Me-109 dest(air) | Brest-Litovsk | P-51 |
| | March 2, 1945 | FW-190 dest(air) | SE Leipzig | P-51 |
| | | FW-190 dam(air) | SE Leipzig | P-51 |
| | April 16 | (3)FW-190 dest(grd) | Ganacker | P-51 |
| | | (2)Ju-87 dest(grd) | see above | P-51 |
| | | Me-109 dest(grd) | see above | P-51 |
| | | Trainer dest(grd) | see above | P-51 |

5.5-0-1 air
14.5-5 ground

[*] - shared with Lt. H.J. Miklajcyk of the 486th Ftr Sqn
[**] - shared with Lt. J.L. Lang of the 4th Ftr Grp

**Henley, Donald, Jr., Lt.** (7.5) Louisville, KY
62nd Ftr Sqn/56th Ftr Grp August 1944-April 1945
69 missions, 301:30 hours

P-47D LM-H 42-75631
P-47M LM-H 44-21233
S/Sgt. Andrew Yourick-c/c
Sgt. Vincent J. Gioielli-ac/c

| Sqn | Date | Claims | Location | A/C |
|---|---|---|---|---|
| 62nd | September 21, 1944 | FW-190 dest(air) | Arnheim | P-47 |
| | December 4 | (.5)u/i a/c dest(grd)[*] | Neuburg | P-47 |
| | January 14, 1945 | (1.5)Me-109 dest(air)[**] | Magdeburg | P-47 |
| | March 10 | (.5)FW-190 dest(air)[@] | Remagen | P-47 |
| | April 10 | Ju-88 dest(grd) | Neuruppin | P-47 |
| | | Ju-88 dam(grd) | Neuruppin | P-47 |
| | April 13 | (2)He-111 dest(grd) | Eggebeck A/F | P-47 |
| | | Ju-87 dest(grd) | Eggebeck A/F | P-47 |
| | | (2)He-111 dam(grd) | Eggebeck A/F | P-47 |

3-0-0 air
4.5-3 ground

[*] - shared with Lt. S.N. Ball of the 62nd Ftr Sqn
[**] - shared with Lt. H.O. Womack of the 62nd Ftr Sqn
[@] - shared with Lt. D.A. Carroll of the 62nd Ftr Sqn

**Henry, Carroll D., Capt.** (6.5) Taylorsville, KY
338th Ftr Sqn/55th Ftr Grp September 1944-June 1945
58 missions, 287 hours

P-51D CL-G 44-63227 "Little Trixie"
S/Sgt. Floyd Padgett-c/c

| Sqn | Date | Claims | Location | A/C |
|---|---|---|---|---|
| 338th | November 26, 1944 | FW-190 dam(grd) | Vorden A/F | P-51 |
| | January 13, 1945 | Me-109 dest(air) | W/Giebelstadt | P-51 |
| | February 15 | (.5)Hs-129 dest(air)* | Scharndau | P-51 |
| | February 25 | FW-190 dest(grd) | Illesheim | P-51 |
| | | FW-190 dam(grd) | Illesheim | P-51 |
| | April 16 | (2)FW-190 dest(grd) | Landshut | P-51 |
| | April 17 | FW-190 dest(grd) | Riess/Canitz | P-51 |
| | | u/i a/c dest(grd) | Riess/Canitz | P-51 |

1.5-0-0 air
5-2 ground

* - shared with Lt. E.H. Duquette of the 338th Ftr Sqn

**Hepner, Neal, Lt.** (5) Detroit, MI
84th Ftr Sqn/78th Ftr Grp March 1945-July 1945
4 missions

No regular a/c or crew

| Sqn | Date | Claims | Location | A/C |
|---|---|---|---|---|
| 84th | April 16, 1945 | (2)Me-109 dest(grd) | Praha/Kakewice | P-51 |
| | | He-111 dest(grd) | see above | P-51 |
| | | Ju-52 dest(grd) | see above | P-51 |
| | | u/i a/c dest(grd) | see above | P-51 |
| | | (2)Ju-52 dam(grd) | see above | P-51 |
| | | Me-109 dam(grd) | see above | P-51 |
| | | Ju-88 dam(grd) | see above | P-51 |

0-0-0 air
5-4 ground

**Hermansen, Cephas, Lt.** Alden Station, PA
504th Ftr Sqn/339th Ftr Grp January 1945-October 1945

P-51D 5Q- "Diane"

| Sqn | Date | Claims | Location | A/C |
|---|---|---|---|---|
| 504th | April 7, 1945 | Me-109 prob(air) | Celle | P-51 |
| | April 10 | (3)Me-410 dest(grd) | N/Neuruppin | P-51 |
| | | (2)Me-410 dam(grd) | N/Neuruppin | P-51 |
| | April 16 | (2)Me-109 dest(grd) | Klatovy | P-51 |

0-1-0 air
5-2 ground

**Herren, James M., Jr., LtCol.** (6) Ashland, AL
434th Ftr Sqn/479th Ftr Grp January 1944-October 30, 1944(KIA)
Collided with a P-51 near Katensen.

P-38J N2-A 42-68008 "Touche'"
P-38J N2-A 44-14396 "Touche'"
S/Sgt. Victor R. Plassenthal-c/c
Sgt. John Wendt-ac/c
Cpl. Regis Marhefky-arm.

| Sqn | Date | Claims | Location | A/C |
|---|---|---|---|---|
| 434th | August 18, 1944 | He-111 dest(grd) | Nancy/Essey A/F | P-38 |
| | | Ju-52 dest(grd) | see above | P-38 |
| | September 26 | (3)Me-109 dest(air) | SW Munster | P-38 |
| | September 28 | Me-109 dest(air) | W/Halberstadt | P-51 |

4-0-0 air
2-0 ground

**Hewett, Sidney H., Capt.** (5) Absecon, NJ
361st Ftr Sqn/356th Ftr Grp February 1943-May 4, 1944(POW)
Downed by a FW-190 near Nienburg.
56 missions, 166 hours

P-47D QI-F 42-76397 "Clarkie"
P-47D QI-F 42-74702 "Clarkie II"
S/Sgt. Bennie F. Giardieniere-c/c
Sgt. Michael Yahwak-ac/c
Sgt. Elwin D. Phillips-arm.

| Sqn | Date | Claims | Location | A/C |
|---|---|---|---|---|
| 361st | January 21, 1944 | (.5)Ju-88 dest(air)* | Cambrai | P-47 |
| | January 24 | FW-190 dam(air) | Bruges-Ostend | P-47 |
| | February 13 | FW-190 dest(air) | SE Paris | P-47 |
| | | (2)FW-190 dam(air) | SE Paris | P-47 |
| | March 6 | Me-109 dest(air) | NW Steinhuder L. | P-47 |
| | April 11 | (2)Ju-88 dest(grd) | Gifhorn | P-47 |
| | | (.5)Ju-52 dest(grd)** | Gifhorn | P-47 |
| | | Ju-52 dam(grd) | Gifhorn | P-47 |

2.5-0-3 air
2.5-1 ground

* - shared with Lt. D.F. Thwaites of the 361st Ftr Sqn
** - shared with Lt. E.M. Parham of the 361st Ftr Sqn

**Hewitt, Richard A., Maj.** (8.33) Lewiston, NY
82nd Ftr Sqn/78th Ftr Grp August 1943-June 1945
127 missions, 426 hours

P-47C MX-R 41-6345 "Miss Tibbie"
P-51D MX-U 44-64147 "Big Dick"
S/Sgt. Philip A. Doloway-c/c
Sgt. Herb Trantham-ac/c
Cpl. John Montgomery-arm.

| Sqn | Date | Claims | Location | A/C |
|---|---|---|---|---|
| 82nd | March 16, 1944 | Me-109 dest(air) | Strasbourg | P-47 |
| | | Me-109 dam(air) | Strasbourg | P-47 |
| | April 5 | Go-242 dam(grd) | Ruwer | P-47 |
| | April 8 | Ju-52 dest(grd) | Trier | P-47 |
| | | (.33)Ar-196 dest(grd)* | Trier | P-47 |
| | September 10 | (2)Ju-88 dest(grd) | Meinbullen | P-47 |
| | November 21 | Me-109 dest(air) | Hanover | P-47 |
| | March 19, 1945 | (2)Me-109 dest(air) | Osnabruck | P-51 |
| | April 17 | Me-262 dest(grd) | Prague | P-51 |

4-0-1 air
4.33-1 ground

* - shared with Capt. N.D. Munson and Lt. J.E. Brasher of the 82nd Ftr Sqn

**Higgins, Donald H., Maj.** (5.5) New Orleans, LA
486th Ftr Sqn/352nd Ftr Grp States-September 1945
84 missions

P-47D PZ-B 42-75076
P-51B PZ-B 43-6436 "Bayou Baby"
P-51K PZ-B 44-11365

| Sqn | Date | Claims | Location | A/C |
|---|---|---|---|---|
| 486th | May 13, 1944 | Me-109 dest(air) | Tribsees | P-51 |
| | July 2 | FW-190 dest(air) | W/Budapest | P-51 |
| | | (.5)Me-109 dest(air)* | W/Budapest | P-51 |
| | April 17, 1945 | (2)Ju-52 dest(grd) | Plattling | P-51 |
| | | Me-109 dest(grd) | Plattling | P-51 |
| | | Me-109 dam(grd) | Plattling | P-51 |

2.5-0-0 air
3-1 ground

* - shared with Lt. D.R. Emerson of the 4th Ftr Grp

**Hightshoe, Melville W., Capt.** (14.5) West Memphis, AR
350th Ftr Sqn/353rd Ftr Grp July 1944-EOW
72 missions, 320:20 hours

P-47D LH-X
P-51D LH-X 44-11167 "Danny Boy"
P-51D LH-X 44-15516 "Danny Boy 2nd"
S/Sgt. Richard Davidowski-c/c

| Sqn | Date | Claims | Location | A/C |
|---|---|---|---|---|
| 350th | August 7, 1944 | Me-109 dam(grd) | SE Amiens | P-47 |
| | | Me-410 dam(grd) | SE Amiens | P-47 |
| | August 29 | (2)Me-109 dest(grd) | Diest | P-47 |
| | | Me-410 dest(grd) | Diest | P-47 |
| | | (2)Me-109 dam(grd) | Diest | P-47 |
| | September 9 | Do-217 dam(grd) | Hesepe | P-47 |
| | November 18 | (2)He-177 dest(grd) | Lechfeld | P-51 |
| | | u/i a/c dest(grd) | Lechfeld | P-51 |
| | February 28, 1945 | (1.5)Me-110 dest(grd)* | S/Gotha | P-51 |
| | | Me-109 dest(grd) | S/Gotha | P-51 |
| | | Me-410 dest(grd) | S/Gotha | P-51 |
| | April 16 | (4)FW-190 dest(grd) | Pocking | P-51 |
| | | Me-109 dest(grd) | Pocking | P-51 |

0-0-0 air
14.5-5 ground

* - shared with Lt. J.D. McMullen of the 350th Ftr Sqn

**Hiro, Edwin W., Maj.** (5) Chisolm, MN
363rd Ftr Sqn/357th Ftr Grp February 1943-September 19, 1944(KIA)
Hit by e/a near Vreden.

P-51B B6-D "Horse's Itch"
P-51D B6-D 44-13518 "Horse's Itch"

| Sqn | Date | Claims | Location | A/C |
|---|---|---|---|---|
| 363rd | February 22, 1944 | Me-109 dam(air) | Leopoldshall | P-51 |
| | April 24 | Me-109 dest(air) | SW Munich | P-51 |
| | May 19 | (2)Me-109 dest(air) | NW Brandenburg | P-51 |
| | | Me-109 dam(air) | NW Brandenburg | P-51 |
| | May 24 | FW-190 prob(air) | SE Berlin | P-51 |
| | May 28 | Me-109 prob(air) | N/Magdeburg | P-51 |
| | July 30 | Me-109 dest(air) | W/Paris | P-51 |
| | September 19 | Me-109 dest(air) | W/Arnheim | P-51 |
| | | 5-2-2 air | | |
| | | 0-0 ground | | |

**Hively, Howard D., Maj.** (14.5) Athens, OH
334th Ftr Sqn/4th Ftr Grp September 1942-January 1945
Earlier flew with 71 Sqn, RAF

Spitfire XR-
P-47C QP-J 41-6576
P-51B QP-J 43-6898 "Deacon"
P-51D QP-J 44-13306
P-51D QP-J 44-15347
S/Sgt. Vincent J. Andra-c/c
Sgt. Glen K. Roen-arm.

| Sqn | Date | Claims | Location | A/C |
|---|---|---|---|---|
| 334th | August 16, 1943 | FW-190 dest(air) | NW Paris | P-47 |
| | March 5, 1944 | (2)Me-109 dest(air) | Mont de Marsan | P-51 |
| | March 21 | (.5)Ju-88 dest(grd)[*] | Langen A/F | P-51 |
| | March 23 | FW-190 dam(air) | Herford | P-51 |
| | March 27 | Ju-88 dest(grd) | Cazaux A/F | P-51 |
| | May 9 | (2)Ju-88 dam(grd) | Riems/Champiegne | P-51 |
| | May 12 | Me-109 dest(air) | Plauen | P-51 |
| | May 19 | (3)Me-109 dest(air) | Lubeck-Schwerin | P-51 |
| | May 24 | Me-109 dest(air) | Hamburg | P-51 |
| | July 2 | (3)Me-109 dest(air) | Budapest | P-51 |
| | July 28 | Me-109 prob(air) | Nordhausen | P-51 |
| | November 18 | Me-262 dest(grd) | Leipheim A/F | P-51 |
| | December 5 | FW-190 dest(air) | NW Nordhorn | P-51 |
| | | 12-1-1 air | | |
| | | 2.5-2 ground | | |

* - shared with Lt. J.W. Goodwyn of the 335th Ftr Sqn, 4th Ftr Grp

**Hobert, Robert D., Capt.** (5) Woodland, WA
336th Ftr Sqn/4th Ftr Grp May 1943-April 5, 1944(KIA)
Died of exposure after bailing out over the North Sea.

P-47C VF-I 41-6256 "Blue Goofis"
P-47D VF-I 42-75274
P-51B VF-I 43-6836

| Sqn | Date | Claims | Location | A/C |
|---|---|---|---|---|
| 336th | February 6, 1944 | FW-190 dest(air) | Beauvais-Marigny | P-47 |
| | March 21 | FW-190 dest(air) | SW Evreux | P-51 |
| | March 27 | Ju-88 dam(grd) | Cazaux A/F | P-51 |
| | April 5 | (3)Ju-88 dest(grd) | Stendal | P-51 |
| | | Ju-88 dam(grd) | Stendal | P-51 |
| | | 2-0-0 air | | |
| | | 3-2 ground | | |

**Hockery, John J., Capt.** (7.8) Independence, MO
82nd Ftr Sqn/78th Ftr Grp July 1943-November 26, 1944(POW)
Hit by a FW-190 near Rheine.

P-47D MX-L
P-47D MX-L 44-19950

| Sqn | Date | Claims | Location | A/C |
|---|---|---|---|---|
| 82nd | January 24, 1944 | Me-110 dest(air) | Engheim | P-47 |
| | February 11 | Me-109 dest(air) | NW Luxembourg | P-47 |
| | February 20 | FW-190 dest(air) | Coblenz | P-47 |
| | March 24 | Ju-188 dest(air) | Paris | P-47 |
| | April 1 | (.13)Do-217 dest(grd)[*] | Verdun | P-47 |
| | April 5 | (.33)Go-242 dest(grd)[**] | Ruwer | P-47 |
| | | (.33)DFS-230 dest(grd)[**] | Ruwer | P-47 |
| | April 12 | Ju-87 dest(air) | Sedan | P-47 |
| | November 26 | (2)Me-109 dest(air) | Rheine | P-47 |
| | | FW-190 prob(air) | Rheine | P-47 |
| | | 7-1-0 air | | |
| | | 0.8-0 ground | | |

* - shared with Capt. W.L. Boone, Capt. W.E. May, Lt. B.M. Watkins, Lt. C.R. Clark, Lt. H.L. Eakes, Lt. R.V. Hearn, and F/O C.W. DeWitt of the 82nd Ftr Sqn
** - both shared with Lt. H.L. Eakes and F/O C.W. DeWitt of the 82nd Ftr Sqn

**Hodges, William R., Capt.** (5) Winston-Salem, NC
370th Ftr Sqn/359th Ftr Grp April 1943-May 11, 1944(MIA-E)
Hit by flak at Rheims-Champagne A/F
370th Ftr Sqn/359th Ftr Grp September 1944-December 1944

P-47D CS-O 42-74719
P-51B CS-O
P-51D CS-O 44-14518

| Sqn | Date | Claims | Location | A/C |
|---|---|---|---|---|
| 370th | February 10, 1944 | (2)Me-109 dest(air) | E/Zuider Zee | P-47 |
| | March 4 | Me-109 prob(air) | Bonn | P-47 |
| | November 21 | (2)FW-190 dest(air) | SE Kassel | P-51 |
| | | FW-190 prob(air) | SE Kassel | P-51 |
| | | FW-190 dam(air) | SE Kassel | P-51 |
| | December 24 | FW-190 dest(air) | Bonn | P-51 |
| | | 5-2-1 air | | |
| | | 0-0 ground | | |

**Hofer, Ralph K., Lt.** (28.5) Salem, MO
334th Ftr Sqn/4th Ftr Grp September 1943-July 2, 1944(KIA)
Hit by a Me-109 near Budapest.
Earlier served with 236 Sqn, RAF
72 missions, 286 hours

P-47C QP-L 41-6484 "Missouri Kid"
P-51B QP-L 42-106924 "Salem Representative"
S/Sgt. Robert Kellett-c/c

| Sqn | Date | Claims | Location | A/C |
|---|---|---|---|---|
| 334th | October 8, 1943 | Me-109 dest(air) | NE Amsterdam | P-47 |
| | February 6, 1944 | Me-109 dest(air) | W/Paris | P-47 |
| | March 16 | Me-110 dest(air) | Munich | P-51 |
| | March 18 | (2)Me-109 dest(air) | SE Mannheim | P-51 |
| | March 21 | He-177 dest(grd) | Langen A/F | P-51 |
| | March 23 | FW-190 dest(air) | E/Hamm | P-51 |
| | | Me-109 dam(air) | E/Hamm | P-51 |
| | April 1 | Me-109 dest(air) | NW Lake Constance | P-51 |
| | April 8 | Me-109 dest(air) | Celle | P-51 |
| | April 11 | Me-110 dest(air) | SE Stettin | P-51 |
| | April 18 | (2)He-177 dest(grd) | Fassberg A/F | P-51 |
| | May 1 | Me-109 dest(air) | Koln | P-51 |
| | May 12 | (.5)Me-109 dest(air)[*] | N/Coburg | P-51 |
| | May 21 | (.5)Bu-131 dest(air)[**] | Rathenow | P-51 |
| | | Bu-131 dest(grd) | Rathenow | P-51 |
| | May 22 | Me-109 dest(air) | Hamburg | P-51 |
| | May 24 | (2)FW-190 dest(air) | E/Hamburg | P-51 |
| | May 28 | Me-109 dest(air) | Magdeburg | P-51 |
| | May 29 | (4)He-177 dest(grd) | Mackfitz A/F | P-51 |
| | May 30 | (2.5)FW-190 dest(grd)[@] | Oschersleben | P-51 |
| | May 31 | (3)Bu-131 dest(grd) | Luxeuil A/F | P-51 |
| | June 21 | Me-109 dam(air) | Siedlce | P-51 |
| | | 15-0-2 air | | |
| | | 13.5-0 ground | | |

* - shared with Lt. L.R. Pierce of the 334th Ftr Sqn
** - shared with Lt. A.C. Hewatt of the 334th Ftr Sqn
@ - shared with Lt. F.C. Jones of the 335th Ftr Sqn, 4th Ftr Grp

**Hollingsworth, James M., Capt.** (10) Montesano, WA
434th Ftr Sqn/479th Ftr Grp July 1944-September 1944
HdQts/479th Ftr Grp September 1944-November 1944
434th Ftr Sqn/479th Ftr Grp November 1944-December 25, 1944(KIA)
Hit by e/a southwest of Bonn
Earlier flew with the 14th Ftr Grp, 12th Air Force in the MTO claiming 3 kills: a Do-217 on May 23, 1943, and single Me-109's on June 24 and August 19, 1943.

P-51D L2-A 44-14892 "Miss"

| Sqn | Date | Claims | Location | A/C |
|---|---|---|---|---|
| 434th | August 28, 1944 | Do-217 dest(grd) | Sedan/Douzy A/F | P-38 |
| | September 5 | (4)Me-410 dest(grd) | Ettinghausen | P-38 |
| | | (2)Do-217 dest(grd) | Ettinghausen | P-38 |
| | December 25 | Me-109 prob(air) | SW Bonn | P-51 |
| | | Me-109 dam(air) | SW Bonn | P-51 |
| | | 0-1-1 air | | |
| | | 7-0 ground | | |

**Hooker, Verne E., Capt.** (6) Great Falls, MT
435th Ftr Sqn/479th Ftr Grp January 1944-EOW
85 missions

P-38J J2-H
P-51D J2-H 44-14827
P-51D J2-H 44-73138

| *Sqn* | *Date* | *Claims* | *Location* | *A/C* |
|---|---|---|---|---|
| 435th | August 18, 1944 | (.5)He-111 dest(grd)[*] | Nancy/Essey A/F | P-38 |
| | | (.5)He-111 dest(grd)[**] | see above | P-38 |
| | | Ju-88 dam(grd) | see above | P-38 |
| | September 5 | He-111 dam(grd) | Hoehst Oberau | P-38 |
| | April 7, 1945 | Me-109 dest(air) | SE Bremen | P-51 |
| | | Me-262 dest(air) | SE Bremen | P-51 |
| | April 13 | (2)Ju-88 dest(grd) | Tarnewitz | P-51 |
| | | Ju-88 dam(grd) | Tarnewitz | P-51 |
| | April 16 | u/i a/c dest(grd) | S/Pocking | P-51 |
| | | Me-109 dam(grd) | S/Pocking | P-51 |
| | April 17 | u/i a/c dam(grd) | Puchhoff | P-51 |
| | April 18 | (2)u/i a/c dam(grd) | Mettenheim | P-51 |

2-0-0 air
4-7 ground

[*] - shared with Lt. N.W. Butler of the 435th Ftr Sqn
[**] - shared with Lt. C.F. Monsell of the 435th Ftr Sqn

**Hopcroft, Ernest J., Lt.** (7) Bay City, MI
436th Ftr Sqn/479th Ftr Grp October 1944-EOW
56 missions

P-51B 9B-G "Poontang II"
P-51D 9B-G "Daisy II"

| *Sqn* | *Date* | *Claims* | *Location* | *A/C* |
|---|---|---|---|---|
| 436th | February 22, 1945 | He-111 dam(grd) | Halberstadt | P-51 |
| | April 13 | (2)Me-410 dest(grd) | Salzwedel | P-51 |
| | | Me-109 dest(grd) | Salzwedel | P-51 |
| | April 16 | He-111 dest(grd) | Landstadt | P-51 |
| | April 17 | FW-190 dest(grd) | Puchhoff | P-51 |
| | | Me-109 dest(grd) | Puchhoff | P-51 |
| | | Fi-156 dest(grd) | Puchhoff | P-51 |
| | | u/i a/c dam(grd) | Puchhoff | P-51 |

0-0-0 air
7-2 ground

**Hopkins, Wallace E., LtCol.** (8) Washington, GA
HdQts/361st Ftr Grp Spring 1943-September 1944
HdQts/361st Ftr Grp December 1944-May 1945 (non-flying duty)
76 missions

P-47D B7-H
P-51B B7-H 42-106655 "Ferocious Frankie"
P-51D B7-H 44-13704 "Ferocious Frankie"
S/Sgt. H.J. Walker-c/c
Sgt. H.R. Brown-ac/c
Cpl. Joseph Matcha-arm.

| *Sqn* | *Date* | *Claims* | *Location* | *A/C* |
|---|---|---|---|---|
| HdQts | May 29, 1944 | (2)FW-190 dest(air) | Pitka | P-51 |
| | June 29 | (4)FW-190 dest(grd) | Oschersleben | P-51 |
| | | (1.5)FW-190 dam(grd)[*] | see above | P-51 |
| | August 8 | (2)FW-190 dest(air) | Evreux | P-51 |

4-0-0 air
4-1.5 ground

[*] - shared with Lt. V.R. Richards of the 374th Ftr Sqn, 361st Ftr Grp

**Horne, Francis W., Capt.** (6.5) Rucilla, FL
328th Ftr Sqn/352nd Ftr Grp September 1943-September 1944

P-47D PE-C 42-8580 "Hiyo Silver"
P-51B PE-S 42-106703 "Snoot's Sniper"
S/Sgt. Art Snyder-c/c
Sgt. O.J. Pinnell-ac/c

| *Sqn* | *Date* | *Claims* | *Location* | *A/C* |
|---|---|---|---|---|
| 328th | December 22, 1943 | Me-110 dest(air) | Zwolle | P-47 |
| | January 30, 1944 | (.5)FW-190 dest(air)[*] | Emmen | P-47 |
| | February 4 | FW-190 dest(air) | Brussels | P-47 |
| | April 29 | (.5)FW-190 dest(air)[**] | Calvorde | P-51 |
| | May 8 | FW-190 prob(air) | E/Bremen | P-51 |
| | May 13 | (2)FW-190 dest(air) | Demnin | P-51 |
| | May 21 | u/i a/c dest(grd) | Alt Ruppin | P-51 |
| | | He-111 dam(grd) | Alt Ruppin | P-51 |
| | June 6 | (.5)FW-190 dest(air)[@] | SE Rouen | P-51 |

5.5-1-0 air
1-1 ground

[*] - shared with Lt. Q.L. Quinn of the 328th Ftr Sqn
[**] - shared with Lt. S.E. Dyke of the 328th Ftr Sqn
[@] - shared with Lt. L.J. Allain of the 328th Ftr Sqn

**Horner, Kenneth R., Lt.** (6) Laughlintown, PA
385th Ftr Sqn/364th Ftr Grp December 1944-EOW
35 missions

| *Sqn* | *Date* | *Claims* | *Location* | *A/C* |
|---|---|---|---|---|
| 385th | February 26, 1945 | (2)He-111 dest(grd) | SE Jade Bay | P-51 |
| | March 21 | Me-109 dest(grd) | Achmer | P-51 |
| | | Me-109 dam(grd) | Achmer | P-51 |
| | April 16 | Ju-188 dest(grd) | Pocking | P-51 |
| | | FW-190 dest(grd) | Pocking | P-51 |
| | | Ju-87 dest(grd) | Pocking | P-51 |
| | | FW-190 dam(grd) | Pocking | P-51 |

0-0-0 air
6-2 ground

**Hovde, William J., Maj.** (12.5) Crookston, MN
358th Ftr Sqn/355th Ftr Grp April 1943-May 1945
113 missions

P-47D YF-I 42-8368 "Ole"
P-51B YF-I 43-6928 "Ole II"
P-51D YF-I 44-13531 "Ole III"
P-51D YF-I "Ole IV"
P-51D YF-I "Ole V"
P-51D YF-I "Ole VI"
S/Sgt. Perry A. Nebergall-c/c
Sgt. William R. Downing-ac/c
Sgt. Perry S. Wilson-arm.

| *Sqn* | *Date* | *Claims* | *Location* | *A/C* |
|---|---|---|---|---|
| 358th | February 22, 1944 | FW-190 dest(air) | SE Munster | P-47 |
| | March 18 | (2)FW-190 dest(air) | Gunzburg-Augsburg | P-51 |
| | | FW-190 dam(air) | see above | P-51 |
| | March 28 | He-111 dam(grd) | Marigny | P-51 |
| | April 8 | Me-109 dest(air) | E/Brunswick | P-51 |
| | July 19 | Me-109 dest(air) | Augsburg | P-51 |
| | July 24 | Do-217 dest(grd) | Augsburg | P-51 |
| | | Ju-88 dest(grd) | Augsburg | P-51 |
| | December 5 | (4.5)FW-190 dest(air)[*] | Berlin | P-51 |
| | | Me-109 dest(air) | Berlin | P-51 |

10.5-0-1 air
2-1 ground

[*] - shared with Lt. A.K. Alexander of the 358th Ftr Sqn

**Howe, David W., Capt.** (8.5) East Hickory, PA
334th Ftr Sqn/4th Ftr Grp September 1943-March 1945
Earlier served with the RCAF
502:05 hours

P-51B QP-S 43-6717
P-51D QP-G 44-13884
S/Sgt. Larmouth-c/c

| *Sqn* | *Date* | *Claims* | *Location* | *A/C* |
|---|---|---|---|---|
| 334th | February 21, 1944 | FW-190 dest(air) | S/Dummer Lake | P-47 |
| | March 8 | Me-109 dest(air) | S/Berlin | P-51 |
| | March 29 | FW-190 dest(air) | NW Brunswick | P-51 |
| | April 10 | (.5)u/i a/c dest(grd)[*] | Romorantin A/F | P-51 |
| | April 18 | (2)Ju-52 dest(grd) | Juterbog A/F | P-51 |
| | | (.25) of (6)Ju-52 dam(grd)[**] | see above | P-51 |
| | April 24 | Me-109 dest(air) | Darmstadt | P-51 |
| | May 19 | Me-109 dest(air) | Neustadt Bay | P-51 |
| | September 28 | FW-190 dest(air) | NE Kassel | P-51 |

6-0-0 air
2.5-1.5 ground

[*] - shared with an unknwon pilot
[**] - shared with Lt. J.L. Lang, Lt. D.M. Malmsten, and Lt. S.W. Monroe of the 334th Ftr Sqn

**Howes, Bernard H., Lt.** (8) Staughton, PA
343rd Ftr Sqn/55th Ftr Grp September 1944-March 3, 1945(POW)
Landed at Prague/Letnany to rescue a downed pilot and could not take-off.

P-51D CY-C

| *Sqn* | *Date* | *Claims* | *Location* | *A/C* |
|---|---|---|---|---|
| 343rd | December 25, 1944 | (2)Me-109 dest(air) | SW Frankfurt | P-51 |
| | February 3, 1945 | (2)FW-190 dest(air) | Boizenburg | P-51 |
| | | Ju-88 dest(air) | see above | P-51 |
| | February 19 | Me-108 dest(air) | S/Hameln | P-51 |
| | February 28 | FW-190 dest(grd) | SW Nurnburg | P-51 |
| | March 3 | Me-109 dest(grd) | Prague/Letnany | P-51 |
| | | Me-109 dam(grd) | see above | P-51 |
| | | Me-110 dam(grd) | see above | P-51 |
| | | Ju-88 dam(grd) | see above | P-51 |
| | | Ju-52 dam(grd) | see above | P-51 |

6-0-0 air
2-4 ground

**Hubbard, Mark E., LtCol.** (6.5) Wausau, WI
HdQts/20th Ftr Grp February 1944-March 18, 1944(POW)
Hit by flak near Augsburg.
Earlier flew in the MTO with the 33rd Ftr Grp, 12th Air Force, claiming 4 kills: (2)Ju-88's on January 15, 1943; a Ju-87 on February 1, 1943; and a Me-109 on March 24, 1943.
13 missions, 59:20 hours

| *Sqn* | *Date* | *Claims* | *Location* | *A/C* |
|---|---|---|---|---|
| HdQts | March 18, 1944 | (2.5)Me-109 dest(air)* | Memmingen | P-38 |
| | | Me-109 prob(air) | Memmingen | P-38 |

2.5-1-0 air
0-0 ground

* - shared with Lt. A.F. Clark of the 77th Ftr Sqn, 20th Ftr Grp

**Hunt, Harlan F., Lt.** (5) Meriden, CT
504th Ftr Sqn/339th Ftr Grp January 1945-October 1945

| *Sqn* | *Date* | *Claims* | *Location* | *A/C* |
|---|---|---|---|---|
| 504th | April 9, 1945 | Me-262 dam(air) | Leipzig | P-51 |
| | April 16 | FW-190 dest(grd) | Klatovy | P-51 |
| | | FW-190 dam(grd) | Klatovy | P-51 |
| | April 17 | Me-109 dest(grd) | Klatovy-Anberg | P-51 |
| | | FW-190 dest(grd) | see above | P-51 |
| | | Fi-156 dest(grd) | see above | P-51 |
| | | Ju-88 dest(grd) | see above | P-51 |

0-0-1 air
5-1 ground

**Hunter, John C., Capt.** (9) Ann Arbor, MI
383rd Ftr Sqn/364th Ftr Grp September 1944-July 1945
54 missions

P-51D N2-E 44-15578
T/Sgt. Max Phillips-c/c
Sgt. Elmer E. Campbell-ac/c

| *Sqn* | *Date* | *Claims* | *Location* | *A/C* |
|---|---|---|---|---|
| 383rd | November 21, 1944 | (2)FW-190 dest(air) | S/Nordhausen | P-51 |
| | | FW-190 dam(air) | S/Nordhausen | P-51 |
| | March 18, 1945 | FW-190 dest(air) | Schwerin | P-51 |
| | April 13 | (3)FW-190 dest(grd) | Flensburg | P-51 |
| | | (2)Ju-52 dest(grd) | see above | P-51 |
| | | Me-110 dest(grd) | see above | P-51 |
| | | (3)Ju-52 dam(grd) | see above | P-51 |
| | | Me-109 dam(grd) | see above | P-51 |

3-0-1 air
6-4 ground

**Icard, Joseph W., Lt.** (5) Granite Falls, NC
62nd Ftr Sqn/56th Ftr Grp August 1943-March 8, 1944(KIA)
Hit by e/a near Diepholz.

P-47D LM-I 42-75040
P-47D LM-I 42-75241
S/Sgt. Edmund R. Namowicz-c/c

| *Sqn* | *Date* | *Claims* | *Location* | *A/C* |
|---|---|---|---|---|
| 62nd | November 11, 1943 | FW-190 dest(air) | Munster | P-47 |
| | February 6, 1944 | FW-190 dam(air) | Albert | P-47 |
| | February 8 | Me-109 dest(air) | Cambrai | P-47 |
| | February 11 | Me-109 dest(air) | Bierset | P-47 |
| | February 21 | FW-190 dest(air) | Soesterberg | P-47 |
| | March 6 | FW-190 dest(air) | Dummer Lake | P-47 |

5-0-1 air
0-0 ground

**Ilfrey, Jack M., Maj.** (8) Houston, TX
79th Ftr Sqn/20th Ftr Grp April 1944-June 13, 1944(MIA-E)
Hit by flak near Angars
79th Ftr Sqn/20th Ftr Grp June 1944-December 1944
Earlier flew in the MTO with the 1st Ftr Grp, 12th Air Force, claiming six kills; a Me-110 on November 29, 1942; (2)Me-109's on December 2, 1942; (2)FW-190's on December 26, 1942; and a Me-109 on March 3, 1943.
70 missions, 320 hours

P-38J MC-O 43-28431 "Happy Jack's Go Buggy"
P-51D MC-I 44-13761 "Happy Jack's Go Buggy"
T/Sgt. Richard E. Burgess-c/c
Sgt. Roy R. Miller-ac/c
Sgt. Ralph Engelhart-ac/c
Sgt. Orville H. Herm-arm.

| *Sqn* | *Date* | *Claims* | *Location* | *A/C* |
|---|---|---|---|---|
| 79th | May 24, 1944 | (2)Me-109 dest(air) | Eberswalde | P-38 |

2-0-0 air
0-0 ground

**Irion, Robert E., Lt.** (6) Axtel, KS
505th Ftr Sqn/339th Ftr Grp September 1944-July 1945
P-51D 6N-N 44-15001 "Silver Streak"

| *Sqn* | *Date* | *Claims* | *Location* | *A/C* |
|---|---|---|---|---|
| 505th | March 1, 1945 | (.5)Ju-88 dest(grd)* | S/Feldkirchen | P-51 |
| | | (.5)Ju-88 dest(grd)** | S/Feldkirchen | P-51 |
| | March 20 | Me-262 dest(air) | Schwerin | P-51 |
| | April 10 | (2)Ju-188 dest(grd) | Wittstock | P-51 |
| | | Do-217 dest(grd) | Wittstock | P-51 |
| | | Me-110 dam(grd) | Wittstock | P-51 |
| | April 17 | Me-110 dest(grd) | SE Pocking | P-51 |

1-0-0 air
5-1 ground

* - shared with Lt. B.B. Booth of the 505th Ftr Sqn
** - shared with Lt. O.K. Biggs of the 505th Ftr Sqn

**Izor, Edward F., Capt.** (5.5) Farmersville, OH
385th Ftr Sqn/364th Ftr Grp April 1944-December 1944

P-38J 5E-O
P-51D 5E-O 44-13869

| *Sqn* | *Date* | *Claims* | *Location* | *A/C* |
|---|---|---|---|---|
| 385th | May 21, 1944 | (.5)He-111 dest(air)* | SE Luneburg | P-38 |
| | August 25 | Me-210 dest(grd) | Anklam | P-51 |
| | | (2)Me-210 dam(grd) | Anklam | P-51 |
| | September 28 | FW-190 dest(air) | SW Magdeburg | P-51 |
| | November 2 | (3)Me-109 dest(air) | Halle | P-51 |

4.5-0-0 air
1-2 ground

* - shared with Lt. C.S. Hill of the 385th Ftr Sqn

**Jabara, James, Lt.** (7) Wichita, KS
354th Ftr Sqn/355th Ftr Grp February 1945-November 1945
Earlier flew in the ETO with the 363rd Ftr Grp, 9th Air Force and claimed 1.5 kills; a shared FW-190 on June 25, 1944, and a FW-190 on August 13, 1944.
108 total missions

P-51D WR-K 44-14346 "Ceegar Kid"

| *Sqn* | *Date* | *Claims* | *Location* | *A/C* |
|---|---|---|---|---|
| 354th | March 22, 1945 | FW-190 dest(grd) | Wurzburg | P-51 |
| | | FW-190 dam(grd) | Wurzburg | P-51 |
| | April 9 | (.5)Ju-88 dest(grd)* | Memmingen | P-51 |
| | April 10 | (2)Me-410 dest(grd) | Rechlin/Larz | P-51 |
| | | (3)u/i a/c dam(grd) | Rechlin/Larz | P-51 |
| | April 13 | He-111 dest(grd) | Husum | P-51 |
| | | Me-109 dest(grd) | Husum | P-51 |
| | | Me-109 dam(grd) | Husum | P-51 |

0-0-0 air
5.5-5 ground

* - shared with F/O H.W. Falvey of the 354th Ftr Sqn

**Jackson, Boyd O., Lt.** (5) Harlem, MT
505th Ftr Sqn/339th Ftr Grp July 1944-November 21, 1944(KIA)
Hit by flak near Handorf.
38 missions

| Sqn | Date | Claims | Location | A/C |
|---|---|---|---|---|
| 505th | July 31, 1944 | FW-190 dest(grd) | Holzkirchen | P-51 |
| | September 10 | (2)u/i a/c dest(grd) | Weizenburg | P-51 |
| | | Ju-88 dest(grd) | Weizenburg | P-51 |
| | | (4)u/i a/c dam(grd) | Weizenburg | P-51 |
| | November 21 | Ju-88 dest(grd) | NE Munster | P-51 |
| | | 0-0-0 air | | |
| | | 5-4 ground | | |

**Jackson, Michael J., Maj.** (13.5) Plainfield, NJ
62nd Ftr Sqn/56th Ftr Grp June 1944-March 1945
86 missions

P-47D LM-J 44-19790 "Teddy"
P-47M LM-J 44-21117 "Teddy"
S/Sgt. Wiley O. Noah-c/c
Sgt. John F. Price-ac/c
Sgt. Robert E. Helwig-arm.

| Sqn | Date | Claims | Location | A/C |
|---|---|---|---|---|
| 62nd | July 4, 1944 | Me-109 dest(air) | Conches | P-47 |
| | July 5 | FW-190 dam(air) | N/Evreux | P-47 |
| | July 7 | Ju-52 dest(air) | Gardelegen A/F | P-47 |
| | August 28 | Ju-88 dest(air) | Irsch | P-47 |
| | September 5 | (2)Ju-88 dest(grd) | Limburg | P-47 |
| | | (1.5)Me-210 dest(grd)* | Limburg | P-47 |
| | | Me-109 dest(grd) | Limburg | P-47 |
| | | (2)Ju-88 dam(grd) | Limburg | P-47 |
| | September 21 | FW-190 dest(air) | NE Arnheim | P-47 |
| | November 6 | Me-410 dam(air) | Deventer | P-47 |
| | November 18 | FW-190 dest(air) | E/Hanau | P-47 |
| | December 4 | Me-262 dest(grd) | Neuburg | P-47 |
| | | Me-262 dam(grd) | Neuburg | P-47 |
| | | FW-200 dam(grd) | Neuburg | P-47 |
| | December 25 | Me-109 dest(air) | Bonn-Coblenz | P-47 |
| | January 14, 1945 | Me-109 dest(air) | Rheine | P-47 |
| | | FW-190 dest(air) | Rheine | P-47 |
| | | 8-0-2 air | | |
| | | 5.5-4 ground | | |

* - shared with Lt. S.T. Murray of the 62nd Ftr Sqn

**Jackson, Willie O., Jr., LtCol.** (11) Converse, LA
486th Ftr Sqn/352nd Ftr Grp May 1943-March 1944
328th Ftr Sqn/352nd Ftr Grp March 1944-April 1944
486th Ftr Sqn/352nd Ftr Grp April 1944-February 1945
HdQts/352nd Ftr Grp February 1945-September 1945
104 missions

P-47D PZ-J 42-8452
P-51B PZ-J 42-106661 "Hot Stuff"
P-51D PZ-J 44-13398
P-51D PZ-J 44-14709
S/Sgt. J.I. Sullivan-c/c
Sgt. J.R. Sturdevant-ac/c
Cpl. G.J. Peters-arm.

| Sqn | Date | Claims | Location | A/C |
|---|---|---|---|---|
| 486th | February 20, 1944 | Me-109 dest(air) | Charleroi | P-47 |
| | | Me-109 dam(air) | Charleroi | P-47 |
| 328th | April 9 | FW-190 prob(air) | Dummer Lake | P-47 |
| 486th | July 18 | Me-109 dest(air) | N/Warnemunde | P-51 |
| | | Ju-88 dest(air) | N/Warnemunde | P-51 |
| | July 19 | Me-109 dest(air) | E/Munich | P-51 |
| | November 2 | Me-109 dam(air) | N/Merseburg | P-51 |
| | | FW-190 dam(air) | N/Merseburg | P-51 |
| | November 30 | Me-109 dest(air) | W/Chemnitz | P-51 |
| | December 27 | Me-109 dest(air) | SW Bonn | P-51 |
| HdQts | March 2, 1945 | FW-189 dest(air) | Prague | P-51 |
| | | (2)u/i a/c dam(grd) | Prague | P-51 |
| | April 16 | (2)Me-109 dest(grd) | Ganacker | P-51 |
| | | (2)FW-190 dest(grd) | Ganacker | P-51 |
| | | Me-109 dam(grd) | Ganacker | P-51 |
| | | u/i a/c dam(grd) | Ganacker | P-51 |
| | | 7-1-3 air | | |
| | | 4-4 ground | | |

**Jacobson, Gail E., Lt.** (10.5) Des Moines, IA
434th Ftr Sqn/479th Ftr Grp September 1944-EOW

P-51D L2-P 44-15380 "Burn'n Bernie"
S/Sgt. Elsworth Drais-c/c
Cpl. Edward A. Tinker-ac/c

| Sqn | Date | Claims | Location | A/C |
|---|---|---|---|---|
| 434th | December 5, 1944 | (2)FW-190 dest(air) | Neuruppin | P-51 |
| | December 23 | FW-190 dest(air) | SE Bonn | P-51 |
| | December 25 | FW-190 prob(air) | SW Bonn | P-51 |
| | February 21, 1945 | He-111 dest(grd) | Gotha | P-51 |
| | March 19 | (.5)FW-190 dest(air)* | Handorf | P-51 |
| | April 7 | Me-109 dest(air) | Celle | P-51 |
| | April 16 | (2)FW-190 dest(grd) | Reichersberg | P-51 |
| | | FW-190 dam(grd) | see above | P-51 |
| | | Ju-88 dam(grd) | see above | P-51 |
| | April 18 | (2)Ju-88 dest(grd) | Ingolstadt | P-51 |
| | | FW-190 dest(grd) | Ottingen | P-51 |
| | | 4.5-1-0 air | | |
| | | 6-2 ground | | |

* - shared with Lt. F.M. Taylor of the 434th Ftr Sqn

**Jamison, Gilbert L., Capt.** (7) Olympia, WA
385th Ftr Sqn/364th Ftr Grp May 1944-December 1944

P-51D 5E-A 44-15035 "Etta Jane"
T/Sgt. Levi Campbell-c/c

| Sqn | Date | Claims | Location | A/C |
|---|---|---|---|---|
| 385th | September 11, 1944 | (2)FW-190 dest(air) | SW Leipzig | P-51 |
| | September 13 | Me-109 dest(air) | SE Kassel | P-51 |
| | October 12 | FW-190 dest(air) | NE Bremen | P-51 |
| | November 25 | Me-109 dam(grd) | Fulda | P-51 |
| | December 27 | (3)FW-190 dest(air) | SW Bonn | P-51 |
| | | Me-109 dam(air) | E/Liege | P-51 |
| | | 7-0-1 air | | |
| | | 0-1 ground | | |

**Jeffrey, Arthur F., LtCol.** (14) San Francisco, CA
434th Ftr Sqn/479th Ftr Grp September 1943-April 1945
82 missions, 352 hours

P-38J L2-O 42-104425 "Boomerang"
P-51D L2-O 44-14423 "Boomerang Jr."
P-51K L2-O 44-11674 "Boomerang Jr."
T/Sgt. N.G. Hummel-c/c
Cpl. Warren B. Shultz-ac/c
Cpl. William Neeley-arm.

| Sqn | Date | Claims | Location | A/C |
|---|---|---|---|---|
| 434th | July 5, 1944 | FW-200 dest(air) | Cognac/Chateau-Bernard A/F | P-38 |
| | July 29 | Me-163 dest(air) | Wilhelmshaven | P-38 |
| | August 15 | Me-109 dest(air) | Steenwijk A/F | P-38 |
| | August 28 | Ju-52 dest(air) | Sedan/Douzy A/F | P-38 |
| | October 7 | Me-109 dest(air) | S/Leipzig | P-51 |
| | November 2 | Me-109 dest(air) | Zeitz | P-51 |
| | December 5 | (3)FW-190 dest(air) | Neuruppin | P-51 |
| | | FW-190 dam(air) | Neuruppin | P-51 |
| | December 23 | (3)Me-109 dest(air) | SE Bonn | P-51 |
| | December 25 | Me-109 dest(air) | SW Bonn | P-51 |
| | February 14, 1945 | Me-109 dest(air) | SW Berlin | P-51 |
| | | Me-109 dam(air) | SW Berlin | P-51 |
| | | 14-0-2 air | | |
| | | 0-0 ground | | |

**Jenkins, Otto D., Lt.** (10.5) Kermit, TX
362nd Ftr Sqn/357th Ftr Grp August 1944-March 24, 1945(KIA)
Hit trees while buzzing Leiston upon completing his tour.

P-51B G4-P 42-106829 "Floogie"
P-51D G4-P 44-14245 "Floogie II"
P-51K G4-X 44-11689 "Toolin' Fool"
P-51D G4-X 44-63199 "Toolin' Fool's Revenge"
S/Sgt. Ray Morrison-c/c
Sgt. Merle C. Olmsted-ac/c
Sgt. Ray R. Viland-arm.
Sgt. Harry Bailey-arm.

| Sqn | Date | Claims | Location | A/C |
|---|---|---|---|---|
| 362nd | September 13, 1944 | (1.5)Me-109 dest(air)* | S/Nordhausen | P-51 |
| | September 19 | Me-109 dest(air) | SE Ijsselstein | P-51 |
| | | FW-190 dest(air) | Ijsselstein | P-51 |
| | October 6 | FW-190 dest(air) | NW Berlin | P-51 |
| | November 18 | (2)Me-109 dest(grd) | Mengen A/F | P-51 |
| | December 24 | (4)FW-190 dest(air) | Fulda | P-51 |
| | | 8.5-0-0 air | | |
| | | 2-0 ground | | |

[*]- shared with Lt. J.A. Kirla of the 362nd Ftr Sqn

**Jennings, Loton D., Lt.** (6) Waynem ME
335th Ftr Sqn/4th Ftr Grp October 1944-EOW

| *Sqn* | *Date* | *Claims* | *Location* | *A/C* |
|---|---|---|---|---|
| 335th | April 9, 1945 | Ju-88 dest(grd) | Munich-Brunnthal | P-51 |
| | April 13 | He-115 dest(grd) | Ratzeburger Lake | P-51 |
| | | u/i a/c dam(grd) | Ratzeburger Lake | P-51 |
| | April 16 | (2)Me-210 dest(grd) | Praha A/F | P-51 |
| | | (2)Do-217 dest(grd) | Praha A/F | P-51 |

0-0-0 air
6-1 ground

**John, Leedom K., Lt.** (5) Coatesville, PA
338th Ftr Sqn/55th Ftr Grp December 1944-September 1945
47 missions, 233 hours

P-51D CL-K 44-13642 "Ornery"
S/Sgt. Robert W. Clark-c/c
Sgt. Ernesto Gallego-ac/c
Sgt. Toney R. Todey-arm.

| *Sqn* | *Date* | *Claims* | *Location* | *A/C* |
|---|---|---|---|---|
| 338th | February 25, 1945 | Me-109 dest(grd) | Illesheim | P-51 |
| | | FW-190 dest(grd) | Illesheim | P-51 |
| | April 16 | (3)FW-200 dest(grd) | N/Landshut | P-51 |

0-0-0 air
5-0 ground

**Johnson, Clarence O., Capt.** (13) Ada, MN
436th Ftr Sqn/479th Ftr Grp November 1943-August 1944
487th Ftr Sqn/352nd Ftr Grp August 1944-September 23, 1944(KIA)
Hit by a Me-109 near Lusiendorf.
Earlier flew in the MTO with the 82nd Ftr Grp, 12th Air Force, claiming 4 kills; a MC-202 on May 24, 1943; (2)FW-190 on August 20, 1943; and a Me-109 on September 2, 1943.

P-38J 9B-R 43-28697 "Bula B III"
P-51D HO-C 44-13953 "Bula B IV"

| *Sqn* | *Date* | *Claims* | *Location* | *A/C* |
|---|---|---|---|---|
| 436th | June 22, 1944 | Fi-156 dest(air) | Reims | P-38 |
| 487th | August 25 | He-177 dest(grd) | Neubrandenburg | P-51 |
| | | Hs-129 dam(grd) | Neubrandenburg | P-51 |
| | September 10 | (5)Ju-52 dest(grd) | Wertheim | P-51 |
| | September 11 | (2)Me-109 dest(air) | Gottingen | P-51 |

3-0-0 air
6-1 ground

**Johnson, Evan M., V, Capt.** (5) Carlisle, PA
505th Ftr Sqn/339th Ftr Grp States-November 1944

P-51B 6N-J
P-51D 6N-J 44-13741 "The Comet"
P-51D 6N-J 44-15039 "Pistol Packin' Mama"
S/Sgt. Edward LeJunne-c/c

| *Sqn* | *Date* | *Claims* | *Location* | *A/C* |
|---|---|---|---|---|
| 505th | May 19, 1944 | (1.5)FW-190 dest(air)[*] | Gustrow | P-51 |
| | May 24 | FW-190 dest(air) | Berlin | P-51 |
| | June 10 | (.5)Ju-52 dest(air)[**] | Laigle | P-51 |
| | June 29 | (.5)Me-109 dest(air)[@] | Halle-S/Magdeburg | P-51 |
| | | (.5)Me-410 dest(air)[@@] | see above | P-51 |
| | September 5 | Me-410 dam(grd) | Sinsheim | P-51 |
| | November 18 | Me-109 dest(air) | Heilbronn | P-51 |
| | | Me-109 dam(air) | Heilbronn | P-51 |

5-0-1 air
0-1 ground

[*]- shared with Lt. J.R. Starnes of the 505th Ftr Sqn
[**] - shared with Capt. L. Reid of the 505th Ftr Sqn
[@] - shared with Lt. A. Sirochman of the 505th Ftr Sqn
[@@] - shared with Lt. G.E. Graham of the 505th Ftr Sqn

**Johnson, Gerald W., Maj.** (16.5) Owenton, KY
61st Ftr Sqn/ 56th Ftr Grp May 1942-November 1943
360th Ftr Sqn/356th Ftr Grp November 1943-February 1944
63rd Ftr Sqn/56th Ftr Grp February 1944-March 27, 1944(POW)
Hit by flak near Carentan.
88 missions, 196 hours

P-47D HV-D 42-7877 "In The Mood"
P-47D PI-
P-47D UN-V 42-76249
S/Sgt. George S. Baltimore-c/c(HV-D)
Cpl. Jack Kazanijan-ac/c(HV-D)
Pvt. Albert A. Asplint-arm.(HV-D)

| *Sqn* | *Date* | *Claims* | *Location* | *A/C* |
|---|---|---|---|---|
| 61st | May 14, 1943 | FW-190 dam(air) | NE Antwerp | P-47 |
| | June 26 | FW-190 dest(air) | N/Dieppe | P-47 |
| | August 17 | (2)Me-109 dest(air) | Hasselt-Diest | P-47 |
| | | (.5)Me-110 dest(air)[*] | N/Liege | P-47 |
| | | Me-109 dam(air) | Hasselt-Diest | P-47 |
| | August 19 | Me-109 dest(air) | Gilze-Rijen | P-47 |
| | | Me-109 dam(air) | Gilze-Rijen | P-47 |
| | October 10 | Me-110 dest(air) | N/Munster | P-47 |
| | | Me-210 dest(air) | N/Munster | P-47 |
| | October 14 | FW-190 dest(air) | Eupen | P-47 |
| 360th | January 14, 1944 | FW-190 dest(air) | NE Ypres | P-47 |
| | | (.5)FW-190 dam(air)[**] | NE Ypres | P-47 |
| 63rd | February 21 | FW-190 dest(air) | NW Zwolle | P-47 |
| | February 22 | FW-190 prob(air) | SW Gutersloh | P-47 |
| | February 24 | FW-190 dest(air) | Minden | P-47 |
| | February 29 | Ju-52 dest(air) | Horderwijk | P-47 |
| | March 2 | Me-109 dest(air) | SE Aachen | P-47 |
| | March 6 | FW-190 dam(air) | Wenzendorf | P-47 |
| | March 8 | (2)Me-109 dest(air) | Dummer Lake-Celle | P-47 |
| | March 15 | (2)Me-109 dest(air) | Nienburg | P-47 |

16.5-1-4.5 air
0-0 ground

[*]- shared with Lt. F.E. McCauley of the 61st Ftr Sqn
[**] - shared with Lt. W.G. Maxwell of the 360th Ftr Sqn

**Johnson, Martin H., Capt.** (10) Fort Worth, TX
375th Ftr Sqn/361st Ftr Grp Spring 1943-September 1944
75 missions, 268 hours

P-47D E2-H 42-75214
P-51B E2-H 42-106951 "Little Skipper"
P-51D E2-H 44-14103
S/Sgt. Thomas F. Organ-c/c
Sgt. Bailey H. Greedlove-ac/c

| *Sqn* | *Date* | *Claims* | *Location* | *A/C* |
|---|---|---|---|---|
| 375th | March 29, 1944 | FW-190 dest(grd) | Rheine | P-47 |
| | | Ju-88 dest(grd) | Rheine | P-47 |
| | April 18 | Ar-196 dest(grd) | Zwischenaschmer | P-47 |
| | April 24 | FW-190 dest(grd) | Metz | P-47 |
| | | Me-110 dest(grd) | Metz | P-47 |
| | | Me-109 dest(grd) | Metz | P-47 |
| | June 16 | Ju-52 dest(grd) | Toussus/Le Noble | P-51 |
| | June 21 | u/i a/c dest(grd) | Zwischenaschmer | P-51 |
| | August 15 | Ju-88 dest(grd) | Wittmunhofen | P-51 |
| | August 25 | Me-109 dest(air) | SW Rostock | P-51 |

1-0-0 air
9-0 ground

**Johnson, Robert S., Maj.** (27) Lawton, OK
61st Ftr Sqn/56th Ftr Grp July 1942-April 1944
62nd Ftr Sqn/56th Ftr Grp April 1944-May 1944
91 missions

P-47C HV-P 41-6235 "All Hell"
P-47D HV-P 42-8461 "Lucky"
P-47D HV-P 42-76234
P-47D LM-Q 42-25512 "Penrod & Sam"
S/Sgt. Ernest D. Gould-c/c(61st)
S/Sgt. Stan P. Morawski-ac/c(61st)
Cpl. Lawrence E. Baker-arm.(61st)
S/Sgt. J.C. Penrod-c/c(62nd)
Sgt. Frank Bridges-arm.(62nd)

| *Sqn* | *Date* | *Claims* | *Location* | *A/C* |
|---|---|---|---|---|
| 61st | June 13, 1943 | FW-190 dest(air) | SE Bergues | P-47 |
| | August 19 | Me-109 dest(air) | NE Woensdrecht | P-47 |
| | August 24 | FW-190 dam(air) | Evreux | P-47 |
| | October 8 | FW-190 dest(air) | Lingen | P-47 |
| | October 10 | FW-190 dest(air) | N/Munster | P-47 |
| | | Me-110 dest(air) | N/Munster | P-47 |
| | November 3 | Me-109 dest(air) | N/Ameland Island | P-47 |
| | December 22 | Me-109 dest(air) | N/Almelo | P-47 |
| | December 30 | FW-190 dest(air) | Soissons | P-47 |
| | December 31 | (2)FW-190 dest(air) | N/St. Gilles | P-47 |
| | January 5, 1944 | FW-190 dest(air) | N/Liege | P-47 |
| | January 21 | FW-190 dest(air) | N/Rouen | P-47 |

| Sqn | Date | Claims | Location | A/C |
|---|---|---|---|---|
| | January 30 | Me-109 dest(air) | E/Lingen | P-47 |
| | | Me-210 dest(air) | E/Lingen | P-47 |
| | February 20 | (2)Me-110 dest(air) | W/Hanover | P-47 |
| | | (2)Me-110 dam(air) | W/Hanover | P-47 |
| | March 6 | FW-190 dest(air) | N/Dummer Lake | P-47 |
| | March 8 | (2)Me-109 dest(air) | NE Steinhuder L. | P-47 |
| | March 15 | (2)FW-190 dest(air) | Dummer Lake | P-47 |
| | | Me-109 dest(air) | Dummer Lake | P-47 |
| | April 9 | FW-190 dest(air) | NW Kiel | P-47 |
| | April 13 | (2)FW-190 dest(air) | Kaiserlautern | P-47 |
| 62nd | May 8 | Me-109 dest(air) | Brunswick-Hanover | P-47 |
| | | FW-190 dest(air) | Brunswick-Hanover | P-47 |

27-0-3 air
0-0 ground

**Johnson, Wilton W., Maj.** (5.33) Dessel, MN
352nd Ftr Sqn/353rd Ftr Grp February 1943-EOW
114 missions, 365:35 hours

P-47D SX-D
P-47D SX-D 42-26011
P-51D SX-D
S/Sgt. Fred Nasser-c/c
Sgt. Charles B. Perkins-ac/c

| Sqn | Date | Claims | Location | A/C |
|---|---|---|---|---|
| 352nd | December 30, 1943 | FW-190 dest(air) | Charleville | P-47 |
| | January 21, 1944 | (.33)Do-217 dest(grd)* | Albert | P-47 |
| | May 19 | Me-109 dam(air) | SW Brunswick | P-47 |
| | December 5 | FW-190 dest(air) | NE Berlin | P-51 |
| | March 1, 1945 | Bu-181 dest(air) | Nordlingen | P-51 |
| | | (4)u/i a/c dam(grd) | Nordlingen | P-51 |
| | April 17 | (2)FW-190 dest(grd) | Muldorf | P-51 |
| | | (3)FW-190 dam(grd) | Muldorf | P-51 |
| | | Me-109 dam(grd) | Ganacker | P-51 |

3-0-1 air
2.33-8 ground

* - shared with Col. G.E. Duncan of HdQts, 353rd Ftr Grp, and Lt. C.H. Sperry of the 352nd Ftr Sqn

**Johnston, Ben D., Jr., Lt.** (7) Jacksonville, FL
357th Ftr Sqn/355th Ftr Grp February 1943-March 29, 1944(POW)
Suffered m/f near Brunswick.

P-47D OS-I 42-22471
P-51B OS-I

| Sqn | Date | Claims | Location | A/C |
|---|---|---|---|---|
| 357th | December 1, 1943 | Me-109 dest(air) | W/Cologne | P-47 |
| | | Me-109 dam(air) | W/Cologne | P-47 |
| | February 20, 1944 | Me-109 dest(air) | Siegen | P-47 |
| | February 21 | FW-190 dam(air) | Dummer Lake | P-47 |
| | March 28 | (2)Me-210 dest(grd) | Dijon | P-51 |
| | | Ju-88 dest(grd) | Dijon | P-51 |
| | | Me-109 dam(grd) | Dijon | P-51 |
| | | Me-210 dam(grd) | Dijon | P-51 |
| | | Ju-88 dam(grd) | Dijon | P-51 |
| | March 29 | (2)FW-190 dest(air) | Brunswick | P-51 |
| | | FW-190 dam(air) | Brunswick | P-51 |

4-0-3 air
3-3 ground

**Joiner, Joseph H., Capt.** (7.5) Chorpus Christi, FL
336th Ftr Sqn/4th Ftr Grp May 1944-June 1945
85 missions

P-51B VF- 43-6573
P-51D VF- 44-13630
P-51D VF-R 44-14548

| Sqn | Date | Claims | Location | A/C |
|---|---|---|---|---|
| 336th | September 11, 1944 | Me-109 dest(air) | Korbach | P-51 |
| | October 6 | Me-109 dest(air) | W/Berlin | P-51 |
| | November 18 | (.5)Me-262 dam(grd)* | Leipheim | P-51 |
| | | (.5)Me-262 dam(grd)* | Leipheim | P-51 |
| | | (.5)Me-262 dam(grd)* | Leipheim | P-51 |
| | January 16, 1945 | (4)FW-190 dest(grd) | Neuhausen A/F | P-51 |
| | February 20 | (1.5)FW-190 dest(air)** | N/Ingolstadt | P-51 |

3.5-0-0 air
4-1.5 ground

* - all shared with Lt. H.A. Kaul of the 336th Ftr Sqn
** - shared with Capt. K.E. Carlson of the 336th Ftr Sqn

**Jones, Cyril W., Lt.** (11) Athens, TN
370th Ftr Sqn/359th Ftr Grp August 1944-September 12, 1944(KIA)
Hit by flak near Coburg.
16 missions
P-51D CS-W 44-14071 "Dora Dee"

| Sqn | Date | Claims | Location | A/C |
|---|---|---|---|---|
| 370th | August 9, 1944 | Me-109 dest(air) | Gunzburg | P-51 |
| | | Me-109 dam(air) | Gunzburg | P-51 |
| | August 16 | Me-163 dest(air) | SE Leipzig | P-51 |
| | September 11 | (4)Me-109 dest(air) | Gotha | P-51 |
| | | He-177 dest(grd) | Gotha | P-51 |
| | | Ju-88 dest(grd) | Gotha | P-51 |
| | | (2)Me-410 dam(grd) | Gotha | P-51 |
| | | (2)Ju-88 dam(grd) | Gotha | P-51 |
| | | (.5)He-177 dam(grd)* | Gotha | P-51 |
| | September 12 | (3)u/i a/c dest(grd) | S/Memmingen | P-51 |

6-0-1 air
5-4.5 ground

* - shared with Lt. W.C. Murray of the 370th Ftr Sqn

**Jones, Frank C., Capt.** (10.5) Montclair, NJ
335th Ftr Sqn/4th Ftr Grp March 1944-August 8, 1944(KIA)
Hit by flak over Norway and crashed into the North Sea.
62 missions

P-51B WD-P 43-6897
P-51D WD-P 44-13389

| Sqn | Date | Claims | Location | A/C |
|---|---|---|---|---|
| 335th | April 5, 1944 | (2)u/i a/c dest(grd) | SE Berlin | P-51 |
| | April 8 | Me-109 dam(air) | Wolfenbuttel | P-51 |
| | April 10 | (2)u/i a/c dam(grd) | Romorantin A/F | P-51 |
| | April 12 | Me-109 dest(air) | Brunswick | P-51 |
| | April 15 | He-177 dest(grd) | Hagenow | P-51 |
| | April 22 | Me-109 dest(air) | Kassel | P-51 |
| | May 1 | Me-109 dest(air) | Zweibrucken | P-51 |
| | | Me-109 dam(air) | Zweibrucken | P-51 |
| | May 24 | Me-109 prob(air) | Hamburg | P-51 |
| | May 30 | (1.5)FW-190 dest(grd)* | Oschersleben | P-51 |
| | | FW-190 dam(grd) | Oschersleben | P-51 |
| | June 20 | Me-109 dest(air) | Stettin | P-51 |
| | June 21 | Me-109 dest(air) | Kobryn | P-51 |
| | | Me-109 dam(air) | Kobryn | P-51 |
| | August 8 | Ju-88 dest(grd) | Stravanger/Sola | P-51 |

5-1-3 air
5.5-3 ground

* - shared with Lt. R.K. Hofer of the 334th Ftr Sqn, 4th Ftr Grp

**Jones, Reps D., Capt.** (7) Miami Springs, FL
77th Ftr Sqn/20th Ftr Grp September 1944-EOW
60 missions, 315:15 hours

P-51D LC-F 44-14823 "Miss Miami"

| Sqn | Date | Claims | Location | A/C |
|---|---|---|---|---|
| 77th | November 2, 1944 | Me-109 dest(air) | Merseburg | P-51 |
| | | Me-109 prob(air) | Merseburg | P-51 |
| | January 14, 1945 | FW-190 dest(air) | Perleburg | P-51 |
| | February 9 | (4)FW-190 dest(grd) | Esperstadt A/F | P-51 |
| | | Me-109 dest(grd) | Esperstadt A/F | P-51 |
| | February 20 | u/i a/c dam(grd) | Straubing | P-51 |
| | March 2 | FW-190 dam(air) | Chemnitz | P-51 |

2-1-1 air
5-1 ground

**Jones, Thomas W., Lt.** (6.5) Meherin, VA
352nd Ftr Sqn/353rd Ftr Grp May 1944-November 1944
66 missions

P-47D SX-R 42-26665
P-51D SX-Y
S/Sgt. Ralph Moore-c/c
Sgt. Ernest Gardner-ac/c
Cpl. Blake Probert-arm.

| Sqn | Date | Claims | Location | A/C |
|---|---|---|---|---|
| 352nd | July 30, 1944 | u/i a/c dest(grd) | Orleans/Bricy | P-47 |
| | August 4 | (2)He-111 dest(grd) | Plantlunne | P-47 |
| | | u/i a/c dest(grd) | Plantlunne | P-47 |
| | August 12 | (2)He-111 dest(grd) | E/Paris | P-47 |
| | August 28 | (.5)Ju-88 dest(air)* | SE Luxembourg | P-47 |

0.5-0-0 air
6-0 ground

* - shared with Lt. B. Parker of the 352nd Ftr Sqn

**Jones, William A., Lt.** (7) Phoenix, AZ
505th Ftr Sqn/339th Ftr Grp States-September 11, 1944(POW)
Hit by a Me-262 near Ardlingen.
297 hours

P-51C 6N-E 43-25038 "Impatient Virgin"

| Sqn | Date | Claims | Location | A/C |
|---|---|---|---|---|
| 505th | May 9, 1944 | Me-109 dest(air) | Vouziers | P-51 |
| | June 8 | FW-190 dest(air) | Rennes | P-51 |
| | July 29 | (.5)Ju-52 dest(grd)* | NW Naumberg | P-51 |
| | September 10 | Ju-87 dest(grd) | Weizenburg | P-51 |
| | | u/i a/c dest(grd) | see above | P-51 |
| | | (.5)Me-109 dest(grd)** | see above | P-51 |
| | | (2)He-111 dam(grd) | see above | P-51 |
| | September 11 | Ju-88 dest(grd) | Munich | P-51 |
| | | Ju-52 dest(grd) | Munich | P-51 |
| | | Ju-88 dam(grd) | Munich | P-51 |

2-0-0 air
5-3 ground

* - shared with Lt. G.J. Hrico of the 505th Ftr Sqn
** - shared with Lt. C.R. Stewart of the 505th Ftr Sqn

**Jordan, William J., Capt.** (5.5) East Orange, NJ
352nd Ftr Sqn/353rd Ftr Grp December 1942-December 1944
106 missions, 380 hours

P-47D SX-T 42-8396 "Lucky"
P-51D SX-T 44-14631 "Lucky Too"
T/Sgt. F.S. Robosky-c/c
Sgt. H.L. Gibson-ac/c

| Sqn | Date | Claims | Location | A/C |
|---|---|---|---|---|
| 352nd | February 10, 1944 | Me-210 prob(air) | Lingen | P-47 |
| | March 29 | Me-109 dest(air) | SW Bremen | P-47 |
| | July 30 | (2.5)u/i a/c dest(grd)* | Orleans/Bricy | P-47 |
| | August 4 | (.5)u/i a/c dest(grd)** | Plantlunne | P-47 |
| | August 12 | (.5)u/i a/c desy(grd)@ | E/Paris | P-47 |
| | November 18 | FW-190 dest(grd) | Lechfeld | P-51 |

1-1-0 air
4.5-0 ground

* - shared with Capt. L.P. Cles of the 352nd Ftr Sqn
** - shared with Lt. G.N. Porterfield of the 352nd Ftr Sqn
@ - shared with Lt. R. Eluhow of the 352nd Ftr Sqn

**Josey, Danford E., Lt.** (8) Scotland Neck, NC
84th Ftr Sqn/78th Ftr Grp March 1945-July 1945
4 missions

No regular aircraft or crew

| Sqn | Date | Claims | Location | A/C |
|---|---|---|---|---|
| 84th | April 16, 1945 | (2)FW-190 dest(grd) | Praha/Kakewice | P-51 |
| | | Me-109 dest(grd) | see above | P-51 |
| | | He-111 dest(grd) | see above | P-51 |
| | | u/i a/c dest(grd) | see above | P-51 |
| | | (2)FW-190 dam(grd) | see above | P-51 |
| | | Ju-52 dam(grd) | see above | P-51 |
| | | u/i a/c dam(grd) | see above | P-51 |
| | April 17 | FW-190 dest(grd) | W/Dresden | P-51 |
| | | Ju-88 dest(grd) | W/Dresden | P-51 |
| | | u/i a/c dest(grd) | W/Dresden | P-51 |
| | | FW-190 dam(grd) | W/Dresden | P-51 |
| | | Ju-88 dam(grd) | W/Dresden | P-51 |

0-0-0 air
8-6 ground

**Juchheim, Alwin M., Capt.** (15) Grenada, MS
83rd Ftr Sqn/78th Ftr Grp September 1943-May 28, 1944(POW)
Collided with a P-51 near Gardelegen.
76 missions, 237 hours

P-47D HL-J 42-74690
P-47D HL-J 42-26020 "Lady Jane"
S/Sgt. Robert H. McCord-c/c

| Sqn | Date | Claims | Location | A/C |
|---|---|---|---|---|
| 83rd | February 22, 1944 | Me-109 dest(air) | E/Eindhoven | P-47 |
| | | FW-190 dam(air) | E/Eindhoven | P-47 |
| | February 24 | (2)Me-109 dest(air) | Furstenau | P-47 |
| | April 10 | (3)FW-190 dest(grd) | Romorantin A/F | P-47 |
| | | Hs-123 dest(grd) | Romorantin A/F | P-47 |
| | April 11 | FW-190 dest(air) | Luneburg | P-47 |
| | | FW-190 prob(air) | Luneburg | P-47 |
| | April 13 | FW-190 dest(air) | Beuchenbeuren | P-47 |
| | | FW-190 dest(grd) | Beuchenbeuren | P-47 |
| | April 24 | (.5)Me-110 dest(grd)* | Trier | P-47 |
| | | Me-110 dam(grd) | Trier | P-47 |
| | April 30 | (2)FW-190 dest(air) | Dreux | P-47 |
| | | FW-190 prob(air) | Dreux | P-47 |
| | | FW-190 dam(air) | Dreux | P-47 |
| | May 25 | Me-109 dest(air) | St. Dizier | P-47 |
| | | (.5)He-111 dest(grd)** | St. Dizier | P-47 |
| | May 27 | Me-109 dest(air) | Frieburg | P-47 |

9-2-2 air
6-1 ground

* - shared with Lt. V.J. Massa of the 83rd Ftr Sqn
** - shared with Lt. L.R. Casey of the 83rd Ftr Sqn

**Julian, William H., LtCol.** (8) Dallas, TX
83rd Ftr Sqn/ 78th Ftr Grp February 1943-March 1945
504th Ftr Sqn/339th Ftr Grp March 1945-EOW

P-47C HL-R 41-6628
P-51K HL-D 44-12126
P-51D 5Q-

| Sqn | Date | Claims | Location | A/C |
|---|---|---|---|---|
| 83rd | May 14, 1943 | FW-190 dam(air) | St. Nicholas | P-47 |
| | December 30 | Me-109 dest(air) | Reims | P-47 |
| | December 31 | FW-190 dest(air) | NE Lorient | P-47 |
| | July 5, 1944 | FW-190 dest(air) | Evreux | P-47 |
| | March 2, 1945 | (2)Me-109 dest(air) | Burg A/F | P-51 |
| | | Me-109 dam(air) | Burg A/F | P-51 |
| 504th | April 10 | (2)Me-410 dest(grd) | N/Neuruppin | P-51 |
| | | (2)Me-410 dam(grd) | N/Neuruppin | P-51 |
| | April 16 | u/i a/c dest(grd) | Klatovy | P-51 |
| | | Me-109 dam(grd) | Klatovy | P-51 |
| | | FW-190 dam(grd) | Klatovy | P-51 |

5-0-2 air
3-4 ground

**Jure, James M., Lt.** (5) Dallas, TX
61st Ftr Sqn/56th Ftr Grp April 1944-September 1944

| Sqn | Date | Claims | Location | A/C |
|---|---|---|---|---|
| 61st | May 13, 1944 | FW-190 dest(air) | NE Hamburg | P-47 |
| | June 27 | Me-109 dest(air) | Esternay | P-47 |
| | | Me-109 prob(air) | Esternay | P-47 |
| | August 4 | (.5)u/i a/c dest(grd)* | Salenter Lake | P-47 |
| | August 28 | (.5)He-111 dest(air)** | S/Saarbrucken | P-47 |
| | September 5 | He-111 dest(grd) | Merzhausen | P-47 |
| | | Ju-88 dam(grd) | Merzhausen | P-47 |
| | | u/i a/c dam(grd) | Merzhausen | P-47 |
| | September 12 | Me-109 dest(air) | N/Brandenburg | P-47 |

3.5-1-0 air
1.5-2 ground

* - shared with Lt. S.H. Getz of the 61st Ftr Sqn
** - shared with Capt. P.A. Conger of the 61st Ftr Sqn

**Jurgens, Fred H., F/O** (8) Long Island, NY
79th Ftr Sqn/20th Ftr Grp January 1945-EOW
27 missions, 166:05 hours
P-51D MC-K 44-15341 "Brown Eyes"

| Sqn | Date | Claims | Location | A/C |
|---|---|---|---|---|
| 79th | April 10, 1945 | (3)He-111 dest(grd) | Werder | P-51 |
| | | (2)Si-204 dest(grd) | Werder | P-51 |
| | | (2)Caudron dest(grd) | Werder | P-51 |
| | | u/i a/c dest(grd) | Werder | P-51 |

0-0-0 air
8-0 ground

**Karger, Dale E., Lt.** (11.5) McKees Rock, PA
364th Ftr Sqn/357th Ftr Grp September 1944-May 1945
65 missions, 293:45 hours

P-51D C5-U 44-15026 "Cathy Mae"
P-51D C5-U 44-72313 "Cathy Mae II"
S/Sgt. Arthur Krantz-c/c
Sgt. Melvin Black-arm.

| Sqn | Date | Claims | Location | A/C |
|---|---|---|---|---|
| 364th | December 5, 1944 | (2)FW-190 dest(air) | N/Berlin | P-51 |
| | December 24 | Me-109 dest(air) | S/Kassel | P-51 |
| | January 14, 1945 | Me-109 dest(air) | NW Berlin | P-51 |
| | January 20 | Me-262 dest(air) | N/Munich | P-51 |
| | March 2 | (.5)Me-109 dest(air)* | SE Magdeburg | P-51 |
| | | (4)u/i a/c dest(grd) | E/Magdeburg | P-51 |
| | | (2)Ju-88 dam(grd) | see above | P-51 |
| | | Ju-188 dam(grd) | see above | P-51 |
| | | u/i a/c dam(grd) | see above | P-51 |
| | March 24 | (2)Me-109 dest(air) | SW Gutersloh | P-51 |
| | | 7.5-0-0 air | | |
| | | 4-4 ground | | |

* - shared with Capt. R.G. Schimanski of the 364th Ftr Sqn

**Keen, Robert J., Capt.** (10) Jacksonville, FL
61st Ftr Sqn/56th Ftr Grp January 1944-August 1944
62nd Ftr Sqn/56th Ftr Grp August 1944-September 1944

| Sqn | Date | Claims | Location | A/C |
|---|---|---|---|---|
| 61st | May 13, 1944 | (3)FW-190 dest(air) | W/Hagenow | P-47 |
| | | FW-190 prob(air) | W/Hagenow | P-47 |
| | July 5 | (3)Me-109 dest(air) | Evreux | P-47 |
| | | Me-109 dam(air) | Evreux | P-47 |
| | September 5 | (3)FW-190 dest(grd) | Gelnhausen | P-47 |
| | | (3)FW-190 dam(grd) | Gelnhausen | P-47 |
| | September 16 | Ju-88 dest(grd) | Dummer Lake | P-47 |
| | | 6-1-1 air | | |
| | | 4-3 ground | | |

**Kemp, William T., Lt.** (6) East Peoria, IL
375th Ftr Sqn/361st Ftr Grp June 1944-February 1945

P-51C E2-X 42-103749 "Betty Lee"
P-51D E2-X 44-14270 "Betty Lee II"
P-51D E2-X 44-15076 "Betty Lee III"
S/Sgt. Ted Coker-c/c
Sgt. Joseph Redden-ac/c

| Sqn | Date | Claims | Location | A/C |
|---|---|---|---|---|
| 375th | July 20, 1944 | Me-109 dest(air) | N/Leipzig | P-51 |
| | | FW-190 dest(air) | N/Leipzig | P-51 |
| | August 7 | FW-190 dest(air) | Chartres | P-51 |
| | | FW-190 dam(air) | Chartres | P-51 |
| | | (.5)Me-109 dam(grd)* | Chartres | P-51 |
| | September 12 | (3)Me-109 dest(air) | NE Magdeburg | P-51 |
| | | 5-0-1 air | | |
| | | 0-0.5 ground | | |

* - shared with Lt. L.A. Wood of the 375th Ftr Sqn

**Kerr, Warren E., Capt.** (5) New Castle, PA
63rd Ftr Sqn/56th Ftr Grp February 1944-December 1944
68 missions, 270 hours

P-47D UN- 42-75461

| Sqn | Date | Claims | Location | A/C |
|---|---|---|---|---|
| 63rd | April 9 1944 | Ar-196 dest(grd) | Schleswig | P-47 |
| | April 24 | (2)Me-109 dest(grd) | Thalheim A/F | P-47 |
| | | Me-110 dest(grd) | Thalheim A/F | P-47 |
| | | Me-110 dam(grd) | Thalheim A/F | P-47 |
| | October 5 | Me-110 dest(grd) | S/Geseke | P-47 |
| | | 0-0-0 air | | |
| | | 5-1 ground | | |

**Kesler, Gilbert L., Lt.** (5.5) Washington, D.C.
336th Ftr Sqn/4th Ftr Grp September 1944-May 1945
57 missions

P-51C VF-C 42-103602
P-51D VF-Y 44-72285 "Becky"

| Sqn | Date | Claims | Location | A/C |
|---|---|---|---|---|
| 336th | January 1, 1945 | (.5)Me-109 dest(air)* | Ulzen | P-51 |
| | January 16 | FW-190 dest(grd) | Neuhausen | P-51 |
| | | He-177 dest(grd) | Neuhausen | P-51 |
| | February 27 | (2)Ju-52 dest(grd) | Weimar | P-51 |
| | | Me-109 dest(grd) | Weimar | P-51 |
| | | 0.5-0-0 air | | |
| | | 5-0 ground | | |

* - shared with Lt. A.O. Wallace of the 336th Ftr Sqn

**Kier, Edward L., Capt.** (7) Wyandot, CO
55th Ftr Sqn/20th Ftr Grp October 1944-EOW
46 missions, 261 hours

P-51D KI-F 44-14330
T/Sgt. John G. McAdams-c/c
S/Sgt. Calvin A. Purtle-ac/c

| Sqn | Date | Claims | Location | A/C |
|---|---|---|---|---|
| 55th | February 25, 1945 | (2)Me-109 dest(air) | Dummer Lake | P-51 |
| | April 10 | (5)Ju-88 dest(grd) | Berlin | P-51 |
| | | (4)Ju-88 dam(grd) | Berlin | P-51 |
| | | 2-0-0 air | | |
| | | 5-4 ground | | |

**King, Benjamin H., Maj.** (7) Oklahoma City, OK
436th Ftr Sqn/479th Ftr Grp States-August 1944
368th Ftr Sqn/359th Ftr Grp August 1944-December 1944
Earlier flew in the PTO with the 347th Ftr Grp, 13th Air Force, and claimed 3 kills: (2)Zeros on July 17, 1943, and a Zero on November 1, 1943.
122 missions, 470 hours total PTO & ETO

P-38J 9B- "Matilda III"
P-51D CV-A 44-13898 "Matilda IV"

| Sqn | Date | Claims | Location | A/C |
|---|---|---|---|---|
| 368th | September 11, 1944 | (2)FW-190 dest(air) | Eisleben | P-51 |
| | | Me-109 dest(air) | Eisleben | P-51 |
| | September 12 | Me-109 dest(air) | Gransee | P-51 |
| | | 4-0-0 air | | |
| | | 0-0 ground | | |

**Kinnard, Claiborne H., Jr., LtCol.** (25) Franklin, TN
360th Ftr Sqn/356th Ftr Grp May 1943-November 1943
354th Ftr Sqn/355th Ftr Grp November 1943-June 1944
HdQts/355th Ftr Grp June 1944-September 1944
HdQts/ 4th Ftr Grp September 1944-December 1944
HdQts/355th Ftr Grp February 1945-June 1945

P-47D PI-A
P-47D WR-A 42-75275 "Man O'War"
P-51B WR-A 43-6431 "Man O'War"
P-51B WR-A 42-106950 "Man O'War"
P-51D WR-A 44-15625 "Man O'War"
P-51D WR-A 44-72144 "Man O'War"
P-51D QP-A 44-14292 "Man O'War"
S/Sgt. Mirion B. Wells-c/c(356th)
Sgt. Robert S. Bone-arm.(356th)
S/Sgt. A.J. Mocerino-c/c(355th)
S/Sgt. Virgil McAfee-c/c(355th)
Sgt. Darrell-ac/c(355th)
S/Sgt. Roderic Lonier-c/c(4th)

| Sqn | Date | Claims | Location | A/C |
|---|---|---|---|---|
| 354th | March 29, 1944 | FW-190 dest(air) | SW Brunswick | P-51 |
| | April 5 | JW-34 dest(air) | Landsberg | P-51 |
| | | (2)Do-217 dest(grd) | Landsberg | P-51 |
| | | Me-110 dest(grd) | Landsberg | P-51 |
| | | (2)Do-217 dam(grd) | Landsberg | P-51 |
| | April 10 | Ju-88 dest(grd) | Bourges | P-51 |
| | | u/i a/c dam(grd) | Bourges | P-51 |
| | April 13 | (3)Ju-88 dest(grd) | Oberpfaffenhofen | P-51 |
| | | Do-217 dest(grd) | see above | P-51 |
| | | Do-217 dam(grd) | see above | P-51 |
| | June 24 | (3)Me-109 dest(grd) | Seiches | P-51 |
| HdQts | July 5 | (.5)Ju-88 dest(grd)* | Chateauroux | P-51 |
| | July 7 | (2)Me-410 dest(air) | Lingen | P-51 |
| | | Me-109 dest(air) | Lingen | P-51 |
| HdQts (4th) | September 11 | Me-109 dest(air) | Halle | P-51 |
| | | Me-410 dest(grd) | Halle | P-51 |
| | September 13 | (2)Hs-123 dest(grd) | Gelcheim | P-51 |
| | April 13, 1945 | (2.5)He-111 dest(grd)** | Schleswig | P-51 |
| | April 20 | (2)Me-109 dest(air) | Prague/Letnany | P-51 |
| | | Me-109 dam(air) | Prague/Letnany | P-51 |
| | | 8-0-1 air | | |
| | | 17-4 ground | | |

* - shared with Lt. R.E. Hulderman of the 354th Ftr Sqn
** - shared with Lt. V.R. Gore of the 358th Ftr Sqn, 355th Ftr Grp

**Kirby, Henry H., Jr., Maj.** (6) Little Rock, AR
357th Ftr Sqn/355th Ftr Grp Early 1943-June 1944
HdQts/355th Ftr Grp June 1944-EOW

P-47D OS-N 42-8399 "Arkansas Traveler"
P-51B OS-N 43-7140 "Arkansas Traveler"
P-51B OS-N 43-24795 "Arkansas Traveler"
P-51D OS-N 44-13771 "Arkansas Traveler"

| *Sqn* | *Date* | *Claims* | *Location* | *A/C* |
|---|---|---|---|---|
| 357th | March 16, 1944 | Me-109 dam(air) | W/Augsburg | P-51 |
| | April 8 | Do-217 dest(grd) | Gifhorn | P-51 |
| | | Ju-88 dest(grd) | Gifhorn | P-51 |
| HdQts | September 18 | Me-109 dest(air) | NW Warsaw | P-51 |
| | March 1, 1945 | Me-262 dam(air) | Donauworth | P-51 |
| | March 30 | Me-109 dest(grd) | Lowenstadt | P-51 |
| | | FW-190 dest(grd) | see above | P-51 |
| | | (.5)He-111 dam(grd)* | see above | P-51 |
| | April 10 | Ju-88 dest(grd) | Rechlin/Larz | P-51 |
| | | (3)Ju-88 dam(grd) | Rechlin/Larz | P-51 |

1-0-2 air
5-3.5 ground

* - shared with Lt. H.I. Knight of the 357th Ftr Sqn

**Kirk, John A., III, Lt.** (10) Baltimore, MD
83rd Ftr Sqn/78th Ftr Grp October 1944-July 1945
49 missions, 248 hours

P-47D No regular a/c
P-51D HL-C 44-63620 "Small Boy Here"
S/Sgt. Homer D. Carlson-c/c
PFC William J. Keith-ac/c

| *Sqn* | *Date* | *Claims* | *Location* | *A/C* |
|---|---|---|---|---|
| 83rd | December 19, 1944 | Me-109 dest(air) | S/Coblenz | P-47 |
| | | FW-190 dest(air) | S/Coblenz | P-47 |
| | March 19, 1945 | Me-109 dest(air) | Osnabruck | P-51 |
| | March 21 | Me-262 dest(air) | Meiningen | P-51 |
| | April 10 | He-111 dest(grd) | Werder A/F | P-51 |
| | | Bu-133 dest(grd) | Werder A/F | P-51 |
| | April 16 | FW-190 dest(grd) | W/Prague | P-51 |
| | | Ju-88 dest(grd) | see above | P-51 |
| | | Ju-87 dest(grd) | see above | P-51 |
| | | u/i a/c dest(grd) | see above | P-51 |
| | | (3)Ju-87 dam(grd) | see above | P-51 |

4-0-0 air
6-3 ground

**Kirla, John A., Capt.** (12) Port Chester, NY
362nd Ftr Sqn/357th Ftr Grp August 1944-EOW

P-51D G4-H 44-14625 "Spook"
P-51D G4-H 44-72180 "Spook"

| *Sqn* | *Date* | *Claims* | *Location* | *A/C* |
|---|---|---|---|---|
| 362nd | September 13, 1944 | (1.5)Me-109 dest(air)* | S/Nordhausen | P-51 |
| | September 19 | Me-109 dest(air) | Ijsselstein | P-51 |
| | November 18 | (.5)He-111 dest(grd)** | Mengen A/F | P-51 |
| | December 5 | Me-109 dest(air) | Berlin | P-51 |
| | | FW-190 dest(air) | Berlin | P-51 |
| | December 24 | (3)FW-190 dest(air) | Fulda | P-51 |
| | January 14, 1945 | (2)FW-190 dest(air) | NW Berlin | P-51 |
| | | (2)Me-109 dest(air) | NW Berlin | P-51 |

11.5-0-0 air
0.5-0 ground

* - shared with Lt. O.D. Jenkins of the 362nd Ftr Sqn
** - shared with Lt. W.T. Gilbert of the 362nd Ftr Sqn

**Kissel, William F., Capt.** (5) San Mateo, CA
383rd Ftr Sqn/364th Ftr Grp September 1944-July 1945
Earlier flew in the MTO with the 12th Air Force

P-51D N2-G 44-13699

| *Sqn* | *Date* | *Claims* | *Location* | *A/C* |
|---|---|---|---|---|
| 383rd | April 13, 1945 | (4)Ju-52 dest(grd) | Flensburg | P-51 |
| | | (2)Me-109 dam(grd) | Flensburg | P-51 |
| | | Me-110 dam(grd) | Flensburg | P-51 |
| | | Ju-52 dam(grd) | Flensburg | P-51 |
| | April 17 | Me-262 dest(air) | Falkenst | P-51 |

1-0-0 air
4-4 ground

**Klibbe, Frank W., Lt.** (7) Anderson, IN
61st Ftr Sqn/56th Ftr Grp September 1943-May 1944
61 missions

P-47D HV-V 42-76179 "Little Chief"
S/Sgt. Peter Meder-c/c
Sgt. John J. Bailey-ac/c
Sgt. Tom A. Gormley-arm.

| *Sqn* | *Date* | *Claims* | *Location* | *A/C* |
|---|---|---|---|---|
| 61st | November 26, 1943 | Me-109 dest(air) | SE Oldenburg | P-47 |
| | January 30, 1944 | Me-109 dest(air) | Lingen | P-47 |
| | February 21 | Me-109 dest(air) | Zuider Zee | P-47 |
| | March 8 | Me-109 dest(air) | Steinhuder Lake | P-47 |
| | March 15 | FW-190 dest(air) | S/Barenburg | P-47 |
| | May 8 | Me-109 dest(air) | W/Celle | P-47 |
| | | FW-190 dest(air) | W/Celle | P-47 |

7-0-0 air
0-0 ground

**Kolb, Herbert G., Capt.** (14.5) Richmond, VA
350th Ftr Sqn/353rd Ftr Grp August 1944-EOW
48 missions

P-51D LH-R 44-15137 "Baby Duck"
P-51D LH-R 44-72259 "Baby Duck"
S/Sgt. Milford J. Hater-c/c
Sgt. Hartman-ac/c

| *Sqn* | *Date* | *Claims* | *Location* | *A/C* |
|---|---|---|---|---|
| 350th | November 2, 1944 | FW-190 dam(air) | NW Merseburg | P-51 |
| | February 27, 1945 | (3)FW-190 dest(grd) | Rohrensee | P-51 |
| | | (1.5)Me-410 dest(grd)* | see above | P-51 |
| | | (.5)u/i a/c dest(grd)** | see above | P-51 |
| | | FW-190 dam(grd) | see above | P-51 |
| | April 16 | (5)FW-190 dest(grd) | Pocking | P-51 |
| | | (2)Me-109 dest(grd) | Pocking | P-51 |
| | | Fi-156 dest(grd) | Pocking | P-51 |
| | | (.5)Fi-156 dest(grd)@ | Pocking | P-51 |
| | | (.5)Fi-156 dest(grd)@ | Pocking | P-51 |
| | | (.5)Hs-126 dest(grd)@ | Pocking | P-51 |
| | | (2)Ju-87 dam(grd) | Pocking | P-51 |

0-0-1 air
14.5-3 ground

* - shared with Lt. W. Grizzle of the 350th Ftr Sqn
** - shared with Lt. H.H. Hakonen of the 350th Ftr Sqn
@ - all shared with Lt. B.D. McMahan of the 350th Ftr Sqn

**Koraleski, Walter J., Capt.** (5.53)Detroit, MI
354th Ftr Sqn/355th Ftr Grp February 1943-April 15, 1944(POW)
Hit by flak near Utrecht.
60 missions, 189:10 hours

P-47D WR-L "Miss Thunder"
P-51B WR-L 43-6968

| *Sqn* | *Date* | *Claims* | *Location* | *A/C* |
|---|---|---|---|---|
| 354th | March 6, 1944 | (2.33)Me-109 dest(air)* | Dummer Lake | P-47 |
| | March 16 | Me-109 dest(air) | Ulm | P-51 |
| | March 29 | FW-190 dest(air) | Brunswick | P-51 |
| | April 5 | (.5)Me-109 dest(air)** | Landsberg | P-51 |
| | | (.5)FW-44 dest(air)** | Landsberg | P-51 |
| | | (.2)Do-217 dest(air)@ | Landsberg | P-51 |
| | | Me-110 dam(grd) | Landsberg | P-51 |
| | | Do-217 dam(grd) | Landsberg | P-51 |

5.53-0-0 air
0-2 ground

* - shared with Lt. N.J. Fortier and F/O C.R. Barger of the 354th Ftr Sqn
** - both shared with Lt. R.E. Woody of the 354th Ftr Sqn
@ - shared with Capt. C.G. Johnston, Lt. H.W. Brown, Lt. J.E. Duffy, and Lt. B.C. Williamson of the 354th Ftr Sqn

**Krauss, William H., Capt.** (5) Lynchburg, VA
505th Ftr Sqn/339th Ftr Grp June 1944-December 1944

P-51B 6N- "Umbriago"
P-51D 6N- 44-14383 "Umbriago"

| Sqn | Date | Claims | Location | A/C |
|---|---|---|---|---|
| 505th | July 19, 1944 | (.5)Ju-188 dest(grd)* | SW Augsburg | P-51 |
| | July 29 | (.5)Me-109 dest(air)** | NW Naumberg | P-51 |
| | September 10 | Ju-88 dam(grd) | Weizenburg | P-51 |
| | September 11 | (2)Me-410 dest(grd) | Munich | P-51 |
| | | Me-110 dest(grd) | Munich | P-51 |
| | | Ju-88 dest(grd) | Munich | P-51 |
| | | (3)Me-410 dam(grd) | Munich | P-51 |
| | | 0.5-0-0 air | | |
| | | 4.5-4 ground | | |

* - shared with Lt. G. Knight of the 505th Ftr Sqn
** - shared with Lt. J.R. Starnes of the 505th Ftr Sqn

**Kruzel, Joseph J., LtCol.** (6.5) Shalimar, FL
HdQts/361st Ftr Grp March 1943-November 1944
Earlier flew in the PTO with the 17th Pursuit Sqn and 49th Ftr Grp claiming 3 kills; a Nate on February 17, 1942 and single Zeros on February 19 and 20, 1942. Flew 175 hours in PTO.
325 hours

P-47D E9-K 42-25286 "Vi"
P-51B E9-K 43-6498 "Vi"
P-51D E9-K 44-13391 "Vi"
P-51D E9-K 44-14406 "Vi"

| Sqn | Date | Claims | Location | A/C |
|---|---|---|---|---|
| HdQts | February 22, 1944 | FW-190 dam(air) | SW Nijmegen | P-47 |
| | March 8 | (.5)FW-190 dest(air)* | W/Dummer Lake | P-47 |
| | April 29 | Me-109 dest(air) | Steinhuder Lake | P-47 |
| | June 13 | Me-109 dest(air) | St. Brieuc | P-51 |
| | June 25 | FW-190 dest(air) | N/Lisieux | P-51 |
| | | 3.5-0-1 air | | |
| | | 0-0 ground | | |

* - shared with Lt. E.W. Kinnaird of the 375th Ftr Sqn, 361st Ftr Grp

**Kucheman, Henry B., Jr., Maj.** (6) Richmond, VA
354th Ftr Sqn/355th Ftr Grp February 1943-July 1944
82 missions, 302 hours

P-47D WR-U "Lil Lo"
P-51B WR-U 42-106450 "Lil Lo"
P-51D WR-U 44-13571
S/Sgt. Robert J. Barnhouse-c/c

| Sqn | Date | Claims | Location | A/C |
|---|---|---|---|---|
| 354th | April 24, 1944 | (3)Me-109 dest(air) | NW Munich | P-51 |
| | June 20 | Me-410 dest(air) | NW Stettin | P-51 |
| | | Me-410 dam(air) | NW Stettin | P-51 |
| | June 24 | (2)Me-109 dam(grd) | Seiches | P-51 |
| | July 8 | (2)Me-410 dest(grd) | SW Chalons | P-51 |
| | | Me-109 dam(grd) | SW Chalons | P-51 |
| | | 4-0-1 air | | |
| | | 2-3 ground | | |

**Kuhn, Philip G., Jr., Lt.** (5) Dearborn, MI
63rd Ftr Sqn/56th Ftr Grp November 1944-EOW
36 missions

P-47M UN-K 44-21225 "Fireball"

| Sqn | Date | Claims | Location | A/C |
|---|---|---|---|---|
| 63rd | February 3, 1945 | FW-190 dest(air) | Friedersdorf A/F | P-47 |
| | April 13 | (2)Me-410 dest(grd) | Eggebeck A/F | P-47 |
| | | FW-190 dest(grd) | see above | P-47 |
| | | u/i a/c dest(grd) | see above | P-47 |
| | | u/i a/c dam(grd) | see above | P-47 |
| | | 1-0-0 air | | |
| | | 4-1 ground | | |

**Kulik, Edward R., Capt.** (7) Dessemer, MI
83rd Ftr Sqn/78th Ftr Grp July 1944-May 1945
68 missions, 340 hours

P-47D HL-X 42-26449
P-51D HL-X 44-72964
S/Sgt. H. Bates-c/c

| Sqn | Date | Claims | Location | A/C |
|---|---|---|---|---|
| 83rd | April 16, 1945 | (4)FW-190 dest(grd) | N/Prague | P-51 |
| | | Me-109 dest(grd) | N/Prague | P-51 |
| | | Ju-87 dest(grd) | N/Prague | P-51 |
| | | u/i a/c dest(grd) | N/Prague | P-51 |
| | | FW-190 dam(grd) | N/Prague | P-51 |
| | | 0-0-0 air | | |
| | | 7-1 ground | | |

**Kurtz, Robert G., Capt.** (5.5) Denver, CO
354th Ftr Sqn/355th Ftr Grp April 1943-August 3, 1944(POW)
Hit by e/a near Gompelschever.
56 missions, 202:05 hours

P-47D WR-A
P-51B WR-A 43-6895 "Hat Jane"
P-51D WR-A 44-14001

| Sqn | Date | Claims | Location | A/C |
|---|---|---|---|---|
| 354th | April 5, 1944 | Do-217 dest(grd) | Landsberg | P-51 |
| | | (2)Do-217 dam(grd) | Landsberg | P-51 |
| | April 8 | (.5)Me-109 dest(air)* | Sachau A/F | P-51 |
| | April 10 | Do-217 dest(grd) | Bourges | P-51 |
| | | FW-190 dest(grd) | Bourges | P-51 |
| | April 11 | Ju-88 dam(grd) | Madu Lake | P-51 |
| | April 20 | He-111 dest(grd) | Blois A/F | P-51 |
| | | Ju-52 dest(grd) | Blois A/F | P-51 |
| | | 0.5-0-0 air | | |
| | | 5-3 ground | | |

* - shared with Lt. H.W. Brown of the 354th Ftr Sqn

**Kyler, Russell S., Lt.** (10) Huntington, PA
61st Ftr Sqn/56th Ftr Grp August 1944-July 1945
58 missions

P-47D HV-J "Lorene"
P-47M HV-J 44-21116 "Lorene"
S/Sgt. Van C. McGehee-c/c
Sgt. Paul Shipman-ac/c
Sgt. Eugene J. Fournier-arm.

| Sqn | Date | Claims | Location | A/C |
|---|---|---|---|---|
| 61st | September 21, 1944 | FW-190 dest(air) | Deventer | P-47 |
| | November 18 | FW-190 dest(air) | E/Hanau | P-47 |
| | January 14, 1945 | Me-109 dest(air) | E/Rheine | P-47 |
| | April 10 | Me-109 dest(grd) | Muritz Lake | P-47 |
| | | u/i a/c dest(grd) | Muritz Lake | P-47 |
| | April 13 | (4)Ju-88 dest(grd) | Eggebeck A/F | P-47 |
| | | Me-410 dest(grd) | Eggebeck A/F | P-47 |
| | | 3-0-0 air | | |
| | | 7-0 ground | | |

**Lamb, Huie H., Jr., Lt.** (5.5) Abilene, TX
82nd Ftr Sqn/78th Ftr Grp August 1944-July 1945
60 missions, 275:30 hours

P-47D MX-O 42-28422
P-51D MX-V 44-63286 "Etta Jeanne"
P-51K MX-V 44-11631 "Etta Jeanne II"
S/Sgt. George F. Schmitt-c/c
Sgt. Elbert M. Holloway-a/c
Cpl. John M. Worth-arm.

| Sqn | Date | Claims | Location | A/C |
|---|---|---|---|---|
| 82nd | October 12, 1944 | Me-109 dest(air) | Hamburg | P-47 |
| | October 15 | Me-262 dest(air) | Bohmte | P-47 |
| | March 19, 1945 | (.5)Ar-234 dest(air)* | Osnabruck | P-51 |
| | | Me-109 dam(air) | Osnabruck | P-51 |
| | | FW-190 dam(air) | Osnabruck | P-51 |
| | April 10 | Me-110 dest(grd) | Werder A/F | P-51 |
| | | Ju-88 dest(grd) | Werder A/F | P-51 |
| | | Ju-52 dest(grd) | Werder A/F | P-51 |
| | | Ju-52 dam(grd) | Werder A/F | P-51 |
| | | 2.5-0-2 air | | |
| | | 3-1 ground | | |

* - shared with Capt. W.H. Brown of the 82nd Ftr Sqn

**Lamb, Robert A., Maj.** (7) Ridgewood, NJ
61st Ftr Sqn/56th Ftr Grp Mid 1942-March 1944
63rd Ftr Sqn/56th Ftr Grp March 1944-May 1944
275 hours

P-47C HV-L 41-6211 "Jackie"
P-47D HV-L 42-7877
P-47D UN-L
S/Sgt. Bernard P. Ruetten-c/c(61st)

| *Sqn* | *Date* | *Claims* | *Location* | *A/C* |
|---|---|---|---|---|
| 61st | August 19, 1943 | FW-190 dest(air) | Breda | P-47 |
| | November 29 | Me-109 prob(air) | NE Bremen | P-47 |
| | December 11 | (3)Me-110 dest(air) | N/Langeroog Isle | P-47 |
| | December 30 | FW-190 dam(air) | S/Soissons | P-47 |
| | February 6, 1944 | Me-109 dest(air) | Beauvais | P-47 |
| | February 20 | Ju-88 dest(air) | E/Minden | P-47 |
| | February 25 | Me-109 dest(air) | Landau | P-47 |

7-1-1 air
0-0 ground

**Landers, John D., LtCol.** (34.5) Joshua, TX
38th Ftr Sqn/ 55th Ftr Grp March 1944-September 1944
HdQts/357th Ftr Grp October 1944-December 1944
HdQts/ 78th Ftr Grp February 1945-June 1945
Earlier flew in the PTO with the 49th Ftr Grp, 5th Air Force, claiming 6 kills: (2)Sallys on April 4, 1942; single Zeros on June 14 and July 30, 1942; and (2)Zeros on December 26, 1942.

P-38J CG-O "Big Beuatiful Doll"
P-51D CG-O 44-13823 "Big Beautiful Doll"
P-51D B6- 44-13923 "Big Beautiful Doll"
P-51D WZ-I 44-72218 "Big Beautiful Doll"
S/Sgt. James Durnin-c/c(55th)
S/Sgt. Clyde G. Bergman-c/c(78th)
Sgt. Woodrow C. Ferris-ac/c(78th)
Sgt. Dudley D. Riffe-arm.(78th)

| *Sqn* | *Date* | *Claims* | *Location* | *A/C* |
|---|---|---|---|---|
| 38th | May 21, 1944 | (.5)u/i a/c dest(grd)[*] | E/Helmstadt | P-38 |
| | | (.5)u/i a/c dest(grd)[*] | E/Helmstadt | P-38 |
| | June 25 | FW-190 dest(air) | SW Paris | P-38 |
| | | Me-109 dam(air) | SW Paris | P-38 |
| | July 7 | (3)Me-410 dest(air) | Bernburg | P-38 |
| | August 24 | (2)Ju-88 dest(grd) | Burg A/F | P-51 |
| | September 5 | Ju-88 dest(grd) | Stuttgart/Boblingen | P-51 |
| | | u/i a/c dam(grd) | see above | P-51 |
| HdQts | November 18 | Me-109 dest(air) | Villingen A/F | P-51 |
| | | Me-109 dest(grd) | Villingen A/F | P-51 |
| HdQts | March 2, 1945 | (2)Me-109 dest(air) | Burg | P-51 |
| | March 19 | Me-109 dest(air) | Osnabruck | P-51 |
| | March 30 | (.5)Me-262 dest(air)[**] | Rendsburg | P-51 |
| | April 10, 1945 | (2)Me-109 dest(grd) | Werder A/F | P-51 |
| | | FW-190 dest(grd) | see above | P-51 |
| | | He-111 dest(grd) | see above | P-51 |
| | | Ju-188 dest(grd) | see above | P-51 |
| | | Ju-88 dest(grd) | see above | P-51 |
| | April 16 | (9)He-177 dest(grd) | Praha/Kakewice | P-51 |

8.5-0-1 air
20-1 ground

[*]- both shared with Lt. N.R. Tipton of the 38th Ftr Sqn
[**] - shared with Lt. T.V. Thain of the 84th Ftr Sqn, 78th Ftr Grp

**Lang, Joseph L., Capt.** (11.83) Hyde Park, MA
334th Ftr Sqn/4th Ftr Grp December 1943-October 14, 1944(KIA)
Hit by a Me-109 near Eurville.
Earlier served with the RCAF

P-51B QP-Z 43-24841
P-51D QP-Z 44-13352
P-51D QP-Z 44-14123
S/Sgt. Edward Eisler-c/c
Sgt. William Rushing-ac/c

| *Sqn* | *Date* | *Claims* | *Location* | *A/C* |
|---|---|---|---|---|
| 334th | April 18, 1944 | (3)Ju-52 dest(grd) | Juterbog A/F | P-51 |
| | | (.25) of (6)Ju-52 dam(grd)[*] | Juterbog A/F | P-51 |
| | April 30 | (.33)Me-110 dest(air)[**] | N/Lyon | P-51 |
| | | Me-110 dest(grd) | Lyon | P-51 |
| | | (2)Me-110 dam(grd) | Lyon | P-51 |
| | | He-111 dam(grd) | Lyon | P-51 |
| | May 19 | Me-109 dest(air) | Weismar | P-51 |
| | | u/i a/c dest(air) | Weismar | P-51 |
| | | Me-109 dam(air) | Weismar | P-51 |
| | May 24 | Me-109 dest(air) | N/Hamburg | P-51 |
| | May 28 | (1.5)Me-109 dest(air)[@] | Magdeburg | P-51 |
| | June 21 | Me-109 dest(air) | SE Warsaw | P-51 |
| | October 14 | (2)Me-109 dest(air) | Nancy/St. Dizier | P-51 |

7.83-0-1 air
4-4.5 ground

[*]- all shared with Lt. D.W. Howe, Lt. D.M. Malmsten, and Lt. S.W. Monroe of the 334th Ftr Sqn
[**] - shared with Capt. W.M. Sobanski and Lt. S.W. Monroe of the 334th Ftr Sqn
[@] - shared with Lt. E.L. Heller of the 352nd Ftr Grp

**Lanoue, Roland J., Lt.** (12) Lensdale, RI
350th Ftr Sqn/353rd Ftr Grp November 1944-July 1945
44 missions

P-51D LH-H "Fran"
P-51D LH-H 44-15519 "Fran 2nd"
S/Sgt. Ray Hall-c/c

| *Sqn* | *Date* | *Claims* | *Location* | *A/C* |
|---|---|---|---|---|
| 350th | February 27, 1945 | (2)Me-410 dest(grd) | Rohrensee | P-51 |
| | | (2)u/i a/c dest(grd) | see above | P-51 |
| | | FW-190 dest(grd) | see above | P-51 |
| | | FW-190 dam(grd) | see above | P-51 |
| | February 28 | (3)Me-110 dest(grd) | S/Gotha | P-51 |
| | March 2 | Me-109 dest(air) | Ruhland | P-51 |
| | March 21 | (2)Ar-234 dest(grd) | Achmer | P-51 |
| | | He-111 dest(grd) | Achmer | P-51 |

1-0-0 air
11-1 ground

**Larson, Donald A., Maj.** (9) Yakima, WA
505th Ftr Sqn/339th Ftr Grp August 1943-August 4, 1944(KIA)
Collided with a P-51 near Ulzen.

P-51B 6N-B
P-51D 6N-B 44-13609 "Mary, Queen of Scots"
P-51D 6N-B 44-13881
S/Sgt. David Register-c/c
Sgt. Jack Duke-ac/c

| *Sqn* | *Date* | *Claims* | *Location* | *A/C* |
|---|---|---|---|---|
| 505th | May 13, 1944 | FW-190 prob(air) | SE Lubeck | P-51 |
| | May 24 | (2)Me-109 dest(air) | Berlin | P-51 |
| | | FW-190 dest(air) | Berlin | P-51 |
| | | FW-190 dam(air) | Berlin | P-51 |
| | July 28 | Ju-52 dest(air) | Ansbach | P-51 |
| | August 3 | FW-190 dest(grd) | Benestroff | P-51 |
| | | Do-217 dest(grd) | Benestroff | P-51 |
| | August 4 | (2)Me-109 dest(air) | Ulzen | P-51 |
| | | Me-410 dest(grd) | Celle | P-51 |

6-1-1 air
3-0 ground

**Lazear, Earl R., Jr., Capt.** (5) Bluefield, WV
486th Ftr Sqn/352nd Ftr Grp June 1944-March 1945

P-51D PZ-L 44-14877 "Pennie's Earl"

| *Sqn* | *Date* | *Claims* | *Location* | *A/C* |
|---|---|---|---|---|
| 486th | July 19, 1944 | Me-109 prob(air) | NE Munich | P-51 |
| | September 12 | (3)Me-109 dest(air) | Kyritz | P-51 |
| | November 30 | Me-109 dest(air) | S/Merseburg | P-51 |
| | December 27 | Me-109 dest(air) | SW Bonn | P-51 |

5-1-0 air
0-0 ground

**Ledington, Dorian, Capt.** (5) Wichita, KS
84th Ftr Sqn/78th Ftr Grp January 1944-April 21, 1945(KIA)
Crashed in bad weather west of Coblenz.

P-47D WZ-
P-51D WZ-A 44-72772
S/Sgt. James W. Darrall-c/c
Cpl. Frank E. Farzych-arm.

| *Sqn* | *Date* | *Claims* | *Location* | *A/C* |
|---|---|---|---|---|
| 84th | June 7, 1944 | Me-109 dest(air) | Montdidier | P-47 |
| | June 10 | Me-109 dest(air) | La Ferte Mace | P-47 |
| | February 3, 1945 | (2)Me-410 dam(grd) | Luneburg | P-51 |
| | April 16 | (2)Ju-52 dest(grd) | Praha/Kakewice | P-51 |
| | | u/i a/c dest(grd) | see above | P-51 |
| | | Ju-52 dam(grd) | see above | P-51 |

2-0-0 air
3-3 ground

**Lee, Louis W., Lt.** (6) Houston, TX
350th Ftr Sqn/353rd Ftr Grp November 1944-EOW
33 missions

P-51D LH-Q 44-14898

| Sqn | Date | Claims | Location | A/C |
|---|---|---|---|---|
| 350th | March 2, 1945 | Me-109 dest(air) | Ruhland | P-51 |
| | | Me-109 dam(air) | Ruhland | P-51 |
| | March 24 | (2)FW-190 dest(air) | NW Kassel | P-51 |
| | | Me-109 dest(air) | NW Kassel | P-51 |
| | April 16 | (2)FW-190 dest(grd) | Pocking | P-51 |

4-0-1 air
2-0 ground

**Lenfest, Charles W., Maj.** (7.5) Boise, ID
354th Ftr Sqn/355th Ftr Grp April 1943-October 3, 1944(POW)
Landed near Nordlingen to rescue a pilot and got stuck in mud.

P-47D WR-F 42-22464 "Lorie"
P-51B WR-F 43-6948 "Lorie II"
P-51B WR-F 42-106874 "Lorie III"
P-51B WR-F 43-6870 "Lorie IV"
P-51D WR-F 44-14275 "Lorie V"

| Sqn | Date | Claims | Location | A/C |
|---|---|---|---|---|
| 354th | March 16, 1944 | (1.5)Me-109 dest(air)[*] | NW Ulm | P-51 |
| | March 18 | (.5)Me-109 dest(air)[**] | NE Munich | P-51 |
| | | Me-109 dam(air) | NE Munich | P-51 |
| | March 29 | Me-108 dest(air) | Goslar A/F | P-51 |
| | | Trainer dest(grd) | Goslar A/F | P-51 |
| | April 5 | (.5)Me-108 dest(grd)[@] | Landsberg | P-51 |
| | | (4)Do-217 dam(grd) | Landsberg | P-51 |
| | August 3 | Me-109 dest(air) | E/Mannheim | P-51 |
| | August 6 | Me-109 dest(air) | S/Hamburg | P-51 |
| | October 3 | FW-190 dest(grd) | Nordlingen | P-51 |

5.5-0-1 air
2-4 ground

[*] - shared with Lt. T.F. Neal of the 354th Ftr Sqn
[**] - shared with Lt. L.G. Mendenhall of the 354th Ftr Sqn
[@] - shared with Lt. H.W. Brown of the 354th Ftr Sqn

**Lewis, William H., Capt.** (7) Pasadena, CA
343rd Ftr Sqn/55th Ftr Grp June 1944-February 1945
325 hours

P-51D CY-S 44-13907
S/Sgt. Charles Siemson-c/c

| Sqn | Date | Claims | Location | A/C |
|---|---|---|---|---|
| 343rd | September 5, 1944 | (5)Trainers dest(air) | N/Goppingen A/F | P-51 |
| | September 13 | Me-109 dest(air) | Eisenach-Gotha | P-51 |
| | | Me-109 dam(air) | see above | P-51 |
| | February 3, 1945 | Ju-88 dest(air) | Gartow | P-51 |

7-0-1 air
0-0 ground

**Lines, Ted E., Capt.** (10) Mesa, AR
335th Ftr Sqn/4th Ftr Grp April 1944-November 1944

P-51B WD-H 43-7172 "Three Jokers"
P-51D WD-O 44-13555 "Thunderbird"
P-51D WD-O 44-14570
S/Sgt. Sy O. Koenig-c/c

| Sqn | Date | Claims | Location | A/C |
|---|---|---|---|---|
| 335th | May 12, 1944 | Me-109 dest(air) | E/Frankfurt | P-51 |
| | August 24 | (2)Me-109 dest(air) | SE Emden | P-51 |
| | September 10 | (3)Me-109 dest(air) | Strasbourg | P-51 |
| | | Ju-88 dest(air) | S/Kaiserlautern | P-51 |
| | September 17 | (3)FW-190 dest(air) | Bocholt | P-51 |

10-0-0 air
0-0 ground

**Littge, Raymond H., Capt.** (23.5) Altenburg, MO
487th Ftr Sqn/352nd Ftr Grp June 1944-May 1945
91 missions, 391 hours

P-51C HO-M 42-103320 "Silver Dollar"
P-51D HO-M 44-72216 "Miss Helen"
P-51D HO-M 44-11330 "E Pluribus Unum"

| Sqn | Date | Claims | Location | A/C |
|---|---|---|---|---|
| 487th | August 25, 1944 | (2)Me-210 dest(grd) | Neubrandenburg | P-51 |
| | | Me-109 dam(grd) | see above | P-51 |
| | September 11 | (2)Ju-88 dest(grd) | Gotha | P-51 |
| | | (2)Ju-88 dam(grd) | Gotha | P-51 |
| | November 27 | (2)Me-109 dest(air) | Hameln | P-51 |
| | December 26 | Me-109 dest(air) | Ollheim | P-51 |
| | December 27 | (3)FW-190 dest(air) | Mauen | P-51 |
| | January 1, 1945 | (2)FW-190 dest(air) | N/Liege | P-51 |
| | January 24 | Me-109 dest(air) | Bonn | P-51 |
| | February 21 | Ju-88 dam(grd) | SW Kassel | P-51 |
| | March 18 | (.5)Me-109 dest(air)[*] | Bad Frienwalde | P-51 |
| | March 25 | Me-262 dest(air) | Rechlin A/F | P-51 |
| | April 16 | (2)Me-109 dest(grd) | Ganacker | P-51 |
| | | Me-210 dest(grd) | see above | P-51 |
| | | (3)Me-109 dam(grd) | see above | P-51 |
| | | FW-190 dam(grd) | see above | P-51 |
| | April 17 | (4)Me-109 dest(grd) | Plattling | P-51 |
| | | (2)Me-262 dest(grd) | Plattling | P-51 |

10.5-0-0 air
13-8 ground

[*] - shared with Lt. J.N. Wood of the 487th Ftr Sqn

**London, Charles P., Capt.** (5) Long Beach, CA
83rd Ftr Sqn/78th Ftr Grp May 1942-November 1943
65 missions

P-47C HL-B 41-6335 "El Jeepo"
T/Sgt. Percy M. Scott-c/c

| Sqn | Date | Claims | Location | A/C |
|---|---|---|---|---|
| 83rd | May 14, 1943 | FW-190 prob(air) | NW Antwerp | P-47 |
| | June 22 | FW-190 dest(air) | W/Walcheren | P-47 |
| | June 29 | (2)Me-109 dest(air) | Gournay | P-47 |
| | July 14 | Me-109 dam(air) | Le Touquet | P-47 |
| | | FW-190 dam(air) | Le Touquet | P-47 |
| | July 30 | Me-109 dest(air) | Haltern | P-47 |
| | | FW-190 dest(air) | Haltern | P-47 |

5-1-2 air
0-0 ground

**Long, Thurman C., Lt.** (6) Fort Wayne, IN
357th Ftr Sqn/355th Ftr Grp August 1944-April 16, 1945(POW)
Hit by flak in the Linz area.

P-51B OS-L 42-106444 "Baby Bet"
P-51D OS-L

| Sqn | Date | Claims | Location | A/C |
|---|---|---|---|---|
| 357th | November 18, 1944 | (2)Me-262 dest(grd) | Leipheim | P-51 |
| | | (2)Me-262 dam(grd) | Leipheim | P-51 |
| | February 23, 1945 | Me-163 dam(grd) | Neuburg | P-51 |
| | February 25 | Ju-188 dest(grd) | Fassberg | P-51 |
| | March 31 | Ju-88 dest(grd) | Magdeburg | P-51 |
| | April 4 | (2)FW-190 dest(air) | Halberstadt | P-51 |

2-0-0 air
4-3 ground

**Loveless, Philip M., Jr., Capt.** (5.5) Warren, OH
505th Ftr Sqn/339th Ftr Grp October 1944-April 1945

| Sqn | Date | Claims | Location | A/C |
|---|---|---|---|---|
| 505th | November 26, 1944 | (.5)FW-190 dest(air)[*] | S/Hanover | P-51 |
| | April 16, 1945 | FW-190 dest(grd) | NE Prague | P-51 |
| | | Ju-87 dam(grd) | NE Prague | P-51 |
| | April 17 | (3)Do-217 dest(grd) | SE Pocking | P-51 |
| | | Me-109 dest(grd) | SE Pocking | P-51 |
| | | Do-217 dam(grd) | SE Pocking | P-51 |
| | | Ju-88 dam(grd) | SE Pocking | P-51 |

0.5-0-0 air
5-3 ground

[*] - shared with Lt. W.R. Phillippi of the 505th Ftr Sqn

**Lowell, John H., LtCol.** (16.5) Denver, CO
384th Ftr Sqn/364th Ftr Grp June 1943-November 1944
HdQts/364th Ftr Grp November 1944-May 1945
157 missions

P-38J 5Y-L 42-68098 "Penny"
P-38J 5Y-L "Penny 2"
P-51D 5Y-L 44-14992 "Penny 3"
P-51D 5Y-L 44-63262 "Penny 4"
T/Sgt. Joseph Jennings-c/c

| Sqn | Date | Claims | Location | A/C |
|---|---|---|---|---|
| 384th | March 6, 1944 | Me-109 dest(air) | W/Hanover | P-38 |
| | | Me-109 prob(air) | W/Hanover | P-38 |
| | March 8 | (2)FW-190 dest(air) | Stendal-Alt Ruppin | P-38 |
| | March 29 | Ju-52 dest(grd) | Osnabruck | P-38 |
| | | FW-190 dam(grd) | Osnabruck | P-38 |
| | April 9 | FW-190 dest(grd) | Bramsche/Rheine | P-38 |
| | | FW-190 dam(grd) | Bramsche/Rheine | P-38 |
| | May 21 | (2)Ju-52 dest(grd) | Parchim-Ludwigslust-Hagenow | P-38 |
| | | He-111 dest(grd) | see above | P-38 |
| | | Ju-88 dest(grd) | see above | P-38 |
| | | FW-190 dam(grd) | see above | P-38 |
| HdQts | November 21 | FW-190 dest(air) | E/Leipzig | P-51 |
| | December 5 | (3)FW-190 dest(air) | N/Berlin | P-51 |
| | | FW-190 dam(air) | N/Berlin | P-51 |
| | December 27 | (.5)Me-109 dest(air)* | W/Coblenz | P-51 |
| | | Me-109 dam(air) | W/Coblenz | P-51 |
| | April 17, 1945 | He-111 dest(grd) | Karlsbad | P-51 |
| | | Me-262 dest(grd) | Karlsbad | P-51 |
| | | FW-200 dest(grd) | Karlsbad | P-51 |
| | | 7.5-1-2 air | | |
| | | 9-3 ground | | |

* - shared with Lt. S.J. Price of the 384th Ftr Sqn

**Luksic, Carl J., Lt.** (15.5) Joliet, IL
487th Ftr Sqn/352nd Ftr Grp December 1942-May 24, 1944(POW)
Hit by flak in the Stendal area.

P-47D HO-Z 42-75860 "Lucky Boy"
P-51B HO-Z 43-7145 "Elly's Lucky Boy"
P-51B HO-Z 42-106788 "Elly's Lucky Boy"

| Sqn | Date | Claims | Location | A/C |
|---|---|---|---|---|
| 487th | April 9, 1944 | (3)Ju-88 dest(grd) | Dummer Lake | P-51 |
| | April 10 | (.5)FW-190 dest(air)* | SW Rheims | P-51 |
| | April 11 | (2)Ju-88 dest(grd) | W/Berlin | P-51 |
| | | Me-110 dest(grd) | W/Berlin | P-51 |
| | | He-111 dest(grd) | W/Berlin | P-51 |
| | | (3)Ju-88 dam(grd) | W/Berlin | P-51 |
| | April 20 | (1.5)Me-109 dest(air)** | SE Paris | P-51 |
| | May 8 | (3)FW-190 dest(air) | Brunswick | P-51 |
| | | (2)FW-190 dest(air) | Brunswick | P-51 |
| | May 13 | (.5)Ju-88 dest(air)@ | E/Neubrandenburg | P-51 |
| | May 19 | Me-109 dest(air) | Ludwigslust | P-51 |
| | | 8.5-0-0 air | | |
| | | 7-3 ground | | |

* - shared with Maj. J.C. Meyer of the 487th Ftr Sqn
** - shared with Lt. A. Bielok of the 487th Ftr Sqn
@ - shared with Lt. G.T. Moran of the 487th Ftr Sqn

**Lynch, William J., Lt.** (5) Kennedy, TX
358th Ftr Sqn/355th Ftr Grp February 1945-April 16, 1945(POW)
Hit by flak at Straubing Airfield.
8 missions

No regular a/c or crew

| Sqn | Date | Claims | Location | A/C |
|---|---|---|---|---|
| 358th | April 9, 1945 | Me-110 dest(grd) | Heilfingen | P-51 |
| | | He-111 dest(grd) | Heilfingen | P-51 |
| | | u/i a/c dam(grd) | Heilfingen | P-51 |
| | April 16 | (2)FW-190 dest(grd) | Straubing A/F | P-51 |
| | | Ju-88 dest(grd) | Straubing A/F | P-51 |
| | | 0-0-0 air | | |
| | | 5-1 ground | | |

**MacClarence, William R., Lt.** (8) Plainfield, NJ
505th Ftr Sqn/339th Ftr Grp February 1945-July 1945

| Sqn | Date | Claims | Location | A/C |
|---|---|---|---|---|
| 505th | April 4, 1945 | Me-410 dest(grd) | Tribsees | P-51 |
| | April 10 | (3)Ju-88 dest(grd) | N/Neuruppin | P-51 |
| | April 16 | (2)u/i a/c dest(grd) | NE Prague | P-51 |
| | April 17 | Ju-188 dest(grd) | SE Pocking | P-51 |
| | | He-111 dest(grd) | SE Pocking | P-51 |
| | | 0-0-0 air | | |
| | | 8-0 ground | | |

**MacKean, Robert G., Capt.** (5) Yonkers, NY
486th Ftr Sqn/352nd Ftr Grp States-April 24, 1944(KIA)
Hit by flak in the Ingolstadt area.

P-47D PZ-Z 42-8548
P-51B PZ-Z 43-7198

| Sqn | Date | Claims | Location | A/C |
|---|---|---|---|---|
| 486th | April 24, 1944 | (3)Me-110 dest(grd) | Ingolstadt | P-51 |
| | | (2)Ju-88 dest(grd) | Ingolstadt | P-51 |
| | | 0-0-0 air | | |
| | | 5-0 ground | | |

**Maguire, William J., Capt.** (8) Boston, MA
351st Ftr Sqn/353rd Ftr Grp December 1942-May 1945
HdQts/353rd Ftr Grp May 1945-September 11, 1945(KIAc)
124 missions

P-47D YJ-M
P-47D YJ-M 42-26126 "Boston Bull"
P-51D YJ-M 44-14569 "Lil Boston Bull"
P-51D YJ-M 44-14893 "Lil Boston Bull"
S/Sgt. William Morgan-c/c

| Sqn | Date | Claims | Location | A/C |
|---|---|---|---|---|
| 351st | September 27, 1943 | Me-109 dest(air) | W/Emden | P-47 |
| | | Me-109 dam(air) | W/Emden | P-47 |
| | October 14 | FW-190 dest(air) | Flacher | P-47 |
| | June 7, 1944 | (2)Me-109 dest(air) | Beauvais/Tille | P-47 |
| | | Me-109 dam(air) | see above | P-47 |
| | June 25 | Me-410 dest(grd) | Bourges | P-47 |
| | July 9 | Me-109 dest(air) | Argentan | P-47 |
| | March 14, 1945 | (2)Me-109 dest(air) | Luckenwalde | P-51 |
| | | 7-0-2 air | | |
| | | 1-0 ground | | |

**Mahany, Howard, Jr., Lt.** (7) Jersey City, NJ
343rd Ftr Sqn/55th Ftr Grp March 1945-July 1945

P-51D CY-M
S/Sgt. Reuben F. Curtis-c/c
Sgt. Walter Hagen-ac/c
Sgt. Hastead-arm.

| Sqn | Date | Claims | Location | A/C |
|---|---|---|---|---|
| 343rd | April 9, 1945 | Me-262 dest(grd) | Munich-Brunnthal | P-51 |
| | | He-111 dest(grd) | see above | P-51 |
| | | He-111 dam(grd) | see above | P-51 |
| | April 17 | (3)Me-410 dest(grd) | Dresden | P-51 |
| | | (2)FW-190 dest(grd) | Dresden | P-51 |
| | | (2)FW-190 dam(grd) | Dresden | P-51 |
| | | 0-0-0 air | | |
| | | 7-3 ground | | |

**Mahurin, Walker M., Maj.** (19.75) Fort Wayne, IN
63rd Ftr Sqn/56th Ftr Grp May 1942-March 27, 1944(MIA-E)
Downed by a Do-217 south of Chartres.
Later flew in the PTO with the 3rd Air Commando Group, 5th Air Force, claiming 1 kill, a Dinah on January 14, 1945.
85 missions, 192 hours

P-47C UN-M 41-6334
P-47D UN-M 42-8487 "Spirit of Atlantic City, N.J."
S/Sgt. John E. Barnes-c/c
Sgt. David V. Hilstad-ac/c
Cpl. Esca May-arm.

| Sqn | Date | Claims | Location | A/C |
|---|---|---|---|---|
| 63rd | August 17, 1943 | (2)FW-190 dest(air) | Eupen-St. Nicholas | P-47 |
| | September 9 | FW-190 dest(air) | S/Beauvais | P-47 |
| | October 4 | (3)Me-110 dest(air) | E/Duren | P-47 |
| | November 3 | Me-110 dest(air) | N/Juist | P-47 |
| | | (.5)Me-109 dest(air)* | N/Essens | P-47 |
| | November 26 | (3)Me-110 dest(air) | S/Oldenburg-Zuider Zee | P-47 |
| | | Me-110 prob(air) | see above | P-47 |
| | November 29 | Me-109 dest(air) | Leer-Papenburg | P-47 |
| | | Me-109 dam(air) | Leer-Papenburg | P-47 |
| | December 22 | (2)Me-109 dest(air) | Hesepe | P-47 |
| | January 30, 1944 | Ju-88 dest(air) | S/Quackenbruck | P-47 |
| | | Ju-88 prob(air) | see above | P-47 |
| | February 3 | Me-109 dest(air) | SE Ruhlertwist | P-47 |
| | March 6 | FW-190 dest(air) | Wenzendorf A/F | P-47 |
| | | FW-190 prob(air) | see above | P-47 |
| | March 8 | (2)FW-190 dest(air) | Wesendorf A/F | P-47 |
| | | Ju-88 dest(air) | see above | P-47 |
| | March 27 | (.25)Do-217 dest(air)** | S/Chartres | P-47 |
| | | 19.75-3-1 air | | |
| | | 0-0 ground | | |

* - shared with Lt. W.J. O'Connor of the 63rd Ftr Sqn
** - shared with Lt. W.D. Johnson, Lt. I.T. Porowski, and F/O S.J. Lowman of the 63rd Ftr Sqn

**Malmsten, Donald M., Capt.** (10.5) Burwell, NE
334th Ftr Sqn/4th Ftr Grp April 1944-August 7, 1944(MIA-E)
Hit by flak in the Dijon area.
334th Ftr Sqn/4th Ftr Grp September 1944-EOW

P-51B QP-M 43-6957 "Turnip Termite"
P-51D QP-V 44-14560 "Crotch Rot"
Sgt. F. Pelosi-arm.(M)

| *Sqn* | *Date* | *Claims* | *Location* | *A/C* |
|---|---|---|---|---|
| 334th | April 10, 1944 | u/i a/c dam(grd) | Romorantin A/F | P-51 |
| | April 18 | Ju-52 dest(grd) | Juterbog A/F | P-51 |
| | | (.25) of (6)Ju-52 dam(grd)* | Juterbog A/F | P-51 |
| | June 20 | Ju-88 dest(air) | Pasewalk | P-51 |
| | February 25, 1945 | (.5)FW-190 dest(air)** | Dessau | P-51 |
| | February 27 | (3)u/i a/c dest(grd) | Weimar | P-51 |
| | | (2)Ju-88 dest(grd) | Weimar | P-51 |
| | | Me-109 dest(grd) | Weimar | P-51 |
| | March 21 | (2)Me-109 dest(grd) | Achmer | P-51 |

1.5-0-0 air
9-2.5 ground

* - all shared with Lt. D.W. Howe, Lt. J.L. Lang, and Lt. S.W. Monroe of the 334th Ftr Sqn
** - shared with Lt. W.C. O'Bryan of the 334th Ftr Sqn

**Malmstrom, Einar A., Col.** (6.5) Spokane, WA
HdQts/356th Ftr Grp November 1943-April 23, 1944(POW)
Hit by flak at Hagenau Airfield.
49 missions

P-47D QI-R 42-22550 "Kay-J"
P-47D QI-R 42-25513 "Kay-J"
S/Sgt. Henry Yoder-c/c
Sgt. Willis A. Youtsey-ac/c

| *Sqn* | *Date* | *Claims* | *Location* | *A/C* |
|---|---|---|---|---|
| HdQts | March 20, 1944 | Me-109 dest(air) | NW Charleville | P-47 |
| | April 11 | (2)Me-110 dest(grd) | Gifhorn | P-47 |
| | | (.25)Me-109 dest(grd)* | Gifhorn | P-47 |
| | | (.25)Ju-88 dest(grd)* | Gifhorn | P-47 |
| | April 23 | (3)He-111 dest(grd) | Hagenau A/F | P-47 |

1-0-0 air
5.5-0 ground

* - shared with Lt. R. Gibson, Lt. J.V. Jack, and F/O E.L. Decker of the 361st Ftr Sqn, 356th Ftr Grp

**Maloney, John T., Lt.** (5) ????
38th Ftr Sqn/55th Ftr Grp February 1945-November 1945
23 missions
P-51D CG-U

| *Sqn* | *Date* | *Claims* | *Location* | *A/C* |
|---|---|---|---|---|
| 38th | April 9, 1945 | Me-262 dest(grd) | Munich-Brunnthal | P-51 |
| | | (2)u/i a/c dam(grd) | see above | P-51 |
| | April 10 | (2)Me-109 dest(grd) | Wesendorf | P-51 |
| | | FW-190 dest(grd) | Wesendorf | P-51 |
| | April 16 | Ju-52 dest(grd) | Bad Aibling | P-51 |
| | | u/i a/c dam(grd) | Bad Aibling | P-51 |

0-0-0 air
5-3 ground

**Mansker, Joseph L., Capt.** (10) Long Beach, CA
55th Ftr Sqn/20th Ftr Grp July 1944-April 1945
50 missions, 265:55 hours

P-51D KI-X 44-13892 "Idiot's Delite"
P-51D KI-X 44-14749

| *Sqn* | *Date* | *Claims* | *Location* | *A/C* |
|---|---|---|---|---|
| 55th | August 6, 1944 | FW-190 dest(air) | S/Brandenburg | P-51 |
| | August 25 | (5)Ju-88 dest(grd) | Parow A/F | P-51 |
| | | BV-140 dest(grd) | Parow A/F | P-51 |
| | | (3)Ju-88 dam(grd) | Parow A/F | P-51 |
| | October 6 | u/i a/c dest(grd) | Kubitzer Bay | P-51 |
| | November 2 | (2)Me-109 dest(air) | Halle/Merseburg | P-51 |
| | | Me-109 prob(air) | see above | P-51 |

3-1-0 air
7-3 ground

**Markham, Gene E., Capt.** (5) Sebring, FL
351st Ftr Sqn/353rd Ftr Grp October 1944-July 1945
48 missions

P-51D YJ-Q 44-14929 "Mr. Gray"
P-51D YJ-Q 44-72171 "Mr. Gray"
S/Sgt. Reemer Hilton-c/c

| *Sqn* | *Date* | *Claims* | *Location* | *A/C* |
|---|---|---|---|---|
| 351st | November 18, 1944 | Me-262 dam(air) | S/Augsburg | P-51 |
| | November 27 | Me-109 dest(air) | NE Steinhuder L. | P-51 |
| | January 14, 1945 | (.5)Me-262 dam(air)* | E/Hanover | P-51 |
| | February 25 | FW-200 dam(grd) | Lechfeld | P-51 |
| | March 14 | (3)Me-109 dest(air) | Luckenwalde | P-51 |
| | April 7 | Me-109 dest(air) | E/Steinhuder Lake | P-51 |
| | | Me-109 dam(air) | see above | P-51 |

5-0-2.5 air
0-1 ground

* - shared with Lt. M.A. Arnold of the 351st Ftr Sqn

**Marsh, Halbert G., Lt.** (5) Birmingham, AL
358th Ftr Sqn/355th Ftr Grp January 1945-September 1945
30 missions

P-51D YF-U 44-63869 "Passion's Playground"
S/Sgt. Irving G. Petersen-c/c

| *Sqn* | *Date* | *Claims* | *Location* | *A/C* |
|---|---|---|---|---|
| 358th | April 16, 1945 | (5)FW-190 dest(grd) | Landsberg | P-51 |
| | | (2)FW-190 dam(grd) | Landsberg | P-51 |

0-0-0 air
5-2 ground

**Marsh, Lester C., Lt.** (5) Los Angeles, CA
503rd Ftr Sqn/339th Ftr Grp June 1944-December 1944
51 missions
P-51D D7-P 44-14947

| *Sqn* | *Date* | *Claims* | *Location* | *A/C* |
|---|---|---|---|---|
| 503rd | September 23, 1944 | FW-190 dest(air) | SW Wesel | P-51 |
| | November 18 | Me-109 dest(air) | NE Mannheim | P-51 |
| | November 26 | (3)FW-190 dest(air) | SE Dummer Lake | P-51 |
| | | FW-190 prob(air) | see above | P-51 |
| | | FW-190 dam(air) | see above | P-51 |

5-1-1 air
0-0 ground

**Marshall, Bert W., Jr., LtCol.** (10) Greenville, TX
354th Ftr Sqn/355th Ftr Grp May 1944-October 1944
HdQts/355th Ftr Grp October 1944-September 1945

P-51B WR-B 43-6457 "Jane"
P-51D WR-B 44-14293 "Jane II"
P-51D WR-B 44-14409 "Jane III"
P-51D WR-B 44-14799 "Jane IV"
P-51D WR-B 44-15279 "Jane V"
P-51D WR-B 44-72253 "Jane VI"
P-51D WR-B 44-72953 "Jane VII"
S/Sgt. Gerry Thompson-c/c

| *Sqn* | *Date* | *Claims* | *Location* | *A/C* |
|---|---|---|---|---|
| 354th | June 6, 1944 | Ju-87 dest(air) | Chartres-Dire | P-51 |
| | June 20 | (2)Me-109 dest(air) | Bergen | P-51 |
| | July 28 | Me-109 dest(air) | Mulhausen | P-51 |
| | August 6 | Me-109 dest(air) | S/Hamburg | P-51 |
| | September 11 | (2)Me-109 dest(air) | S/Kassel | P-51 |
| | | Me-109 dam(air) | S/Kassel | P-51 |
| HdQts | April 13, 1945 | (2)u/i a/c dest(grd) | Husum | P-51 |
| | | Me-109 dest(grd) | Husum | P-51 |
| | | (2)u/i a/c dam(grd) | Husum | P-51 |
| | | FW-190 dam(grd) | Husum | P-51 |

7-0-1 air
3-3 ground

**Martin, William D., Lt.** (7) Fort Smith, AR
354th Ftr Sqn/355th Ftr Grp April 1944-September 1944
79 missions, 300 hours

P-51C WR-J 42-103334 "Martin's Gloria"
P-51D WR-J 44-13756 "Martin's Gloria"
S/Sgt. Moss-c/c

| *Sqn* | *Date* | *Claims* | *Location* | *A/C* |
|---|---|---|---|---|
| 354th | May 13, 1944 | Hs-129 dest(air) | Landsberg | P-51 |
| | June 20 | (2)Me-109 dest(air) | Rugen | P-51 |
| | June 24 | (2)Me-109 dest(grd) | Angars | P-51 |
| | July 8 | Me-109 dest(grd) | SW Chalons | P-51 |
| | | (2)Me-109 dam(grd) | SW Chalons | P-51 |
| | August 6 | Me-109 dest(air) | S/Hamburg | P-51 |

4-0-0 air
3-2 ground

**Marts, Jay F., Lt.** (5) Salem, NJ
505th Ftr Sqn/339th Ftr Grp August 1944-March 1945

P-51D 6N-J 44-14239 "Junior"
S/Sgt. David Register-c/c

| *Sqn* | *Date* | *Claims* | *Location* | *A/C* |
|---|---|---|---|---|
| 505th | August 28, 1944 | Ju-88 dest(grd) | Savernne | P-51 |
| | September 10 | (2)Me-410 dest(grd) | Weizenburg | P-51 |
| | | (2)He-111 dam(grd) | see above | P-51 |
| | | Ju-88 dam(grd) | see above | P-51 |
| | | u/i a/c dam(grd) | see above | P-51 |
| | March 2, 1945 | (2)Me-109 dest(air) | E/Magdeburg | P-51 |

2-0-0 air
3-4 ground

**Marvei, Thomas W., Lt.** (9) East Orange, NJ
505th Ftr Sqn/339th Ftr Grp September 1944-April 1945

| *Sqn* | *Date* | *Claims* | *Location* | *A/C* |
|---|---|---|---|---|
| 505th | March 1, 1945 | Ju-88 dest(grd) | S/Feldkirchen | P-51 |
| | April 10 | (3)Me-410 dest(grd) | N/Neuruppin | P-51 |
| | | Me-410 dam(grd) | N/Neuruppin | P-51 |
| | April 16 | Me-109 dest(grd) | NE Prague | P-51 |
| | | Ju-88 dest(grd) | NE Prague | P-51 |
| | April 17 | Me-109 dest(grd) | SE Pocking | P-51 |
| | | He-111 dest(grd) | SE Pocking | P-51 |
| | | u/i a/c dest(grd) | SE Pocking | P-51 |

0-0-0 air
9-1 ground

**Mason, Joseph L., Col.** (5) Columbus, OH
HdQts/352nd Ftr Grp May 1943-November 1944

P-47D PZ-M 42-8466 "This Is It!"
P-47D PZ-M 42-22486 "This Is It!"
P-51B PZ-M 43-6776 "This Is It!"
P-51B PZ-M 42-106609 "This Is It!"
P-51D PZ-M 44-13395 "This Is It!"
P-51D PZ-M 44-14911 "This Is It!"
S/Sgt. Wayne Stock-c/c

| *Sqn* | *Date* | *Claims* | *Location* | *A/C* |
|---|---|---|---|---|
| HdQts | February 24, 1944 | Me-109 dest(air) | Schwagstorf | P-47 |
| | May 8 | FW-190 dest(air) | N/Nienburg | P-51 |
| | | FW-190 dam(air) | N/Nienburg | P-51 |
| | May 13 | (2)Me-109 dest(air) | Demnin-Freidland | P-51 |
| | | FW-190 dest(air) | see above | P-51 |
| | | Me-109 dam(air) | see above | P-51 |

5-0-2 air
0-0 ground

**Maxwell, Chester K., Capt.** (5) Alva, OK
364th Ftr Sqn/357th Ftr Grp August 1944-May 1945

P-51D C5-H 44-63861 "Lady Esther"

| *Sqn* | *Date* | *Claims* | *Location* | *A/C* |
|---|---|---|---|---|
| 364th | September 19, 1944 | Me-109 dest(air) | SW Arnheim | P-51 |
| | | FW-190 dest(air) | SW Arnheim | P-51 |
| | January 14, 1945 | (3)FW-190 dest(air) | W/Berlin | P-51 |

5-0-0 air
0-0 ground

**Mayden, James D., Col.** (6) Junction City, KS
HdQts/352nd Ftr Grp July 1944-September 1945

P-51C PE-X 42-103789 "Straw Boss"
P-51D PE-X 44-14111 "Straw Boss 2"
S/Sgt. Robling-c/c

| *Sqn* | *Date* | *Claims* | *Location* | *A/C* |
|---|---|---|---|---|
| HdQts | November 2, 1944 | Me-109 dest(air) | Merseburg | P-51 |
| | April 7, 1945 | Me-109 dest(air) | N/Minden | P-51 |
| | April 17 | (2)Me-109 dest(grd) | Plattling | P-51 |
| | | FW-190 dest(grd) | see above | P-51 |
| | | u/i a/c dest(grd) | see above | P-51 |
| | | (2)Me-109 dam(grd) | see above | P-51 |

2-0-0 air
4-2 ground

**Mayo, Ben I., Jr., LtCol.** (6.5) Little Rock, AR
84th Ftr Sqn/78th Ftr Grp April 1944-June 1944
82nd Ftr Sqn/78th Ftr Grp June 1944-July 1944
84th Ftr Sqn/78th Ftr Grp July 1944-September 1944
62 missions

P-47D WZ-P 42-26551
P-47D WZ-V 42-26567 "No Guts, No Glory!"
P-47D MX-X 42-26671 "No Guts, No Glory!"
S/Sgt. Sam T. Snoddy-c/c(84th)
S/Sgt. John E. Tudor-c/c(82nd)
Cpl. Arthur F. Christensen-ac/c(82nd)
Cpl. Robert L. Thout-arm.(82nd)

| *Sqn* | *Date* | *Claims* | *Location* | *A/C* |
|---|---|---|---|---|
| 84th | June 7, 1944 | Me-109 dest(air) | S/Montdidier | P-47 |
| 82nd | June 20 | Me-109 dest(air) | Montdidier | P-47 |
| | July 1 | FW-190 dam(air) | St. Quentin | P-47 |
| 84th | July 19 | (1.5)Do-217 dest(grd)* | Eutingen | P-47 |
| | | u/i a/c dest(grd) | Eutingen | P-47 |
| | September 9 | (2)FW-190 dest(air) | Giessen | P-47 |

4-0-1 air
2.5-1 ground

* - shared with Capt. A.F. Eaton of the 84th Ftr Sqn

**McCasland, Darwin D., Lt.** (5) Morton, TX
357th Ftr Sqn/355th Ftr Grp February 1944-April 15, 1944(POW)
Hit by flak at Wagonhof Airfield.

| *Sqn* | *Date* | *Claims* | *Location* | *A/C* |
|---|---|---|---|---|
| 357th | March 6, 1944 | Me-109 dest(air) | E/Dummer Lake | P-47 |
| | March 29 | FW-190 dest(air) | Brunswick | P-51 |
| | | FW-190 prob(air) | Brunswick | P-51 |
| | April 8 | Ju-88 dest(grd) | Gifhorn | P-51 |
| | April 11 | (2)Ju-88 dest(grd) | Strasbourg | P-51 |
| | | FW-190 dam(grd) | Wensdorf | P-51 |

2-1-0 air
3-1 ground

**McCauley, Frank E., Lt.** (5.5) Hicksville, OH
61st Ftr Sqn/56th Ftr Grp July 1942-November 1943
46 missions, 84:23 hours

P-47C HV-Z 41-6271 "Rat Racer"
S/Sgt. Peter Meder-c/c
Sgt. Edward Hughes-ac/c
Sgt. Tom A. Gormley-arm.

| *Sqn* | *Date* | *Claims* | *Location* | *A/C* |
|---|---|---|---|---|
| 61st | August 17, 1943 | FW-190 dest(air) | Hasselt | P-47 |
| | | (.5)Me-110 dest(air)* | N/Liege | P-47 |
| | | FW-190 dam(air) | Hasselt | P-47 |
| | August 19 | Me-109 dest(air) | Oosterhout | P-47 |
| | | Me-109 dest(air) | Schoonhoven | P-47 |
| | October 4 | Me-110 dest(air) | E/Aachen | P-47 |
| | | Me-110 prob(air) | E/Aachen | P-47 |
| | October 14 | Me-110 dest(air) | W/Aachen | P-47 |

5.5-1-1 air
0-0 ground

* - shared with Capt. G.W. Johnson of the 61st Ftr Sqn

**McClure, James H., Lt.** (5) Springfield, KY
350th Ftr Sqn/353rd Ftr Grp November 1944-July 1945
31 missions

| *Sqn* | *Date* | *Claims* | *Location* | *A/C* |
|---|---|---|---|---|
| 350th | April 16, 1945 | (2)Me-109 dest(grd) | Pocking | P-51 |
| | | FW-190 dest(grd) | Pocking | P-51 |
| | | FW-200 dest(grd) | Pocking | P-51 |
| | | Ju-88 dest(grd) | Pocking | P-51 |

0-0-0 air
5-0 ground

**McCollom, Francis N., Lt.** (5) Los Angeles, CA
358th Ftr Sqn/355th Ftr Grp September 1944-April 16, 1945(POW)
Hit by flak at Straubing and crash-landed near Regensburg.
52 missions

P-51D YF-N 44-14385 "Wooly Lamb"
S/Sgt. A.K. Smith-c/c
Sgt. Jack Groucutt-ac/c

| Sqn | Date | Claims | Location | A/C |
|---|---|---|---|---|
| 358th | April 9, 1945 | Me-110 dest(grd) | Heilfingen | P-51 |
| | | He-111 dam(grd) | Heilfingen | P-51 |
| | April 16 | (2)FW-190 dest(grd) | Straubing | P-51 |
| | | Ju-88 dest(grd) | Straubing | P-51 |
| | | u/i a/c dest(grd) | Straubing | P-51 |

0-0-0 air
5-1 ground

**McCormick, Arthur B., Jr., Capt.** (10) Fort Riley, KS
385th Ftr Sqn/364th Ftr Grp September 1944-EOW
68 missions

P-51D 5E-L 44-15179 "Look Homeward Angel"
P-51D 5E-L 44-11340 "Look Homeward Angel II"

| Sqn | Date | Claims | Location | A/C |
|---|---|---|---|---|
| 385th | November 2, 1944 | Me-109 dest(air) | Halle | P-51 |
| | | Me-109 dam(air) | Halle | P-51 |
| | November 21 | u/i a/c dest(grd) | Eisleben | P-51 |
| | November 26 | (4)Ju-88 dest(grd) | SE Jade Bay | P-51 |
| | January 29, 1945 | u/i a/c dam(grd) | Darmstadt | P-51 |
| | February 26 | (1.5)He-111 dest(grd)* | SE Jade Bay | P-51 |
| | April 13 | Do-217 dest(grd) | E/Luneburg | P-51 |
| | | Ju-188 dest(grd) | see above | P-51 |
| | | (.5)FW-190 dest(grd)** | see above | P-51 |
| | | Do-217 dam(grd) | see above | P-51 |
| | | FW-190 dam(grd) | see above | P-51 |

1-0-1 air
9-3 ground

* - shared with Lt. C.R. Roesch of the 385th Ftr Sqn
** - shared with Lt. J.G. Johnson of the 385th Ftr Sqn

**McCubbin, James L., Lt.** (5) Kansas City, MO
385th Ftr Sqn/364th Ftr Grp September 1944-February 19, 1945(POW)
Hit by flak near Steinhorst Airfield.
44 missions

P-51D 5E-F 44-11242 "Mary-Al"

| Sqn | Date | Claims | Location | A/C |
|---|---|---|---|---|
| 385th | November 21, 1944 | u/i a/c dest(grd) | SE Eisleben | P-51 |
| | | u/i a/c dam(grd) | SE Eisleben | P-51 |
| | December 2 | Me-109 dest(air) | Mannheim | P-51 |
| | December 5 | (2)FW-190 dest(air) | N/Berlin | P-51 |
| | | (2)FW-190 prob(air) | N/Berlin | P-51 |
| | January 1, 1945 | Me-109 dest(air) | SE Hamburg | P-51 |

4-2-0 air
1-1 ground

**McDuffie, Duncan M., Lt.** (9) Aiken, SC
83rd Ftr Sqn/78th Ftr Grp November 1944-EOW
45 missions

| Sqn | Date | Claims | Location | A/C |
|---|---|---|---|---|
| 83rd | March 2, 1945 | (4)Me-109 dest(air) | Burg A/F | P-51 |
| | April 16 | (2)FW-190 dest(grd) | N/Prague | P-51 |
| | | (2)Me-109 dest(grd) | N/Prague | P-51 |
| | | Ju-87 dest(grd) | N/Prague | P-51 |

4-0-0 air
5-0 ground

**McElroy, James N., Capt.** (11) Orlando, FL
358th Ftr Sqn/355th Ftr Grp March 1944-March 1945
99 missions

P-51B YF-S 43-7023 "Big Stoop"
P-51D YF-S 44-14498 "Big Stoop II"
P-51D YF-S "Big Stoop III"
S/Sgt. Charles M. Jones-c/c

| Sqn | Date | Claims | Location | A/C |
|---|---|---|---|---|
| 358th | April 5, 1944 | Me-110 dest(grd) | Munich | P-51 |
| | | Me-110 dam(grd) | Landsberg | P-51 |
| | April 15 | (5)Do-217 dest(grd) | Glienicke A/F | P-51 |
| | April 19 | Me-109 dam(air) | SW Brunswick | P-51 |
| | July 19 | FW-190 dest(air) | Augsburg | P-51 |
| | | FW-190 dam(air) | Augsburg | P-51 |
| | July 28 | Me-109 dest(air) | S/Merseburg | P-51 |
| | | FW-190 dest(air) | S/Merseburg | P-51 |
| | November 2 | Me-109 dam(air) | Merseburg | P-51 |
| | December 5 | FW-190 dest(air) | Berlin | P-51 |
| | | (3)FW-190 dam(air) | Berlin | P-51 |
| | February 27, 1945 | Do-217 dest(air) | SW Plauen | P-51 |

5-0-6 air
6-1 ground

**McFadden, Jack D., Capt.** (5) Brookville, PA
334th Ftr Sqn/4th Ftr Grp June 1944-EOW

P-51D QP-Q 44-14202

| Sqn | Date | Claims | Location | A/C |
|---|---|---|---|---|
| 334th | July 7, 1944 | Me-109 dam(air) | Aschersleben | P-51 |
| | November 6 | Me-109 dest(air) | Rheine | P-51 |
| | November 18 | (2)Me-262 dam(grd) | Leipheim | P-51 |
| | December 2 | FW-190 dest(air) | Hottenback | P-51 |
| | February 27, 1945 | Me-108 dest(grd) | Weimar | P-51 |
| | | Ju-87 dest(grd) | Weimar | P-51 |
| | April 10 | Ju-88 dest(grd) | Wittstock | P-51 |

2-0-1 air
3-2 ground

**McGee, Donald C., Maj.** (8) Mansfield, OH
364th Ftr Sqn/357th Ftr Grp November 1944-January 1945
363rd Ftr Sqn/357th Ftr Grp January 1945-May 1945
Earlier flew in the PTO with the 8th Ftr Grp, 5th Air Force, claiming 5 kills in 154 missions, 329 hours: a Zero on May 1, 1942; (2)Zeros on May 29, 1942; a Betty on April 12, 1943; and a Tony on September 15, 1943.
62 missions, 278 hours

P-51D B6-J 44-15888 "Whole Hawg"
P-51D C5-
S/Sgt. Arthur E. Krantz-c/c(364th)
S/Sgt. John E. Kunelius-c/c(363rd)

| Sqn | Date | Claims | Location | A/C |
|---|---|---|---|---|
| 363rd | March 2, 1945 | Me-109 dest(air) | NE Magdeburg | P-51 |
| | April 10 | Me-410 dest(grd) | Neuruppin | P-51 |
| | | He-111 dest(grd) | see above | P-51 |
| | | (2)u/i a/c dam(grd) | see above | P-51 |

1-0-0 air
2-2 ground

**McGinn, John L., LtCol.** (5) Los Angeles, CA
338th Ftr Sqn/55th Ftr Grp April 1944-October 1944
Earlier flew in the PTO with the 18th and 347th Ftr Grps, 13th Air Force, claimimg 3 kills: single Zeros on June 16, July 17, and November 1, 1943.
64 missions, 271:40 hours

P-38J CL-P 43-28833 "DaQuake"
P-51D CL-P 44-14291 "DaQuake"
P-51D CL-P 44-14730 "DaQuake"
S/Sgt. James C. Seibert-c/c
Sgt. Ted Alexander-ac/c
Sgt. "Pops" Spalding-arm.

| Sqn | Date | Claims | Location | A/C |
|---|---|---|---|---|
| 338th | September 3, 1944 | FW-190 dest(air) | Brussels | P-51 |
| | September 11 | Me-109 dest(air) | S/Meiningen | P-51 |
| | | (2)Me-109 dam(air) | S/Meiningen | P-51 |

2-0-2 air
0-0 ground

**McGinnis, Keith R., Lt.** (8) Des Moines, IA
38th Ftr Sqn/55th Ftr Grp December 1944-November 1945
47 missions

P-51D CG-N

| Sqn | Date | Claims | Location | A/C |
|---|---|---|---|---|
| 38th | February 3, 1945 | (4)Fi-156 dest(grd) | Templin A/F | P-51 |
| | February 19 | FW-190 dest(air) | NW Ingolstadt | P-51 |
| | April 9 | (2)He-111 dest(grd) | Munich-Brunnthal | P-51 |
| | | He-111 dam(grd) | see above | P-51 |
| | April 10 | Me-262 dest(air) | Galworde | P-51 |

2-0-0 air
6-1 ground

**McGrattan, Bernard L., Capt.** (8.5) Utica, NY
335th Ftr Sqn/4th Ftr Grp September 1943-June 6, 1944(KIA)
Hit by e/a near Rouen.

P-47D WD-D 42-7936
P-51B WD-D 43-6767
P-51B WD-D 42-106576
S/Sgt. Sy Koenig-c/c

| Sqn | Date | Claims | Location | A/C |
|---|---|---|---|---|
| 335th | February 22, 1944 | FW-190 dest(air) | Erkelenz | P-47 |
| | March 6 | Me-110 dest(air) | NE Magdeburg | P-51 |
| | March 18 | He-111 dest(air) | NE Augsburg | P-51 |
| | April 8 | Me-109 dest(air) | Wolfenbuttel | P-51 |
| | April 19 | Me-109 dest(air) | Eschwege | P-51 |
| | | (.5)FW-190 dest(air)[*] | Eschwege | P-51 |
| | April 24 | FW-190 dest(air) | Knocke | P-51 |
| | May 1 | Me-109 dest(air) | Losheim | P-51 |
| | May 29 | FW-190 dest(air) | Laaland Island | P-51 |

8.5-0-0 air
0-0 ground

[*] - shared with Lt. N. Megura of the 334th Ftr Sqn, 4th Ftr Grp

**McGraw, Charles L., Capt.** (5) Warrensburg, MO
351st Ftr Sqn/353rd Ftr Grp August 1944-August 1945
55 missions

P-47D YJ-R 42-75740 "Liberty Queen"
P-51D YJ-R 44-14748 "Kansas City Kitty"

| Sqn | Date | Claims | Location | A/C |
|---|---|---|---|---|
| 351st | September 13, 1944 | Do-217 dest(grd) | NW Stuttgart | P-47 |
| | April 7, 1945 | (3)Me-109 dest(air) | Steinhuder Lake | P-51 |
| | April 16 | He-111 dest(grd) | Reichersberg | P-51 |
| | | (2)He-111 dam(grd) | see above | P-51 |

3-0-0 air
2-2 ground

**McHugh, Philip M.N., Lt.** (5) Trenton, NJ
357th Ftr Sqn/355th Ftr Grp April 1944-September 1944

| Sqn | Date | Claims | Location | A/C |
|---|---|---|---|---|
| 357th | June 24, 1944 | Me-109 dest(grd) | E/Angars | P-51 |
| | July 8 | (2)Me-410 dest(grd) | SW Chalons | P-51 |
| | | (3)Me-410 dam(grd) | SW Chalons | P-51 |
| | July 13 | Me-109 dam(air) | Sarrebourg | P-51 |
| | September 12 | (2)FW-190 dest(air) | E/Muritz Lake | P-51 |

2-0-1 air
3-3 ground

**McKee, Daniel D., LtCol.** (5) Greenville, MS
370th Ftr Sqn/359th Ftr Grp April 1943-October 1943
HdQts/359th Ftr Grp October 1943-February 1944
370th Ftr Sqn/359th Ftr Grp February 1944-April 1945
HdQts/359th Ftr Grp April 1945-September 1945
Earlier flew in the Aleutians with the 343rd Ftr Grp

P-47D CS-Z 42-75118
P-51B CS-A 42-106878
P-51D CS-A 44-14521 "Rayner Shine"
P-51D CS-A 44-72823 "Rayner Shine"

| Sqn | Date | Claims | Location | A/C |
|---|---|---|---|---|
| 370th | March 2, 1944 | FW-190 dam(air) | Neufchateau | P-47 |
| | March 27 | FW-190 prob(air) | Chartres | P-47 |
| | | Me-109 dam(air) | Chartres | P-47 |
| | April 11 | Ju-88 dest(grd) | Volkenrod | P-47 |
| | | (2)Ju-88 dam(grd) | Volkenrod | P-47 |
| | April 15 | (2)Ju-88 dam(grd) | Oldenburg | P-47 |
| | November 21 | FW-190 dest(air) | SW Merseburg | P-51 |
| | April 13, 1945 | (2)Ar-196 dest(grd) | Schwerin Lake | P-51 |
| | April 17 | FW-190 dest(grd) | Ganacker-Plattling | P-51 |

1-1-2 air
4-4 ground

**McKennon, Pierce W., Maj.** (17.67) Fort Smith, AR
335th Ftr Sqn/4th Ftr Grp February 1943-August 28, 1944(MIA-E)
Hit by flak near Niederbronn.
335th Ftr Sqn/4th Ftr Grp September 1944-September 1945
560 hours

P-47C WD-A 41-6582
P-51B WD-A 43-6896
P-51B WD-A 42-106911 "Yippee Joe!!"
P-51D WD-A 44-13883
P-51D WD-A 44-14570 "Ridge Runner"
P-51D WD-A 44-14221 "Ridge Runner II"
P-51D WD-A 44-72398 "Ridge Runner III"
P-51D WD-A 44-63166
S/Sgt. Joe B. Sills-c/c

| Sqn | Date | Claims | Location | A/C |
|---|---|---|---|---|
| 335th | July 30, 1943 | FW-190 dest(air) | Zaltboemel | P-47 |
| | December 11 | Me-109 dam(air) | Leeuwarden | P-47 |
| | February 20, 1944 | FW-190 dest(air) | Marburg | P-47 |
| | February 22 | (.5)Me-109 dest(air)[*] | SW Oolgensplant | P-47 |
| | | (.5)FW-190 dam(air)[*] | Erkelenz | P-47 |
| | February 25 | FW-190 dest(air) | S/Luxembourg | P-47 |
| | March 6 | Me-109 dest(air) | S/Berlin | P-51 |
| | March 21 | FW-190 dest(air) | W/Landes de Bussac | P-51 |
| | March 28 | Ju-88 dam(grd) | S/Dreux | P-51 |
| | March 29 | Me-109 dest(air) | NE Brunswick | P-51 |
| | April 8 | FW-190 dest(air) | NW Brunswick | P-51 |
| | | FW-190 dam(air) | NW Brunswick | P-51 |
| | April 9 | (.33)Ju-88 dest(grd)[**] | Lingen-Plantlunne | P-51 |
| | | (.33)Ju-88 dest(grd)[**] | see above | P-51 |
| | April 10 | u/i a/c dam(grd) | Romorantin A/F | P-51 |
| | April 13 | FW-190 dest(air) | SW Schweinfurt | P-51 |
| | April 18 | FW-190 dest(air) | Rathenow | P-51 |
| | April 19 | Me-109 dest(air) | Eschwege | P-51 |
| | December 25 | (.5)FW-190 dest(air)[@] | S/Bonn | P-51 |
| | February 25, 1945 | (2)u/i a/c dam(grd) | Pretzech | P-51 |
| | April 9 | (2)Ju-52 dest(grd) | Munich-Brunnthal | P-51 |
| | | Me-410 dest(grd) | see above | P-51 |
| | | Ju-52 dam(grd) | see above | P-51 |
| | April 16 | (2)Do-217 dest(grd) | Praha/Letnany | P-51 |
| | | u/i a/c dest(grd) | see above | P-51 |
| | | Me-410 dam(grd) | see above | P-51 |

11-0-2.5 air
6.67-6 ground

[*] - both shared with F/O J. Goetz of the 335th Ftr Sqn
[**] - both shared with Capt. J.R. Happel of the 335th Ftr Sqn and Lt. J.T. Godfrey of the 336th Ftr Sqn, 4th Ftr Grp
[@] - shared with Lt. T.J. Cronin of the 334th Ftr Sqn, 4th Ftr Grp

**McKeon, Joseph T., Capt.** (8) Redlands, CA
77th Ftr Sqn/20th Ftr Grp July 1944-September 1944
55th Ftr Sqn/20th Ftr Grp September 1944-October 7, 1944(POW)
Collided with a P-51 near Stettin.
Earlier flew in the PTO with the 8th and 475th Ftr Grps, 5th Air Force, claiming 5 kills: a Zero on December 7, 1942 with the 8th Ftr Grp; single Zeros on September 4, 22, and 24, 1943; and a Val on October 15, 1943.
37 missions, 190:55 hours

P-51D LC-C 44-13992 "Regina Coeli"
P-51D KI-M 44-14319 "Olivia de"

| Sqn | Date | Claims | Location | A/C |
|---|---|---|---|---|
| 77th | August 16, 1944 | Me-109 dest(air) | Mulhausen | P-51 |
| | | FW-190 dam(air) | Mulhausen | P-51 |
| 55th | October 6 | (2)Do-24 dest(grd) | Kubitzer Bay | P-51 |

1-0-1 air
2-0 ground

**McMahan, Bruce D., Lt.** (6) Houston, TX
350th Ftr Sqn/353rd Ftr Grp February 1945-EOW
14 missions

| Sqn | Date | Claims | Location | A/C |
|---|---|---|---|---|
| 350th | April 10, 1945 | (.5)Me-262 dest(air)[*] | Dessau | P-51 |
| | April 16 | (4)FW-190 dest(grd) | Pocking | P-51 |
| | | (.5)Fi-156 dest(grd)[**] | Pocking | P-51 |
| | | (.5)Fi-156 dest(grd)[**] | Pocking | P-51 |
| | | (.5)Hs-126 dest(grd)[**] | Pocking | P-51 |

0.5-0-0 air
5.5-0 ground

[*] - shared with Lt. J.W. Clark of the 350th Ftr Sqn
[**] - all shared with Capt. H.G. Kolb of the 350th Ftr Sqn

**McMahan, Darrell E., Lt.** (5.5) Paso Robles, CA
62nd Ftr Sqn/56th Ftr Grp June 1944-November 1944

P-47D LM-A 42-26298

| *Sqn* | *Date* | *Claims* | *Location* | *A/C* |
|---|---|---|---|---|
| 62nd | July 4, 1944 | (.5)Me-109 dest(air)[*] | Conches | P-47 |
| | September 5 | (4)FW-190 dest(grd) | Gelnhausen | P-47 |
| | September 12 | Me-109 dest(air) | Sachau A/F | P-47 |
| | | 1.5-0-0 air | | |
| | | 4-0 ground | | |

[*] - shared with Lt. F.C. Newell of the 62nd Ftr Sqn

**McMinn, Evan D., Lt.** (7) Pittsburgh, PA
61st Ftr Sqn/56th Ftr Grp December 1943-June 6, 1944(KIA)
Hit by ground fire near Bernay.

P-47D HV-F 42-8458

| *Sqn* | *Date* | *Claims* | *Location* | *A/C* |
|---|---|---|---|---|
| 61st | February 21, 1944 | Me-109 dest(air) | Zuider Zee | P-47 |
| | February 22 | FW-190 dest(air) | Lippstadt | P-47 |
| | March 6 | (2)Me-109 dam(grd) | Vechta | P-47 |
| | March 15 | Me-109 dam(air) | E/Dummer Lake | P-47 |
| | March 16 | FW-190 dest(air) | St. Dizier | P-47 |
| | April 15 | He-111 dest(grd) | Flensburg | P-47 |
| | | Me-210 dest(grd) | see above | P-47 |
| | | He-111 dam(grd) | see above | P-47 |
| | | Me-210 dam(grd) | see above | P-47 |
| | May 22 | (2)FW-190 dest(air) | Rotenburg | P-47 |
| | | FW-190 dam(air) | Rotenburg | p-47 |
| | | 5-0-2 air | | |
| | | 2-4 ground | | |

**McMullen, Joseph D. Lt.** (10) Victoria, TX
350th Ftr Sqn/353rd Ftr Grp November 1944-EOW
40 missions

| *Sqn* | *Date* | *Claims* | *Location* | *A/C* |
|---|---|---|---|---|
| 350th | February 27, 1945 | (1.5)FW-190 dest(grd)[*] | Rohrensee | P-51 |
| | | Ju-88 dest(grd) | see above | P-51 |
| | | FW-190 dam(grd) | see above | P-51 |
| | | Ju-88 dam(grd) | see above | P-51 |
| | February 28 | (1.5)Me-110 dest(grd)[**] | S/Gotha | P-51 |
| | March 21 | He-111 dest(grd) | Achmer | P-51 |
| | | Ar-234 dam(grd) | Achmer | P-51 |
| | April 16 | (5)FW-190 dest(grd) | Pocking | P-51 |
| | | 0-0-0 air | | |
| | | 10-3 ground | | |

[*] - shared with F/O R.N. Gustke of the 350th Ftr Sqn
[**] - shared with Lt. M.W. Hightshoe of the 350th Ftr Sqn

**Megura, Nicholas, Capt.** (15.58) Ansonia, CT
334th Ftr Sqn/4th Ftr Grp July 1943-May 22, 1944(INT)
Hit by a P-38 and landed in Sweden.

P-47D QP-N "Ill Wind?"
P-51B QP-N 43-6636 "Ill Wind?"
S/Sgt. Paul Fox-c/c
Sgt. Jerome Bryrge-ac/c

| *Sqn* | *Date* | *Claims* | *Location* | *A/C* |
|---|---|---|---|---|
| 334th | February 28, 1944 | (.25)Ju-88 dest(grd)[*] | Soissons | P-51 |
| | March 4 | Me-109 dest(air) | NW Leipzig | P-51 |
| | March 6 | (2)Me-110 dest(air) | SW Berlin | P-51 |
| | | Me-110 dam(air) | SW Berlin | P-51 |
| | March 8 | Me-109 dest(air) | W/Berlin | P-51 |
| | | FW-190 dest(air) | W/Berlin | P-51 |
| | | FW-190 dam(air) | W/Berlin | P-51 |
| | | Ju-88 dam(air) | Ruhr | P-51 |
| | March 18 | Me-109 dest(air) | SE Mannheim | P-51 |
| | March 21 | (.5)FW-190 dest(air)[**] | NE Bordeaux | P-51 |
| | | He-177 dest(grd) | NE Bordeaux | P-51 |
| | March 23 | FW-190 dest(air) | Munster | P-51 |
| | March 27 | Me-109 dam(air) | Angars | P-51 |
| | | (.5)Ju-88 dest(grd)[***] | Cazaux A/F | P-51 |
| | | FW-190 dam(grd) | Cazaux A/F | P-51 |
| | April 1 | Me-109 dam(air) | NW Lake Constance | P-51 |
| | April 13 | FW-190 dest(air) | SE Mannheim | P-51 |
| | April 18 | (.33)Me-109 dest(air)[@] | Fassberg A/F | P-51 |
| | | Ju-88 dam(grd) | see above | P-51 |
| | | u/i a/c dam(grd) | see above | P-51 |
| | April 19 | (.5)FW-190 dest(air)[@@] | Eschwege | P-51 |
| | April 24 | (2)FW-190 dest(air) | S/Frankfurt | P-51 |
| | | FW-190 dam(air) | S/Frankfurt | P-51 |
| | April 29 | Ju-52 dest(grd) | Nordhausen | P-51 |
| | | (.5)Ju-52 dest(grd)[@@@] | Nordhausen | P-51 |
| | | (.5)Ju-52 dest(grd)[#] | Nordhausen | P-51 |
| | May 22 | (.5)Me-109 dest(air)[##] | SW Kiel | P-51 |
| | | 11.83-0-6 air | | |
| | | 3.75-3 ground | | |

[*] - shared with Capt. D.W. Beeson and Lt. W.B. Smith of the 334th Ftr Sqn and Lt. V. Garrison of the 336th Ftr Sqn, 4th Ftr Grp
[**] - shared with Lt. A.W. Chatterly of the 334th Ftr Sqn
[***] - shared with Lt. A.H. Markel of the 334th Ftr Sqn
[@] - shared with Capt. V.J. France and Lt. G.C. Siems of the 334th Ftr Sqn
[@@] - shared with Lt. B.L. McGrattan of the 335th Ftr Sqn, 4th Ftr Grp
[@@@] - shared with Lt. J.L. Barden of the 334th Ftr Sqn
[#] - shared with Lt. S.W. Monroe of the 334th Ftr Sqn
[##] - shared with an unknown P-38 pilot

**Mellen, Joseph E., Capt.** (10) Booneville, IN
354th Ftr Sqn/355th Ftr Grp October 1944-May 1945

P-51D WR-C 44-11359 "Lil Lila Lee"
S/Sgt. Julius Moseley-c/c

| *Sqn* | *Date* | *Claims* | *Location* | *A/C* |
|---|---|---|---|---|
| 354th | November 26, 1944 | FW-190 dest(air) | S/Misburg | P-51 |
| | April 7, 1945 | FW-190 dest(air) | S/Bremen | P-51 |
| | April 13 | (3)u/i a/c dest(grd) | Husum | P-51 |
| | | (2)He-111 dest(grd) | Husum | P-51 |
| | April 16 | He-177 dest(grd) | Eger A/F | P-51 |
| | | He-111 dest(grd) | Eger A/F | P-51 |
| | | Ju-88 dest(grd) | Eger A/F | P-51 |
| | | 2-0-0 air | | |
| | | 8-0 ground | | |

**Meroney, Virgil K., Capt.** (9) Pine Bluff, AR
487th Ftr Sqn/352nd Ftr Grp October 1942-April 8, 1944(POW)
Hit by flak at Bramsche Airfield.

P-47D HO-V 42-8473 "Sweet Louise"
P-51B HO-V 43-7166
S/Sgt. Albert F. Giesting-c/c
Sgt. Jack Gillenwater-ac/c

| *Sqn* | *Date* | *Claims* | *Location* | *A/C* |
|---|---|---|---|---|
| 487th | December 1, 1943 | Me-109 dest(air) | S/Rheydt | P-47 |
| | | (.5)Me-210 dest(air)[*] | S/Rheydt | P-47 |
| | December 4 | Me-109 dest(air) | Rotterdam-Utrecht | P-47 |
| | | (.5)FW-190 dest(air)[**] | see above | P-47 |
| | January 29, 1944 | FW-190 dest(air) | Malmedy | P-47 |
| | January 30 | Me-109 dest(air) | Zwolle | P-47 |
| | | Me-109 dam(air) | Zwolle | P-47 |
| | February 3 | FW-190 dest(air) | Groningen | P-47 |
| | February 10 | Me-109 dest(air) | Hengelo | P-47 |
| | March 8 | FW-190 dest(air) | Meppen | P-47 |
| | March 16 | Me-109 dest(air) | S/Bar de Luc | P-47 |
| | | 9-0-1 air | | |
| | | 0-0 ground | | |

[*] - shared with Lt. R.L. Grow of the 487th Ftr Sqn
[**] - shared with F/O J.L. Sweeney of the 487th Ftr Sqn

**Merritt, George L., Jr., Maj.** (11) Cumming, GA
374th Ftr Sqn/361st Ftr Grp May 1943-August 1943
375th Ftr Sqn/361st Ftr Grp August 1943-June 7, 1944(KIA)
Hit poles while strafing near Roiffe.
95 missions

P-47D E2-A 42-75404 "Dr. I.P. Daily"
P-51C E2-A 42-103347
S/Sgt. Alfred Arruda-c/c
Sgt. Harry R. Anderson-arm.

| *Sqn* | *Date* | *Claims* | *Location* | *A/C* |
|---|---|---|---|---|
| 375th | February 22, 1944 | (2)FW-190 dest(air) | NE Tilburg | P-47 |
| | March 17 | Me-109 dest(grd) | Chartres | P-47 |
| | | Me-109 dam(grd) | Chartres | P-47 |
| | April 18 | Ju-88 dest(grd) | Zwischenaschmer | P-47 |

| | | | | |
|---|---|---|---|---|
| | April 27 | He-111 dest(grd) | Etampes | P-47 |
| | May 8 | FW-190 dest(air) | N/Nienburg | P-47 |
| | May 24 | Me-109 dest(air) | NE Berlin | P-51 |
| | May 27 | FW-190 dest(air) | W/Lille | P-51 |
| | May 29 | (2)He-111 dest(grd) | Lackau-Juterbog | P-51 |
| | June 6 | Ju-88 dest(grd) | Tours | P-51 |

5-0-0 air
6-1 ground

**Meyer, John C., LtCol.** (37) Forest Hills, NY
487th Ftr Sqn/352nd Ftr Grp December 1942-November 1944
HdQts/352nd Ftr Grp November 1944-January 1945
Earlier flew a tour in Iceland with the 33rd Ftr Sqn
135 missions, 462 hours

P-47D HO-M 42-8529 "Lambie"
P-51B HO-M 42-106471 "Lambie/Petie"
P-51D HO-M 44-14151 "Petie 2nd"
P-51D HO-M 44-15041 "Petie 3rd"
S/Sgt. W.F. Conkey-c/c
Sgt. William H. Kohlas-ac/c
Sgt. James D. Bleidner-arm.

| *Sqn* | *Date* | *Claims* | *Location* | *A/C* |
|---|---|---|---|---|
| 487th | November 26, 1943 | Me-109 dest(air) | E/Groningen | P-47 |
| | | Me-109 prob(air) | E/Groningen | P-47 |
| | December 4 | Me-109 dest(air) | W/Utrecht | P-47 |
| | December 22 | Me-109 dest(air) | N/Lingen | P-47 |
| | April 10, 1944 | Me-109 dest(air) | SW Rheims | P-51 |
| | | (.5)FW-190 dest(air)* | SW Rheims | P-51 |
| | April 11 | FW-190 dest(grd) | S/Berlin | P-51 |
| | | Ju-88 dest(grd) | S/Berlin | P-51 |
| | | FW-200 dam(grd) | S/Berlin | P-51 |
| | | Ju-290 dam(grd) | S/Berlin | P-51 |
| | April 13 | (2)He-111 dest(grd) | S/Stuttgart | P-51 |
| | | Ju-52 dest(grd) | S/Stuttgart | P-51 |
| | April 22 | Me-210 dest(grd) | Stade A/F | P-51 |
| | | (2)He-111 dam(grd) | Stade A/F | P-51 |
| | May 8 | (3)Me-109 dest(air) | Brunswick-Hanover | P-51 |
| | May 12 | Me-109 dest(air) | SW Frankfurt | P-51 |
| | | He-177 dest(grd) | SW Frankfurt | P-51 |
| | August 25 | He-177 dest(grd) | Neubrandenburg | P-51 |
| | | Ju-52 dest(grd) | see above | P-51 |
| | | (2)u/i a/c dam(grd) | see above | P-51 |
| | September 10 | (3)Ju-52 dest(grd) | Wertheim | P-51 |
| | | u/i a/c dest(grd) | Wertheim | P-51 |
| | September 11 | (3)Me-109 dest(air) | Gottingen-Nordhausen | P-51 |
| | | FW-190 dest(air) | see above | P-51 |
| HdQts | November 21 | (3)FW-190 dest(air) | SW Merseburg | P-51 |
| | November 27 | Me-109 dest(air) | E/Munster | P-51 |
| | December 26 | (1.5)Me-109 dest(air)** | Ollheim | P-51 |
| | | Me-109 dest(air) | Uxheim | P-51 |
| | December 27 | (2)FW-190 dest(air) | SW Bonn | P-51 |
| | | (2)FW-190 dam(air) | SW Bonn | P-51 |
| | December 31 | Ar-234 dest(air) | Euskirchen | P-51 |
| | January 1, 1945 | (2)FW-190 dest(air) | N/Liege | P-51 |

24-1-2 air
13-6 ground

* - shared with Lt. C.J. Luksic of the 487th Ftr Sqn
** - shared with an unknown P-51 pilot

**Miklajcyk, Henry J., Capt.** (13) Syracuse, NY
486th Ftr Sqn/352nd Ftr Grp States-November 2, 1944(KIA)
Hit by e/a west of Halle.

P-47C PZ-K 41-6531 "The Syracusan"
P-51B PZ-K 42-106430 "The Syracusan II"
P-51D PZ-K 44-13690 "The Syracusan 3"
S/Sgt. R.H. Sprole-c/c
Sgt. Claude C. Thomas-ac/c
Sgt. S.J. Lengieza-arm.

| *Sqn* | *Date* | *Claims* | *Location* | *A/C* |
|---|---|---|---|---|
| 486th | April 15, 1944 | FW-190 dest(air) | Vechta | P-51 |
| | April 23 | (.5)Ju-52 dest(grd)* | SE Paris | P-51 |
| | April 24 | Ju-52 dest(air) | E/Neuburg | P-51 |
| | | (3)Ju-88 dest(grd) | Neuburg | P-51 |
| | April 25 | Hs-129 dest(grd) | Metz | P-51 |
| | August 6 | (2)Me-109 dest(air) | SE Hamburg | P-51 |
| | September 12 | (1.5)FW-190 dest(air)** | Kustrin | P-51 |
| | | Ju-52 dest(grd) | Kustrin | P-51 |
| | November 2 | Me-109 dest(air) | Merseburg | P-51 |
| | | FW-190 dest(air) | Merseburg | P-51 |

7.5-0-0 air
5.5-0 ground

* - shared with Lt. E.L. Heller of the 486th Ftr Sqn
** - shared with Lt. J.D. Carter of the 486th Ftr Sqn

**Miller, Gerald J., Lt.** (11) Lowville, NY
351st Ftr Sqn/353rd Ftr Grp January 1945-EOW
22 missions, 118 hours

P-51D YJ-V 44-14595
S/Sgt. Reemer Hilton-c/c

| *Sqn* | *Date* | *Claims* | *Location* | *A/C* |
|---|---|---|---|---|
| 351st | March 21, 1945 | (2)FW-190 dest(grd) | Achmer | P-51 |
| | | (2)FW-190 dam(grd) | Achmer | P-51 |
| | April 16 | (6)FW-190 dest(grd) | Reichersberg | P-51 |
| | | (2)Me-109 dest(grd) | see above | P-51 |
| | | Do-217 dest(grd) | see above | P-51 |

0-0-0 air
11-2 ground

**Miller, Harold O., Lt.** (5.5) Santa Rosa, CA
352nd Ftr Sqn/353rd Ftr Grp April 1944-September 1944
77 missions, 300 hours

P-47D SX-S "Sniffles"
S/Sgt. James M. Cody-c/c

| *Sqn* | *Date* | *Claims* | *Location* | *A/C* |
|---|---|---|---|---|
| 352nd | June 8, 1944 | FW-190 dest(grd) | Angars | P-47 |
| | | (.5)Ju-88 dest(grd)* | Angars | P-47 |
| | June 12 | Me-109 dest(air) | Dreux | P-47 |
| | June 22 | Me-109 dest(air) | S/Rouen | P-47 |
| | June 27 | (2)Me-109 dam(air) | N/Troyes | P-47 |
| | August 4 | (2)He-111 dest(grd) | Plantlunne | P-47 |

2-0-2 air
3.5-0 ground

* - shared with Lt. C.F. Armstrong of the 352nd Ftr Sqn

**Millikan, Willard W., Capt.** (15) Rockport, MO
336th Ftr Sqn/4th Ftr Grp July 1943-May 30, 1944(POW)
Collided with a P-51 near Wittenburg.

P-47C VF-U 41-6180 "Missouri Mauler"
P-51B VF-U 43-6997 "Missouri Mauler"
P-51B VF-U 43-6630 "Missouri Mauler"
P-51B VF-U 43-24769 "Missouri Mauler"
S/Sgt. Neal Gallagher-c/c

| *Sqn* | *Date* | *Claims* | *Location* | *A/C* |
|---|---|---|---|---|
| 336th | September 27, 1943 | FW-190 dest(air) | Potten | P-47 |
| | December 20 | Me-109 dest(air) | NW Bremen | P-47 |
| | February 10, 1944 | FW-190 dest(air) | N/Dummer Lake | P-47 |
| | March 3 | Me-110 dest(air) | Wittenburg | P-51 |
| | March 27 | He-177 dest(grd) | Cazaux A/F | P-51 |
| | April 8 | (3)Me-109 dest(air) | Ulzen | P-51 |
| | April 15 | He-177 dest(grd) | Hagenow | P-51 |
| | April 19 | Me-109 dest(air) | Eschwege | P-51 |
| | April 22 | (4)Me-109 dest(air) | SW Kassel | P-51 |
| | April 30 | Do-24 dam(grd) | Lyon Anchorage | P-51 |
| | May 22 | Me-109 dest(air) | NW Kiel | P-51 |

13-0-0 air
2-1 ground

**Mills, Henry L., Maj.** (6) New York, NY
334th Ftr Sqn/4th Ftr Grp October 1942-March 6, 1944(POW)
Suffered m/f west of Brandenburg.
Earlier flew with 71 Sqn, RAF

Spitfire XR-
P-47C QP-Q 41-6191
P-47D QP-Q 42-74751
P-51B QP-Q 43-6690
S/Sgt. D. Hall-c/c

| *Sqn* | *Date* | *Claims* | *Location* | *A/C* |
|---|---|---|---|---|
| 334th | July 26, 1943 | FW-190 prob(air) | Brielle-Rotterdam | P-47 |
| | July 28 | FW-190 dam(air) | E/Rotterdam | P-47 |
| | August 16 | (2)FW-190 dest(air) | NW Paris | P-47 |
| | October 8 | Me-109 prob(air) | Meppel-Zwolle | P-47 |
| | January 29, 1944 | (2)Me-109 dest(air) | Aachen | P-47 |
| | February 20 | FW-190 dest(air) | Aachen | P-47 |
| | March 6 | FW-190 dest(air) | W/Brandenburg | P-51 |

6-2-1 air
0-0 ground

**Minchew, Leslie D., Capt.** (6) Miami, FL
354th Ftr Sqn/355th Ftr Grp States-December 1943
357th Ftr Sqn/355th Ftr Grp December 1943-October 1944
HdQts/355th Ftr Grp October 1944-April 1945

P-47D WR-M
P-51B OS-Q
P-51D OS-Q 44-14753
S/Sgt. Eugene J. Liebold-c/c(Q)

| *Sqn* | *Date* | *Claims* | *Location* | *A/C* |
|---|---|---|---|---|
| 357th | March 28, 1944 | (.5)He-111 dest(grd)* | Dijon | P-51 |
| | April 8 | Me-109 dest(air) | W/Brunswick | P-51 |
| | April 24 | Me-109 dam(air) | SW Munich | P-51 |
| | June 6 | Ju-87 dam(air) | NE Janville | P-51 |
| | June 20 | Me-109 dest(air) | Pomeranian Bay | P-51 |
| | July 7 | (2.5)Me-410 dest(air)** | Nordhausen | P-51 |
| | | (2)Me-410 dam(air) | Nordhausen | P-51 |
| | August 3 | Me-109 dest(air) | Baden Baden | P-51 |
| HdQts | February 9, 1945 | FW-190 dam(grd) | Kothen | P-51 |

5.5-0-4 air
0.5-1 ground

* - shared with Capt. T.F. Neal of the 354th Ftr Sqn
** - shared with an unknown P-38 pilot

**Moats, Sanford K., Capt.** (8.5) Mission, KS
487th Ftr Sqn/352nd Ftr Grp June 1944-June 1945
89 missions, 367 hours

P-51B HO-K 42-106751 "Kay"
P-51D HO-K "Kay II"
P-51D HO-K 44-14848 "Kay III"

| *Sqn* | *Date* | *Claims* | *Location* | *A/C* |
|---|---|---|---|---|
| 487th | July 18, 1944 | Ju-88 dest(air) | SE Rostock | P-51 |
| | July 21 | (.5)Me-109 dest(air)* | E/Munich | P-51 |
| | July 29 | Me-109 dest(air) | Merseburg | P-51 |
| | November 27 | Me-109 dest(air) | Munster | P-51 |
| | | Me-109 dam(air) | Munster | P-51 |
| | December 27 | FW-190 dest(air) | SW Bonn | P-51 |
| | January 1, 1945 | (4)FW-190 dest(air) | N/Liege | P-51 |

8.5-0-1 air
0-0 ground

* - shared with Maj. G.E. Preddy of the 487th Ftr Sqn

**Monroe, Shelton W., Maj.** (8.33) Waycross, GA
334th Ftr Sqn/4th Ftr Grp January 1944-January 1945
335th Ftr Sqn/4th Ftr Grp January 1945-April 1945
HdQts/4th Ftr Grp April 1945-September 1945

P-51B QP-O
P-51D QP-O 44-13411

| *Sqn* | *Date* | *Claims* | *Location* | *A/C* |
|---|---|---|---|---|
| 334th | March 27, 1944 | Me-410 dest(grd) | Cazaux A/F | P-51 |
| | April 8 | (1.5)FW-190 dest(air)* | Celle | P-51 |
| | | (.5)Me-109 dest(air)* | Celle | P-51 |
| | April 18 | (2)Ju-52 dest(grd) | Juterbog A/F | P-51 |
| | | (.25) of (6)Ju-52 dam(grd)** | see above | P-51 |
| | April 29 | (1.5)Ju-52 dest(grd)@ | Nordhausen | P-51 |
| | April 30 | (.33)Me-110 dest(air)@@ | N/Lyon | P-51 |
| | June 6 | FW-190 dest(air) | Evreux | P-51 |
| | June 20 | Me-109 dest(air) | E/Pasewalk | P-51 |
| | July 7 | FW-190 dam(air) | E/Nordhausen | P-51 |

4.33-0-1 air
4.5-1.5 ground

* - both shared with Lt. A.L. Schlegel of the 335th Ftr Sqn
** - all shared with Lt. D.W. Howe, Lt. J.L. Lang, and Lt. D.M. Malmsten of the 334th Ftr Sqn
@ - shared with Lt. N. Megura of the 334th Ftr Sqn
@@ - shared with Capt. W.M. Sobanski and Lt. J.L. Lang of the 334th Ftr Sqn

**Montgomery, Gerald E., Maj.** (17.5) Littlefield, TX
334th Ftr Sqn/4th Ftr Grp May 1943-EOW

P-47D QP-H 42-7980 "Texas"
P-51B QP-H 42-106846
P-51D QP-H 44-14119 "Sizzlin Liz"
P-51D QP-H 44-15326 "Sizzlin Liz"
P-51D QP-H 44-72382 "Sizzlin Liz"
S/Sgt. George Fite-c/c(P-47)
Sgt. Edward Nelson-ac/c(P-47)
S/Sgt. Edward Nelson-c/c(P-51)
Sgt. R. Hadden-ac/c(P-51)

| *Sqn* | *Date* | *Claims* | *Location* | *A/C* |
|---|---|---|---|---|
| 334th | January 14, 1944 | FW-190 dest(air) | Soissons | P-47 |
| | February 10 | Me-109 dest(air) | Emmerich | P-47 |
| | March 27 | (2)Ju-88 dest(grd) | Cazaux A/F | P-51 |
| | | FW-190 dest(grd) | see above | P-51 |
| | | Ju-52 dest(grd) | see above | P-51 |
| | | Ju-88 dam(grd) | see above | P-51 |
| | April 5 | (2)Ju-88 dest(grd) | Brandenburg-Briest | P-51 |
| | April 10 | (1.5)Bu-131 dest(grd)* | Romorantin A/F | P-51 |
| | April 15 | He-177 dest(grd) | Hagenow | P-51 |
| | | Ju-88 dest(grd) | Hagenow | P-51 |
| | September 11 | Me-109 dest(air) | Aschersleben | P-51 |
| | November 18 | Me-262 dest(grd) | Leipheim | P-51 |
| | | (4)Me-262 dam(grd) | Leipheim | P-51 |
| | February 27, 1945 | Do-217 dest(grd) | Weimar | P-51 |
| | | Me-108 dest(grd) | Weimar | P-51 |
| | | Ju-87 dest(grd) | Weimar | P-51 |
| | April 10 | Me-410 dest(grd) | Wittstock | P-51 |

3-0-0 air
14.5-5 ground

* - shared with Lt. G.C. Siems of the 334th Ftr Sqn

**Montgomery, Robert P., Col.** (6.33) Bethlehem, PA
77th Ftr Sqn/20th Ftr Grp August 1943-November 1943
HdQts/20th Ftr Grp November 1943-February 11, 1944(MIA-E)
Hit by e/a near Giessen.
HdQts/20th Ftr Grp September 1944-October 1944
56 missions, 274:55 hours

P-38J LC-M 42-68036
P-38J LC-M 42-67478
P-51D LC-D 44-14843 "Gumpy"
P-51D LC-D 44-72519 "Gumpy"
T/Sgt. Hugh E. McDonald-c/c

| *Sqn* | *Date* | *Claims* | *Location* | *A/C* |
|---|---|---|---|---|
| HdQts | January 5, 1944 | FW-190 dam(air) | W/Neumunster | P-38 |
| | February 5 | (.33)FW-200 dest(air)* | Bourges | P-38 |
| | February 10 | FW-190 dam(air) | Nienburg | P-38 |
| | November 2 | (2)Me-109 dest(air) | Halle-Merseburg | P-51 |
| | | FW-190 dest(air) | see above | P-51 |
| | April 10, 1945 | Si-204 dest(grd) | Werder A/F | P-51 |
| | | Ar-196 dest(grd) | see above | P-51 |
| | | Ju-52 dest(grd) | see above | P-51 |
| | | Do-217 dam(grd) | see above | P-51 |
| | | Si-204 dam(grd) | see above | P-51 |

3.33-0-2 air
3-2 ground

* - shared with Capt. P.J. Sabo and Lt. J.E. Davis of the 77th Ftr Sqn

**Moran, Glennon T., Lt.** (16) Granite City, IL
487th Ftr Sqn/352nd Ftr Grp September 1943-August 1944
90 missions

P-47D HO-M 42-22785
P-51B HO-M 43-6912
P-51C HO-M 42-103320 "Miss Ann"

| *Sqn* | *Date* | *Claims* | *Location* | *A/C* |
|---|---|---|---|---|
| 487th | February 24, 1944 | Me-109 dest(air) | Enschede | P-47 |
| | | Me-109 dam(air) | Enschede | P-47 |
| | April 11 | Ju-88 dest(grd) | SW Berlin | P-51 |
| | | Ar-196 dam(grd) | see above | P-51 |
| | | Caudron dam(grd) | see above | P-51 |
| | | u/i a/c dam(grd) | see above | P-51 |
| | April 13 | Ju-88 dest(grd) | S/Stuttgart | P-51 |
| | | FW-190 dam(grd) | S/Stuttgart | P-51 |
| | May 13 | (.5)Ju-88 dest(air)* | E/Neubrandenburg | P-51 |
| | May 19 | Me-109 dest(air) | Ludwigslust | P-51 |
| | May 27 | (2)Me-109 dest(air) | Strasbourg | P-51 |
| | May 29 | (1.5)Me-109 dest(air)** | Wolgast | P-51 |
| | | FW-190 dest(air) | Gustrow | P-51 |
| | May 30 | Me-109 dest(air) | Ulzen | P-51 |
| | | FW-190 dest(air) | Ulzen | P-51 |
| | | FW-190 dam(air) | Ulzen | P-51 |
| | June 12 | Me-109 dest(air) | SW Rennes | P-51 |
| | June 21 | Me-109 dest(air) | E/Magdeburg | P-51 |

| Sqn | Date | Claims | Location | A/C |
|---|---|---|---|---|
| | June 25 | Me-109 dest(air) | Soissons | P-51 |
| | | Me-109 dam(air) | Soissons | P-51 |
| | June 29 | Ju-52 dest(grd) | Burg A/F | P-51 |
| | August 5 | Me-109 dest(air) | S/Hamburg | P-51 |
| | August 25 | Me-210 dam(grd) | Neubrandenburg | P-51 |
| | | Caudron dam(grd) | see above | P-51 |

13-0-3 air
3-6 ground

* - shared with Lt. C.J. Luksic of the 487th Ftr Sqn
** - shared with Lt. J.V. Conard of the 487th Ftr Sqn

**Morgan, Frank A., Capt.** (5.5) Portland, OR
361st Ftr Sqn/356th Ftr Grp March 1944-May 1944; to 5th ERS
361st Ftr Sqn/356th Ftr Grp July 1944-March 1945
60 missions, 321 hours

P-47D QI-N 42-26459 "Portland Rose"
P-51D QI-N 44-15079
P-51D QI-N 44-15585 "Donna"
S/Sgt. Edward J. McCormick-c/c

| *Sqn* | *Date* | *Claims* | *Location* | *A/C* |
|---|---|---|---|---|
| 361st | September 5, 1944 | (.5)He-111 dest(air)* | Twente/Enschede | P-47 |
| | February 20, 1945 | (3)u/i a/c dest(grd) | Windleschenlaibach | P-51 |
| | | Me-110 dest(grd) | see above | P-51 |
| | | Ju-88 dest(grd) | see above | P-51 |

0.5-0-0 air
5-0 ground

* - shared with Capt. D.F. Thwaites of the 361st Ftr Sqn

**Moroney, Edward J., Lt.** (5) Highland Park, IL
357th Ftr Sqn/355th Ftr Grp May 1944-December 1944

P-51D OS-I 44-15595 "Mary Jane"
S/Sgt. Moses-c/c
Sgt. Singleton-arm.

| *Sqn* | *Date* | *Claims* | *Location* | *A/C* |
|---|---|---|---|---|
| 357th | November 2, 1944 | Me-109 dest(air) | Wernigerode | P-51 |
| | | (2)u/i a/c dest(grd) | see above | P-51 |
| | November 18 | (3)Me-262 dam(grd) | Leipheim | P-51 |
| | November 26 | (2)FW-190 dest(air) | W/Gardelegen | P-51 |

3-0-0 air
2-3 ground

**Morrill, Stanley B., Capt.** (9) Willimantic, CT
62nd Ftr Sqn/56th Ftr Grp August 1943-March 29, 1944(KIAc)
Killed in the explosion of B-24 at Halesworth.

P-47C LM-F 41-6387 "Fats"

| *Sqn* | *Date* | *Claims* | *Location* | *A/C* |
|---|---|---|---|---|
| 62nd | November 26, 1943 | Me-109 dest(air) | Papenburg | P-47 |
| | | Me-109 dam(air) | Papenburg | P-47 |
| | December 11 | Me-109 dest(air) | Eelde | P-47 |
| | January 5, 1944 | Me-109 dest(air) | Duren | P-47 |
| | January 11 | Me-109 dest(air) | Bramsche | P-47 |
| | January 30 | (.5)Ju-88 dest(air)* | Twente | P-47 |
| | | Ju-88 dam(air) | Twente | P-47 |
| | February 4 | (2)FW-190 dam(air) | Charleroi | P-47 |
| | February 11 | Me-109 dest(air) | Dison | P-47 |
| | February 20 | Me-110 dest(air) | Steinhuder Lake | P-47 |
| | | (.5)Do-217 dest(air)** | see above | P-47 |
| | | (6)Me-110 dam(grd) | see above | P-47 |
| | February 24 | Me-109 dest(air) | E/Asnabruck | P-47 |
| | March 16 | FW-190 dest(air) | St. Dizier | P-47 |

9-0-4 air
0-6 ground

* - shared with Lt. A.R. Carcione of the 62nd Ftr Sqn
** - shared with Lt. F.J. Christensen of the 62nd Ftr Sqn

**Morris, James M., Capt.** (10.16) Detroit. MI
77th Ftr Sqn/20th Ftr Grp October 1942-July 7, 1944(POW)
Hit by a Me-410 in the Leipzig-Halle area.
65 missions, 287:10 hours

P-38J LC-E 42-67717 "My Dad"
S/Sgt. Joseph H. McFarland-c/c

| *Sqn* | *Date* | *Claims* | *Location* | *A/C* |
|---|---|---|---|---|
| 77th | February 5, 1944 | (.33)He-111 dest(air)* | Bourges A/F | P-38 |
| | February 8 | (2)FW-190 dest(air) | Sedan | P-38 |
| | | Me-109 dest(air) | Denain | P-38 |
| | | Me-109 dest(air) | Losheim | P-38 |
| | February 11 | Me-109 dest(air) | Giessen | P-38 |
| | February 24 | Me-110 dest(air) | Schweinfurt | P-38 |
| | April 8 | Me-410 dest(grd) | Salzwedel | P-38 |
| | | (.5)Ju-88 dest(grd)** | see above | P-38 |
| | | (.33)u/i a/c dest(grd)@ | see above | P-38 |
| | April 30 | He-177 dest(grd) | Orleans/Bricy | P-38 |
| | July 7 | Me-410 dest(air) | Leipzig-Halle | P-38 |

7.33-0-0 air
2.83-0 ground

* - shared with Lt. R.L. Frakes and Lt. M.J. Gilbertson of the 77th Ftr Sqn
** - shared with Lt. B.N. Rader of the 77th Ftr Sqn
@ - shared with Lt. I.W. Ferandes and Lt. W.F. Kuemmerle of the 77th Ftr Sqn

**Morris, Raymond S., Lt.** (13.5) South Birmingham, AL
354th Ftr Sqn/355th Ftr Grp States-July 1944
74 missions, 300:35 hours

P-47D WR-M
P-51B WR-M 42-106437 "Darlin' Doris"
S/Sgt. J.J. Tabacchi-c/c

| *Sqn* | *Date* | *Claims* | *Location* | *A/C* |
|---|---|---|---|---|
| 354th | March 16, 1944 | Me-109 dest(air) | NW Ulm | P-51 |
| | March 28 | He-111 dest(grd) | Dijon | P-51 |
| | April 5 | Me-110 dest(grd) | Landsberg | P-51 |
| | | He-111 dest(grd) | see above | P-51 |
| | | He-111 dam(grd) | see above | P-51 |
| | April 13 | (2)Do-217 dest(grd) | Oberpfaffenhofen | P-51 |
| | | Do-217 dam(grd) | see above | P-51 |
| | May 13 | (2)Me-410 dest(air) | E/Berlin | P-51 |
| | June 6 | (.5)Ju-87 dest(air)* | Chartres-Dire | P-51 |
| | June 24 | (3)Me-109 dest(grd) | Seiches | P-51 |
| | July 8 | Me-109 dest(grd) | SW Chalons | P-51 |
| | | Me-410 dest(grd) | SW Chalons | P-51 |

3.5-0-0 air
10-2 ground

* - shared with Lt. F.K. Taylor of the 354th Ftr Sqn

**Moseley, Mark L., Capt.** (6.5) Atlanta, GA
62nd Ftr Sqn/56th Ftr Grp August 1943-August 1944

P-47D LM-H 42-25522

| *Sqn* | *Date* | *Claims* | *Location* | *A/C* |
|---|---|---|---|---|
| 62nd | January 30, 1944 | Me-210 dam(air) | Hanskamp | P-47 |
| | March 8 | FW-190 dest(air) | Dummer Lake-Steinhuder Lake | P-47 |
| | | FW-190 dam(air) | see above | P-47 |
| | March 15 | FW-190 dest(air) | Dummer Lake | P-47 |
| | June 7 | (.5)Ju-88 dest(air)* | St. Andre de L'Eure | P-47 |
| | June 8 | (2)FW-190 dest(air) | St. Andre de L'Eure | P-47 |
| | July 4 | Me-109 dest(air) | Conches | P-47 |
| | July 6 | Me-109 dest(air) | Beaumont | P-47 |

6.5-0-2 air
0-0 ground

* - shared with Lt. J.W. Pierce of the 62nd Ftr Sqn

**Mudge, William F., Jr., Lt.** (8) Fall River, MA
505th Ftr Sqn/339th Ftr Grp States-September 1944
270 hours

P-51B 6N-
S/Sgt. Kochler-c/c

| *Sqn* | *Date* | *Claims* | *Location* | *A/C* |
|---|---|---|---|---|
| 505th | May 21, 1944 | (.5)Ju-88 dest(air)* | Schwepnitz | P-51 |
| | May 25 | (.5)FW-190 dest(air)** | Paris | P-51 |
| | June 6 | Ju-87 dest(air) | Orleans | P-51 |
| | July 19 | FW-190 dest(grd) | SW Augsburg | P-51 |
| | | Ju-188 dest(grd) | SW Augsburg | P-51 |
| | July 29 | Ju-52 dest(grd) | NW Naumberg | P-51 |
| | July 31 | FW-190 dest(grd) | Holzkirchen | P-51 |
| | | Me-110 dest(grd) | see above | P-51 |
| | | Ju-88 dest(grd) | see above | P-51 |
| | | (2)u/i a/c dam(grd) | see above | P-51 |

2-0-0 air
6-2 ground

* - shared with Lt. H.M. Everett of the 505th Ftr Sqn
** - shared with Lt. G.J. Hrico of the 505th Ftr Sqn

**Murphy, Alva C., Capt.** (8) Knoxville, TN
362nd Ftr Sqn/357th Ftr Grp September 1944-January 1945
364th Ftr Sqn/357th Ftr Grp January 1945-March 2, 1945(KIA)
Hit by flak southwest of Magdeburg.

P-51D G4-U 44-13334 "Bite Me"
P-51D C5- 44-63765

| *Sqn* | *Date* | *Claims* | *Location* | *A/C* |
|---|---|---|---|---|
| 362nd | November 18, 1944 | (2)Me-109 dest(grd) | Villingen A/F | P-51 |
| | November 27 | Me-109 dest(air) | S/Magdeburg | P-51 |
| | | FW-190 dest(air) | S/Magdeburg | P-51 |
| | December 2 | (2)Me-109 dest(air) | Bingen | P-51 |
| 364th | March 2, 1945 | (2)Me-109 dest(air) | SE Magdeburg | P-51 |

6-0-0 air
2-0 ground

**Murphy, Jerome T., Lt.** (7) Brainerd, MN
505th Ftr Sqn/339th Ftr Grp February 1945-July 1945

P-51D 6N-S 44-72384

| *Sqn* | *Date* | *Claims* | *Location* | *A/C* |
|---|---|---|---|---|
| 505th | April 10, 1945 | (3)Do-217 dest(grd) | Wittstock | P-51 |
| | | (2)Ju-88 dest(grd) | see above | P-51 |
| | | (3)u/i a/c dam(grd) | see above | P-51 |
| | April 17 | Me-109 dest(grd) | SE Pocking | P-51 |
| | | He-111 dest(grd) | see above | P-51 |
| | | (2)Me-109 dam(grd) | see above | P-51 |
| | | Ju-88 dam(grd) | see above | P-51 |

0-0-0 air
7-6 ground

**Murphy, John B., LtCol.** (6.75) Darlington, SC
370th Ftr Sqn/359th Ftr Grp March 1943-September 1944
Earlier flew in the Aleutians with the 11th Ftr Sqn and claimed one-half of a Mavis on June 3, 1942.

P-47D CS-A 42-8613
P-51B CS-A 42-106878
P-51D CS-A 44-13513

| *Sqn* | *Date* | *Claims* | *Location* | *A/C* |
|---|---|---|---|---|
| 370th | February 22, 1944 | Me-109 prob(air) | Hamm | P-47 |
| | February 24 | Me-109 dest(air) | Hardenbergh | P-47 |
| | March 4 | (.5)FW-190 dest(air)* | Bonn | P-47 |
| | | (.25)Me-109 dest(air)** | Bonn | P-47 |
| | | Me-109 dam(air) | Bonn | P-47 |
| | May 29 | (1.5)FW-190 dest(air)@ | Stettin | P-51 |
| | July 21 | Me-109 dest(air) | Ammer Lake | P-51 |
| | August 9 | FW-190 dest(air) | Gunzburg | P-51 |
| | August 16 | Me-163 dest(air) | SE Leipzig | P-51 |

6.25-1-1 air
0-0 ground

* - shared with Lt. P.H. Bateman of the 370th Ftr Sqn
** - shared with Lt. P.H. Bateman, Lt. A.C. Porter, and Lt. R.S. Wetmore of the 370th Ftr Sqn
@ - shared with Lt. G.A. Doersch of the 370th Ftr Sqn

**Murphy, Randel L., Lt.** (13) Houston, TX
63rd Ftr Sqn/56th Ftr Grp September 1944-April 1945
62 missions, 225:45 hours

P-47D UN-N 42-29364
P-47M UN-N 44-21141 "The Brat"
S/Sgt. Richard J. Wagner-c/c
Cpl. John M. Kozik-arm.

| *Sqn* | *Date* | *Claims* | *Location* | *A/C* |
|---|---|---|---|---|
| 63rd | November 18, 1944 | FW-190 dest(grd) | Gross Ostheim | P-47 |
| | December 4 | FW-200 dam(grd) | Neuburg | P-47 |
| | December 23 | (2)FW-190 dest(air) | NW Coblenz | P-47 |
| | April 13, 1945 | (5)u/i a/c dest(grd) | Eggebeck A/F | P-47 |
| | | (3)He-111 dest(grd) | see above | P-47 |
| | | FW-200 dest(grd) | see above | P-47 |
| | | Me-210 dest(grd) | see above | P-47 |
| | | u/i a/c dam(grd) | see above | P-47 |

2-0-0 air
11-2 ground

**Murr, John N., Lt.** (5) Oxnard, CA
434th Ftr Sqn/479th Ftr Grp July 1944-January 1945

| *Sqn* | *Date* | *Claims* | *Location* | *A/C* |
|---|---|---|---|---|
| 434th | September 5, 1944 | (3)Me-110 dest(grd) | Ettinghausen | P-38 |
| | September 26 | Me-109 dest(air) | SW Munster | P-38 |
| | December 25 | FW-190 dest(air) | SW Bonn | P-51 |
| | | FW-190 prob(air) | SW Bonn | P-51 |
| | | FW-190 dam(air) | SW Bonn | P-51 |

2-1-1 air
3-0 ground

**Myers, Joseph, Jr., LtCol.** (7.5) Canton, OH
38th Ftr Sqn/55th Ftr Grp April 1942-April 1944
82nd Ftr Sqn/78th Ftr Grp August 1944-December 1944
HdQts/78th Ftr Grp December 1944-February 1945
HdQts/55th Ftr Grp February 1945-June 1945
130 missions, 430 hours

P-38H CG-O
P-38J CG-O "Journey's End"
P-47D MX-S 42-27339
P-51D MX-S
P-51K CG-V
S/Sgt. James D. Durnin-c/c(P-38)
Sgt. Fred Rumley-ac/c(P-38)
Sgt. K.P. Partozeck-arm.(P-38)
T/Sgt. Chester Hanson-c/c(CG-V)

| *Sqn* | *Date* | *Claims* | *Location* | *A/C* |
|---|---|---|---|---|
| 38th | November 3, 1943 | FW-190 dam(air) | Wilhelmshaven | P-38 |
| | November 5 | Me-109 dest(air) | Arnheim | P-38 |
| | November 13 | Me-109 dest(air) | Bremen | P-38 |
| | | Ju-88 dam(air) | Bremen | P-38 |
| | December 31 | Me-109 dest(air) | N/Blaye et St. Luce | P-38 |
| 82nd | August 28, 1944 | (.5)Me-262 dest(air)* | Termonde | P-47 |
| | September 10 | (3)He-111 dest(grd) | Meinbullen | P-47 |
| | | He-111 dam(grd) | Meinbullen | P-47 |
| | October 7 | Me-109 dest(air) | Leipzig | P-47 |

4.5-0-2 air
3-1 ground

* - shared with Lt. M.O. Croy of the 82nd Ftr Sqn

**Myers, Raymond B., LtCol.** (8.5) Dundee, MS
358th Ftr Sqn/355th Ftr Grp February 1943-June 1944
72 missions

P-47D YF-U 42-7991 "Miss Pam"
P-47D YF-U 42-75425 "Miss Pam"
P-51B YF-U 43-6991 "Miss Pam"
S/Sgt. Irving G. Petersen-c/c

| *Sqn* | *Date* | *Claims* | *Location* | *A/C* |
|---|---|---|---|---|
| 358th | October 20, 1943 | FW-190 dest(air) | Ath | P-47 |
| | | FW-190 dam(air) | Ath | P-47 |
| | March 2, 1944 | (.5)Me-109 dest(air)* | NE Liege | P-47 |
| | April 5 | (2)Do-217 dest(grd) | Munich | P-51 |
| | | DFS-230 dest(grd) | Munich | P-51 |
| | | (6)Do-217 dam(grd) | Munich | P-51 |
| | April 11 | Me-410 dest(air) | W/Berlin | P-51 |
| | April 13 | FW-190 dest(air) | Nordlingen | P-51 |
| | April 15 | Do-217 dest(grd) | Glienicke | P-51 |
| | May 24 | Me-109 dest(air) | Berlin | P-51 |
| | | Me-109 dam(air) | Berlin | P-51 |

4.5-0-2 air
4-6 ground

* - shared with F/O W.J. McGinty of the 358th Ftr Sqn

**Nagel, Jerome K., Lt.** (5) Denver, CO
434th Ftr Sqn/479th Ftr Grp September 1944-EOW
62 missions, 283:50 hours

P-51D L2-L "The Brat"

| *Sqn* | *Date* | *Claims* | *Location* | *A/C* |
|---|---|---|---|---|
| 434th | April 7, 1945 | Me-109 dest(air) | Soltau | P-51 |
| | April 13 | Ju-88 dest(grd) | Kaltenkirchen | P-51 |
| | April 18 | Me-109 dest(grd) | Deiningen | P-51 |

| Sqn | Date | Claims | Location | A/C |
|---|---|---|---|---|
| | | FW-190 dest(grd) | Deiningen | P-51 |
| | | Ju-88 dest(grd) | Ottingen | P-51 |

1-0-0 air
4-0 ground

**Neal, Thomas F., Jr., Capt.** (5) Chatham, VA
354th Ftr Sqn/355th Ftr Grp Early 1943-April 29, 1944(KIA)
Hit by a FW-190 near Rathenow
50 missions, 159:55 hours

P-47D WR-J 42-8557
P-51B WR-J 43-6577
S/Sgt. Moss-c/c

| *Sqn* | *Date* | *Claims* | *Location* | *A/C* |
|---|---|---|---|---|
| 354th | November 13, 1943 | Me-109 dest(air) | W/Bremen | P-47 |
| | March 16, 1944 | (2.5)Me-109 dest(air)[*] | NW Ulm | P-51 |
| | March 18 | Me-109 dest(air) | NE Munich | P-51 |
| | March 28 | (.5)He-111 dest(grd)[**] | Dijon | P-51 |
| | April 10 | u/i a/c dam(grd) | Bourges | P-51 |

4.5-0-0 air
0.5-1 ground

* - shared with Lt. C.W. Lenfest of the 354th Ftr Sqn
** - shared with Lt. L.D. Minchew of the 357th Ftr Sqn, 355th Ftr Grp

**Neely, Tom D., Lt.** (6) Edmonds, WA
434th Ftr Sqn/479th Ftr Grp June 1944-December 23, 1944(POW)
Hit by flak southeast of Bonn.

P-38J L2-X
P-51D L2-X 44-14596 "Rumboogie, Jr."
S/Sgt. John Stanovich-c/c

| *Sqn* | *Date* | *Claims* | *Location* | *A/C* |
|---|---|---|---|---|
| 434th | August 9, 1944 | He-111 dest(grd) | Nuneburg | P-38 |
| | | (.5)He-111 dam(grd)[*] | Nuneburg | P-38 |
| | September 5 | (2)Me-110 dest(grd) | Ettinghausen | P-38 |
| | | Ju-88 dest(grd) | Ettinghausen | P-38 |
| | December 23 | (2)FW-190 dest(air) | SE Bonn | P-51 |

2-0-0 air
4-0.5 ground

* - shared with Maj. F.J. Keller of the 434th Ftr Sqn

**Nelson, Robert F., Lt.** (6) Long Beach, CA
336th Ftr Sqn/4th Ftr Grp August 1943-April 22, 1944(POW)
Suffered m/f southeast of Kassel.

P-47D VF-Q
P-51B VF-Q 43-6633
S/Sgt. Frank Blankschaen-c/c

| *Sqn* | *Date* | *Claims* | *Location* | *A/C* |
|---|---|---|---|---|
| 336th | April 1, 1944 | Ju-88 dam(grd) | Belgium | P-51 |
| | April 5 | Ju-88 dest(grd) | Brandenburg | P-51 |
| | | He-177 dam(grd) | see above | P-51 |
| | | Ju-88 dam(grd) | see above | P-51 |
| | April 10 | u/i a/c dest(grd) | Romorantin A/F | P-51 |
| | April 15 | Fi-156 dest(air) | Fassberg A/F | P-51 |
| | | (2)He-177 dest(grd) | Fassberg A/F | P-51 |
| | April 18 | Me-109 dest(grd) | Genthin A/F | P-51 |
| | | Me-109 dam(grd) | see above | P-51 |
| | | Ju-88 dam(grd) | see above | P-51 |
| | | u/i a/c dam(grd) | see above | P-51 |

1-0-0 air
5-6 ground

**Newman, Robert A., Lt.** (5) Goose Creek, TX
352nd Ftr Sqn/353rd Ftr Grp October 1942-March 16, 1944(KIA)
Hit by flak in the Laon area.
37 missions

P-47D SX-N 42-75530 "Wham Bam"

| *Sqn* | *Date* | *Claims* | *Location* | *A/C* |
|---|---|---|---|---|
| 352nd | October 14, 1943 | Me-109 dest(air) | Turnhout | P-47 |
| | | Me-109 dam(air) | Turnhout | P-47 |
| | November 3 | Me-110 dest(air) | Wilhelmshaven | P-47 |
| | December 1 | Me-210 dest(air) | Solingen | P-47 |
| | January 30, 1944 | Ju-88 dest(air) | Quackenbruck | P-47 |
| | February 22 | FW-190 dest(grd) | Antwerp | P-47 |

4-0-1 air
1-0 ground

**Norley, Louis H., Maj.** (15.33) Conrad, MT
336th Ftr Sqn/4th Ftr Grp July 1943-August 1944
335th Ftr Sqn/4th Ftr Grp August 1944-January 1945
334th Ftr Sqn/4th Ftr Grp January 1945-September 1945
160 missions, 554 hours

P-47C VF-O 41-6183 "Red Dog"
P-51B VF-O 43-12416
P-51B VF-O 43-6802
P-51D WD-O 44-15028
P-51D QP-O 44-15347
P-51D QP-O 44-72196
P-51D QP-O 44-73108 "Red Dog XII"
S/Sgt. V. Giovenco-c/c(336th)
S/Sgt. Vincent Andra-c/c(334th)

| *Sqn* | *Date* | *Claims* | *Location* | *A/C* |
|---|---|---|---|---|
| 336th | December 16, 1943 | (.33)Ju-88 dest(air)[*] | E/Zuider Zee | P-47 |
| | February 10, 1944 | Me-109 dest(air) | Dummer Lake | P-47 |
| | March 27 | Ju-88 dest(grd) | Cazaux A/F | P-51 |
| | April 8 | (3)FW-190 dest(air) | Ulzen | P-51 |
| | April 13 | FW-190 dest(air) | Schweinfurt | P-51 |
| | April 22 | (2)Me-109 dest(air) | SW Kassel | P-51 |
| 335th | September 17 | FW-190 dest(air) | Bocholt | P-51 |
| | November 2 | Me-163 dest(air) | SE Leipzig | P-51 |
| 334th | March 19, 1945 | Me-109 dest(air) | SE Frankfurt | P-51 |
| | April 16 | (2)FW-190 dest(grd) | Gablingen | P-51 |
| | | Ju-52 dest(grd) | Gablingen | P-51 |
| | | u/i a/c dest(grd) | Gablingen | P-51 |

10.33-0-0 air
5-0 ground

* - shared with Capt. D.S. Gentile and Lt. V. Garrison of the 336th Ftr Sqn

**North, Albert B., Lt.** (5) Massillon, OH
77th Ftr Sqn/20th Ftr Grp November 1944-EOW
38 missions, 190:05 hours

P-51D LC-W 44-13798 "Kitty B"
S/Sgt. Peter McDermott-c/c

| *Sqn* | *Date* | *Claims* | *Location* | *A/C* |
|---|---|---|---|---|
| 77th | February 20, 1945 | Me-108 dest(air) | Straubing | P-51 |
| | | Me-109 dest(grd) | Straubing | P-51 |
| | | Me-108 dest(grd) | Straubing | P-51 |
| | | u/i a/c dest(grd) | Straubing | P-51 |
| | | u/i a/c dam(grd) | Straubing | P-51 |
| | April 10 | Me-262 dest(air) | Oranienburg | P-51 |

2-0-0 air
3-1 ground

**Oberhansly, Jack J., LtCol.** (7.6) Spanish Fork, UT
82nd Ftr Sqn/78th Ftr Grp May 1942-May 1944
HdQts/78th Ftr Grp August 1944-December 1944
HdQts/ 4th Ftr Grp December 1944-February 1945
150 missions

P-47C MX-X 41-6542 "Iron Ass"
P-47D MX-X 42-7883 "Iron Ass"
P-47D MX-X 44-19566 "Iron Ass"
P-51K QP-X 44-11661 "Iron Ass"
S/Sgt. John M. Kovacevich-c/c(78th)
Sgt. Conrad Gerhardt-ac/c(78th)
S/Sgt. Roderic Lonier-c/c(4th)
Sgt. R. Easley-arm.(4th)

| *Sqn* | *Date* | *Claims* | *Location* | *A/C* |
|---|---|---|---|---|
| 82nd | May 14, 1943 | FW-190 prob(air) | Antwerp | P-47 |
| | September 27 | Me-109 dest(air) | Emden | P-47 |
| | | Me-109 prob(air) | Emden | P-47 |
| | November 30 | FW-190 dest(air) | Eupen | P-47 |
| | February 22, 1944 | Me-109 dest(air) | Cologne | P-47 |
| | | FW-190 dest(air) | Gilze-Rijen | P-47 |
| | | (.5)FW-190 dest(air)[*] | Walcheren | P-47 |
| | | (.5)FW-190 dest(air)[*] | Walcheren | P-47 |
| | | Me-109 dam(air) | Cologne | P-47 |
| | April 8 | Me-109 dest(grd) | Trier | P-47 |
| | | (.2)Me-110 dest(grd)[**] | Trier | P-47 |
| | | (.2)Me-110 dest(grd)[**] | Trier | P-47 |
| | | (.2)Me-110 dest(grd)[**] | Trier | P-47 |
| | | Ju-52 dam(grd) | Trier | P-47 |
| HdQts | August 28 | Ju-88 dest(air) | Charleroi | P-47 |

6-2-1 air
1.6-1 ground

* - both shared with Lt. C.W. Hotchkiss of the 83rd Ftr Sqn, 78th Ftr Grp
** - all shared with Capt. N.D. Munson, Lt. J.E. Brasher, Lt. M.K. Woller, and F/O C.W. DeWitt of the 82nd Ftr Sqn

**O'Brien, Gilbert M., Capt.** (7) Charleston, SC
362nd Ftr Sqn/357th Ftr Grp June 1943-August 1944
69 missions, 268 hours

P-51B G4-Q 43-6787 "Shanty Irish"
S/Sgt. Avery G. Goodrich-c/c
Sgt. Ray A. Smith-ac/c
Sgt. DeWitt-arm.

| *Sqn* | *Date* | *Claims* | *Location* | *A/C* |
|---|---|---|---|---|
| 362nd | March 5, 1944 | FW-190 dest(air) | Bordeaux | P-51 |
| | | (.5)FW-190 dam(air)* | Bordeaux | P-51 |
| | April 11 | Me-109 dest(air) | Magdeburg | P-51 |
| | | (2)Me-109 dam(air) | Magdeburg | P-51 |
| | April 22 | FW-190 dest(air) | N/Dummer Lake | P-51 |
| | April 30 | (.5)Me-109 dest(air)** | S/Paris | P-51 |
| | May 27 | FW-190 dest(air) | N/Strasbourg | P-51 |
| | May 30 | Me-109 dest(air) | Celle | P-51 |
| | | (.5)Me-410 dest(air)@ | W/Bernburg | P-51 |
| | July 29 | Me-109 dest(air) | W/Merseburg | P-51 |

7-0-2.5 air
0-0 ground

* - shared with Lt. A.E. Smith of the 362nd Ftr Sqn
** - shared with Lt. T.M. McKinney of the 364th Ftr Sqn, 357th Ftr Grp
@ - shared with Capt. F.E. Adams of the 362nd Ftr Sqn

**O'Brien, William R., Capt.** (5.5) McPherson, GA
363rd Ftr Sqn/357th Ftr Grp March 1943-August 1944
77 missions

P-51B B6-G
P-51D B6-G 44-13522 "Billy's Bitch"

| *Sqn* | *Date* | *Claims* | *Location* | *A/C* |
|---|---|---|---|---|
| 363rd | February 21, 1944 | Me-109 prob(air) | Bussum | P-51 |
| | March 5 | FW-190 prob(air) | N/Bordeaux | P-51 |
| | | FW-190 dam(air) | N/Bordeaux | P-51 |
| | March 6 | (.5)Me-110 dest(air)* | Berlin | P-51 |
| | May 12 | Me-109 dest(air) | N/Frankfurt | P-51 |
| | May 24 | Me-109 dest(air) | E/Berlin | P-51 |
| | May 27 | Me-109 dest(air) | Strasbourg | P-51 |
| | May 30 | (2)Me-109 dest(air) | NE Schonebeck | P-51 |

5.5-2-1 air
0-0 ground

* - shared with Lt. L.A. Ruder of the 364th Ftr Sqn, 357th Ftr Grp

**Olander, Richard B., Capt.** (6.5) Racine, WI
505th Ftr Sqn/339th Ftr Grp Mid 1943-January 17, 1945(KIA)
Hit by flak in the Gladbeck area.
85 missions, 354 hours

P-51B 6N-S "Therese"
P-51D 6N-S 44-14170 "Therese"
P-51K 6N-S 44-11363 "Therese"

| *Sqn* | *Date* | *Claims* | *Location* | *A/C* |
|---|---|---|---|---|
| 505th | May 27, 1944 | Me-109 dest(grd) | Reims | P-51 |
| | June 8 | (.5)FW-190 dest(air)* | Rennes | P-51 |
| | July 19 | Ju-188 dest(grd) | SW Augsburg | P-51 |
| | July 31 | Ju-87 dest(grd) | Holzkirchen | P-51 |
| | | u/i a/c dest(grd) | see above | P-51 |
| | | u/i a/c dam(grd) | see above | P-51 |
| | September 11 | u/i a/c dest(grd) | Munich | P-51 |
| | | (2)u/i a/c dam(grd) | Munich | P-51 |
| | September 12 | Me-109 dest(air) | Goslar | P-51 |

1.5-0-0 air
5-3 ground

* - shared with Lt. A. Sirochman of the 505th Ftr Sqn

**Olds, Robin, Maj.** (24) Beverly Hills, CA
434th Ftr Sqn/479th Ftr Grp January 1944-October 1945
107 missions

P-38J L2-W "Scat"
P-38J L2-W 43-28341 "Scat II"
P-38J L2-W "Scat III"
P-38J L2-W "Scat IV"
P-51D L2-W 44-14426 "Scat 5"
P-51D L2-W 44-72922 "Scat VI"
S/Sgt. S.A. Wold-c/c

| *Sqn* | *Date* | *Claims* | *Location* | *A/C* |
|---|---|---|---|---|
| 434th | August 14, 1944 | (2)FW-190 dest(air) | Montmirail | P-38 |
| | August 18 | (2)Ju-88 dest(grd) | Nancy/Essey A/F | P-38 |
| | | He-111 dest(grd) | Nancy/Essey A/F | P-38 |
| | August 25 | (3)Me-109 dest(air) | Rostock | P-38 |
| | October 6 | FW-190 dest(air) | W/Berlin | P-51 |
| | February 9, 1945 | Me-109 dest(air) | SE Magdeburg | P-51 |
| | February 14 | (2)Me-109 dest(air) | SW Berlin | P-51 |
| | | FW-190 dest(air) | SW Berlin | P-51 |
| | February 20 | Do-217 dest(grd) | Windleschenlaibach | P-51 |
| | | FW-190 dest(grd) | see above | P-51 |
| | March 19 | Me-109 dest(air) | Handorf A/F | P-51 |
| | | FW-190 dest(air) | Handorf A/F | P-51 |
| | April 7 | Me-109 dest(air) | Dummer Lake-Bremen | P-51 |
| | | Me-262 dam(air) | see above | P-51 |
| | April 13 | Ar-234 dest(grd) | Lubeck | P-51 |
| | | Me-410 dam(grd) | Tarnewitz | P-51 |
| | April 16 | (2)Ju-87 dest(grd) | Reichersberg | P-51 |
| | | Me-109 dest(grd) | see above | P-51 |
| | | Me-110 dest(grd) | see above | P-51 |
| | | He-177 dest(grd) | see above | P-51 |

13-0-1 air
11-1 ground

**Olson, Norman E., Capt.** (8) Fargo, ND
357th Ftr Sqn/355th Ftr Grp February 1943-April 8, 1944(KIA)
Hit by flak in the Hofen-Celle area.

P-47D OS-P 42-8413 "Ma Fran"
P-47D OS-P "Ma Fran 2nd"
P-47D OS-P "Ma Fran 3rd"
P-51B OS-X 43-7176 "Ma Fran 4th"
S/Sgt. Jerome Seidl-c/c
Sgt. Norman-ac/c

| *Sqn* | *Date* | *Claims* | *Location* | *A/C* |
|---|---|---|---|---|
| 357th | November 7, 1943 | Me-210 dest(air) | Amiens | P-47 |
| | November 13 | Me-109 dest(air) | Zwolle | P-47 |
| | December 1 | Me-109 dam(air) | W/Cologne | P-47 |
| | February 5, 1944 | (2)Me-109 dest(air) | W/Vendome | P-47 |
| | February 20 | Me-109 dest(air) | Siegen | P-47 |
| | February 21 | FW-190 dest(air) | Dummer Lake | P-47 |
| | | FW-190 dam(air) | Dummer Lake | P-47 |
| | March 28 | He-111 dest(grd) | Dijon | P-51 |
| | | FW-190 dam(grd) | Dijon | P-51 |
| | April 8 | Ju-88 dest(grd) | Gifhorn | P-51 |

6-0-2 air
2-1 ground

**Olson, Thomas C., Lt.** (10.5) Vancouver, WA
434th Ftr Sqn/479th Ftr Grp January 1944-December 1944

P-38J L2-W "Lelah May"
P-51D L2-W "Lelah May"
T/Sgt. Loy C. Slaton-c/c
Sgt. Alworth D. Larson-ac/c

| *Sqn* | *Date* | *Claims* | *Location* | *A/C* |
|---|---|---|---|---|
| 434th | August 18, 1944 | (1.5)He-111 dest(grd)* | Nancy/Essey A/F | P-38 |
| | | Me-109 dest(grd) | see above | P-38 |
| | | Ju-88 dest(grd) | see above | P-38 |
| | | (.5)FW-190 dest(grd)** | see above | P-38 |
| | | He-111 dam(grd) | see above | P-38 |
| | August 28 | FW-190 dest(air) | Sedan/Douzy A/F | P-38 |
| | | u/i a/c dam(grd) | Sedan/Douzy A/F | P-38 |
| | September 5 | (4)Do-217 dest(grd) | Ettinghausen | P-38 |
| | | Me-110 dest(grd) | Ettinghausen | P-38 |
| | November 6 | (.5)FW-190 dest(grd)@ | Hesepe | P-51 |
| | November 27 | Me-410 dam(grd) | Vechta | P-51 |

1-0-0 air
9.5-3 ground

* - shared with Lt. N.W. Butler of the 435th Ftr Sqn, 479th Ftr Grp
** - shared with Lt. T.J. Sowerby of the 435th Ftr Sqn
@ - shared with Lt. W.H. Marlowe of the 434th Ftr Sqn

**Orcutt, Leon M., Jr., Lt.** (8) Huntington, MA
504th Ftr Sqn/339th Ftr Grp October 1944-July 1945
52 missions

P-51D 5Q-S 44-14672 "Lil Injun"

| *Sqn* | *Date* | *Claims* | *Location* | *A/C* |
|---|---|---|---|---|
| 504th | April 9, 1945 | Me-262 dam(air) | Leipzig | P-51 |
| | April 17 | (6)Me-109 dest(grd) | Klatovy | P-51 |
| | | (2)Ju-88 dest(grd) | Klatvoy | P-51 |
| | | 0-0-1 air | | |
| | | 8-0 ground | | |

**Orndorff, Roy W., Capt.** (8) Casey, IL
383rd Ftr Sqn/364th Ftr Grp September 1944-July 1945

P-51D N2-U 44-14315
P-51D N2-U 44-72423

| *Sqn* | *Date* | *Claims* | *Location* | *A/C* |
|---|---|---|---|---|
| 383rd | December 23, 1944 | (2)FW-190 dest(air) | NW Trier | P-51 |
| | December 31 | FW-190 dest(air) | SW Hamburg | P-51 |
| | April 13, 1945 | (2)Ju-52 dest(grd) | Flensburg | P-51 |
| | | Me-109 dest(grd) | see above | P-51 |
| | | FW-190 dest(grd) | see above | P-51 |
| | | Fi-156 dam(grd) | see above | P-51 |
| | April 17 | Me-262 dest(air) | Praha A/F | P-51 |
| | | 4-0-0 air | | |
| | | 4-1 ground | | |

**Palson, Richard C.J., Lt.** (8) Winchester, MA
436th Ftr Sqn/479th Ftr Grp January 1945-EOW

P-51D 9B-

| *Sqn* | *Date* | *Claims* | *Location* | *A/C* |
|---|---|---|---|---|
| 436th | April 13, 1945 | (2)He-111 dest(grd) | Salzwedel | P-51 |
| | | FW-190 dam(grd) | Salzwedel | P-51 |
| | | He-111 dam(grd) | Salzwedel | P-51 |
| | April 16 | (2)FW-190 dest(grd) | Landstadt | P-51 |
| | April 17 | (2)FW-190 dest(grd) | Puchhoff | P-51 |
| | | (2)Me-109 dest(grd) | Puchhoff | P-51 |
| | | 0-0-0 air | | |
| | | 8-2 ground | | |

**Parmelee, Charles E., Lt.** (5) Lakewood, OH
84th Ftr Sqn/78th Ftr Grp June 1944-September 10, 1944(KIA)
Hit by flak near Wiesbaden.
41 missions

P-47D WZ-I 43-25305
S/Sgt. Clyde G. Bergman-c/c

| *Sqn* | *Date* | *Claims* | *Location* | *A/C* |
|---|---|---|---|---|
| 84th | July 6, 1944 | FW-190 dest(air) | NW Paris | P-47 |
| | July 19 | Do-217 dest(grd) | Eutingen | P-47 |
| | August 11 | (2)Me-109 dest(air) | NW Paris | P-47 |
| | September 1 | FW-190 dest(grd) | SW Antwerp | P-47 |
| | | 3-0-0 air | | |
| | | 2-0 ground | | |

**Pascoe, James J., Lt.** (5.5) Poughkeepsie, NY
385th Ftr Sqn/364th Ftr Grp April 1944-December 1944
69 missions

P-38J 5E-Z 42-67453
P-51D 5E-Z 44-13890 "Green Eyes"

| *Sqn* | *Date* | *Claims* | *Location* | *A/C* |
|---|---|---|---|---|
| 385th | May 24, 1944 | (.5)Do-217 dest(air)* | Gifhorn | P-38 |
| | July 6 | FW-190 prob(air) | S/Chalons | P-38 |
| | September 11 | (2)FW-190 dest(air) | SW Leipzig | P-51 |
| | September 19 | FW-190 dest(air) | Arnheim | P-51 |
| | September 28 | FW-190 dam(air) | W/Magdeburg | P-51 |
| | November 2 | (2)Me-109 dest(air) | Halle | P-51 |
| | | 5.5-1-1 air | | |
| | | 0-0 ground | | |

* - shared with Lt. C.S. Hill of the 385th Ftr Sqn

**Patterson, Roy L., Lt.** (5) Roanoke, VA
62nd Ftr Sqn/56th Ftr Grp July 1944-December 1944

P-47D LM-Y 44-19883

| *Sqn* | *Date* | *Claims* | *Location* | *A/C* |
|---|---|---|---|---|
| 62nd | September 5, 1944 | (2)FW-190 dest(grd) | Gelnhausen | P-47 |
| | | u/i a/c dam(grd) | Gelnhausen | P-47 |
| | September 21 | FW-190 dest(air) | Arnheim | P-47 |
| | October 5 | Me-109 dest(grd) | S/Geseke | P-47 |
| | | Ju-88 dest(grd) | S/Geseke | P-47 |
| | | 1-0-0 air | | |
| | | 4-1 ground | | |

**Pattillo, Charles C., Lt.** (6) Atlanta, GA
486th Ftr Sqn/352nd Ftr Grp December 1944-EOW

P-51D PZ-W 44-13737 "Little Rebel"

| *Sqn* | *Date* | *Claims* | *Location* | *A/C* |
|---|---|---|---|---|
| 486th | March 2, 1945 | (2)u/i a/c dam(grd) | Prague | P-51 |
| | April 16 | (3)FW-190 dest(grd) | Ganacker | P-51 |
| | | (2)Me-109 dest(grd) | Ganacker | P-51 |
| | | Ju-88 dest(grd) | Ganacker | P-51 |
| | | (2)Me-109 dam(grd) | Ganacker | P-51 |
| | | FW-190 dam(grd) | Ganacker | P-51 |
| | | 0-0-0 air | | |
| | | 6-5 ground | | |

**Paul, Robert H., Lt.** (6) Baltimore, MD
505th Ftr Sqn/339th Ftr Grp February 1945-July 1945

P-51D 6N-
S/Sgt. Vito Clappe-c/c

| *Sqn* | *Date* | *Claims* | *Location* | *A/C* |
|---|---|---|---|---|
| 505th | April 10, 1945 | (3)Do-217 dest(grd) | Wittstock | P-51 |
| | | (2)Ju-88 dest(grd) | Wittstock | P-51 |
| | | (2)Ju-52 dam(grd) | Wittstock | P-51 |
| | April 17 | Ju-88 dest(grd) | SE Pocking | P-51 |
| | | 0-0-0 air | | |
| | | 6-2 ground | | |

**Payne, Carl G., Capt.** (5.5) San Antonio, TX
334th Ftr Sqn/4th Ftr Grp September 1944-September 1945

P-51D QP-J 44-72381

| *Sqn* | *Date* | *Claims* | *Location* | *A/C* |
|---|---|---|---|---|
| 334th | November 18, 1944 | Me-262 dest(grd) | Leipheim | P-51 |
| | | Me-262 dam(grd) | Leipheim | P-51 |
| | January 2, 1945 | (.5)Me-109 dest(air)* | Westerburg | P-51 |
| | | (.5)Me-109 dest(air)** | Westerburg | P-51 |
| | February 25 | Me-262 dest(air) | SE Naumberg | P-51 |
| | | (.5)Me-410 dest(grd)@ | Rohrensee | P-51 |
| | February 27 | (2)Me-109 dest(grd) | Weimar | P-51 |
| | | 2-0-0 air | | |
| | | 3.5-1 ground | | |

* - shared with Lt. A.J. Senecal of the 334th Ftr Sqn
** - shared with Lt. V.R.T. Rentschler of the 334th Ftr Sqn
@ - shared with Capt. T.R. Bell of the 334th Ftr Sqn

**Peal, Charles M., Capt.** (10) Nashville, TN
83rd Ftr Sqn/78th Ftr Grp April 1943-August 10, 1944(KIA)
Hit by flak near Noyon.

P-47D HL-P 42-7914 "Miss Norma"
P-47D HL-P 42-76232 "Miss Norma II"
P-47D HL-P "Miss Norma III"

| *Sqn* | *Date* | *Claims* | *Location* | *A/C* |
|---|---|---|---|---|
| 83rd | February 24, 1944 | Me-109 dest(air) | Furstenau | P-47 |
| | March 30 | Me-410 dam(grd) | N/Venlo | P-47 |
| | April 10 | (3)Bu-133 dest(grd) | Romorantin A/F | P-47 |
| | | Me-109 dest(grd) | see above | P-47 |
| | | Bu-133 dam(grd) | see above | P-47 |
| | April 13 | FW-190 dest(air) | Beucenbeuren | P-47 |
| | August 10 | (2.5)Ju-52 dest(grd)* | Chateau Salines | P-47 |
| | | (1.5)He-111 dest(grd)* | Chateau Salines | P-47 |
| | | 2-0-0 air | | |
| | | 8-2 ground | | |

* - both shared with Lt. R.T. Green of the 83rd Ftr Sqn

**Pederson, Douglas P., Lt.** (6) Long Beach, CA
336th Ftr Sqn/4th Ftr Grp November 1944-July 1945
32 missions

P-51D VF-D 44-72789

| Sqn | Date | Claims | Location | A/C |
|---|---|---|---|---|
| 336th | February 27, 1945 | u/i a/c dest(grd) | Weimar | P-51 |
| | April 16 | (5)Ju-52 dest(grd) | Praha A/F | P-51 |
| | | (3)Ju-52 dam(grd) | Praha A/F | P-51 |
| | | 0-0-0 air | | |
| | | 6-3 ground | | |

**Perry, Emil F., Capt.** (5) Lebanon, OH
354th Ftr Sqn/355th Ftr Grp February 1944-August 1944
78 missions, 300:25 hours

P-51B WR-I

| Sqn | Date | Claims | Location | A/C |
|---|---|---|---|---|
| 354th | May 13, 1944 | FW-190 dest(air) | NE Bremen | P-51 |
| | | FW-190 prob(air) | NE Bremen | P-51 |
| | | FW-190 dam(air) | NE Bremen | P-51 |
| | May 24 | FW-190 dest(grd) | Cormeilles-en-Vixen | P-51 |
| | | FW-190 dam(grd) | see above | P-51 |
| | June 24 | (2)Me-109 dest(grd) | Seiches | P-51 |
| | July 7 | Me-410 dest(air) | Lingen | P-51 |
| | | 2-1-1 air | | |
| | | 3-1 ground | | |

**Peterburs, Joseph A., Lt.** (5) West Allis, WI
55th Ftr Sqn/20th Ftr Grp November 1944-April 10, 1945(POW)
Hit by flak near Berlin.
46 missions, 255 hours

P-51D KI-B 44-15078 "Josephine"
T/Sgt. Alois G. Hooyman-c/c
Sgt. Wesley F. Harwood-ac/c
Cpl. Adais S. Bransteitter-arm.

| Sqn | Date | Claims | Location | A/C |
|---|---|---|---|---|
| 55th | April 10, 1945 | (5)u/i a/c dest(grd) | Berlin | P-51 |
| | | 0-0-0 air | | |
| | | 5-0 ground | | |

**Peters, Robert O., Lt.** (5) Bexley, OH
358th Ftr Sqn/355th Ftr Grp June 1944-September 18, 1944(KIA)
Shot down over Warsaw by a P-51.

P-51D YF-X 44-13675
S/Sgt. Henry J. Wnukowski-c/c
Sgt. Warner L. Dale-ac/c

| Sqn | Date | Claims | Location | A/C |
|---|---|---|---|---|
| 358th | July 20, 1944 | (2)FW-190 dest(air) | E/Leipzig | P-51 |
| | | Do-217 dest(air) | E/Leipzig | P-51 |
| | | He-111 dest(grd) | E/Leipzig | P-51 |
| | | Ju-88 dest(grd) | E/Leipzig | P-51 |
| | | 3-0-0 air | | |
| | | 2-0 ground | | |

**Peterson, Chesley G., Col.** (7) Santaquin, UT
HdQts/4th Ftr Grp September 1942-May 1943
HdQts/4th Ftr Grp August 1943-January 1944 (non-flying)
Earlier flew with 71 Sqn, RAF, claiming 6 kills: single Me-109's on September 7 and 18, 1941; (2)FW-190's on April 27, 1942; a FW-190 on June 1, 1942; and a Ju-88 on August 19, 1942.
200 total missions

Spitfire XR-

| Sqn | Date | Claims | Location | A/C |
|---|---|---|---|---|
| HdQts | April 15, 1943 | FW-190 dest(air) | W/Ostend | P-47 |
| | May 14 | FW-190 prob(air) | W/St. Nicholas | P-47 |
| | | FW-190 dam(air) | W/St. Nicholas P-47 | |
| | | 1-1-1 air | | |
| | | 0-0 ground | | |

**Peterson, Richard A., Maj.** (19) Alexandria, MN
364th Ftr Sqn/357th Ftr Grp April 1943-February 1945
118 missions, 500 hours

P-51B C5-T 43-6935 "Hurry Home Honey"
P-51D C5-T 44-13586 "Hurry Home Honey"
P-51D C5-T 44-14868 "Hurry Home Honey"
S/Sgt. Earl Lloyd-c/c
Sgt. Howard Brennan-ac/c
Sgt. Kenneth Arveson-arm.

| Sqn | Date | Claims | Location | A/C |
|---|---|---|---|---|
| 364th | March 5, 1944 | FW-190 dest(air) | Bordeaux | P-51 |
| | March 8 | FW-190 dam(air) | Berlin | P-51 |
| | March 16 | (.5)Me-110 dest(air)* | Ulm | P-51 |
| | March 18 | Me-109 dest(air) | Augsburg | P-51 |
| | March 23 | Me-109 prob(air) | E/Brunswick | P-51 |
| | April 11 | Me-109 dest(air) | Magdeburg | P-51 |
| | April 24 | Me-109 dest(air) | Munich | P-51 |
| | April 30 | (2)FW-190 dest(air) | Auxerre | P-51 |
| | May 12 | (.5)FW-190 dest(air)** | NE Frankfurt | P-51 |
| | | FW-190 dam(air) | NE Frankfurt | P-51 |
| | May 13 | (1.5)Me-410 dest(air)@ | E/Grunberg | P-51 |
| | May 24 | (.5)u/i a/c dest(grd)@@ | St. Leger | P-51 |
| | May 28 | Me-109 dest(air) | NW Magdeburg | P-51 |
| | July 1 | (2)Me-109 dest(air) | E/St. Quentin | P-51 |
| | October 6 | FW-190 dest(air) | W/Berlin | P-51 |
| | October 7 | Me-109 dest(air) | Jena | P-51 |
| | November 2 | FW-190 dest(air) | NW Merseburg | P-51 |
| | November 18 | Me-109 dest(air) | Neuhausen A/F | P-51 |
| | January 5, 1945 | (2)Ju-88 dest(grd) | Alten Stadt | P-51 |
| | | Me-109 dest(grd) | Alten Stadt | P-51 |
| | | 15.5-1-2 air | | |
| | | 3.5-0 ground | | |

* - shared with Capt. G.V. Davis of the 364th Ftr Sqn
** - shared with Capt. J.A. Storch of the 364th Ftr Sqn
@ - shared with Lt. J.G. Sullivan of the 364th Ftr Sqn
@@ - shared with Lt. N.J. Frederick of the 364th Ftr Sqn

**Phaneuf, Richard E., Lt.** (5) Flint, MI
83rd Ftr Sqn/78th Ftr Grp November 1944-EOW
49 missions

P-51D HL-

| Sqn | Date | Claims | Location | A/C |
|---|---|---|---|---|
| 83rd | April 10, 1945 | He-111 dest(grd) | Gardelegen | P-51 |
| | April 16 | (2)Ju-87 dest(grd) | N/Prague | P-51 |
| | | FW-190 dest(grd) | N/Prague | P-51 |
| | | Ju-52 dest(grd) | N/Prague | P-51 |
| | | (2)Ju-87 dam(grd) | N/Prague | P-51 |
| | | Me-109 dam(grd) | N/Prague | P-51 |
| | | He-111 dam(grd) | N/Prague | P-51 |
| | | 0-0-0 air | | |
| | | 5-4 ground | | |

**Phillips, Raymond G., Lt.** (5) Newton, IA
328th Ftr Sqn/352nd Ftr Grp September 1943-June 10, 1944(KIA)
Hit trees while strafing near Bayeux.

P-47D PE-P 42-7997 "Hildegarde"
P-51B PE-P 42-106868 "Hildegarde"
S/Sgt. N. Miller-c/c
Sgt. J.A. Sullivan-ac/c

| Sqn | Date | Claims | Location | A/C |
|---|---|---|---|---|
| 328th | February 20, 1944 | Me-110 dest(air) | Blankenheim | P-47 |
| | | Me-110 dam(air) | see above | P-47 |
| | | FW-190 dam(air) | see above | P-47 |
| | May 8 | Me-109 dest(air) | SE Nienburg | P-51 |
| | May 21 | FW-190 dest(grd) | Alt Ruppin | P-51 |
| | | Ju-52 dest(grd) | Alt Ruppin | P-51 |
| | | u/i a/c dest(grd) | Alt Ruppin | P-51 |
| | May 28 | Me-109 dam(air) | W/Magdeburg | P-51 |
| | | 2-0-3 air | | |
| | | 3-0 ground | | |

**Pickering, Malcolm C., Lt.** (8) Detroit, MI
487th Ftr Sqn/352nd Ftr Grp April 1944-September 1944

P-51B HO-S 43-7094 "Gracie"

| *Sqn* | *Date* | *Claims* | *Location* | *A/C* |
|---|---|---|---|---|
| 487th | April 28, 1944 | Ju-88 dest(grd) | Bourges | P-51 |
| | | He-111 dam(grd) | Bourges | P-51 |
| | May 8 | FW-190 dest(air) | Nienburg | P-51 |
| | May 30 | FW-190 dest(air) | Halberstadt | P-51 |
| | June 29 | He-111 dest(grd) | Burg A/F | P-51 |
| | | Me-110 dam(grd) | Burg A/F | P-51 |
| | July 21 | Me-109 dest(air) | E/Munich | P-51 |
| | August 16 | FW-190 dest(air) | Plauen | P-51 |
| | September 10 | (2)u/i a/c dest(grd) | Wertheim | P-51 |

4-0-0 air
4-2 ground

**Pierce, Donald J., Capt.** (8.5) Alliance, OH
336th Ftr Sqn/ 4th Ftr Grp September 1944-February 1945
434th Ftr Sqn/479th Ftr Grp February 1945-EOW

P-51D VF- 44-13375
P-51D L2-R 44-72336 "Setonia No.3"
S/Sgt. Tom J. O'Grady-c/c(479th)

| *Sqn* | *Date* | *Claims* | *Location* | *A/C* |
|---|---|---|---|---|
| 434th | February 14, 1945 | (2)Me-109 dam(air) | SW Berlin | P-51 |
| | February 20 | (.5)He-111 dest(grd)* | Windleschenlaibach | P-51 |
| | | (.5)He-111 dam(grd)* | see above | P-51 |
| | April 13 | Ar-234 dest(grd) | Lubeck | P-51 |
| | | Ju-88 dam(grd) | Kaltenkirchen | P-51 |
| | April 16 | Me-109 dest(grd) | Kirchen | P-51 |
| | | Me-109 dest(grd) | Reichersberg | P-51 |
| | | FW-190 dest(grd) | Reichersberg | P-51 |
| | | Ju-88 dest(grd) | Reichersberg | P-51 |
| | | (2)Me-109 dam(grd) | Reichersberg | P-51 |
| | April 17 | (2)FW-190 dest(grd) | Puchhoff | P-51 |
| | | Me-109 dest(grd) | Landau | P-51 |
| | | Me-109 dam(grd) | Landau | P-51 |
| | | u/i a/c dam(grd) | Landau | P-51 |

0-0-2 air
8.5-5.5 ground

* - both shared with Lt. P.A. Brown of the 434th Ftr Sqn

**Pierce, Joseph F., Lt.** (8) Duncan, OK
363rd Ftr Sqn/357th Ftr Grp April 1943-May 21, 1944(KIA)
Hit by flak at Stralsund Airfield.

P-51B B6-N 43-6644

| *Sqn* | *Date* | *Claims* | *Location* | *A/C* |
|---|---|---|---|---|
| 363rd | March 6, 1944 | Me-110 dest(air) | W/Berlin | P-51 |
| | April 24 | Me-109 dest(air) | W/Munich | P-51 |
| | | Ju-88 dest(air) | W/Munich | P-51 |
| | April 29 | Me-109 dam(air) | Berlin | P-51 |
| | April 30 | (2)FW-190 dest(air) | NE Orleans | P-51 |
| | May 8 | FW-190 dest(air) | Soltau | P-51 |
| | May 12 | Me-109 dest(air) | NE Frankfurt | P-51 |
| | | Me-109 dest(grd) | NE Frankfurt | P-51 |

7-0-1 air
1-0 ground

**Pissanos, Spiros N., Lt.** (5) Plainfield, NJ
334th Ftr Sqn/4th Ftr Grp October 1942-March 5, 1944(MIA-E)
Suffered m/f south of Le Havre.
Earlier flew with 71 Sqn, RAF
106 missions

Spitfire XR-K EN783
P-47D QP-D 42-7945 "Miss Plainfield"
P-51B QP-D 43-6798
S/Sgt. Paul Fox-c/c

| *Sqn* | *Date* | *Claims* | *Location* | *A/C* |
|---|---|---|---|---|
| 334th | May 21, 1943 | FW-190 dam(air) | Ghent | P-47 |
| | August 12 | Me-109 dest(air) | W/Walcheren | P-47 |
| | January 29, 1944 | (2)Me-109 dest(air) | Aachen | P-47 |
| | March 5 | (2)Me-109 dest(air) | Bordeaux | P-51 |

5-0-1 air
0-0 ground

**Pogue, Edward F., Lt.** (6) Chattanooga, TN
79th Ftr Sqn/20th Ftr Grp November 1944-October 1945
42 missions, 228:10 hours

P-51D MC-R 44-13535 "Chattanooga Choo-Choo"
T/Sgt. Charles Osman-c/c
Sgt. Carl C. Johnson-ac/c
Sgt. Stephen S. Kefalas-arm.

| *Sqn* | *Date* | *Claims* | *Location* | *A/C* |
|---|---|---|---|---|
| 79th | February 20, 1945 | (2)He-111 dest(grd) | Weiden | P-51 |
| | April 10 | (3)He-111 dest(grd) | Werder A/F | P-51 |
| | | Me-109 dest(grd) | see above | P-51 |
| | | He-111 dam(grd) | see above | P-51 |
| | | Me-109 dam(grd) | see above | P-51 |
| | April 13 | Me-109 dam(grd) | Jagel-Hutzfeld | P-51 |
| | | He-177 dam(grd) | Jagel-Hutzfeld | P-51 |

0-0-0 air
6-4 ground

**Poindexter, James N., Maj.** (11) Millville, NJ
352nd Ftr Sqn/353rd Ftr Grp October 1942-January 3, 1945(KIA)
Suffered m/f, aborted, and crashed near Capel St. Mary.
111 missions

P-47D SX-H "Honey"
P-47D SX-G 42-26586 "Honey II"
P-51D SX-G 44-14720 "Honey III"
P-51D SX-G 44-14589 "Honey IV"

| *Sqn* | *Date* | *Claims* | *Location* | *A/C* |
|---|---|---|---|---|
| 352nd | September 23, 1943 | Me-109 dest(air) | NE Nantes | P-47 |
| | November 3 | Me-110 dest(air) | Wilhelmshaven | P-47 |
| | | Me-210 dest(air) | Wilhelmshaven | P-47 |
| | February 22, 1944 | (2)Me-109 dest(air) | NW Koln | P-47 |
| | February 24 | FW-190 dam(air) | Steinhuder Lake | P-47 |
| | May 30 | (2)FW-190 dest(air) | Peine | P-47 |
| | June 7 | Me-109 dest(grd) | Compiegne | P-47 |
| | | (1.5)Me-109 dam(grd)* | Compiegne | P-47 |
| | June 20 | He-111 dest(grd) | Plantlunne | P-47 |
| | August 1 | Me-410 dest(grd) | Laon/Couvron | P-47 |
| | November 18 | He-177 dest(grd) | Lechfeld | P-51 |
| | | He-177 dam(grd) | Lechfeld | P-51 |

7-0-1 air
4-2.5 ground

* - shared with Lt. R.V. Keywan of the 352nd Ftr Sqn

**Pompetti, Peter E., Lt.** (7) Philadelphia, PA
84th Ftr Sqn/78th Ftr Grp February 1943-March 17, 1944(POW)
Hit by flak near Villeteneuse.
95 missions, 226:33 hours

P-47C WZ-R 41-6393 "Axe The Axis"
S/Sgt. Harold W. Cecil-c/c
Sgt. Charles Clark-ac/c
Cpl. Charles Twohig-arm.

| *Sqn* | *Date* | *Claims* | *Location* | *A/C* |
|---|---|---|---|---|
| 84th | July 30, 1943 | Me-109 dest(air) | Didam | P-47 |
| | August 17 | Me-210 dest(air) | SE Aachen | P-47 |
| | September 27 | Me-109 dest(air) | NW Emden | P-47 |
| | | Me-110 dest(air) | NW Emden | P-47 |
| | December 1 | FW-190 dam(air) | Liege-Aachen | P-47 |
| | January 4, 1944 | Me-109 dest(air) | Coesfeld | P-47 |
| | | FW-190 dam(air) | Coesfeld | P-47 |
| | January 14 | Me-109 dam(air) | NE Lille | P-47 |
| | February 5 | (.5)Me-109 dam(air)* | Bernay | P-47 |
| | February 6 | Hs-129 dest(grd) | Orleans/Bricy | P-47 |
| | | Ju-88 dam(grd) | Orleans/Bricy | P-47 |
| | March 2 | (.5)Hs-126 dest(grd)** | Chartres | P-47 |
| | | (.5)Ju-52 dest(grd)** | Chartres | P-47 |
| | March 8 | (.5)FW-190 dam(grd)@ | Bohmte | P-47 |
| | March 16 | Me-109 dam(grd) | S/Nancy | P-47 |
| | March 17 | (.5)He-111 dam(grd)@@ | Beauvais | P-47 |

5-0-3.5 air
2-3 ground

* - shared with Lt. L.J. Abel of the 84th Ftr Sqn
** - both shared with Lt. E.S. Lang of the 84th Ftr Sqn
@ - shared with Lt. E.S. Lang of the 84th Ftr Sqn
@@ - shared with Lt. E.S. Lang of the 84th Ftr Sqn

**Powell, Lawrence J., Jr., Lt.** (6) Southgate, CA
505th Ftr Sqn/339th Ftr Grp June 1944-January 14, 1945(POW)
Hit by flak and flew through power lines in the Dummer Lake area.
68 missions

P-51C 6N- "Happy"
P-51D 6N- "Happy Junior"

| Sqn | Date | Claims | Location | A/C |
|---|---|---|---|---|
| 505th | July 31, 1944 | Me-410 dest(grd) | Holzkirchen | P-51 |
| | | u/i a/c dam(grd) | Holzkirchen | P-51 |
| | August 4 | FW-190 dest(air) | S/Hamburg | P-51 |
| | | (.5)Me-109 dest(air)[*] | S/Hamburg | P-51 |
| | September 10 | Me-410 dest(grd) | Weizenburg | P-51 |
| | | Do-217 dest(grd) | see above | P-51 |
| | | (4)u/i a/c dam(grd) | see above | P-51 |
| | September 13 | (.5)Ju-88 dest(grd)[**] | SE Munich | P-51 |
| | September 23 | FW-190 dest(air) | Geldern-Weeze | P-51 |

2.5-0-0 air
3.5-5 ground

[*] - shared with Lt. A.E. Tongue of the 505th Ftr Sqn
[**] - shared with Lt. W.R. Moore of the 505th Ftr Sqn

**Powers, Joseph H., Capt.** (14.5) Tulsa, OK
61st Ftr Sqn/56th Ftr Grp July 1942-April 1944
62nd Ftr Sqn/56th Ftr Grp April 1944-May 1944

P-47C HV-V 41-6267
P-47D HV-P 42-75163 "Power's Girl"
P-47D LM-P 42-76363
S/Sgt. Joseph J. James-c/c

| Sqn | Date | Claims | Location | A/C |
|---|---|---|---|---|
| 61st | July 30, 1943 | Me-109 dest(air) | Arnheim | P-47 |
| | November 29 | Me-109 dest(air) | NE Bremen | P-47 |
| | December 11 | Me-109 dest(air) | N/Aurich | P-47 |
| | | Me-110 dest(air) | N/Norderney Isle | P-47 |
| | | Me-110 dam(air) | N/Norderney Isle | P-47 |
| | December 20 | Me-109 dest(air) | NE Bremen | P-47 |
| | | (.5)Me-109 dam(air)[*] | NE Bremen | P-47 |
| | | (.5)Me-210 dam(air)[*] | NE Bremen | P-47 |
| | January 30, 1944 | FW-190 dest(air) | Meppen | P-47 |
| | February 6 | Me-109 dest(air) | Beauvais | P-47 |
| | February 24 | FW-190 dest(air) | Minden | P-47 |
| | March 15 | Me-109 dest(air) | Dummer Lake | P-47 |
| | | FW-190 dest(air) | Dummer Lake | P-47 |
| | | FW-190 dam(air) | Dummer Lake | P-47 |
| | March 16 | Me-109 dest(air) | St. Dizier | P-47 |
| | | FW-190 dam(air) | St. Dizier | P-47 |
| | March 18 | FW-190 dest(air) | Cambrai-Givet | P-47 |
| 62nd | April 9 | Me-109 dest(air) | S/Kiel | P-47 |
| | April 13 | Me-109 dam(air) | Ludwigshafen | P-47 |
| | May 4 | Me-109 dest(air) | Quackenbruck | P-47 |
| | May 12 | (.5)Me-109 dest(air)[**] | Frankfurt | P-47 |

14.5-0-5 air
0-0 ground

[*] - both shared with Lt. M.C. Wood of the 61st Ftr Sqn
[**] - shared with F/O J. Vitale of the 62nd Ftr Sqn

**Preddy, George E., Maj.** (31.83) Greensboro, NC
487th Ftr Sqn/352nd Ftr Grp January 1943-August 1944
328th Ftr Sqn/352nd Ftr Grp October 1944-December 25, 1944(KIA)
Hit by Allied groundfire near Liege.
Earlier flew in the PTO with the 49th Ftr Grp and claimed 2 damaged.
143 missions, 532 hours

P-47D HO-P 42-8500 "Cripes A'Mighty"
P-51B HO-P 42-106451 "Cripes A'Mighty 2nd"
P-51D HO-P 44-13321 "Cripes A'Mighty 3rd"
P-51D PE-P 44-14906 "Cripes A'Mighty"
S/Sgt. Lew Lunn-c/c(487th)
Sgt. J.J. McVay-ac/c(487th)
Sgt. M.C. Kultaneck-arm.(487th)
S/Sgt. Art C. Snyder-c/c(328th)

| Sqn | Date | Claims | Location | A/C |
|---|---|---|---|---|
| 487th | December 1, 1943 | Me-109 dest(air) | S/Rheydt | P-47 |
| | December 22 | Me-410 dest(air) | E/Zuider Zee | P-47 |
| | January 29, 1944 | Me-109 dest(air) | Malmedy | P-47 |
| | April 11 | He-111 dest(grd) | SE Berlin | P-51 |
| | | He-111 dam(grd) | SE Berlin | P-51 |
| | April 13 | Bu-133 dest(grd) | S/Stuttgart | P-51 |
| | April 20 | Me-109 dam(air) | Beauvais-Chartres | P-51 |
| | April 22 | (.33)Ju-88 dest(air)[*] | Stade A/F | P-51 |
| | | Ju-52 dest(grd) | Salzwedel | P-51 |
| | April 28 | He-111 dam(grd) | Bourges | P-51 |
| | May 12 | (3)u/i a/c dam(grd) | Frankenhausen | P-51 |
| | May 13 | (2)Me-109 dest(air) | Neubrandenburg | P-51 |
| | May 30 | (2.5)Me-109 dest(air)[**] | Magdeburg | P-51 |
| | June 12 | Me-109 dest(air) | SW Rennes | P-51 |
| | June 20 | FW-190 dest(air) | E/Bernburg | P-51 |
| | | (.5)Me-410 dest(air)[@] | E/Bernburg | P-51 |
| | June 21 | Me-109 dest(air) | E/Magdeburg | P-51 |
| | June 29 | Ju-52 dest(grd) | Burg A/F | P-51 |
| | July 18 | (2)Ju-88 dest(air) | NE Rostock | P-51 |
| | | Me-109 dest(air) | NE Rostock | P-51 |
| | | Ju-88 prob(air) | NE Rostock | P-51 |
| | | (2)Ju-88 dam(air) | NE Rostock | P-51 |
| | July 20 | Me-410 dest(grd) | Nordhausen | P-51 |
| | | He-111 dam(grd) | Nordhausen | P-51 |
| | July 21 | (.5)Me-109 dest(air)[@@] | E/Munich | P-51 |
| | July 29 | Me-109 dest(air) | Naunberg | P-51 |
| | August 5 | Me-109 dest(air) | S/Hamburg | P-51 |
| | | Me-109 prob(air) | S/Hamburg | P-51 |
| | August 6 | (6)Me-109 dest(air) | Luneburg-Havelburg | P-51 |
| 328th | November 2 | Me-109 dest(air) | Merseburg | P-51 |
| | November 21 | FW-190 dest(air) | Merseburg | P-51 |
| | | Me-109 prob(air) | Merseburg | P-51 |
| | | Me-109 dam(air) | Merseburg | P-51 |
| | December 25 | (2)Me-109 dest(air) | SW Coblenz | P-51 |

26.83-3-4 air
5-6 ground

[*] - shared with Lt. D.R. Donahue and Lt. J.P. Kessler of the 487th Ftr Sqn
[**] - shared with Lt. W.T. Whisner of the 487th Ftr Sqn
[@] - shared with Lt. J.N. Wood of the 487th Ftr Sqn
[@@] - shared with Lt. S.K. Moats of the 487th Ftr Sqn

**Prescott, Walter A.S., Lt.** (6) Brooklyn, NY
350th Ftr Sqn/353rd Ftr Grp October 1944-April 16, 1945(MIA)
Hit by flak at Pocking Airfield.
47 missions

P-51D LH-

| Sqn | Date | Claims | Location | A/C |
|---|---|---|---|---|
| 350th | March 21, 1945 | Ju-88 dest(grd) | Achmer | P-51 |
| | | Ar-234 dam(grd) | Achmer | P-51 |
| | March 24 | (2)Me-109 dest(air) | NW Kassel | P-51 |
| | April 16 | (2)FW-190 dest(grd) | Pocking | P-51 |
| | | Me-109 dest(grd) | Pocking | P-51 |

2-0-0 air
4-1 ground

**Price, Jack C., Maj.** (5) Grand Junction, CO
84th Ftr Sqn/78th Ftr Grp July 1942-February 1944
HdQts/20th Ftr Grp February 1945-March 1945
55th Ftr Sqn/20th Ftr Grp March 1945-April 1945
HdQts/20th Ftr Grp April 1945-EOW
99 missions, 281:15 hours

P-47C WZ-A 41-6270 "Feather Merchant"
P-47D WZ-A 42-74641 "Feather Merchant II"
P-51D KI- "Feather Merchant III"
P-51D LC-G 44-14693 "Feather Merchant IV"
S/Sgt. Sam T. Snoddy-c/c(78th)
T/Sgt. Delmon D. Sparks-c/c(20th)

| Sqn | Date | Claims | Location | A/C |
|---|---|---|---|---|
| 84th | July 14, 1943 | FW-190 dest(air) | N/Abbeville | P-47 |
| | July 30 | (2)FW-190 dest(air) | Winterswijk | P-47 |
| | October 20 | Me-109 dam(air) | Dinant | P-47 |
| | November 26 | Me-109 dest(air) | Paris | P-47 |
| | | FW-190 dest(air) | Paris | P-47 |

5-0-1 air
0-0 ground

**Price, William J., Maj.** (7) Pittsburgh, PA
350th Ftr Sqn/353rd Ftr Grp October 1942-December 1944
108 missions

P-47D LH-F 42-8623 "Janie"
P-47D LH-F 42-26477 "Janie"
P-51D LH-F 44-14419 "Janie"
S/Sgt. Patton-c/c
Sgt. Lee-arm.

| Sqn | Date | Claims | Location | A/C |
|---|---|---|---|---|
| 350th | November 5, 1943 | Me-210 dest(air) | Ruhr Valley | P-47 |
| | August 28, 1944 | Me-410 dest(grd) | Wavre | P-47 |
| | | (2)Me-410 dam(grd) | Wavre | P-47 |
| | August 29 | (3)Me-109 dest(grd) | Diest | P-47 |
| | | Me-109 dam(grd) | Diest | P-47 |

| | | | | |
|---|---|---|---|---|
| | September 23 | FW-190 dest(air) | SE Arnheim | P-47 |
| | November 18 | u/i a/c dest(air) | Lechfeld | P-51 |
| | | (.5)u/i a/c dam(grd)* | Lechfeld | P-51 |

3-0-0 air
4-3.5 ground

* - shared with Lt. R.W. Abernathy of the 350th Ftr Sqn

**Priest, Royce W., Lt.** (5) San Antonio, TX
354th Ftr Sqn/355th Ftr Grp May 1944-December 1944
67 missions, 310 hours

P-51B WR-E "Weepin' Deacon"
P-51D WR-E 44-13764 "Weepin' Deacon II"
P-51D WR-E 44-15652 "Weepin' Deacon III"
S/Sgt. Yanavich-c/c

| *Sqn* | *Date* | *Claims* | *Location* | *A/C* |
|---|---|---|---|---|
| 354th | September 11, 1944 | Me-109 dest(air) | S/Kassel | P-51 |
| | September 27 | FW-190 dest(air) | Eschwege | P-51 |
| | November 2 | Me-109 dest(air) | W/Naumberg | P-51 |
| | November 26 | (2)FW-190 dest(air) | Misburg | P-51 |

5-0-0 air
0-0 ground

**Pryor, Thomas P., Jr., Lt.** (5) Joliet, IL
351st Ftr Sqn/353rd Ftr Grp January 1945-EOW
24 missions

P-51D YJ-

| *Sqn* | *Date* | *Claims* | *Location* | *A/C* |
|---|---|---|---|---|
| 351st | April 5, 1945 | (3)Me-410 dest(grd) | Weiden | P-51 |
| | | Me-110 dam(grd) | Weiden | P-51 |
| | April 16 | FW-190 dest(grd) | Reichersberg | P-51 |
| | | Do-217 dest(grd) | Reichersberg | P-51 |

0-0-0 air
5-1 ground

**Pugh, John F., Capt.** (6) Brogan, OR
362nd Ftr Sqn/357th Ftr Grp June 1943-September 1944
72 missions, 300 hours

P-51B G4-N 43-6635
P-51B G4-N 42-106473 "Geronimo"

| *Sqn* | *Date* | *Claims* | *Location* | *A/C* |
|---|---|---|---|---|
| 362nd | April 8, 1944 | Me-109 dest(air) | S/Brunswick | P-51 |
| | April 11 | Me-109 dest(air) | Magdeburg | P-51 |
| | May 27 | FW-190 dest(air) | N/Strasbourg | P-51 |
| | June 29 | Me-109 dest(air) | Naumburg | P-51 |
| | July 25 | Me-109 dest(air) | Versailles | P-51 |
| | August 7 | FW-190 dest(air) | N/Kracow | P-51 |

6-0-0 air
0-0 ground

**Queen, Thomas W., Lt.** (5) San Diego, CA
63rd Ftr Sqn/56th Ftr Grp July 1944-EOW
60 missions, 264:30 hours

P-47D UN-H 42-25317
P-47M UN-H 44-21181

| *Sqn* | *Date* | *Claims* | *Location* | *A/C* |
|---|---|---|---|---|
| 63rd | August 28, 1944 | Ju-88 dam(grd) | Bad Brommach | P-47 |
| | September 5 | Me-109 dam(air) | NE Coblenz | P-47 |
| | | FW-190 dest(grd) | Gelnhausen | P-47 |
| | | FW-190 dam(grd) | Gelnhausen | P-47 |
| | April 13, 1945 | (3)u/i a/c dest(grd) | Eggebeck A/F | P-47 |
| | | Me-410 dest(grd) | Eggebeck A/F | P-47 |

0-0-1 air
5-2 ground

**Quirk, Michael J., Capt.** (16) Washington, D.C.
62nd Ftr Sqn/56th Ftr Grp Mid 1942-September 10, 1944(POW)
Hit by flak at Seligenstadt A/F

P-47C LM-K 41-6215
P-47D LM-K 42-75242
P-47D LM-K 42-27382

| *Sqn* | *Date* | *Claims* | *Location* | *A/C* |
|---|---|---|---|---|
| 62nd | August 19, 1943 | FW-190 dest(air) | Gilze-Rijen | P-47 |
| | October 8 | FW-190 dest(air) | Quackenbruck | P-47 |
| | December 20 | Me-109 dest(air) | S/Bremen | P-47 |
| | January 4, 1944 | FW-190 dest(air) | N/St. Gilles | P-47 |
| | January 11 | Me-109 prob(air) | Lingen | P-47 |
| | January 30 | Me-109 dest(air) | Almelo | P-47 |
| | | Me-109 dam(air) | Almelo | P-47 |
| | February 4 | FW-190 dest(air) | Charleroi | P-47 |
| | | Me-110 dest(air) | St. Omer | P-47 |
| | February 22 | (1.5)FW-190 dest(air)* | Breda | P-47 |
| | February 25 | FW-190 dest(air) | Homburg | P-47 |
| | March 8 | (.5)FW-190 dest(air)** | Celle | P-47 |
| | March 15 | FW-190 dest(air) | Dummer Lake | P-47 |
| | August 4 | (3)He-111 dam(grd) | Plantlunne | P-47 |
| | September 5 | (4)FW-190 dest(grd) | Gelnhausen | P-47 |
| | | (4)FW-190 dam(grd) | Gelnhausen | P-47 |
| | September 10 | He-111 dest(grd) | Seligenstadt | P-47 |

11-1-1 air
5-7 ground

* - shared with Lt. J.E. Fields of the 62nd Ftr Sqn
** - shared with Lt. J.B. Eaves of the 62nd Ftr Sqn

**Rafferty, Vernon G., Capt.** (6) Menomonie, WI
350th Ftr Sqn/353rd Ftr Grp June 1944-December 1944
68 missions, 270 hours

P-47D LH-M 42-266?? "Fern Marie"
P-47D LH-M 42-26659 "Fern Marie II"
P-51D LH-M 44-14770 "Fern Marie III"
S/Sgt. McLain-c/c

| *Sqn* | *Date* | *Claims* | *Location* | *A/C* |
|---|---|---|---|---|
| 350th | June 20, 1944 | (.5)He-111 dest(grd)* | Plantlunne | P-47 |
| | June 27 | Me-109 dam(grd) | Chalons | P-47 |
| | August 4 | (3)He-111 dest(grd) | Plantlunne | P-47 |
| | September 21 | (.5)FW-190 dest(air)** | SE Arnheim | P-47 |
| | September 23 | FW-190 dest(air) | SE Arnheim | P-47 |
| | | Me-109 dest(air) | SE Arnheim | P-47 |

2.5-0-0 air
3.5-1 ground

* - shared with LtCol. B. Rimerman of HdQts, 353rd Ftr Grp
** - shared with Lt. R.W. Hedler of the 350th Ftr Sqn

**Ramm, Albert J., Capt.** (5.5) Jamaica, NY
338th Ftr Sqn/55th Ftr Grp August 1944-April 1945

P-51D CL-F "Ginny"
S/Sgt. Curtis H. Payne-c/c
Sgt. Jack Trout-ac/c

| *Sqn* | *Date* | *Claims* | *Location* | *A/C* |
|---|---|---|---|---|
| 338th | August 28, 1944 | (.5)DFS-230 dest(air)* | Dromersheim | P-51 |
| | November 26 | FW-190 dest(grd) | Vorden A/F | P-51 |
| | January 6, 1945 | (2)Ju-88 dest(grd) | Giebelstadt | P-51 |
| | | (2)u/i a/c dest(grd) | Giebelstadt | P-51 |

0.5-0-0 air
5-0 ground

* - shared with Lt. R.C. Haworth of the 338th Ftr Sqn

**Randolph, John P., Col.** (5) Schertz, TX
HdQts/ 20th Ftr Grp July 1944-November 1944
HdQts/359th Ftr Grp November 1944-April 1945

P-51D MC-N 44-13541 "Nancy"
P-51D CV-N 44-14965 "Nancy"
T/Sgt. Edward Peters-c/c(20th)
S/Sgt. Green-ac/c(20th)

| *Sqn* | *Date* | *Claims* | *Location* | *A/C* |
|---|---|---|---|---|
| HdQts | August 9, 1944 | Me-109 dest(air) | S/Augsburg | P-51 |
| | August 25 | BV-140 dest(grd) | Parow A/F | P-51 |
| | | Ju-88 dest(grd) | Parow A/F | P-51 |
| | | (2)Ju-88 dam(grd) | Parow A/F | P-51 |
| | October 6 | (2)Do-24 dest(grd) | Kubitzer Bay | P-51 |

1-0-0 air
4-2 ground

**Rankin, Robert J., Capt.** (10) Washington, D.C.
61st Ftr Sqn/56th Ftr Grp September 1943-August 1944

P-47D HV-H "Wicked Wacker Weegie"
S/Sgt. John P. Faulkner-c/c
Sgt. John J. Gill-ac/c
Cpl. Vernon R. Pritchett-arm.

| *Sqn* | *Date* | *Claims* | *Location* | *A/C* |
|---|---|---|---|---|
| 61st | February 6, 1944 | Me-109 dest(air) | Paris | P-47 |
| | March 15 | (2)Me-109 dest(air) | Dummer Lake | P-47 |
| | | Me-109 prob(air) | Dummer Lake | P-47 |
| | | FW-190 dam(air) | Dummer Lake | P-47 |
| | March 29 | Me-109 dest(air) | NE Nienburg | P-47 |
| | May 12 | (5)Me-109 dest(air) | NW Marburg | P-47 |
| | June 7 | Me-109 dest(air) | SE Senlis | P-47 |
| | | Me-109 dam(air) | SE Senlis | P-47 |

10-1-2 air
0-0 ground

**Rau, Harold J., Col.** (5) Hempstead, NY
HdQts/356th Ftr Grp February 1943-November 1943
HdQts/ 20th Ftr Grp March 1944-June 1944
HdQts/ 20th Ftr Grp August 1944-December 1944
73 missions, 275 hours

P-47D QI-R 42-8425 "Gentle Annie"
P-47D QI-R 42-22550 "Gentle Annie"
P-38J MC-R 42-68145 "Gentle Annie"
P-38J MC-R 42-67722 "Gentle Annie"
P-51D MC-R 44-14337 "Gentle Annie"
S/Sgt. Henry Yoder-c/c(356th)
Sgt. Willis A. Youtsey-ac/c(356th)
T/Sgt. James Douglas-c/c(20th)
Sgt. Grant Beach-ac/c(20th)
Sgt. Luther Ghent-arm.(20th)
Cpl. George A. Fregone-arm.(20th)

| *Sqn* | *Date* | *Claims* | *Location* | *A/C* |
|---|---|---|---|---|
| HdQts | April 8, 1944 | Me-109 dest(air) | Salzwedel | P-38 |
| | | (3)Ju-88 dest(grd) | Salzwedel | P-38 |
| | | Ju-52 dest(grd) | Salzwedel | P-38 |

1-0-0 air
4-0 ground

**Reese, William C., Lt.** (5) Bear City, UT
364th Ftr Sqn/357th Ftr Grp May 1943-May 21, 1944(KIA)
Hit by flak at Stralsund Airfield.

P-51B C5-F 43-12313 "Bear River Betsy"

| *Sqn* | *Date* | *Claims* | *Location* | *A/C* |
|---|---|---|---|---|
| 364th | March 16, 1944 | Me-110 dest(air) | Augsburg | P-51 |
| | | Do-217 dest(air) | Augsburg | P-51 |
| | April 11 | Me-109 dest(air) | E/Hanover | P-51 |
| | April 24 | Me-109 dest(air) | Munich | P-51 |
| | May 12 | Me-109 dest(air) | N/Schweinfurt | P-51 |

5-0-0 air
0-0 ground

**Reinhardt, Edwin D., Lt.** (5) Brecksville, OH
352nd ftr Sqn/353rd Ftr Grp May 1944-November 1944
70 missions, 255 hours

P-47D SX-Y "O.U. Kid-Rack'em Ohio"
S/Sgt. Commodore Collins-c/c
Sgt. Jack Hagen-arm.

| *Sqn* | *Date* | *Claims* | *Location* | *A/C* |
|---|---|---|---|---|
| 352nd | June 7, 1944 | Me-109 dest(grd) | Compiegne | P-47 |
| | June 20 | He-111 dest(grd) | Twente-Enschede | P-47 |
| | August 4 | Me-410 dest(grd) | Plantlunne | P-47 |
| | | He-111 dest(grd) | Plantlunne | P-47 |
| | August 12 | FW-190 dest(grd) | S/Tournan | P-47 |

0-0-0 air
5-0 ground

**Reynolds, Garth L., Capt.** (6) Omaha, NE
77th Ftr Sqn/20th Ftr Grp September 1944-April 1945
59 missions, 310 hours

P-51D LC-S 44-15321

| *Sqn* | *Date* | *Claims* | *Location* | *A/C* |
|---|---|---|---|---|
| 77th | November 2, 1944 | Me-109 dest(air) | Merseburg | P-51 |
| | February 9, 1945 | (2)FW-190 dest(grd) | Esperstadt A/F | P-51 |
| | | (2)Me-110 dest(grd) | Esperstadt A/F | P-51 |
| | February 20 | Me-108 dest(air) | Straubing | P-51 |

2-0-0 air
4-0 ground

**Rice, John J., F/O** (5) Hartford, CT
505th Ftr Sqn/339th Ftr Grp February 1945-July 1945

| *Sqn* | *Date* | *Claims* | *Location* | *A/C* |
|---|---|---|---|---|
| 505th | April 7, 1945 | Me-262 dam(air) | Ulzen | P-51 |
| | April 10 | (2)Do-217 dest(grd) | N/Neuruppin | P-51 |
| | | Do-217 dam(grd) | N/Neuruppin | P-51 |
| | April 16 | (2)Me-109 dest(grd) | NE Prague | P-51 |
| | | Ju-88 dest(grd) | NE Prague | P-51 |
| | | Me-109 dam(grd) | NE Prague | P-51 |
| | | Ju-88 dam(grd) | NE Prague | P-51 |

0-0-1 air
5-3 ground

**Rich, George T., Capt.** (6.5) Wilmington, NC
505th Ftr Sqn/339th Ftr Grp August 1944-April 1945
63 missions

P-51D 6N- 44-14023 "Chute! You're Faded"

| *Sqn* | *Date* | *Claims* | *Location* | *A/C* |
|---|---|---|---|---|
| 505th | September 10, 1944 | FW-190 dest(grd) | Weizenburg | P-51 |
| | September 11 | (2)u/i a/c dest(grd) | Munich | P-51 |
| | | Me-410 dest(grd) | Munich | P-51 |
| | | Me-410 dam(grd) | Munich | P-51 |
| | November 18 | (.5)Me-109 dest(air)* | Neustadt | P-51 |
| | November 21 | Me-109 dest(air) | Warburg | P-51 |
| | March 30, 1945 | Me-262 dam(grd) | N/Luneburg | P-51 |
| | April 4 | Do-217 dest(grd) | NE Tribsees | P-51 |

1.5-0-1 air
5-1 ground

* - shared with Lt. C. Malarz of the 505th Ftr Sqn

**Richards, Vernon R., Lt.** (5.5) Felt Mills, NY
374th Ftr Sqn/361st Ftr Grp June 1943-September 1944
79 missions, 280 hours

P-47D B7-R 42-75452 "Tika"
P-51B B7-R "Tika II"
P-51B B7-R "Tika III"
P-51D B7-R 44-13357 "Tika IV"
S/Sgt. Robert O. Bland-c/c
Sgt. Claude F. Van Pool-ac/c

| *Sqn* | *Date* | *Claims* | *Location* | *A/C* |
|---|---|---|---|---|
| 374th | June 6, 1944 | (.5)Me-109 dest(grd)* | Vendome | P-51 |
| | June 25 | Me-109 dest(air) | S/Caen | P-51 |
| | | FW-190 dest(air) | S/Caen | P-51 |
| | June 29 | (3)FW-190 dest(grd) | Oschersleben | P-51 |
| | | (2)FW-190 dam(grd) | see above | P-51 |
| | | (.5)FW-190 dam(grd)** | see above | P-51 |
| | | (.5)FW-190 dam(grd)@ | see above | P-51 |

2-0-0 air
3.5-3 ground

* - shared with Capt. G.R. Rew of the 374th Ftr Sqn
** - shared with LtCol. W.E. Hopkins of HdQts, 361st Ftr Grp
@ - shared with Lt. R.T. Eckfeldt of the 374th Ftr Sqn

**Rigby, Alden P., Lt.** (5) Logan, UT
487th Ftr Sqn/352nd Ftr Grp July 1944-March 1945
70 missions

P-51D HO-R 44-15629 "Eleen & Jerry"

| *Sqn* | *Date* | *Claims* | *Location* | *A/C* |
|---|---|---|---|---|
| 487th | September 10, 1944 | FW-190 dest(grd) | Wertheim | P-51 |
| | November 27 | Me-109 dest(air) | Minden | P-51 |
| | January 1, 1945 | (2)FW-190 dest(air) | N/Liege | P-51 |
| | | (.5)Me-109 dest(air)* | N/Liege | P-51 |
| | | (.5)Me-109 dest(air)* | N/Liege | P-51 |

4-0-0 air
1-0 ground

* - both shared with an unknown pilot

**Righetti, Elwyn G., LtCol.** (34.5) San Antonio, TX
338th Ftr Sqn/55th Ftr Grp October 1944-February 1945
HdQts/55th Ftr Grp February 1945-April 17, 1945(KIA)
Hit by flak near Dresden and killed by civilians.

P-51D CL-M 44-14223 "Katydid"
P-51D CL-M 44-72227 "Katydid"
T/Sgt. Millard F. Easton-c/c
Sgt. Wayne A. Hunter-ac/c
Sgt. Ruben Robinson-arm.

| *Sqn* | *Date* | *Claims* | *Location* | *A/C* |
|---|---|---|---|---|
| 338th | November 2, 1944 | (.5)Me-109 dest(air)* | SW Leipzig | P-51 |
| | December 24 | (3)FW-190 dest(air) | SE Munster | P-51 |
| | | (2)FW-190 dam(air) | SE Munster | P-51 |
| | January 6, 1945 | (3)Ju-88 dest(grd) | Giebelstadt | P-51 |
| | January 13 | Me-109 dest(air) | W/Wurzburg | P-51 |
| | | Ju-88 dest(grd) | Giebelstadt | P-51 |
| HdQts | February 3 | (2)Ju-88 dest(air) | Boizenburg | P-51 |
| | | FW-190 dest(air) | see above | P-51 |
| | | Ju-88 prob(air) | see above | P-51 |
| | March 21 | (2)FW-190 dest(grd) | Hopsten A/F | P-51 |
| | April 9 | (3)Me-262 dest(grd) | Munich-Brunnthal | P-51 |
| | | (2)u/i a/c dest(grd) | see above | P-51 |
| | | FW-190 dest(grd) | see above | P-51 |
| | | (2)u/i a/c dam(grd) | see above | P-51 |
| | April 16 | (3)He-111 dest(grd) | Bad Aibling | P-51 |
| | | (2)Ju-88 dest(grd) | Autobahn | P-51 |
| | | Si-204 dest(grd) | Munich-Brunnthal | P-51 |
| | | (5)Si-204 dam(grd) | see above | P-51 |
| | | Fi-156 dam(grd) | see above | P-51 |
| | April 17 | (6)u/i a/c dest(grd) | Riess/Canitz | P-51 |
| | | (3)Me-109 dest(grd) | Riess/Canitz | P-51 |
| | | 7.5-1-2 air | | |
| | | 27-8 ground | | |

* - shared with Capt. D.S. Cramer of the 338th Ftr Sqn

**Riley, Paul S., Lt.** (9.5) York, PA
335th Ftr Sqn/4th Ftr Grp September 1943-April 24, 1944 (POW)
Collided with a FW-190 near Worms.

P-47C WD-Y 41-6369
P-51B WD-Y 43-6922

| *Sqn* | *Date* | *Claims* | *Location* | *A/C* |
|---|---|---|---|---|
| 335th | February 20, 1944 | (.5)Me-110 dest(air)* | Coblenz | P-47 |
| | March 4 | Me-109 prob(air) | NW Berlin | P-51 |
| | March 5 | Me-109 dam(air) | S/Bordeaux | P-51 |
| | March 16 | Me-110 dest(air) | SW Munich | P-51 |
| | | Me-110 dam(air) | SW Munich | P-51 |
| | March 29 | Me-109 dest(air) | E/Ulzen | P-51 |
| | April 5 | (.5)He-111 dest(air)** | N/Brandenburg | P-51 |
| | | (2)He-111 dest(grd) | N/Brandenburg | P-51 |
| | April 8 | FW-190 dest(air) | N/Brunswick | P-51 |
| | April 10 | Bu-131 dest(air) | Romorantin A/F | P-51 |
| | | Bu-131 dest(grd) | Romorantin A/F | P-51 |
| | April 22 | (.5)Me-109 dest(air)@ | SW Kassel | P-51 |
| | April 24 | FW-190 dest(air) | N/Mannheim | P-51 |
| | | FW-190 prob(air) | N/Mannheim | P-51 |
| | | 6.5-2-2 air | | |
| | | 3-0 ground | | |

* - shared with Lt. R.I. Reed of the 335th Ftr Sqn
** - shared with Lt. J.W. Goodwyn of the 335th Ftr Sqn
@ - shared with Lt. W.B. Smith of the 334th Ftr Sqn, 4th Ftr Grp

**Rimerman, Ben, LtCol.** (12.5) Omaha, NE
350th Ftr Sqn/353rd Ftr Grp October 1942-November 1943
HdQts/353rd Ftr Grp November 1943-April 1945
HdQts/ 55th Ftr Grp April 1945-EOW
124 missions

P-47D LH-V 42-8001
P-47D LH-V
P-47D LH-V
P-51K LH-V 44-11646
P-51D CY-V 44-72469

| *Sqn* | *Date* | *Claims* | *Location* | *A/C* |
|---|---|---|---|---|
| 350th | September 27, 1943 | Me-109 dest(air) | S/Emden | P-47 |
| | October 14 | FW-190 dest(air) | Duren | P-47 |
| | November 5 | FW-190 dam(air) | Dusseldorf | P-47 |
| | | FW-190 dam(air) | Munchen-Gladbach | P-47 |
| HdQts | March 8, 1944 | FW-190 prob(air) | Hanover | P-47 |
| (353rd) | June 12 | (1.5)Me-109 dest(air)* | S/Paris | P-47 |
| | June 20 | (.5)He-111 dest(grd)** | Plantlunne | P-47 |
| | | (2)u/i a/c dam(grd) | Plantlunne | P-47 |
| | August 2 | Me-109 dest(air) | S/Compiegne | P-47 |
| | August 12 | Ju-88 dest(grd) | SW Coulommiers | P-47 |
| | August 27 | (.5)FW-190 dest(grd)@ | Metz | P-47 |
| | | (.5)Me-109 dam(grd)@ | Metz | P-47 |
| | April 16, 1945 | (3)FW-190 dest(grd) | Reichersberg | P-51 |
| | | Me-109 dest(grd) | see above | P-51 |
| | | Me-108 dest(grd) | see above | P-51 |
| | | Ju-87 dest(grd) | see above | P-51 |
| | | 4.5-1-2 air | | |
| | | 8-2.5 ground | | |

* - shared with Lt. W.J. Frank of the 351st Ftr Sqn, 353rd Ftr Grp
** - shared with Lt. V.G. Rafferty of the 350th Ftr Sqn
@ - both shared with Lt. T.J. Forkin of the 352nd Ftr Sqn, 353rd Ftr Grp

**Roberson, Arval J., Lt.** (7) Los Angeles, CA
362nd Ftr Sqn/357th Ftr Grp June 1943-September 1944
76 missions

P-51B G4-A 43-6688
P-51D G4-A 44-13691 "Passion Wagon"
S/Sgt. Milton F. Lybarger-c/c

| *Sqn* | *Date* | *Claims* | *Location* | *A/C* |
|---|---|---|---|---|
| 362nd | March 6, 1944 | (.5)Me-110 dest(air)* | Berlin | P-51 |
| | March 16 | FW-190 prob(air) | SE Stuttgart | P-51 |
| | March 28 | Ju-88 dest(grd) | S/Paris | P-51 |
| | April 11 | Me-109 dest(air) | E/Magdeburg | P-51 |
| | May 19 | (.5)Me-109 dest(air)** | Hagenow | P-51 |
| | May 30 | (2)Me-109 dest(air) | NE Bernburg | P-51 |
| | September 19 | (2)Me-109 dest(air) | Ijsselstein | P-51 |
| | | 6-1-0 air | | |
| | | 1-0 ground | | |

* - shared with Lt. K.E. Hagen of the 362nd Ftr Sqn
** - shared with Capt. F.E. Adams of the 362nd Ftr Sqn

**Roberts, Eugene P., LtCol.** (9) Spokane, WA
84th Ftr Sqn/ 78th Ftr Grp July 1942-September 1943
HdQts/ 78th Ftr Grp September 1943-December 1943
HdQts/364th Ftr Grp January 1945-November 1945
116 missions

P-47C WZ-Z 41-6630 "Spokane Chief"
P-51D 5E-O 44-15061 "Jimmy the First"
T/Sgt. Negley H. Sapper-c/c(78th)
Sgt. James W. Darrell-ac/c(78th)
Sgt. Russell J. Brooks-arm.(78th)

| *Sqn* | *Date* | *Claims* | *Location* | *A/C* |
|---|---|---|---|---|
| 84th | July 1, 1943 | FW-190 prob(air) | Goederoode Island | P-47 |
| | July 30 | (2)FW-190 dest(air) | Winterswijk | P-47 |
| | | Me-109 dest(air) | Rhenon | P-47 |
| | August 17 | Me-110 dest(air) | SE Aachen | P-47 |
| | August 24 | Me-109 dest(air) | Rouen-Evreux | P-47 |
| | | FW-190 dest(air) | Rouen-Evreux | P-47 |
| HdQts | October 10 | Me-110 dest(air) | W/Enschede | P-47 |
| | | Me-210 dest(air) | W/Enschede | P-47 |
| | October 20 | Me-109 dest(air) | Dinant | P-47 |
| HdQts | April 16, 1945 | (3)Fi-156 dam(grd) | Marienbad | P-51 |
| | | 9-1-0 air | | |
| | | 0-3 ground | | |

**Ruder, Leroy A., Capt.** (5.5) Mekossa, WI
364th Ftr Sqn/357th Ftr Grp June 1943-June 6, 1944(MIA)
Suffered m/f southeast of Cherbourg.

P-51B C5-X "Linda Lu"
P-51B C5-X 42-106768 "Linda Lu"

| *Sqn* | *Date* | *Claims* | *Location* | *A/C* |
|---|---|---|---|---|
| 364th | March 6, 1944 | (1.5)Me-110 dest(air)* | W/Berlin | P-51 |
| | April 11 | FW-190 dest(air) | NE Brunswick | P-51 |
| | May 19 | FW-190 dest(air) | N/Berlin | P-51 |
| | May 27 | Me-109 dest(air) | Strasbourg | P-51 |
| | May 28 | Me-109 dest(air) | NW Magdeburg | P-51 |
| | | 5.5-0-0 air | | |
| | | 0-0 ground | | |

* - shared with Capt. W.R. O'Brien of the 363rd Ftr Sqn, 357th Ftr Grp

**Schank, Thomas D., Lt.** (5) Greeley, CO
338th Ftr Sqn/55th Ftr Grp April 1944-October 1944

P-38J CL-T 42-104106 "Stinger"
P-51D CL-I 44-13668 "Rocky Mtn. Canary"
T/Sgt. Morris Wegman-c/c

| *Sqn* | *Date* | *Claims* | *Location* | *A/C* |
|---|---|---|---|---|
| 338th | June 11, 1944 | Me-109 dest(air) | Beauvais | P-38 |
| | July 25 | (2)Me-109 dest(air) | Dreux | P-51 |
| | | (3)Me-109 dam(air) | Dreux | P-51 |
| | September 13 | Me-109 dest(air) | Gotha-Eisenach | P-51 |
| | September 19 | Me-109 dest(air) | Cologne | P-51 |

5-0-3 air
0-0 ground

**Scheible, Wilbur R., Maj.** (9) Akron, OH
361st Ftr Sqn/356th Ftr Grp June 1944-March 1945
HdQts/356th Ftr Grp March 1945-EOW
70 missions, 245:05 hours

P-47D QI-Z 42-75426
P-51D QI-F 44-15083
S/Sgt. Kenneth A. Withers-c/c(Z)
S/Sgt. Michael Yahwak-c/c(F)
Sgt. Elwin D. Phillips-ac/c(F)

| *Sqn* | *Date* | *Claims* | *Location* | *A/C* |
|---|---|---|---|---|
| 361st | June 15, 1944 | Me-109 dest(air) | SE Rouen | P-47 |
| | October 7 | (2)Me-110 dest(grd) | Fritzlar | P-47 |
| | | Ju-88 dest(grd) | Fritzlar | P-51 |
| | | (4)Ju-88 dam(grd) | Fritzlar | P-51 |
| | November 26 | (3)Me-109 dest(air) | Osnabruck-Dummer Lake | P-51 |
| | | (2)Me-109 dam(air) | see above | P-51 |
| | December 5 | (2)FW-190 dest(air) | Eberswalde | P-51 |

6-0-2 air
3-4 ground

**Schilling, David C., Col.** (33) Leavenworth, KS
62nd Ftr Sqn/56th Ftr Grp June 1941-August 1943
HdQts/56th Ftr Grp August 1943-January 1945
132 missions, 360 hours

P-47D LM-S 42-7938
P-47D LM-S 42-75388
P-47D LM-S 42-75237 "Whack!"
P-47D LM-S 42-26641
P-47M LM-S 44-21125
S/Sgt. Jack T. Holleman-c/c

| *Sqn* | *Date* | *Claims* | *Location* | *A/C* |
|---|---|---|---|---|
| HdQts | October 2, 1943 | Me-109 dest(air) | SE Groningen | P-47 |
| | | FW-190 dest(air) | NE Emden | P-47 |
| | October 4 | Me-110 dest(air) | E/Duren | P-47 |
| | October 8 | FW-190 dest(air) | Quackenbruck | P-47 |
| | October 10 | FW-190 dest(air) | Altenburg | P-47 |
| | November 26 | (2)FW-190 dest(air) | SE Oldenburg | P-47 |
| | | Me-210 dam(air) | SE Oldenburg | P-47 |
| | November 29 | (.5)FW-190 dest(air)* | S/Oldenburg | P-47 |
| | January 11, 1944 | FW-190 dest(air) | Osnabruck | P-47 |
| | | FW-190 dam(air) | Osnabruck | P-47 |
| | January 29 | Me-109 dest(air) | Bonn | P-47 |
| | March 8 | FW-190 dam(air) | Dummer Lake | P-47 |
| | | Me-210 dest(grd) | Dummer Lake | P-47 |
| | March 27 | Ju-52 dest(grd) | Chateaudun | P-47 |
| | March 29 | Me-109 dest(air) | NE Dummer Lake | P-47 |
| | | Me-109 dam(air) | NE Dummer Lake | P-47 |
| | April 9 | (2)FW-190 dest(air) | NE Schleswig | P-47 |
| | | FW-190 dam(air) | NE Schleswig | P-47 |
| | | W-34 dam(air) | Schleswig | P-47 |
| | | Ar-196 dest(grd) | Schleswig | P-47 |
| | April 13 | Me-109 dest(air) | Ludwigshafen | P-47 |
| | July 24 | (.5)Me-210 dest(grd)** | Villaroche | P-47 |
| | | (.5)Me-210 dam(grd)** | Villaroche | P-47 |
| | August 28 | He-111 dest(air) | S/Trier | P-47 |
| | September 5 | (2)FW-190 dest(grd) | Gelnhausen | P-47 |
| | | (2)u/i a/c dest(grd) | Gelnhausen | P-47 |
| | | FW-190 dam(grd) | Gelnhausen | P-47 |
| | September 21 | (3)FW-190 dest(air) | Lochen | P-47 |
| | October 5 | (3)Me-210 dest(grd) | S/Geseke | P-47 |
| | | (3)Me-210 dam(grd) | S/Geseke | P-47 |
| | December 23 | (3)Me-109 dest(air) | Euskirchen-Bonn | P-47 |
| | | (2)FW-190 dest(air) | Euskirchen-Bonn | P-47 |

22.5-0-6 air
10.5-4.5 ground

* - shared with Lt. F.D. Williamson of the 62nd Ftr Sqn
** - shared with Lt. A.J. Bux of the 61st Ftr Sqn, 56th Ftr Grp

**Schiltz, Glen D., Jr., Capt.** (8) North Canton, OH
63rd Ftr Sqn/56th Ftr Grp July 1942-February 1944
200 hours

P-47D UN-Z 42-8269
P-47D UN-Z 42-75232
S/Sgt. Walter L. Harper-c/c

| *Sqn* | *Date* | *Claims* | *Location* | *A/C* |
|---|---|---|---|---|
| 63rd | August 17, 1943 | (3)FW-190 dest(air) | Ans-St. Nicholas | P-47 |
| | | Me-210 dam(air) | see above | P-47 |
| | October 4 | Me-110 dest(air) | E/Duren | P-47 |
| | October 10 | FW-190 dam(air) | W/Munster | P-47 |
| | December 11 | Me-210 dest(air) | Emden | P-47 |
| | January 11, 1944 | (3)Me-109 dest(air) | N/Osnabruck | P-47 |
| | February 21 | Me-109 dam(air) | Zuider Zee | P-47 |

8-0-3 air
0-0 ground

**Schimanski, Robert G., Capt.** (8) Spokane, WA
364th Ftr Sqn/357th Ftr Grp July 1944-April 1945
70 missions, 300 hours

P-51D C5-O 44-14334
S/Sgt. Wilbur Reich-c/c

| *Sqn* | *Date* | *Claims* | *Location* | *A/C* |
|---|---|---|---|---|
| 364th | September 13, 1944 | (.5)Me-109 dest(air)* | E/Bad Frankenhausen | P-51 |
| | November 27 | Me-109 dest(air) | S/Brandenburg | P-51 |
| | December 5 | FW-190 dest(air) | W/Berlin | P-51 |
| | December 24 | Me-109 dest(air) | Kassel | P-51 |
| | March 2, 1945 | (1.5)Me-109 dest(air)** | SE Magdeburg | P-51 |
| | | (2)He-111 dest(grd) | SE Magdeburg | P-51 |
| | March 24 | Me-109 dest(air) | W/Gutersloh | P-51 |
| | | Me-109 dam(air) | W/Gutersloh | P-51 |

6-0-1 air
2-0 ground

* - shared with Maj. J.A. Storch of the 364th Ftr Sqn
** - shared with Lt. D.E. Karger of the 364th Ftr Sqn

**Schlegel, Albert L., Capt.** (13.5) Cleveland, OH
335th Ftr Sqn/4th Ftr Grp July 1943-August 28, 1944(KIA)
Lost for unknown reasons near Strasbourg.

P-47D WD-O 42-7879
P-51B WD-O 43-6725
P-51B WD-O 42-106464
P-51D WD-O 44-14066

| *Sqn* | *Date* | *Claims* | *Location* | *A/C* |
|---|---|---|---|---|
| 335th | October 2, 1943 | Me-109 dest(air) | SE Emden | P-47 |
| | | Me-109 dam(air) | SE Emden | P-47 |
| | February 10, 1944 | (.5)Me-109 prob(air)* | SW Hanover | P-47 |
| | February 24 | FW-190 prob(air) | NW Coblenz | P-47 |
| | March 8 | Me-109 prob(air) | NE Magdeburg | P-51 |
| | March 21 | He-111 dest(air) | S/Saintes | P-51 |
| | March 27 | (.5)FW-190 dam(air)** | Libourne | P-51 |
| | April 5 | He-111 dest(grd) | Brandenburg | P-51 |
| | | Ju-88 dest(grd) | see above | P-51 |
| | | Ju-52 dam(grd) | see above | P-51 |
| | | u/i a/c dam(grd) | see above | P-51 |
| | April 8 | (1.5)FW-190 dest(air)@ | Celle | P-51 |
| | | (.5)Me-109 dest(air)@@ | Celle | P-51 |
| | | FW-190 dest(grd) | Brunswick | P-51 |
| | | FW-190 dam(grd) | Brunswick | P-51 |
| | April 10 | u/i a/c dest(grd) | Romorantin A/F | P-51 |
| | April 15 | He-177 dest(grd) | Hagenow | P-51 |
| | April 22 | (2)Me-109 dest(air) | S/Kassel | P-51 |
| | April 24 | (2.5)FW-190 dest(air)@@ | N/Worms | P-51 |

8.5-2.5-1.5 air
5-3 ground

* - shared with Lt. C.F. Anderson of the 335th Ftr Sqn
** - shared with Capt. J.R. Happel of the 335th Ftr Sqn
@ - both shared with Lt. S.W. Monroe of the 334th Ftr Sqn, 4th Ftr Grp
@@ - shared with Col. D.J.M. Blakeslee of HdQts, 4th Ftr Grp

**Schreiber, Leroy A., Maj.** (14) Plymouth, MA
61st Ftr Sqn/56th Ftr Grp July 1943-August 1943

62nd Ftr Sqn/56th Ftr Grp August 1943-April 15, 1944(KIA)
Hit by flak at Flensburg.

P-47D LM-T 42-74660
P-47D LM-T 42-22537

| *Sqn* | *Date* | *Claims* | *Location* | *A/C* |
|---|---|---|---|---|
| 61st | July 30, 1943 | (2)Me-109 dest(air) | Arnheim | P-47 |
| 62nd | August 24 | FW-190 dest(air) | S/Paris | P-47 |
| | October 8 | FW-190 dest(air) | Quackenbruck | P-47 |
| | November 11 | FW-190 dam(air) | Munster | P-47 |
| | November 29 | (.5)Me-210 dest(air)* | S/Oldenburg | P-47 |
| | February 8, 1944 | Me-109 prob(air) | Cambrai | P-47 |
| | February 11 | Me-109 dam(air) | Namur | P-47 |
| | February 20 | (3)Me-109 dest(air) | Steinhuder Lake | P-47 |
| | | Me-109 dam(air) | see above | P-47 |
| | | Do-217 dam(grd) | see above | P-47 |
| | February 21 | FW-190 dam(air) | Osnabruck | P-47 |
| | February 22 | (.5)FW-190 dest(air)** | Breda | P-47 |
| | March 8 | Me-109 dest(air) | Steinhuder Lake | P-47 |
| | | FW-190 dest(air) | see above | P-47 |
| | March 16 | Me-109 dest(air) | St. Dizier | P-47 |
| | | (.5)FW-190 dest(air)@ | St. Dizier | P-47 |
| | April 8 | (.5)Me-410 dest(grd)@@ | Quackenbruck | P-47 |
| | | (.5)Me-109 dest(grd)@@ | Quackenbruck | P-47 |
| | April 9 | (.5)Me-109 dest(air)# | Lubeck | P-47 |
| | | (3)Me-109 dam(grd) | Lubeck | P-47 |
| | April 15 | He-111 dest(grd) | Schleswig | P-47 |

12-1-4 air
2-4 ground

* - shared with Lt. H.M. Pruden of the 62nd Ftr Sqn
** - shared with Lt. J.E. Fields of the 62nd Ftr Sqn
@ - shared with Lt. A.W. Canizares of the 62nd Ftr Sqn
@@ - both shared with Lt. A.W. Canizares of the 62nd Ftr Sqn
\# - shared with Lt. A.W. Canizares of the 62nd Ftr Sqn

**Schuh, Duerr H., Capt.** (5) Douglas, WY
487th Ftr Sqn/352nd Ftr Grp July 1944-March 1945
67 missions, 272 hours

P-51D HO-A 44-13530 "Dutchess"

| *Sqn* | *Date* | *Claims* | *Location* | *A/C* |
|---|---|---|---|---|
| 487th | September 11, 1944 | Me-109 dest(air) | Einbeck-Gottingen | P-51 |
| | November 2 | Me-109 dest(air) | Merseburg | P-51 |
| | December 26 | (3)Me-109 dest(air) | Veldenbor | P-51 |

5-0-0 air
0-0 ground

**Sears, Alexander F., Capt.** (6) Abilene, TX
487th Ftr Sqn/352nd Ftr Grp June 1944-June 1945

P-51D HO-E 44-14778 "Sheepherder"

| *Sqn* | *Date* | *Claims* | *Location* | *A/C* |
|---|---|---|---|---|
| 487th | June 27, 1944 | FW-190 dest(air) | Noyon | P-51 |
| | July 29 | Me-109 dest(air) | W/Naumberg | P-51 |
| | August 5 | Me-109 dest(air) | S/Hamburg | P-51 |
| | September 11 | u/i a/c dest(grd) | Langensalza | P-51 |
| | December 26 | Me-109 dest(air) | Ollheim | P-51 |
| | January 1, 1945 | Me-109 dest(air) | N/Liege | P-51 |

5-0-0 air
1-0 ground

**Shafer, Dale E., LtCol.** (9) Waynesville, OH
503rd Ftr Sqn/339th Ftr Grp September 1944-September 1945
Earlier flew with the 31st Ftr Grp, 12th Air Force, in the MTO, flying 128 missions and claiming 4 kills: a Me-109 on April 26, 1943; MC-202's on May 6 and June 10, 1943; and a FW-190 on September 10, 1943.
52 missions

P-51D D7-C 44-14671
P-51D D7-C 44-72147

| *Sqn* | *Date* | *Claims* | *Location* | *A/C* |
|---|---|---|---|---|
| 503rd | November 18, 1944 | Me-109 dest(air) | Mannheim | P-51 |
| | December 5 | FW-190 dam(air) | S/Wittstock | P-51 |
| | March 18, 1945 | FW-190 dest(air) | Dummer Lake | P-51 |
| | | FW-190 dam(air) | Dummer Lake | P-51 |
| | April 10 | Me-109 dest(grd) | N/Neuruppin | P-51 |
| | | Ju-88 dest(grd) | see above | P-51 |
| | | (4)Ju-88 dam(grd) | see above | P-51 |
| | April 18 | Ar-234 dest(air) | Regensburg | P-51 |

3-0-2 air
2-4 ground

**Shane, Presson S., Capt.** (5) Junction City, KS
436th Ftr Sqn/479th Ftr Grp January 1945-July 1945

P-51D 9B- "Jayhawk"

| *Sqn* | *Date* | *Claims* | *Location* | *A/C* |
|---|---|---|---|---|
| 436th | April 13, 1945 | Me-410 dest(grd) | Salzwedel | P-51 |
| | | u/i a/c dest(grd) | Salzwedel | P-51 |
| | | Me-109 dam(grd) | Salzwedel | P-51 |
| | April 16 | (2)FW-190 dest(grd) | Landstadt | P-51 |
| | April 17 | Me-109 dest(grd) | Puchhoff | P-51 |

0-0-0 air
5-1 ground

**Sharbo, Walter J., Lt.** (5) Williston, ND
62nd Ftr Sqn/56th Ftr Grp November 1944-EOW

P-47D LM-C "Marion"
P-47M LM-C 44-21237 "North Dakota Kid"

| *Sqn* | *Date* | *Claims* | *Location* | *A/C* |
|---|---|---|---|---|
| 62nd | December 25, 1944 | (2)Me-109 dest(air) | Bonn-Coblenz | P-47 |
| | April 10, 1945 | Me-262 dest(air) | Muritz Lake | P-47 |
| | | (2)He-111 dest(grd) | Neuruppin | P-47 |
| | | He-177 dam(grd) | see above | P-47 |
| | | Ju-88 dam(grd) | see above | P-47 |

3-0-0 air
2-2 ground

**Shaw, Robert M., Capt.** (8) Pittsburgh, PA
364th Ftr Sqn/357th Ftr Grp June 1943-September 1944

P-51B C5-H
P-51D C5-H 44-13815
S/Sgt. Gilbert Krueger-c/c
Sgt. John Roberts-ac/c

| *Sqn* | *Date* | *Claims* | *Location* | *A/C* |
|---|---|---|---|---|
| 364th | April 11, 1944 | Me-109 dest(air) | NE Brunswick | P-51 |
| | April 13 | Me-109 dest(air) | Frankfurt | P-51 |
| | April 24 | Me-109 prob(air) | SE Munich | P-51 |
| | May 13 | (.5)Me-410 dest(air)* | E/Grunberg | P-51 |
| | May 27 | Me-109 dest(air) | SW Strasbourg | P-51 |
| | | Me-109 dam(air) | see above | P-51 |
| | May 30 | (.5)Me-410 dest(air)** | NW Bernburg | P-51 |
| | June 14 | FW-190 dest(air) | E/Paris | P-51 |
| | | FW-190 dam(air) | E/Paris | P-51 |
| | July 5 | FW-190 dest(air) | SE Rouen | P-51 |
| | July 18 | Me-109 dam(air) | NW Rostock | P-51 |
| | August 6 | Me-109 dest(air) | N/Warsaw | P-51 |
| | September 18 | Me-109 dest(air) | N/Maastricht | P-51 |

8-1-3 air
0-0 ground

* - shared with Lt. C.H. Dooley of the 364th Ftr Sqn
** - shared with Lt. J.C. Howell of the 364th Ftr Sqn

**Shupe, Joseph E., Lt.** (7) Bristol, TN
370th Ftr Sqn/359th Ftr Grp January 1944-May 21, 1944(KIA)
Hit by flak in the Lubeck area.

P-47D CS-R
P-51C CS-R 42-103391

| *Sqn* | *Date* | *Claims* | *Location* | *A/C* |
|---|---|---|---|---|
| 370th | April 11, 1944 | Ju-88 dest(grd) | Volkenrod | P-47 |
| | | Ju-88 dam(grd) | Volkenrod | P-47 |
| | May 8 | (2)FW-190 dest(air) | Eschede | P-51 |
| | May 21 | (4)Ju-88 dest(grd) | Schwerin | P-51 |
| | | (3)Ju-88 dam(grd) | Schwerin | P-51 |

2-0-0 air
5-4 ground

**Siems, Grover C., Jr., Lt.** (7.83) Woodside, NY
334th Ftr Sqn/4th Ftr Grp April 1944-July 1944 (WIA July 2, 1944)

P-51D QP-O 44-13322 "Gloria III"

| Sqn | Date | Claims | Location | A/C |
|---|---|---|---|---|
| 334th | April 10, 1944 | (.5)Bu-131 dest(grd)* | Romorantin A/F | P-51 |
| | April 18 | (.33)Me-109 dest(air)** | Fassberg A/F | P-51 |
| | | u/i a/c dam(grd) | Fassberg A/F | P-51 |
| | May 9 | Ju-88 dest(grd) | Reims-Champiegne | P-51 |
| | May 12 | Me-109 dest(air) | Coburg | P-51 |
| | May 21 | (2)Me-210 dest(grd) | Rathenow | P-51 |
| | | (2)Me-210 dam(grd) | Rathenow | P-51 |
| | May 28 | FW-190 dest(air) | Magdeburg | P-51 |
| | June 6 | FW-190 dest(air) | Evreux | P-51 |
| | July 2 | Me-109 dest(air) | Budapest | P-51 |

4.33-0-0 air
3.5-3 ground

* - shared with Lt. G.E. Montgomery of the 334th Ftr Sqn
** - shared with Capt. V.J. France and Lt. N. Megura of the 334th Ftr Sqn

**Silva, Stanley E., Capt.** (7) Pinole, CA
354th Ftr Sqn/355th Ftr Grp October 1944-June 1945

P-51K WR-B 44-11667 "My Catherine S"

| Sqn | Date | Claims | Location | A/C |
|---|---|---|---|---|
| 354th | December 5, 1944 | FW-190 dest(air) | N/Berlin | P-51 |
| | March 22, 1945 | (2)Me-262 dest(grd) | Kitzingen | P-51 |
| | | Me-109 dest(grd) | see above | P-51 |
| | | (3)Me-262 dam(grd) | see above | P-51 |
| | April 13 | (2)Me-109 dest(grd) | Husum | P-51 |
| | | He-111 dest(grd) | Husum | P-51 |
| | | Me-109 dam(grd) | Husum | P-51 |

1-0-0 air
6-4 ground

**Slack, Henry R., IV, Lt.** (8.5) Baltimore, MD
84th Ftr Sqn/78th Ftr Grp November 1944-July 1945
49 missions

P-51K WZ-K 44-11763

| Sqn | Date | Claims | Location | A/C |
|---|---|---|---|---|
| 84th | March 19, 1945 | Me-109 dest(air) | Osnabruck | P-51 |
| | April 7 | (.5)Me-109 dest(air)* | NE Dummer Lake | P-51 |
| | April 10 | FW-190 dest(grd) | Werder A/F | P-51 |
| | | Ju-87 dest(grd) | see above | P-51 |
| | | Ju-52 dest(grd) | see above | P-51 |
| | April 16 | (4)Ju-52 dest(grd) | Praha/Kakewice | P-51 |
| | | Ju-52 dam(grd) | see above | P-51 |
| | | u/i a/c dam(grd) | see above | P-51 |

1.5-0-0 air
7-2 ground

* - shared with Lt. R.K. Corbett of the 84th Ftr Sqn

**Smeltz, Kenneth C., Lt.** (5) Lancaster, PA
55th Ftr Sqn/20th Ftr Grp April 1944-September 1944
53 missions, 272:10 hours

P-38J KI-V
P-51D KI-V 44-13776 "Nancy Gay"
T/Sgt. Robert Asher-c/c

| Sqn | Date | Claims | Location | A/C |
|---|---|---|---|---|
| 55th | August 6, 1944 | FW-190 dest(air) | Schonfeld A/F | P-51 |
| | August 25 | (3)Ju-88 dest(grd) | Parow A/F | P-51 |
| | | (2)Ju-88 dam(grd) | Parow A/F | P-51 |
| | | BV-140 dam(grd) | Parow A/F | P-51 |
| | August 27 | Ju-88 dest(grd) | Habjeerg A/F | P-51 |

1-0-0 air
4-3 ground

**Smigel, Alfred J., Lt.** (5) Garwood, NJ
436th Ftr Sqn/479th Ftr Grp December 1944-EOW

P-51D 9B-U 44-14758 "Chug-A-Lug"
T/Sgt. Kortis-c/c

| Sqn | Date | Claims | Location | A/C |
|---|---|---|---|---|
| 436th | February 22, 1945 | He-111 dest(grd) | Halberstadt | P-51 |
| | | (2)Ju-88 dam(grd) | Halberstadt | P-51 |
| | April 16 | (2)FW-190 dest(grd) | Landstadt | P-51 |
| | | Me-109 dest(grd) | Landstadt | P-51 |
| | April 17 | u/i a/c dest(grd) | Karlsbad | P-51 |
| | | u/i a/c dam(grd) | Karlsbad | P-51 |

0-0-0 air
5-3 ground

**Smith, Donovan F., Maj.** (7.5) Niles, MI
61st Ftr Sqn/56th Ftr Grp November 1942-January 1945
123 missions, 385 hours

P-47C HV-M 41-6319 "Hun Hunter"
P-47D HV-S 42-75393 "Ole Cock"
P-47D HV-S"Ole Cock II"
P-47D HV-S 42-28382 "Ole Cock III"
S/Sgt. Ira E. Lucas-c/c
PFC Berl J. Delp-ac/c
Sgt. James J. Gaynor-arm.

| Sqn | Date | Claims | Location | A/C |
|---|---|---|---|---|
| 61st | July 30, 1943 | Me-109 prob(air) | Nijmegen | P-47 |
| | December 11 | (2)Me-110 dest(air) | Emden | P-47 |
| | | (.5)FW-190 dest(air)* | Emden | P-47 |
| | | Me-110 dam(air) | Emden | P-47 |
| | February 20, 1944 | (2)Me-110 dest(air) | Steinhuder Lake | P-47 |
| | | Me-110 dam(air) | see above | P-47 |
| | February 22 | FW-190 dest(air) | Lippstadt | P-47 |
| | July 20 | He-111 dest(grd) | Bassenheim | P-47 |
| | | He-111 dam(grd) | Bassenheim | P-47 |
| | September 16 | He-177 dest(grd) | Alhorn A/F | P-47 |

5.5-1-2 air
2-1 ground

* - shared with F/O W.R. Aggers of the 61st Ftr Sqn

**Smith, Kenneth G., Capt.** (5) Boise, ID
335th Ftr Sqn/4th Ftr Grp October 1942-March 21, 1944(POW)
Hit by flak near Bordeaux.
Earlier flew with 121 Sqn, RAF

Spitfire AV-
P-47C WD-X 41-6207 "Mark II"
P-51B WD-X 43-6803

| Sqn | Date | Claims | Location | A/C |
|---|---|---|---|---|
| 335th | July 30, 1943 | FW-190 dest(air) | Schouwen | P-47 |
| | March 5, 1944 | (.5)FW-200 dest(air)* | Bergerac A/F | P-51 |
| | March 8 | Me-110 dest(air) | Magdeburg | P-51 |
| | | Bu-181 dam(air) | Magdeburg | P-51 |
| | March 16 | Me-110 dest(air) | Wurm Lake | P-51 |
| | March 18 | FW-190 dest(air) | Gunzburg | P-51 |
| | March 21 | (.5)Fi-156 dest(air)** | NE Bordeaux | P-51 |

5-0-1 air
0-0 ground

* - shared with Lt. E.P. Freeburger of the 335th Ftr Sqn
** - shared with Lt. J.H. Brandenburg of the 335th Ftr Sqn

**Smith, Leslie C., LtCol.** (11.5) Caruthers, CA
61st Ftr Sqn/56th Ftr Grp July 1942-September 1944
62nd Ftr Sqn/56th Ftr Grp September 1944-January 1945
HdQts/56th Ftr Grp January 1945-March 1945
138 missions, 435:05 hours

P-47C HV-S 41-6337
P-47D HV-U 42-26254
P-47D HV-Z 42-26044 "Silver Lady"
P-47D LM-L 44-19925
P-47D LM-L 44-19745
P-47M LM-L
S/Sgt. Joseph B. Gibson-c/c(61st)
Sgt. Ira E. Lucas-ac/c(61st)
Sgt. Ken H. Carlson-ac/c(61st)
Sgt. Joseph M. Gezo-ac/c(61st)

| Sqn | Date | Claims | Location | A/C |
|---|---|---|---|---|
| 61st | July 30, 1943 | FW-190 dam(air) | Arnheim | P-47 |
| | January 21, 1944 | FW-190 dam(air) | NE Rouen | P-47 |
| | February 22 | (2)FW-190 dest(air) | Lippstadt | P-47 |
| | March 8 | FW-190 dam(air) | Steinhuder Lake | P-47 |
| | March 15 | Me-109 dest(air) | Dummer Lake-Solingen | P-47 |
| | March 27 | u/i a/c dam(grd) | Gael A/F | P-47 |
| | April 9 | Me-109 dest(air) | E/Neumunster | P-47 |
| | April 15 | He-111 dest(grd) | Flensburg | P-47 |
| | | He-111 dam(grd) | Flensburg | P-47 |
| | May 19 | (2)FW-190 dest(air) | N/Wernigerode | P-47 |
| 62nd | December 26 | FW-190 dest(air) | Coblenz | P-47 |
| | January 21, 1945 | Ju-88 dest(grd) | Thalheim | P-47 |
| | | (.5)Ju-52 dest(grd)* | Huntingen A/F | P-47 |

| | | | | |
|---|---|---|---|---|
| HdQts | February 27 | (2)u/i a/c dest(grd) | Weimar | P-47 |
| | | (3)u/i a/c dam(grd) | Weimar | P-47 |

7.5-0-3 air
4.5-5 ground

* - shared with Lt. N.D. Gould of the 62nd Ftr Sqn

**Smith, Raymond E., Maj.** (6) Seney, MI
84th Ftr Sqn/78th Ftr Grp October 1943-April 1945

P-47D WZ-N 42-8537
P-51D WZ-B 44-63712 "Fly'n Time Bomb"

| *Sqn* | *Date* | *Claims* | *Location* | *A/C* |
|---|---|---|---|---|
| 84th | January 5, 1944 | Me-109 dam(air) | La Rochelle | P-47 |
| | February 10 | Ju-88 dam(grd) | Soesterberg | P-47 |
| | March 15 | Me-109 dest(air) | W/Munster | P-47 |
| | April 8 | Glider dam(grd) | NE Frankfurt | P-47 |
| | August 17 | (.5)Me-109 dest(grd)* | W/Chaudun | P-47 |
| | | (.5)Me-109 dam(grd)** | W/Chaudun | P-47 |
| | September 10 | (4.5)He-111 dest(grd)@ | Meinbullen | P-47 |
| | | He-111 dam(grd) | Meinbullen | P-47 |

1-0-1 air
5-3.5 ground

* - shared with Lt. R.L. Baron of the 84th Ftr Sqn
** - shared with Lt. P.H. McKenney of the 84th Ftr Sqn
@ - shared with Lt. A.P. Haning of the 84th Ftr Sqn

**Smith, Robert C., Lt.** (5.5) Davison, MI
364th Ftr Sqn/357th Ftr Grp Mid 1943-July 1944

P-51B C5-K 43-6974 "Mr. Period"
S/Sgt. Donald Lumley-c/c
Sgt. Joseph Minervini-ac/c

| *Sqn* | *Date* | *Claims* | *Location* | *A/C* |
|---|---|---|---|---|
| 364th | April 11, 1944 | Me-109 dest(air) | NE Magdeburg | P-51 |
| | April 13 | (.5)Me-109 dest(air)* | Donauworth | P-51 |
| | | Me-109 prob(air) | Frankfurt | P-51 |
| | May 8 | FW-190 dam(air) | S/Hanover | P-51 |
| | May 12 | FW-190 dest(air) | N/Frankfurt | P-51 |
| | May 21 | (3)Me-109 dest(grd) | S/Eichhoff | P-51 |

2.5-1-1 air
3-0 ground

* - shared with Lt. P.D. Fairweather of the 364th Ftr Sqn

**Smith, Vernon A., Lt.** (5) Phillipsburg, VA
63rd Ftr Sqn/56th Ftr Grp January 1945-EOW
12 missions, 61:40 hours

P-47M UN-V 44-21198

| *Sqn* | *Date* | *Claims* | *Location* | *A/C* |
|---|---|---|---|---|
| 63rd | April 10, 1945 | Ju-88 dest(grd) | Werder A/F | P-47 |
| | | u/i a/c dam(grd) | Werder A/F | P-47 |
| | April 13 | (2)He-111 dest(grd) | Eggebeck A/F | P-47 |
| | | (2)Ju-88 dest(grd) | see above | P-47 |
| | | (2)Ju-88 dam(grd) | see above | P-47 |
| | | (2)u/i a/c dam(grd) | see above | P-47 |

0-0-0 air
5-5 ground

**Smith, William B., Capt.** (7.25) Bluefield, VA
334th Ftr Sqn/4th Ftr Grp May 1943-September 13, 1944(KIA)
Hit by flak in the Ulm area.

P-47C QP-Y 41-6410 "Little Butch"
P-51C QP-Y 42-103781
P-51D QP-Y 44-14281

| *Sqn* | *Date* | *Claims* | *Location* | *A/C* |
|---|---|---|---|---|
| 334th | February 28, 1944 | (.25)Ju-88 dest(grd)* | Soissons | P-51 |
| | March 27 | Me-109 dest(air) | Lake Biscarosse | P-51 |
| | | Me-109 dest(grd) | Angouleme | P-51 |
| | April 8 | FW-190 dest(air) | Celle | P-51 |
| | | FW-190 dam(air) | Celle | P-51 |
| | April 11 | (.5)Do-217 dest(air)** | SE Stettin | P-51 |
| | | Me-410 dam(air) | SE Stettin | P-51 |
| | | (2)FW-190 dest(grd) | Stettin | P-51 |
| | April 22 | (.5)Me-109 dest(air)@ | SW Kassel | P-51 |
| | September 13 | u/i a/c dest(grd) | Schwabisch Hall | P-51 |

3-0-2 air
4.5-0 ground

* - shared with Capt. D.W. Beeson and Lt. N. Megura of the 334th Ftr Sqn and Lt. V. Garrison of the 336th Ftr Sqn, 4th Ftr Grp
** - shared with an unknown pilot
@ - shared with Lt. P.S. Riley of the 334th Ftr Sqn

**Sowerby, Theodore J., Capt.** (8.5) Murray, UT
435th Ftr Sqn/479th Ftr Grp July 1944-EOW

| *Sqn* | *Date* | *Claims* | *Location* | *A/C* |
|---|---|---|---|---|
| 435th | August 18, 1944 | Ju-88 dest(grd) | Nancy/Essey | P-38 |
| | | (.5)FW-190 dest(grd)* | see above | P-38 |
| | | (2)He-111 dam(grd) | see above | P-38 |
| | | Ju-88 dam(grd) | see above | P-38 |
| | November 26 | FW-190 dest(air) | Minden | P-51 |
| | December 25 | FW-190 dest(air) | Bonn | P-51 |
| | January 21, 1945 | Ju-52 dest(grd) | Leipheim | P-51 |
| | | Ju-88 dest(grd) | Leipheim | P-51 |
| | April 13 | Ju-88 dest(grd) | Tarnewitz | P-51 |
| | | (4)Ju-88 dam(grd) | Tarnewitz | P-51 |
| | April 17 | (2)Me-262 dest(grd) | Puchhoff | P-51 |

2-0-0 air
6.5-7 ground

* - shared with Lt. T.C. Olson of the 434th Ftr Sqn, 479th Ftr Grp

**Speer, Frank E., Lt.** (6) Allentown, PA
334th Ftr Sqn/4th Ftr Grp April 1944-May 29, 1944(POW)
Hit by flak at Mackfitz Airfield.

P-51B QP-M 43-6957
Sgt. F. Pelosi-arm.

| *Sqn* | *Date* | *Claims* | *Location* | *A/C* |
|---|---|---|---|---|
| 334th | May 21, 1944 | Ju-52 dest(grd) | Rathenow | P-51 |
| | | Ju-88 dest(grd) | Rathenow | P-51 |
| | May 24 | Me-109 dest(air) | E/Hamburg | P-51 |
| | May 29 | (3)He-177 dest(grd) | Mackfitz A/F | P-51 |

1-0-0 air
5-0 ground

**Spencer, Dale F., Lt.** (10) Corry, PA
376th Ftr Sqn/361st Ftr Grp May 1944-September 1944

P-51B E9-S 42-106538 "Little Luke"

| *Sqn* | *Date* | *Claims* | *Location* | *A/C* |
|---|---|---|---|---|
| 376th | May 29, 1944 | (4)Me-410 dest(air) | E/Schwerin | P-51 |
| | June 20 | (.5)BV-138 dest(grd)* | Putnitz | P-51 |
| | July 5 | (2)Me-109 dest(air) | Rouen-Evreux | P-51 |
| | | Me-109 dam(air) | Rouen-Evreux | P-51 |
| | July 7 | (2)Me-109 dest(air) | Wittenburg | P-51 |
| | September 12 | (1.5)Me-109 dest(air)** | W/Magdeburg | P-51 |

9.5-0-1 air
0.5-0 ground

* - shared with Lt. B.D. Welch of the 376th Ftr Sqn
** - shared with Lt. R.W. Ward of the 376th Ftr Sqn

**Stangel, William J., Capt.** (5) Waubun, MN
328th Ftr Sqn/352nd Ftr Grp August 1944-March 1945
Earlier served with the RCAF

P-51D PE-C "Stinky"
P-51D PE-C 44-14015 "Stinky 2"

| *Sqn* | *Date* | *Claims* | *Location* | *A/C* |
|---|---|---|---|---|
| 328th | November 2, 1944 | (2.5)Me-109 dest(air)* | Merseburg | P-51 |
| | | (.5)Me-109 dest(air)* | Merseburg | P-51 |
| | December 25 | (2)Me-109 dest(air) | SW Coblenz | P-51 |

5-0-0 air
0-0 ground

* - both shared with Lt. E.W. James of the 328th Ftr Sqn

**Stanley, Morris A., Capt.** (6.5) Alvin, TX
364th Ftr Sqn/357th Ftr Grp June 1943-November 1944

P-51B C5-Y
P-51D C5-Y 44-13678 "Linda J"

| Sqn | Date | Claims | Location | A/C |
|---|---|---|---|---|
| 364th | March 5, 1944 | FW-200 dest(air) | Parthenay A/F | P-51 |
| | March 6 | Me-110 dest(air) | Brandenburg | P-51 |
| | April 19 | FW-190 dest(air) | Bliecherode | P-51 |
| | May 21 | (1.5)Me-109 dest(grd)* | S/Eichhof | P-51 |
| | May 27 | (2)FW-190 dest(air) | Strasbourg | P-51 |
| | | 5-0-0 air | | |
| | | 1.5-0 ground | | |

* - shared with Maj. I.H. Dregne of HdQts, 357th Ftr Grp

**Starck, Walter E., Capt.** (7) Milwaukee, WI
487th Ftr Sqn/352nd Ftr Grp November 1942-November 27, 1944(POW)
Hit by debris from a Me-109 near Osnabruck.
106 missions, 361 hours

P-47D HO-X 42-8694
P-51B HO-X 43-6929 "Starck Mad"
P-51B HO-X 43-24807 "Starck Mad"
S/Sgt. Keith Stevens-c/c

| Sqn | Date | Claims | Location | A/C |
|---|---|---|---|---|
| 487th | February 10, 1944 | Me-109 dest(air) | Arnheim | P-47 |
| | May 27 | Me-109 dest(air) | Strasbourg | P-51 |
| | June 20 | FW-190 prob(air) | NW Magdeburg | P-51 |
| | July 1 | Me-109 dest(air) | St. Quentin | P-51 |
| | | Me-109 dam(air) | St. Quentin | P-51 |
| | July 21 | Me-109 dest(air) | E/Munich | P-51 |
| | November 21 | FW-190 dam(air) | SW Leipzig | P-51 |
| | November 27 | (2)Me-109 dest(air) | Hameln | P-51 |
| | | Me-109 dest(air) | Osnabruck | P-51 |
| | | 7-1-2 air | | |
| | | 0-0 ground | | |

**Starnes, James R., Capt.** (12) Wilmington, NC
505th Ftr Sqn/339th Ftr Grp States-September 1945
113 missions, 520 hours

P-51B 6N-X 42-106936 "Tarheel"
P-51D 6N-X 44-14113 "Tarheel"
P-51D 6N-X 44-14387 "Tarheel"
P-51D 6N-X 44-72152 "Tarheel"
S/Sgt. Gabe Cutri-c/c
Sgt. Stone Howell-ac/c
Sgt. Fred Harkey-arm.

| Sqn | Date | Claims | Location | A/C |
|---|---|---|---|---|
| 505th | May 19, 1944 | (.5)FW-190 dest(air)* | Gustrow | P-51 |
| | May 21 | (.5)Trainer dest(air)** | Leipzig-Dresden | P-51 |
| | May 29 | FW-190 dest(air) | NE Stettin | P-51 |
| | June 8 | Me-109 dest(air) | Fourgeres | P-51 |
| | | (.5)FW-190 dest(air)@ | Rennes | P-51 |
| | July 11 | Trainer dest(grd) | NE Lake Constance | P-51 |
| | July 19 | Ju-188 dest(grd) | SW Augsburg | P-51 |
| | July 29 | (.5)Me-109 dest(air)@@ | NW Naumberg | P-51 |
| | July 31 | FW-190 dest(grd) | Holzkirchen | P-51 |
| | | u/i a/c dest(grd) | see above | P-51 |
| | | FW-190 dam(grd) | see above | P-51 |
| | August 4 | Me-109 dest(air) | S/Hamburg | P-51 |
| | March 2, 1945 | Me-109 dest(air) | E/Magdeburg | P-51 |
| | | u/i a/c dam(grd) | E/Magdeburg | P-51 |
| | March 3 | He-111 dest(grd) | E/Magdeburg | P-51 |
| | April 10 | Do-217 dest(grd) | N/Neuruppin | P-51 |
| | | (3)Do-217 dam(grd) | N/Neuruppin | P-51 |
| | | 6-0-0 air | | |
| | | 6-5 ground | | |

* - shared with Lt. E.M. Johnson of the 505th Ftr Sqn
** - shared with Lt. J.R. Hanson of the 505th Ftr Sqn
@ - shared with Lt. P.J. McMahan of the 505th Ftr Sqn
@@ - shared with Lt. W.H. Krauss of the 505th Ftr Sqn

**Stewart, David, Lt.** (7) Dallas, TX
79th Ftr Sqn/20th Ftr Grp November 1944-April 10, 1945(POW)
Hit by flak at Werder Airfield.
38 missions, 206:15 hours

P-51D MC-F 44-13751 "Wanda's Worry"
T/Sgt. Norman I. Rasmussen-c/c
Sgt. Douglas M. Forseman-ac/c

| Sqn | Date | Claims | Location | A/C |
|---|---|---|---|---|
| 79th | April 10, 1945 | (3)Me-110 dest(grd) | Werder A/F | P-51 |
| | | (2)FW-190 dest(grd) | Werder A/F | P-51 |
| | | Me-109 dest(grd) | Werder A/F | P-51 |
| | | He-111 dest(grd) | Werder A/F | P-51 |
| | | 0-0-0 air | | |
| | | 7-0 ground | | |

**Stewart, Everett W., Col.** (9.33) Winfield, KS
328th Ftr Sqn/352nd Ftr Grp Early 1943-January 1944
HdQts/355th Ftr Grp January 1944-February 1945
HdQts/ 4th Ftr Grp February 1945-September 1945
Earlier flew 280 hours in the PTO with the 18th Ftr Grp, 7th Air Force.
180 missions, 510 hours

P-47D PE-S 42-8437 "Sunny IV"
P-51B WR-S "Sunny V"
P-51D WR-S 44-13540 "Sunny VI"
P-51D WR-S 44-15255 "Sunny VII"
P-51D WR-S 44-72181 "Sunny VIII"
S/Sgt, Launer-c/c(355th)
Sgt. Gerry Thompson-ac/c(355th)
S/Sgt. Glessner Weckbacher-c/c(4th)
Sgt. Louis Brown-ac/c(4th)
Cpl. Vervene Young-arm.(4th)

| Sqn | Date | Claims | Location | A/C |
|---|---|---|---|---|
| 328th | December 22, 1943 | (.5)Me-110 dest(air)* | Zwolle | P-47 |
| | | Me-210 dam(air) | Zwolle | P-47 |
| | January 5, 1944 | (.33)He-177 dest(air)** | La Ferte Bernard | P-47 |
| HdQts | March 6 | Me-109 dest(air) | NW Hanover | P-47 |
| | March 16 | Me-109 dest(air) | Augsburg-Luneville | P-51 |
| | | Me-109 prob(air) | see above | P-51 |
| | | Me-109 dam(air) | see above | P-51 |
| | March 18 | Me-109 dest(air) | SW Munich | P-51 |
| | March 29 | (2)Me-108 dest(air) | E/Goslar A/F | P-51 |
| | | FW-190 dam(air) | S/Brunswick | P-51 |
| | | (2)Me-108 dam(grd) | Goslar | P-51 |
| | April 11 | Me-410 dest(air) | NW Pyritz | P-51 |
| | | Ju-188 dest(air) | Schau | P-51 |
| | | (2)FW-190 dam(grd) | Sorau | P-51 |
| | September 27 | (.5)Ju-88 dest(grd)@ | Eschwege | P-51 |
| | February 9, 1945 | Ju-188 dest(grd) | Kothen | P-51 |
| | | (2)Ju-188 dam(grd) | Kothen | P-51 |
| HdQts | March 3 | Me-262 dam(air) | Gardelegen | P-51 |
| | | 7.83-1-4 air | | |
| | | 1.5-6 ground | | |

* - shared with Lt. R.H. Powell of the 328th Ftr Sqn
** - shared with Lt. J.B. Coleman and Lt. R.H. Powell of the 328th Ftr Sqn
@ - shared with Lt. H.R. Mann of the 354th Ftr Sqn, 355th Ftr Grp

**Stewart, Henry M., II, Capt.** (5) South Braintree, MA
487th Ftr Sqn/352nd Ftr Grp June 1944-February 1945
Earlier flew with the 50th Ftr Sqn in Iceland.

P-51D HO-N 44-13321 "The Margarets"
P-51D HO-N 44-14716 "The Margarets"

| Sqn | Date | Claims | Location | A/C |
|---|---|---|---|---|
| 487th | September 11, 1944 | Ju-88 dest(grd) | Gotha | P-51 |
| | | (2)Ju-88 dam(grd) | Gotha | P-51 |
| | November 27 | Me-109 dest(air) | Hameln | P-51 |
| | January 1, 1945 | (3)Me-109 dest(air) | N/Liege | P-51 |
| | | 4-0-0 air | | |
| | | 1-2 ground | | |

**Stewart, James C., LtCol.** (12.5) Corona, CA
HdQts/56th Ftr Grp July 1943-January 1944
61st Ftr Sqn/56th Ftr Grp January 1944-April 1944
HdQts/56th Ftr Grp April 1944-April 1944
200 hours

P-47D HV-Q 42-74650
P-47D HV-S 42-75658

| Sqn | Date | Claims | Location | A/C |
|---|---|---|---|---|
| HdQts | October 14, 1943 | Me-110 dam(air) | W/Aachen | P-47 |
| | October 18 | (.5)Me-210 dest(air)* | NE Maastricht | P-47 |
| | November 26 | Do-217 dest(air) | SE Oldenburg | P-47 |
| | January 5, 1944 | FW-190 dest(air) | SW Bonn | P-47 |
| 61st | February 11 | FW-190 dest(air) | Duren | P-47 |
| | February 22 | Me-109 dest(air) | SW Munster | P-47 |
| | February 24 | FW-190 dest(air) | Kassel | P-47 |

| Sqn | Date | Claims | Location | A/C |
|---|---|---|---|---|
| | March 6 | (2)FW-190 dest(air) | N/Dummer Lake | P-47 |
| | March 8 | FW-190 dest(air) | S/Steinhuder Lake | P-47 |
| | | Me-110 dest(air) | see above | P-47 |
| | March 15 | Me-109 dam(air) | Dummer Lake | P-47 |
| | March 20 | (2)Me-109 dest(air) | S/Charleville | P-47 |
| | | Me-109 prob(air) | see above | P-47 |
| HdQts | April 24 | Ju-87 dest(grd) | Thronville | P-47 |
| | | Ju-87 dam(grd) | Thronville | P-47 |
| | | u/i a/c dam(grd) | Thronville | P-47 |
| | April 29 | Me-109 dam(air) | W/Steinhuder Lake | P-47 |

11.5-1-3 air
1-2 ground

* - shared with Lt. M.C. Wood of the 61st Ftr Sqn

**Storch, John A., LtCol.** (12) Long Beach, CA
364th Ftr Sqn/357th Ftr Grp February 1943-May 1945

P-51B C5-R "The Shillelagh"
P-51D C5-R 44-13546 "The Shillelagh"
P-51D C5-R 44-72164 "The Shillelagh"
S/Sgt. Ardell Fiedler-c/c
Sgt. Joseph Kubarek-ac/c

| *Sqn* | *Date* | *Claims* | *Location* | *A/C* |
|---|---|---|---|---|
| 364th | May 12, 1944 | (.5)FW-190 dest(air)* | NE Frankfurt | P-51 |
| | May 19 | Me-109 dest(air) | NE Salzwedel | P-51 |
| | May 21 | Me-109 dest(grd) | S/Eichhof | P-51 |
| | | (.5)FW-44 dest(grd)** | S/Eichhof | P-51 |
| | May 27 | (2)Me-109 dest(air) | Strasbourg | P-51 |
| | | (.5)FW-190 dest(air)@ | Strasbourg | P-51 |
| | June 20 | (.5)Me-109 dest(air)@@ | Pasewalk | P-51 |
| | August 6 | FW-190 dam(air) | Danzig | P-51 |
| | August 7 | (.5)Me-109 dest(air)# | Oswiecim | P-51 |
| | September 13 | (1.5)Me-109 dest(air)## | E/Bad Frankenhausen | P-51 |
| | January 14, 1945 | (2)FW-190 dest(air) | S/Schwerin | P-51 |
| | | Me-109 dest(air) | S/Schwerin | P-51 |
| | February 28 | (2)u/i a/c dam(grd) | Lubeck-Blankensee | P-51 |
| | March 24 | Me-109 dest(air) | W/Gutersloh | P-51 |

10.5-0-1 air
1.5-2 ground

* - shared with Capt. R.A. Peterson of the 364th Ftr Sqn
** - shared with Lt. C.H. Dooley of the 364th Ftr Sqn
@ - shared with Lt. E. Zellner of the 352nd Ftr Grp
@@ - shared with Lt. L.A. Fecher of the 364th Ftr Sqn
# - shared with Lt. H.R. Nowlin of the 364th Ftr Sqn
## - shared with Lt. R.G. Schimanski of the 364th Ftr Sqn

**Strait, Donald J., Maj.** (13.5) Verona, NJ
361st Ftr Sqn/356th Ftr Grp February 1943-March 1945
120 missions, 429:15 hours

P-47D QI-T 42-8640 "Jersey Jerk"
P-47D QI-T 42-25844 "Jersey Jerk"
P-47D QI-T 42-76564 "Jersey Jerk"
P-47D QI-T 42-28827 "Jersey Jerk"
P-51D QI-T 44-15152 "Jersey Jerk"
S/Sgt. Gilbert T. Watson-c/c
Sgt. Edward Burns-ac/c
Sgt. James W. Shuff-arm.

| *Sqn* | *Date* | *Claims* | *Location* | *A/C* |
|---|---|---|---|---|
| 361st | February 6, 1944 | FW-190 dest(air) | Paris-Soissons | P-47 |
| | February 10 | Me-109 dest(air) | NE Lingen | P-47 |
| | May 19 | Me-109 dest(air) | Quackenbruck | P-47 |
| | November 26 | (1.5)Me-109 dest(air)* | Osnabruck-Dummer Lake | P-51 |
| | December 5 | (2)FW-190 dest(air) | Eberswalde | P-51 |
| | December 25 | Me-109 dest(air) | SW Coblenz | P-51 |
| | January 14, 1945 | FW-190 dest(air) | SW Dummer Lake | P-51 |
| | February 14 | (2)FW-190 dest(air) | S/Chemnitz | P-51 |
| | February 20 | (3)Fi-156 dest(air) | SE Bayreuth | P-51 |

13.5-0-0 air
0-0 ground

* - shared with Lt. S.N. Jett of the 361st Ftr Sqn

**Sublett, John L., Capt.** (9) Odessa, TX
362nd Ftr Sqn/357th Ftr Grp September 1944-April 1945

P-51D G4-Q 44-11190 "Lady Ovella"
S/Sgt. Avery G. Goodrich-c/c

| *Sqn* | *Date* | *Claims* | *Location* | *A/C* |
|---|---|---|---|---|
| 362nd | November 25, 1944 | FW-44 dest(grd) | Marburg | P-51 |
| | November 27 | (3)FW-190 dest(air) | S/Magdeburg | P-51 |
| | January 14, 1945 | (2)Me-109 dest(air) | NW Berlin | P-51 |
| | March 2 | Me-109 dest(air) | NE Leipzig | P-51 |
| | | FW-190 dest(air) | NE Leipzig | P-51 |
| | March 3 | Me-262 dam(air) | NE Magdeburg | P-51 |
| | March 20 | Me-109 dest(air) | Quackenbruck | P-51 |

8-0-1 air
1-0 ground

**Sweat, Dale S., Lt.** (5) Lafayette, IL
83rd Ftr Sqn/78th Ftr Grp March 1945-EOW
7 missions

No regular a/c or crew

| *Sqn* | *Date* | *Claims* | *Location* | *A/C* |
|---|---|---|---|---|
| 83rd | April 16, 1945 | (2)FW-190 dest(grd) | N/Prague | P-51 |
| | | (2)Ju-87 dest(grd) | N/Prague | P-51 |
| | | u/i a/c dest(grd) | N/Prague | P-51 |
| | | (2)FW-190 dam(grd) | N/Prague | P-51 |
| | | Ju-87 dam(grd) | N/Prague | P-51 |

0-0-0 air
5-3 ground

**Sykes, Henry S., Lt.** (5) Burlington, IA
487th Ftr Sqn/352nd Ftr Grp August 1944-July 1945

| *Sqn* | *Date* | *Claims* | *Location* | *A/C* |
|---|---|---|---|---|
| 487th | April 16, 1945 | (3)u/i a/c dest(grd) | Ganacker | P-51 |
| | | Me-109 dest(grd) | Ganacker | P-51 |
| | | Fi-156 dest(grd) | Ganacker | P-51 |
| | | Me-109 dam(grd) | Ganacker | P-51 |
| | | u/i a/c dam(grd) | Ganacker | P-51 |

0-0-0 air
5-2 ground

**Sykes, William J., Lt.** (10) Atlantic City, NJ
376th Ftr Sqn/361st Ftr Grp June 1944-December 24, 1944(POW)
Hit by e/a near Wengerohr.
68 missions, 272 hours

P-51D E9-S 44-14520 "Wilma Lee"
S/Sgt. Ralph A. Nye-c/c

| *Sqn* | *Date* | *Claims* | *Location* | *A/C* |
|---|---|---|---|---|
| 376th | September 27, 1944 | FW-190 dest(air) | Eisenach | P-51 |
| | | (2)Me-410 dest(grd) | Eisenach | P-51 |
| | November 2 | Me-109 dest(air) | Erfurt | P-51 |
| | | FW-190 dest(air) | N/Erfurt | P-51 |
| | November 27 | Me-109 dest(air) | S/Munster | P-51 |
| | | Me-109 prob(air) | S/Munster | P-51 |
| | | (2)Me-410 dest(grd) | Munster | P-51 |
| | | Me-110 dest(grd) | Munster | P-51 |
| | December 24 | Me-109 dest(air) | Wengerohr | P-51 |
| | | Me-109 prob(air) | Wengerohr | P-51 |

5-2-0 air
5-0 ground

**Szaniawski, Edward W., LtCol.** (7.66) Scarsdale, NY
357th Ftr Sqn/355th Ftr Grp February 1943-May 19, 1944(POW)
Hit by flak at Diepholz Airfield.

P-47D OS-A 42-8415 "Available Jones"
P-47D OS-A "Available Jones 2nd"
P-51B OS-A "Available Jones 3rd"
P-51B OS-A "Available Jones 4th"
P-51B OS-A 43-7142 "Available Jones 5th"
S/Sgt. Schultz-c/c

| *Sqn* | *Date* | *Claims* | *Location* | *A/C* |
|---|---|---|---|---|
| 357th | February 11, 1944 | (2)Me-109 dest(air) | S/Koln | P-47 |
| | March 28 | Me-110 dest(grd) | Dijon | P-51 |
| | | Me-410 dest(grd) | Dijon | P-51 |
| | | Ju-88 dest(grd) | Dijon | P-51 |
| | | (3)Ju-88 dam(grd) | Dijon | P-51 |
| | | Me-210 dam(grd) | Dijon | P-51 |
| | April 8 | Me-109 dest(air) | Meppen | P-51 |
| | | Me-109 dam(air) | Meppen | P-51 |
| | April 13 | Me-109 dest(air) | Augsburg | P-51 |
| | | Me-109 prob(air) | Augsburg | P-51 |
| | | Me-109 dam(air) | Augsburg | P-51 |
| | | (.33)Me-110 dest(grd)* | Crailsheim | P-51 |

| Sqn | Date | Claims | Location | A/C |
|---|---|---|---|---|
| | | (.33)Me-323 dest(grd)[**] | Crailsheim | P-51 |

4-1-2 air
3.66-4 ground

[*] - shared with Lt. R.F. DeMers and Lt. R.L. Norman of the 357th Ftr Sqn
[**] - shared with Lt. J.F. Kerch and Lt. R.L. Norman of the 357th Ftr Sqn

**Tanner, William F., Maj.** (6.5) Canastota, NY
350th Ftr Sqn/353rd Ftr Grp December 1942-July 1945
135 missions

P-47D LH-O "Prudence"
P-47D LH-O 42-74669 "Prudence II"
P-47D LH-O "Prudence III"
P-47D LH-O "Prudence IV"
P-47D LH-O 42-26472 "Prudence V"
P-51D LH-O "Prudence VI"
P-51D LH-O 44-72212 "Prudence 7th"
S/Sgt. Leo Flint-c/c

| *Sqn* | *Date* | *Claims* | *Location* | *A/C* |
|---|---|---|---|---|
| 350th | October 10, 1943 | FW-190 dest(air) | Hengelo | P-47 |
| | January 30, 1944 | FW-190 dest(air) | Zuider Zee | P-47 |
| | April 9 | He-115 dam(grd) | Eckenforder Bay | P-47 |
| | May 12 | (.5)Me-109 dest(air)[*] | Selters | P-47 |
| | June 12 | (2)Me-109 dest(air) | SW Paris | P-47 |
| | November 18 | He-177 dest(grd) | Lechfeld | P-51 |
| | December 5 | FW-190 dest(air) | S/Steinhuder Lake | P-51 |
| | | FW-190 dam(air) | S/Steinhuder Lake | P-51 |

5.5-0-1 air
1-1 ground

[*] - shared with Lt. K. Chetwood of the 350th Ftr Sqn

**Taylor, Clyde E., Lt.** (9) Jermyn, PA
84th Ftr Sqn/78th Ftr Grp January 1945-July 1945
25 missions, 137:30 hours

P-51D WZ-C 44-63842
S/Sgt. Brown-c/c

| *Sqn* | *Date* | *Claims* | *Location* | *A/C* |
|---|---|---|---|---|
| 84th | March 1, 1945 | u/i a/c dam(grd) | Boblingen | P-51 |
| | April 16 | (4)Ju-52 dest(grd) | Praha/Kakewice | P-51 |
| | | (3)Me-110 dest(grd) | see above | P-51 |
| | | FW-190 dest(grd) | see above | P-51 |
| | | He-111 dest(grd) | see above | P-51 |
| | | FW-190 dam(grd) | see above | P-51 |

0-0-0 air
9-2 ground

**Taylor, Willis B., Capt.** (5) Sarasota, FL
55th Ftr Sqn/20th Ftr Grp October 1942-October 19, 1944(POW)
Suffered m/f near Boppard.
57 missions, 263:30 hours

P-38J KI-U 42-67482
P-38J KI-U 42-67907
P-51D KI-U

| *Sqn* | *Date* | *Claims* | *Location* | *A/C* |
|---|---|---|---|---|
| 55th | January 7, 1944 | Me-109 dest(air) | Worms | P-38 |
| | February 10 | Me-109 dest(air) | NW Hanover | P-38 |
| | April 24 | Me-109 dest(air) | W/Worms | P-38 |
| | October 6 | Do-24 dest(grd) | Kubitzer Bay | P-51 |
| | | u/i a/c dest(grd) | Kubitzer Bay | P-51 |

3-0-0 air
2-0 ground

**Thornell, John F., Jr., Capt.** (19.25) East Walpole, MA
328th Ftr Sqn/352nd Ftr Grp February 1943-July 1944
90 missions, 290:50 hours

P-47D PE-I 42-22474 "Patti Ann"
P-51B PE-T 42-106872 "Patty Ann"
S/Sgt. G.A. McIndoo-c/c
Sgt. John Walters-ac/c
Sgt. H.J. Whiteley-arm.

| *Sqn* | *Date* | *Claims* | *Location* | *A/C* |
|---|---|---|---|---|
| 328th | January 30, 1944 | Me-109 dest(air) | Ruhlertwist | P-47 |
| | | Me-109 dam(air) | Ruhlertwist | P-47 |
| | March 15 | (2)Me-109 dest(air) | Heusden | P-47 |
| | March 22 | (.25)FW-200 dest(air)[*] | Hesepe | P-47 |
| | April 10 | FW-190 dest(air) | Dormans | P-47 |
| | April 19 | (2)FW-190 dest(air) | SW Kassel | P-51 |
| | | FW-190 dam(air) | SW Kassel | P-51 |
| | May 8 | (3)Me-109 dest(air) | Nienburg | P-51 |
| | May 21 | (2)He-111 dest(grd) | Alt Ruppin | P-51 |
| | | He-177 dam(grd) | Alt Ruppin | P-51 |
| | May 27 | (2)Me-109 dest(air) | S/Strasbourg | P-51 |
| | May 28 | Me-109 dest(air) | W/Magdeburg | P-51 |
| | May 29 | (2)Me-109 dest(air) | N/Neubrandenburg | P-51 |
| | June 10 | (2)Me-109 dest(air) | Bayeux | P-51 |
| | June 12 | (.5)Me-109 dest(air)[**] | S/St. Malo | P-51 |
| | June 21 | (.5)Me-410 dest(air)[@] | Dahmsdorf | P-51 |

17.25-0-2 air
2-1 ground

[*] - shared with Capt. E.L. Abbott, Lt. R.C. Brookins, and Lt. E. Zellner of the 328th Ftr Sqn
[**] - shared with Lt. L.E. McCarthy of the 328th Ftr Sqn
[@] - shared with Lt. S.E. Dyke of the 328th Ftr Sqn

**Thury, Joseph L., LtCol.** (28) Clearwater, FL
505th Ftr Sqn/339th Ftr Grp August 1943-July 1945

P-51B 6N-C "Pauline"
P-51D 6N-C 44-14656 "Pauline"
P-51D 6N-C 44-15616 "Pauline"
P-51D 6N-C 44-72437 "Pauline"
S/Sgt. Thomas Miller-c/c

| *Sqn* | *Date* | *Claims* | *Location* | *A/C* |
|---|---|---|---|---|
| 505th | May 27, 1944 | Fi-156 dest(grd) | Frankfurt | P-51 |
| | | He-111 dest(grd) | Frankfurt | P-51 |
| | | Fi-156 dam(grd) | Frankfurt | P-51 |
| | | u/i a/c dam(grd) | Frankfurt | P-51 |
| | May 29 | FW-190 dest(air) | NE Stettin | P-51 |
| | June 27 | FW-190 dest(air) | SE Paris | P-51 |
| | July 19 | Me-109 dest(grd) | SW Augsburg | P-51 |
| | | u/i a/c dest(grd) | SW Augsburg | P-51 |
| | July 31 | (2)u/i a/c dest(grd) | Holzkirchen | P-51 |
| | | (.5)Me-410 dest(grd)[*] | see above | P-51 |
| | | u/i a/c dam(grd) | see above | P-51 |
| | September 10 | Ju-88 dest(grd) | Weizenburg | P-51 |
| | | Ju-52 dest(grd) | Weizenburg | P-51 |
| | September 11 | (2)Ju-88 dest(grd) | Munich | P-51 |
| | | Me-109 dam(grd) | Munich | P-51 |
| | | Me-410 dam(grd) | Munich | P-51 |
| | | He-111 dam(grd) | Munich | P-51 |
| | | Ju-88 dam(grd) | Munich | P-51 |
| | March 1, 1945 | Ju-88 dest(grd) | S/Feldkirchen | P-51 |
| | March 3 | (3)Ju-88 dest(grd) | Mockburn | P-51 |
| | | Do-217 dest(grd) | Mockburn | P-51 |
| | | Ju-88 dam(grd) | Mockburn | P-51 |
| | April 7 | (.5)Me-109 dest(air)[**] | NE Steinhuder L. | P-51 |
| | April 10 | (2)u/i a/c dest(grd) | N/Neuruppin | P-51 |
| | | Ju-88 dest(grd) | see above | P-51 |
| | | He-111 dam(grd) | see above | P-51 |
| | | u/i a/c dam(grd) | see above | P-51 |
| | April 16 | Me-109 dest(grd) | NE Prague | P-51 |
| | | Me-262 dest(grd) | NE Prague | P-51 |
| | April 17 | (2)Me-109 dest(grd) | SE Pocking | P-51 |
| | | (2)FW-190 dest(grd) | SE Pocking | P-51 |
| | | Ju-88 dest(grd) | SE Pocking | P-51 |
| | April 18 | Me-262 dam(air) | Tabor | P-51 |

2.5-0-1 air
25.5-10 ground

[*] - shared with Lt. G.E. Graham of the 505th Ftr Sqn
[**] - shared with Lt. O.K. Biggs of the 505th Ftr Sqn

**Thwaites, David F., Capt.** (7) Conshohocken, PA
361st Ftr Sqn/356th Ftr Grp December 1943-September 1944
90 missions, 293:50 hours

P-47D QI-L 42-75214 "Polly"
P-47D QI-L 42-26457 "Polly"
S/Sgt. Lionel F. Ratte-c/c
Sgt. Frank Strozzi-ac/c

| *Sqn* | *Date* | *Claims* | *Location* | *A/C* |
|---|---|---|---|---|
| 361st | January 21, 1944 | (.5)Ju-88 dest(air)[*] | Cambrai | P-47 |
| | February 13 | Me-109 dest(air) | SW Paris | P-47 |
| | May 13 | FW-190 dest(air) | Hamburg | P-47 |
| | May 19 | FW-190 dest(air) | Quackenbruck-Brunswick | P-47 |
| | | (3)FW-190 dam(air) | see above | P-47 |
| | May 25 | Me-109 dest(air) | Neufchateau | P-47 |

| | Date | Claims | Location | A/C |
|---|---|---|---|---|
| | June 7 | Ju-52 dest(grd) | Laval | P-47 |
| | August 4 | Me-109 dest(air) | Bremen-Hamburg | P-47 |
| | September 5 | (.5)He-111 dest(air)** | Twente/Enschede | P-47 |

6-0-3 air
1-0 ground

*- shared with Lt. S.H. Hewett of the 361st Ftr Sqn
**- shared with Lt. F.A. Morgan of the 361st Ftr Sqn

**Timony, Eugene J., Lt.** (5) Lakewood, OH
63rd Ftr Sqn/56th Ftr Grp April 1944-September 1944
70 missions, 270 hours

P-47D UN-T 42-26258 "Moptop's Pride"

| Sqn | Date | Claims | Location | A/C |
|---|---|---|---|---|
| 63rd | September 5, 1944 | FW-190 dest(air) | S/Coblenz | P-47 |
| | | (2)Bu-131 dest(grd) | Gelnhausen | P-47 |
| | | FW-190 dest(grd) | Gelnhausen | P-47 |
| | September 8 | Ju-88 dest(grd) | Euskirchen | P-47 |

1-0-0 air
4-0 ground

**Tordoff, Harrison B., Capt.** (9.5) Mechanicsville, NY
352nd Ftr Sqn/353rd Ftr Grp June 1944-EOW
85 missions

P-47D SX-L "Ann"
P-51D SX-L 44-14805 "Upupa E Pops!"
P-51D SX-L 44-72364 "Upupa E Pops!"

| Sqn | Date | Claims | Location | A/C |
|---|---|---|---|---|
| 352nd | August 4, 1944 | (2)Me-109 dest(air) | E/Bremen | P-47 |
| | | He-111 dest(grd) | Plantlunne | P-47 |
| | | u/i a/c dest(grd) | Plantlunne | P-47 |
| | September 27 | Me-109 dest(air) | Hanau | P-47 |
| | March 31, 1945 | Me-262 dest(air) | Dessau | P-51 |
| | April 7 | Me-109 dest(air) | E/Hamburg | P-51 |
| | April 16 | Me-109 dest(grd) | Bad Aibling | P-51 |
| | | Do-217 dest(grd) | see above | P-51 |
| | | (.5)Ju-88 dest(grd)* | see above | P-51 |
| | | u/i a/c dam(grd) | see above | P-51 |

5-0-0 air
4.5-1 ground

*-shared with Lt. J.G. Bartley of the 352nd Ftr Sqn

**Tower, Archie A., Maj.** (19.5) Winthrop, NY
505th Ftr Sqn/339th Ftr Grp January 1944-September 1945

P-51B 6N-D "Lucky Boy"
P-51D 6N-D 44-73074 "Lucky Boy"
S/Sgt. Thad Sulina-c/c
Sgt. Herbert Ward-ac/c

| Sqn | Date | Claims | Location | A/C |
|---|---|---|---|---|
| 505th | June 8, 1944 | FW-190 dest(air) | Laigle | P-51 |
| | | (.5)Do-217 dest(air)* | Laigle | P-51 |
| | July 19 | Ju-188 dest(grd) | SW Augsburg | P-51 |
| | September 10 | Ju-88 dest(grd) | Munich | P-51 |
| | | Ju-52 dest(grd) | Munich | P-51 |
| | | (2)He-111 dam(grd) | Munich | P-51 |
| | | Ju-88 dam(grd) | Munich | P-51 |
| | September 11 | (2)Ju-88 dest(grd) | Munich | P-51 |
| | | He-111 dest(grd) | Munich | P-51 |
| | | Me-410 dest(grd) | Munich | P-51 |
| | | Ju-87 dest(grd) | Munich | P-51 |
| | | (2)Ju-88 dam(grd) | Munich | P-51 |
| | March 24, 1945 | FW-190 dam(grd) | Ziegenhall | P-51 |
| | April 4 | (2)Me-410 dest(grd) | NE Tribsees | P-51 |
| | April 10 | (2)Do-217 dest(grd) | Wittstock | P-51 |
| | | (2)Me-410 dest(grd) | see above | P-51 |
| | | (2)Hs-129 dest(grd) | see above | P-51 |
| | | (2)Ju-88 dest(grd) | see above | P-51 |
| | | Do-217 dam(grd) | see above | P-51 |
| | | Me-410 dam(grd) | see above | P-51 |

1.5-0-0 air
18-8 ground

*- shared with Lt. W.R. Opitz of the 505th Ftr Sqn

**Truett, Jesse L., Capt.** (6.5) Artesia, NM
383rd Ftr Sqn/364th Ftr Grp September 1944-July 1945
60 missions

P-51D N2-Q
T/Sgt. Steven R. Bedice-c/c

| Sqn | Date | Claims | Location | A/C |
|---|---|---|---|---|
| 383rd | April 13, 1945 | (4)Ju-52 dest(grd) | Flensburg | P-51 |
| | | Do-217 dest(grd) | Flensburg | P-51 |
| | | Me-109 dam(grd) | Flensburg | P-51 |
| | | FW-190 dam(grd) | Flensburg | P-51 |
| | April 16 | Fi-156 dest(grd) | Marienbad | P-51 |
| | | (.5)FW-190 dest(grd)* | Marienbad | P-51 |
| | | Do-217 dam(grd) | Marienbad | P-51 |
| | | Fi-156 dam(grd) | Marienbad | P-51 |

0-0-0 air
6.5-4 ground

*- shared with Lt. G.F. Hill of the 383rd Ftr Sqn

**Truluck, John H., Capt.** (8) Lynchburg, SC
63rd Ftr Sqn/56th Ftr Grp May 1943-April 1944
71 missions, 201:30 hours

P-47D UN-L 42-74750 "Lady Jane"
S/Sgt. James Walker-c/c
Pvt. John E. Carbough-ac/c
Sgt. John C. Massey-arm.

| Sqn | Date | Claims | Location | A/C |
|---|---|---|---|---|
| 63rd | August 17, 1943 | FW-190 dest(air) | Ans-St. Nicholas | P-47 |
| | | Me-210 dam(air) | Ans-St. Nicholas | P-47 |
| | September 27 | Me-109 dest(air) | Borkum Island | P-47 |
| | | FW-190 dest(air) | Borkum Island | P-47 |
| | November 26 | FW-190 dest(air) | Friesoythe | P-47 |
| | | Me-110 dam(air) | Friesoythe | P-47 |
| | February 24 | FW-190 dest(air) | Herford | P-47 |
| | March 8 | Me-109 dest(air) | Dummer Lake | P-47 |
| | March 15 | FW-190 dest(air) | Hanover | P-47 |
| | | Me-109 dam(air) | Hanover | P-47 |
| | April 24 | Do-217 dest(grd) | Thalheim A/F | P-47 |
| | | (3)Do-217 dam(grd) | Thalheim A/F | P-47 |

7-0-3 air
1-3 ground

**Turley, Grant M., Lt.** (6) Aripine, AZ
82nd Ftr Sqn/78th Ftr Grp September 1943-March 6, 1944(KIA)
Hit by e/a near Haselvenne.
47 missions, 113 hours

P-47D MX-N 42-7998 "Kitty"
S/Sgt. Alfred Turrow-c/c
Sgt. Albert Costelnik-ac/c
Sgt. James Sterner-arm.

| Sqn | Date | Claims | Location | A/C |
|---|---|---|---|---|
| 82nd | February 10, 1944 | (2)Me-109 dest(air) | Osnabruck | P-47 |
| | February 11 | Me-109 dest(air) | Verdun | P-47 |
| | | FW-190 dest(air) | Verdun | P-47 |
| | February 20 | FW-190 dest(air) | Coblenz | P-47 |
| | February 24 | Me-109 dest(air) | Dummer Lake | P-47 |

6-0-0 air
0-0 ground

**Tyler, Gerald E., Capt.** (7) Houston, TX
364th Ftr Sqn/357th Ftr Grp June 1944-November 1944

P-51B C5-J 43-6376 "Little Duckfoot"
P-51D C5-J 44-14650 "Little Duckfoot"
S/Sgt. Gausky-c/c
Sgt. Stanley Bernotas-ac/c

| Sqn | Date | Claims | Location | A/C |
|---|---|---|---|---|
| 364th | June 29, 1944 | Me-109 dest(air) | SW Leipzig | P-51 |
| | July 5 | FW-190 dest(air) | SE Rouen | P-51 |
| | August 24 | Me-109 dest(air) | S/Brunswick | P-51 |
| | September 18 | (2)Me-109 dest(air) | N/Maastricht | P-51 |
| | | FW-190 dest(air) | N/Maastricht | P-51 |
| | September 19 | Me-109 dest(air) | E/Arnheim | P-51 |

7-0-0 air
0-0 ground

**Tyrrell, Albert R., LtCol.** (5) Fresno, CA
368th Ftr Sqn/359th Ftr Grp March 1943-June 21, 1944(POW)
Hit by flak at Wittstock.
62 missions

P-47D CV-A 42-75111
P-51B CV-A
P-51D CV-A 44-13387
S/Sgt. James Kals-c/c

| *Sqn* | *Date* | *Claims* | *Location* | *A/C* |
|---|---|---|---|---|
| 368th | February 24, 1944 | (2)FW-190 dest(air) | Neuhaus | P-47 |
| | June 21 | Me-110 dest(grd) | Wittstock | P-51 |
| | | Me-410 dest(grd) | Wittstock | P-51 |
| | | FW-189 dest(grd) | Wittstock | P-51 |

2-0-0 air
3-0 ground

**Uttwenweiler, Fred L., Capt.** (6) Bridgeport, CT
352nd Ftr Sqn/353rd Ftr Grp June 1944-January 1945
61 missions

P-47D SX-E
P-51D SX-E 44-14726

| *Sqn* | *Date* | *Claims* | *Location* | *A/C* |
|---|---|---|---|---|
| 352nd | August 4, 1944 | (2)He-111 dest(grd) | Plantlunne | P-47 |
| | October 24 | (4)He-111 dest(grd) | N/Luxembourg | P-51 |
| | | (3)He-111 dam(grd) | N/Luxembourg | P-51 |

0-0-0 air
6-3 ground

**Vanden Heuval, George R., Lt.** (8.5) Staten Island, NY
376th Ftr Sqn/361st Ftr Grp September 1944-October 1945
71 missions, 266:20 hours

P-51D E9-L 44-14685 "Mary Mine"
P-51D E9-Z 44-64005 "Mary Mine"
S/Sgt. Eugene Sullivan-c/c

| *Sqn* | *Date* | *Claims* | *Location* | *A/C* |
|---|---|---|---|---|
| 376th | November 2, 1944 | FW-190 dest(air) | N/Erfurt | P-51 |
| | November 26 | (2)FW-190 dest(air) | S/Ulzen | P-51 |
| | December 24 | Me-109 dest(air) | Wengerohr | P-51 |
| | December 26 | (1.5)FW-190 dest(air)* | Merzig | P-51 |
| | April 16, 1945 | (2)FW-190 dest(grd) | Reichersberg | P-51 |
| | | Me-410 dest(grd) | Kircheim | P-51 |
| | | Ju-52 dam(grd) | Reichersberg | P-51 |

5.5-0-0 air
3-1 ground

* - shared with Capt. J.W. Ruch of the 376th Ftr Sqn

**Visconte, Romildo, Capt.** (9) Redwood City, CA
385th Ftr Sqn/364th Ftr Grp February 1944-December 5, 1944(KIA)
Died in a crash near Liege.

P-38J 5E-G
P-51D 5E-G 44-14254

| *Sqn* | *Date* | *Claims* | *Location* | *A/C* |
|---|---|---|---|---|
| 385th | May 21, 1944 | Ju-88 dest(grd) | Schwerin-Ludwigslust | P-38 |
| | August 9 | (3)Me-109 dest(grd) | Gaukonigshafen | P-51 |
| | | Me-110 dest(grd) | see above | P-51 |
| | | Me-110 dam(grd) | see above | P-51 |
| | | (.5)FW-200 dam(grd)* | see above | P-51 |
| | September 23 | Me-109 dest(air) | Emmerich | P-51 |
| | | FW-190 dam(air) | Emmerich | P-51 |
| | October 12 | FW-190 dest(air) | NE Bremen | P-51 |
| | November 26 | Me-109 dest(air) | Hoyd | P-51 |
| | December 2 | FW-190 dest(air) | NW Ludwigshafen | P-51 |

4-0-1 air
5-1.5 ground

* - shared with Lt. D.J. Hustead of the 385th Ftr Sqn

**Vogt, John W., Jr., Maj.** (8) Elizabeth, NJ
63rd Ftr Sqn/ 56th Ftr Grp Mid 1942-February 1944
360th Ftr Sqn/356th Ftr Grp May 1944-October 1944

P-47C UN-V 41-6325 "Lucky Little Devil"
P-47D UN-V 42-22478
P-47D PI-V 42-26553 "Jersey Mosquito"
S/Sgt. Frank Gydick-c/c(56th)
S/Sgt. Arthur V. Hager-c/c(356th)

| *Sqn* | *Date* | *Claims* | *Location* | *A/C* |
|---|---|---|---|---|
| 63rd | August 19, 1943 | Me-109 dest(air) | Walcheren | P-47 |
| | October 4 | Me-110 dest(air) | E/Duren | P-47 |
| | October 20 | FW-190 dest(air) | N/Ans | P-47 |
| | February 21 | Me-110 dest(air) | N/Munster | P-47 |
| | February 22 | Me-110 dest(air) | Radeborn | P-47 |
| 360th | May 19 | FW-190 dest(air) | SW Celle | P-47 |
| | August 4 | (2)Me-109 dest(air) | SW Hamburg | P-47 |

8-0-0 air
0-0 ground

**Waggoner, Horace Q., Capt.** (12.5) Waggoner, IL
352nd Ftr Sqn/353rd Ftr Grp March 1944-July 1945
114 missions, 492 hours

P-47D SX-M "Miss Illini"
P-47D SX-M 42-26661 "Miss Illini II"
P-51D SX-X 44-14892 "Miss Illini III"
P-51K SX-X 44-11565 "Miss Illini III"
S/Sgt. Otto J. Stopen-c/c(P-47)
Sgt. Emmett C. Wren-ac/c(P-47)
S/Sgt. Edgar S. Welborn-c/c(P-51)

| *Sqn* | *Date* | *Claims* | *Location* | *A/C* |
|---|---|---|---|---|
| 352nd | May 27, 1944 | Do-217 dest(grd) | Saverne | P-47 |
| | June 7 | FW-190 dest(grd) | Cormeiles-en-Vixen | P-47 |
| | | (2)FW-190 dam(grd) | see above | P-47 |
| | June 8 | (1.5)FW-190 dest(grd)* | Angars | P-47 |
| | June 20 | Hs-129 dam(grd) | Twente/Enschede | P-47 |
| | | Ju-88 dam(grd) | Plantlunne | P-47 |
| | December 24 | Me-109 dest(air) | SW Euskirchen | P-51 |
| | December 25 | Me-109 dest(air) | NE St. Vith | P-51 |
| | March 2, 1945 | (2)FW-190 dest(air) | Ruhland | P-51 |
| | | Me-109 dest(air) | Ruhland | P-51 |
| | April 17 | (3)Me-109 dest(grd) | Ganacker | P-51 |
| | | Ju-88 dest(grd) | Ganacker | P-51 |

5-0-0 air
7.5-4 ground

* - shared with Lt. C.F. Armstrong of the 352nd Ftr Sqn

**Waldron, Karl M., Lt.** (10) Hopkins, MN
487th Ftr Sqn/352nd Ftr Grp August 1944-EOW

P-51B HO-U 42-106836
P-51D HO-U 44-15513 "Goliath"

| *Sqn* | *Date* | *Claims* | *Location* | *A/C* |
|---|---|---|---|---|
| 487th | November 2, 1944 | Me-109 dest(air) | Merseburg | P-51 |
| | November 21 | (2)FW-190 dest(air) | SW Merseburg | P-51 |
| | April 10, 1945 | Me-262 dam(air) | Salzwedel | P-51 |
| | April 16 | FW-190 dest(grd) | Ganacker | P-51 |
| | | Me-109 dest(grd) | Ganacker | P-51 |
| | April 17 | (2)FW-190 dest(grd) | Plattling | P-51 |
| | | (2)Me-109 dest(grd) | Plattling | P-51 |
| | | Fi-156 dest(grd) | Plattling | P-51 |
| | | (2)FW-190 dam(grd) | Plattling | P-51 |

3-0-1 air
7-2 ground

**Wallace, Alton J., Capt.** (6) Southington, CT
486th Ftr Sqn/352nd Ftr Grp States-EOW
64 missions

P-47D PZ-W 42-8477 "Little Rebel"
P-51B PZ-W 43-7022 "Little Rebel"
P-51D PZ-W 44-13737 "Little Rebel"

| *Sqn* | *Date* | *Claims* | *Location* | *A/C* |
|---|---|---|---|---|
| 486th | April 15, 1944 | (2)FW-190 dest(air) | NE Vechta | P-51 |
| | April 24 | Do-217 dest(grd) | Neuburg | P-51 |
| | | Ju-88 dest(grd) | Ingolstadt | P-51 |
| | | (4)Ju-88 dam(grd) | Ingolstadt | P-51 |
| | | Me-109 dam(grd) | Neuburg | P-51 |
| | April 25 | Me-109 dest(grd) | Metz | P-51 |
| | August 16 | Me-109 dest(air) | Eisenach | P-51 |

3-0-0 air
3-5 ground

**Warren, Jack R., Capt.** (5) San Jacinto, CA
364th Ftr Sqn/357th Ftr Grp March 1943-March 18, 1944(KIA)
Lost over the North Sea in bad weather.

P-51B C5-F 43-12124

| *Sqn* | *Date* | *Claims* | *Location* | *A/C* |
|---|---|---|---|---|
| 364th | February 22, 1944 | Me-109 dest(air) | Bernburg | P-51 |
| | March 8 | FW-190 dest(air) | SE Berlin | P-51 |
| | March 16 | (2)Me-110 dest(air) | Augsburg | P-51 |
| | | FW-190 dest(air) | Augsburg | P-51 |

5-0-0 air
0-0 ground

**Weaver, Charles E., Maj.** (11) Detroit, MI
362nd Ftr Sqn/357th Ftr Grp September 1944-EOW

P-51D G4-A 44-13691 "Passion Wagon"
P-51D G4-A 44-72199
S/Sgt. Milton F. Lybarger-c/c

| *Sqn* | *Date* | *Claims* | *Location* | *A/C* |
|---|---|---|---|---|
| 362nd | September 19, 1944 | Me-109 dest(air) | S/Zuider Zee | P-51 |
| | November 18 | (2)Me-109 dest(grd) | Mengen | P-51 |
| | November 27 | (2)FW-190 dest(air) | S/Magdeburg | P-51 |
| | | FW-190 prob(air) | S/Magdeburg | P-51 |
| | | FW-190 dam(air) | S/Magdeburg | P-51 |
| | December 23 | Me-109 dest(air) | N/Donauworth | P-51 |
| | January 14, 1945 | Me-109 dest(air) | NW Berlin | P-51 |
| | | FW-190 dest(air) | NW Berlin | P-51 |
| | February 25 | He-111 dest(grd) | Memmingen | P-51 |
| | | FW-190 dam(grd) | Memmingen | P-51 |
| | | Ju-88 dam(grd) | Memmingen | P-51 |
| | March 24 | Me-109 dest(air) | W/Gutersloh | P-51 |
| | April 18 | Me-262 dest(air) | Prague/Ruzny | P-51 |

8-1-1 air
3-2 ground

**Webb, Roy A., LtCol.** (9) Pampa, TX
374th Ftr Sqn/361st Ftr Grp February 1943-July 1944
300 hours

P-47D B7-W 42-76140 "Sweet Thing"
P-47D B7-W 42-75512 "Sweet Thing II"
P-51B B7-W 43-24819 "Sweet Thing III"
P-51D B7-W 44-13537 "Sweet Thing IV"
S/Sgt. G.O. Bentley-c/c
Sgt. Garland R. Thomas-ac/c
Sgt. Robert L. Grubb-arm.

| *Sqn* | *Date* | *Claims* | *Location* | *A/C* |
|---|---|---|---|---|
| 374th | January 30, 1944 | Me-109 dest(air) | Rheine | P-47 |
| | May 29 | FW-190 dest(air) | Pitka | P-51 |
| | June 13 | Me-109 dest(air) | St. Brieuc | P-51 |
| | June 25 | FW-190 dest(air) | S/Caen | P-51 |
| | June 29 | (5)FW-190 dest(grd) | Oschersleben | P-51 |
| | | FW-190 dam(grd) | Oschersleben | P-51 |

4-0-0 air
5-1 ground

**Welch, Robert E., Capt.** (18) Brown City, MI
343rd Ftr Sqn/55th Ftr Grp September 1944-September 1945

P-51D CY-O
P-51D CY-Z 44-72138
S/Sgt. "Red" Norton-c/c(CY-Z)

| *Sqn* | *Date* | *Claims* | *Location* | *A/C* |
|---|---|---|---|---|
| 343rd | September 13, 1944 | Me-109 dest(air) | Eisenach-Gotha | P-51 |
| | | Me-109 dam(air) | Eisenach-Gotha | P-51 |
| | November 2 | Me-109 dest(air) | Naumberg | P-51 |
| | December 24 | Me-109 dest(air) | S/Duren | P-51 |
| | December 25 | (2)Me-109 dest(air) | W/Coblenz | P-51 |
| | March 21, 1945 | (2)FW-190 dest(grd) | Hopsten A/F | P-51 |
| | | Ju-88 dam(grd) | Rheine | P-51 |
| | April 9 | (2)Me-109 dest(grd) | Furtenfeldbruck | P-51 |
| | | (2)Me-410 dest(grd) | Munich-Brunnthal | P-51 |
| | | He-177 dest(grd) | Furtenfeldbruck | P-51 |
| | | Me-262 dest(grd) | Munich-Brunnthal | P-51 |
| | | Me-262 dam(grd) | see above | P-51 |
| | April 10 | (2)He-111 dest(grd) | Burg A/F | P-51 |
| | April 16 | Me-110 dest(grd) | Munich-Brunnthal | P-51 |
| | | Me-410 dest(grd) | see above | P-51 |
| | April 17 | FW-190 dest(air) | Kamenz A/F | P-51 |

6-0-1 air
12-2 ground

**Wesson, Warren M., Capt.** (6) Brooklyn, NY
82nd Ftr Sqn/78th Ftr Grp February 1943-May 1944(Off ops in February)

P-47D MX-E 42-8530 "Jeanie V.O.S."
S/Sgt. Clarence H. Koskela-c/c
Cpl. H.R. Trantham-arm.

| *Sqn* | *Date* | *Claims* | *Location* | *A/C* |
|---|---|---|---|---|
| 82nd | November 26, 1943 | FW-190 dest(air) | Beauvais | P-47 |
| | December 30 | Me-109 dest(air) | Reims | P-47 |
| | February 6, 1944 | FW-190 dest(air) | Orleans | P-47 |
| | | (2)He-111 dam(grd) | Orleans | P-47 |
| | February 8 | He-177 dest(grd) | Paris | P-47 |
| | | He-111 dest(grd) | Paris | P-47 |
| | February 10 | FW-190 dest(air) | Osnabruck | P-47 |
| | February 13 | Ju-88 dam(grd) | Bryes-Sud A/F | P-47 |

4-0-0 air
2-3 ground

**Wetmore, Ray S., Maj.** (24.58) Kerman, CA
370th Ftr Sqn/359th Ftr Grp April 1943-November 1945
142 missions, 563 hours

P-47D CS-P 42-75068
P-51B CS-P 42-106894
P-51D CS-L 44-14733 "Daddy's Girl"
S/Sgt. Harry H. Phillimore-c/c
S/Sgt. George Isaac-c/c
Cpl. Edward J. Zuchowski-ac/c
Sgt. Locklyn Sangster-arm.
Sgt. Aaron M. Munson-arm.

| *Sqn* | *Date* | *Claims* | *Location* | *A/C* |
|---|---|---|---|---|
| 370th | February 10, 1944 | Me-109 dest(air) | E/Zuider Zee | P-47 |
| | March 4 | (.25)Me-109 dest(air)[*] | Bonn | P-47 |
| | | Me-109 dam(air) | Bonn | P-47 |
| | March 16 | (2)FW-190 dest(air) | Sommesous | P-47 |
| | April 11 | (2)Ju-88 dest(grd) | Volkenrod | P-47 |
| | | Ju-88 dam(grd) | Volkenrod | P-47 |
| | April 22 | FW-190 dest(air) | Hamm | P-47 |
| | April 24 | Me-109 dest(grd) | St. Dizier | P-47 |
| | | (.33)u/i a/c dest(grd)[**] | see above | P-47 |
| | | Me-109 dam(grd) | see above | P-47 |
| | May 19 | (2)Me-109 dest(air) | Stendal | P-51 |
| | May 29 | (2)FW-190 dest(air) | Stettin | P-51 |
| | November 2 | (2)Me-109 dest(air) | Erfurt-Weimar | P-51 |
| | November 27 | (3)Me-109 dest(air) | SE Hanover | P-51 |
| | December 31 | (1.5)Me-109 dest(air)[@] | Hanover | P-51 |
| | January 1, 1945 | Me-109 dest(air) | Luneburg | P-51 |
| | January 14 | (4.5)FW-190 dest(air)[@@] | Vorden A/F | P-51 |
| | March 15 | Me-163 dest(air) | Wittenburg | P-51 |

21.25-0-1 air
3.33-2 ground

[*] - shared with Maj. J.B. Murphy, Lt. P.H. Bateman, and Lt. A.C. Porter of the 370th Ftr Sqn
[**] - shared with Capt. S.R. Smith of HdQts, 359th Ftr Grp, and Lt. P.H. Bateman of the 370th Ftr Sqn
[@] - shared with Lt. W.J. Rueschenberg of the 370th Ftr Sqn
[@@] - shared with Lt. W.J. Rueschenberg of the 370th Ftr Sqn

**Whalen, William E., Lt.** (8) Hamilton, NY
334th Ftr Sqn/4th Ftr Grp July 1944-September 1944
2nd Scouting Force September 1944-March 1945

P-51B QP-O 43-6899
P-51D WR-A 44-14300 "Hi Nell"
P-51D WR-A 44-14460 "Hi Nell"

| *Sqn* | *Date* | *Claims* | *Location* | *A/C* |
|---|---|---|---|---|
| 334th | August 18, 1944 | Me-109 dest(air) | Beauvais | P-51 |
| 2nd | November 26 | (3)FW-190 dest(air) | S/Hanover | P-51 |
| | February 9, 1945 | (2)Me-109 dest(air) | Dessau | P-51 |
| | | Me-109 prob(air) | Dessau | P-51 |
| | February 22 | (2)FW-190 dest(grd) | Thale A/F | P-51 |
| | | (3)FW-190 dam(grd) | Thale A/F | P-51 |

6-1-0 air
2-3 ground

**Whinnem, Donald Y., Lt.** (6) Hartford, CT
486th Ftr Sqn/352nd Ftr Grp September 1943-September 1944

P-51B PZ-W 42-106752 "HMS Hellion"

| Sqn | Date | Claims | Location | A/C |
|---|---|---|---|---|
| 486th | February 10, 1944 | Me-109 dam(air) | Enschede | P-47 |
| | April 13 | He-111 dest(grd) | S/Stuttgart | P-51 |
| | April 24 | (2)Ju-88 dest(grd) | Ingolstadt | P-51 |
| | | (6)Ju-88 dam(grd) | Ingolstadt | P-51 |
| | June 8 | (2)FW-190 dest(grd) | Le Mans | P-51 |
| | June 21 | Me-109 dest(air) | E/Warsaw | P-51 |
| | August 5 | Me-109 prob(air) | S/Hamburg | P-51 |
| | | Me-109 dam(air) | S/Hamburg | P-51 |

1-1-2 air
5-6 ground

**Whisner, William T., Capt.** (18.5)Shreveport, LA
487th Ftr Sqn/352nd Ftr Grp September 1943-February 1945
137 missions

P-47D HO-W 42-8400 "Beverly"
P-51B HO-W 42-106449 "Princess Elizabeth"
P-51D HO-W 44-14237 "Moonbeam McSwine"

| Sqn | Date | Claims | Location | A/C |
|---|---|---|---|---|
| 487th | January 29, 1944 | FW-190 dest(air) | Malmedy | P-47 |
| | April 9 | (2)Ju-88 dest(grd) | Diepholz | P-47 |
| | April 30 | FW-190 dest(air) | Clermont-Ferrand | P-51 |
| | May 12 | Ju-52 dest(grd) | Frankenhausen | P-51 |
| | May 29 | FW-190 dest(air) | Gustrow | P-51 |
| | May 30 | (.5)Me-109 dest(air)* | Magdeburg | P-51 |
| | November 2 | Me-109 dest(air) | Merseburg | P-51 |
| | November 21 | (5)FW-190 dest(air) | SW Merseburg | P-51 |
| | | (2)FW-190 prob(air) | SW Merseburg | P-51 |
| | November 27 | (2)Me-109 dest(air) | Hameln | P-51 |
| | January 1, 1945 | (2)Me-109 dest(air) | N/Liege | P-51 |
| | | (2)FW-190 dest(air) | N/Liege | P-51 |

15.5-2-0 air
3-0 ground

* - shared with Maj. G.E. Preddy of the 487th Ftr Sqn

**Wicker, Samuel J., Maj.** (7) Muscogee, OK
383rd Ftr Sqn/364th Ftr Grp August 1943-January 1945

P-38J N2-W 42-67415 "Bettye-Jo"
P-38J N2-W 42-67453 "Bettye-Jo II"
P-51D N2-W 44-13936 "Bettye-Jo III"
P-51D N2-W 44-14243 "Bettye-Jo IV"

| Sqn | Date | Claims | Location | A/C |
|---|---|---|---|---|
| 383rd | May 22, 1944 | (2)FW-190 dest(air) | SW Kiel | P-38 |
| | August 15 | Me-109 dest(air) | Frankfurt | P-51 |
| | December 31 | (4)FW-190 dest(air) | SW Hamburg | P-51 |

7-0-0 air
0-0 ground

**Wiggins, Howard E., Capt.** (6) Tunkhammock, PA
361st Ftr Sqn/356th Ftr Grp May 1944-January 1945
75 missions, 277:50 hours

P-47D QI-M 42-26272 "Angel Eyes"
P-47D QI-M 42-26534
P-51D QI-X 44-15170
S/Sgt. James R. McAfee-c/c(P-47)
Sgt. William H. McCormick-ac/c(P-47)
Cpl. Marion E. Popiel-arm.(P-47)
S/Sgt. Robert E. Venzke-c/c(P-51)

| Sqn | Date | Claims | Location | A/C |
|---|---|---|---|---|
| 361st | June 8, 1944 | (.5)FW-190 dest(air)* | Beauvais/Niviller | P-47 |
| | | (.5)FW-190 dest(grd)** | see above | P-47 |
| | August 4 | (2)Me-109 dest(air) | Bremen-Hamburg | P-47 |
| | November 25 | FW-190 dest(grd) | Zwickau | P-51 |
| | | (3)FW-190 dam(grd) | Zwickau | P-51 |
| | November 26 | (2)Me-109 dest(air) | Osnabruck-Dummer Lake | P-51 |

4.5-0-0 air
1.5-3 ground

*-shared with Lt. G.L. Yoakum of the 361st Ftr Sqn
**-shared with Capt. D.B. Clayton of the 361st Ftr Sqn

**Wilkerson, William F., Capt.** (5) Cincinnati, OH
62nd Ftr Sqn/56th Ftr Grp August 1944-EOW
65 missions, 300 hours

P-47D LM-Y
P-47M LM-Y 44-21214
S/Sgt. Thomas F. Bradshaw-c/c

| Sqn | Date | Claims | Location | A/C |
|---|---|---|---|---|
| 62nd | September 5, 1944 | He-111 dest(grd) | Limburg | P-47 |
| | October 5 | (2)He-111 dam(grd) | S/Geseke | P-47 |
| | | Me-109 dam(grd) | S/Geseke | P-47 |
| | November 18 | FW-190 dest(air) | E/Hanau | P-47 |
| | December 4 | He-111 dest(grd) | Neuburg | P-47 |
| | April 10, 1945 | Me-262 dam(air) | Muritz Lake | P-47 |
| | | (2)He-111 dest(grd) | Rechlin | P-47 |
| | | He-111 dam(grd) | Rechlin | P-47 |

1-0-1 air
4-4 ground

**Wilkinson, James W., Capt.** (8) Swathmore, PA
334th Ftr Sqn/ 4th Ftr Grp January 1943-April 1943 (injured)
82nd Ftr Sqn/78th Ftr Grp November 1943-June 4, 1944(KIAc)
Crashed into a mountain near Llandovery.
87 missions

P-47C QP-S 41-6405
P-47D MX-L 42-7954 "Pin-Up Girl"
S/Sgt. Ismal Boase-c/c(78th)
Sgt. Eugene Carter-ac/c(78th)

| Sqn | Date | Claims | Location | A/C |
|---|---|---|---|---|
| 82nd | December 1, 1943 | Me-109 dest(air) | Eupen | P-47 |
| | February 6, 1944 | FW-190 dest(air) | Orleans | P-47 |
| | | (.5)He-111 dam(grd)* | Orleans | P-47 |
| | | (.5)Ju-52 dam(grd)* | Orleans | P-47 |
| | February 8 | (2)He-111 dam(grd) | Paris | P-47 |
| | February 20 | Me-109 dest(air) | Coblenz | P-47 |
| | March 6 | FW-190 dest(air) | Barenburg | P-47 |
| | March 30 | Glider dam(grd) | Wesel | P-47 |
| | April 5 | Ju-188 dam(grd) | Cambrai | P-47 |
| | April 11 | Ju-88 dest(grd) | Rheine | P-47 |
| | | (2)Ju-88 dam(grd) | Rheine | P-47 |
| | April 12 | (2)Me-109 dam(grd) | Florennes | P-47 |
| | May 11 | (.5)u/i a/c dest(grd)** | Dijon | P-47 |
| | | (2)u/i a/c dam(grd) | Dijon | P-47 |
| | | Go-242 dam(grd) | Dijon | P-47 |
| | May 12 | FW-190 dest(air) | Coblenz | P-47 |
| | May 19 | FW-190 dest(air) | Dummer Lake | P-47 |
| | | FW-190 dam(air) | Dummer Lake | P-47 |
| | May 25 | (.5)FW-190 dest(grd)@ | Metz | P-47 |
| | May 29 | FW-190 dam(grd) | Twente/Enschede | P-47 |

6-0-1 air
2-13 ground

* - both shared with Lt. D.E. Ludwig of the 82nd Ftr Sqn
** - shared with Lt. W.V. Van Dyk of the 82nd Ftr Sqn
@ - shared with Lt. R.E. Wilkinson of the 82nd Ftr Sqn

**Williamson, Brady C., Capt.** (5.7) Parkersburg, WV
354th Ftr Sqn/355th Ftr Grp March 1943-January 1945
98 missions

P-47D WR-H
P-51B WR-H
P-51D WR-H 44-14252 "Palma"
P-51D WR-A 44-14374 "Palma II"
Sgt. Robert L. Marzo-ac/c

| Sqn | Date | Claims | Location | A/C |
|---|---|---|---|---|
| 354th | March 20, 1944 | FW-190 dam(air) | Coxyde | P-51 |
| | March 28 | u/i a/c dam(grd) | Dijon | P-51 |
| | April 5 | W-34 dest(air) | Landsberg | P-51 |
| | | (.5)FW-44 dest(air)* | Landsberg | P-51 |
| | | (.2)Do-217 dest(air)** | Landsberg | P-51 |
| | | Do-217 dam(grd) | Landsberg | P-51 |
| | | FW-44 dam(grd) | Landsberg | P-51 |
| | April 13 | (2)Do-217 dest(grd) | Oberpfaffenhofen | P-51 |
| | | Do-217 dam(grd) | see above | P-51 |
| | | u/i a/c dam(grd) | see above | P-51 |
| | September 11 | FW-190 dest(grd) | S/Kassel | P-51 |
| | September 27 | FW-190 dest(grd) | Eschwege | P-51 |

1.7-0-1 air
4-5 ground

* - shared with Lt. R.E. Woody of the 354th Ftr Sqn
** - shared with Capt. C.G. Johnston, Capt. W.J. Koraleski, Lt. H.W. Brown, and Lt. J.E. Duffy of the 354th Ftr Sqn

**Williamson, Felix D., Maj.** (13) Cordele, GA
62nd Ftr Sqn/56th Ftr Grp May 1943-EOW

P-47D LM-M 42-22541 "Willie"
P-47D LM-M 42-25713
P-47D LM-M 44-20555
P-47M LM-I 44-21219

| *Sqn* | *Date* | *Claims* | *Location* | *A/C* |
|---|---|---|---|---|
| 62nd | November 29, 1943 | (.5)FW-190 dest(air)* | S/Oldenburg | P-47 |
| | December 22 | Me-109 dest(air) | W/Rheims | P-47 |
| | March 8, 1944 | FW-190 dest(air) | Minden | P-47 |
| | March 16 | FW-190 dest(air) | St. Dizier | P-47 |
| | April 20 | (.5)Ju-88 dest(air)** | NE Paris | P-47 |
| | December 23 | Me-109 dest(air) | Euskirchen | P-47 |
| | | FW-190 dest(air) | Euskirchen | P-47 |
| | January 14, 1945 | (4)Me-109 dest(air) | N/Burg | P-47 |
| | | FW-190 dest(air) | N/Burg | P-47 |
| | February 3 | FW-190 dest(air) | Berlin | P-47 |
| | | Me-109 dest(air) | Berlin | P-47 |
| | | FW-190 dam(air) | Berlin | P-47 |
| | | 13-0-1 air | | |
| | | 0-0 ground | | |

* - shared with LtCol. D.C. Schilling of HdQts, 56th Ftr Grp
** - shared with Lt. W.A. McClure of the 62nd Ftr Sqn

**Wilson, John H., Maj.** (7) New Rochelle, NY
357th Ftr Sqn/355th Ftr Grp January 1943-February 14, 1945(KIA)
Spun-in at an airfield in Belgium.

P-47D OS-W 42-8423 "Becky"
P-51B OS-W 43-7101 "Becky"
P-51D OS-W 44-14260 "Becky"

| *Sqn* | *Date* | *Claims* | *Location* | *A/C* |
|---|---|---|---|---|
| 357th | January 29, 1944 | FW-190 dest(air) | W/Frankfurt | P-47 |
| | March 27 | (.5)Me-109 dest(air)* | Biscarosse | P-51 |
| | April 8 | Me-210 dest(grd) | Gifhorn | P-51 |
| | April 13 | Me-109 dest(air) | Augsburg | P-51 |
| | | (.5)Me-323 dest(grd)** | Crailsheim | P-51 |
| | | Me-323 dam(grd) | Crailsheim | P-51 |
| | April 24 | Me-109 dest(air) | NW Munich | P-51 |
| | | Me-109 dam(air) | NW Munich | P-51 |
| | June 6 | Ju-87 dam(air) | NE Janville | P-51 |
| | November 18 | Me-262 dest(grd) | Leipheim | P-51 |
| | | Me-262 dam(grd) | Leipheim | P-51 |
| | January 15, 1945 | u/i a/c dest(grd) | Landsberg | P-51 |
| | | 3.5-0-2 air | | |
| | | 3.5-2 ground | | |

* - shared with Lt. I. Reedy of the 357th Ftr Sqn
** - shared with Lt. J.D. Sturm of the 357th Ftr Sqn

**Wilson, William F., Capt.** (5) Strong City, KS
385th Ftr Sqn/364th Ftr Grp April 1944-December 1944
300:10 hours

P-38J 5E-Y
P-51D 5E-Y 44-14258
P-51D 5E-Y 44-14838

| *Sqn* | *Date* | *Claims* | *Location* | *A/C* |
|---|---|---|---|---|
| 385th | September 11, 1944 | (2)FW-190 dest(air) | W/Leipzig | P-51 |
| | | Me-109 dest(air) | W/Leipzig | P-51 |
| | December 5 | (2)FW-190 dest(air) | NW Berlin | P-51 |
| | | Me-109 dam(air) | NW Berlin | P-51 |
| | | 5-0-1 air | | |
| | | 0-0 ground | | |

**Winks, Robert P., Lt.** (5.5) Sumner, IA
364th Ftr Sqn/357th Ftr Grp July 1944-March 1945
69 missions, 300:45 hours

P-51D C5-W "Trusty Rusty"

| *Sqn* | *Date* | *Claims* | *Location* | *A/C* |
|---|---|---|---|---|
| 364th | November 18, 1944 | Me-109 dest(air) | Neuhausen A/F | P-51 |
| | December 24 | FW-190 dest(air) | Fulda | P-51 |
| | January 14, 1945 | (2)FW-190 dest(air) | SW Ludwigslust | P-51 |
| | | (.5)Me-109 dest(air)* | SW Ludwigslust | P-51 |
| | January 15 | Me-262 dest(air) | Shongau A/F | P-51 |
| | | 5.5-0-0 air | | |
| | | 0-0 ground | | |

* - shared with an unknown P-51 pilot

**Witzel, George H., Lt.** (7) Rochester, NY
436th Ftr Sqn/479th Ftr Grp October 1944-October 1945
51 missions, 261:50 hours

P-51D 9B-B "Bruiser"
P-51D 9B-N 44-15742 "Bruiser"
T/Sgt. Robert E. McCoskey-c/c(B)
T/Sgt. Jessie M. Holloway-c/c(N)

| *Sqn* | *Date* | *Claims* | *Location* | *A/C* |
|---|---|---|---|---|
| 436th | February 21, 1945 | Ju-188 dam(grd) | Nordhausen | P-51 |
| | April 13 | (2)FW-190 dest(grd) | Salzwedel | P-51 |
| | | FW-190 dam(grd) | see above | P-51 |
| | | Me-110 dam(grd) | see above | P-51 |
| | April 16 | (3)FW-190 dest(grd) | Landstadt | P-51 |
| | April 17 | FW-190 dest(grd) | Karlsbad | P-51 |
| | | u/i a/c dest(grd) | Karlsbad | P-51 |
| | | 0-0-0 air | | |
| | | 7-3 ground | | |

**Wolski, Victor, Lt.** (5) Glendale, CA
436th Ftr Sqn/479th Ftr Grp January 1944-October 1944

P-38J 9B-W
P-51D 9B-W

| *Sqn* | *Date* | *Claims* | *Location* | *A/C* |
|---|---|---|---|---|
| 436th | September 5, 1944 | (2)FW-190 dest(grd) | Bad Nauheim | P-38 |
| | | FW-190 dam(grd) | Bad Nauheim | P-38 |
| | September 28 | (3)FW-190 dest(air) | W/Magdeburg | P-51 |
| | | FW-190 dam(air) | W/Magdeburg | P-51 |
| | | 3-0-1 air | | |
| | | 2-1 ground | | |

**Woods, Sidney S., LtCol.** (10) Somerton, AZ
HdQts/479th Ftr Grp Late 1943-December 1944
HdQts/ 4th Ftr Grp February 1945-April 16, 1945(POW)
Hit by flak at Praha/Kbely Airfield.
Earlier flew in the PTO with the 49th Ftr Grp, 5th Air Force, flying 112 missions and claiming 2 kills: a Betty on March 11, 1943, and an Oscar on July 28, 1943.
68 missions

P-38J L2-M 42-67465
P-51D L2-M 44-14416
P-51D QP-A 44-72251
S/Sgt. Roderic Lonier-c/c(4th)
Sgt. R. Easley-arm.(4th)

| *Sqn* | *Date* | *Claims* | *Location* | *A/C* |
|---|---|---|---|---|
| HdQts | September 5, 1944 | Ju-88 dest(grd) | Ettinghausen | P-38 |
| HdQts | March 22, 1945 | (5)FW-190 dest(air) | Furstenwalde-Eggersdorf A/F | P-51 |
| | April 16 | (2)Ju-88 dest(grd) | Praha | P-51 |
| | | (5)Ju-88 dam(grd) | Praha | P-51 |
| | | 5-0-0 air | | |
| | | 3-5 ground | | |

**Woody, Robert E., Capt.** (9) Roanoke, VA
354th Ftr Sqn/355th Ftr Grp Early 1943-May 1944
55 missions, 201:30 hours

P-47D WR-W 42-8493
P-51B WR-W 43-6520 "Woody's Maytag"
S/Sgt. William Gertzen-c/c
Sgt. Bennett-ac/c

| *Sqn* | *Date* | *Claims* | *Location* | *A/C* |
|---|---|---|---|---|
| 354th | April 5, 1944 | (.5)FW-44 dest(air)* | Landsberg | P-51 |
| | | (.5)FW-44 dest(air)** | Landsberg | P-51 |
| | | (.5)Me-109 dest(air)@ | Landsberg | P-51 |
| | | Do-217 dam(grd) | Landsberg | P-51 |
| | | Me-110 dam(grd) | Landsberg | P-51 |
| | April 10 | He-111 dest(grd) | Bourges | P-51 |
| | | He-111 dam(grd) | Bourges | P-51 |
| | April 11 | Me-210 prob(air) | S/Madu Lake | P-51 |
| | | Ju-87 dam(grd) | S/Madu Lake | P-51 |
| | April 13 | Ju-88 dest(grd) | Oberpfaffenhofen | P-51 |
| | | Me-110 dam(grd) | see above | P-51 |
| | April 19 | Me-109 dest(air) | Nordhausen | P-51 |
| | April 24 | (4.5)Me-109 dest(air)@@ | SE Munich | P-51 |
| | | Me-109 dam(air) | SE Munich | P-51 |

7-1-1 air
2-5 ground

* - shared with Capt. W.J. Koraleski of the 354th Ftr Sqn
** - shared with Lt. B.C. Williamson of the 354th Ftr Sqn
@ - shared with Capt. W.J. Koraleski of the 354th Ftr Sqn
@@ - shared with Lt. W.P. Boulet of the 354th Ftr Sqn

**Woolery, James C., Lt.** (6) Bloomington, IN
505th Ftr Sqn/339th Ftr Grp October 1944-July 1945

P-51D 6N-I 44-14433 "Pepper"
P-51D 6N-I 44-72512 "Pepper"
S/Sgt. Roy Myers-c/c
Sgt. Homer Mobley-ac/c

| *Sqn* | *Date* | *Claims* | *Location* | *A/C* |
|---|---|---|---|---|
| 505th | March 1, 1945 | Do-217 dest(grd) | S/Feldkirchen | P-51 |
| | April 16 | (2)u/i a/c dest(grd) | NE Prague | P-51 |
| | | FW-190 dest(grd) | NE Prague | P-51 |
| | April 17 | Me-109 dest(grd) | SE Pocking | P-51 |
| | | Ju-88 dest(grd) | SE Pocking | P-51 |
| | | Me-109 dam(grd) | SE Pocking | P-51 |

0-0-0 air
6-1 ground

**Wright, Robert C., Capt.** (7.5) Holdcroft, VA
375th Ftr Sqn/361st Ftr Grp May 1943-September 1944
83 missions, 317 hours

P-47D E2-K
P-51B E2-K 42-106631 "Toby"
S/Sgt. Charles Upright-c/c
Sgt. Fred Carpenter-ac/c
Sgt. Walter F. Johnson-arm.

| *Sqn* | *Date* | *Claims* | *Location* | *A/C* |
|---|---|---|---|---|
| 375th | May 29, 1944 | (2)Ju-52 dest(grd) | Lackau-Juterbog | P-51 |
| | | He-111 dest(grd) | see above | P-51 |
| | | Ju-88 dest(grd) | see above | P-51 |
| | | Ju-88 dam(grd) | see above | P-51 |
| | June 29 | (1.5)Me-109 dest(air)* | SW Kothen | P-51 |
| | July 7 | (2)Me-109 dest(air) | N/Leipzig | P-51 |

3.5-0-0 air
4-1 ground

* - shared with Lt. S. Armsby of the 375th Ftr Sqn

**Zellner, Edmond, Lt.** (5.25) Hazelton, PA
328th Ftr Sqn/352nd Ftr Grp August 1943-July 31, 1944(MIA-E)
Hit by flak near Charleroi and bailed
out southwest of Brussels.
89 missions

P-47D PE-U 42-22547
P-51B PE-U 42-106832 "We Three"
P-51D PE-U 44-13533 "We Three"
S/Sgt. Kraik-c/c

| *Sqn* | *Date* | *Claims* | *Location* | *A/C* |
|---|---|---|---|---|
| 328th | March 22, 1944 | (.25)FW-200 dest(air)* | Hesepe | P-47 |
| | May 19 | (.5)Me-109 dest(air)** | Wittenburg-Havelburg | P-51 |
| | | Me-109 prob(air) | see above | P-51 |
| | May 21 | (2)He-111 dest(grd) | Alt Ruppin | P-51 |
| | May 24 | Me-109 dest(air) | W/Perleberg | P-51 |
| | May 27 | Me-109 dest(air) | S/Strasbourg | P-51 |
| | | (.5)FW-190 dest(air)@ | S/Strasbourg | P-51 |

3.25-1-0 air
2-0 ground

* - shared with Capt. E.L. Abbott, Lt. R.C. Brookins, and Lt. J.F. Thornell of the 328th Ftr Sqn
** - shared with Capt. C.C. Ettlesen of the 359th Ftr Grp
@ - shared with Maj. J.A. Storch of the 357th Ftr Grp

**Zemke, Hubert, Col.** (26.25) Missoula, MT
HdQts/ 56th Ftr Grp September 1942-November 1943
HdQts/ 56th Ftr Grp January 1944-August 1944
HdQts/479th Ftr Grp August 1944-October 30, 1944(POW)
Lost in bad weather southeast of Hamburg.
155 missions

P-47C LM-Z 41-6330 "Mon Tavarish"
P-47D UN-Z 42-75864
P-47D UN-Z 42-76471
P-47D UN-Z 42-26413 "Happy Warrior"
P-38J J2-Z 43-28823
P-51D 9B-Z 44-14351
S/Sgt. Theron B. Dillon-c/c(LM-Z)
S/Sgt. Damon Itza-c/c(UN-Z)
S/Sgt. Harlan W. Leachman-c/c(J2-Z)
S/Sgt. J.A. Standiford-c/c(9B-Z)

| *Sqn* | *Date* | *Claims* | *Location* | *A/C* |
|---|---|---|---|---|
| HdQts | May 14, 1943 | FW-190 dam(air) | NE Antwerp | P-47 |
| | June 13 | (2)FW-190 dest(air) | Cassel | P-47 |
| | | FW-190 dam(air) | Cassel | P-47 |
| | August 17 | Me-110 dest(air) | St. Trond | P-47 |
| | August 19 | FW-190 dam(air) | Numansdorp | P-47 |
| | September 3 | FW-190 dest(air) | Romilly-Sur-Seine | P-47 |
| | October 2 | FW-190 dest(air) | Groningen | P-47 |
| | October 20 | FW-190 dest(air) | Eindhoven | P-47 |
| | November 5 | FW-190 dest(air) | Enschede-Rheine | P-47 |
| | February 11, 1944 | Me-109 dest(grd) | Rheims | P-47 |
| | | (2)Me-109 dam(grd) | Rheims | P-47 |
| | March 6 | (1.25)Me-109 dest(air)* | Minden-Osnabruck | P-47 |
| | | FW-190 dest(air) | see above | P-47 |
| | | FW-190 prob(air) | see above | P-47 |
| | March 16 | Me-109 dam(air) | Chalons | P-47 |
| | April 15 | (3)He-111 dest(grd) | Flensburg | P-47 |
| | | (3)He-111 dam(grd) | Flensburg | P-47 |
| | April 25 | (2)Ju-88 dest(grd) | Metz | P-47 |
| | May 12 | Me-109 dest(air) | SW Coblenz | P-47 |
| | May 31 | (2)FW-190 dest(air) | Gutersloh-Detmold | P-47 |
| | | FW-190 prob(air) | see above | P-47 |
| | | FW-190 dam(air) | see above | P-47 |
| | June 6 | FW-190 dest(air) | NE Bernay | P-47 |
| | June 7 | (2)FW-190 dest(air) | Chartres/Etampes | P-47 |
| | | FW-190 dam(air) | Chartres/Etampes | P-47 |
| | June 24 | Ju-88 dest(grd) | Sailly-Laurette | P-47 |
| | July 4 | Me-109 dam(air) | N/Conches A/F | P-47 |
| | August 4 | (1.5)He-111 dest(grd)** | Plantlunne | P-47 |
| | | (2)He-111 dam(grd) | Plantlunne | P-47 |
| | September 26 | (2)Me-109 dest(air) | Haltern | P-51 |
| (479th) | | Me-109 dam(air) | Haltern | P-51 |
| | October 7 | (.5)Me-109 dest(air)@ | W/Chemnitz | P-51 |

17.75-2-8 air
8.5-7 ground

* - shared with Lt. M.H. Becker, Lt. D.V. Peters, and Lt. C.W. Reed of the 63rd Ftr Sqn, 56th Ftr Grp
** - shared with Lt. J.W. Ferguson of the 62nd Ftr Sqn, 56th Ftr Grp
@ - shared with Lt. N.R. Benoit of the 435th Ftr Sqn, 479th Ftr Grp

**Zettler, Vincent V., Lt.** (8) Canton, OH
364th Ftr Sqn/357th Ftr Grp November 1944-June 1945
35 missions, 173 hours

P-51D C5-F 44-72927 "Canton Can"
S/Sgt. Robert Mathieson-c/c

| *Sqn* | *Date* | *Claims* | *Location* | *A/C* |
|---|---|---|---|---|
| 364th | January 14, 1945 | Me-109 dam(air) | W/Berlin | P-51 |
| | March 2 | Me-109 dest(air) | SE Magdeburg | P-51 |
| | | (4)He-111 dest(grd) | SE Magdeburg | P-51 |
| | April 10 | (3)Ju-88 dest(grd) | Neuruppin A/F | P-51 |

1-0-1 air
7-0 ground

NOTES

NOTES

NOTES

NOTES

NOTES